Colorado & Utah

W9-AYE-452

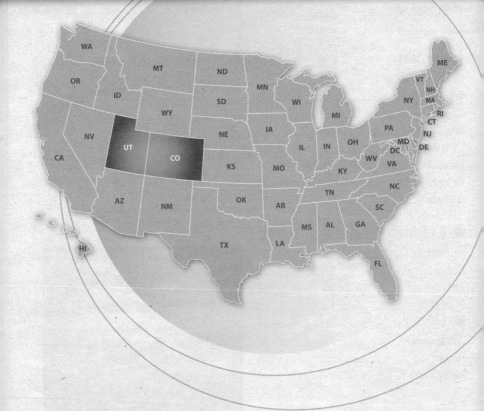

Published by AAA Publishing
1000 AAA Drive, Heathrow, FL 32746-5063
Copyright AAA 2016, All rights reserved

Advertising Rate and Circulation Information: (407) 444-8280

Printed in the USA by Quad/Graphics

This book is printed on paper certified by third-party standards for sustainably managed forestry and production.

Printed on recyclable paper.
Please recycle whenever possible.

Stock #4606 ◆ ◆

CONTENTS

Attractions, hotels, restaurants and other travel experience information are all grouped under the alphabetical listing of the city in which those experiences are physically located—or the nearest recognized city.

Colorado

■ Colorado Springs 80-105

■ Denver 115-165

Utah

Featured Information

Dream.
Plan.
Go.

Picture yourself ...
- At your ideal destination
- In a comfortable hotel
- Eating your favorite meals
- Exploring the sights

Turn your dreams into reality
with **TripTik® Travel Planner.**

Online: AAA.com/ttp | On the go: AAA or CAA Mobile app

We Get You ...

© Sigrid Olsson / Alamy

Going the Extra Mile

Every year AAA experts travel North America to check out places for members to see, stay, dine and play.

Professional Inspectors - conduct in-person hotel and restaurant evaluations, providing ratings, notes and tips to guide your decisions.

Seasoned Travel Writers - gather destination insight, providing itineraries and top picks including AAA GEM attractions.

A to Z City Listings

Cities and places are listed alphabetically within each state or province. Attractions, hotels and restaurants are listed once — under the city in which they are physically located.

Cities that are considered part of a larger destination city or area have an expanded city header. The header identifies the larger region and cross-references pages that contain shared trip planning resources:

- Destination map – outline map of the cities that comprise a destination city or area
- Attraction spotting map – regional street map marked with attraction locations
- Hotel/restaurant spotting map and index – regional street map numbered with hotel and restaurant locations identified in an accompanying index

Cities that are not considered part of a larger destination city or area but have a significant number of listings may have these resources within the individual city section:

- Attraction spotting map
- Hotel/restaurant spotting map and index

Location Abbreviations

Directions are from the center of town unless otherwise specified, using these highway abbreviations:

Bus. Rte.=business route
CR=county road
FM=farm to market
FR=forest road
Hwy.=Canadian highway
I=interstate highway
LR=legislative route
R.R.=rural route
SR/PR=state or provincial route
US=federal highway

Maps

Use the navigable road maps and accompanying legend in the Atlas Section for route planning. Check the destination maps for general location reference. In select cities only, refer to the mass transit overview maps to cross-reference station names and numbers. For attraction and hotel/restaurant spotting maps, see the legend below to identify symbols and color coding.

Map Legend

Roads/Highways

Free / Interchange / Toll	
	Controlled access
	Controlled access toll
	Local toll
	Primary
	Secondary
	Local unpaved
	Under construction
	Tunnel
	Pedestrian only
	Auto ferry
	Passenger ferry
	Scenic byway

Areas of Interest

	Incorporated city
✈ ✈	Int'l/Regional airport
	Park
	Recreation sites
	Forest
	Natural lands
	Military
	Historic
	Native American
	Beach
	Marsh

Route Shields

	Primary	Secondary		Primary	Secondary
Interstate	95	95 Business	Trans-Canada		
Federal	22	22	Provincial Autoroute	22	22
State	1	1	Mexico	1	1
County	1	1	Historic	66	

Boundaries

International	Time zone
State	Continental Divide

Points of Interest

○	Town	⚑	Campground information provided by Woodall's ®
★	National capital	¶	Winery
★	State/Prov capital	Ⓢ	Customs station
■	AAA/CAA club location	▪	Historic
■	Feature of interest	△	Mountain peak
▼	GEM attraction		Rapid transit
12	Hotel listing	Stations	
3	Restaurant listing		Metromover
🎓	College/University		

About Listed Establishments

AAA/CAA Approved hotels and restaurants are listed on the basis of merit alone after careful evaluation and approval by full-time, professionally trained AAA/CAA inspectors. An establishment's decision to advertise in the TourBook guide has no bearing on its evaluation or rating; nor does inclusion of advertising imply AAA endorsement of products and services.

Information in this guide was believed accurate at the time of publication. However, since changes inevitably occur between annual editions, please contact your AAA travel professional, visit AAA.com or download the AAA mobile app to confirm prices and schedules.

Attraction Listings

ATTRACTION NAME, 3 mi. n. off SR 20A (Main Ave.), consists of 250 acres with Olmsted-designed gardens, a 205-foot marble and coquina bell tower and a Mediterranean-style mansion. One of the state's oldest attractions, the tower and gardens were dedicated to the American people in 1929 by President Calvin Coolidge on behalf of their founder, a Dutch immigrant.

Hours: Gardens daily 8-6. Last admission 1 hour before closing. Visitor center daily 9-5. Estate tours are given at noon and 2. Carillon concerts are given at 1 and 3. Phone ahead to confirm schedule. **Cost:** $10; $3 (ages 5-12). Gardens and estate $16; $8 (ages 5-12). **Phone:** (555) 555-5555.
GT ▮▮ ▭ ▯ Dupont Circle,13

AAA/CAA travel experts may designate an attraction of exceptional interest and quality as a AAA GEM — a *Great Experience for Members®. See GEM Attraction Index (listed on CONTENTS page) for a complete list of locations.*

Consult the online travel guides at AAA.com or visit AAA Mobile for additional things to do if you have time.

Cost

Prices are quoted without sales tax in the local currency (U.S. or Canadian dollars). Children under the lowest age specified are admitted free when accompanied by an adult. Most establishments accept credit cards, but a small number require cash, so please call ahead to verify.

Adventure Travel

Activities such as air tours, hiking, skiing and white-water rafting are listed to provide member information and do not imply AAA/CAA endorsement. For your safety, be aware of inherent risks and adhere to all safety instructions.

Icons

SAVE AAA Discounts & Rewards® member discount

▤ Electric vehicle charging station on premises. Domestic station information provided by the U.S. Department of Energy. Canadian station information provided by Plug'n Drive Ontario.

GT Guided Tours available

▲ Camping facilities

▮▮ Food on premises

▢ Recreational activities

▸ Pets on leash allowed

▭ Picnicking allowed

In select cities only:

▯ Mass transit station within 1 mile. Icon is followed by station name and AAA/CAA designated station number within listing.

Information-Only Attraction Listings

Bulleted listings, which include the following categories, are listed for informational purposes as a service to members:

- **Gambling establishments** (even if located in a AAA/CAA Approved hotel)
- **Participatory recreational activities** (those requiring physical exertion or special skills)
- **Wineries that offer tours and tastings**

Mobile Tags

Scan QR codes throughout the TourBook guide to see online offers, menus, videos and more on your smartphone or tablet. If you need a QR scanner app, download one for free from your app store.

If you see a non-QR code in an ad, check the nearby text for details on which app you'll need to scan it.

Hotel and Restaurant Listings

1 Diamond Rating – AAA/CAA Approved hotels and restaurants are assigned a rating of one to five Diamonds. Red Diamonds distinguish establishments that participate in the AAA/CAA logo licensing program. For details, see p. 11 or AAA.com/Diamonds.

fyi indicates hotels and restaurants that are not AAA/CAA Approved and/or Diamond Rated but are listed to provide additional choices for members:

- **Hotels** may be unrated if they are too new to rate, under construction, under major renovation or have not yet been evaluated; or if they do not meet all AAA requirements. Hotels that do not meet all AAA requirements may be included if they offer member value or are the only option; details are noted in the listing.
- **Restaurants** may be unrated if they have not yet been evaluated by AAA.

2 Classification or Cuisine Type – Noted after the Diamond Rating.

- **Hotel Classifications** indicate the style of operation, overall concept and service level. Subclassifications may also be added. (See p. 12.)
- **Restaurant Cuisine Types** identify the food concept from more than 100 categories. If applicable, a classification may also be added. (See p. 13.)

3 Dollar Amounts – Quoted without sales tax in the local currency (U.S. or Canadian dollars), rounded up to the nearest dollar. Most establishments accept credit cards, but a small number require cash, so please call ahead to verify.

- **Hotel Rates** indicate the publicly available two-person rate or rate range for a standard room, applicable all year.
- **Restaurant Prices** represent the minimum and maximum entrée cost per person. Exceptions may include one-of-a-kind or special market priced items.

4 Spotting Symbol – Ovals containing numbers correspond with numbered location markings on hotel and restaurant spotting maps.

5 Parking – Unless otherwise noted, parking is free, on-site self parking.

6 Hotel Value Nationwide – Blue boxes highlight member benefits available at AAA/CAA Approved locations across a hotel chain. (See Just For Members section for details.)

7 Hotel Unit Limited Availability – Unit types, amenities and room features preceded by "some" are available on a limited basis, potentially as few as one.

8 Hotel Terms – Cancellation and minimum stay policies are listed. Unless otherwise noted, most properties offer a full deposit refund with cancellations received at least 48 hours before standard check-in. Properties that require advance payment may not refund the difference for early departures. "Resort fee" indicates a charge may apply above and beyond the quoted room rate.

9 Hotel Check-in/Check-out – Unless otherwise noted, check-in is after 3 p.m. and check-out is before 10 a.m.

10 Restaurant Dress Code – Unless otherwise noted, dress is casual or dressy casual.

11 Restaurant Menu – Where indicated, menus may be viewed in a secure online environment at AAA.com or, if a mobile tag is provided, via the restaurant's website.

12 Hotel Icons – May be preceded by CALL and/or SOME UNITS.

Member Information:

SAVE Member rates: discounted standard room rate or lowest public rate available at time of booking for dates of stay.

ECO Eco-certified by government or private organization.

Electric vehicle charging station on premises. Domestic station information provided by the U.S. Department of Energy. Canadian station information provided by Plug'n Drive Ontario.

Smoke-free premises

In select cities only:

Mass transit station within 1 mile. Icon is followed by station name and AAA/CAA designated station number within listing.

Services:

Airport transportation

Pets allowed (Call property for restrictions.)

Pets allowed (Call property for restrictions and fees.)

Restaurant on premises

Restaurant off premises

Room service for 2 or more meals

Full bar

HOTEL LISTING

HOTEL NAME

(555)555-5555 **50**

AAA Benefit: Members save a minimum 5% off the best available rate.

Hotel
$109-$199

Address: 300 Main St 55555 **Location:** I-275 exit 31 southbound; exit 30 northbound, 1.6 mi w on SR 688 (Oak Rd). Dupont Circle, 13. **Facility:** 149 units, some efficiencies. 3 stories, interior corridors. **Parking:** on-site (fee). **Terms:** check-in 4 pm, cancellation fee imposed, resort fee. **Amenities:** video games. **Pool(s):** heated outdoor. **Activities:** hot tub, exercise room. **Guest Services:** valet and coin laundry. **Featured Amenity:** continental breakfast.

RESTAURANT LISTING

RESTAURANT NAME

555/555-5555

AAA Inspector Notes: *Historic.* A romantic aura punctuates the modern and casual dining room, which is accented with floral arrangements and dramatic, freshly cut branches. The menu features seasonal ingredients. The pastry chef's decadent creations are popular. Semiformal attire. **Features:** full bar, patio dining, happy hour. **Address:** 26 N Main St 55555 **Location:** SR A1A southbound, 2.7 mi s of jct SR 520. Dupont Circle, 13.

Continental
Fine Dining
$15-$35

Menu on AAA.com

Child care

BIZ Business area

Accessible features (Call property for available services and amenities.)

Activities:

Full-service casino

Pool

Health club on premises

In-Room Amenities:

HS High-speed Internet service

sHS High-speed Internet service (Call property for fees.)

Wireless Internet service

Wireless Internet service (Call property for fees.)

No wireless Internet service

Pay movies

Refrigerator

Microwave

Coffee maker

No air conditioning

No TV

No telephones

13 Restaurant Icons

SAVE AAA Discounts & Rewards® member discount

ECO Eco-certified by government or private organization.

Electric vehicle charging station on premises. Domestic station information provided by the U.S. Department of Energy. Canadian station information provided by Plug'n Drive Ontario.

No air conditioning

Accessible features (Call property for available services and amenities.)

Designated smoking section

B Breakfast

L Lunch

D Dinner

24 Open 24 hours

LATE Open after 11 p.m.

Pet-friendly (Call property for restrictions.)

In select cities only:

Mass transit station within 1 mile. Icon is followed by station name and AAA/CAA designated station number within listing.

Just For Members

Understanding the Diamond Ratings

Hotel and restaurant evaluations are unscheduled to ensure our professionally trained inspectors encounter the same experience members do.

- When an establishment is Diamond Rated, it means members can expect a good fit with their needs. The inspector assigns a rating that indicates the type of experience to expect.
- While establishments at high levels must offer increasingly complex personalized services, establishments at every level are subject to the same basic requirements for cleanliness, comfort and hospitality. Learn more at AAA.com/Diamonds.

Hotels

Budget-oriented, offering basic comfort and hospitality.

Affordable, with modestly enhanced facilities, décor and amenities.

Distinguished, multifaceted with enhanced physical attributes, amenities and guest comforts.

Refined, stylish with upscale physical attributes, extensive amenities and high degree of hospitality, service and attention to detail.

Ultimate luxury, sophistication and comfort with extraordinary physical attributes, meticulous personalized service, extensive amenities and impeccable standards of excellence.

Restaurants

Simple, economical food, often self-service, in a functional environment.

Familiar food, often cooked to order, served in relaxed surroundings.

Popular cuisine, skillfully prepared and served, with expanded beverage options, in enhanced setting.

Imaginative, market-fresh food creatively prepared and skillfully served, often with wine steward, amid upscale ambience.

Cutting-edge cuisine of the finest ingredients, uniquely prepared by an acclaimed chef, served by expert service staff led by maître d' in extraordinary surroundings.

What's the difference?

 Red Diamonds mark establishments that participate in the AAA/CAA logo licensing program for increased visibility to members.

 Black Diamonds identify all other AAA/CAA Approved and Diamond Rated establishments.

Hotel Classifications

Quality and comfort are usually consistent across each Diamond Rating level, but décor, facilities and service levels vary by classification.

Berry Manor Inn, Rockland, ME

Bed & Breakfast — Typically owner-operated with a high degree of personal touches. Guests are encouraged to interact during evening and breakfast hours. A continental or full, hot breakfast is included in the room rate.

Killarney Lodge, Algonquin Provincial Park, ON

Cabin — Often located in wooded, rural or waterfront locations. Freestanding units are typically rustic and of basic design. As a rule, essential cleaning supplies, kitchen utensils and complete bed and bath linens are supplied.

Hyatt Regency Clearwater Beach Resort & Spa, Clearwater Beach, FL

Condominium — Apartment-style accommodations of varying design or décor, units often contain one or more bedrooms, a living room, full kitchen and an eating area. As a rule, essential cleaning supplies, kitchen utensils and complete bed and bath linens are supplied.

Montpelier Plantation and Beach, St. Kitts and Nevis

Cottage — Often located in wooded, rural, or waterfront locations. Freestanding units are typically home-style in design and décor. As a rule, essential cleaning supplies, kitchen utensils and complete bed and bath linens are supplied.

Nottoway Plantation & Resort, White Castle, LA

Country Inn — Although similar in definition to a bed and breakfast, country inns are usually larger in scale with spacious public areas and offer a dining facility that serves breakfast and dinner.

The Shores Resort & Spa, Daytona Beach Shores, FL

Hotel — Typically a multistory property with interior room entrances and a variety of guest unit styles. The magnitude of the public areas is determined by the overall theme, location and service level, but may include a variety of facilities such as a restaurant, shops, a fitness center, a spa, a business center and meeting rooms.

All Star Vacation Homes, Kissimmee, FL

House — Freestanding units of varying home-style design. Typically larger scale, often containing two or more bedrooms, a living room, a full kitchen, a dining room and multiple bathrooms. As a rule, essential cleaning supplies, kitchen utensils and complete bed and bath linens are supplied.

Bryce View Lodge, Bryce Canyon City, UT

Motel — A one- or two-story roadside property with exterior room entrances and drive up parking. Public areas and facilities are often limited in size and/or availability.

Vista Verde Guest Ranch, Clark, CO

Ranch — Typically a working ranch featuring an obvious rustic, Western theme, equestrian-related activities and a variety of guest unit styles.

Hotel Subclassifications

These additional descriptives may be added to the classification for more information:

- **Boutique** — Often thematic, typically informal yet highly personalized; may have a luxurious or quirky style that is fashionable or unique.
- **Casino** — Extensive gambling facilities are available, such as blackjack, craps, keno and slot machines.
- **Classic** — Renowned and landmark properties, older than 50 years, well known for their unique style and ambience.
- **Contemporary** — Overall theme reflects characteristics of present mainstream trends.
- **Extended Stay** — Offers a predominance of long-term accommodations with a designated full-service kitchen area within each unit.
- **Historic** — More than 75 years old with one of the following documented historical features: Maintains the integrity of the historical nature, listed on the National Register of Historic Places, designated a National Historic Landmark or located in a National Register Historic District.
- **Resort** — Extensive recreational facilities and programs may include golf, tennis, skiing, fishing, water sports, spa

treatments or professionally guided activities.

- **Retro** — Overall theme reflects a contemporary design that reinterprets styles from a past era.
- **Vacation Rental** — Typically houses, condos, cottages or cabins; these properties are "home away from home" self-catering accommodations.
- **Vintage** — Overall theme reflects upon and maintains the authentic traits and experience of a past era.

Service Animals

Under the Americans with Disabilities Act (ADA), U.S. businesses that serve the public must allow people with disabilities to bring their service animals into all areas of the facility where customers are normally allowed to go.

Businesses may ask if an animal is a service animal and what tasks the animal has been trained to perform. Businesses may not ask about the person's disability, require special identification for the animal or request removal of the animal from the premises except in limited cases that require alternate assistance. Businesses may not charge extra fees for service animals, including standard pet fees, but may charge for damage caused by service animals if guests are normally charged for damage they cause.

Call the U.S. Department of Justice ADA Information Line: (800) 514-0301 or TTY (800) 514-0383, or visit ada.gov. Regulations may differ in Canada.

Restaurant Classifications

If applicable, in addition to the cuisine type noted under the Diamond Rating, restaurant listings may also include one or both classifications:

- **Classic** — Renowned and landmark operation in business for 25 plus years; unique style and ambience.
- **Historic** — Meets one of the following: Listed on National Register of Historic Places, designated a National Historic Landmark or located in a National Register Historic District.

AAA/CAA Approved Hotels

For members, AAA/CAA Approved means quality assured.

- Only properties that meet basic requirements for cleanliness, comfort and hospitality pass inspection.
- Approved hotels receive a Diamond Rating that tells members the type of experience to expect.

Guest Safety

Inspectors view a sampling of rooms during evaluations and, therefore, AAA/CAA cannot guarantee the presence of working locks and operational fire safety equipment in every guest unit.

Member Rates

AAA/CAA members can generally expect to pay no more than the maximum TourBook listed rate for a standard room. Member discounts apply to rates quoted within the rate range and are applicable at the time of booking. Listed rates are usually based on last standard room availability. Rates may fluctuate within the range and vary by season and room type. Obtain current AAA/CAA member rates and make reservations at AAA.com.

Exceptions

- Rates for properties operating as concessionaires for the U.S. National Park Service are not guaranteed due to governing regulations.
- Special advertised rates and short-term promotional rates below the rate range are not subject to additional member discounts.
- During special events, hotels may temporarily increase room rates, not recognize discounts or modify pricing policies. Special events may include Mardi Gras, the Kentucky Derby (including pre-Derby events), college football games, holidays, holiday periods and state fairs. Although some special events are listed in the TourBook guides and on AAA.com, it's always wise to check in advance with AAA travel professionals for specific dates.

If you are charged more than the maximum TourBook listed rate, question the additional charge. If an exception is not in effect and management refuses to adhere to the published rate, pay for the room and contact AAA/CAA. The amount paid above the stated maximum will be refunded if our investigation indicates an unjustified charge.

Reservations and Cancellations

When making your reservation, identify yourself as a AAA/CAA member and request written confirmation of your room type, rate, dates of stay, and cancellation and refund policies. At registration, show your membership card.

To cancel, contact the hotel, your AAA/CAA club office or AAA.com, depending on how you booked your reservation. Request a cancellation number or proof of cancellation.

If your room is not as specified and you have written confirmation of your reservation for a specific room type, you should be given the option of choosing a different room or receiving a refund. If management refuses to issue a refund, contact AAA/CAA.

Contacting AAA/CAA About Approved Properties

If your visit to a AAA/CAA Approved attraction, hotel or restaurant doesn't meet your expectations, please tell us about it — **during your visit or within 30 days**. Be sure to save your receipts and other documentation for reference.

Use the easy online form at AAA.com/TourBookComments to send us the details.

Alternatively, you can email your comments to: memberrelations@national.aaa.com or submit them via postal mail to: AAA Member Comments, 1000 AAA Dr., Box 61, Heathrow, FL 32746.

AAA/CAA Preferred Hotels

All AAA/CAA Approved hotels are committed to providing quality, value and member service. In addition, those designated as AAA/CAA Preferred Hotels also offer these extra values at Approved locations nationwide. Valid AAA/CAA membership required.

- **Best AAA/CAA member rates for your dates of stay.**
- **Seasonal promotions and special member offers.** Visit AAA.com to view current offers.
- **Member benefit.** See the blue boxes in hotel listings for the chains shown in the right-hand column below to find values offered at AAA/CAA Approved locations nationwide, subject to availability. Details valid at the time of publication and may change without notice.

- **Total satisfaction guarantee.** If you book your stay with AAA/CAA Travel and your stay fails to meet your expectations, you can apply for a full refund. Bring the complaint to the hotel's attention during the stay and request resolution; if the complaint is not resolved by the hotel, ask your AAA/CAA travel agent to request resolution through the AAA/CAA Assured Stay program.

	BEST WESTERN®, BEST WESTERN PLUS®, EXECUTIVE RESIDENCY, Vib, BEST WESTERN PREMIER® and BW Premier Collection^{SM}

Hilton	Hilton Hotels & Resorts, Waldorf Astoria™ Hotels & Resorts, Conrad® Hotels & Resorts, Canopy by Hilton, Curio - A Collection by Hilton™, DoubleTree by Hilton™, Embassy Suites Hotels™, Hilton Garden Inn™, Hampton Inn™, Homewood Suites by Hilton™, Home2 Suites by Hilton™ and Hilton Grand Vacations™

HYATT®	Park Hyatt®, Andaz®, Grand Hyatt®, Hyatt Centric®, Hyatt®, Hyatt Regency®, Hyatt Place®, HYATT house®, Hyatt Zilara® and Hyatt Ziva®

	JW Marriott®, Autograph Collection® Hotels, Renaissance® Hotels, Marriott Hotels®, Delta Hotels and Resorts®, Gaylord Hotels®, AC Hotels by Marriott®, Courtyard®, Residence Inn®, SpringHill Suites®, Fairfield Inn & Suites® and TownePlace Suites®

	Bellagio®, ARIA®, Vdara®, MGM Grand®, The Signature at MGM Grand®, Mandalay Bay®, Delano™ Las Vegas, The Mirage®, Monte Carlo™, New York-New York®, Luxor®, Excalibur® and Circus Circus® Las Vegas

 starwood Hotels and Resorts	St. Regis®, The Luxury Collection®, W®, Westin®, Le Méridien®, Sheraton®, Four Points® by Sheraton, Aloft®, element® and Tribute Portfolio™

Landry's Seafood House, The Crab House, Chart House, Oceanaire, Saltgrass Steak House, Muer Seafood Restaurants and Aquarium Restaurants

Member Discounts

Visit AAA.com/searchfordiscounts to find locations and available member discounts. Your AAA/CAA club may offer even greater discounts on theme park tickets. Amtrak and theme park discounts may be used for up to six tickets; restaurant savings may be used for up to six patrons. Other restrictions may apply. All offers subject to change. For complete restrictions, visit your AAA office or AAA.com/restrictions.

- Save 10% on food and nonalcoholic beverages at all of the above restaurants.

- Save 10% on merchandise at Aquarium, Downtown Aquarium and Rainforest Cafe restaurants.

ATTRACTIONS

Six Flags

- Save on admission at the gate, participating AAA/CAA offices or AAA.com/SixFlags.

- Save 10% on merchandise of $15 or more at in-park stores.

Universal Orlando Resort and Universal Studios Hollywood

- Save on tickets at select AAA/CAA offices or AAA.com/Universal. In-park savings available in FL.

- Save 10% on Blue Man Group tickets and at select food and merchandise venues at Universal CityWalk®.

DINING

Hard Rock Cafe

- Save 10% on food, nonalcoholic beverages and merchandise at all locations in the U.S. and Canada, plus select international locations. Visit AAA.com/HardRock for full listing.

SHOPPING

adidas Outlet

- Save 20% on the entire purchase. Visit AAA.com/adidasoutlet for list of locations.

Reebok & Rockport Outlet

- Save 20% on the entire purchase. Visit AAA.com/Reebok for list of locations.

Tanger Outlet Centers

- Receive a free coupon book with discounts up to 50% at select merchants.

TRANSPORTATION

Amtrak

- Save 10% on rail fare booked at least three days in advance of travel date at AAA.com/Amtrak.

Hertz

- Save on daily, weekend, weekly and monthly rentals at AAA.com/Hertz or (800) 654-3080.

RACK UP THE REWARDS

Make membership an even more rewarding experience.

The AAA Member Rewards Visa® credit card lets you earn reward points on all of your purchases. Apply for an account today and let the rewards start rolling in!

- ✓ Earn 1 point for every $1 in purchases with your AAA Member Rewards Visa® card!*

- ✓ Earn 2X points for gas, grocery and drug store purchases!

- ✓ Earn 3X points on qualifying AAA and travel purchases!

- ✓ Redeem for cash or get a AAA Voucher that gives you up to 40% more value!**

- ✓ Exclusive rewards to make you smile!

VISIT AAA.com/creditcard   **STOP BY** any AAA branch

Fall in the Rocky Mountains

Colorado

If you find yourself fed up with the congestion, stress and fast pace of everyday life, change your altitude. In Colorado, people tend to breathe a little easier, focus better and take themselves less seriously.

Geography is a good reason why. Colorado is awe-inspiring: The Continental Divide saws a jagged line through the state, leaving the eastern portion to resemble Kansas with rolling hills and golden plains that expand for miles. But central Colorado gets vertical—its sharp outline reaches for the sky.

The Rocky Mountains resemble a calico quilt in soothing shades of greens. Cathedral-shaped mountains wrap around you under a blanket of blue, and crisp air goes right to your head to sweep out any cobwebs.

Surrounded by a circle of peaks, you'll feel small yet invigorated. John Denver could only describe the oxymoronic feeling as a

"Rocky Mountain High"—a humbling yet empowering drive to find a place for yourself in the midst of such bold surroundings. The sheer majesty of 58 pinnacles surpassing the 14,000-foot mark crowns everyday hassles runners-up.

Purple Peaks and Red Rocks

Pack your suitcase full of bad karma and head for Pikes Peak National Forest, where a cog railway ascends to the tiptop of the magnificent summit. En route, you'll pass bighorn sheep who are just as eager to check you out as you are to snap a photo. It was this peak, named for Col. Zebulon Pike (who never actually made it to the top but admired it during his survey of the Louisiana Purchase), which inspired poet Katherine Lee Bates to write "America the Beautiful." You'll see firsthand at the Garden of the Gods Park in Colorado Springs why early Spanish *conquistadores* called the state *colorado*—meaning "the color red." Giant sandstone rock formations take the shapes of Kissing Camels, a Cathedral and a Sleeping Giant.

Nearby, a mountain of a different sort—fashioned from glass and silver spires—will lift your spirits as well. The Cadet Chapel at the U.S. Air Force Academy, with its pointed aluminum steeples and brightly colored stained glass, contains Catholic, Protestant and Jewish chapels and two All Faiths Rooms, each individually breathtaking.

The Cadet Chapel, U.S. Air Force Academy, Colorado Springs

Golden Days of Ore

Denver, dubbed the "Mile High City" due to its elevation of exactly 5,280 feet, is the gateway to the Rocky Mountains. Early residents came in search of clean air, believed to cure tuberculosis. Others, such as the legendary Buffalo Bill, rode in on the coattails of the Pikes Peak gold rush.

Leadville, the highest city in America—positioned at a whopping 10,152 feet above sea level—is another escape to the past. If the thin air alone doesn't make your head spin, frontier tales of mining, gunfights and love triangles surely will. Wander through the historic district and hear about the "get-rich-quick" story of H.A.W. Tabor and his mine.

Many visitors to this state fall under the spell of its dry air, snowcapped summits, dark canyons, icy mountain streams and dusty ghost towns. A trip here instills a deep appreciation for the power of environmental surroundings. Colorado just might change you, bringing vigor, creativity, solace and emotional riches—and diminishing anxieties.

Recreation

If you're looking for adventure, Colorado is the place. On what might be a lazy Saturday anywhere else, choose from vigorous options like climbing a bluff, tackling river rapids, storming a mountain on a bike or skis, hiking through backwoods to sleep under the stars or observing wildlife.

Aspen, Beaver Creek, Breckenridge, Copper Mountain, Crested Butte, Keystone, Purgatory, Snowmass Village, Steamboat Springs, Telluride, Vail, Winter Park and Wolf Creek are just *some* of the places where you can maneuver the moguls. If skis bore you, try snowboarding down a black diamond or snowmobiling along a mountain trail for an added kick.

Where there are mountains, there are trails. Horseback riding through Devils Canyon provides views of red rocks, while paths at Colorado National Monument snake along 600-foot canyons. Trails suitable for two wheels are nearly everywhere. Hit the ski resorts in summer for mountain biking; you can load your bike onto a ski lift and ride down. Cycle the Rio Grande Trail near Aspen, which skirts the Roaring Fork River and follows the path of the old Denver & Rio Grande Railroad system, or choose from some 600 miles of connecting mountain bike trails at Winter Park in the Fraser River Valley.

Hiking is just as enticing, with thousands of miles of trails winding through nearly every park and national forest. Near Golden, try the Lookout Mountain Trail—it connects Beaver Brook Trail to the top of Lookout Mountain—or the Red Rocks/Dakota Ridge Trail, which meanders through red rock formations and across streams.

The section of Los Pinos River (called "the Pine" by locals) from the wilderness boundary to the Continental Divide offers excellent back country fly fishing. Various streams in the state are stocked with eastern brook, brown and rainbow trout. Walleyed pike, white bass, catfish and perch are hooked from larger lakes and reservoirs.

The Arkansas River is a favored rafting spot. Its upper portion provides for a crazy jaunt, but lower waters are more novice-friendly. The wild at heart will want to tackle the class III and IV waters that charge through Brown Canyon; you'll catch glimpses of some of Colorado's tallest peaks. The Colorado, Dolores, Gunnison and North Platte rivers also cater to rafters. And those who find themselves wandering around downtown Durango are sure to be tempted to slide into a wetsuit and brave the waters of the Animas River.

Hit the slopes in Aspen

Historic Timeline

1540	Francisco de Coronado's expedition begins the journey through what is now southeastern Colorado.
1803	The United States acquires the area as part of the Louisiana Purchase.
1850	Gold is discovered at what is now Arvada; other strikes in 1858 begin Colorado's first gold rush.
1876	Colorado becomes the 38th state in the Union.
1881	Ute tribes are forced onto reservations.
1906	The U.S. Mint at Denver issues its first coins.
1947	Colorado's first commercial ski resort opens for business in Aspen.
1954	The U.S. Air Force Academy is established at Colorado Springs.
1999	Lynxes are reintroduced to Colorado after not being seen in the wild for more than 25 years.
2000	Denver celebrates the news that its public library is named the nation's best.
2013	Flood damage in northern Colorado impacts routes into many communities and Rocky Mountain NP.

What To Pack

Temperature Averages Maximum/Minimum	JANUARY	FEBRUARY	MARCH	APRIL	MAY	JUNE	JULY	AUGUST	SEPTEMBER	OCTOBER	NOVEMBER	DECEMBER
Colorado Springs	43/14	45/17	50/22	59/31	68/41	80/49	85/55	84/54	77/45	66/35	52/23	46/18
Denver	43/17	46/19	51/25	61/34	70/44	81/53	87/59	86/58	78/49	67/38	53/27	46/20
Durango	38/12	43/17	51/24	60/30	69/36	80/43	83/51	82/49	75/42	64/32	53/23	39/13
Grand Junction	35/17	42/23	53/30	65/40	75/49	86/57	93/64	89/62	81/54	67/43	50/28	38/20
Steamboat Springs	28/1	33/4	42/15	53/24	64/32	75/36	82/42	81/41	72/33	59/24	41/13	29/2
Sterling	38/10	44/15	54/21	62/32	70/43	81/52	87/57	86/55	78/45	67/32	53/20	36/11

From the records of The Weather Channel Interactive, Inc.

Good Facts To Know

ABOUT THE STATE

POPULATION: 5,029,196.

AREA: 104,247 square miles; ranks 8th.

CAPITAL: Denver.

HIGHEST POINT: 14,433 ft., Mount Elbert.

LOWEST POINT: 3,315 ft., Arickaree River.

TIME ZONE(S): Mountain. DST.

GAMBLING

MINIMUM AGE FOR GAMBLING: 21.

REGULATIONS

TEEN DRIVING LAWS: No unrelated passengers under age 21 for the first six months; no more than one unrelated passenger under age 21 for the following six months. For the first year as a licensed driver, driving is not permitted midnight-5 a.m. Minimum age for an unrestricted driver's license is 17. For more information about Colorado driver's license regulations, phone (303) 205-5600.

SEAT BELT/CHILD RESTRAINT LAWS: Seat belts are required for driver and front-seat passengers ages 16 and over. Children ages 8-16 are required to be in a seat belt; a booster seat is required for children ages 4-8; child restraints are required for children under age 4 and under 40 pounds; rear-facing car seats are required for children under age 1 and under 20 pounds. AAA recommends the use of seat belts and appropriate child restraints for the driver and all passengers.

CELLPHONE RESTRICTIONS: Drivers under 18 are not permitted to use cell phones. Texting is prohibited for all drivers.

HELMETS FOR MOTORCYCLISTS: Required for all riders under 18.

RADAR DETECTORS: Permitted. Prohibited for use by commercial vehicles.

MOVE OVER LAW: Driver is required to slow down and vacate a lane nearest police, fire and rescue vehicles stopped on the side of the road using audible or flashing signals. Law includes tow trucks.

FIREARMS LAWS: Vary by state and/or county. Contact Colorado Bureau of Investigation, 690 Kipling St., Denver, CO 80215; phone (303) 239-4201.

HOLIDAYS

HOLIDAYS: Jan. 1 ▪ Martin Luther King Jr. Day, Jan. (3rd Mon.) ▪ Washington's Birthday/Presidents Day, Feb. (3rd Mon.); Memorial Day, May (last Mon.) ▪ July 4 ▪ Labor Day, Sept. (first Mon.) ▪ Veterans Day, Nov. 11 ▪ Thanksgiving, Nov. (4th Thurs.) ▪ and Christmas, Dec. 25.

MONEY

TAXES: Colorado's statewide sales tax is 2.9 percent, with local options for additional increments. Cities and counties also may levy a lodging tax. Additional taxes, such as a tribal tax, can be levied.

VISITOR INFORMATION

INFORMATION CENTERS: State welcome centers that provide details about state attractions, accommodations, historic sites, parks and events are at Alamosa, 601 State St. ▪ Burlington, on I-70 between exits 437 and 438 ▪ Cortez, US 160 at 928 E. Main St. ▪ Dinosaur, US 40 at 101 E. Stegosaurus St. ▪ Fort Collins, I-25 at 3745 E. Prospect Rd. ▪ Fruita, I-70 at exit 19 ▪ Julesburg, I-76 exit 180 at 20934 CR 28 ▪ Lamar, US 50 at 109 E. Beech St. ▪ Red Rocks, 18300 W. Alameda Pkwy. at Red Rocks Park and Amphitheatre ▪ and Trinidad, I-25 exit 14 at 309 Nevada Ave.

FURTHER INFORMATION FOR VISITORS:
Colorado Tourism Office
1625 Broadway, Suite 2700
Denver, CO 80202-4729
(303) 892-3840
(800) 265-6723

NATIONAL FOREST INFORMATION:
U.S. Forest Service
Rocky Mountain Region
740 Simms St.
Lakewood, CO 80401
(303) 275-5350
(877) 444-6777 (reservations)

FISHING AND HUNTING REGULATIONS:
Colorado Parks and Wildlife
1313 Sherman St., Room 618
6th Floor
Denver, CO 80203
(303) 297-1192

SKIING INFORMATION:
Colorado Ski Country USA
1444 Wazee St., Suite 320
Denver, CO 80202
(303) 837-0793

Choose real ratings you can trust
from professional inspectors who've been there

Colorado Annual Events
Please call ahead to confirm event details.

JANUARY
- National Western Stock Show / Denver 888-551-5004
- Winterskol / Aspen 970-925-1940
- International Snow Sculpture Championships Breckenridge 888-533-9881

FEBRUARY
- Denver Restaurant Week Denver 303-892-1112
- Colorado Springs Home & Landscape Expo Colorado Springs 952-881-5030
- Winter Carnival Steamboat Springs 970-879-0695

MARCH
- Denver March Powwow Denver 303-934-8045
- Frozen Dead Guy Days Nederland 303-506-1048
- Ski Joring and Crystal Carnival / Leadville 719-486-3900

APRIL
- Breckenridge Spring Fever Festival / Breckenridge 800-936-5573
- Coca-Cola Classic Spring Splash at Winter Park Winter Park 970-726-1564
- Greeley Jazz Festival Greeley 970-351-2394

MAY
- Indian Market and Powwow Morrison 303-839-1671
- Downtown Art + Music Festival / Grand Junction 970-245-9697
- Music and Blossom Festival Cañon City 719-239-1743

JUNE
- Bluegrass and Roots Music Festival / Palisade 970-464-5602
- Colorado Barbecue Challenge / Frisco 800-424-1554
- Colorado Wine Festival Manitou Springs 719-685-5089

JULY
- Crested Butte Wildflower Festival / Crested Butte 970-349-2571
- Colorado Dragon Boat Festival / Denver 877-716-2628
- Pikes Peak or Bust Rodeo Colorado Springs 719-884-1199

AUGUST
- True West Railfest Durango 888-872-4607
- Boom Days and International Pack Burro Race / Leadville 719-486-1182
- Gold Rush Days Buena Vista 719-395-6612

SEPTEMBER
- Blues & Brews Festival Telluride 970-728-8037
- Colorado Balloon Classic Colorado Springs 719-471-4833
- Longs Peak Scottish-Irish Highland Festival Estes Park 970-586-6308

OCTOBER
- Cider Days / Lakewood 303-987-7859
- Glenwood's Historic Ghost Walk / Glenwood Springs 970-945-4448
- Emma Crawford Coffin Races and Parade Manitou Springs 719-685-5089

NOVEMBER
- Victorian Christmas at Miramont Castle Manitou Springs 719-685-1011
- Holiday Food and Gift Festival / Denver 888-412-5015
- Mile High Holidays / Denver 303-892-1505

DECEMBER
- Georgetown Christmas Market / Georgetown 303-569-2840
- New Year's Eve Fireworks Denver 303-534-6161
- Winter Festival and Parade of Lights / Grand Junction 970-245-9697

Colorado Balloon Classic,
Colorado Springs

Red Rocks Park &
Amphitheatre, Morrison

Kayaking in Eldorado
Canyon

Georgetown Loop Railroad

Explore some trails in the Rocky Mountains

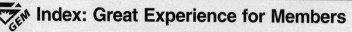 Index: Great Experience for Members

AAA editor's picks of exceptional note

Denver Museum of Nature & Science / Garden of the Gods Park / Mesa Verde National Park / State Capitol

See Orientation map on p. 34 for corresponding grid coordinates, if applicable.

Colorado
Atlas Section

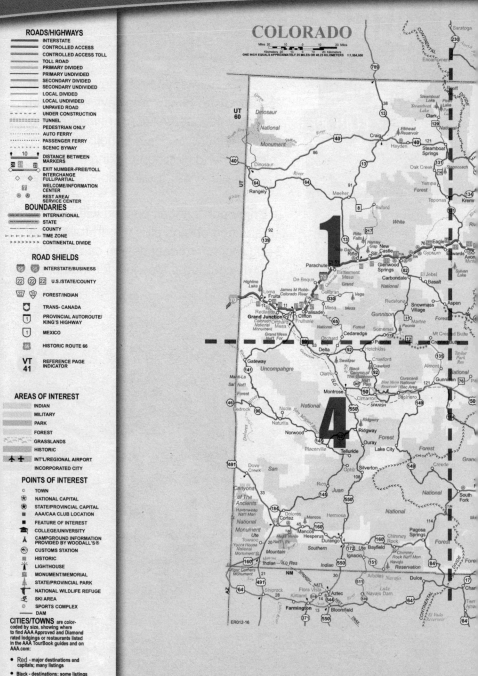

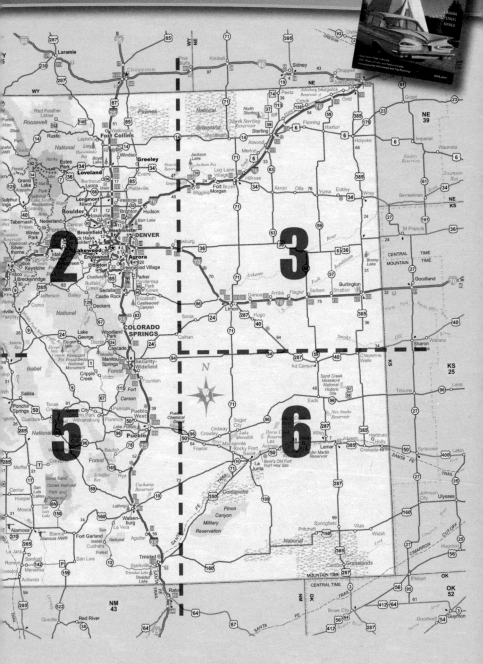

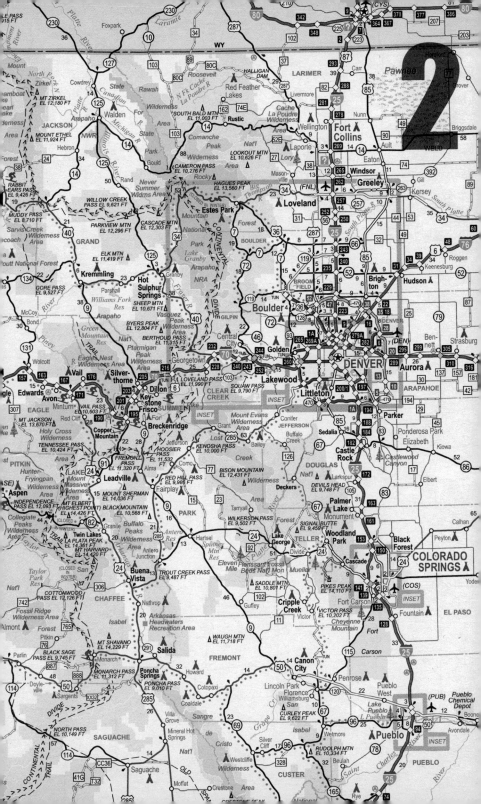

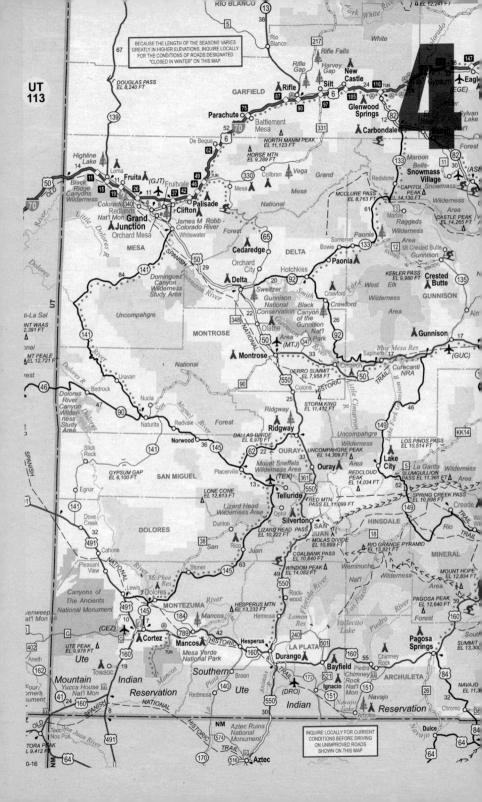

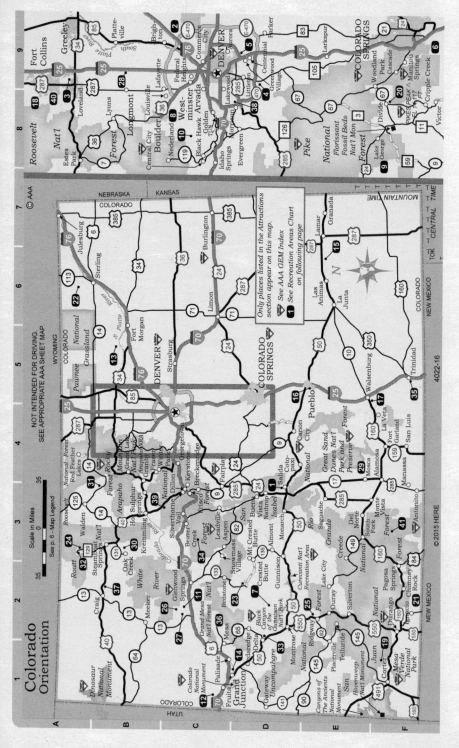

Colorado Orientation

Recreation Areas Chart

The map location numerals in column 2 show an area's location on the preceding map.

	MAP LOCATION	CAMPING	PICNICKING	HIKING TRAILS	BOATING	BOAT RAMP	BOAT RENTAL	FISHING	SWIMMING	PETS ON LEASH	BICYCLE TRAILS	WINTER SPORTS	VISITOR CENTER	LODGE/CABINS	FOOD SERVICE
NATIONAL PARKS *(See place listings.)*															
Black Canyon of the Gunnison (D-2) 30,750 acres. Kayaking, rafting, rock climbing.		•	•	•				•		•			•	•	
Great Sand Dunes National Park and Preserve (E-4) 149,137 acres. Nature programs. Horseback riding; nature trails.		•	•	•						•			•		
Mesa Verde (F-1) 52,000 acres.		•	•	•						•			•	•	•
Rocky Mountain (B-4) 265,800 acres. Cross-country skiing, rock climbing, sledding, snowshoeing; equestrian camping, horse rental.		•	•	•				•		•			•	•	
NATIONAL FORESTS *(See place listings.)*															
Arapaho and Roosevelt/Pawnee National Grassland (A-3, A-4, B-4) 1,280,000 acres. North-central Colorado.		•	•	•	•	•	•	•	•	•	•	•	•		
Grand Mesa—Uncompahgre—Gunnison (D-1) 2,952,549 acres. West-central Colorado.		•	•	•	•	•	•	•		•		•	•		
Pike (E-8) 1,105,704 acres. Central Colorado. Hunting; horse rental.		•	•	•	•	•		•		•		•	•		•
Rio Grande (E-3) 1,851,792 acres. South-central Colorado. Horse camping, hunting, scuba diving, skiing, sledding, snowmobiling, snowtubing; horse trails.		•	•	•	•	•		•	•	•		•	•		
Routt (A-2) 1.26 million acres. Northwest Colorado. Cross-country skiing, horse camping, hunting, snowmobiling, snowshoeing; horseback trails, motorized vehicle trails.		•	•	•	•	•		•	•	•		•	•		
San Isabel (D-3) 1,109,782 acres. South-central Colorado. Hunting; horse rental.		•	•	•	•	•		•		•		•	•		•
San Juan (E-1) 1,881,586 acres. Southwestern Colorado. Bird watching, kayaking; tidal pools		•	•	•	•	•		•		•		•	•		
White River (B-2) 2.3 million acres. Northwestern and north-central Colorado. Horseback riding, hunting, ice skating, skiing, sledding, snowboarding, snowmobiling, snowshoeing, waterskiing, windsurfing; winter sports.		•	•	•	•	•		•		•		•	•		
NATIONAL RECREATION AREAS *(See place listings.)*															
Arapaho (B-4) 36,000 acres. North-central Colorado. Bird watching, horse camping, horse riding, hunting, ice fishing, skiing, snowboarding, snowmobiling, water skiing.		•	•	•	•	•	•	•	•	•	•	•	•		
Curecanti (E-2) 41,971 acres. West-central Colorado. Bird watching, horseback riding, hunting.		•	•	•	•	•	•	•		•		•	•		•
STATE															
Arkansas Headwaters Recreation Area (D-4) 6,190 acres 150 mi. along the Arkansas River from Leadville to Lake Pueblo State Park. Main access roads: US 24, 285 and 50. Nature programs. Cross-country skiing, gold panning, ice fishing, rock climbing, snowmobiling, snowshoeing, white-water rafting and boating, winter camping; horse trails, off-road vehicle trails.	**1**	•	•	•	•	•		•		•		•	•		
Barr Lake (C-9) 2,609 acres n.e. of Denver off I-76 and Bromley Ln. Nature programs. Archery, bird-watching, cross-country skiing, hunting, ice fishing, snowshoeing; horse rental, horse trails.	**2**		•	•	•	•	•		•	•	•	•	•		
Boyd Lake (A-8) 2,186 acres 1 mi. e. of Loveland on US 34. Jet skiing, water skiing; marina, swimming beach.	**3**	•	•	•	•	•	•	•	•	•	•		•		•
Chatfield (D-8) 6,750 acres 8 mi. s.w. of Denver at SR 470 and Wadsworth. Nature programs. Cross-country skiing, hot air ballooning, ice fishing, jet skiing, sailboarding, snowshoeing, water skiing, winter camping; horse rental, horseshoe pits, marina, volleyball courts.	**4**	•	•	•	•	•	•	•	•	•	•	•	•		•
Cherry Creek (D-9) 4,795 acres 10 mi. s.e. of Denver near I-225 and Parker Rd. Nature programs. Bird-watching, cross-country skiing, horseback riding, ice skating, jet skiing, sledding, snow-shoeing, snow tubing, water skiing, winter camping; horse rental, marina.	**5**	•	•	•	•	•	•	•	•	•	•	•	•		

Recreation Areas Chart

The map location numerals in column 2 show an area's location on the preceding map.

	MAP LOCATION	CAMPING	PICNICKING	HIKING TRAILS	BOATING	BOAT RAMP	BOAT RENTAL	FISHING	SWIMMING	PETS ON LEASH	BICYCLE TRAILS	WINTER SPORTS	VISITOR CENTER	LODGE/CABINS	FOOD SERVICE
Cheyenne Mountain (F-9) 1,680 acres on the s.e. side of Colorado Springs off SR 115 across from Fort Carson Gate 1. Nature programs. Archery, geocaching; horse trails.	6	•	•	•							•		•		•
Crawford (D-2) 1,218 acres 1 mi. s. of Crawford on SR 92. Cross-country skiing, hunting, ice fishing, jet skiing, scuba diving, snowshoeing, snow tubing, water skiing. Nature programs.	7	•	•	•	•	•		•	•	•	•	•	•	•	
Eldorado Canyon (C-8) 845 acres 7 mi. s.w. of Boulder on SR 93. Nature programs. Cross-country skiing, hunting, snowshoeing, technical rock climbing; horseback trails, nature trails.	8		•	•				•		•	•	•	•		
Eleven Mile (F-8) 7,662 acres about 11 mi. s.w. of Lake George off US 24 on CR 92. Nature programs. Backcountry camping, bird-watching, cross-country skiing, hunting, ice fishing, ice skating, sailboarding; marina, nature trails.	9	•	•	•	•	•	•	•		•	•	•	•		
Golden Gate Canyon (C-8) 12,000 acres 12 mi. w. of Golden off SR 93. Nature programs. Cross-country skiing, hunting, ice fishing, ice skating, rock climbing, snowshoeing; cabins, horseback trails, nature trails, yurts.	10	•	•	•				•		•	•	•	•	•	
Harvey Gap (C-2) 320 acres 5 mi. n. of Silt off US 6. Cross-country skiing, hunting, ice fishing, snowshoeing, windsurfing.	11		•					•				•			
Highline Lake (C-1) 824 acres 14 mi. n.w. of Grand Junction off I-70 and SR 139. Nature programs. Bird-watching, hunting, ice fishing, ice skating, jet skiing, water skiing; jet ski rental, playground.	12	•	•	•	•	•	•	•	•	•	•	•	•		
Jackson Lake (B-5) 3,350 acres 20 mi. n.w. of Fort Morgan off SR 144. Nature programs. Bird-watching, geocaching, hunting, ice fishing, jet skiing, sailboarding, water skiing, wildlife viewing, winter camping; marina, nature trail, off-road vehicle track.	13	•	•	•	•	•	•	•	•	•	•	•	•	•	
James M. Robb-Colorado River (D-1) 475 acres in five sections along the Colorado River through the Grand Junction area from Island Acres to Fruita. Nature programs. Bird-watching hunting, ice fishing, ice skating, white-water rafting, winter camping, snowmobiling; nature trails.	14	•	•	•	•	•		•	•	•	•	•	•		
John Martin Reservoir (E-7) 5,700 acres 15 mi. e. of Las Animas off US 50. Nature programs. Bird-watching, geocaching, hunting, jet skiing, water skiing, winter camping. (See Las Animas p. 221.)	15	•	•	•	•	•		•	•	•	•	•	•		
Lake Pueblo (D-5) 17,155 acres 6 mi. w. of Pueblo on SR 96. Nature programs. Horseback riding, hunting, jet skiing, sailboarding, water skiing, white-water rafting; marina.	16	•	•	•	•	•	•	•	•	•	•		•		•
Lathrop (F-5) 1,596 acres 3 mi. w. of Walsenburg on US 160. Archery, bird-watching, golf, hunting, jet skiing, kayaking, water skiing, winter camping; horse trails, nature trails.	17	•	•	•	•	•		•	•	•	•	•	•		
Lory (A-8) 2,419 acres 15 mi. n.w. of Fort Collins off US 287. Back-country camping, canoeing, cross-country skiing, geocaching, hunting, kayaking, rafting, rock climbing, snowshoeing, water skiing; horseback trails.	18		•	•	•			•		•	•	•	•		
Mancos (F-2) 577 acres .25 mi. n. of Mancos on SR 184, 4 mi. e. on CR 42, then .5 mi. w. on CR N. Nature programs. Bird-watching, cross-country skiing, hunting, ice fishing, snowmobiling, snowshoeing, snow tubing; cabins, horseback trails, yurts.	19	•	•					•		•	•	•		•	
Mueller (F-9) 5,121 acres 3.5 mi. s. of Divide off SR 67. Nature programs. Cross-country skiing, hunting, sledding, snowshoeing; cabins, horseback trails, yurts.	20	•	•	•							•	•	•	•	
Navajo (F-2) 17,600 acres 2 mi. s. of Arboles on CR 982. Cross-country skiing, hunting, jet skiing, water skiing; cabins, horse-back trails, marina, nature trails, yurts.	21	•	•	•	•	•		•		•	•		•	•	
North Sterling (A-6) 3,000 acres 12 mi. n. of Sterling via N. 7th Ave. Nature programs. Archery, bird-watching, horseback riding, hunting, ice fishing, jet skiing, sailboarding, star gazing, water skiing, winter camping; horseback trails. (See Sterling p. 263.)	22	•	•	•	•	•	•	•	•	•	•	•	•		•
Paonia (D-2) 1,816 acres 14 mi. n. of Paonia on SR 133. Cross-country skiing, horseback riding, hunting, ice fishing, ice skating, jet skiing, water skiing.	23	•	•		•	•		•		•		•	•		

Recreation Areas Chart

The map location numerals in column 2 show an area's location on the preceding map.

	MAP LOCATION	CAMPING	PICNICKING	HIKING TRAILS	BOATING	BOAT RAMP	BOAT RENTAL	FISHING	SWIMMING	PETS ON LEASH	BICYCLE TRAILS	WINTER SPORTS	VISITOR CENTER	LODGE/CABINS	FOOD SERVICE
Pearl Lake (A-3) 274 acres 25 mi. n. of Steamboat Springs off CR 129. Backcountry camping, cross-country skiing, ice fishing, snowmobiling, snowshoeing; cabins, yurts.	24	•	•	•	•	•		•		•		•		•	
Ridgway (E-2) 3,201 acres 4 mi. n. of Ridgway on US 550. Bird-watching, cross-country skiing, geocaching, gold panning, hot-air ballooning, hunting, ice fishing, rock climbing, sailboarding, sledding, snowmobiling, snowshoeing, water skiing, white-water rafting, windsurfing; cabins, volleyball court, yurts.	25	•	•	•	•	•		•	•	•	•	•	•	•	
Rifle Falls (C-2) 93 acres 14 mi. n. of Rifle on SR 325. Nature programs. Cross-country skiing, ice fishing, jet skiing, snowshoeing, water skiing, winter camping; triple waterfall.	26	•	•					•	•	•	•	•			
Rifle Gap (C-2) 2,535 acres 10 mi. n. of Rifle on SR 325. Nature programs. Cross-country skiing, ice fishing, jet skiing, snowmobiling, snowshoeing, water skiing; nature trails.	27	•	•	•				•	•	•		•		•	
St. Vrain (B-9) 130 acres 7 mi. e. of Longmont off I-25. Bird-watching, ice fishing, jet skiing, snowmobiling, water skiing, winter camping; nature trails.	28	•	•	•				•		•	•	•		•	
San Luis (E-4) 586 acres e. of Mosca on Six Mile Ln. Bird-watching, hunting, horse trails; wildlife area.	29	•	•	•				•		•					
Stagecoach (B-3) 1,641 acres 6 mi. w. of Oak Creek off CR 14. Bird-watching, cross-country skiing, hunting, ice fishing, jet skiing, sailboarding, snowmobiling, snowshoeing, water skiing, wildlife viewing, winter camping; sand volleyball court, horse trails.	30	•	•	•	•	•	•	•	•	•	•	•		•	
State Forest (A-4) 72,130 acres 21 mi. s.e. of Walden off SR 14. Nature programs. Bird-watching, cross-country skiing, geocaching, hunting, ice fishing, sledding, snowmobiling, snowshoeing, tubing; cabins, equestrian camping, horseback trails, motorized vehicles trail, nature trails, yurts.	31	•	•	•	•			•		•	•	•	•	•	•
Steamboat Lake (A-2) 2,773 acres 25 mi. n. of Steamboat Springs on CR 129. Nature programs. Backcountry camping, bird-watching, cross-country skiing, hunting, ice fishing, jet skiing, sailboarding, snowmobiling, snowshoeing, water skiing, winter camping; cabins, horseback trails, yurts.	32	•	•	•	•	•	•	•	•	•	•	•	•	•	
Sweitzer Lake (D-1) 210 acres 1.5 mi. s.e. of Delta off US 50. Bird-watching, canoeing, hunting, jet skiing, sailboarding, scuba diving, waterfowl hunting, water skiing; horseback trails.	33		•	•	•	•		•	•	•	•	•			
Sylvan Lake (C-3) 1,272 acres 10 mi. s. of Eagle on Brush Creek Rd. Nature programs. Cross-country skiing, horseback riding, hunting, ice fishing, ice skating, sledding, snowmobiling, snow-shoeing; cabins, horse trails, motorized vehicles trail, yurts.	34	•	•	•	•	•	•	•	•	•	•	•		•	
Trinidad Lake (F-5) 2,800 acres 3 mi. w. of Trinidad on SR 12. Nature programs. Cross-country skiing, ice fishing, jet skiing, snowshoeing, water skiing; horseback trails, volleyball courts.	35	•	•	•	•	•		•		•	•	•	•		
Vega (C-2) 2,730 acres 8 mi. e. of Collbran on CR 330. Historic. Bird-watching, cross-country skiing, horseback riding, hunting, ice fishing, ice skating, jet skiing, sledding, snowmobiling, snow-shoeing, snow tubing, water skiing; cabins, horse corrals, horse trails, motorized vehicles trail, nature trails, yurts.	36	•	•	•	•	•		•		•	•	•		•	
Yampa River (B-2) 70 acres 2 mi. w. of Hayden on US 40, managing 125 mi. of the Yampa River with 13 public access sites. Nature programs. Bird-watching, hunting, white-water rafting; nature trail, sand volleyball courts.	37	•	•	•	•			•		•		•		•	
OTHER															
Bear Creek Lake (D-8) 2,600 acres 14 mi. s.w. of Denver on US 285. Archery range, horse rental, horse trails, swimming beach.	38	•	•	•	•			•	•	•	•				
Green Mountain (B-3) 3,563 acres 17 mi. s. of Kremmling on SR 9. Hunting, ice fishing.	39	•			•	•	•	•	•	•		•			•
Horsetooth Reservoir (A-8) 3,900 acres 3 mi. w. of Fort Collins on CR 52. Rock climbing, scuba diving, waterskiing; nature trails.	40	•	•	•	•	•		•	•	•			•	•	

Recreation Areas Chart The map location numerals in column 2 show an area's location on the preceding map.	MAP LOCATION	CAMPING	PICNICKING	HIKING TRAILS	BOATING	BOAT RAMP	BOAT RENTAL	FISHING	SWIMMING	PETS ON LEASH	BICYCLE TRAILS	WINTER SPORTS	VISITOR CENTER	LODGE/CABINS	FOOD SERVICE
Platoro Reservoir (F-3) 22 mi. w. of Antonito on SR 17, then 23 mi. n.w. on access road. Horse camping, hunting, ice fishing, scuba diving; horseback trails, nature trails.	**41**	•	•	•	•	•	•		•	•	•	•	•		

ALAMOSA (F-4) pop. 8,780, elev. 7,544'
• Restaurants p. 40

When the Denver & Rio Grande Western Railroad reached the stagecoach stop on the cottonwood (alamosa)-blanketed bend of the Rio Grande, it brought with it the houses, stores and churches from its former terminus, Garland City. In a matter of days, Alamosa was in business. As the rails extended beyond the town, Alamosa became the transportation and trading center for the San Luis Valley.

The valley—a high, flat, semiarid plain about 50 miles wide and 125 miles long—once was the bed of an ancient lake. Irrigated by the Rio Grande and artesian wells, it is one of the most productive farming areas in the state. Red McClure potatoes, lettuce and barley are among crops shipped from Alamosa. Many wetlands and lakes make this a popular stopping place for migratory birds, including the 20,000 cranes that grace the valley each spring.

Great Sand Dunes National Park and Preserve (see place listing p. 207) lies 38 miles northeast of Alamosa; recreational opportunities such as camping, hiking and birding are available in the park. Fishing, boating and soaking in hot springs are available in the valley and nearby mountain ranges.

Colorado Welcome Center at Alamosa: 610 State Ave., Alamosa, CO 81101. **Phone:** (719) 589-4840 or (800) 258-7597.

ALAMOSA NATIONAL WILDLIFE REFUGE, 3 mi. e. on US 160, then 2 mi. s. on El Rancho Ln., is a 12,000-acre refuge. Ducks, geese and shorebirds nest on the marshes. Bald eagles are common November through March. A 2-mile nature trail along the Rio Grande, a 3.5-mile driving tour and the Bluff Overlook provide wildlife viewing opportunities. A visitor center offers interpretive displays. **Hours:** Refuge daily dawn-dusk. Visitor center hours vary according to volunteer availability; phone ahead to confirm schedule. Closed major holidays. **Cost:** Free. **Phone:** (719) 589-4021.

RIO GRANDE SCENIC RAILROAD departs from the station at 601 State Ave. at jct. 6th St. The excursion train carries passengers through the Sangre de Cristo mountains, surrounded by dramatic 14,000-foot peaks along the edge of the San Isabel National Forest. Weekday excursions go past serene high mountain meadows and spectacular canyons to eventually arrive in the historic small town of La Veta (see place listing p. 221) for a 1-hour lunch and shopping stop.

Both one-way and round-trips are available. Weekend summer train trips to the summit (June through September) from Alamosa feature outdoor performances at a train and concert venue are offered. **Hours:** Excursion trains depart from Alamosa daily at 9:30 a.m., late May-early Sept. Holiday trains operate Nov.-Dec. Phone ahead to confirm schedule. **Cost:** Round-trip fares $49-$149; $39-$139 (ages 2-12). **Phone:** (719) 587-0520 or (877) 726-7245.

BEST WESTERN ALAMOSA INN (719)589-2567

Motel
$73-$160

AAA Benefit: Save 10% or more every day and earn 10% bonus points!

Address: 2005 W Main St 81101 **Location:** On US 160, 1 mi w of center. **Facility:** 53 units. 2 stories (no elevator); exterior corridors. **Pool(s):** heated indoor. **Activities:** hot tub, picnic facilities, exercise room. **Guest Services:** coin laundry. **Featured Amenity:** full hot breakfast.

COMFORT INN & SUITES (719)587-9000

▼▼▼ Hotel $89-$200 **Address:** 6301 US 160 W 81101 **Location:** 2.3 mi w of center. **Facility:** 68 units. 2 stories, interior corridors. **Pool(s):** heated indoor. **Activities:** hot tub, playground, picnic facilities, exercise room. **Guest Services:** coin laundry, area transportation.

FAIRFIELD INN & SUITES BY MARRIOTT ALAMOSA
(719)587-4000

▼▼▼ Hotel $75-$172 **Address:** 721 Mariposa St 81101 **Location:** 2 mi w of center to Mariposa St, just n, then just w. **Facility:** 57 units. 3 stories, interior corridors. **Pool(s):** heated indoor. **Activities:** hot tub, exercise room. **Guest Services:** valet and coin laundry.

AAA Benefit: Members save 5% or more!

HAMPTON INN ALAMOSA 719/480-6023

▼▼▼ Hotel. Rates not provided. **Address:** 710 Mariposa St 81101 **Location:** 2 mi w of center to Mariposa St, just n. **Facility:** 80 units. 4 stories, interior corridors. **Pool(s):** heated indoor. **Activities:** hot tub, exercise room. **Guest Services:** valet and coin laundry.

AAA Benefit: Members save up to 10%!

HOLIDAY INN EXPRESS 719/589-4026

▼▼▼ Hotel. Rates not provided. **Address:** 3418 Mariposa St 81101 **Location:** On US 160, 2 mi w of center. **Facility:** 74 units. 3 stories, interior corridors. **Pool(s):** heated indoor. **Activities:** sauna, hot tub, exercise room. **Guest Services:** valet and coin laundry.

SUPER 8 OF ALAMOSA (719)589-6447

Motel
$60-$150

Address: 2505 Main St 81101 **Location:** On US 160, 1.3 mi w. **Facility:** 57 units. 2 stories (no elevator); interior corridors. **Pool(s):** heated indoor. **Activities:** hot tub. **Guest Services:** coin laundry.

WHERE TO EAT

BISTRO RIALTO RISTORANTE ITALIANO   719/589-3039
♥♥ Italian. Casual Dining. $6-$19 **AAA Inspector Notes:** Located in a historic building, this charming Italian café offers calzones, sandwiches, pizzas, salads and several types of lasagna. Italian seasoned prime rib and the lobster ravioli with creamy basil pesto are popular. You can create your own entrée by choosing a pasta, sauce and meat. Vegetarian menu items and gluten-free pasta are available. **Features:** full bar. **Address:** 716 Main St 81101 **Location:** West end of Main St; downtown. **Parking:** street only.
Ⓛ Ⓓ

CALVILLO'S MEXICAN RESTAURANT & BAR   719/587-5500
♥♥ Mexican. Casual Dining. $10-$11 **AAA Inspector Notes:** This spacious eatery serves an amazing buffet of flavorful Mexican favorites. Be sure to try the hand-made tortillas that are made fresh in front of you. Sample items include tamales, enchiladas, and build-your-own tacos with fresh made salsas. The dishes may not be labeled, but feel free to ask the friendly staff members if you have questions. **Features:** full bar, patio dining, senior menu, happy hour. **Address:** 400 Main St 81101 **Location:** On US 160, 0.5 mi e.
Ⓑ Ⓛ Ⓓ

ROAST CAFE   719/587-2326
♥ Coffee/Tea. Quick Serve. $6-$10 **AAA Inspector Notes:** Relax and enjoy your favorite espresso drink with breakfast, or sip a pint of craft beer with a gourmet sandwich at this casual eatery. Roasted in house, the joe here might be the best in town. The charming décor mixes touches of the historic building, like exposed brick walls, with colorful paintings of flowers. **Features:** beer only. **Address:** 420 San Juan Ave 81101 **Location:** Jct US 160 westbound, just n. **Parking:** street only. Ⓑ Ⓛ Ⓓ

SAN LUIS VALLEY BREWING   719/587-2337
♥♥ American. Casual Dining. $8-$23 **AAA Inspector Notes:** This is a comfortable spot to enjoy a Colorado microbrew and sample locally made pork sausage. The diverse menu offers a variety of burgers, steaks, entrée salads, pastas and sandwiches. **Features:** full bar. **Address:** 631 Main St 81101 **Location:** US 160 westbound, between San Juan and State aves. **Parking:** street only.
Ⓛ Ⓓ

SAN LUIS VALLEY PIZZA COMPANY   719/589-4749
♥♥ Pizza. Casual Dining. $7-$20 **AAA Inspector Notes:** Loved by locals, this casual eatery offers tasty pizzas, calzones and strombolis. Build your own pizza or choose from the creative gourmet options, such as the buffalo (spicy buffalo-style chicken breast, barbecue sauce and cheddar cheese), or the bandito (homemade chorizo, hot green chile, and cheddar and mozzarella cheese). Kids of all ages will enjoy the arcade games in the back room. **Features:** full bar. **Address:** 2069 W 1st St 81101 **Location:** On US 160, 1.1 mi w of center. Ⓛ Ⓓ

WIZE APPLES   719/937-2204
♥♥ Burgers. Casual Dining. $7-$10 **AAA Inspector Notes:** Locals love this cozy, hole-in-the-wall burger joint. Standard and innovative toppings are available for these giant burgers, which come with a massive portion of savory, crunchy, hand-cut fries. **Features:** full bar. **Address:** 119 Broadway Ave 81101 **Location:** On US 160, jct SR 17. Ⓛ Ⓓ

ALMONT (D-3)

Originally christened Fishers after the man who first settled the area, in 1881 the town was named Almont after a famous stallion of the time. Near the headwaters of the Gunnison River, where the Taylor and East rivers meet, Almont is an outdoor playground with a plethora of activities including fishing, hiking, white-water rafting, kayaking, horseback riding, mountain biking and cross-country skiing.

RECREATIONAL ACTIVITIES
Fishing
- **Almont Anglers Fly Shop and Guide Service** departs from jct. SR 135 and CR 742 at the Almont Resort. **Hours:** Daily dawn-dusk, Mar.-Nov. **Phone:** (970) 641-7404.

White-water Rafting
- **Three Rivers Outfitting** is n. on SR 135, then .25 mi. e. on CR 742 to Three Rivers Resort. Other activities are offered. **Hours:** Daily dawn-dusk, May-Oct. **Phone:** (970) 641-1303 or (888) 761-3474.

ANTONITO (F-3) pop. 781, elev. 7,882'

Originating with the arrival of the railroads, as did many Colorado settlements, Antonito is still a shipping point for perlite and lava rock of the southern San Luis Valley. It also is the Colorado terminal for the Cumbres & Toltec Scenic Railroad and offers many opportunities for recreation including mountain biking, wildlife viewing, sightseeing, hunting and fishing.

Conejos County Museum and Visitors Center: 5045 US 285, P.O. Box 829, Antonito, CO 81120. **Phone:** (719) 376-2049 or (800) 835-1098.

CUMBRES & TOLTEC SCENIC RAILROAD trips depart from the Antonito Depot at jct. US 285 and SR 17. Built in the 1880s, the line connected commercial outposts and mining camps in the Rocky Mountain region and was part of the original Denver & Rio Grande railway system. The 64-mile line, jointly owned by the states of Colorado and New Mexico, has departures from both Antonito, Colo. and Chama, N.M.

All-day trips on vintage, narrow-gauge, coal-burning steam trains afford spectacular views of the scenic San Juan and Sangre de Cristo mountain ranges. Passengers may choose from three types of class: coach, tourist or parlor. The parlor car offers refreshments and the services of an attendant.

Osier, an old stagecoach stop, is the transfer and lunch point. From there, guests can choose to continue on by train to Chama or return to Antonito. Various combinations of train and motor coach transportation are offered; all trips include lunch. One-way and sunset dinner trips also are available.

AAA offices in Colorado and New Mexico can make reservations. **Hours:** Round-trip train excursions depart from Antonito and Chama daily at 10 a.m., late May to mid-Oct. **Cost:** Round-trip, coach-class train or one-way, coach-class train with bus return $95; $49 (ages 2-12). Tourist-class fare $139; $69 (ages 2-12). Round-trip parlor car fare late May-early Sept. $179. Mid-Sept. to mid-Oct. $189. All fares include lunch. Children are permitted in coach and tourist class only.

Reservations are recommended. **Phone:** (888) 286-2737. *(See ad this page.)*

ARAPAHO AND ROOSEVELT NATIONAL FORESTS AND PAWNEE NATIONAL GRASSLAND (A-3, A-4, B-4)

Elevations in the forests range from 4,300 ft. at Pawnee National Grassland to 14,270 ft. at Grays Peak in Arapaho National Forest. Refer to AAA maps for additional elevation information.

In north-central Colorado past and present co-exist within the 1,280,000 mountainous acres of the Arapaho and Roosevelt National Forests, which embrace some of the higher and more visited areas of the region. Creaking ghost towns in the Arapaho region set off lively ski resorts, and the rotted road-beds of abandoned narrow-gauge railways contrast with the well-maintained highways that provide access to this rooftop of the continent.

One of these modern routes, the road to the 14,260-foot summit of Mount Evans, is part of a popular day trip from Denver. The highway, SR 5, is commonly known as Mount Evans Highway or Mount Evans Road. **Note:** There is a $10 fee per private vehicle to use the developed sites located along the Mount Evans Road and the Summit of Mount Evans. The Indian Peaks and Mount Evans wilderness areas can be explored on foot or horseback; camping permits are required at Indian Peaks. Trout fishing is

▼ *See AAA listing this page* ▼

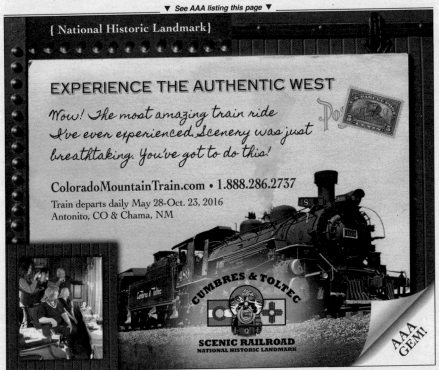

available in the many lakes and streams as well as in Granby and Green Mountain reservoirs. Hunting is available in season with a valid license.

Major winter sports developments within the forests are Eldora Mountain Resort, Loveland Ski Area and Winter Park Resort. An alpine slide, mountain bike trails and chairlift rides also are available.

In a region dotted with alpine lakes and divided by high mountains and deep canyons, Roosevelt National Forest sits along the eastern slope of the Rockies. Numerous small glaciers, remnants of ancient ice fields, and the backcountry areas afford magnificent scenery and varied recreational facilities.

Scenic SR 14, the mountainous route over Cameron Pass and along the Cache La Poudre River, provides access to the adjoining Routt National Forest (see place listing p. 253). A second scenic route, the Peak to Peak National Scenic Byway (SR 7/72/119), connects Estes Park with the mining communities of Black Hawk (see place listing p. 56) and Central City (see place listing p. 77).

Another scenic route, the Colorado River Headwaters, follows the Colorado River 75 miles westward from SR 34 in Grand Lake, SR 40 in Kremmling and along CR 1 in State Bridge.

The fragile uplands of the Rawah Wilderness are accessible only by foot or horseback. Hunting for deer, elk, mountain sheep and bears is permitted in season with a valid license. Other wilderness areas include Byers Peak, Cache La Poudre, Comanche Peak, James Peak, Neota, Never Summer, Ptarmigan Peak, Vasquez Peak and Mount Evans. Motorized vehicles are not permitted in wilderness areas.

The almost 200,000 acres of the Pawnee National Grassland are widely scattered in two units east of Fort Collins. Restored from the devastation of the 1930s dust bowl, the short-grass prairie is inhabited by more than 200 species of wildlife, including falcons, hawks, prairie dogs and coyotes. Hiking, camping, horseback riding and bird-watching are popular activities.

The Pawnee Pioneer Trails is a scenic route that winds 125 miles east from Ault, Colo., along SR 14 and various county roads. In Weld County, contact Pawnee National Grassland, 660 O St., Greeley, CO 80631-3033, for additional information, or phone (970) 346-5000.

The U.S. Forest Service has a visitor information office at 2150 Centre Ave., Building E, Fort Collins, CO 80526. Phone (970) 295-6700 for information or (877) 444-6777 for campground reservations. District offices are also at 2140 Yarmouth Ave. in Boulder, (303) 541-2500; at 101 SR 103 in Idaho Springs, (303) 567-3000; and at 9 Ten Mile Dr. in Granby, (970) 887-4100. See Recreation Areas Chart.

ARAPAHO NATIONAL RECREATION AREA (B-4)

In north-central Colorado, next to Rocky Mountain National Park (see place listing p. 251), Arapaho National Recreation Area comprises more than 36,000 acres. Willow Creek Reservoir, Monarch Lake, Lake Granby, Shadow Mountain Lake and Meadow Creek Reservoir are open for fishing year-round; ice fishing is available December through April. Fishing licenses are required. Boat ramps are located at Arapaho Bay, Green Ridge, Hilltop, Stillwater, Sunset Point and Willow Creek Reservoir locations. (Note: These lakes have tested positive for zebra/quagga mussel larvae. To slow the spread of the mussels to other state lakes and reservoirs, the Colorado Division of Wildlife is conducting boat inspections in the area. Hilltop boat ramp and Willow Creek Reservoir are closed to trailered and motorized boats.)

Other recreational activities include camping, hiking and picnicking. Visitors may ride mountain bikes and horses, and, in winter, cross-country ski, ride snowmobiles or use snowshoes. Hunting also is permitted. Recreation fee $5 per day, $10 for 3 days or $15 for 7 days per private vehicle. Annual pass $30. Phone (970) 887-4100 for information or (877) 444-6777 for campground reservations. See Recreation Areas Chart.

ARVADA (C-9) pop. 106,433, elev. 5,340'
• Hotels & Restaurants map & index p. 136
• Part of Denver area — see map p. 116

It was June 1850 when Lewis Ralston found gold in what is now known as Ralston Creek. His strike was just the beginning, however, as other miners would soon come to Colorado with hopes of finding wealth and fortune. Founded in 1870, 6 years before Colorado achieved statehood, Arvada was initially a trading hub for the surrounding agricultural region.

The town recalls its early days in its Historic Olde Town section, where some of the commercial and residential buildings date to the 19th century, and at Gold Strike Park, the site of the 1850 gold discovery, at the confluence of Ralston and Clear creeks.

Arvada Visitors Center: 7305 Grandview Ave., Arvada, CO 80002. **Phone:** (303) 424-3380.

(See map & index p. 136.)

Self-guiding tours: Brochures describing buildings in Historic Olde Town Arvada are available from many local merchants.

SAVE **ARVADA CENTER FOR THE ARTS AND HUMANITIES**, 6901 Wadsworth Blvd., is the cultural center of the community. Summer concerts are presented under the stars at the 1,500-seat outdoor amphitheater. Two indoor theaters host professional theater productions, concerts and dance events throughout the year. Three galleries feature rotating exhibits of contemporary art by regional, national and international artists. A museum devoted to local history is part of the center.

Time: Allow 1 hour minimum. **Hours:** Mon.-Fri. 9-6, Sat. 10-5, Sun. 1-5. **Cost:** Galleries and museum free. Performances $7-$73. **Phone:** (720) 898-7200.

CUSSLER MUSEUM is at 14959 W. 69th Ave. The museum is owned by Clive Cussler, a best-selling novelist who also is a collector of classic automobiles. Among the more than 75 restored cars on display are a 1913 Marmon, a 1929 Model J Duesenberg, a 1932 Stutz Town Car, a 1952 Allard J2X roadster and a 1932 Auburn Speedster. **Time:** Allow 30 minutes minimum. **Hours:** Mon.-Thurs. 10-5, May-Sept. **Cost:** $10; $8 (ages 65+); $5 (ages 0-11). **Phone:** (303) 420-2795.

BEAU JO'S COLORADO STYLE PIZZA ARVADA
303/420-8376 86

♦♦♦♦ ♦♦♦♦
Pizza
Casual Dining
$6-$12

AAA Inspector Notes: Known for its pizza, this eatery offers a fun atmosphere with a mountain theme. Build your pizza from the crust up. Choices include a mountain pie with a thick, chewy edge; the thin-crust prairie pie; and gluten-free options. Add your favorite toppings or choose a specialty pizza like the sky hawk (pepperoni, Hatch green chiles and feta), or Skier Mike's chicken, Canadian bacon and green pepper pie. **Features:** full bar, patio dining. **Address:** 7525 W 53rd Ave 80002 **Location:** I-70 exit 269A (Wadsworth Blvd), 0.3 mi n, then just e. *(See ad this page.)* L D

"Colorado Style Pizza"
Also Gluten Free Menu

ASPEN (C-3) pop. 6,658, elev. 7,907'
• Hotels p. 47 • Restaurants p. 48
• Hotels & Restaurants map & index p. 45

Mines and mills have given way to beautiful homes on the hillsides above Aspen, a town whose transformation from riches to rags to riches is part of the fabric of Colorado. A 2,350-pound, 93-percent-pure silver nugget taken in three pieces from Aspen's Smuggler Mine was to be displayed at the Chicago Columbian Exposition in 1893 along with the Silver Queen, a sculpture made of silver, gold and minerals from the Aspen area. Yet the nugget never made it, symbolizing both the apex and the beginning of the end of the silver era.

With the repeal of the Sherman Silver Act in 1893, supply exceeded demand and prices fell. As the nation succumbed to the Panic of 1893, Colorado's economy collapsed. Aspen's revival was due to another natural resource, this time a recurrent one—snow. In the late 1930s a simple ski area was built and in 1946 Aspen Ski Corporation launched the ski runs on Aspen Mountain. Seeing the potential, private enterprises quickly turned the little city in the Roaring Fork Valley into a year-round resort and cultural center.

The Ute Indians called the area Shining Mountains, and early pioneers referred to the settlement as Ute City. It wasn't until 1880 that the city officially became known as Aspen, chosen because of the bountiful number of trees of the same name. The city's historic Victorian buildings, its eclectic personality, cultural amenities, nightlife and, of course, the blessing of its natural surroundings have made it an increasingly popular choice for vacationers.

Local events include Wintersköl, Aspen's toast to winter, held in mid-January. In June the Food & Wine Magazine Classic in Aspen is offered. From late June to late August the Aspen Music Festival and School presents classical music concerts and recitals by guest artists. Seminars, lectures and classes also are part of a summer-long festival of the mind at the Aspen Institute. The restored 1889 Wheeler Opera House presents operas, dramas, concerts, films and dances throughout the year.

Concessionaires in Aspen offer hiking, paragliding, bicycle tours, white-water rafting, horseback

(See map & index p. 45.)

riding, river expeditions, back-country jeep excursions, balloon rides, guided rock and mountain climbing, trail rides and overnight pack trips, not to mention the wintry offerings of cross-country and downhill skiing, snowmobiling, sleigh rides and ice-skating.

Guided tours of Victorian homes in the West End are offered by the Aspen Historical Society. Walking tours are available June through October and depart from the Wheeler/Stallard Museum *(see attraction listing)*. For additional information, phone (970) 925-3721.

Aspen Chamber Resort Association: 425 Rio Grande Pl., Aspen, CO 81611. **Phone:** (970) 925-1940 or (800) 670-0792.

ASPEN ART MUSEUM is at 637 E. Hyman Ave. The focus at this museum is on contemporary art; all exhibitions are temporary. Art workshops and lectures are available. **Time:** Allow 30 minutes minimum. **Hours:** Tues.-Sun. 10-8. **Cost:** Free. **Phone:** (970) 925-8050.

GHOST TOWN OF ASHCROFT, 11 mi. s. on Castle Creek Rd., is a weather-beaten vestige of its mining camp heyday. Lack of resources and rail service to the mines caused the town's demise by 1890, although residents had hoped their town would someday rival Aspen in importance. The Aspen Historical Society conducts tours of the town; self-guiding tours also are available. Interpretive signage and brochures are available on site.

Hours: Tours are offered daily 9-5, mid-June through Labor Day. **Cost:** $3; free (ages 0-10). **Phone:** (970) 925-3721.

GHOST TOWN OF INDEPENDENCE, 16 mi. e. on SR 82, is the faded relic of the Roaring Fork Valley's original gold mining community. After the first gold strike in 1879 the town boomed; decline set in by the end of the 1880s when the nearby mines stopped producing. The Aspen Historical Society in the Wheeler/Stallard Museum *(see attraction listing)* offers information about self-guiding tours. Docents are available at the site to answer questions.

Note: Do not enter obviously sagging structures that could collapse. **Hours:** Tours are offered daily 10-6, mid-June through Labor Day; Sat.-Sun. 10-6, day after Labor Day-Sept. 30. **Cost:** $3. **Phone:** (970) 925-3721.

HOLDEN/MAROLT MINING AND RANCHING MUSEUM is at 40180 SR 82. Located in an 1890s barn, this living-history museum tells the story of the silver mining boom in Aspen 1879-93. It also depicts the "quiet years" of ranching between the silver bust and the skiing/cultural boom that began in the

1940s. **Time:** Allow 1 hour minimum. **Hours:** Tues.-Sat. 10:30-4:30 mid-June through Labor Day; 1-5, day after Labor Day-early Oct. **Cost:** (includes Wheeler/Stallard Museum) $6; $5 (ages 65+); free (ages 0-11). **Phone:** (970) 925-3721.

MAROON BELLS is 9 mi. s.w. off SR 82. The jagged peaks of the Maroon Bells are some of the country's most photographed mountains. Many souvenir snapshots feature their reflection in the waters of Maroon Lake. The loftiest of the peaks towers at 14,156 feet. Hiking trails, picnicking and fishing are available in front of the mountain at the lake. Aspen Center for Environmental Studies offers free naturalist-led guided walks along Maroon Lake and up to Crater Lake from early June through Labor Day.

Note: From mid-June through Sept. 30, access to Maroon Creek Road is open daily 8-5 only to private vehicles carrying those staying at the campgrounds, those with children in car seats or those with physically impaired passengers. Round-trip shuttle service from the Aspen Highlands ski area is available. The road reopens to all traffic 5 p.m.-8 a.m. **Hours:** Park 8-5. Shuttle buses depart daily every 20 minutes 8-5, mid-June to Labor Day; Fri.-Sun. every 20 minutes 8-5, Fri. after Labor Day-Sept. 30. **Cost:** Shuttle fare $6. **Phone:** (970) 925-8484, or (800) 854-5588 for bus information.

WHEELER/STALLARD MUSEUM, 620 W. Bleeker St., in an 1888 Queen Anne Revival style house, is dedicated to preserving Roaring Fork Valley history. As home to the Aspen Historical Society, it features rotating exhibits, weekly summer and winter events on Tuesday evenings, and a variety of historic tours, such as walking tours of the historic West End. Activities for all ages are presented June through August. **Hours:** Tues.-Sat. 10:30-4:30, mid-June through Labor Day; 1-5, rest of year. Phone for tour and event schedules. **Cost:** (includes Holden/Marolt Mining and Ranching Museum) $6; $5 (ages 65+); free (ages 0-11). Walking tour $15; $12 (ages 65+); phone for admission costs of other tours. **Phone:** (970) 925-3721.

RECREATIONAL ACTIVITIES
Skiing

- **Aspen Highlands** is 2 mi. w. on SR 82. **Hours:** Daily 9-3:30, early Dec. to mid-Apr. (weather permitting). **Phone:** (970) 925-1227 or (800) 525-6200.
- **Aspen Mountain** is at 601 Dean St. **Hours:** Daily 9-3:30, late Nov. to mid-Apr. (weather permitting). **Phone:** (970) 925-1227 or (800) 525-6200.
- **Buttermilk** is 3 mi. w. on SR 82. **Hours:** Daily 9-3:30, mid-Dec. to early Apr. (weather permitting). **Phone:** (970) 925-1227 or (800) 525-6200.

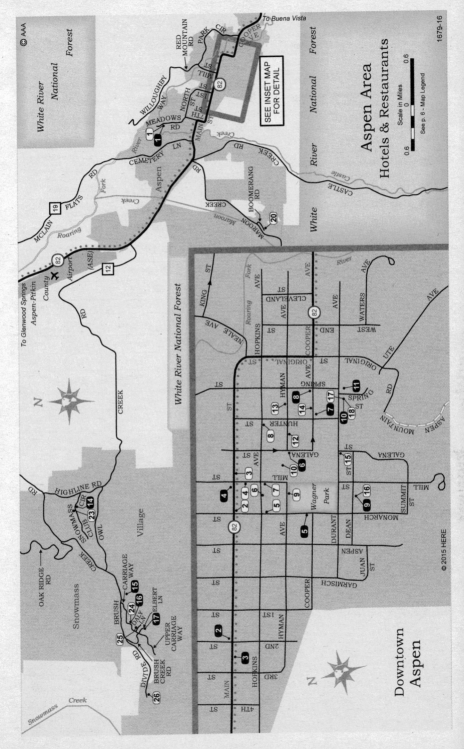

Aspen Area
Hotels & Restaurants

Scale in Miles

See p. 6 - Map Legend

Downtown
Aspen

1679-16

© 2015 HERE

Aspen Area

This index helps you "spot" where approved hotels and restaurants are located on the corresponding detailed maps. Hotel daily rate range is for comparison only. Restaurant price range is a combination of lunch and/or dinner. Turn to the listing page for more detailed rate and price information and consult display ads for special promotions.

ASPEN

Map Page	Hotels	Diamond Rated	Rate Range	Page
1 p. 45	Aspen Meadows Resort, A Dolce Destination Collection	◆◆◆	$109-$799 [SAVE]	47
2 p. 45	Annabelle Inn	◆◆◆	$169-$329	47
3 p. 45	Aspen Mountain Lodge	◆◆	Rates not provided	47
4 p. 45	Hotel Jerome, An Auberge Resort	◆◆◆◆	Rates not provided [SAVE]	47
5 p. 45	The Limelight Hotel	◆◆◆	$115-$2520 [SAVE]	47
6 p. 45	The Residence Hotel	◆◆◆	Rates not provided	48
7 p. 45	Aspen Square Condominium Hotel	◆◆◆	$129-$1500	47
8 p. 45	Chateau Aspen Condominiums	◆◆	Rates not provided	47
9 p. 45	The St. Regis Aspen Resort	◆◆◆◆	$359-$2699 [SAVE]	48
10 p. 45	The Little Nell	◆◆◆◆◆	$325-$1475 [SAVE]	47

Map Page	Restaurants	Diamond Rated	Cuisine	Price Range	Page
1 p. 45	Plato's Restaurant at Aspen Meadows Resort	◆◆◆	American	$25-$45	49
2 p. 45	Matsuhisa	◆◆◆	Japanese	$15-$39	49
3 p. 45	Asie	◆◆◆	Asian	$13-$48	48
4 p. 45	Piñons	◆◆◆	Regional American	$32-$52	49
5 p. 45	Rustique Bistro	◆◆◆	Regional French	$32-$44	49
6 p. 45	Jimmy's, An American Restaurant & Bar	◆◆◆	American	$20-$52	48
7 p. 45	Cache Cache	◆◆◆	French	$31-$63	48
8 p. 45	Kenichi Aspen	◆◆◆	Asian Sushi	$19-$48	48
9 p. 45	The Wild Fig	◆◆	Mediterranean	$23-$38	49
10 p. 45	Zocalito Latin Bistro	◆◆	Latin American	$21-$29	49
12 p. 45	Little Annie's Eating House	◆◆	Comfort Food	$12-$33	49
13 p. 45	L'Hostaria Ristorante	◆◆◆	Italian	$20-$38	49
14 p. 45	Mezzaluna	◆◆	Italian	$15-$36	49
15 p. 45	CP Burger	◆	Burgers	$5-$9	48
16 p. 45	Chefs Club by Food & Wine	◆◆◆	American	$25-$48	48
17 p. 45	Ajax Tavern	◆◆◆	American	$19-$32	48
18 p. 45	Element 47	◆◆◆	Regional American	$18-$50	48
20 p. 45	Willow Creek Bistro	◆◆◆	American	$15-$48	49

SNOWMASS VILLAGE

Map Page	Hotels	Diamond Rated	Rate Range	Page
14 p. 45	Villas at Snowmass Club	◆◆◆	Rates not provided	258
15 p. 45	Viceroy Snowmass	◆◆◆◆	$225-$1350	258
16 p. 45	The Stonebridge Inn	◆◆	Rates not provided	258

SNOWMASS VILLAGE (cont'd)

Map Page	Hotels (cont'd)	Diamond Rated	Rate Range	Page
17 p. 45	**The Westin Snowmass Resort**	▼▼▼	$99-$719 SAVE	259

Map Page	Restaurants	Diamond Rated	Cuisine	Price Range	Page
23 p. 45	Sage Restaurant & Patio	▼▼▼	American	$16-$38	259
24 p. 45	Artisan Restaurant & Bar	▼▼▼	American	$13-$33	259
25 p. 45	Venga Venga	▼▼	Mexican	$15-$22	259
26 p. 45	Krabloonik Restaurant	▼▼	Regional American	$8-$62	259

ANNABELLE INN (970)925-3822 **2**

▼▼▼ **Bed & Breakfast** $169-$329 **Address:** 232 W Main St 81611 **Location:** 0.4 mi w on SR 82; jct W Main and N 2nd sts. **Facility:** Here you'll get the feel of a B&B, but with the amenities of a small-scale hotel. Comfy, well-appointed rooms are individually decorated in a mountain lodge style; some units with fireplace. 34 units. 3 stories, exterior corridors. **Terms:** check-in 4 pm, 2-3 night minimum stay - seasonal and/or weekends, cancellation fee imposed. **Activities:** hot tub, massage. **Guest Services:** coin laundry.

[icons] BIZ HS 🛜 ✕ 💻

ASPEN MEADOWS RESORT, A DOLCE DESTINATION COLLECTION (970)925-4240 **1**

Classic Hotel
$109-$799

Address: 845 Meadows Rd 81611 **Location:** 0.3 mi n of SR 82 via N 7th Ave, just w. Located in a quiet area. **Facility:** Designed by the famous Bauhaus architect, Herbert Bayer, the buildings for this resort and the incorporated Aspen Institute reflect the best design elements of the era. 98 units, some two bedrooms. 2 stories (no elevator), interior/exterior corridors. **Terms:** check-in 4 pm, 30 day cancellation notice-fee imposed, resort fee. **Amenities:** safes. **Dining:** 2 restaurants, also, Plato's Restaurant at Aspen Meadows Resort, see separate listing. **Pool(s):** heated outdoor. **Activities:** hot tub, steamroom, tennis, bicycles, trails, massage. **Guest Services:** valet and coin laundry, area transportation.

SAVE [icons] BIZ HS 🛜 ✕ [icons] / SOME UNITS [icons]

ASPEN MOUNTAIN LODGE 970/925-7650 **3**

▼▼ **Hotel.** Rates not provided. **Address:** 311 W Main St 81611 **Location:** 0.4 mi w on SR 82; between S 2nd and S 3rd sts. **Facility:** 38 units. 3 stories (no elevator), interior corridors. **Terms:** check-in 4 pm. **Amenities:** safes. **Pool(s):** heated outdoor. **Activities:** hot tub.

[icons] BIZ 🛜 ✕ [icons] / SOME UNITS [icons]

ASPEN SQUARE CONDOMINIUM HOTEL (970)925-1000 **7**

▼▼▼ **Condominium** $129-$1500 **Address:** 617 E Cooper Ave 81611 **Location:** Between S Hunter and S Spring sts; downtown. **Facility:** Steps from the gondola, this hotel offers units decorated by individual owners, but they all have wood-burning fireplaces and ski lockers. 101 condominiums. 3-4 stories, interior/exterior corridors. **Parking:** on-site and valet. **Terms:** check-in 4 pm, 1-5 night minimum stay - seasonal, 14 day cancellation notice, 30 day in winter-fee imposed, resort fee. **Amenities:** safes. **Pool(s):** heated outdoor. **Activities:** hot tub, picnic facilities, exercise room, massage. **Guest Services:** valet and coin laundry.

[icons] BIZ HS 🛜 ✕ [icons]

CHATEAU ASPEN CONDOMINIUMS 970/925-8717 **8**

▼▼ **Condominium.** Rates not provided. **Address:** 630 E Cooper Ave 81611 **Location:** Jct E Cooper Ave and S Spring St; downtown. **Facility:** 21 condominiums. 3 stories (no elevator), exterior corridors. **Terms:** off-site registration, check-in 4 pm. **Guest Services:** complimentary laundry.

[icons] / SOME UNITS HS [icons]

HOTEL JEROME, AN AUBERGE RESORT 970/920-1000 **4**

▼▼▼
Historic Boutique Hotel
Rates not provided

Address: 330 E Main St 81611 **Location:** Jct E Main and N Mill sts; downtown. **Facility:** This restored 1889 hotel features elegant public areas decorated with museum-quality paintings, tastefully restored antiques and distinct custom light fixtures. 93 units. 3-4 stories, interior corridors. **Parking:** valet only. **Terms:** check-in 4 pm. **Amenities:** safes. **Dining:** 2 restaurants. **Pool(s):** heated outdoor. **Activities:** hot tub, recreation programs in winter, game room, exercise room, massage. **Guest Services:** valet laundry, area transportation.

SAVE [icons] BIZ HS 🛜 ✕ 💻

/ SOME UNITS [icons]

THE LIMELIGHT HOTEL (970)925-3025 **5**

▼▼▼
Hotel
$115-$2520

Address: 355 S Monarch St 81611 **Location:** Just s of SR 82; at S Monarch and E Cooper sts; downtown. Opposite Wagner Park. **Facility:** 126 units, some two bedrooms and kitchens. 4 stories, interior corridors. **Parking:** on-site (fee). **Terms:** check-in 4 pm, 30 day cancellation notice, resort fee. **Amenities:** safes. **Dining:** entertainment. **Pool(s):** heated outdoor. **Activities:** hot tub, recreation programs, bicycles, trails, exercise room. **Guest Services:** valet and coin laundry, area transportation. **Featured Amenity:** continental breakfast.

SAVE [icons] BIZ HS 🛜 ✕ [icons] / SOME UNITS [icons]

THE LITTLE NELL (970)920-4600 **10**

▼▼▼▼▼
Contemporary Hotel
$325-$1475

Address: 675 E Durant Ave 81611 **Location:** Jct E Durant Ave and S Spring St; downtown. **Facility:** Enjoy ski-in/ski-out privileges at this intimate, modern lodging located beside the gondola at the base of the mountain. Expect room furnishings crafted from luxurious materials in neutral colors. 92 units, some two bedrooms. 4 stories, interior corridors. **Parking:** valet only. **Terms:** closed 4/17-5/11, check-in 4 pm, 3-7 night minimum stay - seasonal and/or weekends, 30 day cancellation notice-fee imposed, resort fee. **Amenities:** safes. **Dining:** Ajax Tavern, Element 47, see separate listings. **Pool(s):** heated outdoor. **Activities:** hot tub, steamroom, downhill & cross country skiing, recreation programs, bicycles, trails, exercise room, massage. **Guest Services:** valet laundry, area transportation.

SAVE [icons] BIZ HS 🛜 ✕ [icons] / SOME UNITS [icons]

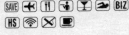

(See map & index p. 45.)

THE RESIDENCE HOTEL   970/920-6532   6

▼▼▼▼ **Boutique Contemporary Hotel.** Rates not provided. **Address:** 305 S Galena St 81611 **Location:** Jct S Galena St and E Hyman Ave; downtown. **Facility:** This unique hotel is located up a steep flight of stairs. Richly furnished with antiques, chandeliers and oil paintings, every room features a different décor theme. 8 units, some two bedrooms and kitchens. 2 stories (no elevator), interior corridors. **Bath:** shower only. **Parking:** street only. **Amenities:** safes. **Guest Services:** coin laundry.

BIZ HS 🛜 ✕ 📷 📶 🍽 📺 / SOME UNITS 🐾

THE ST. REGIS ASPEN RESORT   (970)920-3300   9

▼▼▼▼
Hotel
$359-$2699

ST REGIS

AAA Benefit: Members save up to 15%, plus Starwood Preferred Guest® benefits!

Address: 315 E Dean St 81611 **Location:** Jct S Monarch and E Dean sts; downtown. **Facility:** An elegant setting at the foot of the mountain allows you easy access to skiing and shopping. The courtyard has been outfitted with a snow-melt system and warming fire pits for outdoor relaxation. 179 units. 3-5 stories, interior corridors. **Parking:** valet only. **Terms:** closed 4/24-5/9 & 10/17-11/17, check-in 4 pm. **Amenities:** safes. **Dining:** 2 restaurants, also, Chefs Club by Food & Wine, see separate listing. **Pool(s):** heated indoor. **Activities:** hot tub, downhill & cross country skiing, ice skating, recreation programs in winter, bicycles, trails, spa. **Guest Services:** valet laundry, boarding pass kiosk, area transportation.

SAVE ✈ 🍴 🏋 🍸 🏊 🛁 BIZ HS 🛜 ✕ 🎬 📺 / SOME UNITS 💵 📶

WHERE TO EAT

AJAX TAVERN   970/920-6334   17

▼▼▼▼ **American. Casual Dining.** $19-$32 **AAA Inspector Notes:** Start with the crunchy, fried green tomatoes served with creamy burrata cheese, an herbaceous basil sauce and saba syrup. Skiers can come down the run and stop off for lunch on a gorgeous, slopeside outdoor patio. The lobster roll has a generous amount of lobster, a buttery bun and a light dressing. For a hearty lunch, the double cheeseburger is a famous option. Other choices include Colorado lamb Bolognese, pan-seared striped bass, and steak frites. **Features:** full bar, patio dining. **Reservations:** suggested, for dinner. **Address:** 675 E Durant Ave 81611 **Location:** Jct E Durant Ave and S Spring St; downtown; in The Little Nell. **Parking:** valet only.

L D

ASIE   970/920-9988   3

▼▼▼ **Asian. Casual Dining.** $13-$48 **AAA Inspector Notes:** This popular spot offers artfully presented, varied Asian cuisine. Sushi and tempura dishes sit comfortably next to chicken satay, Thai curry and roasted Peking duck. Friendly, attentive servers and modern décor enhance the dining experience. **Features:** full bar, patio dining, happy hour. **Address:** 413 E Main St 81611 **Location:** Between S Mill and S Galena sts. **Parking:** street only. L D

CACHE CACHE   970/925-3835   7

▼▼▼ **French. Fine Dining.** $31-$63 **AAA Inspector Notes:** Enjoy a special meal in an elegant setting. Start with escargot, a marinated beet salad, or a selection of appetizer-sized homemade pasta. Entrées include Bershire pork, Colorado rack of lamb and filet mignon. End with crème brûlée, warm chocolate cake or gourmet ice cream. **Features:** full bar. **Reservations:** suggested. **Address:** 205 S Mill St 81611 **Location:** At Hyman and Mill sts; downtown; in square. **Parking:** street only. D

CHEFS CLUB BY FOOD & WINE   970/429-9581   16

▼▼▼ ▼▼▼ **American. Fine Dining.** $25-$48 **AAA Inspector Notes:** The St. Regis Aspen Resort and Food & Wine magazine have partnered to create this sophisticated dining venue where each year, four to eight guest chefs are chosen from recently awarded 'Best New Chefs' to create and oversee the menu and flavors that will change on a seasonal basis. The three-course tasting menu with wine pairing is a great option. With the variety this menu offers, good luck choosing just three or four courses. **Features:** full bar, happy hour. **Reservations:** suggested. **Address:** 315 E Dean St 81611 **Location:** Jct S Monarch and E Dean sts; downtown; in The St. Regis Aspen Resort. **Parking:** valet only. D CALL 🌙

CP BURGER   970/925-3056   15

▼ **Burgers. Quick Serve.** $5-$9 **AAA Inspector Notes:** First timers' heads turn as the staff calls out, "Denzel Washington, your order's ready." As someone who is decidedly not Denzel Washington picks up her tray, the crowd gets it. Menu items include beef, chicken, tuna and falafel burgers, gourmet hot dogs, and hearty salads. Children will enjoy the shakes, while the adults might choose one of the spiked versions. In front of the restaurant, guests can play miniature golf in the summer and ice skate in the winter. **Features:** full bar. **Address:** 433 E Durant Ave 81611 **Location:** Between Galena and Mill sts. **Parking:** street only. L D 🅰

ELEMENT 47   970/920-6313   18

▼▼▼ ▼▼▼ **Regional American. Fine Dining.** $18-$50 **AAA Inspector Notes:** Element 47 is silver on the periodic table, a precious metal firmly tied to the history of this town. Artistically presented courses feature rabbit, Wagyu beef, oysters, foie gras, veal, peekytoe crab and seasonally fresh vegetables. The luxuriously appointed dining room looks out onto the patio garden, where seating is also available. **Features:** full bar, patio dining. **Reservations:** suggested. **Address:** 675 E Durant Ave 81611 **Location:** Jct E Durant Ave and S Spring St; downtown; in The Little Nell. **Parking:** valet only. B L D

JIMMY'S, AN AMERICAN RESTAURANT & BAR   970/925-6020   6

▼▼▼ ▼▼ **American. Casual Dining.** $20-$52 **AAA Inspector Notes:** This restaurant and bar offers a great dining room and a large outdoor patio where patrons can feast on tender steaks, wild-caught seafood, Alaskan king crab legs, Chesapeake Bay jumbo lump blue crab and classic comfort dishes such as the popular barbecue meatloaf. Delicious and attractively presented desserts are paired with wines and spirits. **Features:** full bar, patio dining. **Address:** 205 S Mill St 81611 **Location:** Just n of Mill St and Hopkins Ave. **Parking:** street only. D CALL 🌙 🅰

KENICHI ASPEN   970/920-2212   8

▼▼▼ ▼ **Asian Sushi. Fine Dining.** $19-$48 **AAA Inspector Notes:** Start with the "Dynamite Shrimp," a slightly sweet and savory tempura-fried tiger shrimp with masago aioli and teriyaki sauce. Then, select from a variety of dishes, including wagyu beef skewers, torched-salmon sashimi, and lobster rolls. Large plates include Colorado lamb, ahi tuna pepper steak, and pan-seared scallops. The sultry, modern décor makes this the perfect spot for a dinner date. **Features:** full bar, patio dining. **Reservations:** suggested. **Address:** 533 E Hopkins Ave 81611 **Location:** Just s on Galena St, then just e. **Parking:** street only. D

(See map & index p. 45.)

L'HOSTARIA RISTORANTE   970/925-9022   (13)

▼▼▼ Italian. Casual Dining. $20-$38 **AAA Inspector Notes:** Start with the cured-in-house beef, fish or prosciutto carpaccio. Main entrées include fresh pasta, Colorado lamb chops and veal scaloppine. The homemade gelati make the perfect ending to every meal. In the summer and fall, enjoy the Colorado weather on the patio. The décor creates a warm ambience, perfect for a date or for gathering with friends and family. **Features:** full bar, patio dining. **Reservations:** suggested. **Address:** 620 E Hyman Ave 81611 **Location:** Just s of Galena St, then just e. **Parking:** street only. (D)

LITTLE ANNIE'S EATING HOUSE   970/925-1098   (12)

▼▼ Comfort Food. Casual Dining. $12-$33 **AAA Inspector Notes:** This cozy eatery offers a wide variety of delicious items such as daily soups, chili, their famous beef stew, a thick and juicy grilled prime rib sandwich, the spinach pie vegetable plate, curry chicken salad and jumbo shrimp cocktail. Dinner platters include Colorado lamb chops, Caribbean marinated pork rib-eye, fresh Rocky Mountain trout, Annie's rotisserie chicken and tempting homemade desserts. **Features:** beer & wine. **Address:** 517 E Hyman Ave 81611 **Location:** Just s on Galena St, then just e. **Parking:** street only.

(L) (D) (AC)

MATSUHISA   970/544-6628   (2)

▼▼▼ Japanese. Casual Dining. $15-$39 **AAA Inspector Notes:** Created by noted celebrity chef Nobu Matsuhisa and his partner Nobuko Kang, this popular eatery draws locals and tourists alike. The basement of this blue Victorian house transports guests to a warm enclave featuring modern décor. Attractively presented delicious dishes and flavors from around the world are sure to please and surprise. The extensive beverage menu offers various wines and cocktails and even a variety of cocktails with shochu, a Japanese distilled alcohol. **Features:** full bar. **Reservations:** suggested. **Address:** 303 E Main St 81611 **Location:** Jct E Main and S Monarch sts. **Parking:** street only. (D)

MEZZALUNA   970/925-5882   (14)

▼▼ Italian. Casual Dining. $15-$36 **AAA Inspector Notes:** This trendy, high-energy dining room offers internationally flavored cuisine that includes creative appetizers, entrées and pastas. The menu lists crab cakes, oven-fired brie, veal chop Milanese, penne with rock shrimp and wood-fired pizzas. It's a great place for people-watching. **Features:** full bar, patio dining, happy hour. **Address:** 624 E Cooper Ave 81611 **Location:** Opposite Aspen Square; downtown. **Parking:** street only. (L) (D)

PINE CREEK COOKHOUSE   970/925-1044

▼▼▼ American. Fine Dining. $18-$46 **AAA Inspector Notes:** Views of flowers, aspens and mountain scenery creates a special ambience as you dine. Enjoy cocktails and appetizers, like the artisanal cheese and cured meat plate, beside the outdoor wood-burning stove before selecting an entree featuring buffalo, elk or line-caught fresh fish. In winter, the road to the restaurant closes and guests meet at 11399 Castle Creek Rd to take a horse-drawn sleigh to the final destination. The more adventurous can arrive on skis or snowshoes. **Features:** full bar. **Reservations:** suggested. **Address:** 12500 Castle Creek Rd 81611 **Location:** At roundabout, exit Castle Creek Rd (CR 15), then 12.5 mi s. (L) (D) (AC)

PIÑONS   970/920-2021   (4)

▼▼▼ Regional American. Fine Dining. $32-$52 **AAA Inspector Notes:** Relax in a contemporary Western setting as you select entrees featuring bison, Colorado lamb and trout. Start with fried oysters topped with caviar, seared foie gras or sashimi tuna tacos. If you're looking for a great view of Aspen Mountain, the best seats are on the spacious outdoor patio. **Features:** full bar, patio dining. **Reservations:** suggested. **Address:** 105 S Mill St 81611 **Location:** Between E Main St and E Hopkins Ave. **Parking:** street only.

(D)

PLATO'S RESTAURANT AT ASPEN MEADOWS RESORT   970/544-7814   (1)

▼▼▼ American. Fine Dining. $25-$45 **AAA Inspector Notes:** A must for any visitor, this restaurant is a favorite for its flavorful dishes that are artistically presented and perfectly prepared. The talented team of chefs create food for the innovative menu that's more typical of a fine-dining restaurant. The menu changes seasonally. Gorgeous mountain views enhance the dining experience. **Features:** full bar, patio dining. **Reservations:** suggested. **Address:** 845 Meadows Rd 81611 **Location:** 0.3 mi n of SR 82 via N 7th Ave, just w; in Aspen Meadows Resort, A Dolce Destination Collection.

(D)

RUSTIQUE BISTRO   970/920-2555   (5)

▼▼▼ Regional French. Casual Dining. $32-$44 **AAA Inspector Notes:** Hearty fare evokes the feel of country French kitchens, where thick soups, freshly prepared vegetables and great bread are served daily. This bistro is known for fresh salads; a flavorful macaroni and cheese; and truffle fries; as well as traditional French fare like escargot, duck confit and steak au poivre. In nice weather, opt for a table on the patio. Larger groups may reserve private dining in the wine cellar. **Features:** full bar, happy hour. **Address:** 216 S Monarch St 81611 **Location:** Corner of Hopkins Ave and Monarch St; downtown. **Parking:** street only. (D)

THE WILD FIG   970/925-5160   (9)

▼▼ Mediterranean. Casual Dining. $23-$38 **AAA Inspector Notes:** This casual eatery features an open patio, quite popular in the warm summer months. The menu offers a diverse selection of Mediterranean fare such as falafel, hummus with pita bread, panini, and a variety of pasta dishes. Lunch is served June through August only. **Features:** full bar, patio dining. **Address:** 315 E Hyman Ave 81611 **Location:** Between S Monarch and S Mill sts. **Parking:** street only. (D)

WILLOW CREEK BISTRO   970/429-2327   (20)

▼▼▼ American. Fine Dining. $15-$48 **AAA Inspector Notes:** Creative and artistically presented soups, appetizers, salads, sandwiches and entrees are served in secluded surroundings. **Features:** full bar. **Address:** 75 Prospector Rd 81611 **Location:** At roundabout exit Maroon Creek Rd, 1.5 mi sw to Thunderbowl Ln, then just e on Boomerang Rd; in The Ritz-Carlton Club. **Parking:** no self-parking.

(B) (L) (D) (AC)

ZOCALITO LATIN BISTRO   970/920-1991   (10)

▼▼ Latin American. Casual Dining. $21-$29 **AAA Inspector Notes:** Latin specialties and cold cocktails from the rum bar are offered at this colorful eatery. **Features:** full bar. **Address:** 420 E Hyman Ave 81611 **Location:** Corner of S Galena St and E Hyman Ave. **Parking:** no self-parking. (D)

AURORA (C-9) pop. 325,078, elev. 5,435'

- **Hotels p. 50 • Restaurants p. 52**
- **Hotels & Restaurants map & index p. 136**
- **Part of Denver area — see map p. 116**

Aurora is home to the Aurora Reservoir. This municipal park offers recreational activities year-round, including swimming and boating. The city also offers hiking and bicycling trails as well as 16 golf courses. Saturdays from May through October (also Thursdays, June through September) vendors offer fruit, vegetables, specialty items and baked goods for sale at the Southlands Farmer's Market, at the Southlands Outdoor Retail Center at Smoky Hill Road and E470.

Special events proliferate in Aurora and include Kidspree, in early June. It takes place in the Aurora Municipal Center with live entertainment and hands-on activities for children. Early October brings Punkin' Chunkin' Colorado, held at the Arapahoe County Fairgrounds; festivities include hay rides, music, scarecrow building, a pumpkin patch and a pumpkin launch.

Aurora Chamber of Commerce: 14305 E. Alameda Ave., Suite 300, Aurora, CO 80012. **Phone:** (303) 326-8699.

AURORA HISTORY MUSEUM is at 15051 E. Alameda Pkwy. The museum's permanent exhibit incorporates an original 1913 trolley trailer. Changing exhibits are featured in the second and third galleries. The Children's Hands-on Room includes touchable artifacts, clothes and games. **Time:** Allow

(See map & index p. 136.)

30 minutes minimum. **Hours:** Tues.-Fri. 9-4, Sat.-Sun. 11-4. Closed major holidays. **Cost:** Free. Parking is available. **Phone:** (303) 739-6660.

ALOFT DENVER INTERNATIONAL AIRPORT
(303)371-9500 **76**

Contemporary Hotel
$99-$259

AAA Benefit: Members save up to 15%, plus Starwood Preferred Guest® benefits!

Address: 16470 E 40th Cir 80011 **Location:** I-70 exit 283 (Chambers Rd), just n, 0.7 mi e, then just s. **Facility:** 144 units. 5 stories, interior corridors. *Bath:* shower only. **Amenities:** safes. **Pool(s):** heated indoor. **Activities:** exercise room. **Guest Services:** valet and coin laundry, boarding pass kiosk.

BEST WESTERN PLUS GATEWAY INN & SUITES
(720)748-4800 **80**

Hotel
$80-$300

Best Western PLUS

AAA Benefit: Save 10% or more every day and earn 10% bonus points!

Address: 800 S Abilene St 80012 **Location:** I-225 exit 7 (Mississippi Ave), just e, then 0.3 mi n. **Facility:** 82 units. 4 stories, interior corridors. **Amenities:** safes. **Pool(s):** heated indoor. **Activities:** hot tub, exercise room. **Guest Services:** valet and coin laundry. **Featured Amenity:** full hot breakfast.

CAMBRIA HOTEL & SUITES DENVER AIRPORT
(303)576-9600 **72**

Contemporary Hotel $99-$249 **Address:** 16001 E 40th Cir 80011 **Location:** I-70 exit 283 (Chambers Rd), just n, then 0.4 mi e. **Facility:** 151 units. 6 stories, interior corridors. **Pool(s):** heated indoor. **Activities:** hot tub, exercise room. **Guest Services:** valet and coin laundry, rental car service, area transportation.

DENVER AIRPORT MARRIOTT AT GATEWAY PARK
(303)371-4333 **77**

Hotel
$97-$283

MARRIOTT

AAA Benefit: Members save 5% or more!

Address: 16455 E 40th Cir 80011 **Location:** I-70 exit 283 (Chambers Rd), just n, 0.5 mi e, then just s. **Facility:** 238 units. 4 stories, interior corridors. **Pool(s):** heated indoor. **Activities:** hot tub, exercise room. **Guest Services:** valet laundry, boarding pass kiosk.

DOUBLETREE BY HILTON DENVER - AURORA
(303)337-2800 **82**

Hotel
$89-$249

DOUBLETREE BY HILTON

AAA Benefit: Members save 5% or more!

Address: 13696 E Iliff Pl 80014 **Location:** I-225 exit 5 (E Iliff Ave), just w. **Facility:** 248 units. 6 stories, interior corridors. **Terms:** 1-7 night minimum stay, cancellation fee imposed. **Pool(s):** heated indoor. **Activities:** hot tub, exercise room. **Guest Services:** valet laundry, area transportation. *(See ad p. 51.)*

FAIRFIELD INN & SUITES BY MARRIOTT DENVER AURORA/SOUTHLANDS
(303)928-7500

Hotel $109-$191 **Address:** 24192 E Prospect Ave 80016 **Location:** SR 470 exit 10 (Smoky Hill Rd), 6 mi se, then just ne on Aurora Pkwy; in Southlands Shopping Center. **Facility:** 131 units. 4 stories, interior corridors. **Pool(s):** heated indoor. **Activities:** hot tub, exercise room. **Guest Services:** valet and coin laundry.

AAA Benefit: Members save 5% or more!

HILTON GARDEN INN-DENVER AIRPORT
(303)371-9393 **75**

Hotel
$89-$189

Hilton Garden Inn

AAA Benefit: Members save up to 10%!

Address: 16475 E 40th Cir 80011 **Location:** I-70 exit 283 (Chambers Rd), just n to 40th Ave E, then 0.5 mi e. **Facility:** 157 units. 6 stories, interior corridors. **Terms:** 1-7 night minimum stay, cancellation fee imposed. **Amenities:** *Some:* video games. **Pool(s):** heated indoor. **Activities:** hot tub, exercise room, massage. **Guest Services:** valet and coin laundry, area transportation. *(See ad p. 51.)*

HOLIDAY INN EXPRESS DENVER-AURORA MEDICAL CENTER
303)369-8400 **81**

Hotel. Rates not provided. **Address:** 1500 S Abilene St 80012 **Location:** I-225 exit 7 (Mississippi Ave), just e, then 0.5 mi s. **Facility:** 129 units. 4 stories, interior corridors. **Pool(s):** heated outdoor. **Activities:** exercise room. **Guest Services:** valet and coin laundry.

Before you travel, ask your AAA/CAA club about identity theft monitoring products

(See map & index p. 136.)

HYATT PLACE DENVER AIRPORT
(303)371-0700 **73**

Hotel
$84-$299

HYATT PLACE

AAA Benefit: Members save 10%!

Address: 16250 E 40th Ave 80011 **Location:** I-70 exit 283 (Chambers Rd), just n, then 0.5 mi e. **Facility:** 126 units. 6 stories, interior corridors. **Terms:** cancellation fee imposed. **Amenities:** safes. **Pool(s):** heated indoor. **Activities:** exercise room. **Guest Services:** valet laundry, area transportation. **Featured Amenity:** breakfast buffet. (See ad this page.)

RESIDENCE INN BY MARRIOTT
(303)459-8000 **74**

Extended Stay Hotel $101-$249 **Address:** 16490 E 40th Cir 80011 **Location:** I-70 exit 283 (Chambers Rd), just n, 0.5 mi e, then just s. **Facility:** 124 units, some two bedrooms, efficiencies and kitchens. 4 stories, interior corridors. **Pool(s):** heated indoor. **Activities:** hot tub, picnic facilities, exercise room. **Guest Services:** valet and coin laundry.

AAA Benefit: Members save 5% or more!

Visit AAA.com/searchfordiscounts to save on travel, shopping, dining and attractions

SPRINGHILL SUITES BY MARRIOTT
(720)859-1100 **79**

Hotel $104-$233 **Address:** 13400 E Colfax Ave 80011 **Location:** I-225 exit 10, 0.5 mi w. **Facility:** 153 units. 4 stories, interior corridors. **Pool(s):** heated indoor. **Activities:** hot tub, exercise room. **Guest Services:** valet and coin laundry, area transportation.

AAA Benefit: Members save 5% or more!

WOOLLEY'S CLASSIC SUITES-DENVER AIRPORT
(720)599-3750 **78**

Hotel
$149-$299

Address: 16450 E 40th Cir 80011 **Location:** I-70 exit 283 (Chambers Rd), just n, 0.7 mi e, then just s. **Facility:** 191 units. 4 stories, interior corridors. **Terms:** cancellation fee imposed. **Amenities:** safes. **Pool(s):** heated indoor. **Activities:** exercise room. **Guest Services:** complimentary and valet laundry, rental car service, area transportation. **Featured Amenity:** full hot breakfast.

WHERE TO EAT

BENT FORK THE GRILL 303/337-6600 **126**
American. Casual Dining. $10-$23 **AAA Inspector Notes:** Lamb, buffalo, beef, pork and seafood dishes share menu space with burgers and sandwiches. Among the choices that reflect a modern twist on classic favorites are salmon fish and chips, lobster shell pasta and cheese and buffalo pot roast. Specialty martinis merit a look. **Features:** full bar, happy hour. **Address:** 12191 E Iliff Ave 80014 **Location:** I-225 exit 5 (E Iliff Ave), 0.8 mi w.

▼ See AAA listing this page ▼

HYATT PLACE Denver Airport

- Free shuttle to and from the airport
- Complimentary hotel-wide WiFi Internet access
- 42" flat screen HDTV
- Free a.m. Kitchen Skillet, 24/7 Gallery Menu & Market
- Complimentary 24-hour Stay Fit® fitness center

HYATT PLACE
denver airport

16250 E 40th Ave
Aurora, CO 80011
303-371-0700 · denverairport.place.hyatt.com

(See map & index p. 136.)

CAFÉ PAPRIKA   303/755-4150   125

WV WV Moroccan. Casual Dining. $7-$15 **AAA Inspector Notes:** Tucked away in an unassuming strip mall, this little place has been a local favorite since 1993. Desert-themed murals on the wall, complete with camels and their nomadic masters, add to the ambience. The mouthwatering North African and Middle Eastern dishes include kebabs, hummus, tagine stews and gyros. Among the choices of must-try desserts are flaky baklava and the m'hencha, a pastry filled with almond paste and cinnamon. **Address:** 13160 E Mississippi Ave 80012 **Location:** I-225 exit 7 (Mississippi Ave), 0.4 mi w; in Uvalda Shoppette strip mall. L D

CEDAR CREEK PUB   303/537-4124   122

WV WV American. Casual Dining. $9-$14 **AAA Inspector Notes:** Conveniently located near the University of Colorado Anschutz Medical Campus, this restaurant offers a variety of sandwiches, burgers and salads as well as standard pub fare. The drink menu features Colorado-made microbrews, wines, liquors, sodas and coffee. **Features:** full bar, happy hour. **Address:** 2100 N Ursula St, Suite 20 80045 **Location:** SR 225 exit 287, just w to Fitzsimmons Pkwy, 0.5 mi n to Montview Blvd, 0.4 mi w, then just n. **Parking:** street only. L D

LA CUEVA   303/367-1422   123

WV WV Mexican. Casual Dining. $9-$17 **AAA Inspector Notes:** The two brand new hospitals down the road are starting to gentrify this area. Regardless, this restaurant has survived since 1974 for good reason. The menu consists of recipes passed down through generations. The servers treat their regulars with great warmth. My favorite dish is the chile rellenos, but occasionally branch out. I tried (and enjoyed) one of the new menu items--a healthy fajita dish. **Features:** full bar. **Address:** 9742 E Colfax Ave 80010 **Location:** I-225 exit 10, 2.5 mi w. **Parking:** on-site and street. L D

MONSOON CUISINE OF INDIA   303/627-5444

WV WV Indian. Casual Dining. $11-$17 **AAA Inspector Notes:** This eatery offers classic Indian and Pakistani cuisine in a casual setting with minimalist décor. Start with tandoori chicken wings, vegetable samosas or a cup of puréed dal soup. Entrées include tandoor chicken, shrimp, mahi, vindaloos, curries, and masalas with chicken, lamb and shrimp as well as a wide range of vegetarian options. **Features:** full bar, happy hour. **Address:** 24107 E Commons Ave 80016 **Location:** SR 470 exit 10 (Smoky Hill Rd), just se; in strip mall. L D

PHO 888   303/367-4180   124

WV WV Vietnamese. Casual Dining. $8-$13 **AAA Inspector Notes:** Don't be deterred by the strip mall location, as this casual eatery serves satisfying savory pho and other traditional Vietnamese favorites. Start with steamed shrimp spring rolls in rice paper. If you're not in the mood for soup, the menu also features entrée salads, fried rice, lemongrass chicken and much more. **Address:** 539 Sable Blvd 80011 **Location:** I-225 exit 6th Ave, just e, then just s; in strip mall. L D CALL &M

THE SUMMIT STEAKHOUSE   303/751-2112   127

WV WV Steak Seafood. Fine Dining. $11-$69 **AAA Inspector Notes:** There's a loyal local following for this restaurant's wonderful offerings of USDA Prime aged beef, seafood, chicken and lamb. Meals are served by an attentive, capable staff amid a décor of subdued lighting and bas-relief walls. **Features:** full bar, patio dining, Sunday brunch, happy hour. **Reservations:** suggested. **Address:** 2700 S Havana St 80014 **Location:** I-25 exit E Hampden Ave (which becomes S Havana St), 3.5 mi e; I-225 exit 5 (E Iliff Ave), w to S Havana St, then 0.3 mi s on east side. L D

AVON pop. 6,447

THE CHRISTIE LODGE   (970)949-7700

WV WV Hotel $79-$299 **Address:** 47 E Beaver Creek Blvd 81620 **Location:** I-70 exit 167, just s, then just e. **Facility:** 280 condominiums. 3 stories, interior corridors. **Terms:** check-in 5 pm, 2-3 night minimum stay - seasonal and/or weekends, 14 day cancellation notice-fee imposed. **Amenities:** safes. **Pool(s):** heated outdoor, heated indoor. **Activities:** hot tub, recreation programs, game room, exercise room. **Guest Services:** valet and coin laundry.

[icon row]

FALCON POINT RESORT   970/949-4416

WV WV WV Condominium. Rates not provided. **Address:** 175 Lake St 81620 **Location:** I-70 exit 167, just s on Avon Rd, just w on W Beaver Creek Blvd, just s on Benchmark Rd, then just w. **Facility:** Nestled in a quiet, residential neighborhood surround by pines, this property offers studios, one- and three- bedroom condos. Every unit has a pull-out sofa with a foam mattress pad. 58 condominiums. 5 stories, interior corridors. **Terms:** check-in 4 pm. **Amenities:** Some: safes. **Pool(s):** heated outdoor. **Activities:** sauna, hot tub, recreation programs in season, picnic facilities, trails, exercise room. **Guest Services:** coin laundry.

SHERATON MOUNTAIN VISTA   970/748-6000

WV WV WV
Condominium
Rates not provided

(S) Sheraton HOTELS & RESORTS

AAA Benefit: Members save up to 15%, plus Starwood Preferred Guest® benefits!

Address: 160 W Beaver Creek Blvd 81620 **Location:** I-70 exit 167, just s on Avon Rd, then just w. **Facility:** You'll feel at home in these apartment-style units, which feature balconies with barbecue grills. Enjoy mountain views as you work out in the fitness center or soak in the outdoor hot tub. 158 condominiums. 8 stories, interior corridors. **Terms:** check-in 4 pm. **Amenities:** safes. **Pool(s):** heated outdoor. **Activities:** sauna, hot tub, steamroom, bicycles, game room, trails, exercise room, massage. **Guest Services:** complimentary and valet laundry.

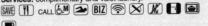

WESTIN RIVERFRONT RESORT & SPA, AT BEAVER CREEK MOUNTAIN   (970)790-6000

WV WV WV WV WV
Condominium
$129-$999

WESTIN® HOTELS & RESORTS

AAA Benefit: Members save up to 15%, plus Starwood Preferred Guest® benefits!

Address: 126 Riverfront Ln 81620 **Location:** Waterfront. I-70 exit 167, 0.6 mi s on Avon Rd, then just w. **Facility:** This upscale riverside hotel offers easy access to the Beaver Creek Village via the Riverfront Express Gondola. The modern-style décor features subtle, mountain-themed accents. 346 condominiums. 9 stories, interior corridors. **Parking:** valet only. **Terms:** check-in 4 pm, cancellation fee imposed, resort fee. **Amenities:** safes. **Dining:** 3 restaurants. **Pool(s):** heated outdoor. **Activities:** hot tub, downhill & cross country skiing, recreation programs in season, kids club, bicycles, game room, trails, spa. **Guest Services:** valet and coin laundry.

WHERE TO EAT

AVON BAKERY & DELI   970/949-3354

WV Deli. Quick Serve. $6-$14 **AAA Inspector Notes:** This small and busy bakery serves freshly-made soups, salads, cold and hot sandwiches and offers a nice selection of combination lunches featuring delicious daily lunch specials. The artisan bread is baked fresh daily on the premises using 100% organic flour. **Address:** 0025 Hurd Ln, Suite 4 81620 **Location:** I-70 exit 167, 0.4 mi s on Avon Rd, then just e. B L

BLUE PLATE BISTRO 970/845-2252

WWW American. Casual Dining. $8-$27 **AAA Inspector Notes:** This chef-owned eatery offers a seasonally changing menu drawing from international influences. Start with the tempura shrimp served with a sweet chili sauce. For a dinner entrée, try the lamb kebab, pork schnitzel or Mediterranean trout. The lunch menu features a variety of salads, burgers and sandwiches as well as a few larger entrées. The patio is a popular spot to enjoy a drink or a meal during the summer. If you're on a budget, head to the bar during happy hour for some great deals. **Features:** full bar, patio dining, happy hour. **Address:** 48 E Beaver Creek Blvd 81620 **Location:** I-70 exit 167, 0.4 mi s, take third exit at 2nd roundabout, then just e; in Boat Building. L D

COLUMBINE CAFE & BAKERY 970/949-1400

W Breads/Pastries. Casual Dining. $7-$12 **AAA Inspector Notes:** This European-style café and bakery is a must stop for quiche, hot and cold sandwiches, and pastries. Dine in or take a sandwich to enjoy on the slopes or hiking trails. Special occasion? This is the perfect spot to pick up a Linzer tart, wildberry mousse torte, or a German chocolate cake. Although a little difficult to find as it's hidden in a strip mall, this cozy eatery is worth seeking out. **Features:** wine only. **Address:** 51 Beaver Creek Pl 81620 **Location:** I-70 exit 167, just s, then just e; across from King Soopers. B L AC

GONDOLA PIZZA BAR & GRILL 970/845-6000

W Pizza. Quick Serve. $9-$13 **AAA Inspector Notes:** Locals and families flock to this casual eatery for a quick meal at affordable prices. For lunch, the pizza and salad buffet allows you to sample a variety of slices. Specialty pizzas include the "Gondola" (creamy garlic sauce, pastrami, sauerkraut and Thousand Island dressing) and the "Fire Chicken" (spiced with hot sauce and jalapeños). If that's not your speed, make your own favorite pizza or select from salads, hamburgers and pasta dishes. **Features:** full bar, patio dining. **Address:** 240 Chapel Pl 81620 **Location:** I-70 exit 167, 0.3 mi s, just s on Benchmark Rd, then just se; in strip mall. L D AC

HOOKED 970/949-4321

WW Seafood. Casual Dining. $9-$35 **AAA Inspector Notes:** This restaurant's name is a reference to its focus on freshly caught fish, which makes up the majority of the menu. The innovative dishes have an international influence. Sample menu items include ceviche, tiradito and sushi rolls. Large plates include rack of lamb, buffalo, buttermilk fried chicken, and steak. **Features:** full bar. **Address:** 122 Beaver Creek Pl 81620 **Location:** I-70 exit 167, 0.4 mi s, take 2nd exit to third roundabout to welcome gate, then 2.5 mi s; in Beaver Creek Village. L D AC

NORTHSIDE COFFEE & KITCHEN 970/949-1423

WW American. Casual Dining. $8-$20 **AAA Inspector Notes:** This unique eatery offers a menu ranging from comfort foods, such as biscuits and gravy and pot pie, to more sophisticated options like pulled lamb shank hash. You'll also find entrées of prime rib, salmon and halibut. Try one of the cake donuts, which feature fun flavors like maple-bacon or fruity pebbles. While you eat, enjoy the mountain views and natural light streaming through the windows. **Features:** full bar. **Address:** 20 Nottingham Rd 81620 **Location:** I-70 exit 167, just ne. B L D AC

PAZZO'S PIZZERIA 970/949-9900

WW Italian. Casual Dining. $10-$15 **AAA Inspector Notes:** Colorful Day of the Dead-inspired murals of cartoon skeletons making pizza add a bit of fun to the décor. Select from specialty pizzas like the Aztec, topped with jalapeños, cilantro and pepperoni, or build your own pie. The menu also features hearty sandwiches like the meatball, chicken Parmesan and Philly cheesesteak as well as a variety of calzones. Enjoy summer and fall weather on the patio. **Features:** full bar, happy hour. **Address:** 82 E Beaver Creek Blvd 81620 **Location:** I-70 exit 167, 0.3 mi s to 2nd roundabout, take third exit, then just e; in Benchmark Shopping Center. L D

VIN 48 RESTAURANT & WINE BAR 970/748-9463

WWW Northern American. Casual Dining. $24-$30 **AAA Inspector Notes:** This upscale eatery features an ever-changing, seasonal menu of small and large plates. Examples include the warm goat cheese salad served with thinly sliced beets and an orange truffle vinaigrette, grilled gulf shrimp, braised goat, Colorado striped bass, and Colorado Angus beef. The wine bar features 40 wines by the glass and distinctive flights. The rosette aperitif, made of prosecco and St. Germain, is a nice, light start. For something heavier, try one of the specialty cocktails. **Features:** full bar, patio dining. **Reservations:** suggested. **Address:** 48 E Beaver Creek Blvd 81620 **Location:** I-70 exit 167, 0.4 mi s, take third exit at 2nd roundabout, then just e; in Boat Building. D

BASALT pop. 3,857

ASPENALT LODGE (970)927-3191

WW Motel $80-$150 **Address:** 157 Basalt Center Cir 81621 **Location:** Jct Two Rivers Rd and Midland Ave, just ne; center. **Facility:** 35 units. 2 stories (no elevator), exterior corridors. **Terms:** cancellation fee imposed. **Activities:** hot tub, fishing.

[icons] 🍴 BIZ 📶 ✕ 🚼 🛏 📺 / SOME UNITS HS AC

WHERE TO EAT

CAFE BERNARD 970/927-4292

WW American. Casual Dining. $8-$29 **AAA Inspector Notes:** This charming French bistro features popular seasonal soups, truffle mousse pate, filet mignon, osso buco, smoked trout or salmon pasta, curry shrimp and a variety of delicious dessert selections. Vegetarian entrées are also available. **Features:** beer & wine. **Reservations:** suggested, for dinner. **Address:** 200 Midland Ave 81621 **Location:** Off SR 82; just e of Two Rivers Rd; downtown. **Parking:** street only. B L D

TEMPRANILLO 970/927-3342

WWW Spanish. Casual Dining. $12-$35 **AAA Inspector Notes:** Rich colors, high ceilings and warm fireplaces enhance the atmosphere at this charming Old World-style home, where food from Spain and Italy pairs with more than 100 wine choices. Guests can sit in the softly lit dining room or the lively bar to feast on delicious Spanish tapas, grilled calamari with arugula and aioli, classic Caesar or Greek salad, fettuccine mambo with jamon serrano, chicken, mushrooms and cream or grilled salmon with Mediterranean olives and citrus and basil pesto. **Features:** full bar. **Reservations:** suggested. **Address:** 165 Midland Ave 81621 **Location:** Off SR 82, just n at Basalt Ave traffic light, w at roundabout toward downtown. D CALL 💪M AC

BEAVER CREEK (C-3) elev. 8,100'

RECREATIONAL ACTIVITIES
Skiing

• **Beaver Creek Resort** is 3 mi. s. of I-70 exit 167. Winter and summer activities are offered. Hours: Daily 8-6, mid.-Nov. to mid-Apr. (weather permitting); daily 9:30-4:30, July 1-early Sept.; Sat.-Sun. 9:30-4:30, weekend after Labor Day to Sept. 30. **Phone:** (970) 754-4636.

BEAVER CREEK LODGE

(970)845-9800

Boutique Hotel
$169-$1599

Address: 26 Avondale Ln 81620 **Location:** I-70 exit 167, 3 mi s on Avon and Village rds, then just e. Located in Beaver Creek Village. **Facility:** The unique lobby feels like an art gallery with original paintings adorning the walls. Guests ready to hit the slopes will appreciate the ski valet and ski lockers. 72 units, some condominiums. 6 stories, interior corridors. **Parking:** valet only. **Terms:** closed 4/9-4/15, 5/1-5/26 & 10/9-11/17, 90 day cancellation notice-fee imposed, resort fee. **Amenities:** safes. **Pool(s):** heated outdoor. **Activities:** sauna, hot tub, steamroom, downhill & cross country skiing, ice skating, recreation programs in season, trails, exercise room, massage. **Guest Services:** valet and coin laundry, area transportation. Affiliated with Preferred Hotels & Resorts.

PARK HYATT BEAVER CREEK RESORT & SPA

(970)949-1234

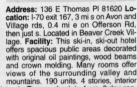

Resort Hotel
$159-$1099

PARK HYATT®

AAA Benefit: Members save 10%!

Address: 136 E Thomas Pl 81620 **Location:** I-70 exit 167, 3 mi s on Avon and Village rds, 0.4 mi e on Offerson Rd, then just s. Located in Beaver Creek Village. **Facility:** This ski-in, ski-out hotel offers spacious public areas decorated with original oil paintings, wood beams and crown molding. Many rooms offer views of the surrounding valley and mountains. 190 units. 4 stories, interior corridors. **Parking:** valet only. **Terms:** check-in 4 pm, 3 day cancellation notice-fee imposed, resort fee. **Amenities:** safes. **Dining:** 2 restaurants. **Pool(s):** heated outdoor. **Activities:** sauna, hot tub, steamroom, downhill & cross country skiing, ice skating, recreation programs, bicycles, playground, lawn sports, trails, spa. **Guest Services:** valet and coin laundry, boarding pass kiosk.

THE RITZ-CARLTON, BACHELOR GULCH

(970)748-6200

Resort Hotel
$259-$1599

AAA Benefit: Unequaled service at special member savings!

Address: 0130 Daybreak Ridge 81620 **Location:** I-70 exit 167, just s past the Beaver Creek Village gatehouse to Prater Rd, then just w; follow signs to Bachelor Gulch Village; in The Ritz-Carlton, Bachelor Gulch. **Facility:** This upscale, ski-in/ski-out resort enjoys a secluded location with its own gondola. After a long day of skiing, unwind with your favorite cocktail next to the roaring stone fireplace. 180 units, some two bedrooms, efficiencies and kitchens. 11 stories, interior corridors. **Parking:** valet only. **Terms:** closed 4/3-5/5, check-in 4 pm, 60 day cancellation notice-fee imposed, resort fee. **Amenities:** safes. **Dining:** 3 restaurants, also, Spago, see separate listing. **Pool(s):** heated outdoor. **Activities:** sauna, hot tub, steamroom, tennis, downhill & cross country skiing, recreation programs in season, kids club, game room, trails, spa. **Guest Services:** valet laundry, boarding pass kiosk, area transportation.

THE OSPREY AT BEAVER CREEK, A ROCKRESORT
970/754-7400

fyi Not evaluated. **Address:** 10 Elk Track Ln 81620 **Location:** I-80 exit 167, 0.4 mi s, take 2nd exit at third roundabout to welcome gate, then 2.5 mi s. Facilities, services, and décor characterize an upscale property.

GOLDEN EAGLE INN
970/949-1940

American. Casual Dining. $12-$35 **AAA Inspector Notes:** Fresh fish and wild game entrées, such as elk fillet and caribou medallions, are menu highlights at this family-friendly restaurant, which sits at the base of the Beaver Creek ski area. The atmosphere is casual, yet the décor is upscale. **Features:** full bar. **Address:** 118 Beaver Creek Plaza 81620 **Location:** I-70 exit 167, 3 mi s on Avon and Village rds; in Beaver Creek Village.

GROUSE MOUNTAIN GRILL
970/949-0600

Regional American. Fine Dining. $40-$45 **AAA Inspector Notes:** Set in an elegant alpine atmosphere, this restaurant offers seasonally focused preparations of fine meats and fish. Panoramic views and capable service enhance your dining experience. **Features:** full bar, patio dining. **Reservations:** suggested. **Address:** 141 Scott Hill Rd 81620 **Location:** I-70 exit 167, 3 mi s via Avon and Village rds; in The Pines Lodge. **Parking:** valet only.

MIRABELLE AT BEAVER CREEK
970/949-7728

Continental. Fine Dining. $30-$44 **AAA Inspector Notes:** *Historic.* At the gatehouse entry to Beaver Creek, this restored 1898 farmhouse has charming decor and a lounge area with a fireplace. Belgian master chef Daniel Joly prepares creative European cuisine featuring entrées of duck, Colorado lamb and elk. **Features:** full bar, patio dining. **Reservations:** suggested. **Address:** 55 Village Rd 81620 **Location:** I-70 exit 167, s to gatehouse; entrance to Beaver Creek Resort.

SPAGO
970/343-1555

American. Fine Dining. $30-$60 **AAA Inspector Notes:** Famed celebrity chef Wolfgang Puck decided to expand his restaurant brand with this location in Beaver Creek. Artful presentations and fresh, high-quality ingredients make every mouthwatering bite enjoyable. The menu changes seasonally but includes such local meats as Colorado lamb as well as fresh seafood that's flown in daily. Discussing wine options with the knowledgeable sommelier is a delight. **Features:** full bar, patio dining. **Reservations:** suggested. **Address:** 0130 Daybreak Ridge 81620 **Location:** I-70 exit 167, just s past the Beaver Creek Village gatehouse to Prater Rd, then just w; follow signs to Bachelor Gulch Village; in The Ritz-Carlton, Bachelor Gulch. **Parking:** valet only.

SPLENDIDO AT THE CHATEAU
970/845-8808

American. Fine Dining. $37-$52 **AAA Inspector Notes:** Chef David Walford delights patrons with his creative, innovative and contemporary cuisine that exhibits global influences. The menu changes seasonally, but if elk or any dish with handmade pasta is available, that's a highly recommended choice. Other options include Scottish salmon, Berkshire pork and Colorado lamb. The extensive wine list features wines from 17 countries. Indulgent desserts include a rich chocolate pudding cake, lemon-blueberry soufflé and a peach tart. **Features:** full bar. **Reservations:** suggested. **Address:** 17 Chateau Ln 81620 **Location:** I-70 exit 167, s on Avon and Village rds (beyond gatehouse), 2.4 mi s on Village Rd, then just nw on Scott Hill Rd; in Chateau at Beaver Creek. **Parking:** valet only.

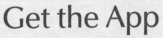

Get the App

Stay mobile with maps, travel information and road service on the go.

AAA.com/mobile • CAA.ca/mobile

BLACK CANYON OF THE GUNNISON NATIONAL PARK (D-2)

Elevations in the park range from 6,547 ft. at East Portal to 9,040 ft. at Poison Spring Hill. Refer to AAA maps for additional elevation information.

Black Canyon of the Gunnison National Park has several observation points on the South Rim, reached via SR 347, leading off US 50, 8 miles east of Montrose; the North Rim is reached by an 11-mile road (the last half is gravel) from SR 92 east of Crawford.

Embracing approximately 30,000 acres, the park contains 14 miles of the deepest portion of the Black Canyon of the Gunnison. Some of Earth's oldest base rocks have been cut by the river to a depth of 2,722 feet. At the narrowest point along the top of the canyon, the distance between the canyon walls measures about 1,100 feet across, but narrows to only 40 feet near the riverbed below.

The name Black Canyon comes from the many shadows cast on the cliff walls due to the narrowness of the canyon and from the dark-colored schists, granites and other Precambrian rocks. Descent into the canyon is arduous and hazardous; do not attempt it without consulting a ranger.

Summer recreational options include camping, hiking along the canyon rim, picnicking, fishing, rock climbing and extreme kayaking. Winter recreation offers cross-country skiing and snowshoeing.

The South Rim Visitor Center at Gunnison Point provides information about current interpretive programs and houses exhibits and a video describing the park's history, geology, flora and fauna. Recreational activities taking place in the inner gorge require a permit, which can be obtained from the visitor center. Programs are held daily, mid-June through Labor Day. Camping and rangers are available year-round at the South Rim, and in summer at the North Rim.

The park provides several options for scenic drives. South Rim Drive is a 7-mile paved road; 12 overlooks provide grand views of the canyon and the river. East Portal Road is a very steep paved drive; vehicles longer than 22 feet are prohibited. The road ends at the Gunnison River, a popular spot for camping, fishing and sightseeing.

The South Rim Visitor Center is open daily 8-6, late May-early Sept.; 8:30-4, late Oct.-late Apr.; 8-5, rest of year. South Rim Drive and East Portal Road are open early April to mid-Nov. (weather permitting). North Rim Road is open intermittently May-Oct. (weather permitting). Admission $15 per private vehicle or $7 per person arriving by other means (valid for 7 days); free (ages 0-16). Camping $12-$18. Phone (970) 641-2337. *See Recreation Areas Chart.*

BLACK FOREST pop. 13,116
• Part of Colorado Springs area — see map p. 81

BLACK FOREST BED & BREAKFAST LODGE   (719)495-4208

 Bed & Breakfast $75-$375 Address: 11170 Black Forest Rd 80908 Location: Jct Shoup and Black Forest rds, 1.3 mi s, then w at stone columns. Located in a quiet area. Facility: 5 units, some efficiencies and kitchens. 1-2 stories (no elevator), interior/exterior corridors. Terms: check-in 4 pm, 2 night minimum stay - seasonal, 30 day cancellation notice-fee imposed. Activities: playground. Guest Services: complimentary laundry.

BLACK HAWK (C-8) pop. 118, elev. 8,056'

GAMBLING ESTABLISHMENTS

• **Ameristar Casino** is at 111 Richman St. **Hours:** Daily 24 hours. **Phone:** (720) 946-4000 or (866) 667-3386.

• **Bullwhackers Casinos** is at 101 Gregory St. **Hours:** Fri.-Sat. 24 hours; Sun.-Thurs. 8 a.m.-2 a.m. **Phone:** (303) 271-2500 or (800) 426-2855.

• **Canyon Casino** is at 131 Main St. **Hours:** Fri.-Sat. 24 hours; Sun.-Thurs. 8 a.m.-2:30 a.m. **Phone:** (303) 777-1111.

• **The Gilpin Casino** is at 111 Main St. **Hours:** Daily 24 hours. **Phone:** (303) 582-1133.

• **Golden Gates Casino** is at 261 Main St. **Hours:** Daily 24 hours. Phone ahead to confirm schedule. **Phone:** (303) 582-2600.

• **Golden Mardi Gras Casino** is at 300 Main St. **Hours:** Daily 24 hours. Phone ahead to confirm schedule. **Phone:** (303) 582-1650.

• **Isle Casino Hotel Black Hawk** is at 401 Main St. **Hours:** Daily 24 hours. **Phone:** (303) 998-7777 or (877) 590-2240.

• **Lady Luck Casino** is at 340 Main St. **Hours:** Daily 24 hours. **Phone:** (303) 582-3000 or (877) 855-2616.

• **The Lodge Casino** is at 240 Main St. **Hours:** Daily 24 hours. **Phone:** (303) 582-1771.

• **Monarch Casino Black Hawk** is at 444 Main St. **Hours:** Daily 24 hours. **Phone:** (303) 582-1000.

• **Saratoga Casino Black Hawk** is at 101 Main St. **Hours:** Fri.-Sat. 24 hours, Sun.-Wed. 9 a.m.-3 a.m., Thurs. 9 a.m.-midnight. **Phone:** (303) 582-6100 or (800) 538-5825.

AMERISTAR CASINO RESORT SPA BLACK HAWK, COLORADO   720/946-4000

Resort Hotel
Rates not provided

Address: 111 Richman St 80422 Location: Just w of jct SR 119. Facility: Touring the public areas of this hotel is akin to visiting an art gallery with unique sculptures, paintings and prints of various styles. 536 units. 34 stories, interior corridors. Parking: on-site and valet. Terms: check-in 4 pm. Amenities: safes. Dining: 4 restaurants, also, Timberline Grill, see separate listing. Pool(s): heated indoor. Activities: sauna, hot tub, steamroom, exercise room, spa. Guest Services: valet laundry.

WHERE TO EAT

TIMBERLINE GRILL   720/946-4000

▼▼▼▼ American. Fine Dining. $14-$36 **AAA Inspector Notes:** Escape the hustle and bustle of the casino by walking into this inviting mountain lodge restaurant, complete with Western-themed oil paintings, wood accents and a fireplace. Menu items include a variety of steaks, pasta dishes, chicken, ribs, and fish. Try to save room for the decadent desserts-the sampler includes a shot of lemon berry trifle, a small hot cocoa with homemade marshmallows and an amazing chocolate hazelnut torte. **Features:** full bar. **Address:** 111 Richman St 80422 **Location:** Just w of jct SR 119; in Ameristar Casino Resort Spa Black Hawk, Colorado. **Parking:** on-site and valet. D

BOULDER (B-8) pop. 97,385, elev. 5,344'
- **Hotels p. 61 • Restaurants p. 62**
- **Hotels & Restaurants map & index p. 59**

Boulder was settled on the outwash plain of Boulder Creek in 1858 because, according to Capt. Thomas A. Aikens, "the mountains look right for gold, and the valleys ... rich for grazing." It has since grown from a cluster of crude log houses into one of the leading educational and scientific research and development centers in the Rocky Mountain states.

The combination of climate, scenery and the 25,000-student University of Colorado attracted such agencies as the National Center for Atmospheric Research, the laboratories of the National Institute of Standards and Technology and the Joint Institute for Laboratory Astrophysics as well as other large corporate installations.

The University of Colorado's establishment in 1876 spurred the struggling gold and agricultural community, then called Boulder City, to a new vigor. The 1,590-acre campus has a computer center, the Fiske Planetarium/Sommers-Bausch Observatory and the Mary Rippon Outdoor Theatre. The theater hosts the Colorado Shakespeare Festival from early June to early August; box office (303) 492-8008. Campus tours are offered Mon.-Sat.; phone (303) 492-6301, ext. 2.

The Dushanbe Teahouse, presented as a gift from its sister city of Dushanbe, Tajikistan, is a traditionally decorated Tajik teahouse that sits at 13th Street in Boulder. The hand-carved, hand-painted structure, which arrived in 200 crates, was assembled by Tajik artisans; phone (303) 442-4993.

An 8,555-acre system of mountain parks includes Boulder Creek Path, Boulder Falls, Colorado Chautauqua (see attraction listing), Flagstaff Mountain and the Flatirons. Boulder Creek, which flows through the city, offers a multitude of recreational activities. In combination with Boulder Creek Path, which winds for 16 miles alongside the creek, opportunities exist for casual strolling, picnicking, tubing and fishing.

Boulder obtains its water supply from a municipally owned glacier. Twenty-eight miles of pipe channel the clear, soft water from Arapaho Glacier to the town's taps.

You'll find both residents and visitors gathering at the Boulder County Farmers' Market to shop for fresh produce from local growers as well as baked goods, flowers and crafts. The market, on 13th Street adjacent to Central Park, is open Wed. 4-8, early May-early Oct. and Sat. 8-2, early Apr.-late Nov.

Boulder Convention and Visitors Bureau: 2440 Pearl St., Boulder, CO 80302. **Phone:** (303) 442-2911 or (800) 444-0447.

Shopping: In Boulder's downtown historic area, not far from the University of Colorado campus, is Pearl Street, a four-block, pedestrian-only outdoor mall lined with bookstores, art galleries, coffeehouses, boutiques and restaurants. Street performers and seasonal arts and crafts shows help contribute to a fun atmosphere.

Just east of 28th Street (US 36) between Arapahoe Avenue and Walnut Street is Twenty Ninth Street, an open-air lifestyle center combining retail establishments with dining and outdoor gathering spots. Joining Macy's are shops such as LOFT, Anthropologie, Apple Store, Victoria's Secret and a J. Crew Factory Store.

BOULDER BEER COMPANY TOUR is at 2880 Wilderness Place. The facility offers interactive tours of Colorado's first microbrewery. Visitors learn about the company's history as well as the science behind making beer and the production process. Free samples are offered to those 21+. **Time:** Allow 1 hour minimum. **Hours:** Guided tours, given on a first-come, first-served basis, depart Mon.-Fri. at 2, Sat. at 2 and 4. Closed Jan. 1, Thanksgiving and Christmas. **Cost:** Free. **Phone:** (303) 444-8448. GT

BOULDER MUSEUM OF CONTEMPORARY ART, 1750 13th St., presents a rotating collection of local, national and international exhibits of contemporary art in its three galleries. **Time:** Allow 45 minutes minimum. **Hours:** Mon.-Fri. 9-5 (also Wed. 5-8 during the Boulder County Farmers' Market). **Cost:** $1. **Phone:** (303) 443-2122.

CELESTIAL SEASONINGS FREE TOUR OF TEA, 4600 Sleepytime Dr., offers complimentary tours of the company's manufacturing facility. Highlights of the facility, which produces more than 75 varieties of tea, include a gallery of original Celestial Seasonings artwork, marketing displays, a tea tasting, a guided tour of the production and packaging facilities, plus the aromatic mint room and herb garden.

Food is available Mon.-Fri. **Time:** Allow 1 hour minimum. **Hours:** Guided 45-minute tours are given Mon.-Sat. on the hour 10-4, Sun. 11-3. Closed major holidays. **Cost:** Free. Ages 0-4 are not permitted in the production area. **Phone:** (303) 581-1202 or (800) 525-0347. ⑪

COLORADO CHAUTAUQUA, 1 mi. w. of US 36 at 900 Baseline Rd., occupies 26 acres at the base of Boulder's iconic mountain. Founded in 1898, the park was part of the Chautauqua movement, which sought to bring culture to rural areas of the country. Music, dance, theater, silent films and lectures are presented during summer in the historic auditorium.

(See map & index p. 59.)

Cultural and educational programs are given year-round. Most of the original buildings remain intact and are still being used for their original intent. Self-guiding tours via mobile phone are available.

Hiking, rock climbing and a playground can be enjoyed. Overnight accommodations are available year-round in cottages and lodges. **Hours:** Daily 24 hours. **Cost:** Free. **Phone:** (303) 442-3282.

FLAGSTAFF SCENIC HIGHWAY leaves Baseline Rd. and winds to the summit of Flagstaff Mountain, 1,600 feet above Boulder. It affords splendid views of the Continental Divide, city, valley and plains. Picnic tables are provided at Panorama Point; hiking trails wind around the summit. **Note:** Drivers should use caution due to the numerous rock-climbers and bicyclists. **Phone:** (303) 442-2911.

LEANIN' TREE MUSEUM AND SCULPTURE GARDEN OF WESTERN ART, n.e. on SR 119, e. on Jay Rd., n. on 63rd St., then w. to 6055 Longbow Dr., is housed in the corporate headquarters of the Leanin' Tree greeting card company. Some 250 paintings and 150 bronze sculptures illustrate the landscape, cowboys, Native Americans and wildlife of the American West. An outdoor sculpture garden contains more than 20 large bronze creations. Free guided tours of the greeting card facility are available.

Time: Allow 1 hour minimum. **Hours:** Mon.-Fri. 8-6, Sat.-Sun. 9-5. Greeting card facility tours Mon.-Fri. 10-2. Closed Jan. 1, Easter, Memorial Day, July 4, Labor Day, Thanksgiving and Christmas. **Cost:** Free. **Phone:** (303) 729-3412, ext. 5. GT

NATIONAL CENTER FOR ATMOSPHERIC RESEARCH (NCAR), 1850 Table Mesa Dr., is a National Science Foundation-sponsored scientific research laboratory offering interactive exhibits and informational displays on such topics as weather; past, present and future climate; Earth's atmosphere and Sun; and NCAR supercomputing capabilities including weather and climate modeling. The building, designed by renowned architect I.M. Pei, is nestled against Boulder's Flatiron mountains, overlooking the city in a picturesque setting. An interpretive .25-mile outdoor weather trail, art galleries, a weather gallery and an exhibit about the relationship between the Sun and Earth are offered.

Guided 1-hour tours are available Mon., Wed., and Fri. at noon or by appointment. Self-guiding tours via personal cell phone or computer tablets available for loan, in both adult and child versions, are offered in English and Spanish daily. **Hours:** Visitor center Mon.-Fri. 8-5, Sat.-Sun. and some holidays 9-4. Guided tours depart Mon. and Wed. at noon. **Cost:** Admission and audio tours free. Computer tablet tours free with ID. **Phone:** (303) 497-1000.

UNIVERSITY OF COLORADO MUSEUM OF NATURAL HISTORY is in the Henderson Building at 15th St. and Broadway. The museum offers exhibits and activities that focus on the natural and cultural history of the Rocky Mountain west. Subjects include dinosaurs and other fossils, southwestern archeology and Colorado's plants and wildlife. A children's Discovery Corner also is available. **Time:** Allow 1 hour minimum. **Hours:** Mon.-Fri. 9-5, Sat. 9-4, Sun. 10-4. Closed major holidays. **Cost:** Donations. **Phone:** (303) 492-6892.

WINERIES

• **Redstone Meadery** is e. on Pearl St. past Foothills Pkwy. (SR 157), then n. on 47th St. to 4700 Pearl St. **Hours:** Tasting room open Mon.-Fri. noon-6:30, Sat. noon-5. Tours are offered Mon.-Fri. at 1 and 3, Sat. at 12:30. **Phone:** (720) 406-1215. GT

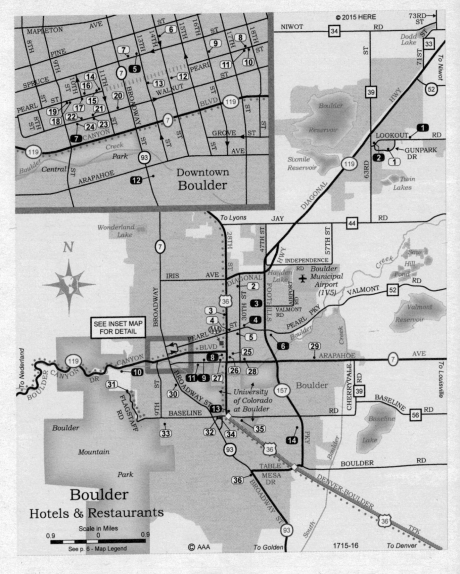

Boulder

This index helps you "spot" where approved hotels and restaurants are located on the corresponding detailed maps. Hotel daily rate range is for comparison only. Restaurant price range is a combination of lunch and/or dinner. Turn to the listing page for more detailed rate and price information and consult display ads for special promotions.

BOULDER

Map Page	Hotels	Diamond Rated	Rate Range	Page
1 this page	Lookout Inn Guesthouse & Suites	▼▼	Rates not provided	62
2 this page	Hampton Inn & Suites Boulder- North	▼▼▼	Rates not provided	61
3 this page	Residence Inn by Marriott	▼▼▼	$160-$333	62
4 this page	Hyatt Place Boulder/Pearl Street	▼▼▼	$129-$329 [SAVE]	62

BOULDER (cont'd)

Map Page	Hotels (cont'd)	Diamond Rated	Rate Range	Page
5 p. 59	**Hotel Boulderado**	◈◈◈	$224-$429 SAVE	62
6 p. 59	Courtyard by Marriott-Boulder	◈◈◈	$119-$302	61
7 p. 59	**St Julien Hotel & Spa**	◈◈◈◈	$259-$599 SAVE	62
8 p. 59	Boulder Marriott	◈◈◈	$156-$355	61
9 p. 59	The Briar Rose Bed & Breakfast	◈◈	$164-$219	61
10 p. 59	**Foot of The Mountain Motel**	◈	$99-$175 SAVE	61
11 p. 59	Quality Inn & Suites Boulder Creek	◈◈	$110-$210	62
12 p. 59	**Boulder University Inn**	◈◈	$109-$249 SAVE	61
13 p. 59	**BEST WESTERN PLUS Boulder Inn**	◈◈	$129-$229 SAVE	61
14 p. 59	Homewood Suites by Hilton	◈◈◈	Rates not provided	62

Map Page	Restaurants	Diamond Rated	Cuisine	Price Range	Page
1 p. 59	Gunbarrel Deli	◈	Deli	$6-$9	64
2 p. 59	Boulder Cork	◈◈◈	American	$12-$40	63
3 p. 59	Chez Thuy Vietnamese Restaurant	◈◈	Vietnamese	$8-$30	64
4 p. 59	Turley's	◈◈	Natural/Organic	$12-$18	65
5 p. 59	Ras Kassa's Ethiopian Restaurant	◈◈	Ethiopian	$10-$18	65
6 p. 59	Lucile's Creole Cafe	◈◈	Creole	$8-$13	64
7 p. 59	Sushi Zanmai	◈◈	Sushi	$10-$25	65
8 p. 59	L'Atelier	◈◈◈	French	$12-$29	64
9 p. 59	Leaf Vegetarian Restaurant	◈◈◈	Vegetarian	$10-$17	64
10 p. 59	Frasca	◈◈◈◈	Regional Italian	$28-$38	64
11 p. 59	Pizzeria Locale	◈◈◈	Pizza	$9-$17	65
12 p. 59	Oak at Fourteenth	◈◈◈	Small Plates	$12-$30	65
13 p. 59	Black Cat	◈◈◈	Natural/Organic	$24-$35	63
14 p. 59	Salt	◈◈◈	Natural/Organic	$12-$28	65
15 p. 59	The Kitchen	◈◈◈	Natural/Organic	$14-$34	64
16 p. 59	Pasta Jay's	◈◈	Italian	$8-$18	65
17 p. 59	Centro Latin Kitchen & Refreshment Palace	◈◈◈	Latin American	$11-$24	63
18 p. 59	Jax Fish House & Oyster Bar	◈◈◈	Seafood	$15-$35	64
19 p. 59	West End Tavern	◈◈	American	$8-$22	65
20 p. 59	Walnut Brewery	◈◈	American	$9-$17	65
21 p. 59	Brasserie Ten Ten	◈◈◈	French	$9-$30	63
22 p. 59	Boulder Chophouse & Tavern	◈◈◈	Steak	$14-$35	63
23 p. 59	The Mediterranean	◈◈◈	Mediterranean	$7-$24	64
24 p. 59	Jill's	◈◈◈	American	$11-$37	64
25 p. 59	**Cantina Laredo**	◈◈	Mexican	$9-$22	63
26 p. 59	Modmarket	◈	American	$5-$14	64
27 p. 59	Zolo Grill	◈◈◈	Southwestern	$10-$28	65

Map Page	Restaurants (cont'd)	Diamond Rated	Cuisine	Price Range	Page
28 p. 59	Moe's Broadway Bagel	◆	Deli	$6-$11	64
29 p. 59	Blackbelly Market	◆◆	American	$8-$27	62
30 p. 59	Cafe Aion	◆◆	Spanish Small Plates	$10-$21	63
31 p. 59	The Flagstaff House Restaurant	◆◆◆	New American	$35-$68	64
32 p. 59	Taj Indian Cuisine	◆◆	Indian	$10-$16	65
33 p. 59	Chautauqua Dining Hall	◆◆	American	$10-$18	63
34 p. 59	Beau Jo's Colorado Style Pizza (See ad p. 63.)	◆	Pizza	$8-$12	62
35 p. 59	Carelli's of Boulder	◆◆	Italian	$11-$30	63
36 p. 59	Tandoori Grill	◆◆	Indian	$10-$17	65

BEST WESTERN PLUS BOULDER INN
(303)449-3800 **13**

Hotel $129-$229

AAA Benefit: Save 10% or more every day and earn 10% bonus points!

Address: 770 28th St 80303 **Location:** US 36 (28th St) exit Baseline Rd via Frontage Rd. Opposite University of Colorado. **Facility:** 98 units. 2 stories, interior corridors. **Pool(s):** heated outdoor. **Activities:** sauna, hot tub, bicycles, trails, exercise room. **Guest Services:** valet and coin laundry.

BOULDER MARRIOTT
(303)440-8877 **8**

Hotel $156-$355 **Address:** 2660 Canyon Blvd 80302 **Location:** US 36 (28th St), just w on Canyon Blvd, s on 26th St. **Facility:** 157 units. 5 stories, interior corridors. **Terms:** check-in 4 pm. **Amenities:** safes. **Pool(s):** heated indoor. **Activities:** exercise room. **Guest Services:** valet and coin laundry, boarding pass kiosk.

AAA Benefit: Members save 5% or more!

BOULDER UNIVERSITY INN
(303)417-1700 **12**

Motel $109-$249

Address: 1632 Broadway 80302 **Location:** US 36 (28th St) exit Baseline Rd, 0.3 mi s, then 3 mi nw. **Facility:** 40 units. 2 stories (no elevator), exterior corridors. *Bath:* shower only. **Terms:** cancellation fee imposed. **Pool(s):** heated outdoor. **Guest Services:** valet and coin laundry. **Featured Amenity:** continental breakfast.

THE BRIAR ROSE BED & BREAKFAST
(303)442-3007 **9**

Bed & Breakfast $164-$219 **Address:** 2151 Arapahoe Ave 80302 **Location:** 0.5 mi w of US 36 (28th St). Located in a residential area. **Facility:** 10 units. 2 stories (no elevator), interior/exterior corridors. **Terms:** 5 day cancellation notice-fee imposed.

COURTYARD BY MARRIOTT-BOULDER
(303)440-4700 **6**

Hotel $119-$302 **Address:** 4710 Pearl East Cir 80301 **Location:** Just e of SR 157 (Foothills Pkwy) exit Pearl St, just e to Pearl East Cir, just s, then just w. **Facility:** 149 units. 3 stories, interior corridors. **Terms:** check-in 4 pm. **Pool(s):** heated indoor. **Activities:** hot tub, exercise room. **Guest Services:** valet and coin laundry, boarding pass kiosk.

AAA Benefit: Members save 5% or more!

FOOT OF THE MOUNTAIN MOTEL
303/442-5688 **10**

Vintage Motel $99-$175

Address: 200 Arapahoe Ave 80302 **Location:** 1.8 mi w of US 36 (28th St). **Facility:** Built in 1936, this charming rustic-style motel features cozy rooms with knotty pine wood paneling, retro style fridges, and fluffy white bedding. 20 units, some two bedrooms and kitchens. 1 story, exterior corridors. **Terms:** 14 day cancellation notice-fee imposed. **Activities:** trails. **Featured Amenity:** continental breakfast.

HAMPTON INN & SUITES BOULDER- NORTH
303/530-3300 **2**

Hotel. Rates not provided. **Address:** 6333 Lookout Rd 80301 **Location:** SR 119 exit 63rd St, just s, then just w. **Facility:** 100 units. 3 stories, interior corridors. **Pool(s):** heated indoor. **Activities:** hot tub, bicycles, exercise room. **Guest Services:** valet and coin laundry, area transportation.

AAA Benefit: Members save up to 10%!

HOLIDAY INN EXPRESS
(303)442-6600

Hotel $120-$230

Address: 4777 N Broadway 80304 **Location:** 3 mi n of Pearl Street Pedestrian Mall. **Facility:** 106 units. 3 stories, interior corridors. **Terms:** cancellation fee imposed. **Pool(s):** heated outdoor. **Activities:** hot tub, bicycles, picnic facilities, exercise room. **Guest Services:** complimentary and valet laundry. **Featured Amenity:** full hot breakfast.

(See map & index p. 59.)

HOMEWOOD SUITES BY HILTON   303/499-9922   14

WWW   **Extended Stay Hotel.**
Rates not provided. **Address:** 4950
Baseline Rd 80303 **Location:** 1.2 mi e of
US 36 (28th St); jct SR 157 (Foothills
Pkwy), just w; entry off Baseline Rd. Lo-
cated behind Meadows Shopping Center. **Facility:** 112 efficiencies,
some two bedrooms. 2 stories, interior/exterior corridors. **Pool(s):**
heated outdoor. **Activities:** exercise room. **Guest Services:** valet
and coin laundry, area transportation.

AAA Benefit:
Members save up to
10%!

HOTEL BOULDERADO   (303)442-4344   5

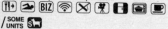

Classic Historic
Hotel
$224-$429

Address: 2115 13th St 80302 **Location:**
At 13th and Spruce sts, just n of Pearl
Street Pedestrian Mall. **Facility:** The
stunning stained glass ceiling in the
lobby, historic displays and carved-wood
crown molding add character to this
hotel. 160 units. 4-5 stories, interior corridors. **Parking:** valet only. **Terms:**
check-in 4 pm, cancellation fee imposed.
Amenities: *Some:* safes. **Dining:** 2 restaurants. **Activities:** exercise room, massage. **Guest Services:** valet laundry.

HYATT PLACE BOULDER/PEARL STREET
(303)442-0160   4

WWW
Hotel
$129-$329

 HYATT PLACE
AAA Benefit: Members save 10%!

Address: 2280 Junction Pl 80301 **Location:** Jct US 36 and Pearl St, just e. **Facility:** 150 units. 5 stories, interior
corridors. **Parking:** on-site (fee) and
valet. **Pool(s):** indoor. **Activities:** hot
tub, bicycles, trails, exercise room.
Guest Services: valet and coin laundry.
Featured Amenity: breakfast buffet.

LOOKOUT INN GUESTHOUSE & SUITES   303/530-1513   1

WW WW **Hotel.** Rates not provided. **Address:** 6901 Lookout Rd
80301 **Location:** SR 119 exit 63rd St, just s, 0.7 mi e on Lookout Rd,
then just n on Idylwild Tr. **Facility:** 13 units. 1-2 stories (no elevator),
exterior corridors. **Activities:** exercise room.

QUALITY INN & SUITES BOULDER CREEK
(303)449-7550   11

WWW **Hotel** $110-$210 **Address:** 2020 Arapahoe Ave 80302
Location: US 36 (28th St), 0.5 mi w. **Facility:** 49 units. 1-2 stories
(no elevator), interior/exterior corridors. **Activities:** sauna, hot tub, exercise room. **Guest Services:** valet and coin laundry.

RESIDENCE INN BY MARRIOTT   (303)449-5545   3

WWW   **Extended Stay Hotel**
$160-$333 **Address:** 3030 Center
Green Dr 80301 **Location:** 0.5 mi w of
US 36 (28th St), e on Valmont Rd; from
Foothills Pkwy, just w on Valmont Rd.
Facility: 128 units, some efficiencies and kitchens. 2 stories (no ele-
vator), exterior corridors. **Pool(s):** heated outdoor. **Activities:** exer-
cise room. **Guest Services:** valet and coin laundry.

AAA Benefit:
Members save 5%
or more!

ST JULIEN HOTEL & SPA   (720)406-9696   7

Hotel
$259-$599

Address: 900 Walnut St 80302 **Location:** Jct 9th and Walnut sts; downtown.
Facility: This attractively designed, full-
service hotel's prime location is just a
short walk from the Pearl Street Pedestrian Mall and popular hiking trails. 201
units. 4 stories, interior corridors.
Parking: on-site (fee) and valet. **Terms:**
cancellation fee imposed. **Amenities:**
safes. **Dining:** Jill's, see separate listing,
entertainment. **Pool(s):** heated indoor.
Activities: sauna, hot tub, steamroom,
bicycles, trails, exercise room, spa.
Guest Services: valet laundry, area
transportation. Affiliated with Preferred

Hotels & Resorts.

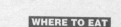

WHERE TO EAT

BEAU JO'S COLORADO STYLE PIZZA
303/554-5312   34

Pizza
Casual Dining
$8-$12

AAA Inspector Notes: Known for its
pizza, this eatery offers a fun atmosphere with a mountain theme. Build
your pizza from the crust up. Choices
include a mountain pie with a thick,
chewy edge; the thin-crust prairie pie;
and gluten-free options. Add your fa-
vorite toppings or choose a specialty pizza like the sky hawk
(a pepperoni pie with Hatch green chiles and feta), or Skier
Mike's chicken, Canadian bacon and green pepper pie. **Features:** full bar. **Address:** 2690 Baseline Rd 80305 **Location:**
US 36 exit Baseline Rd, just w. (See ad p. 63.)

"Colorado Style Pizza"
Also Gluten Free Menu

BLACKBELLY MARKET   303/247-1000   29

WWW   **American. Quick Serve.** $8-$27 **AAA Inspector Notes:**
This eatery has a unique concept. During breakfast and lunch, it's a
fast, casual eatery; dinner is a more formal experience. All menus
feature farm-fresh ingredients, including pork and lamb raised by the
restaurant. For lunch, try a gourmet sandwich like the house-smoked
ham club, pork Cubano, and meatball grinder. Start dinner with hatch
green chile posole, Spanish octopus salad, and Colorado wagyu beef
tartare. Entrées include duck breast, pan-seared barramundi and rotisserie chicken. **Features:** full bar, patio dining, happy hour. **Address:** 1606 Conestoga St 80301 **Location:** Foothills Pkwy exit SR
7 (Arapahoe Ave), 0.6 mi e, then just n.

(See map & index p. 59.)

BLACK CAT   303/444-5500 ⑬
▼▼▼ Natural/Organic. Fine Dining. $24-$35 **AAA Inspector Notes:** The highlight of this cozy restaurant is the innovative cuisine of chef/owner Eric Skokan. The menu changes based on what is available from the restaurant's organic farm, located just northwest of Boulder. Fresh ingredients, chef Skokan's inspired dishes, and an enthusiastic, knowledgeable staff make for an unforgettable meal. Sample dishes include heirloom beet salad, cassoulet of quail and sumac, Columbia River sturgeon, and orange-glazed donuts with salted caramel ice cream. **Features:** full bar. **Reservations:** suggested. **Address:** 1964 13th St 80302 **Location:** Just s of Pearl Street Pedestrian Mall. **Parking:** street only. Ⓓ

BOULDER CHOPHOUSE & TAVERN   303/443-1188 ㉒
▼▼▼ Steak. Casual Dining. $14-$35 **AAA Inspector Notes:** This popular eatery offers various steaks, seafood and other meats, as well as sides and appetizers; you can have tavern fare until midnight. The main dining room offers subdued lighting and interesting historic photos of Boulder. **Features:** full bar, patio dining, happy hour. **Reservations:** suggested. **Address:** 921 Walnut St 80302 **Location:** Just s of Pearl Street Pedestrian Mall. **Parking:** street only. Ⓓ CALL🅶🅼

BOULDER CORK   303/443-9505 ②
▼▼▼ American. Casual Dining. $12-$40 **AAA Inspector Notes:** A favorite spot for delicious steaks since 1969, the restaurant presents a Southwestern menu that also features prime rib, seafood, salad, sandwiches, artichokes and lighter fare. Patio dining is a nice seasonal option. **Features:** full bar, patio dining, early bird specials, happy hour. **Reservations:** suggested. **Address:** 3295 30th St 80301 **Location:** US 36 (28th St) exit SR 157 (Foothills Pkwy) to Valmont Rd, 0.4 mi w, then 0.3 mi n. Ⓛ Ⓓ

BRASSERIE TEN TEN   303/998-1010 ㉑
▼▼ French. Casual Dining. $9-$30 **AAA Inspector Notes:** Although the cuisine is French based, this restaurant has a more casual, bistro feel. The brique poulet, served in beurre blanc sauce with Kennebec frites, is highly recommended. The sauce is buttery, but not overwhelmingly rich. The frites are thin and savory. The happy hour menu has reasonably priced small plates allowing patrons to sample a variety of items in one sitting. **Features:** full bar, Sunday brunch, happy hour. **Address:** 1011 Walnut St 80302 **Location:** Between 9th and 11th sts. **Parking:** on-site and street. Ⓛ Ⓓ

CAFE AION   303/993-8131 ㉚
▼▼▼ Spanish Small Plates. Casual Dining. $10-$21 **AAA Inspector Notes:** Locals love this restaurant for its simple food presentation, use of fresh local ingredients, and tapas-style small plates. All menu items are meant to be shared, so be sure to order accordingly. Plates include duck, scallops, mussels, chicken, pork and Colorado lamb. Vegetarian options are plentiful. **Features:** full bar, Sunday brunch, happy hour. **Address:** 1235 Pennsylvania Ave, Suite A 80302 **Location:** Between 12th and 13th sts; opposite University of Colorado. **Parking:** street only. Ⓛ Ⓓ CALL🅶🅼

CANTINA LAREDO   303/444-2260 ㉕
▼▼ ▼▼
Mexican
Casual Dining
$9-$22
AAA Inspector Notes: Sophisticated yet relaxed, this eatery features authentic Mexican fare with a creative twist. A great starter is the top-shelf guacamole, which is prepared tableside and primes the palate for the entree. The menu features traditional favorites such as tacos, enchiladas, fajitas, carnitas and chiles rellenos. Also featured are vegetarian and gluten-free dishes. **Features:** full bar, Sunday brunch, happy hour. **Address:** 1680 29th St 80301 **Location:** Just n of Arapahoe Ave. Ⓛ Ⓓ

Gourmet Mexican food, fresh-squeezed lime margaritas

CARELLI'S OF BOULDER   303/938-9300 ㉟
▼▼▼ Italian. Fine Dining. $11-$30 **AAA Inspector Notes:** The centerpiece of this inviting dining room is a large fireplace that makes you feel at home and comfortable. Start with a traditional dish like the poached mussels or the more exotic salmon carpaccio. Extensive entrée options include grilled salmon, veal parmigiana, ravioli, fettuccine Alfredo, and pollo saltimbocca as well as artisan pizzas with Hazel Dell mushrooms, fresh mozzarella and San Danielle prosciutto. **Features:** full bar, patio dining, happy hour. **Reservations:** suggested. **Address:** 645 30th St 80303 **Location:** Jct Baseline Rd (SR 93); in Williams Village Shopping Center. Ⓛ Ⓓ

CENTRO LATIN KITCHEN & REFRESHMENT PALACE   303/442-7771 ⑰
▼▼▼ Latin American. Casual Dining. $11-$24 **AAA Inspector Notes:** The lively atmosphere and friendly staff draw locals and visitors in droves, so making reservations at dinner would be wise. The menu features a variety of Mexican-style dishes including tacos, carne asada and chicken enchiladas as well as dishes from other Latin American countries, such as shrimp and sea bass ceviche and picadillo empanadas. The menu changes seasonally, but if it's available, try the dulce de leche flan with grapefruit. **Features:** full bar, patio dining, Sunday brunch, happy hour. **Reservations:** suggested. **Address:** 950 Pearl St 80302 **Location:** West end of Pearl Street Pedestrian Mall. **Parking:** street only. Ⓓ CALL🅶🅼

CHAUTAUQUA DINING HALL   303/440-3776 ㉝
▼▼ ▼ American. Casual Dining. $10-$18 **AAA Inspector Notes:** *Historic.* Built in 1898, the restaurant is part of one of the few surviving Chautauqua meeting places, which was first instituted in the late 19th century as a way to educate communities through seasonal lectures, plays and other forms of entertainment. Although the restaurant recalls a time in the past, the menu reflects modern tastes by offering hamburgers, pasta and comfort food. **Features:** full bar, Sunday brunch, happy hour. **Address:** 900 Baseline Rd 80302 **Location:** US 36 (28th St) exit Baseline Rd, 1.2 mi w. **Parking:** on-site and street. 🍽 Ⓑ Ⓛ Ⓓ

▼ See AAA listing p. 62 ▼

(See map & index p. 59.)

CHEZ THUY VIETNAMESE RESTAURANT 303/442-1700 ③
▼▼▼ Vietnamese. Casual Dining. $8-$30 **AAA Inspector Notes:** This popular eatery features traditional Vietnamese favorites such as pho, stir fries, curries and hot pots, as well as some Chinese-, Thai- and Indonesian-influenced dishes. The service is fast and straightforward. **Features:** full bar. **Address:** 2655 28th St 80301 **Location:** US 36 (28th St), 0.4 mi n of Walnut St. Ⓛ Ⓓ

THE FLAGSTAFF HOUSE RESTAURANT
303/442-4640 ㉛
▼▼▼▼ **AAA Inspector Notes:** You'll enjoy fine dining and marvelous views at this mountainside restaurant offering an extraordinary wine list, ever-changing New American cuisine, wild game, fresh fish and vegetarian selections, a tasting menu and a terrace. Family-owned and operated since 1971, this reputable establishment has hosted the royal family of Japan, Paul Bocuse and other prominent chefs. **Features:** full bar. **Reservations:** suggested. **Address:** 1138 Flagstaff Rd 80302 **Location:** US 36 (28th St), 2.5 mi w on Baseline Rd. **Parking:** valet only. Ⓓ

New
American
Fine Dining
$35-$68

FRASCA 303/442-6966 ⑩
▼▼▼ ▼▼▼ Regional Italian. Fine Dining. $28-$38 **AAA Inspector Notes:** Translated as 'branch' in Italian, Frasca evokes a traditional neighborhood gathering spot in Italy's Friuli-Venezia Giulia region, where a branch typically marks the entrance to one of its dining and socializing hubs. On Monday, your only option is the prix fixe wine tasting menu, which you can order with or without pairings, but on other days, a seasonal menu nudges you toward sampling four small-portioned courses (although you may order fewer or more) for a discounted price. **Features:** full bar. **Reservations:** suggested. **Address:** 1738 Pearl St 80302 **Location:** Just w of jct 18th St; just e of Pearl Street Pedestrian Mall; downtown. **Parking:** on-site and street. Ⓓ

THE GREENBRIAR INN 303/440-7979
▼▼▼ American. Fine Dining. $23-$39 **AAA Inspector Notes:** Historic. Nestled in the foothills north of town, this restaurant sits on 20 acres with attractive flowers, ponds and vegetable gardens. Start with some fresh oysters or the sweet-and-savory shaved beet and arugula tiramisu, which is also a feast for the eyes. The roasted lamb sirloin features Mediterranean accompaniments. Other options include bison, Arctic char and Colorado striped bass. Mountain photos and fresh flowers add color to the dark wood décor. **Features:** full bar, patio dining, Sunday brunch. **Reservations:** suggested. **Address:** 8735 N Foothills Hwy 80302 **Location:** North of town on US 36 (28th St), west side of highway. Ⓓ 🐾

GUNBARREL DELI 303/530-5595 ①
▼ Deli. Quick Serve. $6-$9 **AAA Inspector Notes:** This eatery serves freshly made sandwiches, soups and salads as well as some baked goods. **Address:** 6545 Gun Park Dr, #280 80301 **Location:** Jct SR 119 (Diagonal Hwy) and 63rd St, just s to Lookout Rd, then w; jct Spine and Lookout rds; in Gunbarrel Square. Ⓑ Ⓛ

JAX FISH HOUSE & OYSTER BAR 303/444-1811 ⑱
▼▼▼ Seafood. Casual Dining. $15-$35 **AAA Inspector Notes:** A hot spot for Boulder dining, Jax looks like a New England fish house splashed with touches of New Orleans. Order up some bivalves from the oyster bar or choose a delicious fresh seafood entrée and pair it with a great microbrew or excellent martini. Then, sit back in the snug restaurant and enjoy the people-watching. A young, friendly waitstaff makes it all come together here. **Features:** full bar, happy hour. **Address:** 928 Pearl St 80302 **Location:** West end of Pearl Street Pedestrian Mall. **Parking:** street only. Ⓓ

JILL'S 720/406-7399 ㉔
▼▼▼ American. Casual Dining. $11-$37 **AAA Inspector Notes:** Especially popular on weekends, this casual eatery offers a combination of standard comfort food and more creative options. Gourmet sandwiches, pasta dishes and steaks share space with duck and Colorado Lamb. The flavorful spice-rubbed salmon is a standout entrée. Artful décor, expert tableside preparations, and friendly service add to the dining experience. **Features:** full bar, Sunday brunch, happy hour. **Reservations:** suggested. **Address:** 900 Walnut St 80302 **Location:** Jct 9th and Walnut sts; downtown; in St Julien Hotel & Spa. **Parking:** on-site (fee) and valet. Ⓑ Ⓛ Ⓓ

THE KITCHEN 303/544-5973 ⑮
▼▼▼ Natural/Organic. Casual Dining. $14-$34 **AAA Inspector Notes:** Well-suited to the vast list of wines, beers and cocktails, the frequently changing menu reflects the seasonal availability of ingredients. Local purveyors deliver many organic ingredients. Entrees may include lamb chops, bolognese and Colorado striped bass. End your meal with a duck egg custard tart and sticky toffee pudding. Original flooring and exposed brick walls define the dining room, where the distinctive décor blends simplicity with elegance. **Features:** full bar, Sunday brunch, happy hour. **Address:** 1039 Pearl St 80302 **Location:** Between 10th and 11th sts; downtown. **Parking:** street only. Ⓛ Ⓓ

L'ATELIER 303/442-7233 ⑧
▼▼▼ French. Fine Dining. $12-$29 **AAA Inspector Notes:** Although service may slip when this spot gets busy, you won't mind when you get a taste of the excellent, gorgeously presented French brasserie fare. The décor features custom displays of French figurines. At lunchtime, the tuna carpaccio with house-made crackers is a delicious treat. The sophisticated dinner menu includes duck, rack of lamb, filet mignon and lobster. It's difficult to choose from the extensive list of decadent desserts. **Features:** full bar. **Reservations:** suggested. **Address:** 1739 Pearl St 80302 **Location:** Between 17th and 18th sts. **Parking:** street only. Ⓛ Ⓓ

LEAF VEGETARIAN RESTAURANT 303/442-1485 ⑨
▼▼▼ Vegetarian. Fine Dining. $10-$17 **AAA Inspector Notes:** This eatery does more than serve vegetables, it honors them. Ingredients are grown and gathered on the restaurant farm nearby. For a light meal, choose a mushroom burger, brie sandwich or a "sushi" salad, which offers ingredients found in sushi, except the fish. Larger dishes include huevos rancheros, Jamaican jerk tempeh and spaghetti squash pad thai. The flavors and visual appeal of the vegan carrot cake add a level of sophistication not typically seen at a vegetarian restaurant. **Features:** full bar, Sunday brunch, happy hour. **Address:** 2010 16th St 80302 **Location:** Just n of jct Pearl St. **Parking:** street only. Ⓛ Ⓓ

LUCILE'S CREOLE CAFE 303/442-4743 ⑥
▼ Creole. Casual Dining. $8-$13 **AAA Inspector Notes:** This eatery features friendly folks serving up large portions of a Cajun-influenced, home-style menu. The beignets are a true treat—hot, fresh and covered in powdered sugar. Known for their creative, hearty breakfasts, many locals choose to eat breakfast for lunch. Adventurous eaters might try the eggs Pontchartrain (featuring mountain trout, poached eggs and Bearnaise) or the eggs New Orleans (fried eggplant slices with creole sauce, poached eggs and hollandaise). **Features:** patio dining. **Address:** 2124 14th St 80302 **Location:** 1 blk n of Pearl Street Pedestrian Mall. **Parking:** street only. Ⓑ Ⓛ

THE MEDITERRANEAN 303/444-5335 ㉓
▼▼▼ Mediterranean. Casual Dining. $7-$24 **AAA Inspector Notes:** This bustling restaurant is located close to the popular Pearl Street Pedestrian Mall. Lamb kebabs are on the menu along with gourmet pizzas, like the burrata and prosciutto, and paella. Try one of the tapas: the burrata al tartufo stands out. The creamy, salty burrata cheese pairs well with the tart marinara and earthy black truffles. Knowledgeable servers help you navigate the extensive offerings. **Features:** full bar, patio dining, happy hour. **Address:** 1002 Walnut St 80302 **Location:** Between 9th and 10th sts. **Parking:** street only. Ⓛ Ⓓ

MODMARKET 303/440-0476 ㉖
▼ American. Quick Serve. $5-$14 **AAA Inspector Notes:** This eatery allows you to quickly grab a healthy, farm-fresh meal. In this case, healthy doesn't mean boring or flavorless. In fact, just the opposite. You'll choose from a variety of hearty salads, sandwiches and pizzas. Examples include flat iron steak salad, mushroom-pear salad, a basil chicken sandwich, prosciutto pizza and a sesame tofu plate. Calorie counters will be happy to see a calorie total on their receipt. **Features:** beer & wine. **Address:** 1600 28th St, Suite 1212 80301 **Location:** Jct US 36 and Arapahoe Ave, just e, just n on 29th St, then just w; in strip mall. Ⓑ Ⓛ Ⓓ

MOE'S BROADWAY BAGEL 303/442-4427 ㉘
▼ Deli. Quick Serve. $6-$11 **AAA Inspector Notes:** Like their outlet on North Broadway, this one is popular with the locals, but is closer to nearby lodgings. It offers a wide variety of bagels and juices as well as breakfast, coffees, soup and sandwiches. **Address:** 3075 Arapahoe Ave 80301 **Location:** Just e of jct 30th St and Arapahoe Ave; in Sunrise Center. Ⓑ Ⓛ

(See map & index p. 59.)

OAK AT FOURTEENTH   303/444-3622 (12)

▼▼▼ Small Plates. Fine Dining. $12-$30 **AAA Inspector Notes:** The menu at this stylish restaurant focuses on unique small plates consisting of locally sourced ingredients. Some highlights include the tomato braised meatballs topped with burrata, the hamachi crudo, and, for dessert, the salted caramel budino. Pork tenderloin, scallops, chicken and steak are featured in the larger plates. The spacious windows allow for people-watching near Pearl Street and offer a hint of a mountain view. **Features:** full bar. **Address:** 1400 Pearl St 80302 **Location:** Corner of 14th St. **Parking:** street only.

 L D

PASTA JAY'S   303/444-5800 (16)

▼▼ Italian. Casual Dining. $8-$18 **AAA Inspector Notes:** Enjoying pizza and pasta here is a Boulder tradition. The dining rooms may be small, but the food flavors are big. Service is friendly, and people-watching is an event on the patio. Takeout is available. **Features:** full bar. **Address:** 1001 Pearl St 80302 **Location:** On Pearl Street Pedestrian Mall. **Parking:** street only. L D

PIZZERIA LOCALE   303/442-3003 (11)

▼▼▼ Pizza. Casual Dining. $9-$17 **AAA Inspector Notes:** The gourmet menu indicates an intimate knowledge of authentic Napoli pizzerias. The key ingredient to all menu items is flavor. The tuna wrapped in roasted red peppers and drizzled with olive oil and the Diavola pizza with provola di bufala cheese, basil and salame piccante are highly recommended. Enlarged photos of modern Italy enhance the décor. **Features:** full bar, patio dining. **Address:** 1730 Pearl St 80302 **Location:** Between 17th and 18th sts, just e of 16th St; in the Pearl Street Pedestrian Mall. **Parking:** street only.

 L D

RAS KASSA'S ETHIOPIAN RESTAURANT   303/447-2919 (5)

▼▼ Ethiopian. Casual Dining. $10-$18 **AAA Inspector Notes:** Operating in the area for more than 20 years, this ethnic establishment remains a favorite for locals looking for something different. Diners sit at low tables and eat a variety of stews, vegetarian dishes, meats, chicken and salads with a spongy bread. **Features:** full bar, patio dining, happy hour. **Address:** 2111 30th St, Unit E 80301 **Location:** SR 157 (Foothills Pkwy) exit Pearl St, w to 30th St, then just s.

 L D

SALT   303/444-7258 (14)

▼▼▼ Natural/Organic. Casual Dining. $12-$28 **AAA Inspector Notes:** Flavorful, innovative dishes have earned chef/co-owner Bradford Heap well-deserved local and national attention. The menu changes seasonally and focuses on local, organic ingredients. Sample items include tomato soup with goat cheese, steak salad with avocado and summer vegetables, tender pork belly risotto, local lamb sausage, Tom's Tavern burger, and grilled Southwestern lane snapper. Many of the tasty craft cocktails feature Colorado spirits. **Features:** full bar, patio dining, Sunday brunch, happy hour. **Address:** 1047 Pearl St 80302 **Location:** Between 10th and 11th sts; downtown. **Parking:** street only. L D

SUSHI ZANMAI   303/440-0733 (7)

▼▼ Sushi. Casual Dining. $10-$25 **AAA Inspector Notes:** A convivial and noisy atmosphere pervades this eatery, an established downtown favorite for super sushi. **Features:** full bar, happy hour. **Reservations:** suggested, weekends. **Address:** 1221 Spruce St 80302 **Location:** Just n of Pearl Street Pedestrian Mall; 1 blk e of Broadway. **Parking:** street only. L D

TAJ INDIAN CUISINE   303/494-5216 (32)

▼▼ Indian. Casual Dining. $10-$16 **AAA Inspector Notes:** Located on the second level of a strip mall, this eatery has windows with views of the Flatiron Mountains. The buffet offers traditional favorites like pyaji pakora (chickpea-battered onions), curry chicken, and fluffy naan bread. For a dish with satisfying heat, try the lightly breaded chili chicken. **Features:** full bar. **Address:** 2630 Baseline Rd 80305 **Location:** Baseline Rd (SR 93) exit US 36 (28th St), just w; in Basemar Shopping Plaza, 2nd Floor. L D

TANDOORI GRILL   303/543-7339 (36)

▼▼ Indian. Casual Dining. $10-$17 **AAA Inspector Notes:** In a shopping center near the corner of Broadway and Table Mesa, this restaurant offers Indian cuisine on its full menu and on the popular daily buffet. **Features:** full bar. **Address:** 619 S Broadway St 80305 **Location:** US 36 (28th St) exit Table Mesa Dr, 1 mi w; in Table Mesa Shopping Center. L D

TURLEY'S   303/442-2800 (4)

▼▼ Natural/Organic. Casual Dining. $12-$18 **AAA Inspector Notes:** Decorated with colorful, modern art, this eatery focuses on healthy eating. The menu features many organic vegetables and all-natural chicken and beef, as well as vegan and gluten-free items. Sample dishes include a kale and mixed-green salad topped with pears and maple-balsamic dressing; a braised brisket sandwich; tacos de adobada; buffalo meat loaf; and a natural beef-bacon cheddar burger. **Features:** full bar, happy hour. **Address:** 2805 Pearl St 80301 **Location:** Jct SR 119, just e. B L D

WALNUT BREWERY   303/447-1345 (20)

▼▼ American. Casual Dining. $9-$17 **AAA Inspector Notes:** This upscale, trendy and very popular pub features tasty dishes and several homemade brews, some of which are part of the food recipes. Brunch is offered on Saturday and Sunday. Service is friendly and attentive. **Features:** full bar, happy hour. **Address:** 1123 Walnut St 80302 **Location:** Between 11th St and Broadway. **Parking:** on-site and street. L D

WEST END TAVERN   303/444-3535 (19)

▼▼ American. Casual Dining. $8-$22 **AAA Inspector Notes:** This popular local eatery offers rooftop dining and a great view of the Flatirons. The menu features all natural beef, chicken and pork. All of the cooking oil is recycled into biodiesel that fuels their mobile smoker. The smoked barbecue ribs, served with a crunchy fennel coleslaw, is a highlight. Other menu items include burgers, gourmet sandwiches, fried chicken, and much more. Rich, flavorful sauces enhance every meal. Wash everything down with a microbrew or unique cocktail. **Features:** full bar, Sunday brunch, happy hour. **Address:** 926 Pearl St 80302 **Location:** On west end of Pearl Street Pedestrian Mall. **Parking:** street only. L D

ZOLO GRILL   303/449-0444 (27)

▼▼▼ Southwestern. Casual Dining. $10-$28 **AAA Inspector Notes:** The chef prepares an imaginative and flavorful cuisine that joins with the fun atmosphere to create a great place to dine. The restaurant also offers the best guacamole in town, a variety of tequila drinks and patio dining. **Features:** full bar, patio dining, Sunday brunch, happy hour. **Address:** 2525 Arapahoe Ave 80302 **Location:** Between 28th and Folsom sts; in Village Shopping Center.

 L D

BRECKENRIDGE (C-3) pop. 4,540, elev. 9,602'
• Hotels p. 67 • Restaurants p. 67

Breckenridge offers all the perks of a high-altitude environment and then some. With the winter months comes the thrill of snowboarding, downhill skiing, snowmobiling and dog-sledding. There are also more laid-back snow-related activities to indulge in, like snowshoeing and cross-country skiing; those ready to explore these pursuits on scenic trails can visit the Breckenridge Nordic Center, where the varied terrain satisfies beginners and experts alike. If gliding across the ice is more your style, hit Maggie Pond at the Village at Breckenridge for some quality outdoor skating.

When the summer months arrive, locals stash their cold-weather gear to bike the area's trail system or hike through meadows dotted with wildflowers. The Breckenridge Welcome Center provides visitors with information on trails suitable for hiking and mountain biking. For less-strenuous bicycle touring, a popular choice is the Blue River Bikeway, a 10-mile paved stretch between Breckenridge and Frisco—if you get tired, you can ride the Summit Stage bus back to "Breck." Fly-fishers cast their lines in the meandering Blue River year-round to hopefully snare some trout, and duffers hit the links at the Breckenridge Golf Club, a 27-hole course designed by Jack Nicklaus that's nestled in a valley.

This recreational paradise traces its roots to the gold rush, when prospectors panned gold from the Blue River in 1859. Nearly 250 historic structures reminiscent of the mining era are preserved in one of Colorado's largest National Historic Districts, and Breckenridge's charming Main Street houses galleries, shops, eateries and nightspots within these colorfully restored Victorians. Weary shoppers can hop on the free Breckenridge Trolley, which travels down the main drag and provides access to the ski slopes and other points throughout town.

For those inclined to learn more about the town's storied past, the Breckenridge Heritage Alliance, (970) 453-9767, conducts historic walking and mine tours; athletically oriented individuals also can take advantage of their guided ski and snowshoe excursions. If you prefer to do your sightseeing behind the wheel, catch Boreas Pass Road (FR 223) south of town, a route traveling along an old narrow-gauge railroad bed and cresting at 11,482 feet; you'll see stunning views of the Blue River Valley and an old railroad camp perched at the summit.

Breckenridge presents a medley of enticing events throughout the year. One of the most unique is the Budweiser International Snow Sculpture Championships in late January, when teams from throughout the globe create frosty works of art from massive 20-ton snow blocks. Plenty of activities are packed into 4 weeks from mid-March to late April during Spring Fever; outdoor concerts, competitions, family events, comedy shows and a beer festival are all part of the agenda. Mid-July to mid-August brings the sounds of classical music at the internationally acclaimed Breckenridge Music Festival—Classical Orchestra Summer Series, offering a variety of styles including chamber music, country and jazz.

Breckenridge Welcome Center: 203 S. Main St., P.O. Box 1909, Breckenridge, CO 80424. **Phone:** (970) 453-5579 or (877) 864-0868.

Self-guiding tours: Information about a walking tour through Breckenridge's historic district is available at the Breckenridge Welcome Center.

INSIDER INFO:
High Altitude Health

Temples throbbing, gasping for breath and nauseated, you barely notice the scudding clouds or the spectacular view.

You might be suffering from Acute Mountain Sickness (AMS). Usually striking at around 8,000 feet (2,450 m) in altitude, AMS is your body's way of coping with the reduced oxygen and humidity of high altitudes. Among the symptoms are headaches, shortness of breath, loss of appetite, insomnia and lethargy. Some people complain of temporary weight gain or swelling in the face, hands and feet.

You can reduce the effect of high altitude by being in top condition. If you smoke or suffer from heart or lung ailments, consult your physician before your trip. Certain drugs will intensify the symptoms. To avoid Acute Mountain Sickness, adjust to elevations slowly; a gradual ascent with a couple days of acclimatization is best if you have time. For example, if you are planning a trip to the Rocky Mountains of Colorado, you might want to spend the first night in a lower altitude city such as Denver as opposed to heading directly to an environment with extreme elevations.

On the way up, eat light, nutritious meals and stay hydrated by drinking a large amount of water, taking care to avoid caffeine, alcohol and salt. In addition, your doctor may be able to prescribe medication that can offset the effects of high-altitude.

If you develop AMS, you should stop ascending; you will recover in a few days. If the AMS is mild, a quick descent will end the suffering immediately.

Other high-altitude health problems include sunburn and hypothermia. Dress in layers to protect yourself from the intense sun and wide fluctuations in temperature.

Finally, after you lounge in the sauna or whirlpool bath at your lodgings, remember to stand up carefully, for the heat has relaxed your blood vessels and lowered your blood pressure.

BARNEY FORD HOUSE MUSEUM is at 111 E. Washington Ave. The museum depicts the life of Ford, a former slave that escaped via the Underground Railroad. His travels eventually led him to Colorado, where he became a civil rights pioneer and a successful restaurant and hotel owner. Exhibits focus on Ford and other African-Americans of the era. An 1800's schoolroom exhibit and articles from the period also are displayed. **Time:** Allow 30 minutes minimum. **Hours:** Tues.-Sun. 11-4, mid-June to early Sept.; Tues.-Sun. 11-3, early Sept. to mid-Oct. and mid-Dec. to late Apr.; Fri.-Sun. 11-3, rest of year. Phone ahead to confirm schedule. **Cost:** Donations. **Phone:** (970) 453-9767. GT

COUNTRY BOY MINE, off Wellington Rd. at 0542 French Gulch Rd., offers 45-minute guided underground tours of a late 1800s gold mine deeper than 1,000 feet, as well as mining exhibits and old buildings. Gold panning activities also are offered. Roaming miniature donkeys add to the mining camp environment.

Hard hats are provided. **Time:** Allow 1 hour minimum. **Hours:** Daily 9:30-5:15, Memorial Day weekend-Labor Day weekend; Mon.-Fri. 10:30-2:15, day after Labor Day to late Oct. **Cost:** Mine tour and gold panning $25.95; $19.95 (ages 4-12). Gold panning only $12.95. **Phone:** (970) 453-4405.

RECREATIONAL ACTIVITIES
Skiing
- **Breckenridge Resort** is at 1599C Summit County Rd. within the Arapaho and Roosevelt National Forests. Other activities are offered. **Hours:** Daily mid-Nov. to mid-Apr. (weather permitting). **Phone:** (970) 453-5000 or (800) 789-7669.

Snowmobiling

- **Good Times Adventure Tours and Dog Sledding** is 2.5 mi. n. on SR 9, e. at Breckenridge Golf Course, then 6.5 mi. to 6061 Tiger Rd. **Hours:** Daily 8-5, early Dec. to mid-Apr. Phone ahead to confirm schedule. **Phone:** (970) 453-7604 or (800) 477-0144.

White-water Rafting

- **Good Times Rafting** offers guided rafting trips down the Colorado River from various launch points. **Hours:** Daily 9-5, mid-May to mid-Aug. **Phone:** (719) 395-4200 or (877) 947-7238.

BEAVER RUN RESORT & CONFERENCE CENTER
(970)453-6000

Resort
Condominium
$145-$735

Address: 620 Village Rd 80424 **Location:** 0.4 mi sw of SR 9 and Village Rd; at base of Peak 9. **Facility:** This resort offers standard hotel rooms and condominium-style units with up to six bedrooms, each with a ceiling fan and humidifier. Underground parking is available. 500 condominiums. 5-8 stories, interior corridors. **Parking:** on-site (fee). **Terms:** check-in 4 pm, 1-7 night minimum stay - seasonal and/or weekends, 7 day cancellation notice-fee imposed, resort fee. **Dining:** 4 restaurants. **Pool(s):** heated outdoor, heated indoor. **Activities:** sauna, hot tub, steamroom, miniature golf, tennis, downhill & cross country skiing, ice skating, game room, picnic facilities, trails, exercise room, spa. **Guest Services:** valet and coin laundry, area transportation.

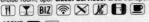

DOUBLETREE BY HILTON BRECKENRIDGE
970/547-5550

Hotel. Rates not provided.
Address: 550 Village Rd 80424 **Location:** Jct Main St, just w on S Park Ave, just sw. **Facility:** 207 units. 8 stories, interior corridors. **Parking:** on-site and valet. **Terms:** check-in 4 pm. **Amenities:** safes. **Dining:** 2 restaurants. **Pool(s):** heated indoor. **Activities:** sauna, hot tub, downhill & cross country skiing, recreation programs, trails, exercise room, massage. **Guest Services:** valet laundry, area transportation.

AAA Benefit:
Members save 5% or more!

THE LODGE AT BRECKENRIDGE
(970)453-9300

Hotel $129-$340 **Address:** 112 Overlook Dr 80424 **Location:** 0.3 m s of Main St and Ski Hill Rd to Boreas Pass Rd, then 2.2 mi w (uphill) to Overlook Rd. **Facility:** 47 units, some houses. 2 stories, interior/exterior corridors. **Terms:** check-in 4 pm, 30 day cancellation notice-fee imposed, resort fee. **Activities:** hot tub, trails, exercise room, spa. **Guest Services:** area transportation.

MAIN STREET STATION
970/453-4000

Condominium. Rates not provided. **Address:** 505 S Main St 80424 **Location:** 0.4 mi s of center; south end of downtown. **Facility:** The lodge-like exterior and lobby décor create a feeling of intimacy at this spacious resort. Swim or soak while gazing at the ski slopes in the outdoor pool and hot tub, which are open year-round. 60 condominiums. 4-5 stories, interior corridors. **Terms:** check-in 4 pm. **Dining:** Quandary Grille, see separate listing. **Pool(s):** heated outdoor. **Activities:** hot tub, steamroom, downhill skiing, exercise room. **Guest Services:** complimentary laundry, area transportation.

MARRIOTT'S MOUNTAIN VALLEY LODGE
(970)453-8500

Condominium $72-$406 **Address:** 655 Columbine Rd 80424 **Location:** 0.5 mi s of downtown (Ski Hill Rd and Lincoln Ave) to Broken Lance Dr, just w, then just n. **Facility:** Situated next to a river and lake, this resort offers picturesque views. Walk a short distance to reach shops, restaurants and the gondola. 111 condominiums. 3-7 stories, interior corridors. **Terms:** check-in 4 pm, 7 day cancellation notice. **Amenities:** safes. **Pool(s):** heated outdoor. **Activities:** hot tub, downhill skiing, recreation programs, bicycles, game room, picnic facilities, trails, exercise room. **Guest Services:** complimentary and valet laundry.

AAA Benefit:
Members save 5% or more!

MOUNTAIN STREAM LODGE
(970)453-2975

Bed & Breakfast $159-$269 **Address:** 303B N Main St 80424 **Location:** 0.3 mi n of center; north end of downtown. 5 units. 2 stories (no elevator), interior corridors. **Bath:** shower only. **Terms:** closed 5/1-5/24 & 10/20-12/4, check-in 4 pm, 45 day cancellation notice-fee imposed. **Activities:** hot tub.

MOUNTAIN THUNDER LODGE
970/547-5650

Condominium. Rates not provided. **Address:** 50 Mountain Thunder Dr 80424 **Location:** Jct Main St, 0.5 mi w on Park Ave. **Facility:** This property offers individually decorated accommodations in a peaceful, residential setting. Guests walk to the gondola but can ski down directly to their townhome or condominium building. 100 condominiums. 2-4 stories, interior/exterior corridors. **Terms:** check-in 4 pm. **Amenities:** safes. **Pool(s):** heated outdoor. **Activities:** hot tub, downhill skiing, playground, picnic facilities, trails, exercise room. **Guest Services:** complimentary and valet laundry, area transportation.

VALDORO MOUNTAIN LODGE BY HILTON GRAND VACATIONS
970/453-4880

Hotel. Rates not provided. **Address:** 500 Village Rd 80424 **Location:** Just off SR 9 via Village Park Ave, then s. **Facility:** 70 condominiums. 5 stories, interior corridors. **Terms:** check-in 4 pm. **Amenities:** safes. **Pool(s):** heated outdoor, heated indoor. **Activities:** hot tub, steamroom, recreation programs in summer, playground, game room, trails, exercise room, massage. **Guest Services:** complimentary and valet laundry.

AAA Benefit:
Members save 5% or more!

GOLD POINT RESORT
970/453-1910

[fyi] Condominium Did not meet all AAA rating requirements for viewports/peepholes in some guest rooms at time of last evaluation on 08/11/2015. **Address:** 53 View Ln 80424 **Location:** Jct SR 9 and Boreas Pass Rd, 1.9 mi se, 1.1 mi e on Baldy Rd. Facilities, services, and décor characterize a mid-scale property.

WHERE TO EAT

AMAZING GRACE NATURAL EATERY
970/453-1445

Natural/Organic Vegan. Quick Serve. $9-$10 **AAA Inspector Notes:** Heated by an antique woodstove, this adorable historic cabin is an old-fashioned gathering place to enjoy a hearty breakfast, spicy tofu salad, hummus and natural turkey, hearty winter soups, blue chip nachos, turkey veggie and turkey berry sandwiches. Scones, biscuits, muffins and oversize vegan chocolate chip cookies are made fresh daily. Gluten and dairy-free options are available. Look for the yellow cabin on the corner. **Features:** Sunday brunch. **Address:** 213 Lincoln Ave 80424 **Location:** Just e of Main St; corner of Lincoln Ave and French St; downtown. **Parking:** street only.

Take your imagination to new destinations with the online AAA/CAA Travel Guides

BLUE RIVER BISTRO 970/453-6974

▼▼▼ American. Casual Dining. $8-$36 **AAA Inspector Notes:** This bistro sustains a lively, energetic atmosphere, in part due to the live entertainment. On this creekside eatery's menu is a wide selection of appetizers, salads, pasta and seafood dishes, including Kobe beef or roasted Kurobuta pork sliders, classic escargot, grilled New York strip steak finished with tarragon and shallot compound butter, shellfish cioppino, chicken Parmesan, and gourmet mac and cheese. The servers are friendly, casual and knowledgeable. **Features:** full bar, patio dining, Sunday brunch, happy hour. **Address:** 305 N Main St 80424 **Location:** Just n of center. [L] [D] [AC]

BRECKENRIDGE BREWERY & PUB 970/453-1550

▼▼ American. Casual Dining. $9-$23 **AAA Inspector Notes:** This place has an airy, inviting and fun atmosphere in which guests can watch the brewing process, then sample a handcrafted ale. The menu includes soups and salads, fish and chips, pork spare ribs and country-fried steak. Sandwiches include barbecued pulled pork, hot turkey and Swiss, and steak and cheese. Burgers, grilled chicken sandwiches and Boca burgers can be ordered in such styles as Las Vegas, Alpine or Tijuana. Entertainment is occasionally provided. **Features:** full bar, patio dining, happy hour. **Address:** 600 S Main St 80424 **Location:** On SR 9, south end of town; corner of S Main and Ridge sts. [L] [D] [LATE] [AC]

BRIAR ROSE CHOPHOUSE & SALOON 970/453-9948

▼▼▼ Steak Seafood. Fine Dining. $20-$44 **AAA Inspector Notes:** Visiting this elegant downtown landmark is a must. Menu items include creatively presented shrimp cocktail with horseradish panna cotta, escargot with parsley-garlic butter, a popular roasted beet and arugula salad served with Colorado goat cheese crisps, mustard herb-crusted Colorado rack of lamb, and roasted duck with cranberry orange demi-glace. **Features:** full bar, happy hour. **Reservations:** suggested. **Address:** 109 E Lincoln Ave 80424 **Location:** Just e of Main St and Lincoln Ave; downtown. [D]

THE DREDGE RESTAURANT & BAR 970/453-4877

▼▼ American. Casual Dining. $12-$29 **AAA Inspector Notes:** Patrons must walk across a small bridge to reach the floating "dredge," which is right in the heart of town. Dredges were used for mining in Breckenridge from 1898 to 1942. Enjoy your meal with a lakeside view. Start with the Thai mussels served in a curry broth, or go for the fried calamari. Entrées include burgers, steaks, Alaskan king crab and pasta dishes. **Features:** full bar, patio dining, happy hour. **Address:** 180 W Jefferson Ave 80424 **Location:** Jct S Main St and W Jefferson Ave, just w; on Blue River. **Parking:** street only. [D] [AC]

EMBER 970/547-9595

▼▼▼ International. Fine Dining. $18-$32 **AAA Inspector Notes:** Chef Scott's vision to share globally-inspired cuisine happens in a historic Victorian home with upscale, contemporary style. Creative, seasonal menu items may feature pork loin, sweet potato pasta, scallops, beef rib-eye and buffalo tenderloin. **Features:** full bar, happy hour. **Reservations:** suggested. **Address:** 106 E Adams Ave 80424 **Location:** Just s of Main St. **Parking:** street only. [D] [AC]

THE HEARTHSTONE RESTAURANT 970/453-1148

▼▼▼ Regional American. Casual Dining. $18-$40 **AAA Inspector Notes:** Historic. Contemporary and regional dishes are served in a century-old Victorian home with gorgeous wall-mounted sconces and dark barn-wood walls. Seasonal menu items—such as prosciutto-wrapped scallops, crispy lobster and baby granola-crusted blackberry elk—are complemented by an excellent wine list. After-dinner wines and ports go well with the decadent desserts. Gluten-free items are available. **Features:** full bar, patio dining, happy hour. **Reservations:** suggested. **Address:** 130 S Ridge St 80424 **Location:** At Washington and Ridge sts, just e of Main St; downtown. **Parking:** street only. [D] CALL [M] [AC]

KENOSHA STEAKHOUSE 970/453-7313

▼▼ Steak Barbecue. Casual Dining. $9-$34 **AAA Inspector Notes:** Start with beer-steamed shrimp, Bavarian pretzel sticks or a fresh salad. Entrées include house-smoked pulled pork sandwiches, bison burgers, and steaks topped with crab stuffing or haystack onions. In warm weather, most diners prefer sitting on the patio. **Features:** full bar, patio dining, happy hour. **Address:** 301 S Main St 80424 **Location:** Corner of Main St and Adams Ave. **Parking:** street only. [L] [D] [AC]

LA FRANCAISE FRENCH BAKERY 970/547-7173

▼ Breads/Pastries. Quick Serve. $7-$13 **AAA Inspector Notes:** Those who appreciate the simplicity of a crunchy baguette with a soft center, the tangy flavor of Brie and the decadence of French pastries must stop in this tiny, quick-serve restaurant. The menu features savory and sweet crepes, quiches, sandwiches, omelets, specialty coffees and a variety of tarts and pastries. When picking out a tart or baked good, it's a good idea to peek around the deli case to view all the options. **Features:** patio dining. **Address:** 411 S Main St 80424 **Location:** 0.3 mi s; in Four Seasons Plaza; lower level. **Parking:** street only. [B] [L] [D] [AC]

LE PETIT PARIS 970/547-5335

▼▼▼ French. Fine Dining. $22-$35 **AAA Inspector Notes:** Spend a night in Paris at this charming bistro, which serves traditional French cuisine in an elegant setting. The dining room is cozy with French decorations and music, pink tablecloths, wine-colored cloth napkins and fresh-cut flowers throughout. The seasonal menu changes often and may feature almond-crusted ruby red trout, pan-roasted chicken, mussels, grilled Colorado lamb chop and pan-roasted pork loin. With advance notice, vegetarian options are available. **Features:** full bar. **Reservations:** suggested. **Address:** 161 E Adams Ave 80424 **Location:** Just e of Main St and Adams Ave; downtown. **Parking:** street only. [D] [AC]

MI CASA MEXICAN RESTAURANT & CANTINA 970/453-2071

▼▼ Mexican. Casual Dining. $9-$20 **AAA Inspector Notes:** This eatery specializes in innovative Mexican dishes like mango duck quesadillas, achiote-lime-marinated dorado, and a fried avocado filled with shrimp. More traditional fare includes chile rellenos, pork tamales and chicken burritos. The patio overlooks a lake. **Features:** full bar, patio dining, happy hour. **Address:** 600 S Park Ave 80424 **Location:** Just w of Main St; center. [L] [D]

MICHAEL'S ITALIAN RESTAURANT 970/453-5800

▼▼ Italian. Casual Dining. $13-$16 **AAA Inspector Notes:** At this casual eatery you'll enjoy pizza and pasta in a relaxed, family-friendly atmosphere. The menu includes favorites like chicken parmigiana, homemade meat lasagna, and orecchiette with sausage and fennel. You'll also find nightly dinner specials and an extensive list of beer and wine. **Features:** full bar, patio dining, happy hour. **Address:** 326 S Main St 80424 **Location:** Jct S Main St and Jefferson Ave, just e; in Centennial Square. **Parking:** street only. [D] [AC]

MODIS 970/453-4330

▼▼▼ American. Casual Dining. $20-$33 **AAA Inspector Notes:** One of the more upscale restaurants in this casual ski town, they focus on elegant, flavorful cuisine. Heartier dishes feature pork, steak, lamb and duck, while less rich options include the vegetable tower, yellowfin tuna or grilled salmon. Among decadent items are butternut squash with brown butter cream and port wine reduction, as well as the chocolate-glazed chocolate tart for dessert. The decor blends modern colors and historic Victorian accents. **Features:** full bar. **Reservations:** suggested. **Address:** 113 S Main St 80424 **Location:** Just s of Ski Hill Rd/Lincoln Ave; downtown. **Parking:** street only. [D] [AC]

MOUNTAIN FLYING FISH 970/453-1502

▼▼ Japanese. Casual Dining. $19-$33 **AAA Inspector Notes:** Chef/owner Tetsuo Shimoda, who trained in Japan, has worked in sushi restaurants in both Japan and New York City. Fresh fish is flown in from Japan and all over the world. The extensive sake menu will please both beginners and connoisseurs. The parking lot is in the back of the mall on South Ridge Street, not on Main Street. **Features:** full bar. **Address:** 500 S Main St 80424 **Location:** At Town Center; in La Cima Mall, 3rd Floor. [D]

QUANDARY GRILLE 970/547-5969

▼▼ American. Casual Dining. $11-$32 **AAA Inspector Notes:** This eatery, with its excellent views of Peak Nine, is a favorite in winter and summer alike. In summer, the patio fills up quickly. Start with the chicken wings, which comes plain or with barbecue, hot or sweet Thai chili. Entrees include steaks, trout amandine and rotisserie chicken. **Features:** full bar, patio dining, happy hour. **Address:** 505 S Main St 80424 **Location:** 0.4 mi s of center; south end of downtown; in Main Street Station. [L] [D]

RELISH
970/453-0989

▼▼▼ American. Casual Dining. $20-$39 **AAA Inspector Notes:** Competent servers assist you through a meal with innovative elements and satisfying flavors. The seasonal menu focuses on ingredients that have been raised or grown locally. Sample items include a Colorado artisanal cheese plate, buffalo New York strip, jalapeño bacon-wrapped quails, and braised Colorado lamb shank. If available, the baked Alaska is a must; the strawberry ice cream complements the fluffy, crunchy meringue. Large windows looking out into town offer natural light. **Features:** full bar, happy hour. **Reservations:** suggested. **Address:** 137 S Main St 80424 **Location:** At Main and E Washington sts; downtown. **Parking:** street only. D AC

SALT CREEK STEAK HOUSE
970/453-4949

▼▼ Steak Barbecue. Casual Dining. $21-$34 **AAA Inspector Notes:** Steaks, seafood, pasta and Texas-style barbecue are on the menu at this casual eatery with a mountain-lodge theme. It also offers an extensive, award-winning wine list; live music can be heard in the upstairs nightclub. **Features:** full bar, patio dining, happy hour. **Address:** 110 E Lincoln Ave 80424 **Location:** Just e of corner of Main St and Lincoln Ave; downtown. D

SOUTHRIDGE SEAFOOD GRILL
970/547-0063

▼▼ Seafood Steak. Casual Dining. $13-$26 **AAA Inspector Notes:** The casual and familiar vibe of this eatery makes it feel like an ordinary neighborhood grill, while the menu makes it a special place to dine. Items such as grilled Norwegian salmon marinated in lemon grass and ginger and Colorado lamb with brown rice and shiitake mushroom salad illustrate just a few of the innovative menu offerings. **Features:** full bar. **Reservations:** suggested. **Address:** 215 S Ridge St 80424 **Location:** Just e of Main St and Washington Ave, then just s. **Parking:** street only. D AC

THE SWISS HAVEN
970/453-6969

▼▼ Swiss. Casual Dining. $16-$35 **AAA Inspector Notes:** This restaurant offers tasty fondue combinations using imported cheeses like Appenzeller, Gruyère and Emmentaler. Start with kaseschnitte, provincial mushrooms, baked Brie or beef carpaccio. Follow with a meat, seafood or cheese fondue or select from a variety of other Swiss staples such as Jungfrau, zuriberg and weisshorn. The menu also includes pasta and wild game. The owner and staff have a passion for food, wine, beer and other alcoholic beverages. **Features:** full bar. **Reservations:** suggested. **Address:** 325 S Main St 80424 **Location:** 0.3 m s of center at Jefferson Ave; downtown; in Columbine Square Building. **Parking:** street only. D

TWIST - ON CLASSIC COMFORT FOOD
970/547-7100

▼▼▼ New American. Casual Dining. $15-$32 **AAA Inspector Notes:** This eatery offers redefined comfort food. Creative and attractively presented items include savory white bean hummus with truffle oil and addictive veggie chips, pork shoulder tacos to die for, potato-wrapped organic salmon and almond seared cod topped with grilled red onion pomegranate molasses tartar. While desserts will vary seasonally, you need to try the chocolate-cherry waffle or the trio of sorbets and ice cream. **Features:** full bar, happy hour. **Address:** 200 S Ridge St 80424 **Location:** At Washington and Ridge sts, just e of Main St; downtown. **Parking:** street only. D AC

BRIGHTON (C-9) pop. 33,352, elev. 4,983'
• Part of Denver area — see map p. 116

ADAMS COUNTY MUSEUM COMPLEX is at 9601 Henderson Rd. Adams County and Colorado history, from prehistoric times to the early 20th century, is presented in three galleries. Buildings include a restored 1887 Victorian house; a working blacksmith's shop; and replicas of a one-room schoolhouse, a 1920s-era Conoco service station and a fire station with a restored antique fire truck inside. A restored early 1940s-era red caboose also can be seen.

Hoffman Hall includes an antique printing press, collections of military equipment, scales and western artifacts. The Heritage Center features displays on earth sciences and fluorescents. The Carlson Cultural Center displays quilts, art, vintage cameras and rotating exhibits. **Time:** Allow 1 hour

minimum. **Hours:** Tues.-Sat. 10-4. Last tour is at 2:30. Closed Jan. 1, July 4, Thanksgiving and Dec. 21-Jan. 2. **Cost:** Museum building free. Guided tour of other buildings $3. **Phone:** (303) 659-7103. GT

BEST WESTERN BRIGHTON INN
(303)637-7710

▼▼▼ Hotel $139-$169

AAA Benefit: Save 10% or more every day and earn 10% bonus points!

Address: 15151 Brighton Rd 80601 **Location:** US 85, 1 mi s of jct SR 7, just w. **Facility:** 58 units. 3 stories, interior corridors. **Terms:** cancellation fee imposed. **Pool(s):** heated indoor. **Activities:** hot tub, picnic facilities, limited exercise equipment. **Guest Services:** valet and coin laundry. **Featured Amenity:** full hot breakfast.

COMFORT INN OF BRIGHTON
(303)654-1400

▼▼ Hotel $159-$169 **Address:** 15150 Brighton Rd 80601 **Location:** I-76 exit 12, 7.3 mi n on US 85. **Facility:** 52 units. 3 stories, interior corridors. **Pool(s):** heated indoor. **Activities:** hot tub. **Guest Services:** valet and coin laundry.

HAMPTON INN
303/654-8055

▼▼▼ Hotel. Rates not provided. **Address:** 992 Platte River Blvd 80601 **Location:** I-76 exit 12, 7.3 mi n on US 85, just w, then just s. **Facility:** 76 units. 4 stories, interior corridors. **Pool(s):** heated indoor. **Activities:** hot tub, exercise room. **Guest Services:** valet and coin laundry.

AAA Benefit: Members save up to 10%!

HOLIDAY INN EXPRESS HOTEL & SUITES DENVER NORTHEAST- BRIGHTON
720/685-1500

fyi Not evaluated. **Address:** 2180 S Medical Center Dr 80601 **Location:** I-76 exit 21, just nw, just n, then just e. Facilities, services, and décor characterize a mid-scale property.

WHERE TO EAT

LA ESTRELLITA
303/654-9900

▼▼ Mexican. Casual Dining. $8-$14 **AAA Inspector Notes:** Although the location inside a small shopping center is a little odd, it's worth wandering down to this family-owned eatery to taste recipes from the owners' grandparents, who also owned a restaurant. Diners have come to expect large portions of stuffed sopaipillas, Mayan enchiladas, carnitas and fajitas. The homemade flan is delicious. Due to high demand from customers, the owners began bottling their salsas, so it's possible to take a little taste of Colorado home. **Features:** full bar, patio dining, happy hour. **Address:** 45 N Main St, Suite 9 80601 **Location:** I-76 exit 12, 8 mi ne on US 85 exit SR 7/Brighton, 0.3 mi e, then just n; in Old Town Shops building. **Parking:** on-site and street. L D

BROOMFIELD pop. 55,889

ALOFT BROOMFIELD DENVER   (303)635-2000

Contemporary Hotel
$79-$299

AAA Benefit: Members save up to 15%, plus Starwood Preferred Guest® benefits!

Address: 8300 Arista Pl 80021 **Location:** US 36 (Boulder Tpke) exit US 287/CR 121, 0.6 mi s, then 0.4 mi w on Uptown Ave. **Facility:** 139 units. 5 stories, interior corridors. *Bath:* shower only. **Terms:** cancellation fee imposed. **Amenities:** safes. **Pool(s):** heated indoor. **Activities:** trails, exercise room. **Guest Services:** valet and coin laundry, area transportation.

(See ad this page.)

HYATT HOUSE BOULDER/BROOMFIELD   (720)890-4811

Extended Stay Hotel
$99-$239

H HYATT house

AAA Benefit: Members save 10%!

Address: 13351 W Midway Blvd 80020 **Location:** US 36 (Boulder Tpke) exit Storagetek Dr/Interlocken Loop, 0.3 mi n, then just e on Via Varra Rd. **Facility:** 123 units, some two bedrooms, efficiencies and kitchens. 4 stories, interior corridors. *Bath:* shower only. **Terms:** cancellation fee imposed. **Pool(s):** heated outdoor. **Activities:** picnic facilities, exercise room. **Guest Services:** valet and coin laundry, area transportation. **Featured Amenity:** breakfast buffet.

OMNI INTERLOCKEN RESORT   303/438-6600

Resort Hotel. Rates not provided. **Address:** 500 Interlocken Blvd 80021 **Location:** US 36 (Boulder Tpke) exit Interlocken Loop, 0.4 mi s, then 0.4 mi e. **Facility:** Public areas feature artwork by Colorado artists, and spacious guest units offer golf course or mountain views. Two large pools and a sunbathing area with waterfalls serves as a great oasis. 390 units. 11 stories, interior corridors. **Parking:** on-site and valet. **Amenities:** safes. **Dining:** 2 restaurants, also, Meritage, see separate listing. **Pool(s):** heated outdoor. **Activities:** hot tub, steamroom, regulation golf, bicycles, trails, spa. **Guest Services:** valet laundry, boarding pass kiosk, area transportation.

RENAISSANCE BOULDER FLATIRON HOTEL
                                     (303)464-8400

Hotel
$108-$310

R RENAISSANCE® HOTELS

AAA Benefit: Members save 5% or more!

Address: 500 Flatiron Blvd 80021 **Location:** US 36 (Boulder Tpke) exit Interlocken Loop, 0.4 mi s, just w on Interlocken Blvd, then just s. **Facility:** 232 units. 10 stories, interior corridors. **Parking:** on-site and valet. **Terms:** check-in 4 pm. **Pool(s):** heated indoor. **Activities:** hot tub, exercise room, massage. **Guest Services:** valet and coin laundry, boarding pass kiosk, area transportation.

AAA.com/ TourBook Comments

Let Your Voice Be Heard

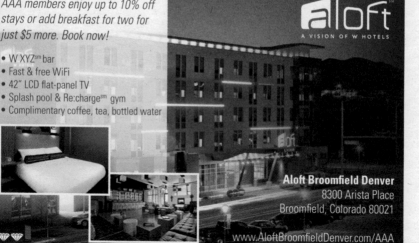

TOWNEPLACE SUITES BY MARRIOTT
BOULDER/BROOMFIELD   (303)466-2200

▼▼▼ **Extended Stay Hotel**
$95-$201 **Address:** 480 Flatiron Blvd
80021 **Location:** US 36 (Boulder Tpke)
exit Interlocken Loop, 0.4 mi s, just w on
Interlocken Blvd, then just s. **Facility:**
150 kitchen units, some two bedrooms. 4 stories, interior corridors.
Pool(s): heated outdoor. **Activities:** exercise room. **Guest Services:**
valet and coin laundry, area transportation.

AAA Benefit:
Members save 5%
or more!

[icons]

WHERE TO EAT

AZITRA   303/465-4444

▼▼ ▼▼ Indian. Casual Dining. $10-$23 **AAA Inspector Notes:** As
you walk in the door, the modern décor hints that this is not a typical
Indian restaurant. There's a bit more sophistication to the menu as
well. Start with the chaat, a daily changing Indian street-food appetizer. In addition to the usual favorites (think saag, tikka masala,
korma and vindaloo), the menu also features masala rack of lamb,
goat curry and tulsi-scented salmon. **Features:** full bar. **Address:**
535 Zang St 80021 **Location:** US 36 (Boulder Tpke) exit Interlocken Loop, 0.8 mi se; in Flatiron Crossing Mall. [L] [D]

MERITAGE   303/464-3330

▼▼▼▼ American. Fine Dining. $11-$42 **AAA Inspector Notes:**
Accomplished service matched with innovative food combinations
makes dinner at this sophisticated restaurant more than just a special
occasion. Creative flavorings mingled with a wide variety of seafood
and meats will satisfy any palate. **Features:** full bar, Sunday brunch.
Reservations: suggested. **Address:** 500 Interlocken Blvd 80021 **Location:** US 36 (Boulder Tpke) exit Interlocken Loop, 0.4 mi s, then
0.4 mi e; in Omni Interlocken Resort. **Parking:** on-site and valet.

[B] [L] [D]

P.F. CHANG'S CHINA BISTRO   720/887-6200

▼▼▼▼ Chinese. Fine Dining. $10-$25 **AAA Inspector Notes:**
Trendy, upscale decor provides a pleasant backdrop for New Age
Chinese dining. Appetizers, soups and salads are a meal by themselves. Vegetarian plates and sides, noodles, chow meins, chicken
and meat dishes are created from exotic, fresh ingredients. **Features:** full bar, happy hour. **Address:** 1 W Flatiron Crossing Dr 80021
Location: US 36 (Boulder Tpke) exit Flatiron Cir, 0.9 mi n, then just
n on Interlocken Blvd. [L] [D] CALL

VILLAGE TAVERN   720/887-6900

▼▼▼▼ American. Casual Dining. $9-$30 **AAA Inspector
Notes:** Attentive, personable servers bring out fresh entrees of steak,
seafood, chicken, wood-oven pizzas, sandwiches, soups, salads and
some downright tasty made-in-house potato chips. The comprehen-
sive offerings, including a children's menu, ensure there is something
for everyone. **Features:** full bar, patio dining, Sunday brunch, happy
hour. **Address:** 100 W Flatiron Crossing Dr 80021 **Location:** US 36
(Boulder Tpke) exit Interlocken Loop/Storagetek Dr; in Flatiron Shopping District. [L] [D] [icon]

BUENA VISTA (D-3) pop. 2,617, elev. 7,955'

Buena Vista means "beautiful view." The
Sawatch Range, which includes the Collegiate
Peaks—mounts Yale, Harvard and Princeton, all
more than 14,000 feet in elevation—forms a backdrop for this pastoral community. An overlook 1.5
miles east of the junction of US 24 and US 285 provides a view of the range.

Though rooted in ranching and mining, Buena
Vista's economic base also includes tourism and
recreation. The area is popular for hot springs,
scenic drives, hiking, skiing, off-road driving, backpacking, hunting, fishing and gold panning. Horseback, snowmobile and mountain bicycle tours are
available from local tour providers.

Often referred to as the "Whitewater Capital of
Colorado," the town is one of the main gateways to
the 148-mile Arkansas Headwaters Recreation Area
(see Recreation Areas Chart) which is favored by
rafters and kayakers.

Buena Vista Chamber of Commerce: 343 US
24S, P.O. Box 2021, Buena Vista, CO 81211.
Phone: (719) 395-6612.

RECREATIONAL ACTIVITIES
White-water Rafting

- **American Adventure Expeditions** is off US 24 to
12844 US 285 on the Arkansas River. **Hours:**
Trips depart daily May-Sept. **Phone:** (719)
395-2409.

- **Buffalo Joe's Whitewater Rafting** is at 801
Front Loop. **Hours:** Daily 7-7, Apr.-Sept. **Phone:**
(719) 395-8757 or (866) 283-3563.

- **Good Times Rafting** offers guided rafting trips
down the Arkansas River from various launch
points. **Hours:** Daily 9-5, mid-May to mid-Aug.
Phone: (970) 402-6081 or (719) 395-4200.

- **Performance Tours** is 1 mi. s. at 115 Gregg Dr.
Hours: Daily May 1-Labor Day. **Phone:** (800)
328-7238.

- **River Runners Riverside Resort** is at jct. US
285 and CR 301. **Hours:** Daily 7 a.m.-9 p.m., May
1-Labor Day. **Phone:** (719) 395-2466 or (800)
723-8987.

- **Wilderness Aware Rafting** is at 12600 US 285.
Hours: Daily 7:30 a.m.-8 p.m., mid-May to Labor
Day. **Phone:** (719) 395-2112 or (800) 462-7238.

BEST WESTERN VISTA INN   (719)395-8009

▼▼▼▼ Hotel
$99-$189

AAA Benefit:
Save 10% or more every
day and earn 10% bonus
points!

Address: 733 US Hwy 24 N 81211 **Location:** 0.5 mi n of center. **Facility:** 52
units. 2 stories (no elevator), interior corridors. **Parking:** winter plug-ins. **Terms:**
check-in 4 pm. **Pool(s):** heated indoor.
Activities: hot tub, exercise room.
Guest Services: coin laundry.

[icons]

WHERE TO EAT

BROWN DOG COFFEE CO   719/395-2634

▼ Deli. Quick Serve. $5-$9 **AAA Inspector Notes:** This eatery
is a great place to stop while biking or traveling for a delicious bite
to eat. The daily quiche selection is a treat. Chicken, tuna, turkey
and veggie sandwiches go well with the daily made-in-house soup
and bow-tie, green leaf, multi-bean or tortellini salad. Espressos,
cappuccinos, lattes, teas and hot chocolate warm patrons in the
winter, and their iced counterparts satisfy during the summer. **Address:** 713 S US 24 81211 **Location:** 0.6 mi s of center.

[B] [L] [D]

CASA DEL SOL   719/395-8810

▼▼ ▼▼
Mexican
Casual Dining
$7-$16

AAA Inspector Notes: *Historic.* This popular eatery has several colorful and nicely appointed dining nooks and a lovely garden patio. **Features:** full bar, patio dining. **Reservations:** suggested, in summer. **Address:** 303 US 24 N 81211 **Location:** Corner of E Arkansas St and US 24. 〔L〕〔D〕

EDDYLINE RESTAURANT & BREWERY   719/966-6000

▼▼ ▼▼ American. Casual Dining. $9-$23 **AAA Inspector Notes:** This restaurant serves a variety of salads, burgers, and pasta dishes; however, the unique microbrews remain the big draw. **Features:** full bar, patio dining. **Address:** 926 S Main St 81211 **Location:** 0.6 mi e on E Main St, 0.3 mi s. **Parking:** street only. 〔L〕〔D〕

BURLINGTON (C-7) pop. 4,254, elev. 4,163'

KIT CARSON COUNTY CAROUSEL is off I-70 exit 437, following signs to Kit Carson County Fairgrounds. Forty-six carved animals adorn the restored 1905 carousel. Visitors may choose from a lion, giraffe, camel or other whimsical creatures for a nostalgic ride, accompanied by music from a Wurlitzer band organ. A museum offers a historical perspective, from the early years of the Philadelphia Toboggan Co. to how carousel animals are crafted. **Time:** Allow 30 minutes minimum. **Hours:** Daily 11-6, Memorial Day weekend-Labor Day. **Cost:** Museum $1; free (ages 0-9); rides 25¢. **Phone:** (800) 825-0208.

◆GEM **OLD TOWN MUSEUM,** 420 S. 14th St., is a 6.5-acre site with a collection of original and re-created buildings furnished with early 1900s artifacts. The 21 buildings include a schoolhouse, church, sod house, train depot, grocery store, jail, saloon, drugstore, soda fountain, Texaco station and blacksmith shop as well as a museum.

Time: Allow 1 hour minimum. **Hours:** Mon.-Sat. 9-5, Sun. noon-5. **Cost:** $6; $5 (ages 60+); $4 (ages 12-17); $2 (ages 3-11). **Phone:** (719) 346-7382 or (800) 288-1334.

BEST WESTERN PLUS CAROUSEL INN & SUITES
(719)346-7777

▼▼ ▼▼ ▼▼
Hotel
$124-$139

Best Western PLUS

AAA Benefit: Save 10% or more every day and earn 10% bonus points!

Address: 605 S Lincoln St 80807 **Location:** I-70 exit 437, just s. **Facility:** 66 units. 3 stories, interior corridors. **Pool(s):** heated indoor. **Activities:** hot tub, exercise room. **Guest Services:** coin laundry.

SAVE CALL ⬇M ➽ BIZ HS 📶 ✕ 🍴 🖥 💻 / SOME UNITS 🐾

COMFORT INN BURLINGTON   (719)346-7676

▼▼ ▼▼ Hotel $104-$149 **Address:** 282 S Lincoln St 80807 **Location:** I-70 exit 437, just n on US 385. **Facility:** 57 units. 2 stories (no elevator), interior corridors. **Pool(s):** heated indoor. **Activities:** hot tub, exercise room. **Guest Services:** coin laundry.

🆓➕ ➽ BIZ 📶 ✕ 🍴 🖥 💻 / SOME UNITS 🐾

WHERE TO EAT

CHEN VUONG THAI   719/346-6033

▼▼ Asian. Casual Dining. $7-$16 **AAA Inspector Notes:** Ignore the sketchy exterior and head straight into this cozy eatery. The menu focuses on Southeast Asian cuisine and is a bit eclectic, pairing steamed-shrimp spring rolls with sesame chicken, pad thai and Vietnamese rice bowls. **Features:** full bar. **Address:** 2160 Rose Ave 80807 **Location:** I-70 exit 437, 1.6 mi n, then just e. 〔L〕〔D〕

RESTAURANT PANADERIA, MEXICO #2   719/346-4660

▼▼ Mexican. Casual Dining. $7-$13 **AAA Inspector Notes:** Find all of your favorites here--enchiladas, rellenos, tamales, tacos, burritos, and much more. Lots of combo plates and reasonable prices allow for sampling of multiple items. Copies of famous Mexican paintings line the walls. **Address:** 460 14th St 80807 **Location:** Jct Rose and Lincoln sts, 0.5 mi e, just n. **Parking:** street only. 〔L〕〔D〕

CAÑON CITY (D-4) pop. 16,400, elev. 5,332'
• Hotels p. 74 • Restaurants p. 74

Shadowed and sheltered by a close ring of mountains, Cañon City is at the head of the Arkansas Valley, where the Arkansas River bursts from its canyon confines to begin a 1,900-mile open-country run to the Mississippi. The canyon scenery attracted filmmakers to Cañon City in the early 20th century. Tom Mix, hero of silent Westerns, launched his career in Cañon City in 1910. Such films as "Cat Ballou" and "True Grit" as well as "Conagher," a made-for-television movie, were made in the vicinity.

Stock raising, agriculture, mining, 13 correctional facilities and tourism provide a broad economic base. The Music and Blossom Festival and the Royal Gorge Rodeo are held the first weekend in May.

Greater Cañon City Chamber of Commerce: 403 Royal Gorge Blvd., Cañon City, CO 81212. **Phone:** (719) 275-2331 or (800) 876-7922.

MUSEUM OF COLORADO PRISONS, off US 50 at 201 N. 1st St., is located in the original women's prison built in 1935. Displays feature the noose used for the last hanging execution in Colorado, a gas chamber, confiscated inmate weapons, disciplinary paraphernalia and inmates' original photographs and art work. Other displays feature Roy Best, one of the prison's most famous wardens, and other inmates such as cannibal Alfred Packer and 11-year-old murderer Anton Wood.

MP3 players are available for self-guiding audio tours. **Time:** Allow 1 hour minimum. **Hours:** Daily 10-6, mid-May through Labor Day; daily 10-5, day after Labor Day to mid-Oct.; Wed.-Sun. 10-5, rest of year. Closed Easter, Thanksgiving and Christmas. **Cost:** $7; $6 (ages 65+); $5 (ages 6-12, military with ID and department of corrections employees with ID). **Phone:** (719) 269-3015.

PHANTOM CANYON ROAD (SR 67), 6 mi. e. on US 50 to SR 67, twists and turns for 35 miles through a canyon leading to Cripple Creek *(see place listing p. 111).* Several old train tunnels cut through red rock formations. Phantom Canyon Road is part of the "Gold Belt Tour," a national historical route. Another one of the legs of the tour is Shelf Road, also departing from the north side of Cañon City. **Note:** This gravel road is narrow and winding and should not be attempted in an RV or by those unaccustomed to mountain driving. The posted speed limit is 20 mph; the drive takes 1.5 to 2 hours. Check road conditions before starting. **Phone:** (719) 275-2331 or (800) 876-7922.

ROYAL GORGE BRIDGE AND PARK is 8 mi. w. on US 50, then 4.3 mi. s. on CR 3A. The bridge is the highest suspension bridge in the United States. Built in 1929, the bridge spans the scenic Royal Gorge nearly 1,000 feet above the Arkansas River.

The park offers more than 360 acres of scenery, history and rides, including the Royal Rush Skycoaster, an aerial tram across the canyon, a zipline, several children's attractions, a theater, a trolley, a miniature train, a carousel and scenic trails for walking and bicycling. The bridge, aerial tram and theater are open year-round; other attractions are available May through Sept.

Note: Park admission is charged before crossing the bridge. Motorcycles and larger vehicles including SUVs, passenger vans and RVs are not permitted to cross the bridge between 10 a.m. and dusk and are subject to pedestrian traffic. Over-size vehicles including campers, buses or large trucks are not permitted on the bridge at any time. Parking is free, and transportation across the bridge is provided May through Sept. Allow 3 hours, 30 minutes minimum during peak season. **Hours:** Bridge open daily 7-dusk (weather permitting). Park opens daily at 10. Closing times vary. Phone ahead to confirm schedule.

Cost: (includes park and all attractions except the Skycoaster, zipline and trail rides) $25; $22 (ages 60+); $20 (ages 4-11). Skycoaster or zipline $25. Discounted admission is available mid-Oct. to late Apr.; phone ahead for updates. **Phone:** (719) 275-7507 or (888) 333-5597. *(See ad this page.)*

ROYAL GORGE REGIONAL MUSEUM & HISTORY CENTER, 612 Royal Gorge Blvd., depicts the history of the Royal Gorge region. Exhibits include dinosaur fossils, a natural history bison diorama, an interactive video display and an 1860s log cabin.

The History Center contains genealogical and research material related to the area. **Hours:** Wed.-Sat. 10-4. **Cost:** Free. **Phone:** (719) 269-9036.

ROYAL GORGE ROUTE RAILROAD departs from the historic Santa Fe Depot at 401 Water St. (3rd St. and US 50). The 20-mile journey follows the Arkansas River through the scenic Royal Gorge and crosses a hanging bridge where the gorge narrows to 30 feet wide. Passengers select from several classes of service including Coach, Vista Dome,

▼ *See AAA listing this page* ▼

Parlor, Club and Cab. Special events include Mother's Day, Murder Mystery, Oktoberfest, a wine train and dinner train. The Santa Express, with afternoon and evening departures Nov. through Dec., features Santa, gifts for kids, cookies and hot cocoa. Breakfast and lunch train rides also are available.

Time: Allow 3 hours minimum. **Hours:** Train rides are offered year-round. Call for schedules of other theme train rides. **Cost:** Coach fare $39; $28 (ages 3-12). Other prices vary with class and type of service; check ahead for ticket information. Reservations are recommended. **Phone:** (719) 276-4000 or (888) 724-5748.

SKYLINE DRIVE, starting 3 mi. w. off US 50, is a 3-mile, paved, one-way road that traverses the crest of a "hogback" ridge 800 feet above town. The view from Skyline Drive is spectacular and includes actual dinosaur tracks in the rocks. **Note:** Motor homes, vans, campers and vehicles towing trailers are not permitted on the narrow, steep and winding road. **Hours:** The road is closed in inclement weather.

WHITEWATER ADVENTURE OUTFITTERS is 1 mi. w. of Cañon City at 50905 US 50W. Half-day, full-day and overnight trips are available on the Arkansas River. Experienced, professional guides provide narrated highlights along the route.

Time: Allow 3 hours minimum. **Hours:** Daily 8-8, mid-Apr. through Labor Day. **Cost:** Fare $69-$115; $35-$75 (ages 6-12). Reservations are recommended. **Phone:** (719) 275-5344 or (800) 530-8212.

RECREATIONAL ACTIVITIES
White-water Rafting
- **American Adventure Expeditions** is at 41746 US 50W on the Arkansas River. **Hours:** Trips depart daily 9-4, May-Sept. **Phone:** (719) 395-2409.
- **Bill Dvorak Rafting & Kayak Expeditions** meets at Parkdale State River Site, 12 mi. w. of Cañon City off US 50W. **Hours:** Daily 7 a.m.-8 p.m., May-Sept. **Phone:** (719) 539-6851 or (800) 824-3795.
- **Buffalo Joe's Whitewater Rafting** is at 45000 US 50. **Hours:** Daily 7-7, early May-early Sept. **Phone:** (719) 395-8757 or (866) 283-3563.
- **Clear Creek Rafting Co.** is 8 mi. w. at 44650 US 50W. **Hours:** Daily 7 a.m.-9 p.m., May 1-Labor Day. **Phone:** (303) 567-1000 or (800) 353-9901.
- **Echo Canyon River Expeditions** is 8 mi. w. at 45000 US 50W. **Hours:** Daily 7-7, May 1-Sept. 15. Times may vary. **Phone:** (719) 275-3154 or (800) 755-3246.
- **Performance Tours** is 8 mi. w. on US 50 at 35 CR 3A. **Hours:** Daily May 1-Labor Day. Phone ahead to confirm schedule. **Phone:** (970) 453-0661 or (800) 328-7238.
- **Raft Masters** is at 2315 E. Main St. **Hours:** Daily 8-6, mid-Mar. to mid-Oct. **Phone:** (719) 275-6645 or (800) 568-7238.

- **River Runners Royal Gorge Rafting Center** is 8 mi. w. at the turnoff for the Royal Gorge Bridge and Park at 44641 US 50W. **Hours:** Daily 7 a.m.-9 p.m., May 1-Labor Day. **Phone:** (719) 275-2291 or (800) 723-8987.
- **Wilderness Aware Rafting** departs from Pinnacle Rock Recreation Area, 11.6 mi. w. of jct. US 50 and SR 9. **Hours:** Trips depart daily at 9, early May-Labor Day. **Phone:** (719) 395-2112 or (800) 462-7238.

BEST WESTERN CAÑON CITY   (719)275-2400

Hotel
$84-$219

AAA Benefit: Save 10% or more every day and earn 10% bonus points!

Address: 110 Latigo Ln 81212 **Location:** From 9th St, 3 mi e on US 50, just n. **Facility:** 82 units. 2 stories, interior corridors. **Pool(s):** heated indoor. **Activities:** sauna, hot tub, exercise room. **Guest Services:** valet and coin laundry. **Featured Amenity:** full hot breakfast.

HAMPTON INN   719/269-1112

Hotel. Rates not provided. **Address:** 102 McCormick Pkwy 81212 **Location:** From 9th St, 2.7 mi e on US 50. **Facility:** 64 units. 3 stories, interior corridors. **Pool(s):** heated indoor. **Activities:** hot tub, exercise room. **Guest Services:** coin laundry.

AAA Benefit: Members save up to 10%!

WHERE TO EAT

DI RITO'S ITALIAN RESTAURANT   719/276-7240

Italian. Casual Dining. $7-$23 **AAA Inspector Notes:** Family-owned and operated, this eatery serves traditional Italian favorites in a casual atmosphere. Menu items include homemade gnocchi, calzone, fettuccine Alfredo, meatball sandwiches, steaks and pizzas. For something different, try the bianco pollo pizza topped with chicken, artichoke hearts, roasted garlic and white sauce. Homemade desserts include tiramisu, lemon chiffon cake and chocolate cake. **Features:** full bar, patio dining, happy hour. **Address:** 231 Main St 81212 **Location:** Jct 3rd St, west end of downtown. **Parking:** street only.

EL CAPORAL   719/276-2001

Mexican. Casual Dining. $7-$20 **AAA Inspector Notes:** Colorful décor sets the stage for this dining experience. The local favorite features daily lunch and dinner specials and offers many authentic dishes to choose from, including meat, seafood and vegetarian options. You also can create your own combo. The enchiladas suizas have a mild, smoky flavor and are the perfect option for those who don't like spicy food. **Features:** beer & wine. **Address:** 1028 Main St 81212 **Location:** Just e of 10th and Main sts; downtown.

LE PETIT CHABLIS   719/269-3333

French. Casual Dining. $9-$32 **AAA Inspector Notes:** If you're yearning for a touch of elegance in the heart of the west, enjoy dining at this hidden jewel. The restaurant sits behind a quaint white picket fence and features a three-course special for lunch and dinner. Menu items include salads, quiche, croissant sandwiches, fish, lamb, duck and a variety of homemade desserts. **Features:** full bar. **Reservations:** suggested, for dinner. **Address:** 512 Royal Gorge Blvd 81212 **Location:** On US 50, between 5th and 6th sts; downtown.

MICHAEL'S ON MAIN 719/276-2233

🔷🔷 American. Casual Dining. $10-$29 **AAA Inspector Notes:** You can't miss at the classy café, which features a coffee and gelato bar and chocolate shoppe. In addition to delicious soups and salads, try the cranberry-tapenade-stuffed mushroom appetizer. Tasty dinners include beef medallions, lamb cheese tortellini and lasagna. **Features:** full bar. **Reservations:** suggested. **Address:** 605 Main St 81212 **Location:** At 6th and Main sts; downtown. **Parking:** street only. [L] [D]

CANYONS OF THE ANCIENTS NATIONAL MONUMENT (E-1)

In the Four Corners region 15 miles northwest of Cortez and west of US 491, Canyons of the Ancients National Monument preserves one of the richest archeological areas in the United States, covering 166,000 acres of remote and difficult terrain. More than 6,000 archeological sites, including dwellings, shrines, hunting camps and petroglyphs, preserve the remnants of cultures and traditions spanning thousands of years.

The 12th-century Lowry Pueblo, a National Historic Landmark containing 40 rooms and ceremonial kivas, is among the largest and most easily accessible of the ruins. Visitors are advised to stop at the Anasazi Heritage Center in Dolores prior to visiting the national monument for maps, advice and current road conditions.

Note: The monument is a backcountry area with gravel and dirt roads, minimal facilities and no permanent source of water. Visitors are advised to bring sufficient water, fuel and maps, and to stay on existing roads and trails. Daily 24 hours. Free. Phone (970) 882-5600.

ANASAZI HERITAGE CENTER, 3.5 mi. w. of Dolores on SR 184, interprets the history and native culture of the Four Corners region, including Canyons of the Ancients National Monument. Ancient pottery displays, interactive exhibits, two 12th-century village sites, changing special exhibits and events are presented. Visitors can try their hand at weaving on a Pueblo-style loom or grinding corn.

As the visitor center for Canyons of the Ancients National Monument, the museum offers maps, brochures and orientation, as well as two short video programs about the ancient culture: "Visit With Respect" is an appeal from Native Americans to protect their ancestral places; "The Cultural History of the Great Sage Plain" focuses on archaeologists' discoveries during the 19th- and 20th centuries. A paved, half-mile nature trail leads to the hilltop Escalante Pueblo.

Time: Allow 1 hour minimum. **Hours:** Daily 9-5, Mar.-Oct.; 10-4, rest of year. Closed Jan. 1, Thanksgiving and Christmas. **Cost:** Mar.-Oct. $3; free (ages 0-17). Rest of year, free. **Phone:** (970) 882-5600.

CARBONDALE pop. 6,427

COMFORT INN & SUITES (970)963-8880

🔷🔷 Hotel $159-$219 **Address:** 920 Cowen Dr 81623 **Location:** Jct SR 82 and 133, just sw. **Facility:** 76 units. 2 stories (no elevator), interior corridors. **Terms:** check-in 4 pm. **Pool(s):** heated indoor. **Activities:** hot tub, fishing. **Guest Services:** valet and coin laundry, boarding pass kiosk.

🛎 BIZ 📶 ✖ 🛏 💻 / SOME UNITS 🏊 🖨

WHERE TO EAT

PHAT THAI 970/963-7001

🔷🔷🔷 Thai. Casual Dining. $9-$16 **AAA Inspector Notes:** This eatery is the sister property to Chef Mark Fischer's Carbondale Restaurant Six89 and offers a delicious selection of salads, soups, small and large plates, curries, noodles, rice and stir-fries such as a northern Thai herb salad, beef satay, spring rolls with tofu, coconut pumpkin soup, asparagus fried rice with pineapple, chicken basil and more. **Features:** full bar. **Address:** 343 Main St 81623 **Location:** East end of downtown. **Parking:** street only. [D]

VILLAGE SMITHY RESTAURANT 970/963-9990

🔷🔷 American. Casual Dining. $5-$18 **AAA Inspector Notes:** *Historic.* This family-owned restaurant must be doing something right as it's been in business since 1975. The menu includes daily specials, Mexican dishes, salads, pasta, a popular Asian chicken salad, sandwiches, espresso, cappuccino, lattes and limited cocktails. Vegetarian items also are available. **Features:** full bar, patio dining, senior menu, Sunday brunch. **Address:** 26 S 3rd St 81623 **Location:** At 3rd and Main sts; downtown. **Parking:** street only. [B] [L] 🐾

WHITE HOUSE PIZZA & PASTA 970/704-9400

🔷🔷 Italian. Casual Dining. $9-$16 **AAA Inspector Notes:** Patrons can enjoy dining upstairs, outside on the patio, in a cozy booth in the bar or in the sunroom. Menu offerings include a variety of tasty appetizers, salads, two types of delicious lasagna, oven-baked sandwiches, pulled pork, noodles galore and last but not least, pizza pies. **Features:** full bar, patio dining, early bird specials, happy hour. **Address:** 801 Main Ct 81623 **Location:** West end of Main St; downtown. [L] [D]

CASCADE (F-9) elev. 7,375'
• Part of Colorado Springs area — see map p. 81

SANTA'S WORKSHOP—NORTH POLE, 10 mi. w. on US 24, is a 27-acre theme park. Highlights include a 60-foot Ferris wheel, children's rides and Santa's house. Inquire about weather policies. **Time:** Allow 2 hours minimum. **Hours:** Daily 10-5, late May to mid-Aug.; Thurs.-Mon. 10-5, mid-Aug. to late Dec. Phone ahead to confirm schedule. **Cost:** $21; $16 (military with ID); free (ages 0-1 and 60+). Prices may vary; phone ahead for updates. **Phone:** (719) 684-9432.

THE WINES OF COLORADO 719/684-0900

🔷🔷 American. Casual Dining. $9-$22 **AAA Inspector Notes:** Arrive a little early for a complimentary tasting of wines made in Colorado, which might help you decide on a meal pairing. Menu items range from hot sandwiches and burgers to bison lasagna and steaks. Located near a mountain stream. **Features:** wine only, patio dining. **Address:** 8045 W US Hwy 24 80809 **Location:** Just nw on Fountain Ave, then just s on frontage road. [L] [D] 🅐🅒

Choose real ratings you can trust
from professional inspectors who've been there

CASTLE ROCK pop. 48,231

BEST WESTERN PLUS CASTLE ROCK   (303)814-8800

Hotel
$89-$189

AAA Benefit:
Save 10% or more every
day and earn 10% bonus
points!

Address: 595 Genoa Way 80109 **Location:** I-25 exit 184 (Meadows Pkwy), just w to Castleton Way, just s, then e. Opposite an outlet mall. **Facility:** 69 units, some efficiencies. 4 stories, interior corridors. **Terms:** check-in 4 pm. **Amenities:** *Some:* safes. **Pool(s):** heated indoor. **Activities:** hot tub, exercise room. **Guest Services:** valet and coin laundry.

SAVE 📞➕ 🏊 BIZ HS 📶 ✕

🛗 📺 🖥 / SOME UNITS 🔒

HAMPTON INN   303/660-9800

▿▿▿ **Hotel.** Rates not provided. **Address:** 4830 Castleton Way 80109 **Location:** I-25 exit 184 (Meadows Pkwy), sw to N Castleton Rd, just s, then e. **Facility:** 72 units. 4 stories, interior corridors. **Pool(s):** heated indoor. **Activities:** hot tub, exercise room. **Guest Services:** valet and coin laundry.

AAA Benefit:
Members save up to
10%!

📞➕ CALL 📞M 🏊 BIZ 📶 ✕ 🛗 📺 🖥

HOLIDAY INN EXPRESS & SUITES CASTLE ROCK
(303)688-0888

Hotel
$100-$200

Address: 610 Genoa Way 80109 **Location:** I-25 exit 184 (Meadows Pkwy), just w to Castleton Way, just s, then e. **Facility:** 84 units. 4 stories, interior corridors. **Pool(s):** indoor. **Activities:** hot tub, exercise room. **Guest Services:** coin laundry. **Featured Amenity:** full hot breakfast.

SAVE CALL 📞M 🏊 BIZ HS 📶

✕ 🖥 / SOME UNITS 🛗 📺

WHERE TO EAT

AUGUSTINE GRILL   303/814-3663

▿▿▿ American. Fine Dining. $8-$36 **AAA Inspector Notes:** Converted from a historic Victorian house into a cheerful restaurant, the Augustine Grill offers a mix of seafood, pasta and meat dishes. Lunch offers more casual fare with a variety of soups, salads and sandwiches. Dinner fare consists of more elaborate entrées, including steak au poivre, duck leg confit and rack of lamb. **Features:** full bar, patio dining. **Reservations:** suggested. **Address:** 519 Wilcox St 80104 **Location:** I-25 exit 182, just w to Park St, 0.6 mi se, then just n. **Parking:** street only. L D

CASTLE CAFE   303/814-2233

▿▿▿ American. Casual Dining. $9-$20 **AAA Inspector Notes:** *Historic.* This Western-style café is located in a tastefully renovated 1910 hotel. Walls are adorned with taxidermy and oil paintings of iconic Western scenes. Delicious fried chicken, Yankee pot roast, mashed potatoes with homemade gravy, burgers, sandwiches and even some Mexican items are among the menu choices. **Features:** full bar. **Address:** 403 Wilcox St 80104 **Location:** I-25 exit 182, just e to Wilcox St, then 0.4 mi s; corner of 4th and Wilcox sts. **Parking:** street only. L D

PEGASUS ON THE SQUARE   303/688-6746

▿▿▿ American. Casual Dining. $9-$20 **AAA Inspector Notes:** The diverse menu is sure to please a variety of tastes. Entrées include Greek, Mexican and American fare. The chile rellenos had a nice flavor and a traditional batter. The charming décor features hardwood floors, decorative wood beams and interesting artwork. **Features:** full bar. **Address:** 313 Jerry St 80104 **Location:** I-25 exit 182, just e, 0.4 mi s to 5th St, just e, then just s. **Parking:** street only.

B L D

ROCKYARD AMERICAN GRILL & BREWING COMPANY
303/814-9273

▿▿▿ American. Casual Dining. $9-$19 **AAA Inspector Notes:** Just off the interstate, this popular brewpub has a high, beamed ceiling, patio seating and a fireplace that separates the lounge from the main dining room. A variety of handcrafted beers complements the typical pub grub. Try the signature cream of jalapeño soup; it's rich and creamy with a mild kick. **Features:** full bar. **Address:** 880 W Castleton Rd 80109 **Location:** I-25 exit 184 (Meadows Pkwy), w to Castleton Rd. L D CALL 📞M

SIENA AT THE COURTYARD   303/688-2622

◇▿▿ Italian. Casual Dining. $11-$31 **AAA Inspector Notes:** This casual eatery offers flavorful Italian-inspired cuisine. The specialty pizza features a thin crust, spicy sausage and a generous amount of cheese. The extensive menu also features more complex dishes such as pappardelle pasta with braised short rib, pan-roasted scallops served in a lobster-mascarpone-cream sauce, veal parmigiana and a New York strip topped with garlic-herb butter served with truffle fries. **Features:** full bar, patio dining, happy hour. **Address:** 333 Perry St 80104 **Location:** I-25 exit 182, 0.6 mi w, then just s. **Parking:** on-site and street. L D

UNION AN AMERICAN BISTRO   303/688-8159

▿▿▿ American. Fine Dining. $10-$26 **AAA Inspector Notes:** Perusing the menu at this innovative restaurant, everything looked interesting. I opted for the seared scallops with bacon apple risotto. A modern take on bacon-wrapped scallops, this dish had a nice combination of sweet and salty flavors; the scallops were perfectly prepared. I also enjoyed the mixed green salad with a tart red wine vinaigrette. The cookie bar sundae with salted caramel ice cream was simply delicious. **Features:** full bar, patio dining, happy hour. **Address:** 3 Wilcox St 80104 **Location:** I-25 exit 181, just e, then just n. **Parking:** on-site and street. L D

CEDAREDGE (D-2) pop. 2,253, elev. 6,264'

PIONEER TOWN MUSEUM AND GIFT SHOP is 2 blks. s. of Main St. on SR 65 at 400 2nd St. This 5-acre site includes more than 20 buildings depicting turn-of-the-20th-century life. Wooden sidewalks line the old Main Street, which features barn silos, a 1906 jail, a schoolhouse, a general store, a depot, a saloon, a fruit-packing shed and a log cabin. The Doris Doll and Toy House, a working blacksmith shop, a railroad depot and the Chapel of the Cross also are featured. The Sutherland Indian Museum displays Indian arrowheads, kachina dolls and other artifacts. **Time:** Allow 1 hour minimum. **Hours:** Mon.-Sat. 10-4, Sun. 1-4, Memorial Day weekend-early Oct. **Cost:** $5; $4 (ages 62+); $3 (ages 8-17). **Phone:** (970) 856-7554.

APPLE SHED   970/856-7007

▿ Deli. Casual Dining. $9-$11 **AAA Inspector Notes:** Located inside a commercial space with art galleries and boutique shops, this eatery offers gourmet sandwiches, salads and burgers. Many of the entrées include unique, freshly made salsas and sauces like the raspberry chipotle sauce and peach salsa. Try the turkey, bacon and avocado sandwich with cranberry relish, which is served hot. For beverages, it doesn't get any more local than the homemade hard cider and wine. Enjoy your meal while soaking in nice weather on the patio. **Features:** wine only, patio dining. **Address:** 250 S Grand Mesa Dr 81413 **Location:** Just s on SR 65. L

CENTENNIAL pop. 100,377, elev. 5,833'
- **Hotels & Restaurants map & index p. 136**
- **Part of Denver area — see map p. 116**

Incorporated in 2001, Centennial is one of the state's newest cities, but being a part of the Denver metro area, it's hardly a small town. More than 100,000 people call Centennial home, yet the area is also known for its recreation trails and parkland. Centennial Center Park, 13133 E. Arapahoe Rd., features a water play area, a playground, a climbing wall, fountains, an amphitheater and a native plant demonstration garden.

COMFORT SUITES DENVER TECH CENTER
(303)858-0700 **102**

▼▼◆◆ **Hotel** $99-$199 **Address:** 7374 S Clinton St 80112 **Location:** I-25 exit 196 (Dry Creek Rd), just e, then n. **Facility:** 78 units. 3 stories, interior corridors. **Amenities:** safes. **Pool(s):** heated indoor. **Activities:** hot tub, exercise room. **Guest Services:** valet and coin laundry.

DRURY INN & SUITES-DENVER NEAR THE TECH CENTER
(303)694-3400 **104**

▼▼◆ **Hotel** $90-$170 **Address:** 9445 E Dry Creek Rd 80112 **Location:** I-25 exit 196 (Dry Creek Rd), just w; on northwest corner. **Facility:** 160 units. 6 stories, interior corridors. **Terms:** cancellation fee imposed. **Pool(s):** heated outdoor, heated indoor. **Activities:** hot tub, exercise room. **Guest Services:** valet and coin laundry, area transportation.

EMBASSY SUITES BY HILTON DENVER TECH CENTER
303/792-0433 **100**

▼▼◆◆
Hotel
Rates not provided

AAA Benefit:
Members save 5% or more!

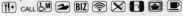

Address: 10250 E Costilla Ave 80112 **Location:** I-25 exit 197 (Arapahoe Rd), 1 mi e, 0.3 mi s then w. **Facility:** 236 units, some two bedrooms. 9 stories, interior corridors. **Pool(s):** heated indoor. **Activities:** hot tub, exercise room. **Guest Services:** valet and coin laundry, area transportation. **Featured Amenity:** full hot breakfast.

HOLIDAY INN EXPRESS HOTEL & SUITES
303/662-0777 **103**

▼▼ **Hotel.** Rates not provided. **Address:** 7380 S Clinton St 80112 **Location:** I-25 exit 196 (Dry Creek Rd), e to S Clinton St, then just n. **Facility:** 91 units. 4 stories, interior corridors. **Pool(s):** heated indoor. **Activities:** hot tub, exercise room. **Guest Services:** valet and coin laundry, area transportation.

STAYBRIDGE SUITES DENVER TECH CENTER
303/858-9990 **101**

▼▼◆▼ **Extended Stay Hotel.** Rates not provided. **Address:** 7150 S Clinton St 80112 **Location:** I-25 exit 197 (Arapahoe Rd), just e to Clinton St, 0.5 mi s, then just e. **Facility:** 128 efficiencies. 3 stories, interior corridors. **Pool(s):** heated outdoor. **Activities:** hot tub, exercise room. **Guest Services:** complimentary and valet laundry, area transportation.

TOWNEPLACE SUITES BY MARRIOTT DENVER TECH CENTER
(720)875-1113 **105**

▼▼◆ **Extended Stay Hotel** $75-$222 **Address:** 7877 S Chester St 80112 **Location:** I-25 exit 196 (Dry Creek Rd), just w to Chester St, then 0.3 mi s. **Facility:** 94 kitchen units, some two bedrooms. 3 stories, interior corridors. **Terms:** check-in 4 pm. **Pool(s):** heated outdoor. **Activities:** picnic facilities, exercise room. **Guest Services:** valet and coin laundry.

AAA Benefit:
Members save 5% or more!

WHERE TO EAT

THE EGG & I
303/804-0902 **152**

▼▼ ▼▼ Breakfast. Family Dining. $9-$10 **AAA Inspector Notes:** Near the Denver Tech Center, this location of a small chain prepares a wide variety of popular breakfast items, including eggs Benedict, frittatas, crepes, waffles and pancakes. The lunch menu includes creative sandwiches, soups and salads. The sophisticated country style decor adds a touch of elegance to an otherwise casual eatery. **Features:** senior menu. **Address:** 6818 S Yosemite St 80112 **Location:** I-25 exit 197 (Arapahoe Rd), just w to S Yosemite St, then just w; in Southgate Center. B L

MAGGIANO'S LITTLE ITALY
303/858-1405 **153**

▼▼▼ Italian. Fine Dining. $11-$40 **AAA Inspector Notes:** Diners savor scrumptious, traditional favorites served in a bustling atmosphere reminiscent of Little Italy. The dining area projects an early-20th-century feel; loud conversations bouncing off high ceilings evoke a sense of the Roaring 20's. **Features:** full bar. **Reservations:** suggested. **Address:** 7401 S Clinton St 80112 **Location:** I-25 exit 196 (Dry Creek Rd), just e, then just n. L D

MARCO'S COAL-FIRED PIZZERIA
303/790-9000 **154**

▼▼ ▼ Pizza. Casual Dining. $9-$17 **AAA Inspector Notes:** Many pizzerias claim to serve authentic cuisine; however, few have their staff members trained by the Associazione Pizzaiuoli Napoletani, a school dedicated to teaching the art of Napolese pizza-making. The combination of high quality ingredients from Italy with local fresh produce makes each bite unforgettable. **Features:** full bar, patio dining, Sunday brunch, happy hour. **Address:** 10111 Inverness Main St 80112 **Location:** I-25 exit 196 (Dry Creek Rd), 0.4 mi e, just s on Inverness Blvd, then just w. **Parking:** on-site and street. L D

CENTRAL CITY (C-8) pop. 663, elev. 8,496'

Within weeks of John Gregory's discovery of gold in 1859, hordes of prospectors were swarming over the steep sides of Gregory Gulch, which soon earned the title "the richest square mile on Earth." Although later eclipsed by the lodes at Cripple Creek, the gold dug from Gregory Gulch amounted to more than $67 million.

Central City, the middle camp among several that sprang up along the precipitous gulch, soon absorbed its immediate neighbors. Train loads of theatergoers came from Denver to enjoy Central City's cultural advantages. In 1932 the Opera Festival featured Lillian Gish in "Camille." The festival still attracts crowds every summer in July and August.

With its preserved 1870s main street, Central City is part of a national historic district that is surrounded by hills and dotted with Victorian houses. Outdoor enthusiasts enjoy camping, hiking, hunting, mountain biking and cross-country skiing. The city offers a variety of museums, casinos and summer festivals.

City of Central Visitors Center: 103 Eureka St., Central City, CO 80427. **Phone:** (303) 582-3345.

CENTRAL CITY OPERA HOUSE, w. of jct. Lawrence and Main sts. on Eureka St., was built in 1878 by the Welsh and Cornish as a reminder of the musical heritage of their homeland. The elaborate 550-seat opera house fell into disrepair when area mines closed shortly thereafter. Volunteers fortunately came to the rescue, and in 1932 the opera house was restored to its original Victorian splendor. Traditional operas have been presented in the grand theater each summer since its reopening. Tours feature the opera house and the adjoining 1872 Teller House hotel.

Tours are arranged at the Gilpin History tour office at Washington Hall across from the opera house. **Hours:** Guided tours are offered Tues.-Sun. 10-5, Memorial Day weekend-Labor Day; 10-4, rest of year. Tour times may vary; phone ahead. Opera season runs late June-early Aug. **Cost:** Tour $6 for opera house or for Teller House hotel; free (ages 0-12). Combination ticket with The Gilpin History Museum, Teller House and Thomas House Museum $10. Opera performance prices vary; phone box office for information. **Phone:** (303) 582-5283 for tour information, or (303) 292-6500 for ticket information.

THE GILPIN HISTORY MUSEUM, 1 blk. from Lawrence at 228 E. High St., is in a restored 2-story 1870 schoolhouse. Displays include a miniature mining town, mining memorabilia, a re-created Main Street and rotating displays on regional and national history. Also featured is the Mountain Submarine, a vessel that was raised from Missouri Lake in 1944 that is believed to have been constructed in the late 1890s. In winter months, tours can be arranged by appointment at the Gilpin History tour office at Washington Hall across from the Central City Opera House. **Time:** Allow 1 hour minimum. **Hours:** Tues.-Sun. 10-4, Memorial Day-Labor Day weekend; by appointment, rest of year. **Cost:** $6; free (ages 0-11). Combination ticket with Central City Opera House, Teller House and Thomas House Museum $10. **Phone:** (303) 582-5283.

Thomas House Museum is at 209 Eureka St. Constructed in 1867 and virtually unchanged since 1897 when Ben Thomas bought it for his bride, the Colorado Greek Revival house contains family memorabilia, including quilts, clothes, calendars, clocks, kitchen items and family photographs.

Tours begin at the Gilpin History tour office at Washington Hall across from the Central City Opera House. **Time:** Allow 30 minutes minimum. **Hours:** Tours are offered Tues.-Sun. 10-5, Memorial Day weekend through Labor Day, 10-4, rest of year. **Cost:** $6; free (ages 0-11). Combination ticket with Central City Opera House, The Gilpin History Museum and Teller House $10. **Phone:** (303) 582-5283. GT

"OH MY GAWD" ROAD (CR 279), s. on Spring St. out of town to the dirt road entering Virginia Canyon, is a half-hour drive to Idaho Springs that offers spectacular views of Mount Evans and the Continental Divide. The bumpy gravel road, with intermittent paved areas, passes through old mining towns, including Russell Gulch, Old Glory Hole and Central City. **Note:** This road is narrow and winding and should not be attempted by camping vehicles or drivers unaccustomed to mountain driving. Check road conditions with the visitor center before starting. **Phone:** (303) 567-4382.

GAMBLING ESTABLISHMENTS

• **Easy Street Casino** is at 120 Main St. **Hours:** Daily 8 a.m.-2 a.m. **Phone:** (303) 582-5914, ext. 235.

• **Reserve Casino and Hotel** is at 321 Gregory St. **Hours:** Daily 24 hours. **Phone:** (303) 582-0800 or (800) 924-6646.

CHIMNEY ROCK (F-2)

CHIMNEY ROCK NATIONAL MONUMENT is between Pagosa Springs and Durango, 3 mi. s. of SR 160 at 3179 SR 151. The site, in the San Juan National Forest, is surrounded by the Southern Ute Indian Reservation. Home to the ancestors of the modern Pueblo Indians 1,000 years ago, Chimney Rock is of great spiritual significance to these tribes. As visitors explore the remains of the ancestral Puebloan village atop a mesa, they see spectacular panoramas, birds of prey and other wildlife, and colorful wildflowers. Guided tours include the Pueblo and Kiva trails. Self-guiding tours and several night sky viewing programs also are available.

Guided tours average 2.5 hours, include 1 mile of hiking with a 200-foot elevation gain and depart at 9:30, 10:30, 1 and 2. Water, sturdy shoes, hats and sunscreen are advised. The only self-guiding tour is a barrier-free trail. **Time:** Allow 2 hours, 30 minutes minimum. **Hours:** Daily 9-4:30, May 15-Sept. 30. Tour times vary. Phone ahead to confirm schedule. **Cost:** $12; $5 (ages 5-11). Tour and program fees vary. **Phone:** (970) 883-5359 May 15-Sept. 30, or (970) 731-7133 rest of year.

CHIPITA PARK
• Part of Colorado Springs area — see map p. 81

CHIPITA LODGE B & B   (719)684-8454

WWWW **Bed & Breakfast** $125-$160 **Address:** 9090 Chipita Park Rd 80809 **Location:** Jct US 24, just s on Fountain Blvd (Pine Peak Hwy), then 1.5 mi w; right at fork. **Facility:** Relax in the great room of this pine-shrouded 1927 log lodge, which has a stone fireplace, overstuffed furniture and a large mounted elk head. 5 units, some cabins. 1 story, interior/exterior corridors. **Terms:** closed 11/15-4/30, check-in 4 pm, 2 night minimum stay - weekends, age restrictions may apply, 7 day cancellation notice. **Activities:** hot tub.

 / SOME UNITS

CLARK

VISTA VERDE GUEST RANCH   970/879-3858

WWWW WWW
Resort Ranch
$850-$1400

Address: 58000 Cowboy Way 80428 **Location:** 1.8 mi nw of center on US 40 to Elk River Rd (CR 129), 17.5 mi n to Slavonia and CR 64 (Seedhouse Rd), 4.5 mi ne, then 1 mi on dirt road, follow sign. **Facility:** This all-inclusive luxury guest ranch has one- to three-bedroom luxury cabins and smaller modern lodge rooms, each with a deck and outdoor hot tub. 12 units, some cabins. 1-2 stories (no elevator), interior/exterior corridors. **Terms:** closed 3/19-6/5 & 10/19-12/12, check-in 4 pm, check-out 9:30 am, 3-7 night minimum stay - seasonal and/or weekends, 90 day cancellation notice-fee imposed. **Pool(s):** heated outdoor. **Activities:** hot tub, fishing, cross country skiing, snowmobiling, recreation programs, kids club, bicycles, trails, exercise room, massage. **Guest Services:** valet laundry, area transportation.

CLIFTON pop. 19,889

BEST WESTERN GRANDE RIVER INN & SUITES
(970)434-3400

WWWW
Hotel
$110-$180

AAA Benefit: Save 10% or more every day and earn 10% bonus points!

Address: 3228 I-70 Business Loop 81520 **Location:** I-70 exit 37, 0.8 mi s; east of Grand Junction. **Facility:** 49 units. 2 stories, exterior corridors. **Pool(s):** heated indoor. **Activities:** hot tub, exercise room. **Guest Services:** coin laundry. **Featured Amenity:** full hot breakfast.

DOS HOMBRES   970/434-5078

WWWW Mexican. Casual Dining. $7-$16 **AAA Inspector Notes:** There are several comfortable dining rooms in which diners sample many appetizers, salads and build-your-own combinations. Favorites include white bean chili, Navajo tacos, seafood enchiladas and Southwest pasta with grilled chicken and jalapeno cream sauce. A daily lunch special is made seven days a week, along with a poquito and New Mexican combination. **Features:** full bar, patio dining, happy hour. **Address:** 3245 I-70 Business Loop 81520 **Location:** I-70 exit 37, 0.8 mi s, east corner of US 6.

L D

COLORADO NATIONAL MONUMENT (D-1)

Colorado National Monument is reached from Fruita via I-70 exit 19 or Grand Junction via SR 340 (Broadway). This bold, big and brilliantly colored canyon country, with its towering and fascinating rock sculptures, covers 32 square miles of rugged terrain. Rim Rock Drive is one of the grandest scenic drives in the American West and offers both motorists and bicyclists access to 23 miles of breathtaking scenery. The drive also provides access to the visitor center and campground, several interpretive viewpoints and 14 hiking trails varying in length and difficulty.

It is a semi-desert landscape of pinyon pines and Utah juniper; low-growing plants and wildflowers grace the area in spring. Camping and picnicking areas, self-guiding nature trails and longer hiking paths are available. Back-country camping requires a permit, available free at the visitor center.

Allow 2 hours, 30 minutes minimum. Daily 24 hours. Entrance fee $10 per private vehicle or $5 per person arriving by other means (valid for 7 days). Camping $20. Phone (970) 858-3617.

COLORADO NATIONAL MONUMENT VISITOR CENTER, near the Fruita entrance, presents cultural and natural history exhibits as well as two 12-minute video programs. **Hours:** Visitor center hours vary. Closed Christmas. Phone ahead to confirm schedule. **Cost:** Free. **Phone:** (970) 858-3617, ext. 360.

Colorado Springs

Then & Now

Gen. William J. Palmer, forging westward with his Denver & Rio Grande Railroad in 1871, saw the area's potential early on and formulated a plan of creating a playground for the wealthy on what was essentially a sagebrush flat. The village already at the site, a miners' and millers' town called Colorado City, hardly met his stringent requirements. Palmer and his associates moved a few miles away and drove the first stake at what is now Pikes Peak and Cascade avenues.

Within the year there were more than 150 temporary and two permanent structures, irrigation ditches, countless seedling cottonwoods and land donated for a college. All were placed according to an orderly plan with broad boulevards, school lots and parks.

A road linked the new town with the mineral springs at Manitou Springs, 6 miles west. Colorado Springs, its name derived from the spa and from Colorado City, was on the way to becoming everything Palmer wanted, and more.

Many of the younger sons of the English gentry arrived. Polo, riding to hounds, gentlemen's clubs and Tudor architecture became so much a part of the Springs that it was soon known as Little London.

When not playing cricket or attending social functions, these Britons and their American counterparts speculated in mining. They made millions, especially after the bonanza in Cripple Creek. The city benefited in the form of parks, office buildings, mansions and hotels. By the first decade of the 20th century, Colorado Springs ranked among the wealthiest cities per capita in the country.

Meanwhile, Colorado City flourished, partly because of liquor trafficking and other temptations prohibited by its neighbor. Allegedly, tunnels ran between the two communities to protect the anonymity of those citizens who liked to visit the other side of the tracks. Colorado City was ultimately absorbed by the Springs and its respectability.

Some of the old buildings still exist, particularly in the Old Colorado City Historic District between 24th and 28th streets. They house specialty shops, restaurants, galleries and municipal offices.

Today, Colorado Springs continues to enjoy the reputation it received upon its creation—a destination for recreation, relaxation and bountiful sightseeing opportunities. A few miles west, scenic US 24 climbs to the 14,100-foot summit of Pikes Peak; the journey to the top offers stunning panoramas, ranging from lush alpine forest to the stark beauty above the timberline. And, if the prospect of driving the twisting route makes you a bit nervous, you can hop on a train at the Manitou Springs depot and travel upward via the cog railway.

(Continued on p. 82.)

Take the Pikes Peak Cog Railway to the summit

Destination Colorado Springs

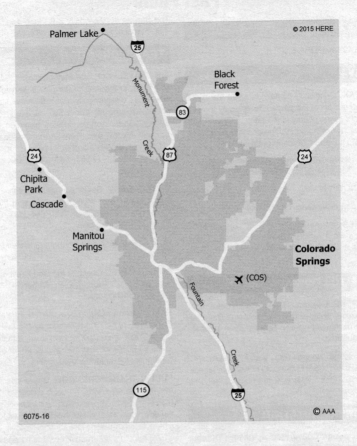

This map shows cities in the Colorado Springs vicinity where you will find attractions, hotels and restaurants. Cities are listed alphabetically in this book on the following pages.

Fast Facts

ABOUT THE CITY

POP: 416,427 ▪ **ELEV:** 6,008 ft.

MONEY

SALES TAX: Colorado's statewide sales tax is 2.9 percent; an additional 2.5 percent is levied by the city, 1.23 percent by the county and 1 percent by the Pikes Peak Rural Transit Authority. The county has a 2 percent lodging tax and 1 percent rental car tax.

WHOM TO CALL

EMERGENCY: 911

POLICE (non-emergency): (719) 444-7000

HOSPITALS: Memorial Hospital, (719) 365-5000 ▪ Penrose-St. Francis Health Services, (719) 776-5000 ▪ St. Francis Medical Center, (719) 571-1000.

WHERE TO LOOK AND LISTEN

NEWSPAPERS: Colorado Springs' major newspaper is The Gazette, distributed in the morning. The Independent is distributed weekly. Special-interest papers also are published.

RADIO: Colorado Springs radio stations KVOR (740 AM) and KRDO (105.5 FM) are all-news/weather stations ▪ KRCC (91.5 FM) is a member of National Public Radio.

VISITOR INFORMATION

Colorado Springs Convention & Visitors Bureau: 515 S. Cascade Ave., Colorado Springs, CO 80903. **Phone:** (800) 368-4748.

The bureau is open daily 8-6, June-Aug.; Mon.-Fri. 8:30-5, rest of year. *(See ad p. 88.)*

TRANSPORTATION

AIR TRAVEL: Colorado Springs Airport (COS), (719) 550-1900, to the east of the city, is served by major airlines. Taxi service is available from the airport to the downtown area for about $35 each way. Colorado Springs Shuttle offers service between Colorado Springs Airport and Denver International Airport (DEN), with drop-offs and pick-ups at designated area hotels; phone (719) 687-3456 for schedule information.

RENTAL CARS: Rental car agencies serve the Colorado Springs area from downtown and the airport. Hertz, (719) 596-1863 or (800) 654-3131, offers discounts to AAA members.

RAIL SERVICE: No passenger trains serve Colorado Springs.

BUSES: TNM&O Coaches Inc. and Greyhound Lines Inc., (719) 635-1505, 120 S. Weber St., serve the Colorado Springs area.

TAXIS: Colorado Springs is served by Yellow Cab Co., (719) 777-7777. It is best to request cabs by phone. Taxis are on the meter system, with the charge about $4.90 for the first mile and $2.90 for each additional mile, for up to four passengers.

PUBLIC TRANSPORTATION: Buses operate in the metropolitan area Mon.-Fri. 5:35 a.m.-9:35 p.m.; Sat. 6:35 a.m.-6:35 p.m.; and Sun. 7:30 a.m.-5:35 p.m. in the downtown area; check individual routes for current schedule information. The fare for in-town routes is $1.75, transfers are free with paid fares and are good for 2 hours and 2 one way trips. Day passes are $4. Phone (719) 385-7433.

(Continued from p. 80.)

Garden of the Gods Park, another must-see, offers dramatic views of towering sandstone rock formations with Pikes Peak looming in the background. The erosion-sculpted, red-hued marvels have morphed into such shapes as Kissing Camels, Siamese Twins and a Sleeping Giant, and depending on the time of day you visit, the light produces a vast array of mesmerizing effects. The park is a natural playground for hikers, rock climbers and those just happy to snap photos of the impressive birdlife and geologic wonders. Given the environment, mountain bikers, golfers and horseback riders find the community a perfect setting in which to indulge their passions.

The city has become an important military center. The North American Air Defense Command (NORAD), sequestered in the granite heart of Cheyenne Mountain, was command-central for American defensive troops during the Desert Storm conflict. More visible are the U.S. Air Force Academy, Fort Carson Army Base, Peterson Air Force Base and U.S. Space Command.

Especially prominent is the Air Force Academy's Cadet Chapel: Majestic glass and silver spires jutting skyward resemble 17 swept-wing, vertical-takeoff planes poised to break Earth's bonds. The academy's visitor center welcomes guests, who are typically free to explore the chapel and such sites as Arnold Hall, the Field House and the Honor Court, but they should inquire first due to fluctuating security levels.

Southwest of the city via SRs 115 and 122 is The Broadmoor resort. Since its opening in 1918 as a grand hotel, it has grown into a recreational retreat and includes two spas, three 18-hole golf courses, 16 tennis courts, squash courts, hiking trails and horseback riding.

Must Do: AAA Editor's Picks

- Visit  **Garden of the Gods Park** (1805 30th St.) to be inspired by the rustic beauty of majestic sandstone pinnacles jutting skyward. Take a free naturalist-guided walk to learn about wildflowers, snakes and other interesting tidbits about Colorado, or go it alone on one of the easy-to-moderate scenic trails. Don't leave your camera behind.

- Take a scenic drive to **Pikes Peak**. Travel 19 miles along the twisting **Pikes Peak Highway** to the summit, where you'll be rewarded with a magnificent panorama. If you'd rather not take on the dizzying mountain route yourself, leave the driving to someone else and board the **Pikes Peak Cog Railway** (515 Ruxton Ave.) in Manitou Springs.

- Spend some time at **The Broadmoor** (1 Lake Ave.). The resort, which opened in 1918 as the "Grand Dame of the Rockies," is nestled in a valley with a spectacular mountain backdrop. Take a guided trail ride at the Broadmoor Stables, relax with a spa treatment, peruse the boutiques or dine in one of the property's restaurants.

- The most stunning structure at the **U.S. Air Force Academy** (2306 Academy Dr.) is the Cadet Chapel, with its 17 futuristic glass and silver spires soaring skyward. You can tour the chapel, along with the Honor Court, Field House, Arnold Hall and other sites; maps are available at the academy's visitor center, which also presents a movie showcasing the cadet experience.

- Explore underground wonders at **Cave of the Winds** (100 Cave of the Winds Rd.) in nearby Manitou Springs. Guides lead you through the winding passageways either by flashlight or hand-held lantern, depending on the tour. Either way, you'll be mesmerized by the play of light on the jagged geological formations and will even experience total cave darkness.

- Hunt for souvenirs in the **Old Colorado City** historic district (W. Colorado Ave. & S. 21st St.). This is where the rowdy Wild West town of Colorado City sprang to life in 1859. Now, instead of saloons, jails and brothels, you'll find quaint boutiques, eclectic galleries and bistros. On summer Saturdays, you can shop for goods at the farmers market on the main drag.

- Wander through the **Colorado Springs Fine Arts Center** (30 W. Dale St.) on your own, or sign up for one of the docent-led tours. An impressive array of modern works in a pueblo-style space is supplemented by traveling exhibits and a varied permanent collection, including Western, Southwestern and Native American art. The sculpture garden is an additional highlight.

- Guided tours of the **U.S. Olympic Complex** (1750 E. Boulder St.) will provide you with an inside peek at where the country's elite athletes live and train prior to the games—you might even witness a practice session. The visitor center presents a video about the Olympics prior to the tours, which are mostly conducted outdoors.

- If you're up for a little **recreation** or fresh air, check out one of the area's parks. Hikers like **North Cheyenne Cañon Park** (2120 S. Cheyenne Canyon Rd.), with its miles of trails, lovely scenic vistas and waterfalls. A favorite with trekkers, horseback riders and mountain bikers, **Palmer Park** (Academy Blvd. & Maizeland Rd.) also has play areas, picnic grounds and a dog park.

- **Cheyenne Mountain Zoo** (4250 Cheyenne Mountain Zoo Rd.) houses more than 1,200 amazing creatures in an invigorating mountain environment highlighting wildlife in natural settings—a favorite is the Rocky Mountain Wild exhibit, with moose, mountain lions and grizzly bears among the residents. You can also take the kids on a carousel or pony ride and soar above the zoo on a chairlift.

Garden of the Gods Park

Colorado Springs 1-day Itinerary

AAA editors suggest these activities for a great short vacation experience.

Morning

- You'll be enchanted by the community of Colorado Springs, tucked into a valley with the Front Range looming in the background. The crowning glory of this rugged mountain panorama is Pikes Peak, rising some 8,000 feet above the city. Naturally, those visiting will want to explore the area's striking scenic wonders. With that said, spend the morning at **Garden of the Gods Park**, at 30th Street and Garden of the Gods Road. Plan to hit the **Garden of the Gods Visitor & Nature Center** first, where you can view the multimedia show "How Did Those Red Rocks Get There?" You'll also be able to view a topographical map as well as interactive and educational exhibits focusing on the region's ecology and geology.

- Ready to enter the park? You can choose to wander the trails on your own, or sign up for a naturalist-led walk; during the summer, van and jeep tours depart from the front of the visitor center. Maps highlighting the terrain will allow you to choose from a variety of easy and moderate routes, from which you will be well-positioned to see stunning sandstone formations that have morphed into otherworldly shapes. The changing position of the sun throughout the day creates dramatic effects.

- If you have time you can also drop by **Rock Ledge Ranch Historic Site** (30th St. & Gateway Rd.), at the park's east entrance. This living-history farm provides insight into such aspects of early Pikes Peak life as homesteading, farming and managing a country estate.

Afternoon

- It's probably a good time to stop for lunch. You can grab a bite at **Marigold Cafe & Bakery** (4605 Centennial Blvd.), just off Garden of the Gods Road. This little bistro offers contemporary cuisine, including sandwiches, salads, pizzas and delectable freshly baked pastries.

- Continuing east on Garden of the Gods Road to I-25, travel north less than a mile to exit 148 to reach your next destination, the **ProRodeo Hall of Fame and Museum of the American Cowboy** (101 ProRodeo Dr.). Through the use of photos and multimedia presentations, the museum pays tribute to great bronco busters, their animals and key contributors to the sport of professional rodeo. You can also spy Western art displays, belt buckles, saddles and other paraphernalia.

- Backtrack to I-25, where you will travel north to exit 150 to visit the next point of interest, the **U.S. Air Force Academy** (2306 Academy Dr.). But, do call in advance to ensure that the

ProRodeo Hall of Fame and Museum of the American Cowboy

academy can receive visitors, since fluctuating security levels can impact public access. You can learn about cadet life at **The Barry Goldwater Air Force Academy Visitor Center** and pick up a brochure outlining a self-guiding tour. An absolute must-see is the Cadet Chapel, which you can access from a nature trail adjacent to the visitor center. This architectural wonder resembles a tight formation of planes ready to take off into the wild blue yonder.

Evening

- For dinner head to Old Colorado City, just west of downtown. The outlaw-infested saloons that once stood in the notorious 1859 Old West town have been replaced with charming galleries, shops and sidewalk cafés housed in renovated historic structures. For hearty Italian fare in a cozy yet casual setting, try **Paravicini's Italian Bistro** (2802 W. Colorado Ave.). Families find all the comforts of home at **The Mason Jar**, (2925 W. Colorado Ave.) with traditional American fare like fried chicken, catfish, buttermilk biscuits and other soul-satisfying dishes.

- Locals who want to relax with a libation or listen to some music usually gravitate to Tejon Street, a hubbub of pubs, taverns and lounges in the downtown area. Those with a passion for the performing arts should check the roster at Pikes Peak Center (190 S. Cascade Ave.), which features the Colorado Springs Philharmonic and Opera Theatre of the Rockies in addition to plays and top-name performers.

Arriving
By Car

North-south access is via I-25, which skirts the eastern face of the Rocky Mountains and is concurrent with US 85/87 through much of Colorado. I-25 is the fast route into or through Colorado Springs, with interchanges at major streets; US 85/87 leaves the interstate briefly in favor of downtown streets. Another major north-south thoroughfare is Powers Boulevard (SR 21), which runs near the airport in the eastern section of the city.

Yet another north-south route leading into town is Nevada Avenue (SR 115 in the southern part of the city), which offers a shortcut from US 50 between Cañon City and Pueblo. East-west travel is via US 24, which comes into the city from the eastern plains as Platte Avenue and from the western mountains through Ute Pass.

Getting Around
Street System

I-25 is the major north-south artery and fastest means of travel through Colorado Springs. Nevada Avenue (SR 115 in the southern section of the city) runs parallel to I-25 and provides access to many downtown streets.

US 24 (Martin Luther King, Jr. Bypass) travels east to west, becoming Platte Avenue when it crosses I-25 into the eastern section of the city; it leads to Manitou Springs and Pikes Peak in the west. East-west roads that interchange with I-25 are Garden of the Gods Road, Fillmore Street, Woodmen Road and Uintah Street.

Parking

Downtown on-street parking is metered, 75c-$1 per hour. Commercial garages and lots are available for 75c-$1 per hour, with a daily maximum of $6.75-$7.50. Prepaid "Easy Park" cards are accepted at most meters and can be purchased at the City Administration Building at Nevada and Colorado avenues.

Shopping

Malls and shopping centers provide most of the shopping opportunities in Colorado Springs. Some of the popular centers include **Chapel Hills Mall,** with anchor stores Burlington Coat Factory, Dillard's, Macy's and Sears, at Academy and Briargate boulevards; **The Citadel,** with anchors Dillard's and JCPenney, N. Academy Boulevard and US 24; **The Promenade Shops at Briargate,** Briargate Parkway and SR 87; and University Village at S. Nevada Ave. and US 25.

A 19th-century haven of fur trappers, cowboys, gamblers and a few outlaws and gunfighters, **Old Colorado City Historic District,** between 24th and 28th streets, now houses specialty shops. The **Garden of the Gods Trading Post,** built in the late 1920s to resemble Pueblo Indian houses, offers Native American arts, crafts, jewelry, rugs and pottery as well as signed prints by well-known artists.

Shop Old Colorado City Historic District

Big Events

Two street festivals featuring local vendors and entertainment herald the arrival of spring to Colorado Springs. **Territory Days** in Old Colorado City takes place in late May, and June brings **Springs Spree** to **Memorial Park.**

Colorado Springs' sports facilities play host to athletic events throughout the year, but the major events take place in summer. The **Ride for the Brand Championship Ranch Rodeo** and the **Pikes Peak or Bust Rodeo** at the **Norris-Penrose Events Center,** both held in early July, attract top rodeo cowboys from around the country. The event kicks off with a **Rodeo Parade** the day before Rodeo Week begins in downtown Colorado Springs. Sports fans also will enjoy the **Pikes Peak International Hill Climb** motor sports race in late June on **Pikes Peak Highway** and the **Pikes Peak Ascent and Marathon** at **Pikes Peak** in August.

Over the Labor Day weekend, watch more than 100 colorful balloons ascend in Memorial Park during the **Colorado Balloon Classic.** The **Festival of Lights Parade** downtown ushers in the holiday season in early December.

Sports & Rec

The surrounding lands of the **Pike National Forest** *(see Pikes Peak and Pike National Forest p. 245)* provide opportunities for outdoor recreation. **Green Mountain Falls** and **Woodland Park** are northwest of the city. **Hiking** and **horseback riding** on the **Barr National Recreation Trail** are enjoyable ways to travel to the summit of Pikes Peak. **Camping** also is popular in this area.

Horseback riding through **Garden of the Gods Park, North Cheyenne Cañon Park** or at area dude ranches can be arranged at a variety of locations in the area. A list is available at the convention and visitors bureau; phone (719) 634-6666.

Golf enthusiasts have their choice of three 18-hole championship golf courses at **The Broadmoor** resort, (719) 577-5790, or the 18-hole championship Pete Dye course at the **Cheyenne Mountain Resort,** (719) 538-4095. Golfers also can tee off at the **Patty Jewett Municipal Golf Course** (18 holes), E. Española and N. Prospect streets, (719) 385-6935, or the **Pine Creek Golf Course** (18 holes), 9850 Divot Tr., (719) 594-9999. The **Valley Hi Municipal Course** (18 holes), 610 Chelton Rd., (719) 385-6911, also has a swimming pool and driving range.

Most city parks have **tennis** courts and **bicycling** trails. The Broadmoor resort also has tennis courts. Guided 20-mile **mountain biking** trips from the 14,110-summit of Pikes Peak are offered daily May 1 through mid-October (weather permitting) by Challenge Unlimited; phone (719) 633-6399 or (800) 798-5954. **Swimming** is available at several indoor and outdoor aquatic facilities operated by the Pikes Peak Region YMCA. **Memorial Park,** at the corner of Pikes Peak and Union, is home to a 40,000-square-foot Skate Park that welcomes skateboarders, in-line skaters and BMX riders.

Hometown fans come out to cheer the **Air Force Academy football** team, phone (719) 472-1895, the **Colorado Sky Sox baseball** team, phone (719) 591-7699, and the **Colorado College Tigers hockey** team, phone (719) 389-6324.

Memorial Park welcomes skateboarders, in-line skaters and BMX riders

Performing Arts

The **Colorado Springs Fine Arts Center** *(see attraction listing p. 87),* 30 W. Dale St., is the scene of permanent and traveling art exhibits, theatrical performances, concerts, dance productions and film showings. The **Civic Music Theater** also holds performances at the fine arts center throughout the year.

Pikes Peak Center, 190 S. Cascade Ave., plays host to more than 200 performances a year, running the gamut from ballet, opera, theater and the symphony to country and rock music; phone (719) 799-4139. The **Colorado Springs Philharmonic** plays its September through May season here; phone (719) 520-7469 for ticket information. The center is also the home of **Broadway in Colorado Springs;** phone (719) 799-4132.

Colorado Springs World Arena features top-name performers in both theatrical productions and concerts, ice hockey and skating shows; phone (719) 477-2100. The **Iron Springs Chateau and Playhouse** dinner theater is at 444 Ruxton Ave; phone (719) 685-5104. Plays also are staged at **Colorado College** and the **University of Colorado-Colorado Springs.** Check the local newspapers for complete listings of current events.

⚑ ATTRACTIONS

AMERICAN NUMISMATIC ASSOCIATION MONEY MUSEUM, 818 N. Cascade Ave., claims to be the country's largest museum dedicated to coins, paper money, medals and related items. The museum presents changing and permanent exhibits featuring coins from ancient civilizations to the present. Of special interest is a collection of American gold coins. A library features more than 40,000 volumes related to numismatics.

Time: Allow 1 hour minimum. **Hours:** Museum and library Tues.-Sat. 10:30-5. Closed major holidays. **Cost:** $5; $4 (ages 55+, students and military with ID); free (third Sat. of the month). **Phone:** (719) 632-2646, Ext. 134 or (800) 367-9723.

BEAR CREEK NATURE CENTER, off 26th St. at 245 Bear Creek Rd. in Bear Creek Regional Park, features hands-on, interactive Colorado wildlife exhibits. Self-guiding nature trails begin at the center. **Time:** Allow 1 hour minimum. **Hours:** Wed.-Sat. 9-4. Park and nature trails daily dawn-dusk. Closed major holidays. **Cost:** Free. **Phone:** (719) 520-6387.

CAVE OF THE WINDS—see Manitou Springs p. 231.

CHEYENNE MOUNTAIN ZOO, 2.75 mi. w. of I-25 exit 138, then 2 mi. s.w. following signs to 4250 Cheyenne Mountain Zoo Rd., claims the distinction of being America's only mountain zoo. The Rocky Mountain Wild exhibit features grizzly bears, river otters, mountain lions and moose among many other animals. The African Rift Valley exhibit highlights the zoo's noted giraffe herd. More than 950 animals, including many endangered species, are featured.

The landscaped grounds also contain an antique carousel and a tot train as well as the Mountaineer Sky Ride, an open-air chairlift providing spectacular views of the Pikes Peak region.

Time: Allow 3 hours minimum. **Hours:** Daily 9-5. Last admission is at 4. Mountaineer Sky Ride daily 9-5, (last ride at 4:30) May 1-Labor Day. Sat.-Sun. 10-4 (last ride at 3:30), rest of year (weather permitting). **Cost:** May 1-Labor Day (includes Will Rogers Shrine of the Sun) $17.25; $15.25 (ages 65+); $14.25 (military with ID); $12.25 (ages 3-11); $9.25 (military children). Rest of year $14.25; $12.25 (ages 65+); $11.25 (military with ID); $10.25 (ages 3-11); $7.25 (military children). Mountaineer Sky Ride $5; $4 (ages 3-11). **Phone:** (719) 633-9925.

Will Rogers Shrine of the Sun, reached via Cheyenne Mountain Zoo Rd., which runs through the zoo, is a stone tower memorial to the 20th-century humorist. Built at an elevation of 8,136 feet, the shrine provides spectacular views of Colorado Springs and the surrounding area. **Time:** Allow 1 hour minimum. **Hours:** Daily 9-5, May-Labor Day; 9-4, rest of year (weather permitting). Admission ends one hour before closing. Closed Jan. 1, Thanksgiving and Christmas. **Cost:** Included with Cheyenne Mountain Zoo. **Phone:** (719) 578-5367.

COLORADO SPRINGS FINE ARTS CENTER is at 30 W. Dale St. The center's fine permanent collection includes works by late 19th- and early 20th-century American artists; Colorado landscape paintings; photography; modern art; Hispanic art, including works from Central and South America, Mexico and the Caribbean as well as the United States. Artists represented include Ansel Adams, Dale Chihuly, Richard Diebenkorn, Walt Kuhn, Georgia O'Keeffe, John Singer Sargent and John Waters.

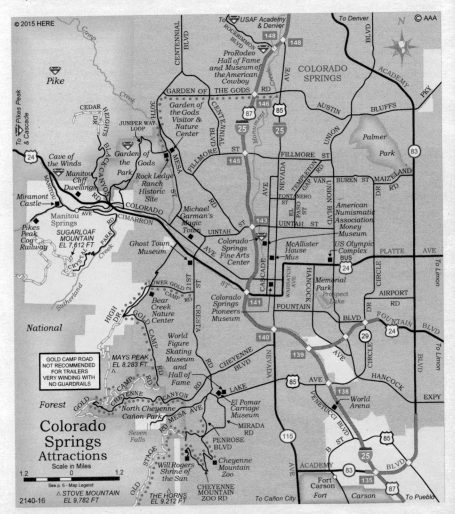

© 2015 HERE   © AAA

Colorado Springs Attractions

Scale in Miles
1.2   0   1.2

See p. 6 - Map Legend

2140-16

The center also features a tactile gallery for the visually impaired, a 400-seat theater, an art school and a courtyard. Additional galleries feature traveling exhibits. Docent-led tours are available. **Time:** Allow 2 hours minimum. **Hours:** Tues.-Sun. 10-5. Closed major holidays. **Cost:** $20-$25; $15 (military and students with ID); free (ages 0-12). An additional fee is charged for special exhibitions. Tactile gallery free. **Phone:** (719) 634-5581. GT ⁙

COLORADO SPRINGS PIONEERS MUSEUM, 215 S. Tejon St., is housed in the 1903 El Paso County Courthouse. The museum contains exhibits about Colorado Springs and Pikes Peak heritage and Native Americans. Changing exhibits and programs also are featured. **Time:** Allow 1 hour minimum. **Hours:** Tues.-Sat. 10-5. **Cost:** Free. **Phone:** (719) 385-5990.

EL POMAR CARRIAGE MUSEUM is at The Broadmoor resort at 11 Lake Cir. Two presidential inaugural coaches, a collection of horse-drawn vehicles, riding accessories, Native American clothing and artifacts, and firearms are displayed. **Time:** Allow 30 minutes minimum. **Hours:** Mon.-Sat. 9-5, Sun. 1-5. Closed Jan. 1, Easter, Thanksgiving and Christmas. **Cost:** Free. **Phone:** (719) 577-7065.

FOCUS ON THE FAMILY WELCOME CENTER is off I-25 exit 151, then 1 mi. e. on Briargate Pkwy. to 8685 Explorer Dr. The organization, dedicated to preserving and promoting traditional values in the home, publishes magazines and books and produces radio broadcasts, films and CDs. The Welcome Center includes interactive displays, a theater and a children's area.

Time: Allow 1 hour, 30 minutes minimum. **Hours:** Mon.-Sat. 9-5, day after Memorial Day-Sat. before Labor Day; Mon.-Fri. 9-5, Sat. 9-4, rest of year. Tours Mon.-Fri.; phone ahead for schedule. **Cost:** Free. **Phone:** (719) 531-3400, or (719) 531-3328 for tour reservations. GT ⁙

GARDEN OF THE GODS PARK, n.w. off US 24 on 31st St. or w. off I-25 on Garden of the Gods Rd. to 30th St., is a 1,323-acre city park at the base of Pikes Peak, where the Great Plains meet the Rockies. Flora and fauna within the park reflect the rich diversity of this crossroad. In 1909, railroad magnate Charles Elliot Perkins bequeathed to the city the parkland he purchased in 1879 with the stipulation that it remain open and free to the public.

The park is known for its towering red sandstone formations, which include Kissing Camels and Balanced Rock. The soft sunlight of early morning and late afternoon enhances the beauty of the formations. Beautifully framed snapshots of Pikes Peak are available from many viewpoints.

In addition, the park offers a diverse list of recreational options. Visitors can explore miles of both paved and unpaved trails and try mountain biking, horseback riding and guided nature walks. The

▼ See AAA listing p. 82 ▼

park's many footpaths have easy slopes. Visitors safe on the ground can watch climbers scale the cliffs. Guided nature walks are offered daily. **Time:** Allow 1 hour minimum. **Hours:** Visitor center open daily 8-7, Memorial Day-Labor Day; 9-5, rest of year. Park hours 5 a.m.-11 p.m., May-Oct.; 5 a.m.-9 p.m., rest of year. Nature walks at 10 a.m. and 2 p.m. **Cost:** Free. **Phone:** (719) 634-6666. 🎡

Garden of the Gods Visitor & Nature Center, 1805 N. 30th St., offers a museum with interactive exhibits; a 14-minute multimedia show featuring park history; guided nature walks and rock-climbing excursions; guided jeep and Segway tours; interactive natural history exhibits; and free maps, brochures and information about the area.

Time: Allow 1 hour minimum. **Hours:** Daily 8-7, Memorial Day-Labor Day; 9-5, rest of year. Guided nature walks are given daily at 10 and 2. Jeep and Segway hours vary; phone ahead for hours and rates. Closed Jan. 1, Thanksgiving and Christmas. **Cost:** Museum and nature walks free. Multimedia show $6; $4 (ages 5-10). **Phone:** (719) 634-6666. GT 🍴

GHOST TOWN MUSEUM is off I-25 exit 141, then 1.5 mi. w. to 400 S. 21st St. at US 24, next to the Colorado Midland railroad roundhouse. This 1800s Old West town, relocated and preserved within one of the last remaining Colorado Midland buildings, is comprised of structures abandoned after the gold rush era. Included are a general store, saloon, Victorian house, blacksmith shop, jail, livery stable, rooming house and other buildings, each containing artifacts of the period. Gold panning and other hands-on activities are offered.

Hours: Daily 9-6, June-Aug.; daily 10-5, rest of year. **Cost:** (includes gold panning and activities) $8.50; $5 (ages 6-16). **Phone:** (719) 634-0696.

GOLD CAMP ROAD is 1 mi. e. off US 115 on Cheyenne Blvd., then 2 mi. n. on 21st St. The road is a narrow, twisting, 36-mile gravel trail that follows the Cripple Creek Short Line Railroad roadbed through North Cheyenne Canyon. President Theodore Roosevelt described it as the "trip that bankrupts the English language." It is a favorite scenic route for cyclists.

Note: The road has no guardrails and is unsuitable for trailers and some RVs. Only experienced mountain drivers should attempt it. Phone ahead for road conditions. An 8-mile section of the road is closed due to a tunnel collapse; Old Stage Road provides a detour. **Time:** Allow 1 hour, 30 minutes minimum. **Phone:** (719) 636-1602 for the Pikes Peak U.S. Forest Service office.

MAY NATURAL HISTORY MUSEUM, 8 mi. s.w. on SR 115 (Nevada Ave.) to 710 Rock Creek Canyon Rd., exhibits more than 7,000 giant and exotic insects and arachnids from the jungles of the world. Self-guiding tours are available. **Time:** Allow 1 hour, 30 minutes minimum. **Hours:** Daily 9-6, May-Sept. **Cost:** $6; $5 (ages 60+ and military with ID); $3 (ages 6-12). **Phone:** (719) 576-0450 or (800) 666-3841.

MANITOU CLIFF DWELLINGS—see Manitou Springs p. 232.

MCALLISTER HOUSE MUSEUM, 423 N. Cascade Ave., was built for Maj. Henry McAllister, who assisted Gen. William Palmer in developing Colorado Springs. The restored 1873 house contains original and period furnishings. **Time:** Allow 30 minutes minimum. **Hours:** Tues.-Sat. 10-4, mid-May through Aug. 31; Thurs.-Sat. 10-4, rest of year. Last tour begins 1 hour before closing. **Cost:** $5; $4 (ages 62+); $3 (ages 6-12). **Phone:** (719) 635-7925.

MICHAEL GARMAN'S MAGIC TOWN, 2418 W. Colorado Ave., is a 3-D cityscape sculpted by artist Michael Garman. Through the use of mirrors, holographs, video projection and illusion, Garman has designed a miniature city of yesterday, complete with mom-and-pop cafés, pool halls, flophouses and saloons. **Time:** Allow 30 minutes minimum. **Hours:** Daily 10-5:30, Mar.-Sept.; Mon.-Sat. 10-5:30, Sun. noon-5. **Cost:** (includes scavenger hunt and popcorn) $5; $4.50 (military, police and firefighters with ID); $4 (ages 55+); $3 (ages 6-12). **Phone:** (719) 471-9391 or (800) 731-3908.

MIRAMONT CASTLE—see Manitou Springs p. 232.

NORTH CHEYENNE CAÑON PARK is reached via Cheyenne Blvd. Striking rock formations and waterfalls, notably Helen Hunt Falls and Silver Cascade Falls, characterize the canyon. Hiking and biking trails, some challenging, are available. A permit is required for technical rock climbing.

Starsmore Discovery Center, at the east entrance of the park, is a visitor center with exhibits about area wildlife, the history of the park and nature programs. Another visitor center is at Helen Hunt Falls, 3 miles up the canyon. Both centers offer special

Hike the stairs at Seven Falls for a spectacular view

youth programs and hummingbird watching in summer. **Hours:** Starsmore Discovery Center daily 9-5, June-Aug.; Tues.-Sat. 9-3, Apr.-May and Sept.-Oct. Helen Hunt Falls Visitor Center 9-5, June-Aug. Phone ahead to confirm schedule and to see if trails are open. **Cost:** Free. **Phone:** (719) 385-6086. 🏕

High Drive begins at the end of N. Cheyenne Cañon Rd. The one-way dirt route ascends a steep mountain for 1 mile, then descends 2.4 miles, eventually intersecting with Gold Camp Road. Maps and information about the drive are available at the Starsmore Discovery Center at the base of N. Cheyenne Canon Road.

Note: The route has no guardrails, and drivers should expect hairpin turns and loose gravel; only experienced mountain drivers should attempt the drive. **Time:** Allow 1 hour minimum. **Hours:** Daily 5 a.m.-dusk, May-Sept. (weather permitting). Phone ahead to confirm road status. **Cost:** Free. **Phone:** (719) 385-6086.

PALMER PARK, about 3 mi. n.e., has entrances off Maizeland and Paseo rds. Comprising 737 acres on Austin Bluffs, the park affords a view of the mountains and offers scenic drives and hiking trails. **Time:** Allow 30 minutes minimum. **Hours:** Daily 5 a.m.-11 p.m., May-Oct.; 5 a.m.-9 p.m., rest of year. **Cost:** Free. **Phone:** (719) 385-5940. 🏕

PETERSON AIR AND SPACE MUSEUM, 7 mi. e. on US 24 (use the west gate into Peterson AFB) to 150 E. Ent Ave., has exhibits about North American air defense, Colorado Springs' aviation heritage and the missions of the Air Force Space Command and

the North American Aerospace Defense Command (NORAD). Displays include 21 historic aircraft and missiles. Museum tours begin in the Colorado Springs Municipal Airport historic district terminal at Peterson Air Force Base.

Note: Visitor passes are required for those without a military or Department of Defense ID. Visitors must provide full names of visitors ages 18+, driver's license number and dates of birth. This information is required at least 24 hours prior to arrival; for Saturday visits, information is required 48 hours prior to visit. Those driving on the base must have a valid driver's license, current vehicle registration and proof of insurance to enter. Base security levels may fluctuate; phone ahead for updates. Photo ID is required for all adults. **Hours:** Tues.-Sat. 9-4. **Cost:** Free. **Phone:** (719) 556-4915.

PIKES PEAK—see Pikes Peak and Pike National Forest p. 245.

PRORODEO HALL OF FAME AND MUSEUM OF THE AMERICAN COWBOY, w. of I-25 exit 148 at 101 ProRodeo Dr., depicts the history of rodeo and honors the sport's champions through multimedia presentations, art, audiovisual programs and artifacts. Setting the tone, a statue of legendary world champion bronc rider Casey Tibbs resides at the entrance to the hall.

The attraction, appropriately enough, is adjacent to the national headquarters of the Professional Rodeo Cowboys Association. Exhibits in Heritage Hall trace the evolution of the modern rodeo. The Hall of Champions honors rodeo greats, both human and equine, and displays statues, trophies and tack belonging to the sport's heroes. A garden, bronzes, an arena and a corral can be found outdoors.

Time: Allow 1 hour, 30 minutes minimum. **Hours:** Daily 9-5, May-Aug.; Wed.-Sun. 9-5, rest of year. Closed major holidays. **Cost:** $8; $7 (ages 55+); $6 (military with ID); $5 (ages 6-12). **Phone:** (719) 528-4732.

ROCK LEDGE RANCH HISTORIC SITE, at the e. entrance to Garden of the Gods Park off 30th St., is a living-history museum and working farm where interpreters in period clothing depict Native American and pioneer life in the Pikes Peak region. Displays include an 1860s homestead, an 1880s farm, a 1907 estate house, a 19th-century blacksmith shop and a Native American camp and general store.

Time: Allow 1 hour minimum. **Hours:** Wed.-Sat. 10-5, early June to mid-Aug. **Cost:** $8; $5 (ages 55+); $4 (ages 6-17). **Phone:** (719) 578-6777.

SEVEN FALLS, 7 mi. w. on Cheyenne Blvd., cascade down a steep canyon in seven distinct falls. The most spectacular view of the falls is seen from the Eagle's Nest platform, reached by an in-mountain elevator or by walking up a 224-step stairway alongside the falls. Self-guiding audio tours highlight features found along two nature trails, one leading to Midnight Falls. Native wildlife abounds

▼ *See AAA listing p. 90* ▼

Visit Cadet Chapel at the U.S. Air Force Academy

with deer and hummingbirds. On summer nights and during the Christmas season, the falls are illuminated in the evening.

Time: Allow 1 hour, 30 minutes minimum. **Hours:** Daily 9-9, May-Sept.; 9-7, Mar.-Apr. and Oct.-Nov.; 9-5, rest of year. Hours subject to change; phone ahead to confirm schedule. Closed Jan. 1, Thanksgiving and Christmas Eve. **Cost:** $14; $8 (ages 2-12). **Phone:** (719) 476-6708. *(See ad p. 91.)*

U.S. AIR FORCE ACADEMY, 14 mi. n. on I-25 to exit 156, prepares cadets for careers in the Air Force. Guests may visit the Cadet Chapel, Field House, Arnold Hall, the Honor Court and the Visitor Center. The newest of the nation's service academies, the U.S. Air Force Academy graduated its first class in 1959.

The strikingly modern aluminum, glass and steel Cadet Chapel and its 17 spires are a campus landmark. The chapel provides worship facilities for cadets of all faiths. The AOG building (Doolittle Hall) is where new cadets begin their careers. The Field House is the site of cadet athletic events and Arnold Hall is a concert and entertainment venue. The academy's Honor Court, between the chapel and Arnold Hall, includes bronze statues and Air Force memorials. Polaris Hall—a 46,000-square-foot glass tower built to align with the North Star—houses the Center for Character and Leadership Development. Throughout the academy grounds are static displays of aircraft.

Note: Fluctuating security levels may affect public access; phone ahead to verify status. **Time:** Allow 2 hours minimum. **Hours:** Academy daily 9-5. Visitor center daily 9-5. Chapel Mon.-Sat. 9-5, Sun. 1-5. Chapel hours may vary due to services and events.

Cost: Free. **Phone:** (719) 333-2636 for chapel information.

The Barry Goldwater Air Force Academy Visitor Center is off I-25 exit 156, 4 mi. from the north entrance. The center presents a short film about cadet life at the academy. There also are displays and an information desk. A .3-mile nature walk connects the visitor center with the chapel. **Hours:** Daily 9-5; closed Jan. 1, Thanksgiving, Christmas Eve, Christmas and Dec. 31. **Cost:** Free. **Phone:** (719) 333-2025.

U.S. OLYMPIC COMPLEX, 1750 E. Boulder St., is a 37-acre sports training center for the U.S. Olympic Committee. Nearly 130 athletes representing nine sports live and train at the complex on a full-time basis; thousands train here part-time. Guided tours feature an Olympic highlights film and a walking tour that includes the multisport gymnasium, the Olympic-size swimming pool and the indoor shooting center. **Time:** Allow 1 hour, 15 minutes minimum. **Hours:** Tours are offered every half-hour, Mon.-Sat. 9-4:30, June-July; hourly 9-4, rest of year. **Cost:** Free. **Phone:** (719) 866-4618 or (888) 659-8687.

WESTERN MUSEUM OF MINING AND INDUSTRY, e. of I-25 exit 156A (Northgate Blvd.) at 225 Northgate Blvd., displays restored, operating steam engines and mining equipment used in early Western mines on its 27 acres. The museum offers a 20-minute film, a rock and mineral display, gold panning demonstrations, exhibits about mining life and a re-created mine drift as well as hands-on exhibits. Guests may pan for gold, visit with the museum's mascot burros and see machinery, a stamp mill and a reclamation project. Special exhibits and events are featured during the year. A research library is available with advance notice.

Hours: Mon.-Sat. 9-4. Guided tours are offered at 10 and 1. Closed major holidays. **Cost:** $8; $7 (military with ID); $6 (ages 60+ and students with ID); $4 (ages 3-12). **Phone:** (719) 488-0880 or (800) 752-6558. 🅷

WORLD FIGURE SKATING MUSEUM AND HALL OF FAME, .5 mi. n.e. of The Broadmoor resort at 20 First St., describes figure skating history and honors the members of both the World and U.S. figure skating Halls of Fame. Exhibits feature American champions Brian Boitano, Scott Hamilton, Kristi Yamaguchi, Michelle Kwan and international skating legend Sonja Henie. Displays include videos, costumes, Olympic medals and other memorabilia.

Time: Allow 1 hour minimum. **Hours:** Tues.-Fri. 10-4. Closed major holidays. **Cost:** $5; $3 (ages 6-12 and 60+). **Phone:** (719) 635-5200.

Sightseeing

Sightseeing tours of the Pikes Peak region with stops at attractions in and around Colorado Springs are offered by Gray Line, (303) 394-6920 or (800) 472-9546. Some excursions include a trek to the summit of Pikes Peak.

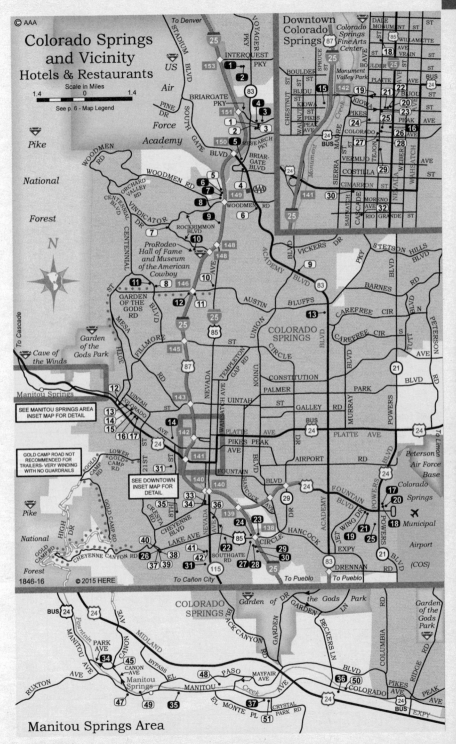

Colorado Springs and Vicinity
Hotels & Restaurants

Scale in Miles
1.4   0   1.4
See p. 6 - Map Legend

Downtown Colorado Springs

Manitou Springs Area

✈ Airport Hotels

Map Page	COLORADO SPRINGS AIRPORT (Maximum driving distance from airport: 4.4 mi)	Diamond Rated	Rate Range	Page
25 p. 93	Hampton Inn Airport, 3.7 mi	◆◆	Rates not provided	100
21 p. 93	Holiday Inn Airport, 4.2 mi	◆◆◆	$99-$189	100
19 p. 93	Holiday Inn Express-Airport, 4.4 mi	◆◆	Rates not provided	100
20 p. 93	**Radisson Hotel Colorado Springs Airport, 4.2 mi**	◆◆◆	$119-$185 SAVE	101
18 p. 93	SpringHill Suites by Marriott Colorado Springs South, 4.3 mi	◆◆◆	$87-$178	101
17 p. 93	TownePlace Suites by Marriott Colorado Springs South, 4.4 mi	◆◆◆	$85-$209	102

Colorado Springs and Vicinity

This index helps you "spot" where approved hotels and restaurants are located on the corresponding detailed maps. Hotel daily rate range is for comparison only. Restaurant price range is a combination of lunch and/or dinner. Turn to the listing page for more detailed rate and price information and consult display ads for special promotions.

COLORADO SPRINGS

Map Page	Hotels	Diamond Rated	Rate Range	Page
1 p. 93	Residence Inn by Marriott Air Force Academy	◆◆◆	$96-$220	101
2 p. 93	Hampton Inn & Suites Colorado Springs Air Force Academy/I-25 North @ Interquest	◆◆◆	Rates not provided	100
3 p. 93	Homewood Suites by Hilton Colorado Springs-North	◆◆◆	Rates not provided	100
4 p. 93	Hilton Garden Inn	◆◆◆	Rates not provided	100
5 p. 93	Plaza Inn	◆◆	Rates not provided	101
6 p. 93	**BEST WESTERN PLUS Peak Vista Inn & Suites** (See ad p. 97.)	◆◆◆	$89-$299 SAVE	96
7 p. 93	Hampton Inn Colorado Springs Central Air Force Academy	◆◆◆	Rates not provided	100
8 p. 93	Colorado Springs Fairfield Inn by Marriott Air Force Academy	◆◆	$73-$159	98
9 p. 93	**Comfort Inn North**	◆◆	$64-$139 SAVE	98
10 p. 93	Colorado Springs Marriott	◆◆◆	$96-$200	98
11 p. 93	TownePlace Suites by Marriott Colorado Springs/Garden of the Gods	◆◆	$94-$207	102
12 p. 93	**Hyatt Place Colorado Springs/Garden of the Gods**	◆◆◆	$69-$179 SAVE	100
13 p. 93	Sonesta ES Suites	◆◆	$199-$259	101
14 p. 93	**Holden House 1902 Bed & Breakfast Inn**	◆◆◆	$175 SAVE	100
15 p. 93	Holiday Inn Express & Suites- Colorado Springs Central	◆◆◆	Rates not provided	100
16 p. 93	**The Mining Exchange, a Wyndham Grand Hotel & Spa**	◆◆◆◆	$119-$249 SAVE	101
17 p. 93	TownePlace Suites by Marriott Colorado Springs South	◆◆◆	$85-$209	102
18 p. 93	SpringHill Suites by Marriott Colorado Springs South	◆◆◆	$87-$178	101
19 p. 93	Holiday Inn Express-Airport	◆◆	Rates not provided	100
20 p. 93	**Radisson Hotel Colorado Springs Airport** (See ad p. 101.)	◆◆◆	$119-$185 SAVE	101
21 p. 93	Holiday Inn Airport	◆◆◆	$99-$189	100
22 p. 93	Courtyard by Marriott	◆◆◆	$92-$183	98

COLORADO SPRINGS (cont'd)

Map Page	Hotels (cont'd)	Diamond Rated	Rate Range	Page
23 p. 93	Hotel Eleganté Conference & Event Center	◆◆◆	$99-$219 [SAVE]	100
24 p. 93	BEST WESTERN Executive Inn & Suites (See ad p. 97.)	◆◆	$79-$159 [SAVE]	96
25 p. 93	Hampton Inn Airport	◆◆	Rates not provided	100
26 p. 93	The Broadmoor	◆◆◆◆◆	$385-$7800 [SAVE]	98
27 p. 93	DoubleTree by Hilton Colorado Springs	◆◆◆	Rates not provided [SAVE]	98
28 p. 93	Fairfield Inn & Suites by Marriott Colorado Springs/South	◆◆	$86-$164	98
29 p. 93	Residence Inn by Marriott-Colorado Springs South	◆◆◆	$123-$246	101
30 p. 93	Hampton Inn & Suites by Hilton I-25 South-Colorado Springs	◆◆◆	Rates not provided	100
31 p. 93	Cheyenne Mountain Resort (See ad p. 99.)	◆◆◆◆	Rates not provided [SAVE]	98

Map Page	Restaurants	Diamond Rated	Cuisine	Price Range	Page
1 p. 93	P.F. Chang's China Bistro	◆◆◆	Chinese	$9-$20	104
2 p. 93	Biaggi's Ristorante Italiano	◆◆◆	Italian	$9-$25	102
3 p. 93	Bird Dog BBQ	◆	Barbecue	$6-$14	102
4 p. 93	La Tartine French Bistro Cafe	◆	Breads/Pastries	$8-$12	103
5 p. 93	The Margarita at Pine Creek	◆◆◆	American	$13-$42	103
6 p. 93	Lemongrass Bistro	◆◆	Vietnamese	$8-$14	103
7 p. 93	Salsa Brava Fresh Mexican Grill	◆◆	Mexican	$9-$18	104
8 p. 93	Marigold Cafe & Bakery	◆◆◆	French	$8-$30	103
9 p. 93	Mirch Masala-Kabab & Curry Dining	◆◆	Indian	$9-$21	103
10 p. 93	Señor Manuel Mexican Cuisine	◆	Mexican	$6-$18	104
11 p. 93	Caspian Cafe Mediterranean Restaurant	◆◆	Mediterranean	$9-$27	102
12 p. 93	The Mason Jar	◆◆	American	$8-$19	103
13 p. 93	Paravicini's Italian Bistro	◆◆	Italian	$8-$25	104
14 p. 93	Jake and Telly's Greek Taverna	◆◆	Greek	$9-$25	103
15 p. 93	Pizzeria Rustica	◆◆	Pizza	$11-$14	104
16 p. 93	Uchenna Ethiopian Restaurant	◆◆	Ethiopian	$10-$15	105
17 p. 93	La Baguette French Bakery and Espresso Cafe	◆	French Breads/Pastries	$6-$9	103
18 p. 93	Panino's Restaurant Downtown	◆◆	Italian	$8-$18	104
19 p. 93	Everest Nepal Restaurant	◆◆	Nepali	$12-$19	102
20 p. 93	Fratelli Ristorante Italiano	◆◆◆	Italian	$17-$20	102
21 p. 93	The Rabbit Hole	◆◆	American	$12-$29	104
22 p. 93	Mediterranean Cafe	◆◆	Mediterranean	$6-$14	103
23 p. 93	The Famous "A Steak House"	◆◆◆	Steak	$13-$52	102
24 p. 93	Phantom Canyon Brewing Co	◆◆	American	$10-$18	104
25 p. 93	The Ritz Grill	◆◆	American	$10-$23	104
26 p. 93	Jack Quinn Irish Alehouse & Pub	◆◆	Irish	$9-$20	103
27 p. 93	Sonterra Innovative Southwest Grill	◆◆◆	Southwestern	$10-$24	105
28 p. 93	MacKenzie's Chop House	◆◆	Steak	$10-$40	103

Map Page	Restaurants (cont'd)	Diamond Rated	Cuisine	Price Range	Page
㉙ p. 93	Nosh	▽▽▽	American	$9-$14	104
㉚ p. 93	The Warehouse	▽▽▽	American	$11-$45	105
㉛ p. 93	The Pepper Tree Restaurant	▽▽▽	Continental	$20-$67	104
㉜ p. 93	Shuga's Restaurant & Bar	▽▽	American	$8-$10	105
㉝ p. 93	The Blue Star	▽▽▽	American	$13-$35	102
㉞ p. 93	**Edelweiss Restaurant**	▽▽	German	$9-$28	102
㉟ p. 93	Little Nepal Indian Restaurant & Bar	▽▽	Indian	$11-$19	103
㊱ p. 93	Larkburger	▽	Burgers	$5-$10	103
㊲ p. 93	**The Penrose Room**	▽▽▽▽▽	Continental	$72-$102	104
㊳ p. 93	The Tavern	▽▽▽	American	$10-$55	105
㊴ p. 93	**Summit**	▽▽▽▽	American	$16-$28	105
㊵ p. 93	Ristorante Del Lago	▽▽▽	Northern Italian	$16-$36	104
㊶ p. 93	Carlos Miguel's Mexican Bar & Grill	▽▽	Mexican	$8-$14	102
㊷ p. 93	Walter's Bistro	▽▽▽	American	$12-$42	105

MANITOU SPRINGS

Map Page	Hotels	Diamond Rated	Rate Range	Page
34 p. 93	**The Cliff House at Pikes Peak**	▽▽▽▽	$109-$440 [SAVE]	232
35 p. 93	**Americas Best Value Inn Villa Motel**	▽▽	$79-$139 [SAVE]	232
36 p. 93	Comfort Inn	▽▽	$79-$164	232
37 p. 93	Magnuson Hotel Manitou Springs	▽▽	Rates not provided	232

Map Page	Restaurants	Diamond Rated	Cuisine	Price Range	Page
45 p. 93	**The Cliff House Dining Room**	▽▽▽▽	New Continental	$8-$35	233
47 p. 93	The Mona Lisa Fondue Restaurant	▽▽	Fondue	$25-$30	233
48 p. 93	**Briarhurst Manor**	▽▽▽	Regional American	$22-$43	233
49 p. 93	Stagecoach Inn	▽▽	Regional American	$9-$25	233
50 p. 93	Adam's Mountain Cafe	▽▽	American	$9-$18	232
51 p. 93	Savelli's	▽▽	Italian	$7-$14	233

COLORADO SPRINGS (F-9)

- **Restaurants p. 102**
- **Hotels & Restaurants map & index p. 93**

BEST WESTERN EXECUTIVE INN & SUITES
(719)576-2371 24

Hotel
$79-$159

AAA Benefit: Save 10% or more every day and earn 10% bonus points!

Address: 1440 Harrison Rd 80905 **Location:** I-25 exit 138, just w; on northwest corner of interchange; entrance through restaurant. **Facility:** 84 units. 2 stories (no elevator), interior corridors. **Pool(s):** heated indoor. **Activities:** hot tub, exercise room. **Guest Services:** valet and coin laundry. *(See ad p. 97.)*

BEST WESTERN PLUS PEAK VISTA INN & SUITES
(719)598-7500 6

Hotel
$89-$299

AAA Benefit: Save 10% or more every day and earn 10% bonus points!

Address: 7265 Commerce Center Dr 80919 **Location:** I-25 exit 149 (Woodmen Rd), just w, then n. **Facility:** 99 units. 4 stories, interior corridors. **Pool(s):** heated indoor. **Activities:** hot tub, exercise room. **Guest Services:** valet and coin laundry. **Featured Amenity:** full hot breakfast. *(See ad p. 97.)*

Ask about AAA/CAA Associate membership
to share the benefits you value

(See map & index p. 93.)

THE BROADMOOR
(719)634-7711 **26**

▽▽▽▽▽
Classic Historic
Resort Hotel
$385-$7800

Address: 1 Lake Ave 80906 **Location:** I-25 exit 138, 3 mi w on Circle Dr (which becomes Lake Ave). **Facility:** This grand hotel has managed to evolve over the years to incorporate contemporary tastes while maintaining its historic character. 774 units, some two bedrooms, three bedrooms and cottages. 1-8 stories, interior/exterior corridors. **Parking:** valet only. **Terms:** check-in 4 pm, 7 day cancellation notice-fee imposed, resort fee. **Amenities:** video games, safes. **Dining:** 10 restaurants, also, The Penrose Room, Ristorante Del Lago, Summit, The Tavern, see separate listings, entertainment. **Pool(s):** heated outdoor, heated indoor. **Activities:** sauna, hot tub, steamroom, regulation golf, tennis, recreation programs, bicycles, playground, trails, spa. **Guest Services:** valet laundry, boarding pass kiosk, area transportation. Affiliated with Preferred Hotels & Resorts.

[SAVE] [🍴] [▥] [▽] [♿] CALL [&M] [🏊] [🛁] [BIZ]
[HS] [📶] [✕] [🎥] [💻] / SOME UNITS [S🐾] [🍴] [📷]

CHEYENNE MOUNTAIN RESORT
719/538-4000 **31**

▽▽▽▽▽▽
Resort Hotel
Rates not provided

Address: 3225 Broadmoor Valley Rd 80906 **Location:** I-25 exit 138, 1.4 mi w to SR 115, 0.5 mi s, just w on Cheyenne Mountain Blvd, then just s. **Facility:** Associated with the Country Club of Colorado, this expansive resort features a lovely golf course surrounded by mountains, a lake with a sandy beach and a variety of meeting spaces. 316 units. 3 stories (no elevator), interior/exterior corridors. **Parking:** on-site and valet. **Terms:** check-in 4 pm. **Amenities:** video games, safes. **Dining:** 3 restaurants. **Pool(s):** heated outdoor, heated indoor. **Activities:** sauna, hot tub, steamroom, self-propelled boats, regulation golf, tennis, recreation programs, playground, spa. **Guest Services:** valet laundry, area transportation. (See ad p. 99.)

[SAVE] [ECO] [✈] [🍴] [♿] [▽] CALL [&M] [🏊] [🛁] [BIZ]
[📶] [✕] [🎥] [🍴] [💻] / SOME UNITS [S🐾] [📷]

COLORADO SPRINGS FAIRFIELD INN BY MARRIOTT AIR FORCE ACADEMY
(719)533-1903 **8**

▽▽▽ Hotel $73-$159 **Address:** 7085 Commerce Center Dr 80919 **Location:** I-25 exit 149 (Woodmen Rd), just w, then just n. **Facility:** 67 units. 4 stories, interior corridors. **Pool(s):** heated indoor. **Activities:** hot tub. **Guest Services:** valet laundry.

AAA Benefit:
Members save 5% or more!

[🍴+] CALL [&M] [🏊] [BIZ] [📶] [✕] [💻] / SOME UNITS [🍴] [📷]

COLORADO SPRINGS MARRIOTT
(719)260-1800 **10**

▽▽▽ Hotel $96-$200 **Address:** 5580 Tech Center Dr 80919 **Location:** I-25 exit 148 (Rockrimmon Blvd), 0.5 mi w, then just s. **Facility:** 309 units. 9 stories, interior corridors. **Terms:** check-in 4 pm. **Amenities:** safes. **Pool(s):** heated outdoor, heated indoor. **Activities:** sauna, hot tub, trails, exercise room. **Guest Services:** valet and coin laundry, boarding pass kiosk, area transportation.

AAA Benefit:
Members save 5% or more!

[🍴] [♿] [▽] [🏊] [BIZ] [📶] [✕] [🎥] [💻]
/ SOME UNITS [🍴] [📷]

COMFORT INN NORTH
(719)262-9000 **9**

▽▽▽
Hotel
$64-$139

Address: 6450 Corporate Dr 80919 **Location:** I-25 exit 149 (Woodmen Rd), just w, then 0.3 mi s. **Facility:** 70 units. 4 stories, interior corridors. **Pool(s):** heated indoor. **Activities:** hot tub, trails, exercise room. **Guest Services:** valet and coin laundry. **Featured Amenity:** full hot breakfast.

[SAVE] CALL [&M] [🏊] [BIZ] [📶] [✕]
[🍴] [📷] [💻] / SOME UNITS [S🐾]

COURTYARD BY MARRIOTT
(719)226-5006 **22**

▽▽▽ Hotel $92-$183 **Address:** 2570 Tenderfoot Hill St 80906 **Location:** I-25 exit 138, just w on Lake Ave, then s. **Facility:** 90 units. 3 stories, interior corridors. **Pool(s):** heated indoor. **Activities:** exercise room. **Guest Services:** valet and coin laundry.

AAA Benefit:
Members save 5% or more!

[🍴] CALL [&M] [🏊] [BIZ] [📶] [✕] [🍴] [📷] [💻]
/ SOME UNITS [HS]

DOUBLETREE BY HILTON COLORADO SPRINGS
719/576-8900 **27**

▽▽▽
Hotel
Rates not provided

DOUBLETREE
BY HILTON

AAA Benefit:
Members save 5% or more!

Address: 1775 E Cheyenne Mountain Blvd 80906 **Location:** I-25 exit 138, just w. **Facility:** 299 units. 4 stories, interior corridors. **Pool(s):** heated indoor. **Activities:** hot tub, game room, exercise room. **Guest Services:** valet and coin laundry.

[SAVE] [✈] [🍴] [▽] CALL [&M] [🏊]
[BIZ] [📶] [✕] [💻]
/ SOME UNITS [S🐾] [🍴] [📷]

FAIRFIELD INN & SUITES BY MARRIOTT COLORADO SPRINGS NORTH AIR FORCE ACADEMY
(719)488-4644

▽▽▽
Hotel
$74-$171

FAIRFIELD
INN & SUITES
Marriott

AAA Benefit:
Members save 5% or more!

Address: 15275 W Struthers Rd 80921 **Location:** I-25 exit 158, just e on Baptist Rd, then just s. **Facility:** 85 units. 3 stories, interior corridors. **Pool(s):** heated indoor. **Activities:** hot tub, exercise room. **Guest Services:** valet and coin laundry. **Featured Amenity:** breakfast buffet.

[SAVE] [🍴+] CALL [&M] [🏊] [BIZ] [HS]
[📶] [✕] [🍴] [💻]
/ SOME UNITS [S🐾] [📷]

FAIRFIELD INN & SUITES BY MARRIOTT COLORADO SPRINGS/SOUTH
(719)576-1717 **28**

▽▽▽ Hotel $86-$164 **Address:** 2725 Geyser Dr 80906 **Location:** I-25 exit 138, just w to E Cheyenne Mountain Blvd, then just s. **Facility:** 84 units. 3 stories, interior corridors. **Pool(s):** heated indoor. **Activities:** picnic facilities, exercise room. **Guest Services:** valet and coin laundry.

AAA Benefit:
Members save 5% or more!

[🍴+] [🏊] [BIZ] [📶] [✕] [🎥] [🍴] [📷] [💻]
/ SOME UNITS [S🐾]

▼ See AAA listing p. 98 ▼

Forge YOUR ADVENTURE

Get an eagle's-eye view

Escape the ordinary and discover the unexpected at Cheyenne Mountain Resort. Experience our four-season Colorado escape featuring a Pete Dye designed golf course, Alluvia Spa , indoor and outdoor tennis, aquatics center, sandy beach, boating activities and gateway access to the best of outdoor Colorado.

ENJOY EXCLUSIVE AAA MEMBER-ONLY SAVINGS!

Book with the promo code "AAA" to enjoy exclusive AAA member-only discounts on room rates.
800.588.0250 | www.cheyennemountain.com/AAA

Your stepping stone to an Authentic Colorado Experience.
SPA PAMPERING · TENNIS · GOLFING · SWIMMING
PADDLE BOARDING · BEACH VOLLEYBALL
CASUAL DINING · S'MORES BY THE FIRE

CHEYENNE MOUNTAIN RESORT
colorado springs

#CMRadventure

BENCHMARK®
RESORTS & HOTELS

3225 Broadmoor Valley Road
Colorado Springs, CO 80906
p. 800.588.0250
cheyennemountain.com

AAA
Four Diamond
Award

(See map & index p. 93.)

HAMPTON INN AIRPORT   719/591-1100   **25**

▼▼ ▼▼ **Hotel.** Rates not provided. **Address:** 2077 Aerotech Dr 80916 **Location:** I-25 exit 139, 4.2 mi e on US 24 Bypass, 0.4 mi s on Powers Blvd, just w on Astrozon Blvd, then just n. **Facility:** 80 units. 3 stories, interior corridors. **Pool(s):** heated indoor. **Activities:** hot tub, exercise room. **Guest Services:** valet and coin laundry, area transportation.

AAA Benefit: Members save up to 10%!

[icons]

HAMPTON INN & SUITES BY HILTON I-25 SOUTH-COLORADO SPRINGS   719/884-0330   **30**

▼▼▼▼ **Hotel.** Rates not provided. **Address:** 2910 Geyser Dr 80906 **Location:** I-25 exit 138, just w, just s on Cheyenne Mountain Blvd, then just e. **Facility:** 101 units. 4 stories, interior corridors. **Pool(s):** heated indoor. **Activities:** hot tub, exercise room. **Guest Services:** valet and coin laundry.

AAA Benefit: Members save up to 10%!

[icons]

HAMPTON INN & SUITES COLORADO SPRINGS AIR FORCE ACADEMY/I-25 NORTH @ INTERQUEST   719/598-6911   **2**

▼▼▼▼ **Hotel.** Rates not provided. **Address:** 1307 Republic Dr 80921 **Location:** I-25 exit 153, 0.5 mi n, then just s. **Facility:** 75 units. 3 stories, interior corridors. **Pool(s):** heated indoor. **Activities:** hot tub, exercise room. **Guest Services:** valet and coin laundry.

AAA Benefit: Members save up to 10%!

[icons]

HAMPTON INN COLORADO SPRINGS CENTRAL AIR FORCE ACADEMY   719/593-9700   **7**

▼▼▼▼ **Hotel.** Rates not provided. **Address:** 7245 Commerce Center Dr 80919 **Location:** I-25 exit 149 (Woodmen Rd), just w, then n. **Facility:** 125 units. 4 stories, interior corridors. **Pool(s):** heated indoor. **Activities:** exercise room. **Guest Services:** valet and coin laundry.

AAA Benefit: Members save up to 10%!

[icons] / SOME UNITS

HILTON GARDEN INN   719/598-6866   **4**

▼▼▼▼ **Hotel.** Rates not provided. **Address:** 1810 Briargate Pkwy 80920 **Location:** I-25 exit 151 (Briargate Pkwy), 0.7 mi e. **Facility:** 154 units. 3 stories, interior corridors. **Terms:** check-in 4 pm. **Pool(s):** heated indoor. **Activities:** hot tub, exercise room. **Guest Services:** valet and coin laundry.

AAA Benefit: Members save up to 10%!

[icons]

HOLDEN HOUSE 1902 BED & BREAKFAST INN
    719/471-3980   **14**

▼▼▼▼
Historic Bed & Breakfast
$175

Address: 1102 W Pikes Peak Ave 80904 **Location:** I-25 exit 141, 0.3 mi w on US 24, just n on 8th St, just w on Colorado Ave, then just n on 11th St. **Facility:** Victorian furnishings, in-room fireplaces and lace curtains impart a sense of traditional charm to the restored homes and carriage house. 6 units. 2 stories (no elevator), interior/exterior corridors. **Terms:** check-in 4 pm, 2-3 night minimum stay - seasonal and/or weekends, 30 day cancellation notice-fee imposed. **Featured Amenity:** full hot breakfast.

[icons] / SOME UNITS

HOLIDAY INN AIRPORT   (719)380-8516   **21**

▼▼ ▼▼ **Hotel** $99-$189 **Address:** 1855 Aeroplaza Dr 80916 **Location:** I-25 exit 139, 4.5 mi e on US 24 Bypass, then just w. **Facility:** 115 units. 4 stories, interior corridors. **Terms:** cancellation fee imposed. **Amenities:** safes. **Pool(s):** heated indoor. **Activities:** hot tub, exercise room. **Guest Services:** valet and coin laundry.

[icons]

HOLIDAY INN EXPRESS-AIRPORT   719/591-6000   **19**

▼▼ ▼▼ **Hotel.** Rates not provided. **Address:** 1815 Aeroplaza Dr 80916 **Location:** I-25 exit 139, 4.5 mi e on US 24 Bypass, then just w. **Facility:** 94 units. 4 stories, interior corridors. **Pool(s):** heated indoor. **Activities:** hot tub, picnic facilities, exercise room. **Guest Services:** valet and coin laundry, area transportation.

[icons]

HOLIDAY INN EXPRESS & SUITES- COLORADO SPRINGS CENTRAL   719/424-4300   **15**

▼▼ ▼▼ **Hotel.** Rates not provided. **Address:** 105 N Spruce St 80905 **Location:** I-25 exit 142, just w, then just s. **Facility:** 80 units. 4 stories, interior corridors. **Pool(s):** heated indoor. **Activities:** hot tub, exercise room. **Guest Services:** valet and coin laundry, area transportation.

[icons]

HOMEWOOD SUITES BY HILTON COLORADO SPRINGS-NORTH   719/265-6600   **3**

▼▼ ▼▼ **Extended Stay Hotel.** Rates not provided. **Address:** 9130 Explorer Dr 80920 **Location:** I-25 exit 151 (Briargate Pkwy), 0.8 mi e. Across from Focus on the Family. **Facility:** 127 efficiencies. 3 stories, interior corridors. **Pool(s):** heated outdoor. **Activities:** picnic facilities, exercise room. **Guest Services:** valet and coin laundry.

AAA Benefit: Members save up to 10%!

[icons] / SOME UNITS

HOTEL ELEGANTÉ CONFERENCE & EVENT CENTER
    (719)576-5900   **23**

▼▼▼▼
Hotel
$99-$219

Address: 2886 S Circle Dr 80906 **Location:** I-25 exit 138, just e. **Facility:** 500 units. 2-3 stories (no elevator), interior corridors. **Terms:** cancellation fee imposed. **Amenities:** video games. **Dining:** 2 restaurants. **Pool(s):** heated outdoor, heated indoor. **Activities:** hot tub, exercise room, massage. **Guest Services:** valet and coin laundry, boarding pass kiosk.

[icons] / SOME UNITS

HYATT PLACE COLORADO SPRINGS/GARDEN OF THE GODS   (719)265-9385   **12**

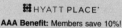

▼▼▼▼
Hotel
$69-$179

HYATT PLACE
AAA Benefit: Members save 10%!

Address: 503 W Garden of the Gods Rd 80907 **Location:** I-25 exit 146 (Garden of the Gods Rd), just w. **Facility:** 124 units. 4 stories, interior corridors. **Terms:** cancellation fee imposed. **Pool(s):** heated outdoor. **Activities:** exercise room. **Guest Services:** valet laundry. **Featured Amenity:** breakfast buffet.

[icons] / SOME UNITS [HS]

(See map & index p. 93.)

THE MINING EXCHANGE, A WYNDHAM GRAND HOTEL & SPA   (719)323-2000 [16]

Historic Hotel
$119-$249

Address: 8 S Nevada Ave 80903 **Location:** Between Colorado and Pikes Peak aves; downtown. **Facility:** Although housed in a 1902 building, this hotel balances unique historic features with modern room amenities, such as 42-inch HDTVs, iHomes and a pillowtop mattress with a plush bedding package. 117 units. 5 stories, interior corridors. **Parking:** valet only. **Amenities:** safes. **Activities:** sauna, steamroom, exercise room, spa. **Guest Services:** valet laundry.

[SAVE] [🍴] [👤] [Y] CALL [ᘓM] [BIZ]
[HS] [📶] [✕] [🖥]
/ SOME UNITS [🛁] [🛗] [🖨]

PLAZA INN   719/598-2500 [5]

Hotel. Rates not provided. **Address:** 8155 N Academy Blvd 80920 **Location:** I-25 exit 150, just s, then e. **Facility:** 117 units. 4 stories, interior corridors. **Pool(s):** heated outdoor, heated indoor. **Activities:** hot tub, exercise room. **Guest Services:** coin laundry.

[🍴] [🏊] [BIZ] [HS] [📶] [✕] [🛗] [🖨] [🖥]
/ SOME UNITS [🛁]

RADISSON HOTEL COLORADO SPRINGS AIRPORT   (719)597-7000 [20]

Hotel
$119-$185

Address: 1645 N Newport Rd 80916 **Location:** I-25 exit 139, 4.5 mi e on US 24 Bypass. **Facility:** 200 units. 2 stories, interior corridors. **Terms:** check-in 4 pm, 7 day cancellation notice. **Amenities:** Some: safes. **Pool(s):** heated indoor. **Activities:** hot tub, game room, exercise room. **Guest Services:** valet and coin laundry. **Featured Amenity:** breakfast buffet. (See ad this page.)

[SAVE] [✈] [🍴] [👤] [Y]
CALL [ᘓM] [🏊] [BIZ] [📶] [✕]
[🖥] [🛗] [🖨] [🖥] / SOME UNITS [🛁]

RESIDENCE INN BY MARRIOTT AIR FORCE ACADEMY   (719)388-9300 [1]

Extended Stay Hotel
$96-$220 **Address:** 9805 Federal Dr 80921 **Location:** I-25 exit 153, just e, then s. **Facility:** 113 units, some two bedrooms, efficiencies and kitchens. 4 stories, interior corridors. **Pool(s):** heated indoor. **Activities:** miniature golf, picnic facilities, exercise room. **Guest Services:** valet and coin laundry.

AAA Benefit: Members save 5% or more!

[🏊] [BIZ] [HS] [📶] [✕] [🎥] [🛗] [🖨] [🖥]
/ SOME UNITS [🛁]

RESIDENCE INN BY MARRIOTT-COLORADO SPRINGS SOUTH   (719)576-0101 [29]

Extended Stay Hotel
$123-$246 **Address:** 2765 Geyser Dr 80906 **Location:** I-25 exit 138, just w to E Cheyenne Mountain Blvd, then just s. **Facility:** 72 units, some two bedrooms, efficiencies and kitchens. 3 stories, interior corridors. **Pool(s):** heated indoor. **Activities:** exercise room. **Guest Services:** valet and coin laundry.

AAA Benefit: Members save 5% or more!

[🍴] [🏊] [BIZ] [HS] [📶] [✕] [🎥] [🛗] [🖨] [🖥]
/ SOME UNITS [🛁]

SONESTA ES SUITES   (719)574-0370 [13]

Extended Stay Hotel $199-$259 **Address:** 3880 N Academy Blvd 80917 **Location:** I-25 exit 146 (Garden of the Gods Rd), 4.5 mi e, then 0.3 mi s. **Facility:** 96 kitchen units. 2 stories (no elevator), exterior corridors. **Terms:** cancellation fee imposed. **Pool(s):** heated outdoor. **Activities:** playground, picnic facilities, exercise room. **Guest Services:** valet and coin laundry.

[🏊] [BIZ] [📶] [✕] [🛗] [🖨] [🖥] / SOME UNITS [🛁] [HS]

SPRINGHILL SUITES BY MARRIOTT COLORADO SPRINGS SOUTH   (719)637-0800 [18]

Hotel $87-$178 **Address:** 1570 N Newport Rd 80916 **Location:** I-25 exit 139, 5 mi e on US 24 Bypass, then just n. **Facility:** 101 units. 4 stories, interior corridors. **Pool(s):** heated indoor. **Activities:** exercise room. **Guest Services:** valet and coin laundry.

AAA Benefit: Members save 5% or more!

[🏊] [BIZ] [HS] [📶] [✕] [🎥] [🛗] [🖨] [🖥]

▼ See AAA listing this page ▼

(See map & index p. 93.)

TOWNEPLACE SUITES BY MARRIOTT COLORADO SPRINGS/ GARDEN OF THE GODS   (719)594-4447 **11**

▼▼ **Extended Stay Hotel** $94-$207 **Address:** 4760 Centennial Blvd 80919 **Location:** I-25 exit 146 (Garden of the Gods Rd), 1 mi w, then just n. **Facility:** 94 kitchen units, some two bedrooms. 3 stories, interior corridors. **Pool(s):** heated outdoor. **Activities:** exercise room. **Guest Services:** valet and coin laundry.

AAA Benefit: Members save 5% or more!

[icons] / SOME UNITS

TOWNEPLACE SUITES BY MARRIOTT COLORADO SPRINGS SOUTH   (719)638-0800 **17**

▼▼ **Extended Stay Hotel** $85-$209 **Address:** 1530 N Newport Rd 80916 **Location:** I-25 exit 139, 5 mi e on US 24 Bypass, then just n. **Facility:** 97 units, some two bedrooms, efficiencies and kitchens. 4 stories, interior corridors. **Pool(s):** heated indoor. **Activities:** exercise room. **Guest Services:** valet and coin laundry.

AAA Benefit: Members save 5% or more!

[icons] / SOME UNITS

THE BROADMOOR'S CLOUD CAMP   719/634-7711

fyi Not evaluated. **Address:** 1 Lake Ave 80906 **Location:** I-25 exit 138, 3 mi w on Circle Dr (which becomes Lake Ave); registration at The Broadmoor. Facilities, services, and décor characterize an upscale property.

THE BROADMOOR'S RANCH AT EMERALD VALLEY   719/634-7711

fyi Not evaluated. **Address:** 1 Lake Ave 80906 **Location:** I-25 exit 138, 3 mi w on Circle Dr (which becomes Lake Ave); registration at The Broadmoor. Facilities, services, and décor characterize an upscale property.

WHERE TO EAT

BIAGGI'S RISTORANTE ITALIANO   719/262-9500 **2**

▼▼▼ Italian. Fine Dining. $9-$25 **AAA Inspector Notes:** Cool, upscale decor surrounds diners who savor freshly prepared creations. Delicious combinations of quality and unusual ingredients make for an adventurous dining experience. **Features:** full bar. **Address:** 1805 Briargate Pkwy 80920 **Location:** I-25 exit 151 (Briargate Pkwy), 0.7 mi e. [L] [D]

BIRD DOG BBQ   719/599-4655 **3**

▼ Barbecue. Quick Serve. $6-$14 **AAA Inspector Notes:** I never know what I'll find walking into a Colorado barbecue joint. Bird Dog came highly recommended and has won awards from local papers. I wasn't disappointed. I dug into the tender, Oklahoma-style brisket with gusto. House-made sauces added the right amount of sweetness and kick. The baked beans and coleslaw were also quite tasty. I polished off the meal with peach cobbler, which had a nice vanilla flavor. As a dog lover, I enjoyed looking at the dog photos given to the restaurant by patrons. **Features:** beer only. **Address:** 1645 Briargate Pkwy, Suite 243 80920 **Location:** I-25 exit 151 (Briargate Pkwy), 0.8 mi e. [L] [D]

THE BLUE STAR   719/632-1086 **33**

▼▼▼ American. Casual Dining. $13-$35 **AAA Inspector Notes:** Local, seasonal cuisine is highlighted on a weekly changing menu. Entrées, which may feature scallops, pork tenderloin, steak and antelope, are well-complemented by a great wine and port list. Vegetarian options also are available. A loyal local following comes for the bustling, sometimes noisy bar atmosphere. Parking is limited and reservations are required for the formal dining room. Walk-ins are welcome in the bar area. **Features:** full bar, happy hour. **Reservations:** suggested. **Address:** 1645 S Tejon St 80906 **Location:** I-25 exit 140, just s to Blue Star neon sign. [D]

CARLOS MIGUEL'S MEXICAN BAR & GRILL   719/527-0500 **41**

▼▼ Mexican. Casual Dining. $8-$14 **AAA Inspector Notes:** A local favorite, this casual eatery features a variety of favorites, including pork carnitas, burritos, steak tacos, fajitas, enchiladas and chimichangas. There are vegetarian options available. The cheerful Southwestern décor is enhanced by natural light from large picture windows. **Features:** full bar. **Address:** 110 E Cheyenne Mountain Blvd 80906 **Location:** I-25 exit 140 (Nevada Ave), 1.7 mi s, then just w; in Country Club Corners. [L] [D]

CASPIAN CAFE MEDITERRANEAN RESTAURANT   719/528-1155 **11**

▼▼ Mediterranean. Casual Dining. $9-$27 **AAA Inspector Notes:** The menu focuses on cuisine from throughout the Mediterranean, everywhere from Morocco to France to Turkey. The chef artistically combines sweet and savory flavors, balancing both to perfection. For example, the pomegranate salad dressing has a nice fruit flavor, but isn't overly sweet and is balanced with spices. The ground beef and lamb kebab comes with a tomato-honey sauce that only has a hint of sweetness. **Features:** full bar, happy hour. **Address:** 4375 Sinton Rd 80907 **Location:** I-25 exit 146 (Garden of the Gods Rd), just e, then just s. [L] [D]

EDELWEISS RESTAURANT   719/633-2220 **34**

▼▼▼ German Casual Dining $9-$28

AAA Inspector Notes: Located in a 100-year-old former schoolhouse, this restaurant has a charming Old World setting with a German hunting lodge theme. The menu offers Wiener schnitzel, sauerbraten, and bratwurst as well as German beer and wine. **Features:** full bar. **Address:** 34 E Ramona Ave 80906 **Location:** I-25 exit 140 southbound, just s on Nevada Ave, then just w. *Menu on AAA.com* [L] [D]

EVEREST NEPAL RESTAURANT   719/473-3890 **19**

▼▼ Nepali. Casual Dining. $12-$19 **AAA Inspector Notes:** Expect to find Indian and Nepalese favorites like samosas, naan, lamb biryani, chicken tikka masala, and tandoori chicken. I enjoyed the saag chicken; the juices from the chicken added flavor to the spinach. During the busy season, the menu also features dishes made with yak. The Tibetan-style décor features Buddha statues and depictions of Ganesha. **Features:** beer & wine, patio dining, happy hour. **Address:** 28 E Bijou St 80903 **Location:** I-25 exit 142 (Bijou St), 0.5 mi e, just n on Tejon St, then just e. **Parking:** street only. [L] [D]

THE FAMOUS "A STEAK HOUSE"   719/227-7333 **23**

▼▼▼ Steak. Casual Dining. $13-$52 **AAA Inspector Notes:** This steakhouse offers an understated elegance, masculine decor, USDA Prime beef, fresh seafood, classic cocktails and a nightly piano bar. Sandwiches and salads make up much of the lunch menu, and sides on the dinner menu are large. Comfortable booths embrace diners, but the large U-shaped bar is the focus of the restaurant. This place is popular with downtown businessmen and those ready to enjoy an after-work drink by the piano. **Features:** full bar. **Address:** 31 N Tejon St 80903 **Location:** I-25 exit 142 (Bijou St), just e to Tejon St, then s. **Parking:** street only. [L] [D] CALL [icons]

FRATELLI RISTORANTE ITALIANO   719/575-9571 **20**

▼▼▼ Italian Casual Dining $17-$20

AAA Inspector Notes: This family-owned restaurant presents Northern and Southern Italian meals prepared in the tradition of the Mediterranean countryside. The ambience is comfortable, with gallery-style artwork and soft music. Italian is spoken here, so don't be surprised to hear Chef Armando yell out, buon appetito! Fine domestic and imported ingredients enhance each recipe of veal, chicken, seafood and pasta. **Features:** full bar, early bird specials. **Reservations:** suggested. **Address:** 124 N Nevada Ave 80903 **Location:** I-25 exit 142 (Bijou St), 0.5 mi e on Kiowa St, then just n. **Parking:** street only. *Menu on AAA.com* [D]

(See map & index p. 93.)

JACK QUINN IRISH ALEHOUSE & PUB 719/385-0766 26
▼▼ Irish. Casual Dining. $9-$20 **AAA Inspector Notes:** This pub's décor appears genuine because it was made and installed by Irish artisans. The menu features a variety of boxties, flavorful stuffed Irish pancakes. Other traditional fare includes fish and chips, lamb stew, corned beef and cabbage, and bangers and mash. Hearty sandwiches, salads and steaks complete the menu. **Features:** full bar, patio dining, Sunday brunch, happy hour. **Address:** 21 S Tejon St 80903 **Location:** Between Colorado and Pikes Peak aves. **Parking:** street only. L D LATE

JAKE AND TELLY'S GREEK TAVERNA 719/633-0406 14
▼▼ Greek. Casual Dining. $9-$25 **AAA Inspector Notes:** This restaurant offers quality food in a beautiful Mediterranean atmosphere. Traditional Greek menu options include a gyro plate, moussaka, lamb kebabs and shrimp makaronada. The almond, citrus and olive oil cake has a light, savory flavor with a hint of orange and is accompanied by a creamy, sweet homemade vanilla ice cream. The outstanding wine list features more than 40 choices, including quality reds and whites from various regions in Greece as well as wines from around the world. **Features:** full bar, happy hour. **Address:** 2616 W Colorado Ave, Suite 24 80904 **Location:** I-25 exit 141, 2.1 mi w, just n on 26th St, then just w. L D

LA BAGUETTE FRENCH BAKERY AND ESPRESSO CAFE 719/577-4818 17
▼ French Breads/Pastries. Quick Serve. $6-$9 **AAA Inspector Notes:** Relax in this quaint café and order from the breakfast or lunch menu. Offering an assortment of coffee delights and pastries for you to enjoy inside the rustic old town shop, the eatery is best known for their French onion soup and almond croissants. **Features:** beer & wine, patio dining, Sunday brunch. **Address:** 2417 W Colorado Ave 80904 **Location:** I-25 exit 141, 1.4 mi w on US 24, just n on 21st St, then just w. **Parking:** street only. B L CALL ▲M

LARKBURGER 719/466-6111 36
▼ Burgers. Quick Serve. $5-$10 **AAA Inspector Notes:** This story began when chef Thomas Salamunovich put his gourmet Larkburger on the menu at Larkspur, his fine dining restaurant in Vail. The burger became so popular Salamunovich created a fast-food restaurant around it; now it's a small chain. The juicy, all-natural Angus beef and turkey burgers are heavenly. Fries seasoned with Parmesan and truffle oil are the perfect accompaniment. **Features:** beer only, patio dining. **Address:** 1904 Southgate Rd 80906 **Location:** Jct CR 115 (Nevada Ave), just se; in strip mall. L D CALL ▲M

LA TARTINE FRENCH BISTRO CAFE 719/598-5550 4
▼ Breads/Pastries. Quick Serve. $8-$12 **AAA Inspector Notes:** Once you sample the French onion soup with a fresh baguette, you'll know this place isn't a typical quick-serve restaurant. The bread is made daily and is used for the delicious sandwiches. Make sure you leave room for dessert, as the display case is filled with tantalizing pastries. **Features:** beer & wine, Sunday brunch. **Address:** 1420 Kelly Johnson Dr 80920 **Location:** I-25 exit 150, 0.5 mi se on Academy Blvd, then just w; in a strip mall. B L D

LEMONGRASS BISTRO 719/592-1391 6
▼ Vietnamese. Casual Dining. $8-$14 **AAA Inspector Notes:** The cheerful yellow walls and modern Asian art pieces help provide a welcoming dining environment. On the menu are various Vietnamese and Chinese dishes, including stir-fries, noodle salads ("bun"), pho, lo mein, chow mein and fried rice. Distinctive desserts incorporate sweet coconut milk, gelatin and tropical fruit. **Features:** full bar. **Address:** 6840 N Academy Blvd 80918 **Location:** I-25 exit 149 (Woodmen Rd), 0.5 mi e, then just s. L D

LITTLE NEPAL INDIAN RESTAURANT & BAR 719/477-6997 35
▼▼ Indian. Casual Dining. $11-$19 **AAA Inspector Notes:** Although this restaurant is off the main drag, it's worth the drive. The large portions of delicious, aromatic entrées and puffy naan bread satisfy even the heartiest appetite. Friendly staff members get to know their regulars and make newcomers feel at home. Patio seating is available in summer. **Features:** full bar, patio dining, happy hour. **Address:** 1747 S 8th St 80905 **Location:** I-25 exit 140, 0.4 mi s on Tejon St to Cheyenne Blvd, 0.8 mi sw, then just n. L D

MACKENZIE'S CHOP HOUSE 719/635-3536 28
▼▼ Steak. Casual Dining. $10-$40 **AAA Inspector Notes:** Exposed-brick walls, dark wood accents and historic photos add to the ambience. Start with a cup of the French onion soup, a shrimp cocktail or the peppered ahi tuna. Select from a variety of steaks, bison and lamb as well as a variety of seafood dishes. **Features:** full bar, happy hour. **Reservations:** suggested. **Address:** 128 S Tejon St 80903 **Location:** I-25 exit 142 (Bijou St), e to Tejon St, then 0.5 mi s; between Colorado and Vermijo sts. **Parking:** street only. L D

THE MARGARITA AT PINE CREEK 719/598-8667 5
▼▼▼ American. Fine Dining. $13-$42 **AAA Inspector Notes:** Before the cluster of hotels just south of it were built, the land where this restaurant now sits was the owner's family picnic spot. The unusual Southwestern-inspired white building was erected in 1974 for exclusive use as a restaurant. Despite its long history, the menu features contemporary cuisine such as beet gratin with gorgonzola dulce and caramelized leeks, sauteed seabass and a grilled honey brined pork chop. You may not see these items as the menu changes weekly. **Features:** full bar, patio dining, Sunday brunch. **Address:** 7350 Pine Creek Rd 80919 **Location:** I-25 exit 149 (Woodmen Rd), just w, then 0.5 mi n on Commerce Center Dr. L D

MARIGOLD CAFE & BAKERY 719/599-4776 8
▼▼▼ French Casual Dining $8-$30 **AAA Inspector Notes:** This popular eatery features an eclectic menu and varied wine list with an upscale ambiance. Fresh-baked goods, pizza, salads, pasta and rotisserie-cooked meats are just a few of the offerings. Take a sandwich to go before heading to the nearby Garden of the Gods or celebrate a special occasion in the more formal dining area. **Features:** full bar. **Reservations:** suggested, for dinner. **Address:** 4605 Centennial Blvd 80919 **Location:** I-25 exit 146 (Garden of the Gods Rd), 1.1 mi w, then just n. L D

THE MASON JAR 719/632-4820 12
▼▼ American Casual Dining $8-$19 **AAA Inspector Notes:** Dig into juicy, hand-breaded fried chicken, real mashed potatoes and other comfort food favorites as well as prime rib, steak, seafood and homemade desserts. Informal, lively and family-friendly, this restaurant offers fireside dining in winter. **Features:** full bar. **Address:** 2925 W Colorado Ave 80904 **Location:** I-25 exit 141, 2.5 mi nw on US 24, just n on 31st St, then just e. L D

MEDITERRANEAN CAFE 719/633-0115 22
▼▼ Mediterranean. Casual Dining. $6-$14 **AAA Inspector Notes:** Delicious food, large portions and reasonable prices make this small cafe a huge hit with the locals. The menu is dominated by traditional Middle Eastern and Greek dishes, including gyro sandwiches, chicken kebabs, falafel, spanakopita, moussaka and hummus. Service is quick and friendly. **Address:** 118 E Kiowa St 80903 **Location:** In historic town center. **Parking:** street only. L D

MIRCH MASALA-KABAB & CURRY DINING 719/599-0003 9
▼▼ Indian. Casual Dining. $9-$21 **AAA Inspector Notes:** The name means "chilies and spices," and guests find plenty of both on the extensive menu. The food is presented with understated elegance. The owner recommends rava masala dhosa, saag paneer, navratan korma, baluchi kebab, goan fish vindaloo and lamb rogan josh. Varied preparations of naan include garlic and cilantro, cheddar cheese, and fruit and nut. The daily buffet is a popular offering. Lending to the inviting atmosphere are interesting murals depicting life in India. **Features:** full bar. **Address:** 5047 N Academy Blvd 80918 **Location:** Between Union Blvd and Flintridge Dr; in Union Square Shopping Plaza. L D

Use travel time to share driving tips

and rules of the road with your teens

(See map & index p. 93.)

NOSH 719/634-6674 ㉙
▼▼▼▼ American. Casual Dining. $9-$14 **AAA Inspector Notes:** The creatively conceived menu allows patrons the option of ordering multiple tapas-sized items or larger, entrée-sized portions. This flexibility makes Nosh the perfect place to grab a specialty cocktail and a small bite during happy hour or to relax and enjoy a full meal. Menu items include calamari, burgers, steak, mac and cheese, and curry coconut mussels. Soups, salads and desserts also are featured. The sultry décor features a large mural of koi fish. **Features:** full bar, patio dining, happy hour. **Address:** 121 S Tejon St, Suite 100 80903 **Location:** I-25 exit 142 (Bijou St), e to Tejon St, 0.5 mi s, then just e on Colorado Ave; in Plaza of the Rockies. L D

PANINO'S RESTAURANT DOWNTOWN 719/635-7452 ⑱
▼▼ Italian. Casual Dining. $8-$18 **AAA Inspector Notes:** This popular eatery has been family owned and operated since 1974. The décor includes interesting historic photos. The menu has a wide variety of panino sandwiches, pizzas, pastas, subs, soup and salads, to name a few options. **Features:** beer & wine. **Address:** 604 N Tejon St 80903 **Location:** Just s of Colorado College, n of downtown; corner of Willamette Ave. **Parking:** street only. L D

PARAVICINI'S ITALIAN BISTRO 719/471-8200 ⑬
▼▼▼ Italian. Casual Dining. $8-$25 **AAA Inspector Notes:** In a vintage 1895 building, this cozy eatery boasts a neighborhood atmosphere and a menu of Italian favorites as well as creative specialties. Selections from the lengthy wine list complement the pasta, chicken, veal and seafood dishes. **Features:** full bar. **Address:** 2802 W Colorado Ave 80904 **Location:** I-25 exit 141, 2.5 mi w on US 24, just n on 31st St, then just e. L D

THE PENROSE ROOM 719/577-5773 ㊲
▼▼▼▼▼ **AAA Inspector Notes:** The panoramic rooftop view is one splendid element of this restaurant's elegant ambiance. The seasonally changing menu features local vegetables and meats, such as Colorado lamb, as well as more exotic items like Oestra caviar and foie gras.
Continental Fine Dining $72-$102
Knowledgeable staff assist with recommendations and present courses with a flourish. Select either a three or four course prix fixe meal with multiple offerings for each course. A seven-course chef's tasting menu with or without wine pairing is available. **Features:** full bar. **Reservations:** suggested. Semiformal attire. **Address:** 1 Lake Ave 80906 **Location:** I-25 exit 138, 3 mi w on Circle Dr (which becomes Lake Ave); in The Broadmoor. **Parking:** valet only. D

THE PEPPER TREE RESTAURANT 719/471-4888 ㉛
▼▼▼ Continental. Fine Dining. $20-$67 **AAA Inspector Notes:** This restaurant offers elegant dining overlooking the downtown skyline. House specialties are served with expert tableside preparation and servers are attentive and professional. Menu items include pepper steak, steak Diane, Colorado rack of lamb, chicken piccata, Chilean sea bass, English Dover sole and Maine lobster tail. **Features:** full bar. **Reservations:** suggested. **Address:** 888 W Moreno Ave 80905 **Location:** I-25 exit 141, 0.3 mi sw on US 24, 0.3 mi s on 8th St, then just w. D

P.F. CHANG'S CHINA BISTRO 719/593-8580 ①
▼▼▼ Chinese. Casual Dining. $9-$20 **AAA Inspector Notes:** Trendy, upscale decor provides a pleasant backdrop for New Age Chinese dining. Appetizers, soups and salads are a meal by themselves. Vegetarian plates and sides, noodles, chow meins, chicken and meat dishes are created from exotic, fresh ingredients. **Features:** full bar, happy hour. **Address:** 1725 Briargate Pkwy 80920 **Location:** I-25 exit 151 (Briargate Pkwy), 0.9 mi e.
L D CALL &M

PHANTOM CANYON BREWING CO 719/635-2800 ㉔
▼▼ American. Casual Dining. $10-$18 **AAA Inspector Notes:** In a restored 1901 building, this popular spot has a bustling atmosphere and massive windows offering impressive views of downtown. The menu features several home brews. The blonde lager and smoked gouda soup provide a rich, creamy dose of comfort during a cold day. The lemon Tabasco fried chicken has a slight kick balanced by the tangy broccoli served with it. Other entrées include a bison burger, fish and chips, and pork chops with bacon-cheddar waffles. **Features:** full bar, happy hour. **Address:** 2 E Pikes Peak Ave 80903 **Location:** I-25 exit 142 (Bijou St) to Cascade Ave, just s. **Parking:** street only. L D LATE

PIZZERIA RUSTICA 719/632-8121 ⑮
▼▼▼ Pizza. Casual Dining. $11-$14 **AAA Inspector Notes:** This rustic bistro imports some ingredients from Italy but also buys fresh vegetables from local farmers. Neapolitan, uncut and regular round pizzas, as well as calzones, are baked in a pecan wood-fired oven. Cured meats, cheeses, marinated vegetables, pickles and olives also are available. Desserts include cookies, gelato, spumoni and sorbetto. Drink selections include artisan Italian beers and wines from Italy and California (some are organic). **Features:** full bar. **Reservations:** suggested. **Address:** 2527 W Colorado Ave 80904 **Location:** I-25 exit 141, just n, then 0.4 mi w. **Parking:** street only.
ECO L D

THE RABBIT HOLE 719/203-5072 ㉑
▼▼▼ American. Casual Dining. $12-$29 **AAA Inspector Notes:** Follow the white rabbit down the stairs into a secret grotto filled with Alice in Wonderland-themed artwork, stone walls, and decorative glass lighting. The creative menu here features game, duck, mussels, pork belly and some vegetarian options. The carrot cake is exceptional. **Features:** full bar, happy hour. **Address:** 101 N Tejon St 80903 **Location:** I-25 exit 142 (Bijou St), just e to Tejon St, just s, then just e on Kiowa St. **Parking:** street only.
D LATE

RISTORANTE DEL LAGO 719/577-5733 ㊵
▼▼▼ Northern Italian. Fine Dining. $16-$36 **AAA Inspector Notes:** Arrive early and start your evening by unwinding with a cocktail next to the fireplace in the lavish lounge. The chef toured Italy, visiting famous culinary centers, to create an authentic menu featuring homemade pastas, braised lamb, and pizzas baked in a wood-burning oven. Starters include imported cheeses and salumi, charred octopus, and marinated beets with hazelnuts. End the evening by selecting tiramisu, a cannoli or a lemon torta from the dessert trolley. **Features:** full bar, patio dining. **Reservations:** suggested. **Address:** 1 Lake Ave 80906 **Location:** I-25 exit 138, 3 mi w on Circle Dr (which becomes Lake Ave); in The Broadmoor. **Parking:** valet only.
B D

THE RITZ GRILL 719/635-8484 ㉕
▼▼ American. Casual Dining. $10-$23 **AAA Inspector Notes:** Distinctive Art Deco appointments lend to this restaurant's warm, inviting atmosphere. New American preparations of chicken, steak and fish appeal to both locals and out-of-towners. **Features:** full bar, happy hour. **Reservations:** suggested. **Address:** 15 S Tejon St 80903 **Location:** I-25 exit 142 (Bijou St), 0.3 mi e, then just s; at Pikes Peak Ave. **Parking:** street only. L D

SALSA BRAVA FRESH MEXICAN GRILL 719/266-9244 ⑦
▼▼ Mexican. Casual Dining. $9-$18 **AAA Inspector Notes:** This friendly and inviting hacienda is equipped with staff that will make you feel right at home. The made-from-scratch salsa will make your taste buds dance, but don't eat too much! Save room for fish tacos, enchiladas and fajitas, or you can go the not-so-traditional route with smoky ribs slathered in a chipotle-fired barbecue sauce, as well as shrimp tossed with Cajun seasonings. **Features:** full bar. **Address:** 802 Village Center Dr 80919 **Location:** I-25 exit 148 (Rockrimmon Blvd), 1.4 mi w, then just s. L D

SALSA BRAVA FRESH MEXICAN GRILL 719/955-6650
▼▼ Mexican. Casual Dining. $9-$19 **AAA Inspector Notes:** This popular eatery features flavorful salsas, sauces and dips. Entrées include enchiladas, fish tacos and rellenos. A warm welcoming décor, friendly staff and delicious food make this restaurant a favorite with locals. **Features:** full bar, happy hour. **Address:** 9420 Briar Village Point 80920 **Location:** I-25 exit 151 (Briargate Pkwy), 1.4 mi e, just n on Pine Village Way, then just w; in Pine Creek strip mall.
L D

SEÑOR MANUEL MEXICAN CUISINE 719/598-3033 ⑩
▼ Mexican. Casual Dining. $6-$18 **AAA Inspector Notes:** Family owned and operated since 1970, this popular eatery prepares menudo, posole, tamales, carnitas and traditional home-style Mexican favorites. The surroundings are unpretentious and the décor is modest. Friendly staffers enhance the experience. **Features:** full bar. **Address:** 4660 N Nevada Ave 80918 **Location:** I-25 exit 146 (Garden of the Gods Rd), 0.5 mi e to Nevada Ave, then just n.
 L D CALL &M

(See map & index p. 93.)

SHUGA'S RESTAURANT & BAR 719/328-1412 (32)

▼▼▼ American. Casual Dining. $8-$10 **AAA Inspector Notes:** This artful café appeals to a diverse clientèle, including fashionable hipsters, workers in business casual attire and military officers. The unique menu combines flavors from all over the world and offers meat as well as vegetarian dishes. The Shuga's favorite café tray is a perfect sampling of customer favorites, including the famous almond butter cake. Service tends to be slow, which doesn't matter too much as this is a popular spot to hang out for hours. **Features:** full bar. **Address:** 702 S Cascade Ave 80903 **Location:** 0.5 mi s of historic downtown; jct Rio Grande Ave. **Parking:** street only.

[L] [D] [LATE]

SONTERRA INNOVATIVE SOUTHWEST GRILL 719/471-9222 (27)

▼▼▼ Southwestern. Casual Dining. $10-$24 **AAA Inspector Notes:** This restaurant proves Southwestern cuisine can be innovative and upscale. Get your taste buds jumping with the signature strawberry jalapeño margarita. The house salad has pecans, dried cranberries, blue cheese, green apple slices and a maple vinaigrette. Entrées include pan-roasted sustainable salmon, adobo chicken tacos, and blue-corn shrimp and lobster enchiladas. Servers are cheerful, friendly and enthusiastic about the food. **Features:** full bar, patio dining, happy hour. **Address:** 28B S Tejon St 80903 **Location:** Between Colorado and Pikes Peak aves. **Parking:** street only. [L] [D]

SUMMIT 719/577-5733 (39)

▼▼▼▼
American Fine Dining
$16-$28

AAA Inspector Notes: The bright, modern ambience sets the Summit apart from other Broadmoor restaurants, but you can expect the same high level of service and food quality. Staple menu items include the whole angry trout, escargots Persillade and beef tenderloin au poivre. Seasonal menu items feature house made charcuterie, duck, pork and Maine diver scallops. Staff members help you choose from expertly crafted cocktails and an excellent wine selection to find the perfect pairing for your meal. **Features:** full bar. **Reservations:** suggested. **Address:** 1 Lake Ave 80906 **Location:** I-25 exit 138, 3 mi w on Circle Dr (which becomes Lake Ave); in The Broadmoor. **Parking:** valet only. [D]

THE TAVERN 719/577-5772 (38)

▼▼▼ American. Casual Dining. $10-$55 **AAA Inspector Notes:** A gracious atmosphere prevails in a handsome room appointed with Henri de Toulouse-Lautrec prints. Arrangements of steak, prime rib, chicken, seafood and pasta are prepared on the display grill. The front room is intimate, the garden room bright and lush. Nightly dancing contributes to the lively feel of the non-smoking bar. **Features:** full bar. **Reservations:** suggested. **Address:** 1 Lake Ave 80906 **Location:** I-25 exit 138, 3 mi w on Circle Dr (which becomes Lake Ave); in The Broadmoor. **Parking:** valet only. [L] [D]

UCHENNA ETHIOPIAN RESTAURANT 719/634-5070 (16)

▼▼ Ethiopian. Casual Dining. $10-$15 **AAA Inspector Notes:** This popular restaurant offers fresh, fragrant dishes of lamb, chicken and beef. In addition to traditional Ethiopian cuisine, there are a few Mediterranean options. **Address:** 2501 W Colorado Ave 80904 **Location:** I-25 exit 141, 1.4 mi w on US 24, just n on 21st St, then just w. [L] [D]

WALTER'S BISTRO 719/630-0201 (42)

▼▼▼ American. Fine Dining. $12-$42 **AAA Inspector Notes:** Ignore the strip mall location, which may seem off-putting; inside, you'll find an elegant, sophisticated setting. Start with the rich, creamy lobster bisque, a dish this restaurant is known for. Entrées range from Chilean sea bass and New York strip steak to slow-braised short ribs. For a more casual experience, opt to dine in the separate bar area with the locals. **Features:** full bar, happy hour. **Reservations:** suggested, weekends. **Address:** 146 E Cheyenne Mountain Blvd 80906 **Location:** I-25 exit 140 (Nevada Ave), 1.7 mi s, then just w; in Country Club Corners retail complex. [L] [D]

THE WAREHOUSE 719/475-8880 (30)

▼▼▼ American. Casual Dining. $11-$45 **AAA Inspector Notes:** Owner and chef Lawrence Johnson has received awards from local and national organizations for his innovative cuisine. Many dishes feature ingredients found in the west such as bison, elk and lamb. Other entrées include rabbit, duck, monkfish and wild boar. Colorado produced wines dominate the wine menu. Located in a converted warehouse, the décor features oil paintings from a variety of local artists. **Features:** full bar. **Reservations:** suggested. **Address:** 25 W Cimarron St 80903 **Location:** I-25 exit 141, 0.4 mi e. [L] [D]

ZIO'S ITALIAN KITCHEN 719/593-9999

▼▼ Italian. Casual Dining. $9-$19 **AAA Inspector Notes:** The warm, comfortable atmosphere and Old World décor complement the menu. Meals are a good value, and so is the service. This small chain specializes in Italian cuisine, including oven-baked pizzas and pasta dishes. Guests are encouraged to get creative with their pizzas by mixing and matching from a list of 24 toppings. Particularly tempting dishes are artichoke spinach pasta, chicken parmigiana and shrimp limone. **Features:** full bar. **Address:** 6650 Corporate Dr 80919 **Location:** I-25 exit 149 (Woodmen Rd), just w, then 0.5 mi s. [L] [D] CALL [&M]

COMMERCE CITY (C-9) pop. 45,913, elev. 5,184'
- **Hotels & Restaurants map & index p. 136**
- **Part of Denver area — see map p. 116**

DICK'S SPORTING GOODS PARK STADIUM TOURS is at 6000 Victory Way. The stadium is the home of Denver's Major League Soccer team, the Rapids. Tours provide visitors a chance to see what goes on behind the scenes at the stadium, park and soccer complex. **Time:** Allow 45 minutes minimum. **Hours:** Tours are given Mon.-Fri. 9-6 (weather permitting). **Cost:** Free; tickets are first-come, first-served, available at box office. **Phone:** (303) 727-3599.

EL JARDIN 303/288-3500 (93)

▼▼ Mexican. Casual Dining. $9-$18 **AAA Inspector Notes:** Okay, so the location isn't very exciting, but this restaurant is worth the trip through a rather industrial town. The unexpected hacienda-style building stands out from its surroundings. The menu features standard Mexican fare like burritos, tostadas and tacos as well as some specialty items like mango-margarita chicken, grilled tacorito and Pablo's chicken enchilada especial, smothered with a secret sauce. Complete your meal with an order of the rich, creamy flan. **Features:** full bar, patio dining, happy hour. **Address:** 6460 E 73rd Ave 80022 **Location:** Jct SR 2 and 72nd Ave, just ne, s on Monaco St, then just w. [B] [L] [D]

COPPER MOUNTAIN pop. 385

CARBONATE CONDOS 970/968-6854

[fyi] Not evaluated. **Address:** 35 Wheeler Pl, #102 80443 **Location:** I-70 exit 195, just s, then just w; corner of Copper Rd and Wheeler Pl. Facilities, services, and décor characterize an economy property. These individually owned lodgings offer a wide selection of apartment-style units, ranging from studios to four bedrooms.

WHERE TO EAT

C.B. GRILLE 970/968-3113

▼▼▼ American. Fine Dining. $15-$33 **AAA Inspector Notes:** This warm and intimate restaurant features an ever-changing menu. Entrées may include beef tenderloin, wood-grilled pork chop, lamb T-bone steak or grilled Atlantic salmon. **Features:** full bar, early fish specials, happy hour. **Address:** 910 Copper Rd, #114 80443 **Location:** I-70 exit 195, just s, then 0.5 mi w; located just inside Copper Mountain Village entrance; park at Beeler Lot. [D] [X]

CORTEZ (F-1) pop. 8,482, elev. 6,201'

Among the mesas and open expanses of land in the Four Corners region, Cortez has been a trading center for more than 2,000 years. Ranching, tourism and light manufacturing support today's economy.

Ten miles east on US 160 is the entrance to Mesa Verde National Park (see place listing p. 234). Hovenweep National Monument (see place listing p. 213) is about 48 miles west.

Native American dances and an outdoor drama are performed at the Cortez Cultural Center, 25 N. Market St., throughout the summer; phone (970) 565-1151. The ☷ Mesa Verde Country Indian Arts and Culture Festival takes place in Cortez and the surrounding area, including Mesa Verde National Park, starting Memorial Day weekend. Highlights of the celebration include a Native American art market, cultural programs and dances; a featured artist; concerts and archeological tours and exhibits.

Mesa Verde Country Visitor Information: 928 E. Main St., P.O. Box HH, Cortez, CO 81321. **Phone:** (970) 565-8227.

CROW CANYON ARCHAEOLOGICAL CENTER is 1.2 mi. w. off US 491 on Rd. L, then 1.4 mi. s. to 23390 Rd. K. The center offers an all-day tour during which visitors examine artifacts and learn about Ancestral Pueblo Indian history, then tour Crow Canyon's archeology laboratory and current excavation site. Lunch is included. A 75-minute tour and other programs also are available. Allow a full day. **Hours:** Mon.-Fri. 8-5. Tours Wed.-Thurs. 8:45-4:30, May-Sept. **Cost:** Fee $60; $35 (ages 10-17). Under 10 are not permitted. **Phone:** (970) 565-8975 or (800) 422-8975. [GT]

FOUR CORNERS MONUMENT, about 35 mi. s.w., is the only place in the country where four states meet. The juncture of Arizona, Utah, Colorado and New Mexico is marked by a monument bearing each state's seal. The original marker erected in 1912 was a simple concrete pad but is now made of granite and brass. The visitor center features a demonstration center with Navajo artisans. Navajo vendors sell their wares near the site.

Hours: Daily 8-7, May-Sept.; 8-5, rest of year. Closed Jan. 1, Thanksgiving and Christmas. **Cost:** $5; free (ages 0-6). Cash only. **Phone:** (928) 871-6647. ⛩

BEST WESTERN TURQUOISE INN & SUITES
(970)565-3778

Motel
$109-$179

AAA Benefit: Save 10% or more every day and earn 10% bonus points!

Address: 535 E Main St 81321 **Location:** 0.6 mi e of center on US 160. **Facility:** 77 units. 2 stories (no elevator), exterior corridors. **Pool(s):** heated outdoor. **Activities:** hot tub, picnic facilities. **Guest Services:** valet and coin laundry. **Featured Amenity:** breakfast buffet.

Free expanded breakfast, high speed internet year round large hot tub seasonal pool May to Sept.

HOLIDAY INN EXPRESS
(970)565-6000

Hotel
$99-$229

Address: 2121 E Main St 81321 **Location:** 1.3 mi e of center on US 160. **Facility:** 100 units. 3 stories, interior corridors. **Pool(s):** heated indoor. **Activities:** hot tub, picnic facilities, exercise room. **Guest Services:** valet and coin laundry. **Featured Amenity:** breakfast buffet.

TOMAHAWK LODGE
(970)565-8521

Vintage Motel $49-$99 **Address:** 728 S Broadway 81321 **Location:** 1 mi w of center on US 160. **Facility:** This no-frills property has a unique retro sign. 37 units. 1 story, exterior corridors. **Terms:** resort fee.

WHITE EAGLE INN & FAMILY LODGE
970/565-3333

Motel. Rates not provided. **Address:** 2110 S Broadway 81321 **Location:** 1.3 mi s of jct US 160 and 491. **Facility:** 16 units, some houses. 1 story, exterior corridors. **Activities:** playground, lawn sports.

HAMPTON INN MESA VERDE / CORTEZ
970/564-5924

[fyi] Not evaluated. **Address:** 2244 E Hawkins St 81321 **Location:** On US 160, 1.4 mi e of center. Facilities, services, and décor characterize a midscale property.

AAA Benefit: Members save up to 10%!

RETRO INN AT MESA VERDE
970/565-3738

[fyi] Not evaluated. **Address:** 2040 E Main St 81321 **Location:** 1.3 mi e of center on US 160. Facilities, services, and décor characterize an economy property.

WHERE TO EAT

THE FARM BISTRO
970/565-3834

Natural/Organic. Casual Dining. $8-$11 **AAA Inspector Notes:** This farm-to-table restaurant serves local and organic food whenever possible. Travelers will enjoy the relaxed atmosphere, which makes this a popular local spot. A nice selection of soups, salads and pita sandwiches are available as well as vegan and gluten-free options. Expect minimal service. **Features:** wine only. **Address:** 34 W Main St 81321 **Location:** Center. **Parking:** street only.

LOTSA PASTA & THAT 'ZA PIZZA   970/564-9131
◈◈ Italian. Casual Dining. $7-$20 **AAA Inspector Notes:** This restaurant offers fresh, hearty Italian dishes in a casual atmosphere. Friendly servers will make you feel at home. **Features:** full bar, happy hour. **Address:** 1020 S Broadway 81321 **Location:** 1 mi s of jct US 160 and 491. [D]

MAIN STREET BREWERY   970/564-9112
◈◈◈ ◈◈ **AAA Inspector Notes:** The extensive menu will please even the pickiest diner. Start by sharing a round of green chile cheese fries, hot wings or nachos. Wash down your pizza, burger or steak with one of the 12 microbrews or blends crafted in the on-site brewery. When available, the chewy "Cowboy Blondies" topped with crunchy pecans satisfy your sweet tooth. After eating, play a round of pool, foosball or air hockey in the game room. The funky murals and unique statues add an artsy flair to the bar area. **Features:** full bar. **Address:** 21 E Main St 81321 **Location:** Center. **Parking:** street only. [L] [D] [AC]

American Casual Dining $9-$26

NERO'S ITALIAN RESTAURANT   970/565-7366
◈◈ Italian. Casual Dining. $10-$27 **AAA Inspector Notes:** This casual, intimate eatery serves Italian dishes prepared with a Southwestern flair. Begin with the stuffed artichokes served in a lemon-garlic sauce. Then, choose from favorites like lasagna, chicken Parmesan, shrimp scampi and veal scallopini. Other options include house-smoked salmon, grilled tuna and steak au poivre. **Features:** full bar, patio dining, happy hour. **Address:** 303 W Main St 81321 **Location:** Jct US 160 and 491. **Parking:** street only. [D]

ONCE UPON A SANDWICH   970/565-8292
◈◈ Deli Comfort Food. Casual Dining. $8-$10 **AAA Inspector Notes:** This eatery is a good choice for a quick, hearty meal. In addition to sandwiches, menu items include burgers, wraps and some Mexican dishes. The homemade posole soup is a hit! **Address:** 7 W Main St 81321 **Location:** Corner of Main and Market sts; downtown. **Parking:** street only. [L] [AC]

PEPPERHEAD RESTAURANT   970/565-3303
◈◈ Mexican. Casual Dining. $8-$14 **AAA Inspector Notes:** This restaurant features made-from-scratch, Southwest cuisine with a focus on local ingredients. Signature dishes include chicken mole, carnitas and the stuffie—a fresh sopaipilla stuffed with chicken, beef or pork and smothered with savory red or green chile. **Features:** beer & wine. **Address:** 44 W Main St 81321 **Location:** At Main and Chestnut sts; downtown. **Parking:** street only. [L] [D]

SHILOH STEAKHOUSE   970/565-6560
◈◈ Steak Seafood. Casual Dining. $9-$29 **AAA Inspector Notes:** In a small, converted residential home on Main Street, this casual restaurant offers a selection of steak and seafood entrées as well as local microbrews and an extensive list of local wines. Try the grilled salmon served with an avocado butter, the country fried elk steak, or the NY strip. **Features:** full bar, patio dining. **Address:** 5 S Veach St 81321 **Location:** 0.5 mi e; corner of Sligo and Main sts. [L] [D]

COTOPAXI (D-4) pop. 47, elev. 6,364'

RECREATIONAL ACTIVITIES
White-water Rafting
• Arkansas River Tours is w. on US 50. **Hours:** Daily 7-7, mid-Apr. to Labor Day. **Phone:** (719) 942-4362 or (800) 321-4352.

CRAIG (B-2) pop. 9,464, elev. 6,186'
• Restaurants p. 108

In the Yampa River Valley, Craig is a starting point for exploring the meandering canyons of the Yampa and Green rivers. It is the western terminus of the 207-mile scenic stretch of US 40 from Denver. Elk, antelopes, deer and eagles are present in the surrounding mountains.

The Colorado entrance to 🦕 Dinosaur National Monument *(see place listing in Utah p. 307)* is 90 miles west of Craig on US 40. North of the monument lies Browns Park National Wildlife Refuge. The refuge offers boating, camping and hunting.

Chainsaw artists converge on Craig City Park each June to create elaborate masterpieces from cottonwood logs; visitors are welcome to watch the competition progress. Tours of a private Pullman railroad car once owned by Denver banker David Moffat can be arranged through the chamber of commerce.

Craig Chamber of Commerce & Moffat County Visitor Center: 360 E. Victory Way, Craig, CO 81625. **Phone:** (970) 824-5689 or (800) 864-4405.

MUSEUM OF NORTHWEST COLORADO, in the old State Armory at 590 Yampa (SR 13), contains Native American artifacts, rock collections and items pertaining to local history. Displays of railroad memorabilia and turn-of-the-20th-century photographs are included. The museum also features one of the largest collections of cowboy and gunfighter memorabilia in the country. **Hours:** Mon.-Fri. 9-5, Sat. 10-4. **Cost:** Free. **Phone:** (970) 824-6360.

BEST WESTERN PLUS DEER PARK INN & SUITES
(970)824-9282
◈◈◈ Hotel $99-$149

AAA Benefit: Save 10% or more every day and earn 10% bonus points!

Address: 262 Commerce St 81625 **Location:** 0.3 mi s of jct US 40 and SR 13. **Facility:** 42 units, some efficiencies. 2 stories, interior corridors. **Pool(s):** heated indoor. **Activities:** hot tub, picnic facilities. **Guest Services:** valet and coin laundry. **Featured Amenity: full hot breakfast.**

CANDLEWOOD SUITES   970/824-8400
◈◈ Extended Stay Hotel. Rates not provided. **Address:** 92 Commerce St 81625 **Location:** 0.4 mi s of jct US 40 and SR 13. **Facility:** 75 efficiencies. 3 stories, interior corridors. **Terms:** check-in 4 pm. **Activities:** picnic facilities, exercise room. **Guest Services:** complimentary and valet laundry.

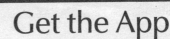

HAMPTON INN & SUITES   970/826-9900

Hotel
Rates not provided

AAA Benefit: Members save up to 10%!

Address: 377 Cedar Ct 81625 **Location:** 0.4 mi s of jct US 40 and SR 13, just w. **Facility:** 89 units. 4 stories, interior corridors. **Terms:** check-in 4 pm. **Pool(s):** heated indoor. **Activities:** hot tub, picnic facilities, exercise room. **Guest Services:** valet and coin laundry. **Featured Amenity:** continental breakfast.

WHERE TO EAT

CARELLI'S PIZZERIA & PASTA   970/824-6868

Italian. Casual Dining. $8-$24 **AAA Inspector Notes:** Locals flock to this restaurant during lunch for the homemade pizzas and calzones. For a more formal dinner experience, head to the back and try one of the hearty pasta dishes. The menu includes spinach lasagna, shrimp scampi and steak Carelli. **Features:** full bar. **Address:** 465 Yampa Ave 81625 **Location:** Just n of US 40 and Yampa Ave; downtown. **Parking:** street only. [L] [D]

JW SNACKS GULF COAST BAR & GRILL   970/826-0468

Cajun. Casual Dining. $6-$14 **AAA Inspector Notes:** This relaxed eatery is outfitted in corrugated tin, plywood, shipping container stamps and parrots. Known for its hot wings, this Louisiana-style restaurant also offers spicy catfish po'boys, fried chicken, blackened catfish and sliced pork sandwiches as well as burgers and dry-rubbed pork spareribs. **Features:** full bar. **Address:** 210 E Victory Way 81625 **Location:** On US 40, between Tucker and Rose sts.

[L] [D]

CREEDE (E-3) elev. 8,838'

A relative latecomer to Colorado's roster of boomtowns—the first silver lode was uncovered in 1889—Creede remained the only silver camp in production during the silver panic of 1893; its mines consistently produced $10 million annually. The industry continued for nearly 100 years until the last mine closed in 1985.

Characters such as Bob Ford (who killed Jesse James), Martha ("Calamity Jane") Cannary and her pal Poker Alice, Bat Masterson and bunco artist "Soapy" Smith gave the town its reputation as one of the wildest camps in the state.

Plays at the nationally acclaimed Creede Repertory Theatre occur from the end of May through September; phone (719) 658-2540. The town also hosts festivals, concerts, bike rallies, mountain runs and art exhibits. The nearby San Juan Mountains and Rio Grande National Forest *(see place listing p. 250)* provide outdoor recreational opportunities throughout the year.

Creede-Mineral County Chamber of Commerce: 904 S. Main St., P.O. Box 580, Creede, CO 81130. **Phone:** (719) 658-2374 or (800) 327-2102.

Self-guiding tours: Brochures outlining a 17-mile driving tour of the historic mining district, as well as walking tours featuring Victorian-era buildings and art galleries are available for $2 at the chamber of commerce.

CREEDE MUSEUM is in the old train depot at 117 Main St. The history of Mineral County is depicted along with the prospectors, miners and entrepreneurs who helped settle the region. Exhibits feature the town's first hand-drawn fire wagon, a horse-drawn hearse, pioneer artifacts, gambling devices, early newspapers, vintage photographs and other memorabilia. **Time:** Allow 30 minutes minimum. **Hours:** Mon.-Sat. 10-4, Sun. 1-4, Memorial Day-Labor Day. **Cost:** $2; $1 (ages 60+); free (ages 0-11); $5 (family). **Phone:** (719) 658-2004 or (719) 658-2303.

CREEDE UNDERGROUND MINING MUSEUM, .5 mi. n. of jct. SR 149 and Creede Ave., is housed in rooms blasted out of solid rock. Exhibits trace the history of mining from the 19th century to the present. A 30-minute narrated self-guiding audio tour is available. Retired miners lead guided tours, explaining equipment and methods of mining; reservations are required. . **Note:** The temperature in the cave is 51 degrees Fahrenheit; warm clothing is recommended. **Time:** Allow 1 hour minimum. **Hours:** Guided tours daily at 10 and 3, late May to mid-Sept. Audio tours Mon.-Fri. 10:30-2:15. Closed major holidays. **Cost:** (including audio tour) $12.50; $6 (ages 60+); $5 (ages 6-12). Guided tour $15. Prices are subject to change; phone ahead for updates. **Phone:** (719) 658-0811. [GT]

RECREATIONAL ACTIVITIES
Fishing

• **Rio Grande Anglers** is at 13 S. Main St. Guided fly fishing trips are offered Apr.-Oct. **Hours:** Daily dawn-dusk. Phone ahead to confirm schedule. **Phone:** (719) 658-2955 or (877) 656-3474.

CRESTED BUTTE (D-3) pop. 1,487, elev. 8,908'

The Elk Mountain Lodge, dating from 1881, and the Old Town Hall and Union Congregational Church, both built in 1883, are reminders of the town's origins as a supply town and coal-mining camp. Another reminder, a two-story outhouse, is behind the shops of the renovated Company Store building on Third Street. The privy's upper level made it usable during the winters when more than 20 feet of snow fell.

More elegant landmarks from the town's past are found along Elk Avenue, where restored Victorian buildings feature shops, eateries and outfitters. Culturally speaking, the Crested Butte Center for the Arts is the town's destination for music, dance, theater and art; phone (970) 349-7487.

The Gunnison National Forest, Elk Mountains and Raggeds Wilderness surround the town. Jagged peaks, glacial valleys and aspen-covered slopes provide a scenic backdrop for golfing, mountain biking and hiking. Three miles from Crested Butte, the resort community of Mt. Crested Butte has become a center for recreation, especially skiing, snowboarding, tubing, mountain biking, hiking and horseback riding in Gunnison National Forest *(see Grand Mesa-Uncompahgre-Gunnison National Forests p. 206).*

Crested Butte/Mount Crested Butte Chamber of Commerce and Visitor Center: 601 Elk Ave., P.O. Box 1288, Crested Butte, CO 81224. **Phone:** (970) 349-6438 or (855) 681-0941.

Self-guiding tours: A walking tour map of the town's historical attractions is available from the Crested Butte Mountain Heritage Museum.

CRESTED BUTTE MOUNTAIN HERITAGE MUSEUM is at 331 Elk Ave. The front of the museum functioned as a hardware store 1883-1996; a coal stove and original cases filled with goods representing items sold in the past are on display. Exhibits about the local Ute population and the geology, mining, ranching, railroad and domestic history of Crested Butte may be seen as well as a model railroad, a mining diorama and a gondola. **Time:** Allow 30 minutes minimum. **Hours:** Daily 10-8, Memorial Day weekend-early Oct. Phone ahead to confirm schedule. **Cost:** $4; free (ages 0-11). **Phone:** (970) 349-1880.

PARAGON GALLERY, 132 Elk Ave. at 2nd St., is in the old town hall. The cooperative gallery displays the works of 14 local artists as well as works by guest artists. Included are fine arts, photographs, ceramics, jewelry, handmade paper, leatherwork, mosaics, stained glass and sculpture. **Hours:** Daily 11-9. Phone ahead to confirm schedule. **Cost:** Free. **Phone:** (970) 349-6484.

ELEVATION HOTEL & SPA   970/251-3000

▼▼▼ **Resort Hotel.** Rates not provided. **Address:** 500 Gothic Rd 81225 **Location:** 5.9 mi n of Elk Ave. Located at Mt. Crested Butte. **Facility:** This ski-in, ski-out hotel offers a warm and inviting lobby, underground parking, and complimentary ski valet and storage. Enjoy an après-ski beverage at the lounge right next to the gondola. 262 units, some kitchens. 6 stories, interior corridors. **Parking:** on-site (fee) and valet. **Terms:** check-in 4 pm. **Amenities:** safes. **Pool(s):** heated indoor. **Activities:** sauna, hot tub, steamroom, miniature golf, downhill & cross country skiing, bicycles, spa. **Guest Services:** coin laundry, area transportation.

ELK MOUNTAIN LODGE   (970)349-7533

▼▼ **Historic Bed & Breakfast** $129-$219 **Address:** 129 Gothic Ave 81224 **Location:** 0.3 mi w on Elk Ave to 2nd St, just n. **Facility:** Built in 1919, this lodge used to cater to local miners and has maintained some aspects of its historic character, including hardwood floors, stained glass and antique pieces. 19 units. 3 stories (no elevator), interior corridors. **Terms:** closed 4/6-5/15 & 11/1-11/20, 2 night minimum stay - weekends, 14 day cancellation notice. **Activities:** hot tub, cross country skiing, bicycles, trails, massage. **Guest Services:** coin laundry.

THE GRAND LODGE   (970)349-8000

▼▼▼▼
Hotel
$99-$289

Address: 6 Emmons Loop 81225 **Location:** 2.3 mi n of center. Located at Mt. Crested Butte. **Facility:** 226 units, some efficiencies. 5 stories, interior corridors. **Terms:** check-in 4 pm, 1-4 night minimum stay - seasonal, 3 day cancellation notice-fee imposed, resort fee. **Amenities:** safes. **Pool(s):** heated outdoor. **Activities:** hot tub, steamroom, downhill & cross country skiing, exercise room, spa. **Guest Services:** coin laundry.

THE LODGE AT MOUNTAINEER SQUARE   970/349-4000

▼▼▼ **Resort Hotel.** Rates not provided. **Address:** 620 Gothic Rd 81225 **Location:** 3 mi n of Elk Ave. Located at Mt. Crested Butte. **Facility:** Located just steps from the ski lifts, the residential units here range from king rooms to a 4-bedroom condo. Rooms have humidifiers and some feature a gas fireplace, balcony, and washer and dryer. 120 units, some efficiencies and condominiums. 6 stories, interior corridors. **Parking:** on-site (fee) and valet. **Terms:** check-in 4 pm. **Amenities:** video games, safes. **Dining:** 2 restaurants, also, Django's Restaurant & Wine Bar, see separate listing. **Pool(s):** heated outdoor, heated indoor. **Activities:** sauna, hot tub, downhill & cross country skiing, recreation programs in season, trails, exercise room. **Guest Services:** area transportation.

OLD TOWN INN   (970)349-6184

▼▼ **Hotel** $99-$139 **Address:** 708 Sixth St 81224 **Location:** On SR 135, just s of Elk Ave. **Facility:** 33 units. 2 stories (no elevator), interior corridors. **Terms:** cancellation fee imposed. **Activities:** hot tub. **Guest Services:** coin laundry.

WESTWALL LODGE   970/349-1280

▼▼▼ **Condominium.** Rates not provided. **Address:** 14 Hunter Hill Rd 81225 **Location:** 2.2 mi n, just e; at Mt. Crested Butte. **Facility:** Experience a high degree of luxury and numerous amenities, including an in-room washer and dryer. This ski-in/ski-out residential lodge offers heated underground parking. 23 condominiums. 3-4 stories, interior corridors. **Pool(s):** heated outdoor. **Activities:** hot tub, steamroom, downhill skiing, exercise room, massage. **Guest Services:** complimentary laundry.

THE INN AT CRESTED BUTTE   970/349-2111

(fyi) Not evaluated. **Address:** 510 Whiterock Ave 81224 **Location:** Just w of SR 145 (6th St) at 5th St and Whiterock Ave; downtown. Facilities, services, and décor characterize a mid-scale property. After a day of hitting the slopes or hiking the trails, sink into a leather sofa in front of the cozy fireplace in this hotel's lobby. Walk a few blocks to shop and eat in the historic downtown area.

NORDIC INN   970/349-5542

(fyi) **Bed & Breakfast** Did not meet all AAA rating requirements for locking devices in some guest rooms at time of last evaluation on 03/04/2015. **Address:** 14 Treasury Rd 81225 **Location:** 2.9 mi n of Elk Ave to Treasury Rd, then just e. Facilities, services, and décor characterize a mid-scale property.

WHERE TO EAT

DJANGO'S RESTAURANT & WINE BAR   970/349-7574

▼▼ Small Plates. Fine Dining. $11-$25 **AAA Inspector Notes:** This stylish restaurant offers an extensive wine list and an interesting selection of scrumptious, creatively presented small plates. Although inspired by the cuisines of Southern Europe, mouth-watering menu items change often (sometimes nightly) and can include steamed Prince Edward Island mussels, pomegranate-glazed quail, masa-dusted diver scallops and encrusted elk tenderloin. **Features:** full bar, patio dining. **Reservations:** suggested. **Address:** 620 Gothic Rd 81225 **Location:** 3 mi n of Elk Ave; in The Lodge at Mountaineer Square. **Parking:** on-site (fee). [D] [🐕]

GINGER CAFE   970/349-7291

▼▼ Asian. Casual Dining. $13-$20 **AAA Inspector Notes:** Among the offerings of the freshly made Pan Asian cuisine are a fiery tom yum goong soup, Vietnamese spring rolls, pot stickers served with a green onion soy dipping sauce, green and red curries and krapow, a favorite dish that pairs fresh green cilantro with local vegetables. Beef, chicken, seafood or tofu are available in most dishes. Rich and filling green tea cheesecake or a mango lassi add delicious sweet touches. **Features:** full bar, happy hour. **Address:** 425 Elk Ave 81224 **Location:** 0.3 mi w. **Parking:** street only. [L] [D] [AC]

IZZYS   970/349-5630

▼ Breakfast. Quick Serve. $5-$10 **AAA Inspector Notes:** Be prepared to wait at this popular eatery, which features homemade bagels, pancakes, crepes and latke Reuben sandwiches. **Features:** patio dining. **Address:** 218 Maroon Ave 81224 **Location:** Between Maroon and Elk aves; in the alley. **Parking:** street only. [B] [L] [AC]

THE LAST STEEP BAR & GRILL   970/349-7007

▼▼ American. Casual Dining. $9-$18 **AAA Inspector Notes:** Named for the owner's favorite north-face ski run, this popular eatery serves appetizers such as Ms. Ann's famous crab cakes, which are grilled and then fried; freshly made soups served in hollowed-out bread bowls; salads; veggie, chicken Caesar and crab cake wraps; award-winning burgers; and creative sandwiches such as Kansas City-style pulled pork, Jamaican-style marinated chicken breast, Cajun-grilled ahi, and a Santa Fe veggie burger. The cozy space has a bohemian vibe. **Features:** full bar, patio dining. **Address:** 208 Elk Ave 81224 **Location:** 0.3 mi w of center. **Parking:** street only. [L] [D] [AC]

LE BOSQUET RESTAURANT FRANCAIS   970/349-5808

▼▼▼ French. Casual Dining. $18-$36 **AAA Inspector Notes:** This popular restaurant for more than 25 years offers a warm ambiance with tasteful artwork throughout. Enjoy mountain views as you savor delectable French favorites such as escargot, baked onion soup, rack of lamb and other entrées of beef, pork and fowl. The Hungarian mushroom soup is a standout. **Features:** full bar. **Reservations:** suggested. **Address:** 525 Red Lady Ave 81224 **Location:** SR 135 (6th St), just w on Belleview Ave, then just s; in Majestic Plaza. [D] [AC]

LIL'S SUSHI BAR & GRILL   970/349-5457

▼▼▼ Sushi. Casual Dining. $8-$37 **AAA Inspector Notes:** This is the place to go for seafood, steak, pasta and a prickly pear margarita. Start with the tuna and avocado poke, served with ponzu, sesame oil and satisfyingly crunchy wonton chips. Try one of the robatayaki, grilled meats and fish, for a small treat, or sample one of the innovative sushi rolls. Larger entrées include filet mignon, diver scallops, Rocky Mountain trout, and salmon. **Features:** full bar, happy hour. **Address:** 321 Elk Ave 81224 **Location:** 0.3 mi w; in the back building. **Parking:** street only. [D] [AC]

MARCHITELLI'S GOURMET NOODLE   970/349-7401

▼▼▼ Regional Italian. Casual Dining. $11-$33 **AAA Inspector Notes:** This intimate family-owned restaurant offers generations-old recipes, like wedding soup, and Italian favorites, such as ravioli of the day, seafood, veal, chicken, meat and game dishes. Diners can pair pasta choices with Nico's hot sausage, Rocky's vodka sauce, Alfredo and white clams, pesto genovese or a hearty red sauce. Smaller portions are available. The Italian cream cake is a lovely dessert choice. **Features:** full bar. **Address:** 411 3rd St 81224 **Location:** Jct SR 135, 0.3 mi w on Elk Ave, just s. **Parking:** street only. [D] [AC]

MCGILL'S   970/349-5240

▼▼ American. Casual Dining. $9-$12 **AAA Inspector Notes:** This popular eatery serves delicious breakfasts all day; homemade soups; blackened steak salad; a chicken Cobb sandwich; Mediterranean grilled ham with roasted red pepper, caramelized onion and marinated artichoke hearts; and a popular create-your-own burger. The long, comfortable soda fountain is the perfect spot for an ice cream float, malt, shake or good old-fashioned sundae. **Features:** full bar. **Address:** 228 Elk Ave 81224 **Location:** 0.3 mi w. **Parking:** street only. [B] [L]

PITAS IN PARADISE   970/349-0897

▼▼ Greek. Casual Dining. $6-$12 **AAA Inspector Notes:** The uninitiated may not think a falafel and hummus fix exists, but after a meal at this spot, they'll be addicted. Try the soup bar- options range from green chile to Hungarian mushroom, which has a tomato base brightened by fresh dill. Entrées include a lamb gyro, a Bombay rice bowl, and a Greek wrap. Leaving this place without trying the baklava would be criminal. **Features:** full bar, patio dining, happy hour. **Address:** 302 Elk Ave 81224 **Location:** Between 3rd and 4th sts. **Parking:** street only. [L] [D] [AC]

RYCE ASIAN BISTRO   970/349-9888

▼▼ Asian. Casual Dining. $13-$20 **AAA Inspector Notes:** This charming eatery offers a riverside dining room and seasonal patio. The menu features a wide selection of Chinese, Japanese, Thai and Vietnamese dishes and creative sake concoctions. Vegetarian and gluten-free options are available. **Features:** full bar, patio dining. **Address:** 120 Elk Ave 81224 **Location:** Between 1st and 2nd sts. **Parking:** street only. [L] [D] [AC]

THE SECRET STASH   970/349-6245

▼▼ Pizza. Casual Dining. $10-$19 **AAA Inspector Notes:** The secret's out on this popular local hangout. After a day of hitting the slopes or exploring the mountains, patrons come to this little gem for great specialty meat or veggie pizzas, calzones, or pasta dishes. Settle in with a starter such as stuffed mushrooms and a local brew or a fancy cocktail. The upstairs offers a more family friendly vibe. Head downstairs if you prefer a sultry lounge scene. **Features:** full bar. **Address:** 303 Elk Ave 81224 **Location:** Corner of 3rd St. **Parking:** street only. [L] [D] [AC]

SLOGAR BAR & RESTAURANT   970/349-5765

▼▼ Comfort Food. Casual Dining. $15-$25 **AAA Inspector Notes:** Famous for skillet-fried chicken dinners and grilled steaks with generous portions of creamed corn and biscuits, experience family-style service in a unique historic Victorian setting. **Features:** full bar. **Address:** 517 2nd St 81225 **Location:** Downtown. **Parking:** street only. [D] [AC]

SOUPCON BISTRO   970/349-5448

▼▼▼ French. Fine Dining. $33-$47 **AAA Inspector Notes:** In an old miner's cabin, this quaint and petite romantic bistro offers traditional French cuisine, incorporating local, seasonal ingredients. Sample dishes include escargot in white wine and garlic, pan-seared lump crab tower, seared foie gras, crispy seared duck breast, all-natural Colorado filet mignon, and grilled Colorado rack of lamb. Try the traditional vanilla soufflé with dark chocolate ganache for a sweet ending. **Features:** full bar. **Reservations:** suggested. **Address:** 127A Elk Ave 81224 **Location:** 0.3 mi w, just n on 2nd St. **Parking:** on-site and street. [D] [AC]

THE SUNFLOWER   970/349-6866

▼ American. Quick Serve. $8-$32 **AAA Inspector Notes:** Stop in for a cup of coffee and a chocolate croissant before heading to the slopes or hitting the local hiking trails. Stick around for a gourmet sandwich, such as the ham and fig panini, pastrami Reuben, or tuna salad and cheddar. The décor is a rough take on a miner's cabin with unfinished wood walls and a jackalope with turquoise antlers. **Features:** full bar. **Address:** 214 Elk Ave 81224 **Location:** Between 2nd and 3rd sts. **Parking:** street only. [B] [L] [D] [AC]

TEOCALLI TAMALE   970/349-2005

▼ Mexican. Quick Serve. $8-$13 **AAA Inspector Notes:** As the name implies, this restaurant is well known for its savory tamales. Try one before leaving, or you'll be missing out. Other options include tacos or burritos filled with mahi mahi, spicy shredded beef, chicken, steak or veggies. Kick up the heat and flavor with one of the homemade salsas. Prepared to order and served up quickly, the flavorful food here will satisfy your hunger in no time. **Features:** full bar. **Address:** 311 1/2 Elk Ave 81224 **Location:** Just w of center. **Parking:** street only. [L] [D] [AC]

THE ICE BAR AT ULEY'S CABIN   970/349-2275

(fyi) Not evaluated. Ski or snowboard in and out for an elegant lunch at this famous ice bar, and choose from an exciting array of cocktails. Or snuggle in for a fun-filled 35-minute sleigh ride up the mountain to a warm and spacious cabin featuring high ceilings and chandeliers, where an eager staff awaits to treat you to a Colorado gourmet dinner. Mesmerizing views of the rugged and majestic mountains will leave you spellbound. The ride down is just 15 minutes. **Address:** 12 Snowmass Rd 81224 **Location:** Mid-mountain near the base of the Twister chairlift; in front of the restaurant at Elevations Hotel & Spa.

CRIPPLE CREEK (F-8) pop. 1,189, elev. 9,508'
• Hotels p. 112 • Restaurants p. 112

Rumors of "color" on the Womack Ranch were largely ignored until the rancher's nephew, Bob, made the first major gold strike in the spring of 1891. Young Womack rode to Colorado City (now Colorado Springs) and went on a binge, celebrating his new wealth. He sold his claim for $500, never dreaming that more than $350 million in gold ultimately would come from it and the claims that followed.

By late 1891 the "$300 million cow pasture" was crawling with prospectors. A town was platted and grew to a population of about 18,000 within 2 years. Town buildings were rebuilt with brick after a fire in 1896; most of the present-day structures date from this period. Although the boom ended in 1904, the shafts that yielded $25 million in a single year were reactivated when gold mining once again became profitable in the 1930s during the Great Depression.

Cripple Creek is reached from Colorado Springs by US 24 and SR 67; the adventurous can take the Gold Camp Road (see attraction listing p. 89) over the mountains. The Phantom Canyon Highway runs south from Cripple Creek to US 50, 7 miles east of Cañon City (see place listing p. 72). Only experienced mountain drivers should attempt the Gold Camp and Phantom Canyon routes; check road conditions before starting.

BUTTE THEATER is at 139 E. Bennett Ave. Live performances include traditional melodramas, dramas, musicals and comedies presented in the 1896 opera house that has been restored to its Victorian heyday, complete with grand chandeliers and period wallpaper. Guests enjoy booing the villains and rooting for the heroes at the melodramas, which feature hand-painted sets and era-appropriate costumes.

Time: Allow 2 hours minimum. **Hours:** Matinee and evening performances are offered year-round; phone for schedule. **Cost:** $18; $14 (ages 62+); $12 (ages 0-18). Prices may vary; phone ahead. **Phone:** (719) 689-3247. (TI)

CRIPPLE CREEK AND VICTOR NARROW GAUGE RAILROAD, at 520 E. Carr St., offers a 45-minute trip through the mining district of Cripple Creek aboard a 2-foot-gauge, coal-fired steam locomotive. **Hours:** Trains depart daily every 40 minutes 10-5, Memorial Day weekend-early Oct. Ticket office opens at 9:30. Phone ahead to confirm schedule. **Cost:** Fare $14; $13 (ages 66+); $8 (ages 3-12). Fares may vary; phone ahead. **Phone:** (719) 689-2640.

CRIPPLE CREEK DISTRICT MUSEUM, at Bennett Ave. and Fifth St., is housed in five original historic buildings. The museum includes the original Midland Terminal Railroad Depot, a turn-of-the-20th-century assay office, two Victorian apartments, mining equipment, an art gallery and two fully furnished historic cabins. **Time:** Allow 30 minutes minimum. **Hours:** Daily 10-5, mid-May to mid-Oct.; Sat.-Sun. 10-4, rest of year. **Cost:** $7; $5 (ages 60+ and military with ID); free (ages 0-12). **Phone:** (719) 689-9540. (GT)

CRIPPLE CREEK HERITAGE CENTER is at 9283 S. SR 67. Historical and interactive exhibits about the Pikes Peak region are on display at the center, recognizable by a front facade resembling a mine entrance. Visitors also can enjoy a stunning panorama of seven mountain ranges and obtain area information. **Time:** Allow 1 hour minimum. **Hours:** Daily 9-5, May-Oct.; 9-4, rest of year. **Cost:** Free. **Phone:** (719) 689-3315 or (877) 858-4653.

MOLLIE KATHLEEN GOLD MINE, 1 mi. n. of Cripple Creek on SR 67, was discovered by Mollie Kathleen Gortner in 1891 and has been maintained as a mine ever since. Tours 1,000 feet underground allow visitors to understand the lives of the late 19th- and 20th-century hard rock gold miners and the nation's mining legacy. Jackets are supplied.

Time: Allow 1 hour minimum. **Hours:** Tours depart every 30 minutes daily 9-5, mid-May to early Sept.; on the hour 10-4, early Sept.-early Oct. Phone ahead to confirm schedule. **Cost:** $20; $12 (ages 3-12). Prices may vary. **Phone:** (719) 689-2466.

THE OLD HOMESTEAD HOUSE MUSEUM is at 353 E. Meyers Ave. Cripple Creek's most famous madam, Pearl DeVere, built the Old Homestead House in 1896. The restored brothel, said to have been the town's finest and most luxurious, features velvet bedspreads and vintage furniture. Guided tours provide information about the house, the lives of the women who lived and worked there, and the gold rush era. **Time:** Allow 30 minutes minimum. **Hours:** Daily 11-5, June-Sept.; Sat.-Sun. 11-4 in May. **Cost:** $5; $2 (ages 8-11). **Phone:** (719) 689-9090.

GAMBLING ESTABLISHMENTS
• **Bronco Billy's** is at 233 E. Bennett Ave. **Hours:** Daily 24 hours. **Phone:** (719) 689-2142 or (877) 989-2142.

- **Century Casino Cripple Creek** is at 200-220 E. Bennett Ave. **Hours:** Daily 24 hours. **Phone:** (719) 689-0333.
- **McGills Casino** is at 232 E. Bennett Ave. **Hours:** Daily 24 hours. **Phone:** (719) 689-2446 or (800) 635-3825.

CARR MANOR   (719)689-3709

▼▼▼▼ **Historic Boutique Bed & Breakfast** $110-$450 **Address:** 350 E Carr Ave 80813 **Location:** Corner of 4th St and E Carr Ave; center. **Facility:** Once a high school, this boutique-style inn has a classroom feel. Blackboards in the rooms feature messages from past guests. Guest rooms offer unique decor with luxurious linens and modern amenities. 14 units, some efficiencies. 2 stories (no elevator), interior corridors. **Parking:** on-site and street. **Terms:** check-in 4 pm, 2-3 night minimum stay - seasonal and/or weekends, age restrictions may apply, 14 day cancellation notice-fee imposed, resort fee. **Activities:** exercise room, massage.

[🍴] [BIZ] [📶] [✕] [🅰] [/SOME UNITS] [🛏] [🖥] [📖]

WHERE TO EAT

MAGGIE'S   719/689-3977

[fyi] Not evaluated. This restaurant offers a nice selection of soups, salads, burgers and popular entrées such as fried chicken and a hearty seafood platter. **Address:** 300 E Bennett Dr 80813 **Location:** Center.

Take Your **Imagination** to New Destinations

Use AAA Travel Guides online to explore the possibilities.

Go to AAA.com/travelguide today.

CURECANTI NATIONAL RECREATION AREA (E-2)

The Curecanti National Recreation Area parallels US 50 between Gunnison and Montrose. It contains three reservoirs formed by dams on the Gunnison River—Blue Mesa, Morrow Point and Crystal.

Blue Mesa Reservoir, 20 miles long, offers 10 vehicular-access and four boat-access campgrounds, boat ramps and water sports. Two marinas rent boats mid-May through September. Boat permits are required. A $4 fee provides boating access at the reservoir for 2 days; for 14 days the fee is $10; an annual pass is $30.

Fishing at Blue Mesa Reservoir yields kokanee salmon and rainbow, brown and Mackinaw trout. The largest Mackinaw trout are caught in April and May. Shore fishing for brown and rainbow trout is best in early spring and late fall. The best salmon fishing is usually late June through August. A Colorado fishing license is required.

Morrow Point and Crystal reservoirs, along US 50, offer backcountry hiking, fishing and hand-carried boating. Additional summer recreational activities include camping, seven hiking trails through Colorado's high country and a number of scenic overlooks and picnic areas for motorists. Winter recreation offers cross-country skiing, snowmobiling, snowshoeing and ice fishing. Facilities are limited in winter. Admission to the recreation area is free. Phone (970) 641-2337. *See Recreation Areas Chart.*

CIMARRON VISITOR CENTER, 20 mi. e. of Montrose just off US 50, has a narrow-gauge railroad engine, coal tender, freight car and caboose displayed on an 1895 trestle. Next to the visitor center are sheep- and cattle-loading corrals, a work car, railroad stock cars, a crane car and other historical displays.

Note: The visitor center will be closed throughout 2016; phone for updates. **Hours:** Daily 9-4, mid-May through Sept. 30; otherwise varies. **Cost:** Free. Camping fee $12. **Phone:** (970) 641-2337. [🔺] [🏕]

ELK CREEK VISITOR CENTER, 16 mi. w. of Gunnison, milepost 142 at 24830 US 50, has seasonal exhibits on natural and cultural history, as well as area information, on summer weekend evenings at the Elk Creek Campground. Occasional ranger-led programs are offered in summer; complimentary Junior Ranger information is available. Picnicking is permitted in summer. **Hours:** Daily 8-6, late May-Sept. 30; daily 8-4, Apr. 1-late May and in Oct.; Mon.-Fri. 8-4, rest of year. **Cost:** Free. Camping fee $12-$18. **Phone:** (970) 641-2337. [🔺]

MORROW POINT BOAT TOURS depart from Pine Creek Trail, 26 mi. w. of Gunnison off US 50. A ranger narrates the 90-minute cruise, noting scenic, historical and geological features of the reservoir's canyon setting.

Note: The hike to the boat dock is 1 mile and includes 232 stairs. Those with physical limitations should consider their ability to hike this trail before making reservations. Allow at least 1 hour for the hike. **Hours:** Trips depart Wed.-Mon. at 10 and 12:30, June 1-Labor Day. Phone ahead to confirm schedule. **Cost:** Fare $16; $8 (ages 0-12 and Senior/Access Pass holders). Pre-paid reservations are required. **Phone:** (970) 641-2337 for information and reservations.

MORROW POINT DAM, 1.5 mi. off US 50 near mile marker 112, is reached from the Cimarron turnoff. The dam, 469 feet high, is reputed to be the first double-curvature, thin-arch concrete dam in the country. The Mesa Creek trail leads to a footbridge that crosses Crystal Reservoir. Photography is permitted. **Hours:** Daily 24 hours. **Cost:** Free. **Phone:** (970) 641-2337. 🏕

DECKERS

LOST VALLEY RANCH   303/647-2311

Resort Ranch
$870-$3536

Address: 29555 Goose Creek Rd 80135 **Location:** From Deckers sign, 3 mi w on CR 126, 9 mi s on gravel road (Forest Service Rd 211), follow signs. Located in a secluded rural area. **Facility:** Nestled in a valley setting, this ranch offers individual and duplex cabins with living rooms, wood-burning fireplaces and luxurious bedding. 23 cabins. 1 story, exterior corridors. **Terms:** closed 11/27-3/6, 2-7 night minimum stay - seasonal and/or weekends, 60 day cancellation notice-fee imposed. **Pool(s):** heated outdoor. **Activities:** hot tub, fishing, tennis, recreation programs, playground, trails, massage. **Guest Services:** valet and coin laundry.

DEL NORTE (E-3) pop. 1,686, elev. 7,879'

RIO GRANDE COUNTY MUSEUM AND CULTURAL CENTER, a half-blk. s. of US 160 at 580 Oak St., offers visitors a glimpse of the San Luis Valley's cultural and natural history. Artifacts displayed include those of Native Americans, pioneers, Hispanic settlers and gold miners. The museum also houses an exhibit about explorer John C. Fremont, a rock art display and changing art exhibits.

Time: Allow 30 minutes minimum. **Hours:** Tues.-Fri. 10-4, Sat. 10-3. Closed major holidays. **Cost:** Donations. $2; $1 (ages 0-12). **Phone:** (719) 657-2847.

DOUBLE SPUR LODGE & RANCH   719/657-2920

Vacation Rental House
$145-$870

Location: On SR 160, 3.2 mi w of center. **Facility:** This upscale, rustic lodge is situated on 16 acres. Its three beautifully appointed private wings can accommodate up to 28 guests; it's ideal for corporate retreats, family reunions and small groups. 3 houses. 1 story, interior/exterior corridors. **Terms:** check-in 4 pm, 2-3 night minimum stay - seasonal. **Activities:** game room, picnic facilities. **Guest Services:** complimentary laundry.

THE WINDSOR HOTEL   719/657-9031

fyi Not evaluated. **Address:** 605 Grand Ave 81132 **Location:** Center. Facilities, services, and décor characterize a mid-scale property. Built in 1874, this hotel has been restored to its original grandeur. It features modern amenities and well-appointed guest rooms with courtyard or mountain views.

WHERE TO EAT

PEACE OF ART CAFE   719/657-3223

◆◆ Natural/Organic Sandwiches. Casual Dining. $8-$13 **AAA Inspector Notes:** Patrons will enjoy this eatery offering healthy and delicious soups, salads, sandwiches, quiches, coffee, smoothies and teas. Baked goods include mouth-watering mini scones, muffins and moist carrot cake. The peace keepers menu is just for kids and their meals come with peeled baby carrots or corn chips. The café features unique architecture and one-of-a-kind cordwood construction. The outdoor covered courtyard features ample seating and a cozy bar made from the front end of a truck. **Features:** beer & wine, patio dining. **Address:** 14475 W Hwy 160 81132 **Location:** Center.

THREE BARREL BREWING   719/657-0681

◆◆ Italian. Casual Dining. $8-$12 **AAA Inspector Notes:** Known for its hand-crafted, small batch beers, this brewery offers a regular stash of IPAs and ales as well as seasonal brews and sour ales. Available sizes range from a small taster to a keg. If you're the designated driver, try one of the home-brewed sodas. The menu features stromboli, calzones and personal-size pizzas. **Features:** beer only. **Address:** 475 Grand Ave 81132 **Location:** Just s of US 160. **Parking:** street only.

THE WINDSOR HOTEL DINING ROOM   719/657-9031

◆◆◆ American. Fine Dining. $10-$28 **AAA Inspector Notes:** *Historic.* In a Victorian-era building, this restaurant offers a menu that changes seasonally. Start with a fresh salad, such as heirloom tomato and cheese, or baby beet with duck prosciutto. Entrées may include bone-in local lamb, grilled flank steak, and hoisin-glazed short ribs. When the weather cooperates, relax with a cocktail in the outdoor courtyard. **Features:** full bar, patio dining, Sunday brunch. **Address:** 605 Grand Ave 81132 **Location:** Center. **Parking:** street only.

DELTA (D-2) pop. 8,915, elev. 4,953'
• Restaurants p. 114

Unlike many Colorado towns, Delta started and stayed small but prosperous. The town owes its stability to agriculture; fruit has always been Delta's economic mainstay. Livestock, mining, lumbering and industry also contribute.

Laid out in 1882 by the Uncompahgre Town Company and named Uncompahgre, the name was later changed to Delta because the shape of the town site resembled that of the Greek letter.

The area is rich in an unusual resource: dinosaur bones. Bones from some of the largest dinosaur skeletons ever found—dubbed supersaurus and brachiosaurus—were unearthed southwest of Delta. The animals are believed to have tipped the scales at nearly 80 tons and to have stood almost five stories tall. The fossilized remains of other prehistoric creatures have been excavated at Dry Mesa Dinosaur Quarry.

Delta is near Grand Mesa, Gunnison and Uncompahgre national forests and the Black Canyon of the Gunnison National Park. It also is the western terminus for the 20-mile scenic stretch of SR 92, which continues northeast as SR 133.

Delta Area Chamber of Commerce & Visitors Center: 301 Main St., Delta, CO 81416. **Phone:** (970) 874-8616.

DELTA COUNTY MUSEUM, 1 blk. e. of US 50 at 251 Meeker St., displays ranching and farming implements, photographs, a collection of 10 large bells, household appliances and historical artifacts. The museum's butterfly collection includes examples of species now extinct. A dinosaur exhibit also is featured. Visitors ages twelve and under must be accompanied by an adult. **Hours:** Tues.-Fri. 10-4, May-Sept.; Tues.-Wed. 10-4, rest of year. **Cost:** $2; $1 (ages 65+); free (ages 0-12 with an adult). **Phone:** (970) 874-8721.

FORT UNCOMPAHGRE, n. on US 50, then n. on Gunnison River Dr. to Confluence Dr., is a history museum consisting of seven re-created cabins on the banks of the Gunnison River. The fort depicts the original 1830s-era civilian trading post. **Time:** Allow 1 hour, 30 minutes minimum. **Hours:** Mon.-Sat. 9-4, Sun. noon-4, June-Sept. Closed major holidays. **Cost:** $4.50; $3.50 (ages 65+); $2.50 (ages 6-16). Cash only. **Phone:** (970) 874-8349.

RECREATIONAL ACTIVITIES
White-water Rafting
- **Wilderness Aware Rafting** departs 14.2 mi. e. on SR 92, passing Milepost 14, s. on LN 2810 (dirt road) to the sign for Gunnison Gorge National Conservation Area, then right into parking lot. **Hours:** Trips depart daily at 9, early May-Labor Day. **Phone:** (719) 395-2112 or (800) 462-7238.

DAVETO'S ITALIAN RESTAURANT   970/874-8277

◆◆ Italian. Casual Dining. $5-$14 **AAA Inspector Notes:** Enjoy half or full-size orders of baked ravioli, or try a Sicilian deep-dish pizza, a meatball sandwich or more. The vegetable tray and Italian spumone are popular. **Features:** beer & wine. **Address:** 520 Main St 81416 **Location:** 0.5 mi s of town. **Parking:** street only.
Ⓛ Ⓓ

FIESTA VALLARTA   970/874-6877

◆◆ Mexican. Casual Dining. $6-$13 **AAA Inspector Notes:** This family-owned restaurant serves traditional favorites, including chile rellenos, enchiladas and flan. The freshly made salsa has a nice kick. Try the egg-battered rellenos or the Colorado chile, a savory beef stew. **Features:** beer & wine. **Address:** 447 Main St 81416 **Location:** 0.3 mi s of town. **Parking:** street only.
Ⓛ Ⓓ

LE BISTRO AT THE GARDEN CENTER   970/874-3073

◆◆ American. Casual Dining. $8-$18 **AAA Inspector Notes:** This charming café serves local wine and offers a variety of menu items such as charred pineapple bourbon ham, the portobello mushroom sandwich with heirloom balsamic vinegar, cranberry chicken salad and a nice selection of salads and soups served with warm, homemade apple bread. Be sure to sample the seasonal fruit pies. **Features:** beer & wine, patio dining, Sunday brunch. **Address:** 1970 S Main St 81416 **Location:** 2 mi s on US 50.
Ⓛ Ⓐ

Denver

Then & Now

It's hard not to think of the John Denver song "Rocky Mountain High" in tandem with Colorado. And, when you arrive in the Mile High City, not only will you see "high" in the soaring backdrop of gorgeous, snowcapped peaks, but you may feel it as a result of the temporary shortness of breath that comes with the 5,280-foot altitude. At one time, out-of-state travelers arriving at Denver International Airport typically bypassed the metropolis and headed west for a bout of skiing or an excursion into Rocky Mountain National Park. But these days, Denver itself is a destination for those who wish to explore its culture, beauty and vibrant shopping and nightlife scenes.

In fact, Denver has the best of both worlds—urban sophistication complemented by easy access to a stunning alpine playground. Locals providing directions to lost tourists frequently advise, "If you get turned around, just look for the mountains and you'll know which way is west." Denverites work hard in such industries as aerospace, telecommunications and energy re-

search, but they like to play hard, too. A health-conscious lot, residents are reputed to be among the nation's thinnest according to a federal study. While prime recreational pursuits like skiing, hiking and rock climbing are a short drive away, city dwellers need not leave their own backyard to indulge in outdoor fun—they can play some golf in City Park, bike on the Platte River Greenway Trail, ride horseback in Cherry Creek State Park or fish one of the area's reservoirs.

Today sleek skyscrapers stand in place of the bustling frontier town of Denver City, which once lured prospectors into its saloons. Indeed, vestiges of the Gold Rush days remain in the refurbished Victorian storefronts of Larimer Square. Other Old West legacies are preserved at sites like Buffalo Bill's Grave and Museum; Four Mile House, once a stagecoach stop along the Cherokee Trail; and Civic Center Park, where murals honor wilderness pioneers and bronze sculptures depict such subjects as a bronco buster and a Native American. Just as REI's flagship store holds court for adventurists seeking the latest and greatest in technical outdoor gear, Rockmount Ranch Wear—inventors of the iconic snap-button shirt—has been tantalizing both cowboys and city folk with Western apparel since the 1940s.

Several chic urban pockets in addition to gracious neighborhoods have emerged from Denver's Cowtown beginnings. The LoDo (Lower Downtown) district, once chock-full of dilapidated warehouses and unsavory characters, has been revitalized with loft apartments, galleries, and trendy nightspots and restaurants attracting hipsters, young professionals and baby boomers alike. The upscale Cherry Creek area,

The Denver skyline at dusk

(Continued on p. 117.)

Destination Denver

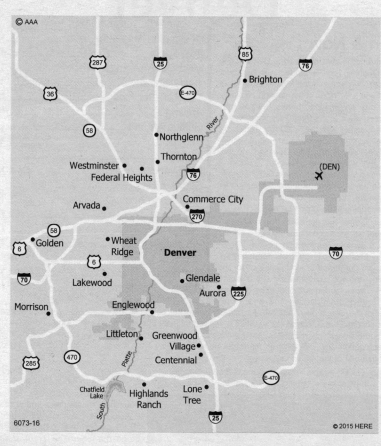

© AAA

This map shows cities in the Denver vicinity where you will find attractions, hotels and restaurants. Cities are listed alphabetically in this book on the following pages.

Fast Facts

ABOUT THE CITY

POP: 600,158 ▪ **ELEV:** 5,280 ft.

MONEY

SALES TAX: Colorado's statewide sales tax is 2.9 percent. Additional fees and taxes bring the total sales tax for the city and county of Denver to 7.62 percent. There also is a 14.75 percent city/county lodging tax, an 11.25 percent rental car tax and an 8.1 percent food and beverage tax.

WHOM TO CALL

EMERGENCY: 911

POLICE (non-emergency): (720) 913-2000

FIRE (non-emergency): (720) 913-2400

TIME AND TEMPERATURE: (303) 337-2500

HOSPITALS: Denver Health Medical Center, (303) 436-6000 ▪ Exempla St. Joseph Hospital, (303) 812-2000 ▪ Porter Adventist Hospital, (303) 778-1955 ▪ Rose Medical Center, (303) 320-2121.

WHERE TO LOOK AND LISTEN

NEWSPAPERS: Denver's major newspaper, *The Denver Post*, is published daily. *The Denver Business Journal* is available weekly.

RADIO: Denver radio station KOA (850 AM) is an all-news/weather station ▪ KCFR (90.1 FM) is a member of National Public Radio.

VISITOR INFORMATION

VISIT DENVER, The Convention & Visitors Bureau's Visitor Information Center: 1600 California St., Denver, CO 80202. **Phone:** (800) 233-6837.

TRANSPORTATION

AIR TRAVEL: Denver International Airport (DEN) is in northeastern Denver. There is a flat fee of $51 for taxi service to downtown. SuperShuttle ($25) provides van service to the downtown area. In addition, the RTD-Sky Ride provides transportation to and from the airport at the Market Street Station for $11 each way.

RENTAL CARS: Most of the numerous car rental agencies serving the Denver area have facilities both downtown and at Denver International Airport. Hertz, (303) 342-3800, offers discounts to AAA members.

RAIL SERVICE: Union Station, 17th and Wynkoop streets, (303) 592-6712, serves Amtrak.

BUSES: Denver's bus terminal complex at 19th and Arapahoe streets houses Greyhound Lines Inc., (303) 293-6555. The Regional Transportation District's Denver-Broomfield-Boulder Bus Service, (303) 299-6000, offers downtown shuttles and local service from the Market Street Station at 16th and Blake.

TAXIS: Cabs in Denver can be requested by phone or, less commonly, hailed on the street. Major companies are Freedom Cab Co., (303) 444-4444 ▪ Metro Taxi Co., (303) 333-3333 ▪ Union Taxi, (303) 922-2222 ▪ and Yellow Cab Co., (303) 777-7777. Taxis are metered, with basic charges that vary from company to company.

PUBLIC TRANSPORTATION: The Regional Transportation District (RTD) operates a fleet of buses in the metropolitan area. In general, buses run 5:30 a.m.-10:30 p.m. One-way fare is $2.25. For information phone (303) 299-6000.

Free shuttle buses known as the 16th Street MallRide traverse the mile-long 16th Street Mall, a pedestrian promenade in downtown Denver.

Light Rail express trains travel from either downtown Denver (D Line/Green) or Union Station (C Line/Orange) to the suburb of Littleton. One-way fare is $2.25-$5, depending on the route. Another line offers service between downtown Denver and many hotels in the Denver Technological Center area along I-25; one-way fares range from $2.75-$4.50.

(Continued from p. 115.)
graced by lovely stone mansions, is a high-end retail mecca sure to inspire the savviest shoppers. Denverites delight in Washington Park's Victorian masterpieces and flower gardens.

Denver also celebrates diversity in its neighborhoods, attractions and events. Far East Center is the hub of the Asian population, Hispanic culture prevails in the La Alma/Lincoln Park sector and the black community thrives in Five Points. While the Black American West Museum pays tribute to the black cowboy—a key figure in helping to mold the West—the Museo de las Americas honors Latin-American history and arts. The Colorado Dragon

Boat Festival's Asian marketplace and Cinco de Mayo Festival's carnival are ethnic celebrations that captivate all races and religions.

Sports fans find bliss at a variety of venues. Sports Authority Field at Mile High is the hallowed gridiron occupied by Denver's beloved Broncos, and Nuggets basketball sets Pepsi Center on fire. Coors Field, home of the Colorado Rockies baseball team, reigns proudly over LoDo and is credited with its rebirth. A sophisticated classical entertainment scene at the Denver Performing Arts Complex mesmerizes opera, ballet and symphony aficionados, while the metro area's robust selection of innovative restaurants and trendy clubs entertain the masses.

Must Do: AAA Editor's Picks

- Savor a heart-thumping panorama from the Mile High City's **Cheesman Park** (1599 E. 8th Ave.)—the view extends 150 miles from Pikes Peak to Mount Evans. Enormous shade trees, wide-open grassy areas and meandering walkways make this urban oasis a great picnic spot. The park's most recognized landmark is the neoclassical Cheesman Pavilion, which serves as both a lovely focal point for photographers and as the setting for events of all types, particularly weddings.

- Relish the excitement of a **Denver Broncos** football game. Fans support their beloved Super Bowl champs by proudly donning orange and blue on game days at Sports Authority Field at Mile High (1701 Bryant St.). If you can't snag game tickets, consider a stadium tour to sneak an inside peek at such features as the TV production area, visiting team's locker room, press box and playing field.

- Stroll through **LoDo** (Lower Downtown), a vibrant enclave dotted with historic Victorians as well as stylish lofts converted from early 20th-century warehouses. Larimer Square (1430 Larimer St.) serves as a gateway to this bustling hub of restaurants, shops, galleries and nightspots.

- Relax and have a cold one—Denver reputedly brews more **beer** than any other city in the world. Visit the Wynkoop Brewing Company (1634 18th St.), one of the nation's largest brewpubs, or sidle over to Great Divide Brewing Co. (2201 Arapahoe St.), a small outfit with seriously good suds (try the Lasso IPA). To learn about the brewing process, head to **Coors Brewing Co.** (13th and Ford sts.) in nearby Golden for a guided tour.

- Explore the **Capitol Hill** neighborhood, once home to *Titanic* survivor Molly Brown and site of opulent Victorian, Tudor and Greek Revival mansions. The 🏛 **State Capitol** (200 E. Colfax Ave.) and Governor's Mansion (400 8th Ave.) are in this district along with the 🏛 **Denver Botanic Gardens** (1007 York St.).

- Lunch in a quaint outdoor café or peruse upscale specialty boutiques in the tree-shaded shopping area known as **Cherry Creek North** (299 Milwaukee St.). If you're happiest in a department store, the adjacent Cherry Creek Shopping Center provides such high-end anchors as Macy's, Neiman Marcus and Nordstrom.

- **Hike, ski, bike or climb**. Cradled in the foothills of the Rockies, Denver offers easy access to recreation areas, ski resorts and trails for an endless supply of year-round fun. And Rocky Mountain National Park is just an hour-and-a-half drive; in winter, cross-country skiing and snowshoeing are the preferred means of navigating the snowy landscape. Warmer months lure hikers, bikers and anglers eager to enjoy their preferred sport amid vibrant wildflowers, starkly beautiful alpine tundra and an amazing backdrop of snow-capped peaks.

- **Drive a scenic route**. You can stop at any one of a number of parks on **The Lariat Loop National Scenic Byway**, which climbs up the Lariat Trail to stunning mountain vistas and descends into Bear Creek Canyon. If time isn't an issue, take the Colorado Heart of the Rockies drive trip on AAA.com to venture more deeply into the mountains.

- Be entertained in the **Denver Performing Arts Complex** (1345 Champa St.), the second largest events center in the United States—its 10 performance venues seat more than 10,000 people. Home to the Denver Center Theatre Company, Opera Colorado, the Colorado Ballet and the Colorado Symphony, this is also the place to catch a Broadway show, a Vegas act or special holiday performances.

- Hunt for souvenirs downtown along the **16th Street Mall**. A free shuttle transports passengers up and down this nicely decorated thoroughfare, which presents a diverse selection of shops and plentiful dining options. Loaf in a comfy chair and sip a cappuccino at The Tattered Cover (1628 16th St.), one of the country's largest independent bookstores.

Stop and smell the flowers at the Denver Botanic Gardens

Denver 1-day Itinerary

AAA editors suggest these activities for a great short vacation experience. Those staying in the area for a longer visit can access a 3-day itinerary at AAA.com/TravelGuide.

Morning

- It's best to rent a car in the Mile High City, especially if you have time to explore the nearby Rocky Mountains. Most downtown attractions have parking facilities, and commercial garages and lots are plentiful. While riding the bus is an option, cabs aren't readily available.

- Spend your first day in Denver exploring the Capitol Hill/Civic Center Park area, chock full of attractions all within walking distance. Get a jump-start by breakfasting at **The Delectable Egg** (1625 Court Pl.), a couple of blocks north of Civic Center Park and home to everything from decadent Belgian waffles to hearty huevos rancheros. If you'd like to obtain maps, brochures and other tourist information, the VISIT DENVER visitor center is nearby at 1600 California St.

- After breakfast, take a guided tour of the ▽ **U.S. Mint** (320 W. Colfax Ave.). Be sure to call first, since fluctuating security levels may restrict access. You'll see the presses in action as they create shiny U.S. coins. You'll also get to ogle an impressive stack of glistening gold bars.

- If the Mint is inaccessible, a nice alternative is the **Denver Firefighters Museum** (1326 Tremont Pl.). Kids are enticed by the child-size firefighting gear, while all ages enjoy viewing the display of fire trucks.

Afternoon

- For lunch spots near the park, try **Watercourse Foods** (837 E. 17th Ave.) for innovative vegetarian selections, or **Pints Pub** (221 W. 13th Ave.) for a burger or robust British fare. You also can have a bite at the café in the ▽ **Denver Art Museum** (100 W. 14th Avenue Pkwy.), your next stop at the park's south end. The museum is comprised of the Hamilton Building and the 24-sided, two-towered North Building, a work of art in itself. African, Asian, pre-Columbian, Native American and contemporary art are among the collections. Be sure to budget some time; you may wish to linger over some of the pieces, which number close to 68,000.

- If you are running short on time, you may opt to visit a smaller attraction, the **Byers-Evans House Museum** (1310 Bannock St.), about a block south of the Denver Art Museum. Guided tours of this 1883 Italianate home provide insight into the lives of the prominent families that lived within over the course of a century.

- Crowned by a gold-leaf dome, the Colorado ▽ **State Capitol** (200 E. Colfax Ave.) overlooks Civic Center Park. As tour guides usher you across elegant marble floors, you'll notice such

The Colorado State Capitol

impressive architectural details as a grand staircase, rose onyx wainscoting and stained-glass renderings of state leaders.

Evening

- For an evening of wining and dining, consider the elegant **Palace Arms** in the Brown Palace Hotel and Spa (321 17th St.), a Denver tradition in the heart of downtown. For a casual, yet cozy approach, try the hotel's **Ship Tavern** for a buffalo burger or some soul-satisfying seafood.

- There's a plentiful array of casual dining options in LoDo (lower downtown), with pricier establishments holding court in the Larimer Square pocket. A fringe benefit of dining in LoDo is that you will be well positioned for some post-dinner fun in this epicenter of Denver nightlife. Wander through the thriving district and poke into one of the trendy art galleries or sizzling nightspots. Many of LoDo's businesses are in fashionably restored warehouses. If you're in the mood for a cold one, Denver supposedly brews more beer than any other city in the world and brims with quality brewpubs. Stop by **Wynkoop Brewing Company** (1634 18th St.), one of the nation's largest. Coors Field also is in LoDo, so baseball fans might be able to catch the Colorado Rockies in action.

- The Denver Coliseum (4600 Humboldt St.) is the staging ground for rodeos, circuses and other evening events. Indoor concert venues include Fillmore Auditorium (1510 Clarkson St.) and the Denver Performing Arts Complex (1345 Champa St.). And the natural sandstone **Red Rocks Park & Amphitheatre** (18300 W. Alameda Pkwy.) is an otherworldly place to see a show.

Top Picks for Kids

Under 13

- Designed to engage kids under age 9, **The Children's Museum of Denver at Marsico Campus** (2121 Children's Museum Dr.) stimulates learning with an array of fun, hands-on exhibits including a real fire truck and an outdoor playground with tunnels, hills and a zipline. The museum even has an area dedicated to newborns and toddlers.

- Lush, open aviaries; cage-less enclosures; and interconnected habitats keep the ▽▽ **Denver Zoo** (2300 Steele St.) interesting for both its diverse animal residents and young visitors. Gorillas and orangutans are zoo stars, as are the elephants, who have their own bridge allowing them to pass between habitats right above visitors' heads.

- Science museums are deadly dull places filled with dusty displays and bored kids, right? Not if you're talking about the ▽▽ **Denver Museum of Nature & Science** (2001 Colorado Blvd.)! Inside dinosaurs stand poised for combat, a whale skeleton seems to swim overhead and silent Egyptian mummies captivate young imaginations. There are plenty of interactive exhibits to occupy antsy children, and the 4th-floor Sky Terrace offers picture postcard views of downtown.

- Ever feel like you're being watched? You will at the ▽▽ **Downtown Aquarium** (700 Water St.), where huge floor-to-ceiling Plexiglas walls look into tanks stocked with a wild assortment of sea life, including sharks, stingrays, eels and anemones. The bug-eyed marine animals swimming by will make you wonder who's watching whom. Highlights include a mermaid show and the Aquarium Restaurant where schools of fish are part of the décor.

Teens

- If your teen will watch anything on TV as long as it's on ESPN, then downtown Denver makes it easy to plan an entertaining itinerary, with three major sporting venues all within a few miles of each other. In addition to the NFL's Broncos, **Sports Authority Field** is home of the **Colorado Sports Hall of Fame Museum** (1701 Bryant St.), where the Centennial State's legendary athletes are celebrated. You can also go behind-the-scenes during the **Sports Authority Field at Mile High Stadium Tours,** which reveals the press boxes, club level and visiting team's locker room.

- At **Coors Field,** major league baseball fans will enjoy a similar backstage peek. **Coors Field Tours** (2001 Blake St.) take visitors into the dugout, suite level and visitor's clubhouse. And if you'd like to peer behind the curtains at **Pepsi Center** where the NBA Denver Nuggets play, **Pepsi Center Tours** (1000 Chopper Cir.) offers that experience.

- Gear up for adventure in Colorado's mountains at **REI Denver** (1416 Platte St.) in the renovated Denver Tramway building. Whether its camping, cycling, hiking, skiing or just about any other recreational pursuit, REI has the latest gear and all-weather clothing. And the store's 47-foot climbing pinnacle will provide a challenge to any daredevil teen who loses interest in shopping.

All Ages

- Denver is a destination for all seasons, with a changing menu of recreational activities throughout the year. In summer, nothing beats a splash in the pool, and **Water World** (1800 W. 89th Ave.) in Federal Heights offers plenty of splashing with thrilling speed slides, low-key lazy rivers, family tube rides, wave pools and play areas for younger children.

- Winter not only means ski season in the Rockies, it's also when Denverites celebrate ▽▽ **Mile High Holidays,** which is held in various locales throughout December. Festivities include a parade, fireworks, wildlife-themed light displays at the **Denver Zoo** and cheerful holiday lights and decorations throughout downtown.

- Only an hour-and-a-half drive from Denver, ▽▽ **Rocky Mountain National Park** preserves some of Colorado's loveliest alpine scenery just waiting to be photographed and added to your family photo album. Trail Ridge Road, the park's main byway, winds high up across the Continental Divide with plenty of turnouts for enjoying the views.

Ride the Conservation Carousel at the Denver Zoo

Arriving
By Car

The main access to Denver from either the east or west is via I-70 and US 40/287; from the north I-25 (US 87); from the south I-25 (US 87) and US 85 (all three are the same highway in Denver: the Valley Highway); and from the northeast by I-76.

Other major freeways are 6th Avenue (US 6) in west-central Denver; SR 470 south, east and west of Denver; I-270 northeast of Denver; and I-225, connecting I-70 in the east with I-25 south of the city.

Getting Around
Street System

All avenues run east-west. Streets generally run north-south except those in the downtown area, where arteries are one-way diagonals with *numbered* streets running southeast-northwest and *named* streets, courts and places running southwest-northeast. The Valley Highway (I-25) is the fastest southeast-northwest route, except during rush hours when it is usually congested.

The main east-west arteries are I-70 in north Denver; Colfax Avenue (US 40), 6th Avenue (US 6) and 8th Avenue in central Denver; Alameda and Evans avenues in south Denver; Hampden Avenue (US 285) in the southern suburbs; and Belleview Avenue and Arapahoe Road in the extreme south.

The main north-south highways are Wadsworth (SR 121), Sheridan (SR 95) and Federal (US 287) boulevards in the west; Broadway, from central downtown south to Englewood and Littleton; University Boulevard (which becomes Josephine and York streets, both one-way, north of E. 1st Avenue) in the southeast; Colorado Boulevard and Monaco Parkway in the east; Havana Street in the eastern suburb of Aurora; and Chambers Road in the extreme east.

Diagonal arteries are I-270 northwest to I-76 and US 36 to Boulder from I-25; I-225, east of I-70, from the southeast suburbs to south I-25; Speer Boulevard, from University Boulevard southeast-northwest to Federal Boulevard; and Leetsdale Drive, southeast from Colorado Boulevard and becoming Parker Road (SR 83) to the extreme southeastern suburbs of Denver.

Broadway, which runs north-south through most of the city, is the dividing line for the east and west designations of all cross streets. It is one-way south from the downtown area to I-25. Nearby Lincoln Street is one-way north from I-25 to the downtown area. Ellsworth Avenue, running east-west through most of the city, is the dividing line for the north and south designations of all cross streets.

The speed limit is generally 30 mph in residential districts and 25 mph in business districts. Right turns on red are permitted, unless otherwise posted, as are left turns on red from the extreme left lane of a one-way street into the extreme left lane of another one-way street.

Rush hours are 7 to 9 and 3:30 to 6. Ramp metering signals help control morning rush-hour traffic

Check out the shopping at the 16th Street Mall

on the south portion of I-25 (the Valley Highway) in Denver and the south and middle portions of I-225 in Aurora.

Parking

Parking is in accordance with posted signs. Downtown on-street parking is metered and limited; the cost is 25c per quarter-hour. Some meters have a "Tow Away Zone" sign; if you park too long, you are subject to a $25 fine. Commercial garages and lots are plentiful downtown, with rates ranging from $1.50 to $5 per hour or $5 to $22 per day.

Shopping

Denver's prime hunting ground for shoppers is concentrated in **LoDo**—that's Denverite speak for Lower Downtown. The Mile High City sprang forth from this 23-block district where Gen. William Larimer settled in 1858, and now it's retail history that's being made amid LoDo's hip urban scene.

The **16th Street Mall**—a tad touristy, yet a definite to-do on your shopping list—serves as LoDo's hub, a pedestrian thoroughfare brimming with retail opportunities and graced with trees, flowers (in summer) and eclectic sculptures. Free shuttle buses whisk passengers along the mall between Union and Civic Center stations, alleviating the hassle and expense of parking.

Traveling south from the Civic Center, you'll encounter **Denver Pavilions** at 500 16th St., an outdoor complex that also indulges shoppers with dining and entertainment options, including [SAVE] Hard Rock Cafe, which offers a collection of rock 'n' roll merchandise. Continuing north, the **Jeweler's Center** in the University Building at 919 16th St. is Denver's "Diamond District," with several floors of jewelry stores and diamond wholesalers that dazzle gem aficionados. The **Shops at Tabor Center,** Arapahoe and Larimer streets, is a three-level, glass-enclosed galleria flanked by the Westin Hotel. Across the street, brick walkways meander through a hodge-podge of stores and outdoor eateries known as **Writer Square.** Near the intersection of 16th and Wazee, cowboys and urbanites alike enjoy perusing the racks of spiffy Western duds at **Rockmount Ranch Wear.** Be sure to stop in the **Tattered Cover Bookstore** at 16th and Wynkoop, where you can settle into a cozy seat by the fireplace and ponder your book purchase.

As the state's colorful history maintains, LoDo gave birth to modern-day Denver, but it was **Larimer Square** that gave birth to LoDo. It all started here with Larimer Street being Denver City's main drag in the 1860s, housing the first bank and post office along with saloons and hotels frequented by weary (and sometimes rowdy) pioneers. Renovated storefronts offer a glimpse into the city's Wild West heyday in addition to providing retail recreation; shops tout a nice selection of crafts, Western wear and jewelry.

The **Lower Downtown Arts District** extends roughly from Larimer to Wynkoop between 14th and 20th streets. Those eager to score that extraordinary conversation piece for their home will have fun browsing the multitude of galleries scattered about, with many situated on Wazee Street. Art objects run the gamut from traditional to modern, including Western-themed paintings, Americana, abstract works, contemporary furnishings and sculpture.

Just south of downtown, art lovers also can check out the **ArtDistrict on Santa Fe Drive** between 7th

Take a tour of the Great Divide Brewing Company

and 10th streets. More than 30 galleries are dotted throughout the area, which also contains a smattering of shops and restaurants. During Art Walks, held the first Friday of every month, the galleries host an open-house wine event from 6-9, offering a pleasant evening with a delightful dose of culture. Antique hounds will find bliss in the shops clustered along 1000-2000 South Broadway, referred to as **Antique Row.** You can spend hours searching for buried treasure in this multi-block enclave, where dealers are often willing to bargain on everything from bric-a-brac to high-quality collectibles.

The Cherry Creek neighborhood, also south of downtown, is Denver's preeminent shopping destination. An outdoor shopping area dubbed **Cherry Creek North** provides a unique mix of boutiques, galleries, coffeehouses and cafes in a setting perfect for strolling. If scouting an indoor complex is more your style, the **Cherry Creek Shopping Center** is one of the Mile High City's best—standouts Neiman Marcus, Nordstrom and Macy's lure those with plenty of cash, but some 150 shops within the posh behemoth usually manage to satisfy all budgets.

The shopping mall is alive and well in Denver's suburbs, and visitors will find no shortage to satisfy their whims. If your top priority is finding great deals, the outlets at **Colorado Mills,** at Colfax and Indiana near I-70 in Lakewood, are the base of operations for bargain hunters. For novelty's sake, you can explore what is reputedly Colorado's largest shopping center, **Park Meadows,** on I-25 at SR 470 and County Line Road in Littleton. Striking a perfect balance between high-end and affordable merchandise, its décor reflects a mountain lodge theme, complete with fireplaces, comfy leather sofas and timber ceilings.

Nightlife

Whether your idea of nighttime entertainment is listening to live music, doing some country line dancing or simply sipping a libation while people-watching, the Mile High City delights with a broad spectrum of offerings. Clubs providing entertainment usually charge a cover fee and may require drink minimums; phone ahead to confirm prices, opening hours, scheduled acts and dress codes.

Denver is said to brew more beer than any other city in the world, and individuals from all walks of life enjoy sampling the suds at the area's quality brewpubs. Try one of the handcrafted ales at **Bull and Bush** (4700 Cherry Creek Dr. S./303-759-0333), a homey neighborhood pub complete with leather sofas and a fireplace, modeled after its namesake in England. If you're interested in learning about the brewing process, take the tour at **Great Divide Brewing Company** (2201 Arapahoe St./303-296-9460); for connoisseurs, the offer of free samples before ordering offsets the rather sterile digs. At **Wynkoop Brewing Company** (1634 18th St./303-297-2700), Denver's first microbrewery and one of the nation's largest, you can play darts or pool in addition to savoring such tempting selections as Cowtown Milk Stout and Patty's Chile

Beer—and the pub grub isn't bad, either. Some aficionados define bliss as a pale ale paired with a tasty mound of nachos at **Rock Bottom Brewery** (1001 16th St./303-534-7616).

Brewpubs aren't the only option for Denver's nightlife scene; a number of comfy spots are perfect for a nightcap or hanging out with friends. The **Whiskey Bar** (2203 Larimer St./303-297-0303) draws an eclectic mix of folks and can be low-key or high-energy, depending on what's happening in downtown that evening; the list of around 115 premium whiskeys has something for every taste. If you prefer to nurse your single-malt scotch—or perhaps an after-dinner brandy or port—in a cigar bar with a more mature, sophisticated clientele, then the **Churchill Bar** (321 17th St./303-297-3111) in the Brown Palace Hotel is just the ticket.

If you come alive on a crowded dance floor, check out one of Denver's clubs. For the alternative rock/emo scene, head to **The Church** (1160 Lincoln St. /303-832-5328), where you'll find 18-year-olds in addition to plenty of professionals in their 30s and 40s gyrating to the beat or having a nibble at the sushi bar. A 20s set wooed by hot DJs and techno/trance music moves to the thump of an unrivaled sound system at **Beta** (1909 Blake St./303-383-1909). All ages with an ear for country music amble up to **Grizzly Rose** (5450 N. Valley Hwy./303-295-1330) for live acts and the free line dance lessons on Sunday night.

Up-and-coming indie bands crank out their latest tunes at **Hi-Dive** (7 S. Broadway/720-570-4500), a friendly, trashy-trendy spot frequented by young, well-behaved hipsters. **Herman's Hideaway** (1578 S. Broadway/303-777-5840), a bare-bones club with a "come as you are" vibe, appeals to an age-diverse blend who like decent (and loud) rock 'n' roll. **Bluebird Theater** (3317 E. Colfax Ave./303-377-1666), an intimate venue that opened as a movie house in 1913, hosts hometown bands as well as emerging national artists; the audience depends on the gig.

Denver also has a healthy jazz and blues scene. For the stereotypical hole-in-the-wall joint serving up red-hot jazz nightly, visit cozy and usually crowded **El Chapultepec** (1962 Market St./303-295-9126), appreciated by all ages for its soulful sounds. You can grab a highly touted burrito or some chili if you're hungry. **DazzleJazz** (930 Lincoln St./303-839-5100), a funky retro lounge with a more mature following, offers a relaxed, supper-club setting and top-notch talent. Known for its smokin' house band, **Jazz at Jacks** (500 16th St./303-433-1000) is another Mile High City favorite, mostly appealing to post-30 Denverites; young professionals patronize Friday's live jazz happy hour.

Big Events

Denver kicks off the year in romping, stomping Old West style at the ⛏ **National Western Stock Show**, held at the **National Western Complex** in early January. Amateur and professional rodeos and livestock demonstrations take place at this event, one of the world's largest in this category. A petting

Celebrate Native American culture at the Denver March Powwow

farm, children's activities and a barn tour add to the down-home fun.

In honor of Denver's mile-high altitude of 5,280 feet above sea level, the city celebrates its burgeoning culinary scene in late February and early March when more than 250 restaurants participate in **Denver Restaurant Week;** multicourse meals come with the "mile high" price tag of $30 per person.

Some 70 tribes honor their legacy at the **Denver March Powwow**, reputedly the nation's largest and most diversified Native American gathering. Jingling bells, beating drums and sweet herbal scents permeate the air of the **Denver Coliseum**, site of this colorful 3-day gathering. Enjoy tribal storytelling, singing and dancing, along with the opportunity to browse arts and crafts booths and sample Fry Bread, a traditional treat.

In early May, Denver celebrates Mexican culture at the ⛏ **Cinco de Mayo Festival. Civic Center Park** comes alive with the rhythm of mariachi and salsa music, supplemented by parades, storytelling and dancing. Food and crafts round out the celebration, which draws a half million folks. Soon after, Civic Center Park also hosts the ⛏ **People's Fair Art and Music Festival** during the first weekend in June. Subject matter ranging from politics and technology to herbal products makes for an interesting mix at this somewhat eclectic neighborhood fest. If face painting, massages, philosophical discussion and New Age pursuits aren't your thing, wander over to one of the several musical venues, ethnic food stands or more than 500 art displays.

⛏ **Cherry Creek Arts Festival,** with some 260 booths adorned with quality arts and crafts, occurs during Fourth of July weekend. When you're not appreciating the goods, savor the entertainment on three performance stages or simply indulge in first-rate people watching at this event. The second weekend of July brings the **Colorado Black Arts Festival** to **City Park.** Dance troupes, a parade, and drum and drill teams entertain visitors, while museum, cultural and gallery exhibits serve to educate. A visual arts pavilion presents works created by African-Americans, including sculpture, painting and photography.

Also in July, the 🐉 **Colorado Dragon Boat Festival** is celebrated in **Sloan's Lake Park.** The event showcases the culture and heritage of the city's Asian Pacific American citizens through performing artists, ethnic cuisine and arts and crafts as well as 2 days of dragon boat races.

Labor Day weekend means it's time for **A Taste of Colorado.** More than 500,000 flock to **Civic Center Park** to honor the region's diverse cultural and Western heritage. This 4-day extravaganza includes culinary delights from local restaurants, top-name musical entertainment, an arts and crafts marketplace and a kiddie carnival. Considered "the Napa Valley of beer" by connoisseurs, Denver upholds that distinction by hosting the **Great American Beer Festival** in October. Brew lovers from throughout the world travel to the 3-day spectacle at the **Colorado Convention Center,** where roughly 3,500 beers are on the sampling roster.

Denver celebrates all of the arts—performing to visual—during **Denver Arts Week.** This November event provides occasion to explore Denver's neighborhood studios and galleries, and its world-class museums and events at the nation's second largest performing arts complex.

🐉 **Mile High Holidays** rounds out the year's event schedule. Festivities, which take place in a variety of locations from late November through the end of January, include fireworks, visits with Santa, sparkling light displays, the Christkindlmarket and Winterfest. Area shops and restaurants, decorated in seasonal finery, add to the merriment by inspiring holiday shoppers.

Sports & Rec

With 300 days of sunshine a year, year-round recreational opportunities are almost unlimited in Denver and the surrounding area and include **swimming, boating, golf, tennis, kayaking, hiking, climbing, fishing, sailing, mountain biking, hunting** and **horseback riding.**

Denver has more than 850 miles of paved trails to accommodate bikers, hikers and joggers. Running along the South Platte River for about 30 miles, the **Greenway Trail** is popular with cyclists—signage depicts the area's history, wildlife and geology. **Cherry Creek Bike Path,** traveling along the creek for some 40 miles to Franktown, is known for its splendid scenery. The 20-mile-long **Clear Creek Bike Path** meanders through neighborhoods and countryside as it follows the creek from the South Platte River to Golden, affording views of high buttes as it nears the town. **Bear Creek Bike Trail** is also 20 miles in length, running along the creek from the South Platte River to Morrison, home to Red Rocks Park and Amphitheatre.

Renowned for its winter sports facilities, Denver offers cold season fun either in the city or just a few minutes away; the closest area for **snow skiing** is within 45 miles. For **ice skating** enthusiasts the Ice Centre, in the Westminster Promenade off US 36 104th Avenue exit in Westminster, offers triple ice sheet facilities. Skate rentals are available. Phone (303) 469-2100 for public skating times.

Auto racing enthusiasts frequent **Bandimere Speedway** in Morrison and **Colorado National Speedway** in Erie.

Note: Policies concerning admittance of children to pari-mutuel betting facilities vary. Phone for information.

At Denver's Coors Field, 2001 Blake St., **baseball** fans can watch the National League **Colorado Rockies;** phone (303) 762-5437 or (800) 388-7625. **Football** season brings the National Football League's **Denver Broncos** to **Sports Authority Field at Mile High,** 1701 Bryant St.; phone (303) 405-1111 or Altitude Tickets at (866) 461-6556. The **Colorado Rapids,** a major league **soccer** team, play at **Dick's Sporting Goods Park,** 6000 Victory Way in Commerce City; phone (303) 405-6066 for ticket information. For **basketball** fans the **Pepsi Center,** 1000 Chopper Cir., hosts the National Basketball Association's **Denver Nuggets;** phone (303) 405-1111 for information or Altitude Tickets at (866) 461-6556.

Sports Authority Field at Mile High

At the Pepsi Center, **hockey** enthusiasts cheer on the National Hockey League's **Colorado Avalanche**, and **lacrosse** lovers catch matches for the National Lacrosse League's **Colorado Mammoth**; for ticket information phone TicketHorse at (866) 461-6556. The area's Major League Lacrosse team, the **Denver Outlaws**, play their games at Sports Authority Field; phone (303) 688-5297. College sports fans have the opportunity to watch the **University of Denver Pioneers** play basketball, soccer, lacrosse and hockey at **Ritchie Center,** 2240 E. Buchtel Blvd.; for ticket information phone (303) 871-2336.

Performing Arts

The **Denver Performing Arts Complex,** occupying four blocks at Curtis and 14th streets, is the second largest performing arts center in the nation. Its 10 performance venues seat a total of more than 10,000 people. During the main concert season from October through May, the **Colorado Symphony Orchestra** usually performs weekly in the **Boettcher Concert Hall; Opera Colorado** and the **Colorado Ballet** perform in the **Ellie Caulkins Opera House.** "The Ellie," as it's called by the locals, features an electronic screen on the back of its seats from which operagoers may view the current performance's text in eight languages.

The **Temple Hoyne Buell Theatre** features Broadway productions and ballet. The **Helen Bonfils Theatre Complex** hosts the **Denver Center Theatre Company.** The 12-acre complex also includes the **Galleria Theater.**

Free band concerts are held in various city parks from May to September. **Fiddlers Green Amphitheater,** in Greenwood Village south of Denver, also has a summer concert series. A little farther out near Morrison, the natural amphitheater in **Red Rocks Park and Amphitheatre***(see Morrison p. 239)* offers summer musical entertainment as well as films.

Family entertainment can be found at the **Paramount Theatre,** downtown at 16th and Glenarm streets. If you prefer drama or comedy while dining, try a dinner theater.

■ ATTRACTIONS

BABI YAR PARK, 1 blk. s. on Havana St. from jct. with Parker Rd. (SR 83), with entry on Yale Ave., is a 26-acre memorial to the 200,000 people killed by the Nazis in Kiev, Ukraine, beginning in 1941. Black granite stones mark the entrance to the park, which serves as a place of remembrance. **Hours:** Daily 5 a.m.-11 p.m. **Cost:** Free. **Phone:** (720) 913-1311.

BLACK AMERICAN WEST MUSEUM, 3091 California St. across from the 30th and Downing Light Rail Station, is in the former home of the first female African-American doctor in Colorado, Justina L. Ford, who began practice in Denver in 1902. This museum houses changing exhibits and displays pertaining to the history of African-American soldiers, pioneers, mountain men, miners and cowboys in the Old West.

Time: Allow 30 minutes minimum. **Hours:** Fri.-Sat. 10-2, or by appointment. Closed Jan. 1, Thanksgiving and Christmas. **Cost:** $10; $9 (ages 65+); $8 (students with ID); $6 (ages 0-12). **Phone:** (720) 242-7428.

BYERS-EVANS HOUSE MUSEUM, near Civic Center Park at 1310 Bannock St., reflects the character of two important Denver families. *Rocky Mountain News* publisher William Byers built the home in 1883 and sold it in 1889 to William Gray Evans, a transportation executive. The elegant two-story Victorian house is restored to reflect the years 1912-24; it contains original Evans family furnishings. The Byers-Evans House Gallery features art related to Denver and the Rocky Mountain West.

The interior of the house can be seen only by guided tour; self-guiding tours are not available. **Time:** Allow 1 hour minimum. **Hours:** Museum Mon.-Sat. 10-4. Guided tours depart at 10:30, 11:30, 12:30, 1:30 and 2:30 (also 3:30 May-Aug.). **Cost:** Gallery free. House tour $6; $5 (ages 65+ and students with ID); $4 (ages 6-12). **Phone:** (303) 620-4933. GT

CHEESMAN PARK, 8th Ave. and Franklin St., offers a panorama that on clear days extends 150 miles from Pikes Peak to Mount Evans. **Hours:** Daily 5 a.m.-11 p.m. **Cost:** Free. **Phone:** (720) 913-1311.

THE CHILDREN'S MUSEUM OF DENVER AT MARSICO CAMPUS is at I-25 exit 211 and 23rd Ave. This is a hands-on environment, geared to newborns through age 8 and their grown-ups, where youngsters can scramble up a 3-story climbing structure, become an artist in a 2300 square-foot gallery, build rockets or power a hot air balloon. Kids also can crawl through an ant tunnel, flash the lights on a real fire truck, shop in a farmers market or explore the science of bubbles.

Hours: Mon.-Fri. 9-4 (also Wed. 4-7:30), Sat.-Sun. 10-5. Closed Jan. 1, Easter, Thanksgiving, Christmas Eve and Christmas. **Cost:** $13 (ages 2-59); $11 (age 1 and ages 60+); free (ages 0-1). **Phone:** (303) 361-0111.

CITY PARK is bounded by 17th and 23rd aves. and York St. and Colorado Blvd. Gardens, pools, fountains and monuments adorn what was a sagebrush flat. Band concerts are presented in the summer. **Hours:** Daily 5 a.m.-11 p.m. **Cost:** Free. **Phone:** (720) 913-1311.

Denver Museum of Nature & Science, 2001 Colorado Blvd. in City Park, is one of the largest natural history museums in the country. Hands-on activities in the Expedition Health exhibit demonstrate how the body functions and changes. Prehistoric Journey contains a working fossil lab as well as exhibits of the sights, sounds and vegetation existing on Earth millions of years ago.

Other exhibits feature wildlife dioramas, Egyptian mummies, Native American cultures, gems and minerals, and sections devoted to the South Pacific islands, Australia and Africa. Explore galaxies at the

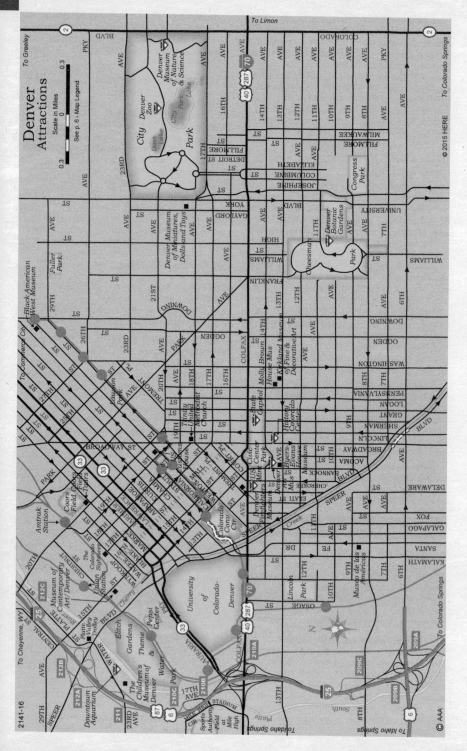

Denver Attractions

Scale in Miles

See p. 6 - Map Legend

0.3 0 0.3

© 2015 HERE

© AAA

2141-16

Space Odyssey exhibit and take a 3-D look at the stars at Gates Planetarium. Traveling exhibits are featured frequently at the three-story museum. The Phipps IMAX Theater and Gates Planetarium present a variety of shows; phone ahead for schedule.

Time: Allow 2 hours minimum. **Hours:** Museum daily 9-5. Closed Christmas. **Cost:** Museum $14.95; $11.95 (ages 65+); $9.95 (ages 3-18). IMAX theater $9.95; $7.95 (ages 3-18 and 65+). Combination ticket for museum and IMAX theater $21.95; $17.95 (ages 65+); $15.95 (ages 3-18). Combination ticket for museum and planetarium $19.95; $15.95 (ages 65+); $13.95 (ages 3-18). All three attractions $26.95; $21.95 (ages 65+); $19.95 (ages 3-18). Reservations are recommended for IMAX and planetarium shows. **Phone:** (303) 370-6000.

Denver Zoo, in City Park at 2300 Steele St., emphasizes the use of natural habitats to showcase their captivating residents. Rare animals such as Amur tigers, endangered cheetahs and greater one-horned rhinos thrive in this spacious setting, which represents more than 650 species. Dramatically landscaped special exhibits provide realistic homes for inhabitants, providing an entertaining and educational viewing experience for all ages. Kids are enticed by the Conservation Carousel, featuring wooden animal carvings, and the natural gas-powered Pioneer Train, which takes passengers for a brief spin through a shady stretch of the grounds.

Black and grizzly bears lumber amid replicated craggy boulders at Bear Mountain, while birds fly freely in unencumbered air space at Bird World. Monkeys frolic and climb twisting vines while gorillas lazily nap in swinging hammocks at Primate Panorama, where you'll also spot orangutans, mandrills and lemurs. The curious can wander past settings enhanced with caves, mangroves, waterfalls and coral reefs at Tropical Discovery, the site of one of the world's largest indoor Komodo dragon exhibits.

At Toyota Elephant Passage, observe elephants, rhinos, tapirs and fishing cats from a village in tropical Asia, stroll a boardwalk under trees populated by acrobatic gibbons or visit one of the exhibits exploring the culture and challenges of village life in rural Asia. Predator Ridge provides a glimpse into African wildlife and presents an opportunity to learn about the continent's chief predators—lions, wild dogs and hyenas—with up-close views and educational material. Zookeepers can be seen interacting with wild dogs and lions daily. The Pachyderm Habitat's hippos intrigue zoo visitors, as does the camel exhibit with its one- and two-humped occupants. In addition to observing the nearly 4,000 animals cared for at the zoo, you'll also encounter a variety of bronze sculptures interspersed throughout the grounds. **Time:** Allow 1 hour minimum. **Hours:** Daily 9-6, Mar.-Oct.; 10-5, rest of year. Last admission 1 hour before closing. **Cost:** Mar.-Oct. $17; $14 (ages 65+); $12 (ages 3-11). Rest of year $13; $11 (ages 65+); $9 (ages 3-11). Ages 0-16 must be with an adult. **Phone:** (303) 337-1400. 🍽 🎢

COLORADO SPORTS HALL OF FAME MUSEUM is at 1701 Bryant St., Suite 500, at Gate 1 on the west side of Sports Authority Field. The Hall of Fame honors the state's leading athletes, coaches and sports leaders. Exhibits include a timeline; photographs; biographies of people in sports; information about sports conditioning; the achievements of sportswomen; information about the Denver Broncos and a kids play area. **Time:** Allow 1 hour minimum. **Hours:** Mon.-Sat. 10-3, June-Aug.; Thurs.-Sat. 10-3, rest of year. **Cost:** Free. **Phone:** (720) 258-3888.

Sports Authority Field at Mile High Stadium Tours depart from the Colorado Sports Hall of Fame Museum at 1701 Bryant St., Suite 500, at Gate 1 on the west side of the field. A 75-minute, half-mile walking tour of the Denver Broncos' stadium allows participants access to the club level, the visitors' locker room, the perimeter of the field and the press boxes. **Time:** Allow 1 hour, 15 minutes minimum. **Hours:** Tours are given Mon.-Sat. on the hour 10-2, June-Aug.; Thurs.-Sat. on the hour 10-2, rest of year. Closed major holidays and the day before any Broncos home game. **Cost:** $15; $12 (65+ and ages 5-12). Reservations are required. **Phone:** (720) 258-3000 or (720) 258-3888.

COORS FIELD TOURS is at 2001 Blake St.; tours begin at Gate D. Guided tours offer a behind-the-scenes look at the home of the Colorado Rockies major league baseball team. Highlights of the tour include the field, rooftop, dugout, press box, visitors' clubhouse, suite level and club level. The ballpark was built to fit in with the historic downtown area and uses the Rocky Mountain scenery as a backdrop.

Time: Allow 1 hour, 30 minutes minimum. **Hours:** On game days, tours are given Mon.-Sat. at 10 and noon, Apr.-Sept. (at 10 and 2 on days with evening games scheduled); Mon., Wed. and Fri.-Sat. at noon and 2, rest of year. Tours are not available when afternoon games are scheduled and are limited when evening games take place. **Cost:** $10; $8 (ages 55+); $7 (ages 3-12). Reservations are recommended. **Phone:** (303) 762-5437.

CRANMER PARK, E. 1st Ave. and Bellaire St., has a Chinese sundial and a terrazzo profile of the Continental Divide. **Hours:** Daily 5 a.m.-11 p.m. **Cost:** Free. **Phone:** (720) 913-1311.

DENVER ART MUSEUM is at the s. end of Civic Center on 14th Avenue Pkwy., 1 blk. w. of Broadway. More than 1 million faceted glass tiles cover the 24-sided North Building, designed by Gio Ponti. The Frederic C. Hamilton Building, designed by Daniel Libeskind, is clad in titanium and resembles the jagged peaks of the nearby Rocky Mountains. A glass-enclosed bridge stretching across 13th Avenue connects the buildings.

The museum has a collection of more than 70,000 art objects from around the world with exhibits of American, Asian, European, Native American, pre-Columbian, Spanish Colonial, Western, African, Oceanic and modern and contemporary works. Additional

Downtown Aquarium

galleries focus on photography, architecture, design and graphics, and textile art. Artists represented include Albert Bierstadt, Alexander Calder, Mary Cassatt, Edgar Degas, Georgia O'Keeffe, Henri Matisse, Claude Monet, Pablo Picasso, Frederic Remington, Charles Russell and Andy Warhol.

The Hamilton Building's modern and contemporary art display includes massive paintings and sculptures enhanced with vibrant hues and composed of a variety of materials, including wood, plaster, fiberglass, steel and vinyl. Masks of all sizes, oils on canvas and enchanting acrylic works characterize the African art collection, while Yipwon spirit, pig and tree-fern figurines capture the imagination in the Oceanic art section.

The North Building's Western American collection entices with works depicting dramatic landscapes, the Gold Rush and the Hispanic West. Buddhist sculptures and bronzes, a Japanese Samurai suit of armor and a portion of a wooden palace facade can be discovered in the Asian galleries; the Everyday Traditions exhibit has such captivating features as a monkey god from India, a guardian lion from Thailand and other colorful works. Ceremonial dress, jewelry, basketry, totems, an 1884 tipi, and elaborate pottery and weavings intrigue all ages on the Native American floor. **Hours:** Tues.-Sun. 10-5 (also Fri. 5-8). Closed Thanksgiving and Christmas. **Cost:** $13; $10 (ages 65+, military with ID and college students with ID); free (ages 0-18). An additional $5 is charged for special exhibitions. **Phone:** (720) 865-5000. GT ⓘ

DENVER BOTANIC GARDENS, 1007 York St. between Cheesman and Congress parks, covers 24 acres. More than 45 formal gardens include rare and endangered plants from around the world, plants native to Colorado, those brought to the state by pioneers, Great Plains grasses and wildflowers, bristlecone and ponderosa pines, an outstanding orchid collection and the Monet Pool, with flowers and water lilies inspired by the French Impressionist.

Rock alpine, herb, romantic and Asian gardens also are displayed. The domed Boettcher Memorial Tropical Conservatory contains thousands of tropical and subtropical plants. A myriad of holiday lights illuminate the gardens during ⚡ Blossoms of Light in December.

Time: Allow 1 hour minimum. **Hours:** Daily 9-9, Mother's Day-Sept. 27; 9-5, rest of year. Some extended hours during Blossoms of Light. Schedule and admission rates subject to change; phone ahead for updates. Closed Jan. 1, Thanksgiving and Christmas. **Cost:** $12.50; $9.50 (ages 65+ and military with ID); $9 (ages 3-15 and students with ID). **Phone:** (720) 865-3500, or (720) 865-3585 for Information Desk. ⓘ

DENVER FIREFIGHTERS MUSEUM is at 1326 Tremont Pl.; take I-25 exit 210, .5 mi. e. on Colfax Ave., .1 mi. n. on Glenarm St. and s. on 14th St. to Tremont Pl. Presented in a 1909 firehouse, the collection features artifacts, tools and photographs, from 1866 to the present, that tell the history of the Denver Fire Department.

Hands-on activities for children and adults focus on fire safety and prevention. **Time:** Allow 30 minutes minimum. **Hours:** Mon.-Sat. 10-4. Closed major holidays. **Cost:** $6; $5 (ages 65+ and students with ID); $4 (ages 2-12). **Phone:** (303) 892-1436.

DENVER MUSEUM OF MINIATURES, DOLLS AND TOYS is at 1880 Gaylord St. The museum is in the historic Pearce-McAllister Cottage, built in 1899 and designed in Dutch Colonial Revival style. The collection includes more than 10,000 items from 1680 to the present.

Displays include artisan-created miniature replicas, handmade wooden toys, manufactured metal and plastic cars, historic dollhouses, dolls and teddy bears. Changing exhibits also are featured. **Hours:** Wed.-Sat. 10-4, Sun. 1-4. Closed major holidays. **Cost:** $6; $5 (ages 62+); $4 (ages 5-16). **Phone:** (303) 322-1053.

DOWNTOWN AQUARIUM, at 700 Water St., is an underwater adventure featuring more than 500 species of fascinating sea creatures, including sharks, snakes, otters, sea anemones, birds and Sumatran tigers. The Aquarium Adventure exhibit tells a tale of various ecosystems, including wetlands, oceans, deserts, barrier reefs, beaches, rain forests and mangrove-fringed lagoons. Scuba and snorkeling programs allow participants to swim with the fish and dive with the sharks. The interactive Stingray Reef touch tank as well as naturalistic sounds and settings complete the experience. The mermaid-themed Under the Sea is an underwater presentation about the environment. For an additional fee, educational programs and tours led by marine biologists are available.

Time: Allow 1 hour, 30 minutes minimum. **Hours:** Sun.-Thurs. 10-9, Fri.-Sat. 10-9:30. Closed Christmas. **Cost:** $18.99; $17.99 (ages 65+); $12.99 (ages 3-11). **Parking:** $7. **Phone:** (303) 561-4450. [11]

SAVE **ELITCH GARDENS THEME & WATER PARK,** downtown off I-25 exit 212A (Speer Blvd. S.), has more than 50 rides, shows and attractions, including roller coasters, family rides, an area dedicated to rides especially for children, the Island Kingdom Water Park, gardens and games. Seasonal festivals include Fright Fest weekends in October.

Hours: Park open Mon.-Thurs. 10-7, late May-Sept. 1; Fri.-Sun. 10-10, rest of year. Water Park daily 10-6, Memorial Day weekend-late Aug. Phone ahead to confirm schedule. **Cost:** $46.99; $31.99 (under 48 inches tall, ages 62+ and restricted use); free (ages 0-3). **Parking:** $15 per private vehicle. **Phone:** (303) 595-4386. [11]

FORNEY MUSEUM OF TRANSPORTATION is off I-70 exit 275B (Brighton Blvd.), then 2 blks. s. to 4303 Brighton Blvd., near the Denver Coliseum. The museum features more than 100 antique and classic cars, carriages, bicycles and other vehicles. Rail equipment and hundreds of die-cast models also are on display. Notable exhibits include "Big Boy," said to be the world's largest successfully operated steam locomotive at 134 feet long and weighing more than 1 million pounds; Amelia Earhart's first car; Denver's only surviving cable-operated trolley; and an 1817 Draisienne, one of the first bicycles ever made.

Time: Allow 1 hour minimum. **Hours:** Mon.-Sat. 10-4, Sun. noon-4. Closed New Year's Eve, Jan. 1, Thanksgiving, Christmas Eve and Christmas Day. Closed July 4. **Cost:** $9.75; $7.75 (ages 65+); $5 (ages 3-12). **Phone:** (303) 297-1113.

FOUR MILE HISTORIC PARK, at 715 S. Forest St. in s.e. Denver, is a 12-acre farm and the site of Denver's oldest standing structure, Four Mile House. Built of hand-hewn pine logs in 1859, the clapboard house reflects the era when it served as a ranch and stage stop along the Cherokee Trail. Barns have been reconstructed to the original design specifications. Horse-drawn wagon rides are offered throughout the year, while quilters, seamstresses and blacksmiths demonstrate their craft on the first Friday of each month.

Gold panning and guided tour of the historic house included with admission. **Hours:** Guided 45-minute tours depart on the half-hour Wed.-Fri. noon-4, Sat.-Sun. 10-4, Apr.-Sept.; Wed.-Sun. noon-4, rest of year. Last tour begins at 2:30. **Cost:** Park $5; $4 (ages 65+ and military with ID); $3 (ages 7-17). Park admission is free first Friday of every month. **Phone:** (720) 865-0800.

GEM **HISTORY COLORADO CENTER** is at 1200 Broadway near Civic Center Park. A destination for exploration, self-discovery, inspiration and fun, the center is designed to ignite the imaginations of all ages about Colorado history. Exhibits share the stories and spirit of Colorado's people over the past 10,000 years. The central exhibit, Living West, includes nearly 200 Mesa Verde artifacts and presentations given in the Dust Bowl Theater. High-tech and hands-on highlights include soaring off a virtual ski jump, taking a virtual ride across the plains in a Model T and pushing an interactive "time machine" on a 60-foot floor map of Colorado. Public programs, activities, and special events for children, families and adults are also available. **Time:** Allow 1 hour, 30 minutes minimum. **Hours:** Daily 10-5. Stephen H. Hart Library Mon.-Sat. 10-5. Closed Jan. 1, Thanksgiving and Christmas. **Cost:** $12; $10 (ages 13-22 with student ID and 65+); $8 (ages 6-12). **Phone:** (303) 447-8679.

KIRKLAND MUSEUM OF FINE & DECORATIVE ART, 1311 Pearl St., is housed in an expanded 1911 Arts and Crafts-style building with two windows by Frank Lloyd Wright. An extensive decorative arts collection of more than 3,500 works, including examples from the Arts & Crafts movement through the Post-Modern period is on display. Works by Colorado painters, ceramists, sculptors and furniture designers as well as works by painter Vance Kirkland are featured, and range from traditional/realist to abstract.

Note: The museum will close after May 1, 2016, as it prepares to move to a new location near the Denver Art Museum. It is scheduled to reopen sometime in 2017. Phone ahead for updates. **Hours:** Tues.-Sun. 11-5. Guided tours are given Wed.-Sat. at 1:30. Closed major holidays. **Cost:** $8; $6 (ages 62+ and students or teachers with ID). Ages 13-17 must be accompanied by an adult. Ages 0-12 are not permitted. **Phone:** (303) 832-8576. [GT]

LOOKOUT MOUNTAIN PARK—see Golden p. 200.

MOLLY BROWN HOUSE MUSEUM, 2 blks. s. of Colfax Ave. at 1340 Pennsylvania St., was the home of Margaret Tobin Brown, who was known for her political activism and philanthropy as well as for surviving the *Titanic* disaster. The socially prominent Mrs. Brown moved into the home in 1889 after her husband struck gold in Leadville. She was later immortalized in the musical "The Unsinkable Molly Brown." Built in 1889, the house has been restored to its original Victorian splendor.

Hours: Guided 45-minute tours are offered every 30 minutes Tues.-Sat. 10-3:30, Sun. noon-3:30 (also Mon. 10-3:30, June 15-Aug. 15). Closed major holidays. **Cost:** $8; $7 (ages 65+ and military and students with ID); $5 (ages 6-12). **Phone:** (303) 832-4092. [GT]

MUSEO DE LAS AMÉRICAS, 861 Santa Fe Dr., houses changing historical, cultural and visual arts exhibits from Latin America and includes works by regional artists. The museum aims to educate visitors about the diversity of Latin American art and culture, from ancient to contemporary. **Time:** Allow 30 minutes minimum. **Hours:** Tues.-Sat. noon-5 (also 5-9 first Fri. of each month). Closed major holidays and during exhibit installations. Phone ahead to confirm schedule. **Cost:** $5; $3 (ages 66+ and students with ID); free (ages 0-12 and first Fri.). **Phone:** (303) 571-4401.

MUSEUM OF CONTEMPORARY ART/DENVER is at 1485 Delgany St. at jct. with 15th St. Designed by noted architect David Adjaye, the environmentally sustainable glass-walled facility has five exhibition spaces that feature contemporary works by both established and emerging artists. A garden on the roof provides a scenic view of downtown Denver.

On-street parking is limited; visitors are encouraged to use public transportation. **Time:** Allow 1 hour minimum. **Hours:** Tues.-Fri. noon-7, Sat.-Sun. 10-5. Closed Jan. 1 and Christmas. **Cost:** $8; $5 (ages 65+ and military with ID); $free (ages 0-18); $1 (ages 7-11). Cash only. **Parking:** $6 for 2 hours weekdays; $5 weekends. **Phone:** (303) 298-7554. [🍴]

PEPSI CENTER TOURS depart from 1000 Chopper Cir. The All Access VIP Tour of Pepsi Center takes visitors behind the scenes of the home arena for the NBA Denver Nuggets, the NHL Colorado Avalanche and the National Lacrosse League Colorado Mammoth. The arena hosts hundreds of events throughout the year, and tour guides explain how the multi-purpose facility can be converted from ice rink to basketball court to concert venue. **Time:** Allow 1 hour, 30 minutes minimum. **Hours:** Mon., Wed. and Fri. at 10, noon and 2, Sat. at 10 and noon, mid-Oct. through early May; Mon., Wed. and Fri. at 10, noon and 2, rest of year. Closed major holidays. Phone ahead to confirm schedule. **Cost:** $10; $8 (ages 2-12 and 55+); $5 (military with ID). **Phone:** (303) 405-8556. [GT]

RED ROCKS PARK & AMPHITHEATRE—see Morrison p. 239.

[GEM] **STATE CAPITOL,** between E. 14th and E. Colfax aves. facing Lincoln St., is a 1908 neoclassic building that resembles the U.S. Capitol in Washington, D.C. The imposing structure is built of Colorado granite and topped with a gold-leafed dome, which commemorates the state's mid-19th-century gold rush days. The floors are made of marble from the Yule Marble Quarry in Marble, Colo. On display is the Women's Gold tapestry, honoring 18 Colorado women who were instrumental in the settlement of the state.

The interior wainscoting and pillar facings are of Colorado rose onyx. In keeping with Denver's identity as the Mile High City, the 13th step on the building's west entrance measures exactly 1 mile above sea level. In addition to the above highlights, guided tours provide insights into Colorado's history and the state's legislative process.

Note: Phone ahead for information about security procedures. **Time:** Allow 1 hour minimum. **Hours:** Guided tours of the Capitol including the dome are given on the hour Mon.-Fri. 10-3. Closed major holidays. **Cost:** Free. **Phone:** (303) 866-2604 for information about the Capitol and for building tours. [GT]

TRINITY UNITED METHODIST CHURCH is at 1820 Broadway opposite the Brown Palace Hotel. The 1888 church, designed by the state's first licensed architect, Robert Roeschlaub, features original stained-glass windows designed by Healy and Millet of Chicago. A Roosevelt organ with 4,275 pipes dominates the sanctuary. Sixty-six small lights above the organ symbolize the 66 books of the Bible. The church's congregation was established in 1859 as Denver's first church. Visitors enter through the church office. **Time:** Allow 30 minutes minimum. **Hours:** Mon.-Fri. 8-4:30. Guided tours are given Sun. at 12:15. **Cost:** Free. **Phone:** (303) 839-1493.

[GEM] **U.S. MINT** is at 320 W. Colfax Ave.; the tour entrance is on Cherokee St. Built 1898-1904, the building reflects its turn-of-the-20th-century grandeur; the Grand Hallway has murals, nine stained glass chandeliers and marble floors and walls. Guided tours enable participants to see a display of solid gold bars and the presses that produce up to 24 million coins each day.

Note: Visitors must arrive 30 minutes before their scheduled tour. Coin production is not guaranteed to occur during tours; phone ahead for schedule. Visitors may only bring a palm-sized wallet or change

Museum of Contemporary Art/Denver

purse; handbags, purses, fanny packs, tote bags, strollers, food, drink, tobacco products, backpacks, lighters, matches, personal grooming items and weapons—including pocket knives and personal protective devices—are not permitted. Storage for personal items is not available. Pets are not allowed. **Time:** Allow 1 hour minimum. **Hours:** Guided tours are offered every 90 minutes Mon.-Thurs. 8-3:30. Closed federal holidays. **Cost:** Free. Reservations must be made online at the United States Mint website. **Phone:** (303) 405-4761. GT

WASHINGTON PARK, extending along Downing St., has tennis, croquet and horseshoe courts, flower gardens, two lakes, lawn bowling, jogging paths, boating, bicycle and walking trails, fishing and a recreation center with a swimming pool. Tennis and basketballs courts as well as a playground also are available. **Hours:** Daily 5 a.m.-11 p.m. **Cost:** Park free. Fees apply to recreational activities. **Phone:** (720) 865-3400 or (720) 913-1311.

WATER WORLD—see Federal Heights p. 186.

WINGS OVER THE ROCKIES AIR & SPACE MUSEUM is .25 mi. e. on 1st Ave., then s. on Roslyn St. to 7711 E. Academy Blvd. (Hangar No. 1 on the former Lowry Air Force Base). The museum displays more than three dozen historic airplanes and space vehicles.

Included are one of only four B-1A bombers ever built, a B-18 Bolo, five Century series fighters and a Star Wars X-Wing fighter. Aviation memorabilia as well as exhibits about the science of flight and Lowry history are featured. **Time:** Allow 1 hour minimum. **Hours:** Mon.-Sat. 10-5, Sun. noon-5. Closed Jan. 1, Easter, Thanksgiving, and December 24-25 and 31. Closed major holidays. **Cost:** $11; $9 (ages 65+ and military with ID); $6 (ages 4-12). **Phone:** (303) 360-5360.

Sightseeing

With aspects both Victorian and modern, Denver and its environs offer much to explore. Information about possible sightseeing itineraries can be obtained at VISIT DENVER, The Convention & Visitors Bureau's Visitor Information Center *(see The Fast Facts box)* and from AAA Colorado.

Gray Line offers a choice of sightseeing tours of Denver and the surrounding area; phone (303) 289-2841 or (800) 348-6877. Blue Moon Carriages, Denver Carriage and Irish Rose Carriages are operators that offer horse-drawn carriage tours of the city; phone (303) 489-7299, (303) 271-1065, or (720) 883-5325, respectively.

Driving Tours

THE LARIAT LOOP NATIONAL SCENIC BYWAY links a number of parks and attractions in the foothills west of Denver. Beginning at US 6 w. of SR 470, the tour passes through Golden and follows the Lariat Trail up Lookout Mountain *(see Golden p. 200),* then continues south along mountaintops via Lookout Mountain Road. After descending to Evergreen, the route follows Bear Creek Canyon to Morrison, goes north to Red Rocks Park and Amphitheatre and Dinosaur Ridge *(see Morrison p. 239),* then back to US 6 and Golden. The 40-mile route is marked by blue and white Scenic Byway columbine signs.

Brochures with maps are available at the Golden Visitors Center, the Buffalo Bill Museum on Lookout Mountain, Dinosaur Ridge in Morrison, Hiwan Homestead Museum in Evergreen *(see attraction listings)* and other sites along the Loop. **Phone:** (720) 971-9649.

Industrial Tours

HAMMOND'S CANDIES FACTORY TOURS is n. off I-25 exit 215 (58th Ave.), then 2 blks. e. to the Mapleton Distribution Center at 5735 N. Washington St. This candy factory, founded in 1920, produces old-fashioned handmade hard candy and chocolates. Guided factory tours highlight the production process. **Time:** Allow 30 minutes minimum. **Hours:** Tours are given Mon.-Fri. every 30 minutes 9-3, Sat. 10-3. Closed Jan. 1, Memorial Day, Labor Day, Thanksgiving, Christmas and day after Christmas. **Cost:** Free. **Phone:** (303) 333-5588, ext. 110.

Trolley and Van Tours

THE COLORADO SIGHTSEER adventure tours depart from downtown hotels and Union Station. Adventures range from a 5-hour Foothills Tour that includes stops at the Coors Brewery and Red Rocks Park and Amphitheatre to a 10-hour journey through Rocky Mountain National Park. Other tours include the Ultimate Mountain Trip, Pikes Peak Region Tour, Rocky Mountain Gold Tour and Historic Denver Tour. Ski area tours also are available. Customized tours can be arranged.

Hours: Daily 7-7. Ski tours are available Nov. 15-Apr. 15. **Cost:** Fare $40-$95; free (ages 0-4). Reservations are required. **Phone:** (303) 423-8200.

PLATTE VALLEY TROLLEY can be boarded at Confluence Park, from behind the REI store at 1416 Platte St., the Downtown Aquarium or The Children's Museum of Denver at Marsico Campus. Narrated 25-minute tours traverse former railroad tracks on a vintage trolley that is a reproduction of an early 1900s open-sided "breezer" streetcar. The 3-mile riverfront route travels through parkland along the South Platte Greenway.

Time: Allow 30 minutes minimum. **Hours:** Departures Thurs.-Mon. every half-hour 11-4:30 (weather permitting), Memorial Day weekend-Labor Day. Phone ahead to confirm schedule. **Cost:** Fare $5; $2 (ages 4-12); free (ages 0-3). **Phone:** (303) 458-6255. GT

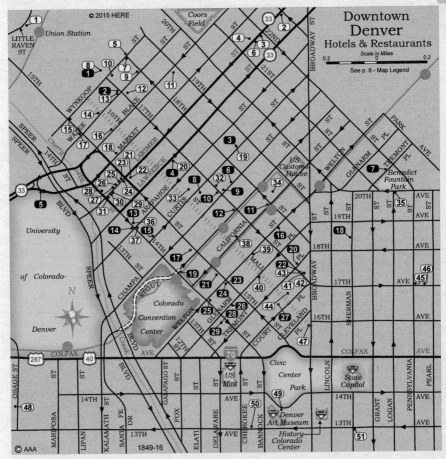

Downtown Denver

This index helps you "spot" where approved hotels and restaurants are located on the corresponding detailed maps. Hotel daily rate range is for comparison only. Restaurant price range is a combination of lunch and/or dinner. Turn to the listing page for more detailed rate and price information and consult display ads for special promotions.

DOWNTOWN DENVER

Map Page	Hotels	Diamond Rated	Rate Range	Page
1 this page	The Crawford Hotel	▼▼▼▼	$289-$529	145
2 this page	The Oxford Hotel	▼▼▼	$209-$409 SAVE	148
3 this page	The Ritz-Carlton, Denver	▼▼▼▼	$329-$449 SAVE	148
4 this page	The Westin Denver Downtown	▼▼▼▼	$149-$399 SAVE	149
5 this page	SpringHill Suites by Marriott Denver Downtown	▼▼▼	$142-$337	149
6 this page	Residence Inn by Marriott Denver City Center	▼▼▼	$132-$339	148
7 this page	Queen Anne Urban Bed & Breakfast	▼▼▼	Rates not provided	148
8 this page	Courtyard by Marriott Denver Downtown	▼▼▼	$143-$381	145
9 this page	Hotel Monaco Denver	▼▼▼	Rates not provided SAVE	147
10 this page	Renaissance Denver Downtown City Center	▼▼▼	$164-$400 SAVE	148

DOWNTOWN DENVER (cont'd)

Map Page	Hotels (cont'd)	Diamond Rated	Rate Range	Page
11 p. 133	Denver Marriott City Center	◇◇◇	$144-$376	146
12 p. 133	**Magnolia Hotel-Downtown Denver**	◇◇◇	$129-$499 [SAVE]	148
13 p. 133	**Four Seasons Hotel Denver**	◇◇◇◇◇	Rates not provided [SAVE]	146
14 p. 133	**Hotel Teatro** *(See ad p. 147.)*	◇◇◇◇	$199-$699 [SAVE]	147
15 p. 133	the Curtis - a DoubleTree by Hilton Hotel	◇◇◇	Rates not provided	146
16 p. 133	**Grand Hyatt Denver**	◇◇◇◇	$99-$399 [SAVE]	146
17 p. 133	**Aloft Denver Downtown**	◇◇◇	$169-$499 [SAVE]	145
18 p. 133	Hampton Inn & Suites Downtown Denver	◇◇◇	Rates not provided	146
19 p. 133	Embassy Suites by Hilton Denver-Downtown	◇◇◇	Rates not provided	146
20 p. 133	**Holiday Inn Express Denver Downtown**	◇◇◇	Rates not provided [SAVE]	146
21 p. 133	**Hyatt Regency Denver at Colorado Convention Center**	◇◇◇◇	$89-$409 [SAVE]	148
22 p. 133	**The Brown Palace Hotel and Spa, Autograph Collection**	◇◇◇	$219-$466 [SAVE]	145
23 p. 133	**Homewood Suites by Hilton-Denver Downtown Convention Center**	◇◇◇	Rates not provided [SAVE]	147
24 p. 133	Hampton Inn & Suites Denver Downtown Convention Center	◇◇◇	Rates not provided	146
25 p. 133	**Hilton Garden Inn Denver Downtown**	◇◇◇	Rates not provided [SAVE]	146
26 p. 133	Crowne Plaza Denver	◇◇◇	Rates not provided	145
27 p. 133	**Sheraton Denver Downtown Hotel**	◇◇◇	Rates not provided [SAVE]	148
28 p. 133	**Hyatt Place Denver/Downtown**	◇◇◇	$99-$499 [SAVE]	147
29 p. 133	**HYATT house Denver/Downtown**	◇◇◇	$99-$499 [SAVE]	147

Map Page	Restaurants	Diamond Rated	Cuisine	Price Range	Page
1 p. 133	Zengo	◇◇◇	Fusion	$18-$36	153
2 p. 133	Snooze	◇◇	Breakfast	$8-$12	152
3 p. 133	Biker Jim's Dogs	◇	Hot Dogs	$7-$9	149
4 p. 133	Marco's Coal- Fired Pizzeria	◇◇	Pizza	$9-$19	151
5 p. 133	Rodizio Grill	◇◇	Brazilian	$19-$35	152
6 p. 133	Trillium	◇◇◇	New Scandinavian	$20-$30	152
7 p. 133	Wynkoop Brewing Company	◇◇	American	$10-$20	153
8 p. 133	Stoic & Genuine	◇◇◇	Seafood	$13-$38	152
9 p. 133	Sullivan's Steakhouse	◇◇◇	Steak	$25-$60	152
10 p. 133	Morton's The Steakhouse	◇◇◇	Steak	$28-$58	151
11 p. 133	Vesta Dipping Grill	◇◇◇	International	$18-$40	152
12 p. 133	Jax Fish House	◇◇◇	Seafood	$10-$46	150
13 p. 133	McCormick's Fish House & Bar	◇◇◇	Regional Seafood	$13-$40	151
14 p. 133	Lucky Pie Pizza & Tap House	◇◇	Pizza	$8-$15	150

Map Page	Restaurants (cont'd)	Diamond Rated	Cuisine	Price Range	Page
⑮ p. 133	The Squeaky Bean	◆◆◆	American	$21-$36	152
⑯ p. 133	ChoLon Modern Asian Bistro	◆◆◆	Asian Fusion	$11-$36	149
⑰ p. 133	Wazee Supper Club	◆◆	American	$8-$16	152
⑱ p. 133	1515 Restaurant	◆◆◆	American	$10-$40	149
⑲ p. 133	Elway's Downtown	◆◆◆	Steak	$15-$60	150
⑳ p. 133	The Palm Restaurant	◆◆◆	American	$22-$57	151
㉑ p. 133	Red Square Euro Bistro	◆◆◆	Russian	$18-$29	151
㉒ p. 133	Cafe Colore	◆◆	Italian	$9-$20	149
㉓ p. 133	Osteria Marco	◆◆◆	Italian	$10-$27	151
㉔ p. 133	The Capital Grille	◆◆◆	Steak	$16-$51	149
㉕ p. 133	The Market	◆	Deli	$6-$13	151
㉖ p. 133	TAG	◆◆◆	Fusion	$14-$32	152
㉗ p. 133	**Rioja**	◆◆◆◆	American	$13-$31	151
㉘ p. 133	Euclid Hall Bar & Kitchen	◆◆	American	$10-$23	150
㉙ p. 133	Russell's Smokehouse	◆◆◆	Barbecue	$14-$26	152
㉚ p. 133	Bistro Vendome	◆◆◆	French	$17-$26	149
㉛ p. 133	Tamayo	◆◆◆	Mexican	$12-$28	152
㉜ p. 133	**Panzano**	◆◆◆◆	Northern Italian	$14-$32	151
㉝ p. 133	Rock Bottom Brewery	◆◆	American	$9-$25	152
㉞ p. 133	Guard and Grace	◆◆◆◆	Steak	$25-$63	150
㉟ p. 133	The Centennial Tavern	◆◆	American	$10-$19	149
㊱ p. 133	**Edge Restaurant & Bar**	◆◆◆◆	Steak	$12-$46	150
㊲ p. 133	The Oceanaire Seafood Room	◆◆◆	Seafood	$26-$60 SAVE	151
㊳ p. 133	Larkburger	◆	Burgers	$4-$10	150
㊴ p. 133	Wild Bangkok Bar and Grill	◆◆	Thai	$8-$16	153
㊵ p. 133	Hard Rock Cafe	◆◆	American	$9-$18 SAVE	150
㊶ p. 133	**Palace Arms**	◆◆◆◆	Continental	$29-$60	151
㊷ p. 133	Ellyngton's at the Brown Palace	◆◆◆	American	$11-$26	150
㊸ p. 133	Ship Tavern	◆◆	American	$15-$45	152
㊹ p. 133	The Delectable Egg	◆◆	Breakfast	$5-$11	150
㊺ p. 133	Ace	◆◆	Asian Fusion	$10-$15	149
㊻ p. 133	Steuben's	◆◆	American	$5-$18	152
㊼ p. 133	Green Fine Salad Co.	◆	Natural/Organic	$7-$10	150
㊽ p. 133	Domo	◆◆	Japanese	$9-$25	150
㊾ p. 133	Palettes	◆◆◆	American	$12-$18	151
㊿ p. 133	Pints Pub	◆◆	British	$10-$14	151
(51) p. 133	City O' City	◆◆	Pizza Vegetarian	$11-$13	150

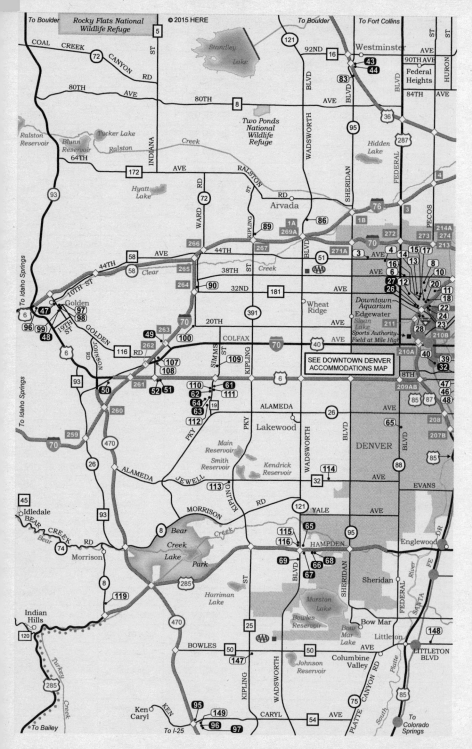

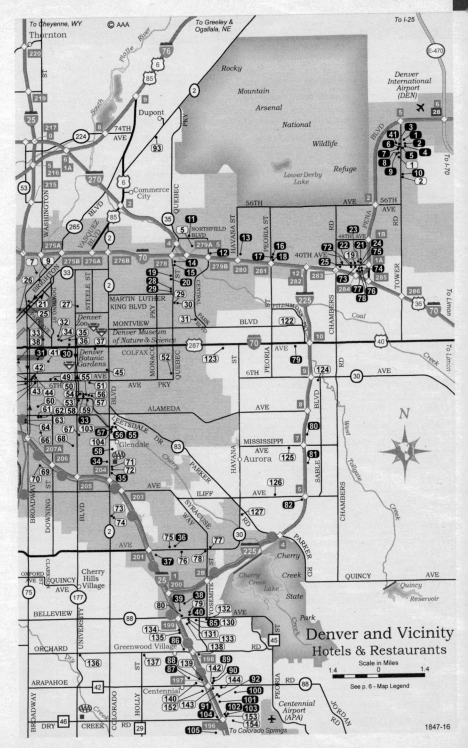

Denver and Vicinity
Hotels & Restaurants

Scale in Miles
1.4   0   1.4

See p. 6 - Map Legend

1847-16

✈ Airport Hotels

Map Page	DENVER INTERNATIONAL (Maximum driving distance from airport: 8.6 mi)	Diamond Rated	Rate Range	Page
76 p. 136	Aloft Denver International Airport, 11.8 mi	▽▽▽	$99-$259 SAVE	50
77 p. 136	Denver Airport Marriott at Gateway Park, 11.9 mi	▽▽▽	$97-$283 SAVE	50
75 p. 136	Hilton Garden Inn-Denver Airport, 11.7 mi	▽▽▽	$89-$189 SAVE	50
73 p. 136	Hyatt Place Denver Airport, 11.8 mi	▽▽▽	$84-$299 SAVE	52
74 p. 136	Residence Inn by Marriott, 11.7 mi	▽▽▽	$101-$249	52
78 p. 136	Woolley's Classic Suites-Denver Airport, 11.8 mi	▽▽▽	$149-$299 SAVE	52
2 p. 136	BEST WESTERN PLUS Denver International Airport Inn & Suites, 7.7 mi	▽▽	$79-$209 SAVE	153
23 p. 136	Country Inn & Suites By Carlson, Denver International Airport, 11.7 mi	▽▽	$109-$209 SAVE	153
6 p. 136	Courtyard by Marriott Denver Airport, 7.7 mi	▽▽▽	$96-$337 SAVE	153
41 p. 136	Embassy Suites by Hilton Denver International Airport, 7.7 mi	▽▽▽	$109-$209 SAVE	155
7 p. 136	Fairfield Inn & Suites by Marriott Denver Airport, 7.8 mi	▽▽▽	$83-$225	155
21 p. 136	Hampton Inn & Suites Denver Airport Gateway Park, 11.7 mi	▽▽▽	Rates not provided	156
10 p. 136	Hampton Inn DIA, 8.6 mi	▽▽▽	Rates not provided SAVE	156
5 p. 136	Holiday Inn & Suites, 7.8 mi	▽▽▽	Rates not provided	156
4 p. 136	Holiday Inn Express & Suites, 7.8 mi	▽▽▽	Rates not provided	156
24 p. 136	Homewood Suites by Hilton Denver International Airport, 11.6 mi	▽▽▽	Rates not provided	156
1 p. 136	HYATT house Denver Airport, 8.1 mi	▽▽▽	$79-$209 SAVE	156
8 p. 136	La Quinta Inn & Suites Denver Airport DIA, 7.9 mi	▽▽	$68-$213	157
9 p. 136	SpringHill Suites by Marriott Denver Airport, 7.9 mi	▽▽▽	$92-$239	157
3 p. 136	Staybridge Suites, 7.6 mi	▽▽▽	$99-$220	157
22 p. 136	TownePlace Suites by Marriott Gateway Park / Denver Airport, 11.9 mi	▽▽▽	$94-$209	158

Denver and Vicinity

This index helps you "spot" where approved hotels and restaurants are located on the corresponding detailed maps. Hotel daily rate range is for comparison only. Restaurant price range is a combination of lunch and/or dinner. Turn to the listing page for more detailed rate and price information and consult display ads for special promotions.

DENVER

Map Page	Hotels	Diamond Rated	Rate Range	Page
1 p. 136	HYATT house Denver Airport	▽▽▽	$79-$209 SAVE	156
2 p. 136	BEST WESTERN PLUS Denver International Airport Inn & Suites	▽▽	$79-$209 SAVE	153
3 p. 136	Staybridge Suites	▽▽▽	$99-$220	157
4 p. 136	Holiday Inn Express & Suites	▽▽▽	Rates not provided	156
5 p. 136	Holiday Inn & Suites	▽▽▽	Rates not provided	156
6 p. 136	Courtyard by Marriott Denver Airport	▽▽▽	$96-$337 SAVE	153
7 p. 136	Fairfield Inn & Suites by Marriott Denver Airport	▽▽▽	$83-$225	155
8 p. 136	La Quinta Inn & Suites Denver Airport DIA	▽▽	$68-$213	157

DENVER (cont'd)

Map Page	Hotels (cont'd)	Diamond Rated	Rate Range	Page
9 p. 136	SpringHill Suites by Marriott Denver Airport	♦♦♦	$92-$239	157
10 p. 136	**Hampton Inn DIA**	♦♦♦	Rates not provided (SAVE)	156
11 p. 136	Staybridge Suites Denver Stapleton	♦♦♦	$114-$194	158
12 p. 136	Drury Inn & Suites Denver Stapleton	♦♦♦	$100-$180	154
13 p. 136	**Embassy Suites by Hilton Denver-Stapleton**	♦♦♦	Rates not provided (SAVE)	155
14 p. 136	**Courtyard by Marriott Denver Stapleton**	♦♦	$89-$210 (SAVE)	154
15 p. 136	DoubleTree by Hilton Denver-Stapleton North	♦♦♦	Rates not provided	154
16 p. 136	Holiday Inn Express & Suites Denver East-Peoria Street	♦♦♦	Rates not provided	156
17 p. 136	La Quinta Inn & Suites Denver Gateway Park	♦♦♦	$98-$252	157
18 p. 136	Comfort Inn Denver East	♦♦	$79-$129	153
19 p. 136	**Renaissance Denver Hotel**	♦♦♦	$97-$225 (SAVE)	157
20 p. 136	Quality Inn & Suites	♦♦	Rates not provided	157
21 p. 136	Hampton Inn & Suites Denver Airport Gateway Park	♦♦♦	Rates not provided	156
22 p. 136	TownePlace Suites by Marriott Gateway Park / Denver Airport	♦♦♦	$94-$209	158
23 p. 136	**Country Inn & Suites By Carlson, Denver International Airport**	♦♦	$109-$209 (SAVE)	153
24 p. 136	Homewood Suites by Hilton Denver International Airport	♦♦♦	Rates not provided	156
25 p. 136	Crowne Plaza Denver Airport - Convention Center	♦♦♦	$99-$309	154
26 p. 136	Residence Inn by Marriott Denver Downtown	♦♦♦	$143-$268	157
27 p. 136	Hampton Inn & Suites Denver /Speer	[fyi]	Rates not provided	156
28 p. 136	Holiday Inn Denver East - Stapleton	♦♦♦	$99-$229	156
29 p. 136	DoubleTree by Hilton Hotel Denver	♦♦♦	Rates not provided	154
30 p. 136	Castle Marne Bed and Breakfast	♦♦♦	Rates not provided	153
31 p. 136	Capitol Hill Mansion Bed & Breakfast Inn	♦♦♦	$154-$229	153
32 p. 136	TownePlace Suites by Marriott Downtown Denver	♦♦	$121-$238	158
33 p. 136	**JW Marriott Denver Cherry Creek**	♦♦♦♦	$217-$531 (SAVE)	157
34 p. 136	**Courtyard by Marriott Denver Cherry Creek**	♦♦♦	$106-$249 (SAVE)	153
35 p. 136	**Fairfield Inn & Suites by Marriott Denver Cherry Creek**	♦♦♦	$98-$193 (SAVE)	155
36 p. 136	**Embassy Suites by Hilton Denver Southeast**	♦♦♦	Rates not provided (SAVE)	155
37 p. 136	TownePlace Suites by Marriott-Denver Southeast	♦♦	$80-$211	158
38 p. 136	**Hyatt Regency Denver Tech Center**	♦♦♦	$99-$429 (SAVE)	156
39 p. 136	Denver Marriott Tech Center	♦♦♦	$85-$297	154
40 p. 136	Hampton Inn & Suites Denver Tech Center	♦♦♦	Rates not provided	156
41 p. 136	**Embassy Suites by Hilton Denver International Airport**	♦♦♦	$109-$209 (SAVE)	155

Map Page	Restaurants	Diamond Rated	Cuisine	Price Range	Page
1 p. 136	DiCicco's Italian Restaurant	♦♦	Italian	$10-$30	160

Map Page	Restaurants (cont'd)	Diamond Rated	Cuisine	Price Range	Page
② p. 136	Moonlight Diner	◆◆	American	$9-$15	162
③ p. 136	Parisi	◆◆	Italian	$9-$19	163
④ p. 136	Tocabe: An American Indian Eatery	◆	Native American	$8-$15	164
⑤ p. 136	La Sandia Tequila Cantina	◆◆◆	Mexican	$8-$19	161
⑥ p. 136	The Universal	◆◆	American	$8-$9	164
⑦ p. 136	Fuel Cafe	◆◆	American	$10-$20	160
⑧ p. 136	Tamales at La Casita	◆	Mexican	$3-$11	164
⑨ p. 136	Acorn	◆◆◆	Small Plates	$13-$27	158
⑩ p. 136	Old Major	◆◆◆	American	$23-$34	162
⑪ p. 136	Root Down	◆◆◆	Natural/Organic	$13-$31	163
⑫ p. 136	Spuntino	◆◆◆	Italian	$9-$23	164
⑬ p. 136	Duo Restaurant	◆◆◆	American	$10-$26	160
⑭ p. 136	Uncle	◆◆	Asian Soup Small Plates	$10-$16	164
⑮ p. 136	Highland Tap & Burger	◆◆	Burgers	$9-$23	161
⑯ p. 136	Z Cuisine Bistrot	◆◆◆	French	$12-$22	165
⑰ p. 136	Linger	◆◆◆	Small Plates	$12-$24	161
⑱ p. 136	Ale House at Amato's	◆◆	American	$7-$24	158
⑲ p. 136	Thai Chili & Sushi	◆◆	Asian	$7-$16	164
⑳ p. 136	Masterpiece Delicatessen	◆	Sandwiches	$6-$13	162
㉑ p. 136	Osaka Ramen	◆◆	Japanese Noodles	$14	162
㉒ p. 136	**Colt & Gray**	◆◆◆◆	American	$20-$40	160
㉓ p. 136	Sushi Sasa	◆◆◆	Japanese	$8-$20	164
㉔ p. 136	My Brother's Bar	◆◆	Burgers	$6-$10	162
㉕ p. 136	Work & Class	◆◆	Small Plates	$11-$28	165
㉖ p. 136	Breckenridge Colorado Craft	◆◆	American	$10-$17	159
㉗ p. 136	Plimoth	◆◆◆	American	$17-$19	163
㉘ p. 136	Aquarium Restaurant	◆◆	Seafood	$10-$35 SAVE	159
㉙ p. 136	Casey's Bistro & Pub	◆◆	American	$8-$19	159
㉚ p. 136	The Berkshire	◆◆	American	$11-$32	159
㉛ p. 136	Mici Handcrafted Italian	◆	Italian	$9-$20	162
㉜ p. 136	Hot Cakes Breakfast and Lunch	◆◆	American	$7-$12	161
㉝ p. 136	Watercourse Foods	◆◆	Vegan	$11-$16	165
㉞ p. 136	Humbolt: Farm Fish Wine	◆◆◆	Seafood	$13-$35	161
㉟ p. 136	Parallel Seventeen	◆◆◆	Vietnamese	$9-$24	163
㊱ p. 136	Il Posto	◆◆◆	Italian	$11-$35	161
㊲ p. 136	Mezcal	◆◆	Mexican	$9-$18	162
㊳ p. 136	Cuba Cuba Cafe & Bar	◆◆	Cuban	$13-$24	160
㊴ p. 136	Parsley	◆	Sandwiches Natural/Organic	$6-$11	163

Map Page	Restaurants (cont'd)	Diamond Rated	Cuisine	Price Range	Page
40 p. 136	**Buckhorn Exchange**	◆◆	Steak	$10-$53	159
41 p. 136	Potager	◆◆◆	American	$18-$29	163
42 p. 136	Luca	◆◆◆	Italian	$13-$33	162
43 p. 136	Mizuna	◆◆◆◆	New American	$37-$39	162
44 p. 136	Bones	◆◆	Asian Noodles	$13-$20	159
45 p. 136	Swing Thai	◆◆	Thai	$5-$14	164
46 p. 136	Racines Restaurant	◆◆	American	$9-$17	163
47 p. 136	Pizzeria Locale	◆	Pizza	$6-$9	163
48 p. 136	Little India Restaurant	◆◆	Indian	$11-$19	162
49 p. 136	Table 6	◆◆◆	American	$18-$30	164
50 p. 136	Fruition Restaurant	◆◆◆	American	$26-$29	160
51 p. 136	Barolo Grill	◆◆◆	Northern Italian	$20-$35	159
52 p. 136	Moongate Asian Grill	◆◆	Asian	$7-$17	162
53 p. 136	Opus Fine Dining & Aria Wine Bar	◆◆◆	American	$13-$40	162
54 p. 136	The Cherry Cricket	◆◆	American	$6-$10	160
55 p. 136	True Food Kitchen	◆◆	Natural/Organic	$12-$26	164
56 p. 136	Harman's Eat & Drink	◆◆	American	$12-$25	161
57 p. 136	Piatti Italian Restaurant & Bar	◆◆	Italian	$13-$22	163
58 p. 136	Elway's	◆◆◆	Steak	$14-$49	160
59 p. 136	Kona Grill	◆◆◆	Pacific Rim Fusion	$10-$33	161
60 p. 136	Carmine's on Penn	◆◆◆	Italian	$24-$47	159
61 p. 136	Bittersweet	◆◆◆	Natural/Organic	$25-$35	159
62 p. 136	Pete's Central One	◆◆	Greek	$10-$21	163
63 p. 136	Imperial Chinese Restaurant	◆◆	Chinese	$6-$42	161
64 p. 136	The Blue Bonnet Mexican Cafe	◆◆	Mexican	$5-$16	159
65 p. 136	New Saigon Restaurant	◆◆	Vietnamese	$7-$25	162
66 p. 136	Vert Kitchen	◆◆	Sandwiches	$11-$14	165
67 p. 136	Bonnie Brae Tavern	◆◆	American	$7-$18	159
68 p. 136	Devil's Food	◆◆	American	$11-$26	160
69 p. 136	Sushi Den	◆◆◆	Japanese	$13-$35	164
70 p. 136	Izakaya Den	◆◆◆	Japanese Sushi	$12-$35	161
71 p. 136	Saigon Terrace Vietnamese & Chinese Restaurant	◆◆	Vietnamese	$7-$15	164
72 p. 136	Royal India	◆◆	Indian	$9-$19	163
73 p. 136	**Beau Jo's Colorado Style Pizza Denver** *(See ad p. 158.)*	◆◆	Pizza	$6-$12	159
74 p. 136	Slotted Spoon	◆	Specialty	$8-$14	164
75 p. 136	**New York Deli News**	◆◆	American	$7-$15	162
76 p. 136	The Fresh Fish Company & Black Pearl Oyster Bar	◆◆	Seafood	$9-$48	160
77 p. 136	**India's Restaurant**	◆◆	Indian	$10-$21	161

Map Page	Restaurants (cont'd)	Diamond Rated	Cuisine	Price Range	Page
78 p. 136	Citron Bistro	▼▼	American	$9-$23	160
79 p. 136	Darcy's Bistro & Pub	▼▼	American	$7-$15	160
80 p. 136	Shanahan's	▼▼▼	Steak	$26-$58	164

WESTMINSTER

Map Page	Hotels	Diamond Rated	Rate Range	Page
43 p. 136	Hampton Inn by Hilton	▼▼▼	Rates not provided	273
44 p. 136	Residence Inn by Marriott	▼▼▼	$116-$227	273

Map Page	Restaurant	Diamond Rated	Cuisine	Price Range	Page
83 p. 136	Yak & Yeti Restaurant & Brewpub	▼▼	Indian	$10-$16	273

GOLDEN

Map Page	Hotels	Diamond Rated	Rate Range	Page
47 p. 136	The Golden Hotel, an Ascend Hotel Collection Member	▼▼▼	Rates not provided	200
48 p. 136	**Table Mountain Inn**	▼▼▼	$184-$269 SAVE	201
49 p. 136	Denver Marriott West	▼▼▼	$115-$300	200
50 p. 136	Hampton Inn Denver West/Golden	▼▼▼	Rates not provided	200
51 p. 136	Residence Inn by Marriott Denver West/Golden	▼▼▼	$123-$260	201
52 p. 136	Courtyard by Marriott Denver West/Golden	▼▼▼	$113-$224	200

Map Page	Restaurants	Diamond Rated	Cuisine	Price Range	Page
96 p. 136	The Briarwood Inn	▼▼▼	Continental	$26-$80	201
97 p. 136	Indulge Bistro & Wine Bar	▼▼▼	Mediterranean	$10-$32	201
98 p. 136	Woody's Wood Fired Pizza & Watering Hole	▼▼	American	$9-$16	201
99 p. 136	**Table Mountain Grill & Cantina**	▼▼▼	Southwestern	$8-$26	201
100 p. 136	Tafolino's	▼▼	Mexican	$7-$15	201

GLENDALE

Map Page	Hotels	Diamond Rated	Rate Range	Page
55 p. 136	**Staybridge Suites Denver/Cherry Creek**	▼▼▼	Rates not provided SAVE	196
56 p. 136	Residence Inn by Marriott	▼▼▼	$128-$252	196
57 p. 136	Hilton Garden Inn Denver/Cherry Creek	▼▼▼	Rates not provided	195
58 p. 136	**Hyatt Place Denver Cherry Creek**	▼▼▼	$79-$219 SAVE	195

Map Page	Restaurants	Diamond Rated	Cuisine	Price Range	Page
103 p. 136	Cuba Cuba Sandwicheria	▼	Cuban	$7-$8	196
104 p. 136	Silvi's Kitchen	▼▼	American	$9-$19	196

LAKEWOOD

Map Page	Hotels	Diamond Rated	Rate Range	Page
61 p. 136	**Sheraton-Denver West Hotel**	▼▼▼	$109-$359 SAVE	220
62 p. 136	Hampton Inn Denver West/Federal Center	▼▼▼	Rates not provided	219
63 p. 136	Homewood Suites by Hilton Denver West/Federal Center	▼▼▼	Rates not provided	219
64 p. 136	Home2 Suites by Hilton Denver West/Federal Center	▼▼▼	Rates not provided	219
65 p. 136	**BEST WESTERN Denver Southwest**	▼▼▼	$72-$165 SAVE	219
66 p. 136	Courtyard by Marriott Denver SW/Lakewood	▼▼▼	$94-$213	219

LAKEWOOD (cont'd)

Map Page	Hotels (cont'd)	Diamond Rated	Rate Range	Page
67 p. 136	**Holiday Inn Denver Lakewood**	◆◆◆	$89-$169 SAVE	219
68 p. 136	Residence Inn by Marriott Denver SW/Lakewood	◆◆◆	$112-$257	220
69 p. 136	Hampton Inn Denver- Southwest-Lakewood	◆◆	Rates not provided	219

Map Page	Restaurants	Diamond Rated	Cuisine	Price Range	Page
107 p. 136	Blue Sky Cafe	◆◆	Natural/Organic	$9-$13	220
108 p. 136	Modmarket	◆	American	$5-$11	220
109 p. 136	**Jus Cookin's Restaurant**	◆◆	Comfort Food	$9-$14	220
110 p. 136	Chad's Grill	◆◆	American	$9-$19	220
111 p. 136	240 Union Restaurant	◆◆◆	American	$12-$35	220
112 p. 136	Kobe An	◆◆	Japanese	$9-$27	220
113 p. 136	Cafe Jordano	◆◆	Italian	$8-$15	220
114 p. 136	**White Fence Farm Restaurant**	◆◆	American	$11-$30	221
115 p. 136	Pad Thai	◆◆	Thai	$7-$12	220
116 p. 136	Namaste	◆◆	Indian	$11-$21	220

AURORA

Map Page	Hotels	Diamond Rated	Rate Range	Page
72 p. 136	Cambria Hotel & Suites Denver Airport	◆◆◆	$99-$249	50
73 p. 136	**Hyatt Place Denver Airport** (See ad p. 52.)	◆◆◆	$84-$299 SAVE	52
74 p. 136	Residence Inn by Marriott	◆◆◆	$101-$249	52
75 p. 136	**Hilton Garden Inn-Denver Airport** (See ad p. 51.)	◆◆◆	$89-$189 SAVE	50
76 p. 136	**Aloft Denver International Airport**	◆◆◆	$99-$259 SAVE	50
77 p. 136	**Denver Airport Marriott at Gateway Park**	◆◆◆	$97-$283 SAVE	50
78 p. 136	**Woolley's Classic Suites-Denver Airport**	◆◆◆	$149-$299 SAVE	52
79 p. 136	SpringHill Suites by Marriott	◆◆◆	$104-$233	52
80 p. 136	**BEST WESTERN PLUS Gateway Inn & Suites**	◆◆◆	$80-$300 SAVE	50
81 p. 136	Holiday Inn Express Denver-Aurora Medical Center	◆◆	Rates not provided	50
82 p. 136	**DoubleTree by Hilton Denver - Aurora** (See ad p. 51.)	◆◆◆	$89-$249 SAVE	50

Map Page	Restaurants	Diamond Rated	Cuisine	Price Range	Page
122 p. 136	Cedar Creek Pub	◆◆	American	$9-$14	53
123 p. 136	La Cueva	◆◆	Mexican	$9-$17	53
124 p. 136	Pho 888	◆◆	Vietnamese	$8-$13	53
125 p. 136	Café Paprika	◆◆	Moroccan	$7-$15	53
126 p. 136	Bent Fork The Grill	◆◆◆	American	$10-$23	52
127 p. 136	The Summit Steakhouse	◆◆◆	Steak Seafood	$11-$69	53

GREENWOOD VILLAGE

Map Page	Hotels	Diamond Rated	Rate Range	Page
85 p. 136	**Hyatt Place Denver Tech Center**	◆◆◆	$99-$229 SAVE	209
86 p. 136	DoubleTree by Hilton Denver Tech Center	◆◆◆	Rates not provided	209
87 p. 136	Wingate by Wyndham	◆◆◆	$81-$189	209

GREENWOOD VILLAGE (cont'd)

Map Page	Hotels (cont'd)	Diamond Rated	Rate Range	Page
88 p. 136	Residence Inn by Marriott-Denver Tech Center	◆◆	$103-$238	209
89 p. 136	Courtyard by Marriott-Denver Tech Center	◆◆◆	$71-$240	209
90 p. 136	BEST WESTERN PLUS Denver Tech Center Hotel	◆◆◆	$89-$199 SAVE	209
91 p. 136	HYATT house Denver Tech Center	◆◆◆	$89-$259 SAVE	209
92 p. 136	Sheraton Denver Tech Center	◆◆◆	Rates not provided SAVE	209

Map Page	Restaurants	Diamond Rated	Cuisine	Price Range	Page
130 p. 136	Larkburger	◆	Burgers	$7-$10	210
131 p. 136	Bara Sushi & Grill	◆◆	Sushi	$9-$25	209
132 p. 136	Chianti Ristorante & Wine Bar	◆◆◆	Italian	$12-$16	210
133 p. 136	Cool River Cafe	◆◆◆	Steak Seafood	$12-$45	210
134 p. 136	Jing	◆◆◆	Asian	$13-$35	210
135 p. 136	Yanni's Greek Restaurant	◆◆	Greek	$11-$30	211
136 p. 136	Sazza	◆	Pizza	$6-$15	210
137 p. 136	Venice Ristorante Italiano	◆◆◆	Italian	$12-$31	210
138 p. 136	Del Frisco's Double Eagle Steak House	◆◆◆	Steak	$14-$89	210
139 p. 136	Brook's Steak House & Cellar	◆◆◆	Steak	$28-$64	210
140 p. 136	Garbanzo Mediterranean Grill	◆	Mediterranean	$6-$10	210
142 p. 136	Brother's BBQ	◆	Barbecue	$8-$19	210
143 p. 136	Gunther Toody's Diner	◆◆	American	$8-$13	210
144 p. 136	Sahara Authentic Moroccan & Lebanese Restaurant	◆◆	Middle Eastern	$9-$19	210

LITTLETON

Map Page	Hotels	Diamond Rated	Rate Range	Page
95 p. 136	Holiday Inn Express Hotel & Suites Denver SW-Littleton	◆◆	$99-$250	226
96 p. 136	Hampton Inn & Suites Denver Littleton	◆◆◆	Rates not provided	226
97 p. 136	Homewood Suites by Hilton-Denver Littleton	◆◆◆	Rates not provided	226

Map Page	Restaurants	Diamond Rated	Cuisine	Price Range	Page
147 p. 136	Thai Bistro	◆◆	Southern Thai	$8-$17	226
148 p. 136	Romano's Italian Restaurant	◆◆	Italian	$9-$19	226
149 p. 136	Lil' Ricci's NY Pizza	◆◆	Italian	$7-$14	226

CENTENNIAL

Map Page	Hotels	Diamond Rated	Rate Range	Page
100 p. 136	Embassy Suites by Hilton Denver Tech Center	◆◆◆	Rates not provided SAVE	77
101 p. 136	Staybridge Suites Denver Tech Center	◆◆◆	Rates not provided	77
102 p. 136	Comfort Suites Denver Tech Center	◆◆◆	$99-$199	77
103 p. 136	Holiday Inn Express Hotel & Suites	◆◆	Rates not provided	77
104 p. 136	Drury Inn & Suites-Denver Near the Tech Center	◆◆	$90-$170	77
105 p. 136	TownePlace Suites by Marriott Denver Tech Center	◆◆	$75-$222	77

Map Page	Restaurants	Diamond Rated	Cuisine	Price Range	Page
(152) p. 136	The Egg & I	♦♦	Breakfast	$9-$10	77
(153) p. 136	Maggiano's Little Italy	♦♦♦	Italian	$11-$40	77
(154) p. 136	Marco's Coal-Fired Pizzeria	♦♦	Pizza	$9-$17	77

ARVADA

Map Page	Restaurant	Diamond Rated	Cuisine	Price Range	Page
(86) p. 136	Beau Jo's Colorado Style Pizza Arvada (See ad p. 43.)	♦♦	Pizza	$6-$12	43

WHEAT RIDGE

Map Page	Restaurants	Diamond Rated	Cuisine	Price Range	Page
(89) p. 136	Luke's A Steak Place	♦♦	Steak	$25-$43	273
(90) p. 136	Abrusci's	♦♦	Italian	$10-$34	273

COMMERCE CITY

Map Page	Restaurant	Diamond Rated	Cuisine	Price Range	Page
(93) p. 136	El Jardin	♦♦	Mexican	$9-$18	105

MORRISON

Map Page	Restaurant	Diamond Rated	Cuisine	Price Range	Page
(119) p. 136	The Fort	♦♦♦	Steak	$29-$49	239

DOWNTOWN DENVER
• Restaurants p. 149
• Hotels & Restaurants map & index p. 133

ALOFT DENVER DOWNTOWN   (303)623-3063 17
♦♦♦♦ Contemporary Hotel $169-$499

AAA Benefit: Members save up to 15%, plus Starwood Preferred Guest® benefits!

Address: 800 15th St 80202 **Location:** Between Champa and Stout sts. **Facility:** 140 units. 6 stories, interior corridors. *Bath:* shower only. **Parking:** valet only. **Terms:** 2 night minimum stay - seasonal, cancellation fee imposed. **Amenities:** safes. **Pool(s):** heated indoor. **Activities:** exercise room. **Guest Services:** valet and coin laundry, boarding pass kiosk.

THE BROWN PALACE HOTEL AND SPA, AUTOGRAPH COLLECTION   (303)297-3111 22
♦♦♦♦ Classic Historic Hotel $219-$466

AAA Benefit: Members save 5% or more!

Address: 321 17th St 80202 **Location:** From Broadway and Tremont Pl, just sw. **Facility:** Visitors to Denver are immediately drawn to this triangular-shaped, historic red stone building. 241 units. 9 stories, interior corridors. **Parking:** valet only. **Amenities:** safes. **Dining:** 2 restaurants, also, Ellyngton's at the Brown Palace, Palace Arms, Ship Tavern, see separate listings, entertainment. **Activities:** exercise room, spa. **Guest Services:** valet laundry, area transportation.

COURTYARD BY MARRIOTT DENVER DOWNTOWN   (303)571-1114 8
♦♦♦ Hotel $143-$381 **Address:** 934 16th St 80202 **Location:** Jct Curtis St. **Facility:** 177 units. 6 stories, interior corridors. **Parking:** valet only. **Terms:** check-in 4 pm. **Activities:** exercise room. **Guest Services:** valet and coin laundry, boarding pass kiosk.

AAA Benefit: Members save 5% or more!

THE CRAWFORD HOTEL   (720)460-3700 1
♦♦♦ ♦♦♦ Historic Boutique Hotel $289-$529 **Address:** 1701 Wynkoop St 80202 **Location:** Corner of 17th St; in Union Station. **Facility:** Located in the spectacularly restored Union Station, Denver's historic train station, this hotel shares its lobby with restaurants, shops and rail travelers. 112 units. 4 stories, interior corridors. **Parking:** valet only. **Terms:** cancellation fee imposed, resort fee. **Amenities:** safes. **Activities:** exercise room, massage. **Guest Services:** valet laundry, area transportation.

CROWNE PLAZA DENVER   303/573-1450 26
♦♦♦ Hotel. Rates not provided. **Address:** 1450 Glenarm Pl 80202 **Location:** I-25 exit 210 (W Colfax Ave) to Glenarm Pl, then 0.3 mi n. **Facility:** 364 units. 20 stories, interior corridors. **Parking:** on-site (fee). **Terms:** check-in 4 pm. **Amenities:** safes. **Pool(s):** heated outdoor. **Activities:** exercise room. **Guest Services:** valet laundry, boarding pass kiosk.

(See map & index p. 133.)

THE CURTIS - A DOUBLETREE BY HILTON HOTEL
303/571-0300 **15**

▼◆▼ **Boutique Contemporary Retro Hotel.** Rates not provided. **Address:** 1405 Curtis St 80202 **Location:** Between 14th and 15th sts. **Facility:** The mod-style lobby features a retro toy theme, which includes the world's largest Lite-Brite. Each floor has a specific theme with artwork reflecting that theme. 336 units. 30 stories, interior corridors. **Parking:** on-site (fee) and valet. **Amenities:** safes. **Activities:** recreation programs, exercise room, massage. **Guest Services:** valet laundry.

AAA Benefit: Members save 5% or more!

DENVER MARRIOTT CITY CENTER
(303)297-1300 **11**

▼◆▼ **Hotel** $144-$376 **Address:** 1701 California St 80202 **Location:** Between 17th and 18th sts. **Facility:** 613 units. 20 stories, interior corridors. **Parking:** valet only. **Terms:** check-in 4 pm. **Pool(s):** heated indoor. **Activities:** bicycles, exercise room. **Guest Services:** valet and coin laundry, boarding pass kiosk, area transportation.

AAA Benefit: Members save 5% or more!

EMBASSY SUITES BY HILTON DENVER-DOWNTOWN
303/592-1000 **19**

▼◆▼ **Hotel.** Rates not provided. **Address:** 1420 Stout St 80202 **Location:** Between 14th and 15th sts. **Facility:** 403 units. 17 stories, interior corridors. **Parking:** valet only. **Terms:** check-in 4 pm. **Amenities:** safes. **Pool(s):** heated indoor. **Activities:** exercise room, massage. **Guest Services:** valet and coin laundry.

AAA Benefit: Members save 5% or more!

FOUR SEASONS HOTEL DENVER
303/389-3000 **13**

▼◆▼◆▼ Hotel Rates not provided

Address: 1111 14th St 80202 **Location:** Between Lawrence and Arapahoe sts. **Facility:** Large windows letting in natural light and sleek, modern décor are the hallmarks of this grand hotel. Rooms feature luxurious bedding of soft thick sheets, pillow top mattresses and down duvets. 239 units, some two bedrooms. 45 stories, interior corridors. **Parking:** valet only. **Amenities:** video games, safes. **Dining:** Edge Restaurant & Bar, see separate listing. **Pool(s):** heated outdoor. **Activities:** hot tub, steamroom, spa. **Guest Services:** valet laundry, area transportation.

GRAND HYATT DENVER
(303)295-1234 **16**

▼◆▼◆▼ Hotel $99-$399

GRAND HYATT

AAA Benefit: Members save 10%!

Address: 1750 Welton St 80202 **Location:** Between 17th and 18th sts. **Facility:** The spacious lobby includes stunning decor with sleek gas fireplaces, textured wall treatments, and modern, Western-influenced artwork. 516 units. 26 stories, interior corridors. **Parking:** valet only. **Terms:** cancellation fee imposed. **Amenities:** video games, safes. **Dining:** entertainment. **Pool(s):** heated indoor. **Activities:** tennis, exercise room, massage. **Guest Services:** valet laundry.

HAMPTON INN & SUITES DENVER DOWNTOWN CONVENTION CENTER
303/623-5900 **24**

▼◆▼ **Hotel.** Rates not provided. **Address:** 550 15th St 80202 **Location:** Between Glenarm Pl and Welton St. **Facility:** 120 units. 12 stories, interior corridors. **Parking:** valet only. **Pool(s):** heated indoor. **Activities:** hot tub, exercise room. **Guest Services:** valet and coin laundry.

AAA Benefit: Members save up to 10%!

HAMPTON INN & SUITES DOWNTOWN DENVER
303/864-8000 **18**

▼◆▼ **Hotel.** Rates not provided. **Address:** 1845 Sherman St 80203 **Location:** Between 18th and 19th aves. **Facility:** 148 units. 6 stories, interior corridors. **Parking:** valet only. **Pool(s):** heated indoor. **Activities:** hot tub, exercise room. **Guest Services:** valet and coin laundry.

AAA Benefit: Members save up to 10%!

HILTON GARDEN INN DENVER DOWNTOWN
303/603-8000 **25**

▼◆▼ Hotel Rates not provided

Hilton Garden Inn

AAA Benefit: Members save up to 10%!

Address: 1400 Welton St 80202 **Location:** Corner of 14th St. **Facility:** 221 units. 12 stories, interior corridors. **Parking:** valet only. **Pool(s):** heated indoor. **Activities:** hot tub, exercise room. **Guest Services:** valet and coin laundry.

HOLIDAY INN EXPRESS DENVER DOWNTOWN
303/296-0400 **20**

▼◆▼ Hotel Rates not provided

Address: 401 17th St 80202 **Location:** From Broadway and Tremont Pl, just sw. **Facility:** 231 units, some two bedrooms. 22 stories, interior corridors. **Parking:** valet only. **Terms:** check-in 4 pm. **Activities:** exercise room. **Guest Services:** valet laundry. **Featured Amenity:** breakfast buffet.

(See map & index p. 133.)

HOMEWOOD SUITES BY HILTON-DENVER DOWNTOWN CONVENTION CENTER
303/534-7800 **23**

Extended Stay Hotel

Rates not provided

HOMEWOOD SUITES BY HILTON

AAA Benefit: Members save up to 10%!

Address: 550 15th St 80202 **Location:** Between Glenarm Pl and Welton St. **Facility:** 182 units, some efficiencies. 12 stories, interior corridors. **Parking:** valet only. **Pool(s):** heated indoor. **Activities:** hot tub, exercise room. **Guest Services:** valet and coin laundry. **Featured Amenity:** full hot breakfast.

SAVE ☎ CALL ♿M 🏊 BIZ HS
📶 ✕ 🔌 🛏 🖨

HOTEL MONACO DENVER
303/296-1717 **9**

Boutique Hotel

Rates not provided

Address: 1717 Champa St 80202 **Location:** Between 17th and 18th sts. **Facility:** Expect to depart this hotel in a different state of mind. Unwind with a chair massage during the nightly wine hour. If you want a pet during your stay, request a goldfish to be put in your room. 189 units. 7 stories, interior corridors. **Parking:** valet only. **Amenities:** video games, safes. **Dining:** Panzano, see separate listing. **Activities:** bicycles, exercise room, spa. **Guest Services:** valet laundry.

SAVE ECO 🍴 🧖 ☎ CALL ♿M
BIZ HS 📶 ✕ 📽

/SOME UNITS 🐕 🔌

HOTEL TEATRO
(303)228-1100 **14**

Historic Boutique Hotel

$199-$699

Address: 1100 14th St 80202 **Location:** Between Lawrence and Arapahoe sts. **Facility:** Centrally located near the Denver Center for the Performing Arts, rooms at this small, upscale hotel feature clean lines, understated elegance and original artwork. 110 units. 9 stories, interior corridors. **Parking:** valet only. **Terms:** cancellation fee imposed. **Amenities:** safes. **Activities:** bicycles, exercise room, massage. **Guest Services:** valet laundry, area transportation. *(See ad this page.)*

SAVE ✈ 🍴 🧖 📶 ✕
📽 🔌 🖨 /SOME UNITS 🐕

HYATT HOUSE DENVER/DOWNTOWN
(303)893-3100 **29**

Extended Stay Hotel

$99-$499

HYATT house

AAA Benefit: Members save 10%!

Address: 440 14th St 80202 **Location:** Between Glenarm Pl and Tremont Pl. **Facility:** 113 units, some efficiencies. 22 stories, interior corridors. **Parking:** valet only. **Pool(s):** heated indoor. **Activities:** exercise room. **Guest Services:** valet and coin laundry. **Featured Amenity:** breakfast buffet.

SAVE ☎ CALL ♿M 🏊 BIZ HS
📶 ✕ 🔌 🛏 🖨

/SOME UNITS 🔌

HYATT PLACE DENVER/DOWNTOWN
(303)893-2900 **28**

Hotel

$99-$499

HYATT PLACE

AAA Benefit: Members save 10%!

Address: 440 14th St 80202 **Location:** Between Glenarm Pl and Tremont Pl. **Facility:** 248 units. 22 stories, interior corridors. **Parking:** valet only. **Pool(s):** heated indoor. **Activities:** exercise room. **Guest Services:** valet and coin laundry. **Featured Amenity:** breakfast buffet.

SAVE ☎ CALL ♿M 🏊 BIZ HS
📶 ✕ 🔌 🛏

▼ See AAA listing this page ▼

(See map & index p. 133.)

HYATT REGENCY DENVER AT COLORADO CONVENTION CENTER (303)436-1234 21

Hotel
$89-$409

AAA Benefit: Members save 10%!

Address: 650 15th St 80202 **Location:** Between California and Welton sts. **Facility:** 1100 units. 37 stories, interior corridors. **Parking:** on-site (fee) and valet. **Terms:** cancellation fee imposed. **Amenities:** safes. **Dining:** 2 restaurants. **Pool(s):** heated indoor. **Activities:** hot tub, exercise room, spa. **Guest Services:** valet laundry, boarding pass kiosk.

MAGNOLIA HOTEL-DOWNTOWN DENVER (303)607-9000 12

Hotel
$129-$499

Address: 818 17th St 80202 **Location:** Jct Stout St. **Facility:** 297 units, some kitchens. 12 stories, interior corridors. **Parking:** valet only. **Terms:** cancellation fee imposed. **Amenities:** safes. **Activities:** exercise room, massage. **Guest Services:** valet and coin laundry, area transportation. **Featured Amenity:** breakfast buffet.

THE OXFORD HOTEL (303)628-5400 2

Historic Hotel
$209-$409

Address: 1600 17th St 80202 **Location:** Corner of 17th and Wazee sts. **Facility:** Antiques and original artwork decorate this restored 1891 hotel, which is located in LoDo near the train station and within quick access of many restaurants, boutiques and event venues. 80 units. 5 stories, interior corridors. **Parking:** valet only. **Terms:** cancellation fee imposed, resort fee. **Dining:** McCormick's Fish House & Bar, see separate listing. **Activities:** steamroom, spa. **Guest Services:** valet laundry, area transportation.

QUEEN ANNE URBAN BED & BREAKFAST 303/296-6666 7

Historic Bed & Breakfast. Rates not provided. **Address:** 2147 Tremont Pl 80205 **Location:** Jct Broadway and Colfax Ave, just e to Logan St, 0.5 mi n to 20th Ave, just w, then just ne. Opposite Benedict Fountain Park. **Facility:** Within walking distance of downtown and across from a park, this B&B is located in the residential section of the Clements Historic District. Bedding is made from 100% organic cotton. 13 units. 2-3 stories (no elevator), interior corridors. **Activities:** bicycles. **Guest Services:** valet laundry.

Before you travel, ask your
AAA/CAA club about identity
theft monitoring products

RENAISSANCE DENVER DOWNTOWN CITY CENTER (303)867-8100 10

Historic Boutique Hotel
$164-$400

AAA Benefit: Members save 5% or more!

Address: 918 17th St 80202 **Location:** Between Curtis and Champa sts. **Facility:** Formerly the Colorado National Bank building, this hotel maintains the opulence of the historic building while adding modern flavor to the décor. 230 units. 8 stories, interior corridors. **Parking:** valet only. **Dining:** 2 restaurants. **Activities:** recreation programs, bicycles, exercise room. **Guest Services:** valet laundry, boarding pass kiosk, area transportation.

RESIDENCE INN BY MARRIOTT DENVER CITY CENTER (303)296-3444 6

Extended Stay Hotel
$132-$339

AAA Benefit: Members save 5% or more!

Address: 1725 Champa St 80202 **Location:** Between 17th and 18th sts. **Facility:** 228 units, some two bedrooms, efficiencies and kitchens. 14 stories, interior corridors. **Parking:** on-site (fee). **Terms:** check-in 4 pm. **Activities:** picnic facilities, exercise room. **Guest Services:** valet and coin laundry, boarding pass kiosk.

THE RITZ-CARLTON, DENVER (303)312-3800 3

Hotel
$329-$449

AAA Benefit: Unequaled service at special member savings!

Address: 1881 Curtis St 80202 **Location:** Between 18th and 19th sts. **Facility:** Luxurious rooms feature hardwood floors in the foyer, bathrooms enhanced with marble and many amenities, including single-serve espresso machines and TVs that offer streaming of movies and tv shows. 202 units. 14 stories, interior corridors. **Parking:** valet only. **Amenities:** safes. **Dining:** Elway's Downtown, see separate listing. **Pool(s):** heated indoor. **Activities:** sauna, hot tub, steamroom, spa. **Guest Services:** valet laundry, area transportation.

SHERATON DENVER DOWNTOWN HOTEL 303/893-3333 27

Hotel
Rates not provided

AAA Benefit: Members save up to 15%, plus Starwood Preferred Guest® benefits!

Address: 1550 Court Pl 80202 **Location:** Between 15th and 16th sts. Located near 16th Street Pedestrian Mall. **Facility:** 1231 units. 8-22 stories, interior corridors. **Parking:** on-site (fee) and valet. **Amenities:** safes. **Dining:** 5 restaurants. **Pool(s):** heated outdoor. **Guest Services:** valet laundry.

(See map & index p. 133.)

SPRINGHILL SUITES BY MARRIOTT DENVER DOWNTOWN
(303)705-7300 **5**

▼▼▼ **Hotel** $142-$337 **Address:** 1190 Auraria Pkwy 80204 **Location:** I-25 exit 212B (Speer Blvd) southbound, just w; exit 212B (Alameda Pkwy), 0.9 mi nw. **Facility:** 150 units. 6 stories, interior corridors. **Parking:** valet and coin laundry, area transportation.

AAA Benefit: Members save 5% or more!

THE WESTIN DENVER DOWNTOWN
(303)572-9100 **4**

▼▼▼▼ **Hotel** $149-$399

WESTIN HOTELS & RESORTS **AAA Benefit:** Members save up to 15%, plus Starwood Preferred Guest® benefits!

Address: 1672 Lawrence St 80202 **Location:** Between 16th and 17th sts. **Facility:** Find luxurious public areas and city- and mountain-view accommodations at this downtown hotel, where contemporary rooms are decorated in muted earth tones. 430 units. 19 stories, interior corridors. **Parking:** on-site (fee) and valet. **Amenities:** safes. **Dining:** The Palm Restaurant, see separate listing. **Pool(s):** heated outdoor. **Activities:** exercise room, massage. **Guest Services:** valet laundry, boarding pass kiosk.

WHERE TO EAT

1515 RESTAURANT
303/571-0011 **18**

▼▼▼ American. Fine Dining. $10-$40 **AAA Inspector Notes:** The exposed brick walls, historic photos, fresh flowers and light wood wine storage combine to create a classy, casual atmosphere. A bar fills the lower level, but the upstairs has a quieter dining area. Entrées include Colorado lamb, bison, lobster, elk, chicken and fish. **Features:** full bar. **Reservations:** suggested. **Address:** 1515 Market St 80202 **Location:** Just ne of jct 15th and Market sts.

ACE
303/242-8520 **45**

▼▼ Asian Fusion. Casual Dining. $10-$15 **AAA Inspector Notes:** Here you'll enjoy simple fusion cuisine in a lively atmosphere. Menu items include pork belly banh mi, kung pao chicken and Mongolian beef. Chicken dumplings and crispy beef make a great start to the meal, and the specialty cocktails will please the adventurous imbiber. In addition, patrons can pay to play ping-pong in an adjoining room. Be sure to reserve a spot in advance as the tables fill up fast. This place is perfect for a first date or a fun evening with friends. **Features:** full bar, patio dining, happy hour. **Address:** 501 E 17th Ave 80203 **Location:** Between Pennsylvania and Pearl sts. **Parking:** on-site (fee) and street.

BIKER JIM'S DOGS
720/746-9355 **3**

▼ Hot Dogs. Quick Serve. $7-$9 **AAA Inspector Notes:** The lowly hot dog, although an American staple, often appears as a punchline in jokes about bad food. Luckily, Denver has Biker Jim, a man with a mission to elevate street food to the level of gourmet cuisine. He succeeded. The Southwest buffalo dog is spicy, meaty and topped with cream cheese and caramelized onions. Delicious! **Features:** full bar. **Address:** 2148 Larimer St 80205 **Location:** Between 21st and 22nd sts. **Parking:** street only.

BISTRO VENDOME
303/825-3232 **30**

▼▼▼ French. Casual Dining. $17-$26 **AAA Inspector Notes:** This restaurant evokes the air of a family-owned Parisian eatery. Skilled staffers knowledgeably explain the French wine choices, which you can appreciate with varied courses of hearty French food. Start with the foie gras, escargot, or mussels, served in a savory broth. Entrees include duck confit, roasted chicken, and steak frites. On weekends, the brunch has an ardent following with the eggs Benedict; it's a major highlight. **Features:** full bar, patio dining, Sunday brunch, happy hour. **Reservations:** suggested. **Address:** 1420 Larimer St 80202 **Location:** Between 14th and 15th sts. **Parking:** valet and street only.

CAFE COLORE
303/534-6844 **22**

▼▼ Italian. Casual Dining. $9-$20 **AAA Inspector Notes:** Located in Larimer Square, an outdoor retail area close to LODO (lower downtown), the eatery features a menu centering on gourmet pizzas and calzones, creative panini, salads and pasta. Sample dishes include the prosciutto arugula pizza, chicken Parmesan panini, salmon pappardelle, and braised beef short rib. Patrons can choose from a selection of local draft beers and an ample wine list. The patio, a popular place to dine in good weather, gives the restaurant a bistro feel. **Features:** full bar, happy hour. **Address:** 1512 Larimer St, Unit R12 80202 **Location:** Corner of 15th and Larimer sts. **Parking:** on-site (fee) and street.

THE CAPITAL GRILLE
303/539-2500 **24**

▼▼▼ Steak. Fine Dining. $16-$51 **AAA Inspector Notes:** This is by far one of the most popular steakhouses in the city. It's a bit pricey, but certainly worth it for a special night out on the town. Start with the jumbo shrimp cocktail. The spinach salad is served with a slightly sweet and salty warm bacon dressing. You can't go wrong with any of the steaks. Try the porcini-rubbed Delmonico glazed with aged balsamic vinegar. The masculine décor filled with dark woods, framed oil paintings and tasteful taxidermy creates a warm and inviting ambience. **Features:** full bar. **Reservations:** suggested. **Address:** 1450 Larimer St 80202 **Location:** Between 14th and 15th sts. **Parking:** valet and street only.

THE CENTENNIAL TAVERN
303/863-7473 **35**

▼▼ American. Gastropub. $10-$19 **AAA Inspector Notes:** Beware, this restaurant is extremely popular, especially on weekends, but for good reason. The pub portion of the menu features the perfect wine list and a generous selection of craft beers, many from Colorado. Plenty of wines by the glass as well as some low- and high-end bottle options are available. Not to be outdone, the gastro part of the menu touts upscale comfort food like the "lamby joe" (a sloppy joe with lamb meat), the "blue plate roast" and Lowcountry grits. **Features:** full bar, happy hour. **Address:** 400 E 20th Ave 80205 **Location:** Jct Logan St. **Parking:** street only.

CHOLON MODERN ASIAN BISTRO
303/353-5223 **16**

▼▼ Asian Fusion. Casual Dining. $11-$36 **AAA Inspector Notes:** Chef and co-owner, Lon Symensma, traveled to France, Spain and Asia in order to hone his culinary skills. Luckily for us, he settled in Denver. The exciting menu features fusion at its best. The standout dish for the evening was actually a "small bite," the soup dumplings with sweet onions and Gruyère. Basically, this is the best French onion soup I've ever had. The soup is carefully packaged in dough and steamed in a bamboo basket—a traditional Chinese technique, but with European ingredients. **Features:** full bar, happy hour. **Reservations:** suggested. **Address:** 1555 Blake St, Suite 101 80202 **Location:** Between 15th and 16th sts. **Parking:** valet and street only.

CHOPHOUSE & BREWERY
303/296-0800

▼▼ Steak. Casual Dining. $12-$39 **AAA Inspector Notes:** In a 1923 train depot adjacent to Coors Field, this place carries out a railroad theme in its dining room. When the casually upscale LoDo hot spot is busy, which is often, the restaurant can get noisy. Watch the activity in the open kitchen as the chefs whip up contemporary dishes, including flavorful tenderloin tips with mushrooms, in addition to various cuts of beef, lamb and pork, and wood-oven pizzas, chicken and salads. Beers brewed on site provide just the right refreshment. **Features:** full bar, Sunday brunch, happy hour. **Reservations:** suggested. **Address:** 1735 19th St, Suite 100 80202 **Location:** I-25 exit 212C (20th St), just e; at Wynkoop St. **Parking:** valet only.

Visit the AAA/CAA senior driver sites for resources to help you drive safely longer

(See map & index p. 133.)

CITY O' CITY   303/831-6443 **51**

💎💎 Pizza Vegetarian. Casual Dining. $11-$13 **AAA Inspector Notes:** This restaurant is known for its vegetarian pizzas and vegan baked goods, although the menu includes an eclectic range of vegetarian starters, salads and sandwiches, too. The vegan desserts feature crumbly scones and rich chocolate cupcakes, a must for anyone with a sweet tooth. This café is a popular hangout for those seeking a dark, hipster coffeehouse during the day. After dark, it livens up for late-night drinks. The service is on the slow side. The restroom has excessive graffiti. **Features:** full bar, patio dining, happy hour. **Address:** 206 E 13th Ave 80203 **Location:** Just e of jct Lincoln Ave. **Parking:** street only.

B   L   D   LATE

THE DELECTABLE EGG   303/892-5720 **44**

💎💎 Breakfast. Casual Dining. $5-$11 **AAA Inspector Notes:** In a busy area with a devoted core of regular patrons, this restaurant is a great breakfast option. Diners can munch on oversize portions of freshly made Belgian waffles, light, fluffy pancakes smothered in butter, savory Benedicts and scrambles. Lunch options include sandwiches, burgers and salads. **Address:** 1625 Court Pl 80202 **Location:** Just ne of 16th Street Pedestrian Mall. **Parking:** street only.

B   L

DOMO   303/595-3666 **48**

💎 Japanese. Casual Dining. $9-$25 **AAA Inspector Notes:** Step into Domo and step into another country. Evocative of a traditional Japanese country house, the setting incorporates padded log stools, stone tables, and tree branch and paper lanterns. You won't be offered additional soy sauce, salt or pepper for your food so you can taste it in the authentic tradition that chef/owner Gaku Homma intends. Select from items such as wanko sushi, nabemono soups, teriyaki, noodle dishes or donburi bowls. **Features:** full bar. **Address:** 1365 Osage St 80204 **Location:** I-25 exit 210A (Colfax Ave), just e, then just s.

L   D

EDGE RESTAURANT & BAR   303/389-3343 **36**

💎💎💎   **Steak**   **Fine Dining**   **$12-$46**

AAA Inspector Notes: Of course, a truly great steak house must have high-quality, flavorful, tender beef—that's a given. This one, however, excels in so many other areas. The artful presentations of the salads, appetizers and desserts delight the senses. Start with the snow crab claws and shrimp served with atomic cocktail sauce. The perfectly seasoned, bone-in steaks may be topped with classic Béarnaise sauce or something more creative like yuzu butter or bruleed bone marrow. **Features:** full bar, Sunday brunch. **Reservations:** suggested. **Address:** 1111 14th St 80202 **Location:** Between Lawrence and Arapahoe sts; in Four Seasons Hotel Denver. **Parking:** valet only.

B   L   D

ELLYNGTON'S AT THE BROWN PALACE   303/297-3111 **42**

💎💎💎 American. Fine Dining. $11-$26 **AAA Inspector Notes:** The city's business elite dine here for breakfast and lunch, so you can expect a lot of suits. Sumptuous breakfasts and lunches with salads, sandwiches, steaks, seafood and pasta are served in elegant surroundings. This place is known for its Dom Perignon Sunday brunch. Sample items include made-to-order omelets, raw oysters, smoked fish, imported cheeses, carved meats, and rich desserts, including a chocolate fountain. **Reservations:** suggested. **Address:** 321 17th St 80202 **Location:** From Broadway and Tremont Pl, just sw; in The Brown Palace Hotel and Spa, Autograph Collection. **Parking:** valet only. B   L

ELWAY'S DOWNTOWN   303/312-3107 **19**

💎💎💎 Steak. Casual Dining. $15-$60 **AAA Inspector Notes:** Named after former Broncos quarterback John Elway, one of the owners, this restaurant takes the concept of a standard Colorado steakhouse and adds sophisticated decor, refined staff and high-quality ingredients. The menu consists of innovative appetizers, such as lamb chop fondue, and top-quality steaks and seafood. **Features:** full bar, patio dining, Sunday brunch, happy hour. **Reservations:** suggested. **Address:** 1881 Curtis St 80202 **Location:** Between 18th and 19th sts; in The Ritz-Carlton, Denver. **Parking:** valet only.

B   L   D

EUCLID HALL BAR & KITCHEN   303/595-4255 **28**

💎💎 American. Gastropub. $10-$23 **AAA Inspector Notes:** In addition to creative pub food like hand-cranked sausage, Dan Dan noodles, schnitzel, poutine, and po'boys, diners will find an extensive beer and wine list as well as hand-crafted cocktails. The sticky, sweet s'mores pot de creme is filled with nostalgia. Housed in an 1883 building with a unique history, the restaurant is located near a popular shopping district. Valet parking is available on Friday and Saturday evenings. **Features:** full bar, patio dining, happy hour. **Address:** 1317 14th St 80202 **Location:** Jct 14th and Larimer sts, just w; in historic Larimer Square. **Parking:** street only.

L   D   LATE

GREEN FINE SALAD CO.   303/629-9127 **47**

💎 Natural/Organic. Quick Serve. $7-$10 **AAA Inspector Notes:** Redefining fast food, this restaurant focuses on quality ingredients, quick service and attractive, modern décor. Patrons may choose from a variety of specialty salads or create their own. Soups, cookies and salads wrapped in a tortilla also are available. **Address:** 110 16th St 80202 **Location:** Jct Broadway; at beginning of 16th Street Pedestrian Mall. **Parking:** street only.

L

GUARD AND GRACE   303/293-8500 **34**

💎💎💎 Steak. Fine Dining. $25-$63 **AAA Inspector Notes:** Live plants, wood ceiling beams and hardwood floors add to the contemporary, urban décor. Select a premium Prime, Angus or grass-fed steak and top it with a rich foie gras butter, crab-heavy Oscar, or traditional brandy peppercorn sauce. Start with the perfectly balanced sweet-and-tart beet salad with charred cauliflower, pistachios, and a blood orange vinaigrette. Other standout starters include tuna from the raw bar, and the charcuterie and cheese plate. **Features:** full bar, happy hour. **Reservations:** suggested. **Address:** 1801 California St 80202 **Location:** Between 18th and 19th sts. **Parking:** valet and street only.

L   D

HARD ROCK CAFE   303/623-3191 **40**

💎💎 American. Casual Dining. $9-$18 **AAA Inspector Notes:** Rock 'n' roll memorabilia decorates the walls of the popular theme restaurant. Live music on the weekends contributes to the bustling atmosphere. On the menu is a wide variety of American cuisine—from burgers and sandwiches to salads, steaks and pasta. **Features:** full bar. **Address:** 500 16th St, Suite 120 80202 **Location:** Jct Glenarm St; in 16th Street Pedestrian Mall. **Parking:** street only.

SAVE   L   D   LATE

JAX FISH HOUSE   303/292-5767 **12**

💎💎💎 Seafood. Casual Dining. $10-$46 **AAA Inspector Notes:** Popular area chef David Query adds this busy fish house to his successful roster of Boulder eateries, which include another Jax restaurant and Zolo Grill. The establishment flies in fresh fish. The colorful décor adds to the upbeat ambiance. It can get noisy when the place is full. Valet parking is offered Friday and Saturday evenings. **Features:** full bar, patio dining, happy hour. **Reservations:** suggested. **Address:** 1539 17th St 80202 **Location:** Corner of 17th and Wazee sts. **Parking:** valet and street only. D

LARKBURGER   720/250-0533 **38**

💎 Burgers. Quick Serve. $4-$10 **AAA Inspector Notes:** Flavorful burgers, shakes, and fries have drawn a large and devoted following to this cozy, quick-serve restaurant. The tasty menu benefits from high quality, 100-percent-natural ingredients, including all-natural turkey, chicken and black Angus beef. The casual, modern décor features wall panels made from reclaimed timber. **Features:** beer only. **Address:** 1617 California St, Unit B 80202 **Location:** Between 16th and 17th sts. **Parking:** street only. L   D

LUCKY PIE PIZZA & TAP HOUSE   303/825-1021 **14**

💎💎 Pizza. Casual Dining. $8-$15 **AAA Inspector Notes:** The perfect place to stop after a stroll along 16th Street Pedestrian Mall, this casual eatery serves pizza made with all natural, organic and local products. The quality comes through in every bite. Interesting starters include the braised lamb meatballs, fried cheese curds, and the savory, sweet bacon peanut brittle. Gourmet sandwiches offer an alternative to pizza. **Features:** full bar, patio dining, happy hour. **Address:** 1610 16th St 80202 **Location:** Between Wazee and Wynkoop sts. **Parking:** street only.

L   D

(See map & index p. 133.)

MARCO'S COAL- FIRED PIZZERIA   303/296-7000 4

 Pizza. Casual Dining. $9-$19 **AAA Inspector Notes:** Located in the LoDo neighborhood, a few blocks from Coors Field, this eatery serves gourmet pizzas in a modern, bistro-style setting. Feeling adventurous? Try the Del Re, a creamy white pizza with fresh mozzarella, pecorino Sardo truffle spread, mushrooms, and thinly sliced prosciutto di Parma. High-quality ingredients ensure that even the traditional New York pies—featuring Italian sausage, pepperoni, spicy salami, coppa and a variety of vegetables—stand out. **Features:** full bar, Sunday brunch, happy hour. **Address:** 2129 Larimer St 80205 **Location:** Between 21st and 22nd sts. **Parking:** street only.

L D

THE MARKET   303/534-5140 25

Deli. Quick Serve. $6-$13 **AAA Inspector Notes:** The Market draws a diverse crowd. Patrons stop in for a cup of coffee, a quick lunch or dinner from the deli, or a luscious dessert. **Features:** beer & wine. **Address:** 1445 Larimer St 80202 **Location:** Between 14th and 15th sts. **Parking:** street only.   B L D

MCCORMICK'S FISH HOUSE & BAR   303/825-1107 13

Regional Seafood. Fine Dining. $13-$40 **AAA Inspector Notes:** This restaurant features a good variety of fresh seafood from both coasts and Victorian-style décor reflecting the building's past. The lump crab tower had the perfect blend of flavors using avocado, mango and crab. Though seafood is the main attraction, the filet mignon was tender and had great flavor. For a before- or after-dinner drink, waltz over to one of Denver's most unusual lounges, the Art Deco-style Cruise Room, which is across the corridor. **Features:** full bar, happy hour. **Reservations:** suggested. **Address:** 1659 Wazee St 80202 **Location:** Corner of 17th and Wazee sts; in The Oxford Hotel. **Parking:** valet and street only.   B L D LATE

MORTON'S THE STEAKHOUSE   303/825-3353 10

Steak. Fine Dining. $28-$58 **AAA Inspector Notes:** Patrons should make sure to reserve ahead for the popular, well-known steakhouse. Large portions, including huge cuts of fine beef and plentiful seafood, are the norm. Even the vegetables are oversized, with baked potatoes big enough for sharing. **Features:** full bar. **Reservations:** suggested. **Address:** 1710 Wynkoop St 80202 **Location:** Between 17th and 18th sts. **Parking:** on-site (fee) and valet.

D CALL M

THE OCEANAIRE SEAFOOD ROOM   303/991-2277 37

Seafood. Fine Dining. $26-$60 **AAA Inspector Notes:** Fresh fish and shellfish are flown in daily from around the globe. The sleek, handsomely designed dining room has a raw bar and is tastefully appointed in an Art Deco/nautical theme. The menu notes the seafood available daily and the varied preparation styles, such as broiled, grilled and blackened. **Features:** full bar, happy hour. **Reservations:** suggested. **Address:** 1400 Arapahoe St 80202 **Location:** Between 14th and 15th sts. **Parking:** valet and street only. SAVE D

OSTERIA MARCO   303/534-5855 23

Italian. Casual Dining. $10-$27 **AAA Inspector Notes:** As a cheese lover, I couldn't resist trying the homemade mozzarella accompanied by the sopressata picante. Wow! It was possibly the best cheese and salumi combo I've ever tasted. If I had known, I would have just ordered a huge plate of it and skipped the entrée. I'm glad I didn't, though, because the beet salad and scallops were also delicious. The unique location allows you to enter at street level, but you're led down into the restaurant below ground. It makes it feel a bit secretive. **Features:** full bar, patio dining, happy hour. **Address:** 1453 Larimer St 80202 **Location:** Between 14th and 15th sts. **Parking:** street only.   L D

PALACE ARMS   303/297-3111 41

Continental Fine Dining $29-$60

AAA Inspector Notes: *Historic.* For a truly magnificent dining experience, patrons must spend an evening here. In addition to being located in a legendary hotel, the restaurant offers creative cuisine to make this fine dining experience truly exceptional. The complex flavors of a layered bed of foie gras, truffle, Swiss chard and brioche make the tender Colorado bison simply outstanding. **Features:** full bar. **Reservations:** suggested. **Address:** 321 17th St 80202 **Location:** From Broadway and Tremont Pl, just sw; in The Brown Palace Hotel and Spa, Autograph Collection. **Parking:** valet only. D

PALETTES   303/534-1455 49

American. Casual Dining. $12-$18 **AAA Inspector Notes:** The warm, contemporary décor fits well with this restaurant's location in the Denver Art Museum. The glass windows allow diners to gaze at the newest wing of the museum and the sculptures outside. This artistic theme transcends the walls and appears on your plate. The light and savory ahi tuna wonton tacos provide the perfect starter. Entrées include seared diver scallops, pork loin schnitzel sandwich, grilled Angus, beef tenderloin, and a charbroiled sirloin burger. **Features:** full bar, Sunday brunch. **Address:** 100 W 14th Ave Pkwy 80204 **Location:** 1 blk w of Broadway; south end of Civic Center; in Denver Art Museum. **Parking:** on-site (fee).

L CALL M

THE PALM RESTAURANT   303/825-7256 20

American. Fine Dining. $22-$57 **AAA Inspector Notes:** This bustling restaurant is noted for Prime, dry-aged steaks and Nova Scotia lobsters. The huge portions are delivered by an attentive staff in an atmosphere that is fun and lively. At the end of the meal, servers present tempting pastries tableside. Caricature-lined walls lend to the feeling that patrons are dining in an art gallery. Even if you bring a big appetite you still may leave with a doggy bag. **Features:** full bar. **Address:** 1672 Lawrence St 80202 **Location:** Between 16th and 17th sts; in The Westin Denver Downtown. **Parking:** valet only.

L D CALL M

PANZANO   303/296-3525 32

Northern Italian Fine Dining $14-$32

AAA Inspector Notes: Talented, innovative chef Elise Wiggins specializes in Northern Italian cuisine. Focusing on fresh, organic, local and naturally raised ingredients, every artfully presented dish delights the senses. Her crespelle ai funghi (mushroom-stuffed crepes) whets the appetite for pasta, seasonal fish, sea scallops, grass-fed veal and rabbit entrées. The bold gray, red and black décor provides an atmosphere of class and elegance. The knowledgeable, friendly staff puts you at ease. **Features:** full bar, Sunday brunch, happy hour. **Reservations:** suggested. **Address:** 909 17th St 80202 **Location:** Between 17th and 18th sts; in Hotel Monaco Denver. **Parking:** valet only.

B L D

PINTS PUB   303/534-7543 50

British. Casual Dining. $10-$14 **AAA Inspector Notes:** Contributing to this brewpub's good local reputation are 22 draft beers, 200 single-malt scotches and six beers made in the on-site brewery. The menu includes burgers, sandwiches, fish and chips, and bangers and mash. **Features:** full bar, happy hour. **Address:** 221 W 13th Ave 80204 **Location:** Between Bannock and Cherokee sts; just w of Denver Art Museum. L D

RED SQUARE EURO BISTRO   303/595-8600 21

Russian. Fine Dining. $18-$29 **AAA Inspector Notes:** This cozy café offers European cuisine with a Russian twist. Entrées include the signature Red Square stroganoff, grilled New York strip, grilled rack of lamb, seared duck and pan-seared halibut. In true Russian fashion, there are more than 50 different vodkas to sample. Patio dining is available when weather permits. **Reservations:** suggested. **Address:** 1512 Larimer St, Suite R38 80202 **Location:** Jct 15th and Larimer sts; just e of historic Larimer Square; in Writer Square. **Parking:** on-site (fee).

D CALL M

RIOJA   303/820-2282 27

American Fine Dining $13-$31

AAA Inspector Notes: After spending 10 years working with Wolfgang Puck, chef Jennifer Jasinski brought her culinary talent to Colorado, where she met her current business partner and sommelier, Beth Gruitch. They opened Rioja in 2004 and have been receiving numerous awards and accolades ever since, including a James Beard Foundation award for Best Chef Southwest. The seasonal menu consists of delicious handmade pastas, seafood, Colorado lamb, duck and steak entrées. **Features:** full bar, patio dining, Sunday brunch. **Reservations:** suggested. **Address:** 1431 Larimer St 80202 **Location:** Between 14th and 15th sts; in historic Larimer Square. **Parking:** valet and street only. L D

(See map & index p. 133.)

ROCK BOTTOM BREWERY
303/534-7616 (33)

▼▼ American. Casual Dining. $9-$25 **AAA Inspector Notes:** Highlights of this brewery include flavorful chicken wings, seasonal beers and a famous patio. The excellent location, on the 16th St. Mall, makes the patio perfect for people-watching. Entrées include everything from burgers to baby back ribs. **Features:** full bar, patio dining. **Address:** 1001 16th Street Mall, Unit 100 80265 **Location:** Between Arapahoe and Curtis sts. **Parking:** street only.

L D LATE CALL M

RODIZIO GRILL
303/294-9277 (5)

▼▼ Brazilian. Casual Dining. $19-$35 **AAA Inspector Notes:** This Brazilian-style restaurant is fun, festive and a meat-eater's paradise. They feature up to 15 types of beef, turkey, pork, chicken, lamb and fish options. Meals are grilled in an open kitchen and removed from the skewer by a server dressed in gaucho attire. An extensive salad bar is included in the meal price. **Features:** full bar, Sunday brunch. **Address:** 1801 Wynkoop St 80202 **Location:** Corner of 18th and Wynkoop sts. **Parking:** street only. L D

RUSSELL'S SMOKEHOUSE
720/524-8050 (29)

▼▼ Barbecue. Casual Dining. $14-$26 **AAA Inspector Notes:** Homemade barbecue sauces, house-smoked meats and specialty cocktails make this restaurant a standout. The combination of smoke and tang come together in the smoked potted trout, a dip accented with fresh pesto. The pork shoulder creates the perfect base for sampling the sweet, spicy and vinegar barbecue sauces. Located on historic Larimer Square, walk down the stairs to a surprisingly sophisticated space filled with dark wood, modern Western oil paintings, and reclaimed stained glass windows. **Features:** full bar, happy hour. **Reservations:** suggested. **Address:** 1422 Larimer St 80202 **Location:** Between 14th and 15th sts. **Parking:** street only. L D

SHIP TAVERN
303/297-3111 (43)

▼▼ American. Casual Dining. $15-$45 **AAA Inspector Notes:** Cape Cod model ships and other nautical accents, as well as closely spaced tables, create a cozy, comfortable ambiance. Prime rib is the signature dish. Among other favorite choices are fresh seafood (try the lobster roll), Kobe beef burgers, Rocky Mountain trout and French onion soup. Longtime bartenders serve more than 30 microbrews. **Features:** full bar. **Reservations:** suggested. **Address:** 321 17th St 80202 **Location:** From Broadway and Tremont Pl, just sw; in The Brown Palace Hotel and Spa, Autograph Collection. **Parking:** valet only. L D

SNOOZE
303/297-0700 (2)

▼ Breakfast. Casual Dining. $8-$12 **AAA Inspector Notes:** Enter and you'll immediately feel this place is special. Reminiscent of a '50s diner, this popular eatery sports mod décor that appeals to its diverse clientele. After just one bite, you'll taste what makes this place stand out. The menu is breakfast-centric and entrées include the savory and the sweet: Juan's breakfast tacos, eggs Benedict, sweet potato pancakes and sticky bun French toast. Brunch items include gourmet sandwiches, a 'ballpark' burger, and fish tacos. **Features:** full bar. **Address:** 2262 Larimer St 80205 **Location:** From Market St, just se on 23rd St, just sw; jct W Park Ave. **Parking:** street only.

B L

THE SQUEAKY BEAN
303/623-2665 (15)

▼▼▼ American. Casual Dining. $21-$36 **AAA Inspector Notes:** Imaginative cuisine, specialty cocktails and warm décor are hallmarks of this foodie favorite. The menu changes seasonally and incorporates vegetables grown in the owners' organic, urban farm. **Features:** full bar, Sunday brunch. **Reservations:** suggested. **Address:** 1500 Wynkoop St, Suite 101 80202 **Location:** Corner of 15th St. **Parking:** street only. D

STEUBEN'S
303/830-1001 (46)

▼▼ American. Casual Dining. $5-$18 **AAA Inspector Notes:** Locals head to this restaurant to indulge in comfort food, decadent desserts and interesting cocktails. The retro, casually upscale décor is slightly fancy for a diner, but it's still a diner. Menu options reflect a creative flair enhanced by higher quality ingredients. Fried chicken, macaroni and cheese and pot roast sidle up next to cayenne étouffée, trout amandine, and a lobster roll. It would be a sin to skip a milk shake, lemon icebox bar, or chocolate cake. **Features:** full bar, Sunday brunch, happy hour. **Address:** 523 E 17th Ave 80203 **Location:** Corner of Pearl St. and 17th Ave. L D

STOIC & GENUINE
303/640-3474 (8)

▼▼ Seafood. Fine Dining. $13-$38 **AAA Inspector Notes:** The fourth restaurant from the James Beard Award-winning chef Jennifer Jasinski and her business partner Beth Gruitch, this place takes seafood to a different level. Start with the octopus, served warm with a nice char, complemented by a slightly sweet pickled onion and dill pistachio pesto. The paella moderna takes all of the elements of a traditional paella, deconstructed for something new. The fried triangle of saffron rice would make an amazing meal even without the seafood accompanying it. **Features:** full bar, happy hour. **Address:** 1701 Wynkoop St 80202 **Location:** At 17th St; in historic Union Train Station. **Parking:** valet and street only. L D CALL M

SULLIVAN'S STEAKHOUSE
303/295-2664 (9)

▼▼ Steak. Fine Dining. $25-$60 **AAA Inspector Notes:** Named for John L. Sullivan, heavyweight champion of the world in the 1880s, the upscale steakhouse prepares a wide selection of steaks, chops and seafood. The décor features black-and-white photographs of Sullivan, Jack Dempsey and other boxing legends. **Features:** full bar. **Reservations:** suggested. **Address:** 1745 Wazee St 80202 **Location:** Just sw of jct 18th and Wazee sts. **Parking:** valet only. D CALL M

TAG
303/996-9985 (26)

▼▼▼ Fusion. Casual Dining. $14-$32 **AAA Inspector Notes:** This place offers a unique style of cuisine, blending local and Asian ingredients and styles to create something new. The Kobe beef sliders served with duck fat fries are the perfect start to any meal. Entrées feature duck, pork rib chops and an ever-changing selection of fresh fish. The specialty cocktails, such as the Jalapeño kumquat mojito, draw many locals during the social hour. **Features:** full bar, patio dining, happy hour. **Reservations:** suggested. **Address:** 1441 Larimer St 80202 **Location:** Between 14th and 15th sts; in historic Larimer Square. **Parking:** valet and street only. L D

TAMAYO
720/946-1433 (31)

▼▼▼ Mexican. Casual Dining. $12-$28 **AAA Inspector Notes:** With an excellent location on historic Larimer Square, this upscale eatery offers traditional Mexican flavors with a modern twist. Famous for its freshly made guacamole and specialty margaritas, this restaurant also features creative entrées, such as crab and shrimp enchiladas, slow-roasted pork carnitas, and beef tenderloin skewers. Weather permitting, the upstairs patio offers outstanding mountain views. **Features:** full bar, patio dining, Sunday brunch, happy hour. **Reservations:** suggested. **Address:** 1400 Larimer St 80202 **Location:** Corner of 14th and Larimer sts. **Parking:** street only.

L D

TRILLIUM
303/379-9759 (6)

▼▼▼ New Scandinavian. Casual Dining. $20-$30 **AAA Inspector Notes:** The unique cuisine at this modern eatery has earned many accolades from local critics. The Smörgåsbord features small tastes of delectable items, such as the highly recommended air-cured beef tenderloin, caviar and fresh oysters. Creative entrées include the open-faced ravioli with grilled blue prawns, seared duck breast, steelhead trout and New York strip steak. **Features:** full bar, happy hour. **Address:** 2134 Larimer St 80205 **Location:** Between 21st and 22nd sts. **Parking:** street only. D

VESTA DIPPING GRILL
303/296-1970 (11)

▼▼▼ International. Fine Dining. $18-$40 **AAA Inspector Notes:** Named after the Roman Goddess of the Hearth, this popular LoDo restaurant features delicious, innovative cuisine and knowledgeable staff who are enthusiastic about the food. The attractive mix of unique light fixtures, exposed brick walls and worn Victorian-era hardwood floors creates a warm, inviting atmosphere. Entrées consist of grilled meats such as beef, lamb, duck, chicken, fish and pork. There are also vegetarian options. **Features:** full bar, happy hour. **Reservations:** suggested. **Address:** 1822 Blake St 80202 **Location:** Between 18th and 19th sts. **Parking:** street only. D

WAZEE SUPPER CLUB
303/623-9518 (17)

▼▼ American. Casual Dining. $8-$16 **AAA Inspector Notes:** Built in 1910, a plumbing supply house initially occupied this space. Reincarnated in 1974 into a restaurant, Wazee's is now one of LoDo's weekend hot spots. Locals and visitors descend upon this cozy eatery for flavorful, thin-crust pizzas and microbrews. The Amazeballs—breaded and fried mac 'n' cheese with jalapeños, bacon and queso—is a popular starter. The diverse menu also includes salads, burgers and calzones. The eclectic, unique décor enhances any meal. **Features:** full bar, happy hour. **Address:** 1600 15th St 80202 **Location:** Corner of Wazee and 15th sts. **Parking:** street only. L D LATE

(See map & index p. 133.)

WILD BANGKOK BAR AND GRILL 303/623-4999 ㊴
◆◆◆ Thai. Casual Dining. $8-$16 **AAA Inspector Notes:** The modern Thai décor glitters with sparkling gold and purple artwork. The extensive menu has traditional items such as pad thai, drunken noodles and panang curry. However, there are many more adventurous offerings, including Thai barbecue chicken and pork, pumpkin soup and pineapple fried rice with salmon. **Features:** full bar, happy hour. **Address:** 1630 Welton St 80202 **Location:** Between 16th and 17th sts. **Parking:** street only. L D

WILLIE G'S 303/575-9000
◆◆◆ Seafood. Fine Dining. $9-$36 **AAA Inspector Notes:** Conveniently located on the 16th Street Pedestrian Mall, this restaurant offers a wide selection of seafood and beef dishes. Specialties include bacon-wrapped scallops, American Kobe beef sliders and brown butter mahi mahi. The masculine, dark wood interior is softened by red and gold accents. **Features:** full bar, happy hour. **Address:** 1585 Lawrence St 80202 **Location:** Corner of Lawrence St and 16th Street Pedestrian Mall. **Parking:** street only. L D

WYNKOOP BREWING COMPANY 303/297-2700 ⑦
◆◆ American. Casual Dining. $10-$20 **AAA Inspector Notes:** Founded in 1988 in a historic building, this brewery has the distinction of being the first in Denver. Today, the brewmaster continues the tradition of using unique ingredients in the beer, including green chiles and Rocky Mountain oysters. Start your evening by sharing some oven-glazed chicken wings, or the beer and cheese dip. For a hearty entrée, try the mac and cheese or the buffalo meatloaf. Lighter fare includes green chile soup, bison burgers and grilled shrimp salad. **Features:** full bar, Sunday brunch, happy hour. **Address:** 1634 18th St 80202 **Location:** Jct Wynkoop St; opposite Union Station. **Parking:** street only. L D LATE

ZENGO 720/904-0965 ①
◆◆◆ Fusion. Casual Dining. $18-$36 **AAA Inspector Notes:** Chef/owner Richard Sandoval went in a new direction with this place by blending Asian and Latin American cuisine. Although it sounds unusual, chef de cuisine Clint Wangsnes artfully fuses the flavors from these two areas of the world in a variety of delicious, delightful dishes. Enjoy Thai chicken empanadas, arepas de puerco, crispy Peking duck confit with daikon tortillas and orange coriander sauce, and much more. The sleek, modern décor enhances the dining experience. **Features:** full bar, Sunday brunch, happy hour. **Reservations:** suggested. **Address:** 1610 Little Raven St 80202 **Location:** Just ne of jct 15th St. **Parking:** valet and street only. D

DENVER (C-9)
- **Restaurants p. 158**
- **Hotels & Restaurants map & index p. 136**

BEST WESTERN PLUS DENVER INTERNATIONAL AIRPORT INN & SUITES (303)373-1600 ②
◆◆ Hotel $79-$209

Best Western PLUS AAA Benefit: Save 10% or more every day and earn 10% bonus points!

Address: 7020 Tower Rd 80249 **Location:** I-70 exit 286 (Tower Rd), 4.5 mi n. **Facility:** 101 units. 3 stories, interior corridors. **Pool(s):** heated indoor. **Activities:** hot tub, limited exercise equipment. **Guest Services:** valet and coin laundry.
SAVE ⊞ ⊞ ➔ BIZ 🛜 ✕
🖥 🖨 💻

CAPITOL HILL MANSION BED & BREAKFAST INN (303)839-5221 ㉛
◆◆◆ Historic Bed & Breakfast $154-$229 **Address:** 1207 Pennsylvania St 80203 **Location:** Jct 12th Ave. **Facility:** Turrets and a balcony add architectural interest to this red sandstone mansion located in a historic residential neighborhood. 8 units, some kitchens. 3 stories (no elevator), interior/exterior corridors. **Terms:** 14 day cancellation notice-fee imposed. **Guest Services:** valet laundry.
BIZ 🛜 ✕ 🖥 💻 /SOME UNITS 🖨

CASTLE MARNE BED AND BREAKFAST 303/331-0621 ㉚
◆◆◆ Historic Bed & Breakfast. Rates not provided. **Address:** 1572 Race St 80206 **Location:** 1.3 mi e of jct Colfax Ave and Broadway, then just n. Located in Wyman Historic District. **Facility:** Built in 1889, this Victorian-era home features an impressive lavastone exterior, intricate stained glass windows, and carved wood accents. Enjoy your breakfast next to the lovingly tended garden. 9 units. 3 stories (no elevator), interior corridors. **Parking:** on-site and street. **Terms:** check-in 4 pm. **Guest Services:** valet laundry.
BIZ 🛜 ✕ 🅦

COMFORT INN DENVER EAST (303)375-1500 ⑱
◆◆ Hotel $79-$129 **Address:** 4380 Peoria St 80239 **Location:** I-70 exit 281 eastbound; exit 282 westbound, just n. **Facility:** 137 units. 4 stories, interior corridors. **Pool(s):** heated indoor. **Activities:** hot tub, exercise room. **Guest Services:** valet and coin laundry.
⊞ ➔ BIZ HS 🛜 ✕ 🖥 🖨 💻
/SOME UNITS 🅢

COUNTRY INN & SUITES BY CARLSON, DENVER INTERNATIONAL AIRPORT (303)375-1105 ㉓
◆◆◆ Hotel $109-$209

Address: 4343 N Airport Way 80239 **Location:** I-70 exit 283 (Chambers Rd), just n to 40th Ave, 0.5 mi e, then just n. **Facility:** 193 units. 6 stories, interior corridors. **Terms:** 7 day cancellation notice. **Pool(s):** heated indoor. **Activities:** hot tub, exercise room. **Guest Services:** valet and coin laundry. **Featured Amenity:** breakfast buffet.
SAVE ⊞ ⊞ CALL 🛗 ➔ BIZ
HS 🛜 ✕ 🖥 🖨 💻

COURTYARD BY MARRIOTT DENVER AIRPORT (303)371-0300 ⑥
◆◆◆ Hotel $96-$337

COURTYARD Marriott AAA Benefit: Members save 5% or more!

Address: 6901 Tower Rd 80249 **Location:** I-70 exit 286 (Tower Rd), 4.3 mi n; 0.8 mi s of Pena Blvd. **Facility:** 202 units. 8 stories, interior corridors. **Pool(s):** heated indoor. **Activities:** hot tub, exercise room. **Guest Services:** valet and coin laundry, boarding pass kiosk.
SAVE ECO ⊞ ⊞ CALL 🛗
➔ BIZ 🛜 ✕ 🍴 🖥 💻
/SOME UNITS 🖨

COURTYARD BY MARRIOTT DENVER CHERRY CREEK (303)757-8797 ㉞
◆◆◆ Hotel $106-$249

COURTYARD Marriott AAA Benefit: Members save 5% or more!

Address: 1475 S Colorado Blvd 80222 **Location:** I-25 exit 204, 0.5 mi n; entrance on Arkansas St. **Facility:** 240 units. 11 stories, interior corridors. **Pool(s):** heated indoor. **Activities:** hot tub, exercise room. **Guest Services:** valet and coin laundry, boarding pass kiosk.
SAVE ⊞ 🍴 🍸 CALL 🛗 ➔ BIZ
🛜 ✕ 🖥 🖨 💻

(See map & index p. 136.)

COURTYARD BY MARRIOTT DENVER STAPLETON

(303)333-3303 **14**

Hotel
$89-$210

COURTYARD® Marriott.

AAA Benefit: Members save 5% or more!

Address: 7415 E 41st Ave 80216 **Location:** I-70 exit 278, s on Quebec St exit Smith Rd, then e to Frontage Rd; I-270 exit 4. **Facility:** 146 units. 3 stories, interior corridors. **Pool(s):** heated indoor. **Activities:** hot tub, exercise room. **Guest Services:** valet and coin laundry, boarding pass kiosk.

CROWNE PLAZA DENVER AIRPORT - CONVENTION CENTER

(303)371-9494 **25**

Hotel $99-$309 **Address:** 15500 E 40th Ave 80239 **Location:** I-70 exit 283 (Chambers Rd), just n, then just e. **Facility:** 255 units. 6 stories, interior corridors. **Terms:** check-in 4 pm, cancellation fee imposed. **Pool(s):** heated indoor. **Activities:** hot tub, exercise room. **Guest Services:** valet laundry, boarding pass kiosk, area transportation.

DENVER MARRIOTT TECH CENTER

(303)779-1100 **39**

Hotel $85-$297 **Address:** 4900 S Syracuse St 80237 **Location:** I-25 exit 199, exit Belleview Ave E to Syracuse St, then just n. **Facility:** 628 units. 5-11 stories, interior corridors. **Parking:** on-site (fee) and valet. **Pool(s):** heated outdoor, heated indoor. **Activities:** hot tub, exercise room. **Guest Services:** valet and coin laundry, area transportation.

AAA Benefit: Members save 5% or more!

DOUBLETREE BY HILTON DENVER-STAPLETON NORTH

303/321-6666 **15**

Hotel. Rates not provided. **Address:** 4040 Quebec St 80216 **Location:** I-70 exit 278, s on Quebec St to Smith Rd exit, then e to Frontage Rd. **Facility:** 299 units. 5 stories, interior corridors. **Amenities:** Some: safes. **Pool(s):** heated outdoor. **Activities:** exercise room. **Guest Services:** valet and coin laundry, area transportation.

AAA Benefit: Members save 5% or more!

DOUBLETREE BY HILTON HOTEL DENVER

303/321-3333 **29**

Hotel. Rates not provided. **Address:** 3203 Quebec St 80207 **Location:** I-70 exit 278, 0.5 mi s; I-270 exit 4. **Facility:** 561 units. 9 stories, interior corridors. **Amenities:** Some: safes. **Pool(s):** heated indoor. **Activities:** sauna, hot tub, exercise room. **Guest Services:** valet and coin laundry, rental car service, area transportation.

AAA Benefit: Members save 5% or more!

DRURY INN & SUITES DENVER STAPLETON

(303)373-1983 **12**

Hotel $100-$180 **Address:** 4550 N Central Park Blvd 80238 **Location:** I-70 exit 279B westbound; exit 279 eastbound, just n. **Facility:** 181 units. 7 stories, interior corridors. **Terms:** cancellation fee imposed. **Pool(s):** heated indoor. **Activities:** hot tub, exercise room. **Guest Services:** coin laundry, area transportation.

Pick up colorful, top-quality travel guides and atlases at AAA/CAA offices

▼ See AAA listing p. 226 ▼

(See map & index p. 136.)

EMBASSY SUITES BY HILTON DENVER INTERNATIONAL AIRPORT (303)574-3000 **41**

▼▼▼▼ Hotel
$109-$209

AAA Benefit: Members save 5% or more!

Address: 7001 Yampa St 80249 **Location:** I-70 exit 286 (Tower Rd), 4.5 mi n, then just w on 71st Ave; from Pena Blvd, 0.3 mi s, then just w on 71st St. **Facility:** 174 units. 7 stories, interior corridors. **Terms:** 1-7 night minimum stay, cancellation fee imposed. **Pool(s):** heated indoor. **Activities:** hot tub, exercise room. **Guest Services:** complimentary and valet laundry, boarding pass kiosk, area transportation. *(See ad this page.)*

SAVE ✈ ❘❙ 🚼 ❤ CALL 🖐M 🏊 BIZ 📶 ✕ 🍴 🛗 📶 📼 / SOME UNITS $ HS

EMBASSY SUITES BY HILTON DENVER SOUTHEAST 303/696-6644 **36**

▼▼▼ Hotel
Rates not provided

AAA Benefit: Members save 5% or more!

Address: 7525 E Hampden Ave 80231 **Location:** I-25 exit 201, 1 mi e. **Facility:** 205 units. 7 stories, interior corridors. **Pool(s):** heated indoor. **Activities:** hot tub, exercise room. **Guest Services:** valet and coin laundry, area transportation. **Featured Amenity:** full hot breakfast.

SAVE ❘❙ 🚼 ❤ 🏊 BIZ 📶 ✕ 🛗 📼 📶

Discover a wealth of savings and offers on the AAA/CAA travel websites

EMBASSY SUITES BY HILTON DENVER-STAPLETON 303/375-0400 **13**

▼▼▼▼ Hotel
Rates not provided

AAA Benefit: Members save 5% or more!

Address: 4444 N Havana St 80239 **Location:** I-70 exit 280, just n. **Facility:** 210 units. 7 stories, interior corridors. **Pool(s):** heated indoor. **Activities:** sauna, hot tub, exercise room. **Guest Services:** valet and coin laundry, area transportation.

SAVE ✈ ❘❙ ❤ CALL 🖐M 🏊 BIZ 📶 ✕ 🍴 🛗 📼 📶

FAIRFIELD INN & SUITES BY MARRIOTT DENVER AIRPORT (303)576-9640 **7**

▼▼▼ Hotel $83-$225 **Address:** 6851 Tower Rd 80249 **Location:** I-70 exit 286 (Tower Rd), 4.3 mi n; 0.8 mi s of Pena Blvd. **Facility:** 160 units. 3 stories, interior corridors. **Pool(s):** heated indoor.

AAA Benefit: Members save 5% or more!

Activities: hot tub, picnic facilities, exercise room. **Guest Services:** valet and coin laundry.

✈ ❘❙ CALL 🖐M 🏊 BIZ 📶 ✕ 🛗 📼 📶

FAIRFIELD INN & SUITES BY MARRIOTT DENVER CHERRY CREEK (303)691-2223 **35**

▼▼▼ Hotel $98-$193

FAIRFIELD INN & SUITES Marriott.

AAA Benefit: Members save 5% or more!

Address: 1680 S Colorado Blvd 80222 **Location:** I-25 exit 204, just n, then just e on Mexico Ave. **Facility:** 134 units. 10 stories, interior corridors. **Pool(s):** heated indoor. **Activities:** exercise room. **Guest Services:** valet and coin laundry.

SAVE ❘❙ CALL 🖐M 🏊 BIZ 📶 ✕ 🍴 🛗 📼 / SOME UNITS HS 📼

▼ See AAA listing this page ▼

(See map & index p. 136.)

HAMPTON INN & SUITES DENVER AIRPORT GATEWAY PARK
303/375-8118 **21**

▼▼▼▼ **Hotel.** Rates not provided. **Address:** 4310 Airport Way 80239 **Location:** I-70 exit 283 (Chambers Rd), just n to 40th Ave E, 0.5 mi e, then just n. **Facility:** 115 units. 6 stories, interior corridors. **Pool(s):** heated indoor. **Activities:** hot tub, exercise room. **Guest Services:** valet and coin laundry.

AAA Benefit: Members save up to 10%!

HAMPTON INN & SUITES DENVER /SPEER
303/455-4588 **27**

fyi **Hotel.** Rates not provided. Under major renovation, scheduled to be completed September 2015. **Last Rated:** ▼▼▼ **Address:** 2728 Zuni St 80211 **Location:** I-25 exit 212B (Speer Blvd) southbound; exit 212A northbound, just w, then just n. **Facility:** 74 units. 4 stories, interior corridors. **Amenities:** safes. **Pool(s):** heated indoor. **Activities:** hot tub, exercise room. **Guest Services:** complimentary and valet laundry.

AAA Benefit: Members save up to 10%!

HAMPTON INN & SUITES DENVER TECH CENTER
303/804-9900 **40**

▼▼▼ **Hotel.** Rates not provided. **Address:** 5001 S Ulster St 80237 **Location:** I-25 exit 199, e to Ulster St, then just n. **Facility:** 123 units, some efficiencies and kitchens. 3 stories, interior corridors. **Pool(s):** heated indoor. **Activities:** hot tub, exercise room. **Guest Services:** valet and coin laundry, area transportation.

AAA Benefit: Members save up to 10%!

HAMPTON INN DIA
303/371-0200 **10**

▼▼▼ **Hotel** Rates not provided

AAA Benefit: Members save up to 10%!

Address: 6290 Tower Rd 80249 **Location:** I-70 exit 286 (Tower Rd), 3.5 mi n. **Facility:** 122 units. 5 stories, interior corridors. **Pool(s):** heated indoor. **Activities:** exercise room. **Guest Services:** valet laundry. **Featured Amenity:** full hot breakfast.

HOLIDAY INN & SUITES
303/574-1300 **5**

▼▼▼ **Hotel.** Rates not provided. **Address:** 6900 Tower Rd 80249 **Location:** I-70 exit 286 (Tower Rd), 4.3 mi n. **Facility:** 161 units, some kitchens. 6 stories, interior corridors. **Amenities:** safes. **Pool(s):** heated indoor. **Activities:** hot tub, exercise room. **Guest Services:** valet and coin laundry, rental car service.

HOLIDAY INN DENVER EAST - STAPLETON
(303)321-3500 **28**

▼▼▼ **Hotel** $99-$229 **Address:** 3333 Quebec St 80207 **Location:** I-70 exit 278, 0.3 mi s; I-270 exit 4. **Facility:** 299 units. 11 stories, interior corridors. **Terms:** check-in 4 pm, cancellation fee imposed. **Pool(s):** heated outdoor. **Activities:** hot tub, exercise room, massage. **Guest Services:** valet and coin laundry, area transportation.

HOLIDAY INN EXPRESS & SUITES
303/373-4100 **4**

▼▼▼ **Hotel.** Rates not provided. **Address:** 6910 Tower Rd 80249 **Location:** I-70 exit 286 (Tower Rd), 4.3 mi n; from Pena Blvd, 0.7 mi s. **Facility:** 139 units. 4 stories, interior corridors. **Pool(s):** heated indoor. **Activities:** hot tub, exercise room. **Guest Services:** valet and coin laundry.

HOLIDAY INN EXPRESS & SUITES DENVER EAST-PEORIA STREET
303/371-9498 **16**

▼▼▼ **Hotel.** Rates not provided. **Address:** 12140 E 45th Ave 80239 **Location:** I-70 exit 281, just n. **Facility:** 81 units. 5 stories, interior corridors. **Pool(s):** heated indoor. **Activities:** hot tub, exercise room. **Guest Services:** valet and coin laundry.

HOMEWOOD SUITES BY HILTON DENVER INTERNATIONAL AIRPORT
303/371-4555 **24**

▼▼▼ **Extended Stay Hotel.** Rates not provided. **Address:** 4210 Airport Way 80239 **Location:** I-70 exit 283 (Chambers Rd), just n to 40th Ave E, 0.5 mi e, then just n. **Facility:** 117 efficiencies, some two bedrooms. 4 stories, interior corridors. **Pool(s):** heated indoor. **Activities:** hot tub, picnic facilities, exercise room. **Guest Services:** valet and coin laundry.

AAA Benefit: Members save up to 10%!

HYATT HOUSE DENVER AIRPORT
(303)628-7777 **1**

▼▼▼ **Extended Stay Hotel** $79-$209

H HYATT house™

AAA Benefit: Members save 10%!

Address: 18741 E 71st Ave 80249 **Location:** I-70 exit 286 (Tower Rd), 4.6 mi n, then just e; from Pena Blvd exit 5 (Tower Rd/SR 32), just s. **Facility:** 123 units, some two bedrooms, efficiencies and kitchens. 4 stories, interior corridors. *Bath:* shower only. **Terms:** cancellation fee imposed. **Pool(s):** heated indoor. **Activities:** hot tub, picnic facilities, exercise room. **Guest Services:** valet and coin laundry, area transportation. **Featured Amenity:** breakfast buffet.

HYATT REGENCY DENVER TECH CENTER
(303)779-1234 **38**

▼▼▼ **Hotel** $99-$429

HYATT REGENCY®

AAA Benefit: Members save 10%!

Address: 7800 E Tufts Ave 80237 **Location:** I-225 exit 2 (Tamarac St), just s to Tufts Ave; I-25 exit 199 (Belleview Ave), e to S Ulster St, then 0.5 mi n. **Facility:** 451 units. 12 stories, interior corridors. **Parking:** on-site (fee) and valet. **Terms:** cancellation fee imposed. **Amenities:** safes. **Pool(s):** heated indoor. **Activities:** sauna, hot tub, bicycles, exercise room, massage. **Guest Services:** valet laundry, boarding pass kiosk, area transportation.

(See map & index p. 136.)

JW MARRIOTT DENVER CHERRY CREEK
(303)316-2700 **33**

▼▼▼▼
Hotel
$217-$531

JW MARRIOTT.

AAA Benefit:
Members save 5%
or more!

Address: 150 Clayton Ln 80206 **Location:** I-25 exit 205 (University Blvd), 2.4 mi n to 1st Ave, just e, then just n. **Facility:** Experience the modern elegance of the hotel lobby by lounging in front of the fireplace. Rich oil paintings, marble floors and cowhide chairs add a luxurious feel to the decor. 196 units. 11 stories, interior corridors. **Parking:** valet only. **Amenities:** safes. **Activities:** bicycles, exercise room, spa. **Guest Services:** valet laundry, boarding pass kiosk, area transportation.

LA QUINTA INN & SUITES DENVER AIRPORT DIA
(303)371-0888 **8**

▼▼ Hotel $68-$213 **Address:** 6801 Tower Rd 80249 **Location:** I-70 exit 286 (Tower Rd), 4.2 mi n; 0.8 mi s of Pena Blvd. **Facility:** 169 units. 5 stories, interior corridors. **Pool(s):** heated indoor. **Activities:** hot tub, exercise room. **Guest Services:** coin laundry.

LA QUINTA INN & SUITES DENVER GATEWAY PARK
(303)373-2525 **17**

▼▼▼ Hotel $98-$252 **Address:** 4460 Peoria St 80239 **Location:** I-70 exit 281, just n. **Facility:** 81 units. 4 stories, interior corridors. **Pool(s):** hot tub, exercise room. **Guest Services:** valet and coin laundry.

QUALITY INN & SUITES
303/388-6161 **20**

▼▼▼ Hotel. Rates not provided. **Address:** 3737 Quebec St 80207 **Location:** I-70 exit 278, just s. **Facility:** 139 units. 4 stories, interior corridors. **Amenities:** safes. **Pool(s):** heated outdoor. **Activities:** exercise room. **Guest Services:** valet and coin laundry.

RENAISSANCE DENVER HOTEL
(303)399-7500 **19**

▼▼▼
Hotel
$97-$225

R
RENAISSANCE®
HOTELS

AAA Benefit:
Members save 5%
or more!

Address: 3801 Quebec St 80207 **Location:** I-70 exit 278, just s via Smith Rd exit. **Facility:** 400 units. 12 stories, interior corridors. **Amenities:** Some: safes. **Dining:** 2 restaurants. **Pool(s):** heated outdoor, heated indoor. **Activities:** hot tub, exercise room. **Guest Services:** complimentary and valet laundry, boarding pass kiosk, area transportation.

RESIDENCE INN BY MARRIOTT DENVER DOWNTOWN
(303)458-5318 **26**

▼▼▼ Extended Stay Hotel $143-$268 **Address:** 2777 Zuni St 80211 **Location:** I-25 exit 212B (Speer Blvd) southbound; exit 212A northbound, just w, then just n. **Facility:** 160 kitchen

AAA Benefit:
Members save 5%
or more!

units. 2 stories (no elevator), exterior corridors. **Terms:** check-in 4 pm. **Pool(s):** heated outdoor. **Activities:** picnic facilities, exercise room. **Guest Services:** valet and coin laundry, area transportation.

SPRINGHILL SUITES BY MARRIOTT DENVER AIRPORT
(303)371-9400 **9**

▼▼▼ Hotel $92-$239 **Address:** 18350 E 68th Ave 80249 **Location:** I-70 exit 286 (Tower Rd), 4.3 mi n, then just w. **Facility:** 124 units. 4 stories, interior corridors. **Amenities:** safes. **Pool(s):**

AAA Benefit:
Members save 5%
or more!

heated indoor. **Activities:** hot tub, exercise room. **Guest Services:** valet and coin laundry.

STAYBRIDGE SUITES
(303)574-0888 **3**

▼▼▼ Extended Stay Hotel $99-$220 **Address:** 6951 Tower Rd 80249 **Location:** Just s of jct Pena Blvd. **Facility:** 147 efficiencies, some two bedrooms. 6 stories, interior corridors. **Pool(s):** heated indoor. **Activities:** picnic facilities, exercise room. **Guest Services:** complimentary and valet laundry.

STAYBRIDGE SUITES DENVER STAPLETON
(303)227-3000 **11**

▼▼▼▼ Extended Stay Hotel $114-$194 **Address:** 8101 E Northfield Blvd 80238 **Location:** I-70 exit 278, 0.4 mi nw, then just e. **Facility:** 102 efficiencies, some two bedrooms. 4 stories, interior corridors. **Terms:** cancellation fee imposed. **Pool(s):** indoor. **Activities:** hot tub, exercise room. **Guest Services:** complimentary and valet laundry.

TOWNEPLACE SUITES BY MARRIOTT-DENVER SOUTHEAST
(303)759-9393 **37**

▼▼▼ Extended Stay Hotel $80-$211 **Address:** 3699 S Monaco Pkwy 80237 **Location:** I-25 exit 201, just e to Monaco Pkwy, then s. **Facility:** 112 kitchen units, some two bedrooms. 3 stories, interior corridors. **Pool(s):** heated outdoor. **Activities:** exercise room. **Guest Services:** valet and coin laundry, area transportation.

AAA Benefit:
Members save 5% or more!

TOWNEPLACE SUITES BY MARRIOTT DOWNTOWN DENVER
(303)722-2322 **32**

▼▼▼ Extended Stay Hotel $121-$238 **Address:** 685 Speer Blvd 80204 **Location:** I-25 exit 209A (6th Ave), 1.4 mi w, then just n on Acoma St. **Facility:** 122 kitchen units, some two bedrooms. 4 stories, interior corridors. **Activities:** exercise room. **Guest Services:** valet and coin laundry, area transportation.

AAA Benefit:
Members save 5% or more!

TOWNEPLACE SUITES BY MARRIOTT GATEWAY PARK / DENVER AIRPORT
(303)373-4243 **22**

▼▼▼ Extended Stay Hotel $94-$209 **Address:** 4100 N Kittredge St 80239 **Location:** I-70 exit 283 (Chambers Rd), just n to 40th Ave, 0.3 mi e, then just n. **Facility:** 99 units, some two bedrooms, efficiencies and kitchens. 4 stories, interior corridors. **Pool(s):** heated indoor. **Activities:** picnic facilities, exercise room. **Guest Services:** valet and coin laundry, area transportation.

AAA Benefit:
Members save 5% or more!

WHERE TO EAT

ACORN
720/542-3721 **9**

▼▼▼ Small Plates. Casual Dining. $13-$27 **AAA Inspector Notes:** Housed in a former refinery, this foodie haven has an industrial look, complete with exposed brick walls with graffiti. Explore the menu by ordering a few small plates. The staff might steer you toward the kale salad, but only order it if you really love kale. Otherwise, the lamb shwarma, meatballs served on butter grits with burrata, and the butterscotch dishes stand out. Cocktail enthusiasts will enjoy the extensive list of creative craft beverages. **Features:** full bar. **Address:** 3350 Brighton Blvd 80216 **Location:** I-70 exit 275B, 1 mi sw; in The Source. L D CALL M

ALE HOUSE AT AMATO'S
303/433-9734 **18**

▼▼ American. Casual Dining. $7-$24 **AAA Inspector Notes:** Located in the Lower Highlands neighborhood, this pub offers outstanding views of the Denver skyline from its rooftop patio. With over 42 beers on tap, the extensive list of craft brews is mind-blowing. Servers exhibit knowledge of the beers and offer potential food pairings. The menu consists of beer-friendly favorites, including boar sliders, chicken wings, IPA-battered fish and chips, and Colorado beef or lamb burgers. **Features:** full bar, patio dining, Sunday brunch, happy hour. **Address:** 2501 16th St 80211 **Location:** I-25 exit 212C (20th St), just w to Central St, then 0.3 mi s. **Parking:** street only. L D LATE CALL M

(See map & index p. 136.)

AQUARIUM RESTAURANT 303/561-4450 (28)
⬥⬥ Seafood. Family Dining. $10-$35 **AAA Inspector Notes:** A 150,000-gallon saltwater aquarium dominates the dining room. There is a lot to see with a myriad of fish large and small, including some sharks. Seafood dishes such as grilled mahi mahi & shrimp, sauteed gulf snapper, and the fried seafood platter dominate the menu. **Features:** full bar, happy hour. **Address:** 700 Water St 80211 **Location:** I-25 exit 211, just e; in Downtown Aquarium. **Parking:** on-site (fee) and valet. (SAVE) L D

BAROLO GRILL 303/393-1040 (51)
⬥⬥⬥ Northern Italian. Fine Dining. $20-$35 **AAA Inspector Notes:** Enjoy a drink as you wait in the bar, then visit the sophisticated dining room, which evokes a country inn feeling. The seasonal menu features excellent preparations of Northern Italian cuisine from Tuscany and Piedmont. The cheese soufflé appetizer stands out. Entrées may include New Caledonia blue prawns, rabbit, veal, duck, salmon, steak and pork. **Features:** full bar. **Reservations:** suggested. **Address:** 3030 E 6th Ave 80206 **Location:** 0.5 mi e of Josephine St. **Parking:** valet and street only. D

BEAU JO'S COLORADO STYLE PIZZA DENVER
303/758-1519 (73)
⬥⬥⬥ Pizza Casual Dining $6-$12
AAA Inspector Notes: Known for its pizza, this eatery offers a fun atmosphere with a mountain theme. Build your pizza from the crust up. Choices include the mountain pie with a thick, chewy edge; the thin-crust prairie pie; and gluten-free options. Add your favorite toppings or choose a specialty pizza like the sky hawk (a pepperoni pie with Hatch green chiles and feta), or Skier Mike's chicken, Canadian bacon and green pepper pie. **Features:** full bar, happy hour. **Reservations:** suggested. **Address:** 2710 S Colorado Blvd 80222 **Location:** I-25 exit 204, 1 mi s, then just e on Yale Ave. *(See ad p. 158.)* L D

"Colorado Style Pizza"
Also Gluten Free Menu

THE BERKSHIRE 303/321-4010 (30)
⬥⬥ American. Casual Dining. $11-$32 **AAA Inspector Notes:** Prepare yourself for a pork extravaganza at this pig-focused eatery. Start with the fun-to-share bacon flight, four slices of individually spiced bacon. Move on to the Porky's Inferno, a pulled pork sandwich. If bacon is as porky as you get, other options include blackened tilapia tacos, a jalapeño cream cheese burger, fried chicken, and duck breast. **Features:** full bar, Sunday brunch, happy hour. **Address:** 7352 E 29th Ave 80238 **Location:** I-70 exit 278, 1 mi s, then just e. **Parking:** on-site and street. L D

BITTERSWEET 303/942-0320 (61)
⬥⬥⬥ Natural/Organic. Fine Dining. $25-$35 **AAA Inspector Notes:** Adventurous diners will appreciate the innovative cuisine at this foodie haven. The menu changes seasonally and features organic vegetables from the restaurant's garden. **Features:** full bar, patio dining. **Reservations:** suggested. **Address:** 500 E Alameda Ave 80209 **Location:** Between Pennsylvania and Pearl sts. **Parking:** on-site and street. D

THE BLUE BONNET MEXICAN CAFE 303/778-0147 (64)
⬥⬥ Mexican. Casual Dining. $5-$16 **AAA Inspector Notes:** One dining room of this popular, well-established café has close table spacing, while the other is a well-lighted and picturesque patio. Reasonably priced entrées include tamales, burritos, menudo and rellenos, which are served in combinations and with side dishes. Margaritas are memorable, and servers are friendly. **Features:** full bar, patio dining, happy hour. **Address:** 457 S Broadway 80209 **Location:** Just s of jct Alameda Ave. L D

BONES 303/860-2929 (44)
⬥⬥ Asian Noodles. Casual Dining. $13-$20 **AAA Inspector Notes:** Famous for his upscale Italian restaurants, acclaimed chef Frank Bonanno forages into new territory with this casual Asian-fusion eatery. The lunch menu consists of unique appetizers, salads, noodle dishes and desserts while the dinner menu has a few additional offerings. Start with the pork steamed buns; portions are large enough to share. **Features:** full bar, patio dining, happy hour. **Address:** 701 Grant St 80203 **Location:** Jct Speer Blvd and 6th Ave, just n on Sherman St, then just e. **Parking:** valet and street only. L D

BONNIE BRAE TAVERN 303/777-2262 (67)
⬥⬥ American. Casual Dining. $7-$18 **AAA Inspector Notes:** The family-friendly eatery recalls a bygone era with its vintage, vinyl-upholstered booths. Although such favorites as meatloaf, juicy hamburgers, and pork chops with applesauce are a hit, the delicious pizza is what keeps locals coming back for more. **Features:** full bar. **Address:** 740 S University Blvd 80209 **Location:** I-25 exit 205 (University Blvd), 1.2 mi n. L D

BRECKENRIDGE COLORADO CRAFT 303/297-3644 (26)
⬥⬥ American. Casual Dining. $10-$17 **AAA Inspector Notes:** Known for its homemade Colorado brews, this casual eatery is located in a large, restored warehouse adjacent to Coors Field. Start with the ancho-apricot barbecued chicken wings, which have a slight sweetness combined with nice heat. Entrées include burgers, specialty sandwiches and larger plates, including Avalanche Ale braised chicken, short ribs, fish and chips, and mac and cheese. **Features:** full bar, happy hour. **Address:** 2220 Blake St 80205 **Location:** Jct 22nd St. **Parking:** on-site and street. L D

BUCKHORN EXCHANGE 303/534-9505 (40)

⬥⬥ Steak Casual Dining $10-$53
AAA Inspector Notes: *Historic.* First opened in 1893, this popular eatery has the prestige of being Denver's oldest restaurant and is filled with Western charm. The décor features Old West memorabilia, a 150-year-old hand-carved oak bar upstairs and an extensive taxidermy collection of local and exotic animals. The menu features standard Western fare, but also includes an exotic flair. Cowhands may start with a serving of rattlesnake, alligator tail or Rocky Mountain oysters. **Features:** full bar, happy hour. **Reservations:** suggested. **Address:** 1000 Osage St 80204 **Location:** I-25 exit 210A (Colfax Ave), 0.4 mi e, then 0.5 mi s. *Menu on AAA.com* L D

CARMINE'S ON PENN 303/777-6443 (60)
⬥⬥ Italian. Casual Dining. $24-$47 **AAA Inspector Notes:** In a quiet residential neighborhood, the restaurant offers a warm décor and is a local favorite for flavorful Italian cuisine, including veal, seafood and pasta. All meals are served family-style, which means portions are large enough to be shared among three to four people. Seating is available inside in several dining rooms and on a patio. **Features:** full bar, patio dining. **Reservations:** suggested. **Address:** 92 S Pennsylvania St 80209 **Location:** Jct Bayaud Ave and Pennsylvania St; just n of Alameda Ave. **Parking:** valet only. D

CASEY'S BISTRO & PUB 720/974-7350 (29)
⬥⬥ American. Casual Dining. $8-$19 **AAA Inspector Notes:** Named for Sean O'Casey, a famous Irish playwright, this distinguished neighborhood eatery is casual but with a more sophisticated pub décor. The menu features limited Irish dishes, such as bangers and mash, fish and chips, and shepherd's pie, along with American fare such as grilled Atlantic salmon and 'adult' mac and cheese. The creamy potato leek soup, flavored with pieces of bacon, brings comfort on a cold day. **Features:** full bar, patio dining, Sunday brunch, happy hour. **Address:** 7301 E 29th Ave, Unit 100 80238 **Location:** I-70 exit 278, 1 mi s, then just e. **Parking:** on-site and street. L D (LATE) CALL (&M)

(See map & index p. 136.)

THE CHERRY CRICKET
303/322-7666 [54]

 American. Casual Dining. $6-$10 **AAA Inspector Notes:** Since it opened in 1945, this eatery has survived major neighborhood changes and manages to offer reasonable prices considering its ritzy Cherry Creek location. The cricket burger remains at the top of many locals' "best burger" lists. The juicy patty sits on a soft sesame seed bun with whatever combination of toppings you choose. Besides burgers, the menu features a spicy green chile soup, chicken wings and burritos. This restaurant also has a popular late-night bar. **Features:** full bar, happy hour. **Address:** 2641 E 2nd Ave 80206 **Location:** Between Columbine and Clayton sts; in Cherry Creek Village.

[L] [D] [LATE]

CITRON BISTRO
303/771-5800 [78]

American. Casual Dining. $9-$23 **AAA Inspector Notes:** The eclectic menu features everything from hamburgers to lamb shank. Portions are hearty. Small plates include mussels, fried calamari and carnitas pork sliders. The inviting bar is the perfect place to enjoy an after-work cocktail. **Features:** full bar, Sunday brunch, happy hour. **Address:** 3535 S Yosemite St 80237 **Location:** Just s of jct Hampden Ave. [L] [D]

COLT & GRAY
303/477-1447 [22]

American Fine Dining $20-$40

AAA Inspector Notes: This intimate restaurant has received much praise during the time it has been open—deservedly so. Each dish exudes artistry, creativity, and, most importantly, flavor. Adventurous diners will appreciate more exotic offerings such as snail risotto, marrow bones, and pig trotters. Entrées feature Colorado lamb, Hudson Valley duck, local pork, trout and a bone-in New York strip. **Features:** full bar, patio dining, happy hour. **Reservations:** suggested. **Address:** 1553 Platte St, Suite 120 80202 **Location:** Jct 15th St, just ne. **Parking:** on-site and street. [D]

CUBA CUBA CAFE & BAR
303/605-2822 [38]

Cuban. Casual Dining. $13-$24 **AAA Inspector Notes:** Celebrate Cuban culture at this tiny eatery. While the weather isn't quite as tropical, the patio allows you to dine afuera. Start with the shrimp ceviche. The fried plantain chip balances out the tart lime flavor. Follow up with a classic sandwich Cubano or churrasco skirt steak. End with the standout tres leches cake. **Features:** full bar, patio dining, happy hour. **Address:** 1173 Delaware St 80204 **Location:** I-25 exit 210A (Colfax Ave), just e to Delaware St, then s at U.S. Mint to 12th St. **Parking:** street only. [D]

DARCY'S BISTRO & PUB
303/770-0477 [79]

American. Casual Dining. $7-$15 **AAA Inspector Notes:** Meet up with friends to enjoy one of the 30 beers on tap and a meal of traditional pub fare, including fish and chips, shepherd's pie, burgers, and sandwiches. Handsome accents of dark wood enhance the visual appeal, where you'll find a private library room and a casual patio seating area. **Features:** full bar, patio dining, Sunday brunch, happy hour. **Address:** 4955 S Ulster St, Unit 103 80237 **Location:** I-25 exit 199, 3 mi e to Ulster St, then just n. [L] [D] [LATE]

DEVIL'S FOOD
303/733-7448 [68]

American. Casual Dining. $11-$26 **AAA Inspector Notes:** An eclectic neighborhood café, Devil's Food will tempt you with much more than good coffee and a charming atmosphere. When you first step in the door you are greeted by perfect pastries and chocolate delicacies. Don't stop there, order some of the innovative creations like the challah French toast, salmon Benedict, and the eggs and corn bread or something more traditional like buttermilk pancakes, omelets and quiche. **Features:** beer & wine, patio dining, Sunday brunch. **Address:** 1020 S Gaylord St 80209 **Location:** Jct University Blvd, just w on Tennessee Ave, then just s; in Gaylord Shopping District; near Washington Park. **Parking:** street only.

[B] [L] [D]

DICICCO'S ITALIAN RESTAURANT
303/574-1956 [1]

Italian. Casual Dining. $10-$30 **AAA Inspector Notes:** The delightful decor is reminiscent of an Italian opera theater. A short drive from Denver International Airport, this spacious restaurant can accommodate large groups as well as parties of one or two. The menu features Italian favorites such as manicotti, veal parmigiana, ravioli and chicken fettuccine. Lighter fare includes sandwiches, salads and pizzas. **Features:** full bar. **Address:** 6701 Tower Rd 80249 **Location:** I-70 exit 286 (Tower Rd), 4.2 mi n; from jct Pena Blvd, 0.8 mi s. [L] [D]

DUO RESTAURANT
303/477-4141 [13]

American. Casual Dining. $10-$26 **AAA Inspector Notes:** Find out for yourself why locals flock to this spot in the city's trendy Highlands neighborhood. The creative, flavorful dishes consisting of local and organic ingredients make this restaurant a must during any visit to Denver. The menu changes seasonally, but the Berkshire pork chop is consistently juicy and flavorful, no matter the rendition. Other favorites include fried chicken, the fresh fish of the day, and bison or beef steaks. **Features:** full bar, Sunday brunch, happy hour. **Address:** 2413 W 32nd Ave 80211 **Location:** I-25 exit 212B (Speer Blvd) southbound; exit 212A (Speer Blvd S) northbound, just w to Zuni St, then 0.5 mi n. **Parking:** street only. [D]

ELWAY'S
303/399-5353 [58]

Steak. Fine Dining. $14-$49 **AAA Inspector Notes:** Indeed, the restaurant's name refers to former Broncos star John Elway, who co-owns this upscale steak house. His fellow owners have extensive restaurant experience, guaranteeing fresh ingredients and memorable dishes. The lunch and dinner menus focus on standard steak and seafood choices, but some creative selections can be found in the "starters" section. Try the lamb chop fondue. The extensive wine list will please even the pickiest connoisseur. **Features:** full bar, patio dining, Sunday brunch. **Reservations:** suggested. **Address:** 2500 E 1st Ave, Suite 101 80206 **Location:** I-25 exit 205 (University Ave), just e. [L] [D] CALL [&][M]

THE FRESH FISH COMPANY & BLACK PEARL OYSTER BAR
303/740-9556 [76]

Seafood. Casual Dining. $9-$48 **AAA Inspector Notes:** The extensive menu features everything from Dungeness crab to black grouper. Start with a crab claw cocktail or fresh oysters. Then, build your own dish by selecting from 20 varieties of fish and picking a spice and sauce. Need help? Try the Cajun-spiced, grilled red snapper served with buttery chive beurre blanc. Other entrées include sesame seared ahi tuna, shrimp scampi and filet mignon. The nautical theme, complete with aquariums, creates a fun atmosphere. **Features:** full bar, Sunday brunch, happy hour. **Address:** 7800 E Hampden Ave 80231 **Location:** I-25 exit 201, 1.3 mi e; in Tiffany Square Plaza, east side. [L] [D]

FRUITION RESTAURANT
303/831-1962 [50]

American. Fine Dining. $26-$29 **AAA Inspector Notes:** Critically acclaimed chef Alex Seidel deserves every accolade he has received and there have been many. Each dish is presented at the table with artistry and precision, and each bite bursts with flavor. The menu changes seasonally, but you can count on Seidel's consistent innovation. His passion for farm-fresh ingredients led him to start his own farm, which includes a spacious green house and chickens. Entrées feature pork, Colorado lamb, duck, beef, fish and scallops. **Features:** full bar. **Reservations:** suggested. **Address:** 1313 E 6th Ave 80203 **Location:** I-25 exit 209A, 2.3 mi e. **Parking:** street only. [D]

FUEL CAFE
303/296-4642 [7]

American. Casual Dining. $10-$20 **AAA Inspector Notes:** Located in a forgotten corner of industrial Denver, this is a hidden foodie haven worth seeking out. In addition to this restaurant, the TAXI development houses loft-style apartments, galleries and shops. Chef/owner Bob Blair serves casual, creative cuisine featuring local, seasonal, high-quality ingredients. The menu changes monthly. **Features:** full bar, patio dining, Sunday brunch, happy hour. **Address:** 3455 Ringsby Ct, Suite 105 80216 **Location:** I-70 exit 274 to Washington St, just s, then just w; in TAXI development. [L] [D]

(See map & index p. 136.)

HARMAN'S EAT & DRINK   303/388-7428 (56)

▼▼ American. Casual Dining. $12-$25 **AAA Inspector Notes:** Expect high-quality food and friendly, casual service at this popular eatery. For lunch try the porchetta sandwich, served hot on a pretzel bun with a slightly sweet red pepper mostarda and pickled onions. Small plates like spicy Brussels sprouts, mac and cheese, and braised pork belly allow you to sample more of the menu. Dinner offers more sophisticated choices, such as foie gras johnnycakes, duck confit cassoulet and pan-roasted local striped bass. **Features:** full bar, patio dining, Sunday brunch. **Address:** 2900 E 2nd Ave 80206 **Location:** Between Fillmore and Milwaukee sts; in Cherry Creek North neighborhood. **Parking:** street only. [L] [D]

HIGHLAND TAP & BURGER   720/287-4493 (15)

▼▼ Burgers. Casual Dining. $9-$23 **AAA Inspector Notes:** This classy but casual neighborhood sports bar has quickly made itself a destination spot for high-quality burgers and local craft beers. The menu features all-natural, locally sourced Angus beef, which makes a strong foundation for all the burgers. The creamy Avery IPA mac 'n cheese is listed under the category 'sharing,' but if you decide not to share, it makes a rich, decadent entrée. **Features:** full bar, patio dining, Sunday brunch, happy hour. **Address:** 2219 W 32nd Ave 80211 **Location:** I-25 exit 213 (20th St), just ne on Central St, just n on Osage St, then just w. **Parking:** street only. [L] [D]

HOT CAKES BREAKFAST AND LUNCH   303/832-4351 (32)

▼ American. Casual Dining. $7-$12 **AAA Inspector Notes:** This casual eatery is well known for its delicious, hearty breakfasts. The menu includes innovative variations, as well as traditional morning favorites. Reasonable prices and quick service make this place a hot spot. **Address:** 1400 E 18th Ave 80218 **Location:** Jct Humbolt St; across from St. Joseph's Hospital. **Parking:** on-site and street. [B] [L]

HUMBOLT: FARM FISH WINE   303/813-1700 (34)

▼▼▼ Seafood. Fine Dining. $13-$35 **AAA Inspector Notes:** The menu consists of sustainably caught seafood, all-natural meats and produce from family-run farms. Sample items include Japanese hamachi crudo, smoked trout, lobster risotto, filet mignon and the Humbolt burger. For a more social experience, try a craft cocktail in the lively bar while waiting for a table. The soft color palette, fish murals and decorative glass bubble lights are reminiscent of the sea. **Features:** full bar, Sunday brunch, happy hour. **Address:** 1700 Humboldt St 80218 **Location:** Corner of 17th Ave. **Parking:** valet and street only. [L] [D]

IL POSTO   303/394-0100 (36)

▼▼▼ Italian. Fine Dining. $11-$35 **AAA Inspector Notes:** Andrea Frizzi, head chef and owner of this cozy restaurant, was born and raised in Milan, Italy, where he worked for many years before moving to the United States. His cuisine focuses on fresh ingredients; the menu changes daily. Servers are enthusiastic about the food and incredibly friendly. **Features:** full bar. **Address:** 2011 E 17th Ave 80206 **Location:** Between Race and Vine sts. **Parking:** street only. [L] [D]

IMPERIAL CHINESE RESTAURANT   303/698-2800 (63)

▼▼ Chinese. Casual Dining. $6-$42 **AAA Inspector Notes:** Colorful presentations add another appealing dimension to the offerings of delicious seafood, chicken and beef. You'll be in the company of plenty of locals who frequent this welcoming spot, where the service is skilled, quick and attentive. **Features:** full bar. **Address:** 431 S Broadway 80209 **Location:** Corner of Dakota Ave and Broadway. [L] [D] CALL [&M]

INDIA'S RESTAURANT   303/755-4284 (77)

▼▼▼
Indian
Casual Dining
$10-$21

AAA Inspector Notes: This restaurant is known for its Mughlai cuisine. In addition to a daily lunch buffet, the menu offers tandoori plates, curries, naan and vegetarian dishes. End your meal with some jalebi, a sweet pretzel shaped candy. The colorful door adds a festive air to the dining room. **Features:** full bar. **Address:** 8921 E Hampden Ave 80231 **Location:** Jct Yosemite St, just e. **Menu on AAA.com**

[L] [D]

IZAKAYA DEN   303/777-0691 (70)

▼▼▼ Japanese Sushi. Casual Dining. $12-$35 **AAA Inspector Notes:** This sleek, modern restaurant offers fresh sushigrade fish flown in from Japan, plus creative takes on Japanese small plates. Share some steamed lobster wontons, gyoza pork dumplings or shrimp and vegetable tempura. In addition to popular sushi rolls, the menu includes noodle dishes like duck udon, pork tantan-men and lobster ramen. **Features:** full bar, patio dining, happy hour. **Address:** 1487A S Pearl St 80210 **Location:** Between Florida and Arkansas aves. **Parking:** valet and street only. [D]

KONA GRILL   720/974-1300 (59)

▼▼▼ Pacific Rim Fusion. Casual Dining. $10-$33 **AAA Inspector Notes:** The eclectic menu reflects Pacific influences. In addition to noodle dishes and sushi, it lists specialties of macadamia nut chicken and lemon grass-encrusted swordfish. The dining room has a large aquarium, a private area and a sushi bar. The patio opens during warm weather. **Features:** full bar, patio dining, happy hour. **Address:** 3000 E 1st Ave, Suite 260 80206 **Location:** Jct Speer Blvd (which becomes 1st Ave) and University Blvd, just e; in Cherry Creek Mall. **Parking:** on-site and valet. [L] [D] CALL [&M]

LA SANDIA TEQUILA CANTINA   303/373-9100 (5)

▼▼▼ Mexican. Casual Dining. $8-$19 **AAA Inspector Notes:** While creating La Sandia's menu, acclaimed chef Richard Sandoval found inspiration from his childhood in Acapulco. Local patrons who flock to this restaurant may not recognize his name, but they certainly appreciate his talent. Quality ingredients, colorful presentation, and bold flavors attract fans of Mexican cuisine as well as foodies. The menu includes fajitas, chicken mole, and Chile Relleno Capeado. The banana empanadas are delicious. **Features:** full bar, patio dining, Sunday brunch, happy hour. **Address:** 8340 Northfield Blvd, Unit 1690 80238 **Location:** I-70 exit 278, 0.5 mi n; exit Northfield Blvd, just e, just s on Uinta St, then just e. **Parking:** street only. [L] [D]

LINGER   303/993-3120 (17)

▼▼▼ Small Plates. Fine Dining. $12-$24 **AAA Inspector Notes:** Make dinner reservations well in advance to enjoy this creative eatery. The menu consists of upscale street food from around the world. Sample a few small plates like the Wagyu beef sliders, ginger chili shrimp and Mongolian bbq duck buns. Friendly waiters help diners navigate the extensive menu options. Flavorful desserts and specialty cocktails are a highlight. **Features:** full bar, patio dining, Sunday brunch, happy hour. **Reservations:** suggested. **Address:** 2030 W 30th Ave 80211 **Location:** I-25 exit 213 (20th St), just nw on 20th St, sw on Central St, just nw on 16th St, then just w. **Parking:** valet and street only. [L] [D]

LITTLE ANITA'S   303/691-3337

▼ New Mexican. Quick Serve. $6-$11 **AAA Inspector Notes:** Authentic New Mexican recipes are on the menu at this quaint, quick-serve eatery. A la carte burritos, calabacitas, enchiladas, tacos, quesadillas and tostadas, as well as a variety of combination plates and hamburgers, are available. **Address:** 1550 S Colorado Blvd, Suite 103 80222 **Location:** I-25 exit 204, just n; in Florida Shopping Center. [B] [L] [D]

(See map & index p. 136.)

LITTLE INDIA RESTAURANT 303/871-9777 48
🔻 Indian. Casual Dining. $11–$19 **AAA Inspector Notes:** From the outside this restaurant doesn't look very special. If ordering off the menu rather than the buffet, try the momo, which is a fried chicken or vegetable dumpling served with a creamy, sweet dipping sauce. For a lighter dish, try the shrimp tandoori. Choose from chicken, lamb and shrimp to top your curry, vindaloo or masala. **Features:** full bar. **Address:** 330 E 6th Ave 80203 **Location:** Jct Speer Blvd, just e; near downtown. L D

LUCA 303/832-6600 42
🔻🔻🔻 Italian. Fine Dining. $13–$33 **AAA Inspector Notes:** The sophisticated menu focuses on contemporary Italian fare. The menu changes seasonally, but always features a selection of homemade pastas. The braised meatballs, tagliatelle fra diavola with poached Maine lobster, and the almond-toasted almond cake with cinnamon caramel sauce, all recommended, have staying power. Other dishes feature scallops, steak, duck and wild boar. **Features:** full bar. **Reservations:** suggested. **Address:** 711 Grant St 80203 **Location:** Jct 7th Ave. **Parking:** valet and street only. D

MASTERPIECE DELICATESSEN 303/561-3354 20
🔻 Sandwiches. Quick Serve. $6–$13 **AAA Inspector Notes:** This tiny eatery houses a wonderment of gourmet sandwiches. In warm weather the patio is the perfect place to gaze across the Highland Bridge, which joins the lower highlands to downtown across I-25. The setup is mainly for a quick lunch or to grab and go. The tables are close together. If you arrive during the lunch hour on a weekday, be prepared for a line and limited to no seating. I had the braised beef brisket. Doesn't sound impressive, but it's possibly the best sandwich I've ever had. **Features:** full bar, patio dining. **Address:** 1575 Central St 80211 **Location:** Just ne of jct 15th St; across from northwest entrance to Highland Bridge. **Parking:** street only. B L D

MEZCAL 303/322-5219 37
🔻🔻 Mexican. Casual Dining. $9–$18 **AAA Inspector Notes:** Although relaxed during the day, this restaurant becomes lively at night and is a popular weekend hangout for locals. Savory and flavorful soups are the perfect way to begin a meal. The tortilla soup is a thick tomato with a little heat and topped with avocado. Entrées include specialty tacos, chicken mole, chiles rellenos, and burritos. The distinctive décor features murals of vintage Mexican movie posters and comic book covers. Saturday brunch is available. **Features:** full bar, casual dining, Sunday brunch, happy hour. **Address:** 3230 E Colfax Ave 80206 **Location:** Jct Broadway, 2 mi e. **Parking:** street only. L D LATE

MICI HANDCRAFTED ITALIAN 303/355-6424 31
🔻 Italian. Quick Serve. $9–$20 **AAA Inspector Notes:** Mici is short for Miceli, the last name of the family that owns this cozy eatery. They use recipes handed down from their ancestors, served up fast and conveniently. Enjoy a gourmet pizza with Italian sausage, a custom-made calzone, or tortellini alla Miceli, tortellini pasta in Alfredo sauce with peas and prosciutto. **Features:** wine only, patio dining. **Address:** 2373 Central Park Blvd 80238 **Location:** I-70 exit 279, 2 mi s. **Parking:** on-site and street. L D

MIZUNA 303/832-4778 43
🔻🔻🔻 New American. Fine Dining. $37–$39 **AAA Inspector Notes:** Locals head to this hot spot for cuisine prepared with an emphasis on flavors. The lobster macaroni and cheese lives up to the hype—it is truly sensational. The menu changes seasonally, but often features duck, Colorado lamb and Chilean sea bass. The five-course prix fixe menu is one of the best values in town. Be sure to take advantage of the outstanding sommelier for wine recommendations. **Features:** full bar. **Reservations:** suggested. **Address:** 225 E 7th Ave 80203 **Location:** I-25 exit 209, e to Sherman St, just n to 7th Ave, then just e. **Parking:** valet and street only. D

MOONGATE ASIAN GRILL 303/329-2921 52
🔻 Asian. Casual Dining. $7–$17 **AAA Inspector Notes:** Less than two miles from the Stapleton hotels, this strip-mall eatery is worth the drive or cab ride. The small, unpretentious dining room is tastefully decorated. On the menu is an interesting variety of Thai, Chinese and Japanese entrées. **Features:** wine only. **Address:** 745 Quebec St 80220 **Location:** 0.7 mi s of Colfax Ave. L D

MOONLIGHT DINER 303/307-1750 2
🔻🔻 American. Casual Dining. $9–$15 **AAA Inspector Notes:** A fun place to eat, the diner has 1950s and aircraft décor in the lounge. The menu lists breakfast items, as well as meatloaf, hot and cold sandwiches and burgers. This place provides room service to nearby hotels. **Features:** full bar, patio dining. **Address:** 6250 Tower Rd 80249 **Location:** I-70 exit 286 (Tower Rd), 3.5 mi n; 0.7 mi s of Pena Blvd. B L D

MY BROTHER'S BAR 303/455-9991 24
🔻🔻 Burgers. Casual Dining. $6–$10 **AAA Inspector Notes:** The city's oldest bar has been continuously operating since 1873. I can picture Jack Kerouac and Neal Cassady tossing back a few during a grittier time, as they were reported to do. Hidden behind the humble, unidentified facade are delicious burgers. They're really why people seek out this hard-to-find spot. In the summer, I like to chill on the patio. In the winter, the masculine woodwork feels cozy. Either way, the juicy, made-to-order bison, ground beef and vegetarian burgers hit the spot. **Features:** full bar, patio dining. **Address:** 2376 15th St 80202 **Location:** Southwest corner of 15th and Platte sts. L D LATE

NEW SAIGON RESTAURANT 303/936-4954 65
🔻🔻 Vietnamese. Casual Dining. $7–$25 **AAA Inspector Notes:** Although the plain appearance might not suggest much, this well-established family restaurant provides a comfortable setting for relaxed dining. Colorful pictures of Vietnam decorate the walls of the unpretentious dining room, which has somewhat tight table spacing. The menu's varied dishes, which have won local and national awards, include grilled lamb, duck salad, beef skewers and rice noodles, in addition to chicken and pork concoctions. **Features:** beer & wine. **Address:** 630 S Federal Blvd 80219 **Location:** 1.4 mi s of jct US 6 and Federal Blvd. L D

NEW YORK DELI NEWS 303/759-4741 75
🔻🔻🔻 **American Casual Dining** $7–$15 **AAA Inspector Notes:** This very popular, authentic New York-style deli offers matzo ball soup, pastrami sandwiches, fish platters and eggs served all day. It also features great variety, ample portions and unlimited refills on soda and pickles. Service is prompt and friendly. **Features:** full bar, early bird specials. **Address:** 7105 E Hampden Ave 80224 **Location:** I-25 exit 201, 0.6 mi e. *Menu on AAA.com* B L D

OLD MAJOR 720/420-0622 10
🔻🔻🔻 American. Fine Dining. $23–$34 **AAA Inspector Notes:** This nationally acclaimed restaurant incorporates a nose-to-tail, farm-to-table philosophy, which results in rich, succulent dishes made from scratch. Every week, the chefs butcher a pig in house for use in dishes such as the pork gyro, the chef's ham plate, and the amazing nose to tail plate—a combination of confit rib, pork chop, ham, pork belly, and pig ear. Other options include pan-seared sea scallops, beef tartare, and Colorado lamb chops. A three-course vegetarian menu is also available. **Features:** full bar, patio dining, Sunday brunch, happy hour. **Address:** 3316 Tejon St 80211 **Location:** Between 34th and 33rd aves. **Parking:** valet and street only. D

OPUS FINE DINING & ARIA WINE BAR 303/355-5853 53
🔻🔻🔻 American. Fine Dining. $13–$40 **AAA Inspector Notes:** Recently relocated to the Cherry Creek shopping area from Littleton, this local favorite continues to serve high quality cuisine in a relaxed atmosphere. Expect artful food presentation, phenomenal flavor combinations, and servers with excellent menu knowledge. Sample menu items include parmiganno gnocchi with truffle honey and poached apple, prime beef rib eye with potato pavé and white cheddar, and oatmeal pie served with a butterscotch caramel sauce. **Features:** full bar, Sunday brunch, happy hour. **Address:** 250 Josephine St 80206 **Location:** Between 2nd and 3rd aves. **Parking:** street only. L D

OSAKA RAMEN 303/319-0948 21
🔻🔻 Japanese Noodles. Casual Dining. $14 **AAA Inspector Notes:** Located down a flight of stairs, this casual eatery offers vegetarian and pork-based ramen soups; beef; chicken; bass; and tofu bento boxes. Unique small plates include chilled green beans with sesame seeds and a sweet sauce, plus bacon-fried rice and shoe-string fries with Japanese flavorings. End with the savory-sweet "My Wife's Donuts," made with mochi, dusted with sugar and served with salted butter. **Features:** full bar. **Address:** 2611 Walnut St 80205 **Location:** Jct Broadway, just ne. **Parking:** street only. L D

(See map & index p. 136.)

PARALLEL SEVENTEEN 303/399-0988 ⟨35⟩
💎💎💎💎 Vietnamese. Casual Dining. $9-$24 **AAA Inspector Notes:** Although Chef Mary Nguyen's menu features some traditional Vietnamese dishes, she is also skilled in traditional French cooking. This diversity will please the palate of even the pickiest patron. The Northern-style pho is delicious. The menu changes seasonally. Sample items include Colorado lamb burger, gnocchi a la Parisienne, braised short ribs and grilled pork tenderloin. The thoughtful wine list has a variety of offerings compatible with any food choice. **Features:** full bar, patio dining, Sunday brunch, happy hour. **Address:** 1600 E 17th Ave 80218 **Location:** Jct Colfax Ave and Franklin St, just n. **Parking:** street only. ⟨L⟩ ⟨D⟩

PARISI 303/561-0234 ⟨3⟩
💎💎 Italian. Casual Dining. $9-$19 **AAA Inspector Notes:** Located in the popular Highlands neighborhood, this casual eatery is reminiscent of an Italian bistro. Co-owner Simone Parisi grew up in Italy and learned to cook from his mother and extended family. The concept is a little different, as the service is limited. However, the food is outstanding, making this affordable restaurant worth finding. The menu consists of authentic pasta dishes, pizzas and paninis. **Features:** full bar, happy hour. **Address:** 4401 Tennyson St 80212 **Location:** I-70 exit 270, 0.3 mi s on Sheridan Blvd to 44th St, 0.5 mi e, then just n. ⟨L⟩ ⟨D⟩

PARSLEY 303/893-7914 ⟨39⟩
💎 Sandwiches Natural/Organic. Quick Serve. $6-$11 **AAA Inspector Notes:** Stop into this eatery for a quick, healthy lunch. Roasted turkey, albacore tuna and organic vegetables make up most of the salads and sandwiches. Try the sweet, salty fig and Brie sandwich with a side of potato and leek soup as a comforting meal on a cold day. **Address:** 303 W 11th Ave 80204 **Location:** Corner of Cherokee St. **Parking:** street only. ⟨L⟩

PETE'S CENTRAL ONE 303/778-6675 ⟨62⟩
💎💎 Greek. Casual Dining. $10-$21 **AAA Inspector Notes:** This popular neighborhood café features traditional Greek favorites such as leg of lamb, spanakopita, gyros, kabobs, and much more. Every bite is filled with flavor. Colorful seaside murals adorn the walls, making the cozy dining room appear larger. Servers are friendly and efficient. **Features:** full bar, patio dining. **Address:** 300 S Pearl St 80209 **Location:** Southeast corner of jct Alameda Ave. **Parking:** street only. ⟨L⟩ ⟨D⟩

PIATTI ITALIAN RESTAURANT & BAR 303/321-1919 ⟨57⟩
💎💎 Italian. Casual Dining. $13-$22 **AAA Inspector Notes:** This bistro features rustic Italian food. Menu items include pork-ricotta meatballs, fried calamari, gourmet pizzas and unique pasta dishes, such as the saffron pappardelle served with shrimp, chili flake and arugula. **Features:** full bar, patio dining. **Address:** 190 St Paul St 80206 **Location:** I-25 exit 205 (University Blvd), 2.4 mi n to 1st Ave, then 0.5 mi e. ⟨L⟩ ⟨D⟩

PIZZERIA LOCALE 720/508-8828 ⟨47⟩
💎 Pizza. Quick Serve. $6-$9 **AAA Inspector Notes:** At this Naples-inspired eatery, expect gourmet pizza at its best. The owners have a popular fine dining restaurant in Boulder and travel to Italy frequently. Here, they've created a special "dough room" that mimics the weather and humidity of Naples. The dough is on the thinner side, but has a nice, chewy crust. Unlike American-style pizza, the cheese is on the lighter side; ask for more if you prefer. **Features:** beer & wine. **Address:** 550 Broadway 80203 **Location:** Jct 6th Ave. **Parking:** on-site and street. ⟨L⟩ ⟨D⟩

PLIMOTH 303/297-1215 ⟨27⟩
💎💎💎 American. Casual Dining. $17-$19 **AAA Inspector Notes:** This popular eatery focuses on seasonal and farm-fresh ingredients. Entrées may include rabbit, chicken and pork dishes. Try one of the specialty cocktails or craft beers. Located in an up-and-coming neighborhood, this restaurant has modern, sleek décor. **Features:** full bar, patio dining. **Address:** 2335 28th Ave 80205 **Location:** I-70 exit 278, 1.5 mi s, then just e. **Parking:** street only. ⟨D⟩

POTAGER 303/832-5788 ⟨41⟩
💎💎💎 American. Casual Dining. $18-$29 **AAA Inspector Notes:** Acclaimed chef Teri Rippeto strips down her food to the most basic of pleasing elements. The fresh, high-quality ingredients are locally produced and perfectly prepared. A frequent fixture at all the local farmers' markets, Rippeto changes the menu monthly in order to use food that reflects the season. The décor features exposed brick and bistro-like features, giving a rustic, earthy atmosphere that complements the street life. **Features:** beer & wine, patio dining. **Address:** 1109 Ogden St 80218 **Location:** From Colfax Ave, 0.4 mi s. **Parking:** on-site and street. ⟨D⟩

PROTO'S PIZZERIA NAPOLETANA 720/855-9400
💎💎 Pizza. Casual Dining. $6-$15 **AAA Inspector Notes:** The creator of this small regional chain, Pam Proto, had a simple dream: to bring Neapolitan pizza to Colorado. The original restaurant in Longmont was so successful that Proto expanded the business to six locations. This one is on a quiet street a short drive from the more active LoDo area. This cozy restaurant offers delicious gourmet pizzas, flavorful salads and Italy-inspired desserts. **Features:** full bar, patio dining, happy hour. **Address:** 2401 15th St 80202 **Location:** Jct Platte St, just ne. **Parking:** street only. ⟨L⟩ ⟨D⟩

RACINES RESTAURANT 303/595-0418 ⟨46⟩
💎💎 American. Casual Dining. $9-$17 **AAA Inspector Notes:** Diners savor the excellent baked turkey sandwich at this restaurant, which also serves Mexican, pasta and stir-fry dishes and foods made in the on-site bakery. Dishes can be washed down with terrific margaritas, microbrews and martinis. The youthful, energetic atmosphere is popular with all ages. **Features:** full bar, Sunday brunch. **Address:** 650 Sherman St 80203 **Location:** Jct Bannock St and Speer Blvd, just n. ⟨B⟩ ⟨L⟩ ⟨D⟩ CALL ⟨🔊M⟩

ROOT DOWN 303/993-4200 ⟨11⟩
💎💎💎 Natural/Organic. Fine Dining. $13-$31 **AAA Inspector Notes:** Located in the Highlands neighborhood, this place is housed in a former car service station. The garage door remains, but you'd never guess at this popular restaurant's former incarnation just by looking at its sophisticated interior. The menu focuses on global flavors and incorporates fresh, seasonal, mostly organic ingredients. **Features:** full bar, patio dining, Sunday brunch, happy hour. **Reservations:** suggested. **Address:** 1600 W 33rd Ave 80211 **Location:** I-25 exit 213 (20th St), just ne on Central St, just n on Osage St, then just w. **Parking:** street only. ⟨D⟩

ROYAL INDIA 303/758-9099 ⟨72⟩
💎💎 Indian. Casual Dining. $9-$19 **AAA Inspector Notes:** This restaurant features traditional vegetarian and meat dishes, including chicken tikka masala, biryani, tandoori or grilled meats and saag paneer. Diners can sample a variety during the lunch buffet or order a la carte during dinner. **Features:** beer & wine. **Address:** 1550 S Colorado Blvd 80222 **Location:** I-25 exit 204, just n; in Florida Shopping Center. ⟨L⟩ ⟨D⟩

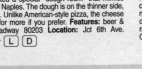

(See map & index p. 136.)

SAIGON TERRACE VIETNAMESE & CHINESE RESTAURANT
303/759-0884 (71)

♥♥ Vietnamese. Casual Dining. $7-$15 **AAA Inspector Notes:** Fresh Vietnamese creations awaken the palate and satisfy the savvy diner. Ingredients in each dish complement each other and create a unique experience. **Features:** full bar. **Address:** 1550 S Colorado Blvd, Suite 106 80222 **Location:** I-25 exit 204, just n; in Florida Shopping Center. [L] [D]

SHANAHAN'S
303/770-7300 (80)

♥♥♥♥ Steak. Fine Dining. $26-$58 **AAA Inspector Notes:** Named after football coach Mike Shanahan, the upscale restaurant adds a modern twist to the traditional steak house. The interior features dark wood accents with modern art and interesting lighting. The glass-encased wine cellar adds visual interest and football fans enjoy seeing Shanahan's Lombardi trophies from his Super Bowl wins. The menu focuses on local and organic produce with a variety of steaks, including three bone-in options, Colorado lamb, red trout, mahi mahi, shellfish and others. **Features:** full bar, patio dining, happy hour. **Address:** 5085 S Syracuse St 80237 **Location:** I-25 exit 199 (Belleview Ave), just e, then just n. **Parking:** on-site and valet. [D]

SLOTTED SPOON
303/756-3072 (74)

♥ Specialty. Quick Serve. $8-$14 **AAA Inspector Notes:** Here, the meatball is king. Choose from pork, salmon, beef, chicken and veggie meatballs, set in creatively flavored pastas, sandwiches and salads. For straight-up Italian, try the old-school zesty penne pasta. For something more adventurous, there's the gyro chicken meatball salad, or the Sonora salmon meatball sandwich. **Features:** full bar. **Address:** 2730 S Colorado Blvd, Unit 19 80222 **Location:** I-25 exit 204, 1 mi s. [L] [D]

SPUNTINO
303/433-0949 (12)

♥♥♥♥ Italian. Casual Dining. $9-$23 **AAA Inspector Notes:** This casual eatery has a clean, modern bistro feel. The menu features fresh, seasonal ingredients, and each course bursts with flavor. Expect gourmet sandwiches, homemade pasta, and entrées featuring organic Berkshire pork, flank steak and chicken. The co-owner is an acclaimed pastry chef, which means dessert is a must. Signature desserts include a chocolate sea salt caramel tart and an orange olive oil cake. **Features:** full bar, patio dining, happy hour. **Reservations:** suggested. **Address:** 2639 W 32nd Ave 80211 **Location:** I-25 exit 212B (Speer Blvd) southbound; exit 212A northbound, just w to Zuni St, 0.5 mi n, then just w. **Parking:** on-site and street. [L] [D]

SUSHI DEN
303/777-0826 (69)

♥♥♥♥ Japanese. Fine Dining. $13-$35 **AAA Inspector Notes:** Artistic presentation, fresh ingredients and heavenly flavors ensure an enjoyable dining experience. This restaurant has possibly the freshest fish in the state, which makes for incredibly delicious sushi worth the high-end prices. In addition to sushi, the menu consists of a roasted duck salad, Wagyu New York strip steak, teriyaki chicken and pork shumai dumplings. Patrons relax while dining in a unique, Asian-inspired, modern industrial setting. **Features:** full bar. **Address:** 1487 S Pearl St 80210 **Location:** Jct Florida Ave. **Parking:** street only. [L] [D]

SUSHI SASA
303/433-7272 (23)

♥♥♥♥ Japanese. Fine Dining. $8-$20 **AAA Inspector Notes:** The extensive sushi menu features fresh fish that is flown in daily. The French onion-style black cod soup may sound a bit strange, but the savory cod pairs well with the Gruyère and rice is substituted for the bread. The artistic presentation of the Japanese small plates such as the Chilean sea bass highlight the chef's creativity. The tempura options include the traditional vegetables and shrimp as well as shiitake mushrooms, oysters and calamari. **Features:** full bar, patio dining, happy hour. **Reservations:** suggested. **Address:** 2401 15th St, Suite 80 80202 **Location:** Just w of jct Platte St. **Parking:** on-site and street. [L] [D]

SWING THAI
303/777-1777 (45)

♥♥ Thai. Casual Dining. $5-$14 **AAA Inspector Notes:** Offering quick-serve Thai cuisine, the menu lists stir-fried, grilled, noodle and curry dishes, including the popular pad thai, drunken noodles and jungle curry entrées. Many choices can be prepared without gluten and in vegetarian or vegan style. The chicken is natural, the beef is from Harris Ranch, and the tofu is organic. **Features:** full bar. **Address:** 845 Colorado Blvd 80206 **Location:** Jct 8th Ave. [L] [D]

TABLE 6
303/831-8800 (49)

♥♥♥ American. Casual Dining. $18-$30 **AAA Inspector Notes:** Near the hip Capitol Hill district, this popular, artsy restaurant exudes casual class. Guests watch from their table as the chef prepares meals in an open kitchen. The daily-changing menu features innovative cuisine with unique flavor combinations. Main courses may feature roast chicken, duck confit, or halibut cheeks. From Philly cheesesteaks to oyster po'boys, the ever-changing sliders consistently stand out. The extensive wine list offers local and international selections. **Features:** beer & wine, Sunday brunch. **Reservations:** suggested. **Address:** 609 Corona St 80218 **Location:** Northwest corner of 6th Ave and Corona St. **Parking:** street only. [D]

TAMALES AT LA CASITA
303/477-2899 (8)

♥ Mexican. Casual Dining. $3-$11 **AAA Inspector Notes:** Since 1975, this family-owned restaurant has served fresh tamales to delighted locals. In addition to tamales, the menu features breakfast burritos, enchiladas, tostatas and beef and bean burritos, all at reasonable prices. Order at the counter, then seat yourself, and the food will quickly follow. The eatery is located a short drive from downtown in a quiet neighborhood. **Address:** 3561 Tejon St 80211 **Location:** I-25 exit 213 (38th Ave/Park Ave), 0.8 mi w on 38th Ave, then just s. [B] [L] [D]

THAI CHILI & SUSHI
303/307-1119 (19)

♥♥ Asian. Casual Dining. $7-$16 **AAA Inspector Notes:** Located near many airport-area hotels, this casual eatery offers a mix of classic Thai and Chinese dishes as well as sushi. Examples include Thai curry, drunken noodles, sesame chicken and kung pao beef. **Address:** 16621 E 40th Ave 80239 **Location:** I-70 exit 283 (Chambers Rd), just n, then 0.5 mi e. [L] [D]

TOCABE: AN AMERICAN INDIAN EATERY
720/524-8282 (4)

♥ Native American. Quick Serve. $8-$15 **AAA Inspector Notes:** Partners Ben Jacobs and Matt Chandra use family recipes to create popular dishes normally found only on or around American Indian reservations. Their modified fry bread, which calls for flash-frying in corn and canola oil instead of deep frying in lard, is amazingly flavorful, puffy, chewy and satisfying. You'll choose your own toppings—High Plains bison, ground beef, chicken, beans, chicken and vegetables—in an assembly line similar to what you've seen at quick-serve Mexican restaurants. **Features:** beer & wine, patio dining. **Address:** 3536 W 44th Ave 80211 **Location:** I-70 exit 272 (US 287/Federal Blvd), 0.5 mi s on Federal Blvd, then 0.4 mi w. [L] [D]

TRUE FOOD KITCHEN
720/509-7661 (55)

♥♥♥ Natural/Organic. Casual Dining. $12-$26 **AAA Inspector Notes:** High quality, healthy ingredients are the focus of this casual eatery. Recommended items include the Tuscan kale salad, the caramelized onion, fig and Gorgonzola tart, and the grass-fed bison burger. **Features:** full bar, patio dining, Sunday brunch. **Reservations:** suggested. **Address:** 2800 E 2nd Ave, Suite 101 80206 **Location:** Corner of Detroit St; in Cherry Creek Village. **Parking:** street only. [L] [D]

UNCLE
303/433-3263 (14)

♥♥ Asian Soup Small Plates. Casual Dining. $10-$16 **AAA Inspector Notes:** This amazing little eatery has instantly become a local favorite. The fresh, handmade egg noodles simply taste better than any noodle in town. Topped with Maple Leaf Farm duck, heirloom pork belly and all-natural chicken, the humble noodle soup is elevated to a more sophisticated level of dining, yet in a laid-back, casual atmosphere. If you're ravenous, start with a pork belly or shrimp steam bun. Otherwise, the rich ramen dishes are pretty substantial. **Features:** full bar, patio dining. **Address:** 2215 W 32nd Ave 80211 **Location:** I-25 exit 212B (Speer Blvd) southbound; exit 212A (Speer Blvd S) northbound, just w to Zuni St, 0.5 mi n, then just e. **Parking:** street only. [D]

THE UNIVERSAL
303/955-0815 (6)

♥♥ American. Casual Dining. $8-$9 **AAA Inspector Notes:** This casual eatery quickly became a local sensation due to its simple menu consisting of high quality, local ingredients. Traditional breakfast dishes like eggs Benedict and buttermilk pancakes share space with unique items such as the cornbread huevos rancheros and custard toast, bread soaked in custard overnight, then grilled. Lunch items feature gourmet sandwiches, a grass-fed beef burger, chicken confit and a revolving grits special. **Features:** full bar. **Address:** 2911 W 38th Ave 80211 **Location:** Just w of jct Federal Blvd. [B] [L]

(See map & index p. 136.)

VERT KITCHEN 303/997-5941 (66)
♦♦ Sandwiches. Quick Serve. $11-$14 **AAA Inspector Notes:** This tiny, cheerful café features items made from organic and local ingredients. All of the innovative menu choices are made from scratch, resulting in bold, flavorful soups, salads and gourmet sandwiches. The roasted turkey sandwich comes with a balanced spread of sweet figs and tart, goat cheese. Try one of the chocolate cookies enhanced with toasted pecans and chewy, dried cherries. **Features:** beer & wine, patio dining. **Address:** 704 S Pearl St 80209 **Location:** Just s of jct Exposition Ave. **Parking:** street only.

[B] [L] [D]

WATERCOURSE FOODS 303/832-7313 (33)
♦♦♦ Vegan. Casual Dining. $11-$16 **AAA Inspector Notes:** Popular with omnivores and herbivores alike, this restaurant specializes in hearty, flavorful vegan cuisine and remains a refuge for those with dietary restrictions. For an early-morning sugar rush, the banana bread French toast is a must. Tofu scrambles and breakfast burritos provide more savory options. At lunch and dinner, popular selections range from fresh soups, salads and sandwiches to pasta and Mexican dishes. The vegan baked goods rival anything grandma whips up (minus the lard). **Features:** beer & wine, patio dining, Sunday brunch. **Address:** 837 E 17th Ave 80218 **Location:** Jct Broadway, 0.5 mi e. **Parking:** street only.

[B] [L] [D]

WORK & CLASS 303/292-0700 (25)
♦♦ Small Plates. Casual Dining. $11-$28 **AAA Inspector Notes:** Surrounded by the bustling din of diners and an open kitchen, you will enjoy sampling a variety of dishes from the unique menu. Start with the creamy grits topped with garlic shrimp or the straightforward pork-and-veal meatballs on polenta. Next, select from catfish, goat, pork, rotisserie chicken, short rib or Colorado lamb. The goat is served carne adovada style. Round out the meal with Brussels sprouts enhanced with salty bacon and sweet apples, or the mac and cheese. **Features:** full bar, patio dining, Sunday brunch. **Address:** 2500 Larimer St 80205 **Location:** At 25th St. **Parking:** street only.

[D]

Z CUISINE BISTROT 303/477-1111 (16)
♦♦♦ French. Fine Dining. $12-$22 **AAA Inspector Notes:** Far removed from the stereotypical stuffy French restaurant, this cozy eatery serves French food at its best. The menu changes daily and features produce from the farmer's market and many local purveyors. The creativity of chef Dupays is remarkable—each bite bursts with unique rich flavors highlighting the freshness of the ingredients. Duck, Colorado grass-fed beef and pork belly frequent the menu. However, the vegetable sides and salads truly shine. **Features:** full bar. **Address:** 2239 W 30th Ave 80211 **Location:** I-25 exit 212B (Speer Blvd) southbound; exit 212A (Speer Blvd S) northbound, just w to Zuni St, just n, then just e. **Parking:** street only. [D]

DILLON (C-3) pop. 904, elev. 9,087'

Dillon is a resort town. Many year-round recreational activities are available along the Dillon Reservoir's 25-mile shoreline. Mountain scenery of the Arapaho and Roosevelt *(see place listing p. 41)* and White River national forests *(see place listing p. 274)* surrounds the community.

East of Dillon on I-70, the 1.5-mile Eisenhower-Johnson Memorial Tunnel Complex burrows through the heart of Mount Trelease. Besides being a milestone in highway engineering, the tunnel bypasses US 6 and the 11,992-foot Loveland Pass, which is often hazardous in winter.

BEST WESTERN PTARMIGAN LODGE   (970)468-2341

Motel
$99-$200

AAA Benefit: Save 10% or more every day and earn 10% bonus points!

Address: 652 Lake Dillon Dr 80435 **Location:** I-70 exit 205, 1.3 mi s on US 6 to Lake Dillon Dr stop light, then 0.3 mi s. Opposite Lake Dillon. **Facility:** 69 units, some efficiencies. 1-2 stories (no elevator), interior/exterior corridors. **Terms:** cancellation fee imposed. **Guest Services:** coin laundry. **Featured Amenity:** breakfast buffet.

DILLON INN   970/262-0801

Hotel. Rates not provided. **Address:** 708 E Anemone Tr 80435 **Location:** I-70 exit 205, 0.5 mi s on US 6 to 2nd Anemone Tr entrance, then just w. **Facility:** 30 units. 2 stories (no elevator), interior corridors. **Pool(s):** heated indoor. **Activities:** sauna, hot tub, playground, exercise room.

WHERE TO EAT

ADRIANO'S BISTRO & DELI   970/468-6111

Northern Italian. Casual Dining. $12-$26 **AAA Inspector Notes:** The entire family shares in the dinner service. The limited menu changes often and might include osso buco, chicken marsala and eggplant parmigiana. Relax after dinner with a glass of wine, coffee, or both, either at the bar or at one of the cozy tables and chairs in front of the fireplace. Share a fresh made cannoli, tiramisù or the chocolate cake with chambord raspberry filling. **Features:** beer & wine, patio dining. **Reservations:** suggested. **Address:** 240 Lake Dillon Dr 80435 **Location:** I-70 exit 205, 1.3 mi e on US 6 to Lake Dillon Dr, then just s.

ARAPAHOE CAFE AND PUB   970/468-0873

American. Casual Dining. $9-$20 **AAA Inspector Notes:** The building was moved from the valley floor to its present location when the Dillon Lake dam was built. The restaurant serves homestyle food with flair. The ruby red mountain trout or roast duckling are popular choices as are the daily soup and lunch specials. **Features:** full bar, happy hour. **Address:** 626 Lake Dillon Dr 80435 **Location:** I-70 exit 205, 1.3 mi e on US 6 to Lake Dillon Dr stop light, then 0.3 mi s.

Check DrivingLaws.AAA.com for local motor vehicle laws when traveling

DILLON DAM BREWERY   970/262-7777

American. Casual Dining. $9-$23 **AAA Inspector Notes:** Having received countless awards for its hand-crafted ales, lagers and root beer, this casual, light-hearted tavern is proud to serve patrons a pint and takes just as much pride in its food. Guests can grab a bowl of hearty stew, enjoy some pasta or tasty beef, pork and chicken dishes. Gluten-free and vegetarian items are available. **Features:** full bar, Sunday brunch, happy hour. **Address:** 100 Little Dam St 80435 **Location:** I-70 exit 205, 0.3 mi s to W Anemone Tr, then just w.

PUG RYAN'S STEAKHOUSE & BREWERY   970/468-2145

Steak Seafood. Casual Dining. $10-$33 **AAA Inspector Notes:** Named after a local outlaw, this restaurant and brewery offers classic pub fare paired with handcrafted beer. Menu options include shepherd's pie, crab cake sliders, burgers, prime rib, rib-eye steak, pan-seared, sushi-grade ahi tuna, hickory-smoked baby back ribs, rainbow trout amandine and a varied selection of salads. **Features:** full bar, happy hour. **Address:** 104 Village Pl 80435 **Location:** I-70 exit 205, 1.3 mi e on US 6 to Lake Dillon Dr, then just s.

DIVIDE (F-8) pop. 127

COLORADO WOLF AND WILDLIFE CENTER is at 4729 Twin Rocks Rd. The center is dedicated to educating the public about wolves, wolf dogs, foxes and coyotes. Guided tours provide the opportunity to see these elusive animals in a natural setting. Visitors can also view endangered species and sign up for special encounters, including a wolf interaction.

Note: Drive slowly on the 0.3 mile dirt road to the center. Arrive at least 15 minutes prior to tour. Noise must be kept to a minimum. Children must be monitored at all times and cannot run, wander or behave loudly. These educational tours may not be appropriate for children under 5. The sanctuary is over 9,000 feet in elevation. **Time:** Allow 1 hour, 30 minutes minimum. **Hours:** Standard guided tours depart Tues.-Sun. at 10, noon, 2 and 4. Feeding tour Fri.-Wed. at 6 p.m., mid-May to mid-Sept. . **Cost:** $15; $8 (ages 0-12). Feeding tour $25; $15 (ages 8-12). **Phone:** (719) 687-9742. GT

DOLORES pop. 936

DUNTON HOT SPRINGS   970/882-4800

fyi Not evaluated. **Address:** 52068 W Road 38 81323 **Location:** 13.3 mi n of center via SR 14 to W Dolores Rd, then 22 mi ne on CR 38 (last 9 mi unpaved). Facilities, services, and décor characterize an upscale property. This former ghost town in the San Juan mountains is now a resort offering luxurious accommodations, fine dining and recreational activities galore.

DURANGO (F-2) pop. 16,887, elev. 6,523'
• Hotels p. 168 • Restaurants p. 172

Durango began as a railroad town with a mining and smelting center during the gold and silver booms. It is now a crossroads for local industry, ranching, commerce and culture. Vestiges of the past accent Durango's Victorian downtown, where visitors can still enjoy the spirit of that colorful era.

Durango is a natural gateway to the San Juan Mountains, one of the more scenic sections of the state. Because they are geologically younger than other Colorado mountain ranges, the San Juans present a more jagged, precipitous appearance.

US 550 runs north from Durango to Silverton and Ouray; the part of the road that is known as the Million Dollar Highway includes many overlooks and is cut from nearly vertical cliff sides *(see Ouray p. 241)*. Because the road has steep drop-offs and no guardrails it should be traveled with caution.

Some of the largest and best preserved Ancestral Puebloan cliff dwellings in the Southwest are 36 miles west in Mesa Verde National Park *(see place listing p. 234)*. Tours to these places and into the back country of the San Juan National Forest can be arranged in Durango; contact the tourism office at (970) 247-3500.

A high mountain hamlet and the Tour of Carvings are 22 miles northeast of Durango at Vallecito Lake Reservoir. Ponderosa pines scattered around the reservoir are carved to represent firefighters and animals who perished in a 2002 forest fire; phone (970) 247-1573.

Other activities available in the Durango area include art gallery tours, golfing, hiking, horseback riding, kayaking, mountain and road biking, rafting, rock climbing, skiing and snowboarding. A convenient year-round way to get around in Durango and avoid parking hassles is to ride the free trolleybus that runs daily every 20 minutes along Main Street 7 a.m.-10 p.m., mid-May to mid-September; Mon.-Fri. 7-7, Sat. 7 a.m.-10 p.m., rest of year.

Durango abounds with more than 100 special events during the year, including ⛄ Snowdown, a wacky celebration held in late January featuring costumes, a parade and a different theme each year. July's Durango Fiesta Days includes a rodeo, parade and barrel races. Music in the Mountains, a classical music festival, is held from mid-July to early August. Durango and Silverton Narrow Gauge Railfest is in August; and Durango Cowboy Poetry Gathering takes place in early October.

Durango Area Tourism Office: 802 Main Ave., P.O. Box 2321, Durango, CO 81302. **Phone:** (970) 247-3500 or (800) 525-8855.

AAM'S MILD TO WILD RAFTING & JEEP TOURS INC. is at 50 Animas View Dr. Full- and half-day guided raft, inflatable kayak, stand-up paddle board and jeep tours explore the surrounding mountains, attractions, ghost towns, waterfalls and nature. A variety of packages combine jeep tours, rafting and one-way railroad excursions on the Durango Train. A guided interpretive tour of Mesa Verde National Park also is available.

Hours: Daily 7:30-8, Memorial Day-Labor Day; Mon.-Sat. 10-5, rest of year. **Cost:** Prices vary by length and type of tour. Full-day jeep fare $135; $115 (children); free (ages 0-4). Half-day jeep fare $84; $64 (children). Rafting full-day fare $89; $69 (children). Half-day rafting fare $49; $38 (children). Economy rafting fare $34; $29 (children). Mesa Verde park tour $129; $89 (children). Combination fare with railroad $164; $114 (children); free (ages 0-4). **Phone:** (970) 247-4789 or (800) 567-6745.

BAR D CHUCKWAGON SUPPERS is 6 mi. n. on US 550, 1 mi. e. on Trimble Lane Rd., then 1.5 mi. n. to 8080 CR 250. Chuck wagon suppers are followed by a Western-style stage show with songs and stories performed by the Bar D Wranglers. The Western village also includes shops and a train ride.

Time: Allow 2 hours minimum. **Hours:** Village and ticket booth open at 5:30, Memorial Day weekend-Labor Day. Dinner at 7:30. Stage show at 8:30. **Cost:** (includes dinner and show) $26-$36 (varies with entrée); $12 (ages 4-10). Reservations are required. **Phone:** (970) 247-5753 or (888) 800-5753.

DURANGO ADVENTURES & TOURS, 555 Main Ave., offers quarter-, half-, three-quarter- and full-day jeep and Hummer excursions to Colorado's scenic San Juan Mountains, featuring ghost towns, mining camps and Native American dwellings. Full-day trips include deli lunches, water and snacks. White-water rafting and snowmobile tours are offered in season. ATV and paddle board rentals also are available.

Hours: Jeep and Hummer quarter-day tours depart daily at 9 and 2, May-Oct. Half-day tours depart daily at 8 and 1, May-Oct. Three-quarter- and full-day tours daily at 8, May-Oct. **Cost:** Quarter-day trips $65; $45 (ages 5-11). Half-day trips $85; $65 (ages 5-11). Three-quarter-day trips $105; $80 (ages 5-11). Full-day trips $145; $115 (ages 5-11). **Phone:** (970) 903-1157 or (877) 259-1800. [GT]

THE DURANGO AND SILVERTON NARROW GAUGE RAILROAD & MUSEUM is at 479 Main Ave. Trains, powered by vintage coal-fired steam locomotives, run through the mountains of the San Juan National Forest following the Animas River to Silverton; the scenery is ruggedly beautiful. The line has been in continuous operation since 1881. Standard-class seating is available in an enclosed coach or open-air car; premium-class cars dating to the 1880s are available on every train.

Least crowded times for the approximately 9-hour round-trip to Silverton are May to early June, late August, October and weekends throughout summer. The 45-mile trip takes 3 1/2 hours each way and allows 30 minutes to 2 1/2 hours in the mining town of Silverton for lunch and shopping. As an upgrade, a bus is available for one direction of the round trip between Durango and Silverton, reducing the trip to 5 1/2 hours; phone for dates and times. A 5-hour, 52-mile round-trip to Cascade Canyon is offered during the winter. Other themed train rides, such as the Polar Express, are schedule throughout the year; call for information. The museum is in a roundhouse in the Durango yard. Rotating displays include vintage locomotives and cars, 1880s photographs, maps and railroad art.

Note: The coal-fired engines may emit cinders and soot. Dark clothing and sunglasses are recommended. Passengers must be in their seats 30 minutes prior to departure or the seat may be sold to waiting passengers. Food is available onboard. **Hours:** Trips to Silverton depart daily at 8 and 8:45

a.m., early May-late Oct. (also at 9:30, early June to mid-Aug.). The winter train to Cascade Canyon departs daily at 10 a.m., day before Thanksgiving-early May. The Polar Express operates late Nov.-early Jan. Closed Christmas. Phone ahead to confirm schedule.

Cost: Fare to Silverton $85; $51 (ages 4-11); free (ages 0-3 not occupying a seat). Premium-class cars $134-$189. Winter train fare $59; $34 (ages 4-11). Museum free. Train fare includes entry to museum. Age requirements for travel in some premium-class cars range from 12 to 21; phone ahead for details. Prices may vary; phone ahead. Reservations are recommended. **Parking:** $9 for RVs/trailers, $7 per private vehicle. **Phone:** (970) 247-2733 or (888) 872-4607.

JAMES RANCH is at 33846 US 550. Electric carts or a tractor-pulled wagon transport visitors past the farm's lush pastures and gardens. During the 2.5-hour tour, visitors see the dairy and cheese making facility as well as a wide variety of livestock. Information is provided about sustainable farming and ranching in addition to the ethical treatment of animals. The tour ends with a sampling of the ranch's own organic cheese and meat in a shady picnic area. **Time:** Allow 2 hours, 30 minutes minimum. **Hours:** Tours depart Mon. and Thurs. 9-11:30, Tues. 4-6:30, mid-June through Aug. 30. **Cost:** $25; free (ages 0-5). Reservations are required. **Phone:** (970) 385-6858. 🍴 🅰️

POWERHOUSE SCIENCE CENTER is at 1333 Camino Del Rio. This interactive science center, within a historic power plant on the banks of the Animas River, educates and entertains all ages relative to the concept of energy. Visitors can take part in a variety of engaging activities, such as designing a playground or a working robot, building a human-powered rocket or race car and using a 3-D printer. The Discovery Kids Zone is designed to inspire creativity in children under five. **Time:** Allow 1 hour minimum. **Hours:** Mon.-Sat. 10-6, Sun. noon-5. Closed major holidays. **Cost:** $7.50; $6.75 (ages 56+, students with ID and military with ID); $6 (ages 3-17). Prices may vary; phone ahead. **Phone:** (970) 259-9234.

RECREATIONAL ACTIVITIES
Horseback Riding
• **Rapp Corral** is .75 mi. past Milepost 41 on US 550 at 51 Haviland Lake Rd. Other activities are offered. **Hours:** Horseback riding daily 8-5, mid-May through Sept. 30. Sleigh rides daily 11-4, mid-Dec. through mid-Feb. **Cost:** Reservations are required. **Phone:** (970) 247-8454.

Skiing
• **Purgatory at Durango Mountain Resort** is off US 550 in the San Juan National Forest. Other activities are offered. **Hours:** Daily 9-4, Thanksgiving-early Apr. (weather permitting). **Phone:** (970) 247-9000 or (800) 982-6103.

Snowmobiling
• **Snowmobile Adventures** departs from Purgatory at Durango Mountain Resort on US 550 in the San

Juan National Forest. **Hours:** Daily 9-4:30, mid-Dec. to late Mar. (weather permitting). **Phone:** (970) 385-2141, or (970) 259-7293 evenings.

White-water Rafting
• **Mountain Waters Rafting** departs from 643 Camino del Rio in the Albertsons parking lot. **Hours:** Rafting trips are offered May 1-Labor Day. Half-day trips depart daily at 8:30, 11 and 1:30. Full-day trips depart daily at 8:30. **Phone:** (970) 259-4191 or (800) 585-8243.

APPLE ORCHARD INN   970/247-0751
 Bed & Breakfast $90-$250 **Address:** 7758 CR 203 81301 **Location:** 8.5 mi n on US 550, just w at Trimble Ln, then 1.3 mi n. **Facility:** Several winding paths and charming wood bridges over streams lead from the main house through postcard-picture-perfect landscaped gardens. Rooms and cottages are individually furnished. 10 units, some cottages. 2 stories (no elevator), interior/exterior corridors. **Terms:** check-in 4 pm, age restrictions may apply, 21 day cancellation notice-fee imposed, resort fee. **Activities:** hot tub. 📶 ❌ 🅰️ / SOME UNITS 🐕 📶 🍴 📷

BEST WESTERN DURANGO INN & SUITES
(970)247-3251

Motel
$89-$169

AAA Benefit: Save 10% or more every day and earn 10% bonus points!

Address: 21382 US Hwy 160 W 81303 **Location:** On US 160, 1 mi w. **Facility:** 71 units. 2 stories (no elevator), exterior corridors. **Pool(s):** heated outdoor. **Activities:** hot tub. **Guest Services:** valet and coin laundry.

SAVE 🍴 🍸 🏊 BIZ 📶 🍴
📠 / SOME UNITS 🐕 HS 📷

BEST WESTERN MOUNTAIN SHADOWS   (970)247-5200

Motel
$99-$189

AAA Benefit: Save 10% or more every day and earn 10% bonus points!

Address: 3255 Main Ave 81301 **Location:** 2.4 mi n on US 550. **Facility:** 65 units, some two bedrooms. 2 stories (no elevator), exterior corridors. **Pool(s):** heated indoor. **Activities:** hot tub. **Guest Services:** coin laundry.

SAVE 🍴 🏊 BIZ 📶 ❌ 🍴
📷 📠

BEST WESTERN PLUS RIO GRANDE INN
(970)385-4980

Hotel
$109-$249

AAA Benefit: Save 10% or more every day and earn 10% bonus points!

Address: 400 E 2nd Ave 81301 **Location:** Just e of Main Ave; just s of 2nd Ave and 5th St. Near Durango and Silverton Narrow Gauge Train Depot. **Facility:** 102 units. 3 stories, interior/exterior corridors. **Amenities:** Some: safes. **Pool(s):** heated indoor. **Activities:** hot tub, exercise room. **Guest Services:** complimentary and valet laundry.

SAVE ECO 🍴 🏊 BIZ 📶 ❌
🍴 📷 📠 / SOME UNITS HS

CABOOSE MOTEL · 970/247-1191
▼ Motel $58-$190 Address: 3363 Main Ave 81301 Location: 2.5 mi n on US 550. Facility: 20 units, some efficiencies and kitchens. 1 story, exterior corridors. Terms: cancellation fee imposed.

DURANGO DOWNTOWN INN · (970)247-5393
Motel $89-$189 Address: 800 Camino Del Rio 81301 Location: On US 550, just n of jct US 160. Facility: 139 units. 2 stories (no elevator), exterior corridors. Terms: check-in 4 pm, cancellation fee imposed. Pool(s): heated indoor. Activities: hot tub, trails, exercise room. Guest Services: valet and coin laundry.

COMFORT INN & SUITES · (970)259-7900
Hotel $75-$300 Address: 455 S Camino Del Rio 81303 Location: On US 160 (Frontage Rd), 1.5 mi e of jct US 550. Facility: 123 units. 3 stories, interior corridors. Amenities: safes. Pool(s): heated indoor. Activities: sauna, exercise room. Guest Services: coin laundry. Featured Amenity: full hot breakfast. (See ad this page.)

DOUBLETREE BY HILTON HOTEL DURANGO · 970/259-6580
▼ Hotel. Rates not provided. Address: 501 Camino Del Rio 81301 Location: Jct US 160 and 550. Facility: 159 units. 4 stories, interior corridors. Dining: 2 restaurants. Pool(s): heated indoor. Activities: hot tub, fishing, trails, exercise room. Guest Services: valet and coin laundry, area transportation.

AAA Benefit:
Members save 5% or more!

Dream. Plan. Go.
TripTik® Travel Planner

AAA.com/ttp

▼ See AAA listing this page ▼

DURANGO LODGE 970/247-0955
🔷🔷🔷 Motel. Rates not provided. **Address:** 150 E 5th St 81301 **Location:** Just e of 5th St and Main Ave. **Facility:** 39 units. 2 stories (no elevator), interior/exterior corridors. **Pool(s):** heated outdoor. **Activities:** hot tub. 🛎️➕ 🏊 📶 ✕ 🍴 🖥️

GENERAL PALMER HOTEL (970)247-4747
🔷🔷🔷 🔷🔷🔷
Historic Hotel
$90-$305
Address: 567 Main Ave 81301 **Location:** At Main Ave and College Dr. Next to Durango and Silverton Narrow Gauge Train Depot. **Facility:** This restored 1898 hotel and adjacent annex building combine rich Victorian elegance and Southwestern hospitality. Puzzles, board games and cards are available. 39 units. 2-3 stories, interior/exterior corridors. **Parking:** on-site and valet. **Terms:** check-in 4 pm, 7 day cancellation notice-fee imposed. **Guest Services:** valet laundry. *(See ad this page.)*
SAVE 🛎️➕ BIZ 📶 ✕ 🖥️
/ SOME UNITS 🍴

HAMPTON INN 970/247-2600
🔷🔷🔷 Hotel. Rates not provided. **Address:** 3777 Main Ave 81301 **Location:** 2.9 mi n on US 550. **Facility:** 76 units. 3 stories, interior corridors. **Pool(s):** heated indoor. **Activities:** hot tub, picnic facilities. **Guest Services:** valet and coin laundry.

AAA Benefit: Members save up to 10%!

🛎️➕ CALL 📞Ⓜ️ 🏊 BIZ 📶 ✕ 🍴 🖥️

HOLIDAY INN HOTEL & SUITES DURANGO CENTRAL
970/385-6400
🔷🔷🔷 Hotel. Rates not provided. **Address:** 21636 Hwy 160 W 81301 **Location:** Just w of jct US 550. **Facility:** 116 units. 4 stories, interior corridors. **Pool(s):** heated indoor. **Activities:** hot tub, exercise room. **Guest Services:** valet and coin laundry, area transportation.
✈️ 🛎️ 🍽️ CALL 📞Ⓜ️ 🏊 BIZ 📶 ✕ 🍴 🖥️ / SOME UNITS 🐾

HOMEWOOD SUITES BY HILTON 970/259-2996
🔷🔷🔷 Extended Stay Hotel. Rates not provided. **Address:** 15 Girard St 81303 **Location:** On US 160 (Frontage Rd), 2.2 mi e of jct US 550. **Facility:** 78 efficiencies. 3 stories, interior corridors. **Terms:** check-in 4 pm. **Pool(s):** heated indoor. **Activities:** hot tub, picnic facilities, trails, exercise room. **Guest Services:** valet and coin laundry.

AAA Benefit: Members save up to 10%!

✈️ CALL 📞Ⓜ️ 🏊 BIZ HS 📶 ✕ 🍴 🖥️ 🖥️
/ SOME UNITS 🐾

LELAND HOUSE BED & BREAKFAST SUITES 970/385-1920
🔷🔷🔷 Historic Bed & Breakfast $159-$449 **Address:** 721 E 2nd Ave 81301 **Location:** Just e of Main Ave via 7th St, then just n. **Facility:** This restored historic inn offers in-room ceiling fans and cozy, charming décor. Three rooms feature a gas fireplace. 12 units, some two bedrooms and kitchens. 2 stories (no elevator), interior/exterior corridors. **Terms:** 14 day cancellation notice. **Activities:** bicycles. **Guest Services:** valet laundry.
🛎️➕ 📶 ✕ 🍴 🖥️ / SOME UNITS 🐾

QUALITY INN (970)259-5373
🔷🔷🔷 Motel. $69-$179 **Address:** 2930 N Main Ave 81301 **Location:** 2 mi n on US 550. Located close to railroad tracks. **Facility:** 48 units. 2 stories (no elevator), exterior corridors. **Pool(s):** heated outdoor. **Activities:** hot tub, bicycles. **Guest Services:** valet laundry.
🛎️➕ 🏊 BIZ 📶 🍴 🖥️ 🖥️ / SOME UNITS 🐾

RESIDENCE INN BY MARRIOTT (970)259-6200
🔷🔷🔷 Extended Stay Hotel $114-$315 **Address:** 21691 Hwy 160 W 81301 **Location:** On US 160, just w. **Facility:** 66 kitchen units, some two bedrooms. 3 stories, interior corridors. **Pool(s):** heated indoor. **Activities:** hot tub, exercise room. **Guest Services:** valet and coin laundry.

AAA Benefit: Members save 5% or more!

🛎️➕ CALL 📞Ⓜ️ 🏊 BIZ 📶 ✕ 🍴 🖥️ 🖥️
/ SOME UNITS 🐾

▼ See AAA listing this page ▼

AAA Vacations® packages ...
exciting itineraries and exclusive values

THE ROCHESTER HOTEL   (970)385-1920

▼▼▼ **Classic Historic Bed & Breakfast** $189-$319 **Address:** 726 E 2nd Ave 81301 **Location:** Just e of Main Ave via 7th St, then just n. **Facility:** The individually decorated rooms at this 1892 hotel reflect a Western theme fashioned after motion pictures filmed in the area. 15 units. 2 stories (no elevator), interior corridors. **Terms:** 14 day cancellation notice-fee imposed. **Activities:** bicycles. **Guest Services:** valet laundry.

SIESTA MOTEL   (970)247-0741

▼ **Motel** $68-$199 **Address:** 3475 N Main Ave 81301 **Location:** 2.6 mi n on US 550. **Facility:** 21 units, some efficiencies and kitchens. 1 story, exterior corridors.

STRATER HOTEL   (970)247-4431

▼▼▼
Classic Historic Hotel
$124-$289

Address: 699 Main 81301 **Location:** Corner of 7th St and Main St; historic downtown. Located near Durango and Silverton Narrow Gauge Train Depot. **Facility:** Carved-wood trim, ornate ceiling details and stained-glass accents add character to this Victorian-era hotel. 93 units. 4 stories, interior corridors. **Terms:** check-in 4 pm, 3 day cancellation notice-fee imposed. **Dining:** Diamond Belle Saloon, The Mahogany Grille, see separate listings, entertainment. **Activities:** hot tub. **Guest Services:** valet laundry. *(See ad p. 171.)*

THE LODGE AT PURGATORY   970/385-2100

fyi **Condominium** Did not meet all AAA rating requirements for locking devices in some guest rooms at time of last evaluation on 08/13/2014. **Address:** 24 Sheol St 81301 **Location:** 27 mi n on US 550; at Durango Mountain Resort. Facilities, services, and décor characterize a mid-scale property. This mountaintop lodge boasts beautifully appointed guest rooms and bathrooms. Guests will appreciate the heated underground parking and the attractive pool area, which features a kiddie slide.

WHERE TO EAT

CHIMAYO   970/259-2749

▼▼ American. Casual Dining. $11-$26 **AAA Inspector Notes:** Exposed brick walls and copper accents create a sophisticated atmosphere at this casual eatery. Enjoy a breeze from the outdoors when the garage door opens in nice weather. Menu items include roasted chicken and date salad, cedar plank Scottish salmon, and stone-fired pizzettes. **Features:** full bar, Sunday brunch, happy hour. **Address:** 862 Main Ave 81301 **Location:** Between 8th and 9th sts; in historic downtown. **Parking:** street only.

CYPRUS CAFE   970/385-6884

▼▼ Mediterranean. Casual Dining. $10-$34 **AAA Inspector Notes:** Located in an elegantly restored Victorian house, this cafe serves flavorful, Mediterranean-inspired cuisine. Seasonal menu items may include wild salmon with goat cheese, grape leaves and olive caper tapenade baked in parchment paper; vegetarian specialties; harissa and lemon-marinated lamb chops served with roasted new potatoes; and a wide variety of farmer's market produce. Desserts such as lavender flan, baklava and chocolate pot de crème can be enjoyed on the beautiful garden patio. **Features:** full bar, patio dining. **Address:** 725 E 2nd Ave 81301 **Location:** Between 7th and 8th sts; center. **Parking:** street only.

DIAMOND BELLE SALOON   970/247-4431

▼▼ American. Casual Dining. $8-$16 **AAA Inspector Notes:** *Historic.* Friendly, costumed dance hall girls and bartenders transport you back to the turn of the last century. Whether you want a fine glass of wine, creative cocktail or frosty mug of beer, this stylish eatery features ragtime music every night. Menu favorites include creamy tomato bisque, bourbon barbecue grilled chicken breast, red chile-rubbed salmon, and chicken pot pie. **Features:** full bar, Sunday brunch. **Address:** 699 Main Ave 81301 **Location:** Corner of 7th St and Main Ave; in historic downtown; in Strater Hotel. **Parking:** street only. *(See ad p. 171.)* L D

DIGS RESTAURANT & BAR   970/259-2344

▼▼ American. Casual Dining. $10-$21 **AAA Inspector Notes:** Located in the Three Springs development near the hospital, this eatery offers casual service in a warm, inviting space. The menu features bison burgers, steaks and pizza. **Features:** full bar, happy hour. **Address:** 125 Mercado St, Unit 107 81301 **Location:** 6 mi e of jct SR 160 and US 550 to Three Springs Blvd, 1 mi e (1st exit at 1st roundabout, 2nd exit at 2nd roundabout). L D

EAST BY SOUTHWEST   970/247-5533

▼▼▼ Japanese. Casual Dining. $12-$45 **AAA Inspector Notes:** The chef prepares traditional Japanese dishes with a twist; some of the innovations include Southwestern spices. Start with steamed pork belly buns, pineapple and jalapeño tiradito, or lollipop lamb chops. Signature rolls include the "Boomshiki," featuring scallops, asparagus and bacon; and the "Lotus Blossom," a riceless roll with a variety of fish and crab. Large plates include tea smoked duck, tofu coconut curry, and filet mignon with a shiitake demi-glace. **Features:** full bar, happy hour. **Address:** 160 E College Dr 81301 **Location:** At College Dr and 2nd Ave; downtown. **Parking:** street only. L D

ENO (WINES, COFFEES, TAPAS)   970/385-0105

▼▼ Small Plates. Casual Dining. $5-$10 **AAA Inspector Notes:** Enjoy a changing selection of wines by the glass presented by very knowledgeable servers. This cozy, casual, contemporary setting also features small plates for sharing such as local artisan cheeses and smoked trout. **Features:** full bar, happy hour. **Address:** 723 E 2nd Ave 81301 **Location:** Between 7th and 8th sts. **Parking:** street only. B L D

GAZPACHO NEW MEXICAN RESTAURANT   970/259-9494

▼▼ Mexican. Casual Dining. $8-$24 **AAA Inspector Notes:** This restaurant features northern New Mexico cooking with carne adovada, homemade tamales, hot chili and vegetarian dishes. The Southwestern dining rooms display skylights and log beams. This popular place has great service and a loyal local following. **Features:** full bar. **Address:** 431 E 2nd Ave 81301 **Location:** Just e of Durango and Silverton Narrow Gauge Train Depot. L D

GUIDO'S FAVORITE FOODS   970/259-5028

▼▼▼
Italian Casual Dining $12-$26

AAA Inspector Notes: When you walk into the gourmet food market, head left to find this authentic Italian trattoria. Start with the rich and creamy burrata cheese served with grilled, marinated eggplant. Entrées include the sea scallops, which comes with bucatini pasta in a light, creamy white wine and mushroom sauce. Other menu items include littleneck clams, sausage and mushroom ragu, lasagna, eggplant Parmesan, and veal loin Bolognese. For a sweet ending, try the homemade gelato or tiramisu. **Features:** full bar, patio dining, happy hour. **Address:** 1201 Main Ave 81301 **Location:** Corner of 12th St and Main Ave. **Parking:** street only. L D

HIMALAYAN KITCHEN   970/259-0956

▼▼ Tibetan. Casual Dining. $10-$20 **AAA Inspector Notes:** Guests can prepare for a distinctive experience centered on flavorful cuisine. Traditional fare includes Indian curry dishes, hearty soups, salads and preparations of beef, chicken, lamb and exotic yak. **Features:** full bar, happy hour. **Address:** 992 Main Ave 81301 **Location:** At 10th St and Main Ave; downtown. **Parking:** street only. L D

HOMESLICE PIZZA
970/422-8337

Pizza. Quick Serve. $8-$16 **AAA Inspector Notes:** Expect creative slices at this casual eatery. Start with a 'holy goat' salad, which has mixed greens, apples, candied walnuts and goat cheese. Feeling experimental? Try the 'fa-gouda-boutit' pizza, a breaded eggplant, smoked Gouda and bacon pie. There's also the 'grow a pear,' topped with prosciutto, arugula and roasted pears. Sound too elaborate? Don't worry, you can also build your own pizza. The fence (made from recycled skis) and gallery art add to the local flavor. **Features:** full bar, patio dining. **Address:** 2915 N Main Ave 81301 **Location:** On US 550, between 14th and 15th sts.

L D

JEAN-PIERRE BAKERY & CAFE
970/247-7700

French. Casual Dining. $8-$24 **AAA Inspector Notes:** Specializing in bistro fare and pastries, this eatery offers a taste of France. Start with a crock of onion soup. Then, select from a hearty country salad with chicken, blue cheese, grapes, apples and pecans; quiche; or a croque-monsieur ham sandwich. Wander over to the display case to pick out a macaroon, chocolate croissant or fruit tart. Oil paintings, antiques and knickknacks give the ambiance a French bistro feel. **Features:** beer & wine, Sunday brunch. **Reservations:** suggested. **Address:** 601 Main Ave 81301 **Location:** Corner of Main Ave and College Dr; downtown. **Parking:** street only.

B L D

KEN & SUE'S
970/385-1810

New American. Casual Dining. $9-$23 **AAA Inspector Notes:** This popular restaurant offers a unique selection of comfort food and international fusion-style cuisine. Appetizers mainly consist of Asian-influenced dishes, such as the ginger-chicken pot stickers, tempura shrimp satays, sesame-seared rare tuna, and spicy shrimp spring rolls. Entrées include Aunt Lydia's meatloaf, pistachio-crusted grouper, filet mignon and grilled pork medallions wrapped in smoked bacon. **Features:** full bar. **Reservations:** suggested. **Address:** 636 Main Ave 81301 **Location:** Just s of 7th St and Main Ave; downtown. **Parking:** street only.

L D

LADY FALCONBURGH'S BARLEY EXCHANGE
970/382-9664

American. Casual Dining. $9-$17 **AAA Inspector Notes:** Serving handcrafted beer and great food in a European pub atmosphere, this lively place features hand-painted murals, an all-brick bar and a sunlit atrium. Favorite dishes include peel-and-eat shrimp, amber ale-battered fish and chips, slow-smoked baby back ribs, grilled salmon with rice and steamed vegetables and a juicy 10-ounce steak. A tasty black and tan soup consists of spicy black bean on one side and creamy cheddar beer on the other. **Features:** full bar. **Address:** 640 Main Ave 81301 **Location:** At E 7th St and Main Ave; downstairs. **Parking:** street only.

L D LATE

THE MAHOGANY GRILLE
970/247-4431

New American Fine Dining $22-$44

AAA Inspector Notes: *Historic.* Served in an intimate Victorian-themed dining room reminiscent of the 1800s are an array of innovative flavors of the west featuring steak, game, seafood, pasta and gourmet salads followed by 'fabulicious' desserts. **Features:** full bar. **Reservations:** suggested. **Address:** 699 Main Ave 81301 **Location:** Corner of 7th St and Main Ave; in historic downtown; in Strater Hotel. **Parking:** street only. *Menu on AAA.com (See ad p. 171.)*

B D

ORE HOUSE
970/247-5707

Steak Seafood Fine Dining $24-$44

AAA Inspector Notes: This rustic, casual dining room displays Old West décor and works by local artists. Menu items include Peruvian-style ceviche, fried calamari and artichokes, wild king salmon, Maine lobster, New York strip steak and Châteaubriand. Vegetarian and non-red meat options are also available. Wash everything down with a local microbrew or a specialty cocktail made with Colorado liquor and liqueurs. **Features:** full bar. **Reservations:** suggested. **Address:** 147 E College Dr 81301 **Location:** Just e of Main Ave and College Dr; downtown. **Parking:** street only.

D

PALACE RESTAURANT
970/247-2018

American. Casual Dining. $9-$32 **AAA Inspector Notes:** This restaurant is known for its outdoor patio. The menu features well-prepared pasta, seafood, beef, poultry and pork entrées. Among the specialty dishes are halibut, almond-honey-roasted duck, Colorado lamb and bison rib-eye. The delicious berry crumble dessert is served hot with a scoop of vanilla ice cream. The friendly, attentive staff enhances the dining experience. **Features:** full bar, happy hour. **Reservations:** suggested. **Address:** 505 Main Ave 81301 **Location:** Next to Durango and Silverton Narrow Gauge Train Depot. **Parking:** street only.

L D

THE RED SNAPPER
970/259-3417

Seafood. Casual Dining. $12-$42 **AAA Inspector Notes:** In a historic building, this eatery has been a local favorite since 1988. The clam chowder or lobster bisque, combined with the salad bar, make a nice, light lunch option. Start with fresh oysters, shrimp cocktail or the ahi tuna tartare. Entrées include ruby red trout, Alaskan king crab legs and sea scallops. If you're not in the mood for seafood, select from one of the premium steaks or try the drunken Hawaiian chicken served with a pineapple-mango chutney. **Features:** full bar, happy hour. **Address:** 144 E 9th St 81301 **Location:** Between Main and 2nd aves; downtown. **Parking:** street only.

L D

SEASON'S ROTISSERIE & GRILL
970/382-9790

American. Fine Dining. $13-$28 **AAA Inspector Notes:** As the name suggests, this restaurant celebrates the changing seasons with local, farm-fresh ingredients and an ever-changing menu. If available, standout dishes include an asparagus salad, topped with crispy, salty pancetta and a fried egg; and the Colorado lamb sirloin served with crispy, cured lamb slices and broccolini. Colorful mountain photos, depicting different seasons, enhance the warm, wood-accented décor. **Features:** full bar, patio dining, happy hour. **Reservations:** suggested. **Address:** 764 Main Ave 81301 **Location:** Between 7th and 8th sts; downtown. **Parking:** street only.

L D

SUSHITARIAN
970/382-0001

Japanese Sushi. Casual Dining. $10-$20 **AAA Inspector Notes:** This relaxed eatery offers creative appetizers—such as the hijiki seaweed salad and striped bass tiradito—noodle bowls and a wide variety of specialty sushi rolls including fried calamari roll and the mango lango roll made of tempura banana, rock shrimp and a mango sauce. Combination meals, similar to a bento box, allow you to sample a number of items and offer a great value. **Features:** full bar, happy hour. **Address:** 601 E 2nd Ave 81301 **Location:** At College Dr and E 2nd Ave; downtown. **Parking:** street only.

L D

EAGLE pop. 6,508
• Restaurants p. 174

AMERICINN LODGE & SUITES OF EAGLE
970/328-5155

Hotel. Rates not provided. **Address:** 0085 Pond Rd 81631 **Location:** I-70 exit 147, just n, then w. **Facility:** 54 units. 3 stories, interior corridors. **Pool(s):** heated indoor. **Activities:** sauna, hot tub, bicycles, exercise room. **Guest Services:** coin laundry.

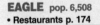

BEST WESTERN PLUS EAGLE LODGE & SUITES
(970)328-6316

Hotel $115-$219

AAA Benefit: Save 10% or more every day and earn 10% bonus points!

Address: 200 Loren Ln 81631 **Location:** I-70 exit 147, just s, then just e. **Facility:** 100 units, some two bedrooms. 2 stories, interior corridors. **Pool(s):** heated indoor. **Activities:** sauna, hot tub, steamroom, exercise room, massage. **Guest Services:** valet and coin laundry.

COMFORT INN VAIL VALLEY   970-328-7878

▼▼ ▼▼ **Hotel.** Rates not provided. **Address:** 0285 Market St 81631 **Location:** I-70 exit 147, just n, then 0.3 mi e. **Facility:** 60 units. 3 stories, interior corridors. **Pool(s):** heated indoor. **Activities:** hot tub. **Guest Services:** coin laundry.

[icons] CALL [icons] BIZ [icons] / SOME UNITS [icons]

GRAND AVE GRILL   970/328-4043

▼▼ ▼▼ American. Casual Dining. $10-$26 **AAA Inspector Notes:** The diverse menu offers everything from gourmet sandwiches to locally made pork tamales. Other options include a grilled ahi tuna salad, roasted meatloaf, and chicken Alfredo. Topped with cheddar cheese and bacon, the rodeo burger comes with a tangy, Asian-style barbecue sauce. Iron chandeliers, Annie Oakley and Calamity Jane advertisements, and hardwood floors add a Western flair to the décor. **Features:** full bar, patio dining, Sunday brunch, happy hour. **Address:** 678 Grand Ave 81631 **Location:** I-70 exit 147, 0.3 mi s, take 1st exit at roundabout, then 0.8 mi w. [L] [D]

PARADIGMS RESTAURANT   970/328-7990

▼▼ ▼▼ American. Casual Dining. $12-$25 **AAA Inspector Notes:** Popular with locals as a place to celebrate a special occasion, this eatery offers more sophisticated fare than other restaurants in town. Try the salmon with the creamy lemon sauce. Other options include pork, Prime sirloin and lamb. Consider sitting in the garden patio when the weather cooperates. Service is more relaxed and casual than the menu might suggest. **Features:** full bar, patio dining. **Reservations:** suggested. **Address:** 343 Capitol St 81631 **Location:** I-70 exit 147, 0.3 mi s on Eby Creek Rd, just w on US 6 (Grand Ave), then just s at 4th St. **Parking:** on-site and street. [D]

PASTATIVELY ROBERTO'S ITALIAN CUISINE   970/328-7324

▼▼ ▼▼ Italian. Casual Dining. $8-$24 **AAA Inspector Notes:** Along with freshly baked bread, each meal begins with assorted olives, red pepper hummus and roasted garlic. The menu features Italian favorites, such as lasagna, chicken parmigiana, and ravioli del giorno. Start with Dave's Italian egg rolls–spinach, sun-dried tomatoes, cheese and prosciutto wrapped in dough and fried. **Features:** beer & wine. **Address:** 94 Market St 81631 **Location:** I-70 exit 147, just n, then just e. [L] [D]

PAZZO'S PIZZERIA   970/337-9900

▼▼ ▼▼ Italian. Casual Dining. $9-$15 **AAA Inspector Notes:** The menu at this lively eatery includes delicious hand-tossed pizzas, strombolis and calzones with a variety of toppings, lasagna, ravioli, rigatoni, spinach manicotti, and chicken and eggplant Parmigiana. The minestrone soup was very good. **Features:** full bar. **Address:** 50 Chambers Ave, Suite C 81631 **Location:** I-70 exit 147, just s to Chambers Ave, then just w. [L] [D]

EDWARDS pop. 10,266

THE LODGE & SPA AT CORDILLERA   (970)926-2200

▼▼ ▼▼ ▼▼
Resort Hotel
$159-$409

Address: 2205 Cordillera Way 81632 **Location:** I-70 exit 163, 0.5 mi s, 2.6 mi w on US 6, then 2 mi nw via Squaw Creek Rd, follow signs; 2.3 mi via paved road from gatehouse. **Facility:** Escape to this resort for a romantic getaway or family vacation. The villa-style façade's ornate woodwork and rich oil paintings give the property a European feel. 56 units. 4 stories, interior corridors. **Parking:** on-site and valet. **Terms:** check-in 4 pm, 3 day cancellation notice-fee imposed, resort fee. **Amenities:** safes. **Dining:** 2 restaurants. **Pool(s):** heated outdoor, heated indoor. **Activities:** sauna, hot tub, steamroom, fishing, regulation golf, tennis, cross country skiing, recreation programs, trails, spa. **Guest Services:** valet laundry, area transportation.

EAT! DRINK!   970/926-1393

▼▼ ▼▼ American. Casual Dining. $9-$15 **AAA Inspector Notes:** The focus of this eatery is gourmet cheese, with most salads and sandwiches featuring a distinct type. The recommended California sandwich features turkey, Tallegio, pear and fig preserves. The second part of the name refers to the wine shop connected to the restaurant. A variety of wines are available by the glass and by the bottle, but the beer selection is limited. The award-winning cupcakes shouldn't be skipped. **Features:** beer & wine, happy hour. **Address:** 56 Edwards Village Blvd, Suite 104 81632 **Location:** I-70 exit 163, 0.5 mi sw to SR 6; in Edwards Village Center; next to post office. [L] [D]

JUNIPER RESTAURANT   970/926-7001

▼▼ ▼▼ ▼▼ American. Fine Dining. $32-$43 **AAA Inspector Notes:** This cozy eatery offers hearty, contemporary American cuisine. If available, start with the fresh berry, arugula and spiced pecan salad. Entrées include bone-in rib-eye, glazed pork chop, and a lump crab-stuffed sole set on a bed of rock shrimp and corn succotash. Locals know to end the meal with Charlie's rich, sticky toffee pudding. When the weather cooperates, request a table overlooking the Eagle River. **Features:** full bar, patio dining. **Reservations:** suggested. **Address:** 97 Main St E, Suite 101 81632 **Location:** I-70 exit 163, 0.5 mi s, then just e; at Riverwalk Plaza. [D] [icon]

LARKBURGER   970/926-9336

▼▼ Burgers. Quick Serve. $7-$9 **AAA Inspector Notes:** Flavorful burgers, shakes and fries have drawn a large and devoted following to this cozy, quick-serve restaurant. The tasty menu benefits from high-quality, 100 percent natural ingredients, including all-natural turkey, chicken and Black Angus beef. The casual, modern décor features wall panels made from reclaimed timber. **Features:** beer only. **Address:** 105 Edwards Village Blvd 81632 **Location:** I-70 exit 163, 0.5 mi sw to SR 6; in Edwards Village Center. [L] [D]

SATO SUSHI   970/926-7684

▼▼ ▼▼ ▼▼ Japanese. Casual Dining. $18-$33 **AAA Inspector Notes:** This eatery specializes in unique sushi, successfully mixing ingredients from other culinary traditions, such as foie gras and white truffle oil with traditional Japanese preparation. Select from traditional nigiri sushi and rolls, or opt for something more adventurous like the Colorado bass nigiri, or the truffle roll (white tuna, cucumber, avocado, shiitake mushroom and a truffle vinaigrette). Entrées include pan-roasted grouper, spicy beef stir-fry, and red curry chicken pot pie. **Features:** full bar, patio dining, happy hour. **Address:** 105 Edwards Village Blvd, Suite 101 81632 **Location:** I-70 exit 163, 0.4 mi s; just sw of jct US 6. [D]

TACORICO   970/926-8226

▼▼ ▼▼ Mexican. Casual Dining. $5-$8 **AAA Inspector Notes:** This fun, festive restaurant offers gourmet street food. The sweet-and-spicy street corn, flavored with ancho powder and Cotija cheese, is a must-order item. Open-face tacos include carnitas, mole chicken and pork belly. Wash everything down with a tequila or mezcal cocktail. **Features:** full bar, happy hour. **Address:** 56 Edwards Village Blvd 81632 **Location:** I-70 exit 163, 0.5 mi sw to SR 6. [D]

VISTA AT ARROWHEAD   970/926-2111

▼▼ ▼▼ ▼▼ American. Fine Dining. $11-$46 **AAA Inspector Notes:** Start with a cup of homemade soup, crostini with burrata, or the Prince Edward Island mussels. Lunch entrées include a variety of salads, pizza, and gourmet sandwiches. The dinner menu consists of more sophisticated fare, such as veal osso buco, pan-seared yellowfin tuna and Colorado rib-eye served with foie gras compound butter. The patio offers picturesque views in the summer and fall. **Features:** full bar, patio dining, early bird specials. **Reservations:** suggested. **Address:** 676 Sawatch Dr 81632 **Location:** I-70 exit 163, 0.4 mi sw, 1.6 mi se on US 6, 0.3 mi s, then just se; in Country Club of the Rockies. **Parking:** valet only. [L] [D]

ZINO RISTORANTE   970/926-0777

▼▼ ▼▼ ▼▼ Italian. Casual Dining. $15-$35 **AAA Inspector Notes:** A spiral staircase leading into the dining room is a focal point of this beautiful restaurant, which also features a large patio overlooking a river. Serving delicious contemporary Italian cuisine and such seasonal menu items as house-made burrata, Maine lobster ravioli, gourmet pizzas, wild boar sausage fettuccine, and Berkshire pork chop Milanese, the restaurant also offers traditional Italian desserts. **Features:** full bar, patio dining, happy hour. **Address:** 27 Main St 81632 **Location:** I-70 exit 163, 0.5 mi s, then just e; at Riverwalk Plaza. [D]

ENGLEWOOD pop. 30,255
• **Part of Denver area — see map p. 116**

COURTYARD BY MARRIOTT DENVER SOUTH/PARK MEADOWS
(720)895-0300

WWW Hotel $84-$252 **Address:** 8320 S Valley Hwy 80112 **Location:** I-25 exit 195 (County Line Rd), just e to S Valley Hwy, then just w. **Facility:** 156 units. 4 stories, interior corridors. **Pool(s):** heated indoor. **Activities:** hot tub, exercise room. **Guest Services:** valet and coin laundry, boarding pass kiosk, area transportation.

AAA Benefit: Members save 5% or more!

[icons] / SOME UNITS

HILTON GARDEN INN DENVER SOUTH/MERIDIAN
303/824-1550

WWW Hotel. Rates not provided. **Address:** 9290 S Meridian Blvd 80112 **Location:** I-25 exit 193 (Lincoln Ave), e to E Havana St, just n, stay in left lane to Meridian Blvd, then 0.5 mi w. **Facility:** 157 units. 6 stories, interior corridors. **Pool(s):** heated indoor. **Activities:** hot tub, exercise room. **Guest Services:** valet and coin laundry, area transportation.

AAA Benefit: Members save up to 10%!

[icons]

HOMEWOOD SUITES BY HILTON - DTC/INVERNESS
303/706-0102

WWW Extended Stay Hotel. Rates not provided. **Address:** 199 Inverness Dr W 80112 **Location:** I-25 exit 195 (County Line Rd), 0.3 mi ne to traffic light, then just n. **Facility:** 113 efficiencies, some two bedrooms. 4 stories, interior corridors. **Pool(s):** heated indoor. **Activities:** trails, exercise room. **Guest Services:** valet and coin laundry, area transportation.

AAA Benefit: Members save up to 10%!

[icons] / SOME UNITS

THE INVERNESS HOTEL AND CONFERENCE CENTER
(303)799-5800

WWW WWW
Resort Hotel
$139-$389

Address: 200 Inverness Dr W 80112 **Location:** I-25 exit 195 (County Line Rd), 0.3 mi ne to traffic light, then just n. **Facility:** Guest rooms overlook either the golf course or the mountains. An expanded spa provides indulgent relaxation after a long day of attending meetings or playing golf. 302 units. 5 stories, interior corridors. **Parking:** on-site and valet. **Terms:** 2-3 night minimum stay, cancellation fee imposed, resort fee. **Amenities:** video games. **Dining:** 5 restaurants. **Pool(s):** heated outdoor, heated indoor. **Activities:** sauna, hot tub, steamroom, regulation golf, tennis, trails, exercise room, spa. **Guest Services:** valet laundry, boarding pass kiosk, area transportation.

[icons] / SOME UNITS

RESIDENCE INN BY MARRIOTT DENVER SOUTH / PARK MEADOWS
(720)895-0200

WWW Extended Stay Hotel $101-$263 **Address:** 8322 S Valley Hwy 80112 **Location:** I-25 exit 195 (County Line Rd), just e to S Valley Hwy, then just w. **Facility:** 112 units, some two bedrooms, efficiencies and kitchens. 4 stories, interior corridors. **Pool(s):** heated indoor. **Activities:** hot tub, picnic facilities, exercise room. **Guest Services:** valet and coin laundry, area transportation.

AAA Benefit: Members save 5% or more!

[icons] / SOME UNITS

WHERE TO EAT

FLEMING'S PRIME STEAKHOUSE & WINE BAR   303/768-0827

WWW Steak. Fine Dining. $28-$48 **AAA Inspector Notes:** The warm, clubby atmosphere is the ideal setting for perfectly grilled steaks and seafood. Side dishes come in hearty portions, and salads are fresh and crisp. More than 100 wine selections are available. **Features:** full bar, patio dining. **Address:** 191 Inverness Dr W 80112 **Location:** I-25 exit 195 (County Line Rd), 0.3 mi ne to traffic light, then just n. **Parking:** on-site and valet. [D]

J. ALEXANDER'S RESTAURANT   303/708-8432

WWW American. Casual Dining. $10-$27 **AAA Inspector Notes:** The busy and casual restaurant prepares classic fare—including steak, grilled fish and prime rib—in the open kitchen. The dessert menu is excellent. **Features:** full bar. **Address:** 9709 E County Line Rd 80112 **Location:** I-25 exit 195 (County Line Rd), just w; in a strip mall. [L] [D] CALL

ESTES PARK (A-8) pop. 5,858, elev. 7,522'
• **Hotels p. 181** • **Restaurants p. 182**
• **Attractions map p. 252**
• **Hotels & Restaurants map & index p. 178**

Estes Park serves as the eastern gateway to Rocky Mountain National Park *(see place listing p. 251)*, and those not roughing it at a campground frequently seek accommodations here. Just as wildlife viewing opportunities attract tourists today, it was nature's bounty that first lured Native American tribes and Kit Carson and his group of trappers. The area was ultimately named for pioneer Joel Estes, who settled in the mountainous hamlet around 1860.

The town is a pleasant surprise; in addition to offering park enthusiasts the usual creature comforts along with a variety of outfitters and gear shops devoted to recreational pursuits, Estes Park has a charm all its own and is a worthy destination in itself. Elkhorn Avenue is the hub of shopping activity, with stores touting souvenirs, clothes, sports equipment, jewelry and crafts. A number of eateries as well as ice cream and candy stores entice visitors, who often stroll along the Estes Park Riverwalk after indulging in culinary delights—the path runs along the Big Thompson River and past an old-fashioned waterwheel through the town center.

The stately white Stanley Hotel *(see attraction listing)* is an impressive landmark, a gracious presence amid a backdrop of craggy mountain peaks. Figuring prominently in Estes Park's history, the owner of the property—who happened to invent the Stanley Steamer—transported his guests to the lodging via his renowned steam cars. Over the years, many elite guests have booked a room at the Stanley and savored the view from its veranda.

For Western-style fun appealing to all ages, head to the evening Cowboy Sing-Along occurring throughout the summer in Bond Park; phone the Estes Park Convention & Visitors Bureau for specific dates. If you're in town in early July, watch modern-day cowboys perform such feats as bronc riding, steer wrestling and barrel racing during the Rooftop Rodeo, a week-long extravaganza including a parade and antique show.

Performance Park, a band shell with great acoustics no doubt aided by its placement below rugged

(See map & index p. 178.)

cliffs, entertains locals and visitors alike with its Thursday night summer concert series; the sounds of jazz, bluegrass and other genres waft through the air in this lovely mountain setting at 417 W. Elkhorn Ave.

If you're up for a scenic drive, you can take advantage of several stunningly beautiful routes that pass through town. US 34 becomes Trail Ridge Road in Rocky Mountain National Park, linking Estes Park with the western gateway town of Granby. Reputed to be the highest continuous paved road in the nation, the route (closed during winter) should be traveled with caution—you'll see lush forest, vibrant summer wildflowers and windswept alpine tundra on this breathtaking mountain drive. The park's Old Fall River Road, also open in summer, provides several pull-offs affording such scenic panoramas as a canyon, waterfall and valley as well as opportunities to spot the park's varied wildlife.

Visit Estes Park: 500 Big Thompson Ave., Estes Park, CO 80517. **Phone:** (970) 577-9900 or (800) 443-7837.

AERIAL TRAMWAY is 1 blk. s. of the post office at 420 E. Riverside Dr. Enclosed 10-passenger tram cars glide to the summit of 8,700-foot Prospect Mountain. **Time:** Allow 1 hour minimum. **Hours:** Daily 9-6, late May-Labor Day (weather permitting). **Cost:** Fare $12; $11 (ages 60+); $8 (ages 6-11). **Phone:** (970) 586-3675.

ESTES PARK MUSEUM, 200 4th St., contains exhibits that emphasize the history of Estes Park and the surrounding region. The museum has displays about local Native Americans, early settlers, floods, tourism, the arts and outdoor recreation as well as a Stanley Steamer automobile and a homestead cabin. **Hours:** Mon.-Sat. 10-5, Sun. 1-5, May-Oct.; Fri.-Sat. 10-5, Sun. 1-5, rest of year. Closed major holidays. **Cost:** Donations. **Phone:** (970) 586-6256.

HISTORIC FALL RIVER HYDROPLANT is 3 mi. w. on US 34 following signs to 1754 Fish Hatchery Rd. Built on the Fall River in 1909, this plant introduced electricity to the region and made the landmark Stanley Hotel the first in the nation to run entirely on electricity. The plant, which operated until damaged by a 1982 flood, has been restored to period. Original equipment and hands-on museum exhibits depict its operation as well as local history.

Guided tours are available by appointment. **Time:** Allow 30 minutes minimum. **Hours:** Tues.-Sun. 1-4, late May-early Sept.; by appointment rest of year. **Cost:** Free. **Phone:** (970) 586-6256.

MACGREGOR RANCH AND MUSEUM, .5 mi. n. of US 34 on MacGregor Ave., is an original 1873 homestead and living-history cattle ranch. The turn-of-the-20th-century ranch house, now a museum, contains furnishings, photographs, clothing, artwork and personal memorabilia from three generations of the MacGregor family. **Hours:** Tues.-Sat. 10-4, June-Aug. **Cost:** $5; free (ages 0-17). **Phone:** (970) 586-3749.

STANLEY HOTEL GHOST TOURS take place at the historic Stanley Hotel, 333 Wonderview Ave. The palatial Georgian-style lodging, which opened in 1909, was built by F.O. Stanley who, with his brother, invented the Stanley Steamer horseless carriage. Several guided tours relate the history of the hotel, which is supposedly haunted by several ghosts. Author Stephen King's stay at the hotel is said to be the inspiration for his novel "The Shining."

Time: Allow 1 hour, 30 minutes minimum. **Hours:** Tours are given daily. Phone ahead to confirm schedule. **Cost:** Night ghost tour $28; $25 (ages 65+ and military with ID). Prices vary with tour selection. Reservations are required. **Parking:** $5. **Phone:** (970) 577-4111. GT ❚❙

RECREATIONAL ACTIVITIES
Fishing
- **Trout Haven Fishing Pond** is 1.2 mi. w. on US 36 at 810 Moraine Ave. **Hours:** Daily 9-dusk, June-Sept. Hours vary rest of year. Phone ahead to confirm schedule. **Phone:** (970) 577-0202 or (800) 794-7857.

Horseback Riding
- **Hi-Country Stables** is at Moraine Park and at Sprague Lake in Glacier Creek within Rocky Mountain National Park. **Hours:** Rides ranging from 2-8 hours are offered daily, mid-May to mid-Sept. (weather permitting). **Phone:** (970) 586-3244 for Glacier Creek, (970) 586-2327 for Moraine Park, or (979) 586-4577 for Estes Park and in the off-season.
- **Sombrero Stables** is on US 34E across from Lake Estes Dam. **Hours:** One- to eight-hour rides are offered daily. Breakfast and dinner rides also are available. Reservations are required for meal rides. **Phone:** (970) 586-4577.

White-water Rafting
- **Rapid Transit Rafting** departs from Estes Park High School. **Hours:** Trips depart daily, Memorial Day weekend-Labor Day. **Phone:** (970) 577-7238 or (800) 367-8523.
- **Rocky Mountain Adventures** is at 380 E. Elkhorn Ave. (US 34). Other activities are offered. **Hours:** Trips depart daily, early May-first week in Sept. **Phone:** (970) 493-4005 or (800) 858-6808.

Enjoy great member rates and benefits
at AAA/CAA Preferred Hotels

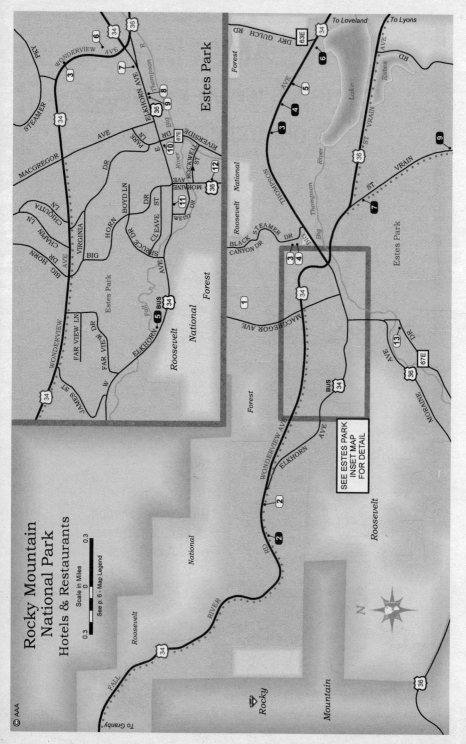

Rocky Mountain
National Park
Hotels & Restaurants

Scale in Miles

See p. 6 - Map Legend

© AAA

Estes Park

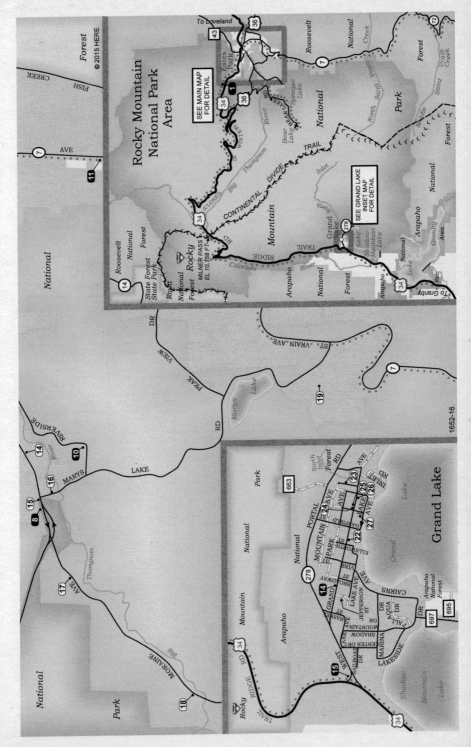

Rocky Mountain National Park Area

Roosevelt National Forest

Fish Creek

Fish Creek

© 2015 HERE

To Loveland

SEE MAIN MAP FOR DETAIL

SEE GRAND LAKE INSET MAP FOR DETAIL

CONTINENTAL DIVIDE

MILNER PASS EL 10,758 FT

Roosevelt National Forest

State Forest State Park

Roosevelt National Forest

Arapaho National Forest

Granby Area

Continental Divide Trail

Colorado River

Arapaho River

Shadow Mountain Lake

Grand Lake

To Granby

1652-16

RIVERSIDE

MARYS LAKE RD

PEAK VIEW DR

ST. VRAIN AVE.

Grand Lake

National Park

Arapaho National Forest

Rocky Ridge Rd

Trail

PORTAL

MOUNTAIN AVE

GRAND AVE

PARK AVE

BROADWAY

GARFIELD

LAKE AVE

ELLSWORTH

VINE ST

LAKE AVE

JEFFERSON ST

AQUA DR

CAIRNS DR

MARINA DR

LAKESIDE DR

SHADOW DR

CENTER DR

MALL DR

WEST

Shadow Mountain Lake

Arapaho National Forest

Rocky Mountain National Park

This index helps you "spot" where approved hotels and restaurants are located on the corresponding detailed maps. Hotel daily rate range is for comparison only. Restaurant price range is a combination of lunch and/or dinner. Turn to the listing page for more detailed rate and price information and consult display ads for special promotions.

ESTES PARK

Map Page	Hotels	Diamond Rated	Rate Range	Page
1 p. 178	**Wildwood Inn**	◆◆	$75-$383 SAVE	182
2 p. 178	**Castle Mountain Lodge LLC**	◆◆	$85-$575 SAVE	182
3 p. 178	**BEST WESTERN PLUS Silver Saddle** (See ad p. 181.)	◆◆◆	$125-$299 SAVE	181
4 p. 178	**Comfort Inn** (See ad p. 183.)	◆◆◆	$100-$400 SAVE	182
5 p. 178	Murphy's River Lodge	◆◆	$129-$239	182
6 p. 178	**The Estes Park Resort**	◆◆◆	Rates not provided SAVE	182
7 p. 178	**Rocky Mountain Park Inn**	◆◆	$99-$289 SAVE	182
8 p. 178	**Alpine Trail Ridge Inn**	◆◆	$91-$267 SAVE	181
9 p. 178	Peak To Peak Lodge	◆	$60-$220	182
10 p. 178	Mountain Shadows Resort	◆◆	Rates not provided	182
11 p. 178	**Saddle & Surrey Motel**	◆◆	$75-$165 SAVE	182

Map Page	Restaurants	Diamond Rated	Cuisine	Price Range	Page
1 p. 178	Twin Owls Steakhouse	◆◆◆	Steak Seafood	$22-$37	185
2 p. 178	Nicky's Steakhouse on the River	◆◆	American	$8-$33	184
3 p. 178	Notchtop Bakery & Cafe	◆◆	Natural/Organic	$7-$11	184
4 p. 178	Mountain Home Cafe	◆◆	American	$5-$15	184
5 p. 178	Grumpy Gringo	◆◆	Mexican	$7-$15	184
6 p. 178	Estes Park Pie Shop	◆◆	Breads/Pastries	$6-$9	184
7 p. 178	The Egg & I	◆◆	Breakfast Sandwiches	$9-$10	184
8 p. 178	Mama Rose's Italian Dining	◆◆	Italian	$8-$19	184
9 p. 178	Poppy's Pizza and Grill	◆◆	Italian Pizza	$7-$13	184
10 p. 178	Nepal's Cafe	◆◆	Nepali	$10-$15	184
11 p. 178	The Grubsteak	◆◆	American	$9-$33	184
12 p. 178	Molly B Restaurant	◆◆	American	$7-$17	184
13 p. 178	Sweet Basilico	◆◆	Italian	$9-$21	185
14 p. 178	Smokin' Dave's BBQ & Tap House	◆◆	Barbecue	$9-$20	184
15 p. 178	Sundeck Restaurant	◆◆	American	$8-$32	185
16 p. 178	The Other Side Restaurant	◆◆	American	$7-$30	184
17 p. 178	Rock Inn Mountain Tavern	◆◆	American	$10-$30	184
18 p. 178	Dunraven Inn Restaurant	◆◆◆	Italian	$14-$32	182
19 p. 178	The Tavern at Marys Lake Lodge	◆◆	American	$12-$34	185

GRAND LAKE

Map Page	Hotels	Diamond Rated	Rate Range	Page
14 p. 178	Americas Best Value Inn Bighorn Lodge	◆◆	$70-$180	206
15 p. 178	Gateway Inn	◆◆	Rates not provided	206

Map Page	Restaurants	Diamond Rated	Cuisine	Price Range	Page
22 p. 178	**Fat Cat Cafe**	◆◆	American	$6-$10	206

Map Page	Restaurants (cont'd)	Diamond Rated	Cuisine	Price Range	Page
23 p. 178	**The Historic Rapids Restaurant**	▽▽▽	American	$10-$42	206
24 p. 178	**Sagebrush BBQ & Grill**	▽▽	American	$8-$26	206
25 p. 178	Grand Pizza	▽▽	Pizza	$7-$15	206
26 p. 178	Pancho & Lefty's	▽▽	Tex-Mex	$6-$25	206
27 p. 178	Miyauchi's Snack Bar	▽	American	$5-$8	206

ALPINE TRAIL RIDGE INN   (970)586-4585 **8**

▽▽▽
Motel
$91-$267

Address: 927 Moraine Ave 80517 **Location:** 1.5 mi sw of jct Elkhorn and Moraine aves; jct SR 66 and Marys Lake Rd. **Facility:** 48 units, some two bedrooms and kitchens. 2 stories (no elevator), exterior corridors. **Terms:** closed 10/12-4/30, check-in 3:30 pm, 2 night minimum stay - seasonal and/or weekends, 14 day cancellation notice-fee imposed. **Pool(s):** heated outdoor.

[SAVE] [⏷] [⇌] [BIZ] [🖥] [✕]
[🏠] [🍽] [🏊]

Mountain views, hiking/photo tips, very high speed free internet/WIFI. Entrance to RMNP/Estes Park.

BEST WESTERN PLUS SILVER SADDLE
(970)586-4476 **3**

▽▽▽
Hotel
$125-$299

AAA Benefit: Save 10% or more every day and earn 10% bonus points!

Address: 1260 Big Thompson Ave 80517 **Location:** 0.9 mi e of jct US 34 and 36. **Facility:** 63 units, some kitchens. 1-2 stories, interior/exterior corridors. **Terms:** check-in 4 pm, 2-3 night minimum stay - seasonal and/or weekends, 3 day cancellation notice. **Pool(s):** heated outdoor. **Activities:** hot tub, playground, exercise room. **Guest Services:** coin laundry. **Featured Amenity:** breakfast buffet. *(See ad this page.)*

[SAVE] [⏷] CALL [♿M] [⇌] [BIZ] [HS] [🖥] [✕] [🏠] [🍽]
[☕]

182 ESTES PARK, CO

(See map & index p. 178.)

CASTLE MOUNTAIN LODGE LLC 970/586-3664 [2]

Cottage
$85-$575

Address: 1520 Fall River Rd 80517 **Location:** 1 mi w on US 34. Located on Fall River. **Facility:** 28 units, some cottages. 1-3 stories (no elevator), exterior corridors. **Terms:** 3 night minimum stay - seasonal and/or weekends, 30 day cancellation notice-fee imposed. **Activities:** hot tub, fishing, playground, picnic facilities. **Guest Services:** coin laundry.

COMFORT INN (970)586-2358 [4]

Hotel
$100-$400

Address: 1450 Big Thompson Ave 80517 **Location:** 1.5 mi e on US 34. **Facility:** 75 units. 2 stories, interior/exterior corridors. **Terms:** check-in 4 pm, 3 day cancellation notice. **Amenities:** safes. **Pool(s):** heated outdoor. **Activities:** hot tub, exercise room. **Guest Services:** coin laundry. **Featured Amenity:** full hot breakfast. *(See ad p. 183.)*

THE ESTES PARK RESORT 970/577-6400 [6]

Hotel
Rates not provided

Address: 1700 Big Thompson Ave 80517 **Location:** 2 mi e on US 34. Adjacent to a marina. **Facility:** 55 units. 3 stories, interior corridors. **Terms:** check-in 4 pm. **Amenities:** safes. **Pool(s):** heated indoor. **Activities:** sauna, hot tub, marina, fishing, recreation programs in summer, game room, picnic facilities, exercise room, massage. **Guest Services:** valet and coin laundry.

MOUNTAIN SHADOWS RESORT 970/577-0397 [10]

Cabin. Rates not provided. **Address:** 871 Riverside Dr 80517 **Location:** Jct Elkhorn and Moraine aves, 1.4 mi sw to Marys Lake Rd, 0.3 mi s, then just e. **Facility:** 8 cabins. 1 story, exterior corridors. **Bath:** shower only. **Activities:** picnic facilities.

MURPHY'S RIVER LODGE (970)480-5081 [5]

Hotel $129-$239 **Address:** 481 W Elkhorn Ave 80517 **Location:** 0.4 mi w of jct Elkhorn and Moraine aves; west end of downtown. **Facility:** 37 units, some kitchens. 2 stories (no elevator), exterior corridors. **Terms:** check-in 4 pm, 2-3 night minimum stay - seasonal and/or weekends, 7 day cancellation notice-fee imposed, resort fee. **Pool(s):** heated indoor. **Activities:** hot tub, picnic facilities, trails. **Guest Services:** valet and coin laundry.

PEAK TO PEAK LODGE (970)586-4451 [9]

Motel $60-$220 **Address:** 760 S Saint Vrain Ave 80517 **Location:** On SR 7, 0.7 mi s of jct US 36. **Facility:** 24 units, some efficiencies and kitchens. 1-2 stories (no elevator), exterior corridors. **Terms:** 2 night minimum stay - weekends, 14 day cancellation notice-fee imposed, resort fee. **Pool(s):** heated outdoor. **Activities:** hot tub, recreation programs, picnic facilities.

ROCKY MOUNTAIN PARK INN (970)586-2332 [7]

Hotel
$99-$289

Address: 101 S Saint Vrain Ave 80517 **Location:** 0.4 mi se on US 36 to SR 7, just s. **Facility:** 150 units. 2-4 stories, interior corridors. **Terms:** check-in 4 pm, cancellation fee imposed. **Pool(s):** heated indoor. **Activities:** hot tub, exercise room. **Guest Services:** coin laundry.

SADDLE & SURREY MOTEL 970/586-3326 [11]

Motel
$75-$165

Address: 1341 S Saint Vrain Ave 80517 **Location:** 0.4 mi se of jct US 34 and 36 to SR 7, then 1.3 mi s on SR 7 (S Saint Vrain Ave). **Facility:** 26 units, some efficiencies. 1 story, exterior corridors. **Terms:** closed 11/1-4/30, 10 day cancellation notice-fee imposed. **Pool(s):** heated outdoor. **Activities:** hot tub, playground, picnic facilities. **Featured Amenity: continental breakfast.**

WILDWOOD INN (970)586-7804 [1]

Motel
$75-$383

Address: 2801 Fall River Rd 80517 **Location:** 3.5 mi w on US 34. Bordering the Rocky Mountain National Park. **Facility:** 34 units, some cabins and condominiums. 1-2 stories (no elevator), exterior corridors. **Terms:** check-in 4 pm, 3-4 night minimum stay - seasonal, 30 day cancellation notice-fee imposed, resort fee. **Activities:** sauna, hot tub, playground, picnic facilities, trails, spa. **Guest Services:** valet laundry.

BLACK CANYON INN 970/586-8113

fyi Not evaluated. **Address:** 800 MacGregor Ave 80517 **Location:** 0.5 mi w on US 34, 0.5 mi n on Devils Gulch Rd. Facilities, services, and décor characterize a mid-scale property.

THE HABER MOTEL 970/449-1660

fyi Not evaluated. **Address:** 397 E Elkhorn Ave 80517 **Location:** Jct US 34 and 36; downtown. Facilities, services, and décor characterize a mid-scale property.

THE STANLEY HOTEL 970/586-3371

fyi Not evaluated. **Address:** 333 Wonderview Ave 80517 **Location:** Just n of jct US 34 and 36. Facilities, services, and décor characterize a mid-scale property. This historic property was built by the famous Freelan Oscar Stanley, co-inventor of the Stanley Steamer car and manufacturer of violins.

WHERE TO EAT

DUNRAVEN INN RESTAURANT 970/586-6409 [18]

Italian. Casual Dining. $14-$32 **AAA Inspector Notes:** On the menu you'll find traditional Italian favorites, plus fresh seafood, charbroiled steaks, veal and chicken entrées. The Mona Lisa-themed artwork adds a touch of whimsy to the décor. **Features:** full bar. **Reservations:** suggested. **Address:** 2470 Hwy 66 80517 **Location:** 1.5 mi sw of Elkhorn and Moraine aves to Marys Lake Rd, then 1.3 mi sw. **D**

▼ *See AAA listing p. 182* ▼

Your Rocky Mountain Headquarters
Estes Park

AAA Approved

Your Morning Hot Breakfast | Fitness Center
Business Center | Meeting Room
Guest Laundry | Free Wi-Fi
Outdoor Seasonal Pool | Whirlpool

Comfort Inn

1450 Big Thompson Ave, Estes Park, CO 80517
970-586-2358 | estescomfortinn.com

Comfort INN
BY CHOICE HOTELS

Choice Hotels Reservations
1-800-228-1222

(See map & index p. 178.)

THE EGG & I   970/586-1173 ⑦

▼▼ Breakfast Sandwiches. Casual Dining. $9-$10 AAA Inspector Notes: The cheerful décor and casual staff create a relaxing environment. Although this restaurant serves lunch, the breakfast menu, served all day, is the main event. Try the eggs Benedict, French toast, or the huevos rancheros. Lunch options include a turkey apple croissant sandwich, cheeseburger, and cobb salad. Features: patio dining, senior menu. Address: 393 E Elkhorn Ave 80517 Location: Just w of jct US 36 and 34.

B L AC

ESTES PARK PIE SHOP   970/577-7437 ⑥

▼▼ Breads/Pastries. Casual Dining. $6-$9 AAA Inspector Notes: "You need pie!" That's the motto of this cozy eatery, where specialties include mixed fruit like blueberry-apple, peach-cherry and raspberry-rhubarb. If you enjoy the occasional slice, you've made it to the right place. No pie for you? Try one of the salads, sandwiches or homemade soups. Features: patio dining. Address: 509 Big Thompson Ave 80517 Location: Jct US 36, just e on US 34.

B L AC

THE GRUBSTEAK   970/586-8838 ⑪

▼▼ American. Casual Dining. $9-$33 AAA Inspector Notes: Guests unwind in small, quaint dining rooms with Western décor as they peruse a serious menu of steaks, barbecue, ribs, fried or blackened trout, and great burgers prepared with elk, buffalo or beef. Be sure to try one of the microbrews. Features: full bar. Address: 134 W Elkhorn Ave 80517 Location: Just w of Elkhorn and Moraine aves; downtown. Parking: street only. L D

GRUMPY GRINGO   970/586-7705 ⑤

▼▼ Mexican. Casual Dining. $7-$15 AAA Inspector Notes: The restaurant's outstanding house margarita tastes great with the flavorful, build-your-own burritos. The mini rellenos wrapped in egg-roll paper and fried are the perfect way to begin a meal. Delicious sopaipillas please the palate at dessert time. Bright, airy décor lends character to several dining areas that offer great views of Longs Peak, the Continental Divide and Lake Estes. Features: full bar, happy hour. Address: 1560 Big Thompson Ave 80517 Location: 1.7 mi e on US 34. L D

MAMA ROSE'S ITALIAN DINING   970/586-3330 ⑧

▼▼ Italian. Casual Dining. $8-$19 AAA Inspector Notes: When the weather cooperates, sit on the outdoor patio next to the river. For a light lunch, consider the lobster Caesar with a homemade dressing. The tart lemon and artichoke ravioli is a nice vegetarian option. Heartier choices include shrimp scampi, chicken Parmesan and lasagna. Most courses—including desserts like tiramisu, cheesecake and brownies—are available in half portions. Large oil paintings with ornate frames enhance the Victorian-style décor. Features: full bar, patio dining. Reservations: suggested. Address: 338 E Elkhorn Ave 80517 Location: On US 36, just e of Elkhorn and Moraine aves; downtown. Parking: street only. L D AC

MOLLY B RESTAURANT   970/586-2766 ⑫

▼▼ American. Casual Dining. $7-$17 AAA Inspector Notes: This hot spot fills up quickly and is easy to find with its white picket fence and outdoor patio. The country-style décor creates a laid-back atmosphere. The breakfast menu includes omelets, huevos rancheros, pancakes, waffles and Molly B's famous homemade "outrageous granola." A good variety of appetizers, soup, salads, sandwiches, seafood, pastas, daily specials and vegetarian items also are available. Features: full bar, patio dining. Address: 200 Moraine Ave 80517 Location: Just w of Elkhorn and Moraine aves; downtown. Parking: street only. B L D

MOUNTAIN HOME CAFE   970/586-6624 ④

▼▼ American. Casual Dining. $5-$15 AAA Inspector Notes: Although the décor is a bit tired, locals and tourists flock to this restaurant for its hearty portions and flavorful menu items. Breakfast includes pancakes, waffles, French toast, egg dishes, eggs Benedict, trout and huevos rancheros. For lunch patrons choose from salad and wraps to chile rellenos and fried chicken. Features: patio dining, Sunday brunch. Address: 457 E Wonderview Ave 80517 Location: Jct US 34 and 36, just n, then just w; in strip mall.

B L AC

NEPAL'S CAFE   970/577-7035 ⑩

▼▼ Nepali. Casual Dining. $10-$15 AAA Inspector Notes: Popular with locals, this cozy eatery offers a variety of traditional Indian and Nepalese dishes. Start with a potato samosa or chicken pokauda. The extensive entrée list includes chicken tandoori, lamb vindaloo, shrimp coconut curry, and saag paneer as well as Nepalese pork noodles and chicken momo, a type of steamed dumpling. Features: full bar, patio dining. Address: 184 E Elkhorn Ave, Unit H 80517 Location: Just w of jct Saint Vrain Ave.

L D AC

NICKY'S STEAKHOUSE ON THE RIVER   970/586-2123 ②

▼▼ American. Casual Dining. $8-$33 AAA Inspector Notes: This spacious steakhouse offers a choice of seating in a casual dining room or more upscale space overlooking the river. Menu selections include beef, chicken, seafood and ribs. Large portions leave diners satisfied. Features: full bar, patio dining. Address: 1350 W Fall River Rd 80517 Location: 1.4 mi w on US 34.

B L D

NOTCHTOP BAKERY & CAFE   970/586-0272 ③

▼▼ Natural/Organic. Casual Dining. $7-$11 AAA Inspector Notes: This cozy eatery specializes in made-from-scratch items using local, natural and organic ingredients. Hearty breakfast items include eggs Benedict, waffles, fruit-topped pancakes and omelets. Lunch ranges from homemade soups, sandwiches, wraps and burgers to specialties like fish and chips, and Polish sausage. Features: patio dining. Address: 459 E Wonderview Ave 80517 Location: Just n of jct US 36; in Upper Stanley Village strip mall.

B L AC

THE OTHER SIDE RESTAURANT   970/586-2171 ⑯

▼▼ American. Casual Dining. $7-$30 AAA Inspector Notes: This restaurant serves flavorful prime rib, steaks and seafood as well as homemade desserts. The comfortable, casual atmosphere offers a nice view of the park and duck pond. Features: full bar, Sunday brunch. Reservations: suggested, in season. Address: 900 Moraine Ave 80517 Location: 1.5 mi w on US 36; at Marys Lake Rd.

B L D

POPPY'S PIZZA AND GRILL   970/586-8282 ⑨

▼▼ Italian Pizza. Casual Dining. $7-$13 AAA Inspector Notes: Recommended by locals, this restaurant offers a variety of specialty pizzas as well as wraps, burgers and salads. Wash down your meal with a unique beer, such as the Trappist Monk Ale from Belgium, or a local microbrew. Features: full bar. Address: 342 E Elkhorn Ave 80517 Location: On US 36, just e of Elkhorn and Moraine aves; downtown. Parking: street only.

L D AC

ROCK INN MOUNTAIN TAVERN   970/586-4116 ⑰

▼▼ American. Casual Dining. $10-$30 AAA Inspector Notes: After a day of exploring Rocky Mountain National Park, patrons revive themselves with a microbrew and hearty meal. The innovative menu appeals to those looking for a perfectly prepared steak as well as foodies searching for something more adventurous. Start with the sweet and savory "Devils on Horseback" (garlic-stuffed dates wrapped in bacon) or the spicy hot wings. For something local, try the pan-seared trout served with dill butter. Features: full bar, Sunday brunch. Address: 1675 Hwy 66 80517 Location: 1.6 mi sw of jct Elkhorn and Moraine aves, then 0.3 mi sw.

D

SMOKIN' DAVE'S BBQ & TAP HOUSE   970/577-7427 ⑭

▼▼ Barbecue. Casual Dining. $9-$20 AAA Inspector Notes: Chef and owner "Smokin" Dave Oehlman prides himself on serving high-quality, traditional American barbecue. The smoky green chile makes the perfect light lunch. You can top hearty portions of beef brisket, roast half-chicken and ribs with your favorite homemade barbecue sauce, including sweet, spicy, tangy and Carolina mustard. Other options include Southern fried catfish, pecan-crusted trout and a wild salmon Reuben. If you have room, try a slice of the Kentucky bourbon pecan pie. Features: full bar. Reservations: suggested. Address: 820 Moraine Ave 80517 Location: Jct Elkhorn Ave, 1.2 mi sw. L D

(See map & index p. 178.)

SUNDECK RESTAURANT   970/586-9832 (15)
♦♦ American. Casual Dining. $8-$32 **AAA Inspector Notes:**
This family-owned operation has been serving diners since 1948. Although the menu is varied, with American offerings as well as a few
Mexican dishes, fresh trout is the specialty. The décor is rustic,
Western, bright and comfortable. A casually attired waitstaff allows for
a relaxing dining experience. **Features:** full bar. **Reservations:** suggested. **Address:** 915 Moraine Ave 80517 **Location:** 1.7 mi w on US
36; near jct SR 66. [L] [D]

SWEET BASILICO   970/586-3899 (13)
♦♦ Italian. Casual Dining. $9-$21 **AAA Inspector Notes:** This
beloved family-owned restaurant serves made-from-scratch Italian
cuisine in a casual, relaxed atmosphere. The flavors are robust and
delightful to your palate. The restaurant has wine only and is closed
its popular status with locals and tourists alike. **Features:** wine only,
Sunday brunch. **Reservations:** suggested. **Address:** 430 Prospect
Village Dr 80517 **Location:** 0.3 mi s on Moraine Ave, just s on Riverside Dr. [L] [D]

THE TAVERN AT MARYS LAKE LODGE   970/586-5958 (19)
♦♦ American. Casual Dining. $12-$34 **AAA Inspector Notes:**
In a lovely, much-talked-about setting, the tavern offers rustic charm
and spectacular views. Menu items include burgers, sandwiches, fish
and chips, lasagna, salmon, elk chops and trout. Wash everything
down with a beer from the on-site brewery. **Features:** full bar, Sunday
brunch. **Reservations:** suggested. **Address:** 2625 Marys Lake Rd
80517 **Location:** 3.4 mi s of jct US 36 and SR 7, just w.

[D]

TWIN OWLS STEAKHOUSE   970/586-9344   (1)
♦♦♦ Steak Seafood. Casual Dining. $22-$37 **AAA Inspector**
Notes: Built in 1929 as a family home, this rustic restaurant nurtures a romantic mountain atmosphere with a fireplace, high-beam
ceiling and oak floors. The sweet and savory beet salad served with
a lemon basil vinaigrette makes a nice light lunch or a shared
starter. For a taste of local flavor, try the Colorado elk medallions,
lamb chops or buffalo rib-eye. Other menu options include roasted
duck, steaks and lobster. **Features:** full bar. **Reservations:** suggested. **Address:** 800 MacGregor Ave 80517 **Location:** 0.5 mi w
on US 34, 0.5 mi n on Devils Gulch Rd; in Black Canyon Inn.

[D] [Ⓐ]

EVERGREEN (D-8) pop. 9,038, elev. 7,040'

In the foothills west of Denver, Evergreen is surrounded by the Denver Mountain Park System and
Jefferson County open space parks. Alderfer/Three
Sisters Open Space Park offers hiking and biking
trails that lead to the unusual rock outcropping
known as Three Sisters and The Brother.

Bergen Peak's subalpine terrain, grasslands,
steep slopes and forests are just outside Elk
Meadow Park. Downtown's Evergreen Lake offers
boating in summer and ice skating in winter. A 1.5-
mile walking path around the lake offers sculptures,
picnic areas and wildlife viewing.

Evergreen Area Chamber of Commerce: 30480
Stagecoach Blvd., Suite C, Evergreen, CO 80439.
Phone: (303) 674-3412.

HIWAN HOMESTEAD MUSEUM, 4208 S. Timber-
vale Dr., is a complex of five historic buildings, including a 25-room log lodge. Once the headquarters
for the Hiwan Ranch, the buildings are known for
their rustic log architecture. Also featured is a collection of Southwestern Indian arts and crafts.

Time: Allow 30 minutes minimum. **Hours:** Tues.-
Sun. noon-5. Closed Jan. 1, July 4, Thanksgiving and
Christmas. **Cost:** Donations. **Phone:** (720) 497-7650.
[GT]

COMFORT SUITES GOLDEN WEST ON EVERGREEN
PARKWAY   (303)526-2000
♦♦♦ Hotel $114-$170 **Address:** 29300 US Hwy 40 80439 **Lo-**
cation: I-70 exit 252 (Evergreen Pkwy) westbound; exit 251 eastbound, just s, then just w. **Facility:** 85 units. 3 stories, interior corridors.
Amenities: safes. **Pool(s):** heated indoor. **Activities:** sauna, hot tub,
exercise room. **Guest Services:** valet and coin laundry.

[icons] / SOME UNITS [icon]

FAIRPLAY (C-3) pop. 679, elev. 9,950'

Fairplay was named by prospectors who settled it in 1859 when they were driven from nearby Tarryall by miners who had staked more claims than they could work. Thereafter scorned and referred to as "Grab-all," Tarryall did not survive beyond its boom times.

Fairplay is now a marketing center for the surrounding South Park ranches. More than 20 log houses, all private residences, survive from the 1800s. The scenic portion of US 285, which runs through Pike National Forest between Poncha Springs and Morrison, passes through town.

Town of Fairplay: 400 Front St., P.O. Box 267, Fairplay, CO 80440. **Phone:** (719) 836-2622.

SOUTH PARK CITY MUSEUM, at 4th and Front sts., is a restored early Colorado goldmining town typical of the 1860s to 1900s. Seven of the more than 40 buildings are on their original sites; the remaining structures were moved from deserted mining camps and ghost towns in nearby areas of Park County.

The buildings, all furnished with period articles, include a newspaper office, drugstore, saloon, assay office and general store. Mining machinery also can be seen, and a narrow-gauge train stands at the depot. Special events feature guides dressed in period clothing along with demonstrations of crafts and arts.

Time: Allow 1 hour minimum. **Hours:** Daily 9-7, Memorial Day weekend-Labor Day; 10-5, mid-May to Fri. before Memorial Day; 10-6, day after Labor Day to mid-Oct. **Cost:** $10; $9 (ages 65+); $4 (ages 6-12). **Phone:** (719) 836-2387.

FEDERAL HEIGHTS (C-9) pop. 11,467, elev. 5,535'
• Part of Denver area — see map p. 116

WATER WORLD is 1 mi. w. off I-25 exit 219, then 4 blks. n. on Pecos St. to 89th Ave. With 70 acres and more than 47 aquatic attractions, Water World is one of the nation's largest family water theme parks. Thrill rides include Warp Speed, The Mile High Flyer, Skyline Speed Slides, Turbo Racer, Lost River of the Pharaohs, Revolution, Voyage to the Center of the Earth, Screamin' Mimi, Storm, Zoomerang and Ragin' Colorado as well as multiple slides, two wave pools and a lazy river. Wally World, a miniature water park for parents and younger children, is another highlight.

Time: Allow 4 hours, 30 minutes minimum. **Hours:** Daily 10-6, Memorial Day weekend-Labor Day weekend. Phone ahead to confirm schedule. **Cost:** $41.99; $36.99 (under 48 inches tall); $10.99 (ages 60+); free (under 40 inches tall). **Phone:** (303) 427-7873.

FIRESTONE pop. 10,147

BEST WESTERN FIRESTONE INN & SUITES
(720)494-1925

Hotel
$100-$170

AAA Benefit: Save 10% or more every day and earn 10% bonus points!

Address: 11228 Business Park Cir 80504 **Location:** I-25 exit 240, just e. **Facility:** 58 units. 3 stories, interior corridors. **Terms:** resort fee. **Pool(s):** heated indoor. **Activities:** hot tub, exercise room. **Guest Services:** valet and coin laundry. **Featured Amenity:** full hot breakfast.

FLORISSANT FOSSIL BEDS NATIONAL MONUMENT (D-3)

Two miles south of Florissant on Teller CR 1, Florissant Fossil Beds National Monument protects an area once covered by a prehistoric lake. As layer after layer of volcanic ash accumulated some 34 to 35 million years ago, the lake vanished, but its plant and animal life were preserved almost intact in paper-thin layers of shale. It is these fossils, dating from the Eocene period and including standing petrified sequoia stumps, that the 6,000-acre monument protects.

The visitor center houses collections of fossils and offers a variety of interpretive programs during the summer, including talks explaining the geology and paleontology of the area. Guided tours of an 1878 homestead also are offered periodically (depending on staff availability). Hiking trails provide access to the back country. Daily 8-6, May 30-Labor Day; 9-5, rest of year (weather permitting). Closed Jan. 1, Thanksgiving and Christmas. Phone ahead to confirm hours. Admission $5; free (ages 0-15). Phone (719) 748-3253.

FORT COLLINS (A-9) pop. 143,986, elev. 5,003'
• Restaurants p. 189

After the 1860s conflicts with Native Americans ended, the Army garrison abandoned its post on the Cache la Poudre River, leaving its buildings and its name, Fort Collins, to the adjoining settlement. The town's economy initially was supported by commerce along the Overland Trail and nearby farms and ranches. More recently, however, Fort Collins has emerged as an industrial, technological and educational center.

Colorado State University, a land-grant institution established in 1879 as an agricultural college, is known for its forestry, veterinary medicine, biotechnology, computer technology and electronic research programs.

The Fort Collins Municipal Railway runs between the city park and downtown on weekends and holidays during summer. Scenic drive SR 14 leaves US 287 3 miles northwest of Fort Collins. The road follows the Cache la Poudre River through narrow

Poudre Canyon—in one place tunneling through solid rock—and traverses the Pawnee National Grassland *(see place listing p. 41)*.

Historic Old Town Square at College and Mountain Avenue is now a retail center. Lincoln Center, a venue for performing and visual arts, hosts plays, musicals, top entertainers and trade shows. Horsetooth Reservoir and Lory State Park *(see Recreation Areas Chart)* offer a variety of recreational activities.

Fort Collins Convention and Visitors Bureau: 19 Old Town Square, Suite 137, Fort Collins, CO 80524. **Phone:** (970) 232-3840 or (800) 274-3678.

ANHEUSER-BUSCH BREWERY TOUR CENTER, 2351 Busch Dr., offers tours covering the brewing and packaging of the company's products as well as a visit to the Budweiser Clydesdale Hamlet to see the renowned draft horses. Visits include a stop at the Hospitality Room for product sampling. Close-up photography of the horses is permitted on Clydesdale Camera Days the first Saturday of each month.

The tour contains a considerable amount of walking. Samples available only to ages 21+. **Time:** Allow 1 hour, 30 minutes minimum. **Hours:** Daily 10-6:30, Sun. 10-4:30. Tours are offered daily; phone for schedule. Closed major holidays. Phone ahead to confirm schedule. **Cost:** Free. **Phone:** (970) 490-4691.

FORT COLLINS MUSEUM OF ART is at 201 S. College Ave. (US 287) between Olive Street and the Oak Street Plaza. The museum, in the 1912 post office building, features changing exhibitions each year. **Time:** Allow 1 hour minimum. **Hours:** Wed.-Fri. 10-5, Sat.-Sun. noon-5. **Cost:** $5; $4 (ages 65+ and college students with ID); $1 (ages 7-18). **Phone:** (970) 482-2787.

FORT COLLINS MUSEUM OF DISCOVERY, 408 Mason Ct., specializes in hands-on science exhibits and the history of northern Colorado. Exhibits include local history and wildlife displays, interactive science exhibits, traveling exhibitions and the Digital Dome theater with IMAX movies. The Schatz Family Exploration Zone features kid-friendly hands-on activities. A local history archive is available to researchers. **Time:** Allow 1 hour minimum. **Hours:** Tues.-Sun. 10-5 (also Thurs. 5-8). Closed Jan. 1, Thanksgiving and Christmas. **Cost:** $9.50; $7 (ages 65+); $6 (ages 3-12). **Phone:** (970) 221-6738.

NEW BELGIUM BREWING CO. is off I-25 exit 269B, 3 mi. w. to Riverside, then n.w. to Linden and just n. over the bridge. Several styles of American craft beers are brewed in this alternatively powered plant. Tours include tastings and a behind-the-scenes look at the facility. **Time:** Allow 1 hour, 30 minutes minimum. **Hours:** Brewery daily, 11-8. Tours are given every half hour, Tues.-Sun. 11:30-4:30. Phone ahead to confirm schedule. **Cost:** Free. Reservations are required. **Phone:** (970) 221-0524 or (888) 622-4044.

BEST WESTERN KIVA INN   (970)484-2444

Hotel $89-$209

AAA Benefit: Save 10% or more every day and earn 10% bonus points!

Address: 1638 E Mulberry St 80524 **Location:** I-25 exit 269B, 1.5 mi w on SR 14. **Facility:** 62 units. 1-2 stories (no elevator), interior/exterior corridors. **Pool(s):** heated outdoor. **Activities:** sauna, hot tub, exercise room. **Guest Services:** coin laundry.

BEST WESTERN UNIVERSITY INN   (970)484-2984

Motel $99-$169

AAA Benefit: Save 10% or more every day and earn 10% bonus points!

Address: 914 S College Ave 80524 **Location:** I-25 exit 268, 4 mi w to College Ave, then just n on US 287. Opposite Colorado State University. **Facility:** 70 units. 2 stories (no elevator), interior/exterior corridors. **Amenities:** safes. **Pool(s):** heated indoor. **Activities:** hot tub, exercise room. **Guest Services:** valet and coin laundry. **Featured Amenity:** continental breakfast.

CAMBRIA HOTEL & SUITES   (970)267-9000

Contemporary Hotel $199-$349 **Address:** 2921 E Harmony Rd 80528 **Location:** I-25 exit 265 (Harmony Rd), 1.5 mi w, then just s on Ziegler Rd. **Facility:** 90 units. 4 stories, interior corridors. **Pool(s):** heated indoor. **Activities:** hot tub, exercise room. **Guest Services:** valet and coin laundry, boarding pass kiosk.

COMFORT INN   (970)407-0100

▼▼▼ **Hotel** $89-$279 **Address:** 601 SW Frontage Rd 80524 **Location:** I-25 exit 269B, just sw. **Facility:** 62 units. 3 stories, interior corridors. **Pool(s):** heated indoor. **Activities:** hot tub, exercise room. **Guest Services:** valet and coin laundry.

COMFORT SUITES FORT COLLINS   970/206-4597

▼▼▼ **Hotel.** Rates not provided. **Address:** 1415 Oakridge Dr 80525 **Location:** I-25 exit 265 (Harmony Rd), 3.3 mi w to McMurry Ave, just s, then w. **Facility:** 66 units. 3 stories, interior corridors. **Amenities:** safes. **Pool(s):** heated indoor. **Activities:** hot tub, exercise room. **Guest Services:** valet laundry.

COURTYARD BY MARRIOTT   (970)282-1700

▼▼▼ **Hotel** $97-$209 **Address:** 1200 Oakridge Dr 80525 **Location:** I-25 exit 265 (Harmony Rd), 3.3 mi w; entry via Lemay Ave. **Facility:** 112 units. 2 stories, interior corridors. **Terms:** check-in 4 pm. **Pool(s):** heated indoor. **Activities:** hot tub, exercise room. **Guest Services:** valet and coin laundry, boarding pass kiosk.

AAA Benefit:
Members save 5% or more!

EDWARDS HOUSE   970/493-9191

▼▼▼ **Classic Bed & Breakfast.** Rates not provided. **Address:** 402 W Mountain Ave 80521 **Location:** Jct College Ave and Mulberry St, just w to Meldrum St, 0.3 mi n. Located in a residential area. **Facility:** In a 1904 neoclassical home a short walk from downtown, this inn features tasteful, sophisticated décor, which mixes the historic character of the building with contemporary design. 8 units. 2-3 stories (no elevator), interior corridors. **Terms:** age restrictions may apply. **Amenities:** safes.

FORT COLLINS MARRIOTT   (970)226-5200

▼▼▼ **Hotel** $113-$222 **Address:** 350 E Horsetooth Rd 80525 **Location:** Jct College Ave and Horsetooth Rd, just e, then just n on John F Kennedy Pkwy. Adjacent to Foothills Fashion Mall. **Facility:** 229 units. 6 stories, interior corridors. **Terms:** check-in 4 pm. **Pool(s):** heated outdoor, heated indoor. **Activities:** hot tub, exercise room. **Guest Services:** valet and coin laundry, boarding pass kiosk.

AAA Benefit:
Members save 5% or more!

HAMPTON INN   970/229-5927

▼▼▼ **Hotel.** Rates not provided. **Address:** 1620 Oakridge Dr 80525 **Location:** I-25 exit 265 (Harmony Rd), 3.3 mi w, just s on McMurry Ave, then just e. Located in a quiet residential area. **Facility:** 75 units. 3 stories, interior corridors. **Pool(s):** heated indoor. **Activities:** hot tub, exercise room. **Guest Services:** valet and coin laundry.

AAA Benefit:
Members save up to 10%!

HILTON FT COLLINS   970/482-2626

▼▼▼ **Hotel**
Rates not provided

Hilton HOTELS & RESORTS

AAA Benefit:
Members save 5% or more!

Address: 425 W Prospect Rd 80526 **Location:** I-25 exit 268, 4.3 mi w. Next to the university. **Facility:** 255 units. 9 stories, interior corridors. **Pool(s):** heated indoor. **Activities:** hot tub, exercise room. **Guest Services:** valet laundry, area transportation.

HILTON GARDEN INN   970/225-2900

▼▼▼ **Hotel.** Rates not provided. **Address:** 2821 E Harmony Rd 80528 **Location:** I-25 exit 265 (Harmony Rd), 1.5 mi w, then just s on Ziegler Rd. **Facility:** 120 units. 4 stories, interior corridors. **Amenities:** safes. **Pool(s):** heated indoor. **Activities:** hot tub, exercise room. **Guest Services:** valet and coin laundry, area transportation.

AAA Benefit:
Members save up to 10%!

HOLIDAY INN EXPRESS & SUITES   970/225-2200

▼▼▼ **Hotel.** Rates not provided. **Address:** 1426 Oakridge Dr 80525 **Location:** I-25 exit 265 (Harmony Rd), 3 mi w, just s on McMurry Ave, then just w. **Facility:** 89 units. 4 stories, interior corridors. **Pool(s):** heated indoor. **Activities:** hot tub, exercise room. **Guest Services:** valet and coin laundry.

HOMEWOOD SUITES BY HILTON FORT COLLINS
970/225-2400

▽▽▽
Extended Stay Hotel
Rates not provided

HOMEWOOD SUITES BY HILTON

AAA Benefit: Members save up to 10%!

Address: 1521 Oakridge Dr 80525 **Location:** I-25 exit 265 (Harmony Rd), 3 mi w, just s on McMurry Ave, then just w. **Facility:** 99 units, some two bedrooms, efficiencies and kitchens. 4 stories, interior corridors. **Pool(s):** heated indoor. **Activities:** hot tub, game room, exercise room. **Guest Services:** valet and coin laundry. **Featured Amenity: breakfast buffet.**

[SAVE] [¶⁺] [🛁] [BIZ] [HS] [📶] [❄] [🖥] [☕] /SOME UNITS [🐕]

QUALITY INN & SUITES
(970)282-9047

▽▽▽▽ **Hotel** $89-$139 **Address:** 4001 S Mason St 80525 **Location:** Jct Harmony Rd and College Ave, just w to Mason St, then 0.5 mi n. **Facility:** 66 units. 3 stories, interior corridors. **Pool(s):** heated indoor. **Activities:** hot tub, exercise room. **Guest Services:** valet and coin laundry.

[¶⁺] CALL[⌖M] [🛁] [BIZ] [📶] [✕] [❄] [🖥] [☕] /SOME UNITS [🐕]

RESIDENCE INN BY MARRIOTT FORT COLLINS
(970)223-5700

▽▽▽▽ **Extended Stay Hotel** $123-$302 **Address:** 1127 Oakridge Dr 80525 **Location:** I-25 exit 265 (Harmony Rd), 3.3 mi w to Lemay Ave, then s to Oakridge Dr. Located in a residential

AAA Benefit: Members save 5% or more!

area. **Facility:** 113 units, some two bedrooms, efficiencies and kitchens. 3 stories, interior corridors. **Terms:** check-in 4 pm. **Pool(s):** heated indoor. **Activities:** hot tub, picnic facilities, exercise room. **Guest Services:** valet and coin laundry.

[ECO] [¶⁺] CALL[⌖M] [🛁] [BIZ] [📶] [✕] [❄] [🖥] [☕] /SOME UNITS [🐕] [HS]

SUPER 8
(970)493-7701

▽▽ **Hotel** $55-$135 **Address:** 409 Centro Way 80524 **Location:** I-25 exit 269B, just w. **Facility:** 71 units. 2 stories (no elevator), interior corridors. **Amenities:** safes. **Activities:** sauna, hot tub, limited exercise equipment. **Guest Services:** valet and coin laundry.

[¶⁺] [📶] [✕] [❄] [🖥] [☕] /SOME UNITS [🐕]

ARMSTRONG HOTEL
970/484-3883

[fyi] Not evaluated. **Address:** 259 S College Ave 80524 **Location:** Corner of Olive St. Facilities, services, and décor characterize a midscale property. Built in 1923, this hotel has a unique and interesting history. The first local AAA chapter made its home in the building.

WHERE TO EAT

ACE GILLETT'S
970/449-4797

▽▽ Small Plates. Casual Dining. $8-$14 **AAA Inspector Notes:** Look for a somewhat hidden staircase halfway up the block and you've found the entrance to this sultry nightclub and eatery. Order a round of specialty cocktails while listening to live jazz. The small plates menu focuses on locally sourced ingredients and ranges from lighter options, such as a beet salad, to crab mac and cheese. **Features:** full bar. **Address:** 239 S College Ave 80524 **Location:** Corner of Olive St; in Armstrong Hotel. **Parking:** street only.

[D] [LATE] CALL[⌖M]

Visit AAA.com/searchfordiscounts to save on travel, shopping, dining and attractions

AUSTIN'S AMERICAN GRILL
970/224-9691

▽▽ American. Casual Dining. $11-$25 **AAA Inspector Notes:** Modern comfort food, warm décor and friendly servers ensure this restaurant receives high marks from locals. Menu items include hearty gourmet sandwiches, rotisserie chicken, steaks, bison pot roast, walleye and salmon. **Features:** full bar, patio dining, Sunday brunch, happy hour. **Address:** 100 W Mountain Ave 80524 **Location:** Jct College Ave. **Parking:** street only. [L] [D]

BANN THAI
970/797-2707

▽▽ Thai. Casual Dining. $11-$16 **AAA Inspector Notes:** When I walked into this restaurant, the earth-toned décor struck me as relaxing and attractive. Out of everything I tried, I enjoyed the tom yum koong, a hot and spicy shrimp soup, the best. The ingredients were fresh, and the chef got my medium-spicy request just right. The homemade coconut ice cream was a light, sweet end to my meal. I can't wait to return and try something new; this seems like the perfect place to experiment. **Features:** beer & wine, patio dining. **Address:** 626 S College Ave 80524 **Location:** I-25 exit 269B, 4 mi w, then 0.3 mi s. **Parking:** street only. [L] [D]

BEAU JO'S COLORADO STYLE PIZZA 970/498-8898

▽▽▽
Pizza Casual Dining $11-$20

AAA Inspector Notes: Known for its pizza, this eatery offers a fun atmosphere with a mountain theme. Build your pizza from the crust up. Choices include a mountain pie with a thick, chewy edge; the thin-crust prairie pie; and gluten-free options. Add your favorite toppings or choose a specialty pizza like the sky hawk (a pepperoni pie with Hatch green chiles and feta), or Skier Mike's chicken, Canadian bacon and green pepper pie. **Features:** full bar, patio dining. **Address:** 205 N College Ave 80524 **Location:** Corner of Laporte Ave. **Parking:** street only. *(See ad p. 188.)* [L] [D]

"Colorado Style Pizza" Also Gluten Free Menu

BISETTI'S RISTORANTE
970/493-0086

▽▽ Italian. Casual Dining. $11-$20 **AAA Inspector Notes:** A favorite among locals since 1979, this family restaurant nurtures a warm, cozy atmosphere. The candlelit dining scene draws couples as well as others celebrating a special night out. Classic entrées include eggplant, veal, chicken parmigiana, gnocchi with vegetables, lasagna, and harvest squash ravioli. For more adventurous spirits, try one of the seasonal dishes. For dessert, don't miss the rich, triple-chocolate cheesecake. Service is knowledgeable and enthusiastic. **Features:** full bar. **Address:** 120 S College Ave 80524 **Location:** I-25 exit 269B, just s of Old Town Square; downtown. **Parking:** street only. [L] [D]

CAFE DE BANGKOK
970/672-8127

▽▽ Thai. Casual Dining. $8-$12 **AAA Inspector Notes:** Although this eatery has an odd location in a strip mall and is a bit too small for its popularity, locals flock here for flavorful, fresh cuisine. Start with a bowl of poh taek, a spicy, sweet-and-sour seafood soup. The noodle dishes have light sauces and brightly colored vegetables. Sample items include pad thai, roasted duck and crispy egg noodles. Other options include a variety of curries and stir-fry dishes. **Address:** 1232 W Elizabeth St, C-7 80521 **Location:** Jct Shields St, just w. [L] [D]

CAFE VINO
970/212-3399

▽▽▽ Small Plates. Casual Dining. $10-$19 **AAA Inspector Notes:** This unique restaurant takes on different personalities throughout the day. In the morning it's a bustling coffee shop. By lunchtime it's a European-style bistro, but by night it turns into a sultry tapas bar. Although eclectic, menu items are delicious and include artisan pizzas, gourmet sandwiches and rich pastas. The tapas menu includes bacon-wrapped dates, ahi tuna tostadas and Colorado lamb "lollipops." Even though the setting is sophisticated, the laid-back staff members lack pretension. **Features:** full bar, Sunday brunch. **Reservations:** suggested. **Address:** 1200 S College Ave 80524 **Location:** On US 287, between Edwards and Pitkin sts. [B] [L] [D] [LATE]

CHARCO BROILER 970/482-1472

▽▽ Steak. Casual Dining. $7-$29 **AAA Inspector Notes:** Owner-operated since 1957, this popular steakhouse is just a short distance from nearby motels and I-25. Friendly servers bring around salads, steaks, burgers, sandwiches, seafood and pasta in a rustic Western setting adorned with eclectic art. **Features:** full bar. **Address:** 1716 E Mulberry St 80524 **Location:** I-25 exit 269B, 1.5 mi w on SR 14. B L D

THE CHOCOLATE CAFE 970/482-2725

▽▽ Desserts. Casual Dining. $6-$10 **AAA Inspector Notes:** This is a delightful little café near the historic center of town. The menu features an eclectic mix of soup, salads, panini, pizza and risotto. The highlight of eating here is, as the name might suggest, dessert. Examples include the sweet ravioli filled with chocolate and hazelnut, the ultimate chocolate cake and Key lime pie. **Features:** full bar. **Reservations:** suggested, weekends. **Address:** 102 W Olive St 80524 **Location:** Jct College Ave. **Parking:** street only. L D

COOPERSMITH'S PUB & BREWING 970/498-0483

▽▽ American. Casual Dining. $9-$20 **AAA Inspector Notes:** Entrées range from hearty pub fare—like fish and chips, chicken pot pie and bangers and mash—to Mexican dishes—such as crab and shrimp enchiladas and ten-mile burrito. Various home-brewed beers are available. The seasonal patio offers comfy seating. Garage parking is across the street. The dining room is divided into a lounge with a variety of pictures of hops and typical pub décor and a casual dining room with a view of the open kitchen. **Features:** full bar, patio dining. **Address:** 5 Old Town Square 80524 **Location:** Just e of College Ave on Mountain Ave; in Old Town Square. **Parking:** street only. L D

JEJU SUSHI AND JAPANESE RESTAURANT 970/416-7733

▽▽ Japanese. Casual Dining. $8-$22 **AAA Inspector Notes:** This casual eatery serves traditional Japanese and Korean favorites. The menu features sushi, teriyaki, udon noodles, Korean barbecue, tempura and bi bim bop. The lunch sushi special is a great bargain. Beverages include local and Japanese beers as well as specialty cocktails. **Features:** full bar, happy hour. **Address:** 238 S College Ave 80524 **Location:** Jct Olive St; downtown. **Parking:** street only. L D

LA CREPERIE 970/224-2640

▽▽▽ French. Casual Dining. $7-$13 **AAA Inspector Notes:** Leave the states behind and step into a true French creperie and bakery. The thin, buttery, crispy buckwheat pancake—gently folded into a square packet with chopped bacon peeking out from the center—is as delightful to look at as it is to eat. For a rich breakfast, try the cocotte brioche-poached eggs in a butter-brioche bowl with a mustard or poblano sauce. Authentic croissants, beignets and tarts—made from scratch without preservatives and artificial flavorings—are fresh, flaky and decadent. **Features:** wine only. **Address:** 2722 S College Ave 80525 **Location:** Jct Drake Rd, just s; on frontage road. **Parking:** street only. B L 🅰

LARKBURGER 970/484-8141

▽ Burgers. Quick Serve. $7-$10 **AAA Inspector Notes:** This story begins when famed chef Thomas Salamunovich put the gourmet Larkburger on the menu at Larkspur, his fine dining restaurant in Vail, Colorado. The delicious, 100% natural burger became so popular, Salamunovich created a fast-food restaurant around it. Now a small chain, the juicy, hand-cut Angus beef and turkey burgers are heavenly. Hand-cut fries, seasoned with grated Parmesan cheese and truffle oil, make the perfect accompaniment. **Features:** beer only, patio dining. **Address:** 2539 S College Ave 80524 **Location:** Jct US 287 (College Ave) and Drake Rd. L D

MAZA KABOB 970/484-6292

▽ Afghan. Quick Serve. $7-$11 **AAA Inspector Notes:** Despite the unassuming location in a strip mall, this no-frills eatery is a must for those looking for a quick, flavorful meal. Well known for its nicely spiced kebabs, it also offers herbed stews and meatballs as well as many vegetarian and gluten-free options. **Features:** none. **Address:** 2427 S College Ave 80525 **Location:** Just n of jct Drake Rd. L D

NYALA ETHIOPIAN CUISINE 970/223-6734

▽▽ Ethiopian. Casual Dining. $8-$20 **AAA Inspector Notes:** If you've never had Ethiopian food, this is the perfect place to try it out. My waitress was patient and informative while explaining the menu items. Both the sambussa, a lentil- or beef-filled pastry, and the chicken alicha, spiced with rosemary and tumeric, were delicious. I enjoyed the spongy texture of the injera pancake, which can be used to scoop up meat and vegetables or be simply eaten by itself. Choose the traditional seating for a more authentic experience. **Features:** beer & wine. **Address:** 2900 Harvard St, Suite A 80525 **Location:** Jct Harmony Rd and College Ave, 1.7 mi n, then just e. **Parking:** street only. L D

RIO GRANDE MEXICAN RESTAURANT 970/224-5428

▽▽ Mexican. Casual Dining. $9-$18 **AAA Inspector Notes:** In a historic building downtown, this casual Tex-Mex eatery offers made-from-scratch guacamole, smothered burritos, enchiladas, open-face tacos and fajitas. The green chile soup features tender pieces of chicken and has a nice kick. Wash everything down with a sweet tart "rio" margarita, happy hour. **Address:** 143 W Mountain Ave 80524 **Location:** Between Mason St and College Ave; downtown. **Parking:** street only. L D

SANFORD'S GRUB & PUB 970/206-0400

▽▽ American. Casual Dining. $9-$22 **AAA Inspector Notes:** Popular with families, this restaurant is adorned with statues of Marilyn Monroe, carousel horses and a cartoonish moose. The $1 domestic beers on tap are a hit. I started with the mild jalapeño hot bites, which were served with a syrupy sauce called berries inferno. The pulled pork sandwich had a sweet sauce with a mild hint of spice. The crunch of the grilled bun provided a nice contrast to the tender meat. The server helped me navigate through the overwhelming menu. Portions are large. **Features:** full bar. **Address:** 1526 Oakridge Dr 80525 **Location:** I-25 exit 265 (Harmony Rd), 3 mi w, just s on McMurry Ave, then just w. L D

SILVER GRILL CAFE 970/484-4656

▽▽ American. Casual Dining. $8-$10 **AAA Inspector Notes:** This eatery opened in 1933, though the building itself is older. Its history (conveyed by hardwood floors, tin ceilings, exposed-brick walls, and black and white photos) gives it character. Yet, character alone isn't what has kept this spot in business so long. It's the signature cinnamon rolls and a cup of coffee with a friend. It's a family gathering for a hearty breakfast of eggs Benedict, blueberry hotcakes, or a green chile-cheddar omelet. **Features:** full bar. **Address:** 218 Walnut St 80524 **Location:** Jct US 287 (College Ave) and Mountain Ave, just n, just se. **Parking:** street only. B L

SNOOZE 970/482-9253

▽ Breakfast. Casual Dining. $10-$15 **AAA Inspector Notes:** Once you enter, you'll immediately see that this place is special. Reminiscent of a '50s diner, this popular eatery sports appealing mod decor. After just one bite, you'll taste what makes this place stand out. The menu is breakfast-centric, and entrées include the savory and the sweet: Juan's breakfast tacos, eggs Benedict, sweet potato pancakes, and sticky bun French toast. Brunch items include gourmet sandwiches and fish tacos. **Features:** full bar. **Address:** 144 W Mountain Ave 80524 **Location:** Just w of jct College Ave. **Parking:** street only. B L

STAR OF INDIA 970/225-1740

▽▽ Indian. Casual Dining. $12-$18 **AAA Inspector Notes:** This cozy restaurant may not look like much from the outside, but it's definitely worth the visit. The menu features standard Indian dishes such as tandoori chicken, lamb vindaloo and saag paneer. The chicken pakora appetizer and naan bread are little treats that should accompany every meal. **Features:** full bar, patio dining. **Address:** 2900 Harvard St, Unit B 80525 **Location:** I-25 exit 265 (Harmony Rd), 4.4 mi w, 1.7 mi n on College Ave, then just e. **Parking:** on-site and street. L D

SUEHIRO JAPANESE RESTAURANT 970/482-3734

▽▽ Japanese. Casual Dining. $8-$20 **AAA Inspector Notes:** The extensive menu includes sushi, teriyaki, hibachi-grilled options, tempura, udon and more. Casual Japanese décor and friendly servers add to the ambience. **Features:** full bar, patio dining, happy hour. **Address:** 223 Linden St 80524 **Location:** Jct College Ave and Walnut St, just se, just ne. **Parking:** street only. L D

TAJ MAHAL RESTAURANT   970/493-1105

♦♦ ♦♦ Indian. Casual Dining. $11-$23 **AAA Inspector Notes:** Guests will enjoy a great variety of delicious lamb, beef and tandoori chicken, which is grilled in a clay oven. Various curries, rice biryanis and fresh tandoori-baked naan bread also are available. They also have a very reasonably priced lunch buffet. **Features:** full bar. **Reservations:** suggested. **Address:** 148 W Oak St 80524 **Location:** Between College Ave and Mason St; downtown. **Parking:** on-site and street. L D

TASTY HARMONY   970/689-3234

♦♦ Vegetarian. Casual Dining. $7-$14 **AAA Inspector Notes:** Dishes served at this cheerful eatery are so flavorful you won't miss the meat. Fresh salads feature homemade dressings, the jackfruit tacos taste just as good as chicken tacos, and the chocolate cake with a hint of toasted coconut is divine. The building reflects some of its Victorian-era heritage with exposed brick walls, hardwood floors and wainscoting. However, the décor has clearly been updated. Servers have extensive knowledge of the menu and take the time to thoroughly answer questions. **Features:** beer & wine. **Reservations:** suggested. **Address:** 130 S Mason St 80524 **Location:** Just n of jct Oak St. **Parking:** on-site (fee) and street. L D

YOUNG'S CAFE VIETNAMESE CUISINE   970/223-8000

♦♦ ♦♦ Vietnamese. Casual Dining. $8-$16 **AAA Inspector Notes:** A popular lunch spot with the local business crowd, this respected restaurant offers delicious dishes such as sesame chicken, seafood delight and several desserts in a casual, open and bright atmosphere. The staff is friendly and prompt. **Features:** full bar. **Address:** 3307 S College Ave, Suite 114 80525 **Location:** 2.8 mi s on US 287; in Crystal Garden Shopping Center. L D

ZQUILA MEXICAN RESTAURANT   970/631-8565

♦♦ ♦♦ Mexican. Casual Dining. $10-$19 **AAA Inspector Notes:** Diners here will enjoy well-prepared, flavorful Mexican cuisine. Menu items include fajitas, burritos, tacos, rellenos, enchiladas, flautas and other favorites. The extensive drink menu is sure to please tequila enthusiasts. The grand, wood bar with a water feature creates a unique focal point for the restaurant. **Features:** full bar, happy hour. **Address:** 2400 E Harmony Rd, Suite 101 80528 **Location:** I-25 exit 265 (Harmony Rd), 2 mi w. L D

FORT GARLAND (F-4) pop. 433, elev. 7,932'

Fort Garland is a farming community on the eastern edge of the San Luis Valley. Great Sand Dunes National Park and Preserve *(see place listing p. 207)* lies 30 miles north via US 160 and SR 150.

FORT GARLAND MUSEUM is at the s. edge of town at 29477 SR 159. The fort was established in 1858 and served as a supply point, a deterrent to hostilities and to facilitate westward expansion. Col. Kit Carson held his last command at the post 1866-67. Abandoned in 1883, the restored fort contains exhibits about the infantry and cavalry barracks, the Buffalo Soldiers and the restoration of the fort. Historic dioramas, military memorabilia and folk art from the San Luis Valley also are on display.

Time: Allow 30 minutes minimum. **Hours:** Daily 9-5, Apr.-Oct.; hours vary rest of year. Phone ahead to confirm schedule. **Cost:** $5; $4.50 (ages 65+); $3.50 (ages 6-16). **Phone:** (719) 379-3512.

FORT GARLAND MOTOR INN   719/379-2993

♦ Hotel $80-$190 **Address:** 411 Hwy 160 81133 **Location:** On US 160; west end of town. **Facility:** 17 units, some kitchens. 2 stories (no elevator), interior corridors. **Terms:** 3 day cancellation notice-fee imposed.

ALL-GON RESTAURANT & PIZZERIA   719/379-2222

♦♦ ♦♦ Italian. Casual Dining. $6-$11 **AAA Inspector Notes:** A stop at this neighborhood eatery rewards you with items from a salad bar, freshly made soups, pizza, calzones, pasta dishes and deli sandwiches. Favorite specialty cakes are the red velvet and the "hummingbird." **Address:** 319 Beaubien Ave 81133 **Location:** On US 160, just w of SR 159; center. L D

SILVER SAGE STEAKHOUSE   719/379-3600

♦♦ ♦♦ American. Casual Dining. $6-$23 **AAA Inspector Notes:** Enjoy a laid-back atmosphere in the tiki bar or Western-theme dining area, which features photos of famous movie cowboys. Menu options include U.S. Choice hand-cut steaks, barbecue pork ribs, and chicken. The fluffy, moderately sweet homemade cake is a must! **Features:** full bar. **Address:** 104 4th St 81133 **Location:** On US 160; center. D

FORT MORGAN (B-6) pop. 11,315, elev. 4,338'
• Restaurants p. 192

Fort Morgan was the childhood home of musician and band leader Glenn Miller. In late June the Dancin' on the Plains festival pays tribute to Miller and his contributions to swing music.

The present city grew out of a military post that was established on the South Platte River in 1864 to protect travelers from hostile Native Americans. It later became a station on the Overland Trail from the Missouri River to Denver. A monument on Riverview Avenue marks the site of the fort. Agriculture, manufacturing, cattle ranching and dairy farming are Fort Morgan's leading industries.

Fort Morgan Area Chamber of Commerce: 300 Main St., P.O. Box 971, Fort Morgan, CO 80701. **Phone:** (970) 867-6702 or (800) 354-8660.

FORT MORGAN MUSEUM is in the library-museum complex in City Park at 414 Main St. Permanent exhibits include a theater dedicated to band leader Glenn Miller and a 1920's soda fountain. Traveling and temporary exhibits also are on display, and a research center is on the grounds. **Time:** Allow 30 minutes minimum. **Hours:** Tues.-Thurs. 9-8, Fri.-Sat. 9-5, Mon. 9-6. Closed major holidays. **Cost:** Donations. **Phone:** (970) 542-4010.

CENTRAL MOTEL   970/867-2401

Motel
Rates not provided

Address: 201 W Platte Ave 80701 **Location:** I-76 exit 80, 0.6 mi s, then w on US 34. **Facility:** 19 units. 1 story, exterior corridors.

SAVE Ⅱ+ ▧ █ ▤ ▣ / SOME UNITS S▬

COMFORT INN   (970)867-6700

♦♦ ♦♦ Hotel $120-$159 **Address:** 1417 Barlow Rd 80701 **Location:** I-76 exit 82 (Barlow Rd), just n. **Facility:** 49 units. 3 stories, interior corridors. **Pool(s):** heated indoor. **Activities:** hot tub, exercise room. **Guest Services:** coin laundry.

Ⅱ+ ➜ BIZ HS ▧ ✕ █ ▤ ▣

FORT MORGAN HAMPTON INN   970/542-2484

▼▼▼▼ **Hotel.** Rates not provided. **Address:** 1152 Main St 80701 **Location:** I-76 exit 80, just s, then just e. **Facility:** 80 units. 4 stories, interior corridors. **Pool(s):** heated indoor. **Activities:** hot tub, exercise room. **Guest Services:** complimentary and valet laundry.

> **AAA Benefit:** Members save up to 10%!

CALL 🄶🄼 ➔ BIZ 🛜 ✕ 🅗 🖥 🖵

RODEWAY INN   (970)867-9481

▼▼▼ **Motel** $89-$99 **Address:** 1409 Barlow Rd 80701 **Location:** I-76 exit 82 (Barlow Rd), just n. **Facility:** 43 units. 1-2 stories (no elevator), interior/exterior corridors. **Dining:** Mavericks Restaurant, see separate listing. **Guest Services:** coin laundry.

🍽 BIZ 🛜 🅗 🖥 🖵 / SOME UNITS 🅢📶

WHERE TO EAT

COUNTRY STEAK OUT   970/867-7887

▼▼
Steak
Casual Dining
$7-$27

AAA Inspector Notes: Guests appreciate the family-oriented restaurant's menu variety and good value. Prime rib, steaks and chicken are served in a Western-themed dining room. A lunch buffet is set up Tuesday through Friday. Service is capable and pleasant. **Features:** full bar. **Address:** 19592 E 8th Ave 80701 **Location:** I-76 exit 82 (Barlow Rd), 0.3 mi s, then 0.4 mi w.

Ⓑ Ⓛ Ⓓ

EL JACAL   970/867-1115

▼▼ Mexican. Casual Dining. $6-$13 **AAA Inspector Notes:** Popular with locals, this eatery is known for its gorditas, fajitas, tamales and tortas. The traditional tacos and unique salsas, especially the jalapeño cream, alone are worth a visit. **Features:** full bar. **Address:** 903 Main St 80701 **Location:** I-76 exit 80, 0.4 mi s.

Ⓛ Ⓓ

LITTLE BAMBOO THAI & CHINESE RESTAURANT   970/867-1827

▼▼ Asian. Casual Dining. $7-$13 **AAA Inspector Notes:** The wonton soup was a highlight with its homemade savory pork wontons and dark beef broth. The menu includes favorites such as Szechuan shrimp, sesame chicken, Mongolian beef, pad thai, drunken noodles and Thai curry. Servers were very attentive throughout the meal. The bright, modern décor is more upscale than most Asian restaurants. **Features:** beer & wine. **Address:** 613 W Platte Ave 80701 **Location:** I-76 exit 80, 0.6 mi s, then 0.4 mi w. Ⓛ Ⓓ

MAVERICKS RESTAURANT   970/542-9482

▼▼ American. Casual Dining. $7-$20 **AAA Inspector Notes:** Specializing in comfort food, the eclectic menu is sure to please most patrons. Burgers, steaks, stuffed potatoes and pizzas are just some of the many offerings. The inviting Western decor, small bar with flat-screen TV and the convenient location enhance the dining experience. **Features:** full bar, Sunday brunch. **Address:** 1409 Barlow Rd 80701 **Location:** I-76 exit 82 (Barlow Rd), just n; in Rodeway Inn.

Ⓛ Ⓓ

O' SOLE MIO   970/867-4836

▼▼ Italian. Casual Dining. $8-$19 **AAA Inspector Notes:** Complete with Italian bistro-style décor, this cozy trattoria quickly became a local favorite as soon as it opened. Entrées include paninis and pizzas as well as an extensive variety of seafood, pork, chicken and beef dishes. **Features:** full bar. **Address:** 322 Ensign St 80701 **Location:** Between Kiowa and Beaver aves; downtown. Ⓛ Ⓓ

FOUR CORNERS MONUMENT—See
Cortez p. 106.

FRASER (B-4) pop. 1,224, elev. 8,574'

Fraser, in north-central Colorado just east of Arapaho National Forest *(see place listing p. 41)* and southwest of Rocky Mountain National Park *(see place listing p. 251)*, offers an abundance of nearby recreational opportunities. When snow begins to accumulate, locals and visitors know they can find ample choices for skiing, snowboarding, snowmobiling and sleigh rides, or in summer for hiking, mountain biking, horseback riding, fishing, white-water rafting and hot-air ballooning.

RECREATIONAL ACTIVITIES
Tubing

- **Fraser Tubing Hill** is .5 mi. n. of jct. US 40 and CR 72 behind the Alco complex. **Hours:** Daily 10-10, Thanksgiving to mid-Mar. Last tube rental is 1 hour before closing. Phone ahead to confirm schedule. **Cost:** Cash only. **Phone:** (970) 726-5954.

FRISCO (C-3) pop. 2,683, elev. 9,042'

Although named by European settlers in 1873, the site of Frisco had served as a favored Ute Indian camp for nearly 7,000 years. The town quickly boomed during the late 19th century as gold and silver mines covered the surrounding mountainsides.

Serving the needs of visiting skiers became Frisco's economic mainstay after World War II. In addition to skiing, the area also offers such recreational activities as bicycling, mountain biking, fishing and sailing. The Lake Dillon Water Taxi provides transportation across the lake between the marinas in Frisco and Dillon. The service is available Mon.-Fri. 10-5, Sat.-Sun. 10-6. Phone (970) 486-0250 for reservations at least 30 minutes in advance.

FRISCO HISTORIC PARK AND MUSEUM, off I-70 exit 203, then .7 mi. s. on Summit Blvd. to jct. 2nd Ave. and Main St., depicts town history during its mining and ranching heydays. Twelve original structures, including furnished homes, depict lifestyles spanning 1880-1930 and include a schoolhouse museum displaying artifacts and photographs, a ranch house, a trappers cabin, a jail, a saloon, a general store and a post office.

Other exhibits feature natural history and a coin-operated train diorama. **Time:** Allow 1 hour minimum. **Hours:** Tues.-Sat. 9-5, Sun 9-3, May-Sept.; Tues.-Sat. 10-4, Sun. 10-2, rest of year. **Cost:** Free. **Phone:** (970) 668-3428.

RECREATIONAL ACTIVITIES
Skiing

- **Copper Mountain Resort** is off I-70 exit 195. Other activities are offered year-round. **Hours:** Mon.-Fri. 9-4, Sat.-Sun. and holidays 8:30-4, June-Sept. and mid-Nov. to mid-Apr. **Phone:** (970) 968-2318 or (866) 841-2481.

Skiing (Cross-country)

- **Frisco Nordic Center** is at 18454 SR 9. **Hours:** Daily 9-4, Nov.-Apr. (weather permitting). **Phone:** (970) 668-0866.

White-water Rafting

- **Colorado Adventure Center** picks up guests at area hotels and offers a range of rafting options. Base camps are located in Buena Vista, Frisco, Glenwood and Idaho Springs. **Hours:** Daily May 1-Labor Day. **Phone:** (970) 668-1228 or (800) 808-0357.

- **Performance Tours** meets at Pioneer Sports, 842 N. Summit Blvd. in Frisco. **Hours:** Daily May 1-Labor Day. **Phone:** (800) 328-7238.

BAYMONT INN & SUITES LAKE DILLON   (970)668-5094

Hotel
$79-$300

Address: 1202 N Summit Blvd 80443 **Location:** I-70 exit 203, just sw. **Facility:** 127 units. 4 stories, interior corridors. **Terms:** check-in 4 pm. **Amenities:** safes. **Pool(s):** heated indoor. **Activities:** hot tub, game room, exercise room. **Guest Services:** coin laundry. **Featured Amenity:** continental breakfast.

FRISCO INN ON GALENA   (970)668-3224

Bed & Breakfast
$159-$279

Address: 106 Galena St 80443 **Location:** I-70 exit 201, 0.6 mi e, then just n on 1st Ave. **Facility:** This charming inn's décor has a Tuscan feel. Each room offers a unique feature, such as a window seat or a balcony with mountain views. Feel like a local and walk to boutique shops and restaurants. 15 units, some two bedrooms. 2 stories (no elevator), interior corridors. **Terms:** 2 night minimum stay - seasonal and/or weekends, 30 day cancellation notice-fee imposed. **Activities:** sauna, hot tub, bicycles, game room, picnic facilities. **Guest Services:** valet laundry. **Featured Amenity:** full hot breakfast.

HOLIDAY INN   970/668-5000

Hotel. Rates not provided. **Address:** 1129 N Summit Blvd 80443 **Location:** I-70 exit 203, just s, then just e. **Facility:** 216 units. 3-6 stories, interior corridors. **Terms:** check-in 4 pm. **Pool(s):** heated indoor. **Activities:** sauna, hot tub, game room, exercise room. **Guest Services:** valet and coin laundry.

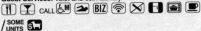

BACKCOUNTRY BREWERY   970/668-2337

American. Casual Dining. $10-$15 **AAA Inspector Notes:** Start with typical bar fare, such as wings, potato skins or a homemade pretzel. Entrées include a grilled chicken mushroom melt, a Tuscan pesto pizza, and the "Santa Fe Burger," served with guacamole, bacon and jalapeño-jack cheese. Delight in the mountain views as you dine on the patio. Try one of their beers, which range from pilsner to porter; they even offer a gluten-free option. **Features:** full bar, patio dining, happy hour. **Address:** 720 Main St 80443 **Location:** I-70 exit 203, 1.3 mi s; southwest corner of Main St and Summit Blvd.

BAGALIS   970/668-0601

Italian. Casual Dining. $8-$26 **AAA Inspector Notes:** This handsome and upscale restaurant's interior is offset by a cozy sidewalk patio. The much-talked-about wine bar offers flights, weekly tastings and wine dinners. Menu selections include cioppino, salads, small meat and cheese plates, and scallops with spring pea and red pepper puree. Patrons can choose a pasta and sauce and combine them with chicken, eggplant or veal Parmesan, Italian sausage, salmon, scallops or shrimp. Artisan pizza can be ordered gluten-free. **Features:** full bar, patio dining, happy hour. **Address:** 320 E Main St 80443 **Location:** I-70 exit 203 westbound, 1.3 mi s to Main St, then 0.3 mi w. **Parking:** street only.

BLUE SPRUCE INN   970/668-5900

Steak Seafood. Casual Dining. $19-$70 **AAA Inspector Notes:** This restaurant offers a lovely dining experience in an 1880s log cabin. Appetizers include baked Brie, blue corn calamari and spinach-artichoke dip. Entrées feature Rocky Mountain trout, king crab legs and steaks. A Western-style saloon is attached and focuses on more casual fare. **Features:** full bar. **Reservations:** suggested. **Address:** 20 W Main St 80443 **Location:** I-70 exit 201, 0.4 mi s.

THE BOATYARD GRILL   970/668-4728

American. Casual Dining. $11-$24 **AAA Inspector Notes:** Select from a wide range of starters, including pizza rolls, jumbo prawn cocktails and pork carnitas tacos. Try one of the flavorful burgers, the almond-crusted trout, or homemade bison meatloaf. The patio is a popular spot in warm weather. **Features:** full bar, patio dining, happy hour. **Address:** 304 Main St 80443 **Location:** I-70 exit 201, 0.7 mi e. **Parking:** on-site and street.

BUTTERHORN BAKERY & CAFE   970/668-3997

American. Casual Dining. $8-$11 **AAA Inspector Notes:** This casual eatery is popular with locals and travelers for the hearty breakfast offerings and tasty hot and cold sandwiches. The glass cases are attractively lined with homemade bread, dainty treats, thick and crunchy cookies and yummy muffins. Patrons waiting to be seated tend to stare trance-like at the gooey cinnamon rolls and pecan-caramel sticky buns. The décor features a changing gallery of art from local artists. **Features:** full bar. **Address:** 408 E Main St 80443 **Location:** I-70 exit 201, 0.9 mi e.

FOOD HEDZ WORLD CAFE   970/668-2000

American. Casual Dining. $12-$33 **AAA Inspector Notes:** Chef/owner David Welch began his career at the Keystone Resort as a dishwasher. After many years of apprenticing, he became executive chef at the famous Keystone Ranch Restaurant. Nine years later, he decided on a new challenge and opened this place, bringing along the quality and artistry of his years in fine dining while leaving the formal atmosphere behind. You'll have to stand in line to order at the cashier stand and then seat yourself, but the food is worth the minor inconvenience. **Features:** wine only. **Address:** 842 Summit Blvd, Suite 19 80443 **Location:** I-70 exit 203, 0.3 mi s; in strip mall.

HIMALAYAN CUISINE   970/668-3330

Indian. Casual Dining. $8-$16 **AAA Inspector Notes:** Serving authentic Indian and Nepalese cuisine, this charming sidewalk eatery serves traditional favorites such as a delicious daal soup, samosas, pakoras, chicken and lamb tikka kabas and masala and many vegetarian entrées. The homemade mango ice cream is soft and sweet. **Features:** full bar, patio dining. **Address:** 409 Main St 80443 **Location:** I-70 exit 201 eastbound; exit 203 westbound, 1.2 mi s to Main St, then 0.5 mi w. **Parking:** street only.

KEMOSABE SUSHI BAR   970/668-2100

Sushi. Casual Dining. $8-$35 **AAA Inspector Notes:** The upscale atmosphere combined with relaxing music goes well with chili garlic edamame, tempura jalapeño shooters wrapped in tuna, spicy miso soup, salads and a variety of sashimi, nigiri and specialty rolls. The sweet, fruity Japanese ice cream wrapped in soft, fluffy dough is dusted with a white powdery coating. The restaurant also offers more than 20 varieties of sake and Japanese beer along with an innovative cocktail menu. **Features:** full bar. **Address:** 605 Main St 80443 **Location:** I-70 exit 203 westbound, 1.2 mi s to Main St, then just w; exit 201 eastbound, then just e. **Parking:** street only.

WHERE TO EAT

LOG CABIN CAFE
970/668-3947

▼▼ Breakfast. Casual Dining. $8-$12 **AAA Inspector Notes:** Built in 1908, this log cabin, whose original walls form part of the kitchen, is a quaint spot in which to enjoy a hearty breakfast, grilled burger, sandwich or Mexican special. A nice shaded patio is streetside. **Features:** full bar, patio dining. **Address:** 121 Main St 80443 **Location:** I-70 exit 201, 0.7 mi e. **Parking:** on-site and street.

B L AC

SILVERHEELS BAR & GRILL
970/668-0345

▼▼▼ Regional American. Casual Dining. $11-$32 **AAA Inspector Notes:** This popular downtown restaurant's upscale Southwestern atmosphere complements a menu featuring an award-winning green chili stew, seafood chowder, a variety of thick choice steaks, wild game, poultry, sizzling crab empanadas, chicken lettuce wraps and pecan-crusted trout. **Features:** full bar. **Address:** 601 Main St 80443 **Location:** I-70 exit 203 westbound, 1.2 mi s to Main St, just w; exit 201 eastbound. **Parking:** street only.

L D

VINNY'S
970/668-0340

▼▼▼ American. Casual Dining. $17-$37 **AAA Inspector Notes:** The Euro-American menu will have you devouring appetizers such as all-natural buffalo jalapeño cheddar sausage and lump blue crab cake. Entrées include chicken Parmesan, prosciutto-wrapped pork tenderloin, lasagna, and crispy duck leg confit served with an apple-smoked bacon white bean cassoulet. House-made desserts feature their signature white chocolate bread pudding with sun-dried cherries and a classic tiramisu. **Features:** full bar, patio dining, happy hour. **Reservations:** suggested. **Address:** 310 Main St, #203 80443 **Location:** I-70 exit 203, 1.3 mi s to Main St, then 0.3 mi e; located upstairs. **Parking:** street only.

D

FRUITA (C-1) pop. 12,646, elev. 4,503'

MUSEUM OF WESTERN COLORADO'S DINO-SAUR JOURNEY is 1 blk. s. of I-70 exit 19 (use caution) to 550 Jurassic Ct. This educational and research facility presents animated re-creations of dinosaurs and other prehistoric creatures in natural settings. A working paleontology laboratory and children's dinosaur quarry also are offered. Dinosaur digs are available in summer.

Time: Allow 1 hour minimum. **Hours:** Mon.-Sat. 9-5, Sun. noon-4, May-Sept.; Mon.-Sat. 10-4, rest of year. Closed Jan. 1, Thanksgiving and Christmas. **Cost:** $7; $6 (ages 55+); $4 (ages 3-12); $20 (family rate). **Phone:** (970) 242-0971 or (888) 488-3466.

COMFORT INN
(970)858-1333

▼▼ Hotel $69-$179 **Address:** 400 Jurassic Ave 81521 **Location:** I-70 exit 19, 0.3 mi s; just e of Dinosaur Journey Museum. **Facility:** 66 units. 3 stories, interior corridors. **Pool(s):** heated indoor. **Activities:** hot tub. **Guest Services:** coin laundry.

[icons] SOME UNITS

WHERE TO EAT

CAMILLA'S KAFFE
970/858-7950

▼▼ American. Casual Dining. $10-$11 **AAA Inspector Notes:** This is the perfect spot for travelers to get off the interstate, take a break, grab a bite and sip an espresso. Menu items include a bleu beef panini, freshly made salads, sandwiches, soups, delicious chimichangas, wraps, a variety of burgers and homemade baked goods. The peanut butter pie is a rich and creamy treat. **Features:** beer & wine, patio dining. **Address:** 206 E Aspen Ave 81521 **Location:** I-70 exit 19, 0.3 mi n, then 0.4 mi e; downtown. **Parking:** street only.

B L

DRAGON TREASURE
970/858-8655

▼▼▼ Chinese. Casual Dining. $8-$15 **AAA Inspector Notes:** Traditional Chinese cuisine makes this restaurant a local favorite. They offer a nice selection of appetizers, soups, sweet and sour chicken or pork, egg foo young, fried rice and pan-fried noodles. Small and large bowls are made fresh at their Mongolian grill. **Features:** full bar, Sunday brunch. **Address:** 576 Kokopelli Blvd 81521 **Location:** I-70 exit 19, 0.3 mi s, then just e.

L D

FIESTA GUADALAJARA
970/858-1228

▼▼ Mexican. Family Dining. $7-$18 **AAA Inspector Notes:** The attentive and courteous staff at this family restaurant enhances the lively atmosphere. Patrons enjoy cold aguas frescas with made-in-house salsa and chips, sizzling fajitas and other traditional Mexican appetizers, entrees and desserts. **Features:** full bar. **Address:** 103 Hwy 6 81521 **Location:** I-70 exit 19, 0.3 mi n, just e, then 0.3 mi s.

L D

HOT TOMATO CAFE & PIZZERIA
970/858-1117

▼ Pizza. Quick Serve. $9-$25 **AAA Inspector Notes:** Patrons gush over the made-to-order calzones, stromboli, sausage rolls, handcrafted pizza dough, fresh-grated mozzarella and the specialty pizzas, which include a white-sauce variety and a mouth-watering basil. The homemade hot and chewy breadsticks go well with the eight distinctly carefully prepared and layered salads. Enjoy beers on tap and craft beers from the New Belgium Brewery. **Features:** beer & wine, patio dining, happy hour. **Address:** 124 N Mulberry St 81521 **Location:** I-70 exit 19, 0.3 mi n, just e (2nd exit at roundabout), then just n; downtown. **Parking:** street only.
L D CALL M

RIB CITY
970/858-6566

▼▼ Barbecue. Casual Dining. $7-$18 **AAA Inspector Notes:** A local favorite, the grill serves Southern-style barbecue and claims its ribs are the best. It's difficult to argue otherwise. The menu also lists barbecue chicken, pork, riblets and beef dinners presented with all the fixings. **Features:** beer & wine. **Address:** 455 Kokopelli Blvd, Suite 5 81521 **Location:** I-70 exit 19, just s to Frontage Rd, just e, then just s.
L D

GATEWAY (D-1)

GATEWAY AUTO MUSEUM is at 43224 SR 141. The museum's multi-car display highlights the history of the American automobile. Themed galleries provide interactive exhibits pertinent to the vehicle's role in industry, pop culture and daily life. Several showpieces are displayed, including a unique 1954 Oldsmobile F-88 and a 1906 Cadillac H Coupe. **Time:** Allow 1 hour, 30 minutes minimum. **Hours:** Daily 10-5. Closed major holidays. **Cost:** $15; $10 (65+). **Phone:** (970) 931-2895 or (866) 671-4733. [icons]

GATEWAY CANYONS RESORT & SPA
(970)931-2458

▼▼▼▼ Resort Hotel $579-$779

Address: 43200 Hwy 141 81522 **Location:** 43 mi w of US 50; 49 mi n of CR 90. **Facility:** You could spend the day driving a Bentley through the mountains, splashing around an outdoor pool, or hiking the red rock Unaweep Canyon while learning about dinosaurs and Native American history. 72 units. 2 stories (no elevator), interior/exterior corridors. **Terms:** check-in 4 pm, 3 day cancellation notice-fee imposed, resort fee. **Amenities:** *Some:* safes. **Dining:** 3 restaurants, also, Entrada Restaurant, see separate listing. **Pool(s):** heated outdoor. **Activities:** hot tub, cabanas, fishing, cross country skiing, snowmobiling, recreation programs, bicycles, game room, lawn sports, trails, exercise room, spa.

[icons] / SOME UNITS

WHERE TO EAT

ENTRADA RESTAURANT   970/931-2458

▼▼▼ Southwestern. Fine Dining. $22-$39 **AAA Inspector Notes:** The chef uses fresh, local ingredients to prepare thoughtful menu selections, all with a Southwestern twist. Enjoy blackened shrimp on creamy truffle grits aside pineapple salsa, broiled Colorado striped bass, lamb rack, or crispy organic chicken in black bean puree. You can dine inside the elegant dining room or on the enormous covered patio. Both offer an intimate ambience overlooking acres of beautiful grounds. **Features:** full bar, patio dining. **Address:** 43200 Hwy 141 81522 **Location:** 43 mi w of US 50; 49 mi n of CR 90; in Gateway Canyons Resort. (D)

GEORGETOWN (C-4) pop. 1,034, elev. 8,512'

Within 2 years of George and Dave Griffith's gold strike at the head of Clear Creek in 1859, the "bust" part of the familiar boom-and-bust story had begun to affect Georgetown. One by one its buildings emptied as the gold ran out and prospectors went elsewhere. In 1864, however, the first large silver discovery in Colorado was made about 5 miles northwest, and Georgetown was in business again.

Until the great strike at Leadville in 1878, Georgetown and its sister camp of Silver Plume, 2 miles up the canyon, comprised the premier silver district. Aptly nicknamed the "Silver Queen of the Rockies," Georgetown blossomed into the third largest city in Colorado.

Unlike other mining towns of the day, it escaped destruction by fire. More than 200 original buildings still stand. Shops now occupy many of the historic downtown structures and the city has been designated the Georgetown/Silver Plume National Historic Landmark District. Outdoor recreational options include fishing, mountain biking and hiking.

Gateway Visitor Center: 1491 Argentine St., Georgetown, CO 80444. **Phone:** (303) 569-0289.

GEORGETOWN LOOP RAILROAD departs from the Devil's Gate station (I-70 Georgetown exit 228) and Silver Plume station (I-70 Silver Plume exit 226). Passengers travel on a historic train over Devil's Gate High Bridge and through silver mining country with views of the Rocky Mountains. A tour of the Lebanon Silver Mine and Everett Silver Mine is available. Tickets may be purchased at the Silver Plume station or the Devil's Gate station. Mine tours are only accessible by train and are only available with the train ride. Gold panning also is available.

Allow 2 hours, 30 minutes for train ride and mine tour. **Hours:** Round-trip trains depart daily, May-Dec. Evening trains depart Sat., mid-June through Sept. 30. North Pole Adventure trains depart mid-Nov. through first weekend in Jan. Departure times vary by station; phone ahead. Mine tours are available daily, early May-early Sept. **Cost:** Train fare $25.95-$34.95; $18.95-$26.95 (ages 3-15). Mine tour $8-$12. Train reservations are strongly recommended. **Phone:** (888) 456-6777.

HAMILL HOUSE, 305 Argentine St., was built in 1879. The restored home of silver mine owner William Arthur Hamill demonstrates the wealth and opulence of the late-19th-century silver boom in

Colorado. The home had central heating, gaslights and running water before most of the community had heard of such things. It also has a six-seat, cupola-topped privy, a granite-constructed stable, a carriage house and an office building.

Time: Allow 30 minutes minimum. **Hours:** Tours are given every 30 minutes Mon.-Fri. 11:30-3:30, Sat.-Sun. 11:30-4:30, Memorial Day-Labor Day. **Cost:** $7; $5 (ages 65+ and ages 0-12). Combination ticket with Hotel de Paris Museum $10. **Phone:** (303) 569-2840. (GT)

HOTEL DE PARIS MUSEUM, 409 6th St., was founded by Frenchman Louis Dupuy in 1875 and became internationally renowned for its architecture, appointments, wine cellar, cuisine and intellectual ambience. A museum since 1954, the hotel retains its Victorian atmosphere. Original collections and furnishings are displayed in restored period rooms. Visitors can take a 40-minute tour of the hotel.

Time: Allow 1 hour minimum. **Hours:** Daily 10-5, May 24-Sept. 30; Sat. 10-5, Sun. noon-5, early Oct. to mid-Dec. Last tour 1 hour before closing. **Cost:** $7; $5 (ages 65+); $3 (ages 7-17). **Phone:** (303) 569-2311. (GT)

RECREATIONAL ACTIVITIES
Skiing

- **Loveland Ski Area** is at I-70 exit 216. **Hours:** Mon.-Fri. 9-4, Sat.-Sun. and holidays 8:30-4, mid-Dec. to mid-Apr. **Phone:** (303) 571-5580 or (800) 736-3754.

GLENDALE pop. 4,184
- **Restaurants p. 196**
- **Hotels & Restaurants map & index p. 136**
- **Part of Denver area — see map p. 116**

HILTON GARDEN INN DENVER/CHERRY CREEK
     303/754-9800 (57)

▼▼▼ Hotel. Rates not provided. **Address:** 600 S Colorado Blvd 80246 **Location:** I-25 exit 204, 1.6 mi n. **Facility:** 210 units. 8 stories, interior corridors. **Pool(s):** heated indoor. **Activities:** hot tub, exercise room. **Guest Services:** valet and coin laundry.

AAA Benefit: Members save up to 10%!

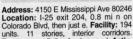

HYATT PLACE DENVER CHERRY CREEK
     (303)782-9300 (58)

▼▼▼ Hotel $79-$219

HYATT PLACE **AAA Benefit:** Members save 10%!

Address: 4150 E Mississippi Ave 80246 **Location:** I-25 exit 204, 0.8 mi n on Colorado Blvd, then just e. **Facility:** 194 units. 11 stories, interior corridors. **Terms:** cancellation fee imposed. **Activities:** exercise room. **Guest Services:** valet laundry. **Featured Amenity:** breakfast buffet.

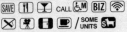

(See map & index p. 136.)

RESIDENCE INN BY MARRIOTT (303)758-6200 [56]

WWW **Extended Stay Hotel**
$128-$252 **Address:** 670 S Colorado
Blvd 80246 **Location:** I-25 exit 204, 1.6
mi n. **Facility:** 135 units, some two bedrooms, efficiencies and kitchens. 4 stories, interior corridors. **Terms:** check-in 4 pm. **Pool(s):** heated indoor. **Activities:** hot tub, picnic facilities, exercise room. **Guest Services:** valet and coin laundry.

AAA Benefit:
Members save 5%
or more!

STAYBRIDGE SUITES DENVER/CHERRY CREEK
303/321-5757 [55]

WWW
Extended Stay
Hotel
Rates not provided

Address: 4220 E Virginia Ave 80246 **Location:** I-25 exit 204, 1.5 mi n on Colorado Blvd to Virginia Ave, then just e. **Facility:** 121 efficiencies, some two bedrooms. 4 stories, interior corridors. **Pool(s):** heated outdoor. **Activities:** hot tub, lawn sports, picnic facilities, trails, exercise room. **Guest Services:** complimentary and valet laundry, area transportation. **Featured Amenity:** continental breakfast.

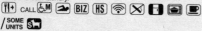
WHERE TO EAT

CUBA CUBA SANDWICHERIA 303/758-1167 [103]

W Cuban. Quick Serve. $7-$8 **AAA Inspector Notes:** The offshoot of a popular AAA three-diamond restaurant, this casual eatery serves authentic Cuban sandwiches featuring pulled pork, chicken and steak. Platters offer similar ingredients, minus the bread, but including a side of rice and beans. The rich, creamy tres leches cake has a hint of coconut. The cozy bar with Caribbean-inspired décor specializes in mojitos and sangrias. **Features:** full bar, happy hour. **Address:** 654 S Colorado Blvd 80246 **Location:** I-25 exit 204, 1.6 mi n, then just e on Cherry Creek S Dr; in strip mall. L D CALL

SILVI'S KITCHEN 303/758-9061 [104]

WW American. Casual Dining. $9-$19 **AAA Inspector Notes:** This family-owned, local chain is known for its gourmet sandwiches served on homemade bread; the French dip is a standout. Other offerings include pizzas, burgers and hearty salads. Be sure to stop by the pastry case and take a look at the house-made pastries and baked goods. If you have trouble deciding, opt for the brown butter pie. **Features:** full bar, Sunday brunch, happy hour. **Address:** 686 S Colorado Blvd 80246 **Location:** I-25 exit 204, 1.6 mi n, then just e on Cherry Creek S Dr; in strip mall. L D

GLENWOOD SPRINGS (C-2) pop. 9,614, elev. 5,763'
• Restaurants p. 198

Hot mineral springs and natural vapor caves have made Glenwood Springs popular since the days of the Ute Indians. During the mining boom the newly rich from Aspen and other bonanza towns came by special train to enjoy the waters at this fashionable spa and stay at the elegant Hotel Colorado. A memorial to Doc Holliday, a dentist with a sideline as a gunslinger, is in nearby Linwood Cemetery.

Ask about on-the-spot
vehicle battery testing and replacement

Ten miles east on I-70 through Glenwood Canyon is a 1.7-mile trail to Hanging Lake, a water-filled rocky bowl literally clinging to the face of a cliff 1,200 feet above the floor of the canyon. Spouting Rock Creek, which feeds the lake, creates Bridal Veil Falls.

Glenwood Springs, at the confluence of the Colorado and Roaring Fork rivers, is a popular rafting and trout fishing destination. The city lies along the scenic stretches of two highways: I-70 from Grand Junction to Georgetown and SR 82 from Glenwood Springs to Aspen, over Independence Pass (sections of the pass are closed in winter).

Glenwood Springs Visitor Center: 802 Grand Ave., Glenwood Springs, CO 81601. **Phone:** (970) 945-6580 or (888) 445-3696.

FRONTIER HISTORICAL MUSEUM is at 1001 Colorado Ave. The museum features exhibits pertaining to the history of Glenwood Springs and Garfield County and historical figures such as Doc Holliday, Kid Curry, Buffalo Bill Cody and Theodore Roosevelt. Included in the collection are a portrait of Doc Holliday, an ornate pump organ, late 19th-century furniture, rock and mineral displays, and a saddle that belonged to Theodore Roosevelt. Guided tours are available by appointment. **Time:** Allow 30 minutes minimum. **Hours:** Mon.-Sat. 10-4, May-Sept.; Mon. and Thurs.-Sat. 1-4, rest of year. **Cost:** $4; $3 (ages 60+); $2 (ages 3-14). **Phone:** (970) 945-4448.

GLENWOOD CAVERNS ADVENTURE PARK is off I-70 exit 116, .3 mi. w. on 6th St., then s. on Devereux Rd. to 51000 Two Rivers Plaza Rd. The Iron Mountain Tramway carries visitors to the caves and Adventure Park. The two 45-minute cave tours feature soda straws and other crystalline formations as well as Exclamation Point, a cliff-side balcony that offers panoramic views. The longer, more adventurous Wild Tour also is available. The park also offers thrill rides including the Cliffhanger roller coaster, the Glenwood Canyon Flyer, an alpine coaster, a zip ride, a giant canyon swing, a Ferris wheel and a family coaster as well as a 4-D motion theater, laser tag arena, gemstone sluice box mining, a maze and a climbing wall.

Time: Allow 2 hours minimum. **Hours:** Daily 9-9, Memorial Day to mid-Aug. Holiday lights display Nov.-Feb.; phone ahead for schedules. **Cost:** Tram or bus rides $14; $12.60 (ages 65+); $9 (ages 3-12). Tram and cave tours $26; $23.70 (ages 65+); $21 (ages 3-12). Day pass (includes tram ride, unlimited thrill rides and cave tours) May-Oct. $49; $44 (ages 3-12). Prices vary during winter months. Phone for details. **Phone:** (970) 945-4228, ext. 111 or (800) 530-1635.

The Iron Mountain Tramway departs from Iron Mountain Station at 51000 Two Rivers Plaza Rd. Visitors travel 4,300 feet to the top of Iron Mountain in glass-enclosed gondolas. An observation area at the top of the mountain offers a panoramic view of Mount Sopris and the Colorado River Valley.

Time: Allow 1 hour minimum. **Hours:** Daily 9-9, Memorial Day to mid-Aug. Schedule varies rest of year; phone ahead. **Cost:** Park entrance and tram fare $14; $9 (ages 3-12). Combination ticket for tram and cave tours $26; $23.70 (ages 65+); $21 (ages 3-12). **Phone:** (970) 945-4228, ext. 111 or (800) 530-1635.

GLENWOOD HOT SPRINGS is off I-70 exit 116 to 401 N. River St. Measuring 2 blocks long, this is the world's largest known outdoor thermal pool. The pool's mineral-rich waters come from Yampah Springs, once considered sacred by the Ute Indians (Yampah means "big medicine"), and are maintained between 93 and 104 degrees Fahrenheit. By the late 19th century the springs had been developed into a resort containing a hot springs pool, bath house and a lodge, which soon became a popular getaway for movie stars, American presidents and other dignitaries.

Exercise lap lanes, a children's wading area, diving boards and two waterslides are featured. A smaller therapy pool is maintained at 104 degrees Fahrenheit. An athletic club, spa and miniature golf also are offered.

Lockers, towels and bathing suits are available for a small fee. **Time:** Allow 1 hour minimum. **Hours:** Pool daily 7:30 a.m.-10 p.m., Memorial Day weekend-Labor Day; 9 a.m.-10 p.m., rest of year. Waterslides daily 10-6, Memorial Day-Labor Day; daily noon-4, Spring Break; Sat.-Sun. 10-6, rest of year (weather permitting). Miniature golf daily noon-10, Memorial Day-Labor Day, Sat.-Sun. noon-8, May 1-day before Memorial Day.

Cost: Memorial Day weekend-Labor Day Mon.-Fri. $18.75; $11.75 (ages 3-12). Sat.-Sun. $20.25; $12.25 (ages 3-12). Rest of year $15.25; $10.25 (ages 3-12). Additional fees apply to athletic club, spa, waterslides and miniature golf. Prices are subject to change; phone ahead. **Phone:** (970) 945-6571 or (800) 537-7946. 🍴

RECREATIONAL ACTIVITIES

Skiing
- **Sunlight Mountain Resort** is at 10901 CR 117. Other activities are offered. **Hours:** Daily 9-4, early Dec.-early Apr. **Phone:** (970) 945-7491 or (800) 445-7931.

White-water Rafting
- **Blue Sky Adventures Inc.** departs from Hotel Colorado, 319 6th St. **Hours:** Daily 8-7. Rafting tips offered May to late Sept. **Phone:** (970) 945-6605 or (877) 945-6605.
- **Rock Gardens Rafting** is at 1308 CR 129. **Hours:** Daily Apr.-Sept. (weather permitting). **Phone:** (970) 945-6737 or (877) 947-7238.
- **Whitewater Rafting** is off I-70 exit 114 at 2000 Devereux Rd. **Hours:** Daily 8-6, May-Sept. **Phone:** (970) 945-8477 or (800) 993-7238.

BEST WESTERN ANTLERS   (970)945-8535

Motel $99-$179

AAA Benefit: Save 10% or more every day and earn 10% bonus points!

Address: 171 W 6th St 81601 **Location:** I-70 exit 116, just n, then just w. **Facility:** 99 units. 2 stories (no elevator), exterior corridors. **Terms:** check-in 4 pm. **Pool(s):** heated outdoor. **Activities:** hot tub, playground. **Guest Services:** valet and coin laundry, area transportation. **Featured Amenity: continental breakfast.**

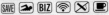

CARAVAN INN   (970)945-7451

Motel $59-$189 **Address:** 1826 Grand Ave 81601 **Location:** I-70 exit 116, 0.9 mi s. **Facility:** 67 units, some efficiencies. 2 stories (no elevator), exterior corridors. **Terms:** cancellation fee imposed. **Amenities:** safes. **Pool(s):** heated outdoor. **Activities:** hot tub. **Guest Services:** coin laundry.

COURTYARD BY MARRIOTT   (970)947-1300

Contemporary Hotel $106-$222 **Address:** 105 Wulfsohn Rd 81601 **Location:** I-70 exit 114, 2nd exit at roundabout, 1.5 mi e on Midland Ave, then just s. **Facility:** 101 units. 3 stories, interior corridors. **Terms:** check-in 4 pm. **Pool(s):** heated indoor. **Activities:** hot tub, trails, exercise room. **Guest Services:** valet and coin laundry, boarding pass kiosk.

AAA Benefit: Members save 5% or more!

GLENWOOD HOT SPRINGS LODGE   (970)945-6571

Hotel $149-$249

Address: 415 E 6th St 81601 **Location:** I-70 exit 116, just ne. Across from Hot Springs Pool. **Facility:** 107 units. 5 stories, interior corridors. **Terms:** check-in 4 pm, 2 night minimum stay - seasonal, 3 day cancellation notice-fee imposed. **Amenities:** safes. **Pool(s):** heated outdoor. **Activities:** miniature golf, spa. **Guest Services:** valet and coin laundry, area transportation.

GLENWOOD SPRINGS CEDAR LODGE   970/945-6579

Motel. Rates not provided. **Address:** 2102 Grand Ave 81601 **Location:** I-70 exit 116, 1.5 mi s on SR 82. **Facility:** 96 units, some two bedrooms and kitchens. 2 stories (no elevator), exterior corridors. **Pool(s):** heated outdoor, heated indoor. **Activities:** sauna, hot tub, exercise room. **Guest Services:** coin laundry.

THE HOTEL DENVER   970/945-6565

Historic Hotel. Rates not provided. **Address:** 402 7th St 81601 **Location:** I-70 exit 116; across from historic train station; in town center. **Facility:** Built in 1915, this hotel references its past while offering modern amenities. Glittering, marble mosaic tiles in the floor catch your eye as you enter the lobby. 68 units. 3-4 stories, interior corridors. **Dining:** Glenwood Canyon Brew Pub, see separate listing. **Guest Services:** valet and coin laundry.

RESIDENCE INN BY MARRIOTT (970)928-0900

▼▼▼▼ **Extended Stay Hotel**
$110-$209 **Address:** 125 Wulfsohn Rd
81601 **Location:** I-70 exit 114, 2nd exit
at roundabout, 1.5 mi e on Midland Ave,
then just s. **Facility:** 124 units, some two
bedrooms, efficiencies and kitchens. 4 stories, interior corridors.
Terms: check-in 4 pm. **Pool(s):** heated indoor. **Activities:** hot tub,
picnic facilities, trails, exercise room. **Guest Services:** valet and coin
laundry.

AAA Benefit:
Members save 5%
or more!

RODEWAY INN (970)945-8817

▼▼ **Motel**
$70-$160

Address: 52039 US 6 & 24 81601 **Location:** I-70 exit 114, 1 mi ne; exit 116, 1 mi
nw. **Facility:** 42 units. 2-3 stories (no elevator), exterior corridors. **Activities:** hot
tub. **Guest Services:** coin laundry. **Featured Amenity:** continental breakfast.

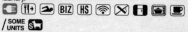
WHERE TO EAT

19TH STREET DINER 970/945-9133

▼ American. Casual Dining. $8-$18 **AAA Inspector Notes:**
A touch of 1950s nostalgia characterizes this breakfast, lunch and
dinner spot, which has a full bar and courteous servers. The eclectic
menu features burgers, sandwiches, fajitas, burritos, chicken fried
steak and meatloaf. **Features:** full bar. **Address:** 1908 Grand Ave
81601 **Location:** I-70 exit 116, just ne, then 1.4 mi s to 19th St.
B L D

FIESTA GUADALAJARA 970/947-1670

▼▼ Mexican. Casual Dining. $7-$15 **AAA Inspector Notes:**
This family restaurant features attractive carved wooden booths, attentive service, traditional Mexican fare and delicious chips and salsa.
Features: full bar. **Address:** 503 Pine St 81601 **Location:** I-70 exit
116, just ne to Pine St, then just n. L D

FIN'S GRILLE & RAW BAR 970/945-4771

▼▼ Seafood. Casual Dining. $14-$39 **AAA Inspector Notes:**
Overlooking the street in the historic downtown area, this restaurant's
menu features a mix of land and sea. Appetizers include calamari, raw
oysters, mussels, chicken wings and escargot. The raw oysters are
served with a traditional cocktail sauce, horseradish and a less traditional tomatillo sauce. Entrées include lobster tail, trout, walleye, filet
mignon and duck breast as well as some pasta dishes. The setting is
appropriate for a special occasion, although the bar is more casual.
Features: full bar, happy hour. **Address:** 710 Grand Ave 81601 **Location:** I-70 exit 116; downtown. **Parking:** street only. D

GLENWOOD CANYON BREW PUB 970/945-1276

▼▼ American. Casual Dining. $9-$23 **AAA Inspector Notes:**
Beer lovers will delight in the seasonal, hand-crafted beers. Start with
a cup of the savory beer-cheese soup. Select from a wide range of
entrées, including burgers, sandwiches and pastas. **Features:** full
bar. **Address:** 402 7th St 81601 **Location:** I-70 exit 116, just se;
across from historic train station; in The Hotel Denver. **Parking:** on-
site and street. L D

GRIND 970/230-9258

▼ Burgers. Quick Serve. $6-$12 **AAA Inspector Notes:** This is
not your usual burger joint. They grind all of their locally raised,
grass-fed and grass-finished meats in house. The beef grind is a
blend of brisket, short rib and chuck, all grass-fed and grass-finished.
A few favorites include the chicken, pepper jack and avocado; black
bean; falafel; and tandoori lamb. **Features:** full bar. **Address:** 701
Grand Ave 81601 **Location:** I-70 exit 116, just ne, then just s; between 7th and 8th sts. **Parking:** street only. L D

ITALIAN UNDERGROUND RESTAURANT 970/945-6422

▼▼ Italian. Casual Dining. $12-$16 **AAA Inspector Notes:**
Downtown under the Grand Avenue Bridge, this local favorite offers
classic Italian fare. Entrees include chicken cacciatore, northern
Italian rotisserie chicken and lasagna. **Features:** full bar. **Reservations:** suggested. **Address:** 715 Grand Ave 81601 **Location:** I-70
exit 116; downtown. D

JH CHEN ASIAN BISTRO 970/945-9898

▼▼ Asian. Casual Dining. $8-$18 **AAA Inspector Notes:**
Order your favorite Chinese dish or select from a range of sushi rolls
and sashimi. Try the fresh, savory chicken lo mein. Wontons are
made from scratch. **Features:** full bar. **Address:** 730 Cooper Ave
81601 **Location:** I-70 exit 116, just e on 8th St, then just n. **Parking:**
street only. L D

JUICY LUCY'S STEAKHOUSE 970/945-4619

▼▼ Seafood Steak. Casual Dining. $10-$42 **AAA Inspector
Notes:** Downtown, below the bridge, this restaurant employs casual, efficient servers who glide through the dining room with appetizers, varied steaks, fresh seafood, salads and sides. **Features:** full
bar, happy hour. **Address:** 308 7th St 81601 **Location:** I-70 exit
116, just ne, then just s on SR 82. **Parking:** street only.
L D

NEPAL RESTAURANT 970/945-8803

▼▼ Indian. Casual Dining. $8-$20 **AAA Inspector Notes:** At
this casual eatery, family recipes offer a delightful Nepali experience.
Settle in with a glass of chai tea as you browse an extensive menu
with a good selection of vegetarian, poultry, lamb and seafood dishes.
I always start with naan fresh from the tandoori oven, then look for a
unique dish like a bowl of Chau Chau (Tibetan-style noodles). Finish
with the Nepalese dessert, khir: basmati rice cooked in milk with raisins and nuts. **Features:** beer & wine. **Address:** 6824 SR 82 81601
Location: I-70 exit 116, 5.5 mi s to CR 114; 5 mi n of Carbondale.
L D

THE PULLMAN FOOD & DRINK 970/230-9234

▼▼▼ American. Casual Dining. $9-$20 **AAA Inspector
Notes:** Appropriately named, this chic neighborhood eatery is across
the street from the train station. Choose from a wonderful array of
unique dishes such as shrimp ceviche with sesame ginger and kimchee, roasted bone marrow, truffled pork rinds, crispy crab cakes with
melon cucumber salsa and rabbit pappardelle. There's also a straight
forward steak, burger and macaroni and cheese for those feeling less
adventurous. **Features:** full bar, Sunday brunch. **Address:** 330 7th St
81601 **Location:** I-70 exit 113, at 7th St and Cooper Ave; downtown.
Parking: street only. L D

RIVERS RESTAURANT 970/928-8813

▼▼▼
**American
Casual Dining**
$14-$27

AAA Inspector Notes: There often is a
wait to take advantage of this restaurant's above-the-river dining deck, which
affords nice views of the nearby cliff.
Diners get a feel for the Southeast in a
setting evocative of a Southern plantation and veranda. On the menu are creative appetizers and entrées featuring Rocky Mountain trout, elk
medallions, prime rib, lamb and salmon. **Features:** full bar, patio
dining, Sunday brunch, happy hour. **Reservations:** suggested,
weekends. **Address:** 2525 S Grand Ave 81601 **Location:** I-70
exit 116, just ne, 1.4 mi s to 23rd St, then 0.3 mi sw; on the
Roaring Fork River. *Menu on AAA.com* D

RIVIERA SUPPER CLUB & WINE BAR 970/945-7692

▼▼ New American. Casual Dining. $12-$28 **AAA Inspector
Notes:** A local institution since 1947, this supper club has evolved
over the years to reflect current tastes. Oil paintings and crystal light
fixtures enhance the inviting décor. The diverse menu offers something for everyone. Starters include escargot, raw oysters, wings and
queso fundido. Entrées include an ahi tuna sandwich, meatball sub,
steaks and duck. If available, try the velvety peanut butter mousse
pie. **Features:** full bar, happy hour. **Reservations:** suggested. **Address:** 702 Grand Ave 81601 **Location:** Just w of jct Cooper Ave and
7th St; downtown. **Parking:** street only. D

RUSSO'S NEW YORK PIZZA   970/945-7437

▼ Pizza. Family Dining. $3-$24 **AAA Inspector Notes:** This friendly family-operated eatery features over 15 specialty pizzas, Italian sandwiches, several selections of pasta and eight family-style salads. You will not be able to resist the warm, chewy garlic knots. **Features:** beer & wine. **Address:** 40 Market St, Suite D 81601 **Location:** I-70 exit 114, just s, take 2nd exit at roundabout; 1 mi e on Midland Ave to W Meadows Dr, then just s to Meadow Ln.

L D

ZHENG ASIAN BISTRO   970/928-9077

▼▼ Asian. Casual Dining. $10-$16 **AAA Inspector Notes:** This cozy and comfortable bistro prepares a variety of Chinese, Korean and Japanese menu items, most notably the atomic shrimp Thai appetizer. You'll also find chicken, garlic pork, and Chinese-style crispy duck. **Features:** full bar, patio dining, happy hour. **Address:** 35 Market St 81601 **Location:** I-70 exit 114, 0.3 mi se; in Glenwood Meadows Mall. L D

GOLDEN (C-8) pop. 18,867, elev. 5,674'
- Hotels p. 200 • Restaurants p. 201
- Hotels & Restaurants map & index p. 136
- Part of Denver area — see map p. 116

Golden was settled in 1859 among the glacial deposits on Clear Creek. Its name recalls an early miner and the local preoccupation with gold prospecting. Golden rivaled Denver in importance for several years. From 1862 to 1867 it served as capital of the Colorado Territory.

The Colorado School of Mines, founded in 1874, is among the oldest institutions devoted to mineral sciences and engineering. The school enrolls more than 3,000 students; phone (303) 273-3815. The National Earthquake Information Center is on the campus; guided tours of this facility are available by appointment Mon. and Thurs.; phone (303) 273-8420.

The Lariat Trail, the first 7 miles of The Lariat Loop National Scenic Byway (see attraction listing p. 131), begins at US 6 and 19th Street and winds into the Denver Mountain Parks, ending near the Buffalo Bill Museum and Grave and Lookout Mountain Park (see attraction listings).

Red Rocks Park and Amphitheatre (see Morrison p. 239), south of Golden, and Hogback Park, off I-70 near the US 40 exit, contain interesting geological formations. Golden Gate Canyon State Park (see Recreation Areas Chart) and White Ranch Park, 9 miles northwest of Golden, offer recreational facilities. Golden celebrates the spirit of the Old West with Buffalo Bill Days on the last weekend in July; highlights include a parade, bands and crafts.

Greater Golden Chamber of Commerce and Visitors Center: 1010 Washington Ave., Golden, CO 80401. **Phone:** (303) 279-3113.

Self-guiding tours: Literature outlining a self-guiding Public Art Walk tour is available from the chamber of commerce.

BRADFORD WASHBURN AMERICAN MOUNTAINEERING MUSEUM is at 710 10th St. Devoted to mountains, rock climbing and mountaineering, the museum features interactive exhibits, multimedia presentations, historic mountaineering and rock climbing gear, and a scale model of Mount Everest. Mountain cultures, safety, conservation and the achievements of mountaineers also are depicted. **Hours:** Mon. and Wed.-Thurs. 9-6, Tues. 9-7, Fri. 9-4, Sat. noon-5. Closed major holidays. Phone ahead to confirm schedule. **Cost:** $5. **Phone:** (303) 996-2755.

BUFFALO BILL MUSEUM AND GRAVE is at the top of Lookout Mountain at 987 1/2 Lookout Mountain Rd. The museum displays artifacts of the Old West and depicts the life of William F. Cody, from his job as a Pony Express rider and buffalo hunter to the world's greatest showman. Exhibits include Native American artifacts, antique firearms and Wild West show posters. Hands-on activities for children and Wild West videos also are offered. A large observation deck provides a spectacular view of the Denver metropolitan area and the Colorado Rockies. Changing exhibits are presented.

Note: The park is best approached from Golden along the Lariat Trail. **Hours:** Daily 9-5, May-Oct.; Tues.-Sun. 9-6, rest of year. Closed Thanksgiving and Christmas. **Cost:** $5; $4 (ages 65+); $1 (ages 6-15). **Phone:** (303) 526-0747. ⏷

CLEAR CREEK HISTORY PARK is 1 blk. w. of Washington Ave. on 11th St. Costumed interpreters depict 19th-century Colorado pioneer life in living history demonstrations, including presentations about foods grown by the pioneers. Historic buildings, originally homesteaded in a nearby canyon, include 1870s cabins, a blacksmith shop and an 1876 one-room schoolhouse. Several heritage gardens include heirloom chickens and a working bee hive.

Time: Allow 1 hour minimum. **Hours:** Park open daily dawn-dusk. Buildings open for paid tours, events and programs on occasion. Closed major holidays. Phone ahead to confirm schedule. **Cost:** Free. $3. Combination ticket with Golden History Center $5. Some programs and events charge an additional fee. **Phone:** (303) 278-3557.

COLORADO RAILROAD MUSEUM, off I-70W exit 265 to 17155 W. 44th Ave., houses records and artifacts of early Colorado railroads. More than 100 locomotives and train cars, some of which can be boarded, are displayed. The main museum building, modeled after an 1880s depot, also contains an extensive model railroad collection and two floors of photographs and artifacts. A coin-operated HO-scale model train layout is on the lower level. A train restoration center in the roundhouse is open for viewing. Rides aboard a 19th-century passenger car are available on Saturdays.

Self-guiding audio cell phone tours are available. **Time:** Allow 1 hour minimum. **Hours:** Daily 9-5. Closed Jan. 1, Thanksgiving and Christmas. **Cost:** $10; $8 (ages 60+); $5 (ages 2-15); $20 (family, two adults and up to five children ages 2-15). During special events $15; $10 (ages 60+); $5 (ages 2-15); $30 (family, two adults and ages 2-15). Saturday train rides $4; $2 (ages 2-15). **Phone:** (303) 279-4591 or (800) 365-6263. ⏢

(See map & index p. 136.)

COLORADO SCHOOL OF MINES GEOLOGY MUSEUM, 1310 Maple St., contains extensive displays of minerals, mining artifacts, meteorites, fossils and gemstones as well as a walk-through mine. Highlights include an introductory video about area geology and a display about ultraviolet minerals. Apollo 15 and 17 moon rocks can also be viewed. Murals originally exhibited at the Golden Gate International Exposition in 1939 by artist Irwin Hoffman depict the history of mining and can be seen in the main gallery. Rotating exhibits also are on display.

An outdoor geologic trail features outcrops containing fossilized dinosaur tracks, logs and leaves. Guided tours are available by reservation. **Hours:** Mon.-Sat. 9-4, Sun. 1-4; closed certain legal and school holidays. Phone ahead to confirm schedule. **Cost:** Donations. **Parking:** $1.50. **Phone:** (303) 273-3815.

COORS BREWING CO., 13th and Ford sts., offers 30-minute self-guiding tours of traditional brewing methods used in the Rocky Mountains since 1873. Visitors learn about the malting, brewing and packaging processes and then may sample products in the hospitality lounge. Nonalcoholic beverages also are available.

Note: Product samples are limited in quantity and are available only to those age 21 or older with a valid ID. Purses, backpacks or large bags of any type are not permitted in the brewery or on tours, and are not able to be stored. Wallets are permitted. Visitors may have to wait in line outside prior to tours and should be prepared for the weather. **Time:** Allow 1 hour, 30 minutes minimum. **Hours:** Mon. and Thurs.-Sat. 10-4, Sun. noon-4; extended hours in summer, phone for schedule. Closed major holidays. **Cost:** Free. Ages 0-17 must be accompanied by an adult. **Phone:** (303) 277-2337 or (866) 812-2337.

GOLDEN HISTORY CENTER, 923 10th St., presents the history of Golden from pioneer to modern times. Interactive exhibits include Made in Golden, focusing on local innovations including the seamless two-piece aluminum can, and Turn it Up, a musical exhibit featuring rare instruments and recordings from Golden's past. Over 100 pieces of labware created by Coors Porcelain also are on display.

Hours: Wed.-Mon. 10-4:30. Closed major holidays. **Cost:** $3; free (ages 0-6). Combination ticket with Clear Creek History Park $5. **Phone:** (303) 278-3557.

LOOKOUT MOUNTAIN NATURE CENTER AND PRESERVE is off I-70E exit 254 or I-70W exit 256, following signs to 910 Colorow Rd. The 110-acre preserve includes 1.4 miles of trails through forest and meadow. The nature center features exhibits about bird migration as well as indigenous plants and animals. Naturalist-led programs are available.

Time: Allow 30 minutes minimum. **Hours:** Preserve daily dawn-dusk. Nature center Tues.-Fri. 10-4, Sat.-Sun. 9-5, Memorial Day weekend-Labor Day; Tues.-Sun. 10-4, rest of year. **Cost:** Free. **Phone:** (720) 497-7600.

LOOKOUT MOUNTAIN PARK, 5 mi. w. off US 6, occupies 66 acres atop Lookout Mountain. It affords a view of snowcapped mountains and Denver's skyline. Buffalo-hunter turned Wild West show entrepreneur William F. Cody—"Buffalo Bill"—is buried here. Picnic pavilions are available. **Phone:** (303) 526-0744.

MOTHER CABRINI SHRINE is 1.5 mi. off I-70E exit 256 at 20189 Cabrini Blvd. A 22-foot statue of Christ at the head of a gradual 373-step stairway is the setting for a panorama of the Denver area. **Time:** Allow 1 hour minimum. **Hours:** Daily 7-5, Memorial Day weekend-Labor Day; 7-5, rest of year. Last admission is 30 minutes before closing. **Cost:** Donations. **Phone:** (303) 526-0758.

THE ROCKY MOUNTAIN QUILT MUSEUM, 1213 Washington Ave., is dedicated to the preservation and promotion of the history and art of quilting. The museum's gallery features four changing exhibitions each year. **Time:** Allow 30 minutes minimum. **Hours:** Mon.-Sat. 10-5, Sun. 11-5. Closed Jan. 1, July 4, Thanksgiving and Christmas. **Cost:** $6; $5 (ages 65+); $4 (ages 6-12 and students with ID). **Phone:** (303) 277-0377. GT

COURTYARD BY MARRIOTT DENVER WEST/GOLDEN (303)271-0776 52
Hotel $113-$224 **Address:** 14700 W 6th Ave, Frontage Rd 80401 **Location:** US 6 exit Indiana Ave, just s to frontage road, then just e. **Facility:** 110 units. 4 stories, interior corridors. **Pool(s):** heated indoor. **Activities:** hot tub, exercise room. **Guest Services:** valet and coin laundry, boarding pass kiosk.
AAA Benefit: Members save 5% or more!

DENVER MARRIOTT WEST (303)279-9100 49
Hotel $115-$300 **Address:** 1717 Denver West Blvd 80401 **Location:** I-70 exit 263, just n, then w. **Facility:** 305 units. 6 stories, interior corridors. **Pool(s):** heated outdoor, heated indoor. **Activities:** exercise room, massage. **Guest Services:** valet and coin laundry, area transportation.
AAA Benefit: Members save 5% or more!

THE GOLDEN HOTEL, AN ASCEND HOTEL COLLECTION MEMBER 303/279-0100 47
Hotel. Rates not provided. **Address:** 800 11th St 80401 **Location:** At 11th St and Washington Ave; downtown. **Facility:** 62 units. 4 stories, interior corridors. **Amenities:** safes. **Activities:** exercise room. **Guest Services:** valet laundry, area transportation.

HAMPTON INN DENVER WEST/GOLDEN 303/278-6600 50
Hotel. Rates not provided. **Address:** 17150 W Colfax St 80401 **Location:** I-70 exit 262 (Colfax Ave), 1.2 mi w. **Facility:** 121 units. 4 stories, interior corridors. **Pool(s):** heated indoor. **Activities:** hot tub, exercise room. **Guest Services:** valet and coin laundry.
AAA Benefit: Members save up to 10%!

(See map & index p. 136.)

RESIDENCE INN BY MARRIOTT DENVER WEST/GOLDEN
(303)271-0909 **51**

WWW **Extended Stay Hotel**
$123-$260 **Address:** 14600 W 6th Ave,
Frontage Rd 80401 **Location:** US 6 exit
Indiana Ave, just s to Frontage Rd, then
just e. **Facility:** 88 units, some two bed-
rooms, efficiencies and kitchens. 4 stories, interior corridors. **Terms:**
check-in 4 pm. **Pool(s):** heated indoor. **Activities:** hot tub, picnic facilities, exercise room. **Guest Services:** valet and coin laundry.

AAA Benefit:
Members save 5%
or more!

[CALL] [&M] [🏊] [BIZ] [📶] [✕] [🎞] [🛏] [▭] [▭]
/ SOME
UNITS [🛏]

TABLE MOUNTAIN INN   (303)277-9898 **48**

WWWW
Boutique Hotel
$184-$269

Address: 1310 Washington Ave 80401
Location: US 6 exit 19th St, 0.5 mi n to
Washington Ave, 0.5 mi w; downtown,
just s of arch. **Facility:** With its iconic
Santa Fe-style building, this hotel has remained one of Golden's most popular
places to stay since it opened in 1925.
Select a cozy standard room, or a larger
suite with a fireplace. 74 units. 5 stories,
interior corridors. **Parking:** on-site and
street. **Terms:** 3 day cancellation
notice-fee imposed. **Dining:** Table
Mountain Grill & Cantina, see separate
listing. **Activities:** exercise room. **Guest
Services:** valet laundry.

[SAVE] [🍴] [🍸] [CALL] [&M] [BIZ] [📶] [✕] [🛏] [▭] [▭]
/ SOME
UNITS [🛏] [▭]

WHERE TO EAT

THE BRIARWOOD INN   303/279-3121 **96**

WWWW Continental. Fine Dining. $26-$80 **AAA Inspector
Notes:** I began with the red and golden beet carpaccio, which had a
layer of thinly sliced beets with arugula and goat cheese. The sweet
beets went well with the tart cheese and spicy greens. The French
onion soup featured savory broth and a thick layer of melted Gruyère.
The main course was a bit of a disappointment. I tried the halibut flavored with a mango and ginger sauce. Although beautifully presented, the halibut was mushy and watery in the center. **Features:**
full bar, patio dining, Sunday brunch, happy hour. **Reservations:** suggested. **Address:** 1630 8th St 80401 **Location:** 1 mi e of jct US 6,
SR 58 and 93, exit s on Washington Ave, w on 8th St, then 1 mi to
end of street. [D]

INDULGE BISTRO & WINE BAR   303/277-9991 **97**

WWWW Mediterranean. Casual Dining. $10-$32 **AAA Inspector
Notes:** Menu items feature high-quality ingredients such as Harris
Ranch Black Angus beef, Polodori Italian sausage and sashimi-
grade ahi tuna. The rich, cheesy gnocchi Piedmontese—topped
with breaded chicken, shaved Parmesan and truffle oil—is a flavorful indulgence. The light, fluffy rum cake is not overpoweringly
sweet and highly recommended. The elegant, modern décor adds
a classy atmosphere to this casual eatery. **Features:** full bar, patio
dining, happy hour. **Address:** 1299 Washington Ave 80401 **Location:** Corner of 13th St and Washington Ave. **Parking:** street only.

[L] [D]

TABLE MOUNTAIN GRILL & CANTINA
303/216-8040 **99**

WWWW
**Southwestern
Casual Dining**
$8-$26

AAA Inspector Notes: *Historic.* Start
with a cup of the spicy green chile, then
try the smoky, slow-roasted chicken enchiladas. Other favorites include elk
burgers, shrimp tacos, and filet mignon
with ancho chile mole. The décor has a
Santa Fe flair, and the staff is prompt
and attentive. Take a short walk to arrive at the Coors Brewery.
Features: full bar, patio dining, Sunday brunch, happy hour. **Address:** 1310 Washington Ave 80401 **Location:** US 6 exit 19th
St, 0.5 mi n to Washington Ave, 0.5 mi w; downtown, just s of
arch; in Table Mountain Inn. **Parking:** on-site and street.

[B] [L] [D] [CALL] [&M]

TAFOLINO'S   303/232-5118 **100**

WW Mexican. Casual Dining. $7-$15 **AAA Inspector Notes:**
This family-owned restaurant focuses on quality, flavorful Mexican
dishes. Chips are homemade and seasoned. Popular entrees include
tamales, fajitas, burritos, soft tacos, enchiladas and rellenos. Those
who can't decide on one item should check out the list of combination plates. Creamy flan is the perfect ending to a meal. **Features:** full
bar. **Address:** 2001 Youngfield St 80401 **Location:** I-70 exit 264, 0.8
mi s. [L] [D]

WESTFALEN HOF   303/642-3180

WWW
**German
Casual Dining**
$14-$29

AAA Inspector Notes: Steins, plates
and pictures lend to the Bavarian look inside this place, where you'll explore the
traditional cuisines of Germany and
other regions in Europe. Choose from
dishes such as frikadellan, rindsroulade,
sauerbraten, stroganoff, spierogis and
goulash, or play it safer with a smattering of American or seafood
dishes. From the dining rooms, you can take in views of the foothills. **Features:** full bar, patio dining. **Reservations:** required.
Address: 32138 Hwy 72 80403 **Location:** 7 mi n on SR 93, 9.3
mi w; up Coal Creek Canyon. [D] [🅰️C]

WOODY'S WOOD FIRED PIZZA & WATERING HOLE
303/277-0443 **98**

WW American. Casual Dining. $9-$16 **AAA Inspector Notes:**
Woody's excels at cooking traditional and specialty pizzas in a wood-
burning oven. The lunch buffet allows you to sample basic and creative slices. Start by sharing some chicken wings with unique sauces
like "303-Colorado" whiskey barbecue and hot honey habanero, or
traditional buffalo sauce. Sandwiches include the "Mack Daddy" tuna
melt, blackened chicken and a build-your-own burger. Among the
specialty pizzas you'll find the "Whiskey King," topped with barbecue
sauce and pulled pork. **Features:** full bar, patio dining. **Address:**
1305 Washington St 80401 **Location:** US 6 exit 19th St, 0.5 mi n to
Washington Ave, then 0.5 mi w; downtown. [L] [D] [LATE]

GOLD HILL pop. 230

GOLD HILL INN   303/443-6461

WW American. Casual Dining. $28-$36 **AAA Inspector Notes:**
Historic. This family-owned restaurant, which is listed in the National
Register of Historic Places, has been in business since 1962. The
menu offers a three or six-course dinner that changes nightly. Entrees
include steak, duck, lamb, and swordfish. There is occasional live entertainment. **Features:** full bar. **Reservations:** suggested. **Address:**
401 Main St 80302 **Location:** US 36 (28th St), 1.3 mi w on Canyon
Ave, 0.3 mi n on 9th St, 6 mi w on Mapleton Ave and CR 52, then 4
mi on dirt road. [D] [🅰️C]

GRANADA (E-7) pop. 517, elev. 3,494'

Less than a half-mile south of US 50 in Granada
are the remains of a Japanese-American internment
camp. From August 1942 to October 1945 the
Granada Relocation Center housed more than
7,000 Japanese-Americans, removed by executive
order from the West Coast during World War II. A
couple of small monuments, a cemetery, building
foundations and roads are all that remain of the
camp. An information kiosk and walking trail with
picnic tables are onsite.

GRANBY (B-4) pop. 1,864, elev. 7,939'
• Hotels p. 202

Granby began as a railroad center serving cattle
ranching and lumbering industries; it is now home to
many dude ranches and golf courses. The town also
is the western gateway to the Arapaho National
Recreation Area (see place listing p. 42) and Rocky
Mountain National Park (see place listing p. 251).

Lake Granby, 6 miles north on US 34 within the recreation area, is an installation of the Colorado-Big Thompson project, which provides irrigation water for portions of northeastern Colorado; it's also a popular fishing spot. Granby lies at the junction of two portions of scenic highway: US 40 from Denver to Craig and US 34 north to Estes Park.

Greater Granby Area Chamber of Commerce: 475 E. Agate Ave., P.O. Box 35, Granby, CO 80446. **Phone:** (970) 887-2311 or (800) 325-1661.

C LAZY U RANCH   970/887-3344

[fyi] Not evaluated. **Address:** 3640 Colorado Hwy 125 80446 **Location:** 4 mi w on US 40, 3.5 mi n. Facilities, services, and décor characterize a mid-scale property. This luxury guest ranch features many amenities and activities, including a spring-fed pool, hot tub, sauna and indoor horseback riding arena.

DROWSY WATER GUEST RANCH   970/725-3456

[fyi] Not evaluated. **Address:** 1454 County Road 219 80446 **Location:** 3 mi w of jct US 40 and SR 34, 1.3 mi n (unpaved road in front of red chuck wagon). Facilities, services, and décor characterize a mid-scale property. Come to this historic dude and guest ranch for a true Colorado ranch vacation for couples, singles, families, groups and special events.

GRAND JUNCTION (D-1) pop. 58,566, elev. 4,597'

• Restaurants p. 204

Two junctions made Grand Junction what it is: that of the Grand—now called the Colorado—and Gunnison rivers, whose waters brought to life the fertile soils of the surrounding valley, and the linking of the railroads from Denver and Salt Lake City.

The surrounding Grand Valley, a major producer of cherries, peaches, grapes and a variety of other crops, is bordered on the east by the Grand Mesa, said to be the largest flat-topped mountain in the world, and the sandstone beauty of the Colorado National Monument on the west. There are more than 18 wineries in the Grand Junction area.

The Colorado Riverfront Trail System consists of a series of trails for biking or walking along the Colorado River; for more information contact the visitor and convention bureau. From US 50 south of the city, a road climbs eastward via a series of spectacular switchbacks to Lands End, the westernmost projection of Grand Mesa. From the summit much of western Colorado is visible.

The Grand Junction Symphony Orchestra offers a concert series August through May as well as a December Christmas program; phone (970) 243-6787. In addition, various performances are presented throughout the year by the Mesa State College Theater at the Moss Performing Arts Center, (970) 248-1604.

Grand Junction Visitor & Convention Bureau: 740 Horizon Dr., Grand Junction, CO 81506. **Phone:** (970) 244-1480 or (800) 962-2547.

ADVENTURE BOUND RIVER EXPEDITIONS picks up guests at the Grand Vista Hotel at 2790 Crossroads Blvd. Professional guides lead 1- and 2-day float trips and white-water rafting expeditions along the Colorado River. Rafters may elect to enjoy the scenery while the guides do all the paddling or use an inflatable kayak if they choose to participate. Longer trips also are available.

Hours: One-and 2-day trips depart several times weekly at 8 a.m., mid-May-Sept.; phone for schedule. **Cost:** One-day fare $95. Two-day fare $325; $250 (ages 0-15). **Phone:** (970) 245-5428 or (800) 423-4668.

THE ART CENTER: WESTERN COLORADO CENTER FOR THE ARTS, w. off I-70 Horizon Dr. exit to 7th St., then .7 mi. s. to 1803 N. 7th St., features a permanent collection of some 300 historic and contemporary works by Western artists, including Paul Pletka lithographs and more than 50 Navajo weavings from the early 1900s. Changing exhibits also are presented including oil, watercolor and pastel pieces as well as clay art. **Time:** Allow 30 minutes minimum. **Hours:** Mon.-Sat. 9-4. Closed major holidays. **Cost:** $3; free (Tues., and ages 0-11). **Phone:** (970) 243-7337.

▼ GEM **COLORADO NATIONAL MONUMENT—** see place listing p. 79.

CROSS ORCHARDS HISTORIC SITE, 3073 Patterson (F) Rd., is a turn-of-the-20th-century apple orchard providing interpretation of the early social and agricultural heritage of western Colorado. Guides in period clothing give tours of the orchard and farm buildings. Also on the grounds are the Uintah Narrow Gauge Railway exhibit, a collection of road-building and related equipment and an agricultural exhibit building.

Special events and workshops are held periodically. **Time:** Allow 1 hour minimum. **Hours:** Thurs.-Sat. 9-4, May-Oct. Phone ahead to confirm schedule. **Cost:** $5; $4 (ages 55+); $3.50 (ages 3-12); $15 (family). **Phone:** (970) 434-9814 or (970) 242-0971.

MUSEUM OF THE WEST AND STERLING T. SMITH EDUCATIONAL TOWER, 462 Ute Ave., presents regional history from prehistoric times to the present. Exhibits include Southwestern pottery, Old West artifacts and a collection of antique firearms. An 1890s schoolhouse and an interactive exhibit about uranium mining also are featured. The 75-foot-tall Sterling T. Smith Educational Tower offers panoramic views of the surrounding mountains and contains a working weather station.

Time: Allow 1 hour minimum. **Hours:** Tues.-Sat. 9-5, May-Sept.; Tues.-Sat. 10-3, rest of year. Closed major holidays. **Cost:** $6.50; $5.50 (ages 55+); $3.75 (ages 3-12); $20 (family rate). **Phone:** (970) 242-0971 or (888) 488-3466.

WESTERN COLORADO BOTANICAL GARDENS is at 641 Struthers Ave. A variety of native and tropical plants is featured in indoor and outdoor settings. The Butterfly House contains butterflies in various stages of development. Outdoor plantings include cacti, herbs, roses and native turf grasses. Orchids and water gardens are featured within the tropical greenhouse. A castle and moat are focal points in the children's garden.

Time: Allow 1 hour minimum. **Hours:** Wed.-Sun. 10-5. Phone ahead to confirm winter schedule. **Cost:** $5; $4 (students and 62+); $3 (ages 3-12). **Phone:** (970) 245-3288.

WINERIES

- **Two Rivers Winery** is 5.3 mi. w. on SR 340. **Hours:** Mon.-Sat. 10:30-6, Sun. noon-5. Tours available on request. **Phone:** (970) 255-1471 or (866) 312-9463. GT

AMERICAS BEST VALUE INN (970)245-1410

Motel
$60-$120

Address: 754 Horizon Dr 81506 **Location:** I-70 exit 31, just n. **Facility:** 97 units. 2 stories (no elevator), exterior corridors. **Pool(s):** heated outdoor. **Activities:** hot tub, playground. **Guest Services:** coin laundry.

CANDLEWOOD SUITES (970)255-8093

Extended Stay Hotel $89-$189 **Address:** 654 Market St 81505 **Location:** I-70 exit 28 (24 Rd), 1.3 mi s to F Rd, just e, then just n. Near Mesa Mall. **Facility:** 97 efficiencies. 4 stories, interior corridors. **Activities:** picnic facilities, exercise room. **Guest Services:** complimentary and valet laundry.

CLARION INN (970)243-6790

Hotel
$79-$109

Address: 755 Horizon Dr 81506 **Location:** I-70 exit 31, just n. **Facility:** 239 units. 2 stories (no elevator), interior/exterior corridors. **Terms:** check-in 4 pm. **Pool(s):** heated outdoor, heated indoor. **Activities:** hot tub, game room, exercise room. **Guest Services:** valet and coin laundry, area transportation.

COMFORT INN (970)245-3335

Hotel $79-$109 **Address:** 750 3/4 Horizon Dr 81506 **Location:** I-70 exit 31, just n. **Facility:** 57 units. 2 stories, interior corridors. **Pool(s):** heated indoor. **Activities:** hot tub, exercise room. **Guest Services:** valet and coin laundry.

Keep your focus safely

on the road when driving

COURTYARD BY MARRIOTT GRAND JUNCTION (970)263-4414

Hotel
$93-$172

 **AAA Benefit:** Members save 5% or more!

Address: 765 Horizon Dr 81506 **Location:** I-70 exit 31, 0.3 mi n. **Facility:** 136 units. 5 stories, interior corridors. **Pool(s):** heated indoor. **Activities:** hot tub, exercise room. **Guest Services:** valet and coin laundry, boarding pass kiosk, area transportation.

DAYS INN GRAND JUNCTION (970)243-4150

Motel
$69-$99

Address: 708 Horizon Dr 81506 **Location:** I-70 exit 31, 0.3 mi s. **Facility:** 80 units. 2 stories (no elevator), exterior corridors. **Terms:** 7 day cancellation notice. **Pool(s):** heated outdoor. **Activities:** hot tub. **Guest Services:** coin laundry, area transportation. **Featured Amenity:** breakfast buffet.

DOUBLETREE BY HILTON GRAND JUNCTION 970-241-8888

Hotel. Rates not provided. **Address:** 743 Horizon Dr 81506 **Location:** I-70 exit 31, just s. Near busy interstate. **Facility:** 273 units. 8 stories, interior corridors. **Dining:** Bistro 743, see separate listing. **Pool(s):** heated outdoor. **Activities:** hot tub, tennis, playground, lawn sports, exercise room. **Guest Services:** valet laundry, area transportation.

AAA Benefit: Members save 5% or more!

ECONO LODGE (970)257-1140

Hotel
$59-$69

Address: 751 Horizon Dr 81506 **Location:** I-70 exit 31, just n. Located behind gas station. **Facility:** 49 units. 2 stories (no elevator), interior corridors. **Terms:** check-in 4 pm.

FAIRFIELD INN & SUITES BY MARRIOTT GRAND JUNCTION DOWNTOWN/HISTORIC MAIN STREET (970)242-2525

Hotel $99-$199 **Address:** 225 Main St 81501 **Location:** At 2nd and Main sts. **Facility:** 70 units. 4 stories, interior corridors. **Parking:** on-site (fee). **Pool(s):** heated indoor. **Activities:** hot tub, exercise room. **Guest Services:** valet and coin laundry, area transportation.

AAA Benefit: Members save 5% or more!

HAMPTON INN DOWNTOWN GRAND JUNCTION
970/243-3222

WWW **Hotel.** Rates not provided. **Address:** 205 Main St 81501 **Location:** At 2nd and Main sts. **Facility:** 80 units. 3 stories, interior corridors. **Parking:** on-site (fee). **Pool(s):** heated outdoor. **Activities:** picnic facilities, exercise room. **Guest Services:** valet laundry, area transportation.

| **AAA Benefit:** Members save up to 10%! |

HOLIDAY INN & SUITES AIRPORT
970/424-5888

WWWW **Contemporary Hotel.** Rates not provided. **Address:** 2751 Crossroads Blvd 81506 **Location:** I-70 exit 31, 0.3 mi n, then 0.5 mi w. **Facility:** 119 units. 4 stories, interior corridors. **Terms:** check-in 4 pm. **Pool(s):** heated indoor. **Activities:** hot tub, exercise room. **Guest Services:** valet and coin laundry, area transportation.

HOLIDAY INN EXPRESS HOTEL & SUITES
970/245-8164

WWW **Hotel.** Rates not provided. **Address:** 625 Rae Lynn St 81505 **Location:** I-70 exit 28 (24 Rd), 1.1 mi s. Near Mesa Mall. **Facility:** 89 units. 4 stories, interior corridors. **Pool(s):** heated indoor. **Activities:** hot tub, exercise room. **Guest Services:** valet and coin laundry.

LA QUINTA INN & SUITES GRAND JUNCTION
(970)241-2929

WW **Hotel** $75-$247 **Address:** 2761 Crossroads Blvd 81506 **Location:** I-70 exit 31, 0.3 mi n, then 0.3 mi w. Next to busy interstate. **Facility:** 108 units. 5 stories, interior corridors. **Pool(s):** heated outdoor. **Activities:** hot tub, exercise room. **Guest Services:** valet and coin laundry, area transportation.

LOS ALTOS BED & BREAKFAST
970/256-0964

WWW **Bed & Breakfast** $125-$129 **Address:** 375 Hill View Dr 81507 **Location:** I-70 exit 28 (Redlands Pkwy), 3.4 mi s to SR 340 (Broadway Rd), 2 mi w to Ridges Blvd, 0.5 mi to Ridge Circle Dr, 0.8 mi to Ridge View Dr, then just sw. **Facility:** From the wraparound porch, this hilltop island in the sky affords spectacular views of the many mountains and natural wonders surrounding the property. Each room has a balcony or porch. 7 units, some kitchens. 2 stories (no elevator), interior/exterior corridors. **Terms:** check-in 4 pm, 2 night minimum stay - seasonal and/or weekends, 14 day cancellation notice-fee imposed. **Activities:** exercise room.

QUALITY INN OF GRAND JUNCTION
(970)245-7200

WWW **Hotel** $75-$159

Address: 733 Horizon Dr 81506 **Location:** I-70 exit 31, just s. **Facility:** 107 units. 3 stories, interior corridors. **Pool(s):** heated outdoor. **Activities:** exercise room. **Guest Services:** valet and coin laundry. **Featured Amenity:** breakfast buffet.

RESIDENCE INN BY MARRIOTT
(970)263-4004

WWW **Extended Stay Hotel** $98-$199

Residence Inn Marriott.

| **AAA Benefit:** Members save 5% or more! |

Address: 767 Horizon Dr 81506 **Location:** I-70 exit 31, 0.3 mi n. **Facility:** 104 units, some efficiencies and kitchens. 4 stories, interior corridors. **Pool(s):** heated indoor. **Activities:** hot tub, picnic facilities, exercise room. **Guest Services:** valet and coin laundry, area transportation. **Featured Amenity:** full hot breakfast.

SPRINGHILL SUITES BY MARRIOTT GRAND JUNCTION DOWNTOWN/HISTORIC MAIN STREET
(970)424-5777

WWW **Hotel** $102-$198 **Address:** 236 Main St 81501 **Location:** At 3rd and Main sts. **Facility:** 100 units. 5 stories, interior corridors. **Parking:** on-site (fee). **Pool(s):** heated indoor. **Activities:** hot tub, exercise room. **Guest Services:** valet and coin laundry, area transportation.

| **AAA Benefit:** Members save 5% or more! |

WHERE TO EAT

626 ON ROOD
970/257-7663

WWW **Seafood Steak. Fine Dining.** $6-$48 **AAA Inspector Notes:** Mediterranean- and Latin-influenced modern cuisine may be paired with interesting wine flights from around the world. Fresh seafood may include sashimi-grade short bill marlin or butter-poached lobster tail. Meats include grilled Berkshire pork loin, porter braised wagyu beef roast, and choice black angus steaks. Fresh, local and organic ingredients are used whenever possible. Stylish, modern décor accented with oil paintings creates a classy atmosphere. **Features:** full bar, patio dining, happy hour. **Reservations:** suggested. **Address:** 626 Rood Ave 81501 **Location:** Just e of Rood Ave and 6th St; downtown. **Parking:** street only. [L] [D]

BIN 707 FOODBAR
970/243-4543

WW **American. Casual Dining.** $10-$24 **AAA Inspector Notes:** On the ground floor of a bank building, this urban restaurant focuses on sophisticated food and casual service. Start your evening with cocktails and small plates or stay for a while enjoying craft beers or wine with a full dinner. Entrées are prepared with high-quality ingredients and include Skuna Bay salmon, duck, lamb, all-natural chicken and heirloom vegetables. Put the fried artichokes served with a creamy lemon and garlic aioli on your small plate list. **Features:** full bar, patio dining, happy hour. **Address:** 225 N 5th St, Suite 105 81501 **Location:** At Rood Ave and N 5th St; downtown. **Parking:** street only. [L] [D] CALL ⅏M

BISTRO 743
970/241-8888

WW **American. Casual Dining.** $6-$27 **AAA Inspector Notes:** This eatery serves steak and seafood dishes, pizzas, a variety of sandwiches and salads. A large patio offers beautiful views of the surrounding mountains. **Features:** full bar, patio dining, happy hour. **Address:** 743 Horizon Dr 81506 **Location:** I-70 exit 31, just s; in DoubleTree by Hilton Grand Junction. [B] [L] [D]

BLUE MOON BAR & GRILLE
970/242-4506

WW **American. Casual Dining.** $7-$27 **AAA Inspector Notes:** This popular eatery offers an eclectic menu with a variety of sandwiches, burgers, steaks and even some Greek favorites. For a bit of entertainment with your meal, start with the flaming-saganaki Greek cheese. **Features:** full bar. **Address:** 120 N 7th St 81501 **Location:** Corner of 7th and Main sts; downtown. **Parking:** street only. [L] [D]

DOS HOMBRES
970/242-8861

▼▼ Mexican. Casual Dining. $8-$16 **AAA Inspector Notes:** This restaurant features a relaxed, family-dining atmosphere and appealing surroundings. The menu offers authentic dishes such as fajitas, tamales, chicken tacos, chiles rellenos, fried ice cream and sopaipillas. **Features:** full bar, patio dining, Sunday brunch, happy hour. **Address:** 421 Brach Dr 81507 **Location:** 1 mi w on Grand Ave; 0.3 mi w of entrance to Colorado National Monument. [L] [D]

DREAM CAFE
970/424-5353

▼▼ American. Casual Dining. $6-$12 **AAA Inspector Notes:** This hip eatery offers a wide variety of light morning fare like specialty pancakes, delicious eggs Benedict and quiche of the day as well as colorful and thoughtfully prepared salads, yummy hot and cold sandwiches, and a small selection of pasta, all creatively presented. **Features:** full bar, patio dining. **Address:** 314 Main St 81501 **Location:** At 3rd and Main sts. **Parking:** street only. [B] [L]

EC'S ASIAN STATION
970/241-7219

▼▼ Chinese. Casual Dining. $8-$17 **AAA Inspector Notes:** Ignore the bland strip mall location and head right in for flavorful Chinese food. The salty, savory wonton soup comes with fresh vegetables. The menu features traditional fare, including teriyaki chicken, lo mein, sesame chicken and kung pao beef. Sushi options also are available. **Address:** 200 W Grand Ave 81501 **Location:** Just w of jct 1st St. [L] [D]

ENZO'S PIZZERIA & ITALIAN CAFE
970/255-8500

▼ Italian. Casual Dining. $9-$15 **AAA Inspector Notes:** Specialty pizzas are addictive at this popular eatery. Favorite appetizers include the asparagus wraps, antipasto plate and fried gouda mac and cheese poppers. Be prepared for a wait as some of the pasta selections are made from scratch. Traditional Italian desserts are prepared on site and go well with an espresso. **Features:** full bar, patio dining. **Address:** 759 Horizon Dr, Suite N 81506 **Location:** I-70 exit 31, 0.3 mi n; in strip mall. [L] [D]

IL BISTRO ITALIANO
970/243-8622

▼▼ Italian. Casual Dining. $10-$30 **AAA Inspector Notes:** Authentic Tuscan recipes served in a casual, bistro-style setting have made this eatery a local favorite for years. The "rosetta" — rosemary ham and provolone cheese rolled in house-made pasta, then baked and covered in a tomato cream sauce — is a standout dish. Other favorites include crispy, thin-crust pizzas and veal saltimbocca. End the evening with tiramisu or a homemade pie. **Features:** full bar, patio dining. **Address:** 400 Main St 81501 **Location:** Corner of 4th St. **Parking:** street only. [L] [D]

LE ROUGE RESTAURANT & PIANO BAR
970/257-1777

▼▼ French. Casual Dining. $20-$37 **AAA Inspector Notes:** An impressive variety of menu offerings is featured at this lovely eatery serving French-American cuisine. Some options include Burgundy onion soup, Montrachet goat cheese salad, crab cakes, rosemary New Zealand lamb chops and flavor-of-the-day creme brûlée. **Features:** full bar, patio dining. **Address:** 317 Main St 81501 **Location:** At 3rd and Main sts; downtown. **Parking:** street only. [D]

MAIN STREET BAGELS, ARTISAN BAKERY & CAFE
970/241-2740

▼ Sandwiches Coffee/Tea. Quick Serve. $6-$9 **AAA Inspector Notes:** This is a perfect stop for coffee, tea, a nutritional fruit smoothie, made-from-scratch bagels with traditional spreads or such bagel sandwiches as the Mesa melt, egg or Waldorf chicken salad. Two seasonal soups are made daily. The eatery also offers a nice selection of panini, signature sandwiches and colorful salads. The cozy outdoor patio and fountain are great for relaxation. **Features:** patio dining. **Address:** 559 Main St 81501 **Location:** At 6th and Main sts. **Parking:** street only. [B] [L]

NEPAL RESTAURANT
970/242-2233

▼▼ Nepali. Casual Dining. $10-$19 **AAA Inspector Notes:** The cozy eatery features authentic Indian and Nepali cuisine such as crispy lentil wafers, ample selections of traditional tandoor-baked flatbreads, a non-vegetarian sampler and a variety of chicken, lamb and seafood biryani and curry dishes. Typical Nepalese desserts include Indian-style ice cream, lal mohan, a type of donut ball with a sweet syrup, and khir, basmati rice cooked in milk with raisins and nuts. **Features:** beer & wine. **Address:** 356 Main St 81501 **Location:** Just e of S 4th and Main sts; downtown. **Parking:** street only. [L] [D]

PABLO'S PIZZA
970/255-8879

▼ Pizza. Quick Serve. $3-$27 **AAA Inspector Notes:** Locals flock to this restaurant for innovative pizzas, gourmet salads and calzones. For something different, try the Spudstacular, a pie with roasted potatoes, sour cream sauce, bacon and green onions. More traditional offerings include the Usual, a pepperoni, sausage and vegetable pizza. Of course, if you don't see something you like, you may opt to build your own gourmet pizza. **Features:** beer & wine. **Address:** 319 Main St 81501 **Location:** Between 3rd and 4th sts; in historic town center. **Parking:** street only. [L] [D]

SPOONS BISTRO & BAKERY
970/255-7237

▼ Breads/Pastries Sandwiches. Quick Serve. $6-$17 **AAA Inspector Notes:** Looking for a quick, healthy lunch? Stop in for sandwiches, Panini and pasta dishes featuring local ingredients. Sample items include a smoked turkey panini with bacon and guacamole, a ham and cheese croissant, and chicken Alfredo. Colorful, modern paintings enhance the décor. **Features:** Sunday brunch. **Address:** 3090 N 12th St 81506 **Location:** I-70 exit 31, 1 mi sw, then 0.5 mi s. [L] [D] CALL [M]

THE WINERY RESTAURANT
970/242-4100

▼▼▼ Seafood Steak. Fine Dining. $25-$66 **AAA Inspector Notes:** Tucked away in a beautifully landscaped breezeway, patrons appreciate the fresh seafood specialties and flavorful prime rib, steak, rack of lamb and elegant desserts. Rough woods, hand-made clay dishware, intimate lighting and stained glass create a comfortable ambience. Dinners include salad, potato or rice and seasonal vegetables. **Features:** full bar, patio dining, happy hour. **Reservations:** suggested. **Address:** 642 Main St 81501 **Location:** Just w of 7th and Main sts, down the breeze way; downtown. **Parking:** street only. [D]

W.W. PEPPERS RESTAURANT & BAR
970/245-9251

◆◆◆ American Casual Dining $9-$31 **AAA Inspector Notes:** Diners may experience a wait at night in the summer, as this is a very popular dining spot with an ideal location for those staying in the nearby hotels. One can enjoy a cocktail on the outdoor patio before entering the dining area featuring handsome woodwork and a very nice Southwestern art collection. While steaks are a specialty here, there is a full page of Southwestern cuisine. **Features:** full bar. **Address:** 753 Horizon Ct 81506 **Location:** I-70 exit 31, 0.3 mi n. [L] [D]

GRAND LAKE (B-4) pop. 471, elev. 8,437'

The resort community of Grand Lake owes its name, as well as its claim as one of the world's highest yacht clubs, to the lake nearby. One mile long and three-quarters of a mile wide, this deep, clear glacial lake is the largest natural body of water in the state. Mount Baldy, with its 12,007-foot-high peak, and the snowcapped Never Summer Range also are nearby.

Adjacent to the Arapaho National Recreation Area (see place listing p. 42), the town is the western gateway to Rocky Mountain National Park (see place listing p. 251). Traversing Trail Ridge Road, the highest continually paved road in the United States, it is just a 48-mile drive to Estes Park (see place listing p. 175), a resort community on the opposite side of the Continental Divide from Grand Lake. Activities popular in Grand Lake include boating, hiking, fishing, cross-country skiing, shopping, horseback riding and attending the Rocky Mountain Repertory Theatre.

Winter Carnival, held in early February, features bed sled races, human bowling, a snow sculpture contest and other events. The Grand Lake Regatta and Lipton Cup Races are held in mid-August.

(See map & index p. 178.)

Grand Lake Area Chamber of Commerce: 14700 SR 34, P.O. Box 429, Grand Lake, CO 80447. **Phone:** (970) 627-3402 or (800) 531-1019.

KAUFFMAN HOUSE MUSEUM, 407 Pitkin Ave., is a restored log hotel built in 1892. It houses a museum of early Grand Lake memorabilia which displays rotating special exhibits. **Hours:** Daily 11-5, Memorial Day weekend-Labor Day; Sat.-Sun. 11-5, day after Labor Day-Sept. 30; by appointment rest of year. **Cost:** $5; free (0-12). **Phone:** (970) 627-9644. GT

AMERICAS BEST VALUE INN BIGHORN LODGE
(970)627-8101 14

▼▼ Motel $70-$180 **Address:** 613 Grand Ave 80447 **Location:** 0.3 mi e to Grand Ave, then just e. **Facility:** 20 units. 2 stories (no elevator), exterior corridors. **Terms:** 7 day cancellation notice-fee imposed. **Activities:** hot tub.

GATEWAY INN   970/627-2400 15

▼▼ Hotel. Rates not provided. **Address:** 200 W Portal Rd 80447 **Location:** Jct US 34 and CR 278. **Facility:** 31 units. 3 stories, interior corridors. **Terms:** check-in 4 pm. **Activities:** sauna, hot tub, exercise room, massage.

SPIRIT LAKE LODGE   970/627-3344

fyi Not evaluated; management refused inspection. **Address:** 829 Grand Ave 80447 **Location:** 0.3 mi e to Grand Ave, then 0.4 mi e. Facilities, services, and décor characterize an economy property.

WHERE TO EAT

FAT CAT CAFE   970/627-0900 22

▼▼
American Casual Dining
$6-$10

AAA Inspector Notes: When leaving this bustling eatery, the owners want you to be as satisfied as a fat cat. Patrons don't mind waiting for the fresh eggs, thick slices of bacon, large English sausages and flavorful quiches. Don't leave without sampling one of the freshly baked pastries. The reasonable entrée portions and matching prices make it easy for you to end a meal with one of the small indulgences. Buffet available on Saturday and Sunday. **Address:** 916 Grand Ave 80447 **Location:** In historic town center. **Parking:** street only. *Menu on AAA.com*
B L

GRAND PIZZA   970/627-8390 25

▼▼ Pizza. Casual Dining. $7-$15 **AAA Inspector Notes:** This quaint eatery is known for its friendly staff and specialty pizzas. Many patrons begin their meals with one of the unusual salads, which can be served in an individual portion or in a family-style serving large enough for the table to share. Gluten and nut-free items are available. **Features:** beer & wine. **Address:** 1131 Grand Ave 80447 **Location:** In historic town center. **Parking:** street only.
L D

THE HISTORIC RAPIDS RESTAURANT
970/627-3707 23

▼▼▼
American Fine Dining
$10-$42

AAA Inspector Notes: *Historic.* This restaurant's log structure, built in 1903, was the first in town to have electricity and running water. The menu offers pasta, beef, fish, elk, lamb and chicken dishes, and the patio by the river is the perfect place to enjoy dessert. **Features:** full bar. **Reservations:** suggested, for dinner. **Address:** 210 Rapids Ln 80447 **Location:** South end of Grand Ave, just e. *Menu on AAA.com* L D

MIYAUCHI'S SNACK BAR   970/627-9319 27

◆ American. Quick Serve. $5-$8 **AAA Inspector Notes:** Nothing says summer like burgers and ice cream. You'll find both here at this outdoor food stand. Ice cream flavors range from plain vanilla bean to unique choices like cotton candy. Enjoy your ice cream while walking along the lake, or try to find a spot at one of the limited picnic tables. **Features:** patio dining. **Address:** 1029 Lake Ave 80447 **Location:** Between Pitkin and Hancock sts; next to marina. **Parking:** street only. L D

PANCHO & LEFTY'S   970/627-8773 26

▼▼ Tex-Mex. Casual Dining. $6-$25 **AAA Inspector Notes:** The highlight of this restaurant is the patio view overlooking the lake. The food is standard Tex-Mex, featuring enchiladas, chile rellenos, fajitas and burritos. In addition, there are bar-food options like jalapeño poppers, chicken tenders, fish and chips, and chicken wings. The bar becomes quite lively in the evenings. **Features:** full bar. **Address:** 1120 Grand Ave 80447 **Location:** Center. **Parking:** street only.
L D

SAGEBRUSH BBQ & GRILL   970/627-1404 24

▼▼
American
Casual Dining
$8-$26

AAA Inspector Notes: Formerly an 1800s jailhouse, this restaurant hangs artifacts from that era on its walls. Barbecue platters consist of pork ribs, smoked pork, beef brisket, buffalo or sausage and come with two sides. The extensive menu also includes steaks, game and seafood, as well as many traditional and Southwest-influenced breakfasts. A full-service bar is adjacent to the dining area. Gluten-free and vegetarian items are also available. **Features:** full bar. **Address:** 1101 Grand Ave 80447 **Location:** At Grand Ave and Pitkin St; downtown. **Parking:** street only. *Menu on AAA.com*
B L D

GRAND MESA—UNCOMPAHGRE—GUNNISON NATIONAL FORESTS (D-1)

Elevations in the forests range from 6,600 ft. at Dominguez Canyon in Uncompahgre National Forest to 14,309 ft. at Uncompahgre Peak, also in Uncompahgre National Forest. Refer to AAA maps for additional elevation information.

In west-central Colorado three separate national forests—Grand Mesa, Uncompahgre and Gunnison—form a multitude of scenic vistas, mountainous terrain and recreation opportunities. The three combined forests total 2,975,647 acres, including more than a half-million acres of state designated wilderness.

The Grand Mesa, one of the world's highest flattop mountains with an average elevation of 10,000 feet, is dotted with about 300 lakes and reservoirs. Crag Crest National Recreation Trail, a 10-mile circular trail, provides scenic views from an elevation of more than 11,000 feet.

The Grand Mesa Scenic and Historic Byway, a 55-mile trip between Cedaredge and the junction of I-70 and SR 65, crosses the Grand Mesa, climbing from the valley to its 11,000-foot crest. Along the way, opportunities exist for fishing, hiking and scenic views. The Powderhorn ski area offers a variety of terrains for snowmobiling, sledding and skiing. The forests are noted for outstanding deer and elk hunting.

The Uncompahgre comprises the Uncompahgre Plateau; a portion of the San Juan Mountains, with many peaks topping 13,000 feet; and the Un-compahgre, Mount Sneffels and Lizard Head state designated wilderness areas. The Uncompahgre is also the site of many old mining towns including Telluride ski resort.

The Gunnison includes 22 peaks of more than 13,000 feet in elevation as well as the Fossil Ridge, La Garita, Collegiate Peaks, Maroon Bells-Snowmass, Powderhorn, Raggeds and West Elk state designated wilderness areas. About 130 miles of the Continental Divide National Scenic Trail and 100 miles of the Colorado Trail wind through the forest. Skiing is available at the Crested Butte ski area.

For additional information contact the Forest Supervisor, Grand Mesa-Uncompahgre-Gunnison National Forests, 2250 US 50, Delta, CO 81416; phone (970) 874-6600. See Recreation Areas Chart.

TAYLOR RESERVOIR, 30 mi. n.e. of Gunnison at the foot of the Sawatch Range, is one of Colorado's largest lakes. The road to the reservoir follows the Taylor River through a 20-mile canyon where the walls reach up to 1,000 feet high. **Phone:** (970) 874-6600.

▽ GREAT SAND DUNES NATIONAL PARK AND PRESERVE (E-4)

Great Sand Dunes National Park and Preserve is 38 miles northeast of Alamosa via US 160 and SR 150. Too heavy to rise over the mountains with the winds that carry it northeastward across the flat, semiarid floor of the San Luis Valley, sand settles at the foot of the Sangre de Cristo Range. Deposits accumulating over the course of thousands of years have created a 30-square-mile, stark yet ever-changing sandscape that forms a vaguely eerie foreground for the rugged mountains.

Local legends maintain that wagon trains vanished among the dunes, some of which are 750 feet high, and that strange creatures inhabit the area's inner reaches.

Two self-guiding nature trails and camping and picnicking facilities are available. Naturalist-conducted walks and nightly amphitheater programs are held in summer. Sleds and sandboards designed for the dunes are available to rent. Visitor center exhibits depict the region's natural and cultural history.

Allow 1 hour minimum for the park. Park open daily 24 hours. Visitor center daily 8:30-6, Memorial Day weekend-Labor Day; hours vary rest of year. Closed Jan. 1, Thanksgiving, Martin Luther King Day and Christmas. Phone ahead to confirm schedule. Admission $3 per person; free (ages 0-15). Phone (719) 378-6399.

GREAT SAND DUNES LODGE   719/378-2900
▽ **Motel.** Rates not provided. **Address:** 7900 State Hwy 150 81146 **Location:** From Alamosa, 16 mi e on US 160, 16 mi n. Located in a quiet area. **Facility:** 14 units. 1 story, exterior corridors. **Pool(s):** heated indoor. **Activities:** picnic facilities.
[icons]

GREELEY (A-9) pop. 92,889, elev. 4,664'
• Hotels p. 208 • Restaurants p. 208

Greeley was founded by a group of visionaries who responded to New York publisher Horace Greeley's renowned exhortation, "Go West, young man!" Greeley's dream to establish an agricultural community in Colorado grew from his visit in 1859. Given power by his newspaper, the New York Tribune, and leadership by his agricultural editor, Nathan Meeker, the dream became a reality with the arrival of the first colonists in 1870.

The location, near the confluence of the Cache la Poudre and South Platte rivers, was well chosen. By 1875 the colony had constructed one of the first large irrigation systems in the territory, and hay and barley were waving in the fields not occupied by cattle. Cattle and crops remain agricultural mainstays.

Many of Greeley's cultural activities are hosted by the University of Northern Colorado and the city's Union Colony Civic Center. The century-old Greeley Philharmonic Orchestra continues to perform concerts throughout the year; phone (970) 356-6406. Featuring one of the largest outdoor rodeos in the nation, the ▽ Greeley Independence Stampede is held each year from late June to early July and includes—in addition to rodeos—a carnival, concerts, a parade and fireworks on the Fourth of July.

Visit Greeley: 902 7th Ave., Greeley, CO 80631-4603. **Phone:** (970) 352-3566 or (800) 449-3866.

CENTENNIAL VILLAGE MUSEUM, 1475 A St., is a living history museum that focuses on the western heritage of Northeastern Colorado, from 1860-1920. The 8-acre landscaped grounds feature more than 30 historic structures including a schoolhouse, blacksmith and print shops, a fire station and a homesteaders shack. Costumed guides lead visitors through various activities related to daily pioneer life including blacksmithing, candle dipping, and livestock care.

Time: Allow 2 hours minimum. **Hours:** Wed.-Sun. 10-5, late May-Oct. 31. Closed July 4. Phone ahead to confirm schedule. **Cost:** $8; $6 (ages 60+); $5 (ages 3-17); $18 (family). **Phone:** (970) 350-9220, or (970) 350-9223 tour information.

COLORADO MODEL RAILROAD AT THE GREELEY FREIGHT STATION is at 680 10th St. This model railroad museum is based on the Oregon, California and Eastern Railroad, a defunct logging railway. It features more than 22.5 scale miles of single track mainline, enhanced by mountain scenes and details such as lakes, bridges, tunnels, towns and miniature people. Visitors can also view railroad-related articles and explore a caboose. **Time:** Allow 45 minutes minimum. **Hours:** Wed.-Sat. 10-4, Sun. 1-4, Memorial Day-Labor Day; Fri.-Sat. 10-4, Sun. 1-4, rest of year. **Cost:** $8; $6 (ages 62+); $4 (ages 3-11). **Phone:** (970) 392-2934.

GREELEY HISTORY MUSEUM, 714 8th St., features permanent and changing exhibits in a renovated 1929 building. The Hazel E. Johnson Research Center contains historical documents and more than

30,000 photographs. Special events and programs are offered. **Time:** Allow 30 minutes minimum. **Hours:** Wed.-Sat. 10-4:30, Sun. noon-4:30. Closed major holidays. **Cost:** Free. Museum free. Hazel E. Johnson Research Center $5; $3 (ages 3-17 and 60+); $15 (family). **Phone:** (970) 350-9220.

COMFORT INN-GREELEY   (970)330-6380

Hotel
$99-$219

Address: 2467 W 29th St 80634 **Location:** US 34 Bypass exit 23rd Ave, just sw. **Facility:** 54 units. 3 stories, interior corridors. **Amenities:** safes. **Pool(s):** heated indoor. **Activities:** hot tub, exercise room. **Guest Services:** valet and coin laundry. **Featured Amenity: full hot breakfast.**

COUNTRY INN & SUITES BY CARLSON   (970)330-3404

Hotel
$99-$189

Address: 2501 W 29th St 80631 **Location:** US 34 Bypass exit 23rd Ave, just s, then w. **Facility:** 63 units. 3 stories, interior corridors. **Terms:** cancellation fee imposed. **Pool(s):** heated indoor. **Activities:** hot tub. **Guest Services:** valet and coin laundry.

FAIRFIELD INN & SUITES BY MARRIOTT   (970)339-5030

Hotel $120-$209 **Address:** 2401 W 29th St 80631 **Location:** US 34 Bypass exit 23rd Ave, just s, then just w. **Facility:** 60 units. 3 stories, interior corridors. **Pool(s):** heated indoor. **Activities:** hot tub, exercise room. **Guest Services:** valet and coin laundry.

AAA Benefit: Members save 5% or more!

GREELEY HAMPTON INN & SUITES   970/339-5525

Hotel. Rates not provided. **Address:** 2350 W 29th St 80631 **Location:** US 34 Bypass exit 23rd Ave, just s, then just w. **Facility:** 74 units. 3 stories, interior corridors. **Pool(s):** heated indoor. **Activities:** hot tub, exercise room. **Guest Services:** valet and coin laundry.

AAA Benefit: Members save up to 10%!

HOLIDAY INN EXPRESS   970/330-7495

Hotel. Rates not provided. **Address:** 2563 W 29th St 80631 **Location:** US 34 Bypass exit 23rd Ave, just s, then just w. **Facility:** 64 units. 3 stories, interior corridors. **Pool(s):** heated indoor. **Activities:** hot tub. **Guest Services:** valet and coin laundry.

Discover a wealth of savings and offers on the AAA/CAA travel websites

---

WHERE TO EAT

COYOTE'S SOUTHWESTERN GRILL   970/336-1725

Southwestern. Casual Dining. $10-$21 **AAA Inspector Notes:** The popular eatery prepares a selection of innovative Southwest-inspired foods, such as Southwestern crab rolls, steak poblano and tequila-lime chicken. The awesome coconut brownie with caramel is just one of the luscious, great-for-sharing desserts. **Features:** full bar. **Address:** 5250 W 9th St Dr 80634 **Location:** 0.5 mi w of 47th Ave on US 34 (10th St), just n on 52nd Ave, just w. L D

THE EGG & I   970/353-7737

Breakfast. Casual Dining. $8-$10 **AAA Inspector Notes:** This restaurant has earned the city newspaper's 'best breakfast in town' nod with creative dishes that emphasize quality. The colorful dining room evokes an inviting garden-like setting. **Features:** senior menu. **Address:** 3830 W 10th St 80634 **Location:** Jct 39th Ave and 10th St; in Market Square Shopping Center. B L

THE EGG & I   970/392-1191

Breakfast. Casual Dining. $7-$9 **AAA Inspector Notes:** This small chain specializes in hearty breakfasts that incorporate fresh ingredients. A to-go cup lets guests pick up freshly brewed coffee, including seasonal flavors. The lunch menu lists popular sandwiches, soups, varied juices and teas and numerous sides. **Features:** senior menu. **Address:** 2305 W 27th St, Unit 509A 80634 **Location:** US 34 Bypass exit 23rd Ave, just n, then just e; in Willow Station. B L CALL M

FAT ALBERT'S FOOD & DRINK   970/356-1999

American Casual Dining $9-$17

AAA Inspector Notes: The casual restaurant presents a wide selection of sandwiches, croissants, interesting salads, full dinners and mouthwatering desserts. Diners who are too late for the outdoor seating in summer might find an adequate substitute amid the plants and fresh flowers inside. **Features:** full bar, patio dining. **Address:** 1717 23rd Ave 80634 **Location:** At 17th St and 23rd Ave; in Cottonwood Square. *Menu on AAA.com* L D

RIO GRANDE MEXICAN RESTAURANT   970/304-9292

Mexican. Casual Dining. $6-$16 **AAA Inspector Notes:** Located in the historic downtown area, this casual eatery serves flavorful Mexican classics. Stop by the bar for steak empanadas or shrimp ceviche and their famous "Rio" margarita. The addition of avocado makes the tortilla soup a standout. Entrées include fajitas, chile rellenos, smothered burritos, open-face tacos and Texas-style enchiladas. **Features:** full bar, Sunday brunch, happy hour. **Address:** 825 9th St 80631 **Location:** Between 8th and 9th sts. **Parking:** street only. L D

SANTERAMO'S PIZZA HOUSE & ITALIAN FOOD

970/353-4844

Italian. Casual Dining. $6-$19 **AAA Inspector Notes:** This family-owned eatery is a local hot spot, with a menu that features made-to-order pizzas and calzones as well as a variety of standard pasta dishes. Although they serve tiramisu, the light and sweet toasted almond cream cake is a nice alternative. Friendly servers and attractive décor add to the experience. **Features:** beer & wine. **Address:** 1229 10th Ave 80631 **Location:** Between 12th and 13th sts; downtown. L D

GREENWOOD VILLAGE pop. 13,925, elev. 5,469'

- Hotels & Restaurants map & index p. 136
- Part of Denver area — see map p. 116

Once a rural community worlds away from urban Denver, Greenwood Village is now a prosperous Denver suburb with tree-lined roads, plenty of parks and recreation trails and a location convenient to the Denver Tech Center, known locally as DTC, a sprawling office park bordered by restaurants and bars. The Greenwood Village city limits also touch on popular Cherry Creek State Park *(see Recreation*

(See map & index p. 136.)

Areas Chart), which features more than 20 trails and an 880-acre reservoir.

BEST WESTERN PLUS DENVER TECH CENTER HOTEL
(303)792-9999 **90**

Hotel
$89-$199

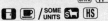

AAA Benefit: Save 10% or more every day and earn 10% bonus points!

Address: 9231 E Arapahoe Rd 80112 **Location:** I-25 exit 197 (Arapahoe Rd), just e. **Facility:** 149 units. 5 stories, interior corridors. **Pool(s):** heated outdoor. **Activities:** exercise room. **Guest Services:** valet and coin laundry, area transportation. **Featured Amenity:** full hot breakfast.

COURTYARD BY MARRIOTT-DENVER TECH CENTER
(303)721-0300 **89**

Hotel $71-$240 **Address:** 6565 S Boston St 80111 **Location:** I-25 exit 197 (Arapahoe Rd), e to Boston St, then e. **Facility:** 155 units. 3 stories, interior corridors. **Pool(s):** heated indoor. **Activities:** exercise room. **Guest Services:** valet and coin laundry, boarding pass kiosk, area transportation.

AAA Benefit: Members save 5% or more!

DOUBLETREE BY HILTON DENVER TECH CENTER
303/779-6161 **86**

Hotel. Rates not provided. **Address:** 7801 E Orchard Rd 80111 **Location:** I-25 exit 198, just w; 1 blk from Denver Tech Center. **Facility:** 305 units. 6 stories, interior/exterior corridors. **Pool(s):** heated outdoor, heated indoor. **Guest Services:** valet laundry, rental car service, area transportation.

AAA Benefit: Members save 5% or more!

HYATT HOUSE DENVER TECH CENTER
(303)706-1945 **91**

Extended Stay Hotel
$89-$259

AAA Benefit: Members save 10%!

Address: 9280 E Costilla Ave 80112 **Location:** I-25 exit 197 (Arapahoe Rd), e to Clinton St, then just s. **Facility:** 135 kitchen units, some two bedrooms. 3 stories, interior corridors. **Terms:** cancellation fee imposed. **Pool(s):** heated outdoor. **Activities:** hot tub, picnic facilities, exercise room. **Guest Services:** valet and coin laundry, area transportation. **Featured Amenity:** breakfast buffet.

AAA Vacations® packages ...

exciting itineraries and exclusive values

HYATT PLACE DENVER TECH CENTER
(303)804-0700 **85**

Contemporary Hotel
$99-$229

HYATT PLACE*

AAA Benefit: Members save 10%!

Address: 8300 E Crescent Pkwy 80111 **Location:** I-25 exit 199, 0.4 mi e to Crescent Pkwy, then just s. **Facility:** 126 units. 6 stories, interior corridors. **Terms:** cancellation fee imposed. **Amenities:** safes. **Pool(s):** heated indoor. **Activities:** exercise room. **Guest Services:** valet laundry, area transportation. **Featured Amenity:** breakfast buffet.

RESIDENCE INN BY MARRIOTT-DENVER TECH CENTER
(303)740-7177 **88**

Extended Stay Hotel $103-$238 **Address:** 6565 S Yosemite St 80111 **Location:** I-25 exit 197 (Arapahoe Rd), just w, then n. **Facility:** 128 kitchen units. 2 stories (no elevator), exterior corridors. **Terms:** check-in 4 pm. **Pool(s):** heated outdoor. **Activities:** picnic facilities, exercise room. **Guest Services:** valet and coin laundry, area transportation.

AAA Benefit: Members save 5% or more!

SHERATON DENVER TECH CENTER
303/799-6200 **92**

Hotel
Rates not provided

AAA Benefit: Members save up to 15%, plus Starwood Preferred Guest® benefits!

Address: 7007 S Clinton St 80112 **Location:** I-25 exit 197 (Arapahoe Rd), just e, then s. **Facility:** 263 units. 10 stories, interior corridors. **Pool(s):** heated outdoor. **Activities:** picnic facilities, exercise room. **Guest Services:** valet and coin laundry, rental car service, area transportation.

WINGATE BY WYNDHAM
(303)221-0383 **87**

Hotel $81-$189 **Address:** 8000 E Peakview Ave 80111 **Location:** I-25 exit 197 (Arapahoe Rd), 0.5 mi w to Greenwood Plaza Blvd, then just n. **Facility:** 86 units. 3 stories, interior corridors. **Terms:** check-in 4 pm, cancellation fee imposed. **Amenities:** safes. **Pool(s):** heated indoor. **Activities:** hot tub, exercise room. **Guest Services:** valet and coin laundry, area transportation.

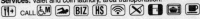

WHERE TO EAT

BARA SUSHI & GRILL
303/221-8880 **131**

Sushi. Casual Dining. $9-$25 **AAA Inspector Notes:** The eatery specializes in decorative rolls, grilled meat and seafood, which patrons enjoy at the sushi bar or in the dining area. Those traveling with children will be pleased with the kid's plate, a smaller version of a bento box. The elegant décor and attentive servers enhance the dining experience. **Features:** full bar. **Address:** 8000 E Belleview Ave, Suite D-50 80111 **Location:** I-25 exit 199, just e; in strip mall.

L D

(See map & index p. 136.)

BROOK'S STEAK HOUSE & CELLAR   303/770-1177   (139)

Steak. Fine Dining. $28-$64 **AAA Inspector Notes:** This popular purveyor of beef offers old world décor accented with polished dark wood and shiny brass. A lounge sits above the large dining room. Dog portraits along one wall are an amusing incongruity. Like other local beef palaces, big food translates into big prices. **Features:** full bar, happy hour. **Reservations:** suggested. **Address:** 6538 S Yosemite Cir 80111 **Location:** I-25 exit 197 (Arapahoe Rd), just w, just n on S Yosemite St to S Yosemite Cir, then just e. D

BROTHER'S BBQ   303/799-9777   (142)

Barbecue. Quick Serve. $8-$19 **AAA Inspector Notes:** The popular barbecue eatery presents a menu that includes Kansas City-style beef brisket, Memphis-style pork shoulder and St. Louis-style pork spare ribs. Among other offerings are the usual sides of slaw, beans and potato salad as well as chicken, hot links, sandwiches and family platters. This place is great for guests of nearby hotels, as it delivers. Car license plates, road signs and sports memorabilia accent the colorful décor. **Features:** full bar, patio dining. **Address:** 9069 E Arapahoe Rd 80112 **Location:** I-25 exit 197 (Arapahoe Rd), just e to Boston St, just n to Southech Dr, then just w to frontage road. L D CALL ✆M

CHIANTI RISTORANTE & WINE BAR   303/796-0611   (132)

Italian. Casual Dining. $12-$16 **AAA Inspector Notes:** This cozy eatery offers an extensive menu of authentic Italian cuisine. Even if you don't like veal, the saltimbocca alla Romana is a must-try. The decadent, buttery Pinot Grigio wine sauce complements the salty Parma prosciutto, creamy fontina and savory sage atop the veal. Another standout is the rich and creamy fettuccine Alfredo. It's the best I've ever tasted. Bonus points if you can guess the secret ingredient. **Features:** full bar. **Address:** 5121 S Yosemite St 80111 **Location:** I-25 exit 199, 0.8 mi e, then just s. L D

COOL RIVER CAFE   303/771-4117   (133)

Steak
Seafood
Fine Dining
$12-$45

AAA Inspector Notes: This popular, upscale steakhouse features Angus beef steak, fresh seafood and poultry. An extensive selection of wine and spirits is available, and live bands play Friday and Saturday nights. **Features:** full bar, happy hour. **Reservations:** suggested. **Address:** 8000 E Belleview Ave, Suite C-10 80111 **Location:** I-25 exit 199, just e. **Parking:** on-site and valet. L D

Steak, seafood, Southwestern fare, world-class bar

DEL FRISCO'S DOUBLE EAGLE STEAK HOUSE   303/796-0100   (138)

Steak. Fine Dining. $14-$89 **AAA Inspector Notes:** This restaurant continues to win awards for its flavorful steaks. The menu also features fresh seafood, veal and lamb. After dinner, guests can relax by the fire in the beautiful cigar lounge, which features nightly live entertainment. **Features:** full bar. **Reservations:** suggested. **Address:** 8100 E Orchard Rd 80111 **Location:** I-25 exit 198, just e, then just s on South Willow Dr. **Parking:** on-site and valet. L D

GARBANZO MEDITERRANEAN GRILL   303/694-7777   (140)

Mediterranean. Quick Serve. $6-$10 **AAA Inspector Notes:** The fresh-baked puffy pitas alone are worth the visit to this popular eatery. The menu features raw, unprocessed, high-quality Middle Eastern options such as hummus, chicken shwarma, beef shwarma, falafel and a variety of salads. Baklava is a must for dessert. The modern décor encourages diners to eat in, yet, many people opt to take their meals to go. **Address:** 8547 E Arapahoe Rd 80112 **Location:** I-25 exit 197 (Arapahoe Rd), just w, then just n; in Arapahoe Marketplace Shopping Center. L D

GUNTHER TOODY'S DINER   303/799-1958   (143)

American. Casual Dining. $8-$13 **AAA Inspector Notes:** This fun 1950s-style family-oriented diner offers salads, burgers, sandwiches, fries, blue-plate specials, shakes and malts. The décor is clean, bright and infused with energy and golden oldies music. A 1956 Corvette hangs above the bar. **Features:** full bar. **Address:** 9220 E Arapahoe Rd 80112 **Location:** I-25 exit 197 (Arapahoe Rd), just e, then s on Clinton St. B L D

JING   303/779-6888   (134)

Asian. Fine Dining. $13-$35 **AAA Inspector Notes:** The calamari here is the perfect texture, not chewy at all with a lighter-style batter. The hoisen-plum sauce that comes with it has a light sweetness, but they serve other dipping sauces with a variety of gorgeous flavors from wasabi to a sweet and sour. Another small plate that is consistently delicious is the ahi Napoleon—a mix of chopped, raw ahi tuna and avocado tiered between layers of deep-fried wonton squares. **Features:** full bar. **Address:** 5370 Greenwood Plaza Blvd 80111 **Location:** I-25 exit 199, just w, just s on Quebec St, just e on Berry Ave, then just n; in strip mall. **Parking:** on-site and valet. L D

LARKBURGER   303/779-0093   (130)

Burgers. Quick Serve. $7-$10 **AAA Inspector Notes:** This story began when chef Thomas Salamunovich put his gourmet Larkburger on the menu at Larkspur, his fine dining restaurant in Vail. The burger became so popular Salamunovich created a fast-food restaurant around it; now it's a small chain. The juicy, all-natural Angus beef and turkey burgers are heavenly. Fries seasoned with Parmesan and truffle oil are the perfect accompaniment. The creamy $5 shakes are made with local ice cream. Reclaimed wood panels complement the modern décor. **Features:** beer only, patio dining. **Address:** 8000 E Belleview Ave, Suite B45 80111 **Location:** I-25 exit 199, just e. L D

PAPPADEAUX SEAFOOD KITCHEN   303/740-9449

Cajun Seafood. Casual Dining. $12-$53 **AAA Inspector Notes:** A seafood lover's delight, the restaurant taps into a little bit of New Orleans with its Cajun dishes and elaborate menu selections. Patrons might start off with a creative choice of blackened oyster and shrimp fondeaux with crayfish and let the feast begin. While music plays in the background, patrons can dig into dirty rice or spicy gumbo loaded with seafood. Well-seasoned shrimp and fish are prepared in varied ways. **Features:** full bar, patio dining, Sunday brunch, happy hour. **Address:** 7520 E Progress Pl 80111 **Location:** I-25 exit 199, just w to Quebec St, just s to Progress Pl, then just e. L D CALL ✆M

SAHARA AUTHENTIC MOROCCAN & LEBANESE RESTAURANT   303/790-4707   (144)

Middle Eastern. Casual Dining. $9-$19 **AAA Inspector Notes:** Expect classic preparations of hummus, baba ghanoush, falafel and shawarma. Seasoned with Mediterranean spices, the rotisserie and grilled lamb, chicken and beef arrive tender and juicy. You can also select from various vegetarian options. **Features:** full bar. **Address:** 9636 E Arapahoe Rd 80112 **Location:** I-25 exit 197 (Arapahoe Rd), 0.3 mi e; in strip mall. L D

SAZZA   303/797 2992   (136)

Pizza. Quick Serve. $6-$15 **AAA Inspector Notes:** Looking for a quick, healthy meal? This is the place. Expect all-natural ingredients with a focus on organic and locally grown ingredients. The pizzas feature an incredibly thin crust and a light layer of cheese, making the ingredients pop. **Features:** beer only. **Address:** 2500 E Orchard Rd 80121 **Location:** Just e of jct University Blvd. L D

VENICE RISTORANTE ITALIANO   720/482-9191   (137)

Italian. Casual Dining. $12-$31 **AAA Inspector Notes:** The degree of Italian charm is somewhat surprising in this strip-mall location. Authentic music, fresco-painted walls and dim lighting envelop patrons in soothing comfort. The expert waitstaff serves artistic, well-seasoned food. **Features:** full bar. **Reservations:** suggested, weekends. **Address:** 5946 S Holly St 80111 **Location:** I-25 exit 198, 1.5 mi n, then just s; in Orchards strip mall. L D

(See map & index p. 136.)

YANNI'S GREEK RESTAURANT   303/692-0404   135

 Greek. Casual Dining. $11-$30 **AAA Inspector Notes:** This local favorite, now located at the Landmark Theatre shopping complex, is cheerfully decorated with artful photos of life in Greece. The menu offers traditional favorites such as dolmades, kalamaria, spanakopita, tzatziki, gyro, moussaka and baklava. **Features:** full bar. **Reservations:** suggested. **Address:** 5425 S Landmark Pl, D109 80111 **Location:** I-25 exit 199, just w, just s on Quebec St, just e on Berry Ave, then just n. L D

GUNNISON (D-3) pop. 5,854, elev. 7,681'

In the broad, fertile valley of the Gunnison River, Gunnison was settled in 1874; the town was founded in 1880 as a mining supply camp. Operating as a trade center for the area's ranching operations as well as home to Western State College, Gunnison serves as a gateway to the Gunnison National Forest *(see Grand Mesa-Uncompahgre-Gunnison National Forests p. 206)* and the Curecanti National Recreation Area *(see place listing p. 112)*.

Summer activities include fishing, horseback riding, camping, mountain biking, kayaking, rafting and boating. Winter offers hockey, snowmobiling, skating, snowshoeing and cross-country skiing. The Gunnison Arts Center features cultural events such as music productions, art exhibits and classes, and theatrical performances; (970) 641-4029.

Gunnison Country Chamber of Commerce and Visitor Center: 500 E. Tomichi Ave., P.O. Box 36, Gunnison, CO 81230. **Phone:** (970) 641-1501 or (800) 274-7580.

GUNNISON PIONEER MUSEUM, jct. S. Adams St. and Tomichi Ave., occupies 26 buildings, including two restored schoolhouses and an 1876 post office. A car barn holds more than 80 antique vehicles; another building houses antique ranch wagons and buggies, a milk wagon, a horse-drawn hearse, a taxi and an antique oxcart. Another building is devoted to military history. Displays of cowboy paraphernalia; antique print shop, carpenter shop and blacksmith shop artifacts; and a collection of taxidermy also are on display.

A narrow-gauge railroad engine and 1881 rail cars are on the grounds. Dolls, china, minerals, arrowheads, photographic equipment and historic clothing are among other items displayed. **Time:** Allow 1 hour minimum. **Hours:** Daily 9-5, mid-May through Sept. 30. **Cost:** $10; $3 (ages 6-12). Cash only. **Phone:** (970) 641-4530.

ALPINE INN   (970)641-2804

 **Hotel** $65-$180 **Address:** 1011 W Rio Grande Rd 81230 **Location:** 0.5 mi w of center, 0.5 mi s; at US 50 and Rio Grande Ave. **Facility:** 36 units. 2 stories (no elevator), interior corridors. **Terms:** cancellation fee imposed. **Pool(s):** heated indoor. **Activities:** hot tub.

ECONO LODGE GUNNISON/CRESTED BUTTE   (970)641-3068

 **Hotel** $79-$119 **Address:** 411 E Tomichi Ave 81230 **Location:** On US 50, 0.3 mi e of center. **Facility:** 52 units. 2 stories (no elevator), interior corridors. **Activities:** hot tub. **Guest Services:** area transportation.

HOLIDAY INN EXPRESS HOTEL & SUITES   (970)641-1288

Hotel
$109-$189

Address: 910 E Tomichi Ave 81230 **Location:** On US 50, 0.5 mi e of center. **Facility:** 107 units. 3 stories, interior corridors. **Terms:** cancellation fee imposed. **Pool(s):** heated indoor. **Activities:** hot tub, picnic facilities, exercise room. **Guest Services:** valet and coin laundry. **Featured Amenity:** full hot breakfast.

THE INN AT TOMICHI VILLAGE   970/641-1131

Motel. Rates not provided. **Address:** 41883 US Hwy 50 E 81230 **Location:** 2 mi e of center. **Facility:** 50 units. 2 stories (no elevator), exterior corridors. **Pool(s):** heated indoor. **Activities:** hot tub, picnic facilities, exercise room. **Guest Services:** coin laundry.

RODEWAY INN   (970)641-0500

Motel $65-$129 **Address:** 37760 W Hwy 50 81230 **Location:** 0.5 mi w of center, 2 mi sw. **Facility:** 38 units. 1 story, exterior corridors. **Activities:** hot tub, picnic facilities. **Guest Services:** coin laundry.

WHERE TO EAT

EL PARAISO FAMILY MEXICAN RESTAURANT   970/641-4957

Mexican. Casual Dining. $8-$17 **AAA Inspector Notes:** Enjoy your favorite Mexican dish in a festive atmosphere. Start with a cup of chicken tortilla soup, served with avocado slices and crunchy tortilla strips. Entrées include cheesy, fried chile rellenos, smothered chicken enchiladas, and seafood chimichangas. **Features:** full bar. **Address:** 112 S Main St 81230 **Location:** Just e of US 50 and Main St; downtown. **Parking:** street only. L D

GARLIC MIKE'S ITALIAN CUISINE   970/641-2493

Italian. Casual Dining. $14-$28 **AAA Inspector Notes:** This locally popular restaurant has menu offerings such as small or bigger salads; three soup choices; fried green tomatoes; traditional steak, veal, seafood and chicken dishes; thin-crust pizza, and tasty desserts that are meant to be shared. The fireplace and open kitchen add to the comfortable log cabin atmosphere. Dining on the deck with its view of the Gunnison River through the willows is offered in the summer. **Features:** full bar, patio dining. **Reservations:** suggested. **Address:** 2674 Hwy 135 81230 **Location:** 3 mi n of center. D

GUNNISACK COWBOY BISTRO   970/641-5445

Southwestern. Casual Dining. $9-$19 **AAA Inspector Notes:** Offering a large vegetarian menu and an array of appetizers, sandwiches and entrées, favorites include their signature jalapeño beer cheese soup and an award-winning chicken-fried rib-eye. Granny's recipe for the chicken pot pie and apple and cherry baked cobblers are the real deal. **Features:** full bar. **Address:** 142 N Main St 81230 **Location:** Just n of US 50 and Main St. **Parking:** street only. L D

MARIO'S PIZZA & PASTA 970/641-1374

▼▼▼ Italian. Casual Dining. $9-$14 **AAA Inspector Notes:** Nothing says comfort like this cozy eatery's savory, cheesy, nine-layer lasagna. Local favorites include the Philly cheesesteak sandwich, "Juicy Lucy" burger, and, of course, the pizzas. **Features:** beer & wine. **Address:** 213 W Tomichi Ave 81230 **Location:** Just w of jct Main St. **Parking:** street only. [L] [D] [Ⓐ]

MOCHA'S COFFEEHOUSE 970/641-2006

▼ Coffee/Tea. Quick Serve. $3-$7 **AAA Inspector Notes:** This inviting coffeehouse serves sweet-and-tangy smoothies made with real fruit, bagel sandwiches, cookies with giant chocolate chunks and, of course, a variety of specialty coffee drinks. It's the perfect spot to hang out with a cup of java or grab a quick bite to go. **Address:** 710 N Main St 81230 **Location:** Jct US 50, 0.5 mi n; in strip mall. [B] [L] [D]

OL' MINER STEAKHOUSE 970/641-5153

▼▼ Steak. Casual Dining. $8-$29 **AAA Inspector Notes:** Most entrée selections start with the salad bar and feature USDA Choice steaks with clever names such as silver cup mine steak, blistered horn flat iron and gold cup mine bone-in rib-eye. Other choices include the "roaring Judy" wild salmon, El Capitan Mine tuna steak and a half or full slab of Robert E. Lee Mine pork ribs. **Features:** full bar. **Address:** 139 N Main St 81230 **Location:** Just n on Main St. **Parking:** street only. [B] [L] [D]

SHERPA CAFE 970/641-7480

▼▼ Nepali. Casual Dining. $10-$15 **AAA Inspector Notes:** The owner of this popular eatery grew up in Nepal and also leads expeditions through the Himalayan mountains. The menu features an extensive range of Nepalese and Indian favorites, including samosas, steamed dumplings, curry, tikka masala and saag paneer. **Features:** wine only. **Address:** 323 E Tomichi Ave 81230 **Location:** Jct Colorado St. [L] [D] CALL [♿M]

TWISTED FORK 970/641-1488

▼▼ American. Casual Dining. $13-$17 **AAA Inspector Notes:** Cuisine and cocktails with an Asian twist are what you can expect at this cute, cozy eatery. Among the plentiful assortment of small plates, snacks, noodle bowls and specialty items you'll find slow-roasted spare ribs served with wasabi mashers and fried Brussels sprouts, lettuce wraps, braised pork sliders, noodle stir-fry, Vietnamese tacos and Kobe beef burgers. Creative, delicious desserts vary with the seasons. Gluten-free items are available. **Features:** full bar. **Address:** 206 N Main St 81230 **Location:** Just n of US 50 and Main St. **Parking:** street only. [D]

HESPERUS

BLUE LAKE RANCH (970)385-4537

▼▼▼▼ Classic Bed & Breakfast $179-$469 **Address:** 16919 Hwy 140 81326 **Location:** Jct US 160 and SR 140, 6.4 mi s. **Facility:** Situated on 90 acres, the grounds of this remarkable property feature a mixture of natural flora and formal landscaping. 16 units, some two bedrooms, efficiencies, kitchens, houses, cabins and cottages. 2-3 stories (no elevator), interior/exterior corridors. **Terms:** 2 night minimum stay - seasonal and/or weekends, 30 day cancellation notice-fee imposed. **Activities:** fishing, trails. **Guest Services:** valet laundry.

[BIZ] [HS] [🛜] [✕] [🛏] [▣] [▣] / SOME UNITS [⊘]

WHERE TO EAT

KENNEBEC CAFE 970/247-5674

▼▼▼▼ Mediterranean. Casual Dining. $12-$36 **AAA Inspector Notes:** The ever-changing seasonal menu may feature fried artichokes, crab cake salad, rib-eye steak, chicken pot pie with shiitake mushrooms, lamb chops, and made-fresh-daily desserts, such as a chocolate custard or tiramisu. An extensive wine list is sure to please. The spectacular mountain views from inside, and on the outdoor courtyard patio, are delightful. **Features:** full bar, patio dining, Sunday brunch, happy hour. **Reservations:** suggested. **Address:** 4 CR 124 81326 **Location:** 10 mi w on US 160 (north side). [L] [D] [🛏]

HIGHLANDS RANCH

• Part of Denver area — see map p. 116

COMFORT SUITES HIGHLAND RANCH DENVER TECH CENTER AREA (303)770-5400

▼▼▼
Hotel
$79-$219

Address: 7060 E County Line Rd 80126 **Location:** SR 470 exit Quebec St, just n to County Line Rd, just w, then just s; at Quebec Highlands Center. **Facility:** 73 units. 4 stories, interior corridors. **Terms:** cancellation fee imposed. **Amenities:** safes. **Activities:** hot tub, exercise room. **Guest Services:** valet and coin laundry. **Featured Amenity:** full hot breakfast.

[SAVE] [🍽️+] CALL [♿M] [BIZ] [🛜] [✕] [🐾] [🛏] [▣] [▣] / SOME UNITS [🔊] [HS]

FAIRFIELD INN & SUITES BY MARRIOTT DENVER TECH SOUTH (303)290-6700

▼▼▼ Hotel $78-$207 **Address:** 7056 E County Line Rd 80126 **Location:** SR 470 exit Quebec St, just n to County Line Rd, just w, then just s; at Quebec Highlands Center. **Facility:** 61 units. 3 stories, interior corridors. **Pool(s):** heated indoor. **Activities:** hot tub, exercise room. **Guest Services:** valet and coin laundry.

AAA Benefit: Members save 5% or more!

[🍽️+] CALL [♿M] [🏊] [BIZ] [🛜] [✕] [▣] / SOME UNITS [🛏] [▣]

HILTON GARDEN INN DENVER/HIGHLANDS RANCH 303/683-4100

▼▼▼ Hotel. Rates not provided. **Address:** 1050 Plaza Dr 80126 **Location:** SR 470 exit Lucent Blvd, just s to Plaza Dr, then 0.4 mi e. **Facility:** 128 units. 5 stories, interior corridors. **Pool(s):** heated indoor. **Activities:** hot tub, exercise room. **Guest Services:** valet and coin laundry, area transportation.

AAA Benefit: Members save up to 10%!

[🍽️] [🍸] [🏊] [BIZ] [HS] [🛜] [✕] [🛏] [▣] [▣]

RESIDENCE INN BY MARRIOTT DENVER HIGHLANDS RANCH (303)683-5500

▼▼▼ Extended Stay Hotel $115-$263 **Address:** 93 W Centennial Blvd 80126 **Location:** SR 470 exit Broadway, just s, then w. **Facility:** 117 units, some two bedrooms, efficiencies and kitchens. 4 stories, interior corridors. **Amenities:** video games. **Pool(s):** heated outdoor. **Activities:** exercise room. **Guest Services:** valet and coin laundry, area transportation.

AAA Benefit: Members save 5% or more!

[🍽️+] CALL [♿M] [🏊] [BIZ] [🛜] [✕] [🐾] [🛏] [▣] [▣] / SOME UNITS [🔊]

WHERE TO EAT

LODO'S BAR AND GRILL 303/346-2930

▼▼ American. Casual Dining. $10-$22 **AAA Inspector Notes:** This hopping local sports bar is best known for its rooftop patio. The 2,500-square-foot terrace offers panoramic views of the front range. Live music is often offered under the Colorado blue sky while you dine. **Features:** full bar, happy hour. **Address:** 8545 S Quebec St 80126 **Location:** SR 470 exit Quebec St, just s, then w. [L] [D] [LATE] CALL [♿M]

Stay connected with #AAA

and #CAA on your favorite

social media sites

OLD BLINKING LIGHT KITCHEN & COCKTAILS   303/346-9797

▼▼ ▼▼ Southwestern. Casual Dining. $12-$29 **AAA Inspector Notes:** The eclectic menu features unique dishes served in large portions. Appetizers include mahi mahi ceviche, chicken queso nachos and New Mexican-style mussels. Entrées range from burgers to duck confit. The modern, Southwest-inspired décor creates an attractive, but casual atmosphere. Staff members exhibit knowledge of the menu and are a great help when ordering. **Features:** full bar, patio dining, happy hour. **Address:** 9344 Dorchester St 80129 **Location:** SR 470 exit Lucent Blvd, 0.5 mi s, 0.6 mi e on Town Center Dr, then just s; in strip mall. L D

HOT SULPHUR SPRINGS (B-3) pop. 663, elev. 7,680'

HOT SULPHUR SPRINGS RESORT AND SPA, off US 40 and across the Colorado River, following signs to 5609 CR 20, offers 24 terraced natural hot springs pools. These mineral waters, used since the days of the Ute Indians, have temperatures of 98 to 112 degrees Fahrenheit. The resort contains 19 outdoor pools and four indoor cave pools; included are a summer swimming pool, four children's pools and a full spa.

Time: Allow 3 hours minimum. **Hours:** Daily 8 a.m.-10 p.m. **Cost:** Outdoor pools $18.50; $11.50 (ages 3-11). Indoor private pools $16 per hour, per person. **Phone:** (970) 725-3306 or (800) 510-6235.

PIONEER VILLAGE MUSEUM, .2 mi. e. on US 40 at CR 55, is in a 1924 schoolhouse. Exhibits about the skiing industry, pioneer families, transportation development and the Windy Gap archeological site are presented. Other exhibits highlight the history and construction of a P.O.W. camp and the Moffat Tunnel, a railroad tunnel running through James Peak. Restored buildings on the grounds include a ranch house, a blacksmith shop, a schoolhouse, a courthouse and a jail. **Hours:** Tues.-Sat. 10-5. **Cost:** $5; $4 (ages 60+); $3 (ages 6-18). **Phone:** (970) 725-3939.

CANYON MOTEL   (970)725-3395

▼ Motel $59-$139 **Address:** 221 Byers Ave 80451 **Location:** On US 40, center. **Facility:** 14 units, some efficiencies. 1 story, exterior corridors. **Terms:** cancellation fee imposed.

[icons] / SOME UNITS

HOVENWEEP NATIONAL MONUMENT (F-1)

Hovenweep National Monument lies in both Colorado and Utah and can be reached from either state. There are two Colorado entrances to the monument. One is the Pleasant View turnoff 18 miles north of Cortez on US 491; the other is the McElmo Canyon Road accessible south of Cortez on US 160.

The Utah approach begins by turning off US 191 onto SR 262 midway between the towns of Blanding and Bluff. Go 14 miles to Hatch Trading Post and continue 16 miles to the Square Tower unit and visitor center.

The name Hovenweep, a Ute Indian word meaning "deserted valley," seems well-suited for the remote mesas and canyons north of the San Juan River. The presence of many standing, structured and tumbled piles of masonry—the remains of many-roomed pueblos, small cliff dwellings and towers—and scattered refuse over canyon slopes tells the story of the sizable population that once lived in this now desolate country.

The early inhabitants of Hovenweep were part of the large group of Ancestral Pueblo Indians who once occupied the Four Corners region of Utah, Colorado, Arizona and New Mexico. For centuries they lived in small villages as peaceful and secure farmers, hunters and gatherers.

Extended droughts in the 12th and 13th centuries gradually reduced their resources. Erosion, failing crops, diminishing water supplies, and perhaps warfare forced the people to abandon their homes by A.D. 1300 and move south and east, never to return.

The Hovenweep National Monument consists of six separate prehistoric village sites: In Utah there are Square Tower, the best preserved and most impressive, and Cajon. Colorado sites include Holly, Hackberry Canyon, Cutthroat Castle and Horseshoe. These landmarks are all noted for their square, oval, circular and D-shaped towers.

The Square Tower visitor center offers interpretive displays as well as maps and brochures for self-guiding tours. With the exception of Square Tower, all the sites are difficult to locate; obtain directions at the visitor center before attempting to find them. Rangers give presentations about the monument May-September (phone visitor center for current schedule).

The monument is open year-round. The visitor center is open daily 8-6, May-Sept.; 8-5 in Apr. and Oct.; 9-5, rest of year. For more information write the Superintendent, Hovenweep National Monument, McElmo Route, Cortez, CO 81321; phone (970) 562-4282, ext. 10.

HUDSON pop. 2,356

PEPPER POD RESTAURANT   303/536-4736

▼▼ ▼▼ ◆◆ American Casual Dining $5-$29 **AAA Inspector Notes:** *Classic.* This popular family-owned roadside eatery features an extensive menu of buffalo steak, burgers, chicken-fried steak and homemade pies. The Old West artwork and wall-mounted buffalo heads are just a part of the country-casual charm. Restaurants come and go, but this place has been in continuous operation for more than 80 years. **Features:** full bar. **Address:** 530 Fir St 80642 **Location:** I-76 exit 31, just s, then immediately w. B L D

Recommend places you'd like us to inspect at AAA.com/TourBookComments

IDAHO SPRINGS (C-8) pop. 1,717, elev. 7,524'

As had the Ute Indians before them, bone-weary miners from the nearby diggings soothed their aches in the mineral springs of Idaho Springs. Known particularly for its radium hot springs, the town has been a popular spa since the 1880s. It retains many Victorian buildings and structures characteristic of the brick and stone architecture of the 1880s.

The first major gold strike in Colorado was made in early 1859 at the juncture of Chicago and Clear creeks; a monument less than one-quarter mile southwest on Chicago Creek Road marks the spot. More than 200 mines in the vicinity once produced silver, uranium, tungsten, zinc, molybdenum, gold and lead.

A relic of the early mining days is "Locomotive 60," which, along with a coal tender and a passenger coach of the Colorado and Southern Railroad, stands on a section of the original narrow-gauge track in the downtown business district. The train made its first run in 1886.

A popular scenic loop is provided by SR 103 south through Chicago Creek Canyon to Echo Lake, then east over Squaw Pass to SR 74 to Bergen Park and Fillius Mountain Park. Follow the highway north to I-70, which returns to Idaho Springs. Another scenic route starts on SR 5 at Echo Lake and goes to the top of 14,260-foot Mount Evans.

Heritage Museum and Visitor Center: 2060 Miner St., P.O. Box 1318, Idaho Springs, CO 80452-1318. **Phone:** (303) 567-4382.

ARGO GOLD MINE AND MILL is off I-70 exit 241A to 2350 Riverside Dr. Self-guiding 45-minute tours begin at the Double Eagle Mine (a hand-dug gold mine), continue through the gold- and silver-processing levels of this late 19th-century mill and conclude in the Clear Creek Mining Museum. The museum displays ore and mineral samples, equipment and early photographs.

Visitors can pan for gold or gemstones. **Hours:** Daily 9-6, mid-Apr. to mid-Oct. (weather permitting); 10-3, rest of year (weather permitting). **Cost:** $16; $8 (ages 6-12). **Phone:** (303) 567-2421.

"OH MY GAWD" ROAD—see Central City p. 77.

PHOENIX MINE, off I-70 exit 239, 1 mi. s.w. on Stanley Rd., then 1 mi. s. on Trail Creek Rd., offers underground guided tours of a working hard-rock gold mine; tours include gold panning. **Time:** Allow 30 minutes minimum. **Hours:** Daily 10-6 (weather permitting). **Cost:** Mine only $10; $5 (ages 0-11). Gold panning, additional $5. Cash only. **Phone:** (303) 567-0422.

SAINT MARY'S GLACIER is accessible by a .7-mile hike from Fall River Rd., .75 mile n. of the ghost town of Alice, which is 12 miles n.w. via I-70 and Fall River Rd. exit 238. St. Mary's Lake is at the foot of the glacier on the flank of James Peak. Parking at the glacier is limited to a small pay lot, north of the glacier trailhead. No parking is permitted on Fall River Rd. or nearby subdivisions. **Cost:** Free. **Parking:** $5. **Phone:** (303) 567-4660.

RECREATIONAL ACTIVITIES

Hiking

- **Mount Goliath Wildflower Hike** departs from the Dos Chappell Nature Center. **Hours:** Tues. and Thurs. (also some Sat.) at 8:45 a.m., mid-June to early Aug. Phone ahead to confirm schedule. Reservations are required and can be made through the Denver Botanic Gardens website. **Cost:** $10 per vehicle (U.S. Forest Service amenity fee). Tours free. **Phone:** (720) 865-3539.

White-water Rafting

- **Clear Creek Rafting Co.** is at 350 Whitewater Rd. **Hours:** Daily 7 a.m.-9 p.m., May 1-Labor Day. **Phone:** (303) 567-1000 or (800) 353-9901.

- **Raft Masters** is at 2804 Colorado Blvd. **Hours:** Daily 8-6, mid-May to Labor Day. **Phone:** (719) 275-6645.

BEAU JO'S COLORADO STYLE PIZZA   303/567-4376

▼▼▼

Pizza
Casual Dining
$11-$20

AAA Inspector Notes: Known for its pizza, this eatery offers a fun atmosphere with a mountain theme. Build your pizza from the crust up. Choices include a mountain pie with a thick, chewy edge; the thin-crust prairie pie; and gluten-free options. Add your favorite toppings or choose a specialty pizza like the Sky Hawk (a pepperoni pie with Hatch green chiles and feta), or Skier Mike's chicken, Canadian bacon and green pepper pie. **Features:** full bar. **Address:** 1517 Miner St 80452 **Location:** I-70 exit 240, just n, then just e. **Parking:** on-site and street. *(See ad p. 214.)*

"Colorado Style Pizza" Also Gluten Free Menu

THE BUFFALO RESTAURANT & BAR   303/567-2729

▼▼ American. Casual Dining. $8-$36 **AAA Inspector Notes:** *Historic.* This fun, popular and well-established place is in an intriguing old mining town. The cuisine features an interesting mix of buffalo, pizza, barbecue and Mexican dishes. Built in 1906, the restaurant's Western décor includes skylights. **Features:** full bar. **Address:** 1617 Miner St 80452 **Location:** I-70 exit 240, just e; exit 241A, just w.

IGNACIO (F-2) pop. 697

SOUTHERN UTE CULTURAL CENTER & MUSEUM, 77 CR 517 at jct. US 172 and CR 517, explores the culture and traditions of the Ute people through interactive and multi-sensory exhibits in a 52,000-square-foot facility with striking contemporary architecture. The permanent gallery offers a historical perspective, while rotating exhibits focus on subjects relating to the Southern Ute tribe. Visitors can explore the surrounding property, which features native trees, plants and flowers of special significance to the Ute. A library and archives contains hundreds of recorded oral histories available to visitors. **Time:** Allow 1 hour minimum. **Hours:** Tues.-Sun. 9-5, Memorial Day-Labor Day. Closed tribal holidays. Last tickets sold 1 hour before closing. **Cost:** $7; $4 (ages 65+); $3 (ages 3-14). **Phone:** (970) 563-9583.

SKY UTE CASINO RESORT   (970)563-7777

▼▼▼

Hotel
$86-$140

Address: 14324 Hwy 172 N 81137 **Location:** Jct US 172 and CR 517. **Facility:** Rooms offer pillowtop mattresses covered in thick duvets, and spacious bathrooms with separate tubs and showers. Unwind or play in the lazy river pool, which features fountain sprays and bubble jets. 140 units. 5 stories, interior corridors. **Terms:** 3 day cancellation notice. **Amenities:** safes. **Dining:** 3 restaurants. **Pool(s):** heated indoor. **Activities:** hot tub, miniature golf, playground, game room, exercise room, massage. **Guest Services:** coin laundry. *(See ad p. 171.)*

FORT SEDGWICK MUSEUM is at 114 E. 1st St. Three buildings, all part of the Fort Sedgwick Historical Society, are dedicated to local history. Fort Sedgwick Museum houses exhibits about the history of the fort and the four incarnations of Julesburg as well as temporary exhibits. The Depot Museum, at 201 W. 1st St., has Pony Express and Union Pacific Railroad memorabilia, period clothing, barbed wire and buggies. The Old Ford Garage, at 112 E. 1st St., features historic photographs, antique cars and gasoline pumps.

Time: Allow 1 hour minimum. **Hours:** Fort Sedgwick Museum and Old Ford Garage Tues.-Sat. 10-4, Sun. 1-4, Memorial Day-Labor Day; Tues.-Fri. 9-1, rest of year. Depot Museum Tues.-Sat. 10-4, Sun. 1-4, Memorial Day-Labor Day; by appointment rest of year. **Cost:** (includes Fort Sedgwick and Depot museums) $1; 50c (ages 6-12). Old Ford Garage free. **Phone:** (970) 474-2061.

KEYSTONE (C-4) pop. 1,079, elev. 9,166'
• Restaurants p. 216

A Pennsylvania prospector searching for gold in the 1880s named the town after his home state's nickname. Great skiing on three mountains—the Outback, Dercum Mountain and North Peak—lure today's visitors. Summer recreation includes boating on Lake Dillon, biking, golfing and hiking.

RECREATIONAL ACTIVITIES
Skiing

- **Arapahoe Basin** is at 28194 US 6. **Hours:** Mon.-Fri. 9-4, Sat.-Sun. and holidays 8:30-4, mid-Oct. to early June. **Phone:** (888) 272-7246.
- **Keystone Resort** is at I-70 exit 205. Other activities are offered. **Hours:** Daily 8:30-4, early Nov.-early Apr. **Phone:** (970) 496-4111 or (888) 697-0785.

THE INN AT KEYSTONE   970/496-4825

▼▼ Hotel $129-$280 **Address:** 23044 Hwy 6 80435 **Location:** I-70 exit 205, 6.5 mi e. **Facility:** 103 units. 6 stories, interior corridors. **Parking:** on-site and valet. **Terms:** check-in 4 pm, 21 day cancellation notice-fee imposed, resort fee. **Amenities:** safes. **Activities:** hot tub, downhill & cross country skiing, bicycles, trails. **Guest Services:** valet and coin laundry, area transportation.

KEYSTONE LODGE & SPA   970/496-2316

▼▼▼ Resort Hotel. Rates not provided. **Address:** 22101 Hwy 6 80435 **Location:** I-70 exit 205, 6 mi e. **Facility:** This lodge is bordered by ski slopes and a national forest. Guests enjoy complete relaxation in the award-winning spa. 152 units. 6 stories, interior corridors. **Parking:** on-site and valet. **Terms:** check-in 4 pm. **Amenities:** safes. **Dining:** 3 restaurants, also, Alpenglow Stube, Bighorn Restaurant, see separate listings. **Pool(s):** heated outdoor. **Activities:** sauna, hot tub, steamroom, fishing, regulation golf, tennis, downhill & cross country skiing, snowmobiling, ice skating, recreation programs in season, bicycles, playground, game room, trails, spa. **Guest Services:** valet laundry, area transportation.

RIVER RUN CONDOMINIUMS AT KEYSTONE   970/496-3390

▼▼▼ **Resort Condominium.** Rates not provided. **Address:** 100 Dercum Square 80435 **Location:** I-70 exit 205, 7.5 mi e on US 6; at base of ski area. **Facility:** Modern and luxury one-bedroom studio to four-bedroom units are located near the gondola. Guests have access to Keystone Resort activities. Registration is at the Buffalo Lodge. 340 condominiums. 4-6 stories, interior corridors. **Terms:** check-in 4 pm. **Amenities:** safes. **Dining:** 6 restaurants. **Pool(s):** heated outdoor. **Activities:** hot tub, fishing, miniature golf, downhill & cross country skiing, ice skating, bicycles, playground, trails. **Guest Services:** valet and coin laundry, area transportation.

🍴 🍸 📶 🏊 BIZ 📶 ✕ 🅰️🅲 🔌 💼 📺

SKI TIP LODGE BED & BREAKFAST   970/496-4950

[fyi] Not evaluated. **Address:** 764 Montezuma Rd 80435 **Location:** I-70 exit 205, 8 mi se on US 6, then 0.8 mi s. Facilities, services, and décor characterize a mid-scale property.

WHERE TO EAT

ALPENGLOW STUBE   970/496-4386

▼▼▼▼ Regional American. Casual Dining. $32-$99 **AAA Inspector Notes:** Looking for a once-in-a-lifetime dining experience? You'll find a memorable one here. Two gondola rides take guests to the highest restaurant in the United States, at 11,444 feet. The view from the front deck is as spectacular as the one talented servers deliver to the table. Winter lunches and rotisserie duck dinners are prepared in the open kitchen's wood-fired oven. The menu changes seasonally. **Features:** full bar. **Reservations:** required, for dinner. **Address:** 22101 Hwy 6 80435 **Location:** I-70 exit 205, 6 mi e; in Keystone Lodge & Spa. L D 🅰️🅲

BIGHORN RESTAURANT   970/496-4386

▼▼▼ Steak Seafood. Casual Dining. $20-$38 **AAA Inspector Notes:** Many local and organic dishes feature game, such as venison, pheasant, elk, antelope and buffalo. Adventurous diners should try the Rocky Mountain Oysters, a culinary experience unique to Colorado. The warm, inviting décor combines elegance with a hint of Western flair. Ask for a mountain or skating rink view in the winter, or a lake view in the summer. **Features:** full bar. **Reservations:** suggested. **Address:** 22101 Hwy 6 80435 **Location:** I-70 exit 205, 6 mi e; in Keystone Lodge & Spa. **Parking:** on-site and valet.

D

DOS LOCOS MEXICAN RESTAURANT & CANTINA
        970/262-9185

▼▼ Mexican. Casual Dining. $9-$17 **AAA Inspector Notes:** The restaurant provides a varied menu consisting of everything from popular chile rellenos and fajitas to harder-to-find fish tacos and chicken mole. While the large bar is suitable for lively groups, the dining rooms provide a quieter backdrop for laid-back dining. **Features:** full bar, patio dining, happy hour. **Address:** 22869 Hwy 6 80435 **Location:** I-70 exit 205, 7.4 mi e; in Mountain View Plaza (north side of US 6). D 🅰️🅲

KEYSTONE RANCH RESTAURANT   970/496-4386

▼▼▼ ▼▼▼ Western American. Fine Dining. $45-$81 **AAA Inspector Notes:** Historic. This restaurant features an expertly prepared three- and five-course dinner set in a refined, rustic dining room. After finishing the main course, you will be escorted into a living room area for after-dinner beverages and dessert. This area is comfortably furnished with overstuffed furniture and a stone fireplace that create a nice, relaxing environment. **Features:** full bar. **Reservations:** suggested. **Address:** 1437 Keystone Ranch Rd 80435 **Location:** I-70 exit 205, 6 mi e, then 3 mi sw, follow signs to Ranch Golf Course. D 🅰️🅲

NEW MOON CAFE   970/262-3772

▼ American. Quick Serve. $7-$10 **AAA Inspector Notes:** Head to this eatery for its famous all-day breakfast options, including jumbo Belgian waffles, chorizo or vegetable burritos, and the egg croissant sandwich. The create-your-own Bloody Mary bar is a big hit. Those not in the mood for breakfast can opt for one of the panini named after famous musicians. **Features:** full bar, happy hour. **Address:** 140 Ida Belle Dr, Suite F25 80435 **Location:** I-70 exit 205, 7.5 mi e on US 6; at base of ski area. B L 🅰️🅲

SKI TIP LODGE RESTAURANT   970/496-4950

▼▼▼▼ Regional American. Fine Dining. $75 **AAA Inspector Notes:** Historic. Creative cuisine is expertly and beautifully presented in a rustic former stagecoach stop. Rotating four-course dinners are offered in quaint and inviting surroundings, and diners may retreat to the cabin sitting room or outdoor patio for dessert. While the setting is ideal for couples, the talented waitstaff will make the single diner and groups feel right at home. **Features:** full bar. **Reservations:** suggested. **Address:** 764 Montezuma Rd 80435 **Location:** I-70 exit 205, 8 mi se on US 6, then 0.8 mi s; in Ski Tip Lodge Bed & Breakfast. D 🅰️🅲

SNAKE RIVER SALOON   970/468-2788

▼▼▼
**American
Casual Dining
$23-$36**

AAA Inspector Notes: In a warm atmosphere, you'll enjoy traditional favorites such as steak, lobster, chicken, pork chops and pasta. The knotty pine-paneled dining room is quite cozy. This is a popular nightspot for a meal and music. **Features:** full bar. **Address:** 23074 Hwy 6 80435 **Location:** I-70 exit 205, 6 mi e. D 🅰️🅲

DER FONDUE CHESSEL   970/496-4386

[fyi] Not evaluated. Enjoy four-course traditional Swiss and Bavarian fondue dinners at 11,444 feet. There are seven beers on tap and Bavarian entertainment. **Address:** 22010 Hwy 6 80435 **Location:** I-70 exit 205, 6 mi e; at The Outpost atop North Peak, take River Run and Outpost gondolas.

KREMMLING (B-3) pop. 1,444, elev. 7,362'

RECREATIONAL ACTIVITIES

White-water Rafting

- **Wilderness Aware Rafting** trips depart from the Pumphouse Recreation Area; go s. on SR 9 crossing the Colorado River to a dirt road (watch for the Pumphouse sign), w. 10.5 mi. to the next Pumphouse sign, then n. 1.3 mi. **Hours:** Trips depart daily at 9:30, mid-May to Labor Day. **Phone:** (719) 395-2112 or (800) 462-7238.

ALLINGTON INN & SUITES   (970)724-9800

▼▼▼
**Hotel
$97-$149**

Address: 215 W Central Ave 80459 **Location:** 0.5 mi w of jct US 40 and SR 9, then just n. **Facility:** 46 units. 2 stories, interior corridors. **Pool(s):** heated indoor. **Activities:** hot tub, limited exercise equipment. **Guest Services:** coin laundry. **Featured Amenity:** continental breakfast.

SAVE 🍴➕ 🏊 BIZ HS 📶 ✕ 🔌 📺 / SOME UNITS 🐾

LAFAYETTE (C-9) pop. 24,453, elev. 5,236'

Lafayette was founded in 1888 by Mary Miller, a prosperous widow who named the town after her husband. In 1884 she discovered coal on her farm; within several years the coal mining industry spurred the town's rapid growth. Mrs. Miller established the Lafayette Bank in 1900, reputedly becoming the only female bank president in the world at the time.

With 20 neighborhood parks, recreational opportunities such as boating, swimming, tennis and picnicking abound. Community events include the Lafayette Quaker Oatmeal Festival in January and the Peach Festival in August.

Lafayette Chamber of Commerce: 1290 S. Public Rd., P.O. Box 1018, Lafayette, CO 80026. **Phone:** (303) 666-9555.

WOW CHILDREN'S MUSEUM is at 110 N. Harrison Ave. Children's activities focus on the arts, music and science. Play areas include a dance studio, an art room and a pirate ship. **Time:** Allow 1 hour minimum. **Hours:** Tues.-Fri. 9-5, Sat. 10-6, Sun. noon-4. Closed Jan. 1, Easter, Memorial Day, July 4, Labor Day, Thanksgiving, Christmas Eve and Christmas. **Cost:** $9 (ages 1-11); $8 (children of military); free (all other ages). **Phone:** (303) 604-2424.

LA JUNTA (E-6) pop. 7,077, elev. 4,052'
• Restaurants p. 218

This was once *la junta*—the junction—where the main and southern routes of the old Santa Fe Trail divided. Bent's Fort, a major trading post, was just to the east. In 1875, with the arrival of the Santa Fe Railroad, La Junta (HUN-ta) became a major hub on the route, and the hoot of the locomotive replaced the rumble of wagon wheels.

La Junta is still a junction, but the term now refers to the numerous state and federal highways that converge in the town. One of these, US 50, is part of the scenic and historic Santa Fe Trail route that continues on as US 350 heading southwest out of La Junta. La Junta also is a major cattle- and produce-shipping center for the lower Arkansas Valley.

Nearby Holbrook Lake provides a setting for water skiing, fishing, boating and camping. The northern unit of Comanche National Grassland lies southwest of town. Vogel Canyon, 13 miles south on SR 109, then following signs, is within the grassland. Several trails beginning at the parking lot lead to scenic overlooks and rock art.

Also part of the grassland is Picket Wire Canyonlands where, in addition to rock art, one of the nation's largest known set of dinosaur tracks (more than 1,300 footprints) can be seen. Picket Wire Canyon is about 13 miles past Vogel Canyon. **Note:** Only experienced hikers in good physical condition should attempt the trek to Picket Wire Canyon. Guided full-day auto tours are offered on Saturdays in May, June, September and October; participants must have their own high-clearance, four-wheel-drive vehicle. These tours are the only way cars may be taken into the canyon. Contact the Comanche National Grasslands office, 1420 E. 3rd. St. in La Junta, (719) 384-2181, for information and reservations.

La Junta Chamber of Commerce: 110 Santa Fe Ave., La Junta, CO 81050. **Phone:** (719) 384-7411.

BENT'S OLD FORT NATIONAL HISTORIC SITE, 6 mi. e. on SR 194E, is a reconstruction of an adobe fur trading post that operated here 1833-49. It figured prominently in westward expansion and maintained friendly relations with many Native American tribes. Kit Carson once worked here as a hunter and trader. The rooms, restored to the 1846 era, include a kitchen, blacksmith shop and trade room. Guides

in period dress demonstrate life in the 1840s (June-Sept.). An orientation film is available.

Time: Allow 1 hour minimum. **Hours:** Daily 8-5:30, June-Aug.; 9-4, rest of year. Guided tours are given daily at 9:30, 11, 1 and 2:30, June-Aug.; at 10:30 and 1, rest of year. Tour schedule may vary; phone ahead. Closed Jan. 1, Thanksgiving and Christmas. **Cost:** $3; $2 (ages 6-12). **Phone:** (719) 383-5010.

KOSHARE INDIAN MUSEUM, 18th St. and Santa Fe Ave., is patterned after the Native American ceremonial kivas of the Southwest. The museum houses fine art and sculpture, pottery, bead and quill work, baskets, rugs and kachinas. The Koshare Indian Dancers perform interpretive Native American dances, preserving the Pueblo and Plains heritage and culture.

Hours: Daily noon-5, June-Aug.; daily noon-5, in Dec.; Fri.-Mon. and Wed. noon-5, rest of year. Winter hours vary; phone ahead. Dances are performed June-July and the week after Christmas to mid-Jan. at 7 p.m. Closed major holidays. Phone ahead to confirm schedule. **Cost:** Museum $5; $3 (ages 7-17 and 65+). Museum and dance performances $10; $5 (ages 3-17). **Phone:** (719) 384-4411.

OTERO MUSEUM is at 218 Anderson Ave. Guides take visitors through the museum, which has memorabilia from La Junta and the surrounding lower Arkansas Valley area dating from 1875-1945. Displays focus on transportation, including an 1867 Old Overland Stage and early fire engines; a home and grocery store furnished in the early 20th-century style; a 19th-century wood-framed structure formerly used as a boarding house; La Junta's first schoolhouse; a mini post office; and a mustache cup collection. **Time:** Allow 1 hour minimum. **Hours:** Mon.-Sat. 1-5, June-Sept.; by appointment, rest of year. Phone ahead to confirm schedule. **Cost:** Free. **Phone:** (719) 384-7500.

STAGECOACH MOTEL   (719)384-5476

Motel
$55-$70

Address: 905 W 3rd St 81050 **Location:** Jct US 50 and 350. **Facility:** 31 units. 2 stories (no elevator), exterior corridors. **Parking:** winter plug-ins. **Terms:** cancellation fee imposed. **Pool(s):** heated outdoor. **Guest Services:** area transportation. **Featured Amenity: continental breakfast.**

SAVE ｜+ 🏊 🛜 ✕ 🖥 📷
▣ / SOME UNITS 🆂⛶

WHERE TO EAT

BOSS HOGG'S SALOON & RESTAURANT   719/384-7879

◆◆ American. Casual Dining. $6-$29 **AAA Inspector Notes:** This restaurant features flavorful, freshly cut steaks and hickory-smoked barbecue. **Features:** full bar, Sunday brunch. **Address:** 808 E 3rd St 81050 **Location:** On SR 109, 0.5 mi e of center. [L] [D]

LUCY'S TACOS   719/384-8333

◆ Mexican. Quick Serve. $3-$9 **AAA Inspector Notes:** Walk right up and order your favorites at this outdoor taco stand. Locals love the menu, which features carnitas, taquitos, carne asada and a variety of Mexican-style tacos—all at reasonable prices. Although there are some tables outside, look for additional seating in a building next to the stand. **Address:** 17 E 3rd St 81050 **Location:** Between Raton and Colorado aves. **Parking:** street only.

[B] [L] [D] CALL 🖝M 🅺

NEW CHINA RESTAURANT   719/384-8504

◆◆ Chinese. Casual Dining. $5-$13 **AAA Inspector Notes:** Family-owned and -operated, this casual eatery offers an extensive list of standard rice and meat dishes. Patrons can expect efficient service and large portions packed with flavor. **Features:** wine only. **Address:** 414 W 1st St 81050 **Location:** On US 50. [L] [D]

THE BARISTA   719/384-2133

[fyi] Not evaluated. This cozy eatery offers a good variety of salads, wraps and sandwiches, such as the Iowan, Wisconsin, road runner and prairie schooner, most served with your choice of chips, fruit, potato salad, side salad or yogurt. Coffee and cookies are available all day. **Address:** 204 Santa Fe Ave 81050 **Location:** Downtown.

LAKE CITY (E-2) pop. 408, elev. 8,658'

Lake City was named for nearby Lake San Cristobal, the second largest natural lake in Colorado. Hidden Treasure and Golden Fleece—the names of local mines—attest to Lake City's early preoccupation. One of the earliest settlements in western Colorado, Lake City served as a supply center for the gold and silver mines of the surrounding San Juan Mountains.

Today the town is a starting point for enjoying two of Colorado's most scenic and historic byways, the Alpine Backcountry Loop and the Silver Thread Scenic Byway. The Alpine Loop's 65 miles of dirt and gravel roads connect the former mining towns of Lake City, Ouray and Silverton. Depending on snowfall, it's open late May to late October; four-wheel-drive, high-clearance vehicles are recommended for some portions, including Engineer and Cinnamon passes.

Weaving over the Continental Divide for some 120 miles, the fully paved Silver Thread (SR 149) links Blue Mesa Reservoir to Creede and South Fork and is open year-round. Mountain peaks, river valleys

and the Gunnison and Rio Grande national forests provide outstanding scenery at nearly every turn.

Five 14,000-foot peaks provide plenty of hiking, biking, fishing, camping, boating, wildlife viewing and horseback riding opportunities; backcountry skiing, snowmobiling, ice climbing, ice fishing and a family ski hill round out the year's recreational activities.

Lake City also is known for its Victorian architecture; most of the town's old buildings have been restored and preserved within a National Historic District.

Lake City/Hinsdale County Chamber of Commerce: 800 N. Gunnison Ave., P.O. Box 430, Lake City, CO 81235. **Phone:** (970) 944-2527 or (800) 569-1874.

Self-guiding tours: A map detailing a walking tour of Lake City is available at the chamber of commerce.

HARD TACK MINE TOURS & MUSEUM is 2.5 mi. w. on CR 20 (Engineer Pass Rd.). The mine, owned and operated by a former hard rock miner, offers 35-minute walking tours that show how hand tools and dynamite were used to blast through the mine's rock. The Hard Tack Mine tunnel was begun more than 100 years ago by employees of the Hidden Treasure Mine, which produced more than $1.5 million in silver ore. Minerals, crystals and gold panning items are displayed. A light jacket is recommended, as the mine temperature is 45 F. **Time:** Allow 45 minutes minimum. **Hours:** Daily 10-5, June-Sept. **Cost:** $13; $9 (ages 1-14). **Phone:** (970) 944-2506.

HINSDALE COUNTY MUSEUM, 130 N. Silver St., traces the history of Lake City and Hinsdale County. Exhibits focus on the cultural development of Lake City, including the Civilian Conservation Corps projects of the 1930s and the transition of the local economy from mining to tourism in the 1940s. Displays include medical equipment, an 1878 hook and ladder truck, old-fashioned gardens utilizing vintage plants, a restored Denver & Rio Grande caboose and a small home depicting late 19th-century family life. Exhibits in the Transportation Building include early transportation memorabilia and a blacksmith shop. In summer, cemetery and ghost tours and tours of historic home interiors are offered. **Time:** Allow 30 minutes minimum. **Hours:** Mon.-Sat. 10-5, Sun. 1-4, Memorial Day to Sept. 30. **Cost:** $4; $2 (ages 8-15); free (military with ID). Tours $5-$10. **Phone:** (970) 944-2050.

POKER ALICE PIZZA   970/944-4100

◆ Pizza Sandwiches. Quick Serve. $6-$13 **AAA Inspector Notes:** Patrons can dine inside or outside on the covered front porch or at a picnic table. Salads, hearty sandwiches, fresh-baked breads, hand-rolled calzones, pasta and stone-baked pizza are offered at this fun eatery. Cake, cookies, pie and good coffee are always available. **Features:** beer & wine. **Address:** 188 S Gunnison Ave 81235 **Location:** On SR 149, south end of town.

[B] [L] [D] 🅺

LAKE GEORGE

RECREATIONAL ACTIVITIES
Horseback Riding
- **M Lazy C Guest Ranch & Mule Creek Outfitters** is at 801 CR 453. **Hours:** Daily, year-round (weather permitting). **Phone:** (719) 748-3398.

M LAZY C GUEST RANCH & MULE CREEK OUTFITTERS
719/748-3398
Ranch. Rates not provided. **Address:** 801 CR 453 80827 **Location:** 5 mi w on US 24, then 1 mi n on dirt road. **Facility:** 11 cabins, some kitchens. 1 story, exterior corridors. **Activities:** hot tub, fishing, cross country skiing, recreation programs, playground, trails. **Guest Services:** coin laundry.

LAKEWOOD pop. 142,980, elev. 5,518'
- Restaurants p. 220
- Hotels & Restaurants map & index p. 136
- Part of Denver area — see map p. 116

Just west of downtown Denver, Lakewood is a sprawling suburb with excellent views of the Front Range Mountains. In the early 2000s, the site of a demolished, 1960s-era shopping mall was transformed into Belmar, a retail and residential development designed to be a pedestrian-friendly village with a central plaza, outdoor cafes and a movie theater complex. William Frederick Hayden Park on Lakewood's western fringe offers a network of trails and 360-degree views from the summit of Green Mountain.

BEST WESTERN DENVER SOUTHWEST
(303)989-5500   65
Hotel
$72-$165
AAA Benefit: Save 10% or more every day and earn 10% bonus points!
Address: 3440 S Vance St 80227 **Location:** Just ne of jct US 285 (Hampden Ave) and S Wadsworth Blvd, e on Girton Dr, then just s. **Facility:** 112 units. 2 stories (no elevator), interior corridors. **Terms:** cancellation fee imposed. **Pool(s):** heated outdoor. **Activities:** hot tub, exercise room. **Guest Services:** valet and coin laundry.

ENJOY THE FREEDOM
Extend your safe driving years.
SENIORDRIVING.AAA.COM
SENIORSDRIVING.CAA.CA

COURTYARD BY MARRIOTT DENVER SW/LAKEWOOD
(303)985-9696   66
Hotel $94-$213 **Address:** 7180 W Hampden Ave 80227 **Location:** Just se of jct US 285 (W Hampden Ave) and S Wadsworth Blvd, e on Jefferson Ave, then n on frontage road. Located in a business park. **Facility:** 90 units. 3 stories, interior corridors. **Pool(s):** heated indoor. **Activities:** hot tub, picnic facilities, exercise room. **Guest Services:** valet and coin laundry, boarding pass kiosk.
AAA Benefit: Members save 5% or more!

HAMPTON INN DENVER- SOUTHWEST-LAKEWOOD
303/989-6900   69
Hotel. Rates not provided. **Address:** 3605 S Wadsworth Blvd 80235 **Location:** Just sw of jct US 285 (Hampden Ave) and S Wadsworth Blvd; entrance on frontage road. **Facility:** 150 units. 4 stories, interior corridors. **Pool(s):** heated outdoor. **Activities:** exercise room. **Guest Services:** valet and coin laundry, area transportation.
AAA Benefit: Members save up to 10%!

HAMPTON INN DENVER WEST/FEDERAL CENTER
303/969-9900   62
Hotel. Rates not provided. **Address:** 137 Union Blvd 80228 **Location:** 0.8 mi s of US 6. **Facility:** 170 units. 6 stories, interior corridors. **Pool(s):** heated outdoor. **Activities:** exercise room. **Guest Services:** valet and coin laundry, area transportation.
AAA Benefit: Members save up to 10%!

HOLIDAY INN DENVER LAKEWOOD
(303)980-9200   67
Hotel $89-$169

Address: 7390 W Hampden Ave 80227 **Location:** US 285 (W Hampden Ave) exit S Wadsworth Blvd, just e on Jefferson Ave, then n on Vance St. **Facility:** 188 units. 6 stories, interior corridors. **Terms:** check-in 4 pm. **Pool(s):** heated outdoor. **Activities:** hot tub, exercise room. **Guest Services:** valet and coin laundry, area transportation.

HOME2 SUITES BY HILTON DENVER WEST/FEDERAL CENTER
303/985-7100   64
Extended Stay Hotel. Rates not provided. **Address:** 50 Van Gordon St 80228 **Location:** US 6 exit Simms St/Union Blvd, 0.6 mi s on Union Blvd to 2nd Pl, just w, then just s. **Facility:** 107 efficiencies, some two bedrooms. 4 stories, interior corridors. **Amenities:** safes. **Pool(s):** heated indoor. **Activities:** hot tub, picnic facilities, exercise room. **Guest Services:** valet and coin laundry.
AAA Benefit: Members save up to 10%!

HOMEWOOD SUITES BY HILTON DENVER WEST/FEDERAL CENTER
303/716-5737   63
Extended Stay Hotel. Rates not provided. **Address:** 139 Union Blvd 80228 **Location:** US 6 exit Simms St/Union Blvd, 0.6 mi s on Union Blvd to 2nd Pl, just w, then just s on Van Gordon St. **Facility:** 110 efficiencies. 4 stories, interior corridors. **Amenities:** safes. **Pool(s):** heated indoor. **Activities:** hot tub, exercise room. **Guest Services:** valet and coin laundry.

(See map & index p. 136.)

RESIDENCE INN BY MARRIOTT DENVER SW/LAKEWOOD
(303)985-7676 **68**

▼▼▼ **Extended Stay Hotel**
$112-$257 **Address:** 7050 W Hampden
Ave 80227 **Location:** Just se of jct US
285 (W Hampden Ave) and Wadsworth
Blvd, e on Jefferson Ave, then n on
frontage road. Located in a business park. **Facility:** 102 units, some
two bedrooms, efficiencies and kitchens. 3 stories, interior corridors.
Terms: check-in 4 pm. **Pool(s):** heated indoor. **Activities:** hot tub,
picnic facilities, exercise room. **Guest Services:** valet and coin
laundry.

AAA Benefit:
Members save 5%
or more!

CALL [ᗷM] [≋] [BIZ] [≋] [✕] [⚏] [◻] [◻] [◻]
/ SOME UNITS [🐕] [HS]

SHERATON-DENVER WEST HOTEL (303)987-2000 **61**

▼▼▼▼
Hotel
$109-$359

Sheraton
HOTELS & RESORTS

AAA Benefit: Members
save up to 15%, plus
Starwood Preferred
Guest® benefits!

Address: 360 Union Blvd 80228 **Location:** US 6 exit Simms St/Union Blvd,
just s. **Facility:** 242 units. 12 stories, interior corridors. **Amenities:** video
games. *Some:* safes. **Pool(s):** heated
indoor. **Activities:** hot tub, exercise
room. **Guest Services:** valet laundry,
area transportation.

[SAVE] [❙❙] [⧠] [≋] [BIZ] [≋] [✕]
[⚏] [◻] / SOME UNITS [🐕] [◻]

WHERE TO EAT

240 UNION RESTAURANT
303/989-3562 **111**

▼▼▼ American. Fine Dining. $12-$35 **AAA Inspector Notes:**
This bustling, well-known restaurant features an open kitchen, a
wood-burning oven and a large, whimsical and flawlessly food-
friendly wine list. Creative appetizers, pasta, pizza and other entrées
get better every season. The well-trained waitstaff offers friendly and
attentive service. **Features:** full bar, Sunday brunch, happy hour.
Reservations: suggested. **Address:** 240 Union Blvd 80228 **Location:** US 6, 0.3 mi s on Union Blvd; I-70 exit 261, 3 mi e.

[L] [D] CALL [ᗷM]

BLUE SKY CAFE
303/216-2670 **107**

▼▼ Natural/Organic. Casual Dining. $9-$13 **AAA Inspector
Notes:** This cozy cafe features menu options that are designed to
promote good health as well as good taste. Breakfast entrees include
Santa Fe huevos rancheros and caramelized banana waffles and a variety of eggs benedicts. For lunch, choose from a wide range of entree salads and sandwiches. Vegetarian options are available as well
as wheat-free pancakes, soy milk and freshly made juices and
smoothies. **Address:** 14403 W Colfax Ave 80401 **Location:** I-70 exit
Colfax, 0.4 mi ne; in Denver West Village strip mall; n of Colorado
Mills Outlet Mall. [B] [L]

CAFE JORDANO
303/988-6863 **113**

▼ Italian. Casual Dining. $8-$15 **AAA Inspector Notes:** The
cuisine served at this popular eatery can be summed up in a few
words: fresh, flavorful and authentic. The menu features classics like
fettuccine Alfredo, ravioli, and gnocchi as well as unique options like
the pollo saporito, chicken in a tomato cream sauce with mushrooms
and artichokes. Expect to wait for a table, but you won't regret it. **Features:** full bar. **Address:** 11068 W Jewell Ave 80227 **Location:** SR
285 exit Kipling Pkwy, 2 mi nw; in strip mall. [L] [D]

Ask about AAA/CAA
Associate membership
to share the benefits you value

CHAD'S GRILL
303/988-5666 **110**

▼▼ American. Casual Dining. $9-$19 **AAA Inspector Notes:**
A good stop for breakfast, lunch or dinner, this restaurant has been a
local favorite since 1982. The menu lineup includes pizzas, pastas,
rotisserie chicken dishes, burgers and sandwiches. More elaborate
options include spicy Cajun jambalaya, grilled salmon and fire-grilled
Gorgonzola steak. Hearty weekend brunch options feature crab
Benedict, huevos rancheros and French toast. When the weather
permits, the covered patio is a nice dining spot. **Features:** full bar,
patio dining, Sunday brunch, happy hour. **Address:** 275 Union Blvd
80228 **Location:** US 6 exit 6th Ave to Union Blvd exit, just s.

[L] [D] CALL [ᗷM]

HACIENDA COLORADO
303/932-0272

▼▼ Mexican. Casual Dining. $7-$19 **AAA Inspector Notes:**
You'll feel right at home the moment you enter this place thanks to its
inviting, upscale décor. Fresh, flavorful salsa is served with thinner-
than-usual chips as you peruse the menu. Try the juicy fajitas or the
unique, mildly spicy poblano de pollo- a roasted poblano stuffed with
chicken, cheese, chipotle aioli and a tomatillo corn relish. Portions are
large and plentiful in this bustling, popular eatery. **Features:** full bar,
patio dining, happy hour. **Address:** 5056 S Wadsworth Way 80123
Location: US 285 exit Wadsworth Blvd, 1.9 mi s; located in a strip
mall. [L] [D]

JUS COOKIN'S RESTAURANT
303/205-0123 **109**

▼▼▼
Comfort Food
Casual Dining
$9-$14

AAA Inspector Notes: This family-
owned and -operated restaurant features home-cooked food such as
meatloaf, turkey, herb-roasted chicken
and real mashed potatoes. The fried
chicken and homemade desserts, like
the cobbler and blueberry pie, are fa-
mous in these parts. Colorful, modern paintings of farm animals
punch up the country-style décor. **Features:** beer & wine. **Address:** 840 Tabor St 80401 **Location:** US 6 exit Simms St/Union
Blvd, just n to 8th St, then w. *Menu on AAA.com*

[L] [D]

KOBE AN
303/989-5907 **112**

▼▼ Japanese. Casual Dining. $9-$27 **AAA Inspector Notes:**
Opened in 1979, this casual eatery enjoys a loyal local following.
Start with the savory beef gyoza or deep-fried tempura. The fresh
sushi includes nigiri as well as creative rolls such as the Bronco
(salmon, shrimp and avocado) and the Heart Attack (jalapeño,
shrimp, spicy tuna, dynamite and no rice). **Features:** full bar. **Address:** 85 S Union Blvd 80228 **Location:** US 6, 0.3 mi s; in strip
mall. [L] [D] CALL [ᗷM]

MODMARKET
303/278-8283 **108**

▼ American. Quick Serve. $5-$11 **AAA Inspector Notes:** This
eatery focuses on creating flavorful, healthy options for a fast meal.
Sample menu items include a basil chicken sandwich, prosciutto pear
pizza, and grilled steak. Vegetarian options include a mushroom pear
salad, three-cheese pizza, and a sesame tofu plate. Plants add life to
the modern-style décor. **Features:** beer & wine. **Address:** 14630 W
Colfax Ave 80401 **Location:** I-70 exit 262, just e; in a strip mall.

[B] [L] [D]

NAMASTE
720/963-4005 **116**

▼▼ Indian. Casual Dining. $11-$21 **AAA Inspector Notes:**
The extensive menu features lamb, chicken, shrimp and vegetarian
options. Start your meal with a crunchy lamb or vegetable samosa.
Vegetarian favorites include saag paneer and veggie curry. Among
the popular meat options are tandoori chicken, lamb vindaloo and
curry shrimp. **Features:** full bar, happy hour. **Address:** 3355 S Wadsworth Blvd 80227 **Location:** I-295 exit Wadsworth Blvd, just n, then
just w; in strip mall. [L] [D]

PAD THAI
303/985-3344 **115**

▼▼▼ Thai. Casual Dining. $7-$12 **AAA Inspector Notes:** The
small kitchen produces amazing amounts of sweet and spicy Thai
classics. Pad thai, curries and other stir-fried entrées share menu
space with some traditional Chinese offerings. Diners might finish
with a bowl of homemade custard or sticky rice topped with mango.
Features: wine only. **Address:** 3333 S Wadsworth Blvd, Suite A101
80227 **Location:** Just nw of jct US 285 (Hampden Ave) and S Wadsworth Blvd. [L] [D]

(See map & index p. 136.)

WHITE FENCE FARM RESTAURANT
303/935-5945 (114)

American Family Dining
$11-$30

AAA Inspector Notes: This delightful Colonial farmhouse restaurant and American barn comes complete with an adjacent animal corral. The famous fried chicken has a crispy batter that stays on the chicken rather than the clumpy type that crumbles off. Every meal comes with sweet pickled beets, a vinegary coleslaw, and, my favorite, the sweet corn fritter. Order the mashed potatoes purely for the gravy flavored with thyme. **Features:** full bar. **Address:** 6263 W Jewell Ave 80232 **Location:** US 6 exit Sheridan Blvd, 3 mi s, then 0.5 mi w; between Sheridan and Wadsworth blvds. *Menu on AAA.com* D CALL

YARD HOUSE
303/278-9273

American. Casual Dining. $10-$32 **AAA Inspector Notes:** This place boasts 250 taps of draft beer, and the menu is a bit massive. I started with a "snack," which is a little like tapas, consisting of shrimp ceviche spoons served with a mango and papaya salsa. The combination of tart lime, sweet fruit and the heat from the spice made this simple dish a hit. Next I tried the sliders with a side salad. The salad was fresh and had mixed greens instead of the typical iceberg or romaine. **Features:** full bar, happy hour. **Address:** 14500 W Colfax Ave, Suite 341 80401 **Location:** I-70 exit 262 (Colfax Ave), 0.9 mi e; in Colorado Mills Outlet Mall. L D CALL

LAMAR (E-7) pop. 7,804, elev. 3,610'

The town of Lamar was born May 24, 1886, when the railroad depot in Blackwell, 3 miles to the east, was surreptitiously moved to the new town site.

"The Madonna of the Trail" monument, at the corner of S. Main and Beech streets, is one of 12 Madonna monuments, each in a different state, which mark one of the old national trails—in this case, the Santa Fe Trail (US 50). It was decided that the "Big Timbers" location in Colorado would be the most appropriate place for that state's monument.

Big Timbers refers to a dense grove of cottonwood trees growing along both banks of the Arkansas River. The trees provided shelter from the heat of summer and from cold winter winds, initially for the Plains Indians and later for pioneers heading west over the Santa Fe Trail.

A state welcome center is in a renovated Santa Fe Railroad Depot next to the Madonna of the Trail monument. About 2 miles north of the chamber of commerce on US 50/287 is a marker commemorating the location of the Santa Fe Trail. Willow Creek Park offers opportunities for bird-watching.

Lamar Chamber of Commerce: 109A E. Beech St., Lamar, CO 81052. **Phone:** (719) 336-4379.

BIG TIMBERS MUSEUM, at jct. US 50/287 and SR 196, contains dresses, photographs, dolls and musical instruments as well as household and farm implements representing the period from the late 1800s to the present. Included among the collection of dresses is an 1893 lace wedding gown. A firearms collection, cowboy gear, artifacts relating to the Sand Creek Massacre, Native American relics, 39 framed World War I posters and a rare Civil War flag are on display. The Transportation Museum features antique wagons, cars and trucks.

Time: Allow 30 minutes minimum. **Hours:** Tues.-Sat. 10-5, June-Aug.; Tues.-Sat. 1-4, rest of year.

Closed county and major holidays. Phone ahead to confirm schedule. **Cost:** $3; $5 (family rate); free (students and military with ID). **Phone:** (719) 336-2472.

HOLIDAY INN EXPRESS & SUITES
719/931-4010

Hotel. Rates not provided. **Address:** 1304 N Main St 81052 **Location:** 0.8 mi n on US 50 and 287. **Facility:** 75 units. 3 stories, interior corridors. **Pool:** heated indoor. **Activities:** hot tub, exercise room. **Guest Services:** coin laundry.

CALL BIZ HS

/ SOME UNITS

WHERE TO EAT

THAI SPICY BASIL ASIAN GRILL
719/336-0688

Thai. Casual Dining. $6-$14 **AAA Inspector Notes:** Attractive contemporary décor and delicious Thai dishes make the restaurant an oasis of hip in this rural locale. **Address:** 10 N Main St 81052 **Location:** Town center. L D

LARKSPUR (E-9) pop. 183, elev. 6,720'

Larkspur hosts the Colorado Renaissance Festival, held weekends in June and July. Drawing inspiration from 16th-century England, festivities include jousting, 7 stages of continuous entertainment, fine arts, crafts and food; for information phone (303) 688-6010.

LAS ANIMAS (E-6) pop. 2,410, elev. 3,886'

In taking the name of the river that flows into the nearby Arkansas River, town founders thought it expedient to shorten the name, since the original title of the Purgatoire River was *Río de las Animas Perdidas en Purgatorio* (River of Souls Lost in Purgatory).

Las Animas flourishes as a trading center for the stock ranches and irrigated farms of the surrounding high plains and as a destination for vacationers at John Martin Reservoir State Park *(see Recreation Areas Chart)*. Two murals highlighting the Western heritage of the Santa Fe Trail can be seen from US 50.

Bent County Development Foundation: 332 Ambassador Thompson Blvd., Las Animas, CO 81054. **Phone:** (719) 456-0452.

LA VETA (F-4) pop. 800, elev. 7,013'

La Veta is a quaint town nestled in the Upper Cuchara Valley. In 1859, John M. Francisco purchased land here and constructed Fort Francisco; the adobe structure soon became the commercial center of the area. The fort now serves as the Francisco Fort Museum *(see attraction listing).*

Twin mountains known as the Spanish Peaks, visible from 100 miles away, serve as landmarks for all who pass this way. The Apache, Cheyenne, Comanche, Navajo and Ute tribes hunted and camped there often. The Comanche Indians named the Spanish Peaks "Wahatoya," meaning "breasts of the world." Giant rock walls (dikes) radiate out from these peaks.

The town, now known for its art galleries and shops, is on the Scenic Highway of Legends (SR 12), which follows the Cucharas River past ranches, aspen groves, clear lakes and the small town of Cuchara. Recreational options include fishing, biking, hiking and hunting. The Rio Grande Scenic Railroad *(see attraction listing p. 39)* schedules daily trips to and from La Veta in the summer and fall seasons over the scenic La Veta Pass.

La Veta-Cuchara Chamber of Commerce Information Center: P.O. Box 32, La Veta, CO 81055. **Phone:** (719) 742-3676.

FRANCISCO FORT MUSEUM, off US 160 to SR 12, following signs to 306 S. Main St., is within an 1862 fort and features seven buildings surrounding an original Spanish-style adobe plaza. The fort contains 11 display rooms, including a kitchen, bedroom, parlor and country store. Fossils, Native American pottery and 19th-century farm equipment are featured.

Other historic buildings include an 1800s saloon, blacksmith shop and log schoolhouse. Guided tours depart from 123 W. Francisco St. **Time:** Allow 1 hour minimum. **Hours:** Tues.-Sat. 10-4, Sun. 11-5, late May-late Oct. Hours may vary. Phone ahead to confirm schedule. **Cost:** $5; $4 (senior citizens and military with ID); free (ages 0-12). **Phone:** (719) 742-5501.

LEADVILLE (C-3) pop. 2,602, elev. 10,152'

Said to be the highest incorporated city in the country, Leadville lies at an altitude that makes its climate rigorous even by Rocky Mountain standards. No less heady is its history, which condenses all the dramatic elements of the mining era into one compact package.

The discovery of gold in California Gulch in 1860 triggered the usual stampede of prospectors; within 4 months of the initial find, Oro City had more than 5,000 miners working a half-mile segment of the gulch. While there was plenty of gold, extracting it was hampered by heavy black sand that clogged sluice boxes. When the easily obtainable ore dwindled, so did Oro City.

By 1870 only a few residents remained. One of these was H.A.W. Tabor, who, in league with the heavy black sand, was to provide the necessary ingredients for a great American saga—the tale of fabulous wealth and flamboyant romance that has been immortalized in the opera "The Ballad of Baby Doe."

The black sand was carbonate of lead, and it was full of silver. By 1880 Leadville—formerly Oro City—was a booming town of 30,000 with storekeeper Tabor as mayor. It was Tabor's financing of a pair of German shoemakers that catapulted him to incredible wealth. He bought up as many claims as he could in the district, including the Matchless, which yielded up to $100,000 a month at its peak.

Drunk with money and generosity, Tabor spent so freely that he alienated his wife, Augusta. He met young, beautiful Baby Doe, whose zest for the pleasures of life matched his own. Tabor divorced Augusta, married Baby Doe and moved to Denver to begin a career as a public servant.

Since the beginning of the silver boom, Leadville district mines have produced nearly $2 billion in gold, silver, lead, zinc, copper, iron, bismuth, manganese and molybdenum.

Colorado's highest peak, 14,433-foot Mount Elbert, is 9 miles south via US 24. The 82-mile Top of the Rockies scenic and historic byway passes through the area. Leadville also is the northern gateway to the Arkansas Headwaters Recreation Area *(see Recreation Areas Chart).*

Leadville/Lake County Chamber of Commerce: 809 Harrison Ave., P.O. Box 861, Leadville, CO 80461. **Phone:** (719) 486-3900 or (888) 532-3845.

Self-guiding tours: Free maps of historic areas and mountain biking, hiking and skiing trails are available from the chamber of commerce.

HEALY HOUSE MUSEUM AND DEXTER CABIN, 912 Harrison Ave., depict Western life in a booming 19th-century silver mining town. Built as a private home in 1878, the three-story, clapboard Greek Revival Healy House is restored to its original Victorian style. Lavish furnishings and collections, including items belonging to silver magnate Horace Tabor and his wife Augusta, depict the late 1800s bonanza mining period. Gardens include heritage plants and native wildflowers.

The 1879 Dexter Cabin—built by James V. Dexter, one of the state's early millionaires— looks like a rustic log cabin from the outside but is finished inside with fine woodwork and hardwood floors.

Guided tours are available by reservation year-round. **Time:** Allow 1 hour minimum. **Hours:** Daily 10-4:30, late May-early Oct. Last tour begins at 3:45. **Cost:** $6; $5.50 (ages 65+); $4.50 (ages 6-16). **Phone:** (719) 486-0487.

HERITAGE MUSEUM, 9th St. and Harrison Ave., depicts Leadville's history with a series of dioramas and mining-era memorabilia. An art gallery, a replica of the town's 19th-century ice palace and an exhibit about the U.S. Army's 10th Mountain Division also are featured.

Time: Allow 30 minutes minimum. **Hours:** Daily 10-5, May-Sept. **Cost:** $6; $3 (ages 6-16). **Phone:** (719) 486-1878.

THE HISTORIC TABOR HOME is at 116 E. 5th St. This was the first home of entrepreneur Horace Tabor, perhaps the most famous of the Silver Kings. Guided tours of the renovated home tell the life story of the Tabor family. **Time:** Allow 45 minutes minimum. **Hours:** Daily 10-4, Memorial Day-Labor Day. Limited winter hours; phone ahead to confirm schedule. **Cost:** $5; $4 (ages 63+); $3 (ages 6-12). **Phone:** (719) 486-0708 for reservations.

LEADVILLE, COLORADO & SOUTHERN RAILROAD COMPANY, 3 blks. e. on 7th St., offers scenic narrated railroad trips through the Colorado Rocky Mountains from Leadville to Climax. Themed trips to see wildflowers and fall colors also are available.

Time: Allow 2 hours, 30 minutes minimum. **Hours:** Trips depart daily at 10 and 2, mid-June to mid-Aug.; Mon.-Fri at 1, Sat.-Sun. at 10 and 2, mid-Aug. to early Oct.; daily at 1, May 1 to mid-June. Phone ahead to confirm schedule. **Cost:** Fare $37; $20 (ages 4-12). **Phone:** (719) 486-3936 or (866) 386-3936.

LEADVILLE NATIONAL FISH HATCHERY is 2 mi. w. off US 24 on SR 300. Established in 1889, this hatchery is one of the oldest in the federal system. It propagates cutthroat and rainbow trout. A visitor center offers educational information and a historic perspective on hatchery operations. Hiking, snowshoeing, cross-country skiing and fish feeding are offered. **Hours:** Grounds dawn-dusk. Hatchery daily 7-3:30. **Cost:** Free. **Phone:** (719) 486-0189. 🔁

THE MATCHLESS MINE AND "BABY DOE'S" CABIN is 1.2 mi. e. on E. 7th St. Sen. H.A.W. Tabor earned his wealth from the Matchless Mine and other claims during Leadville's silver boom of the 1880s. The depletion of high-grade silver ore and extravagant spending combined with the repeal of the Sherman Purchase Act of 1893 dealt the final blow to his fortune. Legend says that on his deathbed in 1899, Tabor instructed his second wife, Baby Doe, to "hang onto the Matchless." She did, living in their cabin in poverty until her death in 1935. The museum has exhibits of Baby Doe memorabilia and displays about 19th-century mining.

Hours: Daily noon-5, Memorial Day weekend-Sept. 30. Guided tours are given at 1 and 3. **Cost:** (includes tour) $10; $8 (students with ID); $free (ages 0-6). Cash only. **Phone:** (719) 486-1229. 🈁

THE NATIONAL MINING HALL OF FAME AND MUSEUM, 120 W. 9th St., is housed in a 70,000-square-foot Victorian school built during the 19th-century silver boom. It offers 17 exhibit rooms portraying the history of mining from the Bronze Age through the present.

Visitors may walk through a replicated underground hard rock mine complete with ore cars and drills. The Gold Rush Room exhibits gold samples and mining artifacts. Illuminated crystals from around the world are presented in the Crystal Room.

Murals, dioramas and sculptures highlight historic mining developments. The Hall of Fame contains plaques honoring individuals who made significant contributions to the industry. **Time:** Allow 2 hours minimum. **Hours:** Daily 9-5, mid-May to mid-Nov.; Tues.-Sun. 9-5, rest of year. **Cost:** $10; $8 (ages 13-19 and 65+); free (ages 0-12). **Phone:** (719) 486-1229.

TABOR OPERA HOUSE, 308 Harrison Ave., opened in 1879. It retains the decor of its "last show," when miners spent huge sums to be entertained by celebrated New York and Chicago artists. A museum on the second floor features opera house memorabilia and traces area history. **Hours:** Mon.-Sat. 10-5, Memorial Day-Labor Day; by appointment rest of year. **Cost:** Donations. **Phone:** (303) 550-1049.

RECREATIONAL ACTIVITIES

Skiing
- **Ski Cooper** is 9 mi. n. of Leadville at 1101 Poplar St. **Hours:** Daily 9-4, mid-Dec. to mid-Apr. **Phone:** (719) 486-2277 or (800) 707-6114.

ALPS MOTEL   719/486-1223

Motel $48-$98

Address: 207 Elm St 80461 **Location:** Just s of center on US 24. **Facility:** 8 units. 1 story, exterior corridors. **Parking:** winter plug-ins. **Terms:** check-in 4 pm, 3 day cancellation notice-fee imposed.

MCGINNIS COTTAGE INN BED & BREAKFAST   719/486-3110

Historic Bed & Breakfast $135-$170 **Address:** 809 Spruce St 80461 **Location:** Just w of US 24 and 8th St, then just n. **Facility:** The amiable owners of this charming Victorian B&B make guests feel at home. Built in 1898, this 'painted lady' features a cozy living room with a carved wood fireplace. 4 units. 3 stories (no elevator), interior/exterior corridors. **Parking:** street only. **Terms:** 15 day cancellation notice-fee imposed.

SUPER 8   (719)486-3637

Motel $66-$210 **Address:** 1128 S Hwy 24 80461 **Location:** On US 24, 1 mi s. **Facility:** 58 units. 3 stories (no elevator), interior corridors. **Parking:** winter plug-ins. **Terms:** cancellation fee imposed. **Activities:** sauna.

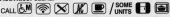

WHERE TO EAT

QUINCY'S STEAK & SPIRITS   719/486-9765

Steak. Casual Dining. $9-$20 **AAA Inspector Notes:** In an age when people feel overwhelmed by too many choices, this restaurant offers relief. Friday and Saturday, find a prime rib or sirloin dinner. The rest of the week is devoted to filet mignon. That's right—there are only one or two options, but patrons know what to expect. Each meal comes with a salad, baked potato, and bread. Dessert options change nightly. The menu also offers a vegetarian lasagna. **Features:** full bar. **Address:** 416 Harrison Ave 80461 **Location:** In historic town center. **Parking:** street only.

TENNESSEE PASS CAFE   719/486-8101

International. Casual Dining. $10-$14 **AAA Inspector Notes:** The brightly painted cafe presents an eclectic menu that picks up on influences from Asia, Mexico, Italy and America. For a light meal, guests might try a flavorful salad or sandwich. Pizza, pasta, stir-fry and Mexican favorites make for a heartier stomach-filler. In summer, patrons head for the patio to enjoy the temperate Leadville weather while dining. **Features:** full bar, patio dining. **Address:** 222 Harrison Ave 80461 **Location:** On US 24 (Harrison Ave) at 2nd St, south end. **Parking:** street only.

LIMON (C-6) pop. 1,880, elev. 5,365'

Limon was named after railroad crew boss John Limon. The town is rich in railroad history; the Union Pacific Railroad and Kyle Railroad in Phillipsburg, Kan., still use the rail yards. Near downtown is the historic Smoky Hill Trail, established in the mid-1800s by gold prospectors seeking a quick route to the Rockies.

Limon Chamber of Commerce: 205 E Ave., P.O. Box 101, Limon, CO 80828. **Phone:** (719) 775-9418.

LIMON HERITAGE MUSEUM, 1 mi. w. of I-70 exit 361, then 2 blks. s. on E Ave., is housed in the restored Union Pacific and Rock Island depot, and an exhibit building featuring a two-room prairie house, a mercantile store, geology displays, a radar weather station, plows, wagons and an 11-foot-high bronze sculpture, "Prairie Odyssey." An extensive Native American collection is a major highlight of the museum. Five rail cars, including a restored dining car and caboose, contain permanent and changing exhibits about area history. Guided tours are available by appointment. **Time:** Allow 30 minutes minimum. **Hours:** Mon.-Sat. 1-8, Sun. 1-4, Memorial Day-Labor Day. **Cost:** Free. **Phone:** (719) 775-8605. *(See ad this page.)*

HOLIDAY INN EXPRESS HOTEL & SUITES (719)775-9033
Hotel $99-$209 **Address:** 803 Hwy 24 80828 **Location:** I-70 exit 359, just s. **Facility:** 68 units. 3 stories, interior corridors. **Terms:** check-in 4 pm, cancellation fee imposed. **Pool(s):** heated indoor. **Activities:** hot tub, exercise room. **Guest Services:** coin laundry.

LIMON COMFORT INN (719)775-2752
Hotel $89-$169 **Address:** 2255 9th St 80828 **Location:** I-70 exit 359, just s. **Facility:** 50 units. 2 stories (no elevator), interior corridors. **Pool(s):** heated indoor. **Activities:** hot tub, limited exercise equipment. **Guest Services:** coin laundry. **Featured Amenity:** full hot breakfast.

SAFARI INN (719)775-2363
Motel $49-$145 **Address:** 637 Main St 80828 **Location:** I-70 exit 361, 0.8 mi w. **Facility:** 28 units. 1-2 stories (no elevator), exterior corridors. **Parking:** winter plug-ins. **Terms:** 3 day cancellation notice-fee imposed. **Pool(s):** heated outdoor. **Activities:** playground. **Guest Services:** coin laundry, area transportation. **Featured Amenity:** continental breakfast.

▼ See AAA listing this page ▼

WHERE TO EAT

OSCAR'S BAR & GRILLE   719/775-2396

▼▼ ▼▼ American. Casual Dining. $7-$20 **AAA Inspector Notes:** The movie posters, photos of Hollywood legends, and entrées named after movies add flair to this comfort-food restaurant. The menu features fried chicken, pot roast and meatloaf as well as a variety of steaks, pasta dishes, sandwiches and even some Mexican food. **Features:** full bar. **Address:** 2295 9th St 80828 **Location:** I-70 exit 359, just s. [L] [D]

RUBY'S   719/775-9564

▼▼ ▼▼ American. Casual Dining. $8-$11 **AAA Inspector Notes:** Locals congregate in this cheerful eatery to enjoy comfort food and friendly conversation. Most of the tables are large, and patrons often share with other parties when it's busy. Menu items include hamburgers, sandwiches, steaks and even some Mexican dishes. Pie-lovers will rejoice! They make the fruit pies from scratch with a homemade crust. **Address:** 197 E Ave 80828 **Location:** I-70 exit 361, 1.2 mi w, then just s. **Parking:** street only. [B] [L]

LITTLETON (D-9) pop. 41,737, elev. 5,389'

On the southern edge of metropolitan Denver, Littleton was settled in the 1860s by farmers homesteading the fertile land along the South Platte River. The arrival of Martin Marietta Corp. in the late 1950s brought rapid growth and economic vitality to this small town.

The city's more than 1,477 acres of parks and open space afford opportunities for picnicking, fishing, hiking and biking. Chatfield State Park *(see Recreation Areas Chart),* a few miles south, is a popular summer recreation spot. Roxborough State Park offers scenic hiking trails that allow for cross-country skiing in winter, opportunities for wildlife viewing and a visitor center featuring historical and geological exhibits; pets are not permitted. Cyclists enjoy riding along the scenic Mary Carter Greenway, with the South Platte River flowing adjacent to the trail. Pedestrians can take a self-guiding walking tour of the historic downtown area with its charming Main Street.

The Columbine Memorial in Clement Park remembers the innocent victims of the 1999 shootings at nearby Columbine High School. It is configured around an inner Ring of Remembrance and an outer Ring of Healing, honoring all those whose lives were affected by the tragedy.

Western Welcome Week, held in mid-August, is a 10-day celebration that includes concerts, fireworks, a parade, an arts and crafts fair, fishing and sports competitions.

South Metro Denver Chamber of Commerce: 2154 E. Commons Ave., Suite 342, Centennial, CO 80122. **Phone:** (303) 795-0142.

DENVER BOTANIC GARDENS AT CHATFIELD is at 8500 W. Deer Creek Canyon Rd. Encompassing 750 acres along Deer Creek, this preserve includes native flora and fauna, wetlands and several distinct ecosystems. A restored 19th-century ranch, farm and one-room schoolhouse also are presented. A children's play area includes a tree house and water features. Nature trails afford views of native wildlife, including coyotes, deer and birds. The Corn Maze is a popular event held in September and October.

Pets are not permitted on the grounds. **Time:** Allow 30 minutes minimum. **Hours:** Daily 9-5; closed Jan. 1, Thanksgiving, day after Thanksgiving, Christmas Eve and Christmas. **Cost:** $5 per passenger vehicle. **Phone:** (720) 865-4336.

THE HUDSON GARDENS & EVENT CENTER is at 6115 S. Santa Fe Dr., 3 mi. n. of jct. SR 470 and US 85, or .5 mi. s. of Bowles Ave. The gardens' 30 acres offer beauty and tranquility, and its grounds feature a multitude of plants, trees and flowers that thrive in Colorado. The setting is complemented by ponds, sculpture, fountains, a miniature railroad and wildlife.

Seasonal events and educational forums are available. **Hours:** Gardens daily 9-5, May-Sept. **Cost:** Free. **Phone:** (303) 797-8565.

LITTLETON MUSEUM is at 6028 S. Gallup St. The museum has a permanent gallery that tells the story of Littleton from its settlement days to the present, a gallery that displays traveling exhibitions, a gallery featuring fine arts and photographs, and a children's area with hands-on exhibits.

The complex also has two living-history farms with costumed interpreters, historic buildings furnished in period, livestock typical of the 19th century, gardens, a blacksmith shop, an 1860s schoolhouse and an icehouse. **Time:** Allow 1 hour minimum. **Hours:** Tues.-Fri. 8-5, Sat. 10-5, Sun. 1-5. Closed major holidays. **Cost:** Donations. **Phone:** (303) 795-3950.

RECREATIONAL ACTIVITIES
Hot Air Ballooning
- **Balloon Rides of the Rockies** meets and departs from Chatfield State Park. **Hours:** Flights depart at dawn (weather permitting). **Phone:** (866) 606-7433.
- **Colorado Hot Air Balloon Rides** departs from Chatfield State Park, .5 mi. s. of SR 470 and Wadsworth Blvd. **Hours:** Flights depart daily at dawn (weather permitting), May-Oct. **Phone:** (888) 468-9280.

HAMPTON INN & SUITES   303/794-1800

▼▼ ▼▼ ▼▼ Hotel. Rates not provided. **Address:** 3095 W County Line Rd 80129 **Location:** SR 470 exit Santa Fe Dr, just n, then 0.3 mi e. **Facility:** 118 units. 6 stories, interior corridors. **Amenities:** *Some:* safes. heated indoor. **Activities:** hot tub, exercise room. **Guest Services:** valet and coin laundry, area transportation.

AAA Benefit: Members save up to 10%!

[icons] [⬛] [BIZ] [HS] [📶] [✕] [⬛] / SOME UNITS [⬛] [⬛]

(See map & index p. 136.)

HAMPTON INN & SUITES DENVER LITTLETON
303/973-2400 **96**

▼▼▼ **Hotel.** Rates not provided. **Address:** 7611 Shaffer Pkwy 80127 **Location:** SR 470 exit Ken Caryl Ave, just e, then just s. **Facility:** 89 units. 4 stories, interior corridors. **Pool(s):** heated indoor. **Activities:** hot tub, exercise room. **Guest Services:** valet and coin laundry.

AAA Benefit:
Members save up to 10%!

HOLIDAY INN EXPRESS HOTEL & SUITES DENVER SW-LITTLETON
(720)981-1000 **95**

▼▼▼ **Hotel** $99-$250 **Address:** 12683 W Indore Pl 80127 **Location:** SR 470 exit Ken Caryl Ave, just e to Shaffer Ave, just n, then w. **Facility:** 76 units. 3 stories, interior corridors. **Terms:** cancellation fee imposed. **Pool(s):** heated indoor. **Activities:** hot tub, exercise room. **Guest Services:** valet and coin laundry.

HOMEWOOD SUITES BY HILTON-DENVER LITTLETON
720/981-4763 **97**

▼▼▼ **Extended Stay Hotel.** Rates not provided. **Address:** 7630 Shaffer Pkwy 80127 **Location:** SR 470 exit Ken Caryl Ave, just e, then just s. **Facility:** 84 efficiencies, some two bedrooms. 4 stories, interior corridors. **Terms:** check-in 4 pm. **Pool(s):** heated indoor. **Activities:** hot tub, exercise room. **Guest Services:** valet and coin laundry.

AAA Benefit:
Members save up to 10%!

TOWNEPLACE SUITES BY MARRIOTT-DENVER SOUTHWEST/LITTLETON
(303)972-0555

▼▼▼ **Extended Stay Hotel** $108-$229

TownePlace SUITES Marriott

AAA Benefit:
Members save 5% or more!

Address: 10902 W Toller Dr 80127 **Location:** SR 470 exit Kipling Pkwy, just s, then 0.4 mi w on Ute St. **Facility:** 99 kitchen units, some two bedrooms. 3 stories, interior corridors. **Pool(s):** heated outdoor. **Activities:** exercise room. **Guest Services:** valet and coin laundry. **Featured Amenity:** breakfast buffet.

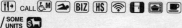
WHERE TO EAT

LIL' RICCI'S NY PIZZA
303/948-0274 **149**

▼▼ Italian. Casual Dining. $7-$14 **AAA Inspector Notes:** Although this restaurant offers a few pasta dishes, most patrons opt for the famous New York-style pizzas. The menu also features calzones, sandwiches and salads. This is the perfect place to stop for a slice and a brew after a long day. **Features:** full bar, happy hour. **Address:** 12652 W Ken Caryl Ave 80127 **Location:** SR 470 exit Ken Caryl Ave, just e, then just s; in strip mall. [L] [D]

NO NO'S CAFE
303/738-8330

▼▼▼ Southern. Cafeteria. $9-$18 **AAA Inspector Notes:** This café specializes in home-style Southern cooking, including lighter dishes and vegetarian selections for particular diets. People return for comfort foods such as shepherd's pie, gumbo and flank steak. Mayme's macaroni and cheese, which makes a delicious side dish or entrée, exemplifies menu items credited to their actual creators. The all-year signature menu is complemented by features that change frequently. **Features:** full bar. **Address:** 3005 W County Line Rd 80129 **Location:** SR 470 exit Santa Fe, just n, then just e. [B] [L] [D]

ROMANO'S ITALIAN RESTAURANT
303/798-4944 **148**

▼▼ Italian. Casual Dining. $9-$19 **AAA Inspector Notes:** It's rare to find a restaurant that's been open since 1967, not to mention owned and operated by the same family. There's a clear reason why the Romano family has been so successful; it's their friendly staff and flavorful Italian American dishes. The extensive menu features sandwiches, pizza and pasta dishes, including stuffed shells, ravioli, spaghetti, tortellini and more. The quaint storefront location hearkens back to a time before the town grew up around it. **Features:** full bar. **Address:** 5666 S Windermere St 80123 **Location:** Jct Littleton Blvd, just n. **Parking:** on-site and street. [L] [D]

THAI BISTRO
720/981-7600 **147**

▼▼ Southern Thai. Casual Dining. $8-$17 **AAA Inspector Notes:** Utilizing robustly flavored recipes from southern Thailand, this restaurant has won numerous awards. Exotic herbs and spices help create unmistakable flavors. The restaurant's exterior is deceiving, as it belies the spacious, tranquil dining room inside. Be sure to try the savory drunken noodles. **Features:** full bar. **Address:** 5924 S Kipling Pkwy, Suite G 80127 **Location:** US 285 exit Kipling Pkwy, 3.2 mi s. [L] [D]

LONE TREE pop. 10,218
• Part of Denver area — see map p. 116

DENVER MARRIOTT SOUTH AT PARK MEADOWS
(303)925-0004

▼▼▼ **Hotel** $93-$297

 MARRIOTT

AAA Benefit:
Members save 5% or more!

Address: 10345 Park Meadows Dr 80124 **Location:** I-25 exit 193 (Lincoln Ave), just w to Park Meadows Dr, just n, then e. **Facility:** 279 units. 6 stories, interior corridors. **Pool(s):** heated indoor. **Activities:** hot tub, exercise room. **Guest Services:** valet and coin laundry, area transportation.

ELEMENT DENVER PARK MEADOWS
(303)790-2100

▼▼▼ **Contemporary Hotel** $99-$199

element

AAA Benefit: Members save up to 15%, plus Starwood Preferred Guest® benefits!

Address: 9985 Park Meadows Dr 80124 **Location:** Jct Yosemite St, 0.4 mi e. **Facility:** 123 units, some efficiencies. 4 stories, interior corridors. *Bath:* shower only. **Terms:** cancellation fee imposed. **Amenities:** safes. **Pool(s):** heated indoor. **Activities:** picnic facilities, exercise room. **Guest Services:** valet and coin laundry, area transportation. (*See ad p. 154.*)

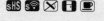

HAMPTON INN & SUITES DENVER/SOUTH-RIDGEGATE
303/790-4100

 Hotel. Rates not provided. **Address:** 10030 Trainstation Cir 80124 **Location:** I-25 exit 193, just w to Park Meadows Blvd, just s to Chatham Dr, just e, then just n. **Facility:** 106 units. 4 stories, interior corridors. **Pool(s):** heated indoor. **Activities:** exercise room. **Guest Services:** valet and coin laundry, area transportation.

AAA Benefit: Members save up to 10%!

CALL ⚒ 🚲 BIZ HS 📶 ❌ 📺 / SOME UNITS 🛗 🖨

HYATT PLACE DENVER - SOUTH/PARK MEADOWS
(303)662-8500

Hotel
$79-$219

HYATT PLACE
AAA Benefit: Members save 10%!

Address: 9030 E Westview Rd 80124 **Location:** I-25 exit 195 (County Line Rd), 0.5 mi w to Yosemite St, just s to Parkland Rd, then just w; SR 470 exit Yosemite St, 0.5 mi nw, just n on Parkland Rd, then just w. Adjacent to Park Meadows. **Facility:** 127 units. 6 stories, interior corridors. **Terms:** cancellation fee imposed. **Amenities:** safes. **Pool(s):** heated indoor. **Activities:** exercise room. **Guest Services:** valet laundry, area transportation. **Featured Amenity:** breakfast buffet.

SAVE ⚒ Y 🚲 BIZ 📶 ❌ 🎿 🛗 📺 / SOME UNITS 🐕

STAYBRIDGE SUITES DENVER SOUTH-LONE TREE
303/649-1010

 **Extended Stay Hotel.** Rates not provided. **Address:** 7820 Park Meadows Dr 80124 **Location:** I-25 exit 195 (County Line Rd), w to Acres Green Dr, s to E Park Meadows Dr, then just w; SR 470 exit Quebec St, just s, then just e. **Facility:** 115 efficiencies, some two bedrooms. 3 stories, interior corridors. **Pool(s):** heated outdoor. **Activities:** picnic facilities, exercise room. **Guest Services:** complimentary and valet laundry, area transportation.

⚒ CALL ⚒ 🚲 BIZ HS 📶 🛗 🖨 📺 / SOME UNITS 🐕

WHERE TO EAT

HACIENDA COLORADO
303/858-8588

🔱🔱 Mexican. Casual Dining. $10-$19 **AAA Inspector Notes:** This restaurant is aptly named; when you walk in it appears to be a large home with bright colors and comfortable décor. Fresh, flavorful salsa is served with thinner-than-usual chips as you peruse the menu. Try the juicy fajitas or the unique, mildly spicy poblano de pollo- a roasted poblano stuffed with chicken, cheese, chipotle aioli and a tomatillo corn relish. The portions are large and plentiful, and the prices are reasonable. **Features:** full bar, happy hour. **Address:** 10500 Bierstadt Way 80112 **Location:** I-25 exit 193 (Lincoln St), 0.4 mi e to Havana St, n to Meridian Blvd (stay in left lane), 0.5 mi w, then just w. L D

JOHN HOLLY'S ASIAN BISTRO
303/768-9088

🔱🔱 Asian. Casual Dining. $8-$25 **AAA Inspector Notes:** This unpretentious yet alluring eatery serves an imaginative and tempting variety of Asian dishes. The dining area has a flair for casual elegance with its contemporary style and excellent service, while the streamlined sushi bar also offers seating. The creative menu appeals to discriminating palates. **Features:** full bar. **Address:** 9232 Park Meadows Dr 80124 **Location:** I-25 exit 195 (County Line Rd), 0.5 mi w to Yosemite St, then s. L D

VIA BACI MODERN ITALIAN BISTRO
303/790-0828

🔱🔱 Italian. Casual Dining. $9-$18 **AAA Inspector Notes:** Although well-known for its gourmet pizzas, this popular restaurant also offers flavorful pasta dishes such as pumpkin ravioli, chicken cavatappi and three-meat lasagna. In addition to pasta, patrons can choose from a list of sandwiches, salads and oven-fired meat entrees. The cheerful decor matches the personality of the friendly staff. **Features:** full bar, happy hour. **Address:** 10005 Commons St, Bldg A 80124 **Location:** I-25 exit 193, 0.7 mi w on E Lincoln Ave, then just s; in shopping complex. L D

LONGMONT (B-9) pop. 86,270, elev. 4,942'
• Restaurants p. 228

Before Longmont was established at the foot of the Rocky Mountains, the area was the haunt of gold seekers, fur traders and adventurers. However, in the mid-19th century, Longmont—in the fertile St. Vrain River Valley—attracted a more stable type of pioneer. The farming community established in 1871 as the Chicago-Colorado Colony was named for Colorado explorer Maj. Steven H. Long, who explored the valley in 1820.

The Golden Rule Store was a Longmont retailer credited with launching JCPenney into the dry goods business; the name was changed accordingly in 1912. Today, the town is an important agricultural center, with sugar beets a chief crop. An appreciation of the arts has resulted in a growing collection of public art pieces placed around town. Outdoor recreational opportunities are plentiful and include hiking, bicycling, horseback riding, hot air balloon rides and skiing.

Longmont Area Visitors Association: 630 Coffman St., Longmont, CO 80501. **Phone:** (303) 776-9011.

LONGMONT MUSEUM is 1 mi. s. on US 287, then e. to 400 Quail Rd. Regional history is exhibited in several galleries, including the Longs Peak Room, which offers panoramic views of the Rocky Mountains and Great Plains. Front Range Rising is an interactive exhibit that guides visitors through 14,000 years of area history featuring maps, re-created habitations and photographs.

A research archive is available. Special exhibits about art, history and technology are offered. A 250-seat auditorium presents concerts, films, lectures and special events. **Time:** Allow 1 hour minimum. **Hours:** Mon.-Sat. 9-5, Sun. 1-5. **Cost:** Free. General admission free. Additional fees for special exhibits. **Phone:** (303) 651-8374.

BEST WESTERN PLUS PLAZA HOTEL
(303)776-2000

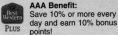
Hotel
$109-$179

AAA Benefit: Save 10% or more every day and earn 10% bonus points!

Address: 1900 Ken Pratt Blvd 80501 **Location:** Jct US 287, 1.3 mi sw on Ken Pratt Blvd (SR 119). **Facility:** 210 units. 2 stories, interior corridors. **Amenities:** safes. **Pool(s):** heated outdoor. **Activities:** sauna, exercise room. **Guest Services:** valet and coin laundry. **Featured Amenity:** breakfast buffet.

SAVE ⚒ Y 🚲 BIZ 📶 ❌ 🛗 📺 / SOME UNITS 🐕 🖨

Remember, car seats, booster seats and seat belts save lives

COURTYARD BY MARRIOTT BOULDER/LONGMONT
(303)682-1166

▼▼▼ Hotel $81-$221 **Address:** 1410 Dry Creek Dr 80503 **Location:** I-25 exit 235 (SR 52), 8 mi w to 95th (Hover Rd), 3.8 mi n to Clover Basin, just w, then s. **Facility:** 78 units. 3 stories, interior corridors. **Pool(s):** heated indoor. **Activities:** hot tub, picnic facilities, exercise room. **Guest Services:** valet and coin laundry, boarding pass kiosk.

AAA Benefit:
Members save 5% or more!

🍴 🍸 CALL 🦽📶 🏊 BIZ 🛜 ✕ 🎥 🔌 🖥 💻 / SOME UNITS 🧳

HOLIDAY INN EXPRESS & SUITES
(303)684-0404

▼▼▼ Hotel $109-$184 **Address:** 1355 Dry Creek Dr 80503 **Location:** Jct Main St and Ken Pratt Blvd (SR 119), 2.2 mi w, just n, then just ne. **Facility:** 75 units. 3 stories, interior corridors. **Pool(s):** heated indoor. **Activities:** hot tub, exercise room. **Guest Services:** valet and coin laundry.

🍴➕ CALL 🦽📶 🏊 BIZ HS 🛜 ✕ 💻 / SOME UNITS 🛏 🔌 🧳

RESIDENCE INN BY MARRIOTT BOULDER/LONGMONT
(303)702-9933

▼▼▼ Extended Stay Hotel $123-$251 **Address:** 1450 Dry Creek Dr 80503 **Location:** Jct Main St and Ken Pratt Blvd (SR 119), 2.2 mi w, just n, then just ne; jct Hoover Rd and SR 119. **Facility:** 84 units, some two bedrooms, efficiencies and kitchens. 3 stories, interior corridors. **Pool(s):** heated indoor. **Activities:** hot tub, picnic facilities, exercise room. **Guest Services:** valet and coin laundry.

AAA Benefit:
Members save 5% or more!

🍴➕ CALL 🦽📶 🏊 BIZ 🛜 ✕ 🎥 🔌 🖥 💻 / SOME UNITS 🛏

SPRINGHILL SUITES BY MARRIOTT BOULDER/LONGMONT
(303)682-2894

▼▼▼ Hotel $89-$206 **Address:** 1470 Dry Creek Dr 80503 **Location:** Jct Ken Pratt Blvd (SR 119) and Hover Rd, just n to Clover Basin Dr, then just w. **Facility:** 90 units. 3 stories, interior corridors. **Pool(s):** heated indoor. **Activities:** hot tub, exercise room. **Guest Services:** valet and coin laundry.

AAA Benefit:
Members save 5% or more!

🍴➕ CALL 🦽📶 🏊 BIZ 🛜 ✕ 🎥 🔌 🖥 💻

SUPER 8 TWIN PEAKS, LONGMONT
(303)772-8106

▼▼▼ Hotel $63-$109

Address: 2446 N Main St 80501 **Location:** I-25 exit 243, 6.4 mi w on SR 66. **Facility:** 64 units. 2 stories (no elevator), interior corridors. **Terms:** cancellation fee imposed. **Amenities:** safes. **Guest Services:** coin laundry. **Featured Amenity:** continental breakfast.

SAVE 🍴➕ BIZ 🛜 🔌 🖥 💻 / SOME UNITS 🛏

WHERE TO EAT

3 MARGARITAS
303/682-0888

▼ Mexican. Casual Dining. $6-$19 **AAA Inspector Notes:** This family-owned place is part of a popular local chain. The menu features a variety of burritos, enchiladas and fajitas, as well as more creative items such as steak tampiquena, pollo culichi and camarones jarochos. Patrons wash down their food with one of the many specialty margaritas. **Features:** full bar, patio dining, happy hour. **Address:** 2350 Main St 80501 **Location:** 2.5 mi n on US 287 at SR 66. L D

FLAVOR OF INDIA
303/682-9010

▼▼▼ Indian. Casual Dining. $10-$25 **AAA Inspector Notes:** In addition to the buffet, patrons may order off an extensive menu that includes traditional Indian dishes featuring lamb, chicken, vegetables and seafood. The paneer pakoras and vegetable samosas are popular appetizers. There are a variety of naan breads to choose from, ranging from garlic to dried fruit and nuts. **Features:** full bar. **Address:** 516 Main St 80501 **Location:** Jct US 287 and Ken Pratt Blvd (SR 119), 1 mi n. **Parking:** street only. L D

MARTINI'S BISTRO
303/651-2772

▼▼▼ American. Fine Dining. $11-$28 **AAA Inspector Notes:** Located in a historic home, this bistro offers a variety of martinis and specialty cocktails. Flavorful entrées include all-natural Colorado rib-eye, Italian-style seafood stew, and grilled salmon. Desserts change nightly, but may include a chocolate hazelnut torte, cheesecake and creme brûlée. **Features:** full bar, patio dining. **Address:** 543 Terry St 80501 **Location:** Just w of US 287 on 3rd St, then 0.3 mi n. **Parking:** street only. L D

MIKE O'SHAYS RESTAURANT & ALE HOUSE
303/772-0252

▼▼ American. Casual Dining. $10-$16 **AAA Inspector Notes:** Patrons don't have to be Irish to appreciate the good food and pub atmosphere of this local favorite. The diversified menu includes salads, sandwiches, fresh fish, scampi and pasta entrées. A city parking lot is in the back. **Features:** full bar, patio dining, happy hour. **Address:** 512 Main St 80501 **Location:** Just n on US 287; downtown. **Parking:** street only. L D LATE

THE RIB HOUSE BY CHEF EXTRAORDINAIRE
303/485-6988

▼ Barbecue. Quick Serve. $6-$26 **AAA Inspector Notes:** Located in "New Town Prospect" (which is worth seeing as it looks like a set from a Disney movie), this barbecue restaurant is worth finding. It features Kansas City-style 'que with pork, brisket, chicken, links and smoked turkey. But the ribs are what live up to the menu's claim of "the best baby back ribs in Colorado" as they are smoked for 12 hours and are tender, lean and delicious. **Features:** beer & wine, patio dining. **Address:** 1920 S Coffman St 80504 **Location:** Jct Ken Pratt Blvd (SR 119) and US 287, 1 mi s on US 287 to Pike Rd, 0.3 mi w to Coffman St, then s. **Parking:** on-site and street. D

SUGARBEET
303/651-3330

▼▼▼ American. Casual Dining. $23-$38 **AAA Inspector Notes:** In a quiet warehouse area close to the historic part of town, this restaurant quickly fills up at night. Chef/owner Seth Witherspoon prefers to work with local ranchers, dairies and farmers, which means the menu features fresh, seasonal ingredients. Knowledgeable staff members, artwork from local artists and a relaxed atmosphere complement the meal. **Features:** full bar, patio dining, happy hour. **Reservations:** suggested. **Address:** 101 Pratt St, Unit A 80501 **Location:** Jct Ken Pratt Blvd (SR 119) and Main St, just n to 2nd Ave, just w, then just s. D

SUSHI HANA
303/485-1055

▼▼▼ Japanese. Casual Dining. $12-$36 **AAA Inspector Notes:** Although the building formerly housed a fast-food joint, the remodeled inside leaves little trace of Sushi Hana's previous incarnation. As the name implies, the menu consists of many sushi and sashimi dishes. Tempura, noodle and teriyaki entrées also are offered. I especially enjoyed the panko-crusted fried oysters. The salmon sushi was competently executed. I was less impressed by the Kobe beef sushi, as it was on the tough side and hard to chew. This made me suspect it wasn't Kobe beef. **Features:** beer & wine. **Address:** 2065 Main St 80501 **Location:** 2.2 mi n on US 287 at SR 66. L D

LOUISVILLE (C-8) pop. 18,376, elev. 5,394'

Although a statue of a miner outside City Hall pays tribute to the coal industry that Louisville was built upon, all traces of the mines have vanished and high-tech and health care now fuel the economy. Situated just east of Boulder and a half-hour from Denver, Louisville embodies small-town charm and is graced with a backdrop of majestic peaks looming in the distance.

The downtown area's rustic early 1900s buildings along Main and Front streets house pubs, thrift stores, boutiques and eateries with a family-friendly vibe, like the occasional ice cream parlor or sandwich shop. During summer Saturdays, a farmer's market takes place on Front and Walnut streets from 9-1; in addition to fresh produce, meats and baked goods, vendors tout such specialty items as chiles, Colorado wildflowers and homemade tamales.

Summer evenings bring the Downtown Street Faire, which runs from 5 to 10. Music, food, arts and crafts displays, fun activities for the kids, and a beer and wine garden are all part of the agenda at this free event. And there's a strong sense of community during winter, too, as the WinterSkate—an old-time ice skating rink—swings into action with the onset of the holidays, when traditional tunes entertain those gliding across the ice.

Louisville holds allure for the outdoor enthusiast, with Estes Park—the gateway to Rocky Mountain National Park—just over an hour's drive and the ski resorts of Summit County about 2 hours away. Coal Creek Golf Course, 585 W. Dillon Rd., offers 18 holes along with spectacular views of the Rockies; phone (303) 666-7888. Cyclists like to follow Coal Creek Trail, a diverse 7-mile trek extending from the golf course to Lafayette that travels through open spaces, cottonwood groves, ranch land and neighborhoods. The area is blessed with an abundance of biking and hiking trails, with most routes originating in nearby Boulder.

Louisville Chamber of Commerce: 901 Main St., Louisville, CO 80027. **Phone:** (303) 666-5747.

LOUISVILLE HISTORICAL MUSEUM is at 1001 Main St. Two historic buildings constructed between 1904 and 1908 feature artifacts and historic photographs reflecting the area's coal mining heritage. The Tomeo House is representative of a coal miner's home during the town's mining heyday. **Time:** Allow 30 minutes minimum. **Hours:** Tues.-Wed. and Sat. 10-3, Fri. 3-8. Closed major holidays. Phone ahead to confirm schedule. **Cost:** Free. **Phone:** (303) 665-9048.

BEST WESTERN PLUS LOUISVILLE INN & SUITES
(303)327-1215

Hotel
$89-$249

AAA Benefit: Save 10% or more every day and earn 10% bonus points!

Address: 960 W Dillon Rd 80027 **Location:** US 36 (Boulder Tpke) exit Superior (SR 170), just n on McCaslin Blvd to Dillon Rd, then just e. **Facility:** 62 units. 2 stories, interior corridors. **Amenities:** *Some:* safes. **Pool(s):** heated outdoor. **Activities:** hot tub, exercise room. **Guest Services:** valet and coin laundry.

COURTYARD BY MARRIOTT BOULDER/LOUISVILLE
(303)604-0007

Hotel $93-$209 **Address:** 948 W Dillon Rd 80027 **Location:** US 36 (Boulder Tpke) exit Superior (SR 170), n on McCaslin Blvd, then e. **Facility:** 154 units. 3 stories, interior corridors. **Pool(s):** heated indoor. **Activities:** hot tub, picnic facilities, exercise room. **Guest Services:** valet and coin laundry, boarding pass kiosk.

AAA Benefit: Members save 5% or more!

RESIDENCE INN BY MARRIOTT-BOULDER/LOUISVILLE
(303)665-2661

Extended Stay Hotel $106-$222 **Address:** 845 Coal Creek Cir 80027 **Location:** US 36 (Boulder Tpke) exit Superior (SR 170), n on McCaslin Blvd to Dillon Rd, then 0.6 mi e. **Facility:** 88 units, some two bedrooms, efficiencies and kitchens. 2 stories, interior corridors. **Amenities:** video games. **Pool(s):** heated indoor. **Activities:** hot tub, picnic facilities, exercise room. **Guest Services:** valet and coin laundry.

AAA Benefit: Members save 5% or more!

WHERE TO EAT

THE EMPIRE LOUNGE & RESTAURANT
303/665-2521

American. Casual Dining. $8-$24 **AAA Inspector Notes:** A food scene has evolved in downtown, and this restaurant is a major part of it. Menu items include homemade mozzarella with roasted red peppers, crispy calamari salad with miso-balsamic dressing and grilled flat iron steak with a tomatillo salsa. Of course, there is a classic burger and a pork and ricotta meatball hoagie for something more traditional. **Features:** full bar, happy hour. **Address:** 816 Main St 80027 **Location:** Between Walnut and Spruce sts; in historic downtown. **Parking:** street only.

LUCKY PIE PIZZA & TAP HOUSE
303/666-5743

Pizza. Casual Dining. $9-$18 **AAA Inspector Notes:** This is not a standard pizza joint. The menu features classic and innovative Italian starters like homemade mozzarella of the moment, pumpkin eggplant caponata, and tomato braised lamb meatballs. The thin-crust pizzas have gourmet toppings and creative combinations. Select from an extensive list of microbrews, many made in Colorado. **Features:** full bar, patio dining. **Address:** 637 Front St 80027 **Location:** Just s of jct Pine St.

LOVELAND (A-9) pop. 66,859, elev. 4,982'
• Hotels p. 230 • Restaurants p. 230

Hundreds of thousands of valentines from around the world are sent to Loveland each year to be hand-stamped by volunteers with the town's postmark and a special poem, which changes annually, and then re-mailed in February from the Sweetheart City.

The town, nestled in the valley at the mouth of Big Thompson Canyon, was named for W.A.H. Loveland, who supervised the building of the Colorado Central Railroad through the valley in 1877. Many who did not strike it rich in the gold fields struck it rich selling vegetables grown in this fertile area. Rocky Mountain National Park *(see place listing p. 251)* is 30 miles west of Loveland.

Several lakes and reservoirs offer water sports. Golf, hiking, bicycling, camping and horseback riding also are popular pastimes. Boyd Lake State Recreation Area *(see Recreation Areas Chart)* is 2 miles east.

Loveland Visitors Center: 5400 Stone Creek Cir., Loveland, CO 80538. **Phone:** (970) 667-3882 or (800) 258-1278.

DESIGNS BY RICKER MUSEUM/SHOWROOM,
6868 N. Franklin Ave., features pewter castings by noted artist and sculptor Michael Anthony Ricker. Staff members provide a detailed tour of the showroom and museum, explaining the process of how the pewter figures are made and giving information about the creations. **Time:** Allow 30 minutes minimum. **Hours:** Mon.-Fri. 8-5:30, Sat. 10-2. Closed Jan. 1, Memorial Day, July 4, Labor Day, Thanksgiving and Christmas. **Cost:** Free. **Phone:** (970) 593-6950 or (800) 373-9837.

LOVELAND MUSEUM/GALLERY, 503 N. Lincoln
Ave. at Fifth St., contains exhibits relating to town history, including a 40- by 50-foot topographic map of the Colorado-Big Thompson water project and a display about Loveland's Great Western Sugar Factory. Objects from the museum's historical collection and private collections are displayed in the Fireside Gallery, and works by regional, national and international artists are exhibited in the art galleries.

Special events take place throughout the year. **Time:** Allow 30 minutes minimum. **Hours:** Tues.-Fri. 10-5 (also Thurs. 5-7), Sat. 10-4, Sun. noon-4. **Cost:** Free. Museum free. $5 Gallery. **Phone:** (970) 962-2410.

RECREATIONAL ACTIVITIES
Horseback Riding
• **Sylvan Dale Guest Ranch** is off US 34 at 2939 N. CR 31-D. Other activities are offered. **Hours:** Daily 8-5 (weather permitting). **Phone:** (970) 667-3915 or (877) 667-3999.

BEST WESTERN PLUS CROSSROADS INN & CONFERENCE CENTER   (970)667-7810

Hotel $119-$199

AAA Benefit: Save 10% or more every day and earn 10% bonus points!

Address: 5542 E US Hwy 34 80537 **Location:** I-25 exit 257B, just w. **Facility:** 87 units, some kitchens. 2 stories, interior/exterior corridors. **Pool(s):** heated outdoor. **Activities:** exercise room. **Guest Services:** valet and coin laundry. **Featured Amenity:** full hot breakfast.

CANDLEWOOD SUITES   970/667-5444
Extended Stay Hotel. Rates not provided. **Address:** 6046 E Crossroads Blvd 80538 **Location:** I-25 exit 259, just e. **Facility:** 63 efficiencies. 3 stories, interior corridors. **Activities:** picnic facilities, exercise room. **Guest Services:** complimentary and valet laundry.

COMFORT INN   970/593-0100
Hotel. Rates not provided. **Address:** 1500 N Cheyenne Ave 80538 **Location:** I-25 exit 257B, 3 mi w on US 34. **Facility:** 62 units. 3 stories, interior corridors. **Amenities:** safes. **Pool(s):** heated indoor. **Activities:** hot tub, exercise room. **Guest Services:** valet and coin laundry.

EMBASSY SUITES BY HILTON LOVELAND   970/593-6200
Hotel. Rates not provided. **Address:** 4705 Clydesdale Pkwy 80538 **Location:** I-25 exit 259, just e, then just n. **Facility:** 263 units. 8 stories, interior corridors. **Amenities:** safes. **Pool(s):** heated indoor. **Activities:** hot tub, steamroom, exercise room, spa. **Guest Services:** valet and coin laundry, area transportation.

AAA Benefit: Members save 5% or more!

HAMPTON INN LOVELAND   970/593-1400
Hotel. Rates not provided. **Address:** 5500 Stone Creek Cir 80538 **Location:** I-25 exit 257B, 0.5 mi to outlet mall entrance, just n, then just e. **Facility:** 80 units. 3 stories, interior corridors. **Pool(s):** heated indoor. **Activities:** hot tub, exercise room. **Guest Services:** valet and coin laundry.

AAA Benefit: Members save up to 10%!

HOLIDAY INN EXPRESS & SUITES   (970)663-0057
Hotel $149-$204 **Address:** 6092 E Crossroads Blvd 80538 **Location:** I-25 exit 259, just e. **Facility:** 82 units. 3 stories, interior corridors. **Terms:** cancellation fee imposed. **Pool(s):** heated indoor. **Activities:** hot tub, picnic facilities, exercise room. **Guest Services:** valet and coin laundry.

WHERE TO EAT

3 MARGARITAS   970/669-4441
Mexican. Casual Dining. $7-$16 **AAA Inspector Notes:** This family-owned place is part of a popular local chain. The menu features a variety of burritos, enchiladas and fajitas, as well as more creative items such as steak tampiquena, pollo culichi and camarones jarochos. Patrons wash down their food with one of the many specialty margaritas. **Features:** full bar. **Address:** 1417 Cheyenne Ave 80538 **Location:** I-25 exit 257B, 3 mi w.

THE BLACK STEER   970/667-6679
Steak. Casual Dining. $9-$25 **AAA Inspector Notes:** Pleasing locals since 1966, the downtown eatery employs friendly servers. The rustic, Western atmosphere incorporates supper club touches. On the menu are traditional appetizers, soups, salads, burgers, chicken, steaks and seafood. **Features:** full bar. **Address:** 436 N Lincoln Ave 80537 **Location:** Jct US 287 and 34, 0.8 mi s on Cleveland Ave, just e, then just n.

DOOR 222 FOOD & DRINK   970/541-3020
American. Fine Dining. $10-$24 **AAA Inspector Notes:** This warm, cozy restaurant offers a classy, yet non-pretentious atmosphere. Specialty cocktails--such as the honey-vodka lemon drop, Colorado gin and tonic, and blood orange margarita--combined with the extensive tapas menu make this the perfect stop for a night on the town. Stay for dinner and treat yourself to Colorado lamb, chicken, beef and striped bass. The fluffy almond cake topped with a sweet-tart blueberry lemon compote is the perfect ending to any evening. **Features:** full bar, happy hour. **Address:** 222 E 4th St 80537 **Location:** Between Cleveland and Lincoln aves. **Parking:** street only.

DOUG'S DAY DINER   970/667-7124
Breakfast. Casual Dining. $9-$12 **AAA Inspector Notes:** Locals flock to this restaurant for hearty breakfasts and no-frills service. Breakfast options include huevos rancheros, omelettes, breakfast burritos and hotcakes. The lunch menu features a variety of unique burgers and sandwiches. **Address:** 532 N Lincoln Ave 80537 **Location:** Between 5th and 6th sts. **Parking:** street only.

HENRY'S PUB   970/613-1896

▼▼ ▼▼ American. Casual Dining. $8-$20 **AAA Inspector Notes:** Warm wood accents give this pub a homey feel. Although traditional pub fare is offered (burgers, fish and chips, bangers and mash), the majority of the menu is more eclectic, featuring pasta dishes, gourmet sandwiches and unique salads. **Features:** full bar. **Address:** 234 E 4th St 80537 **Location:** Between Lincoln and Cleveland aves. **Parking:** street only. [L] [D]

LOVELAND BREAKFAST CLUB   970/461-1261

▼▼ ▼▼ American. Casual Dining. $5-$8 **AAA Inspector Notes:** Hearty breakfasts, friendly servers and a cheerful atmosphere have earned this casual eatery a devoted local following. Served all day, the extensive breakfast options leave little out. Fill up on omelets, steak, eggs Benedict, pancakes, waffles, breakfast burritos and much more. Not in the mood for breakfast? Choose from a variety of burgers, burritos and sandwiches. A senior menu is available. **Features:** wine only. **Address:** 1451 N Boise Ave 80538 **Location:** I-25 exit 257B, 3.1 mi w on US 34, then just n. [B] [L]

MCGRAFF'S AMERICAN GRILL   970/669-8847

▼▼ ▼▼ American. Casual Dining. $9-$18 **AAA Inspector Notes:** Although the dining room is large, it maintains a warm, friendly feel. The diverse menu features pizza, sandwiches and specialty items such as grilled chicken cordon blue and St. Louis-style ribs. **Features:** full bar, patio dining, happy hour. **Address:** 1602 E Eisenhower Blvd 80537 **Location:** I-25 exit 257B, 3.1 mi w. [L] [D]

LYONS (B-8) pop. 2,033, elev. 5,362'

LYONS REDSTONE MUSEUM, 1 blk. n. of US 36 and SR 66 on 3rd Ave., then 1 blk. w. to 340 High St. in the town's 1881 schoolhouse, contains local artifacts, photographs and memorabilia. Brochures are available for a driving tour of the historic district. **Time:** Allow 30 minutes minimum. **Hours:** Mon.-Sat. 9:30-4:30, Sun. 12:30-4:30, May-Sept.; by appointment rest of year. **Cost:** Donations. **Phone:** (303) 823-5271 or (303) 823-5923.

SMOKIN' DAVES BBQ & TAPHOUSE   303/823-7427

▼▼ ▼▼ Barbecue. Casual Dining. $9-$28 **AAA Inspector Notes:** Fill up on ample portions of tender and savory ribs, pulled pork, beef brisket and sausage served with a variety of homemade barbecue sauces. Locals flock to this spot for its high-quality traditional American barbecue. **Features:** full bar, patio dining. **Address:** 228 Main St 80540 **Location:** Just e of jct 3rd Ave. [L] [D]

MANASSA (F-4) pop. 991, elev. 7,683'

THE JACK DEMPSEY MUSEUM, 3 mi. e. of US 285 on SR 142 at 412 Main St., is in the restored home of Jack Dempsey, who earned worldwide fame after winning the 1919 heavyweight boxing championship. Photographs and other memorabilia depicting his life and boxing career are displayed. **Time:** Allow 30 minutes minimum. **Hours:** Tues.-Sat. 9-5, Memorial Day weekend-Labor Day. **Cost:** Free. **Phone:** (719) 580-4346 (town hall).

MANCOS pop. 1,336

MESA VERDE MOTEL   970/533-7741

▼▼ Motel. Rates not provided. **Address:** 191 W Railroad Ave 81328 **Location:** On US 160 at SR 184; 7 mi e of Mesa Verde National Park entrance. **Facility:** 16 units, some two bedrooms. 1 story, exterior corridors. **Activities:** hot tub, picnic facilities.

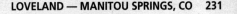

WHERE TO EAT

ABSOLUTE BAKERY & CAFE   970/533-1200

▼▼ ▼▼ American. Casual Dining. $8-$10 **AAA Inspector Notes:** Baked goods are made from scratch using organic ingredients. Fresh soups are made daily, and a nice selection of sandwiches, wraps, salads and pasta dishes are served in this quaint little eatery. Tough decisions will be made when selecting a dessert. **Features:** patio dining. **Address:** 110 S Main St 81328 **Location:** Just s of US 160. [B] [L] [AC]

MANITOU SPRINGS (F-9) pop. 4,992, elev. 6,320'

- Hotels p. 232 • Restaurants p. 232
- Attractions map p. 87
- Hotels & Restaurants map & index p. 93
- Part of Colorado Springs area — see map p. 81

Sitting at the foot of Pikes Peak, Manitou Springs is perhaps best known for the naturally carbonated mineral springs that bubble from the earth. Acknowledging the source of the curative power of the mineral waters, Native Americans named the springs for the Great Spirit Manitou.

Dr. William Bell, an English physician who was convinced that the springs provided "miracle cures," envisioned spas that rivaled those in Europe. He encouraged health seekers, many suffering from consumption, to drink the waters and his patients did, indeed, recover. Little did he or his patients realize, however, that the reason for their cures had more to do with the dry mountain air than the water. Nonetheless, the springs made Manitou a leading spa area and contributed greatly to the successful development of Colorado Springs.

Behind the mineral springs, resort developments and vacation attractions, quaint houses and narrow lanes clamber up the steep hillsides. The town retains an art-colony atmosphere while serving thousands of vacationers each year.

Although once a "summer-only" vacation destination, Manitou Springs draws visitors year-round. The historic district offers numerous shops, eateries and art galleries. Special events include the Pikes Peak International Auto Hill Climb race held in late June; the race begins west of Manitou Springs. Halloween weekend the town celebrates with the Emma Crawford Memorial Coffin Races and Festival.

Manitou Springs Chamber of Commerce and Visitors Bureau: 354 Manitou Ave., Manitou Springs, CO 80829. **Phone:** (719) 685-5089 or (800) 642-2567.

▼ **CAVE OF THE WINDS,** 6 mi. w. of I-25 exit 141 on US 24, offers cave tours through lighted chambers. On the Discovery Tour, a half-mile walking tour, visitors see chambers containing stalactites, stalagmites, helictites and other natural cave formations. On the Lantern Tour visitors light their own way with handheld lanterns while guides tell tales of early cave exploration, ghosts and the history of the cave's first owners. Additional outdoor activities include a rope course, a zip line, an aerial ride and gold panning. Food is available in summer.

(See map & index p. 93.)

Note: Cave temperature is 54 F; jackets are recommended. As of August 2015, the Lantern Tour trail was closed due to flooding. Phone ahead for updates. **Hours:** Daily 9-9, Memorial Day-Labor Day; 10-5, rest of year. Closed Christmas. Phone ahead to confirm schedule. **Cost:** Discovery Tour $20; $12 (ages 6-12); $16 (military with ID); $10 (children of military). Lantern Tour $30; $15 (ages 6-12); $25 (military with ID); $12 (children of military). Ages 5 and under are not permitted on the Lantern Tour. **Phone:** (719) 685-5444. GT

MANITOU CLIFF DWELLINGS is w. on US 24 bypass above Manitou Springs. These dwellings, built in Southern Colorado during the Great Pueblo Period, A.D. 1100-1300, depict the lives, culture and architectural achievements of Southwestern Native Americans. The ruins were moved to this site in 1907 in an effort to preserve them. Two museums feature artifacts and exhibits. **Hours:** Daily 9-6, May-Sept.; 9-5, Mar.-Apr. and Oct.-Nov.; 10-4, rest of year. Closed Thanksgiving and Christmas. **Cost:** $9.50; $7.50 (ages 7-11). **Phone:** (719) 685-5242 or (800) 354-9971.

MIRAMONT CASTLE is at 9 Capitol Hill Ave. off Ruxton Ave. Nine types of architecture are incorporated into the design of the 33-room castle-like mansion. Built of now-rare hand-quarried greenstone into a mountainside in 1895, it "stair-steps" up the mountain with the front door on the first level and the rear door on the fourth. Victorian gardens, a 16-sided room and The Queen's Parlour Tearoom offering high tea, light Victorian tea and lunch by reservation are available. Self-guiding tours are available.

Hours: Daily 9-5, Memorial Day weekend-Labor Day; Tues.-Sat. 10-4, Sun. noon-4, rest of year. Last admission 30 minutes before closing. **Cost:** $9; $8 (ages 60+); $5 (ages 6-12); free (active military and firefighters with ID). **Phone:** (719) 685-1011, (719) 884-4109 for the tearoom or (888) 685-1011. TI

PIKES PEAK—see Pikes Peak and Pike National Forest p. 245.

PIKES PEAK COG RAILWAY leaves from 515 Ruxton Ave. and runs to the summit of Pikes Peak. On a clear day Denver is visible 75 miles to the north, and the Sangre de Cristo Mountains in southern Colorado and New Mexico can be seen on the horizon 100 miles away. During the ride to the top, visitors view cascading streams, aspen and pine forests, and one of the state's largest herds of bighorn sheep.

Note: Distinct altitude and temperature changes from base to peak may cause discomfort for persons with heart or respiratory problems, and for infants under 3 months. Wear warm clothing as temperatures at the 14,115-foot summit are approximately 30 degrees colder than at the base. **Time:** Allow 3 hours, 30 minutes minimum. **Hours:** Train operates year-round, with daily departure times varying; phone

ahead. **Cost:** Fare $38; $20.50 (ages 3-12). Fares may vary; phone ahead. Reservations are required. **Phone:** (719) 685-5401 or (800) 745-3773.

AMERICAS BEST VALUE INN VILLA MOTEL
(719)685-5492 ⟨35⟩

Motel
$79-$139

Address: 481 Manitou Ave 80829 **Location:** I-25 exit 141, 4 mi w on US 24, then 0.8 mi sw on US 24 business route. Opposite Memorial Park. **Facility:** 47 units, some efficiencies. 1-2 stories (no elevator), exterior corridors. **Terms:** cancellation fee imposed. **Pool(s):** heated outdoor. **Activities:** hot tub, picnic facilities. **Guest Services:** coin laundry. **Featured Amenity: continental breakfast.**

SAVE ⟨⟩ ⟨⟩ / SOME UNITS ⟨⟩ ⟨⟩ ⟨⟩

THE CLIFF HOUSE AT PIKES PEAK
(719)685-3000 ⟨34⟩

Historic
Country Inn
$109-$440

Address: 306 Cañon Ave 80829 **Location:** I-25 exit 141, 4 mi w on US 24, 1.2 mi sw on US 24 business route/Manitou Ave, then just w. Opposite post office. **Facility:** Antique furnishings, Impressionist oil paintings in ornate frames, and carved-wood details create an atmosphere of elegance at this inn. 54 units. 5 stories, interior corridors. **Parking:** valet only. **Terms:** cancellation fee imposed, resort fee. **Amenities:** safes. **Dining:** The Cliff House Dining Room, see separate listing. **Activities:** bicycles, trails, exercise room, massage. **Guest Services:** valet laundry, area transportation. **Featured Amenity: full hot breakfast.**

SAVE ⟨⟩ ⟨⟩ ⟨⟩ BIZ HS ⟨⟩ ⟨⟩ ⟨⟩ ⟨⟩

COMFORT INN
(719)685-5455 ⟨36⟩

⟨⟩ ⟨⟩ Hotel $79-$164 **Address:** 45 Manitou Ave 80829 **Location:** I-25 exit 141, 4 mi w on US 24 to Manitou Ave, then just e. **Facility:** 46 units. 2 stories, interior corridors. **Terms:** 3 day cancellation notice. **Pool(s):** heated indoor. **Activities:** hot tub. **Guest Services:** coin laundry.

⟨⟩ ⟨⟩ BIZ HS ⟨⟩ ⟨⟩ ⟨⟩ ⟨⟩ ⟨⟩

MAGNUSON HOTEL MANITOU SPRINGS 719/685-5991 ⟨37⟩

⟨⟩ ⟨⟩ Hotel. Rates not provided. **Address:** 311 Manitou Ave 80829 **Location:** I-25 exit 141, 4 mi w on US 24, then just sw. **Facility:** 38 units. 2 stories (no elevator), exterior corridors. **Pool(s):** heated indoor. **Activities:** hot tub. **Guest Services:** coin laundry.

⟨⟩ ⟨⟩ BIZ ⟨⟩ ⟨⟩ ⟨⟩ ⟨⟩ / SOME UNITS HS

TOWN-N-COUNTRY COTTAGES
719/685-5427

fyi Not evaluated. **Address:** 123 Crystal Park Rd 80829 **Location:** Jct Manitou Ave, 0.3 mi s (curve at entrance). Facilities, services, and décor characterize a mid-scale property.

WHERE TO EAT

ADAM'S MOUNTAIN CAFE
719/685-1430 ⟨50⟩

⟨⟩ ⟨⟩ American. Casual Dining. $9-$18 **AAA Inspector Notes:** Asian, Mediterranean and Southwestern influences punctuate dishes on this restaurant's eclectic menu. Lunch items include a pear and pecan salad, chicken banh mi sandwich, and a vegetarian burger. The dinner menu features a thai chicken satay, pozole verde, and spicy malibari curry. Breakfasts and healthy cuisine are casually served in a charming atmosphere. Sweet and savory, the homemade spiced tea is a must for tea lovers. If tea is not your thing, try one of the specialty cocktails. **Features:** full bar. **Reservations:** suggested. **Address:** 26 Manitou Ave 80829 **Location:** US 24 (Cimarron St) exit Ridge Rd, just n, then 0.4 mi w on Colorado Ave. B L D

(See map & index p. 93.)

BRIARHURST MANOR
719/685-1864 (48)

▼▼▼ ▼▼▼

Regional
American
Fine Dining

$22-$43

AAA Inspector Notes: *Historic.* Housed in a stone mansion built in 1878, this restaurant features many historic details, such as ornately trimmed fireplaces, warm wood accents and exposed-brick walls. Each of the nine dining rooms has its own character. Start with the artistically presented manor greens salad or the rich lobster bisque. Then, select a regionally inspired entrée, such as the wild boar green chile, Rocky Mountain elk or duo of Colorado lamb. **Features:** full bar. **Reservations:** suggested. **Address:** 404 Manitou Ave 80829 **Location:** I-25 exit 141, 5 mi w on US 24 exit Manitou Ave; west side of Manitou Chamber of Commerce. [D]

THE CLIFF HOUSE DINING ROOM
719/785-2415 (45)

▼▼▼ ▼▼▼

New
Continental
Fine Dining

$8-$35

AAA Inspector Notes: The chefs' creative lamb, duck, veal and trout dishes incorporate a wealth of regional ingredients and cross-cultural techniques to provide a distinctive Colorado culinary experience. Oil paintings done by local legend C.H. Rockey add to the ambience. The inn was established in 1873 on the stage line to Leadville. Service is refined, but not pretentious. Desserts are works of art. **Features:** full bar. **Reservations:** suggested. **Address:** 306 Cañon Ave 80829 **Location:** I-25 exit 141, 4 mi w on US 24, 1.2 mi sw on US 24 business route/Manitou Ave, then just w; in The Cliff House at Pikes Peak. **Parking:** valet only.

[B] [L] [D]

THE MONA LISA FONDUE RESTAURANT
719/685-0277 (47)

▼▼ Fondue. Casual Dining. $25-$30 **AAA Inspector Notes:** At this restaurant, guests choose from a selection of shareable four-course fondue meals. For the entrée, pieces of beef, chicken, seafood and wild game are dipped in a variety of flavorful sauces. It's easy to get carried away with the first few courses, but leaving room for the decadent dessert course is a must. **Features:** beer & wine. **Reservations:** suggested. **Address:** 733 Manitou Ave 80829 **Location:** In historic downtown. **Parking:** street only. [D]

SAVELLI'S
719/685-3755 (51)

▼▼ Italian. Casual Dining. $7-$14 **AAA Inspector Notes:** The hearty calzones, homemade meatball sliders and eggplant Parmesan make this casual eatery popular with locals and tourists. Relax and enjoy your meal at the restaurant, or take your order to go. **Features:** beer & wine, patio dining. **Address:** 301 Manitou Ave 80829 **Location:** I-25 exit 141, 4 mi w on US 24 business route, then just w.

[L] [D]

STAGECOACH INN
719/685-9400 (49)

▼▼ Regional American. Casual Dining. $9-$25 **AAA Inspector Notes:** Cozy mountain charm envelops the former stage stop and inn, which has two creekside decks for outdoor dining and inviting fireplaces in various dining rooms. The menu features preparations of slow-roast buffalo, choice beef, seafood, pasta and chicken. Past patrons include President Dwight Eisenhower and the Cartwrights from Bonanza. **Features:** full bar, patio dining, happy hour. **Reservations:** suggested. **Address:** 702 Manitou Ave 80829 **Location:** I-25 exit 141, 4.2 mi nw on Manitou Ave, then 1 mi sw. [L] [D]

MEEKER (B-2) pop. 2,475, elev. 6,239'

In 1868 explorer John Wesley Powell led a 20-person contingent to the area and established winter quarters; that site is now known as Powell Park. Ten years later Nathan C. Meeker arrived at the same site to serve as the agent of the White River Agency of the Bureau of Indian Affairs. The Ute Indians, resentful of Meeker's attempt to make them farmers, ambushed Meeker and 10 agency employees. After the U.S. Army arrived and established a camp on the White River, the Native Americans were banished to a reservation in eastern Utah.

The town of Meeker, the county seat of Rio Blanco County, is near White River National Forest *(see place listing p. 274)* and the Flat Tops Wilderness Area. As a result, recreation opportunities are plentiful and include biking, boating, camping, cross-country skiing, fishing, hiking, horseback riding and snowmobiling.

Meeker Chamber of Commerce: 710 Market St., Meeker, CO 81641. **Phone:** (970) 878-5510.

WHITE RIVER MUSEUM, 2 blks. n. of SR 13 at 565 Park Ave., occupies the original 1880 log U.S. Army

officers' quarters used by the soldiers who came to assist troops pinned down at Milk Creek Battlefield who were helping Bureau of Indian Affairs agent Nathan Meeker, killed in an 1879 Native American uprising. Artifacts, pictures and records document the rich Ute and pioneer history of the White River area. **Hours:** Mon.-Sat. 9-5, Sun. noon-5, mid-Apr. through Nov. 30; Mon.-Sat. 10-4, Sun. noon-4, rest of year. Closed Jan. 1, Thanksgiving and Christmas. Phone ahead to confirm schedule. **Cost:** Donations. **Phone:** (970) 878-9982. GT

MESA (C-1) elev. 5,639'

RECREATIONAL ACTIVITIES
Skiing
- **Powderhorn Ski Resort** is 35 mi. e. on SR 65. **Hours:** Daily 9-4, mid-Dec. to late Mar. **Phone:** (970) 268-5300.

MESA VERDE NATIONAL PARK
(F-1)
- Hotels p. 236 • Restaurants p. 236

Elevations in the park range from 6,954 ft. at Chapin Mesa to 8,572 ft. at Park Point. Refer to AAA maps for additional elevation information.

In southwestern Colorado, 9 miles east of Cortez, Mesa Verde National Park is one of the nation's major archeological preserves. The park consists of nearly 5,000 archeological sites, which include 600 cliff dwellings that were the homes of ancestral Pueblo people. Mesa Verde, Spanish for "green table," is so called because of its comparatively level top, forested with juniper and pinyon trees. The national park encompasses 81 square miles, rises 1,800 to 2,000 feet above the valley along the north side and slopes gradually down to the cliffs bordering the Mancos River Canyon.

A score of large canyons seam the mesa, and in the shelter of the hundreds of alcoves eroded in the cliffs are some of the world's largest and best preserved cliff dwellings. Archeologists have stabilized only a few of the sites; asphalt roads lead to overlooks above the main ones.

The earliest known inhabitants of Mesa Verde were the Ancestral Pueblo people, ancestors of today's modern pueblo tribes. They built subterranean pit houses from about A.D. 500-750, and from A.D. 750 to 1100 they created their living quarters, kivas (ceremonial rooms) and masonry houses around open courts (pueblos).

From A.D. 1100 to 1200 architecture, arts and crafts reached their peak; pottery and cloth were often elaborately decorated. Around 1200 they moved south into the alcoves for reasons that remain unknown and built cliff dwellings. Sometime about 1276 a drought struck and lasted 24 years. The resulting crop failures, depletion of resources, other environmental problems and possible conflict may have driven the people from Mesa Verde in

search of a more reliable water supply and improved living conditions.

Today, some of the Pueblo people living in the Rio Grande pueblos in northwestern New Mexico, Texas and on the Hopi mesas in northern Arizona are descendants of the former occupants of Mesa Verde.

General Information and Activities

Mesa Verde National Park is open all year but some sites are closed in winter. Interpretive activities are held throughout the year (weather permitting). The Chapin Mesa Archeological Museum, with exhibits, artifacts of the Ancestral Puebloans, tour information and ranger program schedules, is open daily 8-6:30, Apr. 1 to mid-Oct.; hours vary rest of the year. A free 25-minute park video can also be viewed; phone (970) 529-4465. The Mesa Verde Visitor and Research Center is open daily 7:30 a.m.-7 p.m., Memorial Day-Labor Day. Closing hours vary; phone for updated schedule.

Half-day ranger-guided tours are available for a fee April through October. Tickets can be purchased at the visitor and research center; phone (800) 449-2288. During summer and fall special events, Hopi dances, cultural demonstrations and lectures are presented. Visitors arriving at other times can inspect the museum, visit mesa-top sites, take a ranger-guided tour of a cliff dwelling and drive along some of the park's scenic routes.

From Memorial Day through Labor Day visitors can drive along a 12-mile access road to Wetherill Mesa, where two cliff dwellings date from the 12th and 13th centuries and four mesa-top villages date from the seventh through 12th centuries.

Phone (970) 529-4465 for the latest information about schedules, weather and road conditions. *See Recreation Areas Chart.*

ADMISSION to the park is $15 per private vehicle, Memorial Day-Labor Day; $10 per private vehicle, rest of year. Admission $8 per person arriving by other means, Memorial Day-Labor Day; $5, rest of year. All admission fees are valid for 7 days.

PETS are permitted in the park only if they are on a leash, crated or otherwise physically restricted at all times. They are not permitted on trails, in public buildings or in the archeological sites.

LODGING is available from mid-April to mid-October at Far View Lodge. For reservations phone (602) 331-5210 or (800) 449-2288.

ADDRESS inquiries to the Superintendent, Mesa Verde National Park, P.O. Box 8, Mesa Verde National Park, CO 81330; phone (970) 529-4465.

ANASAZI HERITAGE CENTER—see Canyons of the Ancients National Monument p. 75.

BALCONY HOUSE, in a high alcove in the west wall of Soda Canyon, is a site that can be reached only by a 32-foot ladder. Careful attention to detail and the skill necessary to construct a village in this particular alcove make Balcony House a classic example of Pueblo architecture. It can be visited only on ranger-guided trips that fill quickly in summer months.

Time: Allow 1 hour minimum. **Hours:** Tours are offered daily every 30 minutes 9-5, late May-Labor Day (weather permitting). Tour hours vary rest of year. Phone ahead to confirm schedule. **Cost:** Fee $4. Tickets are sold at the Visitor and Research Center or the Colorado Welcome Center in Cortez. **Phone:** (970) 529-4465. GT

CLIFF PALACE is in an alcove in the east wall of Cliff Canyon. Though visible from the Sun Temple or the Sun Point overlook directly opposite on the west rim, access is permitted only on ranger-guided tours.

Time: Allow 1 hour minimum. **Hours:** Tours are given every 30 minutes daily 9-6, late May-Labor Day; 9-5, mid-Apr. to late May. Tours are given hourly daily 9-5, day after Labor Day to early Nov. (weather permitting). **Cost:** Fee $4. Tickets are sold at the Visitor and Research Center and the Colorado Welcome Center in Cortez. **Phone:** (970) 529-4465. GT

FAR VIEW SITES, on the entrance highway 4 mi. n. of Chapin Mesa Archeological Museum, exemplify pueblos that were built on the mesa tops during the Developmental and Classic Pueblo periods. The site had been used for centuries before the existing walls were constructed. Self-guiding tours are permitted. **Time:** Allow 1 hour minimum.

FEWKES CANYON SITES are visible from Mesa Top Rd. Near the head of the canyon is Fire Temple, one of the most remarkable of the sites. Nearby is New Fire House, composed of two alcoves. In the upper alcove are a number of living rooms; the lower one contains a few living rooms and three kivas.

Down the canyon a short distance in a deep, arched alcove is Oak Tree House (which was partially excavated by archeologist Jesse Walter Fewkes), with about 50 living rooms and seven kivas. South of this building and directly under Sun Temple is Mummy House, visible from several overlooks and short trails.

LONG HOUSE is in a small side canyon off Rock Canyon on Wetherill Mesa. The second largest cliff dwelling in Mesa Verde National Park, Long House can be visited only on ranger-guided trips in summer. The round-trip hike is 1.3 miles, with a 130-foot gain in elevation upon exiting. During the tour, visitors climb two 15-foot ladders within the site. The tours can be strenuous due to the elevation, steepness and summer heat. **Time:** Allow 1 hour, 30 minutes minimum. **Hours:** Guided tours are available. Schedule varies; phone ahead for times. **Cost:** $4. Tickets must be purchased in advance at the Mesa

Verde Visitor and Research Center or the Colorado Welcome Center in Cortez. **Phone:** (970) 529-4465. GT

MESA TOP LOOP ROAD covers two 6-mi. loops and provides views of about 40 cliff dwellings from canyon-rim lookout points. Two pit houses and six pueblos illustrate the architectural sequence of the Mesa Verde structures. Several cliff dwellings can be viewed at close range from lookout points along the cliff edge. The Cliff Palace-Balcony House Loop Road is closed to car traffic during the winter months, although snowshoeing and skiing are permitted. **Hours:** Daily 8-dusk (weather permitting).

PARK POINT FIRE LOOKOUT, 9 mi. inside the park entrance, has the highest elevation—8,572 feet above sea level—within the park. From this point portions of Colorado, Arizona, New Mexico and Utah are visible. **Time:** Allow 30 minutes minimum.

PETROGLYPH POINT TRAIL starts at the Chapin Mesa Archeological Museum. Nearly a 3-mile round-trip, the trail follows the base of the cliff on the east side of Spruce Tree and Navajo canyons to Petroglyph Point and returns via the mesa top. To use this trail, register at the trailhead or with a ranger in the museum. **Time:** Allow 2 hours minimum. **Hours:** Open mid-May to mid-Oct.

SPRUCE CANYON TRAIL branches off from the Spruce Tree House Trail. The nearly 3-mile round-trip follows the bottom of Spruce Tree Canyon and ends in a picnic area around the headquarters. To use this trail, register at the trailhead near the museum. **Time:** Allow 1 hour, 30 minutes minimum. **Hours:** Open mid-May to mid-Oct.

SPRUCE TREE HOUSE is in an alcove in Spruce Tree Canyon, just behind the museum at park headquarters. It is one of the largest and best preserved cliff dwellings in the park and is easily accessible to visitors. **Time:** Allow 1 hour minimum. **Hours:** Self-guiding tours daily 9-6, Memorial Day-Oct. 31. Guided tour times vary throughout the year. Phone ahead to confirm schedule. **Phone:** (970) 529-4465.

SQUARE TOWER HOUSE is in a shallow alcove in the east wall of Navajo Canyon, opposite Echo Cliff. Its four-story tower stands against the rear wall of the alcove.

SUN TEMPLE is across the canyon from Cliff Palace on Mesa Top Loop Rd., on the promontory formed by the confluence of Cliff and Fewkes canyons. There is no evidence showing how this site was used, but its construction was probably never completed. **Time:** Allow 30 minutes minimum.

FAR VIEW LODGE   970/529-4422

♦♦ **Motel. Rates not provided. Address:** 1 Navajo Hill 81330 **Location:** 14 mi from park gate at MM 15. **Facility:** 150 units. 1-2 stories (no elevator), exterior corridors. **Dining:** Metate Room, see separate listing. **Activities:** recreation programs in summer, trails. *(See ad this page.)*

🍴 🍸 BIZ 📶 ✖ 🏧 📶

💻 / SOME UNITS 🐕

METATE ROOM   970/529-4422

♦♦♦ Southwestern. Fine Dining. $15-$32 **AAA Inspector Notes:** The contemporary Southwestern cuisine is inspired by regional heritage foods and flavorings. Entrée selections include cowboy New York strip with an ancho demi-glace; marinated grilled duck breast served with prickly pear-red pepper jam; and an elk shepherd's pie. Request a window table in order to watch the sun set over the mesa. **Features:** full bar. **Reservations:** required. **Address:** 1 Navajo Hill 81330 **Location:** 14 mi from park gate; in Far View Lodge. B D

▼ *See AAA listing this page* ▼

AAA Vacations® packages ... exciting itineraries and exclusive values

MONARCH (D-3)

MONARCH CREST TRAM is 15 mi. w. on US 50. An enclosed tram car ascends to a height of 12,012 feet for a view of the Rocky Mountains and Pikes Peak, 72 miles to the east. **Hours:** Daily 8:30-5:30, mid-May to mid-Sept. (weather permitting). **Cost:** Fare $10; $7 (ages 55+); $8 (ages 3-12). **Phone:** (719) 539-4091.

RECREATIONAL ACTIVITIES

Skiing

• **Monarch Mountain** is 17 mi. w. on US 50 at 23715 W. US 50. Other activities are offered. **Hours:** Daily 9-4, late Nov. to mid-Apr. **Phone:** (719) 530-5000 or (888) 996-7669.

MONTE VISTA (F-3) pop. 4,444, elev. 7,663'

Monte Vista thrives on the shipping of potatoes and other crops from the surrounding San Luis Valley and on its proximity to the recreational lands of the Rio Grande National Forest *(see place listing p. 250)* to the west.

Monte Vista Chamber of Commerce: 947 1st Ave., Monte Vista, CO 81144. **Phone:** (719) 852-2731.

MONTE VISTA NATIONAL WILDLIFE REFUGE, 6 mi. s. on SR 15, is a 14,800-acre refuge for migratory birds. Ducks, geese, shorebirds and water birds nest in the area, and mallards and geese visit in winter. Sandhill cranes can be seen February through April and mid-September through October; bald eagles are abundant November through March. A 2.5-mile driving route and short walking trail are available. **Hours:** Daily dawn-dusk. **Cost:** Free. **Phone:** (719) 589-4021.

BEST WESTERN MOVIE MANOR   (719)852-5921

Hotel
$89-$159

AAA Benefit: Save 10% or more every day and earn 10% bonus points!

Address: 2830 Hwy 160 W 81144 **Location:** 2 mi w of center. **Facility:** 59 units. 2 stories (no elevator), exterior corridors. **Dining:** Kelloff's Restaurant, see separate listing. **Activities:** regulation golf, playground, exercise room. **Guest Services:** coin laundry.

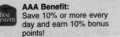

WHERE TO EAT

KELLOFF'S RESTAURANT   719/852-3626

♦♦ American. Casual Dining. $7-$15 **AAA Inspector Notes:** If you are looking for a quiet break from the road, this restaurant is a good option for those traveling east or west on US 160. Menu items will always include a daily special, fresh soup of the day, salads, burgers, hot and cold sandwiches, a popular honey-dipped chicken entrée and a juicy steak. Bicyclists and motorcyclists are welcome. **Features:** full bar. **Address:** 2830 Hwy 160 W 81144 **Location:** 2 mi w of center; in BEST WESTERN Movie Manor.

NINO'S MEXICAN RESTAURANT   719/852-0101

♦ Mexican. Casual Dining. $7-$14 **AAA Inspector Notes:** The quick service and tasty burritos make this casual eatery a favorite with locals. Mixing past and present, one brick wall of this historic building has been left exposed to reveal a Victorian-era advertisement. **Features:** full bar. **Address:** 118 Adams St 81144 **Location:** Just s from 1st Ave (US 160). [L] [D]

MONTROSE (D-2) pop. 19,132, elev. 5,806'

• Hotels p. 238 • Restaurants p. 238

Developed in the 1880s as a supply point for miners following the Uncompahgre River into the silver-laden San Juan Mountains, Montrose now serves a similar purpose for the ranching, farming, mining and recreational interests in the area.

Orchard and truck crops flourish using water diverted from the Gunnison River; the lower portal of the diversion tunnel is 7.5 miles east of Montrose off US 50. The city is headquarters for the power operations segment of the Colorado River storage project.

Black Canyon of the Gunnison National Park *(see place listing p. 56)* is northeast via US 50 and SR 347. In addition to opportunities for a variety of recreational pursuits, the Curecanti National Recreation Area *(see place listing p. 112)* and the Grand Mesa-Uncompahgre-Gunnison National Forests *(see place listing p. 206)* offer beautiful scenery.

Montrose is the western terminus of a scenic stretch of US 50 extending 126 miles from Poncha Springs; it also is the northern end of scenic US 550, which includes the Million Dollar Highway *(see attraction listing p. 241)*, from Durango.

MONTROSE COUNTY HISTORICAL MUSEUM, at Main St. and Rio Grande Ave. in the 1912 D&RG Depot building, displays dolls, toys, quilts, clothing, railroad and mining memorabilia, a stage coach, a Union Pacific caboose and farm equipment from the 18th and 19th centuries. Black and white photographs and documents chronicle town history. A furnished homesteader's cabin and a cowboy cabin are on the grounds.

Hours: Mon.-Fri. 9-5, Sat. 10-2, May-Oct.; by appointment rest of year. Closed major holidays. **Cost:** $6; $2 (students and military with ID). **Phone:** (970) 249-2085.

MUSEUM OF THE MOUNTAIN WEST is at 68169 E. Miami Rd. Visitors learn about the history of western Colorado as trained docents guide them through more than 24 original buildings and 10 re-created structures containing period furnishings. Included among the reconstructed storefronts are a barber shop, saloon, pharmacy, general store, 1880s doctor's office and one-room schoolhouse. The museum also displays some half-million articles, many unusual and rare. **Time:** Allow 2 hours minimum. **Hours:** Guided tours Mon.-Sat. 8:30-4:30. Closed Jan. 1 and Christmas. **Cost:** $10; $5 (ages 5-17). **Phone:** (970) 240-3400. [GT]

UTE INDIAN MUSEUM, 3 mi. s. on US 550, highlights the Ute Indians and early explorers, including the Franciscan missionaries who mapped and named many rivers, valleys and mountains in western Colorado. The museum displays historical dioramas and a gallery with changing exhibits, and medicinal plants are featured in a botanical garden. A monument honors Chief Ouray, peacemaker between the Utes and the settlers, upon whose traditional homeland the museum now stands. The grave of his wife, Chipeta, and her brother Chief John McCook, also are on the grounds.

Time: Allow 45 minutes minimum. **Hours:** Mon.-Sat. 9-4:30, Sun. 11-4:30, July-Oct.; Tues.-Sat. 9-4, Jan.-June; Mon.-Sat. 9-4:30, rest of year. **Cost:** $4.50; $4 (ages 65+); $2 (ages 6-16). **Phone:** (970) 249-3098.

RECREATIONAL ACTIVITIES

Horseback Riding

- **Deb's Livery** is at 31268 US 550S. **Hours:** Daily 9-5. **Phone:** (970) 626-5587 or (970) 729-1266.

DAYS INN   (970)249-4507

Motel $55-$230 **Address:** 1417 E Main St 81401 **Location:** 0.8 mi e on US 50. **Facility:** 70 units. 2 stories (no elevator), exterior corridors. **Terms:** check-in 4 pm. **Amenities:** *Some:* safes. **Pool(s):** heated outdoor. **Activities:** hot tub, picnic facilities. **Guest Services:** coin laundry.

HAMPTON INN   970/252-3300

Hotel. Rates not provided. **Address:** 1980 N Townsend Ave 81401 **Location:** 1.5 mi n on US 550. **Facility:** 64 units. 3 stories, interior corridors. **Pool(s):** heated indoor. **Activities:** hot tub, exercise room. **Guest Services:** valet and coin laundry.

AAA Benefit: Members save up to 10%!

HOLIDAY INN EXPRESS & SUITES   970/240-1800

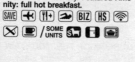

Hotel
Rates not provided

Address: 1391 S Townsend Ave 81401 **Location:** 1 mi s on US 550. **Facility:** 122 units. 3 stories, interior corridors. **Pool(s):** heated indoor. **Activities:** hot tub, exercise room. **Guest Services:** valet and coin laundry. **Featured Amenity:** full hot breakfast.

SUPER 8   (970)240-8200

Hotel $55-$100 **Address:** 1705 E Main St 81401 **Location:** 1 mi e on US 50. **Facility:** 42 units. 2 stories (no elevator), interior corridors. **Guest Services:** coin laundry.

Choose real ratings you can trust

from professional inspectors

who've been there

CAMP ROBBER   970/240-1590

Southwestern
Casual Dining
$11-$23

AAA Inspector Notes: With an inviting outdoor patio and fireplace, lovely photo art adorns the walls of this restaurant, which offers an eclectic selection of menu items such as Asian barbecue chicken salad, chile rellenos, prime rib, vegetarian delight and green chile pistachio-crusted pork medallions. You do not want to miss out on the famous green chili chicken and potato soup, the award-winning desserts or their champagne Sunday brunch. **Features:** full bar, patio dining, early bird specials, Sunday brunch, happy hour. **Reservations:** suggested. **Address:** 1515 Ogden Rd 81401 **Location:** Jct US 50 and Main St, 2.1 mi s on US 550.

CHANG THAI RESTAURANT   970/240-4567

Thai. Casual Dining. $8-$17 **AAA Inspector Notes:** The extensive menu is sure to have your favorite dish. Sample items include drunken noodles, pad thai and green curry. Gold Thai statues enhance the modern décor. **Features:** full bar. **Address:** 1015 S Townsend Ave 81401 **Location:** 0.7 mi s of jct US 50 and 550.

GURU'S RESTAURANT & BAR   970/252-8777

Nepali. Casual Dining. $10-$19 **AAA Inspector Notes:** The restaurant serves a traditional menu of items that have been carefully prepared and seasoned with an exotic blend of curry spices. Options include chicken tikka masala, lamb kawab, shrimp bhuteko and vegetarian fire-roasted eggplant curry. The lunch buffet is a popular local favorite. **Features:** full bar. **Address:** 448 E Main St 81401 **Location:** 0.3 mi e of jct US 50 and 550. **Parking:** street only.

PAHGRE'S PIZZA, PASTA & SALADS   970/249-6442

American Pizza Sandwiches. Casual Dining. $8-$27 **AAA Inspector Notes:** Locally grown and produced ingredients are used whenever possible in the good selection of panini, pastas, small and entrée-size creative salads, stone-baked signature pizza pies and campfire calzones. You can build your own pizza, select a sauce and choose from more than 40 toppings. Gluten-free crust, pasta and beer are available. **Features:** beer only, patio dining. **Address:** 1541 Oxbow Dr, Suite 1800 81401 **Location:** 2.3 mi s of jct US 50 and 550; in Oxbow Crossing.

RED BARN RESTAURANT   970/249-9202

Steak. Casual Dining. $9-$24 **AAA Inspector Notes:** The large cow sign perched on the roof signals that you've arrived at this eatery, where down-home Western cooking is served in a laid-back atmosphere. Peer into the glass case of desserts on the way to your table. **Features:** full bar, Sunday brunch, happy hour. **Address:** 1413 E Main St 81401 **Location:** 0.8 mi e on US 50.

THE STONE HOUSE   970/240-8899

American. Casual Dining. $9-$29 **AAA Inspector Notes:** The upscale bar or cozy seating area in front of the fireplace are ideal spots to enjoy a cocktail before or after lunch or dinner. Soup, salads, burgers and a wide variety of steaks and seafood are offered, including pan-seared sea scallops, baked Caribbean lobster tail and smoke-roasted prime rib. The lightly sweet, lightly tart lemon Italian cream cake is a highlight of the dessert menu. **Features:** full bar, Sunday brunch. **Address:** 1415 Hawk Pkwy 81401 **Location:** On US 550, 2.2 mi s of jct US 50 and 550.

TED NELSON'S STEAK HOUSE   970/252-0262

Steak. Casual Dining. $9-$30 **AAA Inspector Notes:** The menu may change with the season, but you can expect juicy steaks, delicious seafood, a popular portobello stir-fry and great salad in a friendly atmosphere. **Features:** full bar, happy hour. **Address:** 103 Rose Ln 81403 **Location:** 1.2 mi e on US 50.

MORRISON (D-8) pop. 428, elev. 5,766'
- Hotels & Restaurants map & index p. 136
- Part of Denver area — see map p. 116

DINOSAUR RIDGE is w. of SR 470 at 16831 W. Alameda Pkwy. Dinosaur Ridge is the site of such paleontological discoveries as dinosaur bones and tracks, plant and animal fossils, and rock formations from the Jurassic and Cretaceous periods. Twenty interpretive signs help visitors identify these features along the ridge. The visitor center has large murals and interactive exhibits. Shuttle bus tours of the outdoor museum grounds are available.

Time: Allow 1 hour, 30 minutes minimum. **Hours:** Mon.-Sat. 9-5, Sun. 10-5, June-Aug.; Mon.-Sat. 9-5, Sun. 11-5, Apr.-May and Sept.-Oct.; Mon.-Sat. 9-4, Sun. 11-4, rest of year. Forty-minute shuttle bus tours board hourly (half-hourly June-Aug.) at 10 a.m. at the visitor center; last bus leaves at 4 p.m. (May-Oct.) and 3 p.m. (rest of year). Closed Jan. 1, Thanksgiving and Christmas. **Cost:** Free. Shuttle bus tour $5; free (ages 0-3); boarding is first come, first served. **Phone:** (303) 697-3466.

MORRISON NATURAL HISTORY MUSEUM is .25 mi. s. at 501 SR 8 (Morrison Rd.). This museum offers

interactive exhibits highlighting historic and contemporary dinosaur discoveries. Displays include hatchling Jurassic dinosaur fossils from the Denver area. Visitors may help prepare dinosaur bones and encounter live reptiles during guided hour-long tours.

Time: Allow 1 hour minimum. **Hours:** Daily 10-5. Guided tours at 10:15, 12:15 and 2:15. Final tour is given and last tickets are sold 1 hour before closing. **Cost:** (includes guided tour) $8; $6 (ages 3-11). **Phone:** (303) 697-1873.

RED ROCKS PARK & AMPHITHEATRE, I-70W exit 259, then 1.5 mi. s., is an 868-acre park laced with hiking trails at the foot of the Rocky Mountains. The red sandstone formations were created 250 to 300 million years ago and gain their color from varying levels of iron oxide.

Red Rocks Amphitheatre's 9,525 seats are flanked on either side by striking 400-foot-high red sandstone formations. The amphitheater is well known as one of the nation's finest outdoor concert venues. The visitor center has interactive displays about the history of Red Rocks.

Concerts and Easter sunrise services are held seasonally. **Time:** Allow 30 minutes minimum. **Hours:** Park daily dawn-dusk. Visitor center daily 8-7, May-Sept.; 9-4, in Oct. The visitor center closes at 1 p.m. on concert dates and reopens at gate time for patrons with tickets. Closed Thanksgiving and Christmas. **Cost:** Park free. **Phone:** (720) 865-2474 for the amphitheater, or (303) 697-4939 for general information.

TINY TOWN AND RAILROAD is off US 285 at 6249 Turkey Creek Rd. The 10-acre Tiny Town is a miniature children's village begun in 1915. More than 100 buildings in rural, town and mountain settings are featured, including a toy store, grocery, saloon, church, ice cream shop, newspaper office and bank. Town houses are Victorian-style reproductions. Visitors can ride an authentic miniature open-air train through the town, and children can enter some of the buildings.

Time: Allow 1 hour minimum. **Hours:** Daily 10-5, Memorial Day-Labor Day; Sat.-Sun. 10-5, May 1-day before Memorial Day and day after Labor Day-Sept. 30 (weather permitting). **Cost:** $5; $3 (ages 2-12). Train $2. **Phone:** (303) 697-6829.

THE FORT   303/697-4771 (119)
Steak. Casual Dining. $29-$49 **AAA Inspector Notes:** The unique building housing this restaurant is a replica of historic Bent's Old Fort. Influenced by the early American West, the menu focuses on wild game such as buffalo, quail and elk. Hearty steaks, poultry and seafood dishes also are available. The atmosphere of the attractively decorated dining room is warm and inviting, and its Western-attired staff is outgoing. **Features:** full bar. **Reservations:** suggested. **Address:** 19192 Hwy 8 80465 **Location:** 2 mi s; 0.3 mi n of jct US 285. D

MOSCA (E-4) elev. 7,562'

COLORADO GATORS, 17 mi. n. on SR 17, features alligators lolling in the Colorado sun with snow-capped mountain peaks in the background. The unusual nature of this farm grew out of a need to keep the fish hatchery at the site clean of fish remains. The waters of the artesian well are 87 F and allow the alligators to thrive in the otherwise inhospitable Colorado climate. The farm also serves as a refuge for rescued reptiles.

Time: Allow 30 minutes minimum. **Hours:** Daily 9-6, late May-early Sept.; 9-5, early Sept.-Nov. 1. Closed Thanksgiving and Christmas. **Cost:** $15; $7.50 (ages 6-15 and 65-79); free (ages 80+). **Phone:** (719) 378-2612.

MOUNT CRESTED BUTTE (D-3) pop. 801

RECREATIONAL ACTIVITIES
Skiing
- **Crested Butte Mountain Resort** is at 500 Gothic Rd. Other activities are offered. **Hours:** Daily 9-4, mid-Nov. to early Apr. **Phone:** (877) 547-5143.

NATHROP (D-3) elev. 7,690'

RECREATIONAL ACTIVITIES
White-water Rafting
- **Bill Dvorak Rafting & Kayak Expeditions** is at 17921 US 285. **Hours:** Daily 7 a.m.-7 p.m., May-Sept. **Phone:** (800) 824-3795.

NEDERLAND (C-8) pop. 1,445, elev. 8,233'

RECREATIONAL ACTIVITIES
Skiing

- **Eldora Mountain Resort** is 4 mi. w. of CR 119 at 2861 Eldora Ski Rd. **Hours:** Daily 9-4, mid-Nov. to mid-Apr. (weather permitting). **Phone:** (303) 440-8700.

BLACK FOREST RESTAURANT   303/279-2333

▼▼▼
German
Casual Dining
$8-$30

AAA Inspector Notes: Diners will enjoy the homey, comfy décor at this restaurant, which has been serving guests since 1957. The menu features traditional dishes such as sauerbraten, as well as wild game and fowl specialties and American entrees. Entertainment is provided on weekends. **Features:** full bar, patio dining, early bird specials. **Reservations:** suggested. **Address:** 24 Big Springs Dr 80466 **Location:** SR 119 to Peak Hwy, just s of roundabout; above The Village Shopping Center. *Menu on AAA.com*

L D 🎔

NEW CASTLE pop. 4,518

ELK CREEK MINING CO   970/984-0828

▼▼ American. Casual Dining. $10-$27 **AAA Inspector Notes:** The extensive menu features a variety of salads, burgers and sandwiches for lunch. Dinner items also include pork chops, prime rib, fajitas and pasta. The flavorful burgers are made from Certified Angus beef. Adorning the walls are historic mining papers and maps as well as paintings with an Old West theme. **Features:** full bar, happy hour. **Address:** 502 W Main St 81647 **Location:** I-70 exit 105, just n, then 1.1 mi w. **Parking:** on-site and street. L D

NIWOT pop. 4,006

COLTERRA   303/652-0777

▼▼▼ New Continental. Fine Dining. $11-$30 **AAA Inspector Notes:** Seasonal ingredients from local purveyors combine in tempting dishes inspired by the flavors of northern Italy and southern France. Explore the culinary skills of noted chef Bradford Heap, who honed his skills under the guidance of Alain Ducasse, Georges Blanc and Carlo Cioni and received accolades from the James Beard Foundation. Your meal begins with a bite of the perfectly baked rustic bread with a soft middle and a crunchy crust. **Features:** full bar, patio dining, Sunday brunch. **Address:** 210 Franklin St 80544 **Location:** I-25 exit 235, 6.6 mi w to US 287, 1 mi n, then w on Niwot Rd to 2nd Ave; in historic downtown. **Parking:** street only. L D

LEFTY'S GOURMET PIZZA & ICE CREAM   303/652-3100

▼ Pizza. Quick Serve. $6-$27 **AAA Inspector Notes:** A small facility with big ideas, the restaurant offers gourmet pizza prepared according to guests' preferences, tasty chicken wings and fresh-flavored homemade ice cream. **Address:** 364 2nd Ave 80503 **Location:** Center; in historic downtown. **Parking:** street only. L D

NORTHGLENN pop. 35,789
- **Part of Denver area — see map p. 116**

LARKBURGER   720/285-1995

▼ Burgers. Quick Serve. $7-$9 **AAA Inspector Notes:** This story begins when famed chef Thomas Salamunovich put the gourmet "Larkburger" on the menu at Larkspur, his fine dining restaurant in Vail, Colorado. The delicious, 100%-natural burger became so popular, Salamunovich created a fast-food restaurant around it. Nowadays it's a small chain serving juicy, flavorful, Angus beef and turkey burgers that are heavenly. Hand-cut fries, seasoned with grated Parmesan cheese and truffle oil, make the perfect accompaniment. **Address:** 11985 Washington St 80233 **Location:** I-25 exit 223, 0.6 mi e, then just s. L D

NORWOOD pop. 518

BACKCOUNTRY INN   970/327-4232

▼▼ **Motel. Rates not provided. Address:** 1160 Grand Ave 81423 **Location:** 0.3 mi w of town center. **Facility:** 10 units. 1 story, exterior corridors. **Terms:** check-in 4 pm.

🛗 📶 ✕ 🛢 🖥 🖵

OAK CREEK (B-3) pop. 884

TRACKS AND TRAILS MUSEUM is at 129 E. Main St. The museum's collection pertains to the history of coal mining, the railroad and diverse immigration. An outdoor mining display features an 83,000 pound drag-line bucket, while indoor exhibits focus on local railroad and mining artifacts. Rotating exhibits about local culture and history also are featured. **Time:** Allow 1 hour minimum. **Hours:** Tues.-Sat. 10-noon and 1-3. Phone ahead to confirm schedule. **Cost:** Free. **Phone:** (970) 736-8245.

OURAY (E-2) pop. 1,000, elev. 7,811'
- **Restaurants p. 242**

The town draws its name from the Ute chieftain Ouray (you-RAY). Before the miners arrived, the Native Americans came to the area to enjoy the hot springs. The first silver strike was made in 1875. The politics, foibles and personalities of the mining camps were lambasted in the *Solid Muldoon;* the paper became one of the most widely quoted of the time— even Queen Victoria of England was a subscriber.

Not silver but gold stabilized the community after the Panic of 1893. The wealth that poured from Tom Walsh's Camp Bird Mine amounted to $24 million 1896-1902. The fortune bought the family a place in Washington, D.C., society and daughter Evalyn the Hope Diamond. Mining has long since given way to year-round tourism as the leading factor in Ouray's economy.

The springs once enjoyed by the Native Americans now feed the outdoor Ouray Hot Springs Pool; for more information phone (970) 325-7073.

At the end of 8th Avenue is Cascade Falls Park, which features a nature trail and a lovely 300-foot waterfall. Another noteworthy local feature is Ouray Ice Park, one of the only parks in the world dedicated to the sport of ice climbing.

Ouray is the halfway point along the San Juan Skyway, Colorado's first scenic byway. The town also marks the northern terminus of the byway known as the Million Dollar Highway *(see attraction listing).* The surrounding San Juan and Uncompahgre national forests are popular with four-wheel-drive enthusiasts and feature hundreds of hiking trails.

Ouray Chamber Resort Association: 1230 Main St., P.O. Box 145, Ouray, CO 81427. **Phone:** (970) 325-4746 or (800) 228-1876.

Self-guiding tours: Information about a self-guiding historic walking tour of Ouray is available from the visitor information center at the resort association.

BACHELOR-SYRACUSE MINE is 1 mi. n. on US 550, then 1.2 mi. e. on CR 14, following signs. A guided walking tour of Gold Hill, where some $90 million worth of silver and $8 million worth of gold have been removed, is available. The mine temperature is 52 F. Gold panning is available.

Warm clothing is recommended. **Time:** Allow 1 hour minimum. **Hours:** Daily 9-4, May 20-Sept. 30; by appointment, in Oct. **Cost:** Fare $14.99; $7.99 (ages 6-12). **Phone:** (970) 325-0220. 🍽

BOX CAÑON FALLS AND PARK is s. on US 550 to CR 361, following signs. The canyon is 20 feet wide and 285 feet high. Its perpendicular granite walls are roofed by stone. Canyon Creek rushes through the narrow gorge, which is spanned by a high bridge. Interpretive exhibits highlight the canyon's diverse ecosystems. A trail leads from the parking area to a point from which the falls can be seen. **Time:** Allow 30 minutes minimum. **Hours:** Park daily dawn-dusk. Visitor center daily 8-8, May 1 to mid-Oct. **Cost:** $4; $3 (ages 65+); $2 (ages 5-12). **Phone:** (970) 325-7080.

MILLION DOLLAR HIGHWAY is a name often given to all of US 550 s. from Ouray to Silverton, but it technically applies only to the 6-mile section south of Ouray that follows Otto Mears' original toll road. Ranked among the nation's most spectacular automobile routes, it features chasms so deep that neither cliff tops nor canyon bottoms are visible on either side. Bear Creek Falls cascades under the highway into the canyon below and can be viewed from one of the many scenic overlooks along the road.

A few miles from Ouray, a backward look from the portal of a tunnel provides a magnificent view of pyramidal Mount Abrams. Whether the "million dollar" label refers to the cost of rebuilding the road, to the value of the gold in the mine tailings or to the views is uncertain. **Note:** Drivers unfamiliar with mountain roads should use caution.

OURAY COUNTY MUSEUM is at 420 6th Ave. The building that houses this museum was the town's hospital for 77 years. Some 27 rooms contain individual displays about the county's history. Hospital memorabilia remain along with mining relics, ranching and merchant exhibits, Ute Indian artifacts, a replica of the old jail and two restored log cabins.

Time: Allow 1 hour minimum. **Hours:** Mon.-Sat. 10-4:30, Sun. noon-4:30, mid-May through Sept. 30; Thurs.-Sat. 10-4:30, Oct.-Nov.; Thurs.-Sat. 1-4:30, mid-Apr. to mid-May. Phone ahead to confirm schedule. **Cost:** $6; $1 (ages 6-12). **Phone:** (970) 325-4576.

SWITZERLAND OF AMERICA TOURS, 226 7th Ave., offers guided off-road scenic tours of the back country in four-wheel-drive vehicles; sights include ghost towns, mining camps, wildflowers, waterfalls and the San Juan Mountains. Jeep rentals, horseback riding, rafting and hot air balloon rides also are available.

Hours: Daily 8-7, Memorial Day to mid-June and day after Labor Day-Oct. 15. **Cost:** Half-day off-road tours $63; $37 (ages 4-12). Full-day off-road tours $125-$145; $65-$71 (ages 4-12). Reservations are recommended. **Phone:** (970) 325-4484 or (866) 990-5337.

RECREATIONAL ACTIVITIES
Climbing

- **San Juan Mountain Guides** departs from 636 Main St. and various area locations. **Hours:** Daily 7 a.m.-9 p.m. **Phone:** (970) 325-4925 or (800) 642-5389.

BEAUMONT HOTEL & SPA   970/325-7000
▼▼▼▼ **Classic Historic Hotel.** Rates not provided. **Address:** 505 Main St 81427 **Location:** Just s on US 550 (Main St). **Facility:** Built in 1886, this iconic brick building is an architectural delight. Carved wood accents, elaborate wallpaper, and antiques characterize the charming public areas. 13 units, some two bedrooms and efficiencies. 3 stories, interior corridors. **Terms:** check-in 4 pm. **Activities:** sauna, hot tub, spa.

COMFORT INN   (970)325-7203
▼▼ **Motel** $75-$170 **Address:** 191 5th Ave 81427 **Location:** Just w of US 550 (Main St) via 5th Ave. **Facility:** 33 units. 2 stories (no elevator), exterior corridors. **Activities:** hot tub, trails. **Guest Services:** coin laundry.

HOT SPRINGS INN   970/325-7277
▼▼ **Motel** $73-$230 **Address:** 1400 Main St 81427 **Location:** 1 mi n of center on US 550 (Main St). **Facility:** 42 units. 2 stories (no elevator), exterior corridors. **Bath:** shower only. **Terms:** closed 10/20-5/15, 3 day cancellation notice-fee imposed. **Amenities:** safes. **Activities:** hot tub, picnic facilities, trails. **Guest Services:** coin laundry.

MATTERHORN INN OURAY   970/325-4938
▼▼ **Boutique Motel.** Rates not provided. **Address:** 201 6th Ave 81427 **Location:** Just w of US 550 (Main St), at 6th Ave and 2nd St. **Facility:** For travelers who don't need extensive public areas, this motel offers upgraded rooms with hardwood floors, luxurious bedding and flat-screen TVs. Baths have granite vanities and upgraded amenities. 25 units. 2 stories (no elevator), exterior corridors. **Activities:** trails.

OURAY CHALET INN   (970)325-4331
▼▼ **Motel** $65-$175 **Address:** 510 Main St 81427 **Location:** Just s of center on US 550 (Main St). **Facility:** 32 units. 2 stories (no elevator), interior/exterior corridors. **Terms:** cancellation fee imposed, resort fee. **Activities:** hot tub. **Guest Services:** coin laundry.

OURAY RIVERSIDE INN & CABINS   970/325-4061
▼▼▼
Motel
Rates not provided

Address: 1804 N Main St 81427 **Location:** 1 mi n of center on US 550 (Main St). **Facility:** 21 units, some two bedrooms, efficiencies, kitchens and cabins. 2 stories (no elevator), exterior corridors. **Activities:** hot tub, picnic facilities, trails. **Guest Services:** coin laundry.
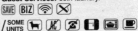

OURAY VICTORIAN INN   970/325-7222

▼▼ Motel. Rates not provided. **Address:** 50 3rd Ave 81427 **Location:** Just w of US 550 (Main St) to 3rd Ave. **Facility:** 38 units. 2 stories (no elevator), exterior corridors. **Activities:** hot tub, playground, trails. **Guest Services:** coin laundry.

ST. ELMO HOTEL   (970)325-4951

▼▼ Historic Country Inn $119-$325 **Address:** 426 Main St 81427 **Location:** Just s of center on US 550 (Main St). **Facility:** Quietly unwind in the Victorian-style lobby, which features ornate wall paper as well as antique and reproduction furniture. 10 units. 2 stories (no elevator), interior corridors. **Parking:** on-site and street. **Terms:** 2 night minimum stay - seasonal, 7 day cancellation notice. **Dining:** Bon Ton Restaurant, see separate listing. **Activities:** sauna, hot tub, trails.

OURAY INN   970/325-4445

[fyi] Not evaluated. **Address:** 120 W 6th Ave 81427 **Location:** Just w of jct US 550. Facilities, services, and décor characterize a midscale property.

WHERE TO EAT

ARTISAN BAKERY & CAFE   970/325-4677

▼ Breads/Pastries Sandwiches. Quick Serve. $6-$10 **AAA Inspector Notes:** This café offers a variety of sandwiches served on freshly-baked bread, pizzas, quiche, soups and pastries. This place is perfect for breakfast or lunch, and you can dine in or take out. **Address:** 460 Main St 81427 **Location:** Just s of center on US 550 (Main St). **Parking:** street only. [B] [L] [🅺]

BON TON RESTAURANT   970/325-4951

▼▼▼ American. Casual Dining. $14-$39 **AAA Inspector Notes:** In the basement of the hotel, this warm and inviting restaurant is surrounded by rock walls, hardwood floors and an elegant martini bar. Menu selections include escargot and crayfish tails, beef Wellington, prime Angus steak, veal piccata, fresh seafood, chicken and pasta dishes. Decadent desserts, such as the galloping goose caboose sundae and the black nasty chocolate fudge pie with graham cracker crust, enhance the dining experience. **Features:** full bar, Sunday brunch. **Reservations:** suggested. **Address:** 426 Main St 81427 **Location:** Just s of center on US 550 (Main St); in St. Elmo Hotel. **Parking:** street only. [D]

BUEN TIEMPO RESTAURANT & CANTINA   970/325-4544

▼▼ Mexican. Casual Dining. $10-$24 **AAA Inspector Notes:** The local favorite prepares Mexican food with flair. Distinctive sauces flavor family-pleasing preparations of fish, chicken and beef. **Features:** full bar. **Address:** 515 Main St 81427 **Location:** Just s of center on US 550 (Main St). **Parking:** street only. [L] [D]

GOLDBELT BAR & GRILL   970/325-7323

▼▼ Sandwiches Pizza. Casual Dining. $8-$13 **AAA Inspector Notes:** Sweet potato fries with curry mayonnaise are addicting, as are the pesto chicken melt sandwich and East Coast-style steak and cheese sub. Popular homemade soup is served daily and patrons can build their own hand-tossed pizzas with homemade sauce, fresh dough and fine, quality cheeses. Postcard-perfect scenery can be viewed from the tall windows inside or from the wraparound outdoor patio with umbrellas. Veggie burgers and gluten-free pizza also are available. **Features:** full bar. **Address:** 800 Main St 81427 **Location:** Just n of center on US 550 (Main St). [L] [D]

OURAY BREWERY   970/325-7388

▼▼ American. Casual Dining. $10-$13 **AAA Inspector Notes:** *Historic.* Located in a charming historic building, this brewery offers a rooftop patio with mountain views. Sidle up to the bar and prepare to swing! Yep. Why sit on a barstool, when you can sit in a swing? The menu consists of burgers, sandwiches and a tangy buffalo chicken wrap as well as ribs, pulled pork and a Southwest pepper steak. **Features:** full bar, patio dining. **Address:** 607 Main St 81427 **Location:** Between 6th and 7th aves. **Parking:** street only. [L] [D]

OUTLAW RESTAURANT   970/325-4366

▼▼ Steak Seafood. Casual Dining. $15-$33 **AAA Inspector Notes:** Experience a taste of the Wild West by dining at this eatery, housed in a historic building. Photos of outlaws and other 19th-century personalities adorn the walls. Cowboy hats, saddles and wagon wheel chandeliers complete the look. Start your meal with a jumbo shrimp cocktail. Entrées include a heavily marbled rib-eye, Rocky Mountain trout and lamb. A piano player entertains with music ranging from classical to modern movie themes. **Features:** full bar. **Reservations:** suggested, in summer. **Address:** 610 Main St 81427 **Location:** On US 550 (Main St); center. **Parking:** street only. [D] [🅺]

TIMBERLINE DELI   970/325-4958

▼ Deli. Quick Serve. $6-$10 **AAA Inspector Notes:** Grab a sandwich, coffee or ice cream to-go, or sit in the cozy dining area. The outdoor patio looks out on Main Street, perfect for enjoying the mountain views as well as people-watching. **Features:** patio dining. **Address:** 803 Main St 81427 **Location:** Between 8th and 9th aves. **Parking:** street only. [L] [D] [🅺]

PAGOSA SPRINGS (F-3) pop. 1,727, elev. 7,105'

Pagosa (healing water) Springs, aptly named by the Ute Indians who vied for possession of the area's thermal springs, became a lumbering center and popular spa in the late 19th century. Bursting from the earth at 140 degrees Fahrenheit, the waters are used to heat some of the community's buildings. Today's bathers enjoy the waters at a variety of pools open to the public.

Numerous lakes and the surrounding lands of the San Juan National Forest *(see place listing p. 255)* and the Weminuche Wilderness Area offer a wide variety of year-round recreational opportunities, including fishing, hiking, horseback riding, bicycling, rafting, hot air ballooning, hunting, alpine and cross-country skiing, ice skating and snowmobiling. Just 17 miles west of the city is the 3,160-acre Chimney Rock National Monument *(see attraction listing p. 78)*, set atop a high mesa that contains hundreds of Ancestral Puebloan sites. Tours and interpretive events are available.

Pagosa Springs Area Visitor Center: 402 San Juan St., P.O. Box 787, Pagosa Springs, CO 81147. **Phone:** (970) 264-2204 or (866) 438-4917.

FRED HARMAN ART MUSEUM is at 85 Harman Park Dr. The work of Western painter and illustrator Fred Harman is displayed. Harman's cowboy comic strip "Red Ryder," drawn 1938-64, was once the nation's most widely syndicated print cartoon. The museum features Harman's studio as well as the oil paintings, pen and ink drawings, and bronze sculptures created in his later years. **Hours:** Mon.-Sat. 10:30-5, early May through Sept. 30; by appointment, rest of year. **Cost:** $3; 50c (ages 0-6). **Phone:** (970) 731-5785.

THE SPRINGS RESORT & SPA, 165 Hot Springs Blvd., offers 23 outdoor naturally hot, therapeutic mineral pools, a geothermal swimming pool and a geothermal whirlpool bath. The pools are arranged in a parklike setting, terraced along the San Juan River. A bath house with towels, robes and lockers is available.

Hours: Daily 7 a.m.-midnight, mid-June to early Sept.; 7 a.m.-11 p.m., rest of year. **Cost:** Single visit $26-$53 (ages 18+); $14-$29 (ages 2-17). Day pass (locker included) $45; $29 (ages 2-10). Prices vary by level of service. Ages 0-13 must be with an adult. Additional fees may apply for some pools. **Phone:** (970) 264-4168 or (800) 225-0934.

RECREATIONAL ACTIVITIES

Fishing

- **Wolf Creek Anglers** departs from 169 Pagosa St. **Hours:** Daily dawn-dusk. Phone ahead to confirm schedule. **Phone:** (719) 873-1414 or (970) 264-1415.

Skiing

- **Wolf Creek Ski Area** is 23 mi. e. on US 160 at the top of Wolf Creek Pass. **Hours:** Daily 8:30-4, early Nov.-early Apr. **Phone:** (970) 264-5639 or (800) 754-9653.

White-water Rafting

- **AAM's Mild to Wild Rafting & Jeep Tours Inc.** departs from the Piedra River Store 15 mi. w. on US 160. Guided jeep trail and Mesa Verde tours and Durango train packages also are available. **Hours:** Full-day trips depart daily at 9, mid-Apr. to late June. **Phone:** (970) 247-4789 or (800) 567-6745.

FIRESIDE INN CABINS   970/264-9204
▼▼ **Cabin.** Rates not provided. **Address:** 1600 E Hwy 160 81147 **Location:** 1.3 mi e of downtown. **Facility:** 15 cabins. 1 story, exterior corridors. *Bath:* shower only. **Activities:** hot tub, fishing, picnic facilities. **Guest Services:** coin laundry.

HIGH COUNTRY LODGE & CABINS   (970)264-4181
▼▼ **Motel** $89-$210 **Address:** 3821 E Hwy 160 81147 **Location:** 3 mi e of downtown. **Facility:** 32 units, some cabins. 1-2 stories (no elevator), exterior corridors. **Terms:** cancellation fee imposed. **Activities:** sauna, hot tub, fishing, playground, picnic facilities, trails. **Guest Services:** coin laundry.

MOUNTAIN LANDING SUITES & R.V. PARK   970/731-5345
▼▼ **Motel** $74-$185 **Address:** 345 Piedra Rd 81147 **Location:** 2.5 mi w of downtown to Piedra Rd, 0.5 mi n. **Facility:** 13 units, some two bedrooms, efficiencies and kitchens. 1 story, exterior corridors. **Terms:** 14 day cancellation notice-fee imposed. **Activities:** hot tub, playground, picnic facilities, limited exercise equipment. **Guest Services:** coin laundry.

WHERE TO EAT

ALLEY HOUSE GRILLE   970/264-0999
▼▼▼ American. Casual Dining. $21-$42 **AAA Inspector Notes:** Guests can enjoy global cuisine served in a casually elegant atmosphere. Continuing selections may include out-of-the-ordinary appetizers such as calamari with wasabi dipping sauce, a tempting Thai Caesar salad, gourmet pizza served on Belgian beer-based sourdough, heartier entrées and scrumptious seasonal dessert selections. **Features:** full bar. **Reservations:** suggested. **Address:** 214 Pagosa St 81157 **Location:** 0.3 mi e of center. **Parking:** street only.

FARRAGO MARKET CAFE   970/264-4600
▼▼ Sandwiches Pizza. Quick Serve. $8-$22 **AAA Inspector Notes:** Build-your-own pizzas with organic crust are a specialty at this colorful eatery. Other menu items include Cajun wings, fish tacos, a grilled lamb gyro, mango Gorgonzola quesadilla, and a selection of gourmet coffees and tea. Cookies, brownies and pastries make great travel companions. **Features:** beer & wine, patio dining, happy hour. **Address:** 175 Pagosa St 81147 **Location:** On US 160, 0.3 mi e of downtown at 2nd St. **Parking:** street only.

KIP'S GRILL & CANTINA   970/264-3663
▼▼ American. Casual Dining. $6-$11 **AAA Inspector Notes:** Enjoy the Colorado outdoors with a meal on the patio. On a cold day, a bowl of the Santa Fe green chile will warm you up. Select from a variety of specialty tacos, such as the spicy grilled shrimp marinated in a cayenne garlic sauce; grilled and marinated pork; or top sirloin and avocado. If you need more heat, add one of the homemade hot sauces to your dish. **Features:** full bar, patio dining. **Address:** 121 Pagosa St 81147 **Location:** On US 160, 0.4 mi e of downtown.

MARCONI'S   970/264-2431
▼▼ Italian. Casual Dining. $7-$23 **AAA Inspector Notes:** This cozy eatery specializes in made-from-scratch Italian favorites like baked ziti, shrimp scampi, chicken saltimbocca, veal Parmesan and pork osso buco. The homemade dressings, such as the garlicky lemon vinaigrette, add spice to the salads. The tiramisu features espresso (rather than rum), soaked cake, white-and-dark chocolate and a slight citrus flavor. **Features:** full bar, happy hour. **Address:** 117 Navajo Trail Dr 81147 **Location:** Jct US 160 and Pagosa Blvd, just nw, just sw.

PAGOSA BAKING COMPANY & CAFE   970/264-9348
▼▼ Breakfast Sandwiches. Casual Dining. $5-$9 **AAA Inspector Notes:** This spot can't be beat for visitors, travelers and skiers looking for some good nourishment. The popular, relaxing eatery offers an assortment of soups, quiches, salads, a few sandwiches and a killer breakfast burrito. Pick up a loaf of artisan bread or some goodies for the road, or for family and friends. **Address:** 238 Pagosa St 81147 **Location:** 0.3 mi e of downtown. **Parking:** street only.

PAGOSA BREWING & GRILL   970/731-2739
▼▼ American. Casual Dining. $8-$15 **AAA Inspector Notes:** This brewery offers some of the best handcrafted beers in the state. Favorites include Poor Richard's Ale, the Chili Verde Cerveza and the Soaker's Stout. The 4-ounce samplers allow you to taste a variety of brews. The salmon fish and chips—made with a light, homemade beer batter—are a must. Other options include pizzas, burgers and sandwiches. **Features:** full bar. **Address:** 118 N Pagosa Blvd 81147 **Location:** Jct US 160 (San Juan St), just nw.

SHANGHAI RESTAURANT   970/731-1688
▼▼ Chinese. Casual Dining. $7-$14 **AAA Inspector Notes:** This casual eatery offers a pleasant dining room and popular outdoor patio. Egg rolls, soup and entrées are made from scratch. Menu items include favorites such as the 'happy family,' Szechuan chicken, moo shu pork, pan-fried noodles and egg foo young. **Features:** full bar, patio dining. **Address:** 20 Village Dr 81147 **Location:** US 160, just n of Pagosa Blvd, just e.

THAI CHILIE   970/731-8440
▼▼ Thai. Casual Dining. $7-$19 **AAA Inspector Notes:** Choose from a variety of Thai staples including shrimp spring rolls, chicken satay, pad thai, drunken noodles, curries, and stir fries. Expect quick service in a casual setting. **Features:** full bar. **Address:** 565 Village Dr, Suite D 81147 **Location:** 4 mi w of downtown to Pinion Cswy, just nw.

PALISADE (C-1) pop. 2,692, elev. 4,724'
- Hotels p. 244 • Restaurants p. 244

A fruit-growing region for more than a century, the East Grand Valley area along the Colorado River at the base of the Book Cliffs and Grand Mesa is known in particular for its peaches. Apples, apricots, cherries and plums also are plentiful, and roadside fruit stands are common sights in season. Vineyards also flourish here. Palisade is home to several wineries producing traditional grape wines as well as those made from other fruits. Bicycling, river floats and hiking are popular choices for outdoor recreation.

Palisade hosts several festivals each year, including the Palisade Peach Festival the third weekend in August, which offers an ice cream social, fruit stands, orchard tours, a pancake breakfast, a recipe contest, live music and a parade. The ☙ Colorado Mountain Winefest celebrates the grape with 4 days of tastings, seminars, jazz, grape stomping, winery tours and an amateur winemaker's competition in September. In early December the Olde-Fashioned Christmas entertains attendees with horse-drawn wagon rides, a soup challenge, music, caroling, arts and crafts and wine tastings.

Palisade Chamber of Commerce: 319 S. Main St., P.O. Box 729, Palisade, CO 81526. **Phone:** (970) 464-7458.

WINERIES

- **Canyon Wind Cellars** is off I-70 exit 44, then .5 mi. s.w. following signs to 3907 North River Rd. **Hours:** Tastings daily 10-5. Guided tours are offered Sat.-Sun. at 11, 1 and 3, Memorial Day-Labor Day. **Phone:** (970) 464-0888. (GT)

- **Carlson Vineyards** is at 461 35 Rd. **Hours:** Daily 10-6. Wine tasting ends at 5:45. Closed Jan. 1, Thanksgiving and Christmas. **Phone:** (970) 464-5554 or (888) 464-5554. (GT)

- **Garfield Estates Vineyard & Winery** is at 3572 G Rd. **Hours:** Tastings daily 11-6, Mar.-Dec.; Mon.-Fri. noon-5, rest of year. Tours available by appointment. Closed Easter, Thanksgiving and Christmas. **Phone:** (970) 464-0941. (GT)

- **Grande River Vineyards** is off I-70 exit 42, then .75 mi. s. to 787 N. Elberta Ave. **Hours:** Daily 9-5. Closed Jan. 1, Thanksgiving and Christmas. **Phone:** (970) 464-5867 or (800) 264-7696. (GT)

- **Plum Creek Cellars** is off I-70 exit 42, s. to US 6, then 5 mi. w. to 3708 G Rd. **Hours:** Daily 10-5. Closed Jan. 1, Thanksgiving and Christmas. Phone ahead to confirm schedule. **Phone:** (970) 464-7586. (GT)

WINE COUNTRY INN   (970)464-5777

◆◆◆◆
Hotel
$104-$429

Address: 777 Grande River Dr 81526 **Location:** I-70 exit 42, 0.3 mi w. **Facility:** 80 units, some two bedrooms and kitchens. 2-3 stories, interior corridors. **Terms:** check-in 4 pm, 2 night minimum stay - weekends, cancellation fee imposed. **Dining:** 2 restaurants; heated outdoor. **Activities:** hot tub, exercise room. **Guest Services:** valet and coin laundry. **Featured Amenity: full hot breakfast.**

WHERE TO EAT

INARI'S, A PALISADE BISTRO   970/464-4911

◆◆◆ American. Casual Dining. $13-$27 **AAA Inspector Notes:** Located in a quaint neighborhood, this bistro offers a sophisticated menu in a casual setting. Selections include Korean tacos with Asian-style braised pork, grilled mahi-mahi, lamb chops, lobster risotto, and rib-eye steak. Save room for a homemade slice of caramel apple pie or chocolate mousse cake. **Features:** beer & wine, patio dining. **Reservations:** suggested. **Address:** 336 Main St 81526 **Location:** I-70 exit 42, 0.5 mi s, 0.5 mi e on W 1st St, then 0.3 mi s. **Parking:** on-site and street. (D)

PALMER LAKE pop. 2,420
- **Part of Colorado Springs area — see map p. 81**

MO ZAIC   719/481-1800

◆◆◆◆ American. Fine Dining. $8-$39 **AAA Inspector Notes:** The varied menu offers something for everyone, including steaks, salmon, chicken, lamb, tofu and veal. The picturesque location features mountain views; request a table by a window. **Features:** full bar, Sunday brunch. **Address:** 443 S Hwy 105 80133 **Location:** I-25 exit 161, 0.3 mi w, then 2.5 mi n. (L)(D)

PAONIA pop. 1,451

BROSS HOTEL BED & BREAKFAST   (970)527-6776

◆◆ Historic Bed & Breakfast $135-$150 **Address:** 312 Onarga Ave 81428 **Location:** At 3rd St and Onarga Ave; downtown. **Facility:** This 1906 B&B combines lovely landscaping and Western charm with modern conveniences, including private baths. 10 units. 3 stories (no elevator), interior corridors. **Terms:** check-in 4 pm, cancellation fee imposed.

WHERE TO EAT

FLYING FORK CAFE   970/527-3203

◆◆◆ Italian. Casual Dining. $9-$23 **AAA Inspector Notes:** Simple elegance describes both the cuisine and ambiance here. The lunch menu includes a grilled lemon chicken salad, rigatoni pomodoro, and a French dip sandwich. Elegant dinner entrées include pasta, steaks, shrimp, pork and Colorado lamb. In the summer, the best seating is in the outdoor garden under the fruit trees. Patrons can choose from a very nice selection of wines and beers from Colorado and Italy. **Features:** full bar, patio dining. **Address:** 101 3rd St 81428 **Location:** From SR 133, 0.7 mi e; corner of 3rd and Main sts. (L)(D)

PARACHUTE pop. 1,085

CANDLEWOOD SUITES   970/285-9880

◆◆ Extended Stay Hotel. Rates not provided. **Address:** 233 Grand Valley Way 81635 **Location:** I-70 exit 75, just se. **Facility:** 73 efficiencies. 4 stories, interior corridors. **Activities:** picnic facilities, exercise room. **Guest Services:** complimentary laundry.

COMFORT INN & SUITES (970)285-1122
Hotel $89-$109 **Address:** 228 Railroad Ave 81635 **Location:** I-70 exit 75, just nw. **Facility:** 71 units. 3 stories, interior corridors. **Pool(s):** heated indoor. **Activities:** hot tub, exercise room. **Guest Services:** coin laundry.

DAYS INN & SUITES (970)285-2330
Hotel $49-$69 **Address:** 221 Grand Valley Way 81635 **Location:** I-70 exit 25, just se. **Facility:** 60 units. 3 stories, interior corridors. **Pool(s):** heated indoor. **Activities:** hot tub, exercise room. **Guest Services:** valet laundry.

WHERE TO EAT

ROCKY MOUNTAIN PIZZA & CONE 970/285-2253
Pizza. Quick Serve. $9-$15 **AAA Inspector Notes:** As the name suggests, the menu primarily consists of pizza and ice cream. Named after Colorado mountain peaks, the specialty pizzas range from familiar combos to more unique options like the Mt. Wilson, a pie topped with chicken, cheese and Alfredo sauce. **Address:** 101 Cardinal Way 81635 **Location:** I-70 exit 75, just se, then 0.4 mi sw.

PARKER (D-9) pop. 45,297, elev. 5,868'

THE WILDLIFE EXPERIENCE is 1 mi. n. on Parker Rd., then 4 mi. w. on Lincoln Ave. to jct. S. Peoria St. The center is dedicated to the preservation and appreciation of wildlife and their habitats. Permanent and traveling interactive exhibits of natural history, film and fine art are featured. Natural history exhibits showcase animals in natural environments. The 315-seat Extreme Screen Theater presents large-screen format adventure films. Education and conservation programs and two interactive children's galleries are available.

Time: Allow 1 hour minimum. **Hours:** Daily 9:30-5. Closed Thanksgiving and Christmas. **Cost:** Museum $10; $9 (ages 65+); $6 (ages 3-12). Extreme Screen Theater $9; $8 (ages 65+); $6 (ages 3-12). Combination ticket $14; $13 (ages 65+); $9 (ages 3-12). **Phone:** (720) 488-3300.

HAMPTON INN & SUITES 303/841-2977
Hotel. Rates not provided. **Address:** 19010 E Cottonwood Dr 80138 **Location:** SR 470 (toll road) exit 5 (Parker Rd/SR 83), 0.4 mi se on Crown Crest Blvd, then just e. **Facility:** 84 units. 4 stories, interior corridors. **Pool(s):** heated indoor. **Activities:** hot tub, exercise room. **Guest Services:** valet laundry.

AAA Benefit: Members save up to 10%!

HOLIDAY INN 303/248-2147
Hotel. Rates not provided. **Address:** 19308 Cottonwood Dr 80138 **Location:** SR 470 (toll road) exit 5 (Parker Rd/SR 83) eastbound, straight at light, follow signs to Cottonwood Dr; exit westbound, just s to Crown Crest Blvd, follow signs to Cottonwood Dr. **Facility:** 100 units. 4 stories, interior corridors. **Terms:** check-in 4 pm. **Amenities:** safes. **Dining:** 2 restaurants. **Pool(s):** heated indoor. **Activities:** hot tub, exercise room. **Guest Services:** valet and coin laundry.

WHERE TO EAT

ARMANDO'S RISTORANTE ITALIANO 720/851-6770
Italian. Casual Dining. $12-$24 **AAA Inspector Notes:** Although it may seem like a common chain on the outside, the owners immigrated from Italy and still assist in the kitchen; they'll occasionally sing opera with the staff. The double-crusted spinach, mozzarella and olive pizza is a local favorite. The hand-breaded chicken Parmesan is also highly recommended. **Features:** full bar. **Address:** 9964 S Twenty Mile Rd 80134 **Location:** SR 470 (toll road) exit 5 (Parker Rd/SR 83), 1.2 mi s, just w on Lincoln Ave, then just s on Dransfeldt Rd.

JUNZ RESTAURANT 720/851-1005
Japanese. Casual Dining. $8-$24 **AAA Inspector Notes:** Chef Jun combines elements of French and Japanese cooking to create his own innovative dishes. The eclectic menu lists delicious tempura, sushi and teriyaki dishes, as well as filet mignon, lamb chops and pasta. Lobster salad makes a delightful light lunch. **Features:** full bar. **Address:** 11211 S Dransfeldt Rd, Suite 100 80134 **Location:** SR 470 (toll road) exit 5 (Parker Rd/SR 83), 2.3 mi s, just w on Main St, then 0.4 mi s; in Parker Valley Center strip mall.

PIKES PEAK AND PIKE NATIONAL FOREST (E-8)

Elevations in the forest range from 7,000 ft. near Colorado Springs to 14,110 ft. at Pikes Peak. Refer to AAA maps for additional elevation information.

West of Denver and Colorado Springs, the 14,110-foot summit of Pikes Peak is visible from a long distance on the Great Plains. The view from the peak inspired poet Katharine Lee Bates in 1893 to write "America the Beautiful." The sentinel of the Front Range is the prime attraction of 1,105,704-acre Pike National Forest. The summit is reached by highway or cog railway; hikers can climb the 11.7-mile Barr National Recreation Trail.

Pike's proximity to the Denver-Colorado Springs corridor makes it one of the most heavily used national forests in the state. The forest has many developed campgrounds and ample opportunities for fishing, hunting, hiking and winter sports. Scenic drives include the Rampart Range Road and the Pikes Peak Highway. Lost Creek and Mount Evans wildernesses are accessible only by foot or horseback.

The Devil's Head Lookout Tower, the last operational fire lookout along the Front Range, stands atop the highest point in the Rampart Range; it is accessible by a 1.3-mile hiking trail. Remnants of early mining activities are evident near Fairplay (see place listing p. 186) in the South Park Valley.

For more information write the Forest Supervisor, Pike National Forest, 2840 Kachina Dr., Pueblo, CO 81008; phone (719) 553-1400. *See Recreation Areas Chart.*

PIKES PEAK COG RAILWAY—see Manitou Springs p. 232.

PIKES PEAK HIGHWAY starts at Cascade, 10 mi. w. of Colorado Springs off US 24. This scenic 19-mile toll road leads to the 14,115-foot summit of one of the nation's tallest mountains. From the gateway at an elevation of 7,400 feet, visitors travel above the timberline and encounter scenic vistas, alpine forests, mountain reservoirs and wildlife habitats. The historic Glen Cove Inn, the North Slope Recreation Area, the Crystal Reservoir Gift Shop and the Summit House offer visitor services.

Caution: Excessive automotive braking is dangerous; use low gear for ascent and descent. An informational handout provides safe driving tips. High altitudes may be hazardous to infants or those with respiratory problems. Fishing and hiking are permitted; a state fishing permit is required. Allow 2 hours, 30 minutes for round-trip travel. **Hours:** Uphill gate open daily 7:30-6, Memorial Day weekend-Labor Day; 7:30-5, day after Labor Day-Sept. 30; 9-3, rest of year (weather permitting).

Cost: May-Nov. $12; $5 (ages 6-15). Maximum charge per private vehicle $40 (up to five people). Dec.-Apr. $10; $4 (ages 6-15). Maximum charge per private vehicle $35 (up to 5 people). A $4 fee is charged for fishing. **Phone:** (719) 385-7325.

PINEWOOD SPRINGS

VILLA TATRA   303/823-6819

(fyi) Not evaluated. This charming restaurant offers Eastern European dishes prepared from scratch, homemade pastry, smoked fish and sausage dishes. Smoked salmon and trout are available by mail. Macrobiotic and vegetarian dinners are available with a two-day reservation. It's open for lunch on Saturday and Sunday. **Address:** 729 Pinewood Dr 80540 **Location:** 12.5 mi se of Estes Park on US 36; town center.

PLACERVILLE (E-2) elev. 7,316'

RECREATIONAL ACTIVITIES
White-water Rafting
- **AAM's Mild to Wild Rafting & Jeep Tours Inc.** departs from Caddis Flats Campground on SR 145. Guided jeep tours, Mesa Verde tours and Durango train packages also are available. **Hours:** Half-day, 1-, 2- and 3-day trips depart daily, early May-late July. **Phone:** (970) 247-4789 or (800) 567-6745.

PLATTEVILLE (B-9) pop. 2,485, elev. 4,825'

FORT VASQUEZ MUSEUM AND VISITOR INFORMATION CENTER, 13412 US 85, features a full-size reconstruction of an early adobe fur-trading post. Built by Louis Vasquez and Andrew Sublette in 1835 to trade with the Cheyenne and Arapaho people, the fort was abandoned in 1842 and eventually worn down by wind, rain and snow. Works Progress Administration (WPA) workers rebuilt the adobe walls 1935-36.

A modern museum features exhibits about the fur-trade era, Native American culture and archeological work completed at the fort in the 1960s. **Hours:** Daily 10-4, Mar.-Sept.; Wed.-Sun. 10-4, rest of year. **Cost:** $3; $2.50 (ages 65+); $2 (ages 6-16). **Phone:** (970) 785-2832.

PONCHA SPRINGS pop. 737

GRIMO'S ITALIAN RESTAURANT   719/539-2903

Italian. Casual Dining. $13-$22 **AAA Inspector Notes:** For a taste of New York Italian cuisine, this is the place to try, especially for those travelers staying in nearby Salida. **Features:** full bar. **Address:** 146 Main St 81242 **Location:** Just s of jct US 50 and 285.

PUEBLO (E-5) pop. 106,595, elev. 4,662'
• Restaurants p. 248

Trader Jim Beckwourth knew a good location when he saw one. He and his party of trappers constructed an adobe fortress at the confluence of Fountain Creek and the Arkansas River in autumn 1842. By the following spring a thriving community had developed and Beckwourth dubbed it Pueblo, meaning "town."

Mountain men, trappers, traders, Native Americans and immigrants convened at this crossroads post. Until a Ute massacre on Christmas Day 1854, Pueblo was the largest settlement in the region. The arrival of the railroad in 1872 and the discovery of coal near Trinidad (see place listing p. 266) made the town a booming workshop for the mines. Foundries manufactured mining equipment; smelters processed the ores.

By 1880 Pueblo's population had increased eightfold, and its present status as Colorado's major industrial center was well established. One of the industrial pioneers of this period was Colorado Coal & Iron Co., now Rocky Mountain Steel, Inc.

Downtown's revitalized waterfront includes the Historic Arkansas Riverwalk of Pueblo, a favorite place for walking, renting paddleboats or enjoying guided boat tours; phone (719) 595-0242 for information and events.

Just west of the city, Lake Pueblo State Park (see Recreation Areas Chart) impounds 17,000-acre Pueblo Reservoir, which is part of the Fryingpan-Arkansas irrigation project. Within the city limits 279 acres of municipal parks provide recreational facilities. Many nature and bicycle trails are available. The Arkansas River is popular for white-water rafting.

The Colorado State Fair is held at the fairgrounds in late August. The third weekend after Labor Day the Chile and Frijoles Festival features cooking contests, a jalapeño-eating competition, a farmers market and live entertainment.

Greater Pueblo Chamber of Commerce: 302 N. Santa Fe Ave., Pueblo, CO 81003. **Phone:** (719) 542-1704 or (800) 233-3446.

Shopping: The Union Avenue Historic District features shopping, galleries, cafés and entertainment in restored brick buildings.

EL PUEBLO HISTORY MUSEUM is off I-25 exit 98B, then 3 blks. w. to 301 N. Union Ave. The museum depicts the history of the region's varied cultures. Permanent exhibits focus on Native Americans, European explorers, trade and settlement, agriculture, industry and natural history. Murals and a hall of international flags also are presented. The museum functions as a visitor information center and a gateway to the city's Historic Arkansas Riverwalk and Union Avenue historic district.

Time: Allow 1 hour minimum. **Hours:** Tues.-Sat. 10-4, Sun. noon-4. Closed Jan. 1, Thanksgiving and Christmas. **Cost:** $5; $4 (ages 6-12, ages 65+ and students or military with ID); free (ages 0-5). Free to ages 0-12 on Sat. **Phone:** (719) 583-0453.

THE NATURE AND RAPTOR CENTER OF PUEBLO, 5200 Nature Center Rd., provides a variety of educational and recreational activities set along the Arkansas River with miles of paved and unpaved trails, xeriscape demonstration gardens, fishing, a watercraft launch, and a raptor rehabilitation center, home to numerous species of predatory birds including eagles, hawks, owls and falcons. Bird of prey demonstrations are given on weekends. **Hours:** Grounds 6:30 a.m.-dusk. Raptor Center Tues.-Sun. 11-4. Bird of prey demonstrations Sat.-Sun. at 11:30 a.m. **Cost:** Free. $3 per vehicle. **Parking:** $3. **Phone:** (719) 549-2414, or (719) 549-2327 for the raptor center.

PUEBLO WEISBROD AIRCRAFT MUSEUM is at 31001 Magnuson Ave., next to the main terminal at Pueblo Memorial Airport. More than 30 war planes from World War I, World War II, the Korean War and the Vietnam War are restored and on display along with uniforms and memorabilia. The B-24 bomber has a special exhibit space, but there's also a B-29, MASH helicopter and modern fighting planes to explore. Researchers can explore the facility's library with historical documents and a collection of photos and video. **Time:** Allow 1 hour, 30 minutes minimum. **Hours:** Mon.-Sat. 10-4, Sun. 1-4. Closed Jan. 1, Easter, Thanksgiving and Christmas. **Cost:** $9; $7 (ages 60+ and military veterans); free (ages 0-8). **Phone:** (719) 948-9219. [GT]

PUEBLO ZOO, in Pueblo City Park, 4 mi. s. of US 50 on SR 45 (Pueblo Blvd.) at jct. Goodnight Ave., houses a collection of animals from around the world, including some threatened or endangered species. Visitors can experience a rainforest, visit the underwater penguin and otter observation areas or view the African lion and Asian monkey exhibits. Wonders of the natural world are explored in the White Discovery Room.

Time: Allow 1 hour, 30 minutes minimum. **Hours:** Daily 9-5, May-Sept.; Mon.-Sat. 9-4, Sun. noon-4, rest of year. Last admission 1 hour before closing. Closes at noon on Christmas Eve and Dec. 31. Closed Jan. 1, Thanksgiving and Christmas. **Cost:** $10; $9 (ages 13-17 and 65+); $8 (ages 3-12); $7 (military with ID); $5 (children of military). **Phone:** (719) 561-1452.

ROSEMOUNT MUSEUM is off I-25 exit 99B, w. on 13th St., then 1 blk. n. on Greenwood to 419 W. 14th St. The 37-room, 1893 Victorian mansion contains original antique furnishings and depicts gracious life in the late 1800s. Built by a wealthy Pueblo entrepreneur, the house is constructed of pink rhyolite stone. **Hours:** Tues.-Sat. 10-3:30, Feb.-Dec. Closed major holidays. **Cost:** $6; $5 (ages 60+); $4 (ages 6-18). **Phone:** (719) 545-5290.

SANGRE DE CRISTO ARTS AND CONFERENCE CENTER, 210 N. Santa Fe Ave., is the scene of cultural and civic events. Six galleries feature changing art exhibits; a children's museum has hands-on activities. Ballet, musical and theatrical productions--including children's productions--are presented in the theater. **Hours:** Galleries Tues.-Thurs. 11-5, Fri. 11-7, Sat.-Sun. noon-5. Box office Mon.-Thurs. 9-6, Fri. 9-7, Sat. 9-5, Sun. noon-5. Closed major holidays. **Cost:** (includes Buell Children's Museum) $8; $6 (ages 3-13, ages 65+ and military with ID). Theater prices vary by production; phone the box office for details. **Phone:** (719) 295-7200.

Buell Children's Museum is at 210 N. Santa Fe Ave. Interactive exhibits for children focus on the arts, history and science. Children may put on a theatrical show, create works of art and participate in a multisensory exhibit. The Buell Baby Barn presents activities for children ages 0-3. **Time:** Allow 2 hours minimum. **Hours:** Tues.-Fri. 11-5, Wed. 9-5, Sat.-Sun. noon-5. Closed major holidays. **Cost:** (includes Sangre de Cristo Arts and Conference Center) $8; $6 (ages 3-16, ages 65+ and military with ID). **Phone:** (719) 295-7200. [T]

STEELWORKS MUSEUM is at 215 Canal St. The museum provides an overview of some 120 years of operations of the Colorado Fuel & Iron Company, which controlled the Western steel and mining industry for many years. The primary exhibit covers the period 1915-1936; topics include the steel mill, coal mines and the C&W Railway. The Mine Rescue Car, just outside the building, is a train car once used as a first-aid training station and rescue car to aid trapped or injured miners. Rotating exhibits from the Colorado Fuel & Iron Company and interactive children's displays also are available. **Time:** Allow 45 minutes minimum. **Hours:** Mon.-Sat. 10-4. Closed federal holidays. **Cost:** $6; $4 (ages 4-12). **Phone:** (719) 564-9086. [GT]

COMFORT INN   (719)542-6868
▼▼ **Hotel** $79-$149 **Address:** 670 N Eagleridge Blvd 81008 **Location:** I-25 exit 102, just w. **Facility:** 59 units. 2 stories. 2 stories, interior corridors. **Pool(s):** heated indoor. **Guest Services:** complimentary and valet laundry.
[ⓘ+] [🏊] [BIZ] [📶] [✕] [🛎] [🖥] [🅿]

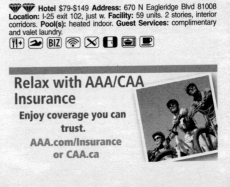

COURTYARD BY MARRIOTT PUEBLO (719)542-3200

Hotel
$97-$173

COURTYARD Marriott.

AAA Benefit: Members save 5% or more!

Address: 110 W City Center Dr 81003 **Location:** I-25 exit 98B, just w. **Facility:** 166 units. 7 stories, interior corridors. **Pool(s):** heated indoor. **Activities:** hot tub, exercise room. **Guest Services:** valet and coin laundry, boarding pass kiosk.

HAMPTON INN & SUITES-NORTH 719/543-6500
Hotel. Rates not provided. **Address:** 4790 Eagleridge Cir 81008 **Location:** I-25 exit 102, just w, then just n. **Facility:** 100 units. 4 stories, interior corridors. **Pool(s):** heated indoor. **Activities:** hot tub, exercise room. **Guest Services:** valet and coin laundry.

AAA Benefit: Members save up to 10%!

HOLIDAY INN EXPRESS & SUITES 719/542-8888
Hotel. Rates not provided. **Address:** 4530 Dillon Dr 81008 **Location:** I-25 exit 102, just e, then just s. **Facility:** 89 units. 4 stories, interior corridors. **Pool(s):** heated indoor. **Activities:** hot tub, exercise room. **Guest Services:** valet and coin laundry.

LA QUINTA INN & SUITES PUEBLO (719)542-3500
Hotel $79-$225 **Address:** 4801 N Elizabeth St 81008 **Location:** I-25 exit 102, just w, then 0.3 mi n. Located next to interstate. **Facility:** 101 units. 4 stories, interior corridors. **Pool(s):** heated outdoor. **Activities:** hot tub, exercise room. **Guest Services:** valet and coin laundry.

MICROTEL INN & SUITES BY WYNDHAM PUEBLO (719)242-2020
Hotel $55-$105 **Address:** 3343 Gateway Dr 81004 **Location:** I-25 exit 94, just w, then just s. **Facility:** 63 units. 3 stories, interior corridors. **Guest Services:** coin laundry.

SPRINGHILL SUITES BY MARRIOTT PUEBLO DOWNTOWN (719)546-1234
Contemporary Hotel $104-$172 **Address:** 150 S Santa Fe Ave 81003 **Location:** I-25 exit 98B, just w, then 0.3 mi s. **Facility:** 105 units. 4 stories, interior corridors. **Pool(s):** heated indoor. **Activities:** hot tub, exercise room. **Guest Services:** valet and coin laundry.

AAA Benefit: Members save 5% or more!

WHERE TO EAT

BINGO BURGER 719/225-8363
Burgers. Quick Serve. $6-$12 **AAA Inspector Notes:** This burger joint has a charming B-I-N-G-O theme with fun wall decorations and order pick-up numbers based on bingo card numbers. Build-your-own burger options include a base of standard ground beef, ground beef with chili peppers, lamb, chicken or portobello mushrooms. Once you've decided, choose from a variety of toppings. Rounding out the menu are field green salads, hand-cut fries or sweet potato fries, and tasty shakes. **Features:** beer only. **Address:** 101 Central Plaza 81003 **Location:** I-25 exit 98B, just w. L D

BLUE OCEAN SUSHI 719/696-8241
Japanese Sushi. Casual Dining. $6-$36 **AAA Inspector Notes:** Locals love the creatively presented sushi rolls, which feature salmon, eel, red snapper and all of your favorite sushi-grade fish. In addition, the menu offers triadic, udon and curry dishes. Start with tempura seafood or vegetables. Before or after dinner, take a stroll along the Historic Arkansas Riverwalk. **Features:** full bar. **Address:** 103 S Union Ave 81003 **Location:** I-25 exit 98B, just w on City Center Dr, then just sw. **Parking:** street only. L D

CACTUS FLOWER RESTAURANT & CANTINA 719/545-8218

Mexican Casual Dining $9-$17

AAA Inspector Notes: The restaurant prepares an assortment of traditional Mexican-American fare in a colorful Southwestern setting. Menu choices include burrito and chimichanga combos, enchiladas, fajitas, rellenos, specialty tacos, tamales and tostadas. Daily economy specials and vegetarian items also are available. Those seeking the perfect margarita have an extensive array of choices. **Features:** full bar. **Address:** 4610 N Elizabeth St 81008 **Location:** I-25 exit 102, just w, then just s. L D

DC'S ON B STREET 719/584-3410
American. Casual Dining. $8-$28 **AAA Inspector Notes:** This restaurant is a must-stop for visitors. The fresh, attractively presented food, including gourmet sandwiches, salads and pasta dishes, tastes delicious, and staff members make guests feel at home. The seasonal dinner menu features beef tenderloin, fresh fish, Colorado lamb and a nice selection of wines. **Features:** full bar, patio dining. **Address:** 115 W B St 81003 **Location:** I-25 exit 98B, just w on 1st St, 0.5 mi s on Union Ave, then just w. **Parking:** street only. L D

HOPSCOTCH BAKERY 719/542-4467
Breads/Pastries Sandwiches. Quick Serve. $9-$12 **AAA Inspector Notes:** Patrons grab gourmet panini sandwiches, salads and desserts to go, then picnic nearby, especially along the Riverfront area. Bakery cases beckon with delicious croissants, cakes, cookies and pastries, which pair great with yummy ice cream. **Address:** 333 S Union Ave 81003 **Location:** Corner of W B St and S Union Ave; in historic downtown. **Parking:** street only. B L

MAGPIES 719/542-5522
American. Casual Dining. $8-$9 **AAA Inspector Notes:** Built in 1883 by Delos Holden, the city's first mayor, this restaurant features warm wood accents that evoke this earlier era. The menu features sandwiches, soup and quiches for lunch. On Friday evening only, you'll find more upscale offerings, such as teriyaki-glazed salmon, grilled lamb chops and rib-eye steak. **Features:** beer & wine, patio dining. **Address:** 229 S Union Ave 81003 **Location:** I-25 exit 98B, 0.3 mi w, then 0.5 mi sw; downtown. **Parking:** street only. L

MR TANDOORI URBAN BAR & GRILL 719/544-3000
Indian. Casual Dining. $10-$23 **AAA Inspector Notes:** At this lovely downtown Pueblo restaurant, expect well-prepared chicken, lamb and shrimp entrées, a large selection of vegetarian specialties and a nice assortment of yummy tandoori breads and rice. Traditional dal and chicken mulligatawny soups are flavorful, as are the pakora and samosa appetizers. **Features:** full bar, patio dining. **Address:** 310 S Victoria Ave, Suite C 81003 **Location:** I-25 exit 98B, 0.3 mi w to Grand Ave, 0.3 mi sw, then just se. **Parking:** street only. L D

NACHO'S 719/544-0733
Mexican. Casual Dining. $7-$12 **AAA Inspector Notes:** This local favorite offers up the usual suspects: tacos, enchiladas, fajitas and more in a hacienda-style setting. Tacos feature a deep-fried, homemade tortilla, which creates a flaky, crunchy shell. Rellenos are prepared with an egg batter. Unfortunately, the store-bought chips and salsa aren't worth the extra charge. **Features:** full bar. **Reservations:** suggested, weekends. **Address:** 409 N Santa Fe Ave 81003 **Location:** I-25 exit 99A, just w on 6th St, then s; downtown. L D

SHAMROCK BREWING CO.   719/542-9974
🔻🔻 Irish. Casual Dining. $9-$17 **AAA Inspector Notes:** This pub features hearty portions, flavorful beers and Irish-themed décor. The menu lines up traditional Irish favorites such as shepherd's pie, fish and chips, and boxties (fluffy potato crepes stuffed with a variety of fillings) along with chicken green chile mac and cheese, a Colorado bison burger and basil pesto salmon. **Features:** full bar, patio dining, Sunday brunch. **Address:** 108 W 3rd St 81003 **Location:** I-25 exit 98B, just w to Santa Fe Ave, n to 3rd St, then just w; downtown. **Parking:** street only. L D LATE

SOLAR ROAST COFFEE   719/544-2008
🔻 Breakfast Coffee/Tea. Quick Serve. $4-$8 **AAA Inspector Notes:** As the name implies, this place roasts its coffee beans using solar power. Take a break, sit down and relax from traveling to nourish yourself with a chicken quesadilla, tasty chicken and pesto croissant, fresh-made quiche, pastry or muffin. Wash it down with a smoothie, or a great "cup of joe." **Features:** patio dining. **Address:** 226 N Main St 81003 **Location:** I-25 exit 98B, just w on 1st St; corner of 3rd and Main sts. **Parking:** street only. B L

RANGELY pop. 2,365

BLUE MOUNTAIN INN & SUITES   (970)675-8888
🔻🔻 Hotel $95-$149 **Address:** 37 Park St 81648 **Location:** On US 64, 0.3 mi w of center. **Facility:** 50 units. 2 stories, interior corridors. **Terms:** cancellation fee imposed. **Pool(s):** heated indoor. **Activities:** hot tub, picnic facilities. **Guest Services:** valet and coin laundry. 🍴 🏊 🛜 ✉ 📶 🖥 🖥

WHERE TO EAT

GIOVANNI'S ITALIAN GRILL   970/675-2670
🔻🔻 Italian. Casual Dining. $8-$16 **AAA Inspector Notes:** In a convenient Main Street location, this colorfully decorated restaurant serves a variety of salads and pasta entrees. **Features:** beer & wine. **Address:** 855 E Main St 81648 **Location:** East end of town. L D

RED FEATHER LAKES (A-4) pop. 343, elev. 8,342'

THE GREAT STUPA is 5 mi. e. on CR 68C (gravel road) to the Shambhala Mountain Center. Rising out of a ponderosa pine forest, this Buddhist shrine is the centerpiece of a 600-acre meditation retreat center. The shrine, said to be one of the world's most significant examples of Buddhist architecture, features a 108-foot-tall gold dome and brightly painted facade. The interior features inlaid marble floors, an intricately painted ceiling and a towering gold statue of Buddha.

Note: Since visitors must walk two-thirds of a mile from the parking lot to the shrine, comfortable shoes are recommended. **Time:** Allow 1 hour minimum. **Hours:** Daily 9-9. Guided tours are offered by appointment only. Phone ahead to confirm schedule. **Cost:** Shrine free. Tours $10; $8 (senior citizens). **Phone:** (888) 788-7221. GT 🍴

REDSTONE (C-2) pop. 130, elev. 7,190'

At the turn of the 20th century, John Cleveland Osgood—cousin to President Grover Cleveland and one of the wealthiest industrialists of his day—created a utopian village in the Crystal River Valley to house the men who worked his coal mines and coke ovens.

Taking its name from the valley's red sandstone cliffs, Redstone was filled with cottages for miners and their families and an inn for bachelors. For his own home Osgood built a magnificent 25,000-square-foot mansion he named Cleveholm Manor, which rivaled some of the finest estates in Europe. The estate is known today as Redstone Castle, and tours recount its history; phone (970) 963-9656 for information. As the mines declined and the workers moved away, the cottages were sold as residences. Many now contain unique shops and boutiques.

Redstone retains much of its Craftsman-era character. A small museum preserves photographs and relics from Redstone's past, and several shops exhibit pottery, jewelry and paintings by local artists.

Carbondale Chamber of Commerce: 520 S. Third St., Suite 3, P.O. Box 1645, Carbondale, CO 81623. **Phone:** (970) 963-1890.

RIDGWAY (E-2) pop. 924, elev. 6,988'
• Hotels p. 250 • Restaurants p. 250

Ridgway is nestled between the verdant San Juan and Uncompahgre national forests with the rugged San Juan Mountains serving as a dramatic backdrop. Recreational activities, including boating, fishing, cross-country skiing, swimming and hiking, abound at Ridgway State Park *(see Recreation Areas Chart)*. The San Juan Skyway begins its southerly route on US 550 in Ridgway, offering scenic views of emerald green pine and golden aspen forests at every turn.

Ridgway Area Chamber of Commerce and Visitors Information Center: 150 Racecourse Rd., Ridgway, CO 81432. **Phone:** (970) 626-5181 or (800) 220-4959.

Self-guiding tours: Historic buildings and homes from the late 19th and the early 20th centuries may be seen on a walking tour of Ridgway. Maps can be picked up at the visitors information center.

RIDGWAY RAILROAD MUSEUM, 150 Racecourse Rd., educates visitors about narrow-gauge railroad history in southwestern Colorado. Featured railroads include the Rio Grande Southern, Silverton Railroad and Ouray Branch Denver and Rio Grande. Indoor and outdoor exhibits include rolling stock and portray the history of the famous RGS "Galloping Geese." Self-guiding tour brochures are contained in a box at the entrance. **Time:** Allow 30 minutes minimum. **Hours:** Daily 9-5, June-Sept.; daily 10-3, in May and Oct.; by appointment rest of year. Closed Thanksgiving and Christmas. **Cost:** Free. **Phone:** (970) 626-5181 or (800) 220-4959.

RECREATIONAL ACTIVITIES
Hot Air Ballooning
• **San Juan Balloon Adventures** departs from various locations in Ridgway. **Hours:** Tours depart daily at dawn, May-Sept. (weather permitting). **Phone:** (970) 626-5495.

RIDGWAY OURAY LODGE & SUITES (970)626-5444

WWW Hotel $86-$117 **Address:** 373 Palomino Tr 81432 **Location:** Just e of jct US 550 and SR 62, just s. **Facility:** 52 units. 2 stories (no elevator), interior corridors. **Terms:** cancellation fee imposed. **Pool(s):** heated indoor. **Activities:** sauna, hot tub, exercise room. **Guest Services:** coin laundry.

LA QUINTA INN & SUITES RIFLE (970)625-2676

WWW Hotel $70-$202 **Address:** 600 Wapiti Ct 81650 **Location:** I-70 exit 90, just s, then just e. **Facility:** 113 units. 3 stories, interior corridors. **Pool(s):** heated indoor. **Activities:** hot tub, picnic facilities, exercise room. **Guest Services:** coin laundry.

WHERE TO EAT

THE ADOBE INN RESTAURANT 970/626-5939

WWW Mexican. Casual Dining. $14-$16 **AAA Inspector Notes:** This restaurant offers homemade salsa with corn and flour tortilla chips, and entrées made from scratch. The healthy cuisine emphasizes flavors from Northern Mexico and New Mexico. The adobe décor provides a comfortable, relaxing ambiance. **Features:** full bar. **Address:** 251 Liddell Dr 81432 **Location:** 0.3 mi w of jct US 550 and SR 62 (Main St), then just s.

KATE'S PLACE 970/626-9800

WWW American. Casual Dining. $9-$11 **AAA Inspector Notes:** Focusing on cuisine from the heart and soul, this charming eatery takes pride in using the finest ingredients available. Breakfast includes French toast, huevos rancheros and your choice of omelettes. For lunch, opt for a panini or sandwich served on freshly baked bread. Try the fluffy, sweet Italian lemon cake. The garden patio features cozy square picnic tables. Guests will find the service efficient and friendly. **Features:** patio dining. **Address:** 615 W Clinton St 81432 **Location:** 0.5 mi w of jct US 550 and SR 62 (Main St) to N Cora St, just n, just w. **Parking:** street only.

THAI PARADISE 970/626-2742

WWW Thai. Casual Dining. $11-$24 **AAA Inspector Notes:** For a light meal, try the spicy tom yum with your choice of chicken, shrimp, scallops or tofu. Hearty entrées include pad thai, tempura and curries. In warm weather, opt for the patio as it may be more comfortable than the non-air-conditioned dining room. **Features:** beer & wine, patio dining. **Address:** 146 N Cora St 81432 **Location:** 0.5 mi w of US 550 and SR 62 (Main St).

TRUE GRIT CAFE 970/626-5739

WWW American. Casual Dining. $8-$22 **AAA Inspector Notes:** Named after the movie featuring John Wayne, this restaurant offers three types of chili and a selection of salads, sandwiches, burgers, steaks and Tex-Mex favorites. Hardwood floors, framed photos of Western movie stars, and a little taxidermy create an old west atmosphere. **Features:** full bar. **Address:** 123 N Lena 81432 **Location:** 0.4 mi w of US 550 and SR 62 (Main St), then just n.

RIFLE pop. 9,172

COMFORT INN & SUITES (970)625-9912

WWWW Hotel $99-$169 **Address:** 301 S 7th St 81650 **Location:** I-70 exit 90, just s, then just w. **Facility:** 82 units. 3 stories, interior corridors. **Pool(s):** heated indoor. **Activities:** hot tub, playground, exercise room. **Guest Services:** valet and coin laundry.

HAMPTON INN & SUITES 970/625-1500

WWWW
Hotel
Rates not provided

Hampton by HILTON

AAA Benefit: Members save up to 10%!

Address: 499 Airport Rd 81650 **Location:** I-70 exit 90, just s, then just e. **Facility:** 92 units. 4 stories, interior corridors. **Pool(s):** heated indoor. **Activities:** picnic facilities, exercise room. **Guest Services:** valet and coin laundry. **Featured Amenity:** continental breakfast.

WHERE TO EAT

LILLY'S KITCHEN 970/625-0165

WW Mexican. Casual Dining. $7-$11 **AAA Inspector Notes:** Since opening, this eatery has become a local favorite. The menu features flavorful sopes, enchiladas and pupusas. In addition, you may order pizza. Choose from Hawaiian, Mexican and veggie specialty pizzas, or build your own. **Features:** full bar. **Address:** 232 W 3rd St 81650 **Location:** I-70 exit 90, 0.5 mi n, just w on US 6, just n on West Ave, then just w.

SAMMY'S ON PARK AVENUE 970/625-8008

WW American. Casual Dining. $10-$40 **AAA Inspector Notes:** This local favorite offers entrées including filet mignon, Colorado lamb T-bones, Alaskan king crab legs, twin lobster tails, Rocky Mountain trout, schnitzel and pasta. Colorado microbrews go down easy with the fare. **Features:** full bar, happy hour. **Address:** 412 Park Ave 81650 **Location:** I-70 exit 90, 0.3 mi n, w on 3rd St, then just n.

THAI CHILI BISTRO 970/625-8888

WW Asian. Casual Dining. $9-$14 **AAA Inspector Notes:** Like the menu, the décor here has an East-meets-West character, with features from the historic Victorian-era building accented with Asian art. Select from Thai dishes, like chicken pad thai, Chinese favorites such as sesame beef, and American-style grilled steaks. **Features:** full bar. **Address:** 115 E 3rd St 81650 **Location:** I-70 exit 90, 0.5 mi n, just n on Railroad Ave, then just e. **Parking:** street only.

RIO GRANDE NATIONAL FOREST (E-3)

Elevations in the forest range from 7,500 ft. at the low end of the Rio Grande to 14,345 ft. at Mount Blanca. Refer to AAA maps for additional elevation information.

Rio Grande National Forest, at the headwaters of the Rio Grande, is characterized by mountain waterways and rugged high country. The 1,851,792-acre forest surrounds the San Luis Valley; its southern tip is along the Colorado-New Mexico boundary.

A majority of the forest lies west of US 285 and is bisected by SR 149 and US 160. The Sangre de Cristo mountain range, now designated a federal wilderness area, lies between SRs 17 and 69. Parts of the San Juan and Sangre de Cristo mountain ranges lie within the forest. The Silver Thread Highway, a 75-mile scenic highway, winds through the San Juan Mountains on SR 149.

Saddle and pack trips can be made into La Garita, Sangre de Cristo, South San Juan and Weminuche wilderness areas. Scenic drives over Wolf Creek Pass on US 160 and Cumbres Pass on SR 17 also are popular. Big-game hunting is allowed in season. Wolf Creek Winter Sports Area is near Wolf Creek Pass on US 160.

For more information write Visitor Information Services, Rio Grande National Forest, 1803 US 160W, Monte Vista, CO 81144; phone (719) 852-5941. *See Recreation Areas Chart.*

ROCKY MOUNTAIN NATIONAL PARK (B-4)

• Attractions map p. 252

Elevations in the park range from 7,840 ft. at the park headquarters to 14,259 ft. at Longs Peak. Refer to AAA maps for additional elevation information.

Rocky Mountain National Park is accessible from the east via SR 7, US 34 and US 36 and from the west via US 34. The park includes about 265,800 acres of the Front Range of the Rocky Mountains. This particular section, one of the highest regions in the country, is truly representative of the grandest in American mountain scenery.

The 240-mile grand loop from Denver via Boulder, Estes Park, Grand Lake and Idaho Springs offers one of the most impressive circular trips in the nation. It cuts across the Continental Divide over one of the country's highest continuous roads, reaches Grand Lake, crosses the Divide again at Berthoud Pass, traverses the Denver Mountain Parks and returns to Denver.

The park's valleys are about 8,000 feet above sea level, with the peaks rising thousands of feet higher. Longs Peak attains a height of 14,259 feet. Within the park, more than 75 named peaks reach elevations of 12,000 feet or higher. The range lies north and south, with the gentler slope on the west. On the east side the descent can be extremely precipitous, with sheer drops of 2,000 and 3,000 feet into rockbound gorges.

Seen from the eastern valleys, the range rises in bold relief, rugged in outline and crowned with snow. The west side, lush with wet meadowland, has many streams and natural lakes. The park is surrounded by the Arapaho and Roosevelt National Forests *(see place listing p. 41)*, while the southwest corner adjoins the Arapaho National Recreation Area *(see place listing p. 42)*.

The records of glacial action on these mountains are so clear that even the untrained eye recognizes them. This is particularly true on the eastern side, where the moraines are enormous. Four of the park's many small alpine cirque glaciers—Tyndall, Andrews, Rowe and Taylor—can be seen at the heads of some of the high mountain canyons at about 12,000 feet.

The park is a wildlife sanctuary. The lofty rocks are the natural home of the Rocky Mountain bighorn sheep. Elk and deer are numerous, and coyotes are often seen by park visitors. Black bears reside in the park and are sometimes seen. Mountain lions, bobcats and smaller carnivores, however, are seldom seen by visitors. Birds also can be observed.

Those bizarre sounds you may hear echoing throughout autumn evenings are more than likely bull elk calling to each other to attract a harem of cow elk during rutting, or mating season. During this time of year, elk descend from the higher elevations to valleys and meadows, and you'll usually see them at dawn and dusk at such locations as Moraine Park, Horseshoe Park and the Kawuneeche Valley.

Observe these animals from a distance, and do not make loud noises in their presence.

Wildflower viewing is spectacular from late May to early August and can be found at varying elevations, with dozens of varieties contributing to a vibrant palette of blue, yellow, pink, purple and white. The Tundra Communities Trail presents the opportunity to view colorful plants and wildflowers unique to the alpine tundra during a half-hour walk. Visitors are required to keep to the marked trails to preserve the fragile alpine plants.

General Information and Activities

The park is never closed, although many facilities are open only from late spring through fall. Trail Ridge Road generally remains open for through travel from late May until the first heavy snowfall, usually in mid-October.

Because Rocky Mountain National Park is primarily a scenic park, motoring, horseback riding, camping, hiking, snowshoeing and mountain climbing are the most popular activities. Horses and camping equipment can be rented in Estes Park and at Grand Lake. There are no accommodations in the park other than camping.

Many beautiful trails of varying lengths and difficulties traverse these mountains, with stunning mountains, lakes, waterfalls and vistas. Dramatic weather changes can occur rapidly at higher elevations so plenty of water and food, plus gloves, hats, appropriate footwear, rain gear and layers of clothing are recommended. Altitude sickness can be a problem; it helps to drink at least a gallon of water a day, and assess how you are feeling as you climb in elevation.

Information about trails and routes is available at all park visitor centers, or by phoning (970) 586-1206. The park has several easy hikes: Bear Lake Trail is a half-mile loop, Adams Falls and Alberta Falls lead to picturesque waterfalls, and Deer Mountain, while more moderate, is a popular summit hike with beautiful panoramas. Those seeking more challenge will have no trouble finding mid-range and strenuous routes.

Fans of winter recreation also can take advantage of several trails geared toward cold-weather sports. Snowshoe enthusiasts will want to check out the Bear Lake area—the invigorating Emerald Lake Trail is a wonderland in winter, with snowy drifts, frozen lakes and glistening peaks. Cross-country skiers gravitate to the west side of the park where there are many trails with a range of difficulty to choose from.

A permit is required for overnight backcountry trips and bivouac climbs; visitors must obtain a permit at the backcountry office near Beaver Meadows Visitor Center, (970) 586-1242, or the Kawuneeche Visitor Center. Special regulations apply to fishing; inquire at any of the visitor centers. A Colorado fishing license is required.

Free ranger-led programs are conducted year-round; see the park newspaper for schedules. An orientation film is shown every half-hour in summer and by request in winter at Beaver Meadows Visitor Center and Kawuneeche Visitor Center.

Ilustrated talks and campfire programs are sometimes presented in the major campgrounds during the summer.

There are lots of sites and activities within the park that mesmerize kids. Short trails like Moraine Park and Sprague Lake captivate youngsters, as does the Beaver Boardwalk near the foot of Trail Ridge Road. Glimpses of wandering elk, scurrying chipmunks and bighorn sheep also entice children, as does scrambling across boulders on Gem Lake Trail, gazing at flowers near Cub Lake or saddling up on a gentle horse for a trail ride. The Junior Ranger program offers a variety of hikes and talks that focus on the park's environment, geology and wildlife—during one talk, kids can touch the skulls and skins of such animals as bighorn sheep, moose and elk. For details about ranger-led programs geared toward youngsters, pick up a park newspaper or inquire at one of the visitor centers.

Schedules of activities are available at ranger stations and visitor centers. *See Recreation Areas Chart.*

Note: Accessibility to roads and trails within the park may be affected by weather conditions. Phone

(970) 586-1242 for the Backcountry Office or (970) 586-1222 for Trail Ridge Road status updates.

ADMISSION to the park is $20 per private vehicle or $10 per person arriving by other means (valid for 7 days).

PETS are prohibited in all areas of the park not accessible by motor vehicles, including all trails and meadows.

ADDRESS inquiries and information requests to the Information Office, Rocky Mountain National Park, 1000 US 36, Estes Park, CO 80517-8397; phone (970) 586-1206.

ALPINE VISITOR CENTER, at Fall River Pass, features exhibits about the alpine tundra environment, its related safety issues, and mountain weather and climate. Information and park literature are available. **Hours:** Open daily 9-5, mid-June through Labor Day; 10:30-4:30, Memorial Day weekend to mid-June and day after Labor Day to mid-Oct. (weather permitting). Phone ahead to confirm schedule. **Cost:** Free with

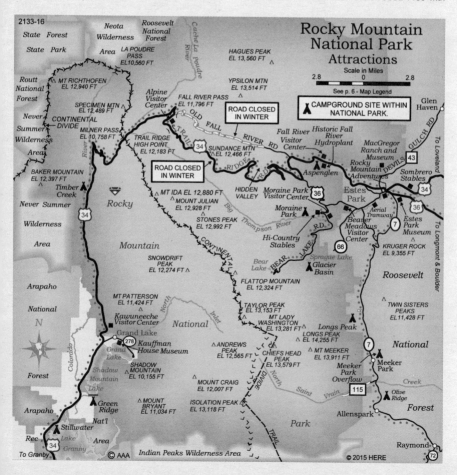

park admission. **Phone:** (970) 586-1206, or (970) 586-1222 for road information.

BEAR LAKE ROAD leads from the Beaver Meadows entrance through Moraine Park to Bear Lake. Several trails offering a range of hiking opportunities begin at Bear Lake, including trails to Dream Lake (1.1 mi.), Emerald Lake (1.8 mi.) and Lake Haiyaha (2.1 mi.). Elk herd sightings are common in the spring and fall in Moraine Park. Horseback riding is available at Sprague Lake and Moraine Park. **Phone:** (970) 586-1206.

BEAVER MEADOWS VISITOR CENTER, 3 mi. w. of Estes Park on US 36, has a large, 3-D topographical map and an orientation film about the park. Ranger-led programs are presented year-round. **Hours:** Daily 8-6, May-Sept.; 8-5, rest of year (weather permitting). Phone ahead to confirm schedule. **Cost:** Free. **Phone:** (970) 586-1206.

FALL RIVER VISITOR CENTER, 5 mi. w. of Estes Park on US 34, contains life-size wildlife displays and a discovery room with exhibits for children. **Hours:** Daily 9-5 (weather permitting). Phone ahead to confirm schedule. **Cost:** Free. **Phone:** (970) 586-1206.

KAWUNEECHE VISITOR CENTER is on the w. side of the park on US 34, 1 mi. n. of the town of Grand Lake. The visitor center has a 20-minute orientation film and exhibits about the plants and animals native to the western portion of the park. **Hours:** Daily 8-5 (weather permitting). Phone ahead to confirm schedule. **Cost:** Free. **Phone:** (970) 586-1206.

MORAINE PARK DISCOVERY CENTER, 1 mi. s. of the Beaver Meadows entrance, contains exhibits that interpret the story of the park environment and the natural elements that shaped it. Park literature, maps and ranger-led activities are available; a half-mile self-guiding nature trail starts at the Discovery Center. **Hours:** Daily 9-4:30 (weather permitting). Phone ahead to confirm schedule. **Cost:** Free with park admission. **Phone:** (970) 586-1206.

TRAIL RIDGE ROAD, (US 34) between Estes Park and Grand Lake, climbs to the crest of the range and crosses the Continental Divide. The 48-mile route reaches elevations of more than 12,000 feet.

Note: The route should be driven with caution by anyone unfamiliar with mountain driving (there are no shoulders or guard rails). Rapid weather changes also can occur; dress appropriately. **Time:** Allow 3 hours minimum. **Hours:** Road open late May to mid-Oct. (weather permitting). **Cost:** Free with park admission. **Phone:** (970) 586-1206 for general information, or (970) 586-1222 for road conditions.

ROUTT NATIONAL FOREST (A-2)

Elevations in the forest range from 6,750 ft. at the Elk River to 12,940 ft. at Mount Richthofen. Refer to AAA maps for additional elevation information.

Accessible via US 40, Routt National Forest lies astride the Continental Divide. The 1.26 million-acre forest offers many scenic areas. Totally within Routt are the 160,000-acre Mount Zirkel Wilderness, surrounding the rugged Park Range, and the 45,190 acres of Sarvis Creek Wilderness.

Other wilderness areas partially within Routt include Flat Tops Wilderness, its 235,214 acres co-administered with the White River National Forest *(see place listing p. 274).* A portion of the 23,492-acre Platte River Wilderness falls into Routt, while the rest is part of Medicine Bow National Forest.

In Routt's eastern section, the 21,090 acres of Never Summer Wilderness spill into the Arapaho and Roosevelt National Forests *(see place listing p. 41).*

In the northeastern section are the 9,924 acres of the Neota Wilderness and the 73,068 acres of the Rawah Wilderness, both part of the Arapaho and Roosevelt National Forests. Pack and saddle trips can be arranged.

Facilities for camping and picnicking are available in the summer; there are recreation areas at Big Creek Lake and Dumont Lake, and along the Elk and Bear River areas. The Fish Creek Falls area offers hiking and picnicking, a trail for the physically challenged and other facilities.

Medicine Bow National Forest and Thunder Basin National Grassland, both in Wyoming, are jointly administered with Routt. For more information write Medicine Bow-Routt National Forest and Thunder Basin National Grassland (Hahns Peak/Bears Ears Ranger District), 925 Weiss Dr., Steamboat Springs, CO 80487; phone (970) 870-2299. Another source for information is the forest's Yampa Ranger District, 300 Roselawn Ave., P.O. Box 7, Yampa, CO 80483; phone (970) 638-4516. *See Recreation Areas Chart.*

RUSTIC

BIGHORN CABINS   970/881-2142

▼▼ ▼▼ **Cabin** $115-$190 **Address:** 31635 Poudre Canyon Rd 80512 **Location:** On SR 14; between MM 90 and 91. **Facility:** 5 cabins. 1 story, exterior corridors. *Bath:* shower only. **Terms:** closed 11/1-4/30, 2-7 night minimum stay - seasonal and/or weekends, 30 day cancellation notice-fee imposed, resort fee. **Activities:** fishing, picnic facilities.

SAGUACHE (E-3) pop. 485, elev. 7,694'

Saguache (Sa-WATCH) lies in a scenic valley between the great Continental Divide and the Sangre de Cristo Range. Some notoriety is associated with Saguache; Alferd Packer, convicted of voluntary manslaughter in the late 1800s, was confined and then escaped from the area before his eventual arrest in Wyoming 9 years later. He was suspected of murdering five men and then engaging in cannibalism.

Saguache Chamber of Commerce: 504 San Juan Ave., P.O. Box 417, Saguache, CO 81149. **Phone:** (719) 655-2232.

SAGUACHE COUNTY MUSEUM, on US 285, depicts life in the mid- to late 1800s. The Memorial Room contains early medical equipment, an antique gun collection and vintage saddles. Other exhibits include a pioneer kitchen, a school, Spanish and Native American artifacts, a parlor and a mineral collection. An old jail features a likeness of the area's infamous killer, Alferd Packer.

Time: Allow 30 minutes minimum. **Hours:** Daily 10-4, Memorial Day weekend-third weekend in Sept. (weather permitting). **Cost:** $5; $1 (ages 1-11). **Phone:** (719) 655-2557.

SALIDA (D-3) pop. 5,236, elev. 7,080'

The thoroughfare provided by the Arkansas River and several passes cutting through the nearby mountain ranges insured that a settlement would develop in this region. Aided by the arrival of the railroad in 1880, Salida (sa-LYE-da)—meaning "exit"—served as an outlet for mines in the Leadville area.

Because of the cool, comfortable summers and relatively mild winters, Salida has been called the "banana belt" of Colorado. It is a fine area for rockhounds; aquamarine, garnet, sapphire, turquoise, topaz and Native American arrowheads can be found in the vicinity. Salida's historic downtown, with its array of galleries, studios and antique shops, draws art lovers and antique collectors.

In spring the melting snow on the flank of 14,239-foot Mount Shavano, about 14 miles northwest, assumes a shape called the "Angel of Shavano." It is said that the angel appeared when the Ute chief Shavano prayed for his dying friend George Beckwith. Tenderfoot Mountain, at the east edge of town off SR 291, offers a good view of the angel as well as the valley and nearby mountains, including 12 peaks over 14,000 feet tall.

The diminishing snows of spring create another Salida hallmark. As the Arkansas River swells from the snowmelt, a variety of rafting and kayaking races are held throughout summer, including the FIBArk Whitewater Festival in mid-June. During the rest of summer, Browns Canyon offers some of the state's best rafting.

Less turbulent are the waters at Salida Hot Springs Aquatic Center piped from Poncha Hot Springs, 5 miles southwest.

Salida Chamber of Commerce and Visitor Center: 406 US 50W, Salida, CO 81201. **Phone:** (719) 539-2068 or (877) 772-5432.

MOUNT SHAVANO STATE FISH HATCHERY, .2 mi. n. on SR 291, then 1 mi. w. on CR 154, covers 25 acres and produces more than 2 million fish each year, including cutthroat and rainbow trout. **Hours:** Daily 8-4. Guided tours are given daily 10-4, Memorial Day-Labor Day. **Cost:** Donations. **Phone:** (719) 539-6877.

SALIDA MUSEUM, US 50 and I St., adjoins the chamber of commerce building. Displays pertain to pioneer and Native American life, railroading and mining.

Time: Allow 30 minutes minimum. **Hours:** Daily 11-5, Memorial Day-Labor Day; Sat.-Sun. 1-5, rest of year. Phone ahead to confirm schedule. **Cost:** $3; $1.50 (ages 12-18); $1 (ages 7-11). **Phone:** (719) 539-7483.

WINERIES

- **Mountain Spirit Winery** is 13 mi. w. at 15750 CR 220. **Hours:** Daily 10-5. **Phone:** (719) 539-1175. GT

CHALETS AT TUDOR ROSE 719/539-2002
 Vacation Rental Cottage. Rates not provided. **Address:** 6720 CR 104 81201 **Location:** East end of US 50, just s on CR 104, then 0.5 mi up the hill. **Facility:** Surrounded by majestic views of the Sangre de Cristo mountains, these spacious chalets include a fireplace, full kitchen, great room and remote skylights. Hiking trails are outside the front door. 5 cottages. 2 stories (no elevator), exterior corridors. **Terms:** off-site registration, check-in 4 pm.

COMFORT INN (719)539-5000
Hotel $75-$199 **Address:** 315 E Rainbow Blvd 81201 **Location:** On US 50, 0.3 mi e of G St. **Facility:** 45 units. 2 stories (no elevator), interior corridors. **Pool(s):** heated indoor. **Activities:** hot tub. **Guest Services:** coin laundry.

DAYS INN (719)539-6651
Motel $57-$100 **Address:** 407 E Hwy 50 81201 **Location:** 0.4 mi e of G St. **Facility:** 28 units. 2 stories (no elevator), interior corridors. **Parking:** winter plug-ins. **Terms:** cancellation fee imposed. **Activities:** hot tub.

HAMPTON INN & SUITES 719/539-0800
Contemporary Hotel. Rates not provided. **Address:** 785 E US 50 81201 **Location:** 0.6 mi e of G St. **Facility:** 107 units. 4 stories, interior corridors. **Pool(s):** heated indoor. **Activities:** hot tub, exercise room. **Guest Services:** coin laundry.

AAA Benefit: Members save up to 10%!

SILVER RIDGE LODGE 719/539-2553
Motel. Rates not provided. **Address:** 545 W Rainbow Blvd 81201 **Location:** On US 50, 0.3 mi w of G St. Opposite Hot Springs Pool. **Facility:** 39 units, some two bedrooms. 1-2 stories (no elevator), exterior corridors. **Pool(s):** heated outdoor. **Activities:** sauna, hot tub.

THOMAS HOUSE BED & BREAKFAST 719/539-7104
Historic Bed & Breakfast. Rates not provided. **Address:** 307 E 1st St 81201 **Location:** Just e of historic downtown; corner of D and 1st sts. **Facility:** Some of these individually decorated rooms feature an antique claw-foot tub, handmade log-cabin quilt and other unique pieces. Relax on roomy decks and near a colorful flower garden. 6 units, some efficiencies and cottages. 2 stories (no elevator), interior/exterior corridors. **Parking:** street only. **Terms:** check-in 4 pm.

TUDOR ROSE BED & BREAKFAST 719/539-2002
Bed & Breakfast. Rates not provided. **Address:** 6720 CR 104 81201 **Location:** East end of US 50, just s on CR 104, then 0.5 mi up the hill. **Facility:** On a hilltop location with scenic mountain views, this B&B is characterized by well-lit guest rooms and a country manor ambiance. The sitting areas on the outdoor deck are inviting. 6 units. 2 stories (no elevator), interior corridors. **Terms:** check-in 4 pm, age restrictions may apply. **Activities:** hot tub.

WOODLAND MOTEL (719)539-4980

Motel
$57-$134

Address: 903 W 1st St 81201 **Location:** 0.5 mi nw on 1st St (SR 291); nw of historic downtown. Across from ballpark. **Facility:** 18 units, some two bedrooms and kitchens. 1-2 stories (no elevator), exterior corridors. **Terms:** 2 night minimum stay - seasonal and/or weekends. **Activities:** hot tub, fishing, picnic facilities. **Guest Services:** coin laundry.

PALACE HOTEL 719/207-4175

[fyi] Not evaluated. **Address:** 204 N F St 81201 **Location:** At F St and Sackett Ave; downtown. Facilities, services, and décor characterize a mid-scale property. With mesmerizing views of the park, mountains or the Arkansas River, this elegant hotel features a nice selection of stylish guest rooms.

WHERE TO EAT

216 FERRARO'S ITALIAN RESTAURANT 719/530-9463
Italian. Casual Dining. $11-$28 **AAA Inspector Notes:** This is a cozy little gathering place where you can enjoy appetizers, Italian wines, specialty cocktails and such martinis as the lemon drop and dirty blue olive. Seasonal menu items may include a tasty mozzarella caprese salad, but you can be sure of Italian classics with chicken, fresh halibut, hand-cut steak and veal. The semi de melone pasta is made in-house, as are the desserts. **Features:** full bar. **Address:** 216 N F St 81201 **Location:** Downtown. **Parking:** street only. [D]

AMICA'S PIZZA, MICROBREWS & MORE 719/539-5219
Italian. Casual Dining. $8-$15 **AAA Inspector Notes:** This warm and inviting local downtown favorite specializes in gourmet pizzas, salads, calzones and more. Microbrews are made on site. For a sweet treat, try the creamy peanut butter mousse pie. **Features:** beer & wine. **Address:** 136 E 2nd St 81201 **Location:** From US 50 and E St, 0.9 mi ne; in historic downtown district. **Parking:** street only. [L] [D]

THE BOUNTY 719/539-3546
American. Casual Dining. $10-$17 **AAA Inspector Notes:** Since 1932, this family-owned eatery has served comfort food to locals and those passing through. For a taste of Thanksgiving, try the open-face hot turkey sandwich, which comes with cranberry sauce and gravy. Heartier options include fried chicken, prime rib, and meatloaf made with ground elk and bison. Historic photos line the walls. If you're looking for a memento or special gift, check out the attached gift shop. **Features:** full bar, Sunday brunch. **Address:** 413 W Rainbow Blvd 81201 **Location:** Just w of H St on US 50. [B] [L] [D]

THE FRITZ 719/539-0364
Small Plates Sandwiches. Gastropub. $9-$12 **AAA Inspector Notes:** This cozy pub serves a variety of creative salads and small and large tapas ranging from simple to complex such as a burger or steak sandwich, bacon-wrapped dates, seared ahi tuna, braised pork with caramelized onions and baked jumbo shells stuffed with ricotta. **Features:** full bar. **Address:** 113 E Sackett St 81201 **Location:** At F and Sackett sts; downtown; across from Riverside Park. **Parking:** street only. [L] [D]

LAUGHING LADIES RESTAURANT 719/539-6209
American. Casual Dining. $9-$23 **AAA Inspector Notes:** Historic. Order a Colorado-brewed beer or scan the vast wine list for an appropriate pairing to your fresh seafood or other creative entrée. Housed in a 1905 building, the restaurant offers Victorian-era charm with hardwood floors and patterned tin ceilings. **Features:** full bar, patio dining, Sunday brunch. **Reservations:** suggested. **Address:** 128 W 1st St 81201 **Location:** US 50 and G St, 1 mi ne to 1st St, then just e; in historic downtown district. **Parking:** street only. [L] [D]

MOONLIGHT PIZZA & BREW PUB 719/539-4277
Pizza Sandwiches. Casual Dining. $5-$14 **AAA Inspector Notes:** Mouthwatering pizzas, salads and sandwiches are served in an easygoing atmosphere. Patrons can choose from the inventive combinations or create their own masterpiece. Microbrews and house-made designer sodas are popular here, and the locals are devoted to the bread sticks. **Features:** full bar, patio dining, happy hour. **Address:** 242 F St 81201 **Location:** Corner of F and 3rd sts; in historic downtown district. [L] [D]

PATIO PANCAKE PLACE 719/539-9905
Breakfast. Casual Dining. $7-$10 **AAA Inspector Notes:** Classic. A neighborhood institution, this eatery has used the same pancake recipe since 1964. Breakfast options include huevos rancheros, eggs Benedict, omelettes, waffles, and the famous, fluffy, fruit-filled or plain buttermilk pancakes. Lunch choices include home-made green chile, burritos and sandwiches. **Address:** 640 E Rainbow Blvd 81201 **Location:** On US 50, between New and State sts. [B] [L]

SAN ISABEL NATIONAL FOREST (D-3)

Elevations in the forest range from 5,860 ft. in the grasslands area to 14,433 ft. at Mount Elbert. Refer to AAA maps for additional elevation information.

Reached via US 24, 50 and 285, and SRs 82, 91 and 165, San Isabel National Forest includes scenic and recreational features within its 1,109,782 acres. A network of roads makes most of the forest easily accessible. The Highway of Legends, starting at Trinidad and traveling through the Cucharas Pass, offers 82 miles of scenic driving on SR 12.

More than 700 miles of trails are available for backpacking and saddle trips into the back country. Twin Lake and Turquoise Lake recreation areas, near Leadville, and the Spanish Peaks National Natural Landmark, near La Veta, provide opportunities for summer activities and camping. Many easy, family-friendly hikes are available in the forest, including the San Carlos Trail near Beulah and the Wachob Trail near Colorado City.

Holy Cross, Mount Massive and Collegiate Peaks wildernesses are accessible by foot or horseback. Numerous ghost towns from Colorado's mining heyday dot the region.

Among the 17 peaks that exceed 14,000 feet in San Isabel National Forest is 14,433-foot Mount Elbert, highest in the state. The high mountain reaches afford summer range for deer, bears, elk, grouse, mountain sheep and turkeys.

For more information write the Forest Superintendent, San Isabel National Forest, 2840 Kachina Dr., Pueblo, CO 81008; phone (719) 553-1400. *See Recreation Areas Chart.*

SAN JUAN NATIONAL FOREST (E-1)

Elevations in the forest range from 6,800 ft. at Junction Creek to 14,246 ft. at Mount Wilson in the Lizard Head Wilderness. Refer to AAA maps for additional elevation information.

West of the Continental Divide in southwestern Colorado, US 550 bisects the forest north/south; US

160 is a major east/west route that borders the southern region. Mountains, canyons, waterfalls, unusual landforms and wide variations in elevation and vegetation characterize the forest, which encompasses 1,881,586 acres.

The Durango and Silverton Narrow Gauge Railroad *(see attraction listing p. 167)* passes through the spectacular canyon of the Rio de Las Animas.

The area around Durango is popular for winter sports; McPhee Reservoir, Vallecito Reservoir, Lemon Reservoir and Williams Creek Reservoir are summer recreation sites. Hunting and fishing are permitted in season. Saddle and pack trips can be made into such backcountry areas as the Lizard Head, South San Juan and Weminuche wildernesses. The San Juan Skyway offers 232 miles of scenic driving through the San Juan and Uncompahgre national forests.

For further information write the USDA Forest Service San Juan National Forest, 15 Burnett Ct., Durango, CO 81301; phone (970) 247-4874. *See Recreation Areas Chart.*

SAN LUIS (F-4) pop. 629, elev. 7,965'

San Luis was founded in 1851 and is one of the oldest towns in Colorado. The area is popular with anglers; nearby Mountain Home Reservoir has trout and Sanchez Reservoir contains pike, walleye and trout.

SHRINE OF THE STATIONS OF THE CROSS, jct. SRs 159 and 142, features two-thirds life-size bronze statues depicting the stations of the cross. The statues, created by sculptor Huberto Maestas, are situated on a .7-mile trail overlooking the community. The Chapel of All Saints is at the end of the trail. **Time:** Allow 30 minutes minimum. **Hours:** Daily dawn-dusk. **Cost:** Free. **Phone:** (719) 672-3685.

SEDALIA pop. 206

GABRIEL'S RESTAURANT & TUSCAN BAR   303/688-2323
♦♦♦ Northern Italian. Fine Dining. $27-$48 **AAA Inspector Notes:** *Historic.* Conspicuously at the center of the foothills in the tiny town of Sedalia, the eatery provides an intimate dining experience set in a Victorian-style home. The menu features flavorful four-course meals served by a polished waitstaff. An excellent selection of wine will definitely complement your meal. A bistro menu, which includes small plates as well as multi-course meals, is available in the Tuscan bar area. **Features:** full bar, patio dining, happy hour. **Reservations:** suggested. **Address:** 5450 Manhart Ave 80135 **Location:** SR 67, just w of jct US 85. [D]

SILT pop. 2,930

HOLIDAY INN EXPRESS & SUITES   970/876-5100
♦♦♦ Hotel. Rates not provided. **Address:** 1535 River Frontage Rd 81652 **Location:** I-70 exit 97, just s, then just e. **Facility:** 80 units. 3 stories, interior corridors. **Pool(s):** heated indoor. **Activities:** hot tub, picnic facilities, trails, exercise room. **Guest Services:** valet and coin laundry.

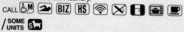

SILVERTHORNE (C-3) pop. 3,887, elev. 8,751'

RECREATIONAL ACTIVITIES
Fishing
• **Cutthroat Anglers** departs from 400 Blue River Pkwy. A variety of full- and half-day trips are available. Rod and gear are provided. **Hours:** Daily 7-7, Memorial Day-Labor Day.; daily 8-6, rest of year. **Phone:** (970) 262-2878.

MOUNTAIN LYON CAFE   970/262-6229
♦ American. Casual Dining. $6-$12 **AAA Inspector Notes:** Popular with the locals, this café serves hearty breakfast items made from fresh ingredients. Eggs Benedict, steak and eggs, omelets (shrimp, spinach and Swiss) and banana-nut pancakes are a few of the samplings. The lunch menu centers on burgers, hot entrées, deli sandwiches, soups and chili. **Features:** Sunday brunch. **Address:** 381 Blue River Pkwy 80498 **Location:** I-70 exit 205, just n.
[B] [L]

SUNSHINE CAFE   970/468-6663
♦♦ Sandwiches Soup. Casual Dining. $8-$12 **AAA Inspector Notes:** Stop in for a hearty breakfast or lunch. Locals sidle up to the counter for eggs Benedict, huevos rancheros, or French toast topped with blueberries and bananas. Lighter fare includes homemade granola, smoothies and oatmeal. Start lunch with a spicy cup of green chile soup. Then, choose from a variety of sandwiches, burgers and pasta dishes. **Features:** beer & wine. **Address:** 250 Summit Pl 80498 **Location:** I-70 exit 205, 0.3 mi s, then just w; in strip mall.
[B] [L] [AC]

SILVERTON (E-2) pop. 637, elev. 9,305'

After the first major silver strike in 1871, Silverton became a prosperous mining community. Between 1882 and 1918, the Las Animas district mines produced $65 million in ore. The Grand Imperial Hotel, an 1880s showplace for silver kings, and the gold-domed San Juan County Courthouse are evidence of the opulence of Silverton's bonanza years.

Blair Street and its assorted 24-hour bordellos thrived. The infamous thoroughfare, with its false-fronted buildings recalling the Wild West, is a tourist attraction and was often used as a movie set.

Other remnants of yesteryear are several ghost towns, including Animas Forks, 12 miles northeast on CR 2. **Note:** CR 2 is mostly a gravel road, passable by two-wheel-drive vehicles. Past Animas Forks a four-wheel-drive vehicle is required.

The rugged San Juan Mountain Range, one of the most scenic parts of the state, is crossed by US 550 through Silverton and is part of the San Juan Skyway, a scenic byway. The section leading from Silverton to Ouray includes the spectacular Million Dollar Highway *(see Ouray p. 241)*. San Juan County is a top destination for off-road adventurers; jeep tours and rentals are available.

Silverton is the terminus of the Durango and Silverton Narrow Gauge Railroad, a historic coal-burning passenger train *(see attraction listing p. 167)*. Much of the surrounding region lies within the San Juan National Forest *(see place listing p. 255)*.

Silverton Chamber of Commerce/Visitor Center: 414 Greene St., P.O. Box 565, Silverton, CO 81433. **Phone:** (970) 387-5654 or (800) 752-4494.

Self-guiding tours: Maps for a walking tour of historic Silverton as well as jeep road maps are available at the chamber of commerce. Gallery and studio literature also is available.

MAYFLOWER GOLD MILL TOUR, 2 mi. e. on CR 2, operates in the Sunnyside Mill, which was one of the town's major employers 1929-91. Former miners demonstrate the mill's original equipment, which remains unchanged since operations ceased. A 30-minute video about the mill's history is shown. **Hours:** Daily 10-5, early June-Labor Day. **Cost:** $8; $7.50 (ages 60+); free (ages 0-12). Guided tours $10; $9 (ages 60+); free (ages 0-12). Reservations are required for guided tours. **Phone:** (970) 387-5838, or (970) 387-5609 for the historical society. GT

OLD HUNDRED GOLD MINE TOUR is 5 mi. e. on CR 2, following signs. An electric mine train takes visitors into the heart of 13,257-foot-tall Galena Mountain. Narrated 1-hour tours through the mine's tunnels provide geological and historical insights as well as demonstrations of early and modern-day mining equipment. Gold panning on the surface is included.

Warm clothing is recommended. **Time:** Allow 1 hour minimum. **Hours:** Tours are given every 90 minutes daily 10-4, mid-May through Sept. 30. **Cost:** Fee (includes gold panning) $18.95; $16.95 (ages 60+); $9.95 (ages 5-12). **Phone:** (970) 387-5444 or (800) 872-3009. GT

SAN JUAN BACKCOUNTRY, 1119 Greene St., offers guided jeep, ATV and SUV tours of the San Juan Mountains. Knowledgeable drivers take passengers on back roads to see mountain views, old mines, wildflowers and wild animals. Rental jeeps and recreational vehicles are available for self-guiding tours. **Time:** Allow 2 hours minimum. **Hours:** Daily 8-6, mid-May through Oct. 31. **Cost:** Two-hour SUV tour $60; $40 (ages 5-17). Four-hour SUV tour (includes snack and water) $80; $45 (ages 5-17). All-day SUV tour (includes lunch) $150; $90 (ages 5-17). ATV and jeep tour prices vary; phone for current prices. **Phone:** (970) 387-5565 or (903) 288-6745. GT

SAN JUAN COUNTY HISTORICAL SOCIETY MUSEUM, 1559 Greene St., is in a 1902 county jail. Displays include artifacts from early mining and railroading days. The upper floor still has all the old jail cells used at the turn of the 20th century. The Mining Heritage Center also includes displays about mining as well as printing and early transportation. **Hours:** Daily 10-5, Memorial Day weekend to mid-Oct. **Cost:** $7; $3 (ages 5-12). **Phone:** (970) 387-5838.

RECREATIONAL ACTIVITIES
Jeep Tours (Self-driving)
- **Silver Summit Jeep Rentals** is at 640 Mineral St. **Hours:** Daily 8-7, May 15-Oct. 15. **Phone:** (970) 387-0240 or (800) 352-1637.

INN OF THE ROCKIES AT THE HISTORIC ALMA HOUSE
970/387-5336

Historic Bed & Breakfast
Rates not provided

Address: 220 E 10th St 81433 **Location:** Just se of 10th and Main sts. **Facility:** Built in 1898, this charming B&B offers a tea room as well as sitting and dining areas. Rooms feature down comforters, feather mattresses and Victorian claw-foot tubs. 9 units. 3 stories (no elevator), interior corridors. *Bath:* some shared. **Parking:** street only. **Activities:** hot tub. **Featured Amenity:** full hot breakfast.

SAVE ⫯⫯ 🛜 ✕ 🚫 📞 / SOME UNITS 🐕

VILLA DALLAVALLE BED & BREAKFAST   970/387-5555

Historic Bed & Breakfast $109-$135 **Address:** 1257 Blair St 81433 **Location:** Corner of 13th and Blair sts. **Facility:** Third-generation innkeepers offer attentive hospitality. Cozy furnishings and unique décor in each unit depicts a different period of history. Guests can enjoy wine and cheese in the evening. 7 units. 2 stories (no elevator), interior corridors. **Parking:** street only. **Terms:** closed 11/1-11/30, 3 day cancellation notice. **Activities:** hot tub, massage.

⫯⫯ 🛜 ✕ 🚫 📞 / SOME UNITS 🐕

THE WYMAN HOTEL & INN   970/387-5372

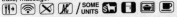
Historic Bed & Breakfast. Rates not provided. **Address:** 1371 Greene St 81433 **Location:** Corner of 14th and Main sts. **Facility:** This historic inn is beautifully decorated with antiques and reproductions. Ceiling fans and feather beds are featured in each of the well-appointed rooms. 17 units, some two bedrooms. 2 stories (no elevator), interior corridors. **Parking:** on-site and street. **Activities:** trails, massage.

⫯⫯ 🛜 ✕ 🚫 / SOME UNITS 🐕 🛏 🍽 🖥

WHERE TO EAT

AVALANCHE BREWING COMPANY   970/387-5282

Coffee/Tea Sandwiches. Quick Serve. $6-$13 **AAA Inspector Notes:** This small eatery has a cozy dining area and seating at an attractive copper bar. It is a traveler's favorite and offers a nice selection of yummy breakfast and sandwich items, seasonal soups and smoothies and make-your-own pizza. Vegan and vegetarian items are available. **Features:** full bar. **Address:** 1067 Blair St 81433 **Location:** Jct 11th and Blair sts. **Parking:** street only. B L D 🚫

BENT ELBOW RESTAURANT AND BAR   970/387-5775

American. Casual Dining. $8-$22 **AAA Inspector Notes:** *Historic.* Located in a historic building, this eatery's décor reflects the town's mining past. Menu items include Colorado elk burgers, shepherd's meat pie and a tilapia fish sandwich. **Features:** full bar. **Address:** 1114 Blair St 81433 **Location:** Jct 11th and Blair sts; in Bent Elbow Hotel. **Parking:** on-site and street. L D 🚫

HANDLEBARS RESTAURANT & SALOON   970/387-5395

American. Casual Dining. $7-$21 **AAA Inspector Notes:** Enjoy a meal in this casual dining area set in rustic décor of days gone by. This popular restaurant features a variety of dishes ranging from salad, sandwiches, steak and prime rib to poultry and burgers. **Features:** full bar. **Address:** 117 W 13th St 81433 **Location:** Corner of Greene (Main St) and 13th sts. **Parking:** street only.

L D AC

THE PICKLE BARREL RESTAURANT   970/387-5713

American Casual Dining $8-$23

AAA Inspector Notes: *Historic.* In a building reminiscent of an Old West saloon, this restaurant is located on Main Street in the town's historic area, within walking distance of the narrow gauge train station. The cuisine features chicken, beef, salads, soups and sandwiches. **Features:** full bar. **Address:** 1304 Greene St 81433 **Location:** At 13th and Greene sts. **Parking:** street only. L D AC

SNOWMASS VILLAGE (C-3) pop. 2,826, elev. 9,100'
• **Hotels & Restaurants map & index p. 45**

Founded in 1967, the ski resort at Snowmass Village was originally dubbed Snowmass-at-Aspen, presumably to distinguish the town from its better-known neighbor. The ski area and all-year resort has since come into its own, however, and lures vacationers from around the world.

First-timers often confuse Snowmass Village with Snowmass, an unincorporated assemblage of ranches and houses on the back side of the ski area's principal mountain. Snowmass Village, incorporated as a town in 1977, is one of several thriving resort communities in the area, as is Aspen *(see place listing p. 43)*, just 9 miles east.

Snowmass Village's 3,100 acres of ski terrain sit within the White River National Forest *(see place listing p. 274)*, a ruggedly mountainous area renowned for spectacular scenery and year-round outdoor recreation. The ski slopes stretch across Baldy and Burnt mountains. The core of Snowmass Village, including lodgings, condominiums, restaurants and boutiques, is centered around the Snowmass Mall and the base village, which both border the beginner slope Fanny Hill.

For those who think ski resorts are only worth visiting in the winter, Snowmass Village has a full slate of warm-weather activities. From June to mid-September, guided nature hikes, free weekly concerts and outdoor theater, golfing, spas, jeep tours, fly-fishing clinics, mountainboarding, horseback riding, mountain biking, chairlift rides, disc golf, white-water rafting and campfire storytelling are popular pastimes. The Anderson Ranch Arts Center, housed on a former sheep ranch, presents workshops and free lectures in painting, ceramics, photography, woodworking and furniture design.

Warm weather also brings with it a host of festivals and special events. The Snowmass Mammoth Festival kicks off the summer season in June with popular music acts, chili competitions and microbrew tastings. From mid-June to early August the Snowmass Summer of Free Music Series presents weekly evening concerts by well-known performers at the resort's slope-side amphitheater on Fanny Hill. The Snowmass Rodeo hosts Wednesday rodeos with calf roping, bronco and bull riding, family activities and a Western barbecue, from mid-June to mid-August.

Labor Day weekend brings the JazzAspen Snowmass Labor Day Festival featuring nationally known acts that attract music connoisseurs. The Snowmass Wine Festival takes place in mid-September, as does the Snowmass Balloon Festival, a wine and jazz festival with 3 days of hot air balloon competitions set against the backdrop of the Elk Mountain Range at sunrise.

Snowmass Village Visitor Information: 130 Kearns Rd., P.O. Box 5566, Snowmass Village, CO 81615. **Phone:** (970) 922-2297 or (800) 766-9627.

RECREATIONAL ACTIVITIES
Skiing

• **Snowmass** is 6 mi. s.w. of SR 82 on Brush Creek Rd. **Hours:** Daily 9-3:30, late Nov. to mid-Apr. (weather permitting). **Phone:** (970) 925-1227 or (800) 525-6200.

THE STONEBRIDGE INN   970/923-2420 **16**

Hotel. Rates not provided. **Address:** 300 Carriage Way 81615 **Location:** 4 mi sw of SR 82 via Brush Creek Rd; Lot 2. Located in Lower Village. **Facility:** 93 units. 7 stories, interior corridors. **Parking:** on-site (fee). **Terms:** check-in 4 pm. **Amenities:** safes. **Dining:** Artisan Restaurant & Bar, see separate listing. **Pool(s):** heated outdoor. **Activities:** sauna, hot tub, steamroom, downhill skiing, picnic facilities, trails, exercise room, massage. **Guest Services:** coin laundry, area transportation.

VICEROY SNOWMASS   (970)923-8000 **15**

Resort Condominium $225-$1350 **Address:** 130 Wood Rd 81615 **Location:** 6 mi sw of SR 82 via Brush Creek Rd, then 0.3 mi to lower Carriage Way. **Facility:** This ski-in/ski-out hotel offers stunning mountain views. The chic rooms feature modern décor with a few western touches, like cowhide pillows and Native American area rugs. 173 condominiums. 8 stories, interior corridors. **Parking:** valet only. **Terms:** closed 4/12-5/29 & 10/26-11/26, check-in 4 pm, 45 day cancellation notice-fee imposed, resort fee. **Amenities:** safes. **Dining:** 2 restaurants. **Pool(s):** heated outdoor. **Activities:** hot tub, downhill skiing, bicycles, trails, exercise room, spa. **Guest Services:** valet laundry, boarding pass kiosk, area transportation.

VILLAS AT SNOWMASS CLUB   970/923-0391 **14**

Resort Condominium. Rates not provided. **Address:** 160 Snowmass Club Cir Dr 81615 **Location:** 2.6 mi n up Brush Creek Rd to roundabout, 2nd exit, 0.3 mi s on Highline Rd, then just w to Welcome Center. **Facility:** This well-established, family-friendly resort offers meticulously manicured landscaping and individually decorated one- to three-bedroom condominiums, many with a Western theme. 44 condominiums. 2-3 stories, interior/exterior corridors. **Terms:** check-in 4 pm. **Dining:** Sage Restaurant & Patio, see separate listing. **Pool(s):** heated outdoor. **Activities:** sauna, hot tub, steamroom, regulation golf, tennis, recreation programs, trails, massage. **Guest Services:** valet and coin laundry, area transportation.

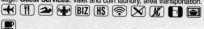

(See map & index p. 45.)

THE WESTIN SNOWMASS RESORT

(970)923-8200 **17**

WESTIN HOTELS & RESORTS

Hotel
$99-$719

AAA Benefit: Members save up to 15%, plus Starwood Preferred Guest® benefits!

Address: 100 Elbert Ln 81615 **Location:** 2.4 mi sw of SR 82 via Brush Creek Rd, 2nd exit at roundabout, then 3 mi to Elbert Ln; Lot 8. Located in Upper Village. **Facility:** 254 units. 5-8 stories, interior corridors. **Parking:** valet and street only. **Terms:** closed 5/1-5/27, check-in 4 pm, cancellation fee imposed, resort fee. **Amenities:** safes. **Pool(s):** heated outdoor. **Activities:** hot tub, downhill skiing, recreation programs in winter, kids club, trails, exercise room, spa. **Guest Services:** valet laundry, area transportation.

POKOLODI LODGE

970/923-4310

(fyi) Motel Did not meet all AAA rating requirements for locking devices in some guest rooms at time of last evaluation on 08/05/2015. **Address:** 25 Daly Ln 81615 **Location:** 4 mi sw of SR 82 via Brush Creek and Lower Village rds; Lot 5. Facilities, services, and décor characterize an economy property.

WHERE TO EAT

ARTISAN RESTAURANT & BAR

970/923-2427 **24**

American. Casual Dining. $13-$33 **AAA Inspector Notes:** The seasonal menu features Colorado lamb, ruby red trout, and local organic chicken. Creative sandwiches include the house porchetta with apple-horseradish slaw and sherry-fig mostarda. When the weather cooperates, sip a specialty cocktail or a glass of wine while watching the sun set from a seat on the patio. **Features:** full bar, happy hour. **Reservations:** suggested. **Address:** 300 Carriage Way 81615 **Location:** 4 mi sw of SR 82 via Brush Creek Rd; Lot 2; in The Stonebridge Inn. **B** **D** **AC**

KRABLOONIK RESTAURANT

970/923-3953 **26**

Regional American. Fine Dining. $8-$62 **AAA Inspector Notes:** Specializing in wild mushroom soup, fresh fish and preparations of seasonal wild game such as caribou, pheasant, wild boar and elk, this restaurant has a log cabin dining room with magnificent mountain views, an intimate sunken fire pit, a warm atmosphere and an excellent wine list. **Features:** full bar. **Reservations:** suggested. **Address:** 4250 Divide Rd 81615 **Location:** 5.3 mi w of SR 82 on Brush Creek Rd, 1 mi on Divide Rd. **L** **D** **AC**

SAGE RESTAURANT & PATIO

970/923-0923 **23**

American. Casual Dining. $16-$38 **AAA Inspector Notes:** During the summer season, bypass the elegant, mountain-style dining room in favor of the expansive patio, where views of Mount Daly will take your breath away. Worry not, though, you'll get your breath back quickly with your first bite of the seasonally changing Colorado bistro fare. Start with a cup of the chicken tortilla soup. For something different, try the kale salad topped with grilled calamari. Entrées may include Colorado lamb, bone-in pork chops, or salmon. **Features:** full bar, Sunday brunch. **Reservations:** suggested. **Address:** 0239 Snowmass Club Cir 81615 **Location:** 2.6 mi n up Brush Creek Rd to roundabout, 2nd exit, 0.3 mi s on Highline Rd, then just w to Welcome Center; in Villas at Snowmass Club. **Parking:** valet only. **L** **D** **AC**

VENGA VENGA

970/923-7777 **25**

Mexican. Casual Dining. $15-$22 **AAA Inspector Notes:** This slope-side cantina features a large outdoor patio with panoramic views. Traditional menu items are prepared with a creative twist, such as pork green-chile burritos, Jalisco shrimp enchiladas, and the achiote salmon. For lighter fare, select from a variety of tacos. Vegetarian items are available. For a fun dessert, try the s'mores, which you make using the outdoor fire pit. **Features:** full bar, patio dining, happy hour. **Address:** 105 Daly Ln 81615 **Location:** East end of Daly Ln. **Parking:** street only. **L** **D** **AC**

SOUTH FORK (E-3) pop. 386, elev. 8,208'

The town of South Fork is named for its proximity to the south fork of the Rio Grande. Since its beginnings as a stagecoach stop in the 1880s, timber processing, agriculture, mining and ranching as well as tourism and recreation have contributed to the town's economy.

South Fork serves as the southern gateway to the Silver Thread Scenic Byway on US 149 as it winds its way 117 miles westward through the San Juan Mountains to Blue Mesa Reservoir. Interpretive signs along the highway give details about the region's history, geology and wildlife.

The area's many lakes and 47 Rio Grande tributaries allow for plentiful fishing and river rafting opportunities. Other recreational activities include hiking, horseback riding, snowmobiling, hunting and skiing.

South Fork Visitors Center: 28 Silver Thread Ln., P.O. Box 1030, South Fork, CO 81154. **Phone:** (719) 873-5512 or (800) 571-0881.

RECREATIONAL ACTIVITIES

Fishing

- **South Fork Anglers** departs from 30359 US 160. **Hours:** Daily dawn-dusk. Phone ahead to confirm schedule. **Phone:** (719) 658-2955 or (877) 656-3474.

Horseback Riding

- **Wolf Creek Ranch Ski Lodge** is at 177022 W. US 160. Other activities are available. **Hours:** Trail rides are offered daily, Memorial Day weekend to mid-Oct. (weather permitting). Phone ahead to confirm schedule. **Phone:** (719) 873-5371 ski lodge and reservations, or (719) 873-5998 for trail ride information.

White-water Rafting

- **Cottonwood Cove Guest Ranch** is at 13046 SR 149 offers self-guided float tours. Rafts and transportation to and from the river are provided. Other activities are available. **Hours:** Daily May-Aug. Phone ahead to confirm schedule. **Phone:** (719) 658-2242 or (855) 216-2683.

STEAMBOAT SPRINGS (B-3) pop. 12,088, elev. 6,728'
- Hotels p. 260 • Restaurants p. 261

Ute Indians, drawn by valuable resources and hot springs, were the area's first inhabitants, but it was French fur trappers who gave Steamboat Springs its name. Legend has it that the rhythmic chugging of the hot spring near the river, from which mineral water spewed 15 feet into the air, sounded like a steamboat chugging down the river.

In the immediate vicinity there are more than 150 mineral springs, both medicinal and recreational. Today Old Town Hot Springs is built on the site of the original Heart Springs; phone (970) 879-1828. Strawberry Park Hot Springs, 7 miles northwest on CR 36, offers rejuvenation in a more natural setting; phone (970) 879-0342.

In addition to the thermal waters, Steamboat Springs has gained prominence as a winter sports playground. Norwegian Carl Howelsen, dubbed the Flying Norseman by Barnum & Bailey, introduced skiing and ski jumping in 1913; by the 1930s Steamboat Springs was internationally known. A number of world ski jump records were set on Howelsen Hill, one of the state's oldest ski areas still in use. Howelsen Ice Arena features an Olympic-size ice rink, which offers hockey and public ice skating from July to May; phone (970) 871-7033.

Howelsen also organized the first Winter Carnival in 1914. Held in February, this ski festival—along with some 69 winter Olympians who have called the town home and the popularity of the Steamboat Ski Area—perpetuate Steamboat Spring's reputation as "Ski Town, U.S.A."

June through August the Strings Music Festival features string ensembles, chamber music, bluegrass, jazz and youth and family concerts at Strings Festival Park; phone the box office at (970) 879-1996. The Steamboat Springs Arts Council hosts a number of cultural events, featuring the Emerald City Opera in August and a free classical music series from June through August.

The Yampa River Core Trail, a 7-mile route that runs the length of the town, provides scenic opportunities for walking, jogging, bicycling and skating. The path winds beside the Yampa River through city parks and wetlands. Kayakers and tubers enjoy the rushing waters of the Yampa River created by the spring snowmelt; tamer currents later in the season lure anglers.

Spectacular Fish Creek Falls, which plunge 283 feet through a geologic fault, is just minutes away. The falls are reached from the parking lot by a footpath along the creek. A footbridge at the bottom of the falls provides an excellent view of the cascades. The overlook trail is paved and is accessible for the physically impaired. Picnic facilities are available.

South of town a scenic route follows SR 131 to Toponas, turns east on SR 134, crosses 9,570-foot Gore Pass and rejoins US 40 at a point 6 miles north of Kremmling. The headquarters for the Routt National Forest (see place listing p. 253), which encompasses much of the neighboring mountain country, is in town. Steamboat Lake State Park lies 25 miles north via CR 129 (see Recreation Areas Chart).

Steamboat Springs Chamber Resort Association: 125 Anglers Dr., P.O. Box 774408, Steamboat Springs, CO 80477. **Phone:** (970) 879-0880.

TREAD OF PIONEERS MUSEUM, 8th and Oak sts., reflects the history and heritage of the Steamboat Springs area. Set in a furnished 1908 Queen Anne-style home, the collection includes early household items; skiing, ranching and mining memorabilia; an extensive collection of firearms; and Native American arts. Displays explore the lives of Native Americans and early settlers. Interactive exhibits and activities for children also are included.

Educational programs and tours are available. **Hours:** Tues.-Sat. 11-5. **Cost:** $5; $4 (ages 62+); $1 (ages 6-12). **Phone:** (970) 879-2214.

YAMPA RIVER BOTANIC PARK, 1 mi. s. on US 40, then w. on Trafalgar Ln. to Pamela Ln., following signs to 1000 Pamela Ln., contains plants, flowers, ornamentals and trees native to the Yampa River basin. Among the gardens are those devoted to day lilies, irises, roses, native plants, spring bulbs and medicinal herbs. A pond complements the surroundings. Pets are not permitted. **Time:** Allow 30 minutes minimum. **Hours:** Daily dawn-dusk, mid-Apr. through Oct. 31. **Cost:** Donations. **Phone:** (970) 846-5172.

RECREATIONAL ACTIVITIES

Fishing

- **Bucking Rainbow Outfitters** is at 730 Lincoln Ave. Guided fly fishing and other activities are offered. **Hours:** Daily 8-8. Phone ahead to confirm schedule. **Phone:** (970) 879-8747 or (888) 810-8747.

Skiing

- **Howelsen Hill** is at 845 Howelsen Pkwy. Other activities are offered. **Hours:** Tues. and Fri. 1-6, Wed.-Thurs. 1-8; Sat.-Sun. 10-4, late Nov. to mid-Mar. Phone ahead to confirm schedule. **Phone:** (970) 879-8499.

- **Steamboat Ski Resort** is 2.3 mi. e. on US 40 in the Routt National Forest. Other activities are offered. **Hours:** Daily 8:30-3:30, mid-Nov. to mid-Apr. **Phone:** (970) 879-6111 for information, or (800) 922-2722 for reservations.

HAMPTON INN & SUITES   970/871-8900

▼▼▼▼ **Hotel.** Rates not provided. **Address:** 725 S Lincoln Ave 80487 **Location:** 1.1 mi e of center on US 40 (Lincoln Ave). Located near railroad tracks. **Facility:** 73 units. 3 stories, interior corridors. **Pool(s):** heated outdoor. **Activities:** hot tub, trails, exercise room. **Guest Services:** valet and coin laundry.

| AAA Benefit: Members save up to 10%! |

HOLIDAY INN STEAMBOAT SPRINGS   970/879-2250

▼▼▼ **Hotel.** Rates not provided. **Address:** 3190 S Lincoln Ave 80487 **Location:** On US 40 (Lincoln Ave), 3 mi s of downtown. **Facility:** 117 units. 2 stories, interior corridors. **Terms:** check-in 4 pm. **Pool(s):** heated outdoor, heated indoor. **Activities:** hot tub, game room, lawn sports, exercise room. **Guest Services:** valet and coin laundry, area transportation.

THE INN AT STEAMBOAT   970/879-2600

▼▼▼ **Hotel.** Rates not provided. **Address:** 3070 Columbine Dr 80487 **Location:** US 40 (Lincoln Ave) and Walton Creek Rd, 0.7 mi e, just s. **Facility:** 34 units. 3 stories (no elevator), interior corridors. **Terms:** check-in 4 pm. **Pool(s):** heated outdoor. **Activities:** sauna, hot tub, exercise room, massage. **Guest Services:** valet laundry, area transportation.

LA QUINTA INN & SUITES STEAMBOAT SPRINGS
(970)871-1219

 **Hotel** $75-$218 **Address:** 3155 Ingles Ln 80487 **Location:** On US 40 (Lincoln Ave), 3 mi s of downtown; near Steamboat Ski Resort. **Facility:** 29 units. 2 stories (no elevator), interior corridors. **Pool(s):** heated indoor. **Activities:** hot tub. **Guest Services:** coin laundry.

NORDIC LODGE
970/879-0531

 **Motel.** Rates not provided. **Address:** 1036 Lincoln Ave 80477 **Location:** On US 40 (Lincoln Ave), just w of 10th St; downtown. **Facility:** 29 units. 1-2 stories (no elevator), exterior corridors. **Pool(s):** heated outdoor. **Activities:** hot tub. **Guest Services:** coin laundry.

RABBIT EARS MOTEL
970/879-1150

Motel. Rates not provided. **Address:** 201 Lincoln Ave 80477 **Location:** On US 40 (Lincoln Ave), just se of 3rd St; downtown. Opposite Municipal Hot Springs Pool and next to park. **Facility:** 65 units. 2 stories (no elevator), exterior corridors. **Activities:** trails. **Guest Services:** coin laundry.

SHERATON STEAMBOAT RESORT
970/879-2220

Resort Hotel
Rates not provided

AAA Benefit: Members save up to 15%, plus Starwood Preferred Guest® benefits!

Address: 2200 Village Inn Ct 80487 **Location:** 2.3 mi s from center on US 40 (Lincoln Ave) to Mt. Werner Rd exit, 0.8 mi e, 0.3 mi ne on Mt. Werner Cir, just ne at Ski Time Square, then just s. **Facility:** This ski-in, ski-out resort offers upscale public areas. Rooms feature balconies with a view of the ski slope, village or valley. Units vary from standard hotel rooms to apartment style condos. 266 units, some condominiums. 8 stories, interior corridors. **Parking:** on-site (fee) and valet. **Terms:** check-in 4 pm. **Amenities:** safes. **Dining:** 3 restaurants. **Pool(s):** heated outdoor. **Activities:** hot tub, steamroom, regulation golf, downhill & cross country skiing, snowmobiling, bicycles, game room, trails, exercise room, spa. **Guest Services:** valet and coin laundry, area transportation.

STEAMBOAT RESORTS BY WYNDHAM VACATION RENTALS
TRAPPEUR'S CROSSING RESORT   970/879-0720

Condominium. Rates not provided. **Address:** 1795 Medicine Springs Dr 80487 **Location:** Off US 40 (Lincoln Ave), take Walton Creek Rd, 0.5 mi e to Village Dr, just n to Medicine Springs Dr, then just e. **Facility:** Surrounding the property's central activity building, these two-, three- and four-bedroom condos vary in style and décor. Select from a variety of outdoor pools and hot tubs to enjoy some relaxation. 120 condominiums. 3 stories, interior corridors. **Terms:** check-in 4 pm. **Pool(s):** heated outdoor, heated indoor. **Activities:** sauna, hot tub, tennis, picnic facilities, exercise room, massage. **Guest Services:** complimentary and valet laundry.

THE ANTLERS
970/879-5548

[fyi] Not evaluated. **Address:** 2085 Ski Time Square Dr 80487 **Location:** US 40 (Lincoln Ave) and Mt. Werner Rd, 0.7 mi e to Mt. Werner Cir, e to Ski Time Square Dr, then just e. Facilities, services, and décor characterize a mid-scale property. This ski-in/ski-out property offers spacious townhomes.

CANYON CREEK AT EAGLE RIDGE
970/879-6606

[fyi] Not evaluated. **Address:** 2740 Eagle Ridge Dr 80487 **Location:** US 40 (Lincoln Ave) and Walton Creek Rd, 0.4 mi e, 0.3 mi n. Facilities, services, and décor characterize a mid-scale property.

EAGLERIDGE LODGE & TOWNHOMES
970/879-5555

[fyi] Not evaluated. **Address:** 1463 Flat Top Cir 80487 **Location:** US 40 (Lincoln Ave) and Mt. Werner Rd, 0.7 mi e to Mt. Werner Cir, 0.3 mi s to Eagle Ridge Dr, then just e. Facilities, services, and décor characterize a mid-scale property.

HIGHMARK STEAMBOAT SPRINGS
970/879-2525

[fyi] Not evaluated. **Address:** 2525 Village Dr 80487 **Location:** US 40 (Lincoln Ave) and Walton Creek Rd, 0.5 mi e to Village Dr, just n. Facilities, services, and décor characterize an upscale property.

HOTEL BRISTOL
970/879-3083

[fyi] Not evaluated. **Address:** 917 Lincoln Ave 80477 **Location:** In historic downtown. Facilities, services, and décor characterize a mid-scale property.

KUTUK CONDOMINIUMS
970/879-6605

[fyi] Not evaluated. **Address:** 2000 Ski Time Square Dr 80487 **Location:** In Ski Time Square. Facilities, services, and décor characterize a mid-scale property.

THE LODGE AT STEAMBOAT SPRINGS
970/879-6000

[fyi] Not evaluated. **Address:** 2700 Village Dr 80487 **Location:** US 40 (Lincoln Ave) and Walton Creek Rd, 0.5 mi e, just n. Facilities, services, and décor characterize a mid-scale property.

PTARMIGAN HOUSE
970/879-6278

[fyi] Not evaluated. **Address:** 2322 Apres Ski Way 80487 **Location:** US 40 (Lincoln Ave) and Walton Creek Rd, 0.5 mi e to Village Dr, 0.3 mi n to Apres Ski Way, just e. Facilities, services, and décor characterize a mid-scale property.

WHERE TO EAT

AZTECA TAQUERIA
970/870-9980

Mexican. Quick Serve. $6-$10 AAA Inspector Notes: This casual eatery features burritos, enchiladas, chimichangas, tacos, quesadillas and salads prepared quickly and made to order. Patrons, who can dine in or take their food to go, can choose their toppings and sauces. Feel like a local and ask for the fish burritos 'the good way,' with cilantro rice, black beans, chipotle sauce, cheese, lettuce and sour cream. Vegetarian options are available. **Features:** full bar, happy hour. **Address:** 116 9th St 80488 **Location:** Just n of Lincoln Ave and 9th St; downtown. **Parking:** street only. [B] [L] [D] [AC]

BEAU JO'S COLORADO STYLE PIZZA
970/870-6401

Pizza. Casual Dining. $11-$16 AAA Inspector Notes: Known for its pizza, this eatery offers a fun atmosphere with a mountain theme. Build your pizza from the crust up. Choices include a mountain pie with a thick, chewy edge; the thin-crust prairie pie; and gluten-free options. Add your favorite toppings or choose a specialty pizza like the sky hawk (a pepperoni pie with Hatch green chiles and feta), or Skier Mike's chicken, Canadian bacon and green pepper pie. **Address:** 704 Lincoln Ave 80487 **Location:** Corner of 7th St and Lincoln Ave; downtown. **Parking:** street only. [L] [D] [AC]

BISTRO C.V.
970/879-4197

Regional American. Fine Dining. $21-$46 AAA Inspector Notes: This upscale bistro adds a touch of class to ski town dining. Some menu items change frequently, but the thoughtfully created menu selections and high-quality ingredients remains consistent. Sample items may include the grilled Caesar salad with truffle-garlic dressing, yellowtail crudo with yuzu foam and summer truffle shavings, Wagyu hanger steak with duck fat potatoes, and the Colorado lamb duo. The wine list includes local, regional and international selections. **Features:** full bar, patio dining. **Reservations:** suggested. **Address:** 345 Lincoln Ave 80487 **Location:** Corner of Lincoln Ave and 4th St; downtown. **Parking:** street only. [D] [AC]

CAFÉ DIVA
970/871-0508

American. Casual Dining. $21-$40 AAA Inspector Notes: This popular restaurant offers an elegant yet relaxed atmosphere at the base of the mountain and is known for its imaginative menu, which includes crab tomato bisque, a taste of Colorado with elk tenderloin and other dishes with out-of-this-world flavors. The accomplished staff can make suggestions from the vast wine list. **Features:** full bar. **Reservations:** suggested. **Address:** 1855 Ski Time Square 80487 **Location:** At the base of Steamboat Ski Area; in Torian Plum Plaza. [D]

CANTINA 970/879-0826

WWW Mexican. Casual Dining. $8-$18 **AAA Inspector Notes:** Flavorful fare and tasty margaritas draw large crowds to this popular hangout. Menu items include a nice selection of appetizers and tapas, pork tamales, buffalo carne asada, chiles rellenos, chicken enchiladas and sizzling tequila-fired fajitas prepared tableside. The cheerful, festive décor enhances the lively atmosphere. **Features:** full bar, patio dining, happy hour. **Address:** 818 Lincoln Ave 80487 **Location:** Just s of center; corner of Lincoln Ave and 8th St; downtown. **Parking:** street only. L D M

CARL'S TAVERN 970/761-2060

WW American. Casual Dining. $12-$19 **AAA Inspector Notes:** This laid-back eatery features juicy burgers packed with flavor and unique toppings, as well as homemade sausage, steaks, and such comfort foods as pot roast and meatloaf. Reclaimed wood and custom wallpaper with historic photos enhance the décor. **Features:** full bar, happy hour. **Address:** 700 Yampa Ave 80487 **Location:** From Lincoln Ave, just s on 10th St; in historic downtown.
L D CALL M M

CREEKSIDE CAFE & GRILL 970/879-4925

WW American. Casual Dining. $11-$13 **AAA Inspector Notes:** Popular with locals and tourists alike, this casual eatery offers hearty portions, so be sure to bring your appetite! Breakfast choices include many variations on traditional eggs Benedict, French toast, pancakes, waffles, breakfast burritos and more, while the lunch menu features creative, flavor-filled sandwiches, wraps, soups and salads. The atmosphere indoors has a bistro feel, and the patio overlooking Soda Creek has a breezier atmosphere. **Features:** full bar, patio dining. **Address:** 131 11th St 80487 **Location:** Corner of US 40 (Lincoln Ave) and 11th St, then just n; downtown. **Parking:** street only.
B L M

CRUISERS SUB SHOP 970/879-1747

W Sandwiches. Quick Serve. $4-$9 **AAA Inspector Notes:** Hang ten at this surf-theme eatery. Grab a salad, smoothie or toasted sub sandwich before heading out on your outdoor adventure. The hearty raw salad makes a fine vegetarian lunch option. For a light sandwich, try the bacon, tomato and cheddar toastie. Larger subs include a pressed Cuban, a Philly and meatball. **Features:** patio dining. **Address:** 685 Marketplace Plaza, Suite C4 80487 **Location:** 2.6 mi s of center to Mt. Werner Rd, 0.3 mi e; in Wildhorse Marketplace.
L D

DRUNKEN ONION GET & GO KITCHEN 970/879-8423

W Deli Soup. Quick Serve. $7-$11 **AAA Inspector Notes:** The chef redefines 'quick serve' with a variety of heat-and-serve meals that patrons can take out. Options include blackened chicken with lemon chive aioli, mac 'n cheese and rotisserie chicken enchiladas. This is an excellent option for members who want a high-quality, home-cooked meal, but also want to relax on vacation. Those wanting to dine in can choose among freshly-made soups, sandwiches, salads and desserts. Desserts include a rich, fudge- like brownie. **Features:** patio dining. **Address:** 685 Marketplace Plaza, Suite 5 80487 **Location:** 2.6 mi s of center to Mt. Werner Rd, 0.3 mi e; in Wildhorse Marketplace. B L D

FRESHIES RESTAURANT 970/879-8099

WW American. Casual Dining. $10-$13 **AAA Inspector Notes:** Well known for its breakfasts, Freshies also offers a wonderful lunch menu filled with tasty soups, sandwiches and salads. As the name implies, fresh ingredients are the key to this eatery's success. Cheerful décor and upbeat staff complete the experience. **Features:** full bar, patio dining. **Address:** 595 S Lincoln Ave 80487 **Location:** 0.6 mi e on US 40 (Lincoln Ave). B L

HARWIGS 970/879-1919

WWW American. Fine Dining. $29-$45 **AAA Inspector Notes:** Creative French and Continental cuisine is served in candlelit ambience. An excellent wine list enhances the menu. Although they change seasonally, entrées often feature Colorado lamb, line-caught fish, duck, chicken, beef and venison. Innovative flavor combinations and artful presentations add to the experience. Lighter fare and more casual dining is offered in Harwigs in a building dating to 1886. **Features:** full bar. **Reservations:** suggested. **Address:** 911 Lincoln Ave 80487 **Location:** US 40 (Lincoln Ave); downtown. **Parking:** street only. D

LA MONTANA 970/879-5800

WWW Southwestern. Casual Dining. $15-$32 **AAA Inspector Notes:** This restaurant specializes in creative Southwestern cuisine. Menu items include the famous camarones de la Montana, jumbo shrimp stuffed with crab, poblano chili and jack cheese and wrapped in hickory-smoked bacon. Other favorites include enchiladas, fajitas, braised chicken mole and black pepper elk medallions. Artful presentations enhance the experience, and the inviting decor has intimate, open dining areas. **Features:** full bar. **Reservations:** suggested. **Address:** 2500 Village Dr, Suite 102 80487 **Location:** 2.3 mi e of center to Mt. Werner Rd, 1 mi n to Apres Ski Way, then just e to Village Dr.
D CALL M

LAUNDRY KITCHEN & COCKTAILS 970/870-0681

WWW Small Plates. Casual Dining. $11-$28 **AAA Inspector Notes:** In its former life, the building served as the town's laundromat for 30 years, a history remembered by the antique washer boards on the walls. The majority of the menu consists of small plates. Standout dishes include a Brussels sprouts, bacon, and cheese and crispy onion hash. Somehow the eclectic sounding flavors come together in a disparate whole. The pow pow Asian-style shrimp has a nice heat. The poke (yellow tail tuna) comes with homemade chips, which lend the dish a satisfying crunch. **Features:** full bar, happy hour. **Reservations:** suggested. **Address:** 127 11th St 80487 **Location:** Just n of US 40 (Lincoln Ave); downtown. **Parking:** street only. D

MAHOGANY RIDGE BREWERY & GRILL 970/879-3773

W Fusion. Casual Dining. $11-$29 **AAA Inspector Notes:** Not your ordinary brewpub, the restaurant gives guests a choice of creative and artistic Asian and Latin-fusion dishes and American comfort food such as a build-your-own satay platter, pork tenderloin, chipotle chicken pot pie, sandwiches, salads and soups, as well as 21 dipping sauces to flavor many of the options. The cozy seasonal outdoor patio is popular in the summer. **Features:** full bar, patio dining, happy hour. **Address:** 435 Lincoln Ave 80487 **Location:** Corner of 5th St and US 40 (Lincoln Ave); downtown. **Parking:** street only. D

MAMBO ITALIANO 970/870-0500

WW Italian. Casual Dining. $9-$26 **AAA Inspector Notes:** In the historic downtown area, this restaurant features specialty pizzas and flavorful pasta dishes. When the weather permits, the outdoor patio is the perfect place to dine. The atmosphere is low-key during the day but amps up to become lively at night. **Features:** full bar, happy hour. **Address:** 521 Lincoln Ave 80477 **Location:** Corner of 5th St and US 40 (Lincoln Ave); downtown. **Parking:** street only. D

MAZZOLA'S MAJESTIC ITALIAN DINER 970/879-2405

WW Italian. Casual Dining. $13-$23 **AAA Inspector Notes:** The red awning indicates you've arrived at this local favorite. The meal starts with an herbaceous pesto and white bean dip served with fresh bread. If you need more starters, choose from garlic shrimp, steamed mussels and fried calamari. The Mazzola salad is tossed tableside with lemon-garlic vinaigrette. The hardest decision is whether to order pasta or a gourmet pizza. For a splurge, try the buttery lobster scampi. **Features:** full bar. **Address:** 917 Lincoln Ave 80487 **Location:** On US 40 (Lincoln Ave) at 9th St; downtown. **Parking:** street only. D LATE M

ORE HOUSE AT THE PINE GROVE 970/879-1190

WW American. Casual Dining. $12-$47 **AAA Inspector Notes:** *Historic.* Western charm abounds in this popular restaurant's converted 100-year-old barn, which is between downtown and the mountain. Specialties include steak, prime rib, wild game and fresh seafood selections. The walls are adorned with historic photographs, and the dining rooms have stone fireplaces and Western appointments such as spurs, chaps and old wagon wheels. **Features:** full bar, patio dining. **Reservations:** suggested. **Address:** 1465 Pine Grove Rd 80487 **Location:** On US 40 (Lincoln Ave), 1.5 mi e of center. D

STEAMBOAT SMOKEHOUSE 970/879-7427

WW Barbecue. Casual Dining. $10-$23 **AAA Inspector Notes:** The floor is covered with peanut shells, and a few peanuts are lodged in mounted animal heads at this quirky haunt. Good barbecue results from a blend of Texas pit, Oklahoma hickory and Colorado beef and pork. **Features:** full bar, happy hour. **Address:** 912 Lincoln Ave 80487 **Location:** On US 40 (Lincoln Ave) at 9th St; downtown. **Parking:** street only. L D

TRUFFLE PIG   970/879-7470

▼▼▼ American. Fine Dining. $15-$38 **AAA Inspector Notes:** Located steps from the gondola, this restaurant offers magnificent views from the upscale bar, spacious dining room and slope-side patio. For apres ski, order a specialty cocktail and some small plates like the fried calamari, bacon-wrapped dates, and braised barbecue pig "wings." If you're on a health kick, fill up on the hearty kale, avocado and farro salad. Entrées include wild mushroom risotto, pork osso buco and Colorado lamb t-bone. **Features:** full bar, patio dining, happy hour. **Reservations:** suggested. **Address:** 2250 Apres Ski Way 80487 **Location:** 3 mi s of center on US 40 (Lincoln Ave) to Walton Creek Rd, 0.5 mi e to Village Dr, 0.3 mi n, then just e; at One Steamboat Place. **Parking:** on-site and valet. ⃞D⃞

WINONA'S   970/879-2483

▼▼ Breads/Pastries Sandwiches. Casual Dining. $9-$11 **AAA Inspector Notes:** Large, thick and covered with tons of gooey white frosting, the homemade cinnamon buns alone have people lining up. The cheerful eatery also offers flavorful fresh sandwiches, soups and hearty breakfasts. **Features:** full bar, patio dining. **Address:** 617 Lincoln Ave 80488 **Location:** Just e of 7th St; in historic downtown. **Parking:** street only. ⃞B⃞ ⃞L⃞

STERLING (B-6) pop. 14,777, elev. 3,940'

Cattle ranchers began arriving in the area in the 1860s, and since then Sterling has grown into a trade center for northeastern Colorado. Agriculture, educational institutions and light industry contribute to its diversified economy.

Fishing, boating, a full-service marina, picnicking, water skiing, swimming and hunting are available at North Sterling State Park *(see Recreation Areas Chart)*, 12 miles north via N. 7th Avenue; phone (970) 522-3657. Types of wildlife that may be found in the area include deer, eagles, pelicans, coyotes, rabbits and many species of waterfowl and shorebirds.

The City of Living Trees is a collection of 12 trees that have been carved into sculptures; some have been bronzed. Located throughout town, the collection includes Skygrazers, a group of five giraffes looking upward.

Tourist Information Center: 12510 CR 370, Sterling, CO 80751. **Phone:** (970) 522-8962 or (800) 544-8609.

OVERLAND TRAIL MUSEUM, e. of the Platte River Bridge at jct. I-76 and US 6, contains historical exhibits including an Evangelical church, blacksmith shop, house, print shop, one-room schoolhouse, barn, general store, barber shop, a 1930s gas station, household goods and Native American artifacts. The Dave Hamil Rural Electric Association building demonstrates how electricity changed rural America. Fossils from northeastern Colorado also are displayed.

Time: Allow 1 hour, 30 minutes minimum. **Hours:** Tues.-Sat. 9-5, Apr.-Oct.; Tues.-Sat. 10-4, rest of year. **Cost:** $3; $1.50 (ages 4-12). **Phone:** (970) 522-3895. ⛱

BEST WESTERN SUNDOWNER   (970)522-6265

▼▼ Motel $120-$199

AAA Benefit: Save 10% or more every day and earn 10% bonus points!

Address: 125 Overland Trail St 80751 **Location:** I-76 exit 125, just w. **Facility:** 58 units. 2 stories (no elevator), interior/exterior corridors. **Pool(s):** heated outdoor, heated indoor. **Activities:** exercise room. **Guest Services:** coin laundry. **Featured Amenity:** breakfast buffet.

⃞SAVE⃞ ⃞➔⃞ ⃞BIZ⃞ 📶 ⃞✕⃞ ⃞📷⃞ ⃞🖨⃞
⃞🖥⃞ / SOME UNITS ⃞🛏⃞ ⃞HS⃞

WHERE TO EAT

GALLAGHER'S RIVER CITY GRILL   970/521-7648

▼▼ American Casual Dining $7-$30

AAA Inspector Notes: This bar and grill is the most popular restaurant in town, and for good reason. The menu features a variety of entrée salads, sandwiches, burgers, steaks and even fajitas. **Features:** full bar. **Address:** 1116 W Main St 80751 **Location:** Between 10th and 11th aves. ⃞L⃞ ⃞D⃞

OLD TOWN BISTRO   970/526-5402

▼▼ American. Casual Dining. $9-$26 **AAA Inspector Notes:** The diverse menu offerings include a barbecue brisket sandwich, seared Chilean sea bass, and dry-aged sirloin steak. Try the creamy chicken fettuccine Alfredo, especially if you like garlic. If you're tempted by the desserts in the deli case, the chocolate peanut butter brownie is a rich option. **Features:** full bar. **Address:** 402 Main St 80751 **Location:** On US 6, between Main and Poplar sts. **Parking:** on-site and street. ⃞B⃞ ⃞L⃞ ⃞D⃞

STRASBURG (C-5) pop. 2,447, elev. 5,386'

Near Strasburg on Aug. 15, 1870, the Kansas Pacific Railroad completed laying the tracks that formed part of a continuous chain of railways connecting the Atlantic and Pacific coasts. A sign and obelisk mark the site of the rail hookup.

COMANCHE CROSSING MUSEUM, 1 blk. n. and 3 blks. w. of I-70 exit 310, portrays the history of the Strasburg area. Exhibits include a doctor's office, cobbler's shop, two relocated school buildings, a railroad station, caboose, antique vehicles, fossils, meteorites and Native American artifacts. **Hours:** Daily 1-4, June-Aug; grounds open dawn-dusk. **Cost:** Donations. **Phone:** (303) 622-4322.

TABERNASH pop. 417

TABERNASH TAVERN   970/726-4430

▼▼ American. Casual Dining. $12-$30 **AAA Inspector Notes:** Locals drive from all over Grand County to dine here. Start with the bison carpaccio and then choose from a variety of steaks, salmon, chicken and wild game. The rustic décor creates a unique atmosphere. **Features:** full bar, happy hour. **Address:** 72287 US Hwy 40 80478 **Location:** Just s of town center. ⃞D⃞ ⃞🍸⃞

TELLURIDE (E-2) pop. 2,325, elev. 8,792'

It seemed logical that the gold and silver veins that were yielding fortunes in Ouray on the east slope of the Uncompahgre Range also would show on the west side. The claims staked in 1875 on the mountainsides above the headwaters of the San Miguel proved the premise. Columbia, the supply camp at the bottom of the narrow gorge, soon changed its name to Telluride after tellurium, the non-metallic matrix in which the precious metals appeared.

Efforts to lend respectability to the brawling camp led to the construction around 1891 of the luxurious Sheridan Hotel and adjacent opera house; the preservation of these structures contributes to the town's Victorian atmosphere.

Although such luminaries as Sarah Bernhardt, William Jennings Bryan and Lillian Gish appeared at the Sheridan Opera House, in 1889 a star of another sort also impressed Telluride: Butch Cassidy "withdrew" $30,000 from a local bank, unauthorized.

In its heyday the mining town boasted a population of 5,000 and included a bowling alley, tennis courts and the highest-altitude YMCA in the country. Once an 1870s mining camp of 250 people, the ghost town of Alta is 5 miles south on SR 145.

A free gondola ride provides a spectacular view of the town and the surrounding mountains. Gondolas stop at Station St. Sophia before continuing on to Mountain Village, where the St. Sophia Nature Center is located a short walk away. Visitors may explore the town's mining past by visiting the Tomboy Mine located near the 13,000-foot summit of Imogene Pass. To get to the mine, take Oak Street north, then continue 6 miles east on Tomboy Road; a four-wheel-drive vehicle is required.

Many local guide services are available. Dave's Mountain Tours provides guided scenic tours of the San Juan Mountains via four-wheel-drive vehicles in the summer; phone (970) 728-9749.

About 2.5 miles east of town Bridal Veil Falls, the longest free-falling waterfall in Colorado, drops 365 feet to become the headwaters of the San Miguel River. Precariously perched at the edge of a cliff above the falls is a renovated 1907 structure that housed one of the oldest Westinghouse generators in the country. The building's machinery has been restored to provide hydroelectric power for Telluride. Hikers, mountain bikers and four-wheelers can take a mining road that dates from the late 1800s up the canyon to the power station and falls. **Note:** The power station is privately owned and not open to the public.

Another dramatic canyon walk begins at the edge of town and climbs 1,040 feet over 2.5 miles to Bear Creek Falls. The hiking and biking trail leads to the waterfall canyon and mining ruins. With more than 350 forested acres, Bear Creek Canyon offers cross-country and back-country skiing during the winter months.

Major summer festivals include Mountainfilm, in late August; the Telluride Bluegrass Festival, the third weekend in June; the Telluride Jazz Celebration, from late July to early August; the Telluride Chamber Music Festival from early to mid-August; the ▼ Telluride Film Festival, Labor Day weekend; and the Telluride Blues & Brews Festival, the third weekend in September.

Telluride Information Center: 700 W. Colorado Ave., Box 1009, Telluride, CO 81435. **Phone:** (970) 728-3041 or (888) 605-2578.

Self-guiding tours: Maps for self-guiding walking tours are available at the visitor information center at the entrance to town.

TELLURIDE HISTORICAL MUSEUM is at 201 W. Gregory St. The history of Telluride from the 1800s to the present is told through exhibits about mining, railroads, home life and healthcare. **Time:** Allow 45 minutes minimum. **Hours:** Mon.-Sat. 11-5 (also Thurs. 5-7), Sun. 1-5, June-Oct.; Tues.-Sat. 11-5, rest of year. **Cost:** $5; $3 (ages 6-17 and 66+). **Phone:** (970) 728-3344.

TELLURIDE OUTSIDE, 121 W. Colorado Ave., offers several guided off-road 4 x 4 tours of the San Juan mountains. Guides are well-versed in local history, flora and fauna, and geology. The Imogene Pass tour passes through mining camps en route to a summit of more than 13,000 feet. Fly fishing, river rafting, mountain bike and photography tours also are offered as well as tours of ghost towns and Ouray. Snowmobiling tours are available in winter months.

Time: Allow 4 hours minimum. **Hours:** Departures require a minimum of 2 people. Daily 7-7, May-Oct.; 8-6, rest of year. **Cost:** Half-day guided 4 x 4 tours $70-$90; $60-$80 (ages 0-12). Full-day guided 4 x 4 tours $155-$175; $130-$145 (ages 0-12). Reservations are required. **Phone:** (970) 728-3895 or (800) 831-6230. [GT]

RECREATIONAL ACTIVITIES
Skiing
• **Telluride Ski Resort** is at 565 Mountain Village Blvd. Other activities are offered. **Hours:** Daily 9-4, Thanksgiving to mid-Apr. **Phone:** (970) 728-6900 or (866) 754-8355.

FAIRMONT HERITAGE PLACE, FRANZ KLAMMER LODGE (970)728-3318
▼▼▼ **Resort Condominium** $350-$2400 **Address:** 567 Mountain Village Blvd 81435 **Location:** 2.3 mi e; in Mountain Village. **Facility:** Admire the ski-slope view from the floor-to-ceiling lobby windows with your favorite après-ski beverage. Feel at home with your friends or family in the spacious two- and three-bedroom condos. 63 condominiums. 5 stories, interior corridors. **Parking:** valet only. **Terms:** closed 4/7-5/23 & 10/20-11/22, check-in 4:30 pm, 2 night minimum stay - seasonal, 45 day cancellation notice-fee imposed. **Pool(s):** heated outdoor. **Activities:** sauna, hot tub, steamroom, downhill & cross country skiing, snowmobiling, ice skating, recreation programs in summer, game room, picnic facilities, trails, exercise room, spa. **Guest Services:** complimentary and valet laundry.

HOTEL COLUMBIA
970/728-0660

Boutique
Contemporary
Retro Hotel
Rates not provided

Address: 301 W San Juan Ave 81435 **Location:** At Aspen St and San Juan Ave; opposite gondola. **Facility:** Opposite the gondola, this hotel offers a variety of rooms, suites and penthouses, most with a balcony and gas fireplace, all with robes and humidifier. 21 units, some condominiums. 4 stories, interior corridors. **Parking:** on-site (fee). **Amenities:** safes. **Dining:** Cosmopolitan of Telluride, see separate listing. **Activities:** downhill & cross country skiing, bicycles, trails, massage. **Guest Services:** valet laundry. **Featured Amenity:** breakfast buffet.

THE HOTEL TELLURIDE
970/369-1188

Boutique Hotel. Rates not provided. **Address:** 199 N Cornet St 81435 **Location:** Just s of roundabout, then just e. **Facility:** This upscale hotel features a spacious, lodge-style lobby with comfortable seating areas and a fireplace. After a day exploring the outdoors, relax on the private balcony or patio in your room. 59 units. 3 stories, interior corridors. **Parking:** on-site (fee) and street. **Terms:** check-in 4 pm. **Amenities:** safes. **Activities:** hot tub, steamroom, bicycles, trails, exercise room, massage. **Guest Services:** valet and coin laundry, area transportation.

LUMIERE HOTEL TELLURIDE
970/369-0400

Boutique Hotel
Rates not provided

Address: 118 Lost Creek Ln 81435 **Location:** 1.5 mi e; in Mountain Village. **Facility:** This small hotel offers personalized services and slope-side ski-in/ski-out facilities. Rooms range from studio units to condos with multiple bedrooms. 29 units, some condominiums. 7 stories, interior corridors. **Parking:** valet only. **Terms:** check-in 4 pm. **Amenities:** safes. **Pool(s):** heated outdoor. **Activities:** sauna, hot tub, downhill & cross country skiing, recreation programs, trails, exercise room, massage. **Guest Services:** valet laundry. **Featured Amenity:** continental breakfast.

MADELINE HOTEL & RESIDENCES
970/369-0880

Resort Hotel
Rates not provided

Address: 568 Mountain Village Blvd 81435 **Location:** 2.2 mi e; in Mountain Village. **Facility:** Richly appointed in contemporary alpine design, this luxury mountain resort offers an impressive selection of one- to four-bedroom condominiums, suites and hotel rooms. 130 units, some condominiums. 7 stories, interior corridors. **Parking:** valet only. **Terms:** check-in 4 pm. **Amenities:** safes. **Dining:** 2 restaurants. **Pool(s):** heated outdoor. **Activities:** hot tub, downhill & cross country skiing, snowmobiling, ice skating, recreation programs in season, bicycles, game room, lawn sports, trails, exercise room, spa. **Guest Services:** valet laundry.

Keep your focus safely
on the road when driving

NEW SHERIDAN HOTEL
970/728-4351

Historic Boutique
Hotel
Rates not provided

Address: 231 W Colorado Ave 81435 **Location:** At SR 145 (Colorado Ave) and Oak St. **Facility:** Built in 1891, this hotel offers attractive rooms with custom furnishings and heated bathroom tile floors. Due to the property's historic nature, standard rooms are on the small side. 26 units. 3 stories, interior corridors. **Parking:** street only. **Terms:** check-in 4 pm. **Amenities:** safes. **Dining:** New Sheridan Chop House, see separate listing. **Activities:** trails, massage. **Guest Services:** valet laundry.

THE PEAKS RESORT & SPA
970/728-6800

Resort Hotel. Rates not provided. **Address:** 136 Country Club Dr 81435 **Location:** 2.5 mi e; in Mountain Village. **Facility:** Enticing features include ski-in/ski-out access, a styling salon, tanning facilities, a rock climbing wall, an oxygen room, a three-lane lap pool and an on-site helipad for heli-skiing. 184 units, some condominiums. 8 stories, interior corridors. **Parking:** valet only. **Terms:** check-in 4 pm. **Amenities:** safes. **Dining:** 3 restaurants. **Pool(s):** heated outdoor, heated indoor. **Activities:** sauna, hot tub, steamroom, regulation golf, tennis, downhill & cross country skiing, recreation programs, playground, game room, trails, spa. **Guest Services:** valet and coin laundry.

RIVER CLUB CONDOMINIUMS
970/239-0140

fyi Not evaluated. **Address:** 550 W Depot Ave 81435 **Location:** Just w of jct Townsend St. Facilities, services, and décor characterize an upscale property. Each upscale condo offers a stone fireplace, local art and steam showers. Relax by soaking in the deep tub or sitting on your balcony, then sink into a luxurious bed with Egyptian cotton sheets.

WHERE TO EAT

221 SOUTH OAK ST BISTRO
970/728-9507

American. Fine Dining. $28-$39 AAA Inspector Notes: This intimate bistro serves creative, quality food in a tastefully furnished historic home just steps from the gondola. The menu changes seasonally. Dishes may include buttermilk-fried quail, seared foie gras, marinated bison hanger steak, Rocky Mountain trout with duo of ravioli and truffle oil, and elk rib-eye with hazelnut and red wine jus. **Features:** full bar, Sunday brunch. **Address:** 221 S Oak St 81435 **Location:** Just s of Aspen St and SR 145 (Colorado Ave) to Pacific Ave, just e to Oak St, then just s. **Parking:** street only.

ALLRED'S RESTAURANT
970/728-7474

Steak Seafood. Fine Dining. $28-$45 AAA Inspector Notes: To enjoy one of Colorado's most unique dining experiences, patrons ride the free gondola up 10,551 feet to this restaurant with exquisite views, impressive décor and a menu that changes seasonally. Past dishes have included Wagyu beef carpaccio, seared scallops, Duroc pork tenderloin and braised pork cheeks, pan-roasted Alaskan halibut, and Angus beef tenderloin. The award-winning wine list and elegant desserts are sure to please. **Features:** full bar, happy hour. **Reservations:** suggested. **Address:** 565 Mountain Village Blvd 81435 **Location:** Gondola Station Saint Sophia; in Mountain Village. **Parking:** no self-parking.

BAKED IN TELLURIDE
970/728-4775

Breads/Pastries Pizza. Quick Serve. $3-$13 AAA Inspector Notes: Before a hike or hitting the ski slopes, drop in for a freshly baked donut or a breakfast burrito. Order your favorite full-size pizza or select individual slices. Other menu options include a roast beef sandwich, fettuccine Alfredo, and enchiladas. Arranged side by side, the tables can accommodate large and small groups. **Features:** beer & wine. **Address:** 127 S Fir St 81435 **Location:** Just s of SR 145/Colorado Ave. **Parking:** street only.

BROWN DOG PIZZA 970/728-8046

▼ Pizza Sandwiches. Casual Dining. $10-$20 **AAA Inspector Notes:** Although specialty pizzas, including the square Detroit style, make this sports bar a popular city institution, the menu also lists pasta, burgers, salads and many other options. Patrons can stop in for a drink or quick meal. **Features:** full bar. **Address:** 110 E Colorado Ave 81435 **Location:** On SR 145, at Pine St; in historic downtown. **Parking:** street only. [L] [D] [AC]

COSMOPOLITAN OF TELLURIDE 970/728-1292

▼▼▼ American. Fine Dining. $21-$49 **AAA Inspector Notes:** Next to the gondola, this classy yet casual restaurant affords wonderful views of the nearby mountains. Start with the house-made burrata, the lobster corn dogs or the raw tuna poke. Entrées include beef filet, duck breast and Colorado lamb. End with the slightly sweet blueberry pie served with tart, sour cream ice cream. **Features:** full bar, happy hour. **Reservations:** suggested. **Address:** 301 W San Juan Ave 81435 **Location:** At Aspen St and San Juan Ave; in Hotel Columbia. **Parking:** street only. [D] [AC]

HONGA'S LOTUS PETAL 970/728-5134

▼▼ Asian. Casual Dining. $16-$32 **AAA Inspector Notes:** Start with some fresh oysters, fennel and pork pot stickers, or beef carpaccio. For a light meal, select from sashimi plates and sushi rolls. Larger entrées include Colorado rack of lamb, pad thai and braised short rib. Unwind with a specialty cocktail like the tart, ginger mojito, or the refreshing cucumber margarita. If you can, opt for a seat next to the window overlooking the main street. **Features:** full bar, patio dining. **Address:** 135 E Colorado Ave 81435 **Location:** Between Pine and Willow sts. **Parking:** street only. [D] [AC]

LA COCINA DE LUZ 970/728-9355

▼ Mexican. Quick Serve. $10-$17 **AAA Inspector Notes:** This restaurant provides mostly organic, Mexican dishes for locals and travelers on the go. You can take your meal to a picnic table outside or to your favorite area destination. **Features:** beer & wine. **Address:** 123 E Colorado Ave 81435 **Location:** On SR 145 (Colorado Ave), just e of Pine St. **Parking:** street only. [B] [L] [D] [AC]

LA MARMOTTE 970/728-6232

▼▼ French. Fine Dining. $20-$49 **AAA Inspector Notes:** Guests can savor a cozy, intimate meal in this French country-style cottage. Professionally prepared, modern French dishes may include lamb, seafood, pork, venison or veal choices. For dessert, try the creatively presented crème brûlée or chocolate molten cake. **Features:** full bar, patio dining. **Address:** 150 W San Juan Ave 81435 **Location:** Just e of San Juan Ave and Fir St. **Parking:** street only. [D] [AC]

NEW SHERIDAN CHOP HOUSE 970/728-9100

▼▼▼ Steak. Fine Dining. $9-$43 **AAA Inspector Notes:** Diners appreciate the convivial ambiance and stylish décor of the chophouse, which presents a menu of excellent-quality beef, wild game, pasta, seafood and nicely presented side dishes. The staff is friendly, hospitable and knowledgeable. **Features:** full bar, patio dining. **Reservations:** suggested. **Address:** 233 W Colorado Ave 81435 **Location:** At SR 145 (Colorado Ave) and Oak St; in New Sheridan Hotel. **Parking:** street only. [B] [L] [D]

RUSTICO RISTORANTE 970/728-4046

▼▼▼ Italian. Fine Dining. $20-$28 **AAA Inspector Notes:** Italian dishes are served in an elegant setting. Wine lovers will delight in sampling something from the extensive list of Italian wines. Start with the light tomato and olive bruschetta, insalata caprese or calamari. Entrees include homemade ravioli, mushroom fettuccine or traditional Italian pizza. Try the lightly sweet, spongy tiramisu. In summer, guests can enjoy their meal on the patio, a popular spot to watch passers-by or enjoy the mountain view. **Features:** full bar, patio dining. **Address:** 114 E Colorado Ave 81435 **Location:** Just e of historic downtown. **Parking:** street only. [L] [D] [AC]

SIAM 970/728-6886

▼▼ Thai. Casual Dining. $14-$29 **AAA Inspector Notes:** Warm, trendy decor complements the spicy and tasty Thai cuisine, including red or green curry and pad thai, and mouthwatering sweet sticky rice with mango. **Features:** full bar. **Address:** 200 S Davis St 81435 **Location:** At Davis St and W Pacific Ave, just s of SR 145 (Colorado Ave). **Parking:** street only. [D] [AC]

TRACKS CAFE & BAR 970/728-0677

▼ American. Quick Serve. $5-$8 **AAA Inspector Notes:** With an excellent location right near the gondola, this eatery makes it easy to grab a quick bite before heading up the mountain. The menu consists of soups, salads and sandwiches as well as pastries. Sit on the patio and enjoy the view. The bar is open later than the café. **Features:** full bar, patio dining. **Address:** 670 Mountain Village Blvd 81435 **Location:** At Mountain Village, the base of Lift 4. [B] [L] [AC]

THORNTON pop. 118,772
• **Part of Denver area — see map p. 116**

HOLIDAY INN EXPRESS HOTEL & SUITES - DENVER NORTH/THORNTON (303)452-0800

▼▼▼ Hotel $129-$275 **Address:** 12030 Grant St 80241 **Location:** I-25 exit 223, just e, then just n. **Parking:** 85 units. 4 stories, interior corridors. **Terms:** cancellation fee imposed. **Amenities:** safes. **Pool(s):** heated indoor. **Activities:** hot tub, exercise room. **Guest Services:** valet and coin laundry.

CALL [&M] [🚗] [BIZ] [HS] [📶] [✕] [🛏] [🖥] [💻]

/ SOME UNITS [S🛎]

WHERE TO EAT

UNITED CHINESE RESTAURANT 720/977-8888

▼ Chinese. Casual Dining. $7-$16 **AAA Inspector Notes:** Expect large portions of your favorite Chinese dishes served piping hot. Entrées include sesame chicken, sweet and sour pork, beef with broccoli, and Peking duck. In addition, the menu offers Thai curries and sushi rolls. **Features:** full bar. **Address:** 4150 E 128th Ave 80241 **Location:** I-25 exit 223, 2.5 mi e to Colorado Blvd, 1 mi n, then just e. [L] [D]

TRINIDAD (F-5) pop. 9,096, elev. 6,019'

Trinidad, below the Santa Fe Trail's landmark Fisher's Peak, began as a supply center for the westward trail. The historic downtown area, designated *Corazon de Trinidad* (Heart of Trinidad), is known for its Victorian architecture, brick streets, shops and restaurants. The town was shaped by the influence of the Spanish, who came from the Southwest, and by the ranching and mining interests to the east and north. An early visitor was scout Kit Carson, whose name and statue mark a park on Kansas Street.

Leading west from the city, SR 12 travels about 35 miles through the Purgatoire Valley to 1,200-acre Monument Lake Park, part of Trinidad's city park system. The route then crosses 9,941-foot Cucharas Pass in a portion of the San Isabel National Forest *(see place listing p. 255)* and passes through La Veta, joining US 160 west of Walsenburg.

Trinidad & Las Animas County Chamber of Commerce: 136 W. Main St., Trinidad, CO 81082. **Phone:** (719) 846-9285.

ARTHUR ROY MITCHELL MEMORIAL MUSEUM OF WESTERN ART is at 150 E. Main St. in the center of the *Corazon de Trinidad* National Historic District. The museum features the work of Arthur Roy Mitchell, known as the "king" of western pulp magazine illustration, as well as works by illustrators Harvey Dunn and Harold Von Schmidt.

Other displays include a collection of early Hispanic religious folk art, Western memorabilia, Native American artifacts and early photographs of Trinidad. **Time:** Allow 1 hour minimum. **Hours:** Wed.-Sun. 11-5. **Cost:** $5 (Mon.-Sat.); $20 (family); free (each Sun.). **Phone:** (719) 846-4224.

TRINIDAD HISTORY MUSEUM, 312 E. Main St., is comprised of several properties that illustrate early settlers' lives. The museum complex includes the Bloom Mansion, Baca House, Santa Fe Trail Museum and the Heritage Gardens. Guided house tours are available by appointment. **Hours:** Museums Mon.-Sat. 10-4, May-Sept. Gardens Mon.-Sat. 9-4, May-Sept.; Mon.-Sat. 10-4, rest of year. Closed on some state holidays. **Cost:** Tours (include Baca House, Bloom Mansion, Santa Fe Trail Museum) $12; $10 (ages 65+); $3 (ages 6-16). Gardens and gallery free. **Phone:** (719) 846-7217. [GT]

Baca House, 312 E. Main St., is a restored 1870s territorial-style adobe structure that was first home to Santa Fe Trail entrepreneur John Hough, who then sold the residence to influential pioneer Felipe Baca. Its Hispanic folk art and Victorian furnishings reflect the lifestyle of Dolores and Felipe Baca, who were among the earliest settlers of Trinidad. The two-story home features a widow's walk and Greek architectural details. The ticket office is at 312 E. Main St. **Hours:** Mon.-Sat. 10-4, May-Sept. Closed state holidays. **Cost:** (includes Bloom Mansion and Santa Fe Trail Museum) $12; $10 (ages 65+); $3 (ages 6-16). **Phone:** (719) 846-7217.

Bloom Mansion, 312 E. Main St., was built in 1882 as a family home for banker and cattle baron Frank G. Bloom. The mansion is currently being restored, and a guided tour about the Bloom family, the boarding house era and the restoration project is available. The ticket office is at 312 E. Main St. **Hours:** Mon.-Sat. 10-4, May-Sept. Closed on state holidays. **Cost:** (includes Baca House and Santa Fe Trail Museum) $12; $10 (ages 65+); $4 (ages 6-16). **Phone:** (719) 846-7217.

Heritage Gardens, 312 E. Main St., surround the Baca House and Bloom Mansion. They contain century-old trees, heirloom herbs, flowers, vegetables and roses, and showcase water wise plants. **Hours:** Mon.-Sat. 9-4, May-Sept.; Mon.-Sat. 10-4, rest of year. Closed on state holidays. **Cost:** Free. **Phone:** (719) 846-7217.

Santa Fe Trail Museum, 120 S. Chestnut St., is a one-story adobe building that originally served as living quarters for the Baca family's domestic workers. It contains exhibits that depict the heydays of the Santa Fe Trail through the railroad and coal mining eras. Historic photographs, commercial goods, family heirlooms and a buckskin coat given to a Trinidad mayor by Kit Carson are among the items presented. Tickets can be purchased directly at the museum or at the main ticket office at 312 E. Main St. **Hours:** Mon.-Sat. 10-4, May-Sept. Closed

on state holidays. **Cost:** (includes Baca House and Bloom Mansion) $12; $10 (ages 65+); $4 (ages 6-16). **Phone:** (719) 846-7217.

DAYS INN & SUITES TRINIDAD   (719)846-2215

Motel
$60-$110

Address: 900 W Adams St 81082 **Location:** I-25 exit 13A northbound; exit 13B southbound, just e to Santa Fe Tr, then 0.3 mi s. **Facility:** 55 units. 2 stories (no elevator), exterior corridors. **Pool(s):** heated outdoor. **Activities:** hot tub. **Guest Services:** coin laundry. **Featured Amenity: full hot breakfast.**

[SAVE] 🏊 [BIZ] 📶 🛏 🖥 🖥 / SOME UNITS 🐕 [HS]

HOLIDAY INN & SUITES   (719)845-8400

Hotel
$130-$175

Address: 3130 Santa Fe Trail Dr 81082 **Location:** I-25 exit 11 (Starkville), just e, then just n. **Facility:** 86 units. 3 stories, interior corridors. **Pool(s):** heated indoor. **Activities:** hot tub, exercise room.
Guest Services: coin laundry.

[SAVE] 🍴 🍸 CALL 🔵M 🏊 [BIZ] [HS] 📶 ✕ 🖥 / SOME UNITS 🐕 🛏 🖥

LA QUINTA INN & SUITES TRINIDAD   (719)845-0102

Hotel $86-$240 **Address:** 2833 Toupal Dr 81082 **Location:** I-25 exit 11 (Starkville), just w, then n. **Facility:** 100 units, interior corridors. **Pool(s):** heated indoor. **Activities:** hot tub, picnic facilities, exercise room, massage. **Guest Services:** valet and coin laundry.

🍴 🏊 [BIZ] [HS] 📶 🛏 🖥 🖥 / SOME UNITS 🐕

WHERE TO EAT

BELLA LUNA PIZZERIA   719/846-2750

Pizza Sandwiches. Casual Dining. $7-$19 **AAA Inspector Notes:** This attractive eatery serves delicious wood-fired gourmet pizza (the oven was imported from Italy) and offers a nice selection of healthy salads. Be forewarned, the breadsticks are addictive. **Features:** beer & wine, patio dining. **Address:** 121 W Main St 81082 **Location:** I-25 exit 13B, just e; downtown. **Parking:** street only.

[L] [D]

THE CAFE   719/846-7119

Breads/Pastries. Quick Serve. $5-$11 **AAA Inspector Notes:** The gourmet sandwiches, salads and baked goods at this cozy café draw locals and visitors from surrounding towns. Fresh ingredients, flavorful food combinations and decadent desserts please even the toughest critic. The unique décor mixes exposed brick with enchanting glass chandeliers. **Features:** patio dining. **Address:** 135 E Main St 81082 **Location:** Historic town center. **Parking:** street only.

[B] [L]

RINO'S ITALIAN RESTAURANT & STEAKHOUSE
719/845-0949

Italian. Casual Dining. $14-$26 **AAA Inspector Notes:** Owner and head chef Frank Cordova clearly loves entertaining and sharing fine food with his patrons. Although born and raised in this city, he spent 25 years in Las Vegas, singing and waiting tables at his brother's Italian restaurant. The Cordovas brought this family tradition back to Colorado, where Frank and his friendly waitstaff still burst into song every evening and Frank makes every effort to befriend his customers. The menu features classic Italian cuisine as well as steaks. **Features:** full bar. **Address:** 400 E Main St 81082 **Location:** In historic downtown. **Parking:** street only. [D]

TWIN LAKES pop. 171

TWIN LAKES ROADHOUSE LODGE   719/486-9345

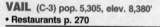

Historic Bed
& Breakfast

$108-$235

Address: 6411 E Hwy 82 81251 **Location:** Center. **Facility:** This quaint lodge offers intimate and elegant rooms overlooking glacial lakes, an adorable cottage, two cabins and a carriage house with a fireplace and front porch. 7 units, some kitchens and cabins. 1 story, interior/exterior corridors. **Terms:** closed 5/21-10/2, check-in 4 pm, 14 day cancellation notice-fee imposed. **Activities:** fishing, trails. **Guest Services:** coin laundry. **Featured Amenity:** continental breakfast.

[icons]
/SOME UNITS [icons]

VAIL (C-3) pop. 5,305, elev. 8,380'
• Restaurants p. 270

Vail is one of Colorado's flourishing resort centers. Internationally known for its extensive winter sports facilities, the Bavarian-style town also offers year-round access to recreation in the surrounding White River National Forest *(see place listing p. 274)*. The resort was founded in 1962 by members of the 10th Mountain Division who trained near Vail at Camp Hale.

Athletes, art and music converge in Vail each June for the annual Teva Mountain Games, which feature trail running, rock climbing, kayaking, adventure racing and mountain biking competitions. In summer, Vail hosts a series of music, theater and dance event that include the Bravo! Vail Valley Music Festival and the Vail International Dance Festival. In mid-September the town celebrates Oktoberfest early with [icon] Vail Oktoberfest, which features traditional German food, music and beer.

Vail Valley Partnership, the Chamber and Tourism Bureau: Vail Village, 101 Fawcett Rd., Ste. 240, Avon, CO 81620; P.O. Box 1130, Vail, CO 81658. **Phone:** (970) 476-1000.

BETTY FORD ALPINE GARDENS is off I-70 exit 176 to 530 S. Frontage Rd. in Ford Park. An alpine rock garden showcases a 120-foot cascading waterfall and hundreds of native plants that depict alpine and subalpine habitats. A perennial garden features more than 1,500 varieties of plants, and a meditation garden combines Asian design and philosophy with Rocky Mountain plantings. Prime viewing season is May through September. A children's garden features a treasure hunt, a discovery cart and a schoolhouse museum. Children's programs also are offered.

Time: Allow 30 minutes minimum. **Hours:** Daily dawn-dusk. Guided tours are offered Mon., Thurs. and Sat. at 10:30, Memorial Day weekend-Labor Day.

Hours and dates may vary; phone ahead. Children's programs Wed. at 10:30, mid-June to mid-Aug. **Cost:** Gardens free. Tours hand children's programs $5. Gardens by donations. **Phone:** (970) 476-0103.

COLORADO SKI AND SNOWBOARD MUSEUM AND HALL OF FAME is 2 blks. e. of I-70 exit 176 at 231 S. Frontage Rd. E., in the Vail Village parking structure. The Hall of Fame honors those who have made significant contributions to skiing and snowboarding in Colorado. Museum exhibits commemorate milestones in Colorado's skiing history and the winter Olympics. A replica of the 10th Mountain Division's Camp Hale is also on display. Videos about skiing are shown.

Time: Allow 30 minutes minimum. **Hours:** Tues.-Sun. 10-5. Closed Thanksgiving and Christmas. **Cost:** Donations. **Phone:** (970) 476-1876 or (800) 950-7410. [GT]

RECREATIONAL ACTIVITIES
Skiing

• **Vail Ski Resort** is off I-70 exit 176 in White River National Forest. Other activities are offered. **Hours:** Daily 8:30-4, mid-Nov. to mid-Apr. **Phone:** (970) 754-4888 for snow conditions, or (800) 500-5155 for general information.

THE ARRABELLE AT VAIL SQUARE, A ROCKRESORT
970/754-7777

Resort Hotel
Rates not provided

Address: 675 Lionshead Pl 81657 **Location:** I-70 exit 176, just s to roundabout, 1 mi w on Frontage Rd to W Lionshead Cir, continue just s past No Outlet sign. Located at base of gondola. **Facility:** This grand ski-in/ski-out hotel exudes European charm. Rich wood furnishings, Picasso marble counters, and oil paintings enhance the guest room décor. Drapery above the bed hides two reading lights. 91 units, some condominiums. 4-7 stories, interior corridors. **Parking:** valet only. **Terms:** check-in 4 pm. **Amenities:** safes. **Pool(s):** heated outdoor. **Activities:** sauna, hot tub, steamroom, downhill & cross country skiing, ice skating, recreation programs, bicycles, trails, exercise room, spa. **Guest Services:** valet laundry, area transportation.

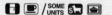

EVERGREEN LODGE AT VAIL   970/476-7810

[icons] **Hotel.** Rates not provided. **Address:** 250 S Frontage Rd W 81657 **Location:** I-70 exit 176, just s, then just w. **Facility:** 128 units. 7 stories, interior corridors. **Terms:** check-in 4 pm. **Pool(s):** heated outdoor. **Activities:** sauna, hot tub, game room, trails, exercise room. **Guest Services:** valet laundry.

[icons]
/SOME UNITS [icons]

FOUR SEASONS RESORT & RESIDENCES VAIL
(970)477-8600

Resort Hotel
$215-$875

Address: One Vail Rd 81657 **Location:** I-70 exit 176, just s, then just w of round-about. **Facility:** Luxurious rooms feature modern, mountain-style décor, a fireplace and a balcony. Marble vanities and tile enhance the spacious bathrooms. 135 units, some two bedrooms, three bed-rooms and kitchens. 10 stories, interior corridors. **Parking:** valet only. **Terms:** check-in 4 pm, 7 day cancellation notice-fee imposed, resort fee. **Amenities:** safes. **Pool(s):** heated outdoor. **Activities:** sauna, hot tub, steamroom, fishing, downhill & cross country skiing, ice skating, kids club, bicycles, game room, trails, spa. **Guest Services:** valet laundry, boarding pass kiosk, area transportation.

HOLIDAY INN APEX VAIL
(970)476-2739

Hotel. $109-$399 **Address:** 2211 N Frontage Rd 81657 **Location:** I-70 exit 173, just n to roundabout, then 0.3 mi e. **Facility:** 115 units, some condominiums. 4 stories, interior corridors. **Terms:** check-in 4 pm, 15 day cancellation notice-fee imposed, resort fee. **Amenities:** safes. **Dining:** 2 restaurants, also, Westside Cafe & Market, see separate listing. **Pool(s):** heated outdoor. **Activities:** hot tub, steamroom, trails, exercise room, massage. **Guest Services:** valet and coin laundry, area transportation.

LION SQUARE LODGE
970/476-2281

Hotel. Rates not provided. **Address:** 660 W Lionshead Pl 81657 **Location:** I-70 exit 176, just s to roundabout, 1 mi w on Frontage Rd to W Lionshead Cir, then just s past No Outlet sign. Located at base of gondola. **Facility:** 133 units, some condominiums. 4-7 stories, interior/exterior corridors. **Parking:** on-site and valet. **Terms:** check-in 4 pm. **Amenities:** safes. **Pool(s):** heated outdoor. **Activities:** sauna, hot tub, fishing, downhill skiing, bicycles, trails, exercise room. **Guest Services:** valet and coin laundry, area transportation.

THE LODGE AT VAIL, A ROCKRESORT & SPA
970/754-7800

Hotel. Rates not provided. **Address:** 174 E Gore Creek Dr 81657 **Location:** I-70 exit 176, 0.3 mi s on Vail Rd to Gore Creek Dr. **Facility:** 165 units, some condominiums. 5 stories, interior/exterior corridors. **Parking:** valet only. **Terms:** check-in 4 pm. **Amenities:** safes. **Dining:** 2 restaurants. **Pool(s):** heated outdoor. **Activities:** sauna, hot tub, steamroom, spa. **Guest Services:** valet and coin laundry, area transportation.

MANOR VAIL LODGE
970/476-5000

Condominium. Rates not provided. **Address:** 595 E Vail Valley Dr 81657 **Location:** I-70 exit 176, just s, take third exit at roundabout, 0.4 mi e to Vail Valley Dr, then 0.3 mi se. **Facility:** This lodge has attractive landscaping and inviting public areas that feature Native American and mountain-theme artwork. Each unit is individually decorated by the owners. 99 condominiums. 2-4 stories, exterior corridors. **Parking:** on-site (fee). **Terms:** check-in 5 pm. **Activities:** sauna, hot tub, steamroom, downhill & cross country skiing, bicycles, trails, exercise room, spa. **Guest Services:** valet and coin laundry.

MARRIOTT'S STREAMSIDE AT VAIL
(970)476-6000

Resort Condominium $58-$461

AAA Benefit: Members save 5% or more!

Address: 2284 S Frontage Rd W 81657 **Location:** I-70 exit 173, 2nd exit at south roundabout. **Facility:** Surrounded by aspen and evergreen trees, each building has its own public sitting area. Head to the club-house to swim in the 9-foot-deep pool, get in a workout, or take a yoga class. 96 condominiums. 3-5 stories, interior corridors. **Terms:** check-in 4 pm, 14 day cancellation notice. **Amenities:** safes. **Pool(s):** heated outdoor, heated indoor. **Activities:** sauna, hot tub, steamroom, recreation programs, playground, game room, trails, exercise room. **Guest Services:** complimentary and valet laundry, area transportation.

MONTANEROS CONDOMINIUMS
970/476-2491

Condominium. Rates not provided. **Address:** 684 W Lionshead Cir 81657 **Location:** I-70 exit 176, just s, take 1st exit at roundabout, 0.3 mi w on S Frontage Rd, then just s. **Facility:** Individually decorated by each owner, units features all the amenities of an apartment, including a balcony or patio with a barbecue grill. You can easily walk to the gondola, shops and restaurants. 36 condominiums. 4 stories, exterior corridors. **Terms:** check-in 4 pm. **Amenities:** safes. **Pool(s):** heated outdoor. **Activities:** sauna, hot tub, downhill skiing. **Guest Services:** valet and coin laundry.

THE SEBASTIAN- VAIL
(970)315-4214

Boutique Resort Hotel
$295-$6250

Address: 16 Vail Rd 81657 **Location:** I-70 exit 176, just s, take 2nd exit at roundabout, then just s. **Facility:** This luxury hotel features stellar suites with fireplaces and Bose speakers, a variety of tastefully appointed guest rooms, and a private on-mountain ski valet with a café at the base of the mountain. 107 units, some condominiums. 6 stories, interior corridors. **Parking:** valet only. **Terms:** check-in 4 pm, 31 day cancellation notice-fee imposed, resort fee. **Amenities:** safes. **Dining:** Leonora, see separate listing. **Pool(s):** heated outdoor. **Activities:** sauna, hot tub, steamroom, downhill & cross country skiing, recreation programs in season, bicycles, trails, exercise room, spa. **Guest Services:** valet laundry, area transportation.

SITZMARK LODGE
970/476-5001

Hotel. Rates not provided. **Address:** 183 Gore Creek Dr 81657 **Location:** I-70 exit 176, s on Vail Rd to center of village through guard check point. **Facility:** 35 units, some kitchens. 3 stories, interior corridors. **Terms:** check-in 4 pm. **Amenities:** safes. **Dining:** The Left Bank, see separate listing. **Pool(s):** heated outdoor. **Activities:** hot tub, bicycles, picnic facilities, trails, exercise room. **Guest Services:** valet and coin laundry.

VAIL CASCADE RESORT & SPA
970/476-7111

Resort Hotel. Rates not provided. **Address:** 1300 Westhaven Dr 81657 **Location:** I-70 exit 176, 1.3 mi w via S Frontage Rd; 1 mi e of exit 173. **Facility:** This spacious, riverside resort sits in a quiet area a short drive or shuttle ride from Vail Village. Since it has its own ski lift, you won't have to leave the property to hit the slopes. 292 units. 5 stories, interior corridors. **Parking:** on-site (fee) and valet. **Terms:** check-in 4 pm. **Amenities:** safes. **Dining:** 2 restaurants. **Pool(s):** heated outdoor. **Activities:** hot tub, steamroom, fishing, tennis, downhill skiing, recreation programs, bicycles, trails, spa. **Guest Services:** valet and coin laundry, area transportation.

VAIL MARRIOTT MOUNTAIN RESORT   (970)476-4444

Resort Hotel
$123-$707

AAA Benefit: Members save 5% or more!

MARRIOTT

Address: 715 W Lionshead Cir 81657 **Location:** I-70 exit 176, just s, take first exit at roundabout, 0.8 mi w on Frontage Rd, then just s. **Facility:** Ski lodge-style common areas and handsomely decorated rooms enhance this large-scale resort. 344 units, some condominiums. 7 stories, interior corridors. **Parking:** valet only. **Terms:** check-in 4 pm, 4 day cancellation notice, resort fee. **Amenities:** video games, safes. **Dining:** 2 restaurants. **Pool(s):** heated outdoor, heated indoor. **Activities:** hot tub, steamroom, fishing, downhill & cross country skiing, snowmobiling, bicycles, game room, trails, exercise room, spa. **Guest Services:** valet and coin laundry, boarding pass kiosk, area transportation.

[SAVE] [Y1] [icons] CALL [icons] [BIZ] [HS] [wifi] [X] [icons] / SOME UNITS [icon]

AUSTRIA HAUS HOTEL   970/754-7850

[fyi] **Hotel** Did not meet all AAA rating requirements for locking devices in some guest rooms at time of last evaluation on 02/25/2014. **Address:** 242 E Meadow Dr 81657 **Location:** I-70 exit 176, just s to roundabout, just e on S Frontage Rd to Village Center Rd, then just s; in Vail Village. This hotel's rooms have excellent appointments, including some with fireplaces, while the bathrooms feature upscale amenities and marble accents.

SIMBA RUN CONDOMINIUMS   970/476-0344

[fyi] Not evaluated. **Address:** 1100 N Frontage Rd 81657 **Location:** I-70 exit 176, just n, then 1.2 mi w. Facilities, services, and décor characterize an economy property.

SOLARIS RESIDENCES   970/476-9000

[fyi] Not evaluated. **Address:** 141 E Meadow Dr, Suite 1000 81657 **Location:** I-70 exit 176, just s, 3rd exit at roundabout, 0.3 mi e to Vail Center Rd, just s, then just w. Facilities, services, and décor characterize an upscale property.

SONNENALP HOTEL   970/476-5656

[fyi] Not evaluated; management refused inspection. **Address:** 20 Vail Rd 81657 **Location:** I-70 exit 176, just s, take 2nd exit at the roundabout, then just s. Facilities, services, and décor characterize a mid-scale property. An international staff strives to pamper and please guests at this resort, which is situated at the entry to Vail Village. Public areas are handsomely appointed with distinct European touches.

VAIL SPA CONDOMINIUMS   970/476-0882

[fyi] Not evaluated. **Address:** 710 W Lionshead Cir 81657 **Location:** I-70 exit 176, 0.4 mi w on S Frontage Rd. Facilities, services, and décor characterize a mid-scale property.

WILLOWS CONDOMINIUMS   970/476-2233

[fyi] Not evaluated. **Address:** 74 Willow Rd 81657 **Location:** I-70 exit 176, just s toward village on Vail Rd, then e. Facilities, services, and décor characterize an upscale property.

AAA.com/ TourBook Comments

Let Your Voice Be Heard

If your visit to a TourBook-listed property doesn't meet your expectations, tell us about it.

AAA.com/TourBookComments

WHERE TO EAT

ALPENROSE   970/476-8899

German. Casual Dining. $14-$19 **AAA Inspector Notes:** Transport yourself to the German Alps with a meal at this casual eatery. Start with some fondue, baked Brie or smoked salmon. Entrées include bratwurst, Wiener Schnitzel and kasespatzle. For a true treat, try one of the freshly made Belgian pastries. **Features:** full bar. **Address:** 100 E Meadow Dr 81657 **Location:** I-70 exit 176, third exit at south roundabout, 0.4 mi e on Frontage Rd to Vail Valley Dr, then just w; in East Vail Village. [L] [D]

THE BLUE MOOSE   970/476-8666

Pizza. Family Dining. $8-$14 **AAA Inspector Notes:** This popular eatery offers hand-tossed, New York-style pizzas, calzones and classic pasta dishes. There is an actual blue moose, and the walls are decorated with children's artwork. **Features:** full bar. **Address:** 675 Lionshead Pl, Suite P170 81657 **Location:** I-70 exit 176, just s to roundabout, 1 mi w on Frontage Rd to W Lionshead Cir, continue just s past no outlet sign; near The Arrabelle at Vail Square, A RockResort. **Parking:** no self-parking. [L] [D] [AC]

BOL VAIL   970/476-5300

American. Casual Dining. $16-$36 **AAA Inspector Notes:** The tasty seasonal menu includes creatively presented dishes such as bibb and beet root salad, olive oil poached salmon with charred onion vinaigrette, steamed pork buns, spicy honeyglazed ribs, bucatini alla Bolognese, American Kobe steak or a two-tier platter of fresh seafood. You can opt to dine and bowl in a separate quiet and upscale area. Each custom white bowling lane comes with a lounge area and oversize couches. **Features:** full bar, patio dining. **Reservations:** suggested. **Address:** 141 E Meadow Dr 81657 **Location:** I-70 exit 176, just s, 3rd exit at roundabout, 0.3 mi e to Vail Center Rd, just s, then just w; in Solaris Residences. **Parking:** on-site (fee) and valet. [D] [AC]

CAMPO DI FIORI   970/476-8994

Italian. Fine Dining. $21-$36 **AAA Inspector Notes:** Popular with locals, this restaurant offers classic cuisine in an intimate setting. Start the evening with beef carpaccio, lightly fried calamari or some fresh burrata cheese. Pasta dishes include homemade pappardelle, mushroom ravioli and gnocchi. Other entrées include steak, chicken, veal and seafood. **Features:** full bar, patio dining. **Address:** 100 East Meadow Dr 81657 **Location:** I-70 exit 176, just s, just e on S Frontage Rd, then just s. **Parking:** no self-parking. [D] [AC]

KELLY LIKEN   970/479-0175

American. Fine Dining. $35-$42 **AAA Inspector Notes:** The eponymous chef uses high-quality, fresh and local ingredients in her innovative menu creations, which changes seasonally. Sample menu items include Rocky Mountain elk carpaccio, Durham Ranch quail, Colorado lamb loin and pan-roasted Berkshire pork tenderloin. **Features:** full bar. **Reservations:** suggested. **Address:** 12 Vail Rd, Suite 100 81657 **Location:** I-70 exit 176, just past south roundabout; in The Gateway Building. **Parking:** valet only. [D]

LA TOUR RESTAURANT & BAR   970/476-4403

French. Fine Dining. $15-$44 **AAA Inspector Notes:** Expect artfully presented, flavorful dishes from this upscale eatery. The seasonally changing menu features a modern twist on French classics like the truffle cheese and braised short rib French onion soup, escargot, and pan-roasted duck breast with a hibiscus confit leg. For something a little different, start with the yellowtail tuna sashimi presented in a container that emits smoke when opened. The herbaceous sprouts and earthy sesame seeds enhance the smoky flavor of the fish. **Features:** full bar, patio dining, Sunday brunch, happy hour. **Reservations:** suggested. **Address:** 122 E Meadow Dr 81657 **Location:** I-70 exit 176, just s, just e on S Frontage Rd, then just s; across from Vail Village parking deck. **Parking:** on-site (fee). [L] [D]

THE LEFT BANK   970/476-3696

French. Fine Dining. $30-$56 **AAA Inspector Notes:** The seasonally changing menu may feature foie gras, Colorado lamb, and organic salmon prepared using classic French techniques. Unique light fixtures and colorful flowers enhance the sleek white and grey décor. In the summer, try to reserve a table near a window and enjoy watching the river flow by as the sun sets. **Features:** full bar. **Reservations:** suggested. **Address:** 183 Gore Creek Dr 81657 **Location:** I-70 exit 176, s on Vail Rd to center of village through guard check point; in Sitzmark Lodge. **Parking:** no self-parking. [D]

LEONORA   970/315-4213

▼▼▼▼ Small Plates. Fine Dining. $15-$38 **AAA Inspector Notes:** The seasonal menu focuses on small plates with tapas, fish crudos and appetizers taking up a full page. Sample items include Parmesan consommé with scallop, Catalan-style potatoes, octopus and Wagyu beef sliders. Entrées feature duck, local lamb, halibut and steak. The rich, warm décor is accented with unique modern sculptures and artistic light fixtures. **Features:** full bar, patio dining. **Reservations:** suggested. **Address:** 16 Vail Rd 81657 **Location:** I-70 exit 176, just s, take 2nd exit at roundabout, then just s; in The Sebastian- Vail. **Parking:** valet only.

[B] [D] CALL [&][M]

THE LITTLE DINER   970/476-4279

▼▼ Breakfast Sandwiches. Casual Dining. $9-$14 **AAA Inspector Notes:** A hidden gem, this old-fashioned style diner has limited seating of about 16 stools set against a counter. The reason for the long lines in the busy season is the made-from-scratch eats comprised of fresh eats. Highlights include the huevos rancheros, corned beef hash, and the eggs Benedict, served with a creamy, tart hollandaise sauce. Lunch options include burgers, Philly cheesesteaks, and Cincinnati chili. **Address:** 616 W Lionshead Cir 81657 **Location:** I-70 exit 176, just s, take 1st exit at roundabout to S Frontage Rd W, then 0.7 mi w; park at Visitor Parking; west end of Lionshead Plaza. **Parking:** no self-parking.

[B] [L] [AC]

MATSUHISA VAIL   970/476-6628

▼▼▼▼ Sushi. Fine Dining. $19-$39 **AAA Inspector Notes:** Created by noted celebrity chef Nobu Matsuhisa, this is not a standard sushi eatery. Start with the bincho with dry miso or a spicy tuna roll. Next, try the meaty sea bass served in a sweet marinade with an earthy eggplant dip. For a unique experience, splurge on the "omakase" chef's tasting menu. Try one of the cocktails made with shōchū, a Japanese distilled alcohol. High ceilings and large glass windows facing the mountains give the restaurant an airy feel. **Features:** full bar, patio dining. **Reservations:** required. **Address:** 141 E Meadow Dr 81657 **Location:** I-70 exit 176, just s, 3rd exit at roundabout, 0.3 mi e to Vail Center Rd, just s, then just w; in Solaris Residences. **Parking:** on-site (fee) and valet. [D]

MOUNTAIN STANDARD   970/476-0123

▼▼▼▼ American. Casual Dining. $13-$38 **AAA Inspector Notes:** Specializing in meats grilled over an open flame, this restaurant offers amazing food in a casual environment. Start with the whiskey-braised pork belly and end with best chocolate you've ever eaten. In between, choose from Alaskan halibut, rotisserie chicken, Colorado lamb, Rocky Mountain trout, and steaks. You'll find standard drinks like Manhattans and margaritas as well as more adventurous cocktails such as the grilled watermelon mint julep. **Features:** full bar, patio dining. **Reservations:** suggested. **Address:** 193 Gore Creek Dr 81657 **Location:** I-70 exit 176, third exit at s roundabout, 0.4 mi e on Frontage Rd to Vail Valley Dr, then just w; in east Vail Village. **Parking:** no self-parking.

[L] [D] [AC]

SWEET BASIL   970/476-0125

▼▼▼▼ American. Casual Dining. $14-$45 **AAA Inspector Notes:** This contemporary restaurant serves creative cuisine utilizing the freshest ingredients wherever possible. An upscale casual ambiance pervades the dining room, which affords a view of a creek. From the patio, diners can watch the passersby at Vail Village. The wine list features more than 500 selections from around the world. **Features:** full bar. **Reservations:** suggested. **Address:** 193 E Gore Creek Dr, Suite 201 81657 **Location:** I-70 exit 176, just s, then just e on Frontage road to public parking; in Vail Village. **Parking:** no self-parking. [L] [D] [AC]

TAVERN ON THE GORE   970/476-2828

▼▼▼▼ American. Casual Dining. $12-$35 **AAA Inspector Notes:** Prime beef, fresh seafood flown in daily for the raw bar and large healthy salads are served to diners at tables that feature private HDTVs for game watching or viewing the crackling fire channel for some ambience. A large wraparound deck is great for al fresco dining with scenic views of the surrounding mountains and babbling Gore Creek. **Features:** full bar, patio dining. **Address:** 223 Gore Creek Dr 81657 **Location:** Just n of Children's Fountain; in Vail Village. **Parking:** no self-parking. [L] [D]

TERRA BISTRO   970/476-6836

▼▼▼ Natural/Organic. Fine Dining. $29-$40 **AAA Inspector Notes:** This elegantly appointed restaurant has been serving sustainable cuisine for more than 20 years. The seasonal menu features artfully presented mussels, Rocky Mountain trout, grass-fed beef, and free-ranch chicken. **Features:** full bar, happy hour. **Address:** 352 E Meadow Dr 81657 **Location:** I-70 exit 176, just s, just e on S Frontage Rd, then just s. **Parking:** valet only.

[D] [AC]

UP THE CREEK   970/476-8141

▼▼▼ American. Fine Dining. $13-$45 **AAA Inspector Notes:** This popular restaurant enjoys a great location next to a creek and the pedestrian mall. Seasonal menu offerings include seared diver scallops, braised short ribs and some game dishes. You should park at the Vail Village public parking lot. **Features:** full bar. **Reservations:** suggested. **Address:** 223 Gore Creek Dr, Suite 103 81657 **Location:** I-70 exit 176, third exit at s roundabout, 0.4 mi e on Frontage Rd to Vail Valley Dr, then just w; in east Vail Village. **Parking:** no self-parking. [L] [D] [AC]

WESTSIDE CAFE & MARKET   970/476-7890

▼▼▼ ▼▼▼ **AAA Inspector Notes:** Hearty, flavorful food at relatively inexpensive prices combine to make this eatery a local favorite. Start with a cup of the tomato-based green chile, a hot pretzel or share the spinach artichoke dip served with naan and veggies. Locally inspired entrées include bison meatloaf, and a Southwest burger topped with green chiles, pepper jack cheese, and jalapeño cream cheese. Other options include mac and cheese with short ribs, Philly cheesesteak and "Grandma's chicken pot pie." **Features:** full bar, patio dining, Sunday brunch, happy hour. **Address:** 2211 N Frontage Rd W 81657 **Location:** I-70 exit 173, just n to roundabout, then 0.3 mi e; in Holiday Inn Apex Vail.

American
Casual Dining
$7-$27

[B] [L] [D]

YAMA SUSHI   970/476-7332

▼▼▼▼ Japanese. Fine Dining. $18-$27 **AAA Inspector Notes:** Settle into the sleek, modern dining room for the evening and enjoy innovative, artistically presented sushi and sashimi. Refreshing cocktails flavored with lychee and passion fruit enhance the dining experience. **Features:** full bar. **Reservations:** suggested. **Address:** 168 E Gore Creek Dr 81657 **Location:** I-70 exit 176, just s, then just e on Frontage road to public parking; in Vail Village. **Parking:** street only.

[D] [AC]

YELLOWBELLY CHICKEN   970/343-4340

▼ Chicken. Quick Serve. $6-$11 **AAA Inspector Notes:** Few spots in the Vail Valley offer fast-food with healthier options. Luckily, this eatery popped up to fill the void. Menu options include juicy, herbed rotisserie and skinless fried chicken. Sides include Brussels sprout slaw, kale salad, smashed potato fries and macaroni pie. Fountain drinks consist of all-natural soda. Considering Vail prices, this is a reasonable option. **Features:** beer only. **Address:** 2161 N Frontage Rd, #14 81657 **Location:** I-70 exit 173, just nw through roundabout, then just ne; in strip mall. [L] [D]

VICTOR (F-8) pop. 397, elev. 9,695'

Victor was founded in 1893 at the base of Battle Mountain, one of the world's richest sources of gold. Some 475 mines in the Cripple Creek-Victor district extracted more than $800 million in gold 1891-1961. In the prime of its mining heyday at the turn of the 20th century, the town's population topped 12,000, and dozens of trains rolled through daily.

More than 300 houses and buildings from Victor's early days still stand, including city hall, where Jack Dempsey once trained, and the *Victor Record* newspaper building, where well-known journalist Lowell Thomas worked as a young man.

Several trails wind past remnants of the 1890s gold mines and mill sites. Hikers, bicyclists and those on horseback take advantage of the sights in summer, while those on skis and snowshoes take over when the weather turns frosty.

Victor can be reached from Colorado Springs via US 24 and SR 67 through Cripple Creek, or by turning southeast onto CR 81 just before reaching Cripple Creek and following the roadbed of the old Midland Terminal Railroad.

Scenic access in summer is by the Gold Camp Road (CR 4) from Colorado Springs or the Phantom Canyon Highway (SR 67) from US 50 west of Pueblo. Only experienced drivers should attempt the Gold Camp and Phantom Canyon routes. Neither one is suitable for trailers and some RVs. Call for road conditions before starting. For Gold Camp Road and Phantom Canyon Highway, phone (719) 636-1602; (719) 275-2331 or (800) 876-7922.

Southern Teller County Focus Group: P.O. Box 328, Victor, CO 80860. **Phone:** (719) 689-2675.

Self-guiding tours: Brochures for a self-guiding walking tour of downtown Victor's historic buildings are available at the Victor Lowell Thomas Museum and at the Victor Hotel, 4th Street and Victor Avenue.

VICTOR LOWELL THOMAS MUSEUM, at jct. 3rd St. and Victor Ave., offers glimpses into the gold rush days of the 1890s as well as the life of the noted journalist, who grew up in Victor. Exhibits also feature World War II memorabilia, a local doctor's office and Victor's mining history. Gold panning and gold mine tours are available.

Time: Allow 30 minutes minimum. **Hours:** Museum and gold panning daily 9:30-5:30, Memorial Day weekend-Labor Day; Fri.-Mon. 10-5, day after Labor Day-Sept. 30. **Cost:** Museum (includes 1 hour gold panning) $6; $5 (ages 60+); $4 (ages 0-12). Mine tours $7.50. **Phone:** (719) 689-5509. GT

WALDEN (A-3) pop. 608, elev. 8,099'

RECREATIONAL ACTIVITIES

White-water Rafting

- **Wilderness Aware Rafting** departs from 4.4 mi. n. of jct. SRs 125 and 127, then e. on first road past the North Platte River to parking area. **Hours:** Trips depart daily at 9:30, mid-May through mid-July. **Phone:** (719) 395-2112 or (800) 462-7238.

WALSENBURG (E-5) pop. 3,068, elev. 6,182'

Walsenburg is a trade and distribution center for an area devoted to farming, ranching and tourism. It began as the Spanish village of Plaza de los Leones, and now bears the name of Fred Walsen, a German merchant who operated the town's first coal mine and general store during the 1870s. Grateful residents showed their gratitude by renaming the town in his honor.

Nearby Lathrop State Park *(see Recreation Areas Chart)* provides water sports, fishing, camping, hiking, skiing and a visitor center. A popular scenic drive along the Highway of Legends follows US 160 and SR 12 west and south through former coal mining towns and the Cucharas Pass area *(see Trinidad p. 266)*.

WALSENBURG MINING MUSEUM, 112 W. 5th St. in the 1896 Huerfano County Jail, depicts coal mining history and the lives of workers who populated camps throughout the region. A mine office, jail cells, vintage photographs, maps, gear, tools and memorabilia are presented. **Time:** Allow 30 minutes minimum. **Hours:** Mon.-Fri. 10-4, Sat. 10-1, early May-Sept. 30. **Cost:** $2; $1 (ages 13-19). Reservations are recommended. **Phone:** (719) 738-1992. GT

BEST WESTERN RAMBLER (719)738-1121

Motel
$89-$125

AAA Benefit: Save 10% or more every day and earn 10% bonus points!

Address: 457 US Hwy 85-87 81089 **Location:** I-25 exit 52, just w. **Facility:** 59 units, some kitchens. 1-2 stories (no elevator), interior/exterior corridors. **Pool(s):** heated indoor. **Activities:** hot tub, exercise room. **Guest Services:** coin laundry. **Featured Amenity: continental breakfast.**

SAVE CALL BIZ HS / SOME UNITS

WESTMINSTER (C-9) pop. 106,114, elev. 5,300'

- **Hotels & Restaurants map & index p. 136**
- **Part of Denver area — see map p. 116**

BUTTERFLY PAVILION is e. off US 36 to 6252 W. 104th Ave. Science education combines with hands-on fun to teach visitors about invertebrates and conservation. The invertebrate zoo offers five interactive exhibits including a 7,000-square-foot tropical rainforest filled with 1,200 free-flying butterflies.

Time: Allow 1 hour, 30 minutes minimum. **Hours:** Daily 9-5. Last admission at 4:15. Closed Thanksgiving and Christmas. **Cost:** $11; $9 (ages 65+); $6 (ages 2-12). **Phone:** (303) 469-5441.

DRURY INN & SUITES (303)460-1220

Hotel $100-$180 **Address:** 10393 Reed St 80021 **Location:** US 36 (Boulder Tpke) exit Church Ranch Blvd W, just s, then just e. **Facility:** 180 units. 7 stories, interior corridors. **Terms:** cancellation fee imposed. **Pool(s):** heated outdoor, heated indoor. **Activities:** hot tub, exercise room. **Guest Services:** valet and coin laundry.

CALL BIZ / SOME UNITS

(See map & index p. 136.)

FAIRFIELD INN & SUITES BY MARRIOTT-DENVER NORTH
(303)255-3100

▼▼ Hotel $105-$184 Address: 12080 Melody Dr 80234 Location: I-25 exit 223, just w to Melody Dr, then n. Facility: 82 units. 3 stories, interior corridors. Pool(s): heated indoor. Activities: hot tub, exercise room. Guest Services: valet and coin laundry.

AAA Benefit: Members save 5% or more!

[icons] CALL 🛗 🏊 BIZ 🛜 ✕ 📺 / SOME UNITS 🛏

HAMPTON INN BY HILTON
303/427-0700 **43**

▼▼▼ Hotel. Rates not provided. Address: 5030 W 88th Pl 80030 Location: US 36 (Boulder Tpke) exit Sheridan Blvd, 0.3 mi n to 92nd Ave, e to Yates Dr, 0.4 mi s, then just w. Facility: 106 units. 3 stories, interior corridors. Pool(s): heated indoor. Activities: hot tub, exercise room. Guest Services: valet laundry.

AAA Benefit: Members save up to 10%!

[icons] CALL 🛗 🏊 BIZ 🛜 ✕ 🛏 📺

RESIDENCE INN BY MARRIOTT
(303)427-9500 **44**

▼▼▼ Extended Stay Hotel $116-$227 Address: 5010 W 88th Pl 80031 Location: US 36 (Boulder Tpke) exit Sheridan Blvd, n to 92nd Ave, e to Yates Dr, then s. Facility: 94 units, some two bedrooms, efficiencies and kitchens. 4 stories, interior corridors. Terms: check-in 4 pm. Pool(s): heated indoor. Activities: hot tub, picnic facilities, exercise room. Guest Services: valet and coin laundry.

AAA Benefit: Members save 5% or more!

[icons] 🍴 🏊 BIZ HS 🛜 ✕ 🛏 📺 / SOME UNITS 🍳

SPRINGHILL SUITES BY MARRIOTT DENVER/WESTMINSTER
(303)464-1999

▼▼▼ Hotel $92-$187 Address: 6845 W 103rd Ave 80021 Location: US 36 (Boulder Tpke) exit Church Ranch Blvd W, just s, then just e. Facility: 164 units. 6 stories, interior corridors. Amenities: safes. Pool(s): heated indoor. Activities: hot tub, exercise room. Guest Services: valet and coin laundry.

AAA Benefit: Members save 5% or more!

CALL 🛗 🏊 BIZ HS 🛜 ✕ 🎥 🛏 📺 🖨

THE WESTIN WESTMINSTER
(303)410-5000

▼▼▼ Hotel $109-$489

WESTIN HOTELS & RESORTS

AAA Benefit: Members save up to 15%, plus Starwood Preferred Guest® benefits!

Address: 10600 Westminster Blvd 80020 Location: US 36 (Boulder Tpke) exit 104th Ave, just n. Opposite a movie plex. Facility: 369 units. 13 stories, interior corridors. Parking: on-site and valet. Amenities: safes. Pool(s): heated indoor. Activities: sauna, hot tub, trails, exercise room, massage. Guest Services: valet laundry, area transportation.

[icons] SAVE 🍴 🍸 CALL 🛗 🏊 BIZ
$HS 🛜 ✕ 🎥 📺 / SOME UNITS 🐾 🛏 🖨

WHERE TO EAT

EAST MOON ASIAN BISTRO
303/635-1888

▼▼ Asian. Casual Dining. $10-$24 AAA Inspector Notes: This casual eatery offers a variety of noodle dishes, stir-fries and sushi. Entrées feature lamb, beef, chicken, shrimp and scallops. Features: full bar. Address: 10431 Town Center Dr, Suite 101C 80021 Location: I-36 exit Church Ranch Blvd/104th Ave, just w, then just n; in strip mall. [L] [D] CALL 🛗

HANA MATSURI
303/404-9888

▼▼ ▼▼ Japanese Sushi. Casual Dining. $9-$15 AAA Inspector Notes: This elegant eatery offers a wide range of sushi rolls, seafood tapas and traditional entrées, such as chicken teriyaki. The flavorful, sliced avocado is large enough to share. Features: full bar, happy hour. Address: 2821 W 120th Ave, #300 80234 Location: Just w of jct Federal Blvd; in a strip mall. [L] [D]

JEWEL OF INDIA RESTAURANT
303/469-7779

▼▼ Indian. Casual Dining. $12-$25 AAA Inspector Notes: Start with a savory fried samosa. Flavorful entrées include spicy chicken kebabs, creamy saag paneer and tandoori lamb. Try the lightly sweet, whipped-mango fruit cream for dessert. Features: full bar. Address: 13443 N Federal Blvd, Unit P 80260 Location: I-25 exit 221, 2.1 mi w; in a strip mall. [L] [D]

KABOB STATION
303/451-1595

▼▼ Mediterranean. Casual Dining. $9-$16 AAA Inspector Notes: Patrons should be sure to arrive early to be seated promptly during the popular eatery's hectic lunch hour. Start with the creamy hummus enhanced with high quality olive oil and paprika. Among the Syrian favorites are kabobs, shawarma (marinated and grilled meat), gyros and falafel. The sweet and nutty baklava is delicious. Address: 12041 Pecos St 80234 Location: I-25 exit 223, 0.8 mi w, then just n. [L] [D]

QUE BUENO! MEXICAN GRILLE
303/464-1171

▼▼▼ Mexican. Casual Dining. $9-$32 AAA Inspector Notes: Lit from behind with changing neon lights, Mayan figures etched in glass adorn the walls of this attractive eatery. Expect to find traditional Mexican cuisine artistically presented in a casual, but elegant atmosphere. Features: full bar, Sunday brunch, happy hour. Address: 10633 Westminster Blvd, Suite 600 80031 Location: US 36 (Boulder Tpke) exit 104th Ave, just n; in Westminster Promenade Shopping Complex. Parking: on-site and valet. [L] [D]

YAK & YETI RESTAURANT & BREWPUB
303/426-1976 **83**

▼▼ Indian. Casual Dining. $10-$16 AAA Inspector Notes: This casual eatery specializes in savory, flavorful Indian and Nepalese dishes. Patrons may choose from the lunch or dinner buffet or order a la carte. Entrees feature salmon, shrimp, chicken, lamb and vegetables prepared in a variety of techniques, including tandoori, masala, korma, saag, vindaloo, biryani, makhani and Rogan Josh. The cheerful staff and colorful décor enhance the experience. Features: full bar. Address: 8665 N Sheridan Blvd 80003 Location: US 36 (Boulder Tpke) exit SR 95/Sheridan Blvd, 0.5 mi s; in a strip mall. [L] [D]

WHEAT RIDGE pop. 30,166
- Hotels & Restaurants map & index p. 136
- Part of Denver area — see map p. 116

ABRUSCI'S
303/232-2424 **90**

▼▼ Italian. Casual Dining. $10-$34 AAA Inspector Notes: This eatery offers individual and family-style classic Italian cuisine. Start with some fried calamari, green-lipped mussels or bruschetta. Famous for a reason, the rigatoni has a creamy tomato sauce that balances out the spicy Italian sausage. Other entrées include a caprese panini with prosciutto di Parma, lamb shank osso buco, and blackened chicken fettuccine Alfredo. Features: full bar, patio dining, Sunday brunch, happy hour. Address: 3244 Youngfield St, Suite G 80033 Location: I-70 exit 264 (32nd Ave), just n. [L] [D]

LUKE'S STEAK PLACE
303/422-3300 **89**

▼▼ Steak. Casual Dining. $25-$43 AAA Inspector Notes: Just a short hop off I-70 in a strip mall, this eatery offers a variety of steaks and some seafood options, served in a warmly decorated dining area by a friendly waitstaff. Features: full bar, Sunday brunch, happy hour. Address: 4990 Kipling St 80033 Location: I-70 exit 267, just n, then just e to Independence Square. [L] [D]

WHITE RIVER NATIONAL FOREST (B-2)

Elevations in the forest range from 5,345 ft. near the town of Rifle to 14,265 ft. at Castle Peak. Refer to AAA maps for additional elevation information.

The White River National Forest is composed of 2.3 million acres of northwestern and north-central Colorado mountains on both sides of I-70; it is entered via US 24 and SRs 13, 82, 131 and 133. The forest was once a favorite hunting ground of the Ute Indians and later of settlers. Highlights include Mount of the Holy Cross, southwest of Vail; Glenwood Canyon; the mountains known as Maroon Bells *(see attraction listing p. 44)*; Ruedi, Dillon and Green Mountain reservoirs; and Trappers Lake.

The Flat Tops, Eagles Nest, Hunter-Fryingpan, Collegiate Peaks, Holy Cross, Ptarmigan Peak, Raggeds and Maroon Bells-Snowmass wildernesses provide opportunities for pack trips, backpacking and mountain climbing. Fishing and big-game hunting also are popular. The forest is home to one of the world's largest elk herds. Camping is available at a number of areas throughout the forest. Some of the world's best-known winter sports areas are found at Aspen, Breckenridge, Copper Mountain, Keystone and Vail.

The following district ranger stations can offer assistance: Aspen, (970) 925-3445; Blanco, (970) 878-4039; Dillon, (970) 468-5400; Eagle, (970) 328-6388; Holy Cross, (970) 827-5715; Rifle, (970) 625-2371; or Sopris, (970) 963-2266. *See Recreation Areas Chart.*

WINDSOR pop. 18,644

PORTER HOUSE BED & BREAKFAST INN   970/686-5793
▼▼▼ **Historic Bed & Breakfast.** Rates not provided. **Address:** 530 Main St 80550 **Location:** I-25 exit 262, 4.5 mi e; center. Located in a commercial area. **Facility:** A hot gourmet breakfast, lush flower gardens and antique furnishings distinguish this restored 1898 Victorian inn. Read a book or have a fireside chat in the cozy living room area. 4 units. 2 stories (no elevator), interior/exterior corridors. **Parking:** on-site and street. **Terms:** check-in 4 pm, age restrictions may apply. **Guest Services:** valet laundry.
🍴⁺ 📶 ✕ ☎

CHIMNEY PARK RESTAURANT & BAR   970/686-1477
▼▼▼ American. Casual Dining. $28-$34 **AAA Inspector Notes:** Located in a historic building adorned with oil paintings, this hidden gem is worth seeking out. The quality of the cuisine is usually found at restaurants with a higher rating. Artfully presented menu items change seasonally, but past items include Hudson Valley foie gras, ricotta cheese gnudi, soy-mirin glazed salmon, truffle stuffed chicken, oven-roasted Colorado lamb, and bison steak. **Features:** full bar, patio dining. **Address:** 406 Main St 80550 **Location:** Downtown. **Parking:** street only. D

OKOLE MALUNA HAWAIIAN GRILL   970/686-8844
▼▼ Hawaiian. Casual Dining. $10-$19 **AAA Inspector Notes:** This cheerful little restaurant brings a touch of the tropics to northern Colorado. The menu features traditional Hawaiian dishes including smoked pork, lomi-lomi salmon and Pulehu sirloin steak. Given that Asia heavily influences Hawaiian cuisine, the menu also lists Korean barbecue beef ribs, Japanese udon noodles and seaweed-crusted ahi tuna. On the dessert menu are pineapple, cheesecake, mango sorbet and haupia, which is made from coconuts. **Features:** full bar. **Address:** 431 Main St 80550 **Location:** I-25 exit 262, 5 mi e on SR 392. **Parking:** street only. L D

WINTER PARK (B-4) pop. 999, elev. 9,040'

Winter Park and the surrounding Fraser Valley offer an extensive network of groomed trails for cross-country skiing, snowshoeing, dog sledding, snow tubing and snowmobiling. One of Colorado's major ski resorts, Winter Park Resort offers three interconnected mountains that cater to a wide variety of skiing abilities.

Summer presents equally diverse activities. More than 600 miles of marked hiking, biking and horseback riding trails offer challenges ranging from novice loops to back-country excursions. The ski resort features some 50 miles of trails that crisscross the mountains.

Visitors can golf at four championship courses, zoom down one of Colorado's longest alpine slides or fish in streams where President Dwight D. Eisenhower once cast a line. White-water rafting on the Colorado River and hiking in the surrounding Arapaho and Roosevelt National Forests *(see place listing p. 41)* present their own fun and adventure.

A major railroad link between the east and west coasts in the early 1900s, Moffat Road was built over 11,600-foot Corona Pass in Winter Park. The Moffat Tunnel, a 6.2-mile-long railroad tunnel, replaced this route in 1927 and still is a major rail route through the Continental Divide.

Winter Park Visitor Center: 78841 US 40, P.O. Box 3236, Winter Park, CO 80482. **Phone:** (970) 726-4221, (303) 422-0666 or (800) 903-7275.

RECREATIONAL ACTIVITIES
Skiing

- **Winter Park Resort** is on US 40 in the Arapaho National Forest. Other activities are offered. **Hours:** Mon.-Fri. 9-4, Sat.-Sun. and holidays 8:30-4, mid-Nov. to mid-Apr. **Phone:** (970) 726-1564 for information, or (800) 979-0332 for reservations.

Snowmobiling

- **Grand Adventures Snowmobiling** is behind the Beaver Village Lodge at 79303 US 40. Other activities are available. **Hours:** Daily 8-6, late Nov. to mid-Apr. **Phone:** (970) 726-9247.

BEST WESTERN ALPENGLO LODGE   (970)726-8088

Hotel
$88-$182

AAA Benefit: Save 10% or more every day and earn 10% bonus points!

Address: 78665 US Hwy 40 80482 **Location:** 0.3 mi n of center. **Facility:** 58 units. 3 stories, interior corridors. **Terms:** check-in 4 pm, 2-3 night minimum stay - seasonal and/or weekends, resort fee. **Activities:** hot tub, picnic facilities.

OLYMPIA MOTOR LODGE   970/726-8843

[fyi] Hotel. Rates not provided. Under major renovation, scheduled to be completed December 2015. **Last Rated:** ▼▼ **Address:** 78572 US Hwy 40 80482 **Location:** 0.4 mi n of center. **Facility:** 40 units, some efficiencies and condominiums. 1-2 stories (no elevator), interior/exterior corridors. **Pool(s):** heated indoor. **Activities:** hot tub. **Guest Services:** area transportation.

WHERE TO EAT

CASA MEXICO   970/726-9674

▼▼ ▼▼ Mexican. Casual Dining. $11-$23 **AAA Inspector Notes:** The extensive menu offers any Mexican dish you can think of, and more! Nice choices include carne asada, pork carnitas, shrimp ceviche, tilapia tacos, burritos and enchiladas. **Features:** full bar, happy hour. **Address:** 78930 US Hwy 40 80482 **Location:** Just off US 40; downtown; at Cooper Creek Square.

DENO'S MOUNTAIN BISTRO   970/726-5332

▼▼ ▼▼ Seafood Steak. Casual Dining. $10-$34 **AAA Inspector Notes:** This former pharmacy and barber shop offers sports, music and good food. With nine TVs, an HD projection screen and satellite coverage, you can watch your favorite sports event while enjoying wine, specialty cocktails or microbrews. The pub menu features hearty soups, sandwiches, pizza, quesadillas and burgers. The dining room menu offers seared sesame-crusted ahi tuna, Alaskan king crab legs, rosemary- and sea salt-crusted rib-eye, and St. Louis fall-off-the-bone barbecue pork ribs. **Features:** full bar, happy hour. **Address:** 78911 US Hwy 40 80482 **Location:** South end of town. **Parking:** on-site and street.

SMOKIN MOE'S RIBHOUSE & SALOON   970/726-4600

▼▼ ▼▼ American. Casual Dining. $9-$27 **AAA Inspector Notes:** Diners can enjoy their favorite games or sporting events while feasting on grilled meats smoked over hickory wood from Osage County, Oklahoma. The menu also includes sandwiches, salads and typical barbecue side dishes. **Features:** full bar, patio dining. **Address:** 65 Cooper Creek Way 80482 **Location:** Just off US 40; downtown; at Cooper Creek Square; lower level of courtyard.

WOODLAND PARK (F-9) pop. 7,200, elev. 8,437'

Incorporated in 1891, Woodland Park's primary industry first took place in its sawmills, where railroad ties and other wood products were made.

Nearby Manitou Lake and Rampart Reservoir provide trout and ice fishing. Other leisure activities include biking, camping, hiking and horseback riding.

The Greater Woodland Park Chamber of Commerce and Visitor Center: 210 E. Midland Ave., P.O. Box 9022, Woodland Park, CO 80866. **Phone:** (719) 687-9885 or (800) 551-7886.

ROCKY MOUNTAIN DINOSAUR RESOURCE CENTER is at 201 S. Fairview St. More than 30 skeletons and life restorations of dinosaurs and other reptiles are on display, including one of the largest Cretaceous sea monster collections in North America. Interactive exhibits, fossils, a viewable fossil laboratory, a children's educational area and theater presentations also are offered.

Time: Allow 30 minutes minimum. **Hours:** Mon.-Sat. 9-6, Sun. 10-5. Closed Jan. 1, Easter, Thanksgiving and Christmas. **Cost:** $11.50; $10.50 (ages 66+); $7.50 (ages 5-12). **Phone:** (719) 686-1820. **[GT]**

BRISTLECONE LODGE   719/687-9518

▼▼▼ Cottage. Rates not provided. **Address:** 510 N Hwy 67 80863 **Location:** 0.5 mi n. **Facility:** These duplex cottage units are nestled between pine trees. Each unit is equipped with a wet bar, has a sitting area separate from the bedroom, and features mountain-style décor. 10 cottages, some two bedrooms and kitchens. 1 story, exterior corridors. **Activities:** hot tub, picnic facilities. **Guest Services:** coin laundry.

WOODLAND COUNTRY LODGE   (719)687-6277

Hotel
$99-$189

Address: 723 US Hwy 24 W 80863 **Location:** Just w of jct SR 67. **Facility:** 60 units. 2 stories (no elevator), interior corridors. **Terms:** cancellation fee imposed. **Dining:** entertainment. **Pool(s):** heated indoor. **Activities:** hot tub. **Guest Services:** coin laundry. **Featured Amenity:** continental breakfast.

WHERE TO EAT

SWISS CHALET RESTAURANT   719/687-2001

▼▼ Continental. Casual Dining. $12-$29 **AAA Inspector Notes:** This family restaurant offers creative menu choices, including Continental cuisine and flambé specialties. The fireplace and candlelight evoke a cozy and charming ambiance. This well-established restaurant is a favorite with locals and tourists alike. **Features:** full bar, patio dining. **Reservations:** suggested, weekends. **Address:** 19263 E US Hwy 24 80863 **Location:** 1.8 mi e of jct SR 67.

Arches National Park

Utah

Utah's spectacular scenery—which ranges from lush Rocky Mountain valleys to desolate, red rock canyons— routinely elicits gasps and exclamations from visitors.

The southern half of the state features terrain carved by wind and water into surreal shapes arrayed in dramatic vistas. Large portions of this many-colored land are preserved within a dozen national parks and monuments.

An area with stunning vistas but little else may seem an unlikely place to establish a homeland, but it suited 19th-century Mormon pioneers who came to the valley of the Great Salt Lake seeking religious freedom. Their hard work transformed a near desert into productive farm country, earning Utah the apt nickname, "The Beehive State."

Today vacationers flock to Utah to admire stately Mormon landmarks and enjoy the urban amenities of fast-growing Salt Lake City, or to explore the canyons, buttes and

The winter skyline of Salt Lake City

natural arches of the south or the snow-capped peaks of the east.

Tales Told in Stone

Due to a seismically active past and a scarcity of terrain-obscuring vegetation, Utah's landscape provides scientists with a remarkable record of the Earth's geologic history. Throughout the state, exposed rock strata billions of years old tell stories of dramatic upheaval. At Dinosaur National Monument on the Colorado-Utah border, the sandstone has yielded thousands of dinosaur bones now displayed in museums around the country.

With fanciful monikers like the Watchman, the Castle, Court of the Patriarchs, Queen Victoria and Fairyland, the countless unusual rock formations obviously inspire human imagination as well. In Capitol Reef National Park, rainbow-hued cliffs form a 100-mile-long barrier reminiscent of an ocean reef, while at Cedar Breaks National Monument, natural columns thrusting upward from the floor of a bowl-shaped valley recall Rome's Coliseum.

In addition to Bryce Canyon's hoodoos— strangely shaped rock formations that inspired Paiute Indian legends—Utah is graced by colorful arches, pinnacles, precipices and gorges. Watch sandstone chimneys change color with the daylight in Kodachrome Basin State Park or marvel at the myriad shades of red as the sun sets over Monument Valley Navajo Tribal Park.

The Right Place

Upon first seeing the Great Salt Lake Valley in 1847, Brigham Young, leader of the Mormon church's westward exodus, proclaimed, "This is the right place." As befitting a man regarded by his followers as a prophet, he was correct.

Salt Lake City is the result of Mormon pioneers' dream to establish a community where adherents could practice their religion free from persecution. Today the city's magnificent six-spired, cathedral-like temple is a symbol and center of Mormonism, a belief system formally referred to as The Church of Jesus Christ of Latter-day Saints.

Although immigration has altered state demographics in recent decades, still more than 70 percent of Utah's citizens are Mormon. Church buildings around Temple Square top Salt Lake City's list of tourist attractions. As an added reminder of the city's spiritual orientation, the central tower of the temple is capped by a nearly 13-foot-tall golden statue of an angel. According to Mormon doctrine, an angel named Moroni appeared to church founder Joseph Smith Jr. and led him to a cache of gold plates etched with text from which the Book of Mormon was translated.

From his lofty setting, Moroni looks out over a state that manages to encompass scenes both ordinary and considerably outside the ordinary—a land of ethereal beauty poised between this world and the next.

Recreation

The Mormon State boasts five national parks and six national forests, more than a half-dozen national monuments, and too many state and local parks to mention, all with their own unique character, and features that change depending on the season.

Spectacular views can be had along hiking and backpacking trails. Standouts include Delicate Arch Trail in Arches National Park, Watchman Viewpoint Trail in Zion National Park, the trail to Hickman Bridge in Capitol Reef National Park, and Queens Garden and Fairyland Loop trails in Bryce Canyon National Park.

East of Salt Lake City, Brighton Lakes Trail ascends 2.5 miles to three lovely lakes and then continues up the summit of Catherine Pass. Near Provo, a 6-mile hike to the top of 11,788-foot Mt. Timpanogos offers dramatic vistas. The High Uintas Wilderness features several trails that wind below the peaks of Utah's tallest mountains.

You can easily arrange an equestrian journey through Utah's unforgettable terrain.

The state also serves up some of the most challenging bike trails in the country. At the end of the scenic drive through Salt Lake City's Mill Creek Canyon, Wasatch Crest Trail, a 10-mile section of the Great Western Trail that runs from Canada to Mexico, attracts bikers with its gorgeous alpine views. Nearby Antelope Island, the largest of the 10 Great Salt Lake islands, features nearly 20 miles of trails. The 4-mile ride to Powell Point, 23 miles northeast of Bryce Canyon National Park, culminates with a precipitous drop and an awesome view of Grand Staircase-Escalante National Monument. Near Nephi, there's the 66-mile Mt. Nebo Loop, while Moab's Slickrock Bike Trail draws hard-core bikers from all over.

Those who know snow perennially place Utah powder at the top of their lists. Four miles north of Park City stands Utah Olympic Park, the world-class training facility that played host to the bobsled, luge and ski jumping competitions for the 2002 Olympic Winter Games. Minutes away from Park City nightlife, The Canyons ski resort, now part of Park City Mountain Resort, features 155 runs. The Alta Ski Area also has a reputation for being a die-hard skiers' retreat. And nearby Snowbird Ski and Summer Resort offers expert slopes wisely avoided by the fainthearted.

Challenge yourself on a Utah trail

Historic Timeline

1776	Franciscan priests Escalante and Dominguez explore Utah in their search for a route from New Mexico to California.
1824	Trapper James Bridger reaches the Great Salt Lake.
1847	Mormons led by Brigham Young reach the Salt Lake Valley.
1848	The United States gains the region from Mexico through the Treaty of Guadalupe Hidalgo.
1850	The Territory of Utah is created, with Brigham Young serving as governor.
1869	The Union Pacific and Central Pacific rails meet at Promontory to form the nation's first transcontinental railroad.
1896	Utah becomes the 45th state.
1952	Uranium deposits are discovered near Moab.
1964	Two dams—Flaming Gorge and Glen Canyon—are completed.
1998	The state of Utah and the federal government conclude one of the largest U.S. land exchanges since the acquisition of Alaska.
2002	Salt Lake City hosts the Winter Olympics.

What To Pack

Temperature Averages Maximum/Minimum	JANUARY	FEBRUARY	MARCH	APRIL	MAY	JUNE	JULY	AUGUST	SEPTEMBER	OCTOBER	NOVEMBER	DECEMBER
Cedar City	43/20	46/24	52/29	60/35	70/44	81/54	86/60	83/58	76/50	64/38	53/29	42/20
Delta	39/14	46/20	56/27	65/33	74/41	86/49	94/56	92/55	82/45	68/34	52/23	40/14
Mexican Hat	42/17	51/23	62/30	70/36	79/45	90/51	95/60	92/59	84/49	71/36	55/25	44/17
Moab	41/16	50/23	62/31	72/39	81/47	91/54	96/61	93/59	84/50	71/38	57/27	43/19
Salt Lake City	37/20	42/24	51/30	62/37	72/45	82/52	92/61	90/59	80/50	66/39	49/28	40/23
Vernal	29/5	36/11	49/23	62/32	72/39	83/46	88/52	85/51	76/41	62/30	48/22	31/7

From the records of The Weather Channel Interactive, Inc.

Good Facts To Know

ABOUT THE STATE

POPULATION: 2,763,885.

AREA: 84,897 square miles; ranks 13th.

CAPITAL: Salt Lake City.

HIGHEST POINT: 13,528 ft., Kings Peak.

LOWEST POINT: 2,200 ft., Beaver Wash Dam.

TIME ZONE(S): Mountain. DST.

REGULATIONS

TEEN DRIVING LAWS: No passengers under 21 except family members are permitted for the first 6 months. Driving is not permitted daily midnight-5 a.m. The minimum age for an unrestricted driver's license is 17. Phone (801) 965-4437 for more information about Utah driver's license regulations.

SEAT BELT/CHILD RESTRAINT LAWS: Seat belts are required for driver and all passengers ages 16 and older. Children ages 8-15 and more than 57 inches tall must use a child restraint or seat belt; child restraints are required for children under age 8 and less than 57 inches tall. AAA recommends the use of seat belts and appropriate child restraints for the driver and all passengers.

CELLPHONE RESTRICTIONS: All drivers are prohibited from text messaging while driving. Drivers under 18 are not permitted to use cell phones. In addition, Utah has a law against careless driving; a person can be charged if they commit a moving violation other than speeding while using a handheld cell phone or engaging in other distracting activities.

HELMETS FOR MOTORCYCLISTS: Required for all riders under age 18.

RADAR DETECTORS: Permitted. Prohibited for use by commercial vehicles.

MOVE OVER LAW: Driver is required to slow down and vacate the lane nearest stopped police, fire and rescue vehicles using audible or flashing signals. The law also includes tow trucks.

FIREARMS LAWS: Vary by state and/or county. Contact Firearms Laws Bureau of Criminal Identification, 3888 West 5400 South, Taylorsville, UT 84118; phone (801) 965-4445.

HOLIDAYS

HOLIDAYS: Jan. 1 ■ Martin Luther King Jr. Day, Jan. (3rd Mon.) ■ Washington's Birthday/Presidents Day, Feb. (3rd Mon.) ■ Memorial Day, May (last Mon.) ■ July 4 ■ Pioneer Day, July 24 ■ Labor Day, Sept. (1st Mon.) ■ Columbus Day, Oct. (2nd Mon.) ■ Veterans Day, Nov. 11 ■ Thanksgiving, Nov. (4th Thurs.) ■ Christmas, Dec. 25.

MONEY

TAXES: Utah's statewide general sales tax is 4.7 percent. Local options allow additional increments up to 1.5 percent. Qualified localities may add an additional resort sales tax of 1 percent. Counties are authorized to levy a lodgings tax of up to 4.25 percent.

VISITOR INFORMATION

INFORMATION CENTERS: State welcome centers are off I-15 southbound 1.5 mi. n. of Brigham City ■ on I-80 westbound at Echo, 6 mi. e. of Coalville ■ in Jensen at jct. US 40 and SR 149 ■ off I-15 northbound 4 mi. s. of exit 6 near St. George ■ and on I-70 westbound 26 mi. e. of Green River at Thompson Springs.

FURTHER INFORMATION FOR VISITORS:
Utah Office of Tourism
300 N. State St.
Salt Lake City, UT 84114
(801) 538-1030
(800) 200-1160

NATIONAL FOREST INFORMATION:
USDA Forest Service, Ogden Ranger District
507 25th St.
Ogden, UT 84401
(801) 625-5112
(877) 444-6777 (reservations)

FISHING AND HUNTING REGULATIONS:
Utah Division of Wildlife Resources
1594 W. North Temple, Suite 2110
Salt Lake City, UT 84114
(801) 538-4700

RECREATION INFORMATION:
Utah Division of Parks and Recreation
1594 W. North Temple, Suite 116
Salt Lake City, UT 84114
(801) 538-7220

Utah Annual Events

Please call ahead to confirm event details.

JANUARY

- HOF Germanfest / Ogden
  801-399-8711
- Sundance Film Festival
  Park City
  801-907-4050
- Bluff International Balloon
  Festival / Bluff
  435-672-2360

FEBRUARY

- Utah Sportsmen's Vacation
  and RV Show / Sandy
  801-485-7399
- Utah Boat Show and
  Watersports Expo / Sandy
  801-485-7399
- NASC (Native American
  Student Council) Pow-Wow
  Logan
  435-797-1728

MARCH

- St. Patrick's Day Parade
  Salt Lake City
  801-467-6268
- St. Patrick's Day
  Celebration / Springdale
  888-518-7070
- Red, White and Snow
  Park City
  435-200-0990

APRIL

- Dixie Kite Festival
  St. George
  435-673-3297
- Baby Animal Days Festival
  Wellsville
  435-245-6050
- April Action Car Show
  Moab
  435-260-1948

MAY

- The Great Salt Lake Bird
  Festival / Farmington
  801-451-3286
- Scandinavian Heritage
  Festival / Ephraim
  435-283-4631
- Moab Arts Festival / Moab
  435-259-2742

JUNE

- Canyonlands PRCA Rodeo
  Moab
  435-259-8825
- Utah Arts Festival
  Salt Lake City
  801-322-2428
- Groovefest American
  Music Festival / Cedar City
  435-867-9800

JULY

- American Fork Steel Days
  American Fork
  801-763-3000
- America's Freedom Festival
  at Provo / Provo
  801-818-1776
- Utah Mid-Summer
  Renaissance Faire
  Cedar City
  435-531-9327

AUGUST

- Western Legends Roundup
  Kanab
  435-644-3444
- Raspberry Days Festival
  Garden City
  800-448-2327
- Park City Kimball Arts
  Festival / Park City
  435-649-8882

SEPTEMBER

- Peach Days Celebration
  Brigham City
  435-723-3931
- Utah State Fair / Salt Lake
  City
  801-538-8440
- Salt Lake City Greek
  Festival / Salt Lake City
  801-328-9681

OCTOBER

- Cedar City Livestock and
  Heritage Festival
  Cedar City
  435-586-8132
- Utah Humanities Book
  Festival / Salt Lake City
  801-359-9670, ext. 104
- Fall Harvest Festival and
  Corn Maze Days / Wellsville
  435-245-6050

NOVEMBER

- Moab Folk Music Festival
  Moab
  435-259-3198
- Navajo Rug Show and Sale:
  Honoring Our Weavers
  Park City
  435-649-0535
- Christmas Lighting of
  Temple Square / Salt Lake
  City / 801-240-4872

DECEMBER

- Festival of Trees / Sandy
  801-201-3755
- ZooLights / Salt Lake City
  801-584-1750
- Dickens' Christmas Festival
  St. George
  435-688-2990

Zion National Park

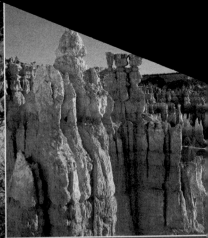
Bryce Canyon National Park

Check out the Alta Ski Area

Owachomo Bridge, Natural Bridges National Monument

State Capitol, Salt Lake City

...at Experience for Members

...editor's picks of exceptional note

Cap... ...National Park

Dinosaur National Monument

Salt Lake Temple

Cedar Breaks National Monument

See Orientation map on p. 288 for corresponding grid coordinates, if applicable.

Utah

Atlas Section

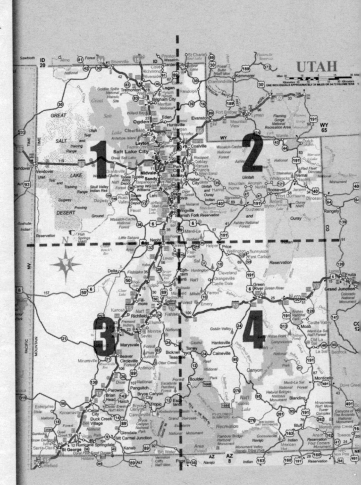

ROADS/HIGHWAYS

- INTERSTATE
- CONTROLLED ACCESS
- CONTROLLED ACCESS TOLL
- TOLL ROAD
- PRIMARY DIVIDED
- PRIMARY UNDIVIDED
- SECONDARY DIVIDED
- SECONDARY UNDIVIDED
- LOCAL DIVIDED
- LOCAL UNDIVIDED
- UNPAVED ROAD
- UNDER CONSTRUCTION
- TUNNEL
- PEDESTRIAN ONLY
- AUTO FERRY
- PASSENGER FERRY
- SCENIC BYWAY
- DISTANCE BETWEEN MARKERS
- EXIT NUMBER-FREE/TOLL
- INTERCHANGE FULL/PARTIAL
- WELCOME/INFORMATION CENTER
- REST AREA/SERVICE CENTER

BOUNDARIES

- INTERNATIONAL
- STATE
- COUNTY
- TIME ZONE
- CONTINENTAL DIVIDE

ROAD SHIELDS

- INTERSTATE/BUSINESS
- U.S./STATE/COUNTY
- FOREST/INDIAN
- TRANS- CANADA
- PROVINCIAL AUTOROUTE/ KING'S HIGHWAY
- MEXICO
- HISTORIC ROUTE 66
- REFERENCE PAGE INDICATOR

AREAS OF INTEREST

- INDIAN
- MILITARY
- PARK
- FOREST
- GRASSLANDS
- HISTORIC
- INT'L/REGIONAL AIRPORT
- INCORPORATED CITY

POINTS OF INTEREST

- TOWN
- NATIONAL CAPITAL
- STATE/PROVINCIAL CAPITAL
- AAA/CAA CLUB LOCATION
- FEATURE OF INTEREST
- COLLEGE/UNIVERSITY
- CAMPGROUND INFORMATION PROVIDED BY WOODALL'S®
- CUSTOMS STATION
- HISTORIC
- LIGHTHOUSE
- MONUMENT/MEMORIAL
- STATE/PROVINCIAL PARK
- NATIONAL WILDLIFE REFUGE
- SKI AREA
- SPORTS COMPLEX
- DAM

CITIES/TOWNS are color-coded by size, showing where to find AAA Approved and Diamond rated lodgings or restaurants listed in the AAA TourBook guides and on AAA.com:

- Red - major destinations and capitals; many listings
- Black - destinations; some listings
- Grey - no listings

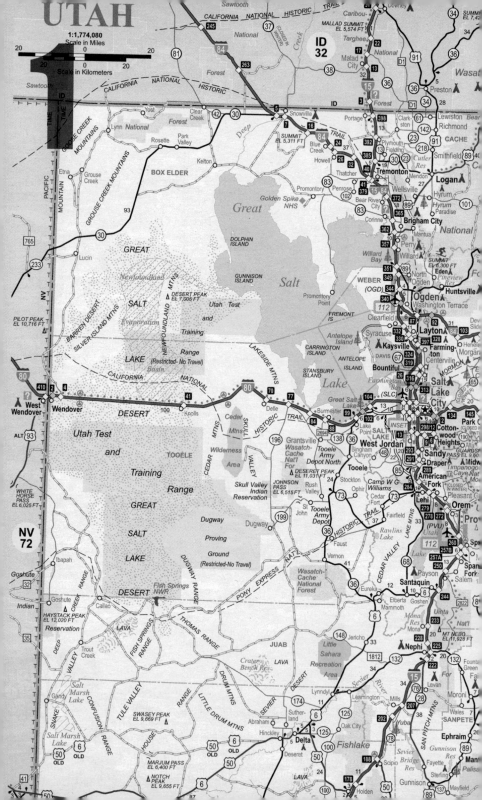

2

Montpelier

Cabou-Targhee
Nat'l For
GENEVA
SUMMIT
EL 7,461 FT

30

Ovid
Paris

89

89

6

232

24

30

30

St Charles

89

Bear
Lake

Cokeville

30

Garden
City

RICH

BEAR LAKE
SUMMIT
EL 7,810 FT

Laketown

Cache

Round
Valley

30 23 8

19

Randolph

16

Woodruff

39

48

MONTE CRISTO
SUMMIT
EL 9,000 FT

Neponset
Reservoir

Woodruff
Narrows
Res

WY
125

23

89

Evanston

TRAIL

HIST

SUMMIT
EL 6,850 FT

5

MORGAN

Croydon
Devils
Slide

111 115

80

191

153

150

150

WY

279

414

Henrys
Fork

295

530

Flaming Gorge
Res

Manila

43

Flaming
Gorge
Lake

44

28

NRA

191

Green

Dutch
John

14

318

CO

Upton

58

National

Forest

Cache

SOUTH BURRO PEAK
EL 12,726 FT

DAGETT

MARSH PEAK
EL 12,240 FT

SUMMIT
EL 8,428 FT

Red
Fleet

2804

Dinosa

Coalville

Hoytsville

SUMMIT

Wasatch

High

MT LOVENIA
EL 13,227 FT

Uintas

Forest

Whiterocks

Steinaker

Maeser

Vernal

149

Rockport

Oakley

32

Kamas

248

32

146

145

Park City

Jordanelle
Res

Midway

Heber City

Francis

150

WOLF CREEK
SUMMIT
EL 9,480 FT

KINGS PEAK
(HIGHEST POINT)
EL 13,520 FT

Wilderness

Lake Fork

UINTA MOUNTAINS

National

Ashley

Moon
Lake

DUCHESNE

Whiterocks

Tridell

121

Naples

45

Jensen

16S

Wasatch
Nat'l
Mon

Deer Creek

WASATCH

Uintah

Hanna

Tabiona

Mountain
Home

Altonah

1566

1567

Neola

Lapoint

40

57

Dinosau

Walls-
burg

DANIELS PASS
EL 7,980 FT

and

Duchesne

Current

Altamont

87

121

1567

Roosevelt

Fort
Duchesne

Ballard

191

Randlett

45

64

River

Provo

PROVO PEAK
EL 11,068 FT

Springville

40 69

Fruitland

208

Starvation Res

Starvation

35

87

Upalco

Myton

1552

Leota

Pelican

Ouray
NWR

188

Ouray

Mapleton

131

Spanish
Fork

Thistle

UTAH

Forest

Duchesne

Ashley

Indian

191

Reservation

National

Forest

Bridge-
land

Uintah

and

Ouray

White

Bonanza

River

21

201

SOLDIER
SUMMIT
EL 7,477 FT

Soldier Summit

96

Colton

42

WEST TAVAPUTS

SUMMIT
EL 9,100 FT

Nine

Mile

Creek

PLATEAU

UINTAH

Ouray

Indian

BAXTER PASS
EL 8,422 FT

25

Manti-
La

Indianola

Scofield

Milburn

Scofield
Res

264

Scofield

Clear
Creek

Helper

10

Kenilworth

CARBON

PATMOS MOUNTAINS

Range

DESOLATION CANYON

Reservation

Fairview

6

116

Mt Pleasant

31

Spring City

Sal

122

Huntington

21

Price

10

Wellington

East
Carbon

Sunnyside

123

124

6

EAST TAVAPUTS PLATEAU

Indian

SOUTH TENT
MTN EL 11,285 FT

SUMMIT
EL 10,200 FT

Huntington

Hiawatha

Elmo

206

Cleveland

River

58

LAVA

Reservation

GRAND

BOOK CLIFFS

89

Manti

29

Palisade

National

Orangeville

Lawrence

215

Castle
Dale

Clawson

48

Ferron

191

Green
River

GRAY CANYON

Green

RIVER VALLEY

227

214

TRAIL

201

HISTORIC

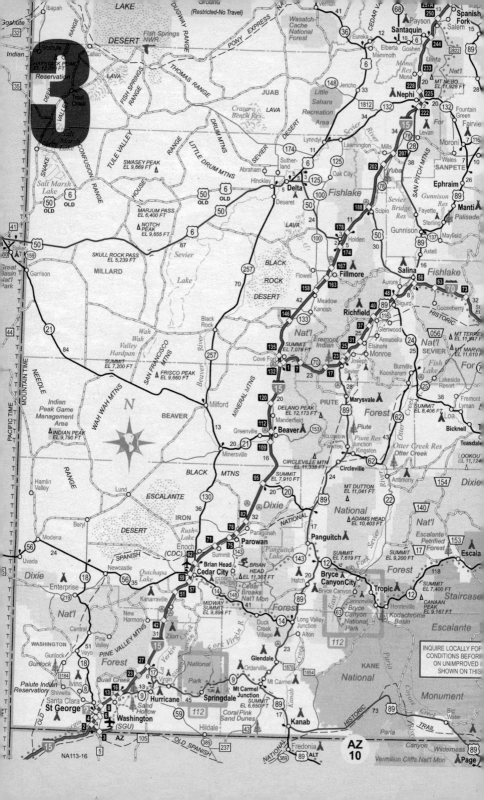

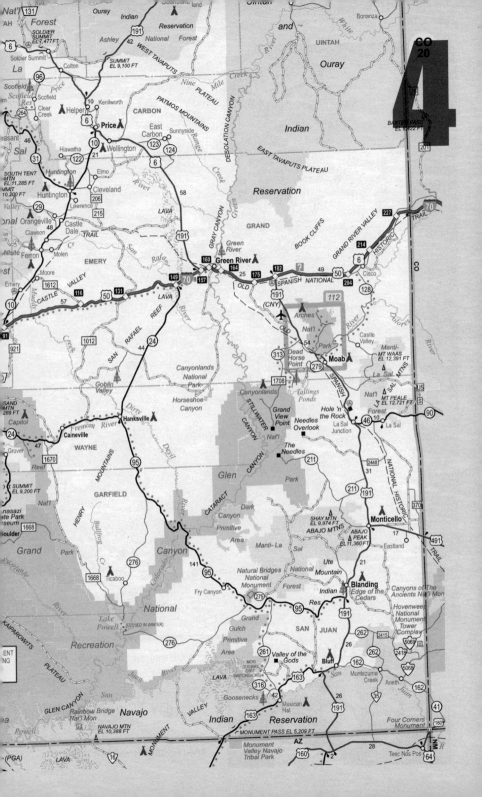

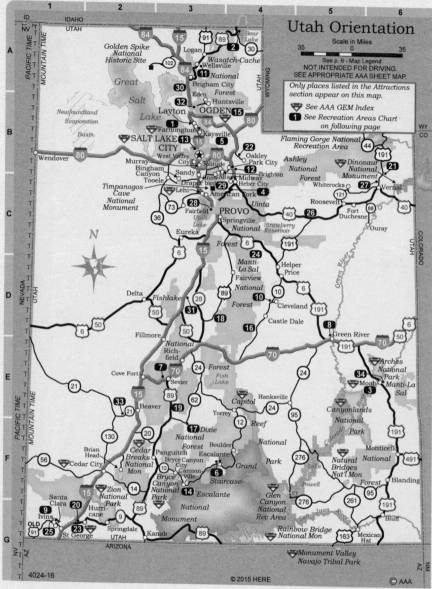

Utah Orientation

Scale in Miles

35   0   35

See p. 6 - Map Legend
NOT INTENDED FOR DRIVING.
SEE APPROPRIATE AAA SHEET MAP.

Only places listed in the Attractions
section appear on this map.

⛊ See AAA GEM Index

1 See Recreation Areas Chart
   on following page

4024-16

© 2015 HERE

© AAA

Recreation Areas Chart

The map location numerals in column 2 show an area's location on the preceding map.

	MAP LOCATION	CAMPING	PICNICKING	HIKING TRAILS	BOATING	BOAT RAMP	BOAT RENTAL	FISHING	SWIMMING	PETS ON LEASH	BICYCLE TRAILS	NATURE PROGS.	VISITOR CENTER	LODGE/CABINS	FOOD SERVICE
NATIONAL PARKS *(See place listings.)*															
Arches (E-6) 76,519 acres. Rock climbing; guided tours.		•	•	•						•			•	•	
Bryce Canyon (F-3) 35,835 acres. Horse and mule rental, interpretive programs.		•	•	•						•			•	•	•
Canyonlands (E-5) 337,598 acres. Canoeing, horseback riding, kayaking, mountain biking, river running, rock climbing.		•	•	•						•			•		
Capitol Reef (E-4) 241,904 acres. Historic. Scenic. Horseback riding, rock climbing; interpretive programs.		•	•	•				•		•			•		
Zion (F-2) 147,551 acres. Bird-watching; guided walks.		•	•	•						•	•	•	•	•	•
NATIONAL FORESTS *(See place listings.)*															
Ashley (B-4) 1,384,132 acres in northeastern Utah. Hunting, kayaking, rock climbing, skiing; horse rental.		•	•	•	•	•	•	•	•	•	•	•	•		
Dixie (F-3) 1,700,000 acres in southwestern Utah. All-terrain vehicle trails, horse rental.		•	•	•	•	•	•	•	•	•	•	•	•		
Fishlake (D-3) 1,434,599 acres in south-central Utah. Hunting, ice fishing, scuba diving, snowmobiling.		•	•	•	•	•	•	•	•	•	•	•	•		
Manti-La Sal (D-4) 1,413,111 acres in southeastern Utah. Cross-country skiing, horseback riding, hunting, snowmobiling; all-terrain vehicle trails.		•	•	•	•	•	•	•	•	•	•	•	•	•	
Uinta (C-4) 949,848 acres in central Utah. Horseback riding, hunting, skiing, snowmobiling, snowshoeing.		•	•	•	•	•	•	•	•	•	•	•	•		
Wasatch-Cache (A-3) 1,259,160 acres in north-central and northeastern Utah. Rock climbing, skiing, snowmobiling; all-terrain vehicle trails, horse rental.		•	•	•	•	•	•	•	•	•	•	•	•		
NATIONAL MONUMENTS *(See place listings.)*															
Dinosaur (B-5) 204,000 acres.		•	•	•				•		•		•	•		
NATIONAL RECREATION AREAS *(See place listings.)*															
Flaming Gorge (B-5) 207,363 acres in northeast Utah and southwest Wyoming. Cross-country skiing, horseback riding, hunting, ice fishing, parasailing, rafting, snowmobiling, water skiing.		•	•	•	•	•	•	•	•	•	•	•	•	•	•
Glen Canyon (F-4) 1,250,000 acres.		•	•	•	•	•	•	•	•	•	•	•	•	•	•
STATE															
Antelope Island (B-3) 28,022 acres in the Great Salt Lake 9.8 mi. w. of Syracuse via West 1700 South and the 7-mi.-long Davis County Cswy. Bird-watching, kayaking; American bison herd. *(See Great Salt Lake p. 317.)*	❶	•	•	•					•	•	•		•		•
Bear Lake (A-4) 69,760 acres 1.5 mi. n. of Garden City on US 89. Scuba diving, water skiing.	❷	•	•		•	•	•	•	•	•			•		•
Dead Horse Point (E-6) 5,362 acres 9 mi. n. of Moab via US 191, then 18 mi. s.w. on SR 313. Scenic. *(See Moab p. 330.)*	❸	•	•	•						•	•	•	•		•
Deer Creek (C-4) 3,000 acres 9 mi. s.w. of Heber City on US 189. Sailing, water skiing, windsurfing.	❹	•	•		•	•	•	•	•	•			•		
East Canyon (B-3) 950 acres 25 mi. n.e. of Salt Lake City on SR 65. Water skiing.	❺	•	•		•	•		•	•	•			•		•
Escalante Petrified Forest (F-3) 1,784 acres 1 mi. w. of Escalante on SR 12, then .5 mi. on an unnamed road, following signs. Historic. *(See Escalante p. 310.)*	❻	•	•	•				•	•	•			•	•	
Fremont Indian (E-3) 1,784 acres 5 mi. s.w. of Sevier off I-70 exit 17. Historic. Archeological site, interpretive trails, museum. *(See Sevier p. 402.)*	❼	•	•	•				•		•	•	•		•	•
Green River (D-5) 53 acres 1 mi. s. of Green River off Main St. Golf (nine holes).	❽	•	•		•	•		•		•					
Gunlock Lake (G-1) 600 acres 1 mi. s. of Gunlock, then n. on Old US 91. Water skiing, wildlife viewing.	❾	•	•		•	•	•	•	•	•					
Huntington (D-4) 350 acres 2 mi. n. of Huntington on SR 10. Bird-watching, ice fishing, water skiing.	❿	•	•		•	•		•	•	•					
Hyrum (A-3) 450 acres s.w. of Hyrum on the n. shore of Hyrum Reservoir. Ice fishing, water skiing, wildlife viewing.	⓫	•	•	•	•	•	•	•	•	•	•		•		

Recreation Areas Chart

The map location numerals in column 2 show an area's location on the preceding map.

	MAP LOCATION	CAMPING	PICNICKING	HIKING TRAILS	BOATING	BOAT RAMP	BOAT RENTAL	FISHING	SWIMMING	PETS ON LEASH	BICYCLE TRAILS	NATURE PROGS.	VISITOR CENTER	LODGE/CABINS	FOOD SERVICE
Jordanelle (B-4) 4,000 acres n. of Heber City on US 40, then 6 mi. s.e. on SR 248. Scenic. Canoeing, ice fishing, kayaking, sailing, wildlife viewing; beaches, interpretive trails, nature center, playground.	12	•	•	•	•	•	•	•	•	•	•	•	•		•
Jordan River (B-3) 500 acres along an 8.5 mi. corridor of the Jordan River from 1700 South in Salt Lake City to the Davis County line. Golf (nine holes), jogging; exercise course, model airplane and helicopter ports, off-highway vehicle and motocross tracks.	13		•	•	•			•		•	•				
Kodachrome Basin (F-3) 4,000 acres 9 mi. s.e. of Cannonville on Kodachrome Rd. Wildlife viewing; horse rental. *(See Cannonville p. 301.)*	14	•	•	•						•	•				
Lost Creek (B-4) 415 acres 10 mi. n.e. of Croydon on Lost Creek Rd. Ice fishing, water skiing. Non-motorized boats only.	15		•		•	•		•	•	•					
Millsite (D-4) 435 acres w. of Ferron off SR 10. Water skiing; all-terrain vehicle and mountain biking trails.	16	•	•		•	•		•	•	•	•	•			
Otter Creek (F-3) 3,120 acres 5 mi. n.w. of Antimony on SR 22.	17	•	•		•	•	•	•	•	•			•		•
Palisade (D-3) 62 acres 10 mi. s. of Manti off US 89. Canoeing, golf (18 holes), ice fishing, water skiing.	18	•	•		•	•	•	•	•	•					•
Piute (E-3) 3,360 acres 12 mi. s. of Marysvale off US 89. Canoeing, ice fishing, kayaking, rock hounding, waterfowl hunting. Electric boats only.	19	•	•		•	•		•	•	•			•		
Quail Creek (G-1) 1,000 acres 14 mi. n.e. of St. George on SR 9. Canoeing, kayaking, winter fishing.	20		•		•	•		•	•	•					
Red Fleet (B-6) 1,963 acres 13 mi. n. of Vernal on US 191. Canoeing, ice fishing, kayaking.	21	•	•		•	•		•		•					
Rockport (B-4) 550 acres 45 mi. e. of Salt Lake City just off I-80. Cross-country skiing, ice fishing, mountain biking, snowshoeing, water skiing.	22	•	•	•	•	•	•	•	•	•	•				•
Sand Hollow (G-1) 20,000 acres 7 mi. e. off I-15 exit 16 (SR 9) near Hurricane. Canoeing, kayaking, mountain biking; sand dunes.	23	•	•	•	•	•		•	•	•			•		
Scofield (C-4) 2,815 acres 35 mi. w. of Price on SR 96. Canoeing, cross-country skiing, ice fishing, kayaking, snowmobiling.	24	•	•		•	•	•	•	•	•			•		
Snow Canyon (G-1) 7,100 acres 3.7 mi. n. of Ivins on SR 8. Mountain biking, rock climbing, wildlife viewing; horseback riding trails. *(See Ivins p. 320.)*	25	•	•	•						•	•				
Starvation (C-5) 3,500 acres 4 mi. n.w. of Duchesne. Ice fishing, water skiing.	26	•	•		•	•	•	•	•	•			•		•
Steinaker (C-6) 750 acres 6 mi. n. of Vernal off SR 191. Ice fishing, water skiing.	27	•	•		•	•		•	•	•			•		
Utah Lake (C-3) 295 acres 4 mi. w. of Provo off I-15. Ice fishing, water skiing; ice-skating rink. *(See American Fork p. 291.)*	28	•	•		•	•		•	•	•			•	•	•
Wasatch Mountain (C-3) 21,592 acres 2 mi. w. of Midway. Historic. Cross-country skiing, golf (54 holes), horseback riding, inline skating, mountain biking, snowmobiling, wildlife viewing; off-highway vehicle trails.	29	•	•	•				•	•	•	•	•	•		•
Willard Bay (A-3) 2,673 acres 15 mi. n. of Ogden. Ice fishing, water skiing; interpretive trails.	30	•	•		•	•	•	•	•	•			•		
Yuba (D-3) 660 acres 25 mi. w. of Nephi off I-15. Ice fishing, mountain biking, water skiing.	31	•	•		•	•		•	•	•			•		
OTHER															
Fort Buenaventura (B-3) 84 acres at 2450 A Ave. in Ogden. Historic. Canoeing. *(See Ogden p. 341.)*	32	•	•	•				•					•	•	
Minersville Lake (E-2) 1,130 acres 12 mi. s.w. of Beaver on SR 21.	33	•	•		•	•		•	•	•					•
Sand Flats Recreation Area (E-5) 7,320 acres .5 mi. e. of Moab on Mill Creek Dr., then 2.5 mi. n.e. on Sand Flats Rd. to entrance booth. *(See Moab p. 332.)*	34	•	•	•						•	•				

ALTA (B-3) pop. 383, elev. 8,583'
• Part of Salt Lake City area — see map p. 368

Alta ballooned into a raucous mining town of 5,000 people with the 1865 discovery of silver. The presence of six breweries and 26 saloons did little to cool the tempers that resulted in more than 100 killings in the town's first few years. The 1873 devaluation of silver put an end to Alta's heyday, and the town languished until the first ski lodge was built in 1940.

The Alta area is now known for many excellent ski areas, all of which offer snow skiing November through May. It also is where the U.S. Forest Service began its avalanche control program, which eliminates such hazards through the use of artillery shells or explosives. The canyon road to the town has alternate routes that avoid these areas.

RECREATIONAL ACTIVITIES
Skiing
• **Alta Ski Area** is off I-215 exit 6 to SR 210, following signs. **Hours:** Daily 9:15-4:30, mid-Nov. to mid-Apr.; Fri.-Sun. 9:15-4:30, mid-Apr. to late Apr. (weather permitting). **Phone:** (801) 359-1078.

AMERICAN FORK (C-3) pop. 26,263, elev. 4,563'

At the foot of the Wasatch Mountains, American Fork lies in the shadow of 11,750-foot Mount Timpanogos. Utah Lake State Park *(see Recreation Areas Chart)*, at the southern edge of town, has the largest body of fresh water in the intermountain region. The lake offers boating, fishing and skiing. Duck hunting is permitted on the lake beyond the state park boundaries.

The Alpine Scenic Loop, a paved highway, encircles Mount Timpanogos; it is especially popular for its spectacular autumn foliage. Points of interest along the 45-minute drive include Bridal Veil Falls, Timpanogos Cave National Monument *(see place listing p. 406)* and American Fork Canyon. This road is narrow and not recommended for RVs.

American Fork Chamber of Commerce: 51 E. Main St., American Fork, UT 84003. **Phone:** (801) 756-5110.

HOLIDAY INN EXPRESS & SUITES AMERICAN FORK
801/763-8500
▼▼▼ **Contemporary Hotel.** Rates not provided. **Address:** 712 S Utah Valley Dr 84003 **Location:** I-15 exit 276, 0.3 mi n on S 500 E, just e on E 620 S, then 0.3 mi s. **Facility:** 80 units. 3 stories, interior corridors. **Pool(s):** heated indoor. **Activities:** hot tub, limited exercise equipment.
CALL &M ⊛ BIZ ⊗ ⊠ ▤ ▤ ▣ / SOME UNITS ⬛

VALUE PLACE   801/492-1600
▼ **Extended Stay Hotel.** Rates not provided. **Address:** 57 N 900 W 84003 **Location:** I-15 exit 278, just w. **Facility:** 121 efficiencies. 4 stories, interior corridors. **Guest Services:** coin laundry.
 ▮▶ ⊛ ▤ ▤

ARCHES NATIONAL PARK (E-6)

Elevations in the park range from 4,500 ft. at the visitor center to 5,200 ft. at Devils Garden. Refer to AAA maps for additional elevation information.

Arches National Park lies 5 miles northwest of Moab on US 191. The rugged area contains the largest number of natural stone arches in the country. Along with more than 2,000 arches are many red rock canyons, spires, fins and balancing rocks. The erosion of the Entrada Sandstone, a 300-foot-thick layer of rock that was deposited as sand 150 million years ago, created these formations.

The arches were formed by the weathering of openings in vertical slabs of sandstone. Opinions vary as to how big an opening must be before it can be classified as an arch, but park officials consider arches to be any opening extending at least 3 feet in any one direction.

General Information and Activities

The park is open year-round. It is particularly photogenic in the morning and evening light, when the sandstone formations take on a fiery glow. Many highlights can be seen from the road, but short foot trails lead to some of the most impressive features. A few trails entail strenuous climbs, and hikers must carry water.

Two miles past the visitor center at the park's entrance, the main road passes the Park Avenue viewpoint. Park Avenue offers an easy 1-mile hike through a red rock canyon whose walls resemble a city skyline. Those who have taken the hike can be picked up farther along the road at the end of the trail.

One of the most accessible areas is the Windows section, where visitors can study the basic geology of arches. Grouped together at the end of a side road 12 miles from the visitor center are Double Arch, Turret Arch, the North Window and the South Window. The route to this area leaves the main road 9 miles past the visitor center.

A paved road passing the Wolfe Ranch and ending at a viewpoint for Delicate Arch *(see attraction listing)* leaves the main road 2.5 miles farther. From the Wolfe Ranch a strenuous, 3-mile roundtrip trail leads to Delicate Arch. At the ranch are the weathered remnants of a homesteader's 20-year sojourn in this barren land in the late 1800s.

The Devils Garden section extends from the end of the paved road 18 miles from the visitor center. Only Skyline Arch is visible from the road, but many more arches, including Landscape Arch *(see attraction listing)*, can be reached by a 1.6-mile round-trip trail. Camping spaces can be reserved March through October and are on a first-come, first-served basis the rest of the year; phone (877) 444-6777, or TTY (877) 833-6777 for reservations. *See Recreation Areas Chart.*

ADMISSION is $25 (per private vehicle); $15 (per person arriving by motorcycle); $10 (per person arriving by other means). The above fees permit entrance to the park for 7 calendar days from date of purchase. An annual pass is $50. The annual permit also is valid for Canyonlands National Park (see place listing p. 301) and Natural Bridges (see place listing p. 339) and Hovenweep (see place listing in Colorado p. 213) national monuments. The camping fee is $25. Fees also are charged for some interpretive programs and ranger-guided walks March through October.

PETS are permitted in parking areas or on roads only if they are on a leash no longer than 6 feet, crated or otherwise physically restricted at all times. Pets are not allowed on trails or in the backcountry areas.

ADDRESS inquiries to the Superintendent, Arches National Park, P.O. Box 907, Moab, UT 84532-0907; phone (435) 719-2100. The superintendent's office is open Mon.-Fri. 8-4:30.

DELICATE ARCH is 15 mi. n.e. from the Arches National Park entrance. Set amid cliffs and slickrock domes, the freestanding arch, with an opening of nearly 35 feet, can be seen from a distant viewpoint 1 mile to the southeast. The viewpoint is accessible by a short hike from the Delicate Arch Viewpoint parking area. The arch is reached by a strenuous 3-mile round-trip trail starting at the Wolfe Ranch parking area. During the morning the arch is silhouetted against the sun; afternoon is the best time to take close-up pictures, but it also is the hottest and most crowded part of the day.

LANDSCAPE ARCH is in the Devils Garden section of Arches National Park. With a span of 306 feet and a height of 105 feet, it is one of the longest natural stone arches in the world; at one point it is only 6 feet thick. The arch can be reached by a 2-mile round-trip trail starting at the Devils Garden trailhead parking area.

VISITOR CENTER is just inside the Arches National Park entrance. The center offers exhibits about the park's cultural and natural history and presents an orientation film. Campfire talks and guided trips take place March through October. **Hours:** Daily 7:30-6, mid-June to early Sept.; 8-4:30, early Sept.-Nov. 1; 9-4, rest of year. Closed Christmas. **Phone:** (435) 719-2299.

ASHLEY NATIONAL FOREST (B-4)

Elevations in the forest range from 6,000 ft. at Antelope Canyon to 13,528 ft. at Kings Peak. Refer to AAA maps for additional elevation information.

In the northeast corner of Utah, Ashley National Forest includes the only major mountain range in the lower 48 states with an east-west alignment—the Uintas. Ashley National Forest embraces this area and the pinion-juniper and ponderosa pine-covered benchland along the Green River. One of the major water-producing areas in the state of Utah, the forest was established by President Theodore Roosevelt in 1908.

The forest contains most of the High Uintas Wilderness (see attraction listing), the spectacular Red Canyon of the Green River, and 13,528-foot Kings Peak, the highest of Utah's mountains. Flaming Gorge Dam and National Recreation Area (see place listing p. 313) provides many recreational and scenic opportunities. This 502-foot-high dam is 1,180 feet long and contains water for 91 miles. Hunting for pronghorn antelopes, mule deer, elk, mountain lions and black bears is allowed in the forest.

Several drives provide access to areas of scenic and geological interest. The Flaming Gorge-Uintas National Scenic Byway (US 191), Utah's first national forest scenic byway, extends from Vernal to the Wyoming border, traversing an area in which a billion years of Earth's history lie exposed. The Sheep Creek Canyon Geological Area, north and west of the byway, is reached via US 191 and another paved road. The Red Cloud Loop, a dirt and gravel road that is rough in spots, is a scenic forest drive that can be accessed near Vernal.

Camping is available in improved sites and backcountry areas throughout the forest. For camping reservations contact the National Recreation Reservation System, P.O. Box 140, Ballston Spa, N.Y. 12020; phone (877) 444-6777, or TTY (877) 833-6777.

For further information contact the Forest Supervisor, Ashley National Forest, 355 N. Vernal Ave., Vernal, UT 84078; phone (435) 789-1181. See Recreation Areas Chart.

INSIDER INFO:
Mountain Driving

Driving through scenic mountains in the western United States can be the high point of your long-awaited vacation—or it can be disastrous. The trick is to know what to expect and to be prepared. By taking a little time before you leave, you can eliminate most potential problems before they happen.

Many tips for safe mountain driving are purely common sense and apply to driving in general: Before you begin your trip, check the weather and road conditions along the way and at your destination; let a member of your family or a friend know where you're going and the route you plan on taking, including stops along the way; keep your gas tank near full, as service stations may be far apart; make sure your car and your tires are in tip-top shape; observe posted speed limits, especially on narrow, winding roads; keep a first-aid kit in your car; and stop every 2-3 hours to stretch and help prevent fatigue.

Remember that high elevations can mean changing weather and road conditions. If you are traveling in winter, make sure you have the following items in your vehicle: a scraper, tire chains, booster cables, shovel, flashlight, blanket, warm clothing and nonperishable food. Be aware that high altitudes (usually above 8,000 feet) can cause headaches, shortness of breath or a lack of energy.

Downshifting to a lower gear when going up or down steep grades will lessen engine and brake stress. Leaving your air conditioner off while ascending a steep hill will also help eliminate strain on your engine. On downhill slopes, tap your brakes instead of applying full pressure in order to avoid overheating and possible brake failure. Consider changing to a brake fluid listed as DOT 4; this grade has a higher boiling point and is recommended for mountain-driving conditions.

Experts advise that it is best to maintain a steady speed whenever possible when driving mountain roads in winter; it is also best not to engage your cruise control in wintry driving situations. Try to avoid starting or stopping suddenly. If you encounter slippery or icy roads, remember the technique of applying gentle pressure on your brakes; this will help avoid skidding or spinning. If you do find yourself in a skid, stay calm, take your foot off the accelerator or brake and steer in the direction you want the front of the car to go. Be aware that it takes longer to stop on snow or ice, so give yourself plenty of time. And when you do stop, be sure to set your emergency brake.

HIGH UINTAS WILDERNESS extends from Mirror Lake eastward beyond Kings Peak to North Pole Pass. It encompasses approximately 456,705 mountainous acres of forests and lakes and offers 545 miles of trails. Ridges divide the region into large scenic basins interspersed with high glacial moraines and drifts. The floors of these basins are a spectacular contrast to the abrupt ridges rising several thousand feet. Many of the hundreds of lakes are stocked with trout.

Backpacking is the most popular way to visit the High Uintas; no motor vehicles are allowed. Visitors should register at a trailhead before entering the area. **Hours:** The wilderness is accessible late June to mid-Sept. **Cost:** Free. **Phone:** (435) 789-1181.

RED CANYON VISITOR CENTER is 40 mi. n. of Vernal via US 44. The center contains exhibits about natural and cultural history. An observation deck overlooks the Flaming Gorge National Recreation Area *(see place listing p. 313)* and the Uinta Mountains. **Hours:** Mon.-Thurs. 10-5, Fri.-Sun. 9-6, mid-May to mid-Sept.; phone for schedule rest of year. **Cost:** Free. **Phone:** (435) 889-3713.

BEAVER (E-2) pop. 3,112, elev. 5,898'

BEAVER COURTHOUSE MUSEUM is at 90 E. Center St. The courthouse, destroyed by fire in 1882, was rebuilt and used through 1975. Now strictly a museum, it contains the U.S. flag that flew on the USS *Utah,* which sank during the attack on Pearl Harbor. Also displayed are re-created judges' chambers, court recorder's and sheriff's offices, and several 19th-century items. The jail in the basement was used through 1976. **Hours:** Tues.-Sat. and holidays 11-5, June 1-Labor Day. **Cost:** Donations. **Phone:** (435) 438-5727.

BEAVER DAYS INN   (435)438-7800

♦♦ Motel $54-$89 **Address:** 646 W 1400 N 84713 **Location:** I-15 exit 112, just w. Across from travel center and truck stop. **Facility:** 29 units. 2 stories (no elevator), interior corridors. **Guest Services:** coin laundry.

BEST WESTERN BUTCH CASSIDY INN   (435)438-2438

◆◆ Motel $72-$119

AAA Benefit: Save 10% or more every day and earn 10% bonus points!

Address: 161 S Main St 84713 **Location:** I-15 exit 109, 1.8 mi e. **Facility:** 35 units, some two bedrooms. 2 stories (no elevator), exterior corridors. **Terms:** cancellation fee imposed. **Pool(s):** heated outdoor. **Featured Amenity:** full hot breakfast.

BEST WESTERN PARADISE INN   (435)438-2455

◆◆ Hotel $79-$149

AAA Benefit: Save 10% or more every day and earn 10% bonus points!

Address: 314 W 1425 N 84713 **Location:** I-15 exit 112, just e. **Facility:** 53 units, some two bedrooms. 2 stories (no elevator), exterior corridors. **Pool(s):** heated indoor. **Activities:** hot tub.

COMFORT INN & SUITES   (435)438-6283

◆◆ Hotel $84-$145

Address: 1540 S Main St 84713 **Location:** I-15 exit 109, just e. **Facility:** 54 units. 2 stories, interior corridors. **Pool(s):** heated indoor. **Activities:** hot tub, limited exercise equipment. **Guest Services:** coin laundry. **Featured Amenity:** full hot breakfast.

QUALITY INN   (435)438-5426

[fyi] Hotel $60-$90 Under major renovation, scheduled to be completed June 2015. Last Rated: ◆◆ **Address:** 781 W 1800 S 84713 **Location:** I-15 exit 109, just w. **Facility:** 52 units. 2 stories (no elevator), interior corridors. **Pool(s):** heated indoor. **Activities:** hot tub.

WHERE TO EAT

ARSHEL'S CAFE   435/438-2977

◆◆ American Family Dining $6-$15

AAA Inspector Notes: *Classic.* Cozy and friendly, family-owned and operated since 1944, the cafe specializes in fresh homemade pies, country-fried chicken and steak. **Address:** 711 N Main St 84713 **Location:** I-15 exit 112, 0.8 mi se.

CRAZY COW CAFE   435/438-6208

▼▼ American. Family Dining. $10-$30 **AAA Inspector Notes:** This restaurant has been converted into a fun atmosphere with a crazy cow décor - which is one of the reasons it is so popular. There is a salad bar open to the small dining room but casual menu. **Address:** 1451 N 300 W 84713 **Location:** I-15 exit 112, just e. B L D

HUNAN GARDEN CHINESE RESTAURANT   435/438-5070

▼ Chinese. Casual Dining. $6-$12 **AAA Inspector Notes:** This basic restaurant offers standard Chinese menu items in a rustic dining room. There is only one server most of the time and if you're craving Chinese food, this is the only place in town. **Address:** 1425 N 400 W 84713 **Location:** I-15 exit 112, just e. L D

TIMBERLINE INN RESTAURANT   435/438-2474

▼▼ American. Family Dining. $9-$26 **AAA Inspector Notes:** Since 1983, the restaurant has been a favorite among families. All day long, guests can order food like Mom used to make, including anytime breakfast items. Servers are friendly. **Address:** 1542 S 450 W 84713 **Location:** I-15 exit 109, just w. B L D

BINGHAM CANYON (C-3) elev. 6,280'
• Part of Salt Lake City area — see map p. 368

Prospectors seeking gold, silver and lead were active in Bingham Canyon as early as 1863, but until the late 1800s they neglected the most promising mineral: copper. About 300,000 tons a year of the nation's refined-grade copper, as well as quantities of gold and silver, come from the open pit mine of Kennecott Utah Copper Corporation's Bingham Canyon Mine.

KENNECOTT'S BINGHAM CANYON MINE is just w. of jct. SR 111 and West 11800 South St., off Kennecott Access Rd. Mining began here in 1906 in what was to become one of the largest open-pit mines in the world. The mine provides 15 percent of the nation's copper needs for medicine, food and technology. The terraced pit is three-quarters of a mile deep and about 2.5 miles wide; the working area covers 1,900 acres. **Note:** The overlook and visitor center is closed indefinitely following a 2013 landslide. Phone for further updates. **Phone:** (801) 204-2025.

BLANDING (F-6) pop. 3,375, elev. 6,000'

Originally a trading center for the surrounding stock ranches, Blanding was settled in 1905 as a result of an irrigation project that still waters abundant crops of hay and grain. Several trading posts deal in Native American arts and crafts.

The town borders some of southeastern Utah's most dramatic canyon country. Natural Bridges National Monument *(see place listing p. 339)* and Glen Canyon National Recreation Area *(see place listing p. 314)* are west via SR 95.

Beginning just southwest of town is the 100-mile loop known as the Trail of the Ancients, along which can be seen many remnants of the Anasazi Indian culture that flourished A.D. 300-1300. The trail begins at Edge of the Cedars State Park *(see attraction listing)* and follows US 191 and US 163 east to Mexican Hat *(see place listing p. 327)*, then north on SR 261 and east again on SR 95. Some sections of SR 261 are unpaved and not recommended for RVs or trailers. Trail of the Ancients also takes a side trip

on SR 262 to Hovenweep National Monument *(see place listing in Colorado p. 213)*.

Blanding Visitor Center: 12 N. Grayson Pkwy., Blanding, UT 84511. **Phone:** (435) 678-3662.

THE DINOSAUR MUSEUM is at 754 South 200 West. The museum displays a 360-pound meteorite, dinosaur skeletons, life-size models and fossil trees that are more than 275 million years old. The History Hall of Hollywood Dinosaur Movies features original movie posters, models and memorabilia. A 3,000-square-foot exhibit hall opened in 2013 with two exhibits: Feathered Dinosaurs and More Dinosaurs in the Movies. **Time:** Allow 1 hour minimum. **Hours:** Mon.-Sat. 9-5, Apr. 15-Oct. 15. **Cost:** $3.50; $2.50 (ages 55+); $2 (ages 4-12). **Phone:** (435) 678-3454.

EDGE OF THE CEDARS STATE PARK, just off US 191 at 660 West 400 North, is the site of a Puebloan Indian village, inhabited A.D. 825-1125, and a museum. The museum features the largest collection of Ancestral Puebloan (Anasazi) pottery on display in the Four Corners area. Visitors can descend a ladder to enter the 1,000-year-old kiva, a ceremonial structure that is partially underground. Archeology and art exhibitions also are offered. **Hours:** Museum Mon.-Sat. 9-5, Sun. 10-4, Apr.-Sept.; Mon.-Sat. 9-5, rest of year. Closed Jan. 1, Thanksgiving and Christmas. **Cost:** $5; $3 (Utah residents ages 62+ with ID). **Phone:** (435) 678-2238.

SUPER 8   (435)678-3880

▼▼ Motel $60-$200 **Address:** 755 S Main St 84511 **Location:** On US 191 (Main St). **Facility:** 59 units. 2 stories (no elevator), interior corridors. **Activities:** hot tub. **Guest Services:** coin laundry.

WHERE TO EAT

HOMESTEAD STEAK HOUSE   435/678-3456

▼▼ American. Family Dining. $6-$20 **AAA Inspector Notes:** Patrons enjoy favorite home-cooked meals in a casual family-friendly setting. **Features:** patio dining. **Address:** 121 E Center 84511 **Location:** Downtown. L D

BLUFF (G-6) pop. 258, elev. 4,320'

Bluff lies in the shadow of the Navajo Twins, two massive sandstone turrets towering over the valley of the San Juan River. Nearby ruins include the Pioneer Cemetery, off US 191 following signs, and the 14-Window Ruin, on a marked trail in the Navajo reservation.

St. Christopher's Mission, a small chapel on SR 162, affords a spectacular view of the surrounding red rock cliffs. Bluff is at the northern end of scenic US 191, which runs southwest through Mexican Hat *(see place listing p. 327)* and continues as US 163 into Arizona.

Bluff Fort Visitors Center: 550 W. Black Locust Ave., Bluff, UT 84512. **Phone:** (435) 672-9995.

RECREATIONAL ACTIVITIES

Hiking

- **Far Out Expeditions** picks up at area lodgings. **Hours:** Half-day, full-day and multi-day hiking trips are offered. **Phone:** (435) 672-2294.

White-water Rafting

- **Wild Rivers Expeditions, LLC** is 1 blk. w. of the post office on US 191 at 101 Main St. **Hours:** One-day raft trips on the San Juan River are offered daily, mid-May to mid-Oct. Two- to 10-day trips also are available. Departure times vary; phone ahead. **Phone:** (435) 672-2244.

DESERT ROSE INN & CABINS   (435)672-2303

▼▼▼◆ **Hotel** $90-$290 **Address:** 701 W Main St 84512 **Location:** On US 191 (Main St), west end of town. **Facility:** 53 units, some cabins. 1-2 stories (no elevator), exterior corridors. **Terms:** check-in 4 pm, resort fee. **Pool(s):** heated indoor. **Activities:** hot tub, exercise room. **Guest Services:** coin laundry.

〖❙〗 ⛵ BIZ 📶 ✕ 🖥 / SOME UNITS 🛗 🖼

KOKOPELLI INN   (435)672-2322

▼ **Motel** $90-$120 **Address:** 160 E Main St 84512 **Location:** On US 191 (Main St). **Facility:** 26 units. 1 story, interior corridors. *Bath:* shower only. **Terms:** closed 11/1-3/31. **Activities:** picnic facilities.

〖❙+〗 📶 ✕ 🖥 🖥

COMB RIDGE COFFEE   435/485-5555

▼ Coffee/Tea Breakfast. Quick Serve. $4-$9 **AAA Inspector Notes:** This special coffeehouse is the perfect spot to take a well-deserved reprieve from driving, biking, hiking—you name it—to check e-mail and enjoy tasty blue corn pancakes and a variety of breads and pastries. **Address:** 680 S Hwy 191 84512 **Location:** On US 191 (Main St), west end of town. B L

COTTONWOOD STEAKHOUSE   435/672-2282

▼▼◆

Steak
Barbecue
Casual Dining
$16-$25

AAA Inspector Notes: Indoor dining in an Old West atmosphere can't get more relaxing, but guests also can enjoy dinner in covered booths beneath a beautiful cottonwood tree beside an evening campfire in the outside courtyard. Entrées are grilled to order over an open flame. In addition to steaks such as the marshal, the deputy and the maverick, the menu lists half or full racks of barbecue ribs, barbecue chicken and grilled salmon. The vegetable stir-fry in spicy Thai peanut sauce is delicious. **Features:** beer & wine, patio dining. **Address:** 409 W Main St 84512 **Location:** Just s of center. D

TWIN ROCKS CAFE & GIFT SHOP   435/672-2341

▼▼ American. Casual Dining. $6-$22 **AAA Inspector Notes:** Located beneath scenic red rock towers, the eatery features indigenous Native American dishes, including fry bread and chicken soup with homemade noodles, Navajo tacos and burgers, smoked meats, vegetarian entrées such as the sautéed vegetable medley or spicy peanut stir-fry, and micro-brewed beers. Special desserts include an apple puff pastry and their famous fruits of the forest pie. The attractive outdoor covered patio with many plants and bird feeders for the hummingbirds is inviting. **Features:** beer & wine, patio dining. **Address:** 913 E Navajo Twins Dr 84512 **Location:** On US 191 (Main St); east end of town. B L D

BOULDER (F-4) pop. 226, elev. 6,640'

Boulder lies on SR 12, a particularly scenic route that runs through Escalante and Cannonville to Panguitch. For 5 miles south of Boulder unusual formations of white slickrock are shot with bursts of red hues.

ANASAZI STATE PARK MUSEUM is on SR 12. The park is the site of an Anasazi Indian village that may have been occupied A.D. 1160-1235. One hundred Ancestral Puebloan structures have been excavated; a self-guiding trail leads visitors through the site. A life-size six-room replica of an Anasazi dwelling depicts village life almost 800 years ago. The museum displays decorated ceramic artifacts that were found in the region. **Hours:** Daily 8-6, May-Oct.; 9-4, rest of year. Closed Jan. 1, Thanksgiving and Christmas. **Cost:** $5; $10 (family, maximum eight people). **Phone:** (435) 335-7308. Ⓐ

BOULDER MOUNTAIN LODGE   435/335-7460

▼▼▼ **Hotel** $115-$325 **Address:** 20 N Hwy 12 84716 **Location:** Just s. **Facility:** 22 units, some two bedrooms. 2 stories (no elevator), interior/exterior corridors. **Terms:** check-in 4 pm, 31 day cancellation notice-fee imposed. **Dining:** Hell's Backbone Grill, see separate listing. **Activities:** hot tub, lawn sports. **Guest Services:** valet laundry.

〖❙〗 BIZ 📶 ✕ 🖥 🖼 🖥 / SOME UNITS 🐾

BOULDER MESA RESTAURANT   435/335-7447

▼▼ American. Family Dining. $10-$20 **AAA Inspector Notes:** The eatery offers meticulously prepared meals including sandwiches, hand-pressed hamburgers, fresh salads and soup; an extensive vegetarian menu is also available as well as breakfast. **Features:** beer & wine. **Address:** 155 E Burr Trail Rd 84716 **Location:** Just e. B L D

HELL'S BACKBONE GRILL   435/335-7464

▼▼▼ Natural/Organic. Casual Dining. $18-$38 **AAA Inspector Notes:** A rugged frontier look gives this place its interesting character. The Western-range menu changes weekly and features locally raised meats and vegetables from an on-site organic garden. **Features:** beer & wine, patio dining. **Reservations:** suggested. **Address:** 20 N Hwy 12 84716 **Location:** Just s; in Boulder Mountain Lodge. B L D

BOUNTIFUL pop. 42,552

- **Hotels & Restaurants map & index p. 385**
- **Part of Salt Lake City area — see map p. 368**

COUNTRY INN & SUITES BY CARLSON - SALT LAKE CITY/ BOUNTIFUL   (801)292-8100 ㉕

▼▼▼ **Hotel** $89-$159 **Address:** 999 N 500 W 84010 **Location:** I-15 exit 317 northbound, just e, then 0.3 mi n; exit southbound, 0.5 mi s. **Facility:** 86 units. 4 stories, interior corridors. **Pool(s):** heated indoor. **Activities:** hot tub, exercise room. **Guest Services:** valet and coin laundry, area transportation.

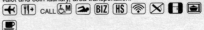

ROBINTINO'S   801/298-1515 ⑲

▼▼ Italian. Casual Dining. $7-$15 **AAA Inspector Notes:** With a simple atmosphere and friendly staff, the eatery serves traditional Italian entrées, pizza, steak and seafood. All entrees are served with garlic bread and one side item. You can't beat the daily specials and guests will appreciate the combination plates and lite dinners offered. A children's menu is available. **Features:** beer only. **Address:** 1385 S 500 W 84010 **Location:** I-15 exit 315 (2600 S), just e, then 1 mi n. L D

BRIAN HEAD (F-2) pop. 83, elev. 9,800'

RECREATIONAL ACTIVITIES
Skiing

- **Brian Head Resort** is at 329 S. SR 143. Other activities are offered. **Hours:** Open daily, mid-Nov. to mid-Apr. Hours vary; phone ahead. **Phone:** (435) 677-2035 or (866) 930-1010.

CEDAR BREAKS LODGE   435/677-3000
 **Resort Hotel.** Rates not provided. **Address:** 223 Hunter Ridge Dr 84719 **Location:** On SR 143. **Facility:** At 9,600 feet and at the bottom of a mountain, this is a skier's paradise. The three buildings have a lodge feel with fireplaces and large hot tubs. 118 units, some two bedrooms, efficiencies and kitchens. 3 stories, interior corridors. **Terms:** check-in 4 pm. **Amenities:** safes. **Pool(s):** heated indoor. **Activities:** sauna, hot tub, steamroom, downhill & cross country skiing, playground, game room, exercise room, spa. **Guest Services:** complimentary laundry.

THE GRAND LODGE AT BRIAN HEAD   435/677-9000
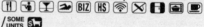 **Resort Hotel.** Rates not provided. **Address:** 314 Hunter Ridge Dr 84719 **Location:** On SR 143. **Facility:** Rustic and elegant, this hotel offers heated sidewalks, beautifully appointed guest rooms with breathtaking views of the surrounding mountains, upscale bathrooms and a covered outdoor deck. 100 units, some two bedrooms. 3 stories, interior corridors. **Terms:** check-in 4 pm. **Amenities:** safes. **Dining:** 2 restaurants. **Pool(s):** heated indoor. **Activities:** hot tub, downhill & cross country skiing, snowmobiling, bicycles, exercise room, spa. **Guest Services:** coin laundry.

BRIGHAM CITY (A-3) pop. 17,899, elev. 4,310'

The Wasatch Range is a towering backdrop for the busy agricultural and manufacturing center of Brigham City. The city began in 1851 as Box Elder. In 1856 it was renamed for Brigham Young, who delivered his last public address in the town in 1877. Relics of the early days of Mormon settlement can be seen in the Community Center, the Brigham City Museum *(see attraction listing)* and the Golden Spike Display. The Golden Spike National Historic Site *(see place listing p. 315)* is 32 miles west.

The city's foundation is a fertile alluvial delta that produces some of Utah's finest peaches as well as apricots, cherries and other crops. From July to mid-September fruit stands flank the 10-mile section of SR 89 known as the Golden Spike Fruitway.

Brigham City Area Chamber of Commerce: 6 N. Main St., Brigham City, UT 84302. **Phone:** (435) 723-3931.

BEAR RIVER MIGRATORY BIRD REFUGE AND JAMES V. HANSEN WILDLIFE EDUCATION CENTER is 15 mi. w. off I-15 exit 363 (Forest St.) and at 2155 W. Forest St., respectively. The 80,000-acre refuge, which consists of pristine marshes, uplands and open water, attracts migrating bald eagles, falcons, hawks and swans and is an important breeding and stopover site for several species of waterfowl.

A 12-mile-long auto tour loop follows a dike road and allows for wildlife viewing. Boasting a modern architectural design, the education center features interactive exhibits as well as a wetland diorama, a video presentation and a .5-mile walking trail. Various activities, including those geared toward children, are offered.

Time: Allow 1 hour minimum. **Hours:** Refuge auto loop accessible daily dawn-dusk (weather permitting). Education center open Mon.-Fri. 8-5, Sat. 10-4. Guided refuge tours are offered seasonally. Closed major holidays. **Cost:** Free. **Phone:** (435) 723-5887.

BOX ELDER STAKE TABERNACLE is at 251 S. Main St. The tabernacle of The Church of Jesus Christ of Latter-day Saints is an effective blend of Gothic and neoclassic architecture. Begun in 1868, it was rebuilt after a fire in 1896. **Hours:** Guided tours Tues.-Sun. noon-8, Mon. noon-6, Memorial Day-Labor Day; phone for schedule, rest of year. **Cost:** Free. **Phone:** (435) 734-3300.

BRIGHAM CITY MUSEUM, 24 North 300 West, displays settlement artifacts and furnishings, items relating to the history of Brigham City 1850-1900, and rotating art exhibits. **Hours:** Tues.-Fri. 11-6, Sat. 1-5. Closed most holidays. **Cost:** Free. **Phone:** (435) 723-6769.

INSPIRATION POINT is near the top of Willard Peak (Mount Baldy). The site offers a view that extends into Idaho and, on a clear day, Nevada. The point is reached by a 16-mile drive from Brigham City; the narrow mountain road from Mantua is hazardous.

CRYSTAL INN BRIGHAM CITY   (435)723-0440

◆◆ **Hotel** $85-$229 **Address:** 480 Westland Dr 84302 **Location:** I-15 exit 362, 1 mi e to S 500 W, then just n. **Facility:** 53 units. 2 stories (no elevator), interior corridors. **Pool(s):** heated indoor. **Activities:** hot tub, picnic facilities, exercise room. **Guest Services:** coin laundry. *(See ad this page.)*

HAMPTON INN BRIGHAM CITY   (435)538-7080

◆◆◆ **Hotel** $89-$139 **Address:** 40 N Main St 84302 **Location:** I-15 exit 362, 2 mi e, then 1.8 mi n; downtown. **Facility:** 73 units. 4 stories, interior corridors. **Parking:** winter plug-ins. **Terms:** 1-7 night minimum stay, cancellation fee imposed. **Pool(s):** heated indoor. **Activities:** hot tub, exercise room. **Guest Services:** coin laundry.

WHERE TO EAT

IDLE ISLE CAFE   435/734-2468

◆◆ American. Casual Dining. $7-$12 **AAA Inspector Notes:** *Classic Historic.* Fresh flowers adorn the tables and original hand-crafted booths year-round. The seasonal menu includes hearty soups, seafood, chicken, chef's salads, fettuccine with grilled salmon or chicken breast and pot roast. Root beer floats and malts are served on the original marble-and-onyx soda fountain that contributes to the 1920s family atmosphere. **Features:** 24 S Main St 84302 **Location:** I-15 exit 363 (Forest St), 2.5 mi e, then just s. L D

MADDOX RANCH HOUSE   435/723-8545

◆◆ American. Family Dining. $10-$29 **AAA Inspector Notes:** What a treat to be treated like family at this genuine ranch house serving thick-cut aged beef that's hand cut on the premises. All-natural bison is a specialty, and the menu also includes skinless fried chicken, a nice selection of premium seafood, and homemade cream pies made in house. The homemade rolls, cornpones with raspberry butter, and the coconut cream pie are habit-forming. Seating is available in several dining rooms. **Features:** patio dining, early bird specials. **Address:** 1900 S Hwy 89 84302 **Location:** I-15 exit 362, 2 mi e to SR 89, then 1 mi s. L D CALL

AAA Vacations® packages ...
exciting itineraries and exclusive values

BRIGHTON (B-3) elev. 8,730'
• Part of Salt Lake City area — see map p. 368

A year-round mountain resort at an elevation of more than 8,700 feet, Brighton is at the head of Big Cottonwood Canyon, 25 miles southeast of Salt Lake City.

RECREATIONAL ACTIVITIES
Skiing
• **Brighton Resort** is off I-215 exit 6, following signs to Big Cottonwood Canyon. **Hours:** Daily 9-4, mid-Nov. to mid-Apr. (also Mon.-Sat. 4-9, early Dec.-Mar. 31). **Phone:** (801) 532-4731 or (855) 201-7669.
• **Solitude Mountain Resort** is at 12000 Big Cottonwood Canyon. Other activities are offered. **Hours:** Winter activities daily 9-4, mid-Nov. to late Apr. Schedule varies rest of year; phone ahead. **Phone:** (801) 534-1400 or (800) 748-4754.

BRYCE CANYON CITY (F-3)
• Part of Bryce Canyon National Park area — see map p. 300

BRYCE MUSEUM AND WILDLIFE ADVENTURE is at 1945 W. SR 12. The museum features more than 450 mounted animals indigenous to North America as well as exotic game from Africa, India and Europe in lifelike dioramas. In addition displays of rare birds and fossils; a collection of Native American artifacts, pottery, tools and weapons; and a large group of butterfly specimens are exhibited. Visitors also can see a live herd of fallow deer. ATV and bicycle rentals also are available.

Time: Allow 30 minutes minimum. **Hours:** Daily 9-9, Apr. 1-Nov. 15. Phone ahead to confirm schedule. **Cost:** Museum $8; $5 (ages 3-13). Phone for ATV and bicycle rental rates. **Phone:** (435) 834-5555.

BEST WESTERN PLUS BRYCE CANYON GRAND HOTEL   (435)834-5700

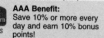
Hotel
$90-$200

Address: 30 N 100 E 84764 **Location:** On SR 63, 1 mi s of SR 12. **Facility:** 164 units. 4 stories, interior corridors. **Terms:** check-in 4 pm. **Pool(s):** heated outdoor. **Activities:** hot tub, fishing, cross country skiing, ice skating, bicycles, playground, exercise room. **Guest Services:** coin laundry, area transportation. **Featured Amenity: breakfast buffet.** *(See ad this page.)*

Choose real ratings you can trust from professional inspectors who've been there

BEST WESTERN PLUS RUBY'S INN   (435)834-5341

Hotel
$70-$150

AAA Benefit:
Save 10% or more every day and earn 10% bonus points!

Address: 26 S Main St 84764 **Location:** On SR 63, 1 mi s of SR 12. **Facility:** 370 units. 1-3 stories, interior/exterior corridors. **Terms:** check-in 4 pm. **Dining:** Canyon Diner, Ruby's Cowboy's Buffet & Steak House, see separate listings, entertainment. **Pool(s):** heated outdoor, heated indoor. **Activities:** hot tub, fishing, cross country skiing, ice skating, bicycles, playground, exercise room. **Guest Services:** coin laundry, area transportation. *(See ad p. 298.)*

BRYCE CANYON PINES   (435)834-5441

Motel
$55-$135

Address: 2476 W Hwy 12, MM 10 84764 **Location:** Jct SR 89, 10 mi e. **Facility:** 50 units, some two bedrooms, three bedrooms, kitchens and cottages. 1-2 stories (no elevator), exterior corridors. **Terms:** check-in 4 pm, 3 day cancellation notice-fee imposed. **Dining:** Bryce Canyon Pines Restaurant, see separate listing. **Pool(s):** heated outdoor. **Activities:** hot tub, cross country skiing.

BRYCE VIEW LODGE   (435)834-5180

Motel
$60-$140

Address: 105 E Center St 84764 **Location:** 1 mi s of SR 12. **Facility:** 160 units. 2 stories (no elevator), exterior corridors. **Terms:** closed 11/1-3/31, check-in 4 pm, cancellation fee imposed, resort fee. **Activities:** fishing, cross country skiing, ice skating, bicycles, playground. **Guest Services:** area transportation. *(See ad p. 298.)*

WHERE TO EAT

BRYCE CANYON PINES RESTAURANT   435/834-5441

Comfort Food. Casual Dining. $5-$30 **AAA Inspector Notes:** This restaurant offers familiar food for hungry hikers. Patrons unwind in a rustic setting with antique-filled walls. Casual cuisine is served such as large cowboy steaks, fresh trout, chicken-fried steak and amazing homemade pies. **Features:** beer & wine. **Address:** 2476 W Hwy 12, MM 10 84764 **Location:** Jct SR 89, 10 mi e; in Bryce Canyon Pines. [B] [L] [D]

CANYON DINER   435/834-8030

Burgers
Pizza
Quick Serve
$4-$20

AAA Inspector Notes: This place caters to on-the-go diners. Basic items, including burgers, nachos and personal pizzas, are served quickly. Everything here is self-service, making it an appealing place to grab a quick bite here or after a hike through the park. **Features:** patio dining. **Address:** 25 N Main St 84764 **Location:** On SR 63, 1 mi s of SR 12; adjacent to BEST WESTERN PLUS Ruby's Inn. [B] [L] [D]

EBENEZER'S BARN AND GRILL   435/834-8003

Western American. Dinner Theatre. $29-$35 **AAA Inspector Notes:** Come and enjoy an authentic Western experience with gun twirling, lassoing and The Bar G Wrangler band. Guests choose rib-eye steak, baked chicken, salmon or pulled pork dishes. The interactive experience is known to be the highlight of some travelers' whole Bryce Canyon experience. **Features:** beer & wine. **Address:** 110 Center St 84764 **Location:** On SR 63, 1 mi s of SR 12. [D]

FOSTER'S FAMILY STEAK HOUSE   435/834-5227

Steak Seafood. Family Dining. $6-$30 **AAA Inspector Notes:** This casual steak house serves fresh steaks, seafood and sandwiches. The western décor features wooden walls and booths along with wildlife art. The boneless grilled chicken is very moist. Desserts are made in the adjacent bakery. **Features:** beer & wine. **Address:** 1150 Hwy 12 84764 **Location:** Jct SR 63, 1.7 mi w. [B] [L] [D]

RUBY'S COWBOY'S BUFFET & STEAK HOUSE   435/834-5341

American
Casual Dining
$8-$26

Menu on AAA.com

AAA Inspector Notes: Steak and seafood specialties are among the choices on the varied menu. Boxed lunches are favorite to-go orders. **Features:** full bar. **Address:** 26 S Main St 84764 **Location:** On SR 63, 1 mi s of SR 12; in BEST WESTERN PLUS Ruby's Inn. [B] [L] [D]

BRYCE CANYON NATIONAL PARK (F-3)

Elevations in the park range from 6,600 ft. at the bottom of the canyon to 9,120 ft. at Rainbow Point. Refer to AAA maps for additional elevation information.

Bryce Canyon National Park is 26 miles southeast of Panguitch via US 89 and SRs 12 and 63. The park includes some of Earth's most colorful rocks, which have been sculpted by erosion into pillars called "hoodoos," and other fantastic forms. Iron oxides give red, yellow and brown tints to the limestone, while manganese oxides lend a lavender hue.

The area's difficult topography led Mormon settler Ebenezer Bryce, whose cattle grazed in the maze-like twists of the canyons' stream beds, to declare it "a hell of a place to lose a cow." Bryce is not a true canyon but a series of horseshoe-shaped amphitheaters carved in the edge of the Paunsaugunt Plateau by tributaries of the Paria River. A Native American name for the area translates as "red rocks standing like men in a bowl-shaped canyon."

General Information and Activities

The park is open all year. The main geological features of the park are easily seen from numerous roadside viewing areas. **Note:** Visitors are advised to avoid using Cottonwood Road to access the park; the road is dangerous and inclement weather may further impair driving conditions. Visitors can take a 37-mile round-trip on a road that follows the high rim to many major vantage points, such as Bryce Point, Inspiration Point, the Natural Bridge, Paria View, Sunrise Point, Sunset Point and Rainbow Point, at the park's end. A free shuttle service with 13 designated stops is available throughout the park late May through September.

Hiking trails descend below the rim, affording close views of colorful formations. Horseback tours provide another way of seeing the park's geology up close. The most brilliant hues in the park come alive with the rising and setting of the sun. Since the park is on an 8,000- to 9,000-foot plateau, hikers should allow for adjustment to the altitude. Camping is available in improved sites and backcountry areas throughout the park; for reservations phone the National Recreation Reservation System at (877) 444-6777, or TTY (877) 833-6777. *See Recreation Areas Chart.*

ADMISSION is $30 (per private vehicle); $25 (per person arriving by motorcycle); $15 (per person arriving by other means). Generally, the above fees permit entrance to the park for 7 calendar days from

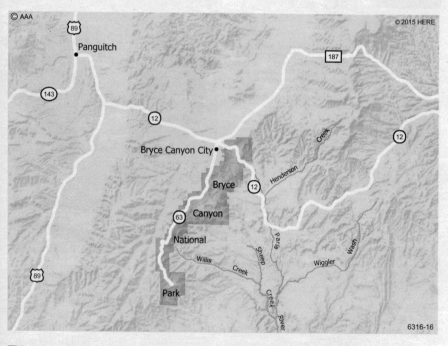

© AAA © 2015 HERE

6316-16

This map shows cities in Bryce Canyon National Park where you will find attractions, hotels and restaurants. Cities are listed alphabetically in this book on the following pages.

date of purchase. An annual pass is $35. A back-country permit, available at the visitor center, is $5-$15. The camping fee is $20.

PETS are permitted in the park only if they are on a leash, crated or otherwise physically restricted at all times. Pets are not allowed on trails or viewpoints or in any of the public buildings.

ADDRESS inquiries to the Superintendent, Bryce Canyon National Park; phone (435) 834-5322. The superintendent's office is open Mon.-Fri. 8-4:30.

BRYCE AMPHITHEATER is s. of the visitor center off Bryce Canyon National Park Rd. (SR 63). Within 3 miles of the park entrance, Bryce Amphitheater is a semicircular area of the canyon filled with the park's signature hoodoo limestone formations. Four overlooks offer some of the park's best views: Sunrise, Sunset, Inspiration and Bryce points. The Rim Trail follows the edge of the canyon, connecting all four overlooks.

BRYCE CANYON NATIONAL PARK VISITOR CENTER is at the park headquarters 1 mi. from the entrance off SR 63. The visitor center contains exhibits pertaining to the geology, biology, archeology and history of the region. Park rangers conduct free hikes and illustrated talks daily Memorial Day through Labor Day. A video presentation is offered every 30 minutes. **Hours:** Daily 8-8, May-Sept.; 8-6 in Apr. and Oct.; 8-4:30, rest of year. Closed Thanksgiving and Christmas. **Phone:** (435) 834-5322.

PARK ROAD is the portion of SR 63 stretching 18 mi. s. from the Bryce Canyon National Park entrance to Rainbow Point. Bryce's main access road runs along a forested plateau near the canyon's edge offering glimpses of the canyon. Drivers can reach 15 viewpoints along the way with either pullouts or parking lots. Since the overlooks are on the east side of the road, it is easier and safer to drive south first and then visit the overlooks on the return trip back to the park entrance.

RECREATIONAL ACTIVITIES
Horseback Riding

- **Canyon Trail Rides** departs from The Lodge at Bryce Canyon off SR 63. **Hours:** Two-hour and half-day trips are offered daily, Apr.-Oct. Departure times vary; phone ahead. **Phone:** (435) 679-8665 or (435) 834-5500.

THE LODGE AT BRYCE CANYON   435/834-8700

▼▼ Historic Hotel. Rates not provided. **Address:** 1 Lodge Way, Hwy 63 84764 **Location:** In Bryce Canyon National Park; at 8000 feet elevation. **Facility:** This lodge, built in 1924, is walking distance from a rim overlook. Motel units with balconies are offered as well as spacious duplex cabins with gas fireplaces and relaxing front porches. 114 units, some cabins. 1-2 stories (no elevator), interior/exterior corridors. **Terms:** check-in 4 pm. **Dining:** 2 restaurants. **Activities:** trails. **Guest Services:** coin laundry.

CAINEVILLE

RODEWAY INN CAPITOL REEF   (435)456-9900

Motel
$80-$116

Address: 25 E SR 24 84775 **Location:** West end of town. **Facility:** 16 units. 2 stories (no elevator), exterior corridors. **Pool(s):** heated outdoor. **Activities:** hot tub. **Guest Services:** coin laundry. **Featured Amenity: continental breakfast.**

CANNONVILLE (F-3) pop. 167, elev. 5,913'

At one time Cannonville was called Gunshot by its residents, who maintained that it was too small to qualify as a cannon.

Irrigation brings water to the farms and orchards surrounding this quiet hamlet on the Paria River. Bryce Canyon National Park *(see place listing p. 300)* is 12 miles northwest. Cannonville is one of several villages along SR 12, a particularly scenic route that connects Panguitch *(see place listing p. 345)* and Boulder *(see place listing p. 295).*

KODACHROME BASIN STATE PARK is 9 mi. s.e. on Kodachrome Rd. The 4,000-acre park contains striking, unusual rock formations that change in color—depending on the time of day and weather conditions—from gray and white to various shades of red. About 10 miles beyond the park entrance via Cottonwood Wash, a dirt road, is Grosvenor Arch. *See Recreation Areas Chart.*

Riding trails are available. **Hours:** Daily 6 a.m.-10 p.m. **Cost:** $8 (per private vehicle, maximum eight people). Camping $16-$28. Extra vehicle on campsite $10-$14. **Phone:** (435) 679-8562, or (800) 322-3770 for camping reservations.

CANYONLANDS NATIONAL PARK (E-5)

Elevations in the park range from 3,720 ft. at Cataract Canyon to 6,987 ft. in the Needles District. Refer to AAA maps for additional elevation information.

In southeastern Utah, Canyonlands National Park encompasses deeply eroded canyons interspersed with sheer-sided mesas and a variety of spires, arches and unusual rock formations. The Green and Colorado rivers join and continue in a series of powerful rapids through the multicolored recesses of Cataract Canyon. The rivers' confluence divides the park into three districts reached by separate accesses.

To reach the entrance to the Island in the Sky District (the easiest district to reach), travel 9 miles north from Moab on US 191, then 26 miles south on SR 313. The entrance to the Needles District is 41 miles south of Moab on US 191, then 34 miles west on SR 211; the entrance to the Maze District is 46 miles from the SR 24 turnoff to the Hans Flat Ranger Station via a rough dirt road.

The northernmost district, Island in the Sky, is a huge, level mesa featuring Upheaval Dome and Grand View Point. Southeast of the rivers' junction lies the Needles District, where multicolored rock spires overshadow meadowlands and natural parks. The Maze District, a remote and rugged section at the western edge of the park, encompasses the Land of Standing Rocks, the Maze and Horseshoe Canyon. The Native American pictograph panels in this area are considered to be among the finest in North America.

General Information and Activities

Although much of the park is backcountry territory, Canyonlands provides paved roads to several of its most scenic areas. The entrance roads to the Needles and the Island in the Sky districts are fully paved, as are the park roads to Grand View Point and Upheaval Dome. The road to the Maze District is passable to high-clearance two-wheel-drive vehicles in good weather conditions; most of the roads within the park are limited to high-clearance four-wheel-drive vehicles. Water is not available in most areas.

The park has many opportunities for backcountry hiking and travel by four-wheel-drive vehicle, mountain bike, horse, canoe, kayak or white-water raft. Permits for overnight backcountry travel must be obtained at a ranger station, visitor center or by mail. River permits for any overnight canoe, kayak or white-water excursions must be obtained from the national park office in Moab or by mail at least 2 weeks in advance. Phone (435) 259-4351 for information about land- or water-based tours. Local tour services provide a variety of guided jeep, air and river tours. Many of these services operate out of Green River (see place listing p. 317), and Moab (see place listing p. 329).

The Island in the Sky Visitor Center (see attraction listing this page) distributes brochures, information and maps daily 9-4:30, March-Dec. The Needles Center is open daily 8-5, March-Nov. The Hans Flat Ranger Station in the Maze District is open daily 8-4:30, year-round. Visitor centers may have extended hours in summer and are closed on some federal holidays. Guided walks are available during the summer and evening programs are offered in spring and fall. See Recreation Areas Chart.

ADMISSION is $25 (per private vehicle); $15 (per person arriving by motorcycle); $10 (per person arriving by other means). Generally, the above fees permit entrance to the park for 7 calendar days from date of purchase. Annual local passes are available for $50 (per private vehicle) and permit entrance into Canyonlands and Arches (see place listing p. 291) national parks as well as Natural Bridges (see place listing p. 339) and Hovenweep (see place listing in Colorado p. 213) national monuments. Backcountry camping fees are $30.

PETS are permitted only if on a leash, crated or otherwise physically restricted at all times. Pets are not allowed in the backcountry, on trails, or in or on rivers within the park.

ADDRESS inquiries to the Superintendent, Canyonlands National Park, 2282 S.W. Resource Blvd., Moab, UT 84532-8000; phone (435) 719-2313.

ISLAND IN THE SKY VISITOR CENTER, 22 mi. s.w. of jct. US 191 and SR 313, offers exhibits, brochures and an orientation video about Canyonlands National Park. From March through October, rangers highlight the area's features through various interpretive programs. **Hours:** Visitor center daily 9-4:30, Mar.-Dec., with extended hours some days. Closed major holidays. Phone ahead to confirm schedule. **Cost:** Visitor center free. **Phone:** (435) 259-4712. 🏕

CAPITOL REEF NATIONAL PARK
(E-4)

Elevations in the park range from 4,000 ft. near Halls Creek to 9,000 ft. at Thousand Lake Mountain. Refer to AAA maps for additional elevation information.

Five miles east of Torrey on SR 24, Capitol Reef National Park was named for reef-like cliffs capped by white Navajo sandstone formations that have eroded and now resemble the dome of the U.S. Capitol. The park contains a spectacular section of the Waterpocket Fold. The fold extends some 100 miles southeastward from Thousand Lake Mountain to Lake Powell and graphically illustrates the way the Earth's surface was built, folded and eroded. Numerous eroded basins or "pockets" can hold critical rainwater necessary to maintain desert life— hence the term "waterpocket fold."

Near the visitor center, brightly colored tiered cliffs rise 1,000 feet above the Fremont River. Pre-Columbian Indian petroglyphs can be seen on the surrounding canyon walls. Amid Capitol Reef's red rock are orchards where fruit may be picked in season. Visitors also can see the remains of Fruita, an early Mormon pioneer settlement.

General Information and Activities

The park is open daily 24 hours; services are reduced in winter. Many hiking trails and drives provide scenic views of the park; a backcountry use permit is required for overnight trips. A trail near the campground leads to Cohab Canyon, where another trail continues to the canyon rim. A nature trail along SR 24 about 2 miles east of the visitor center goes to Hickman Natural Bridge. A scenic drive to Capitol Gorge leaves SR 24 at the visitor center. The Ripple Rock Nature Center, just south of the visitor center, is open Memorial Day-Labor Day. Hours vary; phone ahead for schedule. See Recreation Areas Chart.

ADMISSION to the park is free. Admission to the Capitol Gorge scenic drive is $10 (per private vehicle or motorcycle); $7 (per person arriving by other means). The above fees permit entrance for 7 calendar days from date of purchase. The camping fee is $20.

PETS are not permitted on park trails; they are allowed in specific areas only if on a leash, crated or otherwise physically restricted at all times.

ADDRESS inquiries to the Superintendent, Capitol Reef National Park, HC 70, Box 15, Torrey, UT 84775; phone (435) 425-3791.

GIFFORD HOUSE STORE AND MUSEUM is in Capitol Reef National Park, 1 mi. s. of the visitor center on Scenic Drive. The homestead features a renovated farmhouse, a barn, a smokehouse and a pasture. The site depicts the lifestyle of early 20th-century Mormon settlers in the Fruita Valley. Antiques on display include a treadle sewing machine, Hoosier cupboard and Monarch cookstove. **Time:** Allow 45 minutes minimum. **Hours:** Daily 8-5, Mar. 14-Oct. 31 (also 5-6 in summer). Phone ahead to confirm schedule. **Cost:** Free. **Phone:** (435) 425-3791.

VISITOR CENTER is 6 mi. from Capitol Reef National Park's western entrance on SR 24 at the park's north end. The visitor center offers exhibits about the park's geology and history as well as an orientation program. **Hours:** Daily 8-6, mid-May through Labor Day; 8-4:30, rest of year. Closed Jan. 1, Thanksgiving and Christmas. **Phone:** (435) 425-3791, ext. 3.

RECREATIONAL ACTIVITIES
Horseback Riding
- **Hondoo Rivers & Trails** departs from 90 E. Main St. Other activities—hiking trips and vehicle, rock art and photo tours—are offered. **Hours:** Trips are offered daily with advance reservations. **Phone:** (435) 425-3519 or (800) 332-2696.

CASTLE DALE (D-4) pop. 1,630, elev. 5,771'

The pinnacles and spires of the San Rafael Swell south of Castle Dale were the site of Robbers Roost, the hideout from which Butch Cassidy and other outlaws launched their holdups and rustling activities. The town was settled in 1875 by Orange Seely, a cattleman who gave medical attention to other settlers and was known for weighing more than 300 pounds.

Although the lowlands around Castle Dale eventually became a prosperous farming region, Mrs. Seely allegedly said, "The first time I ever swore was when we arrived ... and I said, 'Damn a man who would bring a woman to such a Godforsaken country.'"

No longer forsaken, the Castle Dale area became industrialized with the building of a Utah Power and Light plant and the development of many coal-mining operations.

San Rafael Country: 75 W. Main St., P.O. Box 907, Castle Dale, UT 84513. **Phone:** (888) 564-3600.

MUSEUM OF THE SAN RAFAEL, 70 North 100 East, has artifacts found in Emery County's caves and rock ledges. Visitors can see dinosaur skeletons, a replica of a fossilized dinosaur egg and rocks from throughout Utah. Also displayed are mounted animals depicted in their natural habitat and such Native American artifacts as the Sitterud Bundle, a knapsack dating from 1250 that was used to hold berries, knives and tools. **Time:** Allow 1 hour minimum. **Hours:** Mon.-Fri. 10-4, Sat. 10-2. Closed major holidays. **Cost:** Donations. **Phone:** (435) 381-3560.

CEDAR BREAKS NATIONAL MONUMENT (F-2)

Cedar Breaks National Monument is off SR 14 between Bryce Canyon National Park (see place listing p. 300) and Cedar City (see place listing p. 304). The park encompasses a 5-mile-wide natural limestone amphitheater eroded to a depth of nearly 2,500 feet. Settlers mistook the junipers at the base of the rock layers for cedars, thus coining the name.

Below the amphitheater's 10,000-foot rim the slopes fall sharply away in ragged walls, spires, columns and arches tinted shades of red, yellow and purple by the manganese and iron oxides in the rock. Bristlecone pines, among the oldest plants on Earth, cling to the windswept ridges above the rim. Hiking trails can be found around the rim.

In summer the meadows and slopes are resplendent wildflower gardens. The area also is a wildlife habitat; mule deer often can be seen grazing in the meadows in the early morning or evening. A self-guiding trail leads from the Chessman Meadow parking area to Alpine Pond, a good spot to take in the view. Guided tours of Spectra Point Trail depart from the trailhead Saturday and Sunday afternoons (phone ahead for tour times); guided tours of Alpine Pond Trail depart from the trailhead Saturdays and Sundays at 10.

A visitor center 1 mile from the south entrance is open daily 9-6, late May to mid-Oct. Camping and picnic facilities are near Point Supreme. The high season is early June-late Oct. (weather permitting). The road may be closed due to snow, rest of year; phone (435) 586-9451 to check conditions.

Admission late May to mid-October is $4 (per person arriving by car, motorcycle, bicycle or foot); free (ages 0-16). Admission rest of year is free. Generally, the above fees permit entrance to the park for 7 calendar days from date of purchase.

For further information contact the Superintendent, Cedar Breaks National Monument, 2390 W. SR 56, Suite 11, Cedar City, UT 84720-4151; phone (435) 586-0787.

CEDAR CITY (F-2) pop. 28,857, elev. 5,840'
• Restaurants p. 306

An abundance of iron ore west of the site of Cedar City induced English, Scottish and Welsh Mormon converts, who were skilled miners, to settle the area. But floods, harsh winters, poor harvests and cheap iron transported by the transcontinental railroad closed the mines, so most of the settlers turned to raising livestock. Since 1920 tourists have been attracted by the town's proximity to scenic areas, making it a prosperous community.

Cedar City-Brian Head Tourism & Convention Bureau/Iron County Visitor Center: 581 N. Main St., Suite A, Cedar City, UT 84720. **Phone:** (435) 586-5124 or (800) 354-4849.

BRAITHWAITE FINE ARTS GALLERY is on the Southern Utah University campus at 351 W. Center St. The gallery presents changing exhibitions of works by state and national artists. The gallery's permanent collection consists of 19th-century and contemporary paintings. Pottery and textile objects also are displayed. **Time:** Allow 30 minutes minimum. **Hours:** Mon.-Sat. 10-8, June-Aug.; Tues.-Sat. noon-7, rest of year. Closed major holidays and between monthly exhibits. **Cost:** Free. **Phone:** (435) 586-5432.

FRONTIER HOMESTEAD STATE PARK MUSEUM is n.w. of Coal Creek Bridge on SR 91 at 635 N. Main St. The first iron foundry west of the Mississippi River was begun here in 1851 by a group of Mormons who answered Brigham Young's call to settle the area and process its extensive iron deposits. A diorama based on descriptions of the foundry; a collection of horse-drawn vehicles such as stagecoaches, surreys and sleighs; and a display of farm machinery can be seen.

The horse-drawn vehicle collection also includes a Stanhope Phaeton and a Studebaker White Top Wagon. One of the stagecoaches, from Utah's Four Corners region, dates from the Butch Cassidy era

and is scarred by bullets. **Hours:** Daily 9-6, June-Aug.; Mon.-Sat. 9-5, rest of year. Closed Jan. 1, Thanksgiving and Christmas. **Cost:** $3. Annual pass $75. **Phone:** (435) 586-9290.

UTAH SHAKESPEARE FESTIVAL, held on the Southern Utah University campus off I-15, presents three Shakespearean plays and works by other playwrights in rotation at several venues: the outdoor Engelstad Shakespeare Theatre, the Eileen and Allen Anes Studio Theatre at the new Beverley Taylor Sorenson Center for the Arts and the Randall L. Jones Theater. Evening performances are preceded by a complimentary Greenshow featuring Elizabethan music, dance of Merrie Olde England, juggling, magic or storytelling. Works from The New American Playwrights Project are performed in August in the Auditorium Theatre.

Day-care services are available on the festival grounds. **Hours:** Season runs June 27-Oct. 22. Matinee and evening performances daily through early Sept., then check schedule. Backstage tours offered some mornings. **Cost:** Tickets $20-$73 plus $4 facilities fee per ticket for some performances. Limited gallery seats $17-$21 (available in person after 10 a.m. on day of performance). New American Playwrights Project $10. Backstage tour $8. Under 6 are not permitted at performances. Reservations are recommended. **Phone:** (435) 586-7878 or (800) 752-9849.

ABBEY INN OF CEDAR CITY (435)586-9966

Motel
$71-$159

Address: 940 W 200 N 84720 **Location:** I-15 exit 59, just e. **Facility:** 85 units, some two bedrooms and kitchens. 2 stories, exterior corridors. **Terms:** cancellation fee imposed. **Pool(s):** heated indoor. **Activities:** hot tub, exercise room. **Guest Services:** valet and coin laundry. **Featured Amenity: full hot breakfast.** *(See ad this page.)*

AMERICAS BEST VALUE INN   (435)867-4700

Hotel
$43-$95

Address: 333 N 1100 W 84720 **Location:** I-15 exit 59, just e. **Facility:** 50 units. 2 stories (no elevator), interior corridors. **Terms:** 2-3 night minimum stay - seasonal, 7 day cancellation notice-fee imposed. **Pool(s):** heated outdoor. **Guest Services:** valet and coin laundry, area transportation. **Featured Amenity: continental breakfast.**

BEST WESTERN TOWN & COUNTRY INN   (435)586-9900

Hotel
$120-$150

AAA Benefit: Save 10% or more every day and earn 10% bonus points!

Address: 189 N Main St 84720 **Location:** I-15 exit 59, 1.2 mi e. **Facility:** 145 units, some two bedrooms. 2 stories, interior/exterior corridors. **Dining:** 2 restaurants, also, Depot Grill Steak & Seafood, see separate listing. **Pool(s):** heated outdoor, heated indoor. **Activities:** hot tub, exercise room. **Guest Services:** coin laundry.

THE BIG YELLOW INN   (435)586-0960

Bed & Breakfast $99-$199 **Address:** 234 S 300 W 84720 **Location:** Jct Main St, 0.6 mi s; downtown. **Facility:** This Georgian Revival home, located a block from the Shakespeare Festival, features a grand staircase, eight fireplaces, a library, four sitting rooms, balconies and two guest kitchens. 12 units. 4 stories (no elevator), interior corridors. **Terms:** 14 day cancellation notice-fee imposed.

COMFORT INN & SUITES   (435)865-0003

Hotel $79-$179 **Address:** 1288 S Main St 84720 **Location:** I-15 exit 57, just e, then just n. **Facility:** 85 units, some two bedrooms. 3 stories, interior corridors. **Amenities:** safes. **Pool(s):** heated indoor. **Activities:** hot tub, exercise room. **Guest Services:** valet and coin laundry.

EL REY INN & SUITES   (435)586-6518

Hotel
$59-$199

Address: 80 S Main St 84720 **Location:** I-15 exit 57, 2 mi n; center. **Facility:** 70 units, some two bedrooms. 2 stories, exterior corridors. **Terms:** cancellation fee imposed. **Pool(s):** heated outdoor. **Activities:** exercise room. **Guest Services:** area transportation. **Featured Amenity: continental breakfast.**

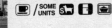

HAMPTON INN CEDAR CITY   (435)586-5000

Hotel $89-$189 **Address:** 1145 S Bentley Blvd 84720 **Location:** I-15 exit 57, just w of off-ramp via Cross Hollow and Royal Hunt. **Facility:** 58 units. 3 stories, interior corridors. **Terms:** 1-7 night minimum stay, cancellation fee imposed. **Pool(s):** heated indoor. **Activities:** exercise room. **Guest Services:** valet and coin laundry.

AAA Benefit: Members save up to 10%!

HOLIDAY INN EXPRESS HOTEL & SUITES   435/865-7799

Hotel. Rates not provided. **Address:** 1555 S Old Hwy 91 84720 **Location:** I-15 exit 57, just e, then s. **Facility:** 80 units. 3 stories, interior corridors. **Pool(s):** heated indoor. **Activities:** hot tub, exercise room. **Guest Services:** valet and coin laundry.

LA QUINTA INN & SUITES DEL SOL   (435)865-0005

Contemporary
Hotel
$89-$235

Address: 1377 S Main St 84720 **Location:** I-15 exit 57, just e. **Facility:** 89 units. 4 stories, interior corridors. **Pool(s):** heated indoor. **Activities:** hot tub, exercise room. **Guest Services:** valet and coin laundry. **Featured Amenity: full hot breakfast.**

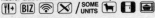

MOTEL 6 OF CEDAR CITY - 4041   435/586-9200

Motel. Rates not provided. **Address:** 1620 W 200 N 84720 **Location:** I-15 exit 59, just w. **Facility:** 79 units. 3 stories, interior corridors. **Guest Services:** coin laundry.

QUALITY INN   (435)586-2082

Motel $80-$105 **Address:** 250 N 1100 W 84720 **Location:** I-15 exit 59, just e. **Facility:** 88 units, some efficiencies. 2 stories (no elevator), exterior corridors. **Pool(s):** heated indoor. **Activities:** hot tub. **Guest Services:** valet and coin laundry, area transportation.

SPRINGHILL SUITES BY MARRIOTT CEDAR CITY   (435)586-1685

Hotel $98-$203 **Address:** 1477 S Old Hwy 91 84720 **Location:** I-15 exit 57, just e, then just s. **Facility:** 72 units. 3 stories, interior corridors. **Pool(s):** heated indoor. **Activities:** hot tub, exercise room. **Guest Services:** valet and coin laundry.

AAA Benefit: Members save 5% or more!

WILLOW GLEN INN
(435)586-3275

Bed & Breakfast $105-$179 **Address:** 3308 N Bulldog Rd 84720 **Location:** I-15 exit 62, 1.5 mi sw via 3000 N. **Facility:** 9 units, some two bedrooms, three bedrooms and efficiencies. 1-2 stories (no elevator), exterior corridors. **Terms:** 14 day cancellation notice-fee imposed. **Activities:** trails.

WHERE TO EAT

BRODY'S
435/531-8773

Mexican. Casual Dining. $7-$23 **AAA Inspector Notes:** This bright and inviting restaurant serves up fresh and tasty traditional cuisine with a casual smile. The chicken fajitas tasted amazing. **Address:** 1166 Sage Dr 84720 **Location:** I-15 exit 57, just w via Cross Hollow Rd and Royal Hunt Dr.

CENTRO WOODFIRED PIZZERIA
435/867-8123

Italian Pizza. Casual Dining. $10-$14 **AAA Inspector Notes:** This is a small trendy place that hand tosses pizza in the middle of the dining room. The menu is limited to large salads, pizza and two desserts, but all are amazing. I had the summer salad, sopressata pizza and vanilla gelato and cannot wait to go back for more. **Features:** beer & wine, patio dining. **Address:** 50 W Center St 84720 **Location:** Downtown. **Parking:** on-site and street.

DEPOT GRILL STEAK & SEAFOOD
435/865-7445

American. Casual Dining. $17-$38 **AAA Inspector Notes:** This is a great name for a restaurant that arose in Cedar City's original train depot. The dining room has elegant train depot décor with dark wood accents and high ceilings. The menu fits right in with American favorites such as filet mignon, fillet of salmon and even maple-lavender duck. **Features:** full bar. **Address:** 241 N Main St 84720 **Location:** I-15 exit 59, 1.2 mi e; in BEST WESTERN Town & Country Inn.

LA CASA DON MIGUEL
435/586-6855

Mexican. Casual Dining. $6-$15 **AAA Inspector Notes:** This small, basic and cramped restaurant serves authentic Mexican cuisine with great flavor. The owner serves the tables herself with only one back-up server, so it can take awhile for dishes to arrive. The line sometimes winds out the door, so it's wise to show up early. **Features:** full bar, patio dining. **Address:** 453 S Main St 84720 **Location:** Center.

LA FIESTA
435/586-4646

Mexican. Casual Dining. $7-$13 **AAA Inspector Notes:** Colorful tropical décor incorporating birds, flowers, monkeys and a large collection of masks lends character to the setting, where guests sit down to delicious homemade cuisine. **Features:** full bar. **Address:** 890 N Main St 84720 **Location:** I-15 exit 62 eastbound, 2 mi s via Main St, then just n of Center St.

LUPITA'S MEXICAN RESTAURANT
435/867-0945

Mexican. Family Dining. $7-$14 **AAA Inspector Notes:** The homemade corn tortillas are just one of the reasons people line up to enjoy very fresh cuisine at this family-run restaurant. The décor is very bright and fun along with very casual service. They can be short-staffed at times, so there can be a wait. **Features:** full bar. **Address:** 453 S Main St 84720 **Location:** I-15 exit 57, just e.

MAIN STREET GRILL
435/586-8389

Breakfast Sandwiches. Casual Dining. $6-$10 **AAA Inspector Notes:** Families sit down together for home-style breakfast and lunch dishes in this relaxed and friendly spot. The owner greets many guests by name and you might hear fun, sarcastic remarks. **Address:** 155 N Main St 84720 **Location:** Downtown. **Parking:** on-site and street.

MARKET GRILL
435/586-9325

American. Family Dining. $7-$19 **AAA Inspector Notes:** An Old West atmosphere awaits diners who want to enjoy a well-rounded menu. Other than breakfast, the menu is limited, but the staff is very friendly. The homemade pies are displayed in a case and taste fantastic. **Address:** 2290 W 400 N 84720 **Location:** I-15 exit 59, 0.5 mi w.

NINJA JAPANESE STEAKHOUSE & SUSHI
435/867-5577

Japanese. Casual Dining. $14-$38 **AAA Inspector Notes:** In a small shopping center, this restaurant lets guests enjoy favorite dishes right at the hibachi grills, at regular tables and even at the sushi bar. The servers are fun and friendly. **Features:** beer & wine. **Address:** 1180 S Sage Dr, Unit A 84720 **Location:** I-15 exit 57, just w via Cross Hollow Rd and Royal Hunt Dr.

THE PASTRY PUB
435/867-1400

Sandwiches Breads/Pastries. Quick Serve. $6-$8 **AAA Inspector Notes:** Choose from bistro tables on the sidewalk or a spacious dining room in which to enjoy specialty drinks, house-brewed tea or coffee. Salads, sandwiches, wraps and croissants are favorites due to homemade breads. **Features:** patio dining. **Address:** 86 W Center St 84720 **Location:** Downtown.

RUSTY'S RANCH HOUSE
435/586-3839

American
Casual Dining
$12-$22

AAA Inspector Notes: Just a short drive up the canyon, the restaurant is surrounded by beautiful mountain scenery. American dishes are served in a rustic setting with log walls and many large animal trophies. **Features:** full bar. **Address:** 2275 E Hwy 14 84720 **Location:** Jct Main St, 1.5 mi e.

SONNY BOY'S BARBECUE
435/867-8010

Barbecue. Quick Serve. $7-$21 **AAA Inspector Notes:** The huge smoker in the parking lot creates long lines for lunch and dinner at this fresh and flavorful BBQ joint. A special is offered daily, and the owner smokes and cuts the meat for everyone to see. This kind of great barbecue is a rare find in this part of the country. **Address:** 126 N Main St 84720 **Location:** Center. **Parking:** on-site and street.

SWEET BASIL THAI CUISINE
435/865-5937

Thai. Casual Dining. $8-$14 **AAA Inspector Notes:** This is a small and basic restaurant that serves fresh Thai cuisine. There is limited staff, so prepare for little attention during your dining experience. The steamed pot stickers were amazing, and dishes seem less spicy than at other Thai restaurants. **Address:** 1322 S Providence Center Dr 84720 **Location:** I-15 exit 37, just w, then just s; in Providence Center.

CIRCLEVILLE pop. 547

BUTCH CASSIDY'S HIDEOUT
(435)577-2008

Motel $60-$90 **Address:** 339 S Hwy 89 84723 **Location:** Just s of center. **Facility:** 11 units. 1 story, exterior corridors. **Terms:** cancellation fee imposed.

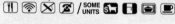

CLEVELAND (D-4) pop. 464, elev. 5,735'

CLEVELAND-LLOYD DINOSAUR QUARRY is 14 mi. s. following signs. Some 12,000 bones representing at least 70 different animals have been recovered from the quarry, which provides bones and complete skeletons to museums throughout the world. The exact reason why the dinosaurs perished here has not been determined. About two-thirds of the bones are from the large carnivore allosaurus. The quarry has a visitor center as well as a nature trail and two hiking trails.

The road to the quarry is graded and unpaved and may be hazardous when wet. Pets on leashes are permitted on trails. **Hours:** Mon.-Sat. 9-5, Sun. noon-5, Memorial Day-Labor Day; Thurs.-Fri. 9-5, Sat. noon-5, late Mar.-day before Memorial Day and day after Labor Day-Oct. 31. Phone ahead to confirm schedule. **Cost:** $5; free (ages 0-15). **Phone:** (435) 636-3600. 🏧

COALVILLE pop. 1,363

BEST WESTERN HOLIDAY HILLS   (435)336-4444

▼▼▼ ▼▼▼
Hotel
$89-$100

AAA Benefit: Save 10% or more every day and earn 10% bonus points!

Address: 500 W 120 S 84017 **Location:** I-80 exit 162, just w. **Facility:** 60 units. 3 stories, interior corridors. **Pool(s):** heated indoor. **Activities:** hot tub, exercise room. **Guest Services:** coin laundry. **Featured Amenity:** breakfast buffet.

SAVE CALL 🔥M 🌫 BIZ HS 🛜 ✕ 💻 / SOME UNITS 🛒 🔋 🗄

COTTONWOOD HEIGHTS pop. 33,433

- **Hotels & Restaurants map & index p. 385**
- **Part of Salt Lake City area — see map p. 368**

RESIDENCE INN BY MARRIOTT - SALT LAKE CITY/ COTTONWOOD HEIGHTS   (801)453-0430 58

▼▼▼ ▼▼▼
Extended Stay Hotel
$104-$237

Residence Inn Marriott

AAA Benefit: Members save 5% or more!

Address: 6425 S 3000 E 84121 **Location:** I-215 S exit 6 (6200 S), 0.4 mi s, then just e. **Facility:** 144 units, some two bedrooms, efficiencies and kitchens. 3 stories, interior corridors. **Parking:** winter plug-ins. **Pool(s):** heated outdoor. **Activities:** hot tub, picnic facilities, exercise room. **Guest Services:** valet and coin laundry, area transportation. **Featured Amenity:** full hot breakfast.

SAVE 🍴 CALL 🔥M 🌫 BIZ HS 🛜 ✕ 🔋 🗄 💻 / SOME UNITS 🛒

WHERE TO EAT

MARKET STREET GRILL & OYSTER BAR COTTONWOOD
801/942-8860 42

▼▼ ▼▼ Seafood. Casual Dining. $11-$37 **AAA Inspector Notes:** After indulging on warm bread, soup and a salad, guests then choose from a variety of blackened or broiled fresh fish and other seafood dishes centered on oysters, clams, mussels, shrimp, Atlantic salmon and lobster. Although it's nowhere close, this place makes patrons feel like they're near the ocean. A delightful selection of mouthwatering desserts rounds out the meal. **Features:** full bar, patio dining, Sunday brunch. **Address:** 2985 E Cottonwood Pkwy 84121 **Location:** I-215 exit 6 (6200 S), 0.8 mi se.

L D CALL 🔥M

PORCUPINE PUB & GRILLE   801/942-5555 44

▼▼ ▼▼ American. Casual Dining. $8-$24 **AAA Inspector Notes:** From November through May you can watch skiers race to a table for the much-talked-about hot chicken soup for the soul. This restaurant also is known for its themed holiday dinners, especially on St. Patrick's Day and during Oktoberfest. Salad specials rotate on weekdays. The signature chocolate porcupine with vanilla bean ice cream is a must. **Features:** full bar, patio dining, Sunday brunch. **Address:** 3698 E Fort Union Blvd 84121 **Location:** I-215 exit 6 (6200 S), 2 mi se.

L D

COVE FORT (E-2) elev. 5,998'

COVE FORT HISTORIC SITE, 1 mi. n. off I-70 exit 1, or 2 mi. s off I-15 exit 135, was built in 1867 by The Church of Jesus Christ of Latter-day Saints. The volcanic rock and limestone fort served as a way station for 19th-century Mormon settlers and travelers and also as a pickup and delivery site for the Pony Express. Period furnishings and artifacts are displayed throughout the restored 12-room fort. **Time:** Allow 30 minutes minimum. **Hours:** Guided tours daily 8-dusk, Apr.-Aug.; 9-dusk, rest of year. **Cost:** Free. **Phone:** (435) 438-5547. 🏧

DELTA (D-2) pop. 3,436, elev. 4,635'

GREAT BASIN MUSEUM is at 45 W. Main St. The museum features exhibits about area history, including mining and pioneer artifacts, photographs, documents and a collection of beryllium. Arrowheads, minerals and fossils also are displayed, as is an exhibit about the Topaz Relocation Center, an internment camp for Japanese Americans during World War II. **Time:** Allow 30 minutes minimum. **Hours:** Mon.-Sat. 10-5, mid-Mar. to mid-Nov. Winter hours vary. **Cost:** Donations. **Phone:** (435) 864-5013.

TOPAZ MUSEUM is at 55 W. Main St. The museum features history and art created at Topaz, a Japanese American Internment Camp during WWII. Also on display is a restored recreation hall as it appeared in 1943 and a typical room for internees at the camp. **Note:** Expansion work continues on the museum, and visitors can drive on the roads around part of the one square mile site. **Hours:** Mon.-Fri. 11-5. Hours may vary in winter. Phone ahead to confirm schedule. **Cost:** Donations. **Phone:** (435) 864-2514.

DAYS INN   (435)864-3882

▼▼ ▼▼ Motel $80-$90 **Address:** 527 E Topaz Blvd 84624 **Location:** Jct US 6 and 50. **Facility:** 83 units. 2 stories (no elevator), exterior corridors. **Pool(s):** heated outdoor. **Guest Services:** coin laundry.

🍴 🌫 BIZ 🛜 🔋 🗄 💻 / SOME UNITS 🛒 HS

💎 DINOSAUR NATIONAL MONUMENT (B-5)

Dinosaur National Monument's Utah section is reached via SR 149, which joins US 40 at Jensen. One of the world's largest concentrations of fossilized dinosaur bones is found in the park, which encompasses about 325 square miles in Utah and Colorado. Fossilized bones of allosaurus and other prehistoric creatures have been revealed in a single sandstone cliff. Several of the region's exhumed skeletons are exhibited in the Carnegie Museum of Natural History in Pittsburgh.

Among the exceptional natural features of the national monument are deep, narrow gorges with strangely carved and delicately tinted sheer sandstone cliffs along the Green and Yampa rivers. The Canyon of Lodore, cut by the Green River, ranges from 1,000 to 3,300 feet deep.

More than 1,500 fossilized bones are on display at the Quarry Exhibit Hall just north of Jensen; shuttles to the cliff face run from the Quarry Visitor Center. Located a half a mile away from the quarry, the visitor center offers exhibits as well as information about recreational activities and ranger-led interpretive programs. A mostly paved 10-mile road that begins nearby leads to petroglyph panels, overlooks and a historic cabin. Several established hiking trails, including Sound of Silence, Desert Voices and Hog Canyon, are accessed from this road.

From the Canyon Area Visitor Center in Dinosaur, Colo., a 31-mile paved road leads north into the heart of the canyon country. There are no fossil bones in this section, but scenic overlooks and a 2-mile-long trail at Harpers Corner provide spectacular views of the Green and Yampa rivers and their confluence at Steamboat Rock 2,500 feet below.

One- to 5-day river trips through the monument can be arranged by contacting private companies mid-May to mid-September. Camping, hiking and fishing are available within the monument.

Admission is $10 (per private vehicle); $5 (per person arriving by other means). Camping fees are $8-$25 (free from late fall to early spring). Backcountry camping is free with permit. For further information contact the Superintendent, Dinosaur National Monument; phone (435) 781-7700. *See Recreation Areas Chart.*

CANYON VISITOR CENTER is at jct. Harpers Corner Rd. and US 40, 2 mi. e. of Dinosaur, Colo. The center offers exhibits about the area's canyon country and an audiovisual program. **Time:** Allow 15 minutes minimum. **Hours:** Daily 9-5, early May-late Sept. Phone ahead to confirm schedule. **Cost:** Free. **Phone:** (970) 374-3000.

QUARRY EXHIBIT HALL, accessible via the Quarry Visitor Center 7 mi. n. of Jensen on SR 149, showcases more than 1,500 dinosaur bones embedded in rock. The remains of allosauruses, apatosauruses and stegosauruses, along with several other prehistoric species, can be seen.

Hours: Access to the exhibit hall fall through spring is by car caravan. Visitors, driving their own vehicles, follow a ranger to the site at 9:30, 10:30, 11:30, 1, 2, 3 and 4. In summer, access is by a shuttle bus that runs from the Quarry Visitor Center on SR 149 every 15 minutes 9:30-5 (the last bus back to the visitor center departs at 5:30); visitors may drive themselves to the quarry prior to 9:30 a.m. Phone for current information about visiting the quarry. Closed Jan. 1, Thanksgiving, Christmas and day after Christmas. Phone ahead to confirm schedule. **Cost:** Free. **Phone:** (435) 781-7700.

QUARRY VISITOR CENTER, 7 mi. n. of Jensen on SR 149, offers displays that illustrate the park's geological and cultural history as well as the nature of the dinosaurs that once roamed the area. An auditorium features educational films. The visitor center

also serves as the gateway to the Quarry Exhibit Hall. Shuttles or car caravans depart from the visitor center and offer access to the cliff face.

Time: Allow 1 hour minimum. **Hours:** Visitor center open daily 8-6, mid-May to mid-Sept.; 9-5, rest of year. Access to the exhibit hall fall through spring is by car caravan. Visitors, driving their own vehicles, follow a ranger to the site at 9:30, 10:30, 11:30, 1, 2, 3 and 4. In summer, access is by a shuttle bus that runs from the Quarry Visitor Center on SR 149 every 15 minutes 9:30-5 (the last bus back to the visitor center departs at 5:30); visitors may drive themselves to the quarry prior to 9:30 a.m. Phone for current information about visiting the quarry. Closed Jan. 1, Thanksgiving, Christmas and day after Christmas. Phone ahead to confirm schedule. **Cost:** Free. **Phone:** (435) 781-7700.

DIXIE NATIONAL FOREST (F-3)

Elevations in the forest range from 2,800 ft. near the town of St. George to 11,310 ft. at Brian Head Peak on Cedar Mountain. Refer to AAA maps for additional elevation information.

In southwestern Utah, Dixie National Forest's warm climate reminded early Mormon settlers of the Deep South, thus its name. The forest, which is the largest in the state, covers approximately 1,700,000 acres. The state's largest trees—predominantly ponderosa pine and spruce—grow in the forest. Bryce Canyon *(see place listing p. 300)*, Capitol Reef *(see place listing p. 302)* and Zion *(see place listing p. 415)* national parks and Cedar Breaks *(see place listing p. 303)* and Grand Staircase-Escalante *(see place listing p. 316)* national monuments are all adjacent to or within the forest.

The Markagunt Plateau, about 9 miles southeast of Cedar City via SR 14, offers many recreational facilities. A fish hatchery west of Hatch raises the fish stocked in the streams and lakes; rainbow trout predominate. Duck Creek Recreation Area has a pond stocked several times yearly. Spring-fed Navajo Lake has outlets in Cascade Falls and Duck Creek, and Panguitch Lake offers excellent fishing. Boat rentals, cabins and camping facilities are available late May to early October.

Brian Head Peak, Strawberry Point and Zion Overlook provide scenic views. Bristlecone pine, one of the oldest forms of plant life on Earth, can be seen on a self-guiding nature trail at Midway Summit.

The Pine Valley Mountains are about 24 miles north of St. George via SR 18 to the town of Central, then east on CR 035 for about 8 miles. The tops of the mountains, which rise some 3,000 feet above the valley floor, are designated as a wilderness area. The cool air at these elevations contrasts sharply with the higher temperatures of the valley. Camping and fishing are available in the valley. More than 100 miles of trails exist for hiking and horseback riding.

The Paunsaugunt and Sevier plateaus parallel SR 89 for 60 miles from Circleville south. The area is known for its panoramic views and distinctive rock formations. Red Canyon along SR 12 affords views, in the heart of the forest, of the pink and red rocks and cliffs. The canyon can be seen by car or by hiking one of the nature trails. Red Canyon Visitor Center and a campground are in the canyon.

Tropic Reservoir, just off SR 12 to the south, is a popular recreation spot that has lake and stream fishing. The reservoir provides a source of water for agricultural land at lower elevations. Additional campsites are at Kings Creek Campground near Kings Creek Lake.

The Boulder Mountain-Aquarius Plateau is a high mountain plateau that lies about 10 miles north of Escalante. SR 12 winds through spectacular slick-rock formations, mountain passes and large areas of aspen that burst with color in the fall. Views from the road take in Capitol Reef National Park and many distant mountain ranges. Small campgrounds are scattered along the way.

Visitor centers Duck Creek, (435) 682-2432, and Red Canyon, (435) 676-2676, are open daily 10-5 (Duck Creek) and 9-6 (Red Canyon), Memorial Day-Labor Day; schedule varies, day after Labor Day-Sept. 30.

For further information contact the Forest Supervisor, Dixie National Forest, 1789 N. Wedgewood Ln., Cedar City, UT 84721; phone (435) 865-3700, or TTY (435) 865-3719. *See Recreation Areas Chart.*

DRAPER (C-3) pop. 42,274, elev. 4,505'
• Part of Salt Lake City area — see map p. 368

LOVELAND LIVING PLANET AQUARIUM is at 12033 S. Lone Peak Pkwy. The museum includes the Discover Utah gallery, exhibiting freshwater aquatic species, amphibians and mammals indigenous to the state. The North American River Otter exhibit showcases these lively animals in indoor and outdoor environments. The Ocean Explorer gallery hosts myriad marine species such as octopus, stingrays, seahorses and other deep-sea creatures, in addition to interactive exhibits and a 300,000-gallon shark tank with a 40-foot walk-through tunnel.

The Journey to South America gallery includes 15 species of freshwater animals from the rivers of the Amazon, including free-flight tropical birds, caimans, anacondas, an electric eel and dozens of other exotic species. The Antarctic Adventure gallery features 15 Gentoo penguins with the potential to house up to 30 birds of three different species in the years to come.

Time: Allow 2 hours minimum. Hours: Daily 10-6. Closed Thanksgiving and Christmas. Cost: $17.95; $14.95 (ages 13-17, ages 65+ and military with ID); $12.95 (ages 3-12). Phone: (801) 355-3474.

FAIRFIELD INN BY MARRIOTT   (801)572-1200

Hotel $85-$153 Address: 12117 S State St 84020 Location: I-15 exit 291, just e, then just n on frontage road. Facility: 66 units. 2 stories (no elevator), interior corridors. Pool(s): heated indoor. Activities: hot tub, exercise room. Guest Services: valet and coin laundry, area transportation.
AAA Benefit: Members save 5% or more!

SPRINGHILL SUITES BY MARRIOTT   (801)572-1800

Contemporary Hotel $86-$207 Address: 12111 S State St 84020 Location: I-15 exit 292, just e, then 0.4 mi n. Facility: 124 units. 4 stories, interior corridors. Pool(s): heated indoor. Activities: hot tub, exercise room. Guest Services: valet and coin laundry, area transportation.
AAA Benefit: Members save 5% or more!

WHERE TO EAT

GUADALAHONKY'S RESTAURANT & CANTINA   801/571-3838
Mexican. Casual Dining. $8-$16 AAA Inspector Notes: This restaurant serves made-from-scratch entrées, including chiles rellenos. Their twist on the seasonal chicken tortilla soup is a good one, and they have hit a home run with their veggie quesadilla. Warm tortilla chips and fresh salsa are served with entrées. Also, gluten-free options are available. Features: full bar, patio dining, senior menu. Address: 136 E 12300 S 84020 Location: I-15 exit 291, 0.3 mi e.
L D

EDEN (B-3) pop. 600
• Hotels p. 310 • Restaurants p. 310

RECREATIONAL ACTIVITIES
Hot Air Ballooning
• **Skywalker Balloon Co.-Ogden Valley** departs from the Maverik gas station at jct. SRs 162 and 158. Time: Allow 3 hours minimum. Hours: Trips generally depart daily at dawn. Phone ahead to confirm schedule. Cost: One-hour flight $250 (per person). Prices may vary. Reservations are required. Phone: (801) 824-3934.

Skiing
• **Powder Mountain Resort** is approximately 7 mi. n. on SR 158, which becomes Powder Mountain Rd. Hours: Open daily 9-9, mid-Nov. to mid-Apr. Hours may vary; phone ahead to confirm schedule. Phone: (801) 745-3772, or (801) 745-3771 for the snow line.
• **Nordic Valley** is 1.9 mi. n. on SR 162, then 1 mi. s. on Nordic Valley Dr. Hours: Open Mon.-Thurs. 11-8, Fri.-Sat. 9-9, Sun. 9-4, mid-Dec. to mid-Mar. Phone ahead to confirm schedule. Phone: (801) 745-3511.

SNOWBERRY INN BED & BREAKFAST   801/745-2634

▼▼▼▼ **Bed & Breakfast. Rates not provided. Address:** 1315 N Hwy 158 84310 **Location:** I-15 exit 344 (12th St), 10 mi e to Pineview Reservoir bridge, then 2.6 mi n. **Facility:** The personal touches throughout this spacious inn, both inside and outside, are endless. The warm hospitality is genuine, and cozy wood decks offer great mountain views. 8 units, some kitchens. 3 stories (no elevator), interior corridors. **Activities:** hot tub, game room, picnic facilities. **Guest Services:** coin laundry.

WHERE TO EAT

CARLOS & HARLEY'S FRESH-MEX CANTINA   801/745-8226

▼▼▼ Mexican. Casual Dining. $10-$22 **AAA Inspector Notes:** Located in a historic general store, favorites at this eatery include Texas-style chili, beef, chicken, shrimp and vegetarian fajitas, and a fun make-your-own plate. The mega chocolate cake and Key lime tart are hard to pass up. Gluten-free and vegetarian items are available. **Features:** full bar, patio dining, Sunday brunch. **Address:** 5510 E 2200 N 84310 **Location:** I-15 exit 344 (12th St), 10 mi e to Pineview Reservoir bridge, then 4 mi n on SR 158. ⓛ ⓓ

EPHRAIM pop. 6,135

WILLOW CREEK INN   435/283-4566

▼▼ **Hotel. Rates not provided. Address:** 450 S Main St 84627 **Location:** On US 89 (Main St); south end of town. **Facility:** 58 units. 3 stories, interior corridors. *Bath:* shower only. **Activities:** hot tub, game room, exercise room. **Guest Services:** coin laundry.

WHERE TO EAT

ROY'S PIZZA & PASTA   435/283-4222

▼ Pizza Sandwiches. Quick Serve. $5-$20 **AAA Inspector Notes:** Patrons enjoy pizza combinations, calzones, salads and a variety of pasta. An old-fashioned ice cream parlor is smack in the middle of the eatery where offerings include malts, milk shakes and banana splits. **Address:** 81 S Main St 84627 **Location:** Center. **Parking:** street only. ⓛ ⓓ

ESCALANTE (F-3) pop. 797, elev. 5,812'

Although Francisco Silvestre Vélez de Escalante came no closer than 150 miles to the present site of Escalante, the town was named for the Spanish priest, who explored sections of Utah in 1776. The Mormons, who settled in Escalante in 1875 because of its mild climate, called it "Potato Valley" for a local wild species of that vegetable.

The town is near the Kaiparowits Plateau, a sparsely settled area of highly eroded rock formations that extends east to the Colorado River and south to Arizona. The nearby Grand Staircase-Escalante National Monument *(see place listing p. 316)* provides recreational opportunities. Highlights of the Escalante Canyons Art Festival, held in late September, include a plein air painting competition, lectures, films and gallery open houses.

Enjoy great member rates and benefits
at AAA/CAA Preferred Hotels

Escalante/Boulder Chamber of Commerce: P.O. Box 175, Escalante, UT 84726. **Phone:** (435) 826-4810.

Self-guiding tours: A brochure describing a walking tour of Escalante's pioneer homes and barns is available at many locations throughout the town.

ESCALANTE PETRIFIED FOREST STATE PARK is 1 mi. w. on SR 12, then .5 mi. on an unnamed road, following signs. The 1,784-acre park contains colorful mineralized wood and fossilized logs. The petrified forest is accessed by a 1.5-mile moderate to strenuous hiking trail. A visitor center has specimens of petrified wood and dinosaur fossils on display. Wide Hollow Reservoir, a freshwater lake, provides many recreational opportunities. A self-guiding nature trail leads through a section of the reserve. *See Recreation Areas Chart.*

Hours: Daily 7 a.m.-10 p.m., June-Aug.; 8 a.m.-10 p.m., rest of year. Closed Jan. 1 and Christmas. **Cost:** $8 (per private vehicle, maximum eight people). Camping fees $19-$25. Extra vehicle on campsite $10-$13. Group campsite $75. **Phone:** (435) 826-4466, (801) 322-3770, or (800) 322-3770 for camping reservations.

ESCALANTE'S GRAND STAIRCASE BED & BREAKFAST INN   (435)826-4890

▼▼▼ **Bed & Breakfast** $142-$182 **Address:** 280 W Main St 84726 **Location:** West end of town. **Facility:** Two separate, attractive one-story buildings behind the property feature eclectic Western décor. The spacious rooms are uniquely decorated with Native American drums, beautiful throws and skylights. 8 units. 1-2 stories (no elevator), exterior corridors. **Terms:** 14 day cancellation notice-fee imposed.

RAINBOW COUNTRY BED & BREAKFAST   435/826-4567

▼▼ **Bed & Breakfast** $84-$114 **Address:** 585 E 300 S 84726 **Location:** Just s of SR 12; east end of town. **Facility:** 4 units. 2 stories (no elevator), interior corridors. **Terms:** closed 11/20-3/15, check-in 4 pm, 3 day cancellation notice, resort fee. **Activities:** hot tub.

WHERE TO EAT

KIVA KOFFEEHOUSE   435/826-4550

▼▼ Natural/Organic. Quick Serve. $7-$10 **AAA Inspector Notes:** An oasis for travelers, hikers and bikers, this oversize restaurant uses organic ingredients whenever feasible. Great breakfasts, salads, muffins, wraps, sandwiches and baked goods are made daily. Many of the seasonal vegetables come right from the on-site organic garden. Wide windows offer views of the Escalante River, and words can't describe the feeling experienced from taking advantage of them from the patio. **Features:** patio dining. **Address:** Hwy 12, MM 73-74 84726 **Location:** SR 12, MM 73-74. ⓑ ⓛ

EUREKA (C-3) pop. 669, elev. 6,430'

You'll find a hodgepodge of wooden and squat brick structures along the once-bustling Main Street of Eureka. Though still an active community, the vicissitudes of more than a century of mining lend the place an air of past glory. Slag heaps, tailings and abandoned mines dot the landscape, and the surrounding mountains, long ago stripped of their forests, look careworn with their cloak of scrub juniper.

Prospectors arrived in the area in 1869. The first mine claim was filed in 1870, triggering a rush. Eureka, straddling an easy east-west pass through the mountains, soon became the focal point of a cluster of rough camps known as the East Tintic Mining District. Mining continued through the 1950s, and some small-scale mining operations remain operational. Since 1870, area mines have produced nearly half a billion dollars in gold, silver, lead, zinc, copper and uranium.

Containing historical photos and newspapers, minerals and mining equipment, the Tintic Mining Museum, on Main Street in the former city hall built in 1899, is open by appointment. Phone (435) 433-6842.

LITTLE SAHARA RECREATION AREA, 27020 Sand Mountain Rd., is a 60,000-acre tract of shifting dunes, juniper-dotted hills and sagebrush flats inhabited by a wide range of animals. Off-road vehicles traverse 124 square miles of dune fields, which were created when strong winds picked up sand from the Sevier Desert and deposited them here.

Sand Mountain, a challenging, nearly 700-foot wall of sand, is Little Sahara's focal point. Attracting riders of all abilities, the White Sand Dunes offer numerous bowls. The Black Mountain includes a network of dirt trails. There also are fenced sand play areas at the White Sands Campground and the Jericho Picnic Area. The Rockwell Outstanding Natural Area is a 9,000-acre unit reserved for non-vehicle use.

Time: Allow 1 hour minimum. **Hours:** Recreation area daily dawn-dusk. Visitor center Thurs.-Mon. 8-4; closed Thanksgiving and Christmas. Phone ahead to confirm visitor center hours. **Cost:** (valid for 2 consecutive days) $18 (per private vehicle). **Phone:** (435) 433-5960. 🔺

FAIRFIELD (C-3) pop. 119, elev. 4,866'

Fairfield flourished during a brief boom 1858-59 when Gen. Albert Sidney Johnston's army forces were at nearby Camp Floyd. The population at that time swelled to about 7,000. About 2,500 of these were soldiers; the rest were camp followers, gamblers and Mormon settlers. Johnston's men were stationed in Fairfield until the beginning of the Civil War, and supplying them with food and goods provided the settlers with a steady cash income, a rarity in pioneer Utah.

CAMP FLOYD/STAGECOACH INN STATE PARK AND MUSEUM, just e. of SR 73 at 18035 W. 1540 N., following signs, was the site of the largest army encampment in the United States 1858-61. More than 3,500 troops were stationed there to suppress a Mormon rebellion that never materialized. The army was recalled back east in 1861 for the Civil War emergency.

Of its 400 structures, only the commissary (now a museum) and the Johnston Army Cemetery, .5 miles west on SR 73, remain. The nearby Stagecoach Inn served as a rest stop for Pony Express riders; it

houses period items. **Hours:** Mon.-Sat. 9-5. Closed Jan. 1, Thanksgiving and Christmas. **Cost:** $3; $9 (family, maximum eight people). **Phone:** (801) 768-8932. 🔓

FAIRVIEW (D-4) pop. 1,247, elev. 6,033'

Settled in 1859, Fairview was named for its impressive view of the Sanpete Valley. Just east of the city on SR 31 is the central point of Skyline Drive, an unpaved road that winds along the Wasatch Plateau for nearly 100 miles. The road is open July through October.

FAIRVIEW MUSEUM OF HISTORY AND ART is at 85 North 100 East. The museum contains Native American and pioneer relics and thousands of miniature woodcarvings. Early farm equipment is displayed on the grounds. The Natural History Building houses a replica of a Columbian mammoth unearthed nearby in 1988. Changing exhibits feature paintings and sculptures by local and regional artists. **Time:** Allow 30 minutes minimum. **Hours:** Mon.-Sat. 10-5. **Cost:** Donations. **Phone:** (435) 427-9216.

FARMINGTON (B-3) pop. 18,275, elev. 4,231'
• Hotels p. 312 • Restaurants p. 312
• Part of Salt Lake City area — see map p. 368

The Farmington area is no longer in the shape William Chandless found it in "A Visit to Salt Lake," published in 1857. Chandless wrote that "though the Mormons are certainly a hospitable people, they have a prodigious number of savage inhospitable dogs about their houses, and worse still, almost impassible ditches, so that the benighted traveler has pretty well as much work to find his way into a house to inquire, as to find the one he is inquiring for without information ...."

Bountiful/Farmington Loop, a 24-mile loop connecting Farmington and Bountiful, offers views of alpine scenery, the Great Salt Lake and Antelope Island. From Bountiful take 400 North east to 1300 East, then north on Ward Canyon Road. Facilities for camping, picnicking and hiking are along the road, which is open May through October.

Note: This route should not be attempted by anyone unfamiliar with mountain driving. Four-wheel-drive vehicles are recommended. Visitors are advised to drive slowly, as the gravel road is rough and washboard-like and the road grades are steep. Inclement weather may further impair road conditions.

🔷 **LAGOON** is off I-15 at 375 N. Lagoon Dr. The amusement park features Pioneer Village, a re-created frontier settlement of the 19th century, where exhibits provide a living-history atmosphere. Ten roller coasters are among the park's more than 55 rides. Also available are a music theater and Kiddieland. In addition the site includes Lagoon A Beach, a water park featuring several waterslides, a kid's play area and a lazy river.

Time: Allow 3 hours minimum. **Hours:** Amusement park open Sun.-Fri. at 11, Sat. at 10, early

June-late Aug.; Sat. at 10, Sun. at 11 (also Memorial Day and Labor Day), early Apr.-early June and late Aug.-late Sept. Lagoon A Beach open daily at 11, Memorial Day weekend to mid-Sept. (weather permitting). Frightmares takes place at the amusement park late Sept.-late Oct.; phone for schedule. Phone ahead to confirm schedule and closing times for both amusement and water parks.

Cost: $49.95; $44.95 (ages 65+); $37.50 (under 48 inches tall); free (ages 0-2). Prices may vary. A photo ID is required for payment by credit card. Checks are not accepted. **Parking:** $10. **Phone:** (801) 451-8000 or (800) 748-5246.

HAMPTON INN & SUITES - SALT LAKE CITY/FARMINGTON
(801)451-7999

Hotel
$99-$169

AAA Benefit: Members save up to 10%!

Address: 332 Park Ln 84025 **Location:** I-15 exit 324 (Lagoon Park), 0.3 mi e on Park Ln. Adjacent to Lagoon Amusement Park. **Facility:** 83 units. 4 stories, interior corridors. **Terms:** 1-7 night minimum stay, cancellation fee imposed. **Pool(s):** heated indoor. **Activities:** hot tub, exercise room. **Guest Services:** valet and coin laundry. **Featured Amenity:** breakfast buffet.

HYATT PLACE SALT LAKE CITY/FARMINGTON/STATION PARK
801/683-4444

[fyi] Hotel Under construction, scheduled to open July 2016. **Address:** 222 N Union Ave 84025 **Location:** I-15 exit 324/325. **Planned Amenities:** 108 units, pets, restaurant, coffeemakers, refrigerators, pool, exercise facility. (See ad this page.)

AAA Benefit: Members save 10%!

SETTEBELLO PIZZERIA NAPOLETANA STATION PARK
801/451-9100

Pizza Small Plates. Casual Dining. $8-$16 **AAA Inspector Notes:** Diners can go healthy with a caprese or arugula salad or instead opt for a traditional Napoli pizza, which can be served sliced or unsliced. Room should be saved for the house sorbet or gelato. This restaurant is a first choice for return visits because in the summer you are steps away from a courtyard that features concerts, daily family fun nights and beautiful water fountains. In the winter, the courtyard is transformed into a Santa's Village with an ice skating rink. **Features:** beer & wine, patio dining. **Address:** 895 W East Promontory Rd 84025 **Location:** I-15 exit 322 (Lagoon Dr), northbound, 1 mi n to W State St, 0.5 mi e, continue on Clark Ln, then just n on Central Ave; exit 325 southbound (Lagoon/Fairgrounds), just w on Park Ln to Station Pkwy, take the 2nd exit at the roundabout; in Station Park. **Parking:** street only.

FILLMORE (E-3) pop. 2,435, elev. 5,700'

Fillmore was selected as the seat of government by the territorial legislature in 1851 and served as the territorial capital until 1856. The city and surrounding Millard County were named for President Millard Fillmore. The town is in generally flat country west of the Pavant Mountains and is a trading center for the surrounding farm and livestock region.

Fillmore Area Chamber of Commerce: 460 N. Main St., Fillmore, UT 84631-5504. **Phone:** (435) 743-7803.

TERRITORIAL STATEHOUSE STATE PARK MUSEUM is on US 91 at 50 W. Capitol Ave. The park was the site of Utah's first territorial government headquarters. Isolation and lack of funds prevented completion of more than one wing of the 1851 statehouse. Pioneer relics, Native American artifacts and early documents are displayed. A small rose gardenis located next to the park grounds. **Hours:** Statehouse Mon.-Sat. 9-5. Closed Jan. 1, Thanksgiving and Christmas. **Cost:** $2; $1 (ages 6-11). **Phone:** (435) 743-5316.

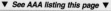

▼ See AAA listing this page ▼

BEST WESTERN PARADISE INN & RESORT
(435)743-6895

Motel
$80-$110

AAA Benefit:
Save 10% or more every day and earn 10% bonus points!

Address: 905 N Main St 84631 **Location:** I-15 exit 167, just e. **Facility:** 74 units. 2 stories (no elevator), exterior corridors. Breakfast is available all day. **Dining:** Garden of Eat'n, see separate listing. **Pool(s):** heated indoor. **Activities:** hot tub, regulation golf.

WHERE TO EAT

GARDEN OF EAT'N   435/743-5414

American. Family Dining. $5-$16 **AAA Inspector Notes:** The eatery offers daily specials and plenty of homemade fruit and cream pies. Breakfast is available all day. **Features:** full bar. **Address:** 915 N Main St 84631 **Location:** I-15 exit 167, just e; next to BEST WESTERN Paradise Inn & Resort. B L D

FISHLAKE NATIONAL FOREST (D-3)

Elevations in the forest range from 5,500 ft. near the town of Kanosh to 12,173 ft. at Delano Peak. Refer to AAA maps for additional elevation information.

In south-central Utah, Fishlake National Forest is divided into four segments by intervening valleys. It covers 1,434,599 acres and includes 76 streams and more than 60 lakes. The forest contains a wide variety of environments, from the alpine of the Tushar Mountains to the red desert of Wayne Wonderland.

The scenic Fish Lake-Johnson Valley area in the southeast includes 2,600-acre Fish Lake and 670-acre Johnson Reservoir, camping and picnicking areas, a boat launch site and three resorts. Another picturesque area is Beaver Mountain in the southwest. The highway to Fish Lake is paved.

Scenic drives from Fish Lake to Salina Canyon and from Beaver to Junction can be taken in good weather; high-clearance vehicles are recommended on most of the forest's 1,700 miles of road. Hunting for deer and elk is permitted, and several species of trout, splake and large mackinaw provide challenging fishing throughout the year. Other possible recreational pursuits include traversing 1,100 miles of trail by foot, horse or mountain bike and ATV. Camping is possible at 29 developed campgrounds and nine undeveloped campgrounds at elevations ranging from 5,500 to 9,300 feet.

For additional information contact the Forest Supervisor, Fishlake National Forest, 115 East 900 North, Richfield, UT 84701; phone (435) 896-9233. *See Recreation Areas Chart.*

FLAMING GORGE NATIONAL RECREATION AREA (B-5)

Reached by SR 530 or US 191 from I-80 in Wyoming or US 191 from Utah, Flaming Gorge National Recreation Area straddles the border between Wyoming and Utah. The area includes a 91-mile-long reservoir and the Flaming Gorge and Red canyons, which were carved through the Uinta Mountains by the Green River.

Lake Flaming Gorge is bounded primarily by Red Canyon to the south and by rolling hills and occasional abrupt cliffs and promontories to the north. Of geologic interest are the exposed strata in Firehole Canyon and the Sheep Creek Geological Loop.

Once belonging to Mexico, Wyoming's portion of the Flaming Gorge region was annexed to the United States after the Mexican War. John Wesley Powell, a one-armed Army major and professor, on his way down the Green River in the late 1860s and early 1870s, naming Flaming Gorge and many other prominent landmarks.

I-80 is connected to SR 530 and US 191. In Utah, US 191 joins with SRs 43 and 44, which then link with SR 530 again, to form a complete 160-mile loop around the recreation area. Along the route are the Flaming Gorge Dam and Visitor Center, off US 191 adjacent to the Bureau of Reclamation offices; the Red Canyon Visitor Center and Overlook, which offers a spectacular view from 1,400 feet above Red Canyon and Flaming Gorge Reservoir off SR 44; the Sheep Creek Geological Loop; and Flaming Gorge.

Known for its bountiful fishing waters, Lake Flaming Gorge also is a popular setting for swimming, boating and water skiing. Large boat ramps are found near campgrounds at convenient access points along the western and eastern sides of the lake.

The western shore, accessible from Buckboard, Wyo., and Lucerne Valley, Utah, has campsites and two marinas that provide boat rentals and supplies. Cedar Springs to the southeast is similarly equipped; the latter has a dock and marina. Other campgrounds are scattered throughout the Utah and Wyoming sections.

The reservoir contains a broad sampling of fish, including German brown, lake, rainbow and cutthroat trout; small-mouth bass; and kokanee salmon. Fishing is permitted all year. A license from either Utah or Wyoming is required.

Seasonal hunting is permitted except near public-use facilities. Cross-country skiing, snowmobiling and ice fishing are popular winter activities. For further information, contact the Flaming Gorge Ranger District, Flaming Gorge National Recreation Area, P.O. Box 279, Manila, UT 84046.

The recreation area is open all year, but most developed facilities are closed during the winter. The Red Canyon Visitor Center is open Mon.-Thurs. 10-5, Fri.-Sun. 9-6, mid-May to mid-Sept.; phone for schedule, rest of year. The Flaming Gorge Dam Visitor Center is open daily 8-6, Memorial Day-Labor Day; daily 9-5, Apr. 1-day before Memorial Day and day after Labor Day to mid-Oct.; Fri.-Mon. 10-4, rest of year. Guided tours of the dam depart from the visitor center daily every 20 minutes 9:10-3:50, mid-Mar. to mid-Oct.; phone ahead to confirm schedule.

A use fee pass is required for all facilities. Passes are $5 (1 day), $15 (16 days) and $35 (annual), beginning from the date of purchase. America the Beautiful–National Parks and Federal Recreational Lands Pass holders enter free. Phone (435) 784-3445 for the ranger district, (435) 889-3713 for the Red Canyon Visitor Center, or (435) 885-3135 for the Flaming Gorge Dam and Visitor Center. *See Recreation Areas Chart.*

FLAMING GORGE DAM is off US 191 near Dutch John, Utah. The dam is a concrete arch structure rising 502 feet above bedrock. **Note:** Pets are allowed only in the parking lot, not on the dam. **Hours:** Guided 1-hour tours are offered every 20 minutes daily 9:10-3:50, mid-Mar. to mid-Oct. Phone ahead to confirm schedule. **Cost:** Free. **Phone:** (435) 885-3135. GT

JOHN JARVIE HISTORIC RANCH is about 8 mi. n.w. of Dutch John, Utah, on US 191, then 22 mi. e. on a gravel road, following signs to Browns Park. A haven for outlaws around the turn of the 20th century, Browns Park formerly was the site of a successful ranching operation started by Scottish immigrant John Jarvie in the 1880s. The ranch today includes a replica of the general store originally built in 1881, a blacksmith shop, a corral and a two-room dugout that was once Jarvie's residence.

A 15-minute orientation video is shown in a historical stone house that now serves as a museum. **Time:** Allow 1 hour minimum. **Hours:** Daily 10-4:30, Memorial Day-Labor Day; Tues.-Sat. 10-4:30, rest of year when staff is available. Phone ahead to confirm schedule. **Cost:** Donations. **Phone:** (435) 885-3307 or (435) 781-4400. GT

FORT DUCHESNE (C-5) pop. 714, elev. 4,988'

Fort Duchesne (doo-SHAYN) is headquarters for the Ute Indian Reservation, home of 1,600 members of the Uinta, White River and Uncompaghre tribes. The tribal organization has encouraged many educational and business enterprises to develop and employ its members. Industry makes use of the vast landholdings.

The Ute Fish and Game Committee runs stocking and conservation programs to ensure supplies of fish. Upland game bird, waterfowl and big game hunting also are available. For further information contact the Ute Indian Tribe Complex at (435) 722-5141.

FOUR CORNERS MONUMENT—See Colorado p. 106.

GARDEN CITY pop. 562

BEAVER CREEK LODGE 435/946-3400
Hotel. Rates not provided. **Address:** 11808 N Hwy 89 84028 **Location:** 12 mi w of Bear Lake Blvd; 25 mi e of Logan; MM 847. **Parking:** winter plug-ins. **Activities:** snowmobiling, playground, lawn sports, picnic facilities. **Facility:** 11 units. 3 stories (no elevator), exterior corridors.

GLEN CANYON NATIONAL RECREATION AREA (F-4)

Along the Colorado River from Grand Canyon National Park in far north-central Arizona to Canyonlands National Park in southeastern Utah, Glen Canyon National Recreation Area is home to one of the highest dams in the United States. Part of the Colorado River storage project, the Glen Canyon Dam generates hydroelectric power that is distributed to cities and industries throughout the West; the dam's main purpose is water storage.

Reaching out to hidden canyons, sandy coves and inlets, and winding through towering red cliffs, 186-mile-long Lake Powell presents an ever-changing array of scenery and such recreational opportunities as water skiing, boating and fishing. Amenities include campsites, marinas, and boat rentals and tours. A copy of fishing regulations can be obtained at the Carl Hayden Visitor Center, the Navajo Bridge Interpretive Center, the Bullfrog Visitor Center or at the administration offices in Page, Ariz.; phone (928) 608-6200.

The Bullfrog Visitor Center, at the Bullfrog Marina in Utah, exhibits the natural and cultural history of Glen Canyon and includes a life-size slot canyon model. The visitor center is open seasonally as staffing allows; phone (435) 684-7423. The Navajo Bridge Interpretive Center, on US 89A near Lees Ferry, Ariz., features a historic pedestrian bridge over the Colorado River at Marble Canyon and outdoor exhibits highlighting the early river crossings. The interpretive center is open daily 9-5, Apr.-Oct., as staffing allows; phone (928) 355-2319.

Exhibits in the Carl Hayden Visitor Center, next to US 89, Glen Canyon Dam and Glen Canyon Bridge in Page illustrate the construction of the dam and bridge and include a relief model of the canyon country. Guided tours of the dam are available throughout the year. The center is open daily 8-6, Memorial Day-Labor Day; 8-5, Mar. 1-day before Memorial Day; 8:30-4:30, rest of year. Closed Jan. 1, Thanksgiving and Christmas. Phone (928) 608-6404.

Ranger-led interpretive programs are offered Memorial Day through Labor Day; phone ahead or stop by the Carl Hayden Visitor Center for program times and locations.

Arrangements for boat tours on Lake Powell can be made at Wahweap Lodge and Marina; facilities, including public launching ramps, boat rentals, camping and boat and automobile fuel, are provided at Wahweap and at four other marinas on the lake.

All facilities may not be available year-round. A boat ramp providing access to 15 miles of the Colorado River below Glen Canyon Dam is available at Lees Ferry, 5 miles north of Marble Canyon.

Boat excursions, which last from 4 to 6.5 hours, are available through Colorado River Discovery; phone (928) 645-9175 or (888) 522-6644. The tours begin near the Glen Canyon Dam and conclude at Lees Ferry. One-day raft trips on the Colorado River below the dam can be arranged in Page. Half-day and full-day trips are available to Rainbow Bridge National Monument, Utah, which is about 50 miles from Wahweap. Trips on the San Juan River leave from Mexican Hat and Bluff, Utah.

Admission, valid for up to 7 days, is $20 (per private vehicle); $10 (per person arriving by foot or bicycle). An annual pass is $40. An additional use fee of $20 is charged for one motorized water vessel and is valid for up to 7 days.

Admission prices are scheduled to increase January 1, 2016, after which admission, valid for up to 7 days, will be $25 (per private vehicle); $12 (per person arriving by foot or bicycle). An annual pass will be $50. An additional use fee of $25 is charged for one motorized water vessel and is valid for up to 7 days.

For further information contact the Superintendent, Glen Canyon National Recreation Area; phone (928) 608-6200. *See Recreation Areas Chart.*

GLENDALE pop. 381

HISTORIC SMITH HOTEL BED & BREAKFAST   (435)648-2156
▼▼▼ ◆◆ **Bed & Breakfast** $69-$120 **Address:** 295 N Main St 84729 **Location:** US 89; north end of town. **Facility:** 6 units. 2 stories (no elevator), interior corridors. **Terms:** closed 11/1-3/1, check-in 4 pm, 4 day cancellation notice.
⊞ 🛜 ✖ ☎ / SOME UNITS 🛏

GOLDEN SPIKE NATIONAL HISTORIC SITE (A-2)

Thirty miles west of Brigham City via SRs 13 and 83, the site marks Promontory Summit, the place where the Union Pacific and Central Pacific rails met to form the nation's first transcontinental railroad on May 10, 1869. A golden spike was placed ceremonially along with three other precious metal spikes in order to commemorate this connection.

The culmination of the nation's dream to unite the East and West coasts brought major changes to the country. The new railroad provided the first practical means of round-trip travel. New opportunities for commerce brought buffalo hunters, who depleted the great bison herds that roamed the plains. The railroad also advanced the settlement of California, Colorado, Nebraska, Nevada, Wyoming and Utah.

Working replicas of the 1869 steam locomotives "119" and "Jupiter" are displayed. Steam demonstrations are given, though no rides are available. The West Auto Tour, a 14-mile looping self-guiding

drive, and the 2-mile-long East Auto Tour take visitors over the old railroad grades. Although the West Auto Tour is closed in winter, the East Auto Tour is accessible daily 9-4:30, year-round (weather permitting). **Note:** Motor homes or vehicles pulling a trailer are not permitted to take either auto tour.

The Big Fill Loop Trail is a 1.5-mile walk on the original Central and Union Pacific railroad grades. Films and museum exhibits are offered daily throughout the year. Allow 2 hours minimum for the historic site and visitor center. The visitor center is open daily 9-5. Steam locomotives are displayed daily, May 1-Columbus Day (schedule varies; phone the visitor center to confirm hours). A re-enactment of the driving of the golden spike ceremony is held Sat. and holidays at 11 and 1:30, May 1-late September. Closed Jan. 1, Thanksgiving and Christmas. Admission is $5-$7 (per private vehicle); $3-$4 (per person arriving by other means). Phone (435) 471-2209, ext. 29, for park information or for the visitor center.

GRAND STAIRCASE-ESCALANTE NATIONAL MONUMENT (F-4)

Between Bryce Canyon National Park and Glen Canyon National Recreation Area, Grand Staircase-Escalante National Monument consists of 1.9 million acres in southern Utah. Established by presidential proclamation in September 1996, the national monument's name is derived from the series of multi-colored cliffs and mesas extending from Bryce Canyon to the Grand Canyon in Arizona. The Escalante and Paria rivers and their tributaries, which run through this area, have created two major canyon systems as well as natural bridges and arches. The majority of monument land remains rugged, remote and undeveloped.

Geological formations found within the monument include red rock canyons, cliffs, rock formations and natural bridges and arches. Highlights include Escalante Natural Bridge, which measures 100 feet across and 130 feet high, and Grosvenor Arch, which are actually two arches reachable from a dirt road off SR 12. Reaching Escalante Natural Bridge entails a 2-mile hike up the Escalante River. Lower Calf Creek Falls, requiring a 6-mile round-trip hike, and Devils Garden are other popular features.

The monument also contains major paleontological and archeological sites, including numerous examples of fossils and petrified wood. Also of significance is the knowledge to be gained from the remains of the area's earliest inhabitants. Prehistoric dwellings and rock art attest to early settlement within the monument's boundaries by antediluvian cultures. Anasazi and Fremont cultures were followed by settlements of Southern Paiutes and Navajos.

The monument's vast acreage, which embraces both deserts and forests, is populated by mountain lions, bighorn sheep, mule deer, coyotes, foxes and more than 200 species of birds, including bald eagles and peregrine falcons.

Access to the monument is by two routes: Scenic SR 12 leads to the monument from the north, and US 89 provides access from the south. Other roads within the monument are partially surfaced or are of gravel, sand or clay; these may present difficult driving conditions in inclement weather.

The monument encompasses one of the country's most remote regions. Driving in the backcountry requires preparation for emergencies and all weather conditions, including flash floods. Services and rescue capabilities are limited. Permits are required for overnight camping or backpacking visitors; these can be obtained for free at trailheads or at the Escalante Interagency Visitor Center.

There are four visitor centers and one information desk within the national monument. Visitor centers are in Kanab, (435) 644-1300, site of the monument's headquarters; in Escalante, (435) 826-5499; in Cannonville, (435) 826-5640; and in Big Water, (435) 675-3200. A contact station is 44 miles east of Kanab at Paria on US 89. The Kanab and Escalante centers are open daily 8-4:30, mid-Mar. to mid-Nov.; Mon.-Fri. 8-4:30, rest of year. The Cannonville center is open daily 8-4:30, mid-Mar. to mid-Nov. The Big Water center is open daily 9-5:30, Apr.-Oct.; Tues.-Sat. 8-4:30, rest of year. Each visitor center offers exhibits and a DVD presentation about the monument. Exhibits vary and range from ecology, biology and archeology to geology, human geography and paleontology.

The monument is open all year (weather permitting), but the best time to visit is March through May and September 1 to early November. Visitors should phone ahead to confirm that weather conditions within the monument are favorable. Closed Jan. 1, Thanksgiving and Christmas.

For additional information contact the Grand Staircase-Escalante National Monument, Kanab Visitor Center, 745 E. US 89, Kanab, UT 84741, (435) 644-1300, or the Escalante Interagency Visitor Center, 755 W. Main St., Escalante, UT 84726, (435) 826-5499.

GREAT SALT LAKE (B-2)
• Part of Salt Lake City area — see map p. 368

With the exception of the Dead Sea, the Great Salt Lake is the saltiest body of water on Earth. Occupying a large part of the northern portion of Utah, the lake is 72 miles long and as wide as 30 miles but only 10 to 28 feet deep. The only crossing over the lake is the 102-mile Southern Pacific Railroad cutoff between Ogden and Lucin.

Centuries ago the northwestern quarter of Utah was covered by Lake Bonneville, a great freshwater lake 10 times the size of the Great Salt Lake. Covering more than 20,000 square miles in Utah, Nevada and Idaho, the lake was 1,000 feet deep where the Great Salt Lake now lies and 900 feet deep at the site of Salt Lake City.

The lake's weight was so great that the Earth's crust in the middle of the basin was depressed more than 150 feet, leaving a shoreline that is still visible.

Because of a change in climate or a volcanic diversion of contributing streams, the huge lake fell below its lowest outlet and shrank to what is now known as the Great Salt Lake.

The Great Salt Lake's salinity varies from 15 to 25 percent (at least six times saltier than the ocean) according to the water level. This salt content can only be tolerated by blue-green algae and brine shrimp.

The lake owes its extreme saltiness to the mineral-laden freshwater streams that feed into it and find no outlet. The evaporation of the streams' waters leaves so much salt behind that the lake will buoy a human body. The water trapped in open, diked lakes near the shores of the larger lake leaves inches of almost pure salt, which is harvested annually for commercial purposes.

On the north side of the lake, at Promontory Summit, the Golden Spike National Historic Site *(see place listing p. 315)* commemorates the place where the first transcontinental railroad linked the east and west coasts in 1869. In the lake itself is Antelope Island State Park *(see attraction listing)*, where visitors can float effortlessly in the lake as well as take advantage of the park's recreational activities.

Great Salt Lake State Park, 16 miles west of Salt Lake City off I-80 exit 104, provides access to the south shore of the lake. The park's marina is a good spot for watching the sun set over the lake. For additional information phone (801) 250-1898.

The Great Salt Lake Desert to the west of the lake is part of the bed of extinct Lake Bonneville and is composed of silt washed into the huge lake hundreds of years ago. Highways crossing the desert follow trails blazed by some of the first Mormon settlers. Also in this region, on the western edge of the Great Salt Lake basin, is the Bonneville Salt Flats. Covering about 46 square miles, the expanse of hard, white salt crust has been popular with racing enthusiasts since the 1930s. Many land speed racing records have been set on the Bonneville Speedway, an area marked out for various motor sports events. Attracting the most gearheads is Speed Week, held in late August.

For additional information contact the Salt Lake Field Office of the Bureau of Land Management at (801) 977-4300.

ANTELOPE ISLAND STATE PARK, within the Great Salt Lake 9.8 mi. w. of Syracuse via West 1700 South and the 7-mi.-long Davis County Cswy., has sand beaches; trails for hiking, horseback riding, mountain biking and cross-country skiing; and a marina. A herd of more than 500 bison as well as mule deer, pronghorn antelopes, bighorn sheep, coyotes and waterfowl are full-time residents.

The Fielding Garr Ranch, Utah's oldest, also can be toured, and the visitor center has a video and information about the island's geology, biology and history. Kayaking, bird-watching, and horseback and wagon rides are available. *See Recreation Areas Chart.*

Time: Allow 2 hours minimum. **Hours:** Park open daily 6 a.m.-10 p.m. Closed Thanksgiving and Christmas. **Cost:** $10 (per private vehicle); $5 (ages 62+ per private vehicle); $3 (per person arriving by other means). Camping $15-$30. **Phone:** (801) 773-2941 for park information, or (800) 322-3770 for camping reservations. 🅰 🍴 🏕 🐾 ⛺

GREEN RIVER (D-5) pop. 952, elev. 4,080'
• Restaurants p. 318

Green River was settled as a mail relay station in 1878 on the site where it was easiest to ford the river. Today it is the center of a melon-growing region.

Crystal Geyser is 5 miles east via US 6/50 to the I-70 overpass, then 7 miles south on a gravel road. The unpredictable eruptions of this rare cold-water geyser can reach as high as 100 feet, though they more typically top out at less than 10 feet. The gravel road to the geyser is in good condition but is not well marked.

About 45 miles west of Green River on I-70, Wedge Overlook affords a view of the San Rafael River 1,000 feet below. The panorama across the San Rafael Swell consists of an impressive 30-by-60-mile hollowed-out red dome marked with buttes, gorges and canyons.

JOHN WESLEY POWELL RIVER HISTORY MUSEUM is at 1765 E. Main St. The museum features photographs, artifacts, models, displays and maps that describe the exploration of the Green and Colorado rivers as well as the geological formation of the rivers' gorges and mountains. Some exhibits focus on the accomplishments of 19th-century explorer John Wesley Powell, whose expeditions contributed to the development of the Colorado Plateau. An art gallery and a visitor center are on the premises.

Hours: Mon.-Sat. 9-7, Sun. noon-5, Apr.-Oct.; Tues.-Sat. 9-5, rest of year. Closed Jan. 1, Thanksgiving and Christmas. Phone ahead to confirm schedule. **Cost:** $6; $2 (ages 5-12); $15 (family). **Phone:** (435) 564-3427.

RECREATIONAL ACTIVITIES
White-water Rafting
• **Holiday River Expeditions** departs from the company's headquarters on the east side of the Green River Bridge behind the Comfort Inn on E. Main St. Other activities and multiday trips are offered. **Hours:** One-day trips on the Green River depart daily May-Aug. **Phone:** (435) 564-3273 or (801) 266-2087.

GREEN RIVER COMFORT INN   (435)564-3300
▼▼ Hotel $79-$119 **Address:** 1975 E Main St 84525 **Location:** I-70 exit 164, 1.5 mi n. **Facility:** 57 units. 2 stories (no elevator), interior corridors. **Pool(s):** heated indoor. **Activities:** hot tub, exercise room. **Guest Services:** coin laundry.
🍴 🛏 🖩 📶 ✖ ▮ 🖵 / SOME UNITS ▯

HOLIDAY INN EXPRESS   435/564-4439

 **Hotel.** Rates not provided. **Address:** 1845 E Main St 84525 **Location:** I-70 exit 164, 1.7 mi nw. **Facility:** 60 units. 2 stories, interior corridors. **Pool(s):** heated indoor. **Activities:** hot tub. **Guest Services:** coin laundry.

 / SOME UNITS

RIVER TERRACE INN   435/564-3401

Hotel. Rates not provided. **Address:** 1740 E Main St 84525 **Location:** I-70 exit 164, 1.7 mi nw. **Facility:** 50 units. 2-3 stories (no elevator), interior corridors. **Pool(s):** heated outdoor. **Activities:** hot tub.

SUPER 8   (435)564-8888

Motel $75-$90 **Address:** 1248 E Main St 84525 **Location:** I-70 exit 164, 1.3 mi n. **Facility:** 67 units. 2 stories (no elevator), interior corridors. **Pool(s):** heated indoor. **Activities:** hot tub, exercise room. **Guest Services:** coin laundry.

 / SOME UNITS

WHERE TO EAT

RAY'S TAVERN   435/564-3511

American. Casual Dining. $8-$27 **AAA Inspector Notes:** Highly recommended by the locals, this no-frills eatery specializes in juicy steaks and burgers but also serves chicken and veggie burgers. Pool tables keep guests busy in the back room. **Features:** beer only. **Address:** 25 S Broadway 84525 **Location:** Downtown. **Parking:** street only. [L] [D]

TAMARISK RESTAURANT   435/564-8109

American. Casual Dining. $7-$20 **AAA Inspector Notes:** Overlooking a bridge and the Green River, which is surrounded by tamarisk trees and bushes, this restaurant is the perfect stop. The menu includes favorites such as charbroiled steaks, fettuccine Alfredo and Navajo tacos. Soups, salads and sandwiches also are available. The homemade fudge is a classic favorite. **Features:** beer only. **Address:** 1710 E Main St 84525 **Location:** I-70 exit 160 eastbound, 3 mi e; exit 164 westbound, 1.7 mi nw. [B] [L] [D]

HANKSVILLE (E-4) pop. 219, elev. 4,288'

GOBLIN VALLEY STATE PARK is 24 mi. s. on SR 24 from I-70, then 12 mi. w. via Temple Mountain Rd., following signs. The reserve contains thousands of colorful rock formations that resemble gnomes. Hiking facilities are available. **Hours:** Daily 6 a.m.-10 p.m. **Cost:** $10 (per private vehicle). Camping $23. Yurt rental $80. **Phone:** (435) 275-4584, (801) 322-3770, or (800) 322-3770 for camping reservations.

WHISPERING SANDS MOTEL   435/542-3238

Motel $99-$119 **Address:** 90 S Hwy 95 84734 **Location:** East end of town. **Facility:** 23 units. 1-2 stories (no elevator), exterior corridors. **Terms:** cancellation fee imposed. **Guest Services:** coin laundry. **Featured Amenity:** continental breakfast.

HATCH pop. 133

MOUNTAIN RIDGE MOTEL   435/735-4300

Motel. Rates not provided. **Address:** 106 S Main St 84735 **Location:** On US 89; center. **Facility:** 8 kitchen units. 1 story, exterior corridors. / SOME UNITS

HEBER CITY (C-4) elev. 5,595'

Founded in 1859 and named for Heber C. Kimball, counselor to Mormon leader Brigham Young, Heber City is the farming and livestock center of the pastoral Heber Valley. Glider and sailplane rides are available spring through fall. Snowmobile and dog sled races are popular winter events.

Heber Valley Office of Tourism and Economic Development: 475 N. Main St., Heber City, UT 84032. **Phone:** (435) 654-3666 or (866) 994-3237.

HEBER VALLEY RAILROAD, at 450 South 600 West, offers scenic, narrated 3-hour Provo Canyon Limited tours aboard historic diesel or steam-powered trains. Passengers see Provo Canyon, Deer Creek Lake and the farmlands of Heber Valley. Other scenic, seasonal and one-way trips also are offered.

Hours: Provo Canyon Limited trips depart Tues.-Sat. at 11, May-Oct. Phone ahead to confirm schedule. **Cost:** Provo Canyon Limited trip $30; $15 (ages 3-12 and veterans and active military with ID). Prices may vary. Reservations are recommended. **Phone:** (435) 654-5601.

RECREATIONAL ACTIVITIES

Hot Air Ballooning

- **Skywalker Balloon Co.-Heber City** departs from The Hub Cafe at 1165 S. Main St. **Time:** Allow 3 hours minimum. **Hours:** Trips generally depart daily at dawn. Phone ahead to confirm schedule. **Cost:** One-hour flight $250 (per person); $150 (ages 4-12). Prices may vary. Reservations are required. **Phone:** (801) 824-3934.

DANIELS SUMMIT LODGE   (435)548-2300

 **Hotel** $129-$395 **Address:** 17000 S Hwy 40 84032 **Location:** I-80 exit 146 (US 40), 34 mi se. **Facility:** 48 units, some cabins. 2 stories, interior/exterior corridors. **Terms:** check-in 4 pm, 3 day cancellation notice-fee imposed. **Pool(s):** heated indoor. **Activities:** hot tub, cross country skiing, snowmobiling, game room, picnic facilities, exercise room, massage.

/ SOME UNITS

HOLIDAY INN EXPRESS   435/654-9990

Hotel. Rates not provided. **Address:** 1268 S Main St 84032 **Location:** I-80 exit 146 (US 40), 17 mi s; south edge of town. **Facility:** 75 units, some kitchens. 3 stories, interior corridors. **Pool(s):** heated indoor. **Activities:** hot tub, limited exercise equipment. **Guest Services:** coin laundry.

WHERE TO EAT

DAIRY KEEN HOME OF THE TRAIN   435/654-5336

◆◆◆

Burgers
Chicken
Quick Serve
$4-$7

AAA Inspector Notes: This is a fun place to bring family for shakes and burgers along with soups made fresh daily, chicken, salads, fish and tacos. While the food is quickly prepared, take a moment to enjoy all of the operating trains and railroad memorabilia located throughout the restaurant. The place can really rock during the local school's short lunch break. **Features:** patio dining. **Address:** 199 S Main St 84032 **Location:** I-80 exit 146 (US 40), 15 mi s; in Swiss Alps Inn. **Parking:** on-site and street. [L] [D]

Come see awesome model trains, famous shakes & burgers

SNAKE CREEK GRILL   435/654-2133

◆◆◆ American. Fine Dining. $20-$31 **AAA Inspector Notes:** Named after a creek that runs nearby, this restaurant serves unpretentious seasonal cuisine, including creative nightly steak and seafood specials such as certified angus beef tenderloin, pan-seared citrus shrimp and roasted salmon served with quinoa and couscous. The yummy black-bottom banana pie is their signature dessert. Along the historic Heber Creeper railway line, the short drive from Park City is worth the trip. **Features:** full bar, patio dining. **Reservations:** suggested. **Address:** 650 W 100 S 84032 **Location:** I-80 exit 146 (US 40), 16.5 mi s to 100 S, then 0.6 mi w. [D]

SPIN CAFE   435/654-0251

◆◆◆

American
Casual Dining
$8-$19

AAA Inspector Notes: At this hip and fun eatery, patrons enjoy Asian pork lettuce wraps, tasty sandwiches and burgers, slow-cooked pulled pork and specialties such as Key West Caesar salad, pork spare ribs and cedar-plank salmon. In addition to great coffee and hot chocolate, tasty homemade gelato and decadent desserts leave guests hooked. **Features:** full bar. **Address:** 220 N Main St 84032 **Location:** I-80 exit 146 (US 40), 16 mi s; on US 40, just n of Center St. [L] [D]

HELPER (D-4) pop. 2,201, elev. 5,840'

Helper was settled in 1870 by a coal prospector who later sold his property to the Denver & Rio Grande Railroad. The extra engines required to push the heavily laden coal trains to Soldier Summit gave the town its name.

WESTERN MINING AND RAILROAD MUSEUM is at 294 S. Main St. in the historic district. The museum depicts area railroad and mining operation history. Exhibits include historical photographs, a video room, 19th-century coal-mining tools, railroad equipment, a hand press used to print payrolls and the wooden steps on which Butch Cassidy robbed the Pleasant Valley Coal Co. in 1897.

The museum also hosts rotating art exhibitions and boasts one of the largest collections of WPA artwork from the Great Depression era. The grounds feature a native plant garden as well as two outdoor display lots showcasing mining equipment and a 1917 railroad caboose. **Time:** Allow 30 minutes minimum. **Hours:** Mon.-Sat. 10-5, mid-May to mid-Sept.; Tues.-Sat. 11-4, rest of year. **Cost:** Donations. **Phone:** (435) 472-3009.

HOLLADAY   pop. 26,472
- Hotels & Restaurants map & index p. 385
- Part of Salt Lake City area — see map p. 368

HYATT PLACE - SALT LAKE CITY/COTTONWOOD
(801)890-1280   **41**

◆◆◆
Hotel
$84-$199

HYATT PLACE·

AAA Benefit: Members save 10%!

Address: 3090 E 6200 S 84121 **Location:** I-215 exit 6 (6200 S), 0.3 mi s; at base of Big Cottonwood Canyon. **Facility:** 124 units, some efficiencies. 4 stories, interior corridors. **Pool(s):** heated outdoor. **Activities:** hot tub, exercise room. **Guest Services:** valet and coin laundry, area transportation. **Featured Amenity:** breakfast buffet.

[SAVE] [🍴] [🍷] CALL [&M] [🛒] [BIZ]

[📶] [✉] [🔌] [📺] / SOME UNITS [🛏] [HS] [🧺]

WHERE TO EAT

CAFE MADRID   801/273-0837   **29**

◆◆◆ Spanish. Fine Dining. $18-$29 **AAA Inspector Notes:** Authentic cuisine, including hot and cold tapas, imported meats, cheeses and accompaniments, entrées such as beef and pork tenderloin, duck breast and poached salmon, are prepared in this distinctive and elegant European bistro. Seafood paella and mixta and tortilla Española are available with advance notice. **Features:** full bar. **Address:** 5244 S Highland Dr 84117 **Location:** I-15 exit 301 (4500 S), 3 mi e, then 1 mi s. [D]

CAFE TRIO - COTTONWOOD   801/944-8746   **33**

◆◆ Italian. Casual Dining. $9-$26 **AAA Inspector Notes:** The neighborhood dining spot offers a seasonally changing menu of simple fresh Italian cuisine and flatbreads served in a warm contemporary setting. Menu items may include tomato braised meatballs, trio steak with piquillo and almond pesto and pasta with grilled chicken, shrimp or seared salmon. Be prepared for a great wine list, dessert wines, creative martinis and decadent desserts such as rhubarb bar with basil ice cream or tollhouse pie. **Features:** full bar, patio dining, Sunday brunch. **Address:** 6405 S 3000 E 84121 **Location:** I-215 exit 6 (6200 S), 0.3 mi e, then just s. [L] [D]

FRANCK'S   801/274-6264   **32**

◆◆◆ French. Fine Dining. $24-$37 **AAA Inspector Notes:** The intimate setting goes perfect with this restaurant's French-inspired cuisine with some twists. Unusual presentations of huckleberry meatloaf and organic Southern fried chicken are offered in addition to scallops with seasonal risotto, sous vide Wagyu sirloin and Hawaiian sea bass. **Features:** full bar, patio dining. **Reservations:** suggested. **Address:** 6263 S Holladay Blvd 84121 **Location:** I-215 exit 6 (6200 S), just w. **Parking:** on-site and valet. [D] CALL [&M]

PRIMO RESTAURANT   801/947-0025   **30**

◆◆◆ Northern Italian. Fine Dining. $15-$39 **AAA Inspector Notes:** Expect a dining experience with attentive and gracious service. The steamed clams and cold antipasto plate with melon and prosciutto are popular appetizers, while entrées consist of several scrumptious preparations each of fish, chicken, steak and veal with a choice of sauces that are specific to each dish. **Features:** full bar, patio dining. **Reservations:** suggested. **Address:** 4699 S Highland Dr 84117 **Location:** I-15 exit 301 (4500 S), 3 mi e, 0.5 mi s. [L] [D]

TUSCANY   801/277-9919   **31**

◆◆◆ Northern Italian. Fine Dining. $18-$32 **AAA Inspector Notes:** Former Utah Jazz star Mark Eaton and partners bring tempting fare to their alpine chalet. The detail-rich décor is very dramatic. Dining on the outdoor patio, with its lush and manicured landscaping, is a must. **Features:** full bar, patio dining. **Address:** 2832 E 6200 S 84121 **Location:** I-215 exit 6 (6200 S), just w. **Parking:** on-site and valet. [D] CALL [&M]

HOVENWEEP NATIONAL MONUMENT—See Colorado p. 213

HUNTSVILLE (B-3) pop. 608, elev. 4,929'

RECREATIONAL ACTIVITIES
Skiing
- **Snowbasin** is 2 mi. s. on SR 39 to SR 167, 6 mi. s. to SR 226 (Snowbasin Rd.), then 3 mi. e. Other activities are offered. **Hours:** Open for winter activities daily, Thanksgiving-early Apr. (weather permitting). Hours vary; phone ahead. **Phone:** (801) 620-1000 or (888) 437-5488.

JACKSON FORK INN (801)745-0051
▼▼ **Country Inn** $100 **Address:** 7345 E 900 S 84317 **Location:** I-15 exit 344 (12th St), 12 mi. e. **Facility:** 7 units. 2 stories (no elevator), interior corridors. **Terms:** check-in 4 pm, 3 day cancellation notice-fee imposed.
🍴 🛜 ✕ 📞 / SOME UNITS 🛗

HURRICANE (G-2) pop. 13,748, elev. 3,254'
- Part of Zion National Park area — see map p. 415

Named for the Hurricane Fault, a jagged escarpment rising 7,000 feet above the town, Hurricane is the center of Utah's fruit-raising region.

Hurricane Valley Chamber of Commerce: 63 South 100 West, Suite 119, Hurricane, UT 84737. **Phone:** (435) 635-3402.

HURRICANE VALLEY HERITAGE PARK, PIONEER AND INDIAN MUSEUM, at the corner of Main and State sts., contains artifacts relating to settlers and Native Americans, displays about local architecture, and an exhibit about the building of the Hurricane Canal. On the grounds are early wagons, farm machinery and a large sculpture of a pioneer family. Across Main Street, the 1906 Bradshaw House was Hurricane's first residence; it contains a doll collection and early medical equipment. **Hours:** Mon.-Sat. 9-5. **Cost:** Donations. **Phone:** (435) 635-3245.

COMFORT INN ZION (435)635-3500
▼▼ **Hotel** $55-$140 **Address:** 43 N 2600 W 84737 **Location:** 1 mi w on SR 9. **Facility:** 53 units. 2 stories (no elevator), interior corridors. **Pool(s):** heated outdoor. **Activities:** hot tub. **Guest Services:** coin laundry.
CALL 📶 M 🚲 BIZ 🛜 ✕ 📶 📺 💻

WHERE TO EAT

SONNY BOY'S BARBECUE 435/215-3011
▼▼ Barbecue. Family Dining. $5-$15 **AAA Inspector Notes:** This is the place to go for all the televised sports action. Located in the middle of town, diners will enjoy amazing Texas barbecue with homemade sauces. **Features:** beer & wine. **Address:** 980 W State St 84737 **Location:** Center. L D

Enjoy peace of mind
with AAA/CAA Insurance products

IVINS (G-1) pop. 6,753

Tuacahn Amphitheatre and Center for the Arts, off SR 91, presents original productions and its ▼▼ Broadway in the Desert series from June through October in a 2,000-seat outdoor venue surrounded by the towering red rock cliffs of *Tuacahn,* the Canyon of the Gods. Other musical performances are offered in spring and late fall. Phone (435) 652-3200 or (800) 746-9882 for tickets.

SNOW CANYON STATE PARK is 3.5 mi. n. on SR 18 from the Snow Canyon Parkway intersection, then rt. on Snow Canyon Drive. Black lava rock formations contrast with the red sandstone walls and white sandstone formations in this canyon. Pictographs still survive on the walls. *See Recreation Areas Chart.* **Hours:** Daily 6 a.m.-10 p.m. **Cost:** $6 (per private vehicle, maximum eight people); $3 (per private vehicle for UT residents 62+ w/ID). Camping $16-$20. **Phone:** (435) 628-2255, (801) 322-3770, or (800) 322-3770 for camping reservations. 🏕 🏕 🏕

RED MOUNTAIN RESORT 435/673-4905
fyi Not evaluated. **Address:** 1275 E Red Mountain Cir 84738. Facilities, services, and décor characterize a mid-scale property.

KANAB (G-2) pop. 4,312, elev. 4,925'
- Restaurants p. 322

Kanab lies south of Bryce Canyon National Park *(see place listing p. 300)* and southeast of Zion National Park *(see place listing p. 415)* in a region of exceptional scenery. Fort Kanab was built in 1864 on the east bank of Kanab Creek for defense and as a base for exploration. Native American attacks forced its abandonment in 1866, but a group of Mormon missionaries reoccupied it and founded the present town in 1870.

Hundreds of movies and TV episodes have been filmed in the area. A favorite set was the Coral Pink Sand Dunes State Park, a windswept area of coral-colored dunes 23 miles northwest of Kanab. The park has camping and picnic facilities as well as a recreation area for off-road vehicles; phone (435) 648-2800.

Kane County Office of Tourism: 78 South 100 East, Kanab, UT 84741. **Phone:** (435) 644-5033 or (800) 733-5263.

Self-guiding tours: Brochures detailing a self-guiding walking tour of Kanab's historic homes are available at Heritage House and at the office of tourism.

BEST FRIENDS ANIMAL SANCTUARY is 5 mi. n. on US 89 to 5001 Angel Canyon Rd., following signs. The sanctuary is the country's largest no-kill refuge for abused, abandoned and neglected animals. About 1,700 domestic animals are at the sanctuary. Standard van tours of the 3,700-acre facility include stops at Dogtown and Cat World. Specialty tours to see other animals like parrots and rabbits also are available.

Time: Allow 1 hour, 30 minutes minimum. Hours: Tours are given daily at 8:30, 10, 1 and 2:30. Closed Christmas. Cost: Donations. Reservations are recommended. Phone: (435) 644-2001.

CRESCENT MOON THEATER, 150 South 100 East, presents traditional western music and comedy in a relaxed, comfortable setting. Classic and blockbuster movies also are featured year-round. Time: Allow 1 hour, 30 minutes minimum. Hours: Schedules vary; phone ahead. Cost: Movie $7; $6 (ages 0-11 and 60+). Phone for music and comedy ticket prices. Phone: (435) 644-2350.

HERITAGE HOUSE, at the corner of East 100 South and Main St., was built in 1894 for Henry Bowman, one of Kanab's first settlers. The Victorian structure exemplifies human ingenuity in using local resources: Rocks for the foundation and cellar walls were quarried from the red ledges just north of town, the lumber was milled locally and the brick was made by a local kiln operator. Inside is a collection of items from the original owners and neighborhood residents.

Guided tours are available by appointment. Time: Allow 30 minutes minimum. Hours: Mon.-Fri. 1-5, May-Sept.; by appointment rest of year. Phone ahead to confirm schedule. Cost: Free. Phone: (435) 644-3506.

LITTLE HOLLYWOOD MUSEUM, 297 W. Center St., features a Western town consisting of original movie sets from a variety of local and big-screen productions filmed in the area. A Chuckwagon Cookout western show called "How the West Was Lost" is also offered at lunch and dinner. Hours: Daily 9-9, Mar.-Oct.; 9-5, Nov.-Dec. Phone ahead to confirm schedule. Cost: Museum admission free. Chuckwagon Cookout show lunch $15; dinner $20. Reservations required for meals. Phone: (435) 644-5337, or (435) 689-0706 for dinner show. 🍴

MOQUI CAVE is 5.5 mi. n. on US 89. The cave has collections of dinosaur tracks, which were removed from their original site and brought to the cave; fluorescent minerals; Native American artifacts; and foreign currency. A replica of nearby cliff dwellings that were inhabited about A.D. 900 is displayed. Hours: Mon.-Sat. 9-7, Memorial Day-Labor Day; 10-4, rest of year. Cost: $5; $4.50 (ages 60+); $3.50 (ages 13-17); $3 (ages 6-12). Phone: (435) 644-8525.

WINDOWS OF THE WEST HUMMER TOURS picks up at area hotels. During these backcountry excursions, friendly, knowledgeable guides maneuver four-wheel-drive Hummer H1s through parts of southern Utah. Drivers point out native plants and towering rock formations and also stop at a variety of natural and cultural sites such as placid lakes and Native American villages. Ranging from 2-hour trips to full-day adventures, the tours offer everything from panoramic views of ponderosa pine-dotted hills to short hikes through narrow slot canyons protecting ancient petroglyphs.

Time: Allow 2 hours minimum. Hours: Daily 9-3. Cost: Tours $30-$130. Reservations are required. Phone: (435) 689-2029 or (888) 687-3006.

AIKENS LODGE (435)644-2625

◆ **Motel** $89-$179 **Address:** 79 W Center St 84741 **Location:** On US 89. **Facility:** 31 units, some two and three bedrooms. 1-2 stories (no elevator), exterior corridors. **Terms:** closed 11/29-2/15, cancellation fee imposed. **Pool(s):** heated outdoor. **Guest Services:** coin laundry.

BEST WESTERN RED HILLS (435)644-2675

Motel
$79-$229

AAA Benefit: Save 10% or more every day and earn 10% bonus points!

Address: 125 W Center St 84741 **Location:** Center. **Facility:** 74 units. 2 stories, interior/exterior corridors. **Pool(s):** heated outdoor. **Activities:** hot tub, exercise room. **Guest Services:** coin laundry. **Featured Amenity:** full hot breakfast.

CANYONS BOUTIQUE HOTEL (435)644-8660

◆◆◆ **Hotel** $89-$239 **Address:** 190 N 300 W 84741 **Location:** North end of town. **Facility:** 28 units. 3 stories (no elevator), interior corridors. **Terms:** 3 day cancellation notice-fee imposed. **Activities:** bicycles.

DAYS INN & SUITES (435)644-2562

◆◆ **Hotel** $54-$97 **Address:** 296 W 100 N 84741 **Location:** On US 89; north of downtown. **Facility:** 116 units. 2-3 stories, interior corridors. **Pool(s):** heated outdoor. **Activities:** hot tub. **Guest Services:** coin laundry.

HOLIDAY INN EXPRESS HOTEL & SUITES 435/644-3100

◆◆◆ **Hotel.** Rates not provided. **Address:** 217 S 100 E 84741 **Location:** On US 89; jct 200 S. **Facility:** 79 units. 3 stories, interior corridors. **Pool(s):** heated indoor. **Activities:** hot tub, exercise room. **Guest Services:** coin laundry.

PARRY LODGE (435)644-2601

◆◆ **Motel** $79-$350 **Address:** 89 E Center St 84741 **Location:** On US 89; corner of 100 E; center. **Facility:** 90 units, some two bedrooms, efficiencies, kitchens and houses. 1-2 stories (no elevator), interior/exterior corridors. **Terms:** cancellation fee imposed. **Dining:** restaurant, see separate listing. **Pool(s):** heated outdoor. **Guest Services:** coin laundry.

QUALITY INN (435)644-8888

◆◆◆ **Hotel** $110-$190 **Address:** 815 E 300 S 84741 **Location:** On US 89, just e. **Facility:** 71 units. 3 stories (no elevator), interior corridors. **Pool(s):** heated outdoor. **Guest Services:** coin laundry.

WHERE TO EAT

ESCOBAR'S MEXICAN RESTAURANT　　435/644-3739

♦ Mexican. Casual Dining. $8-$18 **AAA Inspector Notes:** This very casual restaurant seems to always be busy. Guests return for the fresh authentic cuisine and the very personable owner. The chips and salsa are super fresh and flavorful. **Features:** beer only, patio dining. **Address:** 373 E 300 S 84741 **Location:** Just e. [L] [D]

HOUSTON'S TRAIL'S END RESTAURANT　　435/644-2488

♦♦ American. Family Dining. $8-$25 **AAA Inspector Notes:** Steak and seafood, as well as some Mexican specialties, are served in the Western-style dining room. **Features:** beer only. **Address:** 32 E Center St 84741 **Location:** On US 89. [B] [L] [D]

LUO'S CAFE　　435/644-5592

♦♦ Chinese. Casual Dining. $10-$22 **AAA Inspector Notes:** This family-run restaurant offers casual cuisine with items such as chicken fried rice, tempura shrimp, kung pao chicken and mu shu pork. To-go orders are welcome. **Features:** beer only. **Address:** 365 S 100 E 84741 **Location:** Jct US 89 and SR 89A, just s. [L] [D]

NEDRA'S TOO　　435/644-2030

♦♦ Mexican. Casual Dining. $4-$17 **AAA Inspector Notes:** Just like the first location, this spot offers great Southwestern charm and fresh Mexican food. Friendly servers deliver casual fare to guests in a small dining room covered in Mexican art, old movie pictures and NASCAR collectibles. Just ask and the staff will be proud to inform you about the celebrities who have dined here throughout the years. **Features:** beer & wine. **Address:** 310 S 100 E 84741 **Location:** Jct US 89 and SR 89A. [B] [L] [D]

PARRY LODGE RESTAURANT　　435/644-2601

♦ American. Casual Dining. $5-$10 **AAA Inspector Notes:** Just like the hotel lobby, the dining room is decorated in a casual Victorian style. The basic menu offers breakfast items; for lunch, choose from sandwiches and a salad bar. **Features:** beer & wine. **Address:** 89 E Center St 84741 **Location:** On US 89; corner of 100 E; center; in Parry Lodge. [B] [L]

ROCKING V CAFE　　435/644-8001

♦♦ International. Casual Dining. $9-$43 **AAA Inspector Notes:** Casual food is served in this building which dates back to 1892. The decor is bright red and features local artwork. The varied menu offers made-from-scratch enchiladas, wraps, fresh fish and fine steaks, as well as vegan and vegetarian selections. **Features:** full bar. **Reservations:** suggested. **Address:** 97 W Center St 84741 **Location:** Downtown. [L] [D]

THE THREE BEARS CREAMERY COTTAGE　　435/644-3300

♦ Sandwiches. Casual Dining. $4-$9 **AAA Inspector Notes:** In a city nicknamed "Little Hollywood," this cozy restaurant decorated with bears and a small waterfall serves up sandwiches on homemade bread and many dessert items. The sandwiches are most popular, but large salads and many fried items are served as well. **Address:** 210 S 100 E 84741 **Location:** On US 89; jct 200 S. [L] [D]

KAYSVILLE (B-3) pop. 27,300, elev. 4,357'
• Part of Salt Lake City area — see map p. 368

UTAH STATE UNIVERSITY BOTANICAL CENTER is at 920 South 50 West. The 100-acre site features a wildflower meadow; a variety of themed gardens, including butterfly and teaching gardens; walking and bicycling trails; and an arboretum. Wetlands shelter such wildlife as great blue herons and terns.

Ponds are stocked with largemouth bass, bluegill and channel catfish, and fishing is permitted. At the Utah House, a demonstration and education center, visitors can learn about sustainable living, which aims to reduce an individual's or society's use of the Earth's natural resources. **Time:** Allow 2 hours minimum. **Hours:** Grounds daily dawn-dusk. Utah

House Mon.-Fri. 1-5. **Cost:** Free. **Phone:** (801) 544-3089. [⊠]

PEPPERBELLY'S　　801/444-3132

♦♦ Mexican. Family Dining. $8-$13 **AAA Inspector Notes:** The eatery serves favorite Mexican dishes in a dining room filled with automotive memorabilia celebrating yesteryear and a love of the road. **Address:** 141 N Main St 84037 **Location:** I-15 exit 328, just e, then just s. [L] [D]

LAKE POWELL—See Glen Canyon National Recreation Area p. 314.

LAYTON (B-3) pop. 67,311, elev. 4,350'

HERITAGE MUSEUM OF LAYTON is .4 mi. e. on W. Gentile St., then .3 mi. n. to 403 N. Wasatch Dr. The historical museum displays Native American and pioneer artifacts, documents, newspapers and photographs that tell the story of the cultural, recreational and economic development of northern Davis County. Many displays depict the area at the turn of the 20th century when it was predominately rural and agricultural.

Wheelchairs are available. **Time:** Allow 30 minutes minimum. **Hours:** Tues.-Fri. 11-6, Sat. 1-5. Closed major holidays. **Cost:** Free. **Phone:** (801) 336-3930. [GT] [🏛]

BEST WESTERN PLUS LAYTON PARK HOTEL
(801)896-0271

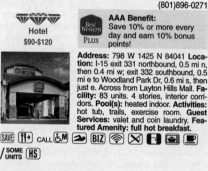

♦♦♦ Hotel $90-$120

AAA Benefit: Save 10% or more every day and earn 10% bonus points!

Address: 798 W 1425 N 84041 **Location:** I-15 exit 331 northbound, 0.5 mi n, then 0.4 mi w; exit 332 southbound, 0.5 mi e to Woodland Park Dr, 0.6 mi s, then just e. Across from Layton Hills Mall. **Facility:** 83 units. 4 stories, interior corridors. **Pool(s):** heated indoor. **Activities:** hot tub, trails, exercise room. **Guest Services:** valet and coin laundry. **Featured Amenity:** full hot breakfast.

[SAVE] [🛎️+] CALL [&M] [🚐] [BIZ] [🛜] [✖] [🛏] [🖥] [💻] /SOME UNITS [HS]

COURTYARD BY MARRIOTT　　(801)217-2300

♦♦♦ Hotel $89-$190 **Address:** 1803 Woodland Park Dr 84041 **Location:** I-15 exit 332 (Antelope Dr), 0.3 mi se. **Facility:** 110 units. 3 stories, interior corridors. **Pool(s):** heated indoor. **Activities:** hot tub, exercise room. **Guest Services:** valet and coin laundry, boarding pass kiosk.

AAA Benefit: Members save 5% or more!

[🛎️+] CALL [&M] [🚐] [BIZ] [🛜] [✖] [🛏] [🖥] [💻] /SOME UNITS [HS]

Remember, car seats, booster seats

and seat belts save lives

HAMPTON INN (801)775-8800

 Hotel $99-$189 **Address:** 1700 N Woodland Park Dr 84041 **Location:** I-15 exit 332 (Antelope Dr), 0.3 mi e, then just s. **Facility:** 98 units. 3 stories, interior corridors. **Parking:** winter plug-ins. **Terms:** 1-7 night minimum stay, cancellation fee imposed. **Pool(s):** heated indoor. **Activities:** hot tub, picnic facilities, exercise room. **Guest Services:** valet and coin laundry.

> **AAA Benefit:** Members save up to 10%!

HILTON GARDEN INN (801)416-8899

Hotel $99-$179 **Address:** 762 W Heritage Park Blvd 84041 **Location:** I-15 exit 332 (Antelope Dr), 0.5 mi e to 700 W, then 0.5 mi s. Located in Davis Conference Center. **Facility:** 147 units. 3 stories, interior corridors. **Terms:** 1-7 night minimum stay, cancellation fee imposed. **Pool(s):** heated indoor. **Activities:** hot tub, exercise room. **Guest Services:** valet and coin laundry.

> **AAA Benefit:** Members save up to 10%!

HOLIDAY INN EXPRESS - LAYTON 801-773-3773

Hotel. Rates not provided. **Address:** 1695 Woodland Park Dr 84041 **Location:** I-15 exit 332 (Antelope Dr), 0.3 mi se. **Facility:** 102 units. 4 stories, interior corridors. **Pool(s):** heated indoor. **Activities:** hot tub, exercise room. **Guest Services:** valet and coin laundry.

HOME2 SUITES BY HILTON - LAYTON (801)820-9222

Extended Stay Contemporary Hotel $99-$159 **Address:** 803 W Heritage Park Blvd 84041 **Location:** I-15 exit 332 (Antelope Dr), 0.6 mi e to 700 W, then 0.5 mi s. **Facility:** 107 units. 4 stories, interior corridors. *Bath:* shower only. **Terms:** 1-7 night minimum stay, cancellation fee imposed. **Pool(s):** heated indoor. **Activities:** hot tub, picnic facilities, exercise room. **Guest Services:** valet and coin laundry.

> **AAA Benefit:** Members save up to 10%!

TOWNEPLACE SUITES BY MARRIOTT (801)779-2422

Extended Stay Hotel $89-$194 **Address:** 1743 Woodland Park Dr 84041 **Location:** I-15 exit 332 (Antelope Dr), 0.3 mi se. **Facility:** 95 kitchen units, some two bedrooms. 3 stories, interior corridors. **Pool(s):** heated outdoor. **Activities:** exercise room. **Guest Services:** valet and coin laundry.

> **AAA Benefit:** Members save 5% or more!

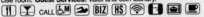
WHERE TO EAT

CORBIN'S GRILLE 801/825-2502

 Steak Seafood. Casual Dining. $8-$34 **AAA Inspector Notes:** Specializing in wood-fired steaks and fresh seafood, the restaurant tempts with choices like surf and turf, seafood martini shakers and pork saltimbocca. Last but not least, the apple strudel and made-in-house desserts satisfy. **Features:** full bar, patio dining. **Reservations:** suggested. **Address:** 748 W Heritage Park Blvd 84041 **Location:** I-15 exit 332 (Antelope Dr), 0.5 mi e, then 0.3 mi s.

GABOR BROTHERS MAIN STREET GRILL 801/544-4344

Italian. Casual Dining. $8-$20 **AAA Inspector Notes:** This funky eatery serves hearty portions of soup, appetizers such as mussels and crab cakes, attractive salads, calzones and a nice selection of pastas and subs. Hand-tossed pizza is prepared in a stone oven. A word of warning, the 11-inch garlic-twisted breadsticks are addictive. **Features:** beer & wine. **Address:** 197 N Main St 84041 **Location:** I-15 exit 330, 1.2 mi nw.

HAPPY HASHI JAPANESE TEPANYAKI & SUSHI BAR 801/779-0204

Japanese. Casual Dining. $9-$36 **AAA Inspector Notes:** Your meal will be prepared by skillful chefs that add an entertaining flair to food preparations. The hibachi grill offers great chicken, filet mignon, shrimp or salmon combinations while the sushi bar and dining room feature more than 40 two-piece and five-piece sushi and sashimi selections from which to choose. **Features:** beer & wine. **Address:** 630 W Ring Rd 84041 **Location:** I-15 exit 331 (Hill Field Rd), 0.4 mi n, then just w.

MACCOOL'S PUBLIC HOUSE RESTAURANT 801/728-9111

Irish. Casual Dining. $6-$18 **AAA Inspector Notes:** Enjoy an authentic Irish dining experience in this friendly pub, which has 7-foot-high carved wooden chairs, stenciled Irish blessings and darts in the game room. Traditional favorites include Guinness stew, corned beef and cabbage, shepherd's pie and chicken pot pie. **Features:** full bar, Sunday brunch. **Address:** 855 W Heritage Park Blvd 84041 **Location:** I-15 exit 332 (Antelope Dr), 0.7 mi e to 700 W, then 0.4 mi s.

ROOSTER'S BREWING CO 801/774-9330

American. Casual Dining. $8-$22 **AAA Inspector Notes:** You can expect cordial service at this brewpub. Menu selections include a variety of starters, pizza, salads, sandwiches and entrées such as baked chicken Milano, broiled salmon and Angus rib-eye topped with Cambozola butter. The center-cut beef tenderloin is delicious. **Features:** full bar, patio dining, Sunday brunch. **Address:** 748 W Heritage Park Blvd 84041 **Location:** I-15 exit 332 (Antelope Dr), 0.5 mi e to 700 W, then just s.

LEHI (C-3) pop. 47,407, elev. 4,550'
• Hotels p. 324 • Restaurants p. 325

Lehi was named for an individual in the Book of Mormon. The polygamous practices of the area's Mormons were vigorously prosecuted by the federal government in the 1870s and '80s; many church members went into hiding. Local legend claims that when federal officers ordered a small boy to take them to a polygamist, he cautiously led them to a chicken run and pointed out a rooster.

JOHN HUTCHING'S MUSEUM OF NATURAL HISTORY is at 55 N. Center St. The museum contains pioneer and Native American artifacts, dinosaur fossils, an extensive rock and mineral collection, military items and bird specimens. Among the highlights are a velociraptor, protoceratops and conchoraptor habitat display; Butch Cassidy's sawed-off shotgun; lawman Porter Rockwell's saddle; and Anasazi Indian artifacts. **Time:** Allow 2 hours minimum. **Hours:** Tues.-Sat. 11-5. Closed major holidays. **Cost:** $4; $3 (ages 3-18 and 60+); $12 (family, maximum six people). **Phone:** (801) 768-7180.

THANKSGIVING POINT is off I-15 exit 284 to Ashton Blvd. The more than 700-acre complex, a dairy farm for close to a century, includes extensive flower and vegetable gardens, a dinosaur museum, an interactive hands-on children's museum, an animal farm, a family science center, a golf course designed by Hall of Fame golfer Johnny Miller, a farmers market, shops, restaurants, a megaplex theater and a 5,000-seat amphitheater.

Farm Country—a working farm that is home to chickens, cows, horses, llamas and peacocks—also has educational displays and pony and wagon rides. Fifty-five acres of themed gardens available for strolling include the Rose Garden, Italian Garden, Butterfly Garden, Monet Garden, Waterfall Garden and Fragrance Garden. The Tulip Festival in spring features 300,00 imported tulips from Holland.

Hours: Grounds Mon.-Sat. and holidays 10-8. Gardens Mon.-Sat. 10-8, late Mar.-late Oct. Farm Country and museums Mon.-Sat. 10-8, Apr.-Oct.; 10-5, rest of year. Closed Thanksgiving and Christmas. **Cost:** Gardens $15; $12 (ages 3-12 and 65+). Farm Country (includes pony and wagon ride) $7. Additional pony ride $2. **Phone:** (801) 768-2300, (801) 768-7401 for golf course or (888) 672-6040.

Museum of Ancient Life is off I-15 exit 284 at Thanksgiving Point. The museum features 60 mounted dinosaur skeletons, hundreds of large and small fossils, various paleontology displays and more than 50 hands-on exhibits geared toward children. The Mammoth Screen Theater features large-format 3-D movies.

Hours: Museum Mon.-Sat. and holidays 10-8; closed Thanksgiving and Christmas. Theater show times Mon.-Sat. 10-5. Closed Thanksgiving and Christmas. **Cost:** Museum $15; $12 (ages 3-12 and 65+). Theater $7.50; $6 (ages 3-12 and 65+). Combination ticket additional $5. **Phone:** (801) 768-2300.

Museum of Natural Curiosity is off I-15 exit 284 at Thanksgiving Point, adjacent to Thanksgiving Point Gardens. The museum features intergenerational-learning experiences exploring science, technology and arts. For adventure seekers, a high ropes course soars over a rainforest canopy. The outdoor portion of the museum's manicured grounds feature acres of colorful botanical gardens. Nearly 2 miles of walking paths wind throughout the bright landscape. Of particular interest to children are the Archimedes Playground, a maze constructed from hedges, and bear caves ready for exploration. Educational programs are offered.

Time: Allow 1 hour minimum. **Hours:** Mon.-Sat. 10-8. Closed Thanksgiving and Christmas. **Cost:** $15; $12 (ages 3-12 and 65+). High ropes $8 (with paid admission); $12 (without paid admission). **Phone:** (801) 768-2300.

BEST WESTERN TIMPANOGOS INN   (801)768-1400

Hotel
$79-$139

AAA Benefit: Save 10% or more every day and earn 10% bonus points!

Address: 195 S 850 E 84043 **Location:** I-15 exit 279, just w, then just s. **Facility:** 59 units. 2 stories (no elevator), interior corridors. **Amenities:** safes. **Pool(s):** heated indoor. **Activities:** hot tub. **Guest Services:** valet and coin laundry.

COURTYARD BY MARRIOTT LEHI AT THANKSGIVING POINT   (801)768-1174

Contemporary   Hotel
$101-$217 **Address:** 2801 W Clubhouse Dr 84043 **Location:** I-15 exit 284 (Highland), just w. **Facility:** 97 units. 4 stories, interior corridors. **Pool(s):** heated indoor. **Activities:** hot tub, exercise room. **Guest Services:** valet and coin laundry, boarding pass kiosk, area transportation.

AAA Benefit: Members save 5% or more!

HAMPTON INN BY HILTON LEHI/THANKSGIVING POINT   (801)766-1186

Hotel $94-$152 **Address:** 3576 N Maple Loop 84043 **Location:** I-15 exit 284 (Highland), just w. **Facility:** 75 units. 3 stories, interior corridors. **Terms:** 1-7 night minimum stay, cancellation fee imposed. **Pool(s):** heated indoor. **Activities:** hot tub, exercise room. **Guest Services:** valet and coin laundry, area transportation.

AAA Benefit: Members save up to 10%!

HOME2 SUITES BY HILTON LEHI-THANKSGIVING POINT   (801)753-5430

Extended Stay Hotel
$89-$189 **Address:** 3051 W Club House Dr 84043 **Location:** I-15 exit 284, 0.5 mi w. **Facility:** 103 units. 4 stories, interior corridors. **Terms:** 1-7 night minimum stay, cancellation fee imposed. **Pool(s):** heated indoor. **Activities:** hot tub, picnic facilities, exercise room. **Guest Services:** valet and coin laundry, area transportation.

AAA Benefit: Members save up to 10%!

HYATT PLACE SALT LAKE CITY/LEHI   (385)345-8300

Contemporary
Hotel
$119-$599

HYATT PLACE
AAA Benefit: Members save 10%!

Address: 3700 N Outlet Pkwy 84043 **Location:** I-15 exit 284 (Highland), 0.3 mi e to Triumph Blvd, just n, then just w. **Facility:** 131 units, some efficiencies. 4 stories, interior corridors. **Pool(s):** heated outdoor. **Activities:** hot tub, exercise room. **Guest Services:** valet and coin laundry, area transportation. **Featured Amenity:** breakfast buffet.

SPRINGHILL SUITES BY MARRIOTT LEHI/THANKSGIVING
POINT   (801)341-6970

WWWW Hotel $99-$196 Address:
2447 W Executive Pkwy 84043 Location: I-15 exit 284 (Highland), just w,
then 0.5 mi s. Next to Thanksgiving
Point. Facility: 94 units. 4 stories, interior
corridors. Pool(s): heated indoor. Activities: hot tub, picnic facilities,
exercise room. Guest Services: valet and coin laundry.

AAA Benefit:
Members save 5%
or more!

[†+] CALL [&M] [�̶] [BIZ] [HS] [📶] [✕] [🖶] [🖳] [🖵]

WHERE TO EAT

BONA VITA ITALIAN BISTRO   801/901-1955

WW Italian. Casual Dining. $10-$19 AAA Inspector Notes:
Patrons have the option of dining on the mezzanine or at ground level
at this busy bistro. The deep-fried cheese ravioli, Mediterranean
salad, chicken pesto sandwich and honey-smoked salmon on a
toasted oat bun are just a few popular items on the menu. A wonderful selection of pasta, pizza and ravioli is available, including a
bacon-wrapped and skewered jumbo shrimp served over savory Alfredo pasta. Gluten-free options and a kids' menu are offered. Features: beer & wine, patio dining. Address: 3700 N Cabelas Blvd
84043 Location: I-15 exit 284 (Highland), 0.3 mi e to Triumph Blvd,
then just n. [L] [D] CALL [&M]

HARVEST RESTAURANT   801/768-4990

WWW Continental. Casual Dining. $11-$32 AAA Inspector
Notes: Seasonal contemporary American and classical French-
inspired dishes incorporate fresh regional ingredients that are either
locally grown or from the restaurant's own gardens and greenhouses.
The shrimp nachos, shepherd's pie and prosciutto-wrapped salmon
are three favorites. Note that alcohol is not served. Address: 3003 N
Thanksgiving Way 84043 Location: I-15 exit 284 (Highland), just w,
then 0.6 mi s; in the Water Tower at Thanksgiving Point. [L] [D]

LOGAN (A-3) pop. 48,174, elev. 4,507'
• Hotels p. 326 • Restaurants p. 326

Built on the terraces of prehistoric Lake Bonneville, Logan lies in the fertile Cache Valley by the
Logan River. A monument to Logan's past and
present is its Mormon Temple. Finished in 1884, the
temple overlooks the town and is one of the state's
earliest and finest; it is not open to visitors.

The Logan Utah Family Search Library, on the
lower level of the Logan Tabernacle at 50 N. Main, is
available for research. The tabernacle has been described as an excellent example of an early Mormon
meeting house. The history center contains computers, microfilm, microfiche, books, periodicals and
manuscripts for reference use; phone (435) 755-5594.
The tabernacle is open for tours in summer. Logan
also is the home of Utah State University.

The Logan area is well known for its Jardine Juniper, believed to be the planet's largest and oldest
juniper tree. An easy 4.4-mile trail to the 1,500-
year-old tree begins 12 miles up Logan Canyon. To
the west are the Wellsville Mountains, said to be the
world's tallest mountains on the narrowest base.

Hardware Ranch, 15 miles up Blacksmith Fork
Canyon on SR 101, is an elk feeding station where
the animals can be viewed during sleigh rides in
winter (weather permitting) or from the visitor center
(see Wasatch-Cache National Forest p. 411); phone
(435) 753-6206.

Logan also is the southeastern terminus of the
Logan Canyon National Scenic Byway (US 89),
which ends at Bear Lake State Park. This road runs
through Logan Canyon beneath cliffs, along a river
and through forests.

Nearby Bear Lake is a turquoise-colored lake with
white sandy beaches. It is 20 miles long, 8 miles
wide and 208 feet deep. Four state parks offer
boating, jet skiing, sailboarding, fishing, swimming,
picnicking and camping facilities. Equipment rentals
are available at the beach or in Garden City. North
of the Bear Lake Marina is a marker along the Oregon Trail. Skiing is available nearby off US 89. A
guide detailing 15 scenic area hiking trails is available at the visitors bureau.

Cache Valley Visitors Bureau: 199 N. Main St.,
Logan, UT 84321. Phone: (435) 755-1890 or (800)
882-4433.

Self-guiding tours: A brochure describing a
walking tour of 19th- and early 20th-century buildings along and near Logan's historic Main Street is
available at the visitors bureau.

Shopping: JCPenney anchors the Cache Valley
Mall, 1300 N. Main St.

AMERICAN WEST HERITAGE CENTER—see
Wellsville p. 412.

DAUGHTERS OF UTAH PIONEERS CACHE MU-
SEUM is at 160 N. Main St. The museum exhibits
Mormon pioneer relics and a collection of musical
instruments, including a melodeon. The museum
also provides wool-dyeing, carding and spinning
demonstrations. Time: Allow 30 minutes minimum.
Hours: Tues.-Fri. 11-5, June-Aug.; by appointment
rest of year. Phone ahead to confirm schedule.
Cost: Donations. Phone: (435) 752-5139.

ELLEN ECCLES THEATRE is at 43 S. Main St.
Completed in 1923, the ornate theater began as a
vaudeville house. Managed and restored in the early
1990s to its former beauty by the Cache Valley
Center for the Arts (CVCA), the theater boasts an
opulent interior and a graceful shape. In addition to
year-round performances by such regional groups
as the Utah Festival Opera & Musical Theatre,
Cache Valley Civic Ballet and Music Theatre West,
CVCA presents dozens of touring productions September to May.

Guided tours are available Sept.-June by appointment. Time: Allow 30 minutes minimum. Hours:
Ticket office open Mon.-Fri. 10-5:30 and 1 hour prior
to curtain. Closed major holidays. Phone ahead to
confirm schedule. Cost: Guided tour free. Performance ticket prices vary. Phone: (435) 752-0026.

NORA ECCLES HARRISON MUSEUM OF ART is
on the Utah State University campus at 650 North
1100 East. The museum offers changing exhibitions
of ceramics, paintings, sculpture, photographs and
prints. It also features a permanent collection of 20th-
century artwork with an emphasis on artists from the
Western United States. Hours: Tues.-Sat. 10-5.
Closed major holidays. Cost: Donations. Parking:

Limited weekday parking at museum. Metered and street parking also is available. **Phone:** (435) 797-0163.

UTAH STATE UNIVERSITY MUSEUM OF ANTHROPOLOGY is in Utah State University's Old Main building at 730 Old Main Hill. Through exhibits, teaching guides and special programs, the museum allows visitors to explore various cultures, including those of the Great Basin Indians, Egyptians, Africans and Peruvians. **Time:** Allow 30 minutes minimum. **Hours:** Tues.-Fri. 9-5, first Sat. of the month 10-2, other times by appointment. Closed major holidays. **Cost:** Free. **Phone:** (435) 797-7545. GT

BEST WESTERN BAUGH MOTEL   (435)752-5220

Motel
$90-$190

AAA Benefit: Save 10% or more every day and earn 10% bonus points!

Address: 153 S Main St 84321 **Location:** Just s of center. **Facility:** 75 units. 1-2 stories (no elevator), exterior corridors. **Parking:** winter plug-ins. **Pool(s):** heated outdoor. **Activities:** hot tub, picnic facilities. **Guest Services:** valet laundry, boarding pass kiosk.

SAVE / SOME UNITS

BEST WESTERN PLUS WESTON INN   (435)752-5700

Motel
$114-$199

AAA Benefit: Save 10% or more every day and earn 10% bonus points!

Address: 250 N Main St 84321 **Location:** 0.3 mi n of center. **Facility:** 89 units. 2 stories, exterior corridors. **Pool(s):** heated indoor. **Activities:** sauna, hot tub, exercise room. **Guest Services:** coin laundry.

SAVE ECO / SOME UNITS

HAMPTON INN   (435)713-4567

Hotel $109-$209 **Address:** 1665 N Main St 84341 **Location:** 1.5 mi n of center. **Facility:** 58 units. 3 stories, interior corridors. **Terms:** check-in 4 pm, 1-7 night minimum stay, cancellation fee imposed. **Pool(s):** heated indoor. **Activities:** hot tub, limited exercise equipment. **Guest Services:** valet and coin laundry.

AAA Benefit: Members save up to 10%!

/ SOME UNITS

HOLIDAY INN EXPRESS & SUITES   (435)752-3444

Hotel $89-$254 **Address:** 2235 N Main St 84341 **Location:** 2.8 mi n of center. **Facility:** 75 units. 3 stories, interior corridors. **Terms:** cancellation fee imposed. **Pool(s):** heated indoor. **Activities:** hot tub, exercise room. **Guest Services:** valet and coin laundry.

/ SOME UNITS

LA QUINTA INN & SUITES   (435)752-0707

Hotel
$64-$202

Address: 853 S Hwy 89 and 91 84321 **Location:** 2 mi s of center. **Facility:** 85 units, some kitchens. 3 stories, interior corridors. **Pool(s):** heated indoor. **Activities:** hot tub, exercise room. **Guest Services:** coin laundry. **Featured Amenity:** breakfast buffet.

SPRINGHILL SUITES BY MARRIOTT THE RIVERWOODS
(435)750-5180

Hotel $105-$233 **Address:** 635 S Riverwoods Pkwy 84321 **Location:** 0.8 mi s of center. **Facility:** 115 units. 4 stories, interior corridors. **Dining:** Elements Restaurant at Riverwoods, see separate listing. **Pool(s):** heated indoor. **Activities:** hot tub, exercise room. **Guest Services:** valet and coin laundry, area transportation.

AAA Benefit: Members save 5% or more!

UNIVERSITY GUEST HOTEL & CONFERENCE CENTER
435/797-0017

Hotel. Rates not provided. **Address:** 850 E 700 N 84322 **Location:** East of US 89 and 91. Located on Utah State University campus. **Facility:** 74 units. 5 stories, interior corridors. **Guest Services:** coin laundry.

WHERE TO EAT

ANGIE'S RESTAURANT   435/752-9252

American. Family Dining. $7-$21 **AAA Inspector Notes:** Patrons can stop in at this established restaurant to enjoy a wide selection of menu offerings served in good-size portions. Friendly servers make their way among the booths, tables and counter. **Address:** 690 N Main St 84321 **Location:** 0.3 mi n of center. B L D

BEEHIVE GRILL   435/753-2600

American. Casual Dining. $8-$22 **AAA Inspector Notes:** Home of a namesake root beer, this pub features hand-crafted sodas, fine ales and large-screen TVs in the lounge. The varied menu includes chili, soup, pub burgers, plenty of poultry favorites, pork ribs, smoked salmon wraps and beer-battered fish and chips. **Features:** full bar. **Address:** 255 S Main St 84321 **Location:** I-15 exit 362, 0.5 mi s of center. L D CALL

CAFE SABOR   435/752-8088

Mexican. Casual Dining. $6-$16 **AAA Inspector Notes:** This eatery, with its comfortable, authentic atmosphere, serves a wide array of traditional enchiladas, burritos, enormous chimichangas and sky-high nachos. The chicken tortilla soup is perfect on a cold day. At the entrance you can see how fresh their tortillas are by watching them come out of the oven. **Features:** full bar. **Address:** 600 W Center St 84321 **Location:** I-15 exit 362, 0.7 mi w; downtown; in Old Rail Depot. L D CALL

THE CREPERY & COFFEE HOUSE   435/752-5766

Specialty. Quick Serve. $6-$9 **AAA Inspector Notes:** This quaint little eatery offers an impressive selection of savory and sweet Parisian crêpes prepared on griddles that were imported from Europe. You also can enjoy a terrific cup of coffee. A small patio by the creek is in the back. Gluten-free items are available. **Features:** patio dining. **Address:** 540 S Main St 84321 **Location:** 1 mi s of center. B L D

CRUMB BROTHERS CAFE 435/792-6063

◆ Breads/Pastries Sandwiches. Quick Serve. $7-$11 **AAA Inspector Notes:** This rustic oasis is a breath of fresh air. Relax, take in the natural light and views of the kitchen while enjoying seasonal salads, gourmet sandwiches, sweet and savory pastries, quiche and specialty crusty artisan organic breads. The trestle wood at the entrance was gathered from the Great Salt Lake. **Features:** patio dining. **Address:** 291 S 300 W 84321 **Location:** 0.4 mi s of center, just w. B L CALL &M

ELEMENTS RESTAURANT AT RIVERWOODS 435/750-5171

◆◆◆ American. Casual Dining. $8-$29 **AAA Inspector Notes:** The upscale restaurant features sleek décor. The extensive menu includes a colorful Thai lettuce wrap, mouthwatering wood-fired pizza, sugar-spiced pork baguette, roasted-chicken fettuccine, turkey chop, Alaskan halibut, kamikaze salmon served with roasted pineapple-ginger coulis and sweet cola-glazed meatloaf. A variety of decadent seasonal desserts is offered. The outdoor patio offers awesome river views. **Features:** full bar, patio dining. **Address:** 640 S 35 E 84321 **Location:** 0.8 mi s of center; at Riverwoods Conference Center; in SpringHill Suites by Marriott. L D CALL &M

EL SOL 435/752-5743

◆◆ Mexican. Casual Dining. $6-$12 **AAA Inspector Notes:** Upbeat service is provided at this colorful eatery, which prepares favorites such as nachos, quesadillas, enchiladas, chimichangas, tostadas, chile verde and marinated fish tacos, in addition to a nice selection of value combination entrées. The attractively garnished fried ice cream is delicious. **Address:** 871 N Main St 84321 **Location:** 1.1 mi n of center. L D

FREDRICO'S PIZZA 435/752-0130

◆ Pizza Sandwiches. Quick Serve. $7-$19 **AAA Inspector Notes:** Enjoy golden-brown calzones, pasta, pizza and salads at this popular eatery that has been around since the 1950s. Everyone will appreciate the lunch and dinner specials. Locals favor the ham and cheese salad and mushroom pizza. **Features:** patio dining. **Address:** 1349 E 700 N 84321 **Location:** Just e of Utah State University. L D

LE NONNE RISTORANTE ITALIANO 435/752-9577

◆◆◆ Northern Italian. Casual Dining. $10-$24 **AAA Inspector Notes:** This charming home-turned-upscale-ristorante serves classic entrées inspired by the Tuscan Alps. Choice selections include Caesar salad for two, mouthwatering rigatoni with bacon and onions, ahi tuna topped with asparagus and tempting desserts. Patrons can relax in the comfortable dining rooms or on a lovely tree-shaded patio. **Features:** full bar, patio dining. **Address:** 129 N 100 E 84321 **Location:** Just e of 100 N, just n; downtown. **Parking:** street only. D

MORTY'S CAFE 435/535-3276

◆ Burgers Sandwiches. Quick Serve. $5-$8 **AAA Inspector Notes:** This cute eatery is easy to find and is located in a new sleek, modern building. Ingredients are locally sourced whenever possible, and menu items consist of garden burgers, quinoa bowls, burgers, limited hot sandwiches, sweet potato fries, onion rings and a killer chocolate peanut butter shake. **Features:** patio dining. **Address:** 780 E 700 N 84321 **Location:** At Darwin Ave; west of Utah State University. **Parking:** on-site and street. B L D LATE CALL &M

MANTI pop. 3,276

MANTI COUNTRY VILLAGE MOTEL 435/835-9300

◆ Motel $69-$99 **Address:** 145 N Main St 84642 **Location:** On US 89 (Main St), just n of center. **Facility:** 23 units. 2 stories (no elevator), exterior corridors. **Terms:** cancellation fee imposed.
🍴 📶 ⊗ 🚭 📦 / SOME UNITS 🛍️

Get maps, travel information and road service with the

AAA and CAA Mobile apps

MANTI-LA SAL NATIONAL FOREST (D-4)

Elevations in the forest range from 5,320 ft. at the San Pete Ranger District to 12,721 ft. at Mount Peale. Refer to AAA maps for additional elevation information.

In southeastern Utah, Manti-La Sal National Forest encompasses 1,413,111 acres in three sections. The largest portion, the Manti Division, is characterized by narrow canyons, mountain meadows and broad rolling ridges covered with aspen and spruce. It lies in central Utah and is part of the Wasatch Plateau.

The La Sal Division, in the spectacular natural bridge and red rock canyon country of southeastern Utah, is made up of two isolated mountain ranges, the La Sals east of Moab and the Blue Mountains west of Monticello. Cross-country skiing and snowmobiling are popular. The forest's La Sal and Abajo mountain ranges provide opportunities for hiking and climbing. Hunting for grouse, waterfowl, turkeys, mule deer, elk, black bears and mountain lions, and fishing for trout are permitted in the forest. A variety of campsites are available.

Skyline Drive Scenic Backway, an 87-mile-long scenic route through the high mountains along the crest of the Wasatch Plateau, affords spectacular views of Nevada to the west and Colorado to the east. Animals are abundant and include elk, deer, bears and moose. Prehistoric animals that once inhabited the area include mammoths, mastodons and short-faced bears.

The narrow, rough, unpaved road, which is open mid-July through September, should be attempted only in good weather. Some sections are open to four-wheel-drive, high clearance vehicles only. Contact a ranger for road conditions before making the drive.

For further information contact the Forest Supervisor, Manti-La Sal National Forest, 599 W. Price River Dr., Price, UT 84501; phone (435) 637-2817. *See Recreation Areas Chart.*

MARYSVALE pop. 408

MOORE'S OLD PINE INN 435/326-4565

◆◆◆ Historic Bed & Breakfast. Rates not provided. **Address:** 110 S Main St 84750 **Location:** Center. **Facility:** After a day on the 275-mile-long Paiute ATV Trail, guests at this 1882 inn can relax and enjoy the swings and the sounds of a creek that runs through the property. 15 units, some efficiencies and cabins. 1-2 stories (no elevator), interior/exterior corridors. **Bath:** some shared. **Guest Services:** coin laundry.
🍴 📶 ⊗ 🚭 / SOME UNITS 📺 🍴 📦 📋

MEXICAN HAT (G-5) pop. 31, elev. 4,400'

Mexican Hat is named for a 2,500-ton boulder that resembles a sombrero. The formation, 60 feet wide and 12 feet thick, balances on a 200-foot cliff and can be seen from a 17-mile looping dirt road.

GOOSENECKS STATE PARK is 9 mi. n.w. off SR 261. The park provides a cliff-top overlook into the scenic "gooseneck" canyons of the San Juan River.

The deep loops are entrenched meanders dug by the silt-laden river. The distance across the goosenecks is 1 mile; the river's course covers 6 miles.

At one point the river makes a 3-mile curve around a ridge only 100 yards wide. Eventually some of the necks will be breached, creating new natural bridges. **Note:** No water, electricity or lighting is available. A cliff with a long drop is immediately adjacent to campsites and there is no barrier. **Cost:** $5 (per private vehicle). Camping $10 (no reservations). **Phone:** (435) 678-2238.

THE VALLEY OF THE GODS is 10 mi. n.e. via SR 261. Nature, by way of water, wind and ice erosion, has carved spectacular, brilliantly colored sandstone monoliths and rock formations over millions of years. A scenic, 17-mile loop road that connects SRs 163 and 261 winds its way through the valley. The dirt road is bumpy and steep in some parts but is suitable for driving during favorable weather.

Note: Visitors should inquire about road conditions during inclement weather. **Time:** Allow 1 hour minimum. **Hours:** Daily dawn-dusk (weather permitting). **Cost:** Free. **Phone:** (435) 587-1500.

MIDVALE pop. 27,964

- **Hotels & Restaurants map & index p. 385**
- **Part of Salt Lake City area — see map p. 368**

HAWTHORN SUITES BY WYNDHAM - SALT LAKE CITY/ MIDVALE   (801)567-0111   **54**
Extended Stay Hotel. $60-$150 **Address:** 6990 S Park Centre Dr 84121 **Location:** I-15 exit 297 (7200 S), 2.4 mi e on 7200 S (Fort Union Blvd) to 1300 E, just e, then just s. **Facility:** 96 efficiencies. 3 stories, interior corridors. **Activities:** picnic facilities, exercise room. **Guest Services:** valet and coin laundry, area transportation.

HOLIDAY INN EXPRESS - SALT LAKE CITY/MIDVALE   801/352-8100   **55**
Contemporary Hotel. Rates not provided. **Address:** 7134 S 700 E 84047 **Location:** I-15 exit 297 (7200 S), 2.3 mi e via 7200 S (Fort Union Blvd) to 700 E, then just n. **Facility:** 66 units. 3 stories, interior corridors. **Amenities:** safes. **Pool(s):** heated indoor. **Activities:** hot tub, exercise room. **Guest Services:** valet and coin laundry.

MIDVALE INN   801/566-4141   **53**
Hotel. Rates not provided. **Address:** 280 W 7200 S 84047 **Location:** I-15 exit 297 (7200 S), just e. **Facility:** 89 units. 2 stories, interior corridors. **Parking:** winter plug-ins. **Amenities:** safes. **Pool(s):** heated outdoor. **Activities:** hot tub, picnic facilities, exercise room. **Guest Services:** valet and coin laundry.

STAYBRIDGE SUITES - MIDVALE   801/871-0871   **52**
Extended Stay Hotel. Rates not provided. **Address:** 747 W Blue Vista Ln 84047 **Location:** I-15 exit 297 (7200 S), 0.4 mi w, then just s. **Facility:** 93 efficiencies. 4 stories, interior corridors. **Pool(s):** heated outdoor. **Activities:** hot tub, picnic facilities, exercise room. **Guest Services:** complimentary and valet laundry, area transportation.

WHERE TO EAT

BOHEMIAN BREWERY   801/566-5474   **36**
Czechoslovakian. Casual Dining. $9-$25 **AAA Inspector Notes:** Enjoy specialty beers aged to perfection alongside authentic Czech and Bohemian pub-style cuisine such as beef goulash, bread dumplings with sauerkraut, schnitzel and blackberry-brandy chicken breast. Gluten-free items are available. **Features:** full bar, patio dining, Sunday brunch. **Address:** 94 E 7200 S 84047 **Location:** I-15 exit 297 (7200 S), 1 mi e; on Fort Union Blvd.

EPIC CASUAL DINING   801/748-1300   **38**
New American. Casual Dining. $14-$24 **AAA Inspector Notes:** This eatery features an array of popular flatbreads such as Kobe skirt steak with portobello mushrooms. Seasonal appetizers, inventive salads named after friends, and creative entrées such as Dungeness crab cakes with balsamic remoulade and seared salmon with tomato-caper butter also are on the menu. The desserts are delicious and meant to be shared. **Features:** beer & wine. **Address:** 707 E 7200 S 84047 **Location:** I-215 exit 9 (Union Park Ave), 0.7 mi s, then 0.7 mi w.

HOPPERS GRILL & BREWING CO   801/566-0424   **37**
American. Casual Dining. $8-$18 **AAA Inspector Notes:** Friends often meet at this fun spot after work or on weekends to watch the big game. Seafood selections are dominant on a menu that also lists a few chicken and beef choices. The handcrafted beers, brewed on site, have won awards. **Features:** full bar, Sunday brunch. **Address:** 890 E Fort Union Blvd 84047 **Location:** I-15 exit 297 (7200 S), 1.6 mi e; southwest corner of 900 E and Fort Union Blvd.

KNEADERS BAKERY & CAFE   801/563-1991   **39**
Breads/Pastries Sandwiches. Quick Serve. $6-$8 **AAA Inspector Notes:** This bakery serves up hearty soups, salads and sandwich fixings with the aromatic breads, homemade pastries and luscious desserts made in the Italian hearthstone oven. **Features:** patio dining. **Address:** 742 E Fort Union Blvd 84047 **Location:** I-15 exit 297 (7200 S), 1.5 mi e.

LANDMARK GRILL   801/566-3664   **40**
American. Casual Dining. $7-$12 **AAA Inspector Notes:** Located in a strip mall, this restaurant offers a bright and inviting atmosphere. You can expect a good selection of burgers (including lamb), hot and cold sandwiches, daily and weekly specials and a variety of salads. Be sure to stop in for their popular breakfasts. **Features:** patio dining. **Address:** 760 E Fort Union Blvd 84047 **Location:** I-15 exit 297 (7200 S), 2.2 mi e.

MIDWAY (C-4) pop. 3,845, elev. 5,640'

HOMESTEAD CRATER is at 700 N. Homestead Dr. at Homestead Resort. The crater, which began forming 10,000 years ago, is filled with warm mineral waters now enjoyed by swimmers, snorkelers and scuba divers. Sunlight enters through a large hole at the top of the hollowed out 55-foot-tall, beehive-shaped limestone rock. After checking in at the Activity Center, visitors enter through a short, lighted tunnel that was dug through the rock wall at ground level. Decks, a soaking area and dressing rooms are available.

Hours: Mon.-Thurs. noon-8, Fri.-Sat. 10-8, Sun. 10-6. Phone for scuba diving schedule and rates. **Cost:** Forty-minute access to the crater and mineral springs for swimming and soaking $16 (Fri.-Sun.); $11 (Mon.-Thurs.). Snorkeling equipment $5. Reservations are required. **Phone:** (435) 657-3840 for the activity center, or (435) 654-1102 for the resort. ⊠

RECREATIONAL ACTIVITIES
Skiing (Cross-country)
• **Soldier Hollow** is at 2002 Soldier Hollow Ln. in Wasatch Mountain State Park. Other activities are offered. **Hours:** Daily 9-4:30, mid-Dec. to late Mar. **Phone:** (435) 654-2002.

BLUE BOAR INN   435/654-1400
▼▼▼▼▼ ▼▼▼▼▼
Country Inn
$175-$295

Address: 1235 Warm Springs Rd 84049 **Location:** I-80 exit 146 (US 40), 13 mi s to River Rd traffic light, then 2.9 mi w to roundabout, follow signs. **Facility:** This charming European-style château is close to world-class resorts and nightlife in Park City. Elegantly appointed rooms are named after literary figures such as Robert Frost and Emily Dickinson. 12 units. 2 stories, interior corridors. **Terms:** 14 day cancellation notice-fee imposed. **Dining:** Blue Boar Inn Restaurant, see separate listing. **Featured Amenity: full hot breakfast.**

SAVE ⑪ ⑦ CALL &M 🛜 ⊠

HOMESTEAD RESORT   435/654-1102
▼▼▼▼
Historic
Resort Hotel
Rates not provided

Address: 700 N Homestead Dr 84049 **Location:** I-80 exit 146 (US 40), 13 mi s to River Rd traffic light, 2.9 mi w to roundabout, 1.2 mi w, follow signs to Homestead Dr, then 0.4 mi s. Located in a quiet area. **Facility:** On an 18-hole championship golf course and set in a broad green valley surrounded by hills and mountains, 19 separate buildings are connected by walkways surrounded by gardens and lawns. 125 units, some kitchens and condominiums. 1-2 stories (no elevator), interior/exterior corridors. **Terms:** check-in 4 pm. **Dining:** 2 restaurants. **Pool(s):** heated outdoor, heated indoor. **Activities:** sauna, hot tub, scuba diving, snorkeling, regulation golf, tennis, recreation programs, bicycles, playground, game room. **Guest Services:** valet and coin laundry.

SAVE ⑪ ⑦ 🛶 🏋️ BIZ 🛜 ⊠ 🖥️ / SOME UNITS 🛏️ 🛗 🖨️

AAA Vacations® packages ...
exciting itineraries and exclusive values

INVITED INN BED & BREAKFAST   435/654-7075
▼▼▼ **Bed & Breakfast.** Rates not provided. **Address:** 1045 N Homestead Dr 84049 **Location:** I-80 exit 146 (US 40), 13 mi s to River Rd traffic light, then 2.9 mi w to roundabout, follow signs. **Facility:** The Swiss-style home overlooks the mountains and Heber Valley. A lovely gazebo, rooms with gas fireplaces, steam showers, hot tubs and saunas make for luxurious stays. 5 units. 2 stories (no elevator), interior corridors. **Terms:** age restrictions may apply.

🛜 ⊠ 🅰️ 🖥️

ZERMATT RESORT & SPA   435/657-0180
▼▼▼ **Resort Hotel.** Rates not provided. **Address:** 784 W Resort Dr 84049 **Location:** I-80 exit 146 (US 40), 13 mi s to River Rd traffic light, then 2.9 mi w, follow signs to Homestead Dr, then 0.3 mi s. **Facility:** Bavarian music is piped in throughout the landscaped gardens to welcome you to this distinctive Alpine village surrounded by breathtaking mountain views. 325 units, some two bedrooms, three bedrooms, efficiencies and kitchens. 3-5 stories, interior corridors. **Parking:** on-site and valet. **Terms:** check-in 4 pm. **Amenities:** safes. **Dining:** 3 restaurants. **Pool(s):** heated outdoor, heated indoor. **Activities:** sauna, hot tub, steamroom, regulation golf, tennis, lawn sports, spa. **Guest Services:** valet and coin laundry, area transportation.

⑪ 🍸 CALL &M 🛶 🏋️ BIZ HS 🛜 ⊠ 🎦 🖥️ / SOME UNITS 🛗 🖨️

WHERE TO EAT

BLUE BOAR INN RESTAURANT   435/654-1400
▼▼▼▼ ▼▼▼▼
Continental
Fine Dining
$8-$36

AAA Inspector Notes: An elegant spot for dignified European dining, the restaurant specializes in wild boar, seasonal cheese and chocolate fondues. Seasonal specialties may include chicken scaloppine with a remarkably light lemon-caper sauce, pork belly with lavender spheres and fresh salads from the on-site garden. **Features:** full bar, patio dining, Sunday brunch. **Reservations:** suggested. **Address:** 1235 Warm Springs Rd 84049 **Location:** I-80 exit 146 (US 40), 13 mi s to River Rd traffic light, then 2.9 mi w to roundabout, follow signs; in Blue Boar Inn.

B L D CALL &M

CAFE GALLERIA   435/657-2002
▼▼ **Pizza Sandwiches.** Casual Dining. $6-$11 **AAA Inspector Notes:** Manicured grounds and beautiful trees and flowers surround this quaint eatery filled with old-school charm where patrons can enjoy wood-fired-oven-baked bagels and pizza, a variety of fresh salads and spaghetti with huge homemade meatballs. The locally named sundaes and homemade cheesecake are sure to please. **Features:** beer & wine, patio dining. **Address:** 101 W Main St 84049 **Location:** West end of Main St. **Parking:** on-site and street.

B L D

MOAB (E-6) pop. 5,046, elev. 4,000'
• Hotels p. 335 • Restaurants p. 337
• Hotels & Restaurants map & index p. 333

Tucked into a valley at the foot of red cliffs and the La Sal Mountains, Moab's mild weather is due to its lower elevation. The town, which overlooks the Colorado River, was familiar to Butch Cassidy's Wild Bunch and other outlaw gangs. Zane Grey made Moab the scene of many of his novels, and it has been used frequently as a setting for movies.

The discovery of uranium in the 1950s changed Moab from a quiet agricultural town into a bustling center for mining and prospecting. Although the uranium boom has passed, the area is still rich in oil and potash. Tourism, however, has become the main industry.

Moab is the starting point for four-wheel-drive, airplane, white-water rafting, canoe, cross-country

(See map & index p. 333.)

skiing, hiking, horseback and mountain biking trips into Arches *(see place listing p. 291)* and Canyonlands *(see place listing p. 301)* national parks. Local tour companies provide hiking, rafting, bicycling, boating, scenic flights, photography and four-wheel-drive tours; other companies provide equipment for such trips. Golf, tennis and fishing in stocked lakes round out the recreational opportunities.

Redtail Aviation offers scenic flight tours of Canyonlands National Park, Monument Valley, Arches National Park and Lake Powell; phone (435) 259-7421 or (800) 842-9251. Moab Adventure Center *(see listing p. 332)* makes sightseeing flights over Canyonlands National Park, Monument Valley, the Colorado and Green rivers, Moab and Island in the Sky; phone (435) 259-7019 or (866) 904-1163.

Canyonlands by Night & Day offers boat trips on the Colorado River. The night trip features illuminated cliff and rock formations and a narrative about the area's history and geology, while the day trip allows visitors to see arches, balanced rocks, birds and wildlife; phone (435) 259-5261 or (800) 394-9978.

The monumental red rock spires of Fisher Towers are 24 miles northeast of Moab off SR 128. Used for many movies and television commercials, the area is accessible via a 3-mile gravel road. Travelers who want a closer look at the towers can make the 2-mile hike from the rest area at the end of the road.

Affording spectacular and contrasting views of the desert floor and the mountain range, the La Sal Mountain Loop Road connects with SR 128 and winds through Castle Valley and up into the La Sal Mountains, returning to the lower end of Moab Valley. SR 128 between Moab and I-70 offers a particularly scenic drive as it parallels the rugged canyons of the Colorado River.

The Slickrock Bike Trail in Moab is prized by mountain bikers. The technically difficult 10.5-mile trail is geared toward skilled riders. Part of the Sand Flats Recreation Area *(see attraction listing)*, the trail is known for its sandpaper-like surface that grips rubber bicycle tires. Geographical features include petrified sand dunes, colorful cliff walls and steep ledges.

In addition to its bounty of outdoor activities, Moab is home to a thriving arts community. Photographers and painters find inspiration in the area's natural beauty; local art is displayed in galleries, cafés and bookstores. The Moab Arts Festival in late May draws attention to local art.

Other festivals of note in Moab include the April Action Car Show in late April, which showcases more than 750 hot rods, classic cars and muscle cars; Canyonlands PRCA Rodeo in late May or early June; the Moab Music Festival, a chamber music festival held late August to mid-September; and November's Moab Folk Festival.

Moab Area Travel Council: P.O. Box 550, Moab, UT 84532. **Phone:** (435) 259-8825 or (800) 635-6622.

A visitor information center at Main and Center streets is open Mon.-Sat. 8-7, Sun. 9-6, Mar. 31-late Oct.; daily 9-5, late Oct.-Dec. 31. *(See ad p. 331.)*

CANYONLANDS FIELD INSTITUTE tours depart from the Moab Information Center, at Main and Center sts. A naturalist leads and narrates guided half-day van tours with short hikes: options are the morning Moab's Ancient Past Rock Art Tour and the afternoon Sunset Tour of Arches National Park. Other educational tours and river trips also are offered. **Hours:** Half-day tours depart Fri.-Sun. at 8:30 and 4, May-Oct. **Cost:** Half-day tours $80 (per person). Phone for fares of other tours. Reservations are required. **Phone:** (435) 259-7750 or (800) 860-5262.

DEAD HORSE POINT STATE PARK is 9 mi. n. via US 191, then about 23 mi. s.w. on SR 313. A band of wild mustangs was once herded into a natural corral created by cliffs and rock formations and inadvertently left to die of thirst in view of the Colorado River—hence the legend of Dead Horse Point.

The point provides a striking panorama of the pinnacles, buttes and sandstone cliffs of the Colorado River canyon and the meandering river 2,000 feet below. The sun and changing weather conditions produce a range of colors on these cliffs. The park offers camping, hiking, mountain biking and a visitor center. *See Recreation Areas Chart.*

Hours: Park open 6 a.m.-10 p.m. Visitor center open daily 8-6, mid-Mar. to mid-Oct.; 9-5, rest of year. Visitor center closed Jan. 1, Thanksgiving and Christmas. **Cost:** $10 (per private vehicle, maximum eight people). Camping $25. **Phone:** (435) 259-2614, (801) 322-3770 or (800) 322-3770.

HOLE 'N THE ROCK is 15 mi. s. via US 191. This 14-room home excavated from solid sandstone by Albert and Gladys Christensen beginning in the early 1940s and continuing for 20 years looks much as it did when the couple lived there; a rock and cactus garden are outside. Mr. Christensen also completed several paintings, including "Sermon on the Mount." A likeness of Franklin D. Roosevelt is carved on the outside face of the home.

An exotic zoo has a camel, a zebra, sheep, goats, pigs, wallabies, emus, alpacas, and miniature donkeys and horses. **Hours:** Tours begin daily every 15-20 minutes 9-5. Closed Thanksgiving and Christmas. **Cost:** Hole 'n the Rock $6.50; $3.50 (ages 5-10). Zoo $4.25; free (ages 0-1). **Phone:** (435) 686-2250.

MOAB MUSEUM OF FILM AND WESTERN HERITAGE is in the Red Cliffs Lodge at Milepost 14 on SR 128. The museum—part of Red Cliffs Ranch, a working ranch since the late 19th century—houses memorabilia detailing Moab's involvement in the film industry, along with displays relating cowboy culture. Since the late 1940s, numerous movies have been shot on location in the region. Its rugged terrain

(See map & index p. 333.)

made it an ideal spot to film Westerns, especially in the eyes of director John Ford, a pioneer of on-location shooting who made "Wagon Master" and "Rio Grande" here.

"Taza, Son of Cochise," with Rock Hudson; "Warlock," which featured Henry Fonda and Anthony Quinn; and "The Comancheros," starring John Wayne, were filmed in and around Moab. In addition to more than 100 commercials, such '90s cinematic productions as "City Slickers" and "Thelma & Louise" also were shot in Moab. The museum's collection includes early pioneer relics as well as photographs of such actors as Maureen O'Hara, Lee

Marvin and James Stewart, all of whom worked on motion pictures at the ranch. **Time:** Allow 45 minutes minimum. **Hours:** Daily 8 a.m.-10 p.m. **Cost:** Free. **Phone:** (435) 259-2002 or (866) 812-2002.

MUSEUM OF MOAB is at 118 E. Center St. The museum has displays about the archeology, geology, mineralogy and history of southeastern Utah. **Hours:** Mon.-Sat. 10-6, Apr. 15-Oct. 15; Mon.-Sat. noon-5, rest of year. Closed Jan. 1, Memorial Day, July 4, Labor Day, Thanksgiving and Christmas. Phone ahead to confirm schedule. **Cost:** $5; free (ages 0-17 and to all Mon.); $10 (family). **Phone:** (435) 259-7985.

▼ *See AAA listing p. 330* ▼

(See map & index p. 333.)

SAND FLATS RECREATION AREA is .5 mi. e. on Mill Creek Dr., then 2.5 mi. n.e. on Sand Flats Rd. to the entrance booth. At the Colorado Plateau's core lies this 9,000-acre recreation area, home to the Slickrock and Porcupine Rim bicycle trails; nearly 40 miles of jeep trails; and varied fauna and flora, including desert cottontail rabbits, bats, mule deer, pinyon pine, juniper and cliff rose shrubs.

The site's spectacular geological features also lure visitors; exposures of Jurassic-aged sedimentary rock layers are encountered by visitors traversing Sand Flats' multitude of foot and vehicle paths. *See Recreation Areas Chart.*

Hours: Daily 24 hours. **Cost:** One-day pass $5 (per private vehicle); $2 (per person arriving by other means). Seven-day pass $10 (per private vehicle); $5 (per person arriving by other means). Vehicle trailer fee $2. **Phone:** (435) 259-2444.

RECREATIONAL ACTIVITIES
Climbing
* **Moab Cliffs & Canyons** is at 253 N. Main St. Canyoneering trips also are offered. **Hours:** Departure days and times vary; phone ahead. **Phone:** (435) 259-3317 or (877) 641-5271.

White-water Rafting
* **AAM's Mild to Wild Rafting & Jeep Trail Tours Inc.** departs from local hotels and campgrounds. **Hours:** Half-day- to 3-day trips on the Colorado River are offered daily, Apr. 1-late Oct. Departure times vary; phone ahead. **Phone:** (970) 247-4789 or (800) 567-6745.
* **Adrift Adventures** is at 378 N. Main St. Other activities, including canyoneering, hiking, horseback riding and jet boat excursions, are offered. **Hours:** Rafting trips are offered daily, Mar.-Oct. Departure times vary; phone ahead. **Phone:** (435) 259-8594 or (800) 874-4483.
* **Canyon Voyages Adventure Co.** is at 211 N. Main St. Other activities are offered. **Hours:** Rafting trips are offered daily, Mar.-Oct. Departure times vary; phone ahead. **Phone:** (435) 259-6007 or (800) 733-6007.
* **Moab Adventure Center** is at 225 S. Main St. Other activities are offered. **Hours:** Open daily, mid-Mar. through Oct. 31. Hours vary; phone ahead. **Phone:** (435) 259-7019 or (866) 904-1163.
* **NAVTEC Expeditions** is at 321 N. Main St. Also offer guided 4x4 tours in Canyonlands and Arches national parks. **Hours:** Rafting trips are offered daily, Mar.-Oct. Departure times vary; phone ahead. **Phone:** (435) 259-7983 or (800) 833-1278.
* **O.A.R.S. Canyonlands Tours** departs from several locations in Moab. Other activities are offered. **Hours:** Rafting trips are offered daily, Apr.-Oct. Departure times vary; phone ahead. **Phone:** (435) 259-5865 or (800) 346-6277.
* **Sheri Griffith Expeditions Inc.** is at 2231 S. US 191. Other activities are offered. **Hours:** Rafting trips are offered daily, Mar.-Oct. Departure times vary; phone ahead. **Phone:** (435) 259-8229 or (800) 332-2439.
* **Tag-A-Long Expeditions** is at 452 N. Main St. Other activities are offered. **Hours:** Rafting trips are offered daily, mid-Apr. to mid-Oct. Departure times vary; phone ahead. **Phone:** (435) 259-8946 or (800) 453-3292.

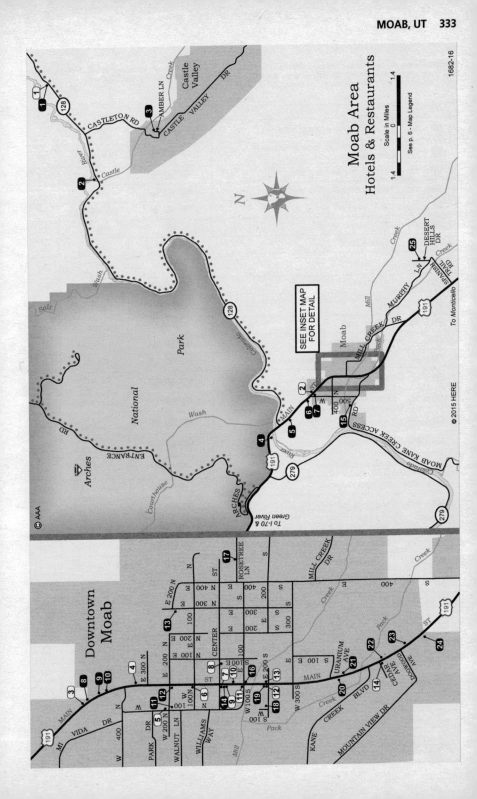

Moab Area
Hotels & Restaurants

Scale in Miles

See p. 6 - Map Legend

Downtown Moab

1682-16

© 2015 HERE

© AAA

Moab Area

This index helps you "spot" where approved hotels and restaurants are located on the corresponding detailed maps. Hotel daily rate range is for comparison only. Restaurant price range is a combination of lunch and/or dinner. Turn to the listing page for more detailed rate and price information and consult display ads for special promotions.

MOAB

Map Page	Hotels	Diamond Rated	Rate Range	Page
1 p. 333	Sorrel River Ranch Resort & Spa	◆◆◆◆	Rates not provided	336
2 p. 333	**Red Cliffs Lodge - Moab's National Park Experience**	◆◆◆	$99-$340 SAVE	336
3 p. 333	Castle Valley Inn Bed & Breakfast	◆◆◆	$110-$195	335
4 p. 333	Fairfield Inn & Suites by Marriott Moab	◆◆◆	$94-$328	335
5 p. 333	**Aarchway Inn**	◆◆◆	$99-$299 SAVE	335
6 p. 333	Motel 6 Moab #4119	◆	$59-$199	336
7 p. 333	Super 8 Moab	◆◆	$60-$300	337
8 p. 333	Inca Inn	◆	Rates not provided	336
10 p. 333	Hampton Inn	◆◆◆	$169-$259	336
11 p. 333	River Canyon Lodge, An Extended Stay Inn & Suites	◆◆	$59-$199	336
12 p. 333	**Bowen Motel**	◆◆	$59-$169 SAVE	335
13 p. 333	Sunflower Hill, A Luxury Inn	◆◆◆	$185-$265	337
14 p. 333	**BEST WESTERN PLUS Canyonlands Inn**	◆◆◆	$119-$269 SAVE	335
15 p. 333	Adobe Abode Moab Bed & Breakfast	◆◆◆	Rates not provided	335
16 p. 333	**BEST WESTERN PLUS Greenwell Inn**	◆◆◆	$89-$309 SAVE	335
17 p. 333	The Mayor's House Bed & Breakfast	◆◆◆	Rates not provided	336
18 p. 333	**The Gonzo Inn**	◆◆◆	Rates not provided SAVE	336
19 p. 333	Hotel Moab Downtown	◆◆	Rates not provided	336
20 p. 333	**Big Horn Lodge**	◆◆	$60-$140 SAVE	335
21 p. 333	**Red Stone Inn**	◆	Rates not provided SAVE	336
22 p. 333	Moab Valley Inn	◆◆	$69-$279	336
23 p. 333	**La Quinta Inn & Suites Moab**	◆◆◆	$75-$345 SAVE	336
24 p. 333	**Silver Sage Inn**	◆	$45-$120 SAVE	336
25 p. 333	Desert Hills Bed & Breakfast	◆◆◆	Rates not provided	335

Map Page	Restaurants	Diamond Rated	Cuisine	Price Range	Page
1 p. 333	Sorrel River Grill	◆◆◆	American	$14-$39	337
2 p. 333	Sunset Grill	◆◆	Steak Seafood	$14-$25	337
3 p. 333	La Hacienda Mexican Restaurant	◆◆	Mexican	$8-$24	337
4 p. 333	**EklectiCafe**	◆	Natural/Organic	$5-$10	337
5 p. 333	Jeffrey's Steakhouse	◆◆◆	Steak	$22-$40	337
6 p. 333	Jailhouse Cafe	◆◆	Breakfast	$7-$10	337
7 p. 333	Pasta Jay's	◆◆	Italian	$8-$19	337
8 p. 333	Singha Thai Cuisine	◆◆	Thai	$11-$18	337
9 p. 333	Peace Tree Juice Cafe	◆◆	Natural/Organic	$6-$25	337

Map Page	Restaurants (cont'd)	Diamond Rated	Cuisine	Price Range	Page
⑩ p. 333	Eddie McStiff's	▽▽	American	$8-$20	337
⑪ p. 333	Zax Restaurant	▽▽	American	$10-$22	337
⑫ p. 333	Pancake Haus	▽	Breakfast	$6-$10	337
⑬ p. 333	Moab Diner	▽	American	$8-$16	337
⑭ p. 333	Moab Brewery	▽▽	American	$8-$22	337

AARCHWAY INN
(435)259-2599 **5**
▽▽▽
Hotel
$99-$299

Address: 1551 N Riverview Dr 84532 **Location:** 2 mi n. **Facility:** 97 units, some kitchens. 2 stories, interior corridors. **Terms:** cancellation fee imposed. **Pool(s):** heated outdoor. **Activities:** hot tub, playground, picnic facilities, trails, exercise room. **Guest Services:** coin laundry, area transportation. **Featured Amenity: full hot breakfast.**

ADOBE ABODE MOAB BED & BREAKFAST
435/259-7716 **15**

▽▽▽ **Bed & Breakfast. Rates not provided. Address:** 778 Kane Creek Blvd 84532 **Location:** 0.4 mi s to Kane Creek Blvd, 1.1 mi nw. Located in a quiet area. **Facility:** Surrounded by red cliffs, these elegant rooms have unusual furnishings made by the creative innkeeper; common areas include secluded spaces. 6 units. 1-2 stories (no elevator), interior corridors. **Terms:** age restrictions may apply. **Activities:** hot tub.

BEST WESTERN PLUS CANYONLANDS INN
(435)259-2300 **14**
▽▽▽
Hotel
$119-$269

AAA Benefit: Save 10% or more every day and earn 10% bonus points!

Address: 16 S Main St 84532 **Location:** Just s of Main and W Center sts. **Facility:** 80 units. 2 stories, interior/exterior corridors. **Terms:** check-in 4 pm. **Pool(s):** heated outdoor. **Activities:** hot tub, playground, exercise room. **Guest Services:** coin laundry. **Featured Amenity: full hot breakfast.**

BEST WESTERN PLUS GREENWELL INN
(435)259-6151 **16**
▽▽▽
Hotel
$89-$309

AAA Benefit: Save 10% or more every day and earn 10% bonus points!

Address: 105 S Main St 84532 **Location:** Just s of jct Main and Center sts. **Facility:** 75 units. 2 stories, exterior corridors. **Terms:** check-in 4 pm, cancellation fee imposed. **Pool(s):** heated outdoor. **Activities:** hot tub, exercise room. **Guest Services:** coin laundry.

BIG HORN LODGE
(435)259-6171 **20**
▽▽ ▽▽
Motel
$60-$140

Address: 550 S Main St 84532 **Location:** 0.5 mi s. **Facility:** 58 units. 2 stories (no elevator), exterior corridors. **Terms:** cancellation fee imposed. **Pool(s):** heated outdoor.

BOWEN MOTEL
(435)259-7132 **12**
▽▽ ▽▽
Motel
$59-$169

Address: 169 N Main St 84532 **Location:** Downtown. **Facility:** 44 units, some three bedrooms and kitchens. 1-2 stories (no elevator), exterior corridors. **Pool(s):** heated outdoor. **Guest Services:** coin laundry.

CASTLE VALLEY INN BED & BREAKFAST
(435)259-6012 **3**

▽▽▽ **Bed & Breakfast** $110-$195 **Address:** 424 Amber Ln 84532 **Location:** Jct US 191 and SR 128, 15.5 mi ne to LaSal Mountain Loop Rd, 1.7 mi se to Castle Valley Dr, 0.7 mi sw to Meadow Ln, just e, then just n. Located in a quiet secluded area. **Facility:** Deer come by to sample the rich grass of this 5-acre property in a secluded green valley surrounded by impressive buttes, mountains and fruit trees. 8 units, some two bedrooms, efficiencies and cabins. 1-2 stories (no elevator), interior/exterior corridors. **Terms:** check-in 4 pm, 2 night minimum stay - weekends, 14 day cancellation notice. **Activities:** hot tub, picnic facilities.

DESERT HILLS BED & BREAKFAST
435/259-3568 **25**

▽▽▽ **Bed & Breakfast. Rates not provided. Address:** 1989 Desert Hills Dr 84532 **Location:** 4.1 mi s to Spanish Trail Rd, 1 mi e to roundabout, take Murphy Ln just n to Desert Hills Dr, then just e. **Facility:** Located in a quiet neighborhood, guests can enjoy peaceful mountain views while relaxing in the hot tub, sitting on the log swing for two or watching the hummingbirds on the garden patio. 5 units, some two bedrooms. 2 stories (no elevator), interior/exterior corridors. **Activities:** hot tub, playground, picnic facilities. **Guest Services:** complimentary laundry.

FAIRFIELD INN & SUITES BY MARRIOTT MOAB
(435)259-5350 **4**

▽▽▽ **Hotel** $94-$328 **Address:** 1863 N Hwy 191 84532 **Location:** 3.6 mi n of center. **Facility:** 89 units. 3 stories, interior corridors. **Amenities:** safes. **Pool(s):** heated outdoor. **Activities:** hot tub, trails, exercise room. **Guest Services:** coin laundry, boarding pass kiosk.

AAA Benefit: Members save 5% or more!

(See map & index p. 333.)

THE GONZO INN
435/259-2515 **18**

Boutique Hotel
Rates not provided

Address: 100 W 200 S 84532 **Location:** Just w of 200 S and S Main St. **Facility:** With beautiful landscaping surrounding the pool area, this boutique hotel successfully blends Southwestern architecture and contemporary décor to create a truly distinctive lodging. 43 units, some two bedrooms. 2 stories (no elevator), interior/exterior corridors. **Terms:** check-in 4 pm. **Amenities:** safes. **Pool(s):** heated outdoor. **Activities:** hot tub. **Guest Services:** coin laundry. **Featured Amenity: continental breakfast.**

[SAVE] [Ⓨ+] [≈] [BIZ] [⤢] [✕] [🍴]
[📷] [💻] / SOME UNITS [🐾]

HAMPTON INN
(435)259-3030 **10**

Hotel $169-$259 **Address:** 488 N Main St 84532 **Location:** 0.5 mi n. **Facility:** 79 units. 3 stories, interior corridors. **Terms:** 1-7 night minimum stay, cancellation fee imposed. **Pool(s):** heated outdoor. **Activities:** hot tub, exercise room. **Guest Services:** coin laundry.

AAA Benefit: Members save up to 10%!

[Ⓨ+] CALL [📶] [≈] [BIZ] [HS] [⤢] [✕] [🍴] [💻]
/ SOME UNITS [📷]

HOTEL MOAB DOWNTOWN
435/259-7141 **19**

Motel. **Rates not provided. Address:** 182 S Main St 84532 **Location:** Center. **Facility:** 81 units, some two bedrooms. 2 stories (no elevator), exterior corridors. **Pool(s):** heated outdoor. **Activities:** hot tub. [Ⓨ+] [≈] [BIZ] [⤢] [✕] [🍴] [📷] [💻]

INCA INN
435/259-7261 **8**

Motel. **Rates not provided. Address:** 570 N Main St 84532 **Location:** 0.6 mi n. **Facility:** 24 units. 1 story, exterior corridors. **Pool(s):** heated outdoor. [Ⓨ+] [≈] [⤢] [✕] [🍴] [📷]

LA QUINTA INN & SUITES MOAB
(435)259-8700 **23**

Hotel
$75-$345

Address: 815 S Main St 84532 **Location:** 0.8 mi s. **Facility:** 100 units. 3 stories, interior corridors. **Pool(s):** heated outdoor. **Activities:** hot tub, playground, picnic facilities, exercise room. **Guest Services:** coin laundry. **Featured Amenity: continental breakfast.**

[SAVE] [Ⓨ+] [≈] [BIZ] [⤢] [✕] [🍴]
[📷] [💻] / SOME UNITS [🐾]

THE MAYOR'S HOUSE BED & BREAKFAST
435/259-6015 **17**

Bed & Breakfast. **Rates not provided. Address:** 505 Rosetree Ln 84532 **Location:** 0.4 mi e on Center St, just s on 400 S, then just e. **Facility:** Once owned by the town mayor, the B&B has a lovely shaded yard and garden with a pool. Breakfast specialties include French toast, blueberry pancakes, strawberry waffles and homemade cinnamon rolls. 5 units. 2 stories (no elevator), interior/exterior corridors. **Terms:** age restrictions may apply. **Pool(s):** heated outdoor. **Activities:** hot tub.

[Ⓨ+] [≈] [BIZ] [⤢] [✕] [🎿] [🍴] / SOME UNITS [📷]

MOAB VALLEY INN
(435)259-4419 **22**

Hotel $69-$279 **Address:** 711 S Main St 84532 **Location:** 0.7 mi s. **Facility:** 126 units. 3 stories, interior corridors. **Terms:** cancellation fee imposed. **Amenities:** safes. **Pool(s):** heated outdoor, heated indoor. **Activities:** hot tub, picnic facilities, exercise room. **Guest Services:** coin laundry.

[Ⓨ+] [≈] [BIZ] [⤢] [✕] [🍴] [💻] / SOME UNITS [📷]

MOTEL 6 MOAB #4119
(435)259-6686 **6**

Motel $59-$199 **Address:** 1089 N Main St 84532 **Location:** 1.5 mi n. **Facility:** 66 units. 3 stories, interior corridors. **Terms:** cancellation fee imposed. **Pool(s):** heated outdoor. **Activities:** hot tub. **Guest Services:** coin laundry. [≈] [⤢] [✕] / SOME UNITS [🐾]

RED CLIFFS LODGE - MOAB'S NATIONAL PARK EXPERIENCE
(435)259-2002 **2**

Resort Ranch
$99-$340

Address: Milepost 14 Hwy 128 84532 **Location:** Waterfront. 2.3 mi n to jct US 191 and SR 128, 14 mi e to MM 14. **Facility:** Creekside and riverfront cabins and a wonderful selection of spacious guest rooms, all with large secluded patios, overlook the Colorado River. A barbecue lunch is served daily on the river deck. 110 units, some cabins. 1 story, exterior corridors. **Terms:** 30 day cancellation notice-fee imposed. **Amenities:** safes. **Pool(s):** heated outdoor. **Activities:** hot tub, tennis, recreation programs in summer, playground, trails, exercise room. **Guest Services:** coin laundry.

[SAVE] [Ⓨ] [Ⓨ] [≈] [BIZ] [HS] [⤢] [✕] [🍴] [📷] [💻]
/ SOME UNITS [🐾]

RED STONE INN
435/259-3500 **21**

Motel
Rates not provided

Address: 535 S Main St 84532 **Location:** 0.5 mi s. **Facility:** 52 units. 1 story, interior corridors. **Activities:** hot tub, picnic facilities. **Guest Services:** coin laundry.

[SAVE] [Ⓨ+] [HS] [⤢] [✕] [🍴] [📷]
[💻] / SOME UNITS [🐾]

RIVER CANYON LODGE, AN EXTENDED STAY INN & SUITES
(435)259-8838 **11**

Extended Stay Motel $59-$199 **Address:** 71 W 200 N 84532 **Location:** Just w of 200 N and Main St. **Facility:** 80 units, some two bedrooms and kitchens. 3 stories, interior corridors. **Terms:** closed 12/1-2/27, cancellation fee imposed. **Pool(s):** heated outdoor. **Activities:** hot tub, recreation programs.

[Ⓨ+] [≈] [BIZ] [⤢] [✕] [🍴] [📷] / SOME UNITS [🐾] [💻]

SILVER SAGE INN
(435)259-4420 **24**

Motel
$45-$120

Address: 840 S Main St 84532 **Location:** 0.9 mi s of the center. **Facility:** 17 units. 1 story, interior corridors. **Activities:** picnic facilities.

[SAVE] [Ⓨ+] [⤢] [✕] [🍴] [📷] [💻]
/ SOME UNITS [🐾]

SORREL RIVER RANCH RESORT & SPA
435/259-4642 **1**

Resort Hotel. **Rates not provided. Address:** Hwy 128 at MM 17 84532 **Location:** Waterfront. 17 mi e of jct US 191 and SR 128; at MM 17. **Facility:** Surrounded by red rocks on the Colorado River, the resort offers upscale rooms, family suites and baths with designer details in a 'rich ranch' style. All rooms have a covered front porch. 59 units, some houses. 1-2 stories (no elevator), exterior corridors. **Parking:** on-site and valet. **Terms:** check-in 4 pm. **Amenities:** safes. **Dining:** Sorrel River Grill, see separate listing. **Pool(s):** heated outdoor. **Activities:** sauna, hot tub, steamroom, tennis, recreation programs, lawn sports, trails, exercise room, spa. **Guest Services:** valet laundry, area transportation.

[🏋] [🍸] [🍽] [Ⓨ] [≈] [BIZ] [⤢] [✕] [🍴] [📷] [💻]
/ SOME UNITS [🐾]

(See map & index p. 333.)

SUNFLOWER HILL, A LUXURY INN   435/259-2974   13

▼▼▼▼ Bed & Breakfast $185-$265 **Address:** 185 N 300 E 84532 **Location:** 0.3 mi e of Main St via 100 N, then just n. Located in a residential area. **Facility:** Guests stay in either a historic farmhouse or a two-story garden cottage, both nestled on an acre of wooded pathways, flower gardens and numerous cozy seating areas. 12 units. 2 stories (no elevator), interior/exterior corridors. **Terms:** 14 day cancellation notice-fee imposed. **Pool(s):** heated outdoor. **Activities:** hot tub, picnic facilities. **Guest Services:** complimentary laundry.

SUPER 8 MOAB   (435)259-8868   7

▼▼ Motel $60-$300 **Address:** 889 N Main St 84532 **Location:** 1.2 mi n of center. **Facility:** 146 units, some kitchens. 2 stories (no elevator), interior corridors. **Pool(s):** heated outdoor. **Activities:** hot tub. **Guest Services:** coin laundry.

WHERE TO EAT

EDDIE MCSTIFF'S   435/259-2337   10

▼▼ American. Casual Dining. $8-$20 **AAA Inspector Notes:** The eatery features handcrafted ales with menu items ranging from steaks to pasta and pizza, all served by a friendly staff. **Features:** full bar, patio dining, Sunday brunch. **Address:** 57 S Main St 84532 **Location:** Just s of center.

EKLECTICAFE   435/259-6896   4

▼ Natural/Organic Quick Serve $5-$10

AAA Inspector Notes: An ideal stop for a quick healthful meal, this café focuses on fresh, organic dishes. Pancakes, eggs, tofu, granola and bagels dominate the breakfast menu, while the lunch menu has a more international flair. Highlights include Indonesian satay, hummus plates, curry wraps and Southwestern veggie burgers. **Features:** patio dining. **Address:** 352 N Main St 84532 **Location:** 0.3 mi n. *Menu on AAA.com*

JAILHOUSE CAFE   435/259-3900   6

▼▼ Breakfast. Casual Dining. $7-$10 **AAA Inspector Notes:** This restaurant serves only breakfast, but it's done exceptionally well with a sophisticated twist. The motto is "good enough for a last meal." Options include a spinach, feta and mushroom omelet, old-fashioned ginger pancakes and Southwestern eggs Florentine. **Features:** patio dining, Sunday brunch. **Address:** 101 N Main St 84532 **Location:** Just n. **Parking:** street only.

JEFFREY'S STEAKHOUSE   435/259-3588   5

▼▼ Steak. Fine Dining. $22-$40 **AAA Inspector Notes:** This elegant new restaurant features a popular lobster, crab and shrimp appetizer, Wagyu steaks, lollipop lamb chops and decadent desserts. **Features:** full bar. **Address:** 218 N 100 W 84532 **Location:** Just n to W 200 N, just w, then just n.

LA HACIENDA MEXICAN RESTAURANT   435/259-6319   3

▼▼ Mexican. Casual Dining. $8-$24 **AAA Inspector Notes:** This family-owned eatery features fresh and tasty Mexican dishes such as enchiladas, chili rellenos, burritos and tacos. Margarita fans won't be disappointed with the variety. Daily lunch specials provide great value for those traveling on a budget. **Features:** full bar. **Address:** 574 N Main St 84532 **Location:** 0.6 mi n; next to Inca Inn.

MOAB BREWERY   435/259-6333   14

▼▼ American. Casual Dining. $8-$22 **AAA Inspector Notes:** Warehouse walls laden with sports regalia surround an enclosed pub in the town's only brewery/restaurant. Seating is available in a large inside dining room or on the patio in season. Standard pub fare goes down easy with the eight hand-crafted ales on tap, which are enough to quench any thirst on a hot Utah day. **Features:** full bar. **Address:** 686 S Main St 84532 **Location:** 0.7 mi s.

MOAB DINER   435/259-4006   13

▼ American. Casual Dining. $8-$16 **AAA Inspector Notes:** Step back in time to the fabulous era of the diner and ice cream shoppe in this establishment, which specializes in Kokopelli chicken and world famous green chili. **Address:** 189 S Main St 84532 **Location:** 0.3 mi s.

PANCAKE HAUS   435/259-7141   12

▼ Breakfast. Family Dining. $6-$10 **AAA Inspector Notes:** The eatery specializes in banana and walnut pancakes, fruit-topped French toast and crêpes, stuffed omelets and country-fried steak with eggs. **Address:** 196 S Main St 84532 **Location:** Just s; next to Ramada Moab Downtown.

PASTA JAY'S   435/259-2900   7

▼▼ Italian. Casual Dining. $8-$19 **AAA Inspector Notes:** A nice selection of pasta, pizza, salads, sandwiches and wine is served on red-and-white-checkered tablecloths. The large covered patio, which is open year-round, surrounds the attractively landscaped exterior, which runs along two downtown sidewalks. **Features:** beer & wine, patio dining. **Address:** 4 S Main St 84532 **Location:** At Main and W Center sts. **Parking:** street only.

PEACE TREE JUICE CAFE   435/259-0101   9

▼▼ Natural/Organic. Casual Dining. $6-$25 **AAA Inspector Notes:** Specializing in fresh juices, healthy salads, chips and hummus, wraps and tasty ice cream, this brightly colored café lifts guests' moods as they sip on delicious smoothies and fresh coffee. Dinners offer more complex dishes like polenta lasagna, baked wahoo with fresh thyme and stuffed chicken breast. **Features:** beer & wine, patio dining. **Address:** 20 S Main St 84532 **Location:** Downtown. **Parking:** street only.

SINGHA THAI CUISINE   435/259-0039   8

▼▼ Thai. Casual Dining. $11-$18 **AAA Inspector Notes:** Well-prepared traditional entrées are served in this charming eatery. The menu includes spring rolls, stuffed angel wings, authentic Thai curry, soups, and house specials such as tamarind duck and volcano shrimp. Gluten-free dishes are available upon request. **Features:** beer & wine. **Address:** 92 E Center St 84532 **Location:** Just e. **Parking:** street only.

SORREL RIVER GRILL   435/259-4642   1

▼▼▼ American. Fine Dining. $14-$39 **AAA Inspector Notes:** The restaurant offers savory meals made from local foods and attentive service in a riverfront setting with covered decks. Patrons might start with grilled marinated shrimp then move on to Colorado wild duck or grilled salmon steak with creamy truffle sauce. **Features:** full bar, patio dining. **Reservations:** required, for dinner. **Address:** Hwy 128, MM 17 84532 **Location:** 17 mi e of jct US 191 and SR 128; at MM 17; in Sorrel River Ranch Resort & Spa.

SUNSET GRILL   435/259-7146   2

▼▼ Steak Seafood. Casual Dining. $14-$25 **AAA Inspector Notes:** The grill occupies the historic former home of Uranium King Charlie Steen. The menu emphasis is on seafood, prime rib, filet mignon and pasta. Patrons will enjoy watching the sunset by candlelight at this cliff-side spot, which affords a million-dollar panoramic view. **Features:** full bar. **Address:** 900 N Hwy 191 84532 **Location:** 1.1 mi n, 0.3 mi e up to bluff; rough road to top of bluff.

ZAX RESTAURANT   435/259-6555   11

▼▼ American. Casual Dining. $10-$22 **AAA Inspector Notes:** This eatery offers much more than delicious pizzas; a variety of creative burgers, sandwiches, steaks and pasta dishes complement the menu. Attractive murals reflect the adventurous spirit of the city and its surroundings. **Features:** full bar, patio dining. **Address:** 96 S Main St 84532 **Location:** At W Center and Main sts. **Parking:** street only.

MONTICELLO (F-6) pop. 1,972, elev. 7,050'

Named for Thomas Jefferson's Virginia home, Monticello is on the edge of the Manti-La Sal National Forest *(see place listing p. 327)* and 14 miles south of the southern entrance to Canyonlands National Park *(see place listing p. 301)*. The surrounding Abajo Mountains (also known as the Blue Mountains) provide many opportunities for backpacking, camping, off-road driving, snowmobiling and cross-country skiing.

Harts Draw Road is a 22-mile scenic drive that connects Monticello to SR 211, passing lakes and pine forests and offering views of Canyonlands National Park.

San Juan County Economic Development & Visitor Services: 117 S. Main St., P.O. Box 490, Monticello, UT 84535. **Phone:** (435) 587-3235 or (800) 574-4386.

NEWSPAPER ROCK is near Indian Creek Canyon, 14 mi. n. on US 191, then 12 mi. w. on SR 211. Newspaper Rock is a large cliff mural consisting of ancient Native American petroglyphs and pictographs from three distinctive periods. **Cost:** Free. **Phone:** (435) 587-1500.

PEACE TREE JUICE CAFE   435/587-5063

Deli. Quick Serve. $8-$9 **AAA Inspector Notes:** Specializing in fresh juice, healthful wraps and tasty ice cream, this brightly colored cafe lifts guests' moods as they sip on delicious smoothies. **Features:** patio dining. **Address:** 516 N Main St 84535 **Location:** Jct US 191 and 491, 0.5 mi n. **Parking:** street only. [B] [L]

MONUMENT VALLEY (G-5)

GOULDING'S MONUMENT VALLEY MUSEUM is 2 mi. w. of US 163 in Goulding's Lodge at 1000 Main St. The first floor is a re-creation of the original 1920s trading post and contains items pertaining to local history. The Gouldings' living quarters on the second floor has displays of photographs and personal items.

The Movie Days Film Gallery has area film memorabilia. Earth Spirit and Among the Monuments, 20-minute multimedia presentations that capture the beauty of Monument Valley, are shown nightly. **Hours:** Daily 8-8. Multimedia shows are offered nightly at 6:10 and 7:10. A movie is shown at 8. Phone ahead to confirm schedule. **Cost:** Donations. **Phone:** (435) 727-3231.

GOULDING'S MONUMENT VALLEY TOURS departs from Goulding's Lodge at 1000 Main St. All-day, 3.5- and 2.5-hour excursions conducted by Navajo Indian guides in four-wheel-drive vehicles highlight such Monument Valley sights as pictographs and petroglyphs, pueblo-style cliff dwellings built by Anasazi Indians about A.D. 1250, natural arches and windows, and monoliths.

Hiking and full moon tours also are offered, as is a 5.5-hour tour of Mystery Valley, located adjacent to Monument Valley. **Hours:** Full-day and Mystery

Valley tours depart daily at 9. Tours lasting 3.5 hours depart daily at 9 and late afternoon (exact time dependent on season). Tours lasting 2.5 hours depart daily at 8, July-Aug.; at 1:30, Apr.-June and Sept.-Oct. Winter tour times vary; phone ahead. **Cost:** Full-day tour $119.10; $85.75 (ages 0-7). Mystery Valley tour $89.55; $68.60 (ages 0-7). Tour lasting 3.5 hours $66.70; $42.90 (ages 0-7). Tour lasting 2.5 hours $53.40; $38.10 (ages 0-7). Phone for hiking and full moon tour prices. **Phone:** (435) 727-3231.

GOULDING'S LODGE & TOURS   (435)727-3231

Hotel $91-$325 **Address:** 1000 Main St 84536 **Location:** 2 mi w of US 163; 0.5 mi n of Arizona border. **Facility:** 113 units, some efficiencies, houses and cabins. 2 stories (no elevator), exterior corridors. **Terms:** 3 day cancellation notice-fee imposed. **Pool(s):** heated indoor. **Activities:** exercise room. **Guest Services:** coin laundry.

MONUMENT VALLEY NAVAJO TRIBAL PARK (G-5)

Reached via scenic US 163, Monument Valley Navajo Tribal Park is a colorful region covering several thousand square miles within the Navajo Indian Reservation. The park contains Mystery Valley, where isolated monoliths of red sandstone tower as much as 1,000 feet above the valley floor.

The visitor center, 4 miles southeast of US 163, provides information about self-guiding tours. Guided tours from the center are offered daily; picnicking is permitted.

Horseback and four-wheel-drive trips through the vicinity can be arranged through agencies in Arizona at Kayenta and in Utah at Bluff, Mexican Hat and Monument Valley. Overnight accommodations also are available in Kayenta, Mexican Hat and Monument Valley; reservations are recommended.

Visitors should not photograph the Navajo people, their homes or their possessions without asking permission; a gratuity is usually requested. Other restrictions apply. For more information contact Monument Valley Navajo Tribal Park, P.O. Box 360289, Monument Valley, UT 84536.

The park is open daily 6 a.m.-8 p.m., May-Sept.; 8-4:30, rest of year (weather permitting). Closed Jan. 1, Thanksgiving and Christmas. Last admission 30 minutes before closing. Recreational vehicles more than 25 feet long and motorcycles are not permitted on the self-guiding tour. A 4-day pass is $20 (per vehicle with 1-4 people; $6 each additional person). Phone (435) 727-5870.

VISITOR CENTER, 4 mi. s.e. of US 163 near the Arizona/Utah border, offers an impressive panorama of the Mitten and Merrick buttes; exhibits about Native Americans; an auditorium; an outdoor amphitheater; a patio; a library; and a Navajo hogan, the traditional housing structure of the Navajo people.

Departing from the center are various guided tours led by Navajo tour operators, who take visitors down into the valley and backcountry. **Time:** Allow 2 hours,

30 minutes minimum. **Hours:** Daily 8-5. Hours may be extended in summer; phone to confirm schedule. Closed Jan. 1, Thanksgiving and Christmas. **Cost:** Free. **Phone:** (435) 727-5870.

MOUNT CARMEL JUNCTION
• Part of Zion National Park area — see map p. 415

BEST WESTERN EAST ZION THUNDERBIRD LODGE
(435)648-2203

Hotel
$70-$199

AAA Benefit: Save 10% or more every day and earn 10% bonus points!

Address: Jct US 89 & SR 9 84755 **Location:** Jct US 89 and SR 9. **Facility:** 61 units. 2 stories (no elevator), exterior corridors. **Dining:** Thunderbird Restaurant, see separate listing. **Pool(s):** heated outdoor. **Activities:** hot tub, regulation golf. **Guest Services:** coin laundry.

WHERE TO EAT

GOLDEN HILLS RESTAURANT   435/648-2602

American. Family Dining. $10-$20 **AAA Inspector Notes:** Long a staple in area dining, the restaurant is a great stop for travelers on their way to or from Zion National Park. The salad bar is an option at lunch or dinner. **Address:** 4475 S State St 84755 **Location:** US 89, jct SR 9. [B] [L] [D]

THUNDERBIRD RESTAURANT   435/648-2262

American. Family Dining. $6-$21 **AAA Inspector Notes:** Right off the lobby, this home-style-cooking restaurant serves casual items such as sandwiches, burgers and some local fare. There's no way anyone should turn down one of the homemade pies. **Features:** beer & wine. **Address:** Jct US 89 & SR 9 84755 **Location:** Jct US 89 and SR 9; in BEST WESTERN East Zion Thunderbird Lodge. [B] [L] [D]

MURRAY pop. 46,746
• Hotels & Restaurants map & index p. 385
• Part of Salt Lake City area — see map p. 368

In the center of scenic Salt Lake Valley, Murray is a bustling suburban community with easy access to recreational activities, skiing areas and Salt Lake City, which sits just 8 miles north. The rugged mountain peaks of the Wasatch Range rise to the east, while the Jordan River flows to the west. Dining and shopping opportunities abound, especially near Fashion Place Mall (6191 State St.), which offers Dillard's and Nordstrom among other retailers.

CRYSTAL INN MIDVALLEY/MURRAY   (801)685-9300 **49**

Hotel $86-$229 **Address:** 818 E Winchester St 84107 **Location:** I-215 exit 9 (Union Park Ave), 1.2 mi nw via 6600 S. **Facility:** 128 units. 4 stories, interior corridors. **Pool(s):** heated indoor. **Activities:** hot tub, picnic facilities, limited exercise equipment. **Guest Services:** valet and coin laundry, area transportation. *(See ad p. 390.)*

FAIRFIELD INN BY MARRIOTT - MURRAY   (801)265-9600 **45**

Hotel $86-$195 **Address:** 594 W 4500 S 84123 **Location:** I-15 exit 301 (4500 S), 0.3 mi w. **Facility:** 60 units. 3 stories, interior corridors. **Pool(s):** heated indoor. **Activities:** hot tub, exercise room. **Guest Services:** complimentary and valet laundry.

AAA Benefit: Members save 5% or more!

HAMPTON INN - MURRAY   (801)293-1300 **44**

Hotel $109-$149 **Address:** 606 W 4500 S 84123 **Location:** I-15 exit 301 (4500 S), 0.3 mi w. **Facility:** 64 units. 3 stories, interior corridors. **Terms:** 1-7 night minimum stay, cancellation fee imposed. **Pool(s):** heated indoor. **Activities:** hot tub, limited exercise equipment. **Guest Services:** valet and coin laundry.

AAA Benefit: Members save up to 10%!

HOLIDAY INN EXPRESS & SUITES - SALT LAKE CITY SOUTH/MURRAY   (801)266-0800 **48**

Hotel $89-$299 **Address:** 5429 S Commerce Dr 84107 **Location:** I-15 exit 300 (5300 S), just e. **Facility:** 83 units. 4 stories, interior corridors. **Terms:** cancellation fee imposed. **Pool(s):** heated indoor. **Activities:** hot tub, exercise room. **Guest Services:** valet and coin laundry.

HOME2 SUITES BY HILTON - SALT LAKE CITY/MURRAY   (801)288-1234 **46**

Extended Stay Contemporary Hotel $99-$169 **Address:** 4927 S State St 84107 **Location:** I-15 exit 300 (5300 S), 0.6 mi e, then 0.6 mi n. **Facility:** 117 units. 4 stories, interior corridors. **Terms:** 1-7 night minimum stay, cancellation fee imposed. **Pool(s):** heated indoor. **Activities:** game room, picnic facilities, exercise room. **Guest Services:** valet and coin laundry.

AAA Benefit: Members save up to 10%!

RESIDENCE INN BY MARRIOTT - SALT LAKE CITY/MURRAY   (801)262-4200 **47**

Extended Stay Hotel $118-$267 **Address:** 171 E 5300 S 84107 **Location:** I-15 exit 300 (5300 S), 0.8 mi e. **Facility:** 136 units, some two bedrooms and efficiencies. 6 stories, interior corridors. **Terms:** check-in 4 pm. **Pool(s):** heated indoor. **Activities:** hot tub, picnic facilities, exercise room. **Guest Services:** valet and coin laundry, boarding pass kiosk, area transportation.

NATURAL BRIDGES NATIONAL MONUMENT (F-5)

Natural Bridges National Monument is 42 miles west of Blanding via SR 95. The park has a scenic 7,780 acres. Within the winding corridors of White and Armstrong canyons, water has eroded the stone walls to form three massive bridges. The natural bridges remained known only to the Anasazi and other Native American tribes until 1883, when Cass Hite, a gold prospector, first entered the area from a remote mining camp on the Colorado River.

All three bridges can be viewed from overlooks accessible by short walks from a scenic 9-mile loop drive. Trails lead down to each bridge, and an 8.6-mile round-trip trail connects the bridges.

The three natural bridges were named after Hopi Indian terms that relate to their characteristics. The Sipapu Bridge, the longest and highest, is 268 feet long, 31 feet wide, 53 feet thick and 220 feet high. The second largest natural bridge in the world, Sipapu represents a mature stage in the evolution of a natural bridge.

Kachina Bridge, 2.5 miles away at the junction of Armstrong and White canyons, crosses the stream bed at a height of 210 feet. The most massive bridge, Kachina is 204 feet long, 44 feet wide and 93 feet thick. Owachomo Bridge, the smallest and oldest, is a narrow strip of rock only 9 feet thick in the center and 27 feet wide. Spanning 180 feet, Owachomo is in a late stage of erosion and is approaching the day when weather and gravity will bring it crashing to the canyon floor.

Bridge View Drive, a scenic, 9-mile-long, one-way loop starting and ending near the visitor center has overlooks for each of the three bridges. Horse Collar Ruin, an ancestral Puebloan cliff dwelling, is visible from the Bridge View Drive overlook. Pets and bicycles are not permitted on trails or off-road areas. Hiking on bridges is not allowed.

Camping is permitted. Visitors should note that there is a 26-foot limit for RVs and any vehicles pulling them and that the closest gas stations are 44 miles away in Mexican Hat from the south and 38 miles away in Blanding from the east.

A visitor center at the monument headquarters presents a slide show and a museum with historical and geological exhibits. The monument is open all year (weather permitting), but the best time to visit is late April to late October. The visitor center is open daily 8-6, May-Sept.; 8-5, Oct. and Apr.; 9-5, rest of year. Closed Jan. 1, Thanksgiving and Christmas. Admission is $10 (per private vehicle); $5 (per person arriving by other means). The above fees permit entrance to the park for 7 calendar days from date of purchase. Annual local passes are available for $50 and permit entrance into Arches *(see place listing p. 291)* and Canyonlands *(see place listing p. 301)* national parks as well as Hovenweep National Monument *(see place listing in Colorado p. 213)*. The camping fee is $10.

For additional information contact the Superintendent, Natural Bridges National Monument, HC-60, Box 1, Lake Powell, UT 84533; phone (435) 692-1234.

NEPHI pop. 5,389

BEST WESTERN PARADISE INN OF NEPHI

(435)623-0624

Motel
$90-$115

AAA Benefit: Save 10% or more every day and earn 10% bonus points!

Address: 1025 S Main St 84648 **Location:** I-15 exit 222, 0.5 mi n. Across from train tracks. **Facility:** 40 units. 2 stories (no elevator), exterior corridors. **Terms:** 2 night minimum stay - seasonal and/or weekends. **Pool(s):** heated indoor. **Activities:** hot tub, playground.

SAVE ▮▮ ▭ BIZ 🛜 ✕ ▯ ▭ ▯ / SOME UNITS 🐾

JC MICKELSON'S RESTAURANT   435/623-0152

American. Family Dining. $6-$20 **AAA Inspector Notes:** Old-fashioned cooking and country-friendly service are to be expected at this eatery. Favorites here include homemade soups and pies as well as made-from-scratch dinner rolls and scones. **Features:** senior menu. **Address:** 2100 S Main St 84648 **Location:** I-15 exit 222, just s. ▭ B L D

NORTH SALT LAKE pop. 16,322

• **Hotels & Restaurants map & index p. 385**
• **Part of Salt Lake City area — see map p. 368**

BEST WESTERN PLUS COTTONTREE INN

(801)292-7666 **22**

Hotel
$99-$159

AAA Benefit: Save 10% or more every day and earn 10% bonus points!

Address: 1030 N 400 E 84054 **Location:** I-15 exit 315 (Woods Cross), just e to Onion St, then just s. **Facility:** 113 units. 2 stories, interior corridors. **Terms:** 2-3 night minimum stay - seasonal and/or weekends. **Amenities:** Some: safes. **Pool(s):** heated indoor. **Activities:** hot tub, recreation programs in season, exercise room. **Guest Services:** valet and coin laundry, area transportation. **Featured Amenity: full hot breakfast.**

SAVE ✚ ▮▮ CALL ▭ ▭ BIZ 🛜 ✕ ▮ ▭ / SOME UNITS 🐾

OAKLEY (B-4) pop. 1,470, elev. 6,434'

ROCKY MOUNTAIN SLEIGH CO. is 10.7 mi. n.e. on Weber Canyon Rd. from jct. SR 32, then just n.w., following signs to the Stillman Ranch. Half-hour sleigh rides in a two-horse sled take passengers along the Weber River and through meadows and woods. The sleigh's destination is a rustic log cabin at the ranch where a sumptuous, homey dinner is served before a huge, roaring fireplace. Snowmobile tours, snowshoeing tours and dog sledding also are offered.

Time: Allow 2 hours, 30 minutes minimum. **Hours:** Sleigh rides depart daily at 5 and 7 p.m., mid-Nov. through Apr. 30. **Cost:** Mid-Dec. to early Jan. sleigh ride with dinner $99; $79 (ages 3-11).Rest of season sleigh ride with dinner $89; $69 (ages 3-11). Sleigh ride only, mid-Dec. to early

Jan. $65; $50 (ages 3-11); $55, $45 (ages 3-11), rest of year. Reservations are required. **Phone:** (435) 645-7256 or (800) 303-7256. [⬛]

OGDEN (B-3) pop. 82,825, elev. 4,300'
• Hotels p. 342 • Restaurants p. 343

Ogden is one of the largest cities in Utah and an important railroad distribution center for products destined for the West Coast. The city's importance as a rail center dates from 1869, when the golden spike uniting the nation by rail was driven at Promontory, northwest of Ogden. The main rail junction was moved to Ogden soon afterward.

Mormon pioneers arrived at the confluence of the Weber and Ogden rivers soon after reaching the Great Salt Lake Valley on July 24, 1847. Named for a noted fur trapper and designed by Brigham Young, Ogden's layout incorporates broad, straight streets lined with box elder, elm and poplar trees. Late July is highlighted by the Pioneer Days Rodeo and Celebration.

Visitors can stroll the grounds of the Ogden Tabernacle and Temple, 350 22nd St. Also of interest in the city is Weber State University's Ott Planetarium, which occasionally presents free planetarium shows; phone (801) 626-6871 for the schedule.

Municipal Gardens is at 25th Street and Washington Boulevard. The park contains 5 acres of gardens, gaslit paths and picnic facilities. Between Thanksgiving and Christmas a Santa's village and an international Christmas display are presented.

Willard Bay State Park*(see Recreation Areas Chart)*, north of Ogden, offers a number of recreational activities March through November. Ogden Canyon, east on 12th Street, is known for numerous faults and erosion patterns that are of interest to both expert and novice explorers.

Golden Spike Event Center, 1000 North 1200 West, hosts rodeos, horse racing, the county fair, outdoor concerts, and soccer and softball games; phone (801) 399-8798.

Ogden/Weber Convention and Visitors Bureau: 2438 Washington Blvd., Ogden, UT 84401. **Phone:** (801) 778-6250 or (866) 867-8824.

DAUGHTERS OF UTAH PIONEERS MUSEUM AND MILES GOODYEAR CABIN is at 2104 Lincoln Ave. The site contains furnishings, clothing and handicrafts reminiscent of pioneer days. Miles Goodyear, a mountain man trapper, established the first permanent settlement in the Basin in 1836. Built in 1845, the cabin is said to be the oldest homestead in Utah. **Time:** Allow 30 minutes minimum. **Hours:** Mon.-Sat. 10-5, mid-May to early Sept. **Cost:** Free. **Phone:** (801) 393-4460.

ECCLES COMMUNITY ART CENTER is at 2580 Jefferson Ave. The center displays visual works in various media by Utah artists. **Hours:** Mon.-Fri. 9-5 (also first Fri. of the month 5-9), Sat. 9-3. Closed major holidays. **Cost:** Free. **Phone:** (801) 392-6935.

FORT BUENAVENTURA is off I-15, then e. to 2450 A Ave. The park contains a replica of the 1836 stockade and cabins built by trapper Miles Goodyear. Wooden pegs and mortise and tenon joints were used instead of nails in the construction of the stockade. Fishing and canoeing are permitted. Hiking trails are available. *See Recreation Areas Chart.*

Time: Allow 30 minutes minimum. **Hours:** Park open daily 8-8, Apr.-Nov. Visitor center open daily 9-5, Apr.-Nov. **Cost:** $1; free (ages 0-5). Camping $18. Canoe rental $5 (1 hour); $3 (half-hour). **Phone:** (801) 399-8099. [🄰] [🄰]

GEORGE S. ECCLES DINOSAUR PARK is at 1544 E. Park Blvd. The park features replicas of prehistoric creatures such as crawlers, dinosaurs, flying reptiles and marine animals from the Permian through the Jurassic and Cretaceous eras. An exhibit hall displays dinosaur bones and other prehistoric objects.

Time: Allow 1 hour, 30 minutes minimum. **Hours:** Mon.-Sat. 10-8, Sun. 10-6, Memorial Day-Labor Day; daily 10-6, late Mar.-day before Memorial Day and day after Labor Day-Oct. 29; Tues.-Sat. 10-5, rest of year. Last admission 1 hour before closing. Closed Jan. 1, Thanksgiving, Christmas Eve and Christmas; closed at 4, July 4. **Cost:** $7; $6 (ages 13-17 and 62+); $5 (ages 2-12). **Phone:** (801) 393-3466.

HILL AEROSPACE MUSEUM, e. of I-15 exit 338 on Hill Air Force Base, displays aircraft, missiles, engines, bombs and other weapons in more than 100 indoor and outdoor exhibits. More than 80 military aircraft, including a B-1 bomber, B-17 bomber, B-29 Superfortress, B-52 bomber, C-47 cargo plane, C-119 Flying Boxcar, HH-3 Jolly Green Giant helicopter and an SR71 Blackbird, are showcased.

Changing films include the story of the recovery and restoration of a P-38 airplane that crashed in Alaska. **Time:** Allow 2 hours minimum. **Hours:** Tues.-Sat. 9-4:30. Closed Jan. 1, July 4, Christmas Eve and Christmas. Phone ahead to confirm schedule. **Cost:** Free. **Phone:** (801) 777-6818 or (801) 777-6868. [🄰]

OGDEN NATURE CENTER, 966 W. 12th St., is a nature preserve and community education center featuring hands-on exhibits as well as native Utah animals and nonreleasable birds of prey. The grounds, gardens and ponds provide shelter and natural habitat for various birds, insects and small mammals. The 152-acre site also has 1.5 miles of easy walking trails, two tree houses, two green buildings and an observation tower. **Time:** Allow 1 hour minimum. **Hours:** Mon.-Fri. 9-5, Sat. 9-4. Closed major holidays. **Cost:** $5; $4 (ages 62+); $3 (ages 2-11). **Phone:** (801) 621-7595. [🄰]

OGDEN UNION STATION MUSEUMS, 2501 Wall Ave., houses four museums and two art galleries in Ogden's former 1924 train station.

The John M. Browning Firearms Museum displays the well-known handguns, rifles and machine guns created by Ogden's Browning family. The Utah State Railroad Museum interprets the state's railroad history and includes the Wattis-Dumke Model Railroad Museum featuring model trains that highlight the transcontinental line from California to Wyoming. The Eccles Rail Center outdoor exhibit features vintage engines and cars. The Browning-Kimball Classic Car Museum exhibits a collection of elegant early 20th-century automobiles. The Utah Cowboy and Western Heritage Museum includes artifacts and photographs. The Archive Hall features the station's permanent art collection.

Time: Allow 1 hour, 30 minutes minimum. **Hours:** Mon.-Sat. 10-5. Closed Jan. 1, Thanksgiving, Christmas Eve and Christmas. **Cost:** $5; $4 (students ages 13+ and ages 62+); $3 (ages 2-12); $15 (family, two adults and up to eight children). **Phone:** (801) 393-9886. GT

TREEHOUSE CHILDREN'S MUSEUM is at 347 22nd St. The hands-on museum offers the younger set interactive exhibits with an emphasis on stories and family literacy. There is also is a tree house to climb, a storybook village to explore and a chance to travel back in time to experience Utah's history. **Time:** Allow 2 hours minimum. **Hours:** Mon.-Sat. 10-5 (also Fri. 5-8), June-Aug. and holidays; Tues.-Sat. 10-5 (also Fri. 5-8), Mon. 10-3, rest of year. Closed Jan. 1, July 4 and 24, 3 weeks in mid-Sept., Thanksgiving and Christmas. **Cost:** $7 (ages 1-12); $5 (adults). **Phone:** (801) 394-9663.

ALASKAN INN BED & BREAKFAST   (801)621-8600
▼▼▼ **Bed & Breakfast** $125-$355 **Address:** 435 Ogden Canyon 84401 **Location:** I-15 exit 344 (12th St), 7.5 mi e. **Facility:** Located in Ogden Canyon among lofty pines and granite-crested mountains, this romantic inn features Arctic-inspired guest rooms and luxuriously appointed cabins. All units have an oversize jetted tub. 23 units, some cabins. 1-2 stories (no elevator), interior/exterior corridors. **Terms:** check-in 4 pm, age restrictions may apply, cancellation fee imposed. [icons]

BEST WESTERN PLUS CANYON PINES - SOUTH OGDEN/UINTAH   (801)675-5534

Hotel
$90-$120

AAA Benefit: Save 10% or more every day and earn 10% bonus points!

Address: 6650 S Hwy 89 84405 **Location:** I-84 exit 87 (US 89/South Ogden), 0.6 mi n. Located in a commercial area. **Facility:** 52 units. 3 stories, interior corridors. **Pool(s):** heated indoor. **Activities:** hot tub, exercise room. **Guest Services:** valet and coin laundry. **Featured Amenity:** full hot breakfast.

[icons]

BEST WESTERN PLUS HIGH COUNTRY INN   (801)394-9474

Hotel
$79-$170

AAA Benefit: Save 10% or more every day and earn 10% bonus points!

Address: 1335 W 12th St 84404 **Location:** I-15 exit 344 (12th St), just e. Located near train tracks. **Facility:** 109 units. 2 stories (no elevator), interior/exterior corridors. **Parking:** winter plug-ins. **Dining:** Jeremiah's Restaurant, see separate listing. **Pool(s):** heated outdoor. **Activities:** hot tub, exercise room. **Guest Services:** valet and coin laundry.

[icons]

COMFORT SUITES   (801)621-2545
▼▼▼ **Hotel** $84-$159 **Address:** 2250 S 1200 W 84401 **Location:** I-15 exit 343 (21st St), 0.3 mi e. **Facility:** 142 units. 3 stories, interior corridors. **Pool(s):** heated indoor. **Activities:** hot tub, exercise room. **Guest Services:** valet and coin laundry.

[icons]

COURTYARD BY MARRIOTT   (801)627-1190
▼▼▼ **Hotel** $91-$186 **Address:** 247 24th St 84401 **Location:** I-15 exit 341 (31st St), 0.7 mi e, 1 mi n, then just e; exit 343 (21st St), 2 mi e to Wall Ave, 0.4 mi s, then just e. **Facility:** 193 units.

AAA Benefit: Members save 5% or more!

8 stories, interior corridors. **Pool(s):** heated indoor. **Activities:** hot tub, exercise room. **Guest Services:** valet and coin laundry, boarding pass kiosk.

[icons]

HAMPTON INN & SUITES   (801)394-9400
▼▼▼ **Historic Hotel** $89-$219 **Address:** 2401 Washington Blvd 84401 **Location:** I-15 exit northbound exit 342 (24th St), 1.5 mi e; southbound exit 343 (21st St), 2 mi e to Wall Ave, 0.4 mi s,

AAA Benefit: Members save up to 10%!

then 0.4 mi e; at 24th St and Washington Blvd. **Facility:** This downtown hotel features a luxurious lobby with fascinating architectural features, an array of well-appointed guest rooms and beautiful bathrooms, some with a jetted bathtub. 124 units. 8 stories, interior corridors. **Parking:** on-site and valet. **Terms:** 1-7 night minimum stay, cancellation fee imposed. **Activities:** hot tub, exercise room. **Guest Services:** valet and coin laundry.

[icons]

HILTON GARDEN INN OGDEN   (801)399-2000
▼▼▼ **Hotel** $109-$179 **Address:** 2271 S Washington Blvd 84401 **Location:** I-15 exit 342 (24th St), 1.5 mi e, then just n. Across from Salomon Entertainment Center. **Facility:** 120 units. 4

AAA Benefit: Members save up to 10%!

stories, interior corridors. **Terms:** 1-7 night minimum stay, cancellation fee imposed. **Pool(s):** heated indoor. **Activities:** hot tub, exercise room. **Guest Services:** valet and coin laundry.

[icons]

HOLIDAY INN EXPRESS & SUITES   (801)392-5000
▼▼▼ **Hotel** $89-$199 **Address:** 2245 S 1200 W 84401 **Location:** I-15 exit 343 (21st St), 0.3 mi e. **Facility:** 75 units. 3 stories, interior corridors. **Pool(s):** heated indoor. **Activities:** hot tub, exercise room. **Guest Services:** valet and coin laundry.

[icons]

SLEEP INN OGDEN   (801)731-6500

WWW WWW ◆◆
Hotel
$65-$125

Address: 1155 S 1700 W 84404 **Location:** I-15 exit 344 (12th St), just w. Across from truck stop. **Facility:** 65 units. 2 stories (no elevator), interior corridors. *Bath:* shower only. **Parking:** winter plug-ins. **Activities:** exercise equipment. **Guest Services:** coin laundry. **Featured Amenity: full hot breakfast.**

SAVE [¶↑] [BIZ] 🛜 [💻]
/ SOME UNITS [🐾] [🗄] [🖨]

VALUE PLACE   801/334-8628

W **Extended Stay Motel.** Rates not provided. **Address:** 2160 S 1200 W 84401 **Location:** I-15 exit 343 (21st St), 0.3 mi e. **Facility:** 124 efficiencies. 4 stories, interior corridors. **Guest Services:** coin laundry. [¶↑] 🛜 [🗄] [🖨]

WHERE TO EAT

A GOOD LIFE CAFE & JUICE BAR   801/394-1020

W W **Natural/Organic. Casual Dining. $7-$14 AAA Inspector Notes:** Using all-natural ingredients, this eatery offers a varied menu that includes whole or half build-your-own sandwiches, a yummy quinoa salad, seasonal winter and summer soups, smoothies and build-your-own juices where you pick a base and then add three items. Locals favor the acai bowls, spinach salad, mac 'n' cheese and the carrot cake. Vegetarian and vegan options are available. **Features:** beer & wine, patio dining. **Address:** 274 25th St 84401 **Location:** Jct 25th St and Grant Ave; downtown. **Parking:** street only.

[B] [L]

BISTRO 258   801/394-1595

W W W **American. Casual Dining. $9-$27 AAA Inspector Notes:** Tucked in along historic 25th Street, this bistro serves certified Angus steak, popular pasta dishes, chicken and seafood entrées in a cozy dining room and on an outdoor patio. Gluten-free and vegetarian items are available. **Features:** full bar, patio dining. **Address:** 258 25th St 84401 **Location:** I-15 exit 343 (21st St), 2.3 mi e, 0.6 mi s on Wall Ave, then just e. [L] [D]

GOLDEN DYNASTY   801/621-6789

W W **Chinese. Family Dining. $6-$10 AAA Inspector Notes:** All the favorites can be savored at both lunch and dinner in a comfortable, friendly setting. **Features:** Sunday brunch. **Address:** 3433 Washington Blvd 84401 **Location:** I-15 exit 341A (31st St), 1.5 mi e, then 0.5 mi s. [L] [D]

GRAY CLIFF LODGE RESTAURANT   801/392-6775

W W **American. Casual Dining. $11-$45 AAA Inspector Notes:** People travel for miles to enjoy the ride up breathtaking Ogden Canyon and to experience the cozy atmosphere in this historic 1912 grand old house. Traditional dinners include a fruit cup or tomato juice, salad or soup, baked potato, cinnamon rolls and a choice of chicken, prime rib, filet mignon, lamb chops, Alaskan king crab legs, fresh local trout filleted at the table and more. Although varied desserts are offered, oatmeal pie is a favorite. **Features:** full bar, senior menu, Sunday brunch. **Address:** 508 Ogden Canyon Rd 84401 **Location:** I-15 exit 344 (12th St), 9 mi e. [D]

THE GREENERY RESTAURANT   801/392-1777

W W **American. Casual Dining. $8-$16 AAA Inspector Notes:** At the mouth of Ogden Canyon, this bright eatery with black-and-white tile and red café chairs is famous for its Mormon muffin and gabby-crabby sandwich. Children have their own menu, and everyone can feast on appetizers, salads, soups and dishes such as chicken penne pesto. **Features:** beer & wine. **Address:** 1875 Valley Dr 84401 **Location:** I-15 exit 344 (12th St), 4.8 mi e. [L] [D]

HARLEY & BUCKS GREAT AMERICAN CUISINE   801/745-2060

W W **American. Casual Dining. $8-$28 AAA Inspector Notes:** In the heart of downtown Ogden, this trendy restaurant offers a fresh oyster bar on select evenings. Choices such as crab cakes, rolled and seared ahi tuna, hardwood smoked beef brisket, buffalo burgers, and fried shrimp lead up to desserts such as apple walnut cobbler a la mode. Lots of gluten-free items are available. **Features:** full bar, Sunday brunch. **Address:** 2432 Washington Blvd 84401 **Location:** I-15 exit 243 (21st St), 1.5 mi e to Wall Ave, 0.6 mi s to 25th St, 0.4 mi e, then just n. **Parking:** on-site and street. [L] [D] CALL[🔊M]

JEREMIAH'S RESTAURANT   801/394-3273

W W **American. Casual Dining. $8-$17 AAA Inspector Notes:** Known for its all-day breakfast menu, the restaurant also serves good-size lunches and dinners to appreciative locals and tourists. Some menu items consist of fresh local trout, bison from Antelope Island and chicken tenders served with coleslaw and beans. Their signature Southwest chicken tortilla soup is a hit! **Features:** full bar. **Address:** 1307 W 12th St 84404 **Location:** I-15 exit 344 (12th St), just e; next to BEST WESTERN PLUS High Country Inn. [B] [L] [D]

PRAIRIE SCHOONER STEAK HOUSE   801/621-5511

W W **Steak Seafood. Casual Dining. $10-$55 AAA Inspector Notes:** Patrons dine inside a real covered wagon next to an open prairie fire as they enjoy popular favorites such as deep-fried mushrooms, country-fried steak, Alaskan snow and king crab, bacon-wrapped filet mignon and signature desserts. All entrées are served with yummy prairie bread, soup or salad, seasonal vegetables and several options for a starch, including baked yam with cinnamon butter. Stop in for their express lunch special. **Features:** full bar. **Reservations:** suggested. **Address:** 445 Park Blvd 84401 **Location:** I-15 exit 342 (24th St), 1.5 mi e to Washington Blvd, 0.3 mi n, then just e. [L] [D] CALL[🔊M]

RICKENBACKER'S STEAK HOUSE   801/627-4100

W W **Seafood Steak. Casual Dining. $9-$29 AAA Inspector Notes:** Watch airplanes take off and land and soak up the amazing views of the mountains while enjoying shepherd's pie, pistachio-crusted halibut or prime-grade bone-in-tenderloin. Several vegetarian and pasta selections are available, and the list of wine has been carefully chosen to complement the cuisine. **Features:** full bar. **Address:** 4282 S 1650 W 84405 **Location:** I-15 exit 341 (31st St), 0.3 mi w, 2 mi s on Airport Rd, 1st exit at roundabout, then just w.
[L] [D] CALL[🔊M]

ROOSTERS 25TH STREET BREWING CO & RESTAURANT   801/627-6171

W W **American. Casual Dining. $7-$22 AAA Inspector Notes:** Located on historic 25th Street, this friendly pub features specialty beers brewed on-site along with chicken, seafood, steak, pasta and beer-battered fish and chips. **Features:** full bar, patio dining. **Address:** 253 25th St 84401 **Location:** I-15 exit 342 (24th St), 1.5 mi e; in historic downtown. [L] [D]

ROVALI'S RISTORANTE ITALIANO   801/394-1070

W W **Italian. Casual Dining. $8-$16 AAA Inspector Notes:** This casual restaurant has an upbeat atmosphere, old-world charm and walls adorned with colorful posters of jazz musicians. Pasta dinners include lasagna, Mizithra, pesto, ravioli, linguine and clams. Watch out for the glass dessert case next to the espresso bar—it's filled with tempting chilled desserts, all made in-house. Gluten-free options, vegetarian sauces and a children's menu are available. **Features:** full bar, patio dining. **Address:** 174 25th St 84401 **Location:** I-15 exit 341 (31st St), 0.8 mi e to Wall Ave, 0.8 mi n, then just e; in historic downtown. **Parking:** street only. [L] [D]

RUBY RIVER STEAKHOUSE   801/622-2320

W **Steak. Family Dining. $10-$30 AAA Inspector Notes:** Guests can nibble on peanuts from the shell before their meal or while watching the game in the lounge. Menu choices range from steaks and ribs to chicken and pasta. The atmosphere is fun. **Features:** full bar. **Address:** 4286 Riverdale Rd 84405 **Location:** I-15 exit 339 (Riverdale Rd), 2.2 mi e. [L] [D]

SLACKWATER PUB & PIZZERIA
801/399-0637

▼▼ ▼▼ American. Gastropub. $9-$14 **AAA Inspector Notes:** Next to the river, this pub will quickly become one of your favorites when passing through Ogden. Whatever they prepare, it is delicious, including more than 90 high-point bottle options. The brick oven-roasted garlic heads are an absolute must. The nice selection of creative and colorful salads, artisan-style pizza, tasty sandwiches and to-die-for desserts are for you to enjoy. **Features:** full bar, patio dining. **Address:** 1895 Washington Blvd 84401 **Location:** I-15 exit 343 (21st St), 2.2 mi e, then 0.3 mi n. L D

SONORA GRILL
801/393-1999

▼▼ ▼▼ Mexican. Casual Dining. $9-$20 **AAA Inspector Notes:** Patrons will enjoy the comfortable ambience where watching the delicious guacamole made tableside and eating the huge tortilla chips with two kinds of salsa is part of the fun. Menu offerings include ceviche, lettuce-wrap tacos, fajitas and achiote salmon, all made with authentic ingredients. Vegan and gluten-free items are available. **Features:** full bar, patio dining. **Address:** 2310 S Kiesel Ave 84401 **Location:** I-15 exit 342 (24th St), 1.5 mi e, then just n; at Kiesel Ave and 23rd St. **Parking:** street only. L D CALL &M

TWO BIT STREET CAFE
801/393-1225

▼▼ ▼▼ American. Casual Dining. $9-$22 **AAA Inspector Notes:** This restaurant also is an antique shop. You can sit at a table or cozy up to the bar where there are plenty of stools. Try the Scottish eggs, smoked salmon crostini, citrus-glazed organic chicken, seared pork tenderloin or a steak with sautéed mushrooms. **Features:** beer & wine, patio dining. **Address:** 126 25th St 84401 **Location:** I-15 exit 341 (31st St), 0.8 mi e to Wall Ave, 0.8 mi n, then just e; in historic downtown. **Parking:** street only. L D

UNION GRILL RESTAURANT
801/621-2830

▼▼ ▼▼ American. Casual Dining. $8-$19 **AAA Inspector Notes:** Classic. In an historic train station, authentic Mexican along with American, Cajun, Greek and Italian specialties are created daily. Popular menu items include the margarita nachos, blackened shrimp spring salad, chicken cucumber lettuce wraps, and a classic meatloaf dinner. Making room for their famous bread pudding or mud pie will be a good decision. **Features:** full bar. **Address:** 2501 Wall Ave 84401 **Location:** I-15 exit 341 (31st St), west end of 25th St; downtown; in Union Station. L D

ZUCCA TRATTORIA
801/475-7077

▼▼ ▼▼ Italian. Casual Dining. $8-$28 **AAA Inspector Notes:** Menu items include rigatoni with house-made fennel sausage, grilled pork loin with porcini mushroom sauce and antipasti with sopressata, pistachio mortadella, pancetta and prosciutto. Neapolitan-style pizza is made in a Valoriani wood-fired oven from Italy. **Features:** full bar. **Address:** 1479 E 5600 S 84403 **Location:** I-15 exit 341 (31st St), just w of Harrison Blvd and 5600 S. L D

OREM pop. 88,328

FAIRFIELD INN & SUITES BY MARRIOTT OREM
(801)225-9009

[fyi] Hotel $85-$187 Too new to rate, opening scheduled for March 2016. **Address:** 901 N 1200 W 84057 **Location:** I-15 exit 272 (800 N), just e, then just n. **Amenities:** 77 units, coffeemakers, microwaves, refrigerators, pool, exercise facility.

AAA Benefit:
Members save 5% or more!

HAMPTON INN & SUITES - PROVO/OREM
(801)426-8500

▼▼ ▼▼ Hotel $79-$199 **Address:** 851 W 1250 S 84058 **Location:** I-15 exit 269 (University Pkwy), 0.3 mi e, then just s. **Facility:** 129 units, some kitchens. 4 stories, interior corridors. **Terms:** 1-7 night minimum stay, cancellation fee imposed. **Pool(s):** heated indoor. **Activities:** hot tub, picnic facilities, exercise room. **Guest Services:** valet and coin laundry.

AAA Benefit:
Members save up to 10%!

[†] CALL &M ⟶ BIZ 🛜 ✕ 🖨 🖼 🖵

Visit AAA.com/searchfordiscounts to save on travel, shopping, dining and attractions

HOLIDAY INN EXPRESS & SUITES - PROVO/OREM
801/655-1515

▼▼ ▼▼ Hotel. Rates not provided. **Address:** 1290 W University Pkwy 84058 **Location:** I-15 exit 269 (University Pkwy), 0.5 mi w. **Facility:** 122 units. 4 stories, interior corridors. **Pool(s):** heated indoor. **Activities:** hot tub, game room, exercise room. **Guest Services:** valet and coin laundry, boarding pass kiosk.

[†] CALL &M ⟶ BIZ HS 🛜 ✕ 🖨 🖼 🖵 / SOME UNITS 🆂

TOWNEPLACE SUITES BY MARRIOTT - PROVO/OREM
(801)225-4477

▼▼ ▼▼ **Extended Stay Hotel** $89-$155 **Address:** 873 N 1200 W 84057 **Location:** I-15 exit 272 (800 N), just e. Located in commercial area. **Facility:** 100 efficiencies, some two bedrooms and kitchens. 4 stories, interior corridors. **Pool(s):** heated indoor. **Activities:** hot tub, picnic facilities, exercise room. **Guest Services:** valet and coin laundry.

AAA Benefit:
Members save 5% or more!

CALL &M ⟶ BIZ HS 🛜 ✕ 🖨 🖼 🖵 / SOME UNITS 🆂

WHERE TO EAT

BANGKOK GRILL
801/434-8424

▼▼ ▼▼ Thai. Casual Dining. $9-$15 **AAA Inspector Notes:** This treat of a restaurant is just off State Street in a small strip mall. The menu is diverse and features affordable lunch specials. The Thai meatballs from the barbecue section are recommended, as is the fried banana with mango ice cream for dessert. **Address:** 338 E 800 S 84097 **Location:** I-15 exit 269 (University Pkwy) northbound, 1.5 mi e, then 0.6 mi n; exit 271 southbound, 1.6 mi e, then 0.3 mi s. L D

KNEADERS BAKERY & CAFE
801/764-9451

▼ Breads/Pastries Sandwiches. Quick Serve. $5-$8 **AAA Inspector Notes:** Prompt, pleasant servers buzz through the dining room with great cups of soup, quality sandwiches on artisan breads and a wide selection of tempting pastries and other desserts. **Features:** patio dining. **Address:** 1960 N State St 84057 **Location:** I-15 exit 273 (1600 N), 1.3 mi e, then 0.5 mi n; at E 200 S and N State St. L D

P.F. CHANG'S CHINA BISTRO
801/426-0900

▼▼ ▼▼ Chinese. Fine Dining. $9-$26 **AAA Inspector Notes:** Trendy, upscale decor provides a pleasant backdrop for New Age Chinese dining. Appetizers, soups and salads are a meal by themselves. Vegetarian plates and sides, noodles, chow meins, chicken and meat dishes are created from exotic, fresh ingredients. **Features:** full bar, patio dining, happy hour. **Address:** 575 E University Pkwy, Suite A-20 84097 **Location:** I-15 exit 269 (University Pkwy), 2.3 mi e; south side of University Mall. L D

PIZZERIA SEVEN TWELVE
801/623-6712

▼▼ ▼▼ Pizza Small Plates. Casual Dining. $9-$16 **AAA Inspector Notes:** Seasonal small-plate selections highlight the menu and may include crunchy polenta beneath tender short ribs braised low and slow in a cooler section of the wood-fired oven or wood-roasted Brussels sprouts with toasted hazelnuts, bacon and vinegar. A wide selection of ingredients is available as toppings on the thin-crust pizza. I chose the pomegranate panna cotta for dessert but will be back to savor the Amano chocolate pudding. **Features:** beer & wine, patio dining. **Reservations:** suggested. **Address:** 320 S State St, Suite 185 84058 **Location:** I-15 exit 272 (800 N), 1.3 mi e to State St, then 1.5 mi s (on west side). L D

TERRA MIA RISTORANTE
801/226-4757

▼ Pizza Sandwiches. Quick Serve. $9-$13 **AAA Inspector Notes:** This restaurant offers casual dining in a simplistic and spacious atmosphere. Menu items include salads, a tasty mushroom dill soup, sandwiches, pizza and traditional Italian desserts. It is easy to become a devoted fan of the gelato bar. **Features:** patio dining. **Address:** 1050 S 750 E 84097 **Location:** I-15 exit 269 (University Pkwy), 2.3 mi e to S 800 E, 0.3 mi n to E 1000 S, just w, then just n; across from the theater. L D CALL &M

OURAY (C-6) elev. 4,650'

Off SR 88 near Ouray is the Ouray National Wildlife Refuge. This largely undeveloped refuge along the Green River is home to large numbers of waterfowl as well as eagles, hawks, pheasants and deer. Visitors can walk or drive through the area, which is open daily; phone (435) 545-2522.

PANGUITCH (F-3) pop. 1,520, elev. 6,560'
• Part of Bryce Canyon National Park area — see map p. 300

The name Panguitch comes from the Paiute Indian word for "big fish," many of which were caught at nearby Panguitch Lake. This ranching community offers access to the colorful and remote "Inner Utah" of the Kaiparowits Plateau region. The city's historic district is peppered with shops and museums as well as historic homes, which feature red bricks fired in the community kiln years ago.

Garfield County Travel Council: 55 S. Main St., P.O. Box 200, Panguitch, UT 84759. **Phone:** (435) 676-1161 or (800) 444-6689.

Self-guiding tours: A self-guiding, 45-minute walking tour of the area, featuring the Garfield County Courthouse and the Social Hall (Panguitch Playhouse) among other notable sights, is available from the travel council.

PANGUITCH-ESCALANTE-BOULDER   SCENIC DRIVE begins off US 89 at SR 12 and traverses Bryce Canyon for 124 miles. SR 12 borders a large, unsurveyed wilderness area. The Kaiparowits Plateau's vividly colored canyons and rock formations contrast with the heavy forest of the Aquarius Plateau; Native American ruins and pictographs can be seen. Near Escalante are extensive deposits of colorful petrified wood. Hells Backbone, between Escalante and Boulder, offers spectacular views.

BLUE SPRINGS LODGE AT PANGUITCH LAKE   435/676-2277
▼▼ Cabin $95-$215 **Address:** 120 W Hwy 143 84759 **Location:** Jct US 89, 18 mi sw. **Facility:** 6 cabins. 1 story, exterior corridors. *Bath:* shower only. **Terms:** 2 night minimum stay - seasonal and/or weekends, 14 day cancellation notice-fee imposed. **Activities:** fishing, playground.

WHERE TO EAT

COWBOY'S SMOKEHOUSE CAFE'   435/676-8030
▼▼ Barbecue. Casual Dining. $6-$20 **AAA Inspector Notes:** A cowboy style complete with Western artifacts and game trophies characterize this restaurant's dining room. On the menu are mesquite-smoked barbecued beef brisket, pork ribs, chicken, turkey and steak. **Features:** beer only. **Address:** 95 N Main St 84759 **Location:** Just n. **Parking:** street only. L D X

FLYING M RESTAURANT   435/676-8008
▼ American. Family Dining. $6-$19 **AAA Inspector Notes:** The restaurant offers a down-home American menu with specialties of homemade turkey pot pie and buttermilk pancakes, in addition to made-from-scratch pastries, breads and sauces. **Features:** beer & wine. **Address:** 614 N Main St 84759 **Location:** 0.5 mi n. B L D

HAROLD'S PLACE RESTAURANT   435/676-2350
▼ American. Casual Dining. $11-$18 **AAA Inspector Notes:** The rustic setting evokes a casual feel with a sampling of varied menu items such as walnut-crusted trout and Southwest chicken breast. **Features:** beer only. **Address:** 3066 E Hwy 12 84759 **Location:** Jct US 89 and SR 12, 0.5 mi e; in Harold's Place Inn & Cabins. B D X

PARK CITY (B-4) pop. 7,558, elev. 6,911'
• Hotels p. 349 • Restaurants p. 352
• Hotels & Restaurants map & index p. 347

When three off-duty soldiers discovered silver in the mountains above Park City in the 1870s, they started a rush that produced millions of dollars' worth of the metal from mines in the surrounding area. Since the early 1960s, another natural resource has made Park City a popular destination for skiers: snow, and lots of it. In 2002 this small town became part of Olympic Winter Games history. Fourteen Olympic medal events, including bobsledding, luge and ski jumping, thrilled more than 300,000 spectators at Utah Olympic Park *(see attraction listing)*. Park City, or P.C. as it's known to locals, also is the home of the U.S. Ski and Snowboard Association.

Park City is a year-round recreational community as well as a resort town. Winter sports include cross-country and downhill skiing, snowboarding and snowshoeing. Horseback riding, mountain biking, golf and hiking are popular in snow-free months. The 28-mile Historic Union Pacific Rail Trail winds its way along I-80 through Coalville and Wanship and is open year-round for hikers, mountain bikers, joggers, skiers and equestrians; phone (435) 649-6839.

A variety of festivals to please many tastes are scattered throughout the year. The Sundance Institute premieres the works of independent filmmakers at the 🎥 Sundance Film Festival in mid- to late January. Wine, culinary and ski festivals are combined in March's Red, White and Snow. Starting in late March, The Canyons resort (now part of Park City Mountain Resort) hosts Spring Grüv, a 10-day festival offering free rock, reggae and R&B concerts.

Celebrate the arts at the Park City Kimball Arts Festival in August. The Miner's Day Parade and Celebration in September pays tribute to Park City's beginnings; mucking and drilling competitions showcase 19th-century mining techniques. The Deer Valley Music Festival in July and August brings a blend of performances by the Utah Symphony and the Utah Opera.

The year ends with a flurry of holiday festivals in December, including Santa on the Slopes; Christmas Eve at Park City Mountain Resort, featuring caroling, synchronized skiing, torchlight parades and sleigh rides; Deer Valley Celebrity Skifest; and a New Year's Celebration.

In a city where a car can be more of a hindrance than a help, a leisurely walk is a stress-free way to while away some time. Head down to Main Street, where a stroll past its shops of brightly painted 19th-century facades that hearken to the Old West provides a pleasant interlude between or prelude to lunch or dinner.

(See map & index p. 347.)

Park City Convention and Visitors Bureau: 1850 Sidewinder Dr., Suite 320, P.O. Box 1630, Park City, UT 84060. **Phone:** (435) 649-6100 or (800) 453-1360.

Shopping: [SAVE] Tanger Outlets, 6699 N. Landmark Dr., offers more than 60 outlet stores including Ann Taylor, Banana Republic, Gap and Tommy Hilfiger.

KIMBALL ART CENTER is at 1401 Kearns Blvd. The center features three galleries and displays the works of local, regional and national professional artists. Changing exhibits are presented every 5 to 7 weeks. **Time:** Allow 30 minutes minimum. **Hours:** Mon.-Thurs. 10-5, Fri. 10-7, Sat. noon-7, Sun. noon-5, Feb.-Dec. Closed major holidays. **Cost:** Free. **Phone:** (435) 649-8882.

PARK CITY MUSEUM is at 528 Main St. The museum explores the town's history and heritage. Exhibits chronicle the local silver boom, the town's days as a mining camp and Park City's skiing history. A territorial jail, or "dungeon," has been preserved in the basement. It once held several of the nation's early labor leaders.

Interactive exhibits and movies are offered, and children may go on a scavenger hunt in search of treasure. **Time:** Allow 1 hour minimum. **Hours:** Mon.-Sat. 10-7, Sun. noon-6, June-Oct. and early Dec.-Mar. 31; phone for schedule, rest of year. Closed Thanksgiving and Christmas. Phone ahead to confirm schedule. **Cost:** $10; $8 (ages 65+ and students and military with ID); $5 (ages 7-17). **Phone:** (435) 649-7457.

UTAH OLYMPIC PARK, 3419 Olympic Pkwy., served as the 2002 Olympic Winter Games venue for bobsled, skeleton, luge and Nordic ski jumping. National and international competitions are held at the 389-acre park, and athletes train here year-round. Self-guiding tours include Olympic competition sites, a ski museum and a museum devoted to the 2002 games. A guided bus tour also includes access to the ski jump and bobsled track. Depending on the season, visitors can see freestyle aerial shows and experience ziplines, adventure ropes courses, a drop tower, an alpine slide and bobsled rides.

Time: Allow 1 hour minimum. **Hours:** Daily 10-6. Guided tours are given daily on the hour 11-3, June 1-Labor Day; at 11, 1 and 3, rest of year. Closed Jan. 1, Easter, Thanksgiving and Christmas. **Cost:** Park and self-guiding tour free. Guided tour $10; $5

(ages 3-12 and 65+). Other activities are an additional fee; phone for schedules, rates and reservations. **Phone:** (435) 658-4200. [TI] [A]

2002 Eccles Winter Olympic Museum is at 3419 Olympic Pkwy. in Utah Olympic Park. The museum showcases officially licensed 2002 Olympic pins as well as 2002 Winter Olympics equipment, uniforms and medals, much of which was donated by athletes. Videos and touch screens also are featured. **Time:** Allow 30 minutes minimum. **Hours:** Daily 10-6. Closed Jan. 1, Easter, Thanksgiving and Christmas. **Cost:** Free. **Phone:** (435) 658-4240. [TI]

Alf Engen Ski Museum is in Utah Olympic Park at the Joe Quinney Winter Sports Center. Utah's ski history is highlighted through interactive displays, videos, virtual reality theaters, games and topographical maps. The museum also features ski equipment from the past as well as trophies and awards. Pictures depicting the skiing prowess of Alf Engen, a Utah native and ski pioneer, are displayed. **Time:** Allow 1 hour minimum. **Hours:** Daily 10-6. Closed Jan. 1, Easter, Thanksgiving and Christmas. **Cost:** Free. **Phone:** (435) 658-4233. [GT] [TI]

RECREATIONAL ACTIVITIES

Alpine Slides

- **Alpine Slide** is at 1345 Lowell Ave. in the Park City Mountain Resort. Other activities are offered. **Hours:** Open daily, late May to mid-Oct. Hours vary; phone ahead. **Phone:** (435) 649-8111 or (800) 222-7275.

Hot Air Ballooning

- **Skywalker Balloon Co.-Park City** departs from the Best Western Plus Landmark Inn at 6560 N. Landmark Dr. **Time:** Allow 3 hours minimum. **Hours:** Trips generally depart daily at dawn. Phone ahead to confirm schedule. **Cost:** One-hour flight $225-$250 (per person); $125-$150 (ages 4-12). Prices may vary. Reservations are required. **Phone:** (801) 824-3934.

Skiing

- **Deer Valley Resort** is at 2250 Deer Valley Dr. S. Other activities are offered. **Hours:** Open daily, early Dec. to mid-Apr. Hours vary; phone ahead. **Phone:** (435) 649-1000 or (800) 424-3337.
- **Park City Mountain Resort** is at 1345 Lowell Ave. Includes Canyons Village. Other activities are offered. **Hours:** Open daily 9-4, mid-Nov. to mid-Apr. **Phone:** (435) 649-8111 or (800) 222-7275.

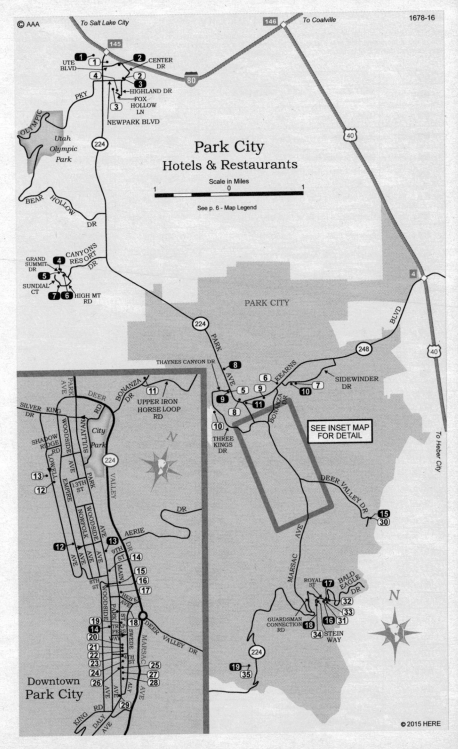

© AAA

1678-16

To Salt Lake City

To Coalville

To Heber City

Park City
Hotels & Restaurants

Scale in Miles
1   0   1

See p. 6 – Map Legend

PARK CITY

Utah
Olympic
Park

OLYMPIC PKY

BEAR HOLLOW DR

CANYONS RESORT DR

GRAND SUMMIT DR

SUNDIAL CT

HIGH MT RD

UTE BLVD

CENTER DR

HIGHLAND DR

FOX HOLLOW LN

NEWPARK BLVD

THAYNES CANYON DR

PARK AVE

KEARNS

SIDEWINDER DR

BONANZA DR

THREE KINGS DR

SEE INSET MAP
FOR DETAIL

DEER VALLEY DR

MARSAC AVE

ROYAL ST

BALD EAGLE DR

GUARDSMAN CONNECTION RD

STEIN WAY

Downtown
Park City

SILVER KING DR

PARK AVE

DEER

BONANZA DR

City
Park

UPPER IRON HORSE LOOP RD

SHADOW RIDGE RD

WOODSIDE AVE

LOWELL AVE

EMPIRE AVE

13TH ST

NORFOLK AVE

WOODSIDE AVE

PARK VALLEY DR

AERIE DR

9TH ST

MAIN ST

HEB'S ST

8TH ST

WOODSIDE

PARK AVE

SWEDE ALY

H ST

TRIPPERS WAY

MARSAC AVE

DEER VALLEY DR

ALY

AVE

KING RD

DALY AVE

N

N

© 2015 HERE

Park City

This index helps you "spot" where approved hotels and restaurants are located on the corresponding detailed maps. Hotel daily rate range is for comparison only. Restaurant price range is a combination of lunch and/or dinner. Turn to the listing page for more detailed rate and price information and consult display ads for special promotions.

PARK CITY

Map Page	Hotels	Diamond Rated	Rate Range	Page
1 p. 347	**BEST WESTERN PLUS Landmark Inn & Pancake House**	◈◈	$129-$239 [SAVE]	349
2 p. 347	Holiday Inn Express & Suites	◈◈◈	Rates not provided	350
3 p. 347	Newpark Resort Hotel & Conference Center	◈◈◈	Rates not provided	350
4 p. 347	**Grand Summit Hotel**	◈◈◈	$131-$4188 [SAVE]	350
5 p. 347	Sundial Lodge, Park City Resort at Canyons Village	◈◈◈	Rates not provided	352
6 p. 347	**Westgate Park City Resort & Spa**	◈◈◈◈	Rates not provided [SAVE]	352
7 p. 347	**Hyatt Escala Lodge at Park City**	◈◈◈◈	$139-$799 [SAVE]	350
8 p. 347	Park City Peaks Hotel	◈◈	Rates not provided	351
9 p. 347	**Hotel Park City, Autograph Collection**	◈◈◈◈	$161-$664 [SAVE]	350
10 p. 347	**Park City Marriott**	◈◈◈	$106-$320 [SAVE]	351
11 p. 347	DoubleTree by Hilton Hotel Park City Â- The Yarrow	◈◈◈	Rates not provided	349
12 p. 347	Old Town Guest House Bed & Breakfast	◈◈	Rates not provided	350
13 p. 347	Park Station Condominium Hotel	◈◈	Rates not provided	351
14 p. 347	Washington School House, A Luxury Boutique Hotel	◈◈◈	Rates not provided	352
15 p. 347	**St. Regis Deer Valley** (See ad p. 351.)	◈◈◈◈◈	$299-$2200 [SAVE]	351
16 p. 347	**Goldener Hirsch Inn**	◈◈◈◈	$169-$1474 [SAVE]	349
17 p. 347	**The Chateaux Deer Valley**	◈◈◈◈	$179-$720 [SAVE]	349
18 p. 347	**Stein Eriksen Lodge Deer Valley**	◈◈◈◈	$235-$850 [SAVE]	352
19 p. 347	Montage Deer Valley	◈◈◈◈◈	$265-$2295	350

Map Page	Restaurants	Diamond Rated	Cuisine	Price Range	Page
1 p. 347	Loco Lizard Cantina	◈◈	Mexican	$8-$18	354
2 p. 347	Maxwell's East Coast Eatery	◈◈	Italian	$12-$21	354
3 p. 347	Sushi Blue	◈◈	Asian Fusion	$10-$22	354
4 p. 347	Ghidotti's Classic Italian Restaurant	◈◈◈	Italian	$12-$37	353
5 p. 347	Ruth's Chris Steak House	◈◈◈	Steak	$35-$70	354
6 p. 347	Adolph's Restaurant	◈◈◈	Swiss	$16-$43	352
7 p. 347	Fuego Bistro & Pizzeria	◈◈	Italian	$9-$20	353
8 p. 347	Squatters Roadhouse Grill & Pub	◈◈	American	$9-$21	354
9 p. 347	Blind Dog Restaurant & Sushi	◈◈◈	Steak Seafood	$16-$35	353
10 p. 347	Silver Star Cafe	◈◈◈	Regional American	$10-$27	354
11 p. 347	Windy Ridge Cafe	◈◈	American	$9-$28	355
12 p. 347	Baja Cantina	◈◈	Mexican	$8-$28	352
13 p. 347	The Viking Yurt at Park City Mountain Resort	◈◈◈	Norwegian	$125-$175	354
14 p. 347	Flying Sumo Sushi Bar & Grill	◈◈	Sushi	$13-$22	353
15 p. 347	Reef's Restaurant & Gallery	◈◈	Mediterranean	$20-$28	354
16 p. 347	High West Distillery & Saloon	◈◈◈	New American	$11-$55	353

Map Page	Restaurants (cont'd)	Diamond Rated	Cuisine	Price Range	Page
⑰ p. 347	Zoom	◈◈	American	$12-$39	355
⑱ p. 347	Wahso Asian Grill	◈◈◈	Asian	$27-$40	354
⑲ p. 347	**Riverhorse on Main**	◈◈◈	American	$32-$55	354
⑳ p. 347	Shabu	◈◈◈	Asian	$10-$45	354
㉑ p. 347	Cafe Terigo	◈◈	American	$10-$32	353
㉒ p. 347	Bistro 412	◈◈	French	$12-$38	353
㉓ p. 347	Chimayo	◈◈◈	Southwestern	$32-$50	353
㉔ p. 347	350 Main New American Brasserie	◈◈◈	American	$23-$39	352
㉕ p. 347	Red Banjo Pizza Parlour	◈	Italian	$7-$20	354
㉖ p. 347	The Eating Establishment	◈◈	American	$8-$25	353
㉗ p. 347	Cisero's Ristorante & Nightclub	◈◈	Italian	$11-$28	353
㉘ p. 347	Wasatch Brew Pub	◈◈	American	$9-$24	355
㉙ p. 347	Grappa Italian Restaurant	◈◈◈	Northern Italian	$11-$49	353
㉚ p. 347	J&G Grill at St. Regis Deer Valley (See ad p. 351.)	◈◈◈◈	New American	$16-$65	353
㉛ p. 347	**Goldener Hirsch Restaurant**	◈◈◈	Continental	$28-$39	353
㉜ p. 347	The Mariposa	◈◈◈	Continental	$20-$32	354
㉝ p. 347	Royal Street Cafe	◈◈	American	$10-$32	354
㉞ p. 347	**Glitretind Restaurant**	◈◈◈	Continental	$12-$38	353
㉟ p. 347	Apex Restaurant	◈◈◈◈	Regional American	$17-$68	352

BEST WESTERN PLUS LANDMARK INN & PANCAKE HOUSE (435)649-7300 ❶

◈◈ Hotel $129-$239

AAA Benefit: Save 10% or more every day and earn 10% bonus points!

Address: 6560 N Landmark Dr 84098 **Location:** I-80 exit 145 (Kimball Jct), 0.3 mi s, then 0.3 mi nw. **Facility:** 106 units, some two bedrooms and kitchens. 3 stories, interior corridors. **Terms:** 3 day cancellation notice-fee imposed. **Amenities:** safes. **Pool(s):** heated indoor. **Activities:** hot tub, game room, exercise room. **Guest Services:** valet and coin laundry, area transportation. Featured **Amenity:** full hot breakfast.

THE CHATEAUX DEER VALLEY (435)658-9500 ❼

◈◈◈ Hotel $179-$720

Address: 7815 Royal St E 84060 **Location:** I-80 exit 145 (Kimball Jct), 6 mi se to Deer Valley Dr, 1 mi e via SR 224 to roundabout, exit Marsac Ave, 2 mi s to Guardsman Connection, then 0.3 mi n, follow signs. **Facility:** This mid-mountain property offers a choice of hotel rooms, studios and multi-bedroom condominiums. The Chateaux enjoys a perfect location for the avid skier at the Deer Valley slopes. 140 units, some two bedrooms, three bedrooms, efficiencies, kitchens and condominiums. 4 stories, interior corridors. **Parking:** on-site and valet. **Terms:** check-in 4 pm, 7 day cancellation notice, 30 day in winter-fee imposed, resort fee. **Amenities:** safes. **Pool(s):** heated outdoor. **Activities:** hot tub, downhill skiing, bicycles, exercise room, massage. **Guest Services:** complimentary and valet laundry, area transportation.

DOUBLETREE BY HILTON HOTEL PARK CITY Â- THE YARROW (435)649-7000 ⓫

◈◈◈ **Hotel.** Rates not provided. **Address:** 1800 Park Ave 84060 **Location:** I-80 exit 145 (Kimball Jct), 6 mi s; jct SR 224 (Park Ave) and Kearns Blvd. **Facility:** 181 units. 2 stories, interior corridors. **Terms:** check-in 4 pm. **Amenities:** safes. **Pool(s):** heated outdoor. **Activities:** hot tub, exercise room. **Guest Services:** valet and coin laundry.

AAA Benefit: Members save 5% or more!

GOLDENER HIRSCH INN (435)649-7770 ⓰

◈◈◈ ◈◈◈ Boutique Hotel $169-$1474

Address: 7570 Royal St E 84060 **Location:** I-80 exit 145 (Kimball Jct), 6 mi se to Deer Valley Dr, 1 mi se via SR 224 to roundabout, take 2nd exit (Marsac Ave), 2.3 mi s to Guardsman Connection, then 0.3 mi n, follow signs. Located in Deer Valley Resort. **Facility:** Nestled up in the resort village, the inn offers a wonderful highland escape. Rooms feature a wood-burning fireplace and an idyllic blend of quality, refinement, comfort and tradition. 20 units. 4 stories, interior corridors. **Parking:** on-site (fee) and valet. **Terms:** closed 4/9-6/16 & 10/2-12/1, check-in 4 pm, 2-4 night minimum stay - seasonal and/or weekends, 60 day cancellation notice-fee imposed. **Amenities:** safes. **Dining:** Goldener Hirsch Restaurant, see separate listing. **Activities:** sauna, hot tub, downhill skiing, limited exercise equipment, massage. **Guest Services:** valet laundry, area transportation. Featured **Amenity:** continental breakfast.

Keep your focus safely
on the road when driving

(See map & index p. 347.)

GRAND SUMMIT HOTEL
(435)615-8040 **4**

Resort Hotel
$131-$4188

Address: 4000 Canyons Resort Dr 84098 **Location:** I-80 exit 145 (Kimball Jct), 3 mi sw on SR 224 (Park Ave), then 0.7 mi w. **Facility:** This resort offers spectacular panoramic mountain views. Situated in a ski-in/ski-out location, the beautifully designed property provides a vast selection of well-appointed rooms to suit everyone. 290 units, some two bedrooms, three bedrooms and kitchens. 7 stories, interior corridors. **Parking:** on-site and valet. **Terms:** check-in 4 pm, 2-4 night minimum stay - seasonal and/or weekends, 45 day cancellation notice-fee imposed. **Amenities:** safes. **Dining:** 4 restaurants. **Pool(s):** heated outdoor. **Activities:** sauna, hot tub, steamroom, fishing, regulation golf, miniature golf, downhill skiing, snowboarding, recreation programs in season, bicycles, trails, exercise room, spa. **Guest Services:** valet and coin laundry, area transportation.

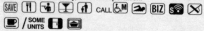

HOLIDAY INN EXPRESS & SUITES
435/658-1600 **2**

Hotel. Rates not provided. **Address:** 1501 W Ute Blvd 84098 **Location:** I-80 exit 145 (Kimball Jct), just s to Ute Blvd, then 0.3 mi e. **Facility:** 76 units. 3 stories, interior corridors. **Pool(s):** heated indoor. **Activities:** sauna, hot tub, exercise room. **Guest Services:** coin laundry.

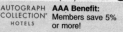

HOTEL PARK CITY, AUTOGRAPH COLLECTION
(435)940-5000 **9**

Resort Hotel
$161-$664

AUTOGRAPH COLLECTION® HOTELS **AAA Benefit:** Members save 5% or more!

Address: 2001 Park Ave 84060 **Location:** I-80 exit 145 (Kimball Jct), 5.6 mi s to corner of Thaynes Canyon Dr and SR 224 (Park Ave). **Facility:** This ski, golf and spa retreat is nestled in the mountains close to three ski resorts. Guests will appreciate the ski-in/ski-out cross-country skiing access. 98 units, some two bedrooms, efficiencies, kitchens and cottages. 3 stories, interior corridors. **Parking:** on-site and valet. **Terms:** check-in 4 pm, 2 night minimum stay - seasonal and/or weekends, 3 day cancellation notice, resort fee. **Amenities:** safes. **Dining:** Ruth's Chris Steak House, see separate listing. **Pool(s):** heated outdoor. **Activities:** sauna, hot tub, regulation golf, cross country skiing, exercise room, spa. **Guest Services:** complimentary and valet laundry, area transportation.

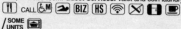

Let Your Voice Be Heard

If your visit to a TourBook-listed property doesn't meet your expectations, tell us about it.

AAA.com/TourBookComments

HYATT ESCALA LODGE AT PARK CITY
(435)940-1234 **7**

Hotel
$139-$799

HYATT
AAA Benefit: Members save 10%!

Address: 3551 N Escala Ct 84098 **Location:** I-80 exit 145 (Kimball Jct), 3 mi sw on SR 224 (Park Ave), then 0.8 mi w; at Canyons. **Facility:** This ski-in/ski-out lodge's residential-style rooms are filled with Old World European charm and luxury amenities. Some units feature a washer and dryer, private patio or balcony and gas fireplace. 139 units, some two bedrooms, three bedrooms, kitchens and condominiums. 3-6 stories, interior corridors. **Parking:** on-site and valet. **Terms:** check-in 4 pm, 7 day cancellation notice-fee imposed, resort fee. **Amenities:** safes. **Pool(s):** heated outdoor. **Activities:** sauna, hot tub, steamroom, downhill skiing, snowboarding, exercise room. **Guest Services:** complimentary and valet laundry, area transportation.

HYATT PLACE PARK CITY
(435)776-1234

[fyi] Hotel $129-$399 Too new to rate, opening scheduled for December 2015. **Address:** 4377 N Hwy 224 84060 **Location:** I-80 exit 145 (Kimball Jct). **Amenities:** 122 units.

AAA Benefit: Members save 10%!

MONTAGE DEER VALLEY
(435)604-1300 **19**

Resort Hotel $265-$2295 **Address:** 9100 Marsac Ave 84060 **Location:** I-80 exit 145 (Kimball Jct), at roundabout, take Marsac Ave exit, 2 mi s to Guardsman Connection, then 2 mi sw. **Facility:** From the winding Empire Pass, your eyes will widen as you catch a glimpse of this enormous and imposing structure. They offer ski-in/ski-out access and endless recreational activities. 220 units, some two bedrooms, three bedrooms, kitchens and condominiums. 10 stories, interior corridors. **Parking:** valet only. **Terms:** check-in 4 pm, 7 day cancellation notice-fee imposed, resort fee. **Amenities:** safes. **Dining:** 5 restaurants, also, Apex Restaurant, see separate listing, entertainment. **Pool(s):** heated outdoor, heated indoor. **Activities:** sauna, hot tub, steamroom, downhill skiing, sledding, recreation programs, kids club, bicycles, game room, lawn sports, trails, spa. **Guest Services:** valet laundry, area transportation.

NEWPARK RESORT HOTEL & CONFERENCE CENTER
435/649-3600 **3**

Hotel. Rates not provided. **Address:** 1456 Newpark Blvd 84098 **Location:** I-80 exit 145 (Kimball Jct), 0.3 mi s to Newpark Blvd, then just e. **Facility:** 150 units, some efficiencies, kitchens and condominiums. 4 stories, interior corridors. **Parking:** winter plug-ins. **Terms:** check-in 4 pm. **Amenities:** safes. **Dining:** Maxwell's East Coast Eatery, see separate listing. **Pool(s):** heated indoor. **Activities:** sauna, hot tub, steamroom, cross country skiing, bicycles, picnic facilities, trails, exercise room. **Guest Services:** valet and coin laundry.

OLD TOWN GUEST HOUSE BED & BREAKFAST
435/649-2642 **12**

Bed & Breakfast. Rates not provided. **Address:** 1011 Empire Ave 84060 **Location:** I-80 exit 145 (Kimball Jct), 6 mi s, then 0.7 mi w. Located in a residential area. **Facility:** 4 units, some two bedrooms. 2 stories (no elevator), interior corridors. **Parking:** street only. **Amenities:** safes. **Activities:** hot tub, recreation programs. **Guest Services:** complimentary laundry.

(See map & index p. 347.)

PARK CITY MARRIOTT   (435)649-2900 **10**

Hotel
$106-$320

AAA Benefit: Members save 5% or more!

Address: 1895 Sidewinder Dr 84060 **Location:** I-80 exit 145 (Kimball Jct), 6 mi s to Kearns Blvd, then 0.6 mi ne to Sidewinder Dr; in Prospector Square. **Facility:** 199 units. 4 stories, interior corridors. **Amenities:** safes. **Dining:** 2 restaurants. **Pool(s):** heated indoor. **Activities:** hot tub, steamroom, bicycles, exercise room. **Guest Services:** valet and coin laundry, boarding pass kiosk, rental car service, area transportation.

PARK CITY PEAKS HOTEL   435/649-5000 **8**

Hotel. Rates not provided. **Address:** 2346 Park Ave 84060 **Location:** I-80 exit 145 (Kimball Jct), 5.5 mi s; jct SR 224 (Park Ave) and Saddle View Way. **Facility:** 131 units. 3 stories, interior corridors. **Amenities:** safes. **Pool(s):** heated outdoor, heated indoor. **Activities:** sauna, hot tub. **Guest Services:** valet and coin laundry.

PARK STATION CONDOMINIUM HOTEL   435/649-7717 **13**

Condominium. Rates not provided. **Address:** 950 Park Ave 84060 **Location:** I-80 exit 145 (Kimball Jct), 6.3 mi s on SR 224 (Park Ave). **Facility:** 35 units, some condominiums. 4 stories, interior corridors. **Terms:** check-in 4 pm. **Pool(s):** heated outdoor, heated indoor. **Activities:** sauna, hot tub. **Guest Services:** coin laundry.

ST. REGIS DEER VALLEY   (435)940-5700 **15**

Resort Hotel
$299-$2200

ST REGIS

AAA Benefit: Members save up to 15%, plus Starwood Preferred Guest® benefits!

Address: 2300 Deer Valley Dr E 84060 **Location:** I-80 exit 145 (Kimball Jct), 6 mi s to Deer Valley Dr, 1 mi se to roundabout, take third exit (Deer Valley Dr), then 1.2 mi se. **Facility:** Located on a ski run with true slopeside ski-in/ski-out access, your experience begins with a peaceful and luxurious funicular tram ride up to the hotel, offering stunning picture-postcard views. 177 units, some two bedrooms, kitchens and condominiums. 11 stories, interior corridors. **Parking:** valet only, winter plug-ins. **Terms:** 14 day cancellation notice-fee imposed. **Amenities:** video games, safes. **Dining:** J&G Grill at St. Regis Deer Valley, see separate listing. **Pool(s):** heated outdoor. **Activities:** sauna, hot tub, steamroom, downhill skiing, recreation programs, bicycles, game room, exercise room, spa. **Guest Services:** valet laundry, area transportation. *(See ad this page.)*

Turn your road trip dreams

into reality with the

TripTik® Travel Planner

▼ See AAA listing this page ▼

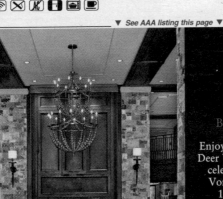

(See map & index p. 347.)

STEIN ERIKSEN LODGE DEER VALLEY
(435)649-3700 **18**

Resort Hotel
$235-$850

Address: 7700 Stein Way 84060 **Location:** I-80 exit 145 (Kimball Jct), 6 mi se to Deer Valley Dr, 1 mi se via SR 224 to roundabout, take 2nd exit (Marsac Ave), 2.3 mi s to Guardsman Connection, then 0.3 mi n, follow signs. Located in Deer Valley. **Facility:** Offering a premier location overlooking a picturesque mountain landscape, this European style year-round mountain lodge offers ski-in/ski-out access and nicely appointed suites. 180 units, some two bedrooms, three bedrooms, kitchens and condominiums. 3 stories, interior/exterior corridors. **Parking:** valet only. **Terms:** check-in 4 pm, 7 day cancellation notice. **Amenities:** safes. **Dining:** Glitretind Restaurant, see separate listing. **Pool(s):** heated outdoor. **Activities:** sauna, hot tub, steamroom, downhill skiing, recreation programs, bicycles, game room, trails, exercise room, spa. **Guest Services:** complimentary and valet laundry, area transportation.

SUNDIAL LODGE, PARK CITY RESORT AT CANYONS VILLAGE
435/615-8070 **5**

Hotel. Rates not provided. **Address:** 3720 Sundial Ct 84098 **Location:** I-80 exit 145 (Kimball Jct), 3 mi s on SR 224 (Park Ave), then 0.5 mi w. **Facility:** 195 units, some two bedrooms, kitchens and condominiums. 6 stories, interior corridors. **Terms:** check-in 4 pm. **Pool(s):** heated outdoor. **Activities:** hot tub, fishing, regulation golf, miniature golf, downhill skiing, snowboarding, playground, picnic facilities, exercise room. **Guest Services:** complimentary and valet laundry, area transportation.

WASHINGTON SCHOOL HOUSE, A LUXURY BOUTIQUE HOTEL
435/649-3800 **14**

Historic Boutique Hotel. Rates not provided. **Address:** 543 Park Ave 84060 **Location:** I-80 exit 145 (Kimball Jct), 6 mi se to Kearns Blvd and SR 224 (Park Ave), then 1.2 mi s; downtown. **Facility:** Stay in school! Transformed into a luxurious hotel, be prepared to be pampered at this hidden gem offering superior service, elegant rooms and ice-white marble bathrooms. 12 units. 4 stories, interior corridors. **Parking:** on-site and street. **Amenities:** safes. **Pool(s):** heated outdoor. **Activities:** hot tub, massage. **Guest Services:** valet laundry, area transportation.

WESTGATE PARK CITY RESORT & SPA
435/940-9444 **6**

Resort Hotel
Rates not provided

Address: 3000 Canyons Resort Dr 84098 **Location:** I-80 exit 145 (Kimball Jct), 3 mi s, then 0.5 mi w up Canyons Resort Dr. **Facility:** The accommodating staff takes great pride in the personalized service and helps make your visit memorable. This mountain resort is in a fabulous location with spectacular views. 350 units, some two bedrooms, three bedrooms, efficiencies and condominiums. 2-9 stories, interior corridors. **Parking:** on-site and valet. **Terms:** check-in 4 pm. **Amenities:** safes. **Dining:** 2 restaurants. **Pool(s):** heated outdoor, heated indoor. **Activities:** sauna, hot tub, steamroom, tennis, downhill skiing, snowboarding, recreation programs, bicycles, playground, game room, picnic facilities, trails, exercise room, spa. **Guest Services:** valet and coin laundry, area transportation.

THE SKY LODGE
435/658-2500

(fyi) Not evaluated. **Address:** 201 Heber Ave 84060 **Location:** At Heber Ave and Main St; in historic downtown. Facilities, services, and décor characterize an upscale property. This intimate luxury hotel offers beautifully appointed guest rooms.

SUNRISE LODGE, A HILTON GRAND VACATIONS CLUB
435/655-9000

(fyi) Not evaluated. **Address:** 2307 W High Mountain Rd 84098 **Location:** I-80 exit 145 (Kimball Jct), 3 mi sw on SR 224 (Park Ave), then 0.8 mi w; at Canyons. Facilities, services, and décor characterize a mid-scale property.

AAA Benefit: Members save 5% or more!

WALDORF ASTORIA PARK CITY
435/647-5500

(fyi) Not evaluated. **Address:** 2100 W Frostwood Blvd 84098 **Location:** I-80 exit 145 (Kimball Jct), 3 mi sw via SR 224 (Park Ave), then 0.3 mi w; at Canyons. Facilities, services, and décor characterize an upscale property.

AAA Benefit: Members save 5% or more!

WHERE TO EAT

350 MAIN NEW AMERICAN BRASSERIE
435/649-3140 **24**

American. Casual Dining. $23-$39 **AAA Inspector Notes:** An innovative menu features organically grown ingredients whenever possible. Diners sit under a copper and tin stamped roof to enjoy flavorful dishes, the likes of which might be the tower of ahi and hamachi appetizer and such entrées as black-pepper-crusted venison medallions, wasabi-seared Pacific ono, black sesame sea scallops and grilled Rocky Mountain red trout. The lemon-mint angel food cake is a must. **Features:** full bar. **Reservations:** suggested. **Address:** 350 Main St 84060 **Location:** Center of historic Main St. [D]

ADOLPH'S RESTAURANT
435/649-7177 **6**

Swiss. Fine Dining. $16-$43 **AAA Inspector Notes:** The menu lines up specialties such as escargot, ahi tuna sashimi, table-side-served Chateaubriand for two, salmon, fondue for two and the chef's nightly specials. Eye-catching made-in-house desserts are beautifully presented. **Features:** full bar, patio dining. **Reservations:** suggested. **Address:** 1500 Kearns Blvd 84060 **Location:** I-80 exit 145 (Kimball Jct), 6 mi se to Kearns Blvd, then 0.5 mi e. **Parking:** on-site and valet. [D]

APEX RESTAURANT
435/604-1300 **35**

Regional American. Fine Dining. $17-$68 **AAA Inspector Notes:** The large fireplace and rich wood trim work enveloping the dining room enhance this upscale dining experience. There is a well-coordinated and unobtrusive team approach to service. A meticulous chef presents flavorful and colorful seasonal menu items such as Niman Ranch strip loin, pork belly, Burgundy truffles and bison. **Features:** full bar, patio dining. **Reservations:** suggested. **Address:** 9100 Marsac Ave 84060 **Location:** I-80 exit 145 (Kimball Jct), at roundabout, take Marsac Ave exit, 2 mi s to Guardsman Connection, then 2 mi sw on SR 224 (Park Ave); in Montage Deer Valley. **Parking:** valet only. [B] [L] [D]

BAJA CANTINA
435/649-2252 **12**

Mexican. Casual Dining. $8-$28 **AAA Inspector Notes:** Colorful décor contributes to the restaurant's lively atmosphere. Seafood specialties stand out on a menu of nicely varied dishes. Patio seating can be requested during the summer season. **Features:** full bar, patio dining, happy hour. **Address:** 1284 Lowell Ave 84060 **Location:** I-80 exit 145 (Kimball Jct), 5.5 mi s on SR 224 (Park Ave) to Empire Ave, 0.3 mi w to Shadow Ridge Rd, just w to Lowell Rd, then just s; upstairs at the base of ski lift. [L] [D]

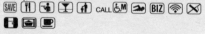

(See map & index p. 347.)

BISTRO 412   435/649-8211   22
WWW French. Fine Dining. $12-$38 **AAA Inspector Notes:**
The efficient staff of this American-style sidewalk bistro brings out
dishes prepared with fresh ingredients and rich sauces. Specialties
include fresh Idaho red trout and French dishes such as braised lamb
shank. Nibbling on pomme frites is a must. An oversize crème brûlée
is a great finishing choice. **Features:** full bar, patio dining. **Address:**
412 Main St 84060 **Location:** Center of historic Main St. **Parking:**
street only. L D

BLIND DOG RESTAURANT & SUSHI   435/655-0800   9
WWW Steak Seafood. Casual Dining. $16-$35 **AAA Inspector
Notes:** Named for the owner's beloved pet, you will find accolades to
canines all throughout the décor. Signature dishes such as the hearty
"dreamloaf" with creamed spinach, lobster bisque, crab cakes and
their infamous mac 'n cheese are served by pleasant waitstaff. **Features:** full bar. **Reservations:** suggested. **Address:** 1251 Kearns
Blvd 84060 **Location:** I-80 exit 145 (Kimball Jct), 6 mi s to Kearns
Blvd, then 0.3 mi e; at The Yard. L D

CAFE TERIGO   435/645-9555   21
WWW American. Casual Dining. $10-$32 **AAA Inspector
Notes:** Whimsical sayings etched on the walls lend to the light, fresh
décor of this casual eatery, which has a large patio. Innovative combinations such as roasted pork tenderloin with grilled polenta and
seafood choices along the lines of trout and diver scallops are expertly prepared. This place is known for its bread pudding. **Features:**
full bar, patio dining. **Address:** 424 Main St 84060 **Location:** I-80 exit
145 (Kimball Jct), center of historic Main St. **Parking:** street only.
L D

CHIMAYO   435/649-6222   23
WWW Southwestern. Fine Dining. $32-$50 **AAA Inspector
Notes:** This restaurant serves distinctive gourmet fare in surround-
ings of terra-cotta and blue and white tiles, suggestive of a hacienda.
Features: full bar. **Reservations:** suggested. **Address:** 368 Main St
84060 **Location:** Upper historic Main St. **Parking:** street only. D

CISERO'S RISTORANTE & NIGHTCLUB   435/649-5044   27
WW Italian. Casual Dining. $11-$28 **AAA Inspector Notes:**
The décor in the main dining room is delightful and the restaurant
puts forth a menu of chicken, veal, steak and a nice selection of
pasta. The capellini pomodoro is simple yet colorful and flavorful. The
tapenade served with the warm bread is habit-forming. A lounge
dining area features live entertainment and is a popular spot for
dancing. **Features:** full bar, patio dining, Sunday brunch. **Address:**
306 Main St 84060 **Location:** On upper historic Main St. **Parking:**
street only. L D

THE EATING ESTABLISHMENT   435/649-8284   26
WW American. Casual Dining. $8-$25 **AAA Inspector Notes:**
Known as the 'Double E' to locals, this cozy eatery has nourished
many skiers since 1972 and features traditional American fare with a
Western flair such as hearty soups, spicy chili, burgers, sandwiches,
steaks and slowly smoked barbecue beef, pork and chicken. The two
cozy dining rooms have plenty of sunlight and warm fires, and the enclosed indoor garden patio opens up to the outside in the summer.
Features: full bar. **Address:** 317 Main St 84060 **Location:** I-80 exit
145 (Kimball Jct); on upper historic Main St. **Parking:** street only.
B L D

FLYING SUMO SUSHI BAR & GRILL   435/649-5522   14
WW WW Sushi. Casual Dining. $13-$22 **AAA Inspector Notes:**
Tucked under a ski lift, this tiny restaurant with a large sumo heart
serves great sushi along with delicate wok-seared fish, chicken and
steak. **Features:** beer & wine. **Reservations:** suggested. **Address:**
838 Park Ave 84060 **Location:** I-80 exit 145 (Kimball Jct), 7 mi se on
SR 224 (Park Ave). **Parking:** on-site and street. D

FUEGO BISTRO & PIZZERIA   435/645-8646   7
WW WW Italian. Casual Dining. $9-$20 **AAA Inspector Notes:** This
brightly colored eatery features more than 13 types of gourmet pizza,
Italian grilled sandwiches, traditional entrées such as baked lasagna,
shrimp and clam linguine, and large house-made meatballs. The daily
lunch and nightly specials are very affordable. **Features:** full bar. **Address:** 2001 Sidewinder Dr 84068 **Location:** I-80 exit 145 (Kimball
Jct), 6 mi se, 0.7 mi ne on Kearns Blvd, then just e; at Prospector
Square. L D

GHIDOTTI'S CLASSIC ITALIAN RESTAURANT
                                         435/658-0669   4
WW WW Italian. Fine Dining. $12-$37 **AAA Inspector Notes:**
Large fires burn at the entrance to this elegant restaurant where the
New World ambience features large linen-covered round tables that
are meant to be shared family-style. With menus that change with the
seasons, classics include minestrone soup with house-made Italian
sausage, clams casino, veal Marsala and cannoli with toasted pistachios and amarena cherries. **Features:** full bar. **Reservations:** suggested. **Address:** 6030 N Market St, Suite 100 84098 **Location:** I-80
exit 145 (Kimball Jct), just s; in Redstone Village. D

GLITRETIND RESTAURANT   435/645-6455   34
WW WW WW   **AAA Inspector Notes:** In an elegant
                      and majestic mountain setting, seasonal
Continental   and beautifully presented appetizers
Fine Dining   might include braised Wagyu short rib in
$12-$38   corn pudding with popcorn and herbed
                      salt with creative entrées such as duck
                      and waffles, honey and lavender chicken
in tomato marmalade or Utah lamb T-bone with lamb and sweet
potato croquettes. **Features:** full bar, patio dining, Sunday
brunch. **Reservations:** suggested. **Address:** 7700 Stein Way
84060 **Location:** I-80 exit 145 (Kimball Jct), 6 mi se to Deer
Valley Dr, 1 mi se via SR 224 to roundabout, take 2nd exit
(Marsac Ave), 2.3 mi s to Guardsman Connection, then 0.3 mi n,
follow signs; in Stein Eriksen Lodge Deer Valley. **Parking:** valet
only. B L D

GOLDENER HIRSCH RESTAURANT   435/649-7770   31
WW WW WW   **AAA Inspector Notes:** Experience au-
                      thentic classics served in a charming
Continental   and romantic setting. Menus typically
Fine Dining   feature fondue with melted Swiss and
$28-$39   French cheeses, house charcuterie and
                      cured meats and their signature pork
                      schnitzel. Seasonal items might include
mouthwatering gazpacho, heirloom-melon salad with prosciutto,
Utah steelhead trout and Wagyu beef bavette steak. **Features:**
full bar, patio dining. **Reservations:** suggested. **Address:** 7570
Royal St E 84060 **Location:** I-80 exit 145 (Kimball Jct), 6 mi se
to Deer Valley Dr, 1 mi se via SR 224 to roundabout, take 2nd
exit (Marsac Ave), 2.3 mi s to Guardsman Connection, then 0.3
mi n, follow signs; in Goldener Hirsch Inn. L D

GRAPPA ITALIAN RESTAURANT   435/645-0636   29
WW WW Northern Italian. Fine Dining. $11-$49 **AAA Inspector
Notes:** This romantic restaurant is in an old country farmhouse at the
top of a hill on historic Main Street. They serve favorites such as osso
buco, dry-aged steak, heirloom vegetables and many fine salads and
pastas. **Features:** full bar, patio dining. **Address:** 151 Main St 84060
Location: At the top of historic Main St. **Parking:** street only.
D

HIGH WEST DISTILLERY & SALOON   435/649-8300   16
WW WW New American. Gastropub. $11-$55 **AAA Inspector
Notes:** This restaurant serves high country cuisine paired with
whiskey and vodka. Diverse seasonal menu items may include deviled eggs with candied bacon, wild arugula and heirloom spinach
salad, braised lamb with chickpeas and apricots, apple smoked Scottish salmon and a pot pie with chicken and wild mushrooms. Order
the s'more for dessert, it's sensational! Vegetarian options are available. Also, children are welcome and have their own menu. **Features:** full bar, patio dining. **Address:** 703 Park Ave 84060 **Location:**
I-80 exit 146 (US 40), 6.5 mi s. **Parking:** street only.
L D

J&G GRILL AT ST. REGIS DEER VALLEY   435/940-5760   30
WW WW WW New American. Fine Dining. $16-$65 **AAA Inspector Notes:** The dining experience begins with amazing views
from a funicular tram ride up the mountain to this Jean-Georges
slope-side restaurant. The kitchen prepares seasonal creations such
as ginger-marinated tuna tartare, charred corn ravioli in a basil
fondue, lime juice and basil-roasted Maine lobster, melt-in-your-
mouth glazed short ribs and black truffle pizza with fontina cheese.
Their wine vault is impressive and the largest in Utah. **Features:** full
bar, patio dining. **Reservations:** suggested. **Address:** 2300 Deer
Valley Dr E 84060 **Location:** I-80 exit 145 (Kimball Jct), 6 mi s to
Deer Valley Dr, 1 mi se to roundabout, take third exit (Deer Valley Dr),
then 1.2 mi se; in St. Regis Deer Valley. **Parking:** valet only. *(See
ad p. 351.)* B L D CALL

(See map & index p. 347.)

LOCO LIZARD CANTINA   435/645-7000 (1)
▼▼▼ Mexican. Casual Dining. $8-$18 AAA Inspector Notes:
The family-friendly Mexican cantina serves good food at reasonable
prices. The menu consists of some non-traditional touches such as
rellenos that are baked, not fried. Features: full bar, patio dining. Address: 1612 Ute Blvd, Suite 101 84098 Location: I-80 exit 145 (Kimball Jct), just s, then just e. [L] [D]

THE MARIPOSA   435/645-6715 (32)
▼▼▼ ▼▼▼ Continental. Fine Dining. $20-$32 AAA Inspector
Notes: The seasonal menu in this elegant, rustic lodge features a
creative small plates tasting menu such as poached wild shrimp and
Brie filling in tender gnocchi dough and Maine lobster chowder. Appetizers and entrees may consist of diver scallop ceviche, nori and
sesame seared ahi tuna, wild mushroom beggar's purse, quail saltimbocca and seared bison filet, all artistically presented. Features: full
bar. Reservations: suggested. Address: 7600 Royal St 84060 Location: I-80 exit 145 (Kimball Jct), in Deer Valley; in Silver Lake Day
Lodge. [D] [AC]

MAXWELL'S EAST COAST EATERY   435/647-0304 (2)
▼▼ Italian. Casual Dining. $12-$21 AAA Inspector Notes:
After a starter of caprese salad, crispy calamari or steamed mussels,
diners can savor homemade pasta with a choice of meat (grilled
chicken, sauteed shrimp, Italian sausage or meatball) and sauce
(marinara, Alfredo, tomato basil cream or brown butter sage with pine
nuts). House specialties include pizza, risotto, chicken piccata, eggplant parmigiana and veal sauteed with pancetta, shallots, spinach
and sun-dried tomatoes. Scrumptious cannoli or cookie pizza satisfy
a sweet tooth. Features: full bar, patio dining. Address: 1456 Newpark Blvd 84098 Location: I-80 exit 145 (Kimball Jct), 0.3 mi s to
Newpark Blvd, then just e; in Newpark Resort Hotel & Conference
Center. Parking: on-site and valet. [L] [D] [LATE]

RED BANJO PIZZA PARLOUR   435/649-9901 (25)
▼▼ Italian. Casual Dining. $7-$20 AAA Inspector Notes: This
eatery on historic Main Street has a lovely upper-level patio that offers spectacular mountain views. The root beer floats are worth the
splurge. Features: beer & wine. Address: 322 Main St 84060 Location: On upper historic Main St. Parking: street only. [L] [D]

REEF'S RESTAURANT & GALLERY   435/658-0323 (15)
▼▼ Mediterranean. Casual Dining. $20-$28 AAA Inspector
Notes: The intimate and distinctive restaurant serves an appetizer
sampler featuring hummus, baba ghanoush, tahini, falafel and roasted
eggplant. Also featured are delicious salads, Morocan salmon, lamb
and fish. I tried the banana leaf wrapped halibut on coconut rice and it
was absolutely delicious! Features: beer & wine, patio dining. Address: 710 Main St 84098 Location: On lower historic Main St; behind
Village Shopping Plaza. Parking: street only. [D]

RIVERHORSE ON MAIN   435/649-3536 (19)

♦♦♦♦ ♦♦♦♦

American
Fine Dining
$32-$55

AAA Inspector Notes: Historic. The
appetizer trilogy of smoked salmon and
potato pancake, goat cheese won tons
and Kobe beef with huckleberry compote served on lovely logo china is a
start, while the roasted tomato bisque
with avocado is a good following. Col-
orful and enticing entrées may include a trio of wild game or
macadamia nut-crusted Alaskan halibut. Features: full bar, patio
dining, Sunday brunch. Reservations: suggested. Address:
540 Main St 84060 Location: On historic Main St, 2nd Floor.
Parking: street only. [D]

ROYAL STREET CAFE   435/645-6724 (33)
▼▼ American. Casual Dining. $10-$32 AAA Inspector Notes:
At an elevation of 8,100 feet with stunning views, this restaurant's
seasonal menu features appetizers and entrées such as a shrimp
and lobster margarita, maple-bacon barbecue bison burger, slow-
roasted chili and coffee-rubbed duck breast. McHenry's frozen lemon
meringue pie and fresh thyme-maple ice cream are just some of the
scrumptious desserts offered daily. Features: full bar, patio dining.
Address: 7600 Royal St 84060 Location: I-80 exit 145 (Kimball Jct),
in Deer Valley; in Silver Lake Village; mid-mountain. Parking: street
only. [L] [D]

RUTH'S CHRIS STEAK HOUSE   435/940-5070 (5)
▼▼▼ ▼▼▼ Steak. Fine Dining. $35-$70 AAA Inspector Notes: The
main fare is steak, which is prepared from several cuts of Prime beef
and cooked to perfection, but the menu also lists lamb, chicken and
seafood dishes. Guests should come hungry because the side dishes,
which are among the a la carte offerings, could make a meal in themselves. Features: full bar. Reservations: suggested. Address: 2001
Park Ave 84068 Location: I-80 exit 145 (Kimball Jct), 5.6 mi s to
corner of Thaynes Canyon Dr and SR 224 (Park Ave); in Hotel Park
City, Autograph Collection. Parking: on-site and valet.
[L] [D]

SHABU   435/645-7253 (20)
▼▼▼ Asian. Casual Dining. $10-$45 AAA Inspector Notes:
They call it "freestyle" Asian food, although the well-balanced blend
of tastes and textures are designed to delight any palate. From sushi
hand rolls to wok-seared diver scallops with mango fried rice, patrons
will be tantalized by the flavors. Features: full bar, patio dining. Reservations: suggested. Address: 442 Main St 84060 Location: On
upper historic Main St; downstairs. Parking: street only.
[L] [D] [LATE]

SILVER STAR CAFE   435/655-3456 (10)
▼▼▼ Regional American. Casual Dining. $10-$27 AAA Inspector Notes: Lunch, dinner, and even breakfast is served during
the height of the ski season. The owner-chef is imaginative, creating
classic dishes such as stroganoff and stews alongside Southwestern-
influenced creations. The huevos rancheros is rich and flavorful, or try
the tasty grilled fish tacos or hearth-fired pizza. The menu changes
with the season and always offers a memorable dining experience.
Features: beer & wine, patio dining. Address: 1825 Three Kings Dr
84060 Location: Just n of SR 224 and Park City Golf Club.
[L] [D]

SQUATTERS ROADHOUSE GRILL & PUB   435/649-9868 (8)
▼▼ American. Casual Dining. $9-$21 AAA Inspector Notes:
Award-winning beers are paired with a large selection of appetizers,
soups, salads, sandwiches and pub favorites. It's a great stop for
breakfast, lunch or dinner. The cheesesteak on ciabatta, stout barbecue chicken pizza and appetizer sampler are good choices. Vegetarian, gluten-free, vegan and low-carb items are available upon
request. Features: full bar, patio dining. Address: 1900 Park Ave
84060 Location: I-80 exit 145 (Kimball Jct), 6 mi se; at Kearns Blvd
and Park Ave (SR 224). [B] [L] [D]

SUSHI BLUE   435/575-4272 (3)
▼▼▼ Asian Fusion. Casual Dining. $10-$22 AAA Inspector
Notes: This spot serves up a fusion of Asian and American cuisine. Try
Korean street tacos, pad thai, sushi rolls, marinated smoked squid
salad as well as traditional burgers and rib-eye. I found the edamame
perfectly seasoned and the citrus prawns amazing. Features: full bar.
Address: 1571 W Redstone Dr, Suite 140 84098 Location: I-80 exit
145 (Kimball Jct), 0.3 mi s to Newpark Blvd, then just e.
[L] [D]

THE VIKING YURT AT PARK CITY MOUNTAIN RESORT
435/615-9878 (13)
▼▼▼ Norwegian. Fine Dining. $125-$175 AAA Inspector
Notes: This four-hour adventure dinner starts with a 23-minute open
sleigh ride (seats 32), or heated cab (seats 8), to the 8,000-foot peak
of the Park City Mountain Resort ski runs. Warm blankets are provided. The views of the valley below and the stars above are stunning, and live music from a baby grand piano is the accompaniment.
Features: full bar. Reservations: required. Address: Park City
Mountain Resort 84098 Location: I-80 exit 145 (Kimball Jct), 6.3 mi
se to Empire and Park aves, 0.3 mi sw to Shadow Ridge Rd, just w
to Lowell Ave, then just se; take stairs up to Legacy Lodge.
[L] [D] [AC]

WAHSO ASIAN GRILL   435/615-0300 (18)
▼▼▼ Asian. Fine Dining. $27-$40 AAA Inspector Notes:
Guests who unwind in the 1930s Shanghai Deco-Victorian setting can
savor traditional Asian meals prepared in a French-cooking-style. Flavors and textures blend for a true culinary delight. Features: full bar,
patio dining. Reservations: suggested. Address: 577 Main St 84060
Location: On lower historic Main St. Parking: street only. [D]

(See map & index p. 347.)

WASATCH BREW PUB   435/649-0900 (28)
▼▼ ▼▼ American. Casual Dining. $9-$24 **AAA Inspector Notes:**
This eatery serves up a wide variety of delicious craft brews. Menu
items include a healthy Cobb salad, fire-fried Monterey Bay calamari,
roasted chicken and mussels paella, fish and chips with Creole coleslaw, shrimp tacos, house-made pizza and decadent desserts. Children will be pleased with their own menu. **Features:** full bar, patio
dining, Sunday brunch. **Address:** 250 S Main St 84060 **Location:** I-80
exit 145 (Kimball Jct), top of historic Main St. **Parking:** street only.

[L] [D]

WINDY RIDGE CAFE   435/647-0880 (11)
▼▼ ▼▼ American. Casual Dining. $9-$28 **AAA Inspector Notes:**
Gourmet influences enhance your lunch and dinner choices at this
comfortable eatery. **Features:** full bar. **Address:** 1250 Iron Horse Dr
84060 **Location:** I-80 exit 145 (Kimball Jct), 6 mi s, then 0.5 mi e.

[L] [D]

ZOOM   435/649-9108 (17)
▼▼ ▼▼ American. Casual Dining. $12-$39 **AAA Inspector Notes:**
In a historic railroad depot, the bar and dining room have a rustic
character that speaks to days gone by. Notice the original wood floors
that have survived two major fires as you slide into your private booth
or sit at the copper-topped show kitchen counter. Choose several
small plates of Asian beef skewers, spicy buffalo onion rings, seafood
ceviche and white cheddar mac 'n' cheese that are perfect for sharing
or a full rack of baby back pork ribs served with cornbread and pop-
pyseed coleslaw. **Features:** full bar. **Reservations:** suggested. **Address:** 660 Main St 84060 **Location:** Corner of Main St and Heber
Ave. **Parking:** street only. [L] [D]

PRIME STEAK HOUSE & PIANO BAR   435/655-9739
[fyi] Not evaluated. If serving Midwestern, custom-aged beef prepared
in a 1800-degree broiler doesn't make your mouth water, try their signature melt-in-your-mouth molten chocolate cake. Patrons will appreciate the free underground parking. **Address:** 804 Main St 84060
Location: Lower Main St; historic downtown; across from town lift.

SILVER RESTAURANT   435/940-1000
[fyi] Not evaluated. This sophisticated establishment serves creative
and artfully prepared dishes in an upscale atmosphere. **Address:**
508 Main St 84060 **Location:** Center of historic downtown.

PRICE (D-4) pop. 8,715, elev. 5,547'

Originally settled as a farming area, Price grew
with the coming of the railroad in the early 1880s.
The discovery of coal brought new wealth and new
residents to the town but also made it popular with
such outlaws as the Brown's Hole Gang and Butch
Cassidy and his Wild Bunch. The Price Mural,
painted by native Lynn Fausett, details the history of
Carbon County and covers 800 square feet in the
Price Municipal Building.

Price is in a large coal-mining and farming district.
Uranium, helium and natural gas deposits have been
discovered in the area. The Manti-La Sal National Forest *(see place listing p. 327)* headquarters is in town.

**Carbon County Office of Tourism and Visitor
Center:** 751 East 100 North, Price, UT 84501.
Phone: (435) 636-3701.

Self-guiding tours: Maps and information about
self-guiding tours to Native American dwellings and
several areas of geological interest—including the
San Rafael Desert, Little Grand Canyon and Nine
Mile Canyon, with its extensive array of petroglyphs
and pictographs—are available from the travel office.

PREHISTORIC MUSEUM, USU EASTERN is at
155 E. Main St. Dinosaurs, the ice age and archeology are explored. Two levels of exhibits include the

museum's signature dinosaur, the Utahraptor. The
Observation Labs offer visitors a glimpse behind the
scenes and the chance to speak to the scientists who
prepare specimens for display. **Hours:** Mon.-Sat. 9-5.
Closed Jan. 1, Thanksgiving, Christmas Eve,
Christmas and Dec. 31. **Cost:** $6; $5 (ages 65+ and
active and reserve military with ID); $3 (ages 2-12);
$17 (family living in same residence); $14 (military
family in same residence). Prices may vary; phone
ahead. **Phone:** (435) 613-5060 or (800) 817-9949.

CARRIAGE HOUSE INN   (435)637-5660
◆◆ ◆◆
Hotel
$76-$100
Address: 590 E Main St 84501 **Location:** Cross streets 600 E and Main St;
downtown. **Facility:** 40 units. 2 stories
(no elevator), interior corridors. **Terms:**
cancellation fee imposed. **Pool(s):**
heated indoor. **Activities:** hot tub. **Featured Amenity: continental breakfast.**

[SAVE] [◊◊+] [≈] [BIZ] [◊] [✕] [◊]
[◊] [◊] /SOME UNITS [HS]

HOLIDAY INN EXPRESS & SUITES   (435)637-7700
▼▼ ▼▼ **Hotel** $99-$129 **Address:** 925 Westwood Blvd 84501
Location: US 6 exit 240 (Business Loop), just e. **Facility:** 82 units. 4
stories, interior corridors. **Terms:** cancellation fee imposed. **Pool(s):**
heated indoor. **Activities:** hot tub, exercise room. **Guest Services:**
valet and coin laundry, area transportation.

[◊◊+] CALL [◊M] [≈] [BIZ] [◊] [✕] [◊] [◊] [◊]

LEGACY INN   435/637-2424
◆◆ ◆◆
Motel
Rates not provided
Address: 145 N Carbonville Rd 84501
Location: US 6 exit 240 (Business
Loop), 0.5 mi se, 0.3 mi e then just ne.
Facility: 31 units, some two bedrooms
and efficiencies. 1 story, exterior corri-
dors. **Guest Services:** coin laundry.

[SAVE] [◊◊+] [◊] [◊] [◊] [◊]

RAMADA PRICE   (435)637-8880
▼▼ ▼▼ **Hotel** $81-$115 **Address:** 838 Westwood Blvd 84501 **Location:** US 6 exit 240 (Business Loop), just e. Near Castleview Hospital. **Facility:** 150 units, some efficiencies. 2 stories (no elevator),
interior corridors. **Amenities:** video games. **Pool(s):** heated indoor.
Activities: exercise room. **Guest Services:** valet and coin laundry,
area transportation.

[◊] [◊] [◊] CALL [◊M] [≈] [BIZ] [◊] [✕] [◊] [◊]
[◊] [◊] /SOME UNITS [◊◊]

WHERE TO EAT

FARLAINO'S CAFE   435/637-9217
▼ Breakfast Sandwiches. Casual Dining. $6-$9 **AAA Inspector
Notes:** Nothing fancy, this casual restaurant is where you will find the
locals, and it's a good stop for a hearty breakfast. Drop in for a sandwich, daily special or tasty soup. **Address:** 87 W Main St 84501 **Location:** At 1st and Main sts; downtown. **Parking:** street only.

[B] [L]

GROGG'S PINNACLE BREWING CO   435/637-2924

▼▼ American. Casual Dining. $9-$24 **AAA Inspector Notes:** Informal, laid-back dining is the norm at this spot, where pine walls wrap around the rooms. Menu items include house-smoked meats, baked salmon, steamed clams, burgers, wraps, pizza and a variety of sandwiches featuring a cheesesteak made with cream cheese, all served with a choice of soup or salad, potato salad, broccoli slaw, chips and salsa or oven-baked fries. **Features:** beer only, patio dining. **Address:** 1653 N Carbonville Rd 84526 **Location:** SR 6 exit 240, 0.3 mi e to W 600 S, then 2 mi n; 1.5 mi se from jct SR 6 and Carbonville Rd. [L] [D]

RICARDO'S RESTAURANT   435/637-2020

▼▼ Mexican. Casual Dining. $5-$25 **AAA Inspector Notes:** This casual family restaurant serves made-from-scratch Mexican food, along with a good selection of American items. **Features:** full bar. **Address:** 655 E Main St 84501 **Location:** At 600 E; downtown; next to Greenwell Inn & Convention Center. [B] [L] [D]

PROVO (C-3) pop. 112,488, elev. 4,549'
• Restaurants p. 358

Provo, on a shelf along the former shoreline of prehistoric Lake Bonneville, is nurtured by the Provo River. Etienne Provost, a French Canadian, explored this area with a trapping expedition in 1825, found it suitable for settlement and gave the river his name. Encouraged by his reports, a colony from Salt Lake City settled in 1849 on the river's south bank, which is overshadowed by Provo Peak, Mount Timpanogos and the Wasatch Range.

By 1851 the village was well established and irrigation was being used successfully. The railroad came to Provo in 1875, linking the settlement to Salt Lake City. Brigham Young University, which was organized by the Mormon colonizer, was established 2 years later to supply trained teachers for the public schools. The area is important industrially for the production of steel, pig iron and foundry products.

The gold-spired Provo Mormon Temple, completed in 1972, overlooks the city from the northeast; it is open to Mormons only.

Various water sports are permitted at Deer Creek Reservoir in Provo Canyon, which irrigates a vast area. Provo is at the southern terminus of scenic US 189, which passes through Uinta National Forest *(see place listing p. 409)* and joins scenic SR 92 just southeast of Deer Creek State Park *(see Recreation Areas Chart)*. SR 92 then runs west, passing through Timpanogos Cave National Monument *(see place listing p. 406)* before terminating at the junction with I-15, 19 miles northwest of Provo.

Between February and November, numerous patriotic events that are part of ▼ America's Freedom Festival at Provo take place in the city. Independence Day highlights include the Grand Parade; the Freedom Run, which encompasses a 1-mile Fun Run as well as 10- and 5-kilometer races; and the Stadium of Fire, a popular extravaganza boasting fireworks, concerts and dance performances.

Utah Valley Convention and Visitors Bureau: 220 W. Center St., Suite 100, Provo, UT 84601. **Phone:** (801) 851-2100 or (800) 222-8824.

BRIGHAM YOUNG UNIVERSITY, at the base of the Wasatch Mountains, is one of the largest church-related private universities in the nation. Its 634-acre campus is dominated by the 112-foot Centennial Carillon Tower, where 52 bells ring at intervals throughout the day. The Hosting Center offers free 45-minute guided riding tours of the campus. Appointments are recommended, though walk-in visitors can be accommodated, based on availability. **Hours:** Tours are given Mon.-Fri. on the hour 9-4 (except Tues. at 11). **Phone:** (801) 422-4678 for tour information.

Brigham Young University Museum of Art is on the n.e. corner of the Brigham Young University campus on N. Campus Dr. The museum houses galleries of European, local and 19th-century American paintings. Additional exhibits include house ceramics, paintings, pottery and sculpture by faculty and students. The center's theaters offer theatrical and musical performances; ticket prices vary by performance. **Time:** Allow 1 hour minimum. **Hours:** Mon.-Sat. 10-6 (also Wed.-Fri. 6-9 p.m.). Closed Jan. 1, July 4, Thanksgiving and Christmas. **Cost:** Free. A fee may be charged for some traveling exhibitions. **Phone:** (801) 422-8287. [¶]

Monte L. Bean Life Science Museum is on the campus of Brigham Young University at 645 E. 1430 N. The museum displays wildlife from around the world; collections of mounted birds, fish, insects, plants and reptiles also can be seen. Free live animal shows are presented. **Time:** Allow 1 hour minimum. **Hours:** Museum Mon.-Fri. 10-9, Sat. 10-5. Animal show is given Mon.-Fri. at 7:30 p.m. (also Mon. at 6:30 p.m.), Sat. at 1 and 3. Closed Jan. 1, July 4, Pioneer Day, Thanksgiving, Christmas Eve, Christmas and Dec. 31. Phone ahead to confirm holiday schedule. **Cost:** Free. **Phone:** (801) 422-5050.

Museum of Paleontology is directly w. of Cougar Stadium on the n.w. edge of the Brigham Young University campus at 1683 N. Canyon Rd. The museum displays what is said to be one of the top five collections of Jurassic dinosaur fossils in the world. **Time:** Allow 1 hour minimum. **Hours:** Mon.-Fri. 9-5. Closed university holidays. **Cost:** Free. **Phone:** (801) 422-3680.

Museum of Peoples and Cultures is at 2201 N. Canyon Rd. The archeology museum has annually rotating exhibitions that feature the cultures of the Great Basin, Mesoamerica, ancient Peru and Polynesia and Southwest. Brigham Young University students serve as curators. **Time:** Allow 1 hour minimum. **Hours:** Mon.-Fri. 9-5 (also Tues. and Thurs. 5-7, Sept.-Apr.). Closed major holidays. **Cost:** Free. **Phone:** (801) 422-0020.

SEVEN PEAKS WATERPARK is .5 mi. e. on East 100 North, .1 mi. s. on North 600 East, .4 mi. e. on E. Center St., then .3 mi. n. on N. Seven Peaks Blvd. to 1330 East 300 North. The park contains tube runs, speed slides, activity pools, a wave pool, a zero-depth entry pool, a 500,000-gallon lazy river, a bowl slide and a 100-foot free-fall drop slide. Also featured are carnival games, a children's play area, a game area, a tadpole pond and a beach volleyball sand pit.

Note: The facility is not wheelchair accessible. Towels are not provided. Cabana, tube, lounge chair, umbrella and barbecue rentals are available. **Time:** Allow 2 hours minimum. **Hours:** Mon.-Sat. noon-8, Memorial Day-Labor Day (weather permitting). Phone ahead to confirm schedule. **Cost:** $24.99; $19.99 (under 48 inches tall); $7.99 (non-participants); free (ages 0-2 and 65+). After 4 p.m. $15.99; free (ages 0-2 and 65+). After 6 p.m. $9.99 (under 48 inches tall); free (ages 0-2 and 65+). Life jacket requires a driver's license or refundable season pass deposit. **Parking:** $7 (full day); $4 (half-day). **Phone:** (801) 373-8777.

RECREATIONAL ACTIVITIES
Skiing
- **Sundance Mountain Resort** is off I-15 exit 272; take US 189 7 mi. n.e., then SR 92 2.3 mi. n.w. Other activities are offered. **Hours:** Open for winter activities daily, mid-Dec. to early Apr. Hours vary; phone ahead. **Phone:** (801) 225-4107 or (888) 974-8501.

BAYMONT INN & SUITES PROVO RIVER (801)373-7044

Hotel $79-$139 **Address:** 2230 N University Pkwy 84604 **Location:** I-15 exit 269 (University Pkwy), 3.2 mi e, then just n; in CottonTree Square. **Facility:** 80 units. 2 stories (no elevator), interior corridors. **Pool(s):** heated indoor. **Activities:** hot tub, picnic facilities, exercise room. **Guest Services:** valet and coin laundry, area transportation.

COURTYARD BY MARRIOTT (801)373-2222

Hotel $92-$176 **Address:** 1600 N Freedom Blvd 84604 **Location:** I-15 exit 269 (University Pkwy), 3.7 mi e to N Freedom Blvd, then just s. **Facility:** 99 units. 5 stories, interior corridors. **Pool(s):** heated indoor. **Activities:** hot tub, picnic facilities, exercise room. **Guest Services:** valet and coin laundry, boarding pass kiosk.

AAA Benefit: Members save 5% or more!

ECONO LODGE (801)373-0099

Motel $50-$80 **Address:** 1625 W Center St 84601 **Location:** I-15 exit 265 (Center St), just w. **Facility:** 28 units. 2 stories (no elevator), exterior corridors.

FAIRFIELD INN BY MARRIOTT PROVO (801)377-9500

Hotel $90-$168 **Address:** 1515 S University Ave 84601 **Location:** I-15 exit 263 (University Ave), just e. **Facility:** 72 units. 3 stories, interior corridors. **Activities:** hot tub, exercise room. **Guest Services:** valet and coin laundry, area transportation.

AAA Benefit: Members save 5% or more!

HAMPTON INN PROVO (801)377-6396

Hotel $119-$249

AAA Benefit: Members save up to 10%!

Address: 1511 S 40 E 84601 **Location:** I-15 exit 263 (University Ave), just e. **Facility:** 87 units. 3 stories, interior corridors. **Parking:** winter plug-ins. **Terms:** 1-7 night minimum stay, cancellation fee imposed. **Pool(s):** heated indoor. **Activities:** hot tub, exercise room. **Guest Services:** valet and coin laundry. **Featured Amenity:** full hot breakfast.

LA QUINTA INN PROVO TOWNE CENTER (801)374-9750

Hotel $71-$153 **Address:** 1460 S University Ave 84601 **Location:** I-15 exit 263 (University Ave), just e. **Facility:** 78 units. 2 stories (no elevator), interior corridors. **Pool(s):** heated outdoor. **Activities:** exercise room. **Guest Services:** valet and coin laundry.

PROVO MARRIOTT HOTEL & CONFERENCE CENTER (801)377-4700

Hotel $106-$191

AAA Benefit: Members save 5% or more!

Address: 101 W 100 N 84601 **Location:** I-15 exit 265 (Center St), 1.2 mi e, just n at 500 W, then 0.3 mi e. **Facility:** 330 units. 9 stories, interior corridors. **Amenities:** Some: safes. **Dining:** 2 restaurants. **Pool(s):** heated outdoor, heated indoor. **Activities:** hot tub, exercise room. **Guest Services:** valet and coin laundry, area transportation.

RESIDENCE INN BY MARRIOTT (801)374-1000

Extended Stay Hotel $94-$217 **Address:** 252 W 2230 N 84604 **Location:** I-15 exit 269 (University Pkwy), 3.2 mi e to W 2230 N, then 0.3 mi n. **Facility:** 114 efficiencies, some two bedrooms. 3 stories, interior corridors. **Pool(s):** heated indoor. **Activities:** picnic facilities, exercise room. **Guest Services:** valet and coin laundry, area transportation.

AAA Benefit: Members save 5% or more!

SLEEP INN (801)377-6597

Hotel $75-$150 **Address:** 1505 S 40 E 84606 **Location:** I-15 exit 263 (University Ave), just e. **Facility:** 82 units. 3 stories, interior corridors. **Terms:** check-in 4 pm. **Pool(s):** heated indoor. **Activities:** hot tub, exercise room. **Guest Services:** coin laundry.

SPRINGHILL SUITES BY MARRIOTT (801)373-0073

Hotel $104-$187 **Address:** 1580 N Freedom Blvd 84604 **Location:** I-15 exit 269 (University Pkwy), 3.9 mi e to N Freedom Blvd, then just s. **Facility:** 82 units. 4 stories, interior corridors. **Pool(s):** heated indoor. **Activities:** exercise room. **Guest Services:** valet and coin laundry.

AAA Benefit: Members save 5% or more!

HINES MANSION BED & BREAKFAST   801/374-8400

[fyi] Not evaluated. **Address:** 383 W 100 S 84601 **Location:** I-15 exit 265 (Center St), 1.2 mi e to 500 W, just s to 100 S, then just e. Facilities, services, and décor characterize a mid-scale property. Focal points of this property include the lovely landscaping, covered entryway and imported Italian marble fireplace, which provides the perfect spot to relax or visit with fellow guests.

SUNDANCE MOUNTAIN RESORT   801/225-4107

[fyi] Not evaluated. **Address:** 8841 N Alpine Loop Rd 84604 **Location:** I-15 exit 272 (800 N/Sundance), 3.7 mi e to US 189, 6.8 mi ne to Alpine Loop Rd, then 2.5 mi n. Facilities, services, and décor characterize a mid-scale property.

WHERE TO EAT

THE BANANA LEAF RESTAURANT   801/205-7619

▼▼ Indian. Casual Dining. $10-$25 **AAA Inspector Notes:** This restaurant is housed in an adorable building on landscaped grounds that features a screened-in gazebo out front. Find a selection of beef, chicken and seafood entrées with a variety of distinctive sauces to accompany each dish. Theme platters would be the perfect choice for a family or group meal. Vegetarian and gluten-free items are available. Try the avocado shake. **Address:** 409 N University Ave 84601 **Location:** I-15 exit 265 (Center St), 1.2 mi e, just n on 500 W, 0.4 mi e on 100 N, then 0.3 mi n. **Parking:** street only. [L] [D]

BLACK SHEEP CAFE   801/607-2485

▼▼ Native American. Casual Dining. $8-$14 **AAA Inspector Notes:** This cozy eatery serves delicious menu items such as bleu-fire shrimp, a popular Navajo taco trio and puree of roasted squash soup. Many items come with fry bread or Navajo flatbread. Try the hand-pressed burger stuffed with goat cheese and served with cumin-garlic sweet potato fries or Southwestern street corn (yum!). **Features:** full bar, patio dining. **Address:** 19 N University Ave 84606 **Location:** I-15 exit 265 (Center St), 1.3 mi e, just n on 500 W, 0.4 mi e on 100 N, then just s; downtown. **Parking:** on-site and street. [L] [D]

BOMBAY HOUSE CUISINE OF INDIA   801/373-6677

▼▼ Indian. Casual Dining. $11-$17 **AAA Inspector Notes:** You will feel like you've stepped into India when you pass through the doors of one of this town's most authentic and outstanding ethnic restaurants. Menu items are centered around flavorful beef, chicken and lamb. **Features:** beer & wine. **Address:** 463 N University Ave 84601 **Location:** I-15 exit 265 (Center St), 1.8 mi e to University Ave, then 0.3 mi n. [D]

COMMUNAL   801/373-8000

▼▼▼ American. Fine Dining. $9-$32 **AAA Inspector Notes:** Introverts can sit at a set table, while extroverts are welcome to join the communal table at this small, elegant eatery. Seasonal menu items may include Berkshire pork chop in persimmon sauce, pan-roasted salmon in a warm leek vinaigrette, gnocchi in a lemon-thyme cream, creamy farro and chanterelles, winter squash gratin or roasted root vegetables. **Features:** beer & wine. **Reservations:** suggested. **Address:** 102 N University Ave 84601 **Location:** I-15 exit 265 (Center St), 1.2 mi e, just n on 500 W, 0.4 mi e on 100 N, then just s; in historic downtown. **Parking:** street only. [L] [D]

GLORIA'S LITTLE ITALY   801/805-4913

▼▼ Italian. Casual Dining. $10-$20 **AAA Inspector Notes:** The corner location of this adorable trattoria is perfect for people-watching. When you order, pick one of the varied sauces, ranging from traditional ragu to aglio olio peperoncino, and a pasta such as fettuccine, penne, spaghetti or ravioli. Vegetarian items are available. **Features:** patio dining. **Address:** 1 E Center St, Suite 100 84606 **Location:** I-15 exit 265 (Center St), 2 mi e; at Center St and University Ave; downtown. **Parking:** on-site and street. [L] [D]

GURU'S CAFE   801/375-4878

▼▼ American. Quick Serve. $6-$15 **AAA Inspector Notes:** You will enjoy this eclectic eatery serving healthy pasta, soup, rice bowls, sandwich wraps, salads, tacos, burritos and delicious desserts. Vegan and vegetarian items are available. **Address:** 45 E Center St 84606 **Location:** I-15 exit 265 (Center St), 2 mi e; downtown. **Parking:** on-site and street. [B] [L] [D]

JOE VERA'S MEXICAN RESTAURANT   801/375-6714

▼▼▼ Mexican. Casual Dining. $7-$15 **AAA Inspector Notes:** The restaurant features very colorful décor. The salsa served with tortilla chips is presented in a small decanter. You can expect traditional Mexican fare such as stuffed jalapeños and beef, chicken or pork fajitas. You also can create well-liked combination platters with one, two or three items. **Features:** beer & wine. **Address:** 250 W Center St 84601 **Location:** I-15 exit 265 (Center St), 1.5 mi e; downtown. **Parking:** street only. [L] [D]

LA DOLCE VITA RISTORANTE ITALIANO   801/373-8482

▼▼ Italian. Casual Dining. $8-$17 **AAA Inspector Notes:** Whether you stop in this locals' favorite restaurant for the lunch or dinner special, you'll enjoy the homemade garlic bread, cannelloni, lasagna, house-made pizza and tasty desserts. **Features:** beer & wine. **Address:** 61 N 100 E St 84606 **Location:** I-15 exit 265 (Center St), 2 mi e to 100 E, then just n; downtown. **Parking:** street only. [L] [D]

LA JOLLA GROVES   801/224-5111

▼▼▼▼ New American. Casual Dining. $10-$19 **AAA Inspector Notes:** Dine under a lemon grove with a yellow rose, lemon linen napkins and mint-colored menus. Healthier ingredients are predominant, featuring organically grown vegetables from their own garden and local greenhouses. Popular selections include slow-roasted portobello and crimini mushroom soup, tomato and fresh Italian mozzarella Caprese, and thyme-and-citrus-roasted chicken breast. **Features:** full bar. **Address:** 4801 N University Ave, Suite 610 84604 **Location:** I-15 exit 271, 3 mi e; in The Shops at Riverwoods (east courtyard). [L] [D]

MALAWI'S PIZZA   801/225-2800

▼▼ Pizza. Casual Dining. $9-$11 **AAA Inspector Notes:** Healthy choices are offered, with pizza on honey-wheat or gluten-free crust. Signature pizzas include a popular herb-roasted chicken and pesto cream with asparagus, spinach and Gorgonzola cheese. Consider the "pastabilities" and choose your own pasta, sauce, vegetables and toppings. **Address:** 4801 N University Pkwy, Suite 110 84604 **Location:** I-15 exit 271, 3 mi e; in The Shops at Riverwoods; east side. [L] [D] CALL [&M]

NICOLITALIA PIZZERIA   801/356-7900

▼ Italian. Quick Serve. $6-$19 **AAA Inspector Notes:** This eatery serves hand-tossed, East Coast-style pizza baked in a hearth brick oven, calzones, soups, salads, sides of meatballs and sausage, chicken and eggplant Parmesan and a small selection of pasta with marinara or Alfredo sauce. The Boston Italian cream pie and cannoli are yummy. **Features:** patio dining. **Address:** 2295 N University Pkwy 84604 **Location:** I-15 exit 269 (University Pkwy), 3 mi e, just s of Carterville Rd; in shopping plaza (west side). [L] [D]

RUBY RIVER STEAKHOUSE   801/371-0648

▼▼ Steak. Family Dining. $9-$30 **AAA Inspector Notes:** The restaurant serves great steaks along with pasta, seafood and chicken, too. The atmosphere is casual and fun with a lively lounge; a pail of peanuts in the shell is on every table. **Features:** full bar. **Address:** 1454 S University Ave 84601 **Location:** I-15 exit 263 (University Ave), 0.5 mi e. [L] [D]

TREE ROOM AT SUNDANCE MOUNTAIN RESORT   801/223-4200

▼▼ ▼▼ American. Fine Dining. $25-$44 **AAA Inspector Notes:** Serving seasonal mountain cuisine, innovate menu items might include scallops with crispy pork belly and quail egg, the signature Tree Room peppered steak, lobster and gnocchi, local steelhead trout with maple bacon or chicken on top of cheddar grits. There is a small but mighty selection of creative salads. **Features:** full bar. **Reservations:** suggested. **Address:** 8841 N Alpine Loop Rd 84604 **Location:** I-15 exit 272 (800 N/Sundance), 3.7 mi e to US 189, 6.8 mi ne to Alpine Loop Rd, then 2.5 mi n; in Sundance Mountain Resort. [D]

◣◢ RAINBOW BRIDGE NATIONAL
GEM MONUMENT (G-4)

Just north of the Arizona-Utah border within Glen Canyon National Recreation Area *(see place listing p. 314)*, Rainbow Bridge is the largest known natural bridge in the world—standing 290 feet above the stream bed and stretching 275 feet wide. It has an enormous and almost perfectly formed arch below and a curved surface above, giving the effect of a rainbow. Rainbow Bridge is considered a sacred place by many Native American tribes.

The bridge is reached by a 14-mile hike over rugged terrain or by boat and, depending on the lake's water level, a 1- to 1.5-mile hike. Backpackers must obtain a permit to hike the 14-mile trail from the Navajo Nation Parks and Recreation Department, P.O. Box 2520, Window Rock, AZ 86515; phone (928) 871-6647.

Regularly scheduled boat tours on Lake Powell provide access to Rainbow Bridge. Tours provided by Lake Powell Resorts & Marina depart from the Wahweap Marina in Arizona; phone (888) 896-3829 for schedule, prices and reservations. Camping and swimming are not permitted within the monument grounds.

For information contact the Superintendent, Rainbow Bridge National Monument, c/o Glen Canyon National Recreation Area, P.O. Box 1507, Page, AZ 86040; phone (928) 608-6200.

RICHFIELD (E-3) pop. 7,551, elev. 5,308'

Big Rock Candy Mountain, 24 miles south on US 89, has multicolored rock formations. Six miles north of the mountain on US 89 are canyons with Native American petroglyphs that predate the birth of Christ. Nearby, in Sevier, Fremont Indian State Park (see attraction listing p. 402) comprises archeological sites, rock art and a museum that houses exhibits relating to the Fremont Anasazi Indian culture.

Richfield Area Chamber of Commerce: 250 N. Main St., Suite B42, Richfield, UT 84701. **Phone:** (435) 896-4241.

BEST WESTERN RICHFIELD INN   (435)893-0100

Hotel $90-$129

AAA Benefit: Save 10% or more every day and earn 10% bonus points!

Address: 1275 N Main St 84701 **Location:** I-70 exit 37, just s. **Facility:** 42 units. 2 stories (no elevator), interior corridors. **Pool(s):** heated indoor. **Activities:** hot tub, exercise room. **Guest Services:** coin laundry. **Featured Amenity:** continental breakfast.

COMFORT INN   (435)893-0119

Hotel $80-$90 **Address:** 1070 W 1250 S 84701 **Location:** I-70 exit 37, just e. **Facility:** 63 units. 3 stories, interior corridors. **Terms:** resort fee. **Pool(s):** heated indoor. **Activities:** hot tub, limited exercise equipment. **Guest Services:** valet and coin laundry.

FAIRFIELD INN & SUITES BY MARRIOTT   (435)896-9191

Hotel $94-$174 **Address:** 990 W 1350 S 84701 **Location:** I-70 exit 37, just e. **Facility:** 65 units. 3 stories, interior corridors. **Pool(s):** heated indoor. **Activities:** hot tub, limited exercise equipment. **Guest Services:** valet and coin laundry.

AAA Benefit: Members save 5% or more!

HAMPTON INN   (435)896-6666

Hotel $109-$189 **Address:** 1100 W 1350 S 84701 **Location:** I-70 exit 37, just e. **Facility:** 52 units. 3 stories, interior corridors. **Terms:** 1-7 night minimum stay, cancellation fee imposed. **Pool(s):** heated indoor. **Activities:** hot tub, exercise room. **Guest Services:** valet and coin laundry.

AAA Benefit: Members save up to 10%!

HOLIDAY INN EXPRESS & SUITES   435/896-8552

Hotel. Rates not provided. **Address:** 20 W 1400 N 84701 **Location:** I-70 exit 40, just s. **Facility:** 64 units. 3 stories, interior corridors. **Pool(s):** heated indoor. **Activities:** hot tub, exercise room. **Guest Services:** coin laundry.

SUPER 8   (435)896-9204

Motel $55-$86 **Address:** 1377 N Main St 84701 **Location:** I-70 exit 40, just s. **Facility:** 42 units. 2 stories (no elevator), interior/exterior corridors. **Terms:** 3 day cancellation notice. **Guest Services:** coin laundry.

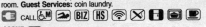
WHERE TO EAT

FRONTIER VILLAGE RESTAURANT   435/893-8361

American. Casual Dining. $9-$26 **AAA Inspector Notes:** This log building has a charming dining room with a country décor. The classic American menu serves large salads, gourmet burgers, barbecue, steaks and some pasta dishes. The friendly service is great but not pretentious. **Features:** beer & wine. **Address:** 1475 N Main St 84701 **Location:** I-70 exit 40, just s.

B L D

IDEAL DAIRY   435/896-5061

Sandwiches Desserts. Quick Serve. $5-$9 **AAA Inspector Notes:** In the center of town, the mom-and-pop creamery offers fresh sandwiches, homemade ice cream, fresh milk and freshly baked bread. It's a great stop for any meal, great dessert or even a gallon of milk to go. **Address:** 490 S Main St 84701 **Location:** I-70 exit 40, 0.9 mi s on US 89.

B L D

LITTLE WONDER CAFE   435/896-8960

American. Family Dining. $7-$14 **AAA Inspector Notes:** Down-home cooking has been going on at this café since 1929. A comfortable country look brightens the interior, and the staff goes out of its way to make patrons feel welcome. **Address:** 101 N Main St 84701 **Location:** On Main St (SR 120); center.

B L D

PEPPERBELLY'S   435/896-2097

Mexican. Casual Dining. $7-$13 **AAA Inspector Notes:** The casual restaurant serves Mexican favorites in a small casual dining room. Some of the favorites include large salads, Mexican pizza, and the sweet pork enchilada. **Address:** 680 S Cove View Rd 84701 **Location:** I-70 exit 37, 0.4 mi e, then 0.8 mi ne.

L D

STEVE'S STEAKHOUSE   435/893-8880

▼▼ Steak. Casual Dining. $12-$31 **AAA Inspector Notes:** Those not in the mood for one of the great selections of steak can contemplate several choices of chicken and seafood. A Western theme punctuates the décor. The experience can fluctuate depending on your server. **Features:** beer & wine. **Address:** 647 S Main St 84701 **Location:** I-70 exit 37, 0.3 mi e to Cove View Rd, then 0.7 mi ne. [D]

RIVERTON pop. 38,753
• Part of Salt Lake City area — see map p. 368

SALSA LEEDOS MEXICAN GRILL   801/565-8818

▼▼ Mexican. Casual Dining. $9-$17 **AAA Inspector Notes:** This eatery combines a very bright and festive atmosphere with flavorful dishes. The chile verde and beef or chicken fajitas are recommended. **Features:** full bar, patio dining. **Address:** 3956 W Innovation Dr S 84096 **Location:** I-15 exit 289 (Bangerter Hwy), 5 mi w to W 13400 S, then just w. [L] [D]

ROOSEVELT (C-5) pop. 6,046, elev. 5,100'

The area south of Roosevelt was the site of the discovery of Gilsonite, a brittle asphalt used in the manufacture of pipe insulation and ink. The Uinta Basin deposit was discovered in 1885 by Samuel H. Gilson, who was told by Native Americans of a substance that would not burn.

Duchesne County Area Chamber of Commerce: 50 East 200 South, P.O. Box 1417, Roosevelt, UT 84066. **Phone:** (435) 722-4598.

Self-guiding tours: Brochures outlining self-guiding tours of the area, including Native American petroglyphs, a 30-mile Rock Creek tour and a 60-mile Elkhorn Loop trip, are available from the chamber of commerce.

AMERICAS BEST VALUE INN - ROOSEVELT/BALLARD
435/722-4644

▼▼ Motel. Rates not provided. **Address:** 2203 E Hwy 40 84066 **Location:** 1 mi e of center on US 40. **Facility:** 40 units. 2 stories (no elevator), exterior corridors.

[¶↑] [HS] [📶] [🔲] [🖥] [💻] / SOME UNITS [🔲]

BALLARD PLAZA HOTEL - ROOSEVELT/BALLARD
435/722-1171

▼▼▼ Hotel. Rates not provided. **Address:** 2197 E Hwy 40 84066 **Location:** 1.2 mi e of downtown on US 40. **Facility:** 46 units, some efficiencies. 3 stories, interior corridors. **Pool(s):** heated indoor. **Activities:** hot tub, exercise room. **Guest Services:** coin laundry.

[¶↑] CALL [♿M] [🏊] [BIZ] [HS] [📶] [✕] [🔲] [🖥] [💻]

BEST WESTERN PLUS LANDMARK HOTEL
(435)725-1800

▼▼▼
Hotel
$109-$169

Best Western PLUS

AAA Benefit: Save 10% or more every day and earn 10% bonus points!

Address: 2477 E Hwy 40 84066 **Location:** 1.2 mi e of downtown on US 40. **Facility:** 49 units. 3 stories, interior corridors. **Pool(s):** heated indoor. **Activities:** hot tub, picnic facilities, exercise room. **Guest Services:** coin laundry.

[SAVE] [¶↑] CALL [♿M] [🏊] [BIZ] [HS] [📶] [✕] [🔲] [🖥] [💻] / SOME UNITS [🔲]

WHERE TO EAT

MI CASA RESTAURANT   435/722-2243

▼▼ Mexican. Casual Dining. $7-$14 **AAA Inspector Notes:** This eatery makes you feel like you are visiting family. The front lawn walkway leads to a door that opens up to a colorful and festive interior filled with thoughtful appointments. The menu consists of traditional burritos, enchiladas, flautas, nachos, quesadillas, tacos, taquitos, a popular sampler platter and a simple tortilla soup. Sandwiches and burgers also are available. **Features:** beer & wine. **Address:** 227 E Hwy 40 84066 **Location:** 1.2 mi e of center. [L] [D]

ST. GEORGE (G-1) pop. 72,897, elev. 2,840'
• Hotels p. 362 • Restaurants p. 365

St. George is in Utah's "Dixie," where summers are warm and winters are mild. The area was settled during the Civil War by Mormons sent by Brigham Young to raise cotton. A textile mill was built and production continued until the South was once again able to supply Utah with cotton.

The St. George Mormon Temple, built 1869-77, was the first Mormon temple built in Utah. The temple and several other early buildings still stand. The red sandstone 1863 tabernacle at Main and Tabernacle streets supports a 140-foot steeple that serves as a town landmark; the tabernacle is open to visitors. Although the temple is not open to the public, guided tours offered by the St. George Temple Visitors Center, 490 South 300 East (on the temple grounds), explain the temple's functions and Mormon beliefs; phone (435) 673-5181.

St. George's temperate weather makes it ideal for all sorts of outdoor recreation, including boating, water skiing, fishing and camping. The area also is popular with golfers and offers a variety of courses that can be played throughout the year.

St. George Area Chamber of Commerce: 97 E. St. George Blvd., St. George, UT 84770. **Phone:** (435) 628-1658. *(See ad p. 361.)*

Self-guiding tours: Many of St. George's late-19th-century buildings can be seen on a walking tour that begins at the chamber of commerce's visitor center at 100 East and St. George Boulevard; a map describing the route and each building is available at the visitor center.

Shopping: Among the more than 65 stores at Red Cliffs Mall, 1770 E. Red Cliffs Dr., are the anchor stores Dillard's, JCPenney and Sears. The Shoppes at Zion, off I-15 exit 8, has more than 33 outlet shops, including Eddie Bauer, Gymboree, Levi's and Pendleton.

BRIGHAM YOUNG WINTER HOME is at 67 West 200 North. Built around 1873, the restored house contains 19th-century furnishings. **Hours:** Guided tours are offered daily 9-7, Apr.-Oct. (also 7-8 in summer); 10-5, rest of year. Last tour begins 30 minutes before closing. Phone ahead to confirm schedule. **Cost:** Free. **Phone:** (435) 673-5181.

DAUGHTERS OF UTAH PIONEERS MUSEUM is in the McQuarrie Memorial Building at 145 North 100

East. The museum contains memorabilia from the pioneer days 1847-70. Clothing, pictures of early settlers and pioneer implements are among the items exhibited. **Time:** Allow 30 minutes minimum. **Hours:** Mon.-Tues. and Thurs.-Sat. 10-5, Jan.-Nov. Closed major holidays. **Cost:** Free. **Phone:** (435) 628-7274.

ROSENBRUCH WILDLIFE MUSEUM is off I-15 exit 6 to 1835 Convention Center Dr. Visitors encounter realistic representations of wildlife habitats that resemble those in Africa, Australia, the Arctic, Europe and Asia as well as North America. Replicas of wildlife are created using fiberglass or foam forms and real animal skin and fur. Among animals represented are several types of antelopes, bears, camels, caribous, cats, crocodiles and deer as well as elk, foxes, kangaroos, monkeys, sheep and wolves.

The museum features an interactive children's area, an exotic insect collection and an art gallery. Video presentations and rotating exhibits also are available. **Time:** Allow 1 hour, 30 minutes minimum. **Hours:** Mon.-Sat. 10-6. Closed Jan. 1, Thanksgiving and Christmas. **Cost:** $8; $6 (ages 55+); $4 (ages 3-12). **Phone:** (435) 656-0033.

ST. GEORGE ART MUSEUM is at 47 East 200 North. The museum's permanent collection consists of approximately 800 items that include all types of

▼ See AAA listing p. 360 ▼
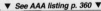

media in both two and three dimensions. A Family Discovery Center and the Adult Study Center also are offered. Changing exhibits are offered throughout the year. Children's cultural classes are available in summer. **Time:** Allow 30 minutes minimum. **Hours:** Mon.-Sat. 10-5 (also third Thurs. of the month 5-9). **Cost:** $3; $1 (ages 3-11). **Phone:** (435) 627-4525.

ST. GEORGE DINOSAUR DISCOVERY SITE AT JOHNSON FARM is at 2180 E. Riverside Dr. Visitors can see 200-million-year-old dinosaur tracks that were uncovered when the property was being cleared. Other exhibits include fossils of dinosaur and fish bones, shells of marine animals, and imprints of leaves and seeds. The new adjacent Dino Park has several hands-on areas for children. **Time:** Allow 1 hour minimum. **Hours:** Mon.-Sat. 10-6, Sun. 11-5, Mar.-Sept.; Mon.-Sat. 10-5, rest of year. Closed Jan. 1, Thanksgiving and Christmas. **Cost:** $6; $3 (ages 4-11). **Phone:** (435) 574-3466.

ST. GEORGE TABERNACLE is at 18 S. Main St. Guided tours offer visitors insight into the history of the church as well as the people who contributed to its development. **Time:** Allow 1 hour minimum. **Hours:** Daily 9-5. Last tour begins at 4:30. Closed Jan. 1, Thanksgiving and Christmas. **Cost:** Free. **Phone:** (435) 628-4072.

RECREATIONAL ACTIVITIES
Hot Air Ballooning
• **Skywalker Balloon Co.-St. George** departs from the Ramada Inn at 1440 E. St. George Blvd. or other area locations. **Time:** Allow 3 hours minimum. **Hours:** Trips generally depart daily at dawn. Phone ahead to confirm schedule. **Cost:** One-hour flight $250 (per person). Prices may vary. Reservations are required. **Phone:** (801) 824-3934.

AMERICA'S BEST INN & SUITES   435/652-3030
▼▼ ▼▼ **Motel.** Rates not provided. **Address:** 245 N Red Cliffs Dr 84790 **Location:** I-15 exit 8, just e. **Facility:** 49 units. 2 stories (no elevator), exterior corridors. **Pool(s):** heated outdoor. **Activities:** hot tub. **Guest Services:** coin laundry.

BEST WESTERN CORAL HILLS   (435)673-4844

Hotel
$72-$199

AAA Benefit: Save 10% or more every day and earn 10% bonus points!

Address: 125 E St. George Blvd 84770 **Location:** I-15 exit 8, 1 mi w. **Facility:** 98 units, some two bedrooms. 2 stories (no elevator), interior/exterior corridors. **Terms:** check-in 4 pm. **Pool(s):** heated outdoor, heated indoor. **Activities:** hot tub, exercise room. **Guest Services:** valet and coin laundry. **Featured Amenity:** breakfast buffet. (See ad this page.)

BEST WESTERN PLUS ABBEY INN   (435)652-1234

Hotel
$90-$175

AAA Benefit: Save 10% or more every day and earn 10% bonus points!

Address: 1129 S Bluff St 84770 **Location:** I-15 exit 6 (Bluff St), just n. **Facility:** 154 units. 2-3 stories, interior corridors. **Terms:** 2-3 night minimum stay - seasonal. **Pool(s):** heated outdoor. **Activities:** hot tub, exercise room. **Guest Services:** valet and coin laundry. **Featured Amenity:** full hot breakfast. (See ad this page.)

BEST WESTERN TRAVEL INN
(435)673-3541

Motel
$63-$119

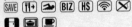

AAA Benefit: Save 10% or more every day and earn 10% bonus points!

Address: 316 E St. George Blvd 84770 **Location:** I-15 exit 8, 0.8 mi w; downtown. **Facility:** 30 units, some two bedrooms. 1 story, exterior corridors. **Pool(s):** heated outdoor. **Activities:** hot tub. **Guest Services:** coin laundry. **Featured Amenity: full hot breakfast.** *(See ad p. 362.)*

CLARION SUITES
(435)673-7000

Hotel
$75-$159

Address: 1239 S Main St 84770 **Location:** I-15 exit 6 (Bluff St), just w. **Facility:** 122 units. 2 stories, exterior corridors. **Pool(s):** heated outdoor. **Activities:** hot tub, exercise room. **Guest Services:** valet and coin laundry.

COMFORT INN
(435)628-8544

Hotel $80-$146 **Address:** 138 E Riverside Dr 84790 **Location:** I-15 exit 6 (Bluff St), just e. **Facility:** 122 units. 3 stories, interior corridors. **Pool(s):** heated outdoor. **Activities:** hot tub, exercise room. **Guest Services:** coin laundry.

COMFORT INN SAINT GEORGE NORTH
(435)251-9600

Hotel $84-$199 **Address:** 974 N 2720 E 84790 **Location:** I-15 exit 10, just e, then just s. **Facility:** 65 units, some two bedrooms. 4 stories, interior corridors. **Terms:** 3 day cancellation notice-fee imposed. **Pool(s):** heated indoor. **Activities:** sauna, hot tub. **Guest Services:** coin laundry.

COURTYARD BY MARRIOTT
(435)986-0555

Hotel
$99-$207

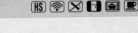

AAA Benefit: Members save 5% or more!

Address: 185 S 1470 E 84790 **Location:** I-15 exit 8, just e, just s, then just e. **Facility:** 131 units. 4 stories, interior corridors. **Pool(s):** heated outdoor, heated indoor. **Activities:** hot tub, exercise room. **Guest Services:** valet and coin laundry, area transportation. *(See ad this page.)*

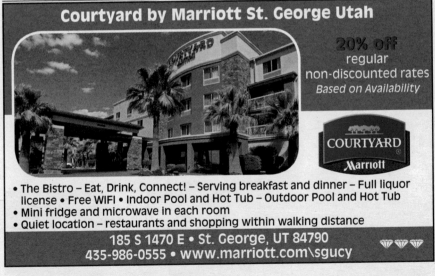
Ask about AAA/CAA Associate membership
to share the benefits you value

CRYSTAL INN ST. GEORGE (435)688-7477

Hotel $84-$209 **Address:** 1450 S Hilton Dr 84770 **Location:** I-15 exit 6 (Bluff St), just w. **Facility:** 101 units. 2 stories, interior corridors. **Terms:** cancellation fee imposed. **Pool(s):** heated outdoor. **Activities:** sauna, hot tub, tennis, exercise room. **Guest Services:** valet and coin laundry. *(See ad this page.)*

FAIRFIELD INN BY MARRIOTT (435)673-6066

Motel $82-$181

AAA Benefit: Members save 5% or more!

Address: 1660 S Convention Center Dr 84790 **Location:** I-15 exit 6 (Bluff St), just e. **Facility:** 99 units. 3 stories, interior corridors. **Pool(s):** heated outdoor. **Activities:** hot tub, exercise room. **Guest Services:** valet and coin laundry. **Featured Amenity:** full hot breakfast.

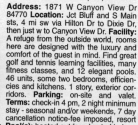

GREEN VALLEY BOUTIQUE HOTEL AND SPA (435)628-8060

Resort Hotel $119-$169

Address: 1871 W Canyon View Dr 84770 **Location:** Jct Bluff and S Main sts, 4 mi sw via Hilton Dr to Dixie Dr, then just w to Canyon View Dr. **Facility:** A refuge from the outside world, rooms here are designed with the luxury and comfort of the guest in mind. Find great golf and tennis learning facilities, many fitness classes, and 12 elegant pools. 46 units, some two bedrooms, efficiencies and kitchens. 1 story, exterior corridors. **Parking:** on-site and valet. **Terms:** check-in 4 pm, 2 night minimum stay - seasonal and/or weekends, 7 day cancellation notice-fee imposed, resort fee. **Amenities:** safes. **Pool(s):** heated outdoor, heated indoor. **Activities:** sauna, hot tub, tennis, recreation programs, playground, game room, spa. **Guest Services:** valet laundry, area transportation.

HAMPTON INN BY HILTON (435)652-1200

Hotel $109-$189 **Address:** 53 N River Rd 84790 **Location:** I-15 exit 8, just e. **Facility:** 125 units. 4 stories, interior corridors. **Terms:** 1-7 night minimum stay, cancellation fee imposed. **Pool(s):** heated outdoor, heated indoor. **Activities:** hot tub, exercise room. **Guest Services:** valet and coin laundry, area transportation.

AAA Benefit: Members save up to 10%!

HILTON GARDEN INN (435)634-4100

Hotel $99-$189

AAA Benefit: Members save up to 10%!

Address: 1731 S Convention Center Dr 84790 **Location:** I-15 exit 6 (Bluff St), just e, then s. **Facility:** 150 units, some two bedrooms. 5 stories. **Terms:** 1-7 night minimum stay, cancellation fee imposed. **Pool(s):** heated outdoor. **Activities:** hot tub, exercise room. **Guest Services:** valet and coin laundry.

HOWARD JOHNSON INN (435)628-8000

Motel $49-$200

Address: 1040 S Main St 84770 **Location:** I-15 exit 6 (Bluff St), just w, then just e. **Facility:** 52 units, some two bedrooms and kitchens. 2 stories (no elevator), exterior corridors. **Terms:** cancellation fee imposed. **Amenities:** safes. **Pool(s):** heated outdoor. **Activities:** hot tub. **Guest Services:** valet and coin laundry. **Featured Amenity:** continental breakfast.

THE INN AT ST. GEORGE (435)673-4666

Motel $47-$129

Address: 60 W St. George Blvd 84770 **Location:** 1 blk w of Main St; downtown. **Facility:** 54 units. 2 stories (no elevator), exterior corridors. **Terms:** cancellation fee imposed. **Pool(s):** outdoor. **Guest Services:** coin laundry. **Featured Amenity:** continental breakfast.

LA QUINTA INN & SUITES - ST. GEORGE   (435)674-2664

Hotel
$75-$251

Address: 91 E 2680 S 84790 Location: I-15 exit 4, just e on Brigham Rd. Facility: 104 units. 3 stories, interior corridors. Pool(s): heated outdoor. Activities: hot tub, exercise room. Guest Services: valet and coin laundry. Featured Amenity: full hot breakfast.

QUALITY INN ST. GEORGE   (435)628-4481

Hotel $61-$250 Address: 1165 S Bluff St 84770 Location: I-15 exit 6 (Bluff St), just w. Facility: 94 units. 2 stories (no elevator), exterior corridors. Pool(s): heated outdoor. Activities: hot tub. Guest Services: coin laundry.

RAMADA ST. GEORGE   (435)628-2828

Hotel $71-$189 Address: 1440 E St. George Blvd 84790 Location: I-15 exit 8, just e. Adjacent to factory outlet stores. Facility: 135 units. 2-3 stories, interior corridors. Pool(s): heated outdoor. Activities: hot tub, exercise room. Guest Services: valet and coin laundry.

ST. GEORGE INN & SUITES   (435)673-6661

Hotel $69-$129 Address: 1221 S Main St 84770 Location: I-15 exit 6 (Bluff St), just w. Facility: 143 units, some efficiencies. 2 stories (no elevator), exterior corridors. Terms: cancellation fee imposed. Pool(s): heated outdoor, heated indoor. Activities: hot tub, playground, exercise room. Guest Services: coin laundry.

SEVEN WIVES INN   (435)628-3737

Historic Bed & Breakfast $105-$195 Address: 217 N 100 W 84770 Location: I-15 exit 8, 2.1 mi w, then n. Facility: The two adjacent Victorian-style homes that make up this property feature bright rooms, some with balconies. The stand-alone cottage has a wet bar open to the room and a large bathroom. 13 units, some cottages. 3 stories (no elevator), interior/exterior corridors. Terms: 7 day cancellation notice-fee imposed. Pool(s): outdoor. Activities: massage.

TOWNEPLACE SUITES BY MARRIOTT   (435)986-9955

Extended Stay Hotel
$109-$238

AAA Benefit: Members save 5% or more!

Address: 251 S 1470 E 84790 Location: I-15 exit 8, just e. Facility: 84 kitchen units, some two bedrooms. 3 stories, interior corridors. Pool(s): heated outdoor. Activities: hot tub, exercise room. Guest Services: valet and coin laundry. Featured Amenity: breakfast buffet. (See ad this page.)

WINGATE BY WYNDHAM   (435)673-9608

Hotel $99-$179 Address: 144 W Brigham Rd, Bldg G 84790 Location: I-15 exit 4, just w. Facility: 77 units. 4 stories, interior corridors. Amenities: safes. Pool(s): heated outdoor. Activities: hot tub, exercise room. Guest Services: valet and coin laundry, area transportation.

WHERE TO EAT

AHI'S 'TASTE OF ASIA'   435/673-6604

Asian. Quick Serve. $7-$15 AAA Inspector Notes: This small restaurant prefers guests to order and pay at the counter. Guests can then grab a seat in the contemporary dining area and wait for items to be brought to the table. Offerings include very fresh and flavorful teriyaki bowls, wraps, orange chicken and beef fried rice. You can't go wrong with the pad Thai. Address: 157 E Riverside Dr, Unit 2 84790 Location: I-15 exit 6 (Bluff St), just e. L D

ANASAZI STEAKHOUSE & GALLERY   435/674-0095

Steak. Casual Dining. $12-$34 AAA Inspector Notes: Guests enjoy great steaks cooked on stones at the table, as well as cheese and dessert fondues, in an art gallery setting. In the dining area are photographs by William Carr and metal works by Darrick Phallon, all of which are available for purchase. Features: full bar. Address: 1234 W Sunset Blvd 84770 Location: Jct N Bluff St, 0.5 mi w. D

▼ See AAA listing this page ▼

BEAR PAW CAFE 435/634-0126

▼▼ Breakfast Sandwiches. Family Dining. $7-$10 **AAA Inspector Notes:** Gourmet coffees and teas are offered at this popular local place. Food specialties include homemade soup, sandwiches and early dinner specials, all served in large portions. **Address:** 75 N Main St 84770 **Location:** Downtown. B L

BENJA THAI & SUSHI 435/628-9538

▼▼ Asian. Casual Dining. $10-$18 **AAA Inspector Notes:** Enjoy many Thai and sushi items made from fresh Thai herbs in a calm and peaceful dining room. Very helpful service is provided. **Features:** beer & wine. **Address:** 2 W St. George Blvd, Suite 12 84770 **Location:** Jct Main St. L D

D.U.B'.S 'DEVEY'S URBAN BARBEQUE' 435/674-1023

▼ Barbecue. Quick Serve. $7-$20 **AAA Inspector Notes:** Great barbecue is hard to find in this part of the country, and this place is amazing due to a mix of regional cooking styles. The restaurant is casual with several TVs, and heart and soul goes into all the comfort food served. **Features:** beer only. **Address:** 1812 W Sunset Blvd, Suite 10 84790 **Location:** Jct N Dixie Dr. L D

THE EGG & I 435/628-0368

▼▼ Breakfast Sandwiches. Casual Dining. $7-$10 **AAA Inspector Notes:** This cozy restaurant invites guests in to enjoy creative breakfast dishes and a few lunch items. Eggs Benedict is the specialty, but the waffles and bacon are very flavorful. Many discounts are offered, so ask if you qualify at the register. **Features:** patio dining. **Address:** 1091 N Bluff St 84770 **Location:** I-15 exit 8, 1.8 mi w, then 1.2 mi n; in Sunset Corner Shopping Ctr. B L CALL ⬛

GEORGE'S CORNER RESTAURANT & PUB 435/216-7311

▼▼ American. Casual Dining. $8-$21 **AAA Inspector Notes:** Located in the center of town, this establishment is characterized by upscale pub décor. The multilevel dining room and varied menu cater to all with large salads, calamari, nachos, a lamb burger and even short rib ragout pasta. A pool table resides in the small basement next to the bustling kitchen. **Features:** full bar. **Address:** 2 W St George Blvd 84770 **Location:** I-15 exit 8, at Main St; in Ancestor Square. L D

THE GUN BARREL STEAK & GAME HOUSE 435/652-0550

▼▼ Steak. Casual Dining. $11-$37 **AAA Inspector Notes:** A sister restaurant to the original Wyoming restaurant. Originally a wild game museum, it's been turned into a steak/game house. The log cabin décor with deer, hog and buffalo trophies pairs well with the menu items. Enjoy a large mashed potato bar with many toppings on Friday and Saturday evenings. **Features:** full bar. **Address:** 1091 N Bluff St, Suite 1400 84770 **Location:** I-15 exit 8, 1.8 mi w, then 1.2 mi n. D

IGGY'S SPORTS GRILL 435/673-3344

▼▼ American. Casual Dining. $9-$19 **AAA Inspector Notes:** A lively atmosphere, good casual food and large-screen TVs make outposts of this small chain great places to watch the game. The menu consists mostly of pub grub burgers, BLTs and rib-eye steaks. **Features:** full bar. **Address:** 148 S 1470 E 84770 **Location:** I-15 exit 8, just e. L D

MAD PITA EXPRESS 435/215-1855

▼ Mediterranean. Quick Serve. $6-$18 **AAA Inspector Notes:** Guest flock to this small eatery for the popular "big fat gyros." All the items are prepared fresh with quick and friendly service. This is a casual and favorite local spot after a nearby movie. **Features:** patio dining. **Address:** 2376 E Red Cliffs Dr, Suite 216 84790 **Location:** I-15 exit 10, just e, then 1 mi s. L D

MONGOLIAN BBQ 435/656-1880

▼ Asian. Casual Dining. $8-$12 **AAA Inspector Notes:** This unique restaurant allows guest to choose their own noodle and meat dish from a long buffet line. After piling your bowl high it is handed to a chef that stir-fries it in front of you. The décor is basic, but the staff is friendly and helpful. **Address:** 250 N Red Cliffs Dr, Suite 3 84790 **Location:** I-15 exit 6 (Bluff St), just e, then just n; in The Outlets at Zion. L D

NINJA JAPANESE STEAKHOUSE & SUSHI 435/656-8628

▼▼ Japanese. Casual Dining. $8-$24 **AAA Inspector Notes:** In a busy shopping center, this restaurant employs talented chefs who prepare Japanese food in front of guests at hibachi tables. On the other side of the dining room, patrons can experience a more traditional style of dining. **Features:** beer & wine, patio dining. **Address:** 245 N Red Cliff Dr, Suite 11 84790 **Location:** I-15 exit 8, just e; in Promenade at Red Cliffs Plaza. L D

PAINTED PONY RESTAURANT 435/634-1700

▼▼▼ American. Fine Dining. $9-$36 **AAA Inspector Notes:** The restaurant is adorned with contemporary Southwestern art and fresh flowers. The menu blends fresh ingredients and delicate flavorings. A simple but varied wine list is available, including their personal label. **Features:** full bar, patio dining. **Reservations:** suggested. **Address:** 2 W St. George Blvd 84770 **Location:** I-15 exit 8, at Main St; in Ancestor Square. L D

THE PASTA FACTORY 435/674-3753

▼▼ Italian. Family Dining. $6-$14 **AAA Inspector Notes:** Downtown in Ancestor's Square, this popular restaurant offers such traditional pasta choices as spaghetti, chicken fettuccine and bow-tie pasta with shrimp. Patrons also can make their own varieties. Those who prefer pizza to pasta can bring over a pie from the pizza factory just next door. **Address:** 2 W St. George Blvd 84770 **Location:** Jct Main St; downtown. L D

PAULA'S CAZUELA MEXICAN FOOD 435/673-6568

▼▼ Mexican. Family Dining. $7-$16 **AAA Inspector Notes:** The amazing panoramic view of the city is a huge hit, along with traditional Mexican cuisine and creative flavored margaritas. The service and décor is very casual and it is very popular with families. **Features:** beer & wine. **Address:** 745 Ridgeview Dr 84770 **Location:** I-15 exit 6 (Bluff St), 2.5 mi nw. L D

PLAYERS SPORTS GRILL 435/634-9211

▼▼ American. Casual Dining. $9-$23 **AAA Inspector Notes:** The upscale sports grill offers a range of pub grub, pasta dishes, steaks and specialty items. Guests can watch the big-game action on many large flat-screen TVs as the friendly staff does their thing. **Features:** full bar. **Address:** 1688 S Convention Center Dr 84790 **Location:** I-15 exit 6 (Bluff St), just e. L D

SALINA pop. 2,489

SCENIC HILLS SUPER 8 (435)529-7483

▼▼ Motel $60-$100

Address: 375 E 1620 S 84654 **Location:** I-70 exit 56, just n. Adjacent to a truck stop. **Facility:** 69 units, some two bedrooms and kitchens. 2 stories (no elevator), exterior corridors. **Pool(s):** heated outdoor. **Guest Services:** coin laundry. **Featured Amenity:** continental breakfast.

SAVE ▦ 🚲 BIZ 🛜 ⬛ ⬛ ⬛ / SOME UNITS ⬛

WHERE TO EAT

EL MEXICANO RESTAURANT 435/529-2132

▼▼ Mexican. Casual Dining. $6-$14 **AAA Inspector Notes:** This popular restaurant serves more than 25 specialty dinners and 30 combination platters, including mole poblano, carne asada, chile verde and coconut shrimp. They are not open in the morning, but if you can wait, tasty breakfast selections are available for lunch and dinner. **Features:** beer only. **Address:** 1535 S State St 84654 **Location:** I-70 exit 56, just n. L D

Ask your AAA/CAA club
about travel money and other
financial services for travelers

Salt Lake City

Then & Now

Founded by Mormons in 1847, Salt Lake City—today the cultural and ecclesiastical as well as the political capital of Utah—lies in a spectacular setting at the foot of the Wasatch Mountains, with the Great Salt Lake visible to the northwest and the Great Salt Lake Desert to the west.

Like many earlier American settlers, adherents of The Church of Jesus Christ of Latter-day Saints (who often are referred to as Mormons) traveled across the country in search of a place where they could practice their religion without persecution. As these Mormon pioneers approached the Salt Lake Valley for the first time, their leader, Brigham Young, proclaimed, "This is the right place."

In 1850, following a failed petition by the settlers for their "State of Deseret" to be recognized by the U.S. government, Congress established the Utah Territory, with Salt Lake City later

named as its capital. A few years after Utah joined the Union in 1896, the decorous Corinthian-style State Capitol was built. Set on a lush site showcasing plants native to the region, the seat of government spotlights Utah's history, people and values in its masterful design.

Still, many of the city's finest buildings are ecclesiastical, and some of its most striking houses were once occupied by Young and his family. With streets designed to be "wide enough for a team of four oxen and a covered wagon to turn around," Salt Lake was laid out in a grid pattern fanning out from what is now known as Temple Square.

The three-block area is home to the most prominent LDS Church edifices. Today, both clued-in and inexperienced sightseers have this square on their list of must-sees, as evidenced by the two visitor centers located here. Most trip itineraries include a tour of the dome-shaped Salt Lake Tabernacle on Temple Square. Outside the Salt Lake Temple, amateur photographers feverishly snap pictures of the dazzling multi-spired edifice, an active and highly revered place of worship whose interior is closed to the public.

South Temple Street has a large concentration of 19th- and early 20th-century designs, including the Gothic-style Cathedral of the Madeleine, completed in 1909, and the 1901 Thomas Kearns Mansion. Architectural evidence of Salt Lake City's mining wealth around the turn of the 20th century can be seen during guided tours at the latter, now the governor's mansion; phone (801) 538-1005.

The Brigham Young Monument, a tribute to the second president of the Mormon Church and the first territorial governor of Utah, is on the corner of South Temple and Main streets. On its

Brigham Young Monument

(Continued on p. 369.)

Destination Salt Lake City

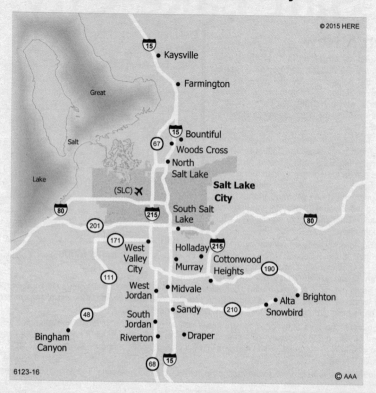

This map shows cities in the Salt Lake City vicinity where you will find attractions, hotels and restaurants. Cities are listed alphabetically in this book on the following pages.

Fast Facts

ABOUT THE CITY

POP: 186,440 ▪ ELEV: 4,390 ft.

MONEY

SALES TAX: The sales tax in Salt Lake County is 6.85 percent. There also is a 4.75 percent tax on lodgings in Salt Lake County, 9.5 percent levied on automobile rentals and a 1 percent restaurant tax.

WHOM TO CALL

EMERGENCY: 911

POLICE (non-emergency): (801) 799-3000

HOSPITALS: LDS Hospital, (801) 408-1100 ▪ St. Mark's Hospital, (801) 268-7111 ▪ Salt Lake Regional Medical Center, (801) 350-4111 ▪ University of Utah Health Care-University Hospital, (801) 581-2121.

WHERE TO LOOK AND LISTEN

NEWSPAPERS: The Salt Lake Tribune and the Deseret News are the city's daily morning newspapers.

RADIO: Salt Lake City radio station KSL (1160 AM/102.7 FM) is an all-news radio station ▪ KCPW (88.3 and 105.3 FM) and KUER (90.1 FM) are members of National Public Radio.

VISITOR INFORMATION

Salt Lake City Visitor Information Center: 90 S. West Temple, Salt Lake City, UT 84101-1406. Phone: (801) 534-4900 or (800) 541-4955.

TRANSPORTATION

AIR TRAVEL: Salt Lake City International Airport (SLC), 7 miles west of the downtown area, is accessible from I-80. Driving time is approximately 10 minutes. Most Salt Lake City hotels offer free shuttle service to and from the airport. Average taxi fare from the airport to the city is $20; limousine fare averages $79 per car. Salt Lake City's light rail system, TRAX, now provides service from the airport to downtown on its green line. The one-way fare is $2.50; $1.25 (ages 65+).

Canyon Transportation provides car and van service from Salt Lake International Airport to hotels and resorts in Alta, Brighton, Park City, Sundance and other destinations throughout the Salt Lake Valley; phone (801) 255-1841 or (800) 255-1841.

RENTAL CARS: Hertz, 775 N. Terminal Dr. at the airport, offers discounts to AAA members; phone (801) 575-2683 or (800) 654-3080.

RAIL SERVICE: The Amtrak station is at 340 South 600 West; phone (800) 872-7245.

BUSES: The Greyhound Lines Inc. terminal is at 300 South 600 West; phone (801) 355-9579 or (800) 231-2222 or TTY (800) 345-3109.

TAXIS: Taxis are on the meter system. Cab companies include City Cab, (801) 363-5550 ▪ Ute Cab, (801) 359-7788 ▪ and Yellow Cab, (801) 521-1862.

PUBLIC TRANSPORTATION: Utah Transit Authority (UTA) provides bus service for Salt Lake City as well as transportation to nearby ski areas. Salt Lake City's light rail system, TRAX, also is operated by UTA. The Blue Line runs from downtown south to Draper. The Red Line connects downtown with Jordan and the University of Utah campus. The Green Line connects downtown with West Valley City and the airport. TRAX arrives at stations within 10-30 minutes. In addition, the FrontRunner commuter rail line connects downtown with Ogden, and a high-speed MAX bus links the Millcreek TRAX station with the town of Magna.

One-way fare, valid on buses and light rail, is $2.50; $1.25 (ages 65+); free (ages 0-5). Round-trip fare is $5; $2.50 (ages 65+). A 1-day pass is $6.25. A round-trip group pass is $10 (up to four people). All fares include a fuel surcharge. Exact change is required.

When traveling within the Free Ride Zone, located downtown from North Temple to 500 South and 400 West to 200 East and including the TRAX library station and the bus stops between 200 East and 300 East on 400 South, passengers may use either the buses or light rail for free, but boarding and unloading must occur within the defined area. Phone (801) 287-4636 for information about either system.

(Continued from p. 367.)

north face, a bronze plaque lists the Mormon pioneers who arrived here on July 24, 1847; their predecessors, Native Americans and enterprising fur trappers, also are commemorated with two bronze figures at the monument's base.

One of Salt Lake City's most interesting structures is the Eagle Gate, erected in 1859 as the entrance to Young's private farm. Spanning State Street in front of the Beehive House, the giant four-legged arch is surmounted by a 4,000-pound bronze statue of an eagle with a wingspread of 20 feet. The gate has been remodeled several times; the original copper-plated eagle, which has a wingspread of 16 feet, is in the Pioneer Memorial Museum on Main Street.

A more modern architectural showpiece is the Salt Palace, an integral part of the city's cultural scene. Officially the Calvin L. Rampton Salt Palace Convention Center, the complex at 90 S. West Temple St. includes Abravanel Hall, the home of the Utah Symphony, and the Utah Museum of Contemporary Art.

Must Do: AAA Editor's Picks

- Encompassing three city blocks in the heart of downtown Salt Lake City, **Temple Square** contains nearly 20 points of interest relating to the Mormon religion and Utah pioneer history. If you're a first-time visitor, take one of the regularly scheduled guided tours led by missionaries and volunteer docents.

- The massive, six-spired, neo-Gothic **Salt Lake Temple,** the worldwide icon of The Church of Jesus Christ of Latter-day Saints, was constructed over a 40-year period by Mormon pioneers who sacrificed time, labor and material goods to create a symbol of their faith and devotion. Only church members may enter, but you can stroll around the grounds and admire the building's sheer scale and stunning exterior workmanship.

- The **State Capitol** overlooks Salt Lake Valley from the vantage point of Capitol Hill. Marvel at the interior ceiling of the building's dome, which soars 165 feet above the floor and is painted with a large mural depicting seagulls flying among clouds—a reference in Mormon folklore to the miraculous 1848 arrival of California gulls that proceeded to devour insects destroying the first crops planted by pioneers.

Tour the State Capitol

- Brigham Young and his followers first entered the Salt Lake Valley at Emigration Canyon, where the Mormon leader allegedly declared that "This is the right place." **"This Is The Place" Heritage Park** commemorates their arrival with a bronze sculpture of Young and two fellow colleagues. Learn about 19th-century pioneer life at the park's **Heritage Village.**

- Across from Heritage Park is **Utah's Hogle Zoo,** a great family destination. Kids love riding the horses, bears and other beasties on the Conservation Carousel and watching as nature's largest land mammals have their toenails trimmed during Elephant Encounter. In summer the Wildlife Theatre Bird Show features performing eagles, hawks, owls and parrots.

- Great Salt Lake is one of the saltiest bodies of water on Earth (only the Dead Sea has a higher saline content). Take a day trip to **Antelope Island State Park,** where you can test the water's incredible buoyancy—even the most committed landlubbers will easily float—go for a hike or tour the state's oldest ranch.

- Utah is famed for rugged mountains and stark landscapes, but there also are greener pleasures like **Red Butte Garden and Arboretum.** Pack a picnic lunch and enjoy nature at one of the "wayside" resting areas; the spring show of color, courtesy of daffodils, lilacs and blooming crab apple trees, is lovely.

- Meet Chilean flamingos, trumpeter swans, turquoise tanagers and Storm the red-tailed hawk at the **Tracy Aviary,** where you can learn lots of cool stuff about our feathered friends via informal, up-close bird encounters.

- Hearing the glorious collective voice of the Mormon Tabernacle Choir is an inspirational experience. Attend one of the choir's free weekly performances at the **Salt Lake Tabernacle on Temple Square,** where the superb acoustics heighten the glory.

- A twinkling wonderland awaits during the **Christmas Lighting of Temple Square.** Hundreds of thousands of white lights cover trees and buildings from the day after Thanksgiving through December.

Salt Lake City 1-day Itinerary

AAA editors suggest these activities for a great short vacation experience.

Morning

- **Market Street Grill & Oyster Bar - Downtown** has a well-earned reputation for seafood dinners, but it's under the radar when it comes to breakfast. Fuel up for a morning of sightseeing with eggs Benedict or an avocado-topped crab omelet; both come with potatoes and toast you can slather with the restaurant's homemade raspberry jam.

- Then explore ▽ **Temple Square,** the headquarters of The Church of Jesus Christ of Latter-Day Saints. The ▽ **Salt Lake Temple,** built by Brigham Young's devoted followers over a 40-year period beginning in 1853, is the massive and inspiring focal point of the square, but there are many other things to see. Take a tour of the ▽ **Salt Lake Tabernacle on Temple Square,** home to the world-famous Mormon Tabernacle Choir. The acoustics are amazing: It's said that a pin dropped at the front of the cavernous interior can be heard all the way at the back. The Church Office Building has an observation deck; visitors are welcome to take the elevator to the 26th floor and enjoy the panoramic city views.

- The **Beehive House,** one of church founder Brigham Young's two Salt Lake City homes, is named for the image of a beehive—the symbol of industriousness—that sits atop the residence. And Young was nothing if not industrious, serving as Utah's territorial governor and, as president of the Mormon church, helping to establish pioneer settlements throughout the West. Tour the house and get a look at how Young and his family lived in the 1850s.

Afternoon

- Salt Lake City's dramatic backdrop of towering mountains sliced by deep canyons offers wonderful scenic drive opportunities, so hit the road. One of the most popular routes is east via I-80 to Parleys Canyon, on the eastern side of the Salt Lake Valley. Side roads off the interstate wind through forests that blaze with color in the fall.

- If you don't feel like a drive trip, spend time at Trolley Square. This isn't just another mall; the brick buildings that house favorites like Lululemon, Pottery Barn and Williams-Sonoma once served as storage barns for the cars that made up the city's trolley system.

- And if you want to spend time outdoors but not behind the wheel, head to **Wheeler Historic Farm.** This restored, turn-of-the-20th-century dairy farm offers cow-milking demonstrations, tractor-pulled wagon rides and tours of the historic Wheeler house, where Henry and Sariah

Visit the Beehive House

Wheeler and their six kids lived when not engaged in wood chopping, butter churning, soap making and various other tasks. You can also take a walk along Little Cottonwood Creek.

Evening

- Locals swear that the **Red Iguana** has the best Mexican food in Salt Lake City. It's a festive, fun place complete with plastic poinsettia-pattern tablecloths and strolling mariachis. The seven different mole sauces include mole amarillo, an unusual blend of golden raisins, yellow tomatoes, zucchini and guajillo chiles, and the strawberry margaritas and Mexican beers pack a potent punch. It's very popular, so reservations are advised.

- The Capitol Theatre, with its ornate decorations and huge crystal chandeliers, is a reminder of when going out to see a show was a special occasion. The home of Ballet West and the Utah Opera is also the place to see touring Broadway productions and holiday perennials like "The Nutcracker."

- The Tavernacle (at 201 East 300 South, within walking distance of Temple Square) is a dueling piano bar that also offers karaoke on Sundays, Mondays and Tuesdays. Reservations are recommended; phone (801) 833-0570.

- Lumpys Downtown, 145 Pierpont Ave., is favored by the college crowd. Expect the usual at this rowdy sports bar—pool tables, foosball and private booths with HDTV for game viewing. There's also an upstairs dance floor with DJ music Friday and Saturday nights.

Arriving
By Car

Salt Lake City is sometimes called the "Crossroads of the West" due to its easy access. I-15 crosses through Salt Lake City in a north-south direction, while I-80 cuts through the city carrying traffic east and west. I-215 provides a loop around all but the northeastern quadrant of the city. US 89 (State Street) is a major north-south thoroughfare, with the State Capitol as its northern terminus. An alternate east-west route through the city is 2100 South Street.

Getting Around
Street System

Getting around Salt Lake City is not difficult once you know how the street system works. Salt Lake City is based on a grid system. Temple Square in downtown Salt Lake is the center of the grid and is the point at which all numbering begins. Addresses in Salt Lake City usually consist of two numbers. For example, the AAA office is at 560 East 500 South. This means that the office is 5 blocks south of the temple and slightly more than 5 blocks east of the temple. Another way of stating this is 560 East on 500 South. Locals tend to drop the last two zeros when giving directions; thus 500 South becomes 5th South. Some streets have a name as well as a number, but most have numbers only.

Parking

Metered parking is available throughout the city, with a 2-hour limit at most meters. After 6 p.m. metered parking is free. Parking is available at the Firestone Building, 175 West 200 South and through Ampco System Parking at various locations; phone (801) 364-7275. Fees range from $3-$5 (hourly rate) to $5-$10 (daily rate).

Shopping

Onetime downtown shopping mainstays Crossroads Plaza, bounded by S. Main, South Temple and West Temple streets, and ZCMI Center Mall, across from Temple Square on S. State Street, closed in early 2007 to make way for the creation of a new mixed-use downtown district, **City Creek Center.** Combining retail, office and residential development, the property is noted for its retractable glass roof and open-air design. Other highlights include a foliage-lined creek that runs throughout the site, a pedestrian skyway, and such anchor stores as Macy's and Nordstrom.

The Gateway, located on South 400 West, features a restored 1908 Union Pacific Depot with French Renaissance architecture and original artwork. In addition to more than 130 stores and restaurants, the area also offers the "dancing waters" of the Olympic Snowflake Fountain at the Olympic Legacy Plaza.

Gardner Village, 1100 West 7800 South in West Jordan, consists of historic cabins and homes from sites throughout Utah that now house old-time stores offering furniture, accessories and collectibles. The Old Gardner Mill, now home to a restaurant and country store, also is featured.

Trolley Square, on 700 East between 500 and 600 South streets, is in a 1908 trolley barn built by railroad magnate E.H. Harriman. The plants, trolley cars, stained-glass windows and antique lighting fixtures create a nostalgic atmosphere. Shops, restaurants and theaters line the mall; some of the businesses are housed in refurbished trolley cars, while the exteriors of others resemble Victorian mansions. Self-guiding walking tours are available; phone (801) 521-9877.

Area malls include **Fashion Place Mall,** at 6191 S. State St. in Murray. Boasting 110 stores and restaurants, it counts Dillard's and Nordstrom as its anchors. **South Towne Center,** with a carousel in the mall's center, claims the title of largest mall in the state. At 10450 S. State St. in Sandy, its 130 stores include Dillard's, JCPenney and Macy's. **Valley Fair Mall,** 3601 South 2700 West, lists JCPenney and Macy's among its 100 retailers.

Big Events

Proud of their heritage, Salt Lake City residents celebrate it throughout the year. The ▽ **Days of '47 Celebration** in July commemorates the arrival of the Mormon pioneers in the Salt Lake Valley. A week of community festivities, which includes a rodeo, ends with floats, bands, horse brigades, clowns and dignitaries marching down **Main Street** in the **Days of '47 Parade.**

Other events include the ▽ **Utah Arts Festival** in late June; the **Hot Air Balloon Festival** in August in Sandy; the **Utah State Fair** and the ▽ **Salt Lake City Greek Festival,** both in September; and, after

Do some shopping at The Gateway

Thanksgiving, the ✈️ **Christmas Lighting of Temple Square.** ✈️ **EVE Winterfest** concludes the year's festivities as residents of all ages join to usher in the new year.

Sports & Rec

Salt Lake City is known for its variety of year-round sports and recreational opportunities. Perhaps most prominent are the major **ski** resorts located within 45 minutes of the Salt Lake City airport. Little Cottonwood and Big Cottonwood canyons are home to **Snowbird, Alta, Brighton and Solitude Mountain ski resorts.** Parleys Canyon is where snow falls on the **Park City Mountain Resort.** With snowfall in excess of 400 inches per year, snow is fresh and falls often. **Snowmobiling** and **cross-country skiing** also are abundant along the **Wasatch Front.** Nearby local mountains also offer **mountain biking.**

Summer activities include both indoor and outdoor sports. Favorite **golf** courses include **Bonneville, Bountiful Ridge, The Country Club, Davis Park, Eaglewood, Glendale, Glenmoor, Mountain Dell, Nibley Park, Old Mill, Rose Park, University of Utah, West Ridge** and **Wingpointe.** Information and reservations for most of these courses can be made by phoning the Utah Golf Association at (801) 563-0400.

Bicycling in the mountains or valleys is a popular activity; trails follow the **Jordan River,** which runs through Salt Lake County. **Hiking, camping** and **fishing** in and around the city also are favorite pastimes. Along Canyon Road in the northeast section of the city is **City Creek Canyon,** a favorite recreational area for hikers, joggers, picnickers and bicyclists. Reservations must be made to drive through or to picnic beyond the main gate, and a fee for picnicking is charged; phone the Watershed Management Division, (801) 483-6705. In summer, on even-numbered days the park is closed to cyclists and joggers; on odd-numbered days the park is closed to all motorized vehicles.

Three large reservoirs provide opportunities for **boating** and water sports. Public **tennis** courts are available in many parks, including **Liberty** and **Murray. Antelope Island State Park** offers sand beaches and **swimming.** The park, about a 30-minute drive north of Salt Lake City, is reachable via a causeway.

The 20,500-seat **Vivint Smart Home Arena** at 301 West and South Temple streets is the home of the NBA's **Utah Jazz;** phone (801) 355-3865. **Baseball** is represented by the **Salt Lake Bees,** the AAA farm team of the Los Angeles Angels of Anaheim. Games are played at **Smith's Ballpark** at 77 West 1300 South; phone (801) 350-6900. **Hockey** fans attend the games of the **Utah Grizzlies** of the ECHL. Their rink, the **Maverik Center,** is at 3200 S. Decker Lake Dr. in West Valley City; phone (801) 988-7825, or (801) 988-8000 for the box office.

Play a round of golf in Salt Lake City

Performing Arts

The **Salt Palace** (officially the Calvin L. Rampton Salt Palace Convention Center), 90 S. West Temple, is known for its striking architectural elements, including delicate snowflake chandeliers and a circular, glass-walled entrance tower framed by HSS (Hollow Structural Steel); phone (801) 534-4900.

Performances of the **Utah Symphony,** (801) 533-6683, are held in **Abravanel Hall,** located within the Salt Lake County Center for the Arts complex at 123 W. South Temple. **Capitol Theatre,** nearby at 50 West 200 South, is the home of **Ballet West,** which stages both classical and modern works. The theater, which has been restored to its original turn-of-the-20th-century opulence, also is the home of **Utah Opera** productions. Phone ArtTix at (801) 355-2787; or (888) 451-2787 or TTY (801) 328-8202 for symphony, ballet or opera tickets.

The **Mormon Tabernacle Choir** presents free weekly performances of inspirational music and thought in the acoustically unique **Salt Lake Tabernacle on Temple Square** (see attraction listing p. 378).

Pioneer Theatre Company, Utah's resident professional theater, is located on the University of Utah campus. The company presents musicals as well as classical and contemporary plays; for ticket information phone (801) 581-6961.

Dance in Salt Lake City is represented by **Repertory Dance Theatre,** which stages American modern dance classics and contemporary masterpieces at 138 West 300 South, and the **Ririe-Woodbury Dance Company,** a modern dance touring company performs at the **Rose Wagner Performing Arts Center** and the Capitol Theatre. Phone the Repertory Dance Theatre at (801) 534-1000 or ArtTix at (801) 355-2787, (888) 451-2787 or TTY (801) 328-8202 for Rose Wagner Performing Arts Center tickets.

INSIDER INFO:
Mormonism

Joseph Smith Jr., the son of a poor upstate New York farmer, is said to have received a visit in 1827 from the angel Moroni. Smith said the angel, who was the son of the prophet Mormon, entrusted him with golden plates inscribed with symbols, which Smith translated into the Book of Mormon.

The name of the church, which began in 1830, is The Church of Jesus Christ of Latter-day Saints, or LDS Church; "Mormon" is a nickname. Mormons believe that Jesus Christ is the son of God and that divine revelation did not end with the disciples but continues today. They place strong emphasis on the family and rely on the leadership of lay members rather than professional clergy.

Smith advocated polygamy and was plurally married himself. Although no more than 4 percent of the Mormon population practiced polygamy at any time, advocacy of it led to strife with non-Mormons wherever the Mormons settled. Smith had designated Missouri as Zion, but persecution there forced the Mormons to move to Illinois, where they established the city of Nauvoo. Smith was arrested and jailed in neighboring towns; in 1844 he was shot to death by a mob that stormed Carthage City Jail.

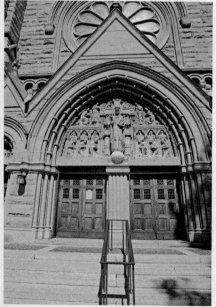
Cathedral of the Madeleine

Soon after Smith's death the church split into two factions. Mormons who rejected polygamy formed a "Reorganized Church" and returned to Missouri. A larger group followed Brigham Young to Utah in 1847, establishing Salt Lake City. Although Utah Mormons applied for statehood as early as 1849, their request was not granted until 1896, after the church abolished polygamy.

ATTRACTIONS

BEEHIVE HOUSE is at 67 E. South Temple St. The 1854 house, the restored official residence of Brigham Young, the second president of the Mormon Church, is decorated with period furnishings. A beehive, the symbol of industry and a reference to Young's work ethic, sits on top of the house. **Hours:** Half-hour guided tours are given daily 9:30-8:30. Last tour begins 15 minutes before closing. Closed Christmas. **Cost:** Free. **Phone:** (801) 240-2681.

BRIGHAM YOUNG'S GRAVE is on First Ave. between State and A sts. The Mormon leader died in 1877. Others buried in the small plot include several family members and Eliza R. Snow, a pioneer songwriter. The Mormon Pioneer Memorial Monument, honoring the 6,000 pioneers who perished during their 1847-69 journey to Utah, also is at the site.

CATHEDRAL OF THE MADELEINE is at 331 E. South Temple St. The cathedral was built by the first bishop of Salt Lake City, Bishop Lawrence Scanlon. Begun in 1900, the cathedral is 190 feet long, 100 feet wide and has two towers 220 feet high. The Gothic interior has Venetian mosaics and Tennessee marble, three main altars of Utah marble and wall niches with oak statues. Above each altar is a painting of St. Mary Magdalene. **Time:** Allow 1 hour minimum. **Hours:** Mon.-Fri. 7:30 a.m.-9 p.m., Sat.-Sun. 7:30-7:30. Guided tours are given Sun. at 12:30, Tues. at 1, when staff is available. Phone ahead to confirm schedule. **Cost:** Free. **Phone:** (801) 328-8941.

CHURCH HISTORY MUSEUM is at 45 N. West Temple St. Parking is available at 103 N. West Temple St. The museum chronicles the history of Mormonism from 1820 to the present through interpretive exhibits, films and demonstrations. Displays include memorabilia, sculpture and paintings from around the world as well as changing exhibits. Guided tours are available by appointment; reservations must be scheduled at least 2 weeks in advance.

Time: Allow 30 minutes minimum. **Hours:** Mon.-Fri. 9-9, Sat.-Sun. and holidays 10-5. Closed Jan. 1, Easter, Thanksgiving, Christmas Eve and Christmas. **Cost:** Free. **Phone:** (801) 240-3310 for recorded information, or (801) 240-4615 for tour reservations.

THE CHURCH OFFICE BUILDING, 50 E. North Temple St., houses the Mormon Church's administrative, communications and missionary departments. A mural of Christ and the Apostles occupies a lobby wall.

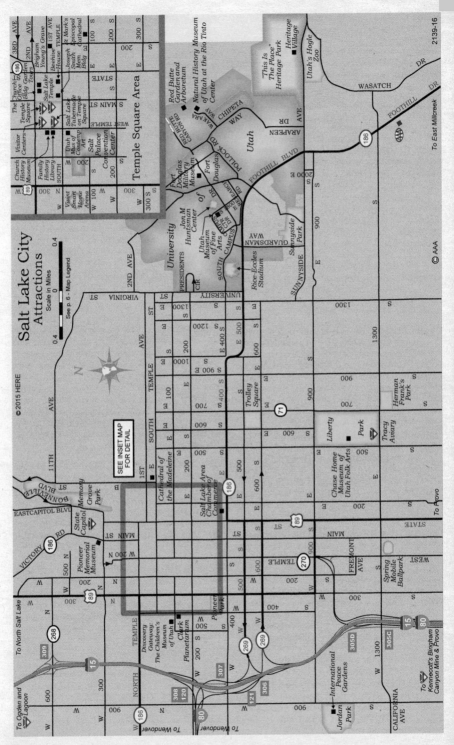

Salt Lake City Attractions

Scale in Miles

See p. 6 · Map Legend

0.4   0.4

©2015 HERE

2139-16

© AAA

Temple Square Area

The Church of Jesus Christ of Latter-day Saints Temple Square
Church Office Bldg
Brigham Young's Grave
Beehive House
Joseph Smith Mem. Bldg
St. Mark's Episcopal Cathedral
Salt Lake Temple
Salt Lake Tabernacle on Temple Square
Museum of Church History and Art
Visitor Centers
Church History Museum
Family History Library
Utah Museum of Contemporary Art
Salt Palace Convention Center
Vivint Smart Home Arena

Red Butte Garden and Arboretum
Natural History Museum of Utah at the Rio Tinto Center
"This Is The Place" Heritage Park
Heritage Village
Utah's Hogle Zoo
University of Utah
Jon M Huntsman Center
Utah Museum of Fine Arts
Fort Douglas Military Museum
Fort Douglas
Rice-Eccles Stadium
Sunnyside Park
Herman Frank's Park
Liberty Park
Chase Home Museum of Utah Folk Arts
Tracy Aviary
Trolley Square
Cathedral of the Madeleine
Salt Lake Area Chamber of Commerce
State Capitol
Memory Grove Park
Pioneer Memorial Museum
Pioneer Park
Discovery Gateway: The Children's Museum of Utah
Clark Planetarium
Spring Mobile Ballpark
International Peace Gardens
Jordan Park

SEE INSET MAP FOR DETAIL

To Ogden and Lagoon
To North Salt Lake
To Wendover
To Provo
To Kennecott's Bingham Canyon Mine & Provo
To East Millcreek

Guided tours include an explanation of the mural and a visit to the 26th-floor observation deck, which offers a panoramic view of the Salt Lake Valley. **Hours:** Building and observation deck Mon.-Fri. 9-5, Apr.-Sept.; Mon.-Fri. 9-4:30, rest of year. Closed major holidays. **Cost:** Free. **Phone:** (801) 240-1000.

Garden Tours is at 50 E. North Temple St. in Temple Square. Visitors may enjoy a leisurely stroll or take a guided tour through spring, summer or autumn gardens that are redesigned and replanted every 6 months. More than 16,500 bedding plants and 250 flower beds surround the plaza, an oval reflecting pool and a fountain. A 4-acre rooftop prairie garden includes hundreds of native flowers, trees and drought-tolerant plants.

Time: Allow 1 hour minimum. **Hours:** Tours are given Mon.-Fri. at 11 (also Wed. at 7 p.m.), Sun. at 10:30, Apr.-Sept. Rooftop tours are given Mon.-Fri. at 10 (also Sun. at 10:30 or 11:30; phone for schedule), Apr.-Sept. Weekday morning tours depart from the southwest lobby. Wed. evening tour departs from the south door. Sun. morning tour begins at the east gate. Rooftop tours begin in the lobby at door 15 (Mon.-Fri.) and at door 20 on Sun. Closed major holidays. Phone ahead to confirm schedule. **Cost:** Free. **Phone:** (801) 240-5916.

CLARK PLANETARIUM is at 110 South 400 West. The Hansen Dome contains high-resolution projectors that take visitors on a simulated trip through the universe. The Museum and Exhibit Hall has a Foucault pendulum, a rotating relief globe, a large lunar hemisphere, a sphere movie screen and photographic transparencies. The IMAX Theater offers various 3-D science and nature films. The planetarium also features hands-on exhibits and laser concerts.

Hours: Planetarium and museum Sun.-Wed. 10:30-7, Thurs. 10:30-10; Fri.-Sat. 10:30 a.m.-11 p.m. Star and laser show times vary; phone ahead for schedule. Closed Thanksgiving and Christmas. Closes at 4 on Christmas Eve. **Cost:** Planetarium and museum free. Hansen Dome or IMAX Theater $9; $7 (ages 0-12 and to all at matinees). **Parking:** $1 (3 hours). **Phone:** (801) 456-7827.

DISCOVERY GATEWAY: THE CHILDREN'S MUSEUM OF UTAH is at 444 West 100 South. The contemporary interactive discovery center, encompassing more than 60,000 square feet on three floors, provides families with hands-on exhibits and workshops. Visitors explore the world of STEM (science, technology, engineering and mathematics), art and humanities. Activities include "piloting" a Life Flight helicopter, performing iPad-enabled operations in the kid-sized Primary Children's Hospital, delivering mail in a kids' town, building a model house and testing its ability to withstand an earthquake and creating an animated film.

Time: Allow 2 hours minimum. **Hours:** Mon.-Sat. 10-6 (also Fri.-Sat. 6-8 p.m.), Sun. noon-6. Closed Easter, Thanksgiving and Christmas. **Cost:** $9.50; $7 (ages 65+); free (ages 0-2). **Parking:** $1 (3 hours). **Phone:** (801) 456-5437. [🍴]

FAMILY HISTORY LIBRARY is at 35 N. West Temple St. The library, founded in 1894, is one of the world's largest genealogical libraries. The collection focuses mainly on the United States, Canada, the British Isles and Europe, including Scandinavia, but there are growing records for other areas of the world. Records date 1550-1920. Research tools include microfilm, microfiche, periodicals, computers and reference books.

Hours: Tues.-Fri. 8 a.m.-9 p.m., Mon. 8-5, Sat. 9-5. Phone ahead to confirm schedule around holidays. Closed major holidays. **Cost:** Free. **Parking:** Lot parking $2/hr. Free parking Tues.-Fri., 4:30-9 and all day Sat. behind the Church History Museum, 45 N. West Temple St. **Phone:** (801) 240-6996.

FORT DOUGLAS is just e. of the University of Utah campus on Wasatch Dr. Spread over 9,000 acres, the former military installation was founded in 1862. Its buildings embrace five architectural styles and include an impressive group of 19th-century red sandstone structures. **Hours:** Daily 24 hours.

Fort Douglas Military Museum, 32 Potter St., has displays about Utah and U.S. military history. Exhibits include military uniforms dating from 1858 through Operation Iraqi Freedom as well as tanks. Key events relating to the fort's history are depicted in the stained glass window panels. Artillery pieces are on display in the Cannon Park. The centerpiece of the Utah Fallen Warrior Memorial is a 9,000-pound concrete slab from an underground slurry wall that kept the Hudson River from flooding Ground Zero on Sept. 11. Note: Exhibit work is ongoing in the museum. **Hours:** Tues.-Sat. noon-5. Closed Thanksgiving and Christmas. **Cost:** Free. **Phone:** (801) 581-1710 or (801) 581-1251.

INTERNATIONAL PEACE GARDENS is at 1000 South 900 West in Jordan Park. Dedicated in 1952 to foster world peace, the park features gardens dotted by buildings, flags and statues that reflect the heritage and culture of 26 countries. Among the statues located throughout the park are miniature Eiffel Tower and Matterhorn replicas. **Hours:** Daily dawn-dusk, May-Sept. **Cost:** Free. **Phone:** (801) 938-5326. [🐾]

JOSEPH SMITH MEMORIAL BUILDING is at 52 N. Main St. Named for the first president of The Church of Jesus Christ of Latter-day Saints, the renovated building, which served as a hotel 1911-87, contains a genealogy center and decorative features such as marble columns, art glass and an elegant staircase. Gardens surround the building, and a 500-seat theater presents a 70-minute film about Smith's life.

Time: Allow 1 hour, 30 minutes minimum. **Hours:** Guided tours Mon.-Fri. 9-9, Sat. 9-5. Film shown every 2 hours. Gardens Mon.-Sat. 11-3:30 (also Mon.-Thurs. 5-9 and Fri.-Sat. 5-10). Closed Jan. 1, Thanksgiving and Christmas. **Cost:** Free. **Phone:** (801) 240-1266. [🍴]

LIBERTY PARK stretches from 500 to 700 East St. and 900 to 1300 South St. The 100-acre park contains an aviary, a museum featuring Utah folk art, a playground, a pool, tennis courts, the Seven Canyons Fountain, and a seasonal children's amusement park and garden. Paddleboat rentals are available Memorial Day weekend through Labor Day.

Hours: Park open daily 6 a.m.-11 p.m. Pool and tennis courts open daily; phone ahead for hours. Amusement park open daily 11-7, Memorial Day weekend-Labor Day. **Cost:** Park free. Pool $2; $1.50 (ages 3-17); free (ages 0-2 and 80+). Amusement park ride prices vary. **Phone:** (801) 521-0962 for concessions, rides and boats, (801) 328-4711 for the tennis courts, or (385) 468-1564 for the pool.

Chase Home Museum of Utah Folk Arts is in the middle of Liberty Park. In a two-story, 1853 adobe Greek-Revival house, the museum showcases traditional folk art crafted by Utahns. Native art such as baskets, cradleboards and jewelry; ethnic pieces, including origami and piñatas; items that are occupational in nature, such as saddles and spurs; and handmade objects from rural areas, such as rugs and furniture help depict Utah's history and culture.

In addition to its exhibits, the museum also has a collection of recordings and photographs and presents concerts and dances in the park. **Hours:** Tues.-Sat. 10-4, Memorial Day-Labor Day; Tues.-Fri. 11-4, rest of year. Closed major holidays. Phone ahead to confirm schedule. **Cost:** Free. **Phone:** (801) 533-5760.

Tracy Aviary is at 589 East 1300 South in the s.w. corner of Liberty Park; access is via the park's north entrance off 900 South at 600 East. One of the world's oldest public aviaries, it was founded in 1938 by banker Russell Tracy. More than 400 birds from around the world can be seen, including more than 135 species (many endangered). Programs featuring free-flying birds entertain guests during several shows daily, as keepers explain how these creatures live.

Time: Allow 2 hours minimum. **Hours:** Daily 9-5 (also Mon. 5-8, June-Aug.). Closed Thanksgiving and Christmas. **Cost:** $7; $6 (ages 65+ and students and military with ID); $5 (ages 3-12). **Phone:** (801) 596-8500.

PIONEER MEMORIAL MUSEUM is w. of the Capitol at 300 N. Main St. The museum is a replica of the old Salt Lake Theater. Displays include doll collections, handmade textiles and 19th-century furniture. The adjacent carriage house contains historic vehicles and antique farm machinery. **Hours:** Mon.-Sat. 9-5 (also Wed. 5-8). **Cost:** Donations. **Phone:** (801) 532-6479.

ST. MARK'S EPISCOPAL CATHEDRAL is at 231 East 100 South. The small 1870 cathedral has thick native sandstone walls and heavy wooden roof trusses. Exquisite stained-glass windows by Louis Comfort Tiffany and painted glass creations by artist

Pioneer Memorial Museum

Charles Connick are highlights. The 1857 Mirrlees chamber organ, said to be the oldest pipe organ in Utah, was built in Glasgow, Scotland. An Opus 35 tracker organ with three manuals and 40 ranks was installed in 2011. **Hours:** Office open Mon.-Fri. 8:30-4. **Cost:** Donations. **Phone:** (801) 322-3400.

SEVEN PEAKS WATERPARK is at 1200 West 1700 South. The 17-acre water park has heated pools, a water roller coaster, waterslides, a lazy river and the Wild Wave pool. A special children's area offers activities for toddlers. **Hours:** Mon.-Sat. noon-8, Memorial Day-Labor Day. **Cost:** $24.99; $19.99 (under 48 inches tall); $7.99 (nonparticipants); free (ages 0-2 and 65+). After 4 p.m. $15.99. After 6 p.m. $9.99. **Parking:** $7 (full day); $4 (half-day). **Phone:** (801) 972-3300.

STATE CAPITOL is at 350 N. State St. on Capitol Hill. The Corinthian-style structure was built in 1916 of Georgia marble and Utah granite. The top consists of a huge copper-covered dome. Inside are a main hall and rotunda as well as historical wall and ceiling murals. The State Reception Room, or "Gold Room," gets its nickname from its lavish furnishings and extensive use of gold leaf.

Hours: Capitol open Mon.-Fri. 7 a.m.-8 p.m., Sat.-Sun. and holidays 8-6. Guided tours are given on the hour Mon.-Fri. 9-4 (also Wed. at 6 and 7 p.m. by appointment). No tours on state or national holidays. **Phone:** (801) 538-1800.

TEMPLE SQUARE is bounded by North Temple, South Temple, West Temple and Main sts. This 35-acre, three-block area contains the most prominent buildings of The Church of

Jesus Christ of Latter-day Saints, the Seagull Monument and several other memorials and statues, including the Handcart Monument. The 1877 Gothic-style Assembly Hall is the site of free 60-minute concerts; phone ahead for schedule.

Hours: Grounds 9-9. Guided 30-minute tours of the square begin at the north and south gates every 15 minutes daily 9:15-8:15; hours vary for tours on Jan. 1, Mormon Conference days (first Sun. in Apr. and Oct.), Thanksgiving and Christmas. **Cost:** Free. Under 8 are not permitted at Assembly Hall concerts. **Phone:** (801) 240-1706, (801) 240-4872, or (801) 240-3323 for Assembly Hall.

Salt Lake Tabernacle on Temple Square is in Temple Square at 50 W. North Temple St. Completed in 1867, the tabernacle seats 6,500 under one of the world's largest domed roofs without center supports. The building has remarkable acoustics, and its 11,623-pipe organ is said to be one of the finest in existence.

The tabernacle has been the home of the renowned Mormon Tabernacle Choir since the group's inception in the mid-19th century. The choir's 360 volunteer singers, all members of The Church of Jesus Christ of Latter-day Saints, practice and perform weekly.

Hours: Tours are given daily on the hour 9-8; hours vary for tours on Jan. 1, Thanksgiving and Christmas. The choir's public rehearsals are Thurs. 7:30-9:30 p.m. The choir's weekly live broadcast starts Sun. at 9:30 a.m.; guests for the broadcast must be seated by 9:15 a.m. Organ recitals are held Mon.-Sat. at noon, Sun. at 2. **Cost:** Free. **Phone:** (801) 240-4150.

Salt Lake Temple, in Temple Square, is the symbol of The Church of Jesus Christ of Latter-day Saints and holds the ordinances sacred to the Mormon faith. Begun in 1853 when Brigham Young laid the cornerstone and completed in 1893, the neo-Gothic temple cost $4 million to build. Atop the 210-foot east tower is a gold leaf-covered statue of the Angel Moroni, an angel that Joseph Smith Jr. said visited him on numerous occasions. **Note:** The building is closed to the public.

Visitor Centers are located in the n.w. and s.e. corners of Temple Square. The starry dome of the North Visitor Center is highlighted by an 11-foot-tall statue of Jesus Christ. Exhibits include Old and New Testament murals, a scale model of Jerusalem as it likely appeared during Jesus' lifetime and examples of the church's humanitarian efforts. Three films are shown on a daily basis.

The South Visitor Center features exhibits and artifacts about the construction of the temple and the importance the religion places on the family. **Hours:** Both visitor centers open daily 9-9. **Cost:** Free. **Phone:** (801) 240-2534 for the South Visitor Center, or (801) 240-4872 for the North Visitor Center. GT

"THIS IS THE PLACE" HERITAGE PARK is e. at the mouth of Emigration Canyon at 2601 E. Sunnyside Ave. The 430-acre park includes the This Is The Place Monument commemorating the Mormons' entrance into the valley; the National Pony Express Monument; the Mormon Battalion Museum; and Heritage Village, a re-created 19th-century pioneer settlement. A visitor center has a video presentation.

Hours: Park open daily 9-5. Visitor center open daily 9-6, Memorial Day-Labor Day; Mon.-Sat. 9-6, Sun. 10-6, early Apr.-day before Memorial Day and day after Labor Day-Dec. 31; daily 10-5, rest of year. **Cost:** Free. **Phone:** (801) 582-1847. [⊤] [⋒]

Heritage Village, e. at the mouth of Emigration Canyon at "This Is The Place" Heritage Park, is a living-history village with more than 50 original and replica structures typical of the 1847-98 Utah pioneer and Native American era. Staff and tradesmen in period costumes demonstrate pioneer crafts, trades and hands-on fun. Visitors can enjoy train rides, panning for gold, pony rides, crafts, the Petting Corral, Irrigation Station Splash Pad and the new Treasure House! Dig in Prospectors Pit.

Time: Allow 1 hour minimum. **Hours:** Daily 9-5. Limited facilities are available on Sun. Phone for Haunted Village and Candlelight Christmas schedule. Phone ahead to confirm schedule. **Cost:** Mon.-Sat. Apr. 1-late Oct. and early Dec.-late Dec. for Candlelight Christmas, $11; $8 (ages 3-11 and 55+). Mon.-Sat. late Oct-early Dec., Jan.-Mar. and Sun. year-round $5; $3 (ages 3-11 and 55+). Haunted Village $20. **Phone:** (801) 582-1847.

UNIVERSITY OF UTAH, e. on 400 South to 13th East, then 1 blk. e. to the campus at University St., occupies 1,494 acres overlooking the city. **Hours:** The Park Building, which houses the university's administrative offices, is open Mon. and Wed.-Fri. 8-5, Tues. 9-5. **Phone:** (801) 581-7200, or (800) 685-8856 for guided tour information. GT

Natural History Museum of Utah at the Rio Tinto Center is on the University of Utah campus at 301 Wakara Way. A 42,000-square-foot ribbon of locally mined copper wraps around the exterior of this sustainable building, a five-level structure whose modern design mimics the topography of the surrounding foothills. An active research institution, the museum presents the natural and cultural history of the Great Basin region.

Ten themed galleries contain such exhibits as dinosaur skeletons, live insect specimens, and gems and minerals. Hands-on displays, wall murals and multimedia presentations enhance visitors' understanding of Utah's landscapes and people. On the fourth level of the facility is an indoor-outdoor interpretive space featuring dazzling views of Salt Lake City and the Salt Lake Valley. In addition, the museum is located on the Bonneville Shoreline Trail, a developing hiking and biking route that, when complete, will stretch from Nephi to the Idaho border.

Time: Allow 1 hour, 30 minutes minimum. **Hours:** Daily 10-5 (also Wed. 5-9). Last admission 30 minutes before closing. Closed Thanksgiving and Christmas. **Cost:** $13; $11 (ages 13-24 and 65+); $9

(ages 3-12); free (ages 0-2 and University of Utah students, faculty and staff with ID). **Phone:** (801) 581-4303 or (801) 581-6927. 🍴

Olympic Cauldron Park is at 451 South 1400 East on the University of Utah campus. The park showcases the authentic 2002 Hoberman Arch and glass-and-steel Olympic cauldron. An 8.5-minute cinematic film featuring memorable images and sounds of the opening ceremonies and athletes in action is shown every 15 minutes. An art gallery contains more than 50 photographs of the 2002 Olympics.

Time: Allow 30 minutes minimum. **Hours:** Mon.-Fri. 10-6. Closed university holidays and during major stadium events. Phone ahead to confirm schedule. **Cost:** Park and visitor center free. Film by donation. **Phone:** (801) 581-5445.

Red Butte Garden and Arboretum, 300 Wakara Way on the University of Utah campus, has hiking trails and paved garden paths, wildlife, waterfalls, a floral walk, a children's garden, and terraced herb, medicinal and fragrance gardens. The garden boasts more than 400,000 blooming bulbs in the spring, and the rose garden features more than 175 varieties. Morning bird-watching tours, evening garden tours and wildflower hikes are available seasonally.

Time: Allow 1 hour minimum. **Hours:** Daily 9-9, May-Aug.; 9-7:30 in Apr. and Sept.; 9-5, rest of year. Closed Thanksgiving and Christmas Eve-Jan. 1. **Cost:** Admission Mar.-Nov. $10; $8 (ages 65+, military, and University of Utah faculty and staff with ID); $6 (ages 3-17); free (ages 0-2 and University of Utah students with ID). Half-price admission, rest of year. **Phone:** (801) 585-0556. ⏰

Utah Museum of Fine Arts is on the University of Utah campus in the Marcia and John Price Museum Building at 410 Campus Center Dr. The permanent collection encompasses some 19,000 paintings, photographs, sculpture and other art objects from around the world—from the art of Utah and the West to the work of internationally acclaimed contemporary artists. A variety of public programs are scheduled year-round.

Time: Allow 1 hour minimum. **Hours:** Tues.-Fri. 10-5 (also Wed. 5-8), Sat.-Sun. 11-5. Closed major holidays. Phone ahead to confirm schedule. **Cost:** $14; $12 (ages 6-18, ages 65+ and out-of-state higher education students); $5 (Wed. after 5); free (higher education students in Utah with ID, military with ID and their dependents, and to all on the first Wed. and third Sat. of the month). **Phone:** (801) 581-5163. GT 🍴

UTAH'S HOGLE ZOO, 2600 E. Sunnyside Ave. (840 South) near the entrance to Emigration Canyon, contains a large collection of birds, mammals and reptiles in natural settings. Offering impressive underwater viewing opportunities, the Rocky Shores exhibit shelters a polar bear, three grizzly bears, seals, sea lions, river otters and bald eagles. At Elephant Encounter, you'll enjoy an up-close look at African elephants. Full-grown male Amur tigers, leopards, lynx and Pallas' cats are the stars of Asian Highlands. The new African Savanna exhibit features giraffes, zebras, nyalas, ostriches and four African lions and can be explored on a miniature locomotive, the Zoofari Express.

The Conservation Carousel features 42 hand-carved wooden animals and two stationary chariots. Lighthouse Point features shooting water, a large lighthouse slide, a shipwreck photo-op and a small "tide pool" where kids can get their feet wet and look for pretend critters while parents rest in the shade. Stroller and wheelchair rentals are available. **Time:** Allow 2 hours minimum. **Hours:** Daily 9-6:30 (last admission at 5), Mar.-Oct.; 9-5 (last admission at 4), rest of year. Closed Jan. 1 and Christmas. **Cost:** Admission May-Sept. $14.95, $12.95 (ages 65+); $10.95 (ages 3-12). Admission rest of year $11.95, $9.95 (ages 65+), $8.95 (ages 3-12).Carousel ride $2. **Phone:** (801) 582-1631. 🍴

UTAH MUSEUM OF CONTEMPORARY ART is at 20 S. West Temple St. This venue for contemporary art offers five galleries featuring changing exhibitions. **Hours:** Tues.-Sat. 11-6 (also Fri. 6-9 p.m.). Closed major holidays. **Cost:** Donations. **Phone:** (801) 328-4201.

WHEELER HISTORIC FARM is at 6351 South 900 East; from I-215 exit 9 take Union Park Ave. n. via 6400 South and 900 East. Visitors to this 75-acre

Red Butte Garden and Arboretum

380 SALT LAKE CITY, UT

working farm and public park can tour the outbuild-
ings, grounds and nature area and see farm animals. Try your hand at milking the cows or take a
1-hour guided tour of the 1898 Victorian House.
Wagon rides are available seasonally. Special activities are held periodically; phone ahead for
schedule.

Hours: Farm grounds daily dawn-dusk. House
tours are given Mon.-Sat. at 11, 1 and 3, May-Oct.;
Mon.-Fri. by appointment, rest of year. Cow milking
takes place Mon.-Sat. at 5. **Cost:** Free. House and
grounds tour $4; $2 (ages 3-12). Wagon ride $3; $2
(ages 2-12). Cow milking $1. **Phone:** (385) 468-1755.

Sightseeing
Carriage Tours

Carriage rides, which begin at Temple Square,
are a popular way to see the downtown area. Reservations are suggested; inquire at your hotel for
recommendations.

Walking and Driving Tours

A free brochure covering self-guiding walking and
driving tours is available at the Salt Lake City Visitor
Information Center *(see Fast Facts)* and at major
area hotels and motels. The Utah Heritage Foundation also provides information about self-guiding
tours of the area; phone (801) 533-0858.

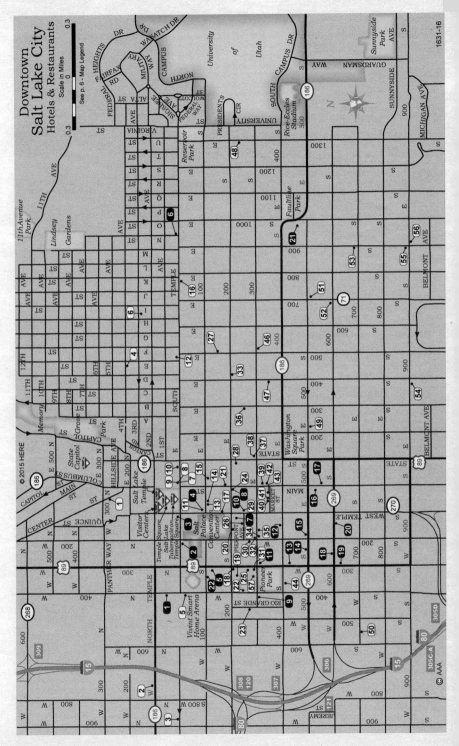

Downtown Salt Lake City

This index helps you "spot" where approved hotels and restaurants are located on the corresponding detailed maps. Hotel daily rate range is for comparison only. Restaurant price range is a combination of lunch and/or dinner. Turn to the listing page for more detailed rate and price information and consult display ads for special promotions.

DOWNTOWN SALT LAKE CITY

Map Page	Hotels	Diamond Rated	Rate Range	Page
1 p. 381	Hyatt Place Salt Lake City - Downtown/The Gateway	◈◈◈	$79-$499 SAVE	391
2 p. 381	Radisson Hotel - Salt Lake City/Downtown	◈◈◈	$99-$259	393
3 p. 381	Salt Lake Plaza Hotel at Temple Square	◈◈	Rates not provided SAVE	393
4 p. 381	Salt Lake Marriott - Downtown at City Creek	◈◈◈	$113-$304	393
5 p. 381	HYATT house Salt Lake City Downtown	◈◈◈	$99-$359 SAVE	391
6 p. 381	Haxton Manor Bed & Breakfast	◈◈◈	Rates not provided	391
7 p. 381	Holiday Inn Express - Salt Lake City/Downtown	◈◈◈	Rates not provided	391
8 p. 381	Hotel Monaco	◈◈◈◈	Rates not provided SAVE	391
9 p. 381	Homewood Suites by Hilton - Downtown/The Gateway	◈◈◈	$129-$199	391
10 p. 381	Hilton Salt Lake City Center	◈◈◈	$109-$249 SAVE	391
11 p. 381	Residence Inn by Marriott - Salt Lake City/Downtown	◈◈◈	$125-$250	393
12 p. 381	Fairfield Inn by Marriott Downtown	◈◈◈	$91-$250	390
13 p. 381	Hampton Inn Downtown	◈◈◈	$109-$189	391
14 p. 381	Crystal Inn Hotel & Suites - Salt Lake City/Downtown (See ad p. 390.)	◈◈	$89-$259	390
15 p. 381	Sheraton Salt Lake City Hotel	◈◈◈	Rates not provided SAVE	393
16 p. 381	Little America Hotel (See ad p. 392.)	◈◈◈◈	$89-$900 SAVE	393
17 p. 381	Grand America Hotel	◈◈◈◈	$209-$5000 SAVE	390
18 p. 381	Hilton Garden Inn Downtown	◈◈◈	$109-$269	391
19 p. 381	SpringHill Suites by Marriott Downtown	◈◈◈	$98-$221	393
20 p. 381	Red Lion Hotel - Salt Lake City/Downtown	◈◈◈	Rates not provided	393
21 p. 381	Anniversary Inn Fifth South	◈◈◈	Rates not provided	390
22 p. 381	Courtyard by Marriott Salt Lake City/Downtown	◈◈◈	$109-$229	390

Map Page	Restaurants	Diamond Rated	Cuisine	Price Range	Page
1 p. 381	Em's Restaurant	◈◈	American	$8-$26	394
2 p. 381	Red Iguana	◈◈	Mexican	$9-$18	396
3 p. 381	Red Iguana 2	◈◈	Mexican	$9-$17	396
4 p. 381	Cafe Shambala	◈	Tibetan	$7-$9	394
5 p. 381	Fleming's Prime Steakhouse & Wine Bar	◈◈◈	Steak Seafood	$20-$49	395
6 p. 381	Avenue's Bistro on Third	◈◈	American	$10-$24	394
7 p. 381	The Garden Restaurant	◈◈	American	$10-$19	395
8 p. 381	Nauvoo Cafe	◈	American	$6-$8	396
9 p. 381	The Roof Restaurant	◈◈◈	American	$40	396
10 p. 381	The Lion House Pantry	◈	American	$7-$13	395
11 p. 381	Elevations	◈◈◈	American	$10-$25	394

Map Page	Restaurants (cont'd)	Diamond Rated	Cuisine	Price Range	Page
⑫ p. 381	Wild Grape Bistro	◆◆◆	New American	$8-$33	397
⑬ p. 381	Naked Fish Japanese Bistro	◆◆◆	Sushi	$9-$39	396
⑭ p. 381	Caffe Molise	◆◆	Italian	$10-$33	394
⑮ p. 381	Martine Cafe & Tapas	◆◆◆	New American	$12-$30	396
⑯ p. 381	Sawadee Thai Restaurant	◆◆	Thai	$8-$20	396
⑰ p. 381	Blue Iguana Downtown	◆◆	Mexican	$7-$16	394
⑱ p. 381	Cafe Trang	◆◆	Chinese	$8-$17	394
⑲ p. 381	Finca	◆◆	Spanish	$7-$34	395
⑳ p. 381	J. Wong's Asian Bistro	◆◆	Asian	$6-$18	395
㉑ p. 381	Lamb's Grill Cafe	◆◆	American	$6-$29	395
㉒ p. 381	Pallet	◆◆	New American	$9-$29	396
㉓ p. 381	Rio Grande Cafe	◆◆	Mexican	$8-$22	396
㉔ p. 381	**Bambara**	◆◆◆	New American	$9-$42	394
㉕ p. 381	Cucina Toscana Tuscan Trattoria	◆◆	Italian	$18-$46	394
㉖ p. 381	Christopher's Prime Steak House & Grill	◆◆◆	Seafood Steak	$8-$51	394
㉗ p. 381	Oasis Cafe	◆◆	New American	$9-$23	396
㉘ p. 381	La Bella Piastra	◆◆◆	Italian	$11-$28	395
㉙ p. 381	Spencer's for Steaks and Chops	◆◆◆	Steak	$15-$67	397
㉚ p. 381	Settebello Pizzeria Napoletana	◆◆	Pizza	$9-$16	397
㉛ p. 381	Tony Caputo's Market & Deli	◆	Deli	$6-$10	397
㉜ p. 381	P.F. Chang's China Bistro	◆◆◆	Chinese	$10-$27	396
㉝ p. 381	Vinto	◆◆	Italian	$8-$13	397
㉞ p. 381	Valter's Osteria	◆◆◆◆	Italian	$20-$32	397
㉟ p. 381	Squatter's Pub Brewery	◆◆	American	$9-$19	397
㊱ p. 381	Gourmandise The Bakery	◆◆	Breads/Pastries Sandwiches	$7-$12	395
㊲ p. 381	Copper Common	◆◆	Small Plates	$8-$16	394
㊳ p. 381	The Copper Onion	◆◆◆	Regional American	$13-$29	394
㊴ p. 381	Eva	◆◆	Mediterranean	$8-$16	395
㊵ p. 381	The New Yorker	◆◆◆	Seafood Steak	$12-$48	396
㊶ p. 381	Market Street Grill & Oyster Bar - Downtown	◆◆	Seafood Steak	$11-$39	395
㊷ p. 381	Whiskey Street Cocktails & Dining	◆◆◆	American	$10-$24	397
㊸ p. 381	Takashi	◆◆	Sushi Small Plates	$9-$24	397
㊹ p. 381	Tin Angel Bistro	◆◆	Regional Natural/Organic	$7-$28	397
㊻ p. 381	Su Casa Mexican Restaurant	◆◆	Mexican	$6-$10	397
㊼ p. 381	Ichiban Sushi	◆◆◆	Sushi	$12-$33	395
㊽ p. 381	Aristo's Greek Restaurant & Cafe	◆◆◆	Greek	$10-$30	394
㊾ p. 381	Les Madeleines Cafe & Patisserie	◆◆	Breads/Pastries Sandwiches	$6-$11	395

Map Page	Restaurants (cont'd)	Diamond Rated	Cuisine	Price Range	Page
50 p. 381	Frida Bistro	◆◆◆	Regional Mexican	$11-$29	395
51 p. 381	Tucci's Cucina Italiana	◆◆	Italian	$9-$28	397
52 p. 381	Rodizio Grill	◆◆	Brazilian	$19-$26	396
53 p. 381	Cafe Trio Downtown	◆◆◆	Italian	$28	394
54 p. 381	Forage Restaurant	◆◆◆◆	Regional American	$89	395
55 p. 381	Pago	◆◆◆	New American	$11-$38	396
56 p. 381	Mazza Cafe at 9th	◆◆	Middle Eastern	$7-$24	396

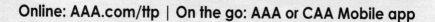

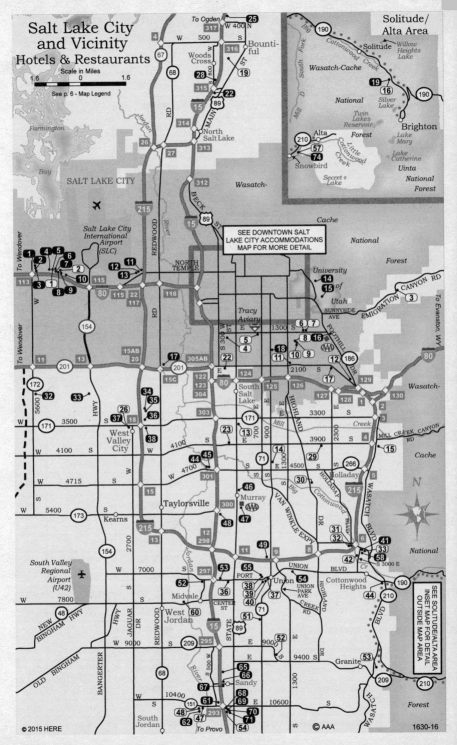

Salt Lake City
and Vicinity
Hotels & Restaurants

Scale in Miles

See p. 6 - Map Legend

© 2015 HERE

© AAA

1630-16

Airport Hotels

Map Page	**SALT LAKE CITY INT'L** (Maximum driving distance from airport: 4.2 mi)	Diamond Rated	Rate Range	Page
2 p. 385	**BEST WESTERN PLUS Airport Inn & Suites, 3.8 mi**	♦♦♦	$79-$99 SAVE	397
12 p. 385	Candlewood Suites - Airport East, 3.8 mi	♦♦	Rates not provided	397
11 p. 385	Comfort Suites, 4.2 mi	♦♦♦	$79-$149	398
9 p. 385	Courtyard by Marriott - Salt Lake City/Airport, 3.1 mi	♦♦♦	$77-$195	398
4 p. 385	**DoubleTree by Hilton - Salt Lake City/Airport, 3.4 mi**	♦♦♦	$79-$279 SAVE	398
3 p. 385	Fairfield Inn & Suites - Airport, 3.9 mi	♦♦♦	$76-$177	398
1 p. 385	**Hampton Inn & Suites - Airport, 3.9 mi**	♦♦♦	$69-$159 SAVE	398
6 p. 385	Hilton Garden Inn - Airport, 3.2 mi	♦♦♦	$140	399
5 p. 385	Holiday Inn & Suites - Salt Lake City/Airport West, 3.3 mi	♦♦♦	Rates not provided	399
10 p. 385	**Hyatt Place - Salt Lake City/Airport, 3.2 mi**	♦♦♦	$70-$210 SAVE	399
13 p. 385	Radisson Hotel - Salt Lake City/Airport, 3.8 mi	♦♦♦	$110-$219	399
8 p. 385	Residence Inn by Marriott - Salt Lake City/Airport, 3.1 mi	♦♦♦	$103-$204	399
7 p. 385	SpringHill Suites by Marriot - Salt Lake City/ Airport, 3.2 mi	♦♦♦	$76-$182	399

Salt Lake City and Vicinity

This index helps you "spot" where approved hotels and restaurants are located on the corresponding detailed maps. Hotel daily rate range is for comparison only. Restaurant price range is a combination of lunch and/or dinner. Turn to the listing page for more detailed rate and price information and consult display ads for special promotions.

SALT LAKE CITY

Map Page	Hotels	Diamond Rated	Rate Range	Page
1 p. 385	**Hampton Inn & Suites - Airport**	♦♦♦	$69-$159 SAVE	398
2 p. 385	**BEST WESTERN PLUS Airport Inn & Suites**	♦♦♦	$79-$99 SAVE	397
3 p. 385	Fairfield Inn & Suites - Airport	♦♦♦	$76-$177	398
4 p. 385	**DoubleTree by Hilton - Salt Lake City/Airport** *(See ad p. 398.)*	♦♦♦	$79-$279 SAVE	398
5 p. 385	Holiday Inn & Suites - Salt Lake City/Airport West	♦♦♦	Rates not provided	399
6 p. 385	Hilton Garden Inn - Airport	♦♦♦	$140	399
7 p. 385	SpringHill Suites by Marriot - Salt Lake City/Airport	♦♦♦	$76-$182	399
8 p. 385	Residence Inn by Marriott - Salt Lake City/Airport	♦♦♦	$103-$204	399
9 p. 385	Courtyard by Marriott - Salt Lake City/Airport	♦♦♦	$77-$195	398
10 p. 385	**Hyatt Place - Salt Lake City/Airport**	♦♦♦	$70-$210 SAVE	399
11 p. 385	Comfort Suites	♦♦♦	$79-$149	398
12 p. 385	Candlewood Suites - Airport East	♦♦	Rates not provided	397
13 p. 385	Radisson Hotel - Salt Lake City/Airport	♦♦♦	$110-$219	399
14 p. 385	University Guest House & Conference Center	♦♦♦	Rates not provided	399
15 p. 385	Marriott Salt Lake City University Park	♦♦♦	$100-$249	399
16 p. 385	Hampton Inn & Suites - Salt Lake City/Foothill	♦♦♦	$99-$189	398
17 p. 385	Hampton Inn - Salt Lake City/Central	♦♦♦	$89-$319	399

SALT LAKE CITY (cont'd)

Map Page	Hotels (cont'd)	Diamond Rated	Rate Range	Page
18 p. 385	Wildflowers Bed & Breakfast	♦♦	$90-$145	399
19 p. 385	The Inn at Solitude	♦♦♦	$149-$449	399

Map Page	Restaurants	Diamond Rated	Cuisine	Price Range	Page
1 p. 385	Wing Tips Bar & Bistro	♦♦	American	$9-$19	401
2 p. 385	Roberts Restaurant	♦♦	American	$6-$18	401
3 p. 385	Ruth's Diner	♦♦	American	$8-$22	401
4 p. 385	Meditrina Small Plates & Wine Bar	♦♦♦	Small Plates	$7-$26	400
5 p. 385	Park Cafe	♦	Breakfast Sandwiches	$6-$9	400
6 p. 385	Eggs in the City	♦♦	Breakfast Sandwiches	$6-$11	400
7 p. 385	Sea Salt	♦♦♦	Southern Italian	$9-$34	401
8 p. 385	The Paris Bistro	♦♦♦	French	$17-$39	400
9 p. 385	Fresco Italian Cafe	♦♦♦	Italian	$20-$32	400
10 p. 385	Mazza Cafe' at 15th	♦♦	Middle Eastern	$7-$24	400
11 p. 385	DoDo Restaurant	♦♦	American	$10-$27	400
12 p. 385	Bombay House Cuisine of India	♦♦	Indian	$9-$17	400
13 p. 385	Oh Mai Vietnamese Sandwich Kitchen	♦	Vietnamese	$5-$8	400
14 p. 385	Stella Grill	♦♦	New American	$10-$21	401
15 p. 385	Citris Grill	♦♦	New American	$8-$21	400
16 p. 385	St. Bernard's at Solitude	♦♦♦	French	$22-$32	401
17 p. 385	Harbor Seafood & Steak Co	♦♦♦	Seafood Steak	$18-$39	400

NORTH SALT LAKE

Map Page	Hotel	Diamond Rated	Rate Range	Page
22 p. 385	**BEST WESTERN PLUS CottonTree Inn**	♦♦♦	$99-$159 [SAVE]	340

BOUNTIFUL

Map Page	Hotel	Diamond Rated	Rate Range	Page
25 p. 385	Country Inn & Suites By Carlson - Salt Lake City/Bountiful	♦♦♦	$89-$159	295

Map Page	Restaurant	Diamond Rated	Cuisine	Price Range	Page
19 p. 385	Robintino's	♦♦	Italian	$7-$15	295

WOODS CROSS

Map Page	Hotel	Diamond Rated	Rate Range	Page
28 p. 385	Hampton Inn - Salt Lake City North/Woods Cross	♦♦♦	$109-$169	414

WEST VALLEY CITY

Map Page	Hotels	Diamond Rated	Rate Range	Page
32 p. 385	TownePlace Suites by Marriott - Salt Lake City/West Valley	♦♦♦	$90-$190	414
33 p. 385	Home2 Suites by Hilton - Salt Lake City/West Valley City	♦♦♦	$89-$209	414
34 p. 385	Holiday Inn Express & Suites Waterpark - West Valley City	♦♦♦	Rates not provided	413
35 p. 385	Staybridge Suites - West Valley City	♦♦♦	Rates not provided	414
36 p. 385	Crystal Inn - Salt Lake City/West Valley City (See ad p. 390.)	♦♦♦	$89-$229	413
37 p. 385	Embassy Suites by Hilton - Salt Lake City/West Valley City	♦♦♦	$129-$199	413

WEST VALLEY CITY (cont'd)

Map Page	Hotels (cont'd)	Diamond Rated	Rate Range	Page
38 p. 385	La Quinta Inn Salt Lake City West	▽▽	$64-$306	414

Map Page	Restaurant	Diamond Rated	Cuisine	Price Range	Page
26 p. 385	Shula's 347	▽▽▽	Steak Seafood	$9-$48	414

HOLLADAY

Map Page	Hotel	Diamond Rated	Rate Range	Page
41 p. 385	**Hyatt Place - Salt Lake City/Cottonwood**	▽▽▽	$84-$199 SAVE	319

Map Page	Restaurants	Diamond Rated	Cuisine	Price Range	Page
29 p. 385	Cafe Madrid	▽▽▽	Spanish	$18-$29	319
30 p. 385	Primo Restaurant	▽▽▽	Northern Italian	$15-$39	319
31 p. 385	Tuscany	▽▽▽	Northern Italian	$18-$32	319
32 p. 385	Franck's	▽▽▽	French	$24-$37	319
33 p. 385	Cafe Trio - Cottonwood	▽▽	Italian	$9-$26	319

MURRAY

Map Page	Hotels	Diamond Rated	Rate Range	Page
44 p. 385	Hampton Inn - Murray	▽▽	$109-$149	339
45 p. 385	Fairfield Inn by Marriott - Murray	▽▽	$86-$195	339
46 p. 385	Home2 Suites by Hilton - Salt Lake City/Murray	▽▽▽	$99-$169	339
47 p. 385	Residence Inn by Marriott - Salt Lake City/Murray	▽▽▽	$118-$267	339
48 p. 385	Holiday Inn Express & Suites - Salt Lake City South/Murray	▽▽▽	$89-$299	339
49 p. 385	Crystal Inn Midvalley/Murray (See ad p. 390.)	▽▽▽	$86-$229	339

MIDVALE

Map Page	Hotels	Diamond Rated	Rate Range	Page
52 p. 385	Staybridge Suites - Midvale	▽▽▽	Rates not provided	328
53 p. 385	Midvale Inn	▽▽▽	Rates not provided	328
54 p. 385	Hawthorn Suites by Wyndham - Salt Lake City/Midvale	▽▽	$60-$150	328
55 p. 385	Holiday Inn Express - Salt Lake City/Midvale	▽▽▽	Rates not provided	328

Map Page	Restaurants	Diamond Rated	Cuisine	Price Range	Page
36 p. 385	Bohemian Brewery	▽▽	Czechoslovakian	$9-$25	328
37 p. 385	Hoppers Grill & Brewing Co	▽▽	American	$8-$18	328
38 p. 385	Epic Casual Dining	▽▽▽	New American	$14-$24	328
39 p. 385	Kneaders Bakery & Cafe	▽	Breads/Pastries Sandwiches	$6-$8	328
40 p. 385	Landmark Grill	▽▽	American	$7-$12	328

COTTONWOOD HEIGHTS

Map Page	Hotel	Diamond Rated	Rate Range	Page
58 p. 385	**Residence Inn by Marriott - Salt Lake City/ Cottonwood Heights**	▽▽▽	$104-$237 SAVE	307

Map Page	Restaurants	Diamond Rated	Cuisine	Price Range	Page
42 p. 385	Market Street Grill & Oyster Bar Cottonwood	▽▽	Seafood	$11-$37	307
44 p. 385	Porcupine Pub & Grille	▽▽	American	$8-$24	307

SOUTH JORDAN

Map Page	Hotels	Diamond Rated	Rate Range	Page
61 p. 385	Country Inn & Suites By Carlson - Salt Lake City/South Towne	▽▽▽	Rates not provided	403
62 p. 385	Home2 Suites by Hilton - Salt Lake City/South Jordan	▽▽▽	$99-$159	403

Map Page	Restaurants	Diamond Rated	Cuisine	Price Range	Page
47 p. 385	Gecko's Mexican Grill	▽▽	Mexican	$7-$16	403
48 p. 385	Market Street Grill & Oyster Bar South Jordan	▽▽	Seafood Steak	$8-$70	403

SANDY

Map Page	Hotels	Diamond Rated	Rate Range	Page
65 p. 385	**HYATT house - Salt Lake City/Sandy**	▽▽▽	$94-$249 SAVE	402
66 p. 385	Residence Inn by Marriott - Sandy	▽▽▽	$117-$238	402
67 p. 385	Hilton Garden Inn - Sandy	▽▽▽	$99-$169	401
68 p. 385	Hampton Inn by Hilton - Salt Lake City/Sandy	▽▽▽	$99-$169	401
69 p. 385	Courtyard by Marriott - Sandy	▽▽▽	$89-$205	401
70 p. 385	**Holiday Inn Express & Suites Sandy**	▽▽▽	Rates not provided SAVE	401
71 p. 385	**BEST WESTERN PLUS CottonTree Inn - Salt Lake City/Sandy**	▽▽▽	$109-$169 SAVE	401

Map Page	Restaurants	Diamond Rated	Cuisine	Price Range	Page
51 p. 385	Tiburon Fine Dining	▽▽▽	New American	$11-$45	402
52 p. 385	Fratelli Ristorante	▽▽	Italian	$10-$26	402
53 p. 385	**La Caille**	▽▽▽	Continental	$29-$52	402
54 p. 385	Carvers Steaks & Seafood	▽▽▽	Steak Seafood	$10-$39	402

SNOWBIRD

Map Page	Hotel	Diamond Rated	Rate Range	Page
74 p. 385	The Cliff Lodge, Spa & Conference Center	▽▽▽	Rates not provided	403

Map Page	Restaurant	Diamond Rated	Cuisine	Price Range	Page
57 p. 385	Aerie Restaurant at Snowbird	▽▽▽	American	$14-$44	403

SOUTH SALT LAKE

Map Page	Restaurants	Diamond Rated	Cuisine	Price Range	Page
22 p. 385	Pat's Barbecue	▽▽	Barbecue	$9-$17	403
23 p. 385	Left Fork Grill	▽▽	Comfort Food	$8-$15	403

WEST JORDAN

Map Page	Restaurant	Diamond Rated	Cuisine	Price Range	Page
60 p. 385	Archibald's Restaurant at Gardner Village	▽▽	American	$7-$26	413

DOWNTOWN SALT LAKE CITY

- Restaurants p. 394
- Hotels & Restaurants map & index p. 381

ANNIVERSARY INN FIFTH SOUTH

801/363-4900 **21**

◈◈◈ **Historic Bed & Breakfast.** Rates not provided. **Address:** 460 S 1000 E 84102 **Location:** I-15 exit 307 (400 S), 2.6 mi e to 1000 E, then just s. Located in a residential area. **Facility:** This distinctive inn offers themed and luxury suites. All rooms have a two-person jetted tub and some offer a fireplace. Upon arrival to your room, you'll find chilled sparkling cider and cheesecake. 36 units. 3 stories (no elevator), interior corridors. **Terms:** check-in 5 pm, age restrictions may apply. CALL 🆓 M 🛜 ✕ 🛄

COURTYARD BY MARRIOTT SALT LAKE CITY/DOWNTOWN

(385)290-6500 **22**

◈◈◈ **Hotel** $109-$229 **Address:** 345 W 100 S 84101 **Location:** I-15 southbound exit 307 (400 S); northbound exit 306 (600 S); at 300 W and 100 S. Across from Vivint SmartHome Arena.

AAA Benefit: Members save 5% or more!

Facility: 175 units. 6 stories, interior corridors. **Parking:** on-site (fee) and street. **Pool(s):** heated indoor. **Activities:** hot tub, exercise room. **Guest Services:** valet and coin laundry, boarding pass kiosk.

🍽 🍸 CALL 🆓 M 🛳 BIZ 🛜 ✕ 🛄 📦 🖥

CRYSTAL INN HOTEL & SUITES - SALT LAKE CITY/DOWNTOWN

(801)328-4466 **14**

◈◈ **Hotel** $89-$259 **Address:** 230 W 500 S 84101 **Location:** Cross streets 500 S and 200 W. **Facility:** 175 units. 4 stories, interior corridors. **Terms:** cancellation fee imposed. **Pool(s):** heated indoor. **Activities:** sauna, hot tub, exercise room. **Guest Services:** valet and coin laundry, area transportation. *(See ad this page.)*

✈ 🍽 CALL 🆓 M 🛳 BIZ 🛜 🛄 📦 🖥 / SOME UNITS 🔕

FAIRFIELD INN BY MARRIOTT DOWNTOWN

(801)531-6000 **12**

◈◈◈ **Hotel** $91-$250 **Address:** 130 W 400 S 84101 **Location:** Just w of S West Temple and 400 S. **Facility:** 120 units. 3 stories, interior corridors. **Pool(s):** heated indoor. **Activities:** hot tub, exercise room. **Guest Services:** valet and coin laundry.

AAA Benefit: Members save 5% or more!

🍽 CALL 🆓 M 🛳 BIZ 🛜 ✕ 🛄 📦 🖥

GRAND AMERICA HOTEL

(801)258-6000 **17**

◈◈◈◈ **Hotel** $209-$5000

Address: 555 S Main St 84111 **Location:** 1 mi s of Temple Square; just s of Main St and 500 S. **Facility:** Inspired by the charm of Europe's classic hotels, the Grand was crafted from the finest materials, such as Italian chandeliers and marble, West African woods and French tapestries. 775 units, some efficiencies. 24 stories, interior corridors. **Parking:** on-site (fee) and valet. **Terms:** cancellation fee imposed. **Amenities:** safes. **Pool(s):** heated outdoor, heated indoor. **Activities:** sauna, hot tub, steamroom, spa. **Guest Services:** valet laundry, boarding pass kiosk, area transportation.

SAVE ✈ 🍽 🧍 🍸 CALL 🆓 M 🛳 🏋 BIZ HS 🛜 ✕ / SOME UNITS 🛄 📦 🖥

Choose real ratings you can trust
from professional inspectors
who've been there

(See map & index p. 381.)

HAMPTON INN DOWNTOWN   (801)741-1110 🔟🛑

▽▽▽▽ **Hotel** $109-$189 **Address:** 425 S 300 W 84101 **Location:** Jct 400 S and 300 W. **Facility:** 158 units. 5 stories, interior corridors. **Terms:** 1-7 night minimum stay, cancellation fee imposed. **Pool(s):** heated indoor. **Activities:** hot tub, picnic facilities, exercise room. **Guest Services:** valet and coin laundry.

AAA Benefit: Members save up to 10%!

🍽️➕ CALL &Ⓜ 🛳 BIZ 🛜 ✕ 💻 / SOME UNITS 🛏 📠

HAXTON MANOR BED & BREAKFAST   801/363-4646 6️⃣

▽▽▽▽ **Historic Bed & Breakfast.** Rates not provided. **Address:** 943 E South Temple St 84102 **Location:** Jct South Temple St and 900E, just e. **Facility:** This manor is elegant and features rooms with upscale bedding and a few with a hot tub. After skiing or meetings, relax on the wraparound porch, in front of the Beehive fireplace, or the library. 7 units. 3 stories (no elevator), interior corridors.

🍽️➕ CALL &Ⓜ 🛜 ✕

HILTON GARDEN INN DOWNTOWN   (801)364-5200 1️⃣8️⃣

▽▽▽▽ **Hotel** $109-$269 **Address:** 250 W 600 S 84101 **Location:** On 600 S, just e of 300 W. **Facility:** 132 units. 4 stories, interior corridors. **Terms:** 1-7 night minimum stay, cancellation fee imposed. **Pool(s):** heated indoor. **Activities:** hot tub, exercise room. **Guest Services:** valet and coin laundry.

AAA Benefit: Members save up to 10%!

✈️ 🍽️ CALL &Ⓜ 🛳 BIZ HS 🛜 ✕ 📠 📟 💻

HILTON SALT LAKE CITY CENTER   (801)328-2000 1️⃣0️⃣

▽▽▽▽ **Hotel** $109-$249

Hilton HOTELS & RESORTS

AAA Benefit: Members save 5% or more!

Address: 255 S West Temple 84101 **Location:** Just s of S West Temple and 200 S. **Facility:** 499 units. 17 stories, interior corridors. **Parking:** on-site (fee) and valet. **Terms:** 1-7 night minimum stay, cancellation fee imposed. **Amenities:** safes. **Dining:** Spencer's for Steaks and Chops, see separate listing. **Pool(s):** heated indoor. **Activities:** hot tub, exercise room. **Guest Services:** valet laundry.

SAVE ✈️ 🍽️ 🛁 Y CALL &Ⓜ 🛳 BIZ 🛜 ✕ 📠 💻 / SOME UNITS 🛏 S🛏

HOLIDAY INN EXPRESS - SALT LAKE CITY/DOWNTOWN   801/521-9500 7️⃣

▽▽▽▽ **Hotel.** Rates not provided. **Address:** 206 S West Temple 84101 **Location:** At S West Temple and 200 S. **Facility:** 212 units. 12 stories, interior corridors. **Pool(s):** heated indoor. **Activities:** sauna, hot tub, exercise room. **Guest Services:** valet and coin laundry, area transportation.

✈️ 🍽️➕ CALL &Ⓜ 🛳 BIZ 🛜 ✕ 📠 📟 💻

HOMEWOOD SUITES BY HILTON - DOWNTOWN/THE GATEWAY   (801)363-6700 9️⃣

▽▽▽▽ **Extended Stay Contemporary Hotel** $129-$199 **Address:** 423 W Broadway (300 S) 84101 **Location:** Jct 400 W and 300 S, just w. Located at the south edge of The Gateway Mall. **Facility:** 124 efficiencies, some two bedrooms. 6 stories, interior corridors. **Terms:** 1-7 night minimum stay, cancellation fee imposed. **Amenities:** safes. **Pool(s):** heated outdoor. **Activities:** hot tub, exercise room. **Guest Services:** valet and coin laundry.

AAA Benefit: Members save up to 10%!

🍽️➕ CALL &Ⓜ 🛳 BIZ HS 🛜 ✕ 📠 📟 💻

HOTEL MONACO   801/595-0000 8️⃣

▽▽▽▽ **Historic Boutique Hotel** Rates not provided

Address: 15 W 200 S 84101 **Location:** Jct Main St and 200 S. **Facility:** Built in 1924, multiple architectural enhancements and distinctive luxurious ceilings, artwork and appointments from around the world inspire a sense of travel and escape at this vibrant hotel. 225 units. 15 stories, interior corridors. **Parking:** on-site (fee) and valet. **Amenities:** safes. **Dining:** Bambara, see separate listing. **Activities:** bicycles, exercise room, massage. **Guest Services:** valet laundry.

SAVE ECO 🍽️ 🛁 Y CALL &Ⓜ BIZ 🛜 ✕ 📹 📠 / SOME UNITS 🛏

HYATT HOUSE SALT LAKE CITY DOWNTOWN   (801)359-4020 5️⃣

▽▽▽▽ **Hotel** $99-$359

H HYATT house

AAA Benefit: Members save 10%!

Address: 140 S 300 W 84101 **Location:** I-15 exit 307 (400 S) southbound; exit 306 (600 S) northbound; jct 100 S and 300 W, just s. **Facility:** 159 units, some efficiencies. 6 stories, interior corridors. **Pool(s):** heated outdoor. **Activities:** hot tub, picnic facilities, exercise room. **Guest Services:** valet and coin laundry. **Featured Amenity:** breakfast buffet.

SAVE 🍽️ Y CALL &Ⓜ 🛳 BIZ HS 🛜 ✕ 📠 🖼️ 📟 / SOME UNITS S🛏

HYATT PLACE SALT LAKE CITY - DOWNTOWN/THE GATEWAY   (801)456-6300 1️⃣

▽▽▽▽ **Hotel** $79-$499

H HYATT PLACE

AAA Benefit: Members save 10%!

Address: 55 N 400 W 84101 **Location:** Jct W North Temple and 400 W, then just s. Located at north edge of The Gateway Mall. **Facility:** 128 units. 6 stories, interior corridors. **Parking:** on-site (fee). **Terms:** cancellation fee imposed. **Pool(s):** heated outdoor. **Activities:** hot tub, exercise room. **Guest Services:** valet and coin laundry. **Featured Amenity:** breakfast buffet.

SAVE 🍽️➕ Y CALL &Ⓜ 🛳 BIZ 🛜 ✕ 📹 📠 📟 / SOME UNITS S🛏

▼ See AAA listing p. 393 ▼

ENJOY LOCALLY OWNED AND OPERATED HOSPITALITY

Visit our website at
SALTLAKE.LITTLEAMERICA.COM
or call 888.594.2261 for more information.

LITTLE AMERICA *Hotel*
SALT LAKE CITY

500 SOUTH MAIN STREET | SALT LAKE CITY, UT 84101

(See map & index p. 381.)

LITTLE AMERICA HOTEL   (801)363-6781   **16**

▽▽▽ ▽▽▽
Hotel
$89-$900

Address: 500 S Main St 84101 **Location:** 1 mi s of Temple Square; just s of Main St and 500 S. **Facility:** The main entrance and lobby are impressive and a sight to behold. Manicured landscaping and fountains surround three separate buildings: the 17-story main tower, the garden and the courtside areas. 849 units. 2-17 stories, interior/exterior corridors. **Parking:** on-site and valet. **Terms:** cancellation fee imposed. **Amenities:** Some: safes. **Dining:** 2 restaurants. **Pool(s):** heated outdoor, heated indoor. **Activities:** sauna, hot tub, exercise room, spa. **Guest Services:** valet laundry, boarding pass kiosk. *(See ad p. 392.)*

[SAVE] [†1] [🛏] [Y] CALL [&M] [≈] [BIZ] [🛜] [✕] [▣]
/ SOME UNITS [HS] [🔲]

RADISSON HOTEL - SALT LAKE CITY/DOWNTOWN
(801)531-7500   **2**

▽▽▽ ▽▽▽ Hotel $99-$259 **Address:** 215 W South Temple 84101 **Location:** Cross streets 200 S and W South Temple. Near Energy Solutions Arena and Salt Palace Convention Center. **Facility:** 381 units. 15 stories, interior corridors. **Parking:** on-site (fee) and valet. **Terms:** cancellation fee imposed. **Amenities:** Some: safes. **Pool(s):** heated indoor. **Activities:** sauna, hot tub, exercise room. **Guest Services:** valet laundry.

[ECO] [†1] [🛏] [Y] CALL [&M] [≈] [BIZ] [HS] [🛜] [✕]
[🔲] [▣] / SOME UNITS [S🔲]

RED LION HOTEL - SALT LAKE CITY/DOWNTOWN
801/521-7373   **20**

▽▽▽ ▽▽▽ Hotel. Rates not provided. **Address:** 161 W 600 S 84101 **Location:** Cross streets S West Temple and 600 S. **Facility:** 394 units. 12 stories, interior corridors. **Dining:** 2 restaurants. **Pool(s):** heated outdoor. **Activities:** hot tub, exercise room. **Guest Services:** valet and coin laundry, area transportation.

[🖐] [†1] [🛏] CALL [&M] [≈] [BIZ] [🛜] [✕] [🔲] [🖼]
[▣] / SOME UNITS [S🔲]

RESIDENCE INN BY MARRIOTT - SALT LAKE CITY/DOWNTOWN
(801)355-3300   **11**

▽▽▽ ▽▽▽ Extended Stay Hotel $125-$250 **Address:** 285 W 300 S (Broadway) 84101 **Location:** At 300 W and 300 S. **Facility:** 189 efficiencies, some two bedrooms and kitchens. 3-4 stories, interior corridors. **Amenities:** safes. **Pool(s):** heated outdoor. **Activities:** hot tub, picnic facilities, exercise room. **Guest Services:** valet and coin laundry.

AAA Benefit: Members save 5% or more!

[†1→] CALL [&M] [≈] [BIZ] [🛜] [✕] [🔲] [🖼] [▣]
/ SOME UNITS [S🔲]

SALT LAKE MARRIOTT - DOWNTOWN AT CITY CREEK
(801)531-0800   **4**

▽▽▽ ▽▽▽ Hotel $113-$304 **Address:** 75 S West Temple 84101 **Location:** Jct S West Temple and 100 S. **Facility:** 515 units. 14 stories, interior corridors. **Parking:** on-site (fee) and valet. **Amenities:** Some: safes. **Dining:** Elevations, see separate listing. **Pool(s):** heated indoor. **Activities:** sauna, hot tub, exercise room. **Guest Services:** valet and coin laundry.

AAA Benefit: Members save 5% or more!

[†1] [🛏] [Y] CALL [&M] [≈] [BIZ] [sHS] [S🛜] [✕] [🐾]
[🔲] [▣]

SALT LAKE PLAZA HOTEL AT TEMPLE SQUARE
801/521-0130   **3**

▽▽▽ ▽▽▽
Hotel
Rates not provided

Address: 122 W South Temple 84101 **Location:** Cross streets W South Temple and S Temple. Across from Temple Square and Salt Palace. **Facility:** 150 units. 13 stories, interior corridors. **Parking:** on-site (fee) and street. **Amenities:** safes. **Pool(s):** heated indoor. **Activities:** hot tub, exercise room. **Guest Services:** valet and coin laundry.

[SAVE] [🖐] [†1] [🛏] [≈] [BIZ] [🛜]
[✕] [🔲] [🖼] [▣]

SHERATON SALT LAKE CITY HOTEL
801/401-2000   **15**

▽▽▽ ▽▽▽
Hotel
Rates not provided

[Sheraton HOTELS & RESORTS] **AAA Benefit:** Members save up to 15%, plus Starwood Preferred Guest® benefits!

Address: 150 W 500 S 84101 **Location:** Jct 200 W and 500 S. **Facility:** 362 units. 10 stories, interior corridors. **Parking:** on-site and valet. **Amenities:** Some: safes. **Dining:** 2 restaurants. **Pool(s):** heated outdoor. **Activities:** hot tub, exercise room. **Guest Services:** valet laundry, boarding pass kiosk, area transportation.

[SAVE] [🖐] [†1] [🛏] [Y] CALL [&M]
[≈] [BIZ] [🛜] [✕] [▣]
/ SOME UNITS [🐾] [🔲]

SPRINGHILL SUITES BY MARRIOTT DOWNTOWN
(801)238-3000   **19**

▽▽▽ ▽▽▽ Hotel $98-$221 **Address:** 625 S 300 W 84101 **Location:** At 600 S and 300 W. **Facility:** 86 units. 4 stories, interior corridors. **Pool(s):** heated indoor. **Activities:** hot tub, exercise room. **Guest Services:** valet and coin laundry.

AAA Benefit: Members save 5% or more!

[🖐] [†1→] CALL [&M] [≈] [BIZ] [HS] [🛜] [✕] [🔲] [🖼]
[▣]

ANNIVERSARY INN SOUTH TEMPLE   801/363-4950

[fyi] Not evaluated. **Address:** 678 E South Temple 84102 **Location:** 1 mi e of Temple Square; just e of 700 E and E South Temple. Facilities, services, and décor characterize a mid-scale property. This distinctive inn offers themed and luxury suites. All rooms have a two-person jetted tub and some offer a fireplace. Upon arrival to your room, you'll find chilled sparkling cider and cheesecake.

DOUBLETREE SUITES BY HILTON - SALT LAKE CITY/DOWNTOWN   801/359-7800

[fyi] Hotel Did not meet all AAA rating requirements for locking devices in some guest rooms at time of last evaluation on 02/27/2015. **Address:** 110 W 600 S 84101 **Location:** Jct 600 S and S West Temple. Facilities, services, and décor characterize a mid-scale property.

AAA Benefit: Members save 5% or more!

SALT LAKE CITY MARRIOTT CITY CENTER   801/961-8700

[fyi] Not evaluated. **Address:** 220 S State St 84111 **Location:** Jct State St and 200 S. Facilities, services, and décor characterize a mid-scale property.

AAA Benefit: Members save 5% or more!

(See map & index p. 381.)

WHERE TO EAT

ARISTO'S GREEK RESTAURANT & CAFE 801/581-0888 (48)
▼▼▼ Greek. Casual Dining. $10-$30 **AAA Inspector Notes:** Traditional authentic soup, salads and entrées are made from generations of family recipes and served in a warm, elegant dining room and on the lovely landscaped outdoor patio. Enjoy many of their specialties by ordering an authentic appetizer platter. Savor a house-made dessert with a demitasse cup of strong Greek coffee. **Features:** full bar, patio dining. **Address:** 224 S 1300 E 84102 **Location:** 1.8 mi e on S Temple, 0.4 mi s. **Parking:** street only.
L D

AVENUE'S BISTRO ON THIRD 801/831-5409 (6)
▼▼ American. Casual Dining. $10-$24 **AAA Inspector Notes:** If you are looking for an off-the-beaten path neighborhood bistro serving creative, seasonal and locally sourced food, look no further. A few favorites are a crispy-on-the-outside vegan lentil rice patty, polenta burger, cold duck salad, manila clams and shallots, lamb chili, Wagyu strip steak and Asian-style noodles. Lunch and dinner menus are different and gluten-free items are available. Tip: Browse the pastry case before ordering. **Features:** full bar, patio dining, Sunday brunch. **Address:** 564 E 3rd Ave A 84103 **Location:** Jct E South Temple St and 700 E, just n, then just w; between H and I sts; Avenues District. **Parking:** street only.
B L D

BAMBARA 801/363-5454 (24)
▼▼▼▼
New American Casual Dining
$9-$42

AAA Inspector Notes: Located in a former bank lobby, the sophisticated restaurant serves colorful creations of local and regional products from an open-air kitchen in a vibrant atmosphere. Relax and enjoy a before- or after-dinner cocktail in the Vault Lounge. Gluten-free items are available. **Features:** full bar, Sunday brunch. **Address:** 202 S Main St 84101 **Location:** Cross streets 200 S and Main St; in Hotel Monaco. **Parking:** on-site (fee) and valet.
B L D

BLUE IGUANA DOWNTOWN 801/533-8900 (17)
▼▼ Mexican. Casual Dining. $7-$16 **AAA Inspector Notes:** Off a courtyard, the restaurant whips up authentic Mexican food, including classic enchiladas and burritos, with tasty mole sauces and other great flavor-enhancers. **Features:** full bar, patio dining. **Address:** 165 S West Temple 84101 **Location:** Just n of S West Temple and 200 S; in Arrow Press Square Shopping Center. **Parking:** street only.
L D

CAFE SHAMBALA 801/364-8558 (4)
▼ Tibetan. Casual Dining. $7-$9 **AAA Inspector Notes:** The café presents a menu of interesting Tibetan preparations. The lunch and dinner buffets are quite popular. **Address:** 382 E 4th Ave N 84103 **Location:** Between D and E sts; in The Avenues. **Parking:** street only.
L D

CAFE TRANG 801/539-1638 (18)
▼▼ Chinese. Casual Dining. $8-$17 **AAA Inspector Notes:** Warm, inviting service is what diners experience at this family-operated restaurant, which serves tasty traditional poultry, beef, pork and seafood entrées; mouthwatering appetizers; and fire-pot or broth soups. **Features:** beer & wine. **Address:** 307 W 200 S 84101 **Location:** Jct 300 W. **Parking:** street only.
L D

CAFE TRIO DOWNTOWN 801/533-8746 (53)
▼▼▼ Italian. Fine Dining. $28 **AAA Inspector Notes:** This upbeat and energetic neighborhood spot features a menu of specialty flatbreads, mouthwatering organic salads, cedar-plank wild salmon and a wide variety of appetizers and pastas. Patrons can expect great service. The decadent desserts include bittersweet chocolate pudding, seasonal cobblers and a Toll House pie with roasted walnuts. **Features:** full bar, patio dining, Sunday brunch. **Address:** 680 S 900 E 84102 **Location:** Corner of 700 S and 900 E.
L D

CAFFE MOLISE 801/364-8833 (14)
▼▼ Italian. Casual Dining. $10-$33 **AAA Inspector Notes:** Featuring fresh Italian cuisine and attentive service, this downtown cafe is the perfect location for dining before or after a theater, concert, opera or sporting event. The garden patio affords intimate seating. **Features:** full bar, patio dining, Sunday brunch. **Reservations:** suggested. **Address:** 55 W 100 S 84101 **Location:** Just e of 100 S and West Temple. **Parking:** street only.
L D

CHRISTOPHER'S PRIME STEAK HOUSE & GRILL 801/519-8515 (26)
▼▼ Seafood Steak. Fine Dining. $8-$51 **AAA Inspector Notes:** Selections include seafood, which is flown in daily, slow-roasted prime rib, free-range chicken and New Zealand lamb. **Features:** full bar, patio dining. **Address:** 134 W Pierpont Ave 84101 **Location:** Just n of 300 S and 200 W, then just e. **Parking:** valet and street only.
D

COPPER COMMON 801/355-0543 (37)
▼▼ Small Plates. Casual Dining. $8-$16 **AAA Inspector Notes:** The bacon-wrapped, Gorgonzola-stuffed dates will be remembered long after you depart this bar and eatery, which serves a wide array of ever-changing seasonal tapas such as deviled eggs, tots with garlic aioli, roasted mussels, lobster spaghetti and duck ravioli. Expect fresh, in-season and flavorful menu items. The bartenders appear to be technical mixologists, which equates to creativity and artistry. **Features:** full bar. **Address:** 111 E 300 S 84111 **Location:** I-15 exit 307 (400 S), 1.5 mi e, just n on State St, then just e. **Parking:** on-site (fee) and street.
D CALL

THE COPPER ONION 801/355-3282 (38)
▼▼▼ Regional American. Fine Dining. $13-$29 **AAA Inspector Notes:** This downtown bistro has a trendy vibe. Well-prepared and tastefully presented seasonal courses include melt-in-your-mouth ricotta dumplings, pork belly salad, roasted heirloom chicken and Wagyu tri-tip steak with watercress salad. The traditional desserts and house-made ice cream make wonderful treats with an after-dinner drink. **Features:** full bar, patio dining, Sunday brunch. **Reservations:** suggested. **Address:** 111 E 300 S, Suite 170 84111 **Location:** Just e of State St and 300 S; 0.4 mi e of Temple Square; next to Broadway Theatre. **Parking:** on-site (fee).
L D

CUCINA TOSCANA TUSCAN TRATTORIA 801/328-3463 (25)
▼▼ Italian. Fine Dining. $18-$46 **AAA Inspector Notes:** Located in the arts and entertainment district and serving authentic Tuscan fare, the chef's special reserve menu includes carefully prepared salads, soups, chicken, veal, seafood and steak, as well as an excellent selection of wine. The Caesar salad and risotto del giorno are served tableside. The knowledgeable staff provides personalized, attentive service. **Features:** full bar. **Reservations:** suggested. **Address:** 307 W Pierpont Ave 84101 **Location:** Just n of 300 S and 300 W.
D

ELEVATIONS 801/531-0800 (11)
▼▼▼ American. Casual Dining. $10-$25 **AAA Inspector Notes:** With a rustic and refined ambience, this restaurant serves classics such as shrimp cocktail, aged steaks, chops, flatbread pizza, piled-high sandwiches and beer-battered fish and chips. **Features:** full bar. **Address:** 75 S West Temple 84101 **Location:** Cross streets 100 S and S West Temple; in Salt Lake Marriott Downtown at City Creek. **Parking:** valet and street only.
B L D

EM'S RESTAURANT 801/596-0566 (1)
▼▼ American. Casual Dining. $8-$26 **AAA Inspector Notes:** This neighborhood bistro is casual and comfortable. Selections, which incorporate local and organic ingredients, may include potato pancakes, phyllo stuffed with goat cheese and duck confit, pear-and-walnut green salad, braised short ribs, leek-stuffed wild salmon and free-range chicken. Seasonal dessert selections always include ice cream and sorbet made in house. **Features:** beer & wine, patio dining, Sunday brunch. **Address:** 271 N Center St 84103 **Location:** 0.3 mi n of State St and E North Temple to 300 N, just w to Center St, then just s; in The Avenues. **Parking:** street only.
L D

(See map & index p. 381.)

EVA   801/359-8447 (39)
▼▼ ▼▼ Mediterranean. Casual Dining. $8-$16 AAA Inspector
Notes: This small eatery features creative specialty drinks and small
and large plates. Some of the menu items include sautéed Brussels
sprouts with toasted hazelnuts and cider vinegar, crab cakes, a variety of salads, wood-fired pizza and pasta. Vegan and vegetarian
items are available. Features: full bar, patio dining, Sunday brunch,
happy hour. Reservations: suggested. Address: 317 S Main St
84111 Location: At 300 S and Main St; 0.6 mi s of South Temple St.
Parking: street only. (D) (LATE)

FINCA   801/487-0699 (19)
▼▼▼▼ Spanish. Fine Dining. $7-$34 AAA Inspector Notes:
Flavors abound at this downtown restaurant, which offers an array of
cold and hot tapas in snack, small, large, and larger size. A well-
thought-out seasonal menu may include popular local potatoes with
paprika and garlic aioli, mussels, pork belly in a minted pea puree,
mouthwatering gazpacho verde or a watermelon gazpacho garnished
with fresh lavender. The house made churros served with a rich chocolate dipping sauce will have you licking the plate. Features: full bar,
patio dining, Sunday brunch. Reservations: suggested. Address:
327 W 200 S 84101 Location: Jct 300 W and 200 S, just w. Parking:
street only. (L) (D)

FLEMING'S PRIME STEAKHOUSE & WINE BAR
                                           801/355-3704 (5)
▼▼▼▼ Steak Seafood. Fine Dining. $20-$49 AAA Inspector
Notes: The warm, clubby atmosphere is the ideal setting for perfectly
grilled steaks and seafood. Side dishes come in hearty portions, and
salads are fresh and crisp. More than 100 wine selections are available. Features: full bar, happy hour. Reservations: suggested. Address: 20 S 400 W 84101 Location: I-15 exit 306 (600 S), 0.4 mi e,
then 1 mi n on S 400 W; exit 309 (600 N) southbound, 0.4 mi e, then
1 mi s on S 400 W; across from Energy Solutions Arena; at The
Gateway. (D)

FORAGE RESTAURANT   801/708-7834 (54)
▼▼▼ ▼▼ Regional American. Fine Dining. $89 AAA In-
spector Notes: In an intimate setting, this restaurant's seasonal
fixed-price tasting menu is filled with flavors and texture. Dishes are
prepared in a distinctive manner utilizing the best local and regional
ingredients available, particularly those gathered by hand. Nightly
menu items might include butter-poached scallops, trout warmed in
cherry wood oil, Idaho sturgeon, marinated elk, black currant and
pork fat, roast Colorado lamb, brown-butter-poached apricots and
chilled passion fruit soup. Features: beer & wine. Reservations: required. Address: 370 E 900 S 84111 Location: Jct State St and 900
S, 0.4 mi e. (D) CALL (&M)

FRIDA BISTRO   801/983-6692 (50)
▼▼▼ Regional Mexican. Fine Dining. $11-$29 AAA Inspector
Notes: The attentive service begins with the initial greeting and seating
where you will experience approachable and modern yet sophisticated
gastronomy. Enticing and flavorful courses might include a mole negro
turkey tamale steamed in a banana leaf or pan-seared duck quesadilla
with orange reduction and menonita cheese. Features: full bar, patio
dining. Reservations: suggested. Address: 545 W 700 S 84101 Location: I-15 exit 306 (600 S) northbound, 0.5 mi e to 400 W, just s to
700 S, then just w; exit 307 (400 S) southbound, 0.5 mi e over ramp to
500 W, 0.5 mi s to 700 S, then just w. (L) (D)

THE GARDEN RESTAURANT   801/539-3170 (7)
▼▼ ▼▼ American. Family Dining. $10-$19 AAA Inspector Notes:
With stunning views of downtown and Temple Square, the restaurant
features a retractable glass roof and offers local favorites such as
fried dill pickles, spinach salad, several pasta dishes, gourmet sandwiches and oven-roasted Pacific salmon drizzled with Thai peanut
sauce. Scrumptious desserts include the restaurant's famous chocolate cinnamon cake. Address: 15 E S Temple 84150 Location: Just
w of State St and South Temple; in Joseph Smith Memorial Building,
10th Floor. (L) (D)

GOURMANDISE THE BAKERY   801/328-9022 (36)
▼▼ ▼▼ Breads/Pastries Sandwiches. Family Dining. $7-$12 AAA
Inspector Notes: The menu lists a plentiful array of grilled panini
sandwiches, daily quiches with flaky and buttery made-from-scratch
crust, hearty soups and traditional or vegetable lasagna. Sweet diver-
sions include feuilletée, English bread pudding and baba au rum
tartlette. Features: patio dining. Address: 250 S 300 E 84111 Location: Between 200 S and 300 S. (B) (L) (D) CALL (&M)

ICHIBAN SUSHI   801/532-7522 (47)
▼▼ ▼▼ Sushi. Casual Dining. $12-$33 AAA Inspector Notes:
Fresh sushi and sashimi, as well as traditional Japanese dishes, are
prepared by skillfully trained chefs in this beautiful historic restaurant,
which was once a cathedral. The saltwater aquarium is mesmerizing.
Features: full bar, happy hour. Address: 336 S 400 E 84111 Location: I-15 exit 307 (400 S), 1 mi e to 400 E, then just n. (D)

IGGY'S SPORTS GRILL   801/532-9999
▼▼ ▼▼ American. Casual Dining. $8-$19 AAA Inspector Notes:
Patrons seeking hearty food in a fun atmosphere will find it at this upbeat sports grill. Among diverse offerings are chicken teriyaki, barbecue ribs, pizza, macadamia nut salmon, Sicilian lasagna, burgers
and rib-eye steak. The turkey meatballs and chili are local favorites
and all beer lovers will delight in a variety of microbrews on tap. Features: full bar. Address: 423 W 300 S 84101 Location: Corner of
300 S and 400 W. Parking: street only. (L) (D)

J. WONG'S ASIAN BISTRO   801/350-0888 (20)
▼▼ ▼▼ Asian. Casual Dining. $6-$18 AAA Inspector Notes:
Named for four brothers, this bistro features a satay bar and a chic
full-service bar with custom-made tabletops. The lunch menu fea-
tures single-meal choices. Features: full bar. Address: 163 W 200 S
84101 Location: Just e of 200 S and 200 W; across from Salt Palace
Convention Center. Parking: valet and street only.
(L) (D)

LA BELLA PIASTRA   801/961-8700 (28)
▼▼ ▼▼ Italian. Casual Dining. $11-$28 AAA Inspector Notes:
Upscale contemporary cuisine hits the mark with appetizers, pasta,
brick-oven pizza, veal scaloppini, cedar plank salmon with a sweet
pea risotto and a tasty chicken piccata with fresh lemon and capers.
Features: full bar. Address: 220 S State St 84111 Location: Cross
streets State and 200 S; in Salt Lake City Marriott City Center.
Parking: on-site (fee) and valet.
(B) (L) (D) CALL (&M)

LAMB'S GRILL CAFE   801/364-7166 (21)
▼▼ ▼▼ American. Casual Dining. $6-$29 AAA Inspector Notes:
Classic Historic. Located in the business district, this restaurant
serves a wide variety of menu items, including seafood, chicken,
lamb, steak, sandwiches, soups and salads and popular pre-theater
dinner specials. Features: full bar, early bird specials. Address: 169
S Main St 84111 Location: 0.3 mi s of Temple Square. Parking: on-
site and street. (B) (L) (D)

LES MADELEINES CAFE & PATISSERIE 801/355-2294 (49)
▼▼ ▼▼ Breads/Pastries Sandwiches. Quick Serve. $6-$11 AAA
Inspector Notes: This delightful patisserie makes cakes, candy,
shortbread and tarts from scratch. Travel-inspired lunches feature
tasty soup, macaroni with white cheddar and Gruyère cheese, delicious sesame-chicken salad wrapped in butter lettuce and rice paper
served with edamame and a ham and cheese on house bread with
unsalted butter and pomme frites. Features: patio dining. Address:
216 E 500 S 84111 Location: At 500 S and 200 E. Parking: street
only. (B) (L)

THE LION HOUSE PANTRY   801/363-5466 (10)
▼▼ American. Cafeteria. $7-$13 AAA Inspector Notes: Patrons
will enjoy home-style food, fresh rolls and pastries served cafeteria
style in the historic home of Brigham Young. Covered validated
parking is available. Features: patio dining. Address: 63 E South
Temple 84150 Location: At Temple Square; next to Joseph Smith
Memorial Building. (B) (L) (D)

MARKET STREET GRILL & OYSTER BAR - DOWNTOWN
                                           801/322-4668 (41)
▼▼ ▼▼ Seafood Steak. Casual Dining. $11-$39 AAA Inspector
Notes: Historic. After warm bread, soup and a salad, guests then
choose from a variety of blackened or broiled fresh fish and other
seafood dishes centered on oysters, clams, mussels, shrimp, Atlantic
salmon and lobster. Although it's nowhere near, this place makes patrons feel they're close to the ocean. A delightful selection of
mouthwatering desserts rounds out the meal. Features: full bar, early
bird specials, Sunday brunch. Address: 48 W Market St 84101 Location: From Temple Square, 0.5 mi s on Main St, then just w.
Parking: valet and street only. (B) (L) (D)

(See map & index p. 381.)

MARTINE CAFE & TAPAS
801/363-9328 (15)

▼▼▼ New American. Fine Dining. $12-$30 **AAA Inspector Notes:** Flavorful creations come together in varied tapas and entrees, including spicy lobster rolls, wild boar ribs with pomegranate barbecue sauce, lavender and sweet pea soup, pepita crusted trout, seared duck breast and wild salmon served with yogurt quinoa and stone fruit chutney. A special pasta salad is served each day of the week. A dessert wine will end the meal on a memorable note. **Features:** full bar. **Reservations:** suggested. **Address:** 22 E 100 S 84111 **Location:** Just e of 100 S and Main St. **Parking:** valet and street only. L D

MAZZA CAFE AT 9TH
801/521-4572 (56)

▼▼ Middle Eastern. Casual Dining. $7-$24 **AAA Inspector Notes:** This neighborhood eatery offers specialty appetizer and entrée sampler platters that include your choice of more than 22 mouthwatering items. Traditional dishes include grape leaves, falafel, muhamara made with pomegranate molasses, and chicken, beef or lamb kebabs. The seafood platter features seasoned and broiled mahi mahi, shrimp and scallops. **Features:** full bar, patio dining. **Address:** 912 E 900 S 84105 **Location:** Just e of Temple Square to State St, 1.3 mi s, 1.3 mi e. **Parking:** street only. L D

NAKED FISH JAPANESE BISTRO
801/595-8888 (13)

▼▼▼ Sushi. Casual Dining. $9-$39 **AAA Inspector Notes:** Expect creative, colorful presentations and high quality ingredients at this bistro which provides an intimate and elegant ambiance. Seating is available at a table, the sushi bar or in private dining areas tatami style. **Features:** full bar, patio dining. **Address:** 67 W 100 S 84101 **Location:** Just e of SW Temple and 100 S. **Parking:** on-site (fee) and street. L D

NAUVOO CAFE
801/539-3346 (8)

▼ American. Cafeteria. $6-$8 **AAA Inspector Notes:** Patrons enjoy hand-carved sandwiches and the famous pot pies. Covered validated parking is available. **Features:** patio dining. **Address:** 15 E South Temple 84150 **Location:** In Joseph Smith Memorial Building. B L D

THE NEW YORKER
801/363-0166 (40)

▼▼▼ Seafood Steak. Fine Dining. $12-$48 **AAA Inspector Notes:** *Historic.* The perfect stop before or after the theater, symphony or sports events, this restaurant offers classy dining with an emphasis on the freshest seafood available and premium steaks. Additional menu items may include spaghetti with Dungeness crab and rack of lamb with mint pesto. Colorful heirloom vegetables are incorporated into many of the salads and entrees. The desserts are beautiful to look at and even better to enjoy. **Features:** full bar. **Reservations:** suggested. **Address:** 60 W Market St 84101 **Location:** Between Main St and West Temple. **Parking:** valet and street only. L D

OASIS CAFE
801/322-0404 (27)

▼▼ New American. Casual Dining. $9-$23 **AAA Inspector Notes:** This popular eatery has a varied selection of creatively presented seasonal menu items ranging from stuffed fillet medallions and grilled salmon to herb-roasted chicken and udon peanut stir-fry. Share the pita tasting plate or an elegant dessert. Be advised, the toasted Brie sandwich on cranberry-walnut bread is addictive. **Features:** full bar, patio dining, Sunday brunch. **Address:** 151 S 500 E 84102 **Location:** Just n of 200 S and 500 E. **Parking:** on-site and street. B L D CALL ⌖M

PAGO
801/532-0777 (55)

▼▼▼ New American. Casual Dining. $11-$38 **AAA Inspector Notes:** In the trendy 9th and 9th neighborhood, this restaurant is known for its farm-to-table ingredients. Menu offerings may include delicious lamb burgers, Wagyu steak salad, shallow-poached Alaskan halibut, roasted quail or pork tenderloin roulade. For dessert, the seasonal mousse tasting is a favorite. Vegan and vegetarian items available. **Features:** full bar, patio dining, Sunday brunch. **Address:** 878 S 900 E 84102 **Location:** I-15 exit 307 (400 S), 2.3 mi e, 0.6 mi s on 700 E, then 0.3 mi e; at 900 S and 900 E. **Parking:** street only. L D

PALLET
801/935-4431 (22)

▼▼▼ New American. Casual Dining. $9-$29 **AAA Inspector Notes:** Careful thought was put into the preservation of this former downtown loading dock including commissioned artwork, reclaimed wood and a repurposed wood ceiling. Seasonal menu offerings may include organic salads, seared scallops with black rice and cherries and a popular bison tri-tip. Creative desserts and a nice selection of spirits also are available. Seasonal house-made tonic or lemonade is a nightly feature. **Features:** full bar, patio dining. **Reservations:** suggested. **Address:** 237 S 400 W 84101 **Location:** Corner of 200 S and 400 W. **Parking:** on-site and street. D

P.F. CHANG'S CHINA BISTRO
801/539-0500 (32)

▼▼▼ Chinese. Fine Dining. $10-$27 **AAA Inspector Notes:** Trendy, upscale decor provides a pleasant backdrop for New Age Chinese dining. Appetizers, soups and salads are a meal by themselves. Vegetarian plates and sides, noodles, chow meins, chicken and meat dishes are created from exotic, fresh ingredients. **Features:** full bar, patio dining, happy hour. **Address:** 174 W 300 S 84101 **Location:** Jct 200 W and 300 S. **Parking:** valet and street only. L D LATE

RED IGUANA
801/322-1489 (2)

▼▼ Mexican. Casual Dining. $9-$18 **AAA Inspector Notes:** Come here rain, shine or snow. In the winter, outdoor heat warmers will keep you toasty on the outdoor seating area while you wait to experience the true taste of authentic moles. Burritos, chimichangas, enchiladas, salads, seafood, soups, steaks, tacos and tostadas also are served at this cozy cucina. Their pozole knocks it out of the park and the desserts are well worth consideration. **Features:** full bar, Sunday brunch. **Address:** 736 W North Temple 84116 **Location:** 1 mi w of Temple Square. L D

RED IGUANA 2
801/214-6050 (3)

▼▼ Mexican. Casual Dining. $9-$17 **AAA Inspector Notes:** Patrons can experience the true taste of authentic mole at this cozy and friendly spot. Burritos, chimichangas, enchiladas, salads, seafood, soups, steaks, tacos, tostadas and desserts also are available. **Features:** full bar, Sunday brunch. **Address:** 866 W South Temple 84101 **Location:** 0.4 mi w of Temple Square via W South Temple, just n on 300 W, 0.7 mi w on W North Temple, s on 800 W, then just w. L D

RIO GRANDE CAFE
801/364-3302 (23)

▼▼ Mexican. Casual Dining. $8-$22 **AAA Inspector Notes:** *Historic.* Located in the historical Rio Grande train depot, the restaurant offers festive dining on consistently great Mexican fare, including carnitas, margaritas and more. Don't miss the model train running overhead. **Features:** full bar. **Address:** 270 S Rio Grande St (455 W) 84101 **Location:** I-15 exit 306 (600 S), just e to 300 W, then 0.3 mi n; in Rio Grande Train Station. L D

RODIZIO GRILL
801/220-0500 (52)

▼▼ Brazilian. Casual Dining. $19-$26 **AAA Inspector Notes:** This authentic Brazilian restaurant, offering unlimited appetizers and salad bar, has more than a dozen selections of delicious meats, which are served tableside and hand carved by Brazilian gauchos. The live drums provide a night-in-Brazil feeling. **Features:** full bar. **Address:** 459 Trolley Square 84102 **Location:** Main building, 2nd Level; in Trolley Square. L D

THE ROOF RESTAURANT
801/539-1911 (9)

▼▼▼ American. Casual Dining. $40 **AAA Inspector Notes:** Breathtaking views of downtown, Temple Square and the surrounding mountains can be seen from this restaurant's 10th-floor location. A gorgeous gourmet buffet of American and international dishes is prepared daily and includes a wide selection of salads, chilled shrimp, poached salmon, prime rib, baked ham, pasta, chef's choice of potatoes, seasonal fruit and vegetables. The mouthwatering desserts are colorfully displayed. **Reservations:** suggested. **Address:** 15 E South Temple 84150 **Location:** Just w of State St and South Temple; in Joseph Smith Memorial Building, 10th Floor. D CALL ⌖M

SAWADEE THAI RESTAURANT
801/328-8424 (16)

▼▼ Thai. Casual Dining. $8-$20 **AAA Inspector Notes:** The popular lunch menu includes soups, salads and curry dishes, all delicious. Enjoy gracious service at this charming downtown café. **Features:** beer & wine. **Address:** 754 E South Temple 84102 **Location:** 1.2 mi e of Temple Square, just e of 700 E. L D

(See map & index p. 381.)

SETTEBELLO PIZZERIA NAPOLETANA   801/322-3556   30
▼▼▼ Pizza. Casual Dining. $9-$16 **AAA Inspector Notes:** Diners can go healthy with a Caprese or arugula salad or instead opt for a traditional Napoli pizza, which can be served sliced or unsliced. The gelato choices are many, but the favorite is pistachio. **Features:** beer & wine. **Address:** 260 S 200 W 84101 **Location:** Jct 200 S and 200 W. **Parking:** on-site and street. L D CALL M

SPENCER'S FOR STEAKS AND CHOPS   801/238-4748   29
▼▼▼ Steak. Fine Dining. $15-$67 **AAA Inspector Notes:** This classic steakhouse offers a sophisticated alternative, with an à la carte menu of classic favorites and impressive world-class wines. Try the fresh seafood such as the sashimi grade ahi tuna or wild-caught salmon. You can't go wrong with the double-layered strawberry shortcake. **Features:** full bar. **Address:** 255 S West Temple 84101 **Location:** Just s of cross streets 200 S and S West Temple; in Hilton Salt Lake City Center. **Parking:** valet and street only. L D CALL M

SQUATTER'S PUB BREWERY   801/363-2739   35
▼▼ American. Casual Dining. $9-$19 **AAA Inspector Notes:** Patrons can enjoy the brewpub atmosphere from seats by the fireplace or on the patio. A variety of award-winning beers taste great paired with the selection of appetizers, soups, salads, sandwiches and pub favorites. Vegetarian and low-carb items are available. **Features:** full bar, patio dining. **Address:** 147 W Broadway (300 S) 84101 **Location:** Cross streets 300 S and 200 W. L D LATE

SU CASA MEXICAN RESTAURANT   801/363-7771   46
▼▼ Mexican. Casual Dining. $6-$10 **AAA Inspector Notes:** Fast, upbeat service is provided at this cute eatery offering favorite dishes such as nachos, enchiladas, burritos and tasty veggie tacos. **Features:** patio dining. **Address:** 516 E 300 S 84102 **Location:** At 500 E and 300 S. **Parking:** on-site and street. L D CALL M

TAKASHI   801/519-9595   43
▼▼▼ Sushi Small Plates. Casual Dining. $9-$24 **AAA Inspector Notes:** Hot small plates include braised Asian barbecue pork ribs brushed with ginger-soy glaze, wok-tossed asparagus in a garlic and shiitake mushroom sauce over glass noodles, assorted seafood in a lemon grass and cilantro broth, and shiitake lamb shank braised in a Japanese yellow curry. Also offered are sashimi and sushi combination plates, vegetarian items and creative and exciting specialty rolls. An excellent selection of sake, beer, wine and spirits is available. **Features:** full bar. **Address:** 18 W Market St 84101 **Location:** From Temple Square, 0.5 mi s on Main St, then just w. **Parking:** valet and street only. L D

TIN ANGEL BISTRO   801/328-4155   44
▼▼ Regional Natural/Organic. Casual Dining. $7-$28 **AAA Inspector Notes:** Tapas may include prosciutto-wrapped shrimp or espresso-crusted beef tenderloin, while entrées trend toward eggplant and seafood torre or chicken saltimbocca. Creative and whimsical desserts are seasonal, and local and organic produce are used whenever possible. **Features:** full bar, patio dining. **Reservations:** suggested. **Address:** 365 W 400 S 84101 **Location:** I-15 exit 307 (400 S), 0.3 mi e; across from Pioneer Park. L D

TONY CAPUTO'S MARKET & DELI   801/531-8669   31
▼ Deli. Quick Serve. $6-$10 **AAA Inspector Notes:** The menu features a good mix of Italian and Southern European dishes. **Features:** patio dining. **Address:** 314 W 300 S 84101 **Location:** Cross streets 300 S and 300 W. **Parking:** street only. L D

TUCCI'S CUCINA ITALIANA   801/533-9111   51
▼▼ Italian. Casual Dining. $9-$28 **AAA Inspector Notes:** Guests see a colorful display of the chef's interesting entrées and desserts as they enter this restaurant, which boasts one of the city's largest covered patios. An attentive staff caters to diners as they enjoy such signature items as pasta mista, shrimp puttanesca, butternut squash ravioli and lamb a la Napoli. A kicky espresso goes great with dessert. **Features:** full bar. **Address:** 515 S 700 E 84102 **Location:** Cross streets 500 S and 700 E; in Trolley Square. L D

VALTER'S OSTERIA   801/521-4563   34
▼▼▼ ▼▼ Italian. Fine Dining. $20-$32 **AAA Inspector Notes:** The gnocchi and ravioli sampler and the free-range chicken sautéed in lemon butter sauce with slivers of oyster mushrooms and caper berries are surprisingly light. The chocolate soufflé and tiramisù are a few of the delectable desserts. Many dishes are prepared and presented tableside. Simply put, be prepared for a memorable dining experience presented to you by a skilled and professional staff. **Features:** full bar, patio dining. **Reservations:** required. **Address:** 173 W Broadway Ave (300 S) 84101 **Location:** Jct 200 W and 300 S. **Parking:** valet and street only. D

VINTO   801/539-9999   33
▼▼ Italian. Casual Dining. $8-$13 **AAA Inspector Notes:** This casual eatery has chic and bright décor. Menu offerings include meatballs the size of golf balls, wood-fired pizzas, attractively presented salads, breadsticks, flatbread and a thoughtful selection of wine, bottled water, teas and coffee. Flights of colorful house-made gelato and sorbetto hit the spot. **Features:** full bar, patio dining. **Address:** 418 E 200 S 84111 **Location:** Cross streets E 200 S and 400 E. L D CALL M

WHISKEY STREET COCKTAILS & DINING   801/433-1371   42
▼▼ American. Gastropub. $10-$24 **AAA Inspector Notes:** Offering extensive whiskey, wine and beer pairings, hand-crafted beer and habit-forming bourbon-bacon-caramel popcorn, the 72-foot-long cherry-wood bar and floor-to-ceiling bottles of whiskey make a jaw-dropping first impression. Menu favorites are the potato logs served with braised short ribs topped with a seasoned flash-fried soft-boiled egg, corn crab chowder, pork-chop-confit-stuffed tomato dressed with bourbon-apricot compote and braised pork belly corn dogs. **Features:** full bar. **Address:** 323 S Main St 84111 **Location:** Jct Main St and 300 S, just s. **Parking:** street only. L D LATE CALL M

WILD GRAPE BISTRO   801/746-5565   12
▼▼▼ New American. Casual Dining. $8-$33 **AAA Inspector Notes:** Creative dishes such as grilled lobster tail with saffron risotto and braised fennel, and spicy butternut squash soup with pear and cranberry chutney combine locally grown organic products whenever possible. Favorite sandwiches include a Colorado bison burger and a lamb burger with glazed onions. **Features:** full bar, Sunday brunch. **Address:** 481 E South Temple 84111 **Location:** Corner of S Temple and E St; 0.7 mi e of Temple Square. B L D CALL M

SALT LAKE CITY (B-3)
- Restaurants p. 400
- Hotels & Restaurants map & index p. 385

BEST WESTERN PLUS AIRPORT INN & SUITES
(801)428-0900   2
▼▼▼ Hotel $79-$99

Address: 5433 W Wiley Post Way 84116 **Location:** I-80 exit 114 (Wright Brothers Dr), 0.5 mi n, just e, then just s. **Facility:** 81 units. 3 stories, interior corridors. **Amenities:** safes. **Pool(s):** heated indoor. **Activities:** hot tub, exercise room. **Guest Services:** valet and coin laundry.

SAVE ⊁ ▐↑▌ CALL M ⊅ BIZ
HS 🛜 ✕ ⊟ ⊡ ⊡

CANDLEWOOD SUITES - AIRPORT EAST   801/359-7500   12
▼▼ Extended Stay Hotel. Rates not provided. **Address:** 2170 W North Temple 84116 **Location:** I-80 exit 118, 0.3 mi n, then 0.7 mi w. **Facility:** 122 efficiencies. 3 stories, interior corridors. **Activities:** picnic facilities, exercise room. **Guest Services:** complimentary laundry.

⊁ ▐↑▌ HS 🛜 ✕ ⊟ ⊡ ⊡ SOME UNITS S▐

(See map & index p. 385.)

COMFORT SUITES (801)715-8688 **11**
▼▼▼ **Hotel** $79-$149 **Address:** 171 N 2100 W 84116 **Location:** I-80 exit 118, 0.3 mi n, 0.7 mi w, then just e. **Facility:** 104 units. 4 stories, interior corridors. **Pool(s):** heated indoor. **Activities:** hot tub, limited exercise equipment. **Guest Services:** valet and coin laundry.

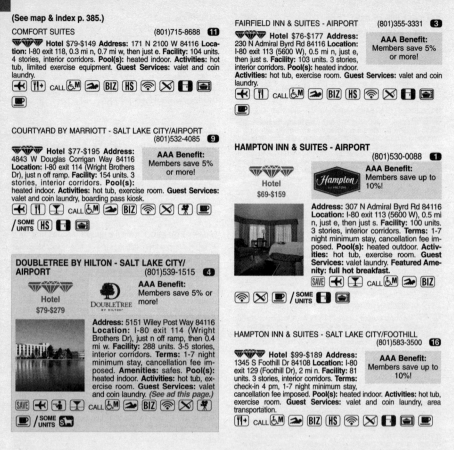

COURTYARD BY MARRIOTT - SALT LAKE CITY/AIRPORT
(801)532-4085 **9**
▼▼▼ **Hotel** $77-$195 **Address:** 4843 W Douglas Corrigan Way 84116 **Location:** I-80 exit 114 (Wright Brothers Dr), just n off ramp. **Facility:** 154 units. 3 stories, interior corridors. **Pool(s):** heated indoor. **Activities:** hot tub, exercise room. **Guest Services:** valet and coin laundry, boarding pass kiosk.

AAA Benefit: Members save 5% or more!

DOUBLETREE BY HILTON - SALT LAKE CITY/AIRPORT (801)539-1515 **4**
▼▼▼ Hotel $79-$279

AAA Benefit: Members save 5% or more!

Address: 5151 Wiley Post Way 84116 **Location:** I-80 exit 114 (Wright Brothers Dr), just n off ramp, then 0.4 mi w. **Facility:** 288 units. 3-5 stories, interior corridors. **Terms:** 1-7 night minimum stay, cancellation fee imposed. **Amenities:** safes. **Pool(s):** heated indoor. **Activities:** hot tub, exercise room. **Guest Services:** valet and coin laundry. *(See ad this page.)*

FAIRFIELD INN & SUITES - AIRPORT (801)355-3331 **3**
▼▼▼ **Hotel** $76-$177 **Address:** 230 N Admiral Byrd Rd 84116 **Location:** I-80 exit 113 (5600 W), 0.5 mi n, just e, then just s. **Facility:** 103 units. 3 stories, interior corridors. **Pool(s):** heated indoor. **Activities:** hot tub, exercise room. **Guest Services:** valet and coin laundry.

AAA Benefit: Members save 5% or more!

HAMPTON INN & SUITES - AIRPORT
(801)530-0088 **1**
◇◇◇ Hotel $69-$159

AAA Benefit: Members save up to 10%!

Hampton by Hilton

Address: 307 N Admiral Byrd Rd 84116 **Location:** I-80 exit 113 (5600 W), 0.5 mi n, just e, then just s. **Facility:** 100 units. 3 stories, interior corridors. **Terms:** 1-7 night minimum stay, cancellation fee imposed. **Pool(s):** heated indoor. **Activities:** hot tub, exercise room. **Guest Services:** valet laundry. **Featured Amenity: full hot breakfast.**

HAMPTON INN & SUITES - SALT LAKE CITY/FOOTHILL
(801)583-3500 **16**
▼▼▼ **Hotel** $99-$189 **Address:** 1345 S Foothill Dr 84108 **Location:** I-80 exit 129 (Foothill Dr), 2 mi n. **Facility:** 81 units. 3 stories, interior corridors. **Terms:** check-in 4 pm, 1-7 night minimum stay, cancellation fee imposed. **Pool(s):** heated indoor. **Activities:** hot tub, exercise room. **Guest Services:** valet and coin laundry, area transportation.

AAA Benefit: Members save up to 10%!

▼ See AAA listing this page ▼

(See map & index p. 385.)

HAMPTON INN - SALT LAKE CITY/CENTRAL
(801)886-0703 **17**

Hotel $89-$319 **Address:** 2055 S Redwood Rd 84104 **Location:** I-15 exit 305C (2100 S), 1.5 mi w; jct S Redwood Rd and W 2100 S. Located in a commercial area. **Facility:** 73 units. 3 stories, interior corridors. **Terms:** 1-7 night minimum stay, cancellation fee imposed. **Pool(s):** heated indoor. **Activities:** hot tub, exercise room. **Guest Services:** valet and coin laundry.

AAA Benefit: Members save up to 10%!

HILTON GARDEN INN - AIRPORT
(801)519-9000 **6**

Hotel $140 **Address:** 4975 Wiley Post Way 84116 **Location:** I-80 exit 114 (Wright Brothers Dr), just n off ramp, then just w. **Facility:** 172 units. 6 stories, interior corridors. **Terms:** 1-7 night minimum stay, cancellation fee imposed. **Pool(s):** heated indoor. **Activities:** exercise room. **Guest Services:** valet and coin laundry.

AAA Benefit: Members save up to 10%!

HOLIDAY INN & SUITES - SALT LAKE CITY/AIRPORT WEST
801/741-1800 **5**

Hotel. Rates not provided. **Address:** 5001 W Wiley Post Way 84116 **Location:** I-80 exit 114 (Wright Brothers Dr), just n off ramp, then 0.4 mi w. **Facility:** 111 units. 4 stories, interior corridors. **Dining:** Wing Tips Bar & Bistro, see separate listing. **Pool(s):** heated indoor. **Activities:** hot tub, exercise room. **Guest Services:** valet and coin laundry, boarding pass kiosk.

HYATT PLACE - SALT LAKE CITY/AIRPORT
(801)363-1400 **10**

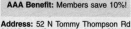

Hotel $70-$210

HYATT PLACE'

AAA Benefit: Members save 10%!

Address: 52 N Tommy Thompson Rd 84116 **Location:** I-80 exit 114 (Wright Brothers Dr), just n off ramp, just e, then just se. **Facility:** 123 units. 5 stories, interior corridors. **Terms:** cancellation fee imposed. **Pool(s):** heated indoor. **Activities:** exercise room. **Guest Services:** valet and coin laundry, area transportation. **Featured Amenity:** breakfast buffet.

THE INN AT SOLITUDE
(801)517-7717 **19**

Hotel $149-$449 **Address:** 12000 Big Cottonwood Canyon 84121 **Location:** I-215 exit 6 (6200 S), 14 mi up Big Cottonwood Canyon, 2nd entrance. **Facility:** 46 units, some efficiencies. 4 stories, interior corridors. **Parking:** on-site and valet. **Terms:** check-in 4 pm. **Amenities:** safes. **Dining:** St. Bernard's at Solitude, see separate listing. **Pool(s):** heated outdoor. **Activities:** sauna, hot tub, downhill & cross country skiing, snowboarding, ice skating, recreation programs in winter, game room, exercise room, spa. **Guest Services:** coin laundry, area transportation.

MARRIOTT SALT LAKE CITY UNIVERSITY PARK
(801)581-1000 **15**

Hotel $100-$249 **Address:** 480 Wakara Way 84108 **Location:** I-80 exit 125 (700 E), 2.5 mi n to 800 S, 2 mi e to Foothill Dr, 0.3 mi n to Wakara Way, then 0.3 mi ne. Next to University of Utah campus and hospitals. **Facility:** 217 units. 6 stories, interior corridors. **Dining:** 2 restaurants. **Pool(s):** heated indoor. **Activities:** hot tub, exercise room. **Guest Services:** valet laundry, area transportation.

AAA Benefit: Members save 5% or more!

RADISSON HOTEL - SALT LAKE CITY/AIRPORT
(801)364-5800 **13**

Hotel $110-$219 **Address:** 2177 W North Temple 84116 **Location:** I-80 exit 118, 0.3 mi n, then 0.8 mi w. **Facility:** 124 units. 3 stories, interior corridors. **Terms:** 3 day cancellation notice. **Amenities:** Some: safes. **Pool(s):** heated outdoor. **Activities:** exercise room. **Guest Services:** valet and coin laundry, area transportation.

RESIDENCE INN BY MARRIOTT - SALT LAKE CITY/AIRPORT
(801)532-4101 **8**

Extended Stay Hotel $103-$204 **Address:** 4883 W Douglas Corrigan Way 84116 **Location:** I-80 exit 114 (Wright Brothers Dr), just n off ramp. **Facility:** 104 efficiencies, some two bedrooms and kitchens. 4 stories, interior corridors. **Pool(s):** heated indoor. **Activities:** hot tub, picnic facilities, exercise room. **Guest Services:** valet and coin laundry.

AAA Benefit: Members save 5% or more!

SPRINGHILL SUITES BY MARRIOT - SALT LAKE CITY/AIRPORT
(801)532-6633 **7**

Hotel $76-$182 **Address:** 4955 Wiley Post Way 84116 **Location:** I-80 exit 114 (Wright Brothers Dr), just n off ramp, then just w. **Facility:** 143 units. 5 stories, interior corridors. **Pool(s):** heated indoor. **Activities:** picnic facilities, exercise room. **Guest Services:** valet and coin laundry.

AAA Benefit: Members save 5% or more!

UNIVERSITY GUEST HOUSE & CONFERENCE CENTER
801/587-1000 **14**

Hotel. Rates not provided. **Address:** 110 S Fort Douglas Blvd 84113 **Location:** I-80 exit 129 (Foothill Dr), 3.5 mi n to Mario Capecchi Dr, 0.5 mi n to Gibbon St, then just e, follow signs. Located on University of Utah campus. **Facility:** 180 units, some efficiencies and kitchens. 4 stories, interior corridors. **Activities:** exercise room. **Guest Services:** coin laundry, boarding pass kiosk, area transportation.

WILDFLOWERS BED & BREAKFAST
801/466-0600 **18**

Historic Bed & Breakfast $90-$145 **Address:** 936 E 1700 S 84105 **Location:** Cross streets 900 E and 1700 S, just e. **Facility:** Guest rooms are comfortably appointed at this older fully restored 1891 Victorian home, which provides beveled and stained-glass windows, a hand-carved staircase, original chandeliers and high ceilings. 5 units. 3 stories (no elevator), interior/exterior corridors. **Terms:** 3 day cancellation notice-fee imposed.

Upgrade to Plus or Premier membership for *more* of the benefits you need most

(See map & index p. 385.)

HOLIDAY INN EXPRESS & SUITES - SALT LAKE CITY/
AIRPORT   801/741-1500
[fyi] Hotel Did not meet all AAA rating requirements for locking devices in some guest rooms at time of last evaluation on 02/20/2015. **Address:** 200 N 2100 W 84116 **Location:** I-80 exit 218, 0.3 mi e, 0.8 mi n, then just e. Facilities, services, and décor characterize a mid-scale property.

WHERE TO EAT

BOMBAY HOUSE CUISINE OF INDIA   801/581-0222 (12)
Indian. Casual Dining. $9-$17 **AAA Inspector Notes:** This enchanting restaurant features an authentic atmosphere and delicate ethnic dishes. The flavor of curry abounds and is quite delightful. Vegetarian and vegan options are available. **Features:** beer & wine. **Address:** 2731 E Parley's Way 84109 **Location:** I-80 exit 129, 0.4 mi nw on Parley's Way off Foothill Dr; in Lamplighter Square. (D)

CITRIS GRILL   801/466-1202 (15)
New American. Casual Dining. $8-$21 **AAA Inspector Notes:** Menu items served in this friendly neighborhood eatery can be ordered in the petite or hearty size. The sweet potato corn chowder is served daily, as are the delicious pepper-crusted risotto cakes. **Features:** full bar, Sunday brunch. **Address:** 3977 S Wasatch Blvd 84124 **Location:** I-215 exit 3 (3300 S/Wasatch Blvd), just e. (B) (L) (D)

DODO RESTAURANT   801/486-2473 (11)
American. Casual Dining. $10-$27 **AAA Inspector Notes:** You won't miss the modern purple building or the 'dodo' birds socializing over drinks when dining at this bistro. The delicious selection of breakfast, lunch, dinner and brunch menu items include the Dodo omelette, lemon-pepper seared ahi medallions, roasted-tomato polenta cake, beef stroganoff, and spinach-mushroom-feta quiche. Seasonal desserts may include a slice of banana cream cheese pie or their signature Toll House pie. **Features:** full bar, patio dining, Sunday brunch. **Address:** 1355 E 2100 S 84105 **Location:** I-80 exit 126 (Sugar House), 0.5 mi n to 2100 S, then just e. (B) (L) (D)

EGGS IN THE CITY   801/581-0809 (6)
Breakfast Sandwiches. Casual Dining. $6-$11 **AAA Inspector Notes:** Formerly a gas station, quality ingredients keep the crowds coming back to this local East Bench eatery. It is appointed in clever and unusual décor. Expect to wait for a table. **Features:** patio dining, Sunday brunch. **Address:** 1675 E 1300 S 84105 **Location:** I-15 exit 305C (1300 S), 3.3 mi e, at 1300 S and 1700 E. **Parking:** on-site and street. (B) (L)

FRESCO ITALIAN CAFE   801/486-1300 (9)
Italian. Fine Dining. $20-$32 **AAA Inspector Notes:** This charming café with its lovely outdoor landscaped patio is a hideaway gem. Architecturally presented seasonal menu items might include the chef's soup of the evening, steamed mussels and clams, pan-seared shrimp with house-made black linguine, potato-crusted sea bass and roasted tomatoes with pearl pasta. **Features:** full bar, patio dining. **Reservations:** suggested. **Address:** 1513 S 1500 E 84105 **Location:** Cross streets 1500 S and 1500 E. (D)

HARBOR SEAFOOD & STEAK CO   801/466-9827 (17)
Seafood Steak. Casual Dining. $18-$39 **AAA Inspector Notes:** This neighborhood eatery offers an ambience that is intimate yet casual and the music hits the spot. The cuisine is simple: dock-to-table fresh seafood flown in daily, local wagyu beef and fresh salads featuring ingredients from an on-site garden. Popular items include clam chowder over garlic mashed potatoes, habit-forming crabcakes topped with celery root slaw and melt-in-your-mouth Korean short ribs. For me, the crème brûlée pound cake is an absolute delight with French press coffee. **Features:** patio dining. **Reservations:** suggested. **Address:** 2302 Parley's Way 84109 **Location:** Jct 2100 S and 2300 E; in Sugar House. (D) CALL [&] [M]

LOG HAVEN   801/272-8255
New American Fine Dining $27-$44

AAA Inspector Notes: Tucked away on a 40-acre site, the restaurant occupies a picture-postcard setting. Seasonal menu offerings include wild game, fresh seafood, steak and a gluten-free, three-course menu. Natural and organic ingredients, including produce from the chef's garden, are used whenever possible. **Features:** full bar, patio dining. **Reservations:** suggested. **Address:** 6451 E Millcreek Canyon Rd 84109 **Location:** I-215 exit 4 (3900 S), just e to Wasatch Blvd, just n to 3800 S/Millcreek Canyon, 0.5 mi e to canyon guard station, then 4.5 mi e up the canyon; north side; in Wasatch National Forest. *Menu on AAA.com* (D)

Historic Wilderness Mansion - Live Entertainment

MAZZA CAFE' AT 15TH   801/484-9259 (10)
Middle Eastern. Casual Dining. $7-$24 **AAA Inspector Notes:** The cozy neighborhood eatery offers specialty appetizer and entrée sampler platters that include a choice of nearly two dozen mouthwatering dishes ranging from grape leaves, falafel, mujaddara and kafta to kabesh, baba ghanoush, muhamara made with pomegranate molasses, and chicken, beef and lamb kebabs. The seafood platter includes seasoned and broiled mahi mahi, shrimp and scallops. Most desserts are served with orange blossom syrup. Gluten-free, vegetarian and vegan options are available. **Features:** beer & wine. **Address:** 1515 S 1500 E 84105 **Location:** I-80 exit 126 (1300 E), 1.1 mi n, then 0.4 mi e. **Parking:** street only. (L) (D)

MEDITRINA SMALL PLATES & WINE BAR 801/485-2055 (4)
Small Plates. Casual Dining. $7-$26 **AAA Inspector Notes:** The carefully selected wines at this cozy spot are meant to complement seasonal small-plate choices such as steamed mussels in tomato-basil wine broth and lamb sirloin with roasted Roma tomatoes in feta butter and mint gastrique. The seasonal house-made desserts are decadent. **Features:** beer & wine, patio dining. **Address:** 1394 S West Temple St 84115 **Location:** 2 mi s of Temple Square. (D)

OH MAI VIETNAMESE SANDWICH KITCHEN
                                  801/467-6882 (13)
Vietnamese. Quick Serve. $5-$8 **AAA Inspector Notes:** Serving addictive toasted banh mi sandwiches that are beautifully dressed with a gazillion flavors and textures; pho available in choices of beef cuts; and jasmine rice dishes, including rice vermicelli noodles loaded with bean sprouts, cucumbers, peanuts, carrots and scallions, this is an eatery you do not want to miss. Order brisket pho (P5) and garlic rib-eye banh mi (S8). Have no doubt, you will be back for more. **Features:** patio dining. **Address:** 3425 S State St 84115 **Location:** I-15 exit 303 (3300 S), 0.7 mi e to State St, then 0.5 mi s. **Parking:** on-site and street. (B) (L) (D)

THE PARIS BISTRO   801/486-5585 (8)
French. Fine Dining. $17-$39 **AAA Inspector Notes:** Inspired by French cuisine and the freshest ingredients available at local farmers' markets, meals are a celebration at this elegant neighborhood bistro. Wine selections complement seasonal hand-crafted salads, charcuteries and cheese courses. All menu items coincide with the season. **Features:** full bar, patio dining. **Reservations:** suggested. **Address:** 1500 S 1500 E 84105 **Location:** I-80 exit 126 (1300 E), 1.2 mi n, then 0.3 mi e. **Parking:** on-site and street. (D)

PARK CAFE   801/487-1670 (5)
Breakfast Sandwiches. Casual Dining. $6-$9 **AAA Inspector Notes:** This little eatery across from Liberty Park is known for serving excellent Michigan hash. You can grab a cup of coffee while you wait in line on their cozy wraparound porch. **Features:** patio dining. **Address:** 604 E 1300 S 84105 **Location:** I-15 exit 305C (1300 S), 1.7 mi e. **Parking:** street only. (B) (L)

ROBERTS RESTAURANT 801/364-3663 ②

▼▼ American. Casual Dining. $6-$18 **AAA Inspector Notes:** Nothing fancy here, just a simple, country-style eatery offering daily soups, sandwiches and grandma's apple pie with cheddar cheese. **Features:** beer & wine, patio dining. **Address:** 145 N Wright Brothers Dr 84116 **Location:** I-80 exit 114 (Wright Brothers Dr), just n.

Ⓑ Ⓛ Ⓓ

RUTH'S DINER 801/582-5807 ③

▼▼ American. Casual Dining. $8-$22 **AAA Inspector Notes:** When the weather is nice, guests can sit under the trees on the creekside patio to enjoy salads, sandwiches and deluxe plates from the varied menu. **Features:** full bar, patio dining. **Address:** 4160 Emigration Canyon Rd 84108 **Location:** I-80 exit 129, 2.6 mi n on Foothill Dr, then 2.8 mi e via Sunnyside Ave and Emigration Canyon Rd.

Ⓑ Ⓛ Ⓓ

ST. BERNARD'S AT SOLITUDE 801/517-7717 ⑯

▼▼▼ French. Casual Dining. $22-$32 **AAA Inspector Notes:** Spend an enchanting evening eating by the fireside. The knowledgeable staff will help you pair fine wine with seasonal courses such as duck confit with butternut squash risotto, sage-brown-butter sauce and caramelized apples with a lavender-cheddar tuile and a fresh fish selection. **Features:** full bar. **Reservations:** suggested. **Address:** 12000 Big Cottonwood Canyon 84121 **Location:** I-215 exit 6 (6200 S), 14 mi on Big Cottonwood Canyon, 2nd entrance; in The Inn at Solitude. **Parking:** on-site and valet.

Ⓑ Ⓓ Ⓚ

SEA SALT 801/349-1480 ⑦

▼▼▼ Southern Italian. Casual Dining. $9-$34 **AAA Inspector Notes:** The restaurant offers a wonderful variety of to-be-shared appetizers, soups, salads, wood-fired Neapolitan-style hand-tossed pizza, pasta with creative twists, grilled salmon, chicken with cream polenta and braised greens. The rhubarb, strawberry, pistachio and buttermilk panna cotta was nice and light, but I'm going back for the budino chocolate cake sprinkled with sea salt and drizzled with olive oil. **Features:** full bar, patio dining. **Reservations:** suggested. **Address:** 1709 E 1300 S 84108 **Location:** I-15 exit 305C (1300 S), 3 mi e; at 1700 E and 1300 S. **Parking:** on-site and street.

Ⓛ Ⓓ

STELLA GRILL 801/288-0051 ⑭

▼▼ New American. Casual Dining. $10-$21 **AAA Inspector Notes:** Soups, daily pasta salads, sandwiches and entrees, such as plank roasted salmon served with quinoa and stone fruit salsa, balsamic marinated steak skewers, oven-roasted chicken, and Mexican dishes served with Southwest corn succotash make up the menu at this neighborhood restaurant. The seasonal desserts are scrumptious. **Features:** full bar, patio dining, Sunday brunch. **Address:** 4291 S 900 E 84107 **Location:** I-15 exit 301 (4500 S), 2 mi e to 900 E, then just n. Ⓛ Ⓓ CALL Ⓖᴹ

WING TIPS BAR & BISTRO 801/741-1800 ①

▼▼ American. Casual Dining. $9-$19 **AAA Inspector Notes:** Energizing and upscale décor paves the way for an enjoyable dinner with selections such as lasagna, soups, salads and New York strip grilled with olive oil and rosemary. The dessert menu is varied. **Features:** full bar, patio dining. **Address:** 5001 W Wiley Post Way 84116 **Location:** I-80 exit 114 (Wright Brothers Dr), just n off ramp, then 0.4 w; in Holiday Inn & Suites Salt Lake City Airport.

Ⓑ Ⓛ Ⓓ CALL Ⓖᴹ

SANDY (B-3) pop. 87,461, elev. 4,465'

Shopping: Scheels, at 11282 S. State St. at Auto Mall Drive, isn't *just* a 220,000-square-foot sporting goods store. Besides a wide selection of fitness apparel and recreational equipment (everything from Nikes to duck calls), the massive showroom flaunts a 16,000-gallon saltwater aquarium, a 16-car Ferris wheel and a retro shooting gallery.

Just north of Scheels is South Towne Center. Anchored by Dillard's, JCPenney and Macy's, the shopping venue is one of the largest in the state, offering 150 stores and restaurants.

BEST WESTERN PLUS COTTONTREE INN - SALT LAKE CITY/SANDY (801)523-8484 ⓱

▼▼▼ Hotel $109-$169

AAA Benefit: Save 10% or more every day and earn 10% bonus points!

Address: 10695 S Auto Mall Dr 84070 **Location:** I-15 exit 293 (10600 S), 0.3 mi e, then just s. **Facility:** 111 units. 4 stories, interior corridors. **Parking:** winter plug-ins. **Pool(s):** heated indoor. **Activities:** hot tub, exercise room. **Guest Services:** valet and coin laundry, area transportation.

SAVE Ⓣⅈ₊ CALL Ⓖᴹ ⌇ BIZ ⇝
✕ 🅱 🖨 💻 / SOME UNITS 🐾

COURTYARD BY MARRIOTT - SANDY (801)571-3600 ⓰

▼▼▼ Hotel $89-$205 **Address:** 10701 S Holiday Park Dr 84070 **Location:** I-15 exit 293 (10600 S), just e, then just s. **Facility:** 124 units. 4 stories, interior corridors. **Pool(s):** heated indoor. **Activities:** hot tub, exercise room. **Guest Services:** valet and coin laundry, boarding pass kiosk, area transportation.

AAA Benefit: Members save 5% or more!

Ⓣⅈ Ⓨ CALL Ⓖᴹ ⇝ BIZ ㎐ ⌇ ✕ 🅱 💻

HAMPTON INN BY HILTON - SALT LAKE CITY/SANDY (801)571-0800 ⓱

▼▼▼ Hotel $99-$169 **Address:** 10690 S Holiday Park Dr 84070 **Location:** I-15 exit 293 (10600 S), just e. **Facility:** 130 units. 4 stories, interior corridors. **Terms:** 1-7 night minimum stay, cancellation fee imposed. **Pool(s):** heated indoor. **Activities:** hot tub, cross country skiing, exercise room. **Guest Services:** valet and coin laundry, area transportation.

AAA Benefit: Members save up to 10%!

Ⓣⅈ₊ CALL Ⓖᴹ ⇝ BIZ ⌇ ✕ 🅱 💻

HILTON GARDEN INN - SANDY (801)352-9400 ⓰

▼▼▼ Hotel $99-$169 **Address:** 277 W Sego Lilly Dr 84070 **Location:** I-15 exit 293 (10600 S), 0.4 mi e to State St, 0.7 mi n to 10000 S, then 0.3 mi w. **Facility:** 150 units. 5 stories, interior corridors. **Terms:** 1-7 night minimum stay, cancellation fee imposed. **Pool(s):** heated indoor. **Activities:** hot tub, exercise room. **Guest Services:** valet and coin laundry, area transportation.

AAA Benefit: Members save up to 10%!

Ⓣⅈ Ⓨ CALL Ⓖᴹ ⇝ BIZ ㏋ ⌇ ✕ 🅱 🖨 💻

HOLIDAY INN EXPRESS & SUITES SANDY 801/495-1317 ⓰

▼▼▼ Hotel Rates not provided

Address: 10680 S Auto Mall Dr 84070 **Location:** I-15 exit 293 (10600 S), 0.3 mi e, then just s. **Facility:** 88 units. 3 stories, interior corridors. **Pool(s):** heated indoor. **Activities:** hot tub, exercise room. **Guest Services:** valet and coin laundry, area transportation. **Featured Amenity:** full hot breakfast.

SAVE Ⓣⅈ₊ CALL Ⓖᴹ ⇝ BIZ ⌇
✕ 🅱 🖨 💻 / SOME UNITS 🐾

(See map & index p. 385.)

HYATT HOUSE - SALT LAKE CITY/SANDY
(801)304-5700 [65]

H HYATT **house™**

AAA Benefit: Members save 10%!

Extended Stay
Contemporary
Hotel
$94-$249

Address: 9685 S Monroe St 84070 **Location:** I-15 exit 295 (9000 S), 0.3 mi e to Frontage Rd, then 1 mi s. **Facility:** 137 units, some two bedrooms, efficiencies and kitchens. 4 stories, interior corridors. **Terms:** cancellation fee imposed. **Pool(s):** heated outdoor. **Activities:** hot tub, picnic facilities, exercise room. **Guest Services:** valet and coin laundry, area transportation. **Featured Amenity:** breakfast buffet.

SAVE CALL &M ➜ BIZ HS 🤶 ✕ ⛽ 🍽 ⬛ / SOME UNITS 🛏

RESIDENCE INN BY MARRIOTT - SANDY
(801)561-5005 [66]

Extended Stay Hotel $117-$238 **Address:** 270 W 10000 S 84070 **Location:** I-15 exit 293 (10600 S), 0.4 mi e to State St, 0.7 mi n to 10000 S, then 0.3 mi w. **Facility:** 153 units, some two bedrooms, efficiencies and kitchens. 3 stories, interior corridors. **Pool(s):** heated indoor. **Activities:** hot tub, picnic facilities, exercise room. **Guest Services:** valet and coin laundry, boarding pass kiosk, area transportation.

AAA Benefit: Members save 5% or more!

CALL &M ➜ BIZ 🤶 ✕ ⛽ 🍽 ⬛ / SOME UNITS 🛏

WHERE TO EAT

CARVERS STEAKS & SEAFOOD
801/572-5177 [54]

Steak Seafood. Fine Dining. $10-$39 **AAA Inspector Notes:** This restaurant offers a very nice dining experience with several distinctive dining rooms to choose from. The ambience is upscale. Juicy steaks, chops, seafood and choice prime rib offerings are available for your dining pleasure in addition to refreshing salads. **Features:** full bar, patio dining. **Reservations:** suggested. **Address:** 10720 S Holiday Park Dr 84070 **Location:** I-15 exit 293 (10600 S), 0.3 mi e, then just s. [D]

FRATELLI RISTORANTE
801/495-4550 [52]

Italian. Casual Dining. $10-$26 **AAA Inspector Notes:** Owned and managed by two brothers, you will be treated to menu items and ingredients using grandmother's secret recipes. Some menu items include an attractive caprese salad, classic pasta dishes like bucatini carbonara and Tuscan steak in a rosemary marinade. **Features:** full bar, patio dining. **Address:** 9236 S Village Shop Dr 84094 **Location:** I-15 exit 295 (9000 S), 3 mi e; in Quarry Bend Shopping Center. [L] [D] CALL &M

IGGY'S SPORTS GRILL
801/495-1885

American. Casual Dining. $9-$19 **AAA Inspector Notes:** Every seat offers a view of the sports action on the multiple TVs. There are lots of choices on the menu, including a variety of salads, soup, steaks, a nice selection of pasta, ribs, chicken and seafood. **Features:** full bar. **Address:** 10631 S Holiday Park Dr 84070 **Location:** I-15 exit 293 (10600 S), 0.3 mi e, then just s. [L] [D]

JOE'S CRAB SHACK
801/255-9571

Seafood. Casual Dining. $8-$32 **AAA Inspector Notes:** The popular seafood restaurant specializes in a year-round variety of crab: Alaskan king, Dungeness, snow and blue. Among other offerings are fresh shrimp, hearty gumbo, clam chowder and classic steaks and chicken. **Features:** full bar. **Address:** 65 E 9400 S 84070 **Location:** I-15 exit 295 (9000 S); jct State St and 9400 S; in Jordan Commons. [L] [D] [LATE]

LA CAILLE
801/942-1751 [53]

Continental Fine Dining $29-$52

AAA Inspector Notes: Cross the château gates and look for the swans, then step into a storybook at this restaurant, where the charming French atmosphere envelops an 18th-century estate surrounded by spacious, well-landscaped grounds. **Features:** full bar, Sunday brunch. **Reservations:** suggested. **Address:** 9565 Wasatch Blvd 84092 **Location:** I-215 exit 6 (6200 S), e toward ski areas, 4 mi s to jct Little Cottonwood Rd, then continue 0.8 mi s. **Parking:** valet only. [D]

TIBURON FINE DINING
801/255-1200 [51]

New American. Fine Dining. $11-$45 **AAA Inspector Notes:** For a tasteful meal, try the charbroiled New Zealand elk tenderloin, black-sesame-crusted ahi tuna or the award-winning sweet crab cakes. The restaurant's ambience signals warmth and class. Sitting on the outside patio enveloped in mature trees is magical. Seasonal desserts are not to be missed. **Features:** full bar, patio dining. **Reservations:** suggested. **Address:** 8256 S 700 E 84070 **Location:** I-15 exit 295 (9000 S), 1 mi e, then 1 mi n. [D]

SANTA CLARA (G-1) pop. 6,003, elev. 2,759'

JACOB HAMBLIN HOME is at Santa Clara Blvd. and Hamblin Dr. The house was the 1863 residence of a Mormon missionary noted for his peacemaking achievements with the Native Americans. The furnishings and implements are from the 1880s. **Time:** Allow 30 minutes minimum. **Hours:** Daily 9-7, Apr.-Sept.; 10-5, rest of year. Last tour begins 30 minutes before closing. **Cost:** Free. **Phone:** (435) 673-2161, or (435) 673-5181 for the Temple Visitor Center Annex to schedule tours.

SANTAQUIN pop. 9,128

LESLIE'S FAMILY TREE RESTAURANT
801/754-3499

American. Casual Dining. $5-$16 **AAA Inspector Notes:** This downtown cafe serves hot lunches, sandwiches, burgers on homemade buns, salads, shrimp and chicken baskets and a few south-of-the-border items. In addition, nice selections of steaks are featured for dinner. Beware, a 15-inch scone with honey butter is presented with entrées. **Address:** 77 W Main St 84655 **Location:** I-15 exit 244, 0.7 mi w. **Parking:** street only. [B] [L] [D]

SEVIER (E-3) elev. 5,542'

FREMONT INDIAN STATE PARK is 5 mi. s.w. off I-70 exit 17. The 1,784-acre park was established to protect the area's heritage of rock art and archeological sites. A museum interprets the evolution of the Fremont Anasazi Indian culture A.D. 500-1300 and displays artifacts and pictographs taken from nearby Five Fingers Hill. *See Recreation Areas Chart.*

Time: Allow 30 minutes minimum. **Hours:** Daily 9-6, mid-May to mid-Sept.; 9-5, rest of year. Closed Jan. 1, Thanksgiving and Christmas. **Cost:** $6 (per private vehicle, maximum eight people) or $3 (per person arriving by other means). Camping $15. **Phone:** (435) 527-4631. 🅰 🍴 🗙 🏕 🅰

SNOWBIRD (B-3) elev. 8,163'
• Hotels & Restaurants map & index p. 385
• Part of Salt Lake City area — see map p. 368

RECREATIONAL ACTIVITIES
Skiing
• **Snowbird Ski and Summer Resort** is off I-215 exit 6; take 6200 South s.e., then SR 210 e. up Little

(See map & index p. 385.)

Cottonwood Canyon. Other activities are offered. **Hours:** Winter activities daily 9-4:45, late Nov.-late May. Schedule varies rest of year; phone ahead. **Phone:** (801) 933-2222 or (800) 232-9542.

THE CLIFF LODGE, SPA & CONFERENCE CENTER
801/933-2222 **74**

▼▼▼▼ **Resort Hotel.** Rates not provided. **Address:** 9320 S Cliff Lodge Drive Rd 84092 **Location:** 8 mi e on Little Cottonwood Canyon Rd, Level 4. **Facility:** Ski enthusiasts appreciate the resorts ski-in, ski-out accessibility and the spacious indoor lockers that can accommodate bulky ski accessories. 500 units, some kitchens. 9 stories, interior corridors. **Parking:** on-site and valet. **Terms:** check-in 4 pm. **Amenities:** safes. **Dining:** 2 restaurants, also, Aerie Restaurant at Snowbird, see separate listing. **Pool(s):** heated outdoor. **Activities:** hot tub, tennis, downhill & cross country skiing, snowmobiling, recreation programs, bicycles, playground, game room, exercise room, spa. **Guest Services:** complimentary laundry, area transportation.

🛬 🍴 🛄 🍽 👤 🚐 BIZ 📶 ✕ 🔲 💻
/ SOME UNITS 🖥

WHERE TO EAT

AERIE RESTAURANT AT SNOWBIRD   801/933-2160 **57**

▼▼▼ **American. Gastropub.** $14-$44 **AAA Inspector Notes:** On the 10th floor, this restaurant offers breathtaking mountain views. Expect innovative and seasonal creations such as mushroom-encrusted scallops set in English pea risotto, bison short ribs served with bleu cheese potato gratin, lobster mac and cheese, corn-flake-pistachio-encrusted chicken breast and a variety of sushi, nigiri and sashimi. **Features:** full bar, early bird specials. **Reservations:** suggested. **Address:** 9320 S Cliff Lodge Dr 84092 **Location:** 8 mi e on Little Cottonwood Canyon Rd, Level 10; in The Cliff Lodge, Spa & Conference Center. **Parking:** on-site and valet. D CALL 🔲M

SOLITUDE

Solitude is a community designed solely around a ski resort in the Big Cottonwood Canyon of the Wasatch Mountains, about 30 miles southeast of Salt Lake City.

RECREATIONAL ACTIVITIES
Skiing

• **Solitude Mountain Resort** is at 12000 Big Cottonwood Canyon. Other activities are offered. **Hours:** Winter activities daily 9-4, mid-Nov. to late Apr. Schedule varies rest of year; phone ahead. **Phone:** (801) 534-1400 or (800) 748-4754.

is at 12000 Big Cottonwood Canyon. Other activities are offered. **Hours:** Winter activities daily 9-4, mid-Nov. to late Apr. Schedule varies rest of year; phone ahead. **Phone:** (801) 534-1400 or (800) 748-4754.

SOUTH JORDAN pop. 50,418
• **Hotels & Restaurants map & index p. 385**
• **Part of Salt Lake City area — see map p. 368**

COUNTRY INN & SUITES BY CARLSON - SALT LAKE CITY/
SOUTH TOWNE   801/553-1151 **61**

▼▼▼▼ **Hotel.** Rates not provided. **Address:** 10499 S Jordan Gateway 84095 **Location:** I-15 exit 293 (10600 S), just w, then just n. **Facility:** 127 units. 6 stories, interior corridors. **Parking:** winter plug-ins. **Pool(s):** heated indoor. **Activities:** hot tub, picnic facilities, exercise room. **Guest Services:** valet and coin laundry, area transportation.

ECO CALL 🔲M 🚐 BIZ HS 📶 ✕ 📷 🔲 🖥
💻

HOME2 SUITES BY HILTON - SALT LAKE CITY/SOUTH
JORDAN   (801)446-8800 **62**

▼▼▼ **Extended Stay Contemporary Hotel** $99-$159 **Address:** 10704 S River Front Park 84095 **Location:** I-15 exit 293 (10600 S), 1 mi w, then just s. **Facility:** 125 units. 4 stories, interior corridors. *Bath:* shower only. **Terms:** 1-7 night minimum stay, cancellation fee imposed. **Pool(s):** heated indoor. **Activities:** picnic facilities, exercise room. **Guest Services:** complimentary and valet laundry, area transportation.

AAA Benefit: Members save up to 10%!

🍴 CALL 🔲M 🚐 BIZ 📶 🔲 🖥 💻 / SOME UNITS 🖥

WHERE TO EAT

GECKO'S MEXICAN GRILL   801/253-8668 **47**

▼▼ **Mexican. Family Dining.** $7-$16 **AAA Inspector Notes:** The cute restaurant offers an authentic atmosphere and a friendly staff. Locals favor the burrito combinations, tamales, chile rellenos, sizzling fajitas, and the daily lunch special! **Features:** patio dining. **Address:** 781 W 10600 S 84095 **Location:** I-15 exit 293 (10600 S), 0.5 mi w, just s at River Park Corporate Center, then just w. L D

MARKET STREET GRILL & OYSTER BAR SOUTH JORDAN
801/302-2262 **48**

▼▼▼ **Seafood Steak. Casual Dining.** $8-$70 **AAA Inspector Notes:** After warm bread, soup and a salad, guests then choose from a variety of blackened or broiled fresh fish and other seafood dishes centered on oysters, clams, mussels, shrimp, Atlantic salmon and lobster. Although it's nowhere near, this place makes patrons feel like they're close to the ocean. A delightful selection of mouthwatering desserts rounds out the meal. **Features:** full bar, patio dining, early bird specials, Sunday brunch. **Address:** 10702 S River Front Pkwy 84095 **Location:** I-15 exit 293 (10600 S), 0.4 mi w; in River Park. L D CALL 🔲M

SOUTH SALT LAKE pop. 23,617
• **Hotels & Restaurants map & index p. 385**
• **Part of Salt Lake City area — see map p. 368**

LEFT FORK GRILL   801/266-4322 **23**

▼▼ **Comfort Food. Casual Dining.** $8-$15 **AAA Inspector Notes:** The diner serves great classic selections, including several soups made fresh daily, meatloaf sandwiches, chicken schnitzel and open-faced hot turkey and steak sandwiches. Fresh seasonal pies such as the banana, apple, blueberry or peach cream are the signature here. Parking can take extra time during peak hours. **Features:** beer & wine. **Address:** 68 W 3900 S 84107 **Location:** I-15 exit 303, just e to 300 W, 1 mi s to 3900 S, then just e. **Parking:** on-site and street. B L D

PAT'S BARBECUE   801/484-5963 **22**

▼▼ **Barbecue. Casual Dining.** $9-$17 **AAA Inspector Notes:** This barbecue joint features state wide award-winning hand-rubbed-and-smoked pulled pork and beef brisket, pork ribs, chicken and Southern comfort food. Daily weekday specials are not to be missed and include burnt ends on Friday. Homemade dessert favorites vary daily, but the sweet potato pie is a hit. **Features:** beer only. **Address:** 155 W Commonwealth Ave 84115 **Location:** 2.8 mi s from Temple Square via S West Temple St, just s of 2100 S; in industrial neighborhood. **Parking:** on-site and street. L D

SPANISH FORK pop. 34,691

WESTERN INN   (801)798-9400

▼
Hotel
$63-$96

Address: 632 Kirby Ln 84660 **Location:** I-15 exit 257B, on US 6. **Facility:** 47 units, some efficiencies. 2 stories (no elevator), interior corridors. **Terms:** cancellation fee imposed. **Guest Services:** coin laundry. **Featured Amenity:** continental breakfast.

SAVE 🍴 BIZ 📶 ✕
/ SOME UNITS 🖥

SPRINGDALE (G-2) pop. 529, elev. 3,912'
• Part of Zion National Park area — see map p. 415

Springdale was founded by Mormon pioneers in the 1850s. Because of its location at the south entrance to Zion National Park *(see place listing p. 415)*, the town supports a number of accommodations and shops for park visitors.

The O.C. Tanner Amphitheater, just outside the entrance to Zion National Park, is a 1,500-seat site of outdoor concerts presented on Saturdays and select other days, Memorial Day through Labor Day. The amphitheater's mountain backdrop provides natural acoustics; phone (435) 652-7800 for ticket information.

ZION CANYON GIANT SCREEN THEATRE is at 145 Zion Park Blvd. Using a six-story-high, 82-foot-wide screen and digital surround sound, "Zion Canyon Treasure of the Gods" showcases Zion National Park and the local area. Other large-format nature films and Hollywood blockbusters also are screened. **Hours:** "Zion Canyon Treasure of the Gods" shown daily at 2, 3 and 5, Apr. 1-late Nov. Hollywood films shown at 7, in summer. Phone ahead to confirm schedule and for off-season schedule. **Cost:** Hollywood movies $10; $8 (ages 0-11 and 60+). "Zion Canyon Treasure of the Gods" $8; $6 (ages 0-11 and 60+). **Phone:** (435) 772-2400 or (888) 256-3456. 🍴

ZION OUTBACK SAFARIS AND JEEP TOURS departs from local hotels. Visitors experience the back-country of Zion National Park in customized 12-passenger open-air safari vehicles. Guides discuss the park's ecosystem, geology, history and wildlife as well as local folklore. Private tours in off-road jeeps that seat up to seven passengers are also offered. **Time:** Allow 3 hours minimum. **Hours:** Two-hour safari outback tours depart daily at 10. Three-hour afternoon Mesa Vista tour departures vary with the season; phone for schedule. **Cost:** Outback safari tour $65; $45 (ages 1-11). Mesa Vista tour $72; $50 (ages 1-11). Combination jeep/ATV/helicopter tours start at $299 per person. **Phone:** (435) 668-3756. 🅰️

BUMBLEBERRY INN (435)772-3224
◈◈ Motel $58-$158 **Address:** 97 Bumbleberry Ln 84767 **Location:** SR 9, 1 mi s of south gate to Zion National Park. **Facility:** 48 units. 2 stories (no elevator), interior corridors. **Terms:** 3 day cancellation notice. **Pool(s):** heated outdoor. **Activities:** hot tub, limited exercise equipment. **Guest Services:** coin laundry.

🍴➕ 🏊 BIZ 🛜 ✕ 🛅 🖨 🖵

CABLE MOUNTAIN LODGE (435)772-3366
◈◈◈ Hotel $129-$279 **Address:** 147 Zion Park Blvd 84767 **Location:** Just s of Zion National Park entrance; in Toaquim's Village. **Facility:** 51 units, some kitchens. 2 stories (no elevator), exterior corridors. **Terms:** 3 day cancellation notice-fee imposed. **Pool(s):** heated outdoor. **Activities:** hot tub. **Guest Services:** coin laundry.

🍴➕ 🏊 BIZ HS 🛜 ✕ 🛅 🖨

CANYON RANCH MOTEL 435/772-3357
◈◈ Motel. Rates not provided. **Address:** 668 Zion Park Blvd 84767 **Location:** SR 9, just s of south gate to Zion National Park. **Facility:** 22 units, some efficiencies. 1 story, exterior corridors. **Pool(s):** outdoor. **Activities:** hot tub.

🍴➕ 🏊 🛜 ✕ 🛅 /SOME UNITS 🐾 🖨 🖵

CLIFFROSE LODGE & GARDENS 435/772-3234
◈◈◈◈
Hotel
Rates not provided

Address: 281 Zion Park Blvd 84767 **Location:** Just s of south gate to Zion National Park. **Facility:** 52 units, some two bedrooms, three bedrooms, efficiencies and kitchens. 2 stories (no elevator), exterior corridors. **Pool(s):** heated outdoor. **Activities:** hot tub, playground, massage. **Guest Services:** coin laundry. **Featured Amenity:** breakfast buffet.

SAVE 🍴 🏊 🍸 🏊 BIZ 🛜 ✕ 🛅 🖨 /SOME UNITS 🖵

DESERT PEARL INN 435/772-8888
◈◈◈ Hotel. Rates not provided. **Address:** 707 Zion Park Blvd 84767 **Location:** SR 9, just s of south gate to Zion National Park. **Facility:** 73 units, some efficiencies and kitchens. 2 stories (no elevator), exterior corridors. **Amenities:** safes. **Pool(s):** heated outdoor. **Activities:** hot tub, massage. **Guest Services:** coin laundry.

🍴➕ 🏊 BIZ 🛜 ✕ 🛅 🖨 🖵

FLANIGAN'S INN & DEEP CANYON ADVENTURE SPA
435/772-3244
◈◈◈◈
Hotel
Rates not provided

Address: 450 Zion Park Blvd 84767 **Location:** Just s of south gate to Zion National Park. Located in a quiet area. **Facility:** 34 units, some two bedrooms. 1-2 stories (no elevator), exterior corridors. **Dining:** Spotted Dog Cafe at Flanigan's Inn, see separate listing. **Pool(s):** heated outdoor. **Activities:** hot tub, spa. **Guest Services:** coin laundry.

SAVE 🍴 🏊 BIZ 🛜 ✕ 🖵 /SOME UNITS 🛅 🖨

HAMPTON INN & SUITES SPRINGDALE ZION NATIONAL PARK (435)627-9191
◈◈◈ Hotel $199-$299 **Address:** 1127 Zion Park Blvd 84767 **Location:** 2 mi s of Zion National Park entrance. **Facility:** 90 units. 2 stories, interior corridors. **Terms:** 1-7 night minimum stay, cancellation fee imposed. **Pool(s):** heated outdoor. **Activities:** hot tub, exercise room. **Guest Services:** coin laundry.

| AAA Benefit: Members save up to 10%! |

🍴➕ CALL 🅼 🏊 BIZ 🛜 ✕ 🛅 🖨 🖵 /SOME UNITS 🐾

HOLIDAY INN EXPRESS ZION NATIONAL PARK 435/772-3200
◈◈◈ Hotel. Rates not provided. **Address:** 1215 Zion Park Blvd 84767 **Location:** 2 mi s of Zion National Park entrance. **Facility:** 117 units, some efficiencies. 2 stories, interior corridors. **Dining:** Switchback Grille, Switchback Jack's Sports Grill, see separate listings. **Pool(s):** heated outdoor. **Activities:** hot tub, exercise room. **Guest Services:** coin laundry.

🍴 🏊 BIZ 🛜 ✕ 🛅 🖨 🖵 /SOME UNITS 🐾

MAJESTIC VIEW LODGE

(435)772-0665

Hotel
$89-$186

Address: 2400 Zion Park Blvd 84767 **Location:** 3.5 mi s of park entrance. **Facility:** 69 units. 2 stories (no elevator), exterior corridors. **Terms:** cancellation fee imposed. **Dining:** Arkansas Al's Pub & Eatery, see separate listing. **Pool(s):** heated outdoor. **Activities:** hot tub. **Guest Services:** coin laundry.

NOVEL HOUSE INN AT ZION

435/772-3650

Bed & Breakfast. Rates not provided. **Address:** 73 Paradise Rd 84767 **Location:** Just off SR 9, 1 mi s of Zion National Park. **Facility:** This romantic getaway, with spacious rooms inspired by famous authors, offers a library with board games and books, a covered porch and a secluded patio. 11 units. 2 stories (no elevator), interior corridors.

RED ROCK INN B & B COTTAGES

435/772-3139

Cottage $119-$269 **Address:** 998 Zion Park Blvd 84767 **Location:** SR 9, just w of center. **Facility:** This property has a shaded lawn with a flower and cactus garden. Rooms are modern and bright with large flat-panel TVs. 6 cottages. 1 story, exterior corridors. **Terms:** check-in 4 pm, 14 day cancellation notice. **Amenities:** safes.

UNDER THE EAVES INN

435/772-3457

Bed & Breakfast. Rates not provided. **Address:** 980 Zion Park Blvd 84767 **Location:** SR 9, just w of center. **Facility:** 7 units. 2 stories (no elevator), interior/exterior corridors.

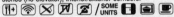

ARKANSAS AL'S PUB & EATERY

435/772-0665

American. Casual Dining. $18-$38 **AAA Inspector Notes:** This restaurant sits on top of a large hill, making the views from the dining room amazing. Enjoy casual cuisine in a rustic log cabin dining room with high ceilings, a stone waterfall and floor-to-ceiling windows giving a panoramic view of the surrounding Zion Mountains. **Features:** beer & wine, patio dining. **Address:** 2400 Zion Park Blvd 84767 **Location:** 3.5 mi s of park entrance; in Majestic View Lodge.
B L D

BIT AND SPUR SALOON & RESTAURANT

435/772-3498

Mexican. Casual Dining. $9-$26 **AAA Inspector Notes:** Near Zion National Park, this youthful and upbeat place offers Southwestern cuisine, baby back ribs and Mexican favorites. A large selection of microbrews and margaritas are offered as well. **Features:** full bar, patio dining. **Reservations:** suggested. **Address:** 1212 Zion Park Blvd 84767 **Location:** 2 mi s of park entrance.
D

BLONDIE'S DINER

435/772-0595

American. Casual Dining. $5-$16 **AAA Inspector Notes:** This small dining room has a diner feel with many signs with joking phrases. The menu features simple home-style cooking options such as burgers, chicken breast and homemade pies. Try a buffalo burger and the homemade banana creme pie. **Address:** 736 Zion Park Blvd 84767 **Location:** SR 9, 0.9 mi s of south gate to Zion National Park.
B L D

CAFE OSCAR'S

435/772-3232

Mexican. Casual Dining. $7-$34 **AAA Inspector Notes:** This small and funky café seems to get better each time I try it. The menu is a fun mix of casual cuisine, featuring large garlic burgers and traditional favorites prepared with free-range chicken. **Features:** beer only, patio dining. **Address:** 948 Zion Park Blvd 84767 **Location:** Jct Winderland Dr.
B L D

CAFE SOLEIL

435/772-0505

Coffee/Tea Sandwiches. Quick Serve. $7-$13 **AAA Inspector Notes:** Just outside the entrance to the park, the small cafe employs friendly staff members who serve guests behind the counter. This place is known for great breakfasts, which might include a fresh bagel, oatmeal or fruit. Fresh coffee gets patrons going in the morning. Packed lunches are available to purchase and take on a hike. **Features:** beer & wine, patio dining. **Address:** 205 Zion Park Blvd 84767 **Location:** Just s of south gate to Zion National Park.
B L D

CASA DE AMIGOS

435/772-0422

Mexican. Casual Dining. $8-$18 **AAA Inspector Notes:** The bright, modern and festive décor draws passers-by inside. The fresh made-to-order cuisine makes them returning guests. The salsa is great, and believe it or not, the ranch dressing is, too. **Features:** beer only. **Address:** 805 Zion Park Blvd 84767 **Location:** Center.
L D

THE FLYING MONKEY

435/772-3333

Pizza. Casual Dining. $9-$15 **AAA Inspector Notes:** After a long hike, this casual and friendly eatery is the perfect place to indulge in fresh wood-fired pizza and a local brew. If you're not in the mood for pizza, burgers, sandwiches and large salads also are served. **Features:** beer only, patio dining. **Address:** 975 Zion Park Blvd 84767 **Location:** Center.
L D

MEME'S CAFE

435/772-0114

Breakfast Barbecue. Casual Dining. $7-$17 **AAA Inspector Notes:** This popular family-run restaurant focuses on creative all-day breakfast items, crepes and barbecue. Guests can enjoy watching their fresh-squeezed orange juice being made at the front of the small and quaint spot. Special homemade baked goods also are prepared daily. **Features:** Sunday brunch. **Address:** 975 Zion Park Blvd 84767 **Location:** Center.
B L D

PIONEER RESTAURANT

435/772-3009

American. Family Dining. $9-$24 **AAA Inspector Notes:** Springdale's historic restaurant features a rustic pioneer atmosphere along with country cooking, prime rib and, on weekends, Navajo tacos. Diners enjoy delicious daily specials and a vegetarian menu, all within the shadows of Zion Mountains. **Features:** beer & wine. **Address:** 838 Zion Park Blvd 84767 **Location:** Center; in Pioneer Lodge.
B L D

SPOTTED DOG CAFE AT FLANIGAN'S INN

435/772-0700

Continental. Casual Dining. $14-$32 **AAA Inspector Notes:** A pearl in the desert just outside Zion National Park, giving fantastic panoramic views of the red mountains. The café offers a seasonal menu with local game, lamb and fresh local vegetables in a soothing, tranquil dining room. **Features:** full bar, patio dining. **Reservations:** suggested. **Address:** 428 Zion Park Blvd 84767 **Location:** Just s of south gate to Zion National Park; in Flanigan's Inn & Deep Canyon Adventure Spa.
B D

SWITCHBACK GRILLE

435/772-3700

Steak Seafood. Fine Dining. $15-$48 **AAA Inspector Notes:** Browse in the gift shop and then come in for a delicious meal in the attractive dining room. Enjoy the attentive service and choose from several selections of beef, seafood and poultry. **Features:** full bar, patio dining. **Reservations:** suggested. **Address:** 1149 Zion Park Blvd 84767 **Location:** 2 mi s of Zion National Park entrance; in Holiday Inn Express Zion National Park.
D

SWITCHBACK JACK'S SPORTS GRILL

435/772-3700

Burgers Sandwiches. Gastropub. $5-$12 **AAA Inspector Notes:** A perfect place to watch the game after a big hike. Locally brewed beer, burgers, sandwiches and rice bowls are simple but have great flavor. Don't be surprised if there is a crowd yelling or laughing at the TV together. **Features:** full bar, patio dining. **Address:** 1149 Zion Park Blvd B 84767 **Location:** 2 mi s of Zion National Park entrance; in Holiday Inn Express Zion National Park.
L D

WILDCAT WILLIE'S RESTAURANT 435/772-0115

American
Casual Dining
$10-$35

AAA Inspector Notes: The bare wood walls, cast-iron chandeliers, wood booths and tables scream the West. The menu is made up of many items with a Western flair such as a rib-eye steak, burgers, St. Louis pork ribs, Red Mountain Utah trout, and you can't forget about the famous bumbleberry pie for dessert. The staff is always willing to make suggestions. **Features:** full bar. **Address:** 897 Zion Park Blvd 84767 **Location:** SR 9, 1 mi s of south gate to Zion National Park; adjacent to Bumbleberry Inn.

[B] [L] [D]

ZION PARK GIFT & DELI 702/772-3843

Deli Desserts. Quick Serve. $5-$8 **AAA Inspector Notes:** Enjoy fresh sandwiches prepared on homemade bread or any of the many assorted chocolates, homemade fudge or ice cream. Make sure to pick up a souvenir in the gift shop on your way out. **Address:** 866 Zion Park Blvd 84767 **Location:** Center. [B] [L]

ZION PIZZA & NOODLE CO. 435/772-3815

Italian Pizza. Quick Serve. $11-$14 **AAA Inspector Notes:** Hungry hikers line up to order from the small counter and then wait for their food to be delivered in the bright and eclectic dining room. Pizza and pasta is obviously the main focus, but seasonal salad specials are a great choice, too. A large selection of bottled and draft beer is offered. **Features:** beer & wine. **Address:** 868 Zion Park Blvd 84767 **Location:** Center. [D]

SPRINGVILLE (C-3) pop. 29,466, elev. 4,571'

Springville, overshadowed by the Wasatch Mountains on the east and bordered by Utah Lake on the west, is an important agricultural center. The town, settled by eight pioneer families in 1850, was originally called Hobble Creek because the pioneers' horses were often hobbled and left along the stream to graze; if they wandered into the creek their hobbles came off.

The Daughters of Utah Pioneers Museum, 175 S. Main St., houses relics of area pioneers; phone the chamber of commerce at (801) 491-7830. Jeep tours, fishing, hunting and snowmobiling are available nearby.

Springville Chamber of Commerce: 110 S. Main St., Springville, UT 84663. **Phone:** (801) 491-7830.

SPRINGVILLE MUSEUM OF ART is at 126 E. 400 South. The museum has six galleries containing works by Utah painters, sculptors and printmakers from 1850 to the present, and seven galleries housing changing exhibitions. The museum, said to be Utah's oldest art museum, contains a collection of Soviet socialist realist paintings and the Utah Photographic Art Reference Archive, which documents the history of Utah art.

The museum grounds contain sculptures. Museum tours and a research library are available. **Hours:** Tues.-Sat. 10-5 (also Wed. 5-9), Sun. 3-6 (also first Mon. of the month 6-8 p.m. except when it falls on a holiday). Closed major holidays. **Cost:** Free. **Phone:** (801) 489-2727.

BEST WESTERN MOUNTAIN VIEW INN (801)489-3641

Hotel
$85-$170

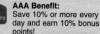

AAA Benefit:
Save 10% or more every day and earn 10% bonus points!

Address: 1455 N 1750 W 84663 **Location:** I-15 exit 261, just e. **Facility:** 55 units. 2 stories (no elevator), interior corridors. **Terms:** check-in 4 pm. **Pool(s):** heated outdoor. **Activities:** hot tub, exercise room. **Guest Services:** coin laundry. **Featured Amenity:** full hot breakfast.

DAYS INN (801)491-0300

Hotel $60-$129 **Address:** 520 S 2000 W 84663 **Location:** I-15 exit 260, just w. **Facility:** 64 units. 3 stories, interior corridors. **Pool(s):** heated outdoor. **Activities:** hot tub.

HOLIDAY INN EXPRESS & SUITES 801/489-5000

Hotel. Rates not provided. **Address:** 1502 N 1750 W 84663 **Location:** I-15 exit 261, just e. **Facility:** 92 units. 4 stories, interior corridors. **Activities:** exercise room. **Guest Services:** coin laundry.

TEASDALE pop. 191

MULEY TWIST INN BED & BREAKFAST 435/425-3640

Bed & Breakfast $105-$155 **Address:** 249 W 125 S 84773 **Location:** 4.5 mi w of jct SR 12 and 24 to Teasdale Rd (CR 3262), 1.5 mi s to 125 S, 0.5 mi w. **Facility:** Specialty omelets, south-rim eggs, homemade bagels and gourmet coffee set the tone for breakfast at this property. Rocking chairs are on the covered porch, displaying amazing mountain views. 5 units. 2 stories (no elevator), interior corridors. **Terms:** closed 10/11-4/8, check-in 4 pm, 10 day cancellation notice-fee imposed. **Activities:** trails.

TIMPANOGOS CAVE NATIONAL MONUMENT (C-2)

Seven miles east of American Fork on SR 92, Timpanogos Cave National Monument covers 250 acres in the American Fork Canyon on the north slope of 11,750-foot Mount Timpanogos. The visitor center is 10 miles east off I-15 exit 287 between Salt Lake City and Provo; a 20-minute introductory film is shown upon request.

Three large limestone caverns are connected by man-made tunnels. About 1,800 feet in length, the limestone caves maintain an average temperature of 45 F with nearly 100 percent humidity. Dripstone is still forming, and spectacular helictites, aragonite crystals, stalagmites and stalactites are found throughout the lighted caverns. The cave entrance, about 1,065 feet above the canyon floor, is reached from the visitor center by a strenuous, 1.5-mile paved foot trail. Wheelchairs and strollers are not permitted on the trail. The round-trip takes about 3 hours, including the cave tour. A self-guiding trail booklet is available at the visitor center.

Visitors must purchase tickets for cave tours at the visitor center before hiking up the 1.5-mile paved trail. Tours are limited to 16 people. Arrive as early as possible or phone ahead, since tours are often filled by mid-morning. Expect to wait several hours on Saturdays and holidays. A caving instructional tour also is available mid-May through Labor Day for ages 14 and older. Tickets can be purchased up to 30 days in advance; phone (877) 444-6777.

Picnicking is permitted. Food is available. The visitor center and the cave are open daily 7-6, mid-May through Labor Day weekend; Mon.-Fri. 7:30-6, Sat.-Sun. 7-6, day after Labor Day-Columbus Day. Cave tours begin every 10-20 minutes 8-3:30. Last tour begins 1 hour before closing, mid-May through Labor Day; 90 minutes before closing, day after Labor Day-Columbus Day. The cave tour is $8; $6 (ages 6-15); $4 (ages 3-5 and ages 62+ with America the Beautiful–National Parks and Federal Recreational Lands Pass–Senior Pass). The Introduction to Caving tour is $16; under 14 are not permitted. There is a fee of $6 (for 3 days) or $12 (for 7 days) to drive the Canyon Road (also known as SR 92 and American Fork Canyon-Alpine Loop Scenic Backway).

For further information contact the Superintendent, Timpanogos Cave National Monument, R.R. 3, Box 200, American Fork, UT 84003; phone (801) 756-5239.

TOOELE (C-3) pop. 31,605, elev. 4,885'

Located on a long, gradual slope at the base of the Oquirrh Mountains, Tooele (pronounced too-ILL-uh) offers sweeping views of Great Salt Lake to the north and, across the Tooele Valley to the west, the Stansbury Mountains. Major employers in this fast-growing, sprawling area include military installations such as the Tooele Army Depot, a government repository for training and war reserve ammunition. At an elevation of 9,400 feet, Oquirrh Overlook, 10.5 miles east of Tooele at the crest of the mountains via Middle Canyon Road, offers a grand perspective of Kennecott's Bingham Canyon Mine *(see attraction listing p. 294)*, one of the largest open-pit mines in the world. **Note:** The road to the overlook is closed in winter.

Tooele County Chamber of Commerce & Tourism: 154 S. Main St., Tooele, UT 87074. **Phone:** (435) 882-0690 or (800) 378-0690.

BENSON GRIST MILL is on SR 138 adjacent to Stansbury Park. The grist mill was built in 1854 under the direction of Ezra Taft Benson, an apostle of The Church of Jesus Christ of Latter-day Saints, to serve the early Mormon settlers in Tooele County. In addition to a working grist mill, the site also includes a blacksmith shop, cabins, a miller's home and a museum. **Time:** Allow 1 hour minimum. **Hours:** Thurs.-Sat. 10-6, May-Oct. **Cost:** Free. **Phone:** (435) 882-7678.

TOOELE VALLEY RAILROAD MUSEUM is at 35 N. Broadway. The area's history is depicted through artifacts pertaining to railroading, smelting and mining. The museum's centerpiece is a 1910 steam locomotive that has been restored and converted into an interpretive display. A miniature train offers rides to visitors on some Saturdays. **Time:** Allow 30 minutes minimum. **Hours:** Tues.-Sat. 1-4, Memorial Day weekend-Labor Day. **Cost:** Donations. **Phone:** (435) 882-2836.

BEST WESTERN INN TOOELE   (435)882-5010

Hotel $95-$120

AAA Benefit: Save 10% or more every day and earn 10% bonus points!

Address: 365 N Main St 84074 **Location:** I-80 exit 99, 11 mi s. **Facility:** 31 units, some houses. 2 stories (no elevator), interior/exterior corridors. **Parking:** winter plug-ins. **Pool(s):** heated indoor. **Activities:** hot tub, exercise room. **Guest Services:** coin laundry. **Featured Amenity:** full hot breakfast.

COMFORT INN & SUITES - TOOELE   (801)250-3600
Hotel $99-$179 **Address:** 8580 N Hwy 36 84074 **Location:** I-80 exit 99, just s. Next to truck stop. **Facility:** 69 units. 3 stories, interior corridors. **Parking:** winter plug-ins. **Pool(s):** heated indoor. **Activities:** hot tub, exercise room. **Guest Services:** coin laundry.

HOLIDAY INN EXPRESS & SUITES - TOOELE   435/833-0500
Hotel. Rates not provided. **Address:** 1531 N Main St 84074 **Location:** I-80 exit 99, 11 mi s. **Facility:** 64 units. 3 stories, interior corridors. **Pool(s):** heated indoor. **Activities:** hot tub, picnic facilities, exercise room. **Guest Services:** coin laundry.

WHERE TO EAT

THAI HOUSE   435/882-7579
Thai. Casual Dining. $8-$17 **AAA Inspector Notes:** Among the many Thai specialties are cashew-nut stir-fry, vegetarian dishes and made-in-house coconut ice cream. The warm ambience and friendly service keep guests coming back. **Features:** beer & wine. **Address:** 297 N Main St 84074 **Location:** I-80 exit 99, 11 mi s; on Main St (SR 36), 0.3 mi n of center.

VISTA LINDA MEXICAN RESTAURANT   435/228-6487
Mexican. Casual Dining. $7-$9 **AAA Inspector Notes:** This eatery has a colorful atmosphere and a relaxing vibe. You can expect traditional entrées such as beef or chicken fajitas, enchiladas, taquitos, tacos and chimichangas. The pozole hit the spot and I enjoyed watching patrons go to the salsa bar even before they ordered. **Address:** 21 E Vine St 84074 **Location:** Just e of Main and Vine sts; downtown. **Parking:** street only.

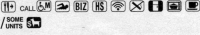

TORREY pop. 182

Torrey is considered a gateway town to Capitol Reef National Park, given its location just 8 miles west of the park's visitor center on SR 24. With a population of fewer than 200 people, Torrey is a tiny town, but it offers spectacular views of red rock formations and plenty of options for dining and accommodations. Hiking, horseback riding, mountain biking, fishing and canyoneering are popular recreational pursuits.

CAPITOL REEF RESORT   435/425-3761

Motel
Rates not provided

Address: 2600 E SR 24 84775 **Location:** 2 mi e of jct SR 12 and 24. **Facility:** 100 units. 1-2 stories (no elevator), exterior corridors. **Terms:** check-in 4 pm. **Dining:** Chimney Rock Restaurant, see separate listing. **Pool(s):** heated outdoor. **Activities:** hot tub. **Guest Services:** coin laundry.

SAVE 🍴 🏊 BIZ 🛜 ✕ 📶 📠 ☕

COWBOY HOMESTEAD CABINS   435/425-3414

Cabin $89-$99 **Address:** 2323 S Hwy 12 84775 **Location:** 3.3 mi s of jct SR 12 and 24. **Facility:** 4 cabins. 1 story, exterior corridors. **Terms:** check-in 4 pm, 2 night minimum stay - seasonal and/or weekends, 7 day cancellation notice. **Activities:** fishing.

🛜 ✕ 🚗 📶 📠 📠 ☕

RED SANDS HOTEL   (435)425-3688

Hotel $79-$140 **Address:** 670 E SR 24 84775 **Location:** 0.3 mi w of jct SR 12 and 24. **Facility:** 35 units. 2 stories (no elevator), interior corridors. **Terms:** closed 11/10-2/13, cancellation fee imposed. **Pool(s):** heated indoor. **Activities:** hot tub. **Guest Services:** coin laundry.

🍴+ CALL 🦽 🏊 BIZ 🛜 ✕ 📶 📠 ☕
/ SOME
/ UNITS 📶

THE RIM ROCK INN & RESTAURANTS   435/425-3398

Motel. Rates not provided. **Address:** 2523 E Hwy 24 84775 **Location:** 2.5 mi ne of jct SR 12 and 24. **Facility:** 19 units. 1 story, exterior corridors. **Dining:** Rim Rock Patio, Rim Rock Restaurant, see separate listings. **Activities:** regulation golf, trails.

🍴 🍸 🛜 ✕ / SOME UNITS 📶

SKYRIDGE INN BED & BREAKFAST   435/425-3222

Bed & Breakfast. Rates not provided. **Address:** 1090 E Hwy 24 84775 **Location:** Just e of jct SR 12 and 24. **Facility:** Casual Southwest sophistication and magnificent views greet visitors to this Territorial-style house on 75 acres overlooking red rock cliffs. Guests can relax on the front porch or back patio. 6 units. 3 stories (no elevator), interior/exterior corridors. **Terms:** check-in 4 pm. **Activities:** hot tub. 🍴+ 🛜 ✕ ☕ / SOME UNITS 📶

TORREY SCHOOLHOUSE BED & BREAKFAST   435/491-0230

Bed & Breakfast. Rates not provided. **Address:** 150 N Center St 84775 **Location:** 1 mi w of jct SR 12 and 24, then just n. **Facility:** At this beautiful inn, the spectacular views are the star attraction. The spacious, school-themed rooms have names like Music, Arithmetic, Reading and Writing. There's a Teacher's Lounge, too. 10 units. 3 stories (no elevator), interior corridors.

🍴+ CALL 🦽 BIZ 🛜 ✕ 🚗

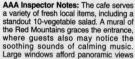

WHERE TO EAT

CAFE DIABLO   435/425-3070

Southwestern. Casual Dining. $11-$32 **AAA Inspector Notes:** Friendly, attentive service are hallmarks of this casually upscale cafe. Among the menu favorites are painted salmon, pecan chicken, empanadas, duck mariachi, rattlesnake cakes and pumpkin seed trout, all innovatively presented. Wonderful homemade ice cream and pastries also are offered. Seating is seasonally available on a patio beside the herb and tulip garden. **Features:** full bar, patio dining. **Address:** 599 W Main St 84775 **Location:** 1 mi w of jct SR 12 and 24. L D

CAPITOL REEF CAFE   435/425-3271

Southwestern
Casual Dining
$6-$19

AAA Inspector Notes: The cafe serves a variety of fresh local items, including a standout 10-vegetable salad. A mural of the Red Mountains graces the entrance, where guests also may notice the soothing sounds of calming music. Large windows afford panoramic views of the mountains themselves. Among the healthful choices are chicken, salmon and trout. **Features:** beer & wine. **Address:** 360 W Main St 84775 **Location:** 1 mi w of jct SR 12 and 24.

B L D

CASTLE ROCK COFFEE & CANDY   435/425-2100

Coffee/Tea Sandwiches. Quick Serve. $7-$9 **AAA Inspector Notes:** Oven-fresh breakfast sandwiches, cinnamon rolls, croissants, English scones, Japanese banana bread, muffins, chicken-pesto sandwiches and incredibly delicious all-grain trail bars are served at this popular eatery made for travelers. Homemade power bagels are served with peanut butter, banana, cranberries and walnuts, and the smoked flaked salmon with cream cheese is a delicious treat. Soups and freshly squeezed juices and smoothies are appropriate thirst-quenchers after a day in the desert. **Address:** 685 Hwy 24 84775 **Location:** Jct SR 12 and 24. B L

CHIMNEY ROCK RESTAURANT   435/425-3797

American. Casual Dining. $8-$15 **AAA Inspector Notes:** Patrons can choose from a good selection of comfort food for both breakfast and dinner. The menu is as basic as the service, with sandwiches and a children's menu. **Features:** full bar. **Address:** 2600 E Hwy 24 84775 **Location:** 2 mi e of jct SR 12 and 24; in Capitol Reef Resort. B D

RIM ROCK PATIO   435/425-3389

Italian
Casual Dining
$7-$20

AAA Inspector Notes: The eatery has mostly patio seating with a small bar area inside. Guests can play darts, disc golf and horseshoes while they wait for their food or after their meal. The menu consists of pizza, sandwiches, beer and prepackaged desserts. **Features:** beer only. **Address:** 2523 E Hwy 24 84775 **Location:** 2.5 mi ne of jct SR 12 and 24; in The Rim Rock Inn & Restaurants. L D

RIM ROCK RESTAURANT   435/425-3388

American
Casual Dining
$15-$30

AAA Inspector Notes: Perched atop a red rock cliff, this restaurant features 10 large windows with stunning views of the rim rocks. The popular nightly seasonal mixed grill might include elk bratwurst, Utah trout and quail. Hummingbirds love to hang outside the large windows in the summer. **Features:** full bar. **Reservations:** suggested. **Address:** 2523 E Hwy 24 84775 **Location:** 2.5 mi ne of jct SR 12 and 24; in Rim Rock Inn. D

THE SADDLERY COWBOY BAR & STEAKHOUSE   435/425-2424

Steak. Gastropub. $12-$38 **AAA Inspector Notes:** If you love live country music, dancing and hearty steak dinners, this is your place. There are several red pool tables and dartboards to enjoy before or after dining. The bison burger, rib eye, and the USDA choice tenderloin are the most sought-after menu items. **Features:** full bar, patio dining. **Address:** 430 W Hwy 24 84775 **Location:** 1 mi w of jct SR 12 and 24. D CALL 🦽

TREMONTON pop. 7,647

HAMPTON INN
(435)257-6000

▼▼▼ **Hotel** $109-$169 **Address:** 2145 W Main St 84337 **Location:** I-84 exit 40, 0.4 mi e. **Facility:** 67 units. 3 stories, interior corridors. **Terms:** 1-7 night minimum stay, cancellation fee imposed. **Pool(s):** heated indoor. **Activities:** hot tub, exercise room. **Guest Services:** valet and coin laundry.

AAA Benefit: Members save up to 10%!

CALL ⬛ 🅜 ➡ BIZ HS 🛜 ✕ 🖥 📷 ▱ / SOME UNITS 🅢

WESTERN INN
(435)257-3399

▽▽▽ Hotel $74-$85

Address: 2301 W Main St 84337 **Location:** I-84 exit 40, just e. **Facility:** 46 units. 2 stories (no elevator), interior corridors. **Featured Amenity: continental breakfast.**

SAVE 🍴 BIZ 🛜 ✕ / SOME UNITS 🅢 🖥

TROPIC pop. 530

BRYCE TRAILS BED & BREAKFAST
435/679-8700

▼▼▼ **Bed & Breakfast.** Rates not provided. **Address:** 1001 W Bryce Way 84776 **Location:** Jct SR 12, 1 mi w. **Facility:** This modern B&B has spacious rooms and spectacular views just under the rim of Bryce Canyon National Park. The furniture is older and rooms still have tube TVs. 7 units. 2 stories (no elevator), interior corridors. **Terms:** age restrictions may apply. 🛜 ✕ ▱

BYBEE'S STEPPING STONE MOTEL
435/679-8998

fyi Not evaluated. **Address:** 21 S Main St 84776 **Location:** 0.3 mi s of center. Facilities, services, and décor characterize an economy property.

WHERE TO EAT

CLARKE'S RESTAURANT
435/679-8383

▼▼ American. Casual Dining. $6-$30 **AAA Inspector Notes:** In the center of town, the rustic restaurant is hard to miss. An old-fashioned candy store at the entrance lends to the inviting ambience. Among the casual American dishes on the varied menu are salmon steak, New York strip and chicken tenders. **Features:** beer & wine, patio dining. **Address:** 141 N Main St 84776 **Location:** On SR 12, 10 mi e of Bryce Canyon National Park; in Americas Best Value Inn & Suites Bryce Valley Inn. B L D

THE PIZZA PLACE
435/679-8888

▼▼ Pizza. Casual Dining. $7-$20 **AAA Inspector Notes:** The bright wood booths, floors and walls make it an inviting place to enjoy homemade pizza. A perfect place for a pizza lover, and the breadsticks are the specialty. **Features:** beer & wine, patio dining. **Address:** 21 N Main St 84776 **Location:** On SR 12. L D

UINTA NATIONAL FOREST (C-4)

Elevations in the forest range from 4,828 ft. at the mouth of the Provo River to 11,877 ft. at Mount Nebo. Refer to AAA maps for additional elevation information.

Extending in a rough semicircle around Provo, Uinta National Forest encompasses 949,848 acres of mountainous timber and rangeland. In 2007, the forest merged with Wasatch-Cache National Forest

(see place listing p. 411) to form an ecologically diverse expanse comprising more than 2 million acres.

One of Uinta's highest points is 11,750-foot Mount Timpanogos; northwest is Timpanogos Cave National Monument (see place listing p. 406). The forest offers scenic drives and has three wilderness areas: Lone Peak and Timpanogos on the north and Nebo on the south.

Mount Nebo Recreation Area lies 10 miles from Nephi in the left fork of Salt Creek Canyon. Nebo Scenic Byway is a 32-mile paved drive through the mountains, passing overlooks of surrounding valleys. The loop begins at Payson and ends near Nephi. Mount Nebo, which can be seen from the highway, is the highest peak in the Wasatch mountain range. In autumn the drive provides a view of brilliant colors.

Twelve miles southeast of Payson on FR 15 are Payson Lakes and Blackhawk recreation areas, where swimming and fishing are permitted. Payson Canyon Road is open when there is no snow. At the other end of the loop is Devil's Kitchen, resembling Bryce Canyon on a smaller scale.

Strawberry Reservoir Recreation Area, 23 miles south of Heber City, is known for its trout fishing and sailing opportunities. The area has boat ramps, a marina and camping facilities. Heber Mountain, 13 miles east of Heber City, provides many miles of groomed snowmobile trails. A visitor center provides exhibits and interpretive trails explaining the natural resources of Strawberry Reservoir. The center is open Thursday through Monday 9-3, mid-May through October; phone (435) 548-2321.

For further information contact the Forest Supervisor's Office, Uinta-Wasatch-Cache National Forest, 857 West S. Jordan Pkwy., South Jordan, UT 84095; phone (801) 999-2103. See Recreation Areas Chart.

VERNAL (C-6) pop. 9,089, elev. 5,050'
• Hotels p. 410 • Restaurants p. 411

The Bank of Vernal building on Main Street was constructed of bricks sent parcel post from Salt Lake City in 1919, when railroad freight charges were $1.70 per pound and parcel post charges were only $1.05. Because the postal code forbade mailing more than 50 pounds in one package and mailing more than 500 pounds in a shipment to the same address, the bricks had to be sent in packages of seven, to a dozen Vernal addresses.

With mineral deposits and Native American petroglyphs nearby, Vernal is in an area of ancient and renewed geologic interest. The Flaming Gorge-Uintas National Scenic Byway, north from Vernal on US 191 and US 44 to Manila, passes geological formations where many different strata are exposed. Wildlife is abundant along the corridor. Signs along the scenic byway explain the sights. Local tour operators offer float trips on the Green and Yampa rivers.

Uintah County Travel & Tourism: 147 E. Main St., Vernal, UT 84078. **Phone:** (435) 781-6765 or (800) 477-5558.

Self-guiding tours: Self-guiding tour brochures are available at most local restaurants, motels and service stations as well as at the travel board. Areas covered by the tours include Dry Fork Canyon, Red Fleet Reservoir, Dinosaur National Monument *(see place listing p. 307)* and other area attractions. The travel board also has information about a walking tour of Vernal's historic sites.

JONES HOLE NATIONAL FISH HATCHERY, 40 mi. n.e. via SR 44 and Jones Hole Rd., raises trout for Utah, Wyoming and Colorado streams, lakes and reservoirs. Indoor hatching pools and outdoor ponds contain trout in various stages of growth. Rainbow trout account for the majority of the stocked fish, but cutthroat, brook and brown trout also are raised.

A trout stream emerges from a hole in the canyon wall nearby, joining the Green River 3.5 miles downstream. A hiking trail connects the hatchery and the river. **Time:** Allow 30 minutes minimum. **Hours:** Daily 7-3:30. Closed major holidays. **Cost:** Free. **Phone:** (435) 789-4481.

MCCONKIE RANCH is 10 mi. n.w. in Dry Fork Canyon to 6228 McConkie Rd. On the property are Fremont Indian petroglyphs thought to have been created A.D. 1000-1200. Self-guiding tour brochures are available at the travel board and at local restaurants, hotels and service stations. **Time:** Allow 1 hour minimum. **Hours:** Daily dawn-dusk. **Cost:** Donations. **Phone:** (435) 789-6733.

UTAH FIELD HOUSE OF NATURAL HISTORY STATE PARK MUSEUM, 496 E. Main St., has hands-on exhibits that depict the prehistoric background of the Uinta Basin. Visitors are greeted by a 90-foot skeleton of a diplodocus, a plant-eating dinosaur, before entering a theater to view a brief film. Several other dinosaur skeletons, a simulated dig site, sights and sounds from millions of years ago, a wall of leaf fossils, and a fenced dinosaur garden with life-size replicas also can be seen. **Time:** Allow 1 hour minimum. **Hours:** Daily 9-5, Mar.-Oct; Mon.-Sat. 9-5, rest of year. **Cost:** $7; $3.50 (ages 6-12 and 62+). **Phone:** (435) 789-3799.

UINTAH COUNTY HERITAGE MUSEUM, 155 E. Main St., has memorabilia from Uintah County and the Uinta Basin. Exhibits depict the lives of the pioneers, particularly early settlers, miners and soldiers. The museum also features one of the largest collections of Fremont and Ute Indian artifacts. Displays include the First Ladies of the White House Doll Exhibit, a mounted wildlife exhibit, an outdoor display of horse-drawn equipment and monthly fine art exhibits. Also on-site are an amphitheater, an arena, an equestrian complex, a convention center and an indoor ice rink.

Pick up colorful, top-quality travel guides and atlases at AAA/CAA offices

Time: Allow 1 hour minimum. **Hours:** Mon.-Thurs. 9-7:30, Fri. 9-6, Sat. 10-4, June-Aug.; Mon.-Fri. 9-6, Sat. 10-4, rest of year. Closed major holidays. **Cost:** Donations. **Phone:** (435) 789-7399.

RECREATIONAL ACTIVITIES
White-water Rafting
- **Don Hatch River Expeditions** departs from 221 North 400 East. **Hours:** Trips are offered daily, mid-May to mid-Sept. Office hours 8-7. **Phone:** (435) 789-4316 or (800) 342-8243.

BEST WESTERN ANTLERS   (435)789-1202

Motel $100-$130
AAA Benefit: Save 10% or more every day and earn 10% bonus points!

Address: 423 W Main St 84078 **Location:** 0.4 mi w of center on US 40. **Facility:** 44 units. 2 stories (no elevator), exterior corridors. **Pool(s):** heated outdoor. **Activities:** hot tub, limited exercise equipment. **Guest Services:** valet and coin laundry. **Featured Amenity:** breakfast buffet.

BEST WESTERN DINOSAUR INN   (435)789-2660

Motel $83-$250
AAA Benefit: Save 10% or more every day and earn 10% bonus points!

Address: 251 E Main St 84078 **Location:** 0.3 mi e of center on US 40. **Facility:** 60 units. 2 stories (no elevator), exterior corridors. **Pool(s):** heated outdoor. **Activities:** playground, picnic facilities. **Guest Services:** valet and coin laundry.

HOLIDAY INN EXPRESS HOTEL & SUITES - VERNAL/DINOSAURLAND   435/789-4654
Hotel. Rates not provided. **Address:** 1515 W US 40 84078 **Location:** 1.8 mi w of center. **Facility:** 69 units. 3 stories, interior corridors. **Terms:** check-in 4 pm. **Pool(s):** heated indoor. **Activities:** hot tub, exercise room. **Guest Services:** valet and coin laundry.

MICROTEL INN & SUITES BY WYNDHAM - VERNAL/NAPLES   (435)781-8141
Hotel $80-$116 **Address:** 1041 S 1500 E 84078 **Location:** 1.8 mi e of center on US 40. Located in Naples. **Facility:** 23 units. 4 stories, interior corridors. **Pool(s):** heated indoor. **Activities:** hot tub, limited exercise equipment. **Guest Services:** coin laundry.

SPRINGHILL SUITES BY MARRIOTT   (435)781-9000
Hotel $98-$196 **Address:** 1205 W Hwy 40 84078 **Location:** 1.3 mi w of center. Located in a commercial area. **Facility:** 97 units. 4 stories, interior corridors. **Parking:** winter plug-ins. **Pool(s):** heated indoor. **Activities:** hot tub, exercise room. **Guest Services:** valet and coin laundry.
AAA Benefit: Members save 5% or more!

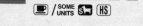

TOWNEPLACE SUITES BY MARRIOTT
(435)789-8050

▼▼▼ **Extended Stay Hotel**
$103-$198 **Address:** 1219 W Hwy 40
84078 **Location:** 1.3 mi w of center. **Fa-**
cility: 85 units, some two bedrooms, efficiencies and kitchens. 4 stories, interior
corridors. **Parking:** winter plug-ins. **Pool(s):** heated indoor. **Activ-**
ities: hot tub, picnic facilities, exercise room. **Guest Services:** valet
and coin laundry.

AAA Benefit:
Members save 5%
or more!

WHERE TO EAT

7-11 RANCH CAFE
435/789-1170

▼▼▼ American. Casual Dining. $7-$21 **AAA Inspector Notes:**
Wagon-wheel chandeliers hang from the ceilings of this Western-
themed restaurant featuring fresh scones with every meal, fruit and
potato salads, soups, chili, blackened steak, fried chicken, prime rib
and a variety of seasonal fruit and cream pies. **Address:** 77 E Main
St 84078 **Location:** On US 40 (Main St), just e of Vernal Ave; downtown. **Parking:** street only. B L D

CLUB XS
435/781-0122

▼▼▼ American. Casual Dining. $8-$34 **AAA Inspector Notes:**
Locals rightly recommend this restaurant for the steaks and lobster.
Other options include a few Mexican and pasta dishes. Family dining
is offered downstairs. **Features:** full bar. **Address:** 1089 US 40
84078 **Location:** Jct US 191 (Vernal Ave), 1.2 mi e.
L D LATE

COUNTRY GRUB CAFE
435/789-7000

▼ Burgers Hot Dogs. Quick Serve. $5-$9 **AAA Inspector Notes:**
There is nothing fancy here, but this cute roadside eatery features
great burgers, hot dogs and milk shakes. Expect a crowd during peak
and even most nonpeak hours. My chocolate malt was worth any
wait. **Address:** 2419 S 1500 E 84078 **Location:** 3.5 mi s of center
on US 40; in Naples. L D

DON PEDRO'S FAMILY MEXICAN RESTAURANT
435/789-3402

▼▼ Mexican. Casual Dining. $7-$14 **AAA Inspector Notes:**
This restaurant has a festive decor. Traditional menu items include a
large bowl of tortilla soup, taco salad, huevos rancheros, chicken taquitos, sizzling fajitas and vegetarian choices. A menu is available for
the little amigos. **Features:** full bar. **Address:** 3340 N Vernal Ave
84078 **Location:** 3.5 mi n of jct US 40 and 191 (Vernal Ave). L D

NAPLES COUNTRY CAFE
435/789-8870

▼▼ American. Casual Dining. $8-$25 **AAA Inspector Notes:**
This is an ideal stop if you are looking for a good meal with servers
that make you feel like you are family. Grilled pork chops, catfish,
chicken-fried steak and ½-pound burgers are the most popular
menu items and kids have their own menu. **Tip:** The popular fruit
and cream pies are first come, first served. **Address:** 1010 S Hwy
40 84078 **Location:** 1.6 mi s on US 40; in Naples.
B L D

THE QUARRY
435/789-2337

▼▼ American. Casual Dining. $9-$36 **AAA Inspector Notes:**
The distinctive décor reflects Vernal's history as a quarry town. The
menu features a variety of sandwiches, steaks, chicken, fish and
pasta dishes. **Features:** full bar. **Address:** 25 S Vernal Ave 84078
Location: Just e of US 191 (Vernal Ave). **Parking:** street only.
L D

VERNAL BREWING COMPANY
435/781-2337

▼▼ American. Casual Dining. $10-$17 **AAA Inspector Notes:**
This brewpub offers attractive modern décor with natural light. The
menu includes burgers, rib-eye, pizzas and mac 'n cheese. Beer offerings include an IPA, porter, kolsch, lager and hefeweizen. **Fea-**
tures: full bar, patio dining. **Address:** 55 S 500 E 84078 **Location:**
Just e of jct US 191 (Vernal Ave). L D CALL

WASATCH-CACHE NATIONAL FOREST
(A-3)

Elevations in the forest range from 5,000 ft.
at the West Desert Salt Lake Valley to
13,512 ft. at Gilbert Peak in the High Uintas
Wilderness. Refer to AAA maps for additional
elevation information.

Wasatch-Cache National Forest lies along the Wasatch, Uinta and Stansbury ranges of north-eastern and north-central Utah. A small portion of the 1,259,160-acre forest, which merged with 949,848-acre Uinta National Forest *(see place listing p. 409)* in 2007, extends into Wyoming, and its northern sector reaches the Idaho border.

Some of the tallest mountains in Utah are found in the Uinta and Wasatch mountain ranges. (Wasatch is a Native American word meaning "high mountain pass.") Among the first white explorers to visit this area of Utah were trapper Jim Bridger, guide Kit Carson, trader and explorer Jedediah Smith, and the Rocky Mountain Fur Co. trappers. They found Paiute and Ute Indians living in the semidesert valleys.

Access throughout Wasatch-Cache is provided by 1,391 miles of road and 1,500 miles of trails. The forest has seven wilderness areas, more than 70 campgrounds and more than 30 picnic areas.

The forest terrain is very diverse, from the dry Great Basin Desert to the lush green meadows and high peaks of the Uinta Mountains. In the forest's easternmost section lies part of the High Uintas Wilderness Area *(see Ashley National Forest p. 292),* with peaks 12,000 to 13,512 feet high. The wilderness area contains hundreds of glacial lakes, many of which are stocked with trout. More than half the people in Utah depend on water produced from the forest's municipal watersheds.

Wasatch-Cache National Forest is an important wildlife and fishery forest, providing a habitat for an estimated 300 species, predominantly birds and mammals. Two endangered species, the peregrine falcon and bald eagle, are seasonal residents. Much of the forest is suitable for livestock grazing.

There are snowmobile trails at Mirror Lake North, Mirror Lake South, Wolf Creek Pass, the Bridger Lake area and between Monte Cristo and Woodruff; because of the high altitudes, snowmobiling is best after the snow has settled. Snowshoeing as well as downhill and cross-country skiing trails also are available.

Other recreational opportunities include deer and elk hunting. A winter feeding ground for elk at Hardware Ranch is managed by the Division of Wildlife Resources. Elk and deer can be observed by telescope from a visitor center November through April. Sleigh rides are offered in winter. Phone (435) 753-6206.

A scenic drive from Provo Canyon via US 189 and SR 150 (Mirror Lake Highway) at Kamas winds through the forest and ends in Evanston, Wyo. Another scenic drive is SR 39 between the Monte Cristo Range and Woodruff. Pineview Lake, about 9 miles up Ogden Canyon, can be reached via SR 39. Logan Canyon is a recreation area east of the college town of Logan. Logan Canyon Scenic Byway, a 45-mile-long winding route, part of US 89, runs between Logan eastward to Bear Lake.

Snowbasin, on the east slope of Mount Ogden, offers year-round recreation. Notable ski areas include Alta and Snowbird, both within the forest.

For further information contact the Forest Supervisor, Uinta-Wasatch-Cache National Forest, 857 West S. Jordan Pkwy., South Jordan, UT 84095; phone (801) 999-2103, (877) 444-6777, or TTY (877) 833-6777 for camping reservations. *See Recreation Areas Chart.*

MIRROR LAKE is 33 mi. from Kamas via Bald Mountain Pass. The 11,943-foot Bald Mountain rises from the lake's western shore, providing views of the Uinta Range. The summit can be reached by trail.

WASHINGTON pop. 18,761

HOLIDAY INN EXPRESS & SUITES   435/986-1313
▼▼▼ **Hotel.** Rates not provided. **Address:** 2450 N Town Center Dr 84780 **Location:** I-15 exit 16, just e. **Facility:** 100 units, some two bedrooms and kitchens. 3 stories, interior corridors. **Terms:** check-in 4 pm. **Pool(s):** heated outdoor. **Activities:** hot tub, exercise room. **Guest Services:** coin laundry.

WELLSVILLE (A-3) pop. 3,432, elev. 4,547'

AMERICAN WEST HERITAGE CENTER is at 4025 S. US 89/91. This 160-acre living-history site includes the Trappers Cabin, Pioneer Encampment and 1917 Farm. Displays highlight pioneer music, folk life, values and other aspects of 1820-1920 American life. Activities such as sheep shearing, gardening, woodworking and threshing are demonstrated. Special events are held throughout the year.

Time: Allow 1 hour minimum. **Hours:** Mon.-Thurs. 10-9, Fri.-Sat. 10-10, late Sept.-late Oct. (historic sites closed); Tues.-Fri. and holidays 9-5, Sat. 10-5 (historic sites open 11-4), June-Aug.; Mon.-Fri. 9-3 (historic sites only open during special events), Sept. 1-late Sept. Phone for schedule rest of year. Closed Jan. 1, Thanksgiving and Christmas. **Cost:** $5-$12; $3-$12 (ages 3-11). Combination tickets are available. Prices vary for special events. **Phone:** (435) 245-6050.

WENDOVER (B-1) pop. 1,400, elev. 4,291'

Located on the Utah-Nevada border at the western edge of the Great Salt Lake Desert, Wendover was established in 1907 as a Western Pacific Railroad stop. In 1940 the Army established an air base just south of town. During World War II it became a major training center for bomber pilots, including the crews that dropped the atomic bombs on Hiroshima and Nagasaki.

From vicinity hillsides it is possible to see the curvature of the earth. Looking east across the vast, level expanse of the Great Salt Lake Desert, the straight lines of the interstate and parallel railroad tracks and utility lines appear to curve away to the horizon.

WENDOVER AIRFIELD MUSEUM is at 345 S. Airport Apron. Operational 1942-69, Wendover is one of the country's most intact World War II-era training airfields. A museum housed in the operations building just south of the control tower has exhibits about the onetime Army airfield and Air Force base. Models of aircraft, vintage flight instruments, and flight gear and military uniforms are displayed. An 8-minute video is shown in the former pilot's lounge on the main floor. One-hour guided tours of the base, which includes an atomic bomb loading pit, are available.

Hours: Guided tours require a minimum of four people, and reservations are recommended. Museum daily 8-6:30. Last admission 1 hour before closing. Closed Thanksgiving and Christmas. **Cost:** Museum admission by donation. Guided tour $10; free (ages 0-12). **Phone:** (435) 665-2308.

BEST WESTERN PLUS WENDOVER INN   (435)665-2215

▼▼▼ Hotel $70-$120
AAA Benefit: Save 10% or more every day and earn 10% bonus points!
Address: 685 E Wendover Blvd 84083 **Location:** I-80 exit 2, east end of town. **Facility:** 79 units. 3 stories, interior corridors. **Activities:** exercise room. **Guest Services:** coin laundry.

SUPER 8 WENDOVER   (435)665-7811
▼▼ Motel $69-$99 **Address:** 935 E Wendover Blvd 84083 **Location:** I-80 exit 2, 2 mi w. **Facility:** 24 units. 2 stories (no elevator), exterior corridors. **Pool(s):** heated outdoor.

Nearby Nevada

WEST WENDOVER pop. 4,410

PEPPERMILL HOTEL & CASINO   775/664-2255

▼▼▼ **Hotel.** Rates not provided. **Address:** 680 Wendover Blvd 89883 **Location:** I-80 exit 410, 0.3 mi s, then just e. **Facility:** Pamper yourself in a variety of comfortable rooms while watching the sunset over the high desert. The bright red and white stone casino is always bustling. 382 units. 4 stories, interior corridors. **Dining:** 3 restaurants. **Guest Services:** area transportation.

🍴 🍽 📞 🅶🅼 📶 💻 / SOME UNITS 🛗

RAINBOW HOTEL & CASINO   775/664-4000

[fyi] Not evaluated. **Address:** 1045 Wendover Blvd 89883 **Location:** I-80 exit 410, 0.3 mi s, then just w. Facilities, services, and décor characterize a mid-scale property. The hotel offers something for everyone.

WHERE TO EAT

ROMANZA RISTORANTE ITALIANO   775/664-9100

▼▼▼ Italian. Casual Dining. $15-$36 **AAA Inspector Notes:** House specialties here include braised halibut Sorrento, wood-grilled Atlantic salmon, braised veal shank, sautéed chicken piccata and a popular Tuscan trio of chicken parmigiana, lasagna and fettuccine Alfredo. Aged steaks are grilled over oak and cherry woods. **Features:** full bar. **Reservations:** suggested. **Address:** 100 Wendover Blvd 89883 **Location:** I-80 exit 410, just s, then 0.8 mi e; in Montego Bay Casino & Resort. [D]

THE STEAK HOUSE   775/664-4000

▼▼▼ Steak Seafood. Fine Dining. $25-$70 **AAA Inspector Notes:** Diners enjoy fresh fish and seafood appetizers and entrées, steak, prime rib or pasta in this eatery's relaxed atmosphere. A glass of wine from an extensive wine list as well as professional, courteous staff members enhance the dining experience. **Features:** full bar. **Address:** 1045 Wendover Blvd 89883 **Location:** I-80 exit 410, 0.3 mi s, then just w; in Rainbow Hotel & Casino. [D]

This ends Nearby Nevada and resumes the alphabetical city listings for Utah.

WEST JORDAN pop. 103,712

- **Hotels & Restaurants map & index p. 385**
- **Part of Salt Lake City area — see map p. 368**

ARCHIBALD'S RESTAURANT AT GARDNER VILLAGE   801/566-6940 (60)

▼▼ American. Family Dining. $7-$26 **AAA Inspector Notes:** Historic. The Gardner Mill, which is part of historic Gardner Village, was built in 1877 and is on the National Register of Historic Places. The restaurant menu includes fried green tomatoes, batter-dipped halibut with chips, and homemade carrot cake. **Features:** beer & wine. **Address:** 1100 W 7800 S 84084 **Location:** I-15 exit 297 (7200 S), 0.4 mi w, 0.7 mi s on 700th W, then just w. [L] [D]

WEST VALLEY CITY pop. 129,480

- **Restaurants p. 414**
- **Hotels & Restaurants map & index p. 385**
- **Part of Salt Lake City area — see map p. 368**

As the name suggests, West Valley City is a quiet suburb of Salt Lake City set on the west side of scenic Salt Lake Valley. The Green Line of the TRAX light rail system connects the community with the airport. Hockey fans cheer on the Utah Grizzlies at Maverik Center (3200 S. Decker Lake Dr.), which served as the official ice hockey venue for the 2002 Winter Olympic Games.

CRYSTAL INN - SALT LAKE CITY/WEST VALLEY CITY   (801)736-2000 36

▼▼▼ Hotel $89-$229 **Address:** 2254 W City Center Ct 84119 **Location:** I-215 exit 18 (3500 S), just e, then 0.3 mi n. **Facility:** 122 units. 3 stories, interior corridors. **Pool(s):** heated indoor. **Activities:** hot tub, exercise room. **Guest Services:** valet and coin laundry, area transportation. *(See ad p. 390.)*

🍴 🚭 📞 🅶🅼 🏊 💼 📶 ✕ 🛗 🍽 💻 / SOME UNITS 🛗 🆑

EMBASSY SUITES BY HILTON - SALT LAKE CITY/WEST VALLEY CITY   (801)963-4760 37

▼▼▼ Hotel $129-$199 **Address:** 3524 S Market St 84119 **Location:** I-215 exit 18, 0.4 mi w. **Facility:** 162 units. 7 stories, interior corridors. **Terms:** 1-7 night minimum stay, cancellation fee imposed. **Dining:** Shula's 347, see separate listing. **Pool(s):** heated indoor. **Activities:** hot tub, exercise room. **Guest Services:** valet and coin laundry.

AAA Benefit: Members save 5% or more!

🍴 🍽 📞 🏊 💼 📶 🛗 🍽 💻

HOLIDAY INN EXPRESS & SUITES WATERPARK - WEST VALLEY CITY   801/517-4000 34

▼▼▼ Contemporary Hotel. Rates not provided. **Address:** 3036 S Decker Lake Dr 84119 **Location:** I-215 exit 18A (3500 S), just e, 0.6 mi n, then just w. Across from Maverik Center. **Facility:** 94 units. 3 stories, interior corridors. **Pool(s):** heated indoor. **Activities:** hot tub, game room, picnic facilities, exercise room. **Guest Services:** valet and coin laundry, area transportation.

🚭 📞 🅶🅼 🏊 💼 📶 ✕ 💻 / SOME UNITS 🆑 🛗 🛗 🍽

(See map & index p. 385.)

HOME2 SUITES BY HILTON WEST VALLEY CITY
(801)679-8222 **33**

▼▼▼ **Extended Stay Contemporary Hotel** $89-$209 **Address:** 4028 Parkway Blvd 84120 **Location:** I-15 exit 305A (West Valley/2100 S), 4.2 mi w on SR 201 exit 13 (Bangerter Hwy), 1.2 mi s to Parkway Blvd, then 0.3 mi w. Located in Lake Park Corporate Center. **Facility:** 90 units. 4 stories, interior corridors. **Terms:** 1-7 night minimum stay, cancellation fee imposed. **Pool(s):** heated indoor. **Activities:** hot tub, picnic facilities, exercise room. **Guest Services:** valet and coin laundry.

AAA Benefit: Members save up to 10%!

〔¶→〕 CALL 〔&M〕 🏊 〔BIZ〕 〔HS〕 📶 📱 📠 ☕
/ SOME UNITS 〔S🔊〕

LA QUINTA INN SALT LAKE CITY WEST
(801)954-9292 **38**

▼▼ **Hotel** $64-$306 **Address:** 3540 S 2200 W 84119 **Location:** I-215 exit 18 (3500 S), just e, then just s. **Facility:** 59 units. 3 stories, interior corridors. **Pool(s):** heated indoor. **Activities:** hot tub, limited exercise equipment. **Guest Services:** valet and coin laundry.

〔¶→〕 CALL 〔&M〕 🏊 〔BIZ〕 📶 ✕ 📱 ☕
/ SOME UNITS 〔S🔊〕 📠

STAYBRIDGE SUITES - WEST VALLEY CITY
801/746-8400 **35**

▼▼▼ **Extended Stay Hotel.** Rates not provided. **Address:** 3038 S Decker Lake Dr 84119 **Location:** I-215 exit 18A (3500 S), just e, 0.6 mi n, then just w. Across from Maverik Center. **Facility:** 97 efficiencies, some two bedrooms. 3 stories, interior corridors. **Pool(s):** heated indoor. **Activities:** hot tub, game room, picnic facilities, exercise room. **Guest Services:** complimentary and valet laundry, area transportation.

✈ CALL 〔&M〕 🏊 〔BIZ〕 📶 📱 📠 ☕
/ SOME UNITS 〔S🔊〕 〔HS〕

TOWNEPLACE SUITES BY MARRIOTT WEST VALLEY CITY
(801)307-3300 **32**

▼▼▼ **Extended Stay Hotel** $90-$190 **Address:** 5473 W High Market Dr 84120 **Location:** I-80 exit 113 (5600 S), 4.7 mi s, then just e; I-15 exit 305A/B (SR 201), 6.5 mi w, exit 11, 1 mi s, then just e. **Facility:** 87 units, some efficiencies and kitchens. 4 stories, interior corridors. **Pool(s):** heated indoor. **Activities:** hot tub, picnic facilities, exercise room. **Guest Services:** valet and coin laundry.

AAA Benefit: Members save 5% or more!

〔¶→〕 CALL 〔&M〕 🏊 〔BIZ〕 📶 ✕ 📱 📠 ☕
/ SOME UNITS 〔S🔊〕

WHERE TO EAT

SHULA'S 347
801/966-3470 **26**

▼▼▼ Steak Seafood. Fine Dining. $9-$48 **AAA Inspector Notes:** The upscale restaurant serves Shula-cut steaks and fresh seafood. This is an ideal spot for a lovely lunch or dinner with colleagues, family or friends. Popular menu items include jumbo lump crab cakes, braised short ribs, pan-seared shrimp and filet mignon. The signature dessert is the Key lime pie which is shipped to Shula's from Florida. **Features:** full bar, patio dining. **Reservations:** suggested. **Address:** 3524 S Market St 84119 **Location:** I-215 exit 18, 0.4 mi w, in Embassy Suites by Hilton Salt Lake West Valley City.

〔L〕 〔D〕 CALL 〔&M〕

WHITEROCKS (C-5) pop. 289, elev. 6,033'

WHITEROCKS STATE FISH HATCHERY is 2 mi. n. on Whiterocks Rd. The hatchery supplies brook, brown, cutthroat and rainbow trout as well as kokanee salmon to Utah waters, including the Green River, Strawberry Reservoir and the lakes in the Uinta Basin and Flaming Gorge National Recreation Area (see place listing p. 313). Nearly 1.5 million trout are raised on the 14-acre site annually. **Time:** Allow 30 minutes minimum. **Hours:** Mon.-Sat. 8-4. **Cost:** Free. **Phone:** (435) 353-4855.

WOODS CROSS pop. 9,761

• **Hotels & Restaurants map & index p. 385**
• **Part of Salt Lake City area — see map p. 368**

HAMPTON INN - SALT LAKE CITY NORTH/WOODS CROSS
(801)296-1211 **28**

▼▼▼ **Hotel** $109-$169 **Address:** 2393 S 800 W 84087 **Location:** I-15 exit 315, just w, then just n. **Facility:** 60 units. 3 stories, interior corridors. **Terms:** 1-7 night minimum stay, cancellation fee imposed. **Pool(s):** heated indoor. **Activities:** hot tub, exercise room. **Guest Services:** valet and coin laundry, area transportation.

AAA Benefit: Members save up to 10%!

✈ CALL 〔&M〕 🏊 〔BIZ〕 📶 ✕ ☕
/ SOME UNITS 🐾 📱 📠

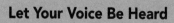

ZION NATIONAL PARK (F-2)
• Hotels p. 417 • Restaurants p. 417

Elevations in the park range from 3,666 ft. at Coalpits Wash to 8,726 ft. at Horse Ranch Mountain. Refer to AAA maps for additional elevation information.

Zion National Park's entrances on the south-western and eastern edges are connected by SR 9 (Zion-Mount Carmel Highway), which joins I-15 on the west and US 89 on the east. The park's north-western entrance is accessible from I-15, but no other road connects this part of the park with the Zion Canyon section.

Desert terrain and huge, sculpted rock formations coexist with hanging gardens. The gigantic stone masses of the West Temple and the Watchman guard the southern entrance to the park. From a multicolored stairway, the red-brown Watchman looms 2,555 feet above the canyon floor. The 7,810-foot West Temple is one of the most prominent for-mations in the southern section.

Just north of the southern entrance is the begin-ning of Zion Canyon, a spectacular gorge being carved through strangely colored sandstones and shale by the Virgin River. About a half-mile deep and a half-mile wide at its mouth, the canyon narrows to about 300 feet at the Temple of Sinawava, the nar-rowest portion of the canyon accessible by car and about 8 miles from the park entrance.

From the west the main park road, a continuation of SR 9 known as Zion-Mount Carmel Highway *(see attraction listing)*, climbs the talus slope of Pine Creek Canyon in six switchbacks, enters 5,607-foot Zion-Mount Carmel Tunnel (completed in 1930) and continues to ascend on a 5-percent grade. This road's construction is considered a remarkable engi-neering feat.

The Kolob Canyons section in the northwest corner of the park contains fingerlike red sandstone canyons at the edge of Kolob Terrace. Within this area is the Hurricane Fault, where layers of ancient rock are clearly exposed. Kolob Arch is accessible via a 14-mile round-trip trail. At 310 feet across, it is one of the largest freestanding arches in the world.

General Information and Activities

The park and its main roads are open all year. Scenic drives include a 13-mile round-trip through Zion Canyon from the southern entrance and a 22-mile round-trip from the eastern entrance to Zion

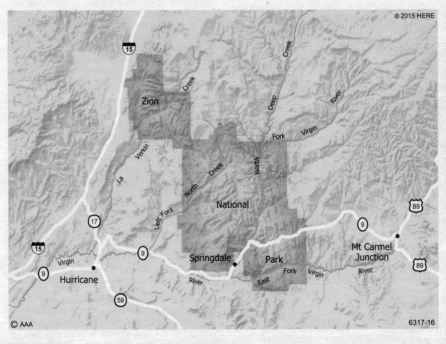

© 2015 HERE

© AAA   6317-16

This map shows cities in Zion National Park where you will find attractions, hotels and restaurants. Cities are listed alphabetically in this book on the following pages.

Canyon. A paved road from SR 9 at Virgin joins an unpaved road leading north to Lava Point and Kolob Reservoir; the unpaved road is closed in the winter. A 5-mile drive from the Kolob Canyons Visitor Center at I-15 exit 40 affords spectacular views. Zion Canyon Scenic Drive stretches from Zion Canyon Visitor Center to the Temple of Sinawava. **Note:** Use caution and good judgment when driving along SR 9 to Bryce Canyon City. The road is not lit at night and contains hairpin turns that are difficult to maneuver; there are no guardrails.

From early April through October, the Zion Canyon Scenic Drive is only accessible by park shuttle bus. Parking at the Zion Canyon Visitor Center fills up quickly during peak summer months; free parking is available throughout the town of Springdale, near the south entrance of the park. A free shuttle provides regular transportation to and from the park from several sites throughout the town daily 6 a.m.-9:15 p.m., mid-May through Labor Day; 7 a.m.-8:30 p.m., in spring and early fall; and 7 a.m.-7:30 p.m., in late fall. Schedule may vary; phone ahead.

The town shuttle drops off its passengers just outside the park entrance. There, visitors enter the park on foot and walk a short distance to the Zion Canyon Visitor Center, where they may board another shuttle for Zion Canyon Scenic Drive. Shuttles run on a continuous loop, making stops at the park's points of interest; visitors may disembark and board another shuttle as many times as they wish 7:10 a.m.-9:45 p.m. in summer, 8:10 a.m.-8:45 p.m. in spring and 8:10 a.m.-7:45 p.m. in fall. Schedule may vary; phone ahead. Shuttles run between 7 and 30 minutes apart and are equipped with storage areas for bicycles. Pets are not permitted on shuttles; a kennel service is available in Springdale.

When private transportation is used, vehicles wider than 7 feet 10 inches (including mirrors) and/or higher than 11 feet 4 inches must be escorted through the Zion-Mount Carmel Tunnel, which is on the park road between the east entrance and Zion Canyon. The fee for this service is $15, which includes two trips for the same vehicle within 7 days from date of purchase. Escorts are stationed at tunnel entrances daily 8-8, Memorial Day-Labor Day; schedule varies rest of year. Phone ahead to check tunnel escort availability, or, upon arrival, confirm hours at the main park entrance stations. Phone (435) 772-3256. Single vehicles more than 40 feet long or combined vehicles longer than 50 feet are prohibited. Vehicles exceeding 19 feet in length may not park in the Weeping Rock Parking Area or at the Temple of Sinawava.

About 65 miles of trails are open all year; some in the canyon may close due to potential danger of ice falling from above. Permits are required for all backcountry camping and day trips going down the Narrows and its tributaries, the Subway and all canyons that require mechanical aid; a fee is charged for the permits. Phone (435) 772-0170 for backcountry information.

Ranger-naturalists offer talks and guided walks April through the summer each year and, most years, through October (weather permitting). The Junior Ranger Program, an outdoor learning experience for ages 6 through 12, is held at the park nature center Memorial Day through Labor Day. *See Recreation Areas Chart.*

ADMISSION is $30 (per private vehicle); $25 (per person arriving by motorcycle); $15 (per person arriving by other means). The above fees permit entrance to the park for 7 calendar days from date of purchase. **Note:** Visitors who do not plan to take the Zion Canyon Scenic Drive are still required to pay the $30 park entrance fee to use SR 9 between Springdale and the east Zion entrance station. The Zion-Mount Carmel Tunnel is within the park boundaries.

PETS must be physically restrained at all times and are not permitted in public buildings, on trails or aboard shuttles.

ADDRESS inquiries to the Superintendent, Zion National Park, Springdale, UT 84767-1099; phone (435) 772-3256.

ANGELS LANDING TRAIL is accessible from the Grotto Picnic Area in Zion National Park. The steep 2.5-mile climb to the top of Angels Landing offers spectacular views of the canyon. **Note:** While portions of the route are paved, the trail is not recommended for those afraid of heights or for young children. The last half-mile of the trail to the summit is strenuous and involves traveling along a narrow ridge flanked by dizzying drop-offs. Support chains are anchored intermittently along the route. Footing can be slippery even when the rock is dry.

BRIDGE MOUNTAIN is in Zion National Park on the eastern flank of the canyon. Named for the natural arch high on its face, the mountain is visible from Zion Canyon Visitor Center. East Temple, Twin Brothers and Mountain of the Sun also are visible. On the opposite side of the canyon are the Altar of Sacrifice, the Beehives and the Sentinel. Farther up is the Court of the Patriarchs, and rising above that are the Three Patriarchs. Lady Mountain, Castle Dome, the Spearhead and Mount Majestic also are visible on the same side of the canyon.

CANYON OVERLOOK TRAIL is in Zion National Park and begins at the parking area at the east end of Zion-Mount Carmel Tunnel. A moderately difficult half-mile nature trail, it offers excellent views of the western side of the canyon.

GREAT WHITE THRONE is beyond Zion Lodge against the east wall. Seen through a saddle in a low red rock wall, this towering monolith gradually changes shade from white at its top to red near the bottom. The iron minerals that produce the red color in the rock have been leached from the upper part of the formation. Opposite the Great White Throne is a smaller monolith, Angels Landing.

KOLOB CANYONS VISITOR CENTER is off I-15 exit 40 at the entrance to the Kolob Canyons area. The center provides Zion National Park information.

Hours: Daily 8-6, Memorial Day-late Sept.; 8-5, rest of year. Closed Thanksgiving and Christmas. Phone ahead to confirm schedule. **Cost:** Free. **Phone:** (435) 586-9548.

TEMPLE OF SINAWAVA is in Zion National Park at the north end of Zion Canyon Dr. In the center of the Temple of Sinawava, which is a huge natural amphitheater, are two large stone pillars known as The Altar and The Pulpit. Many springs trickle from the walls of the canyon, and cascades tumble everywhere in early spring and after summer rains.

RIVERSIDE WALK is in Zion National Park and runs along the Virgin River from the Temple of Sinawava to the beginning of the Narrows. This spectacular section of the canyon at one point is more than 1,000 feet deep and less than 20 feet wide at its bottom. The 1-mile paved trail is Zion's most popular footpath. **Note:** Inquire about potential flood danger before starting out. **Time:** Allow 1 hour, 30 minutes minimum. **Hours:** Daily dawn-dusk (weather permitting).

ZION CANYON VISITOR CENTER is on SR 9 inside Zion National Park's south entrance. The center offers park information and orientation, literature, maps, permits and educational activities. **Hours:** Daily 8-7:30, in summer; 8-6, in fall and spring; 8-5, rest of year. Closed Christmas. Phone ahead to confirm schedule. **Cost:** Free. **Phone:** (435) 772-3256.

ZION HUMAN HISTORY MUSEUM is on SR 9, .5 mi. n. of the south entrance to Zion National Park. This small museum was the park's main visitor center before the larger one was completed at the park's southern boundary in 2000. Inside are panels describing the canyon's human history; a few historic items are on display.

A 22-minute orientation film shown every half-hour introduces visitors to the park, explaining its geological origins and human history. Exhibits focus on early pioneers and Native Americans. **Time:** Allow 30 minutes minimum. **Hours:** Daily 9-7, in summer; 10-5, in spring and late fall; 9-6, in early fall. Closed Nov.-Feb. **Cost:** Free. **Phone:** (435) 772-3256.

ZION-MOUNT CARMEL HIGHWAY connects Zion National Park's east entrance with its south entrance and Zion Canyon Scenic Drive. The 10-mile road ascends from the floor of Zion Canyon through the mile-long Zion-Mount Carmel Tunnel and out into a broad area of slickrock, ancient sand dunes that have been turned to stone and eroded into unusual shapes.

One highlight is Checkerboard Mesa, a weathered sandstone hill crosshatched with fissures in a checkerboard pattern; a turnout allows drivers to take a closer look at the formation. The Canyon Overlook Trail *(see attraction listing)* begins at the tunnel's eastern end.

Note: Vehicles wider than 7 feet 10 inches (including mirrors) and/or higher than 11 feet 4 inches must be escorted through the narrow tunnel for a round-trip fee of $15. **Phone:** (435) 772-3256.

RECREATIONAL ACTIVITIES

Horseback Riding

- **Canyon Trail Rides** departs from the corral near Zion Lodge. **Hours:** One-hour Virgin River and half-day Sand Bench Trail trips are offered daily, Mar.-Oct. Departure times vary. **Phone:** (435) 679-8665 for reservations or (435) 772-3810.

ZION LODGE   435/772-7700

[fyi] Not evaluated. **Address:** Zion Lodge 84767 **Location:** SR 9, 4 mi n of south gate; in Zion Canyon. Facilities, services, and décor characterize an upscale property.

WHERE TO EAT

CASTLE DOME CAFE   435/772-7700

American. Quick Serve. $2-$8 **AAA Inspector Notes:** This is a perfect place for the person on the go to grab a quick bite to eat. Continental breakfast is served in the morning, while burgers, hot dogs, pizza and soft serve ice cream are on tap for the rest of the day and night. This is a great spot for an ice cream cone to cool off on a hot day. **Features:** beer only, patio dining. **Address:** Zion Lodge 84767 **Location:** SR 9, 4 mi n of south gate; in Zion Canyon; in Zion Lodge. B L D

RED ROCK GRILL   435/772-7760

American. Casual Dining. $6-$22 **AAA Inspector Notes:** Inside Zion National Park, the restaurant treats diners to great views. The uniformed full-service staff willingly helps guests with whatever they need. Items on the American menu include prime rib, flat-iron steak, stuffed chicken breast and even a vegan dish. **Features:** full bar, patio dining. **Reservations:** suggested, for dinner. **Address:** Zion Lodge 84767 **Location:** SR 9, 4 mi n of south gate; in Zion Canyon; in Zion Lodge. B L D

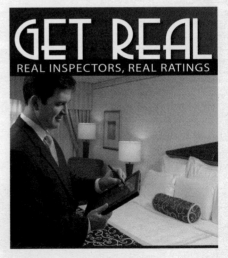

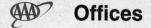 # Offices

Main office listings are shown in **BOLD TYPE** and toll-free member service numbers appear in *ITALIC TYPE*.
All are closed Saturdays, Sundays and holidays unless otherwise indicated.
The addresses, phone numbers and hours for any AAA/CAA office are subject to change.
The type of service provided is designated below the name of the city where the office is located:

✦ Auto travel services, including books and maps, and on-demand TripTik ® routings.
● Auto travel services, including selected books and maps, and on-demand TripTik ® routings.
■ Books/maps only, no marked maps or on-demand TripTik ® routings.
▲ Travel Agency Services, cruise, tour, air, car and rail reservations; domestic and international hotel reservations; passport photo services; international and domestic travel guides and maps; travel money products; and International Driving Permits. In addition, assistance with travel related insurance products including trip cancellation, travel accident, lost luggage, trip delay and assistance products.
✪ Insurance services provided. If only this icon appears, only insurance services are provided at that office.
⌁C Car Care Plus Facility provides car care services.
🔌 Electric vehicle charging station on premises.

AAA NATIONAL OFFICE: 1000 AAA DRIVE, HEATHROW, FLORIDA 32746-5063, (407) 444-7000

COLORADO

BOULDER—AAA COLORADO, 1933 28TH ST #200, 80301. WEEKDAYS (M-F) 8:30-5:30, SAT 9:00-1:00. (303) 753-8800 EXT 8600, *(877) 244-9790.* ✦ ▲ ✪

CENTENNIAL—AAA COLORADO, 19761 E SMOKY HILL RD #A, 80015. WEEKDAYS (M-F) 8:30-5:30, SAT 9:00-1:00. (303) 753-8800 EXT 8300, *(877) 244-9790.* ✦ ▲ ✪

CENTENNIAL—AAA COLORADO, 7400 S UNIVERSITY BLVD, 80122. WEEKDAYS (M-F) 8:30-5:30, SAT 9:00-1:00. (303) 753-8800 EXT 8500, *(877) 244-9790.* ✦ ▲ ✪

COLORADO SPRINGS—AAA COLORADO, 7330 N ACADEMY BLVD, 80920. WEEKDAYS (M-F) 8:30-5:30, SAT 9:00-1:00. (719) 591-2222 EXT 5400, *(877) 244-9790.* ✦ ▲ ✪

DENVER—AAA COLORADO, 4100 E ARKANSAS AVE, 80222. **WEEKDAYS (M-F) 8:30-5:30, SAT 9:00-1:00. (303) 753-8800,** *(877) 244-9790.* ✦ ▲ ✪

DENVER—AAA COLORADO, 4100 E ARKANSAS AVE, 80222. WEEKDAYS (M-F) 8:30-5:30, SAT 9:00-1:00. (303) 753-8800 EXT 8000, *(877) 244-9790.* ✦ ▲ ✪

DURANGO—AAA COLORADO, 16 TOWN PLZ, 81301. WEEKDAYS (M-F) 8:30-5:30. (970) 247-2273 EXT 3900, *(877) 244-9790.* ● ▲

FORT COLLINS—AAA COLORADO, 3636 S COLLEGE AVE UNIT 2, 80525. WEEKDAYS (M-F) 8:30-5:30, SAT 9:00-1:00. (970) 223-1111 EXT 2200, *(877) 244-9790.* ✦ ▲ ✪

GRAND JUNCTION—AAA COLORADO, 2454 US HWY 6 & 50 #109, 81505. WEEKDAYS (M-F) 8:30-5:30. (970) 245-2236 EXT 3800, *(877) 244-9790.* ● ▲ ✪

LITTLETON—AAA COLORADO, 8601 W CROSS DR STE B1, 80123. WEEKDAYS (M-F) 8:30-5:30, SAT 9:00-1:00. (303) 753-8800 EXT 8806, *(877) 244-9790.* ✦ ▲ ✪

WESTMINSTER—AAA COLORADO, 5140 W 120TH AVE UNIT 300, 80020. WEEKDAYS (M-F) 8:30-5:30, SAT 9:00-1:00. (303) 753-8800 EXT 8900, *(877) 244-9790.* ✦ ▲ ✪

WHEAT RIDGE—AAA COLORADO, 3850 WADSWORTH BLVD, 80033. WEEKDAYS (M-F) 8:30-5:30, SAT 9:00-1:00. (303) 753-8800 EXT 8400, *(877) 244-9790.* ✦ ▲ ✪

UTAH

DRAPER—AAA NORTHERN CALIFORNIA NEVADA & UTAH, 185 E 12300 S #100, 84020. WEEKDAYS (M-F) 9:00-6:00 (SAT BY APPOINTMENT ONLY). (801) 878-8500 ✦ ✪

MURRAY—AAA NORTHERN CALIFORNIA NEVADA & UTAH, 5207 S STATE ST STE 2, 84107. WEEKDAYS (M-F) 9:00-6:00 (SAT BY APPOINTMENT ONLY). (801) 266-8472 ✦ ▲ ✪

OGDEN—AAA NORTHERN CALIFORNIA NEVADA & UTAH, 5705 S HARRISON BLVD, 84403. WEEKDAYS (M-F) 9:00-6:00 (SAT BY APPOINTMENT ONLY). (801) 605-0098 ✦ ✪

OREM—AAA NORTHERN CALIFORNIA NEVADA & UTAH, 160 E UNIVERSITY PKY ST F, 84058. WEEKDAYS (M-F) 9:00-6:00 (SAT BY APPOINTMENT ONLY). (801) 788-3300 ✦ ✪

SALT LAKE CITY—AAA NORTHERN CALIFORNIA NEVADA & UTAH, 1400 S FOOTHILL DR ST 154, 84108. WEEKDAYS (M-F) 9:00-6:00 (SAT BY APPOINTMENT ONLY). (801) 238-1250 ✦ ✪

WASHINGTON—AAA NORTHERN CALIFORNIA NEVADA & UTAH, 844 W TELEGRAPH RD STE 4, 84780. WEEKDAYS (M-F) 9:00-6:00 (SAT BY APPOINTMENT ONLY). (435) 656-3990 ● ✪

Metric Equivalents Chart

TEMPERATURE

To convert Fahrenheit to Celsius, subtract 32 from the Fahrenheit temperature, multiply by 5 and divide by 9.
To convert Celsius to Fahrenheit, multiply by 9, divide by 5 and add 32.

ACRES

1 acre = 0.4 hectare (ha)   1 hectare = 2.47 acres

MILES AND KILOMETERS

Note: A kilometer is approximately 5/8 or 0.6 of a mile.
To convert kilometers to miles multiply by 0.6.

Miles/Kilometers		Kilometers/Miles	
15	24.1	30	18.6
20	32.2	35	21.7
25	40.2	40	24.8
30	48.3	45	27.9
35	56.3	50	31.0
40	64.4	55	34.1
45	72.4	60	37.2
50	80.5	65	40.3
55	88.5	70	43.4
60	96.6	75	46.6
65	104.6	80	49.7
70	112.7	85	52.8
75	120.7	90	55.9
80	128.7	95	59.0
85	136.8	100	62.1
90	144.8	105	65.2
95	152.9	110	68.3
100	160.9	115	71.4

Celsius °		Fahrenheit °
100	BOILING	212
37		100
35		95
32		90
29		85
27		80
24		75
21		70
18		65
16		60
13		55
10		50
7		45
4		40
2		35
0	FREEZING	32
-4		25
-7		20
-9		15
-12		10
-15		5
-18		0
-21		-5
-24		-10
-27		-15

LINEAR MEASURE

Customary	Metric
1 inch = 2.54 centimeters	1 centimeter = 0.4 inches
1 foot = 30 centimeters	1 meter = 3.3 feet
1 yard = 0.91 meters	1 meter = 1.09 yards
1 mile = 1.6 kilometers	1 kilometer = .62 miles

LIQUID MEASURE

Customary	Metric
1 fluid ounce = 30 milliliters	1 milliliter = .03 fluid ounces
1 cup = .24 liters	1 liter = 2.1 pints
1 pint = .47 liters	1 liter = 1.06 quarts
1 quart = .95 liters	1 liter = .26 gallons
1 gallon = 3.8 liters	

WEIGHT

If You Know:	Multiply By:	To Find:
Ounces	28	Grams
Pounds	0.45	Kilograms
Grams	0.035	Ounces
Kilograms	2.2	Pounds

PRESSURE

Air pressure in automobile tires is expressed in kilopascals. Multiply pound-force per square inch (psi) by 6.89 to find kilopascals (kPa).

24 psi = 165 kPa   28 psi = 193 kPa
26 psi = 179 kPa   30 psi = 207 kPa

GALLONS AND LITERS

Gallons/Liters		Liters/Gallons			
5	19.0	12	45.6	10	2.6	40	10.4
6	22.8	14	53.2	15	3.9	50	13.0
7	26.6	16	60.8	20	5.2	60	15.6
8	30.4	18	68.4	25	6.5	70	18.2
9	34.2	20	76.0	30	7.8	80	20.8
10	38.0	25	95.0	35	9.1	90	23.4

420

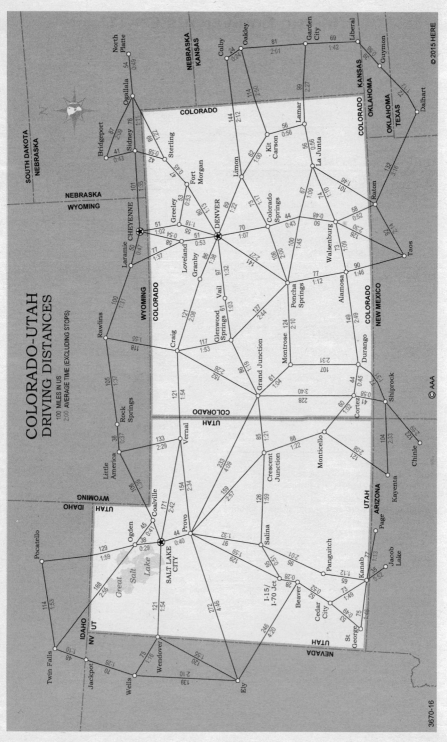

COLORADO-UTAH
DRIVING DISTANCES
100 MILES IN US
2:00 AVERAGE TIME (EXCLUDING STOPS)

© 2015 HERE

© AAA

3670-16

Points of Interest Index

 Attractions appear at the top of each category and offer a Great Experience for Members®.

Index Legend

CHILDREN'S ACTIVITIES

EVENTS & FESTIVALS

HISTORIC SITES & EXHIBITS

SHOPPING & NIGHTLIFE

TOURS & SIGHTSEEING

Photo Credits

Page numbers are in bold type. Picture credit abbreviations are as follows:
- (i) numeric sequence from top to bottom, left to right ▪ (AAA) AAA Travel library.

- (Cover) View from Union Station, Denver, CO / © Blaine Harrington III / Alamy Stock Photo
- **2** (i) Courtesy of VISIT DENVER
- **2** (ii) © Evan Simon / VISIT DENVER
- **12** (i) Courtesy of Berry Manor Inn
- **12** (ii) © Chris Dew / Killarney Lodge
- **12** (iii) Courtesy of Hyatt Hotels
- **12** (iv) Courtesy of Montpelier Plantation and Beach
- **12** (v) © Elisa Rolle / Wikimedia Commons
- **12** (vi) Courtesy of The Shores Resort & Spa
- **12** (vii) Courtesy of All Star Vacation Homes
- **12** (viii) Courtesy of Bryce View Lodge
- **12** (ix) Courtesy of Vista Verde Guest Ranch
- **13** Courtesy of Divi Resorts
- **18** (i) Courtesy of VISIT DENVER
- **18** (ii) © Bryan Mullennix/Space / age fotostock
- **19** © Scott Markewitz / Alamy Stock Photo
- **20** (i) © Billy Hathorn / Wikimedia Commons
- **20** (ii) © Bill Bachmann / Alamy Stock Photo
- **23** (i) © Blaine Harrington III / Alamy Stock Photo
- **23** (ii) Courtesy of VISIT DENVER
- **23** (iii) © BWB - IMAGES / Alamy Stock Photo
- **23** (iv) © Ron Ruhoff / VISIT DENVER
- **23** (v) Courtesy of VISIT DENVER
- **24** (i) © Evan Simon / VISIT DENVER
- **24** (ii) © Mira / Alamy Stock Photo
- **24** (iii) © David Wall / Alamy Stock Photo
- **24** (iv) © Ellen Isaacs / age fotostock
- **80** © Danita Delimont / Alamy Stock Photo
- **83** © Ian Dagnall / Alamy Stock Photo
- **84** © JCPhoto / Alamy Stock Photo
- **85** Courtesy of VisitCOS.com
- **86** Courtesy of VisitCOS.com
- **90** © Richard Cummins / age fotostock
- **92** © Blaine Harrington III / Alamy Stock Photo
- **115** Courtesy of VISIT DENVER
- **118** © Scott Dressel-Martin / VISIT DENVER
- **119** © Stan Obert / VISIT DENVER
- **120** © FOTOSEARCH RM / age fotostock
- **121** © Steve Crecelius / VISIT DENVER
- **122** Courtesy of VISIT DENVER
- **123** © age fotostock / Alamy Stock Photo
- **124** © Greg Throw / VISIT DENVER
- **128** © Stan Obert / VISIT DENVER
- **130** © Danita Delimont / Alamy Stock Photo
- **276** (i) © McPHOTO / age fotostock
- **276** (ii) © JDP Productions / Pur / age fotostock
- **277** © Norbert Eisele-Hein/imageBROKER / age fotostock
- **278** (i) Courtesy of Wikimedia Commons
- **278** (ii) © Philkon Phil Konstantin / Wikimedia Commons
- **281** (i) © Mike Anich / age fotostock
- **281** (ii) © Scott Markewitz / Aur / age fotostock
- **281** (iii) © Brian Jannsen / Alamy Stock Photo
- **281** (iv) © Alan Majchrowicz / age fotostock
- **281** (v) © Chris Hepburn / age fotostock

LET'S GET SOCIAL

Stay connected with #AAA and #CAA

Visit with us on your favorite social media sites for the latest updates on hot discounts, cool destinations and handy automotive know-how.

Talk with us!

 AAA.com/Facebook   AAA.com/Googleplus

AAA.com/Twitter   YouTube.com/AAA

CAA Social Media: CAA.ca/social